Comparative Politics

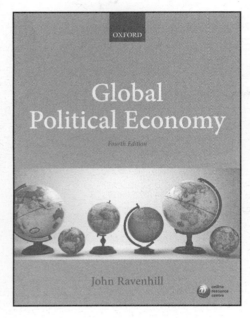

Comparative Politics

Third Edition

Edited by

Daniele Caramani

OXFORD
UNIVERSITY PRESS

OXFORD

UNIVERSITY PRESS

Great Clarendon Street, Oxford, OX2 6DP,
United Kingdom

Oxford University Press is a department of the University of Oxford.
It furthers the University's objective of excellence in research, scholarship,
and education by publishing worldwide. Oxford is a registered trade mark of
Oxford University Press in the UK and in certain other countries

First edition 2008

Second edition 2011

Impression: 1

Published in the United States of America by Oxford University Press
198 Madison Avenue, New York, NY 10016, United States of America

British Library Cataloguing in Publication Data

Data available

Library of Congress Control Number: 2013953963

ISBN 978–0–19–966599–0

Printed in Italy by
L.E.G.O. S.p.A.—Lavis TN

Preface

About the book

In designing this textbook on *Comparative Politics* the ambition was to produce an exciting, authoritative, and up-to-date teaching instrument. We have tried to write chapters of the highest standards in terms of their content, with information presented comparatively and supported by cutting-edge theories and a rigorous methodology. We aimed at comprehensive chapters in their substantive coverage of the field, and a worldwide range of countries.

We hope that the third edition will speak to comparative politics students at all levels, as well as to teachers who will use it for their classes, as did the first and second editions. Our goal was to produce an integrated text with a maximum of cross-references between chapters, an aspect that we have tried to improve in preparing the present edition. On the other hand, the modular structure with self-contained chapters should maximize its appeal to lecturers and students, alongside accessible language enhanced by a number of learning features and a similar format throughout. This structure does not require that it is read cover to cover, thus the book can be used in any order, making it possible to compose courses with a 'variable geometry'. For the same reason, more but shorter chapters have been preferred. With respect to the first edition published in 2008, this third edition is more concise with about 15–20 per cent less text.

Rationale for the book

The first important feature is that the volume aims at a *comprehensive and wide-ranging coverage* of both the *subject areas* of comparative politics and the *geographical spread* of cases. The range of countries includes not only advanced industrial nations but also developing regions and emerging economies (in post-communist countries, Latin America, Asia, the Middle East, and Africa).

The range of topics is also more comprehensive than most commonly taught courses in comparative politics. On the one hand, throughout the book attention is given to *theory and methodology*, and three chapters on the comparative approach deal specifically with these topics in Section 1 on 'Theories and methods'. As far as possible all chapters include the most important theoretical approaches in each field of the discipline and present the most recent advances and current debates. Deliberately no specific approach has been privileged. Methodologically, it is based on rigorous comparative analysis and up-to-date empirical data.

On the other hand, the range of *substantive topics* is reflected in a number of chapters that add to the usual core areas of comparative politics courses. The book devotes a great deal of attention to sub-national institutions and actors (Chapters 11 and 15) and to non-institutional actors such as interest groups, social movements, and media (in Section 4 on 'Actors and processes'). Most importantly, perhaps, the book includes an entire section on 'Public policies'—not only how policies are made but also their impact on economies and societies (with a focus on the welfare state and its undergoing reform). This gives a better balance between the 'input' and 'output' sides of the political system. Finally, the book has an entire section (Section 6 on 'Beyond the nation-state') on, first, new types of political systems (such as the European Union) and, second, on interactions between political systems which take into account transnational and international factors that affect politics at the supra-national, national, and sub-national level. Theoretically this section deals with major challenges to comparative politics.

Despite the wide coverage of topics, a number had to be omitted, namely a larger section on theories, a chapter on political ideologies, and a chapter on institutional engineering and reform. Most of the topics in these fields are dealt with in the chapters of the book as they stand now, as well as in the Online Resource Centre that accompanies this book: **www.oxfordtextbooks.co.uk/ orc/caramani3e/**

The second important feature is the *analytical and comparative* approach of the volume. Information and data are presented thematically rather than country by country and systematic comparison between countries is carried out on specific political, institutional, and socio-economic phenomena. For us, comparative politics should not be reduced to the one-by-one description of single countries. Case studies (see the various 'Country profiles') are theoretically useful only if inserted in a broader comparative framework. We understand comparative politics in analytical terms, as a combination of substance (the study of political systems, actors, and processes) and method, i.e. identifying and explaining differences and similarities between cases through the test of hypotheses about relationships—law-like generalizations—between concepts and variables applicable in more than one context. This thematic, analytical, and comparative approach leads to the basic choice of organizing the book around major substantive themes.

Third, the book presents a large amount of *comparative empirical data.* The analytical approach of the book leads us to present information and data in tables and figures throughout the chapters (as well as in the 'World data' tables and 'Comparative tables'). Many of these data are previously unpublished and have been collected for this textbook.

Particular attention is given to historical trends, longitudinal data, and time series (see 'Trends' figures). The book is comparative and contemporary but, in addition, it includes a long-term perspective allowing a better appreciation of current changes. It thus combines *time and space dimensions.* There is a specific reason for this. The development of the modern nation-state and mass democracies in the nineteenth century is a unique change that has no previous equivalent in history. This change involved a totally new political organization—based on principles of individual equality, civil liberties, voting rights—and social organization, in particular with industrialization and the subsequent development of the welfare state towards the end of the century. Therefore an understanding of contemporary society cannot be complete without a long-term perspective highlighting the scope of these changes.

The empirical approach also allows us to provide students with the possibility of *analysing data* themselves. The Online Resource Centre includes a large amount of *comparative data*, making it not just a learning device but a truly research-oriented data depository. With files in different formats, students can analyse data and teachers prepare exercises. Furthermore, a web directory allows students to look for and collect more data in the internet archives of international and national organizations, official and academic data collections, and websites specializing in elections, referendums, or survey data and opinion polls.

Therefore the Online Resource Centre is not simply the electronic version of the printed book. Although it also includes additional substantial information that could not be fitted on paper— as well as learning devices such as review questions, PowerPoint presentations of each chapter, extra tables and figures, and examination questions—its most important feature is that it allows empirical data analysis. We believe that comparative politics is an empirical discipline and that theories and methods are of no use if they are not combined with data. The website makes this textbook an ongoing and cumulative project with information and material that will be placed on it over the years.

In attempting to achieve these goals, we are aware that we have not produced an 'easy' book. However, we believe that most students are much better, more motivated, and harder working than is often assumed. And we also believe that it is when confronted with challenge and unexplored fields that young people enjoy learning, perform best, and acquire self-confidence. Against what seems to be a trend towards scholarization of university teaching (either to increase numbers of students or degrees awarded), we are convinced that an effort on the part of students will be rewarding and that they will learn from this book and its website. Comparative politics is a broad and fascinating discipline dealing with important current world issues. Studying it will prove a lifetime investment.

Acknowledgements

We very much appreciate that Oxford University Press—our editors in the first two editions, Ruth Anderson and Catherine Page in particular, and the editor of the present edition, Martha Bailes—shared this approach with strong commitment and encouragement, and supported us substantially, technically, and logistically. As editor of the volume, I am very grateful that they agreed to additional chapters not figuring in the initial plan. From the first steps of the project up to its conclusion, their input has been remarkable and crucial to the successful completion of this volume.

When defining the line-up of contributors and bringing on board new contributors in the second edition, the criteria were those of excellence. I am very happy that it has been possible to bring together an outstanding group of highly respected 'comparativists' from a range of nationalities and academic traditions. All are currently engaged in research, and thus are 'research-minded' and in touch with the most recent advances in their fields of expertise. On a personal level, I am honoured that such a prestigious group of scholars has trusted a less experienced colleague to edit this volume since its first edition. I am very thankful to the authors of this volume who have worked with high professional and collaborative spirit.

Finally, I would like to thank my research assistants—Beatrice Eugster, Patrick Lengg, Matthias Meyer-Schwarzenberger, and Alexander Schäfer—for the marvellous job they did in preparing the Online Resource Centre, the 'Country profiles', the data for the 'Trends' and 'Comparative tables', and, more generally, for supporting us throughout the project with extreme professionalism and dedication. Their substantial criticisms, too, allowed us to clarify obscure points in several chapters. I am deeply grateful to them for their engagement.

Daniele Caramani

July 2007, September 2010, September 2013

Remembering Peter Mair (1951–2011)

Professor Peter Mair was a leading political scientist whose sudden and premature death in 2011 has saddened the political science community. The huge intellectual gap left in his wake will prove impossible to fill. The contributors of this volume mourn one of the most influential and inspiring scholars in comparative politics—for many of us also a mentor and a friend.

Peter Mair's scholarly contribution is wide-ranging and includes ground-breaking work on party systems, cleavage structures and electoral behaviour, representative democracy and its institutions, as well as theoretical and normative questions about the functioning of modern democracies. When confronted with the issue of adapting his chapter for the third edition, we instinctively and unanimously decided to keep his original text—one of the most complete, most informative, and clearest treatments of the crucial topic of democracy. It is a sharp and provocative text dealing with most pressing questions. It required only minor updates in the tables, in addition to the editorial cuts as in all chapters in this edition. Throughout his entire career Peter taught, guided, and mentored many students across Europe. We are happy that through this volume his challenging style continues to speak to a new a generation of students.

We dedicate the current edition to Peter's memory.

His colleagues and friends
September 2013

New to this edition

- Covers the events of the Arab Spring, the global financial and economic crises, and the rise of right-wing populism
- Addresses the latest theoretical contributions in the field
- Provides revised empirical data, including figures, tables, graphs, and country profiles, in the text and online.

Contents in brief

Contents in detail

List of figures

List of boxes

List of tables

Abbreviations

The list of abbreviations does not include the names of political parties, trade unions, social movements, interest groups, or other organizations.

2RS	Two-round (electoral) system
AV	Alternative vote (electoral system)
CAP	Common Agricultural Policy (European Union)
CDI	Centre for Democratic Institutions (Australia)
CFSP	Common Foreign and Security Policy (European Union)
CIS	Commonwealth of Independent States
CLRAE	Congress of Local and Regional Authorities of Europe
CMEs	Coordinated Market Economies
CMP	Comparative Manifesto Project
CoR	Committee of the Regions (European Union)
DG	Democracy and Governance, Directorate-General (European Union)
ECB	European Central Bank
ECJ	European Court of Justice
ECSC	European Coal and Steel Community
EEA	European Economic Area
EEC	European Economic Community
EED	European Endowment for Democracy
EIDHR	European Instrument for Democracy and Human Rights (European Union)
EMU	Economic and Monetary Union
ENEP	Effective Number of Elective Parties
ENP	European Neighbourhood Policy (European Union)
ENPP	Effective Number of Parliamentary Parties
EP	Eopean Parliament
EPD	European Partnership for Democracy
ESDP	European Security and Defence Cooperation (European Union)
ESM	European Stability Mechanism
ESS	European Social Survey
EU	European Union
F	Fractionalization index
FAO	United Nations Food and Agriculture Organization
FCO	Foreign and Commonwealth Office (UK)
FDI	Foreign Direct Investment
FPTP	First past the post (electoral system)
GDP	Gross Domestic Product
GEM	Gender Empowerment Measure

GNI	Gross National Income
GNP	Gross National Product
GWP	Gross World Product
ICC	International Criminal Court
ICTs	Information and Communication Technologies
IGO	International Governmental Organization
ILO	International Labour Organization
INGO	International Non-Governmental Organization
IRI	International Republican Institute (US)
IREX	International Research and Exchanges Board
ISO	International Organization for Standardization
ITU	International Telecommunications Union
LMEs	Liberal Market Economies
LSq	Least square index
MDSD	Most Different Systems Design
MEP	Member of European Parliament
MMM	Mixed-member majoritarian (electoral system)
MMP	Mixed-member proportional (electoral system)
MP	Member of Parliament
MSSD	Most Similar Systems Design
NAFTA	North American Free Trade Agreement
NATO	North Atlantic Treaty Organisation
NDI	National Democratic Institute for International Affairs (US)
NED	National Endowment for Democracy (US)
NEPAD	New Partnership for Africa's Development
NGO	Non-Governmental Organization
NIMD	Netherlands Institute for Multiparty Democracy
NPM	New Public Management
OAS	Organization of American States
OCA	Optimal Currency Area
ODA	Official Development Assistance
OECD	Organisation for Economic Co-operation and Development
OMC	Open Method of Coordination
OPEC	Organization of Petroleum Exporting Countries
OSCE	Organization for Security and Co-operation in Europe
PACs	Political Action Committees
PDA	Personal Digital Assistant
PPP	Purchasing Power Parities
PR	Proportional representation (electoral system)
QMV	Qualified Majority Voting (European Union)
RoP	Rules of Procedure (legislatures)
RSS	Really Simple Syndication
SES	Socio-economic status
SGP	Stability and Growth Pact (European Union)
SIDA	Swedish International Development Cooperation Agency

SMEs	Social Market Economies
SMO	Social Movement Organisation
SMP	Single-member plurality (electoral system)
SoP	Separation of powers
STV	Single transferable vote (electoral system)
TNC	Transnational companies
UDHR	Universal Declaration of Human Rights
UFW	United Farm Workers
UN	United Nations
UNCTAD	United Nations Conference on Trade and Development
UNDP	United Nations Development Programme
USAID	United States Agency for International Development
USSR	Union of Soviet Socialist Republics
WEF	World Economic Forum
WFD	Westminster Foundation for Democracy (UK)
WHO	World Health Organization
WTO	World Trade Organization
WVS	World Values Survey

About the contributors

Jørgen Goul Andersen is Professor of Political Sociology at the Department of Political Science, Aarhus University, Denmark. His main research areas are comparative welfare studies, electoral behaviour, and political participation. Among his recent publications in English are authored and co-authored volumes such as *The Changing Face of Welfare: Consequences and Outcomes from a Citizenship Perspective* (Policy Press 2005), *Europe's New State of Welfare: Unemployment, Employment Policies and Citizenship* (Policy Press 2002), and *Democracy and Citizenship in Scandinavia* (Palgrave 2001).

Klaus von Beyme is Emeritus Professor at the Institute of Political Science, University of Heidelberg, Germany. His research interests include the analysis of institutions and political regimes, political parties, and trade unions, as well as political theories and the history of ideologies and political thought. His publications include *Political Parties in Western Democracies* (Gower 1985), *Transitions to Democracy in Eastern Europe* (Macmillan 1996, *Parliamentary Democracy* (Macmillan 2000), *The Legislator: German Parliament as a Decision-Making Centre* (St Martin's Press 1998), *Politische Theorien im Zeitalter der Ideologien: 1789–1945* (Westdeutscher Verlag 2002).

James Bickerton is Professor of Political Science at St Francis Xavier University, Canada. His research interests include nationalism, federalism, regionalism, and regional development in Canada. His publications as co-editor include *Canadian Politics* (University of Toronto Press 2014, 6th edn) and *Governing: Essays in Honour of Donald Savoie* (McGill–Queen's University Press 2013), and he is co-author of *Freedom, Equality, Community: The Political Philosophy of Six Influential Canadians* (McGill–Queen's University Press 2006) and *Ties That Bind: Parties and Voters in Canada* (Oxford University Press 1999). Recently he has been a Visiting Professor at Universitat Pompeu Fabra (Barcelona) and the University of Edinburgh.

Paul Brooker was formerly a visiting professor in the Department of Political Science at the University of Canterbury, New Zealand. His recent publications include *Twentieth-Century Dictatorships: The Ideological One-Party States* (Macmillan 1997), *Defiant Dictatorships: Communist and Middle-Eastern Dictatorships in a Democratic Age* (Macmillan 1997), *Leadership in Democracy* (Palgrave 2010, 2nd edition), *Modern Stateless Warfare* (Palgrave 2010), and *Non-Democratic Regimes* (Palgrave 2014, 3rd edn).

Peter Burnell is Professor of Politics in the Department of Politics and International Studies, University of Warwick, UK. He was founding editor of the journal *Democratization*. He is author, editor, or co-editor of many books, including *Globalizing Democracy: Party Politics in Emerging Democracies* (Routledge 2006), *Evaluating Democracy Support: Methods and Experiences* (International IDEA and SIDA 2007), *New Challenges to Democratization* (Routledge 2009), and *Politics in the Developing World* (Oxford University Press 2011, 3rd edn). His monograph *Promoting Democracy Abroad: Policy and Performance* was published in February 2011 (Transaction Books).

Daniele Caramani is Professor of Comparative Politics at the University of St Gallen, Switzerland. He is the author of *The Nationalization of Politics* (Cambridge University Press 2004)—awarded the Stein Rokkan Prize for Comparative Research in the Social Sciences—and *Introduction to the Comparative Method with Boolean Algebra* (Sage, 'Quantitative Applications in the Social Sciences', 2009), as well as of the handbook and CD-ROM *Elections in Western Europe since 1815* (Palgrave 2000). He is co-director of the Constituency-Level Data Archive (CLEA) which received the APSA 2012 'Dataset Award'.

Roland Erne is Senior Lecturer in Industrial Relations and Human Resources at University College Dublin. His research spans comparative politics, democratic theory, economic and political sociology, and international and comparative industrial relations. In particular, he studies how interest associations and social movements—especially trade unions—respond to processes of European integration and globalization. In *European Unions: Labor's Quest for a Transnational Democracy* (Cornell University Press 2008), he challenged the assertion that no realistic prospect exists for remedying the European Union's democratic deficit, i.e. its domination by corporate interests and lack of a cohesive European people.

Alain-G. Gagnon is Canada Research Chair in Quebec and Canadian Studies at the Université du Québec à Montréal, Canada. In 2007 he received the First Josep Maria Vilaseca i Marcet Award granted by the Institute of Autonomous Studies of Catalonia for his work entitled *Au-delà de la nation unificatrice: Plaidoyer pour le fédéralisme multinational.* He is the director of the Research Group on Multinational Societies (GRSP) as well as of the Centre de Recherche Interdisciplinaire sur la Diversité au Québec (CRIDAQ). Among his other recent publications is *Federalism, Citizenship and Quebec: Debating Multinationalism* (University of Toronto Press 2007).

Michael Gallagher is Professor of Comparative Politics and Head of the Department of Political Science at Trinity College, University of Dublin, Ireland. He has been a visiting professor at New York University, City University of Hong Kong, and Sciences Po Lille. He is co-editor or co-author of *Representative Government in Modern Europe* (McGraw-Hill 2011, 5th edn), *How Ireland Voted 2011* (Palgrave Macmillan 2011), *The Politics of Electoral Systems* (Oxford University Press 2005), *Politics in the Republic of Ireland* (Routledge 2010, 5th edn), *Days of Blue Loyalty* (PSAI Press 2002), and *The Referendum Experience in Europe* (Macmillan 1996).

Simon Hix is Professor of European and Comparative Politics at the London School of Economics and Political Science, UK. He is currently Head of the Department of Government and Associate Editor of *European Union Politics*. He is co-author (with Bjørn Høyland) of *The Political System of the European Union* (Palgrave 2011, 3rd edn) and co-author (with Abdul Noury and Gérard Roland) of *Democratic Politics in the European Parliament* (Cambridge University Press 2007). In 2004 he won a Distinguished Scholar Award from the US–UK Fulbright Commission, in 2007 he won the Fenno Prize of the American Political Science Association (APSA) for the best book on legislative studies, in 2010 he was elected to the APSA Council, and in 2011 he became a Fellow of the British Academy.

Ronald Inglehart is Lowenstein Professor of Political Science and a research professor at the Institute for Social Research at the University of Michigan, US. He helped found the Euro-Barometer surveys and directs the World Values Survey. He is the author of *The Silent Revolution: Changing Values and Political Styles Among Western Publics* (Princeton University Press 1977). His most recent books are *Cosmopolitan Communications: Cultural Diversity in a Globalized World* (Cambridge University Press 2009), *Sacred and Secular: The Secularization Thesis Revisited* (Cambridge University Press 2004), *Rising Tide: Gender Equality in Global Perspective* (Cambridge University Press 2003), all with Pippa Norris, *Democratization* (Oxford University Press 2009), with Christian Haerpfer, Patrick Bernhagen, and Christian Welzel, and *Modernization, Cultural Change and Democracy: The Human Development Sequence* (Cambridge University Press 2005), with Christian Welzel.

Richard S. Katz is Professor and Chairman of Political Science at the Johns Hopkins University, Baltimore, US. He has held faculty appointments at the City University of New York and the State University of New York at Buffalo. From 2006 to 2012 he was co-editor of the *European Journal of Political Research*, and from 1996 until 2006 he was co-editor of the EJPR *Political Data Yearbook*. He has served on the editorial boards of numerous journals, as convenor of the ECPR Standing Group on Political Parties, and as chairman of the APSA Representation and Electoral Systems Organized Section and the Conference Group on Italian Politics and Society. On political parties he co-edited *Party Organizations: A Data Handbook* (Sage 1992) and *How Parties Organize: Change and Adaptation in Party Organizations in Western Democracies* (Sage 1994), as well as *Handbook of Party Politics* (Sage 2006).

Hans Keman is Professor of Comparative Political Science at the Free University of Amsterdam, the Netherlands. His research interests include political parties and government coalitions, comparative research methodologies, labour markets and welfare statism, and parties' policy positions. He has published *Comparative Democratic Politics: A Guide to Contemporary Theory and Research* (Sage 2002), *Party Government in 48 Democracies (1945–98): Composition, Duration, Personnel* (Kluwer Academic 2000), and *Doing Research in Political Science: An Introduction to Comparative Methods and Statistics* (Sage 2006, 2nd edn), and *Organizing Democratic Choice: Party Representation Over Time* (Oxford University Press 2012).

Kees van Kersbergen is Professor of Comparative Politics in the Department of Political Science and Government at Aarhus University, Denmark. His research interests lie in the fields of comparative politics, political sociology, and political economy, particularly focusing on religion and politics and the welfare state. His publications include *Social Capitalism: A Study of Christian Democracy and the Welfare State* (Routledge 1995), which was awarded the Stein Rokkan Prize, and articles in numerous journals. His latest book is *Religion, Class Coalitions, and Welfare States* (Cambridge University Press 2009), edited with Philip Manow.

Herbert Kitschelt is George V. Allen Professor of International Relations in the Department of Political Science at Duke University, US. His research focuses on the role of political parties and party systems in democratic polities. He has written on social democratic party strategies, ecology/left-libertarian parties, and the new radical right in post-industrial democracies. He has also investigated the emerging party systems of post-communist Eastern Europe. His publications include *The Transformation of European Social Democracy* (Cambridge University Press 1994), *The Radical Right in Western Europe: A Comparative Analysis* (University of Michigan Press 1995) and, with others, *Latin American Party Systems* (Cambridge University Press 2010).

Christoph Knill is Professor of Comparative Public Policy and Administration at the University of Konstanz, Germany. His main research interests lie in the areas of comparative policy analysis and public administration. His focus is on policy-making in the European Union, the analysis of processes of international policy convergence, and policy diffusion as well as research on policy implementation. His recent publications include *The Europeanization of National Administrations: Patterns of Institutional Change and Persistence* (Cambridge University Press 2001), *Environmental Politics in the European Union: Policy-Making, Implementation and Patterns of Multilevel Governance* (Manchester University Press 2007), and *Public Policy—A New Introduction* (Palgrave Macmillan 2012).

Amie Kreppel is a Jean Monnet Chair of EU Politics (*ad personam*) and served as the founding Director of the University of Florida's Title VI funded Center for European Studies (CES) from 2003 to 2011 and the European Union funded Jean Monnet Centre of Excellence (2007 to date). She is an Associate Professor in the Department of Political Science. Dr Kreppel has written extensively on the political institutions of Europe in general and the European Union more specifically including *The Development of the European Parliament and Supranational Party System* (Cambridge University Press 2002) as well as articles in a wide variety of journals including *Comparative Political Studies*, *The British Journal of Political Research*, *European Union Politics*, *The European Journal of Political Research*, *Political Research Quarterly*, *The Journal of European Public Policy*, and *The Journal of Common Market Studies*. Dr Kreppel has served as international visiting faculty at the *Université Louis Pasteur (ULP)*, Strasbourg, France, *Institut für Höhere Studien (Institute for Advanced Studies)*, Vienna, Austria, and the *Institut d'Etudes Européennes, Université Libre Bruxelles (ULB)*, Brussels, Belgium. She was President of the European Union Studies Association (EUSA) from 2011 to 2013, is President of the Conference Group on Italian Politics (CONGRIPS) for the 2013–15 term, and she sits on the steering committee of the European Consortia for Political Research Standing Group on the European Union (ECPR-SGEU). In Spring 2011 she was a visiting Fernand Braudel Senior Fellow at the European University Institute (EUI) in Italy.

Hanspeter Kriesi is Professor of Comparative Politics at the European University Institute, Florence, Italy. Previously, he has taught at the universities of Amsterdam, Geneva, and Zurich.

His research interests include the study of social movements, political parties and interest groups, public opinion, the public sphere, and the media, as well as direct democracy. His recent books include (together with co-authors) *Political Conflict in Western Europe* (Cambridge University Press 2012), *Political Communication in Direct-Democratic Campaigns. Enlightening or Manipulating?* (Palgrave 2012), and *Democracy in the Age of Globalization and Mediatization* (Palgrave 2013).

John Loughlin is Fellow and Tutor at St Edmund's College, Cambridge, and Senior Fellow and Affiliated Lecturer in the Department of Politics and International Studies, University of Cambridge. Previously, he was Professor of European Politics at Cardiff University, UK, where he is now an Honorary Professor. He has served as an expert on regional and local democracy for the Committee of the Regions, the United Nations, and the Council of Europe. His publications include authored and edited volumes such as *Subnational Government: The French Experience* (Palgrave 2007), *Subnational Democracy in the European Union: Challenges and Opportunities* (Oxford University Press 2001), and *Culture, Institutions and Regional Development: A Comparative Analysis of Eight European Regions* (Edward Elgar 2003). He has edited the *Oxford Handbook on Local and Regional Democracy* (Oxford University Press 2010) and the *Routledge Handbook of Regionalism and Federalism* (Routledge 2013).

Peter Mair (1951–2011) was Professor of Comparative Politics at the European University Institute, Florence, Italy, and at Leiden University, the Netherlands. During his productive career he authored and co-authored numerous articles in scholarly journals and research monographs among which *Identity, Competition and Electoral Availability* (Cambridge University Press 1990), winner of the Stein Rokkan Prize for Comparative Research in the Social Sciences, and recently republished in the ECPR Classics series, *Party System Change* (Oxford University Press 1997), *Party Organizations: A Data Handbook* (Sage 1992), *How Parties Organize: Change and Adaptation in Party Organizations in Western Democracies*, and the textbook *Representative Government in Modern Europe* (McGraw-Hill 2011, 5th edn).

Philip Manow is Professor of Political Science at the University of Bremen, Germany. His research interests include comparative welfare state research, comparative political economy, political corruption, European integration, and legislative turnover. He was a visiting scholar at the Center for European Studies, Harvard, and at the Centre d'études Européennes, Paris. From 2002 to 2006 he was leader of the research group 'Economic Governance and Democratic Government' at the Max Planck Institute for the Study of Societies, Cologne. He has published in *Legislative Studies Quarterly, Comparative Political Studies, Journal of European Public Policy*, and *West European Politics* among others. He co-edited *Comparing Welfare Capitalism: Social Policy and Political Economy in Europe, Japan and the USA* (Routledge 2001) and co-authored *Religion, Class, Coalitions and Welfare States* (Cambridge University Press 2009).

Wolfgang C. Müller is Professor of Political Science at the University of Vienna, Austria. His book publications include *Policy, Office, or Votes? How Political Parties in Western Europe Make Hard Decisions* (Cambridge University Press 1999), co-editor with Kaare Strøm, *Coalition Governments in Western Europe* (Oxford University Press 2000), co-editor with Kaare Strøm, *Delegation and Accountability in Parliamentary Democracies* (Oxford University Press 2003), co-editor with Kaare Strøm and Torbjörn Bergman, *Political Parties and Electoral Change* (Sage 2004), co-editor with Peter Mair and Fritz Plasser, and *Cabinets and Coalition Bargaining: The Democratic Life Cycle in Western Europe* (Oxford University Press 2008), co-editor with Kaare Strøm and Torbjörn Bergman.

Pippa Norris is the McGuire Lecturer in Comparative Politics at Harvard University. Recent related book publications include *Public Sentinel: News Media and Governance Reform* (edited for the World Bank 2009) and *Cosmopolitan Communications: Cultural Diversity in a Globalized World* (Cambridge University Press 2009), co-authored with Ronald Inglehart.

B. Guy Peters is Maurice Falk Professor of American Government at the University of Pittsburgh, US, and Distinguished Professor of Comparative Governance at Zeppelin University, Germany. His research interests include political theory (with a focus on institutionalism), methodology, American public policy, and the study of bureaucracy. He is the author of numerous volumes including *Comparative Politics: Theory and Methods* (Macmillan 1998), *Institutional Theory in Political Science: The New Institutionalism* (Continuum 2005), *The Politics of Bureaucracy* (Longman 1994, 4th edn), *Handbook of Public Administration* (Sage 2003), and *American Public Policy: Promise and Performance* (Chatham House 1996). He is currently co-editor of the *European Political Science Review* and associate editor of the *International Encyclopedia of Political Science*.

Gianfranco Poggi is Emeritus Professor of Sociology at the University of Virginia, US. He has held posts in sociology or political science in several universities (in the UK, Canada, Australia, Germany, and Italy). Most recently, he held a chair of sociology at the University of Trento, Italy, where he still resides. He has been a Fellow at the Center for Advanced Behavioral Studies in Stanford and at the Wissenschaftskolleg in Berlin. His main research interests are the history of social theory and the analysis of political institutions and the state. His publications include *The Development of the Modern State* (Stanford University Press 1978), *The State: Its Nature, Development and Prospects* (Polity Press 1990), and *Forms of Power* (Polity Press 2001).

Philipp Rehm is Assistant Professor in the Political Science Department at the Ohio State University, US. Previous posts include the Postdoctoral Prize Research Fellowship at Nuffield College, Oxford University. His work is located at the intersection of political economy and political behaviour. In particular, he is interested in the causes and consequences of income dynamics (such as income loss, income volatility, risk exposure, etc.). At the micro-level, his research explores how income dynamics shape individual preferences for redistribution, social policies, and parties. At the macro-level, his work analyses the impact of labour market and income dynamics on polarization, electoral majorities, and coalitions underpinning social policy.

Georg Sørensen is Professor of Political Science at the University of Aarhus, Denmark. He is the author or co-author of *A Liberal World Order in Crisis. Choosing Between Imposition and Restraint* (Cornell University Press 2011), *Introduction to International Relations: Theories and Approaches* (Oxford University Press 2013, 5th edn), *Changes in Statehood: The Transformation of International Relations* (Palgrave 2001), *The Transformation of the State: Beyond the Myth of Retreat* (Palgrave 2004), and *Democracy and Democratization: Processes and Prospects in a Changing World* (Westview Press 2008, 3rd edn).

Alec Stone Sweet is Leitner Professor of Law, Politics, and International Studies at the Yale Law School and the Yale Department of Political Science, US. His research interests are in the fields of comparative law and politics, international law and politics, and European integration. Recent books include *The Judicial Construction of Europe* (Oxford University Press 2004) and *On Law, Politics, and Judicialization* (Oxford University Press 2002).

Jale Tosun is Research Fellow at the Mannheim Centre for European Social Research at the University of Mannheim. Her research interests comprise comparative public policy and comparative political economy, Europeanization research, and risk regulation. Recent books include *Environmental Policy Change in Emerging Market Democracies—Central and Eastern Europe and Latin America Compared* (University of Toronto Press 2013) and *Risk Regulation in Europe: Assessing the Application of the Precautionary Principle* (Springer 2013). She has co-authored *Public Policy—A New Introduction* (Palgrave Macmillan 2012).

Christian Welzel is Professor of Political Culture Research at Leuphana University, Germany. His research interests range from human development and modernization theory to democratization processes, civil society, and social capital. He has contributed widely to the field of political culture. He has co-authored *Modernization, Cultural Change and Democracy: The Human Development Sequence* (Cambridge University Press 2005) and co-edited *Democratization* (Oxford University Press 2009).

Guided tour of learning features

We have developed a number of learning tools to help you develop the essential knowledge and skills you need to study comparative politics. This guided tour shows you how to get the most out of this text.

Reader's guides

Each chapter opens with a reader's guide outlining what you can expect to cover in the chapter.

Boxes

Throughout the book boxes give you extra information on particular topics, define and explain key ideas, and challenge you to think about what you've learned.

Key points

Each main chapter section ends with key points that reinforce your understanding and act as a useful revision tool.

Questions

End-of-chapter questions probe your understanding of each chapter and encourage you to think critically about the material you've just covered.

Further reading

Recommendations for further reading at the end of each chapter identify the key literature in the field, helping you to develop your interest in particular topics in comparative politics.

 Further reading

Classical texts on social movements

Della Porta, D. and Rucht, D. (eds) (2013) *Meeting Democracy. Power and Deliberation in Global Justice Movement* (Cambridge: Cambridge University Press).

Web links

Carefully selected lists of websites direct you to the sites of institutions and organizations that will help develop your knowledge and understanding.

Web links

www.ned.org
The National Endowment for Democracy is the leading private non-profit organization in the US for promoting democracy. The website gives access to *Democracy Newsletter*, World Movement for Democracy, and much more.

Glossary terms

Key terms appear in blue in the text and are defined in a glossary at the end of the book, identifying and defining key terms and ideas as you learn, and acting as a useful prompt when it comes to revision.

GLOSSARY

Conventional and unconventional participation Conventional participation is expressed within accepted institutional channels. Unconventional participation takes place through activities that range from public events to direct physical attacks on property or people.

Comparative data section

Extensive empirical data are presented not only to illustrate ideas and concepts, but also for you to use in your own research and analysis, giving you a real sense of how comparative politics works in practice.

In the book you will find empirical data including:

– twenty **country profiles** with information on state formation, forms of government, legal systems, legislature, and electoral systems

– graphs of **world trends** on matters from military expenditure to urbanization

– **world data** on languages, religions, and socio-economic indicators

– **comparative tables** to directly compare different countries' statistics across a range of important themes and issues.

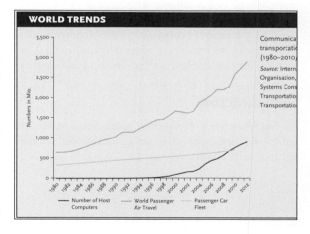

Guided tour of the Online Resource Centre

The Online Resource Centre that accompanies this book provides ready-to-use learning and teaching materials. These resources are free of charge and designed to maximize the learning experience.

www.oxfordtextbooks.co.uk/orc/caramani3e/

For Students

This textbook package has been developed to give you a real sense of how comparative politics works. Extensive empirical data have been gathered by a team of researchers for you to use in your own research and analysis.

Comparative data sets

Comparative data are available for 200 countries, for use in analysis, essay writing, and lab-based exercises. Information is taken from official national sources and international organizations, with indicators including: demography; health; human and social rights; gender equality; education; economy and development; communication and transport; geography and natural resources; the environment; and government and security.

Web directory

A comprehensive web directory points you to databases compiled by international organizations, as well as international and national archives.

Country profiles

An interactive world map presents key information about a selection of countries.

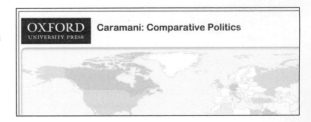

Flashcard glossary

A series of interactive flashcards containing key terms allows you to test your knowledge of important concepts and ideas.

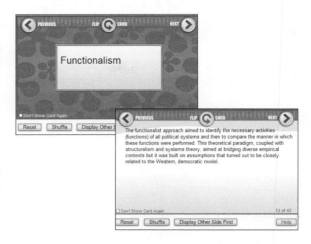

Additional material

Selected topics in the book are explored in more detail online, giving you extra information on particular topics, and defining and explaining key ideas.

Web links

Carefully selected lists of websites direct you to the sites of institutions and organizations that will help develop your knowledge and understanding, and provide useful sources of information in your comparative politics studies.

Review questions

Review questions help you to test your understanding of comparative politics.

For Lecturers

These customisable resources are password protected, but access is available to anyone using the book in their teaching. Complete the short registration form on the site to choose your own username and password.

PowerPoint slides

PowerPoint slides complement each chapter of the book and are a useful resource for preparing lectures and handouts.

Test bank

Over 200 multiple choice and true/false questions can be downloaded to Virtual Learning Environments, or printed out, for use in assessment.

Figures and tables from the book

All figures and tables in the textbook are available to download electronically.

World map

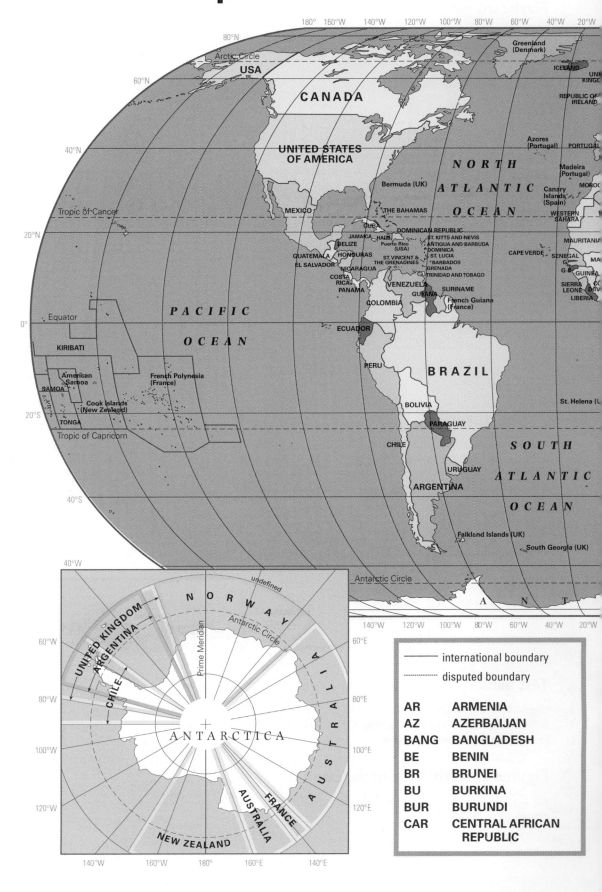

80°N

Arctic Circle

Greenland
(Denmark)

USA

ICELAND

UNI
KINGI

CANADA

60°N

REPUBLIC OF
IRELAND

40°N

UNITED STATES
OF AMERICA

NORTH

Azores
(Portugal)

PORTUGAL

ATLANTIC

Madeira
(Portugal)

MORO

Bermuda (UK)

OCEAN

Canary
Islands
(Spain)

Tropic of Cancer

MEXICO

THE BAHAMAS

WESTERN
SAHARA

20°N

CUBA

DOMINICAN REPUBLIC

MAURITANIA

JAMAICA HAITI

ST. KITTS AND NEVIS

BELIZE

Puerto Rico
(USA)

ANTIGUA AND BARBUDA
DOMINICA

CAPE VERDE

SENEGAL

MA

GUATEMALA

HONDURAS

ST. VINCENT &
THE GRENADINES

ST. LUCIA

BARBADOS

G-
G-B

GUINEA

EL SALVADOR

NICARAGUA

GRENADA

TRINIDAD AND TOBAGO

SIERRA
LEONE

D'IV

COSTA
RICA

VENEZUELA

SURINAME

LIBERIA

PANAMA

GUYANA

COLOMBIA

French Guiana
(France)

Equator

PACIFIC

ECUADOR

0°

KIRIBATI

OCEAN

PERU

BRAZIL

St. Helena (L.

American
Samoa

BOLIVIA

French Polynesia
(France)

SAMOA

Cook Islands
(New Zealand)

PARAGUAY

20°S

TONGA

Tropic of Capricorn

CHILE

SOUTH

URUGUAY

ATLANTIC

ARGENTINA

40°S

OCEAN

Falkland Islands (UK)

South Georgia (UK)

Antarctic Circle

AN

T

UNITED KINGDOM

NORWAY

Antarctic Circle

ARGENTINA

Prime Meridian

CHILE

ANTARCTICA

AUSTRALIA

FRANCE

AUSTRALIA

NEW ZEALAND

———— international boundary

------------ disputed boundary

AR	ARMENIA
AZ	AZERBAIJAN
BANG	BANGLADESH
BE	BENIN
BR	BRUNEI
BU	BURKINA
BUR	BURUNDI
CAR	CENTRAL AFRICAN REPUBLIC

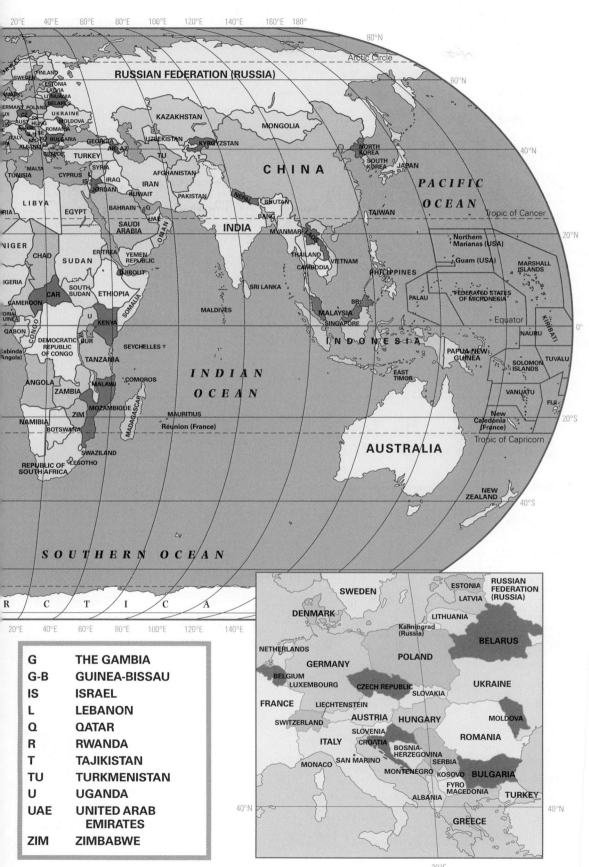

20°E 40°E 60°E 80°E 100°E 120°E 140°E 160°E 180°

80°N

Arctic Circle

60°N

RUSSIAN FEDERATION (RUSSIA)

SWEDEN
FINLAND
ESTONIA
LATVIA
LITHUANIA
BELARUS
POLAND
UKRAINE
MOLDOVA
ROMANIA
BULGARIA
ALBANIA
GREECE
ITALY
MALTA
TUNISIA
CYPRUS
SYRIA
LEBANON

KAZAKHSTAN
MONGOLIA
40°N

GEORGIA
UZBEKISTAN
KYRGYZSTAN
TURKEY
AFGHANISTAN
IRAN
IRAQ
KUWAIT
JORDAN
PAKISTAN

CHINA

NORTH
KOREA
SOUTH
KOREA
JAPAN

PACIFIC

OCEAN

LIBYA
EGYPT
SAUDI
ARABIA
BAHRAIN
UAE
NIGER
CHAD
SUDAN
ERITREA
YEMEN
REPUBLIC
DJIBOUTI
NIGERIA
ORIAL
UINEA
CAMEROON
CAR
SOUTH
SUDAN
ETHIOPIA
GABON
CONGO
DEMOCRATIC
REPUBLIC
OF CONGO
Cabinda
(Angola)
ANGOLA
ZAMBIA
NAMIBIA
ZIM
BOTSWANA
SWAZILAND
REPUBLIC OF
SOUTH AFRICA
LESOTHO

INDIA
NEPAL
BHUTAN
BANG
MYANMAR
LAOS
THAILAND
VIETNAM
CAMBODIA
SRI LANKA
MALDIVES
MALAYSIA
SINGAPORE

TAIWAN

Tropic of Cancer

20°N

Northern
Marianas (USA)
Guam (USA)
MARSHALL
ISLANDS
PALAU
FEDERATED STATES
OF MICRONESIA

Equator 0°

KENYA
SOMALIA
U
BUR
TANZANIA
SEYCHELLES
COMOROS
MALAWI
MOZAMBIQUE
MADAGASCAR
MAURITIUS
Réunion (France)

INDIAN

OCEAN

INDONESIA
EAST
TIMOR
PAPUA NEW
GUINEA
SOLOMON
ISLANDS
NAURU
KIRIBATI
TUVALU
VANUATU
FIJI
New
Caledonia
(France)

Tropic of Capricorn

20°S

AUSTRALIA

NEW
ZEALAND

40°S

SOUTHERN   OCEAN

R   C   T   I   C   A

20°E 40°E 60°E 80°E 100°E 120°E 140°E

G	THE GAMBIA
G-B	GUINEA-BISSAU
IS	ISRAEL
L	LEBANON
Q	QATAR
R	RWANDA
T	TAJIKISTAN
TU	TURKMENISTAN
U	UGANDA
UAE	UNITED ARAB EMIRATES
ZIM	ZIMBABWE

SWEDEN
DENMARK
NETHERLANDS
GERMANY
BELGIUM
LUXEMBOURG
FRANCE
SWITZERLAND
LIECHTENSTEIN
AUSTRIA
SLOVENIA
ITALY
CROATIA
MONACO
SAN MARINO
MONTENEGRO
ALBANIA
GREECE

ESTONIA
LATVIA
LITHUANIA
Kaliningrad
(Russia)
POLAND
CZECH REPUBLIC
SLOVAKIA
HUNGARY
BOSNIA-
HERZEGOVINA
SERBIA
KOSOVO
FYRO
MACEDONIA

RUSSIAN
FEDERATION
(RUSSIA)
BELARUS
UKRAINE
MOLDOVA
ROMANIA
BULGARIA
TURKEY

40°N

40°N

20°E

World data

Languages	Absolute figures (million)	%	Main geographical areas
Mandarin	848	12.3	China
Spanish	406	5.9	Spain, Latin America
English	335	4.8	UK, USA, Canada, New Zealand, Australia
H'indi	260	3.8	India
Arabic	223	3.2	Maghreb, Middle East
Portuguese	202	2.9	Portugal and overseas territories, Brazil, Angola
Bengali	193	2.8	Bangladesh
Russian	162	2.3	Russia
Japanese	122	1.8	Japan
Others	4170	60.3	All remaining areas
Total	6,921	100.0	

Figures are approximate. The table includes languages spoken as a first language by more than 100 million people. The remaining languages are classified under 'Others'.

Source Ethnologue (17th edn), Summer Institute of Linguistics.

Religions	Absolute figures (million)	%
Christianity	2,100	33.3
Islam	1,200	19.1
No religion	900	14.3
Hinduism	850	13.5
Buddhism	375	6.0
Chinese traditionalism	300	4.8
Animism	250	4.0
African traditionalism	90	1.4
Sikhism	24	0.4
Judaism	15	0.2
Spiritism	14	0.2
Confucianism	6	0.1
Jainism	5	0.1
Baha'i	7	0.1
Cao Dai	4	0.1
Shintoism	3	0.0

Zoroastrianism	2	0.0
Tenrikyo	2	0.0
Taoism	2	0.0
Others	150	2.4

Figures are approximate. Christianity includes Roman Catholicism (52.5%), Protestantism (17.6%), Orthodoxy (10.4%), and Anglicanism (3.8%), as well as Pentecostalism, Latter-Day Saints, Evangelicalism, Jehovah's Witnesses, Quakerism, etc. Islam includes Sunnis (83.0%) and Shiites (16.1%).

Sources: See Comparative table 2.

World data 3 Socio-economic indicators

Indicators	Western Europe	Central and Eastern Europe	Latin America	North America	Middle East and Maghreb	Sub-Saharan Africa	Central and Northern Asia	South-East Asia	Oceania	Total
Population (million)	402.8	338.1	460.1	460.9	457.9	874.4	3,293.3	599.1	36.1	6,922.7
Life expectancy (years)	80.6	71.7	73.8	77.8	73.3	55.3	70.0	70.9	77.0	69.9
Aged 65 or above (%)	18.2	14.1	7.2	11.7	4.8	3.2	7.2	5.7	11.0	7.7
Richest to poorest 10%	8.9	9.1	46.3	16.8	10.7	18.9	12.0	10.0	12.7	14.9
GDP per capita 2011 (US$)	42,415	11,575	9,770	38,798	8,904	1,469	5,271	3,826	43,168	10,104
Literacy (%)	99	99	89	99	68	61	76	89	90	80
Carbon dioxide emissions (% share of world total)	9.7	9.9	3.4	20.8	8.2	2.4	40.2	4.1	1.5	100
Female labour force participation rate	51.1	52.4	53.6	54.9	26.0	61.6	49.6	56.8	60.5	51.1
Health expenditure per capita 2010 (PPP US$)	4,169	666	703	6,195	380	84	301	113	3,411	940.69
Unemployment (%)	9.2	9.3	8.5	8.4	10.3	18.7	4.4	6.0	5.4	7.80
Labour force (millions)	196.5	168.5	222.8	226.1	152.4	336.9	1,586.7	301.6	17.9	3,209.40
Agriculture (%)	2.9	12.8	15.2	4.5	22.9	68.0	42.5	37.2	4.3	35.65
Industry (%)	23.9	31.4	21.8	19.3	25.4	10.9	24.3	18.5	20.9	22.01
Services (%)	72.5	59.4	62.7	75.7	51.6	21.1	33.2	4.2	74.6	42.41

Sources: See various comparative tables, additionally: Health expenditure: World Bank Data, http://data.worldbank.org/indicator/SH.XPD.PCAP/countries?display=default

Introduction to comparative politics

Daniele Caramani

Chapter contents

Reader's guide

Comparative politics is one of the three main disciplines in political science, alongside political theory and international relations. It deals with internal political structures (institutions like parliaments and executives), individual and collective actors (voters, parties, social movements, interest groups), and processes (policy-making, communication and socialization processes, and political cultures). The main goal of the discipline is empirical: describe, explain, and predict similarities and differences across political systems, be they countries, regions, or supra-national systems (such as empires or the European Union). This can be done through the intensive analysis of few cases (or one case) or large-scale extensive analyses of many cases, and can be either synchronic or diachronic (including a temporal dimension). Comparative politics uses both quantitative and qualitative data. Increasingly, the analysis of domestic politics is challenged by the growing geographical scope and interdependence between countries through globalization. This brings comparative politics and international relations closer.

Introduction

This book is about politics. It is a book about the most important dimensions of political life, not about one specific aspect (such as elections or policies). Furthermore, it is a *comparative* book, meaning that we look at a variety of countries from all over the world. It is not a book about politics in one place only. Finally, it is not only about politics today, but rather about how politics changed over time, beginning with the transition to mass democracy in the nineteenth century. In sum, it is a book about the long-term comparative study of politics.

But what, precisely, is politics? Politics is the human activity of *making public authoritative decisions.* They are public because they concern the whole of a society. Political decisions apply to everyone who is part of a given citizenship and/or living in a specific territory (a state). They are authoritative because the government that makes such decisions is invested with the authority (and legitimacy) to make them binding, meaning that they are supported by the possibility to sanction individuals who do not comply with them. 'Authorities' have the authority—as it were—to force individuals to comply through coercive means. Politics is thus the activity of *acquiring* (and maintaining) the *power* of making such decisions and of *exercising* this power. It is the *conflict or competition* for power and its use. Who makes political decisions? How did they acquire the power of making them? Where does the authority to make such decisions come from? What decisions have been taken, why, and how do they affect the life of societies? These are the questions that comparative politics seeks to answer.

It goes without saying that these are important questions. *Which decisions are made* concerns our everyday life. The decision to increase taxation is a political decision. So are the decisions to cut welfare benefits such as maternity leave from the workplace, introduce military conscription or carry out military intervention in a foreign country, and invest in nuclear power as a source of energy. But also *how decisions are made* is important. The way in which public and authoritative decisions are made varies a great deal. In democracies we, as citizens, are directly involved through elections or referendums. If we are unhappy with them we can protest through demonstrations, petitions, or letters, or vote differently at the next election. In other types of government individuals are excluded (as in authoritarian regimes). And, finally, *who makes or influences decisions* also counts. Many decisions on the maintenance of generous pension systems today are supported by elderly age cohorts in disagreement with younger ones who pay for them. Or, as another example, take the decision to introduce high taxation for polluting industries. Such a decision is heavily influenced by lobbies and pressure groups and by environmental activists. Configurations of power relationships can be very different, but all point to the basic fact that

Box I.1 Definition of 'comparative politics'

Comparative politics is one of the three main subfields of political science (alongside political theory and international relations) focusing on internal political structures, actors, and processes, and analysing them empirically by describing, explaining, and predicting their variety (similarities and differences) across political systems (and over time)—be they national political systems, regional, municipal, or even supra-national systems.

political decisions are made by individuals or groups who acquired that power against others through either peaceful/democratic or violent means.

KEY POINTS

- Politics is the human activity of making public and authoritative decisions. It is the activity of acquiring the power of making such decisions and of exercising this power. It is the conflict or competition for power and its use.

- Who decides what, and how, is important for the life of societies.

What is comparative politics?

A science of politics

Even though the questions addressed above are very broad, they do not cover the whole spectrum of political science. Comparative politics is one of the three main subfields in political science:

- comparative politics;
- political theory;
- international relations.[1]

Whereas political theory deals with normative and theoretical questions (about equality, democracy, justice, etc.), comparative politics deals with empirical questions. The concern of comparative politics is not primarily whether participation is good or bad, but rather investigates which forms of participation people choose to use, why young people use more unconventional forms than older age groups, and if there are differences in how much groups participate. Even though comparative political scientists are also concerned with normative questions, the discipline as such is empirical and *value-neutral.*

On the other hand, whereas international relations deals with interactions between political systems (balance of power, war, trade), comparative politics deals with *interactions within political systems*. Comparative politics does not analyse wars between nations, but rather investigates which party is in government and why it has decided in favour of military intervention, what kind of electoral constituency has supported this party, how strong the influence of the arms industry has been, and so on. As a subject matter, it is concerned with power relationships between individuals, groups, and organizations, classes, and institutions within political systems. Comparative politics does not ignore external influences on internal structures, but its ultimate concern is power configurations within systems.

As subsequent chapters clarify, the distinction between these three disciplines is not so neat. Many argue that, because of globalization and increasing interdependence and diffusion processes between countries, comparative politics and international relations converge towards one single discipline. Indeed, the brightest scholars bridge the two fields. What is important for the moment is to understand that comparative politics is a discipline that deals with the very essence of politics where sovereignty resides—i.e. in the *state*: questions of power between groups, the institutional organization of political systems, and authoritative decisions that affect the whole of a community. For this reason, over centuries of political thought the state has been at the very heart of political science. Scholars like Aristotle, Machiavelli, and Montesquieu—with many others—were interested in the question 'how does politics work?'

Despite being a vast and variegated discipline, comparative politics constitutes a subdiscipline of political science in its own right and, as Peter Hall has asserted, '[n]o respectable department of political science would be without scholars of comparative politics' (Hall 2004: 1). Similarly, Chapter 1 in this book shows that the most influential political scientists have been 'comparativists', according to two surveys (see Table 1.2).

Types of comparative politics

The term 'comparative politics' originates from the way in which the empirical investigation of the question 'how does politics work?' is carried out. Comparative politics includes three traditions (van Biezen and Caramani 2006).

1. The first tradition is oriented towards the *study of single countries*. This reflects the understanding of comparative politics in its formative years in the US, where it mainly meant the study of political systems outside the US, often in isolation from one another and involving little comparison. Today many courses on comparative politics still include 'German politics', 'Spanish politics', and so on, and many textbooks are structured in 'country chapters'. As discussed in Chapter 3, case studies have a useful purpose, but only when they are put in comparative perspective and

Box I.2 Important works in comparative politics: Aristotle

Aristotle (350 BC), *Ta Politika (Politics)*

The typologies of political systems presented in this work are based on a data compilation of the constitutions and practices in 158 Greek city-states by Aristotle's students. Unfortunately, this collection is now lost (with the exception of *The Constitution of Athens*). This work represents the oldest attempt on record of a comparative empirical data collection and analysis of political institutions. Aristotle distinguished three types of city-states: those ruled by one person, by few persons, and by all citizens. He further separates the corrupt from the non-corrupt ones.

generate hypotheses to be tested in analytical studies involving more than one case, such as implicit comparisons, the analysis of deviant cases, and proving grounds for new techniques.

2. The second tradition is *methodological* and is concerned with establishing rules and standards of comparative analysis. This tradition addresses the question of how comparative analyses should be carried out in order to enhance their potential for the descriptive cumulation of comparative information, causal explanations and associations between key variables, and prediction. This strand is concerned with rigorous conceptual, logical, and statistical techniques of analysis, also involving issues of measurement and case selection.

3. The third tradition of comparative politics is *analytical* in that it combines empirical substance and method. The body of literature in this tradition is primarily concerned with the identification and explanation of differences and similarities between countries and their institutions, actors, and processes through systematic comparison. Its principal goal is explanatory. It aims to go beyond merely ideographic descriptions and aspires to identify *law-like explanations*. Through comparison researchers test (i.e. verify and falsify) whether or not associations and causal relationships between variables hold true empirically across a number of cases. It can be based on 'large-N' or 'small-N' research designs (N indicates the number of cases considered) with either mostly similar or different cases. It can use either qualitative or quantitative data, or logical or statistical techniques, for testing the empirical validity of hypotheses. But ultimately this tradition aims at causal explanation.

This book takes this latter approach.

Thus, like all scientific disciplines, comparative politics is a combination of *substance* (the study of political institutions, actors, and processes) and *method* (identifying and explaining differences and similarities between cases following established rules and standards of analysis). Comparative politics involves the *analysis of similarities and differences* between cases. Are there differences, how large are they, and how can we explain them? Like all sciences, it is only by looking at more than one case that we can say something general about the world, i.e. that generalizations can be reached.

What does comparative politics do in practice?

1. To compare means that similarities and differences are *described*. Comparative politics describes the world and, building on these descriptions, establishes *classifications* and *typologies*. For example, we classify different types of electoral systems.

2. Similarities and differences are *explained*. Why did social revolutions take place in France and Russia but not in Germany and Japan? Why is there no socialist party in the US? Why is electoral turnout in the US and Switzerland so much lower than in any other democracy? As in all scientific disciplines, we formulate *hypotheses* to explain these differences and use empirical data to test them—to check whether or not hypotheses hold true in reality. It is through this method that causality can be inferred, generalizations produced, and theories developed and improved.

3. Comparative politics aims at formulating *predictions*. If we know that PR electoral systems favour the proliferation of parties in the legislature, could we have predicted that the change of electoral law in New Zealand in 1998 from first past the post to PR would lead to a more fragmented party system?

'Comparative politics' as a label stresses the analytical, scientific, and 'quasi-experimental' character of the discipline. It was in the 1950s–60s that the awareness of the need to carry out systematic comparisons for more robust theories increased. The 'comparative' label before 'politics' was added to make a methodological point in a discipline that was not yet fully aware of the importance of explicit comparison. However, single-case studies can be comparative in an implicit way like Tocqueville's *Democracy in America* (1835). As John Stuart Mill noted in his review of the book in 1840, Tocqueville contrasted US specificities with France in a quasi-experimental way. Similarly, books on single countries in the 1960s and early 1970s—on Belgium, Italy, Norway, Spain, Switzerland—not only showed that 'politics works differently over here' but also included systematic, if hidden, comparison with the better-known cases of the US and Britain.

In practice the label 'comparative' was needed as a battle horse. In an established discipline this label could and should be dropped. Today it goes without saying that the analysis of political phenomena is comparative, i.e. entails more than one case. Therefore we should conclude that—since comparative politics covers all aspects

> ### Box I.3 Important works in comparative politics: Machiavelli
>
> **Niccolò Machiavelli (written 1513, published posthumously 1532), *Il Principe* (*The Prince*, Florence: Bernardo di Giunta)**
>
> This book was novel in its time because it told how principalities and republics are governed most successfully from a realist perspective and not how they should be governed in an ideal world. Machiavelli makes his argument through examples taken from empirical observations compared with one another. In *The Prince* he compares mainly different types of principalities (hereditary, new, mixed, and ecclesiastic), whereas in *The Discourses on Livy* (*Discorsi Sopra la Prima Deca di Tito Livio*) his comparison between princely and republican government is more systematic.

of domestic politics—the discipline of comparative politics becomes 'synonymous with the scientific study of politics' (Schmitter 1993: 171). All the dimensions of the political system can be compared, so that all is potentially comparative politics. As Mair noted, '[i]n terms of its substantive concerns the fields of comparative politics seem hardly separable from those of political science *tout court*, in that any focus of inquiry can be approached either comparatively (using cross-national data) or not (using data from just one country)' (Mair 1996: 311). The generality of the scope of coverage of comparative politics leads us now to talk about its substance in more depth.

> **KEY POINTS**
>
> - Comparative politics is one of the three main subfields of political science, alongside international relations and political theory.
> - Comparative politics is an empirical science that studies chiefly domestic politics.
> - The goals of comparative politics are: to describe differences and similarities between political systems and their features; to explain these differences; to predict which factors may cause specific outcomes.

The substance of comparative politics

What is compared?

The classical cases of comparative politics are *national political systems*. These are (still) the most important political units in the contemporary world. However, national systems are not the only cases that comparative politics analyses.

1. First, non-national political systems can be compared: *sub-national regional political systems* (state level in the US or the German *Länder*) or *supra-national units* such as (1) regions (Western Europe, Central-Eastern Europe, North America, Latin America, and so on), (2) empires (Ottoman, Habsburg, Russian, Chinese, Roman, etc.), and (3) supra-national organizations (European Union, NAFTA, etc.).

2. *Types of political systems* can be compared (e.g. a comparison between democratic and authoritarian regimes in terms of, say, economic performance).

3. Comparative politics compares *single elements* of the political system rather than the whole system. Researchers compare the structure of parliaments of different countries or regional governments (or other institutions), the policies (e.g. welfare state or environmental policies), the finances of parties or trade unions, the presence or absence of direct democracy institutions and electoral laws.

The various chapters of this book compare the most important features of national political systems. As can be seen in the Contents list at the beginning of the volume, the variety of topics is very large and comparative politics covers—in principle—all aspects of the political system. It has been argued that precisely because comparative politics encompasses 'everything' from a substantial point of view, it has no substantial specificity, but rather only a methodological one resting on comparison, and its status as a discipline has been questioned (Verba 1985; Dalton 1991; Keman 1993*a*). Yet, there is a substantial specificity which resides in the empirical analysis of internal structures, actors, and processes. But it is also true that comparative politics is a broad discipline and, over the decades, it has had moments in which it focused on particular aspects. This evolution is described in the next two sections.

From institutions to functions ...

Comparative politics before the Second World War was mainly concerned with the analysis of the state and its institutions. Institutions were defined in a narrow sense overlapping with state powers (legislative, executive, judiciary), civil administration, and military bureaucracy. The type of analysis was formal, using as main 'data' constitutional texts and legal documents. The emphasis on the study of formal political institutions focused, naturally, on the geographical areas where they first developed, namely Western Europe and North America.

While the study of state institutions remains important, the reaction against what was perceived as the legalistic study of politics led to one of the major

Box I.4 Important works in comparative politics: Montesquieu

Charles de Secondat, baron de Montesquieu (1748) *De l'Esprit des Loix* (On the Spirit of the Laws, Geneva: Barrillot et fils)

In this influential book, in which the idea of the separation of powers is presented systematically for the first time, Montesquieu distinguishes between republics, monarchies, and despotic regimes. He describes comparatively the working of each type of regime through historical examples. Furthermore, Montesquieu was really a pioneer of 'political sociology' as, first, he analysed the influence of factors such as geography, location, and climate on a nation's culture and, indirectly, its social and political institutions and, second, did so by applying an innovative naturalistic method.

turns in the discipline between the late 1920s and the 1960s—a period considered by some the 'Golden Age' of comparative politics (Dalton 1991). The behavioural revolution—imported from anthropology, biology, and sociology—shifted the substance of comparative politics away from institutions. Pioneers of comparative politics such as Gabriel A. Almond, founder of the Committee on Comparative Politics in 1954 (an organization of the American Social Science Research Council), started analysing other aspects of politics than formal institutions and observing politics in practice rather than as defined in official texts.

What triggered this revolution? Primarily, more attention was devoted to 'new' cases, i.e. a rejection of the almost exclusive focus on the West and the developed world. Early comparativists like James Bryce, Charles Merriam, A. Lawrence Lowell, and Woodrow Wilson—as Philippe Schmitter calls them, 'Dead, White, European Men, but not Boring' (Schmitter 1993: 173)—assumed that the world would converge towards Western models of 'political order'. With this state of mind, it made sense to focus on major Western countries. However, the rise of communist regimes in Eastern Europe (and, later, in China and Central America) and the breakdown of democracy where fascist dictatorships came to power—and in some cases lasted until the 1970s as in Portugal, Spain, and Latin America, and to some extent also in Greece (Stepan 1971; Linz 1978; O'Donnell and Schmitter 1986)—made it clear that other types of 'political order' could exist and needed to be understood. After the Second World War patterns of decolonization spurred analyses beyond Anglo-Saxon-style liberal democratic institutions. New patrimonialist regimes emerged in Africa and the Middle East, and populist ones in South America (Huntington 1968; O'Donnell 1973).

These divergent patterns could not be understood within the narrow categories of Western institutions. New categories and new concepts were required, as was more attention to other actors, such as revolutionary parties and clans under patrimonialistic leadership. The mobilization of the masses that took place in communist and fascist regimes in Europe, as well as under populism in South America, turned attention away from institutions toward ideologies, belief systems, and communication. This motivated comparativists to ask which were the favourable conditions for democratic stability, and thus to look into political cultures, social capital, and traditions of authority.[2]

Finally, the closer analysis of Europe also contributed to a shift away from the formal analysis of institutions. From the 1960s on, European comparative political scientists started to question the supposed 'supremacy'—in terms of stability and efficiency—of Anglo-Saxon democracies based on majoritarian institutions and homogeneous cultures. Other types of democracies were not necessarily the unstable democracies of France, Germany, or Italy. The analyses of Norway by Stein Rokkan (1966), Austria by Gerhard Lehmbruch (1967), Switzerland by Jürg Steiner (1974), Belgium by Val Lorwin (1966a, b), and the Netherlands by Hans Daalder (1966) and Arend Lijphart (1968a)—most published in Robert Dahl's influential volume *Political Oppositions in Western Democracies* (1966)—as well as Canada, South Africa, Lebanon, and India, all showed that politics worked differently than the Anglo-Saxon model.

Although ethnically, linguistically, and religiously divided, these societies were not only stable and peaceful but also wealthy and equal (most remarkably in the case of the Scandinavian welfare states). On the one hand, these new cases showed that *other types of democracies were viable.* Besides the 'Westminster' type of majoritarian democracy, these authors stressed the 'consociational' type with patterns of compromise between elites—rather than competition—'amicable agreement', and 'accommodation'—in short, *alternative practices of politics beyond formal institutions.* On the other hand, these new cases stimulated the investigation of the role of cleavages (overlapping vs. cross-cutting pluralism), as in the case of welfare economies, as well as the role of elite collaboration in the political economy of small countries, which later led to important publications (see e.g. Esping-Andersen 1990; Katzenstein 1985).

What have been the consequences of the broadening of the geographical and historical scope?

First, it increased the *variety of political systems.* Second, it pointed to the *role of agencies* other than institutions, in particular parties and interest groups, civil society organizations, social movements, and media (Almond 1978: 14). Third, it introduced a *new methodology* based on:

- the analysis of behaviour and roles based on empirical observation;
- many cases ('large-N'), i.e. extensive large-scale comparisons;
- statistical techniques for the analysis of large data sets;
- an extraordinary effort of systematic data collection (mostly quantitative),[3] the creation of data archives, combined with the introduction of computerization and machine-readable data sets.

Fourth, a new 'language', namely *systemic functionalism,* was imported in comparative politics. The challenge posed by the extension of the scope of comparison was to elaborate a conceptual body able to encompass the diversity of cases. Concepts, indicators, and measurements that had been developed for a set of Western cases did not fit the new cases. It also soon became clear that 'Western concepts' had a different meaning in other parts of the world. What Sartori has called the 'travelling problem' (Sartori 1970: 1033) is closely related to the expansion of politics and appears when concepts and categories are applied to cases different from those around which they had originally been developed.

The emphasis on institutions and the state was dropped because of the need for *more general and universal concepts.* Since the behavioural revolution we speak of political systems rather than states (Easton 1953, 1965a, b). Concepts were redefined to cover non-Western settings, pre-modern societies, and non-state polities. Most of these categories were taken from the very abstract depiction of the social system by Talcott Parsons (1968). These more general categories could not be institutions that did not exist elsewhere but their functional equivalents.

Functions dealing with the survival of systems were perceived as particularly important. From biology and

Box I.5 Important works in comparative politics: Tocqueville

Alexis Charles Henri Clérel de Tocqueville (1835) *De la Démocratie en Amérique* (On Democracy in America, Paris: C. Gosselin)

Although this book represents a 'case study'—an analysis of democracy in the United States—it is an example of comparison with an 'absent' case, i.e. France and, more generally, Europe. In his implicit comparison Tocqueville analyses the uniqueness of conditions in American society and geography that were favourable to the development of democracy. Tocqueville follows Montesquieu in going beyond public institutions to include social and cultural aspects. He speaks of aristocratic and democratic societies when comparing France with the US. Tocqueville was also strongly influenced by the use of naturalistic methods for political matters by Montesquieu.

cybernetics David Easton and Karl Deutsch (Deutsch 1966*a*, *b*) imported the idea of the *system*—ecological systems, body systems, and so on—and identified 'survival' as its most important function. Similarly, in the 1950s—still in the shadow of the dark memory of the breakdown of democratic systems between the two world wars through fascism and communism—the most important topic was to understand why some democracies survived while others collapsed. Almond and Verba's *The Civic Culture* (1963) is considered as a milestone precisely because it identified specific cultural conditions favourable or unfavourable to democratic stability.

... and back to institutions

It soon also became clear, however, that the price to be paid for encompassing transcultural concepts was an excessive level of abstraction. This framework was not informative enough and remote with regard to the concrete historical context of specific systems. In the 1970s European comparative political scientists like Rokkan, Lehmbruch, and others (and even more so area specialists from Eastern Europe, Latin America, Africa, and Asia) had already noted that the ahistorical categories of systemic functionalism did not allow the understanding of concrete cases. The chapter by Lipset and Rokkan on 'Cleavage structures, party systems, and voter alignments' (Lipset and Rokkan 1967) is the emblematic piece of research that puts history and context back in the equation.

The counter-reaction to systemic functionalism starts precisely in 1967 and involves (1) a shift of *substantial* focus, (2) a narrowing of *geographical* scope, (3) a change of *methodology*, and (4) a *theoretical turn* devoting greater attention to the rationality and strategies of actors (see Table I.1).

Bringing the state back in

The shift of substantial focus consists of a return to the state and its institutions (Skocpol 1985). In recent decades there has been a re-establishment of the centrality of institutions more broadly defined as sets of rules, procedures, and social norms. In the new-institutionalism theory (March and Olsen 1989; Hall and Taylor 1996; Thelen 1999; Ostrom 2007; Pierson and Skocpol 2002; Przeworski 2004) institutions are seen as the most important actors, with autonomy being part of real politics. Institutions, furthermore, are seen as determining the opportunity structures and the limits within which individuals formulate preferences.[4]

Grounded theory

The excessive abstraction of concepts in systemic functionalism was also countered by a return of attention to varying historical structures, cultural elements, and geographic location, in which the specific socio-economic context plays a central role (Thelen and Steinmo 1992). Rather than general universalistic theories, mid-range theories stress the advantages of case studies or in-depth analyses of a few countries.

Some authors argue that the reawakening of attention to the state and its institutions is in fact a consequence of this narrowing of geographical scope (Mair 1996). The general language introduced by systemic functionalism—and which nearly discarded the state and its institutions—was needed to encompass a greater variety of political systems. Institutions have recently been re-appreciated because of a closer focus. Systemic functionalism did not forget institutions; simply, they were 'absorbed upward into the more abstract notions of role, structure and function' (Mair 1996: 317). A regionally more restricted perspective giving up global

Table I.1 Comparative politics before and after the 'behavioural revolution'

Dimensions of analysis	Before	After
Unit	State	Political system
Subject matter	Regimes and their formal institutions, leadership	All actors in the process of decision-making
Cases	Major democracies: US, Britain, France; analysis of democratic breakdown in Germany and Italy; authoritarianism in Spain and Latin America	Objective extension of cases (decolonization) and subjective extension with spread of discipline in various countries
Indicators/ variables	West-centric, qualitative categories, typologies	Abstract concepts (functionalism); empirical universals, quantitative variables
Method	Narrative accounts and juxtapositions between cases	Machine-readable data sets and statistics; quasi-experimental comparative method
Data	Constitutional and legal texts	Survey and aggregate data
Theory	Normative: institutional elitism and pluralism; no elaborate conceptualization	Empirical: structural functionalism, systems theory, neo-institutionalism, rational choice

comparisons does not require the same level of abstraction of concepts. Therefore the shift of substantial focus is a consequence of less ambitious theoretical constructions. The change of substantial focus has been favoured by the narrowing of the geographical focus.

Case-oriented analysis

This narrowing of scope also entailed a methodological change. The counter-reaction to large-scale comparisons came from the development of methods based on few cases ('small-N') (see Ragin 1987). They revitalize today a type of comparative investigation that had long been criticized because few cases did not allow the testing of the impact of large numbers of factors—the problem that Lijphart (1971, 1975) named 'few cases, many variables'. This difficulty made the analysis of rare social phenomena, such as revolutions, impossible with statistical techniques. Hence the great importance of this 'new' comparative method. It provides the tool for analysing rigorously phenomena of which only few instances occur historically (see later in this Introduction and Chapter 3 for more details).

Rational choice theory

At the end of the 1980s another turn took place in comparative politics, strengthening further the place of institutions. It was the turn given by the increasing influence of rational choice theory in comparative politics.

Whereas the behavioural revolution primarily imported models from sociology, the turn at the end of the 1980s was inspired by developments in economics. In addition, the rational choice turn does not revolve around a redefinition of the political, for it applies a more general theory of action that applies equally well to all types of human behaviour, be it in the economic market, the political system, the media sphere, or elsewhere (Munck 2001; Tsebelis 1990).

This theory of action is based on the idea that actors (individuals but also organizations such as political parties) are rational. They are able to order alternative options from most to least preferred and then, through their choice, seek the maximization of their preferences (utility). For example, voters are considered able to identify what their interest is and to distinguish the different alternatives that political parties offer in their programmes with regard to specific policies. Voters then maximize their utility by voting for the political party whose policy promises are closest to their interests. It is rational for political parties to offer programmes that appeal to a large segment of the electorate as this leads to the maximization of votes.

It is clear from these premises that the place for 'sociological' factors on which the behavioural revolution insisted—such as socio-economic status and cultural traits—assume a lower key in rational choice models. These models have been crucial to understanding the behaviour of a number of actors. In the field of party politics, examples include work by Downs (1957), Przeworski (Przeworksi and Sprague 1986), and Cox (1997). Other examples include the work of Popkin (1979) on peasants in Vietnam, Bates (1981) on markets in Africa, Fearon and Laitin (1996) on ethnicity, Przeworski (1991) on democratization, Gambetta (1993, 2005) on the Mafia and suicide missions, and Acemoglou and Robinson (2006) on the origins of political regimes.

Rational choice theory in political science owes a lot to the work of William Riker. He is the founder of the 'Rochester School' (Riker 1990; see also Amadae and Bueno de Mesquita 1999). Today, rational choice theory comes in various forms and degrees of formalization. They range from 'hard' game-theoretical versions, in which the degree of mathematical formalization is very high, to 'softer' versions in which the basic assumptions are maintained but in which there is no formal theorizing. What is important to note is that the rational choice turn did not lead to a redefinition of comparative politics as a subject matter precisely because it does not offer a meta-theory that is specific to politics. The subject matter did not change under the impulse of rational choice theory. On the contrary, *it has reinforced the pre-eminence of institutions in comparative politics*. Rational choice institutionalism, in particular, sees institutions as constraints of actors' behaviour (Weingast 2002). An example of this approach is the concept of 'veto player' developed by Tsebelis (2002).

What is left?

As we have seen, there has been an almost cyclical process.[5] However, comparative politics did not simply return to its starting point.

1. Despite the recent narrowing of scope and the tendency to concentrate on 'grounded theories', the expansion that took place in the 1950s and 1960s left behind an extraordinary variety of topics. A glance at the Contents shows how many *features of the political system* are dealt with in comparative politics.

2. Also the great contribution made by the systemic paradigm has not been lost. We continue to speak of a political system and use this descriptive tool to organize the various dimensions of domestic politics. In fact, the structure and coverage of the book mirrors the political system as described by David Easton (see Figure I.1 and Box I.6). Easton's work is a monumental theoretical construction of the structural-systemic paradigm, still unrivalled and probably the last and most important attempt to build a general empirical theory including all actors and processes of political systems.

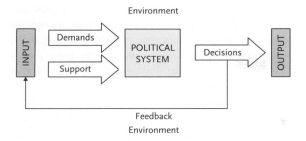

Figure I.1 The political system
Source: Easton (1965).

Easton's concepts have marked the minds of political scientists, as well as those of the wider public. His attempt has been an extremely systematic one, with subsequent and cumulative contributors drafted towards one single goal. His concept of *political system*, as a set of structures (institutions and agencies) whose decision-making function is to reach the collective and authoritative allocation of values (*output*, i.e. public policies) receiving support as well as demands (*inputs*) from the domestic as well as the international environment which it shapes through outputs in the *feedback loop*, includes all aspects of what is described in this book, from communication to culture, socialization and behaviour, interest articulation through parties, movements or pressure groups, institutions in democratic and authoritarian regimes, decision-making and policies, as well as the interaction with other systems—addressed in the last section of this book.

3. The substantive scope has not ceased to grow and this trend has continued over the most recent decades. As discussed in Chapter 1, there has been a change

Box I.6 Important works in comparative politics: Easton

David Easton (1953) *The Political System: An Inquiry into the State of Political Science* **(New York: Alfred A. Knopf)**

This volume is the first of a series of books by Easton on the political system. His work represents the most systematic and encompassing effort on the 'theoretical side' of the behavioural revolution. Scholars like David Easton and Karl W. Deutsch imported the notion of system from other scientific disciplines (biology and cybernetics). This notion soon replaced the formal concept of state and enlarged the field of comparative politics to non-institutional actors. The framework developed by Easton and his colleagues, and its conceptual components (input, output, feedback loop, black box, etc.), are common language today. Easton's work remains the last major attempt to develop a general empirical theory of politics.

in focus from 'input' processes to 'output' processes, namely public policies, policy-making, as well as the outcome and impact of policies. This is the reason why a specific section of this book is devoted to these topics. In particular, recent trends of 'what' is compared include industrial relations, trade, and economic policies (aspects stressed in Chapters 22 and 24), the reawakening of ethnic, religious, and nationalist movements, trends towards regionalization (aspects stressed in Chapters 11, 15, and 17), and the growing role of pressure groups (see Chapter 14).

New trends also include awareness of the interdependence between national systems (discussed below more extensively). Chapter 23 analyses the integration between member-states of the European Union, Chapter 24 addresses the blurring of national boundaries, and Chapter 25 shows how states influence others through democratic promotion and peacekeeping.

KEY POINTS

- Comparative politics is not limited to the comparison of national political systems but includes other units such as sub-national and supra-national organization, single political actors, processes, and policies.

- With the widening of the number of 'cases' (new states or other regions) the need for more general concepts that could 'travel' beyond Western countries led to a focus on functions rather than institutions. In the last two decades, however, a reaction against overly abstract analysis led back to 'grounded theories' limited in space and time.

- As for the behavioural revolution, rational choice also aims at a general and unified theory of politics applicable in all times and places. This paradigm was imported into political science from economics and stresses the role of institutions.

- Comparative politics includes as a subject matter all features of political systems and, recently, has turned its attention towards the interaction between them, approaching international relations.

The method of comparative politics

Having discussed the 'what' of comparison, we turn now to the 'how' of comparison.

A variety of methods

It should be stressed straight away that comparative politics does not rely on a specific method, for four main reasons.

1. Depending on the number of cases included in the analysis (say, two countries or 150), the type of data the analysis deals with (quantitative electoral results or qualitative typologies of administrative systems), and the time period covered (the most recent census or longitudinal trends since the mid-nineteenth century), the methods employed are different. The important point to note is that *the research method depends on the research question*. We address the problem and formulate the research question; then we look for the most appropriate data and methods to analyse it. The choice of cases very often depends on the research question: there are political phenomena that occur rarely, sometimes only once. As explained in Chapter 3, comparative politics may analyse *one single case* (a case study). Research designs can be more or less *intensive or extensive* (depending on the balance between the number of cases and the number of features analysed); they can be *synchronic or diachronic*. What matters is that the research method follows the research question.

2. The dimensions of comparison can be diverse. It is wrong to suppose that comparative politics is always cross-sectional, i.e. that it involves a spatial comparison between countries, areas, or groups of political systems. In fact, *spatial (cross-sectional)* comparison is only one of the possible dimensions of comparison. A second dimension of comparison is the *functional (cross-organizational or cross-process) comparison*. Take, as an example, the comparison of the liberal and the nationalist ideologies in Europe. Or the comparison of policy-making of environmental and military policies in, say, the US. Or the comparison of leadership in social movements such as the civic rights movement, the feminist movement, the green movement, and the pacifist movement. The dimension of comparison here is not territorial. A third dimension is the *longitudinal (cross-temporal) comparison*. We can compare institutions, actors, and processes over time rather than space as, for example, in the comparison of party organizations in the nineteenth century (cadre parties), after the First World War (mass parties), after the Second World War (catch-all parties), and since the 1980s (cartel parties).

3. *Units of analysis* can be diverse. As we have seen earlier, 'what' is compared can be either whole political systems or single actors, institutions, processes, or trends.

4. Comparative research designs can either focus on *similarities* or *differences*. Sometimes we ask questions about similar outcomes, such as 'why did social revolutions take place in France, Russia and China?' (Skocpol 1979) or 'why did democracy resist attacks from anti-system forces in some countries and not in others?' (Capoccia 2005). To explain similar outcomes we look for common factors (something that is present in all the cases in which the outcome occurred—either a revolution or a democratic breakdown) in cases which are otherwise very different from each other. As we will see in Chapter 3, John Stuart Mill called this research design the Method of Agreement (Przeworksi and Teune (1970) called it the 'Most Different Systems Design'). However, sometimes we use the Method of Difference (or 'Most Similar Systems Design'), in which we ask questions about different outcomes, such as 'why did Britain democratize early and Prussia/Germany late?' (Moore 1966). To explain different outcomes we look at factors that vary (something that is either present or absent in the case in which the outcome either occurred or did not—democracy) among otherwise similar cases. We also often combine these two methods.

From cases to variables ...

Comparative politics prior to the behavioural revolution was typically a discipline that compared few cases. Today, we speak of *'small-N'* research designs. As explained earlier, it was thought that the world would converge towards the Anglo-Saxon model of democracy and that, consequently, these were the cases that comparative political scientists should concentrate upon. Therefore the number of cases ('N') was limited to the US, Britain, France, and a few other cases such as Canada, sometimes Australia and New Zealand, and the 'failed' democracies of Germany or Italy.

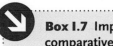

Box I.7 Important works in comparative politics: Lazarsfeld *et al.*

Paul Lazarsfeld, Bernard R. Berelson, and Hazel Gaudet (1944) *The People's Choice: How the Voter Makes up His Mind in a Presidential Campaign* (New York: Columbia University Press)

This book is a marvellous example of the use of statistical methods, and multivariate analysis of elections, public opinion, socialization processes, and communication through large data sets and the employment of rudimentary computing techniques. It is an application of the positivist approach to politics and has paved the way for countless studies of the determinants of people's vote: the crucial questions of what groups of people (classes, professions, age cohorts, gender, and so on) tend to turn out more often and for which parties they tend to vote. A follow-up volume entitled *Voting* (1954) pursued this line of research. This book is an example of the 'empirical side' of the behavioural revolution.

The behavioural revolution involved the widening of cases. On the one hand, this involved a much larger effort of *data collection*. Large data sets were created with the help of the incipient development of computer technology. On the other hand, this involved the need for comparability of indicators and, as it turned out, the most general 'language' was that of *quantities*. It is very difficult to establish whether or not civic culture, honour, patriotism, justice, etc. have the same meaning in different continents. However, it is possible to measure the number of cars, televisions, internet connections, or mobile telephones in all countries of the world. Both factors—the increasing number of cases and the quantification of indicators—led to the development of sophisticated *statistical techniques*, which became the dominant method. Therefore research designs based on a 'large-N' typically employ techniques such as multiple regression and factor analysis based on numerical coefficients which allow the causal association between political phenomena to be 'quantified'.

This trend turned attention away from cases and shifted it towards variables. *Intensive* research designs became *extensive*: many cases and few variables. Ragin (1987) defines the large-N research design as 'variable-oriented', implying that, with many cases, we ultimately know very little about the context of the countries. Not only did concepts become increasingly abstract in the search for the most general, most comparable, and most equivalent concepts, but the analysis itself referred increasingly to abstract relationships between variables (political phenomena). We would know that higher literacy levels are associated with higher turnout rates, but we would be ignorant about patterns in single countries.

Box 1.8 Important works in comparative politics: Downs

Anthony Downs (1957) *An Economic Theory of Democracy* **(New York: Harper & Collins)**

This is a small book (Downs's PhD dissertation) which had an enormous impact, showing the great potential of rational choice theory for the study of politics. It introduced economic models for the analysis of actors' behaviour as well as the deductive analytical rigour in comparative politics. Today, rational choice models are one of the dominant approaches in comparative politics. Although this approach had an impact in all fields of comparative politics, in the field of electoral studies it still remains one of the most important works, alongside that of Maurice Duverger and Giovanni Sartori, inspiring pioneering research such as that of Gary Cox on voting behaviour and the impact of electoral systems on politics.

... and back to cases

More recently there has been a return to 'small-N' and case-oriented research designs and, today, the comparative method is in fact equated with the qualitative techniques based on John Stuart Mill's Methods of Agreement and Difference and on the search for sufficient and necessary conditions. Theda Skocpol (1984), David Collier (1991), and, most prominently, Charles Ragin with his ground-breaking *The Comparative Method* (Ragin 1987), showed that rigorous empirical tests could also be carried out when the number of cases is small (for an overview see Caramani 2009).

This methodological shift stresses the intrinsic advantages of the study of few cases. Case-oriented scholars stress that small-N comparisons allow in-depth analyses in which configurations or combinations of factors are privileged in explanations. Cases are seen as 'wholes' rather than being divided into isolated variables. Constellations of factors represent the explanation rather than the impact of each factor individually.

This is a reaction against the first writings on the comparative method which advanced strong arguments precisely against configurative or combinatorial analyses in which a large number of potential explicative variables were listed (e.g. Przeworski and Teune 1970). On the contrary, the focus was on parsimonious explanatory designs, i.e. a few key variables whose impact should be tested on as many cases as possible. In two famous articles, Arend Lijphart (1971, 1975) suggested increasing the number of cases (e.g. by selecting several time points) and decreasing the number of variables by focusing on similar cases (thus reducing the number of factors that vary across them).

As we have seen, comparative methods developed in a period when social sciences were looking for a general language, i.e. theoretical and operative concepts that could be used without temporal or spatial limitations. Such a move implied 'replacing proper names with variables' (Przeworski and Teune 1970), defining concepts able to 'travel' (Sartori 1970), and using 'sets of universals' applicable to all political systems (Almond 1966a; Lasswell 1968). In addition, because of the small number of cases for many research questions, a parsimonious use of variables was also invoked. This has led to 'a strong argument against ... "configurative" or "contextual" analysis' (Lijphart 1971: 690) unable to give rise to generalizing statements. Thirty years later, a large part of the recent debates around methods in the social sciences has focused on the opposite reaction, namely a swing away from the variable-oriented approach towards 'thick' research designs.

Critiques of case-oriented approaches denounce a return to the past. As John Goldthorpe notes, this represents a revival of holism against which Przeworski and Teune (1970) had directed their work. In addition, even

Box I.9 Important works in comparative politics: Almond and Verba

Gabriel A. Almond and Sidney Verba (1963) *The Civic Culture: Political Attitudes and Democracy in Five Nations* (Princeton, NJ: Princeton University Press)

This book was the seminal attempt to make systematic use of individual-level data collected comparatively through survey techniques. It is a phenomenal effort of individual data collection and analysis, in the US, the UK, Germany, Italy, and Mexico, at the dawn of the computer age. Within the behavioural paradigm, it analyses the function of political culture in political systems and, in particular, the central role that the 'civic culture' plays in the survival of democratic political systems. This book opened the way to studies on values, trust, and social capital pursued most prominently by Ronald Inglehart and Robert Putnam.

if one concentrates on 'whole' cases, one still refers to selected features or attributes. Comparison can take place only when one compares cases' values of shared properties or attributes, i.e. variables (Goldthorpe 2000; see also Bartolini 1993: 137). The accusation is that we are going back to holism. And, again, we see a cyclical pattern in the *method* of comparative politics just as we did for its *subject matter*.

From aggregate to individual data ...

For a long time, the only available data were those collected as official statistics. The term 'statistics' itself goes back to the seventeenth century and the German School of Statistics. Etymologically, the term means 'science of the state' and its purpose is, as it were, to analyse *state* matters. Statistics started developing during the formation of the modern mercantilist nation-states and flourished in the course of the nineteenth century when the great economic transformations (industrialization) and population movements (urbanization) strengthened the need for states to monitor increasingly complex societies.

The same period saw the development of the liberal nation-state, which, as discussed in Chapters 4 and 8, increased its intervention in the society and economy, which was accentuated with the welfare state. To act, states needed knowledge of the society and economy they were supposed to steer. Democratization also gave a big push towards the development of statistics as governments became accountable; they had to perform, which involved a systematic collection of information. To meet this need, i.e. to increase their 'cybernetic

capacity' (Flora 1977: 114), techniques for gathering information greatly improved.

Primarily, statistics were collected for practical reasons linked to the economic and military action of governments. The contents of national statistics relate directly to the activity of the state: security and finance (military and criminal statistics, and statistics relating to income and expense items, taxation, and natural resources). With the growth of welfare states, the transformation of the population and health issues are monitored very closely: birth rates, mortality, health, and mental illness (often linked to crime statistics in the nineteenth century under the heading of 'moral' statistics or 'deviant' behaviour). As far as political statistics are concerned, they were usually included under juridical statistics. However, the presence of political statistics is however less common than that of other categories, in particular electoral statistics which are linked to democratization and attempts to legitimize regimes (see Caramani 2000: 1005–15).

The landmarks of this development have been the organization of censuses—every five or ten years depending on the country—and the establishment of the annual publication of statistical yearbooks. These often include statistics of neighbouring countries requiring a certain degree of standardization of information to allow for comparisons.

These data are called *aggregate data* because they are available at some territorial level: provinces, regions, countries. Typical aggregate data are election results. We never know how individuals vote because voting is secret. However, we have aggregates: the number of voters and the number of votes for parties and candidates in a constituency. These data can be aggregated into upper levels (regions or countries). Similarly, we often have data for unemployment rates, population density, and activity in a given sector (e.g. agriculture) for territorial units.

With the behavioural revolution the approach to data collection changed radically.

1. Scientific researchers became more sceptical about official statistics which, especially in non-democratic states, may be subject to *manipulation*. This concerns data on elections and all aspects of civil rights, but also data on economic performance (unemployment or GDP). Therefore the creation of large data sets by university researchers independent from politics is an important aspect of the behavioural revolution.

2. Official statistics do not include all variables of interest to researchers. On the one hand, official statistics do not include information on political actors. An example is data on political parties, their members, and their finances (very difficult to obtain and rarely reliable). On the other hand, official statistics do not include information on *individuals' values, opinions,*

attitudes and beliefs, competence and trust in political institutions, and differences between elites and masses in political preferences. Through official statistics we would not know whether an individual has authoritarian attitudes or post-material values, and whether he or she is strongly religious. Census data are the closest type of data on this information, but, first, they concern primarily households rather than individuals and, second, they do not include political data. We do not know, for example, what the party preference of a respondent is. The behavioural revolution introduced *surveys* as a systematic instrument to collect *individual data*. As Chapter 17 shows, political culture cannot be analysed without this type of data, which can be found throughout the world in surveys such as the World Value Survey, Eurobarometers, European Social Survey, Latinobarometers, etc.

3. The collection of individual data involved much larger data sets as thousands of individuals are included in a survey. This amount of data can be dealt with only through the *computerization of the social sciences* which began in the 1950s. The behavioural revolution involved the analysis of individual data through a new electronic computing technology. Certainly, in the past there had been examples of extraordinary data analysis without computers. Durkheim's *Le Suicide* (1897) is a breathtaking example of comparative multivariate analysis of a huge amount of data presented in tables and figures without the help of computers. Every social scientist should admire this effort. Yet, computerization put this type of analysis within the reach of all researchers, first through mainframe systems (usually in a university) and, in the late 1980s, through personal computers (PCs) and statistical software designed for them. Today every undergraduate student has Excel, SPSS, R, Stata, or other packages on his or her laptop.

4. The year 1950 proved to be devastating for analysis with aggregate data. This was the year when William S. Robinson published his famous article about 'ecological fallacy' (Robinson 1950). This article undermined the assumption that correlations observed at the level of aggregated units could be inferred at the individual level. Problems of ecological inference arise in the attempt to infer conclusions reached at the level of territorial units down to the individual level. Put simply, what is true on an aggregated level is not necessarily true at the individual level. Robinson showed that through aggregate data (based on counties and states in the US) there was a strong correlation between race and literacy, but this correlation disappeared when individual data were used. The effect of this article was disruptive, the term 'ecological fallacy' became popular, and for a long time analyses based on ecological data were discredited.

> **Box I.10 Important works in comparative politics: Rokkan**
>
> ### Stein Rokkan (1970) *Citizens, Elections, Parties* (Oslo: Universitetsforlaget)
>
> This book is a collection of previously published articles and chapters, complemented by unpublished bits and pieces, and conference papers by Stein Rokkan (who never wrote an authored monograph but preferred to work his writings over and over again). Nonetheless, Rokkan's work provides the most systematic comparative picture of a huge amount of empirical material on similarities and differences between countries in their patterns of state formation, nation-building, democratization, and the structuring of party systems and electoral alignments. In the tradition of 'comparative historical sociology' (with Reinhart Bendix, Otto Hintze, and Barrington Moore, among others), his work encompasses centuries of political development and has inspired generations of scholars such as Theda Skocpol and Charles Tilly.

... and back to aggregate data

The reaction to this 'shock' began almost immediately, with methodological work attempting to find solutions to 'ecological fallacy'. Conferences and meetings led to collective publications (see Merritt and Rokkan 1966; Dogan and Rokkan 1969; for recent discussions of ecological data analysis see Berglund and Thomsen 1990; King 1997; King *et al.* 2004).

Furthermore, the reaction to Robinson's blow to ecological data involved the creation of international networks for comparable 'hard data' worldwide. International data archives were set up. The most important ones today are the Inter-University Consortium for Political and Social Research (ICPSR) (at the University of Michigan), the Data Archive (at the University of Essex), the Mannheim Centre for European Social Research (MZES) (at the University of Mannheim), and the Norwegian Data Archive (at the University of Bergen). Data archives developed in all countries are linked together in a global network (see the Online Resource Centre). Such efforts led to major publications of aggregate data collections with documentation, most notably the three editions of the *World Handbook of Political and Social Indicators* (Russett *et al.* 1964; Taylor and Hudson 1972; Taylor and Jodice 1983), but also other projects (see the 'Yale Political Data Program'; Deutsch *et al.* 1966). These publications are updated today through the internet resources of the ICPSR.

International organizations such as the United Nations (UN), the World Trade Organization (WTO), the World Bank, the International Monetary Fund (IMF),

online resource centre

and World Health Organization (WHO), the Organization for Security and Co-operation in Europe (OSCE), and so forth also contributed to the creation of large comparative data sets with aggregate data in their sectors of competence. The Online Resource Centre provides all the links to these data sets.

online resource centre

But perhaps the main reason for a 'recovery' of ecological data analysis resides in the intrinsic weaknesses of individual-level data. It is more difficult to build long time series with individual data. Only aggregate data that we can collect from the beginning of the nineteenth century allow us to understand topics that need a long-term perspective. This was particularly true during the 1960s and 1970s when modernization approaches were used to understand newly decolonized countries. Panels—surveys carried out with the same group of respondents over protracted periods of time—are extremely costly (and, anyway, do not allow going 'back' in time). And the use of existing surveys for comparative purposes is not straightforward. Intelligence services, especially US ones, carried out a number of surveys in Europe after the Marshall Plan to investigate the public's attitudes, its favour of democratic values, and the potential of a communist menace or fascist return. However, these early studies are fragmented, with different questions asked and different groups or respondents.

Therefore aggregate data have not disappeared and sometimes provide more solid bases than individual-level data for international long-term comparisons.

Box I.11 Important works in comparative politics: Esping-Andersen

Gøsta Esping-Andersen (1990) *The Three Worlds of Welfare Capitalism* **(Cambridge: Polity Press)**

This is the book that best illustrates the shift in comparative politics from input to output and public policies. It presents a typology and an explanation of what can be considered the most encompassing of all public policies after the Second World War—the development of the welfare state as the latest stage in the construction of the modern nation-state and citizenship, where social rights complement political and civic rights (as distinguished by T. H. Marshall). This work is a prominent example among other large research programmes, namely on varieties of capitalism (e.g. Susan Strange's work), comparative political economy (e.g. Peter Hall), and welfare states (e.g. Peter Flora).

KEY POINTS

- Comparative politics employs statistical techniques when research designs include many cases and quantitative indicators (variable-oriented large-N studies), or 'comparative methods' when research designs include few cases and qualitative indicators (case-oriented small-N studies). Case studies can also be carried out in a comparative perspective.

- The dimensions of comparison are multiple: spatial, temporal, and functional.

- The purpose of comparative politics is descriptive, explanatory, and predictory. To this end research designs aim either at selecting similar cases and explaining their different outcomes (Most Similar Systems Designs, the 'Method of Difference'), or at selecting different cases and explain similar outcomes (Most Different Systems Designs, the 'Method of Agreement').

- Comparative politics relies on different types of data.

Conclusion

The variety of comparative politics

The great variety of approaches, methods, and data of comparative politics matches the great variety of the world's societies, economies, cultures, and political systems. At the end of this book we have inserted a number of 'Comparative tables' on various indicators. We have also inserted a number of 'Trends', figures which show how societies and political systems have changed over the recent decades. Readers will also find 'Country profiles', small files on political systems around the world.

The book rests on the principle that 'everything' is comparable. Large-scale comparisons through space and time in this book are based on the idea that there are no limits to comparison. Everything—i.e. any case in the world at any point in time—is, in principle, comparable. Analytical comparison never compares cases as such (say, countries) but rather properties (e.g. turnout levels) and their values for each case—whether turnout levels are high or low according to countries. Obviously, turnout applies only where there are democratic elections, so the level of generality and the spatial and temporal scope of the comparison of turnout is limited (there would be no point in analysing turnout in France under Louis XIV or in China today).

The nineteenth century witnessed what is probably the greatest change in the political organization of human societies with the rise of modern nation-states and democracies. There was no previous experience of mass democracy based on principles of fundamental equality between individuals, civic liberties, political rights, and open participation to the political process and to social welfare. The scope of this change was matched only by the Industrial Revolution during the same period. This is a unique period in our history and we should be aware of its exceptional character but also of its shortness. Therefore it is crucial to cover the development of the nation-state and mass democracy over nearly 200 years.

This Introduction to comparative politics has stressed the great variety of what is a huge field of study covering all aspects of domestic politics, with many areas of specialization and subdisciplines which are reflected in the chapters of *Comparative Politics*. The great variety—and the consequent specialization of the field—is the main reason why it is difficult to single out the most important books (see the various boxes scattered through this Introduction). Each subdiscipline has its 'classic' work: in the field of coalition formation, in that of the study of electoral systems, in that of the formation of modern nations, and so forth.

It is not only the broadness of its *substantial focus* of the topics that gives comparative politics a character of great variety. This variety also appears in the *research design* and in the *theoretical frameworks* we apply (see the five I's distinguished in Chapter 2). Today, this variety becomes even larger as comparative politics increasingly 'invades' the discipline of international relations (and vice versa). Yet, despite fragmentation and current changes towards the overlap with other disciplines, the intent of comparative politics is that of a rigorous scientific and empirical field of study: description, explanation, and prediction.

From divergence to convergence ...

Comparative politics was born out of diversity. There would be no comparative politics without the diversity of political systems and their features. The literature up to the 1950s assumed that there would be a *convergence* towards the model of the major Western liberal democracies. On the contrary, no convergence occurred; rather there has been *divergence* (in the form of alternative models of political order) and this has led to the actual development of comparative politics.

Is it still like that? Currently, trends towards convergence are very strong. The end of the Cold War in 1989 and the disappearance of the leading superpower that embodied one of the major alternative political models, the 'Third Wave' of democratization (the Arab Spring being its latest manifestation), the pressures towards market economy coming from world trade and globalization in a country like China, the numerous initiatives to 'export' and 'promote' democracy in Africa and Asia, democratic consolidation in Latin America—these are all patterns of worldwide convergence.

Thus the role of comparative politics is called into question in a world that is less and less diverse. What is the future of comparative politics in a globalized world? Comparative politics—like all 'quasi-experimental' methods—bases its explanations on the covariation between phenomena which, quite naturally, leads to a focus on *differences* between analytical cases. Yet, how does such a discipline deal with the existence of *commonalities*, patterns of *homogenization*, and *diffusion* effects? Furthermore, comparative politics was built on the methodological assumption that cases—i.e. national political systems—are independent of each other. It has been less concerned with common aspects and interactions.[6]

As Sørensen notes in Chapter 24, '[t]he standard image of the sovereign nation-state is that of an entity within well-defined territorial borders: a national polity, a national economy, and a national community of citizens', and on this premise researchers thought that they could 'safely ignore what takes place outside the borders of the countries they were studying'. Although comparative politics has also considered other types of states (city-states and empires), and although the behavioural revolution replaced the concept of 'state' with that of 'political system', for a long time its main concern has remained the study of the Westphalian territorial state.

However, it is increasingly difficult to maintain such a position and, indeed, the literature has addressed these issues. In recent years there has been a resurgence of interest in the so-called 'Galton problem', i.e. the methodological issue raised at the end of the nineteenth century by the polymath Francis Galton concerning associations between phenomena that are, in fact, the result of diffusion effects between cases. Contagion processes among cases violate the assumption of independence among units of analysis. Units of analysis are not isolated from one another. In temporal developments phenomena spread from one case to the other.

Today, most countries are open systems subject to external influences, borrowing and learning from the practices of others. For example, it is plausible to suppose that the development of welfare states in various countries (see Chapters 20 and 22) is affected by diffusion processes through policy transfers and policy learning. There is coordination when countries belong to overarching integrating organizations (the European Union, for example, as shown in Chapter 23) as well as cases of imposition by conquest, colonialism, and economic dependency (as discussed in Chapter 4, many current states were part of other states before secession). Finally, our current world, more than ever, experiences migrations (see Comparative Table 10 at the end of this volume).

The risk for comparative politics is—methodologically speaking—that of ending up with 'N = 1'. Already, Przeworski and Teune in their classic book on the comparative method have asked: 'How many independent events can we observe? If the similarity within a group of systems is a result of diffusion, there is only one independent observation' (Przeworski and Teune 1970: 52). Is our methodology fit to analyse common developments, changes without variation between cases, and situations of dependence between them? The problem obviously increases with transnationalization processes, amelioration of communication, spread of information, and acceleration of exchanges. In an increasingly interdependent world, comparative political scientists realize that social phenomena are not isolated and self-contained, but rather are affected by events occurring within other, sometimes remote, societies. Within a 'shrinking world' the problem is larger today than in the past.

... and back to divergence?

The last section of the book addresses precisely these questions with chapters on integration, globalization, and promotion of democracy in non-Western parts of the world. This is where comparative politics and international relations become contiguous and their efforts, in the future, will increasingly be common efforts.

Nonetheless, one should not forget that while there are signals of convergence and homogenization, there are also signals pointing in divergent directions. Examples include the renewed role that religion plays in some parts of the world, such as the Muslim areas, but also in the US; the emergence of alternative forms of neopopulist 'Bolivarian' democracies in Latin America, particularly in Bolivia, Ecuador, and Venezuela; differentiation at the sub-national level that points to the resurgence—as a parallel process to the weakening of the Westphalian nation-state caused by supra-national integration—of regionalist phenomena with ethno-linguistic support; also supra-national integration, where it takes place, occurs to different degrees and at different paces.

All this is to say that it is difficult to detect linear, or cyclical, developments in world politics over short periods of time and by looking at few cases only. This is one of the reasons why this book adopts a long-term perspective from the beginning of modern politics—the formation of national states, mass democracies, and industrialization in the nineteenth century—as well as a broad cross-country perspective. The French expression *reculer pour mieux sauter* (to step backwards in order to jump further) was a favourite of Stein Rokkan, one of the founding pioneers of comparative politics. To have a firm ground for looking at the future fits very well with the philosophy of this book as well.

 Further reading

'Classics' of comparative politics are shown in the boxes in this Introduction. These books should be on every comparative political scientist's shelves.

Overviews of the discipline

Blondel, J. (1999) 'Then and Now: Comparative Politics', *Political Studies*, 47(1): 152–60.

Daalder, H. (1993) 'The Development of the Study of Comparative Politics', in H. Keman (ed), *Comparative Politics* (Amsterdam: Free University Press), 11–30.

Dalton, R. J. (1991) 'Comparative Politics of the Industrial Democracies: From the Golden Age to Island Hopping', in W. Crotty (ed.), *Political Science* (Evanston, IL: Northwestern University Press), 15–43.

Eckstein, H. (1963) 'A Perspective on Comparative Politics, Past and Present' in H. Eckstein and D. E. Apter (eds), *Comparative Politics: A Reader* (New York: Free Press), 3–32.

Mair, P. (1996) 'Comparative Politics: An Overview', in R. E. Goodin and H.-D. Klingemann (eds), *A New Handbook of Political Science* (Oxford: Oxford University Press), 309–35.

Rogowski, R. (1993) 'Comparative Politics', in A. W. Finifter (ed.), *Political Science: The State of the Discipline* (Washington, DC: American Political Science Association), 431–50.

Schmitter, P. (1993) 'Comparative Politics', in J. Krieger (ed.), *The Oxford Companion to Politics of the World* (Oxford: Oxford University Press), 171–7.

Verba, S. (1985) 'Comparative Politics: Where Have We Been, Where Are We Going?', in H. J. Wiarda (ed.), *New Directions in Comparative Politics* (Boulder, CO: Westview Press), 26–38.

Recent treatments of comparative politics as a discipline

Almond, G. A. (1990) *A Discipline Divided: Schools and Sects in Political Science* (Newbury Park CA:, Sage).

Chilcote, R. H. (1994) *Theories of Comparative Politics: The Search for a Paradigm Reconsidered* (2nd edn) (Boulder, CO: Westview Press).

Chilcote, R. H. (2000) *Comparative Inquiry in Politics and Political Economy* (Boulder, CO: Westview Press).

Landman, T. (2007) *Issues and Methods in Comparative Politics: An Introduction* (2nd edn) (London: Routledge).

Lichbach, M. I., and Zuckerman, A. S. (1997) *Comparative Politics: Rationality, Culture, and Structure* (Cambridge: Cambridge University Press).

Peters, B. G. (1998) *Comparative Politics: Theory and Methods* (Basingstoke: Macmillan).

Wiarda, H. J. (ed.) (2002) *New Directions in Comparative Politics* (3rd edn) (Boulder, CO: Westview Press).

Reference work

Boix, C., and Stokes, S. C. (2007) *Oxford Handbook of Comparative Politics* (Oxford: Oxford University Press).

See also the other titles in the *Oxford Handbooks of Political Science* series. For specific topics see the 'Further reading' section at the end of each chapter.

Scientific comparative politics research publishes results in a number of specialized journals. The most important scientific journals with a focus on comparative politics are the following: *Comparative Politics, Comparative Political Studies, Comparative European Politics, European Journal of Political Research, West European Politics*, among others.

In addition, most countries have political science journals that publish research in comparative politics. Examples include *American Political Science Review, British Journal of Political Science, Revue Francaise de Science Politique, Scandinavian Political Studies, Politische Vierteljahresschrift, Irish Political Studies, Australian Journal of Politics and History, Swiss Political Science Review*.

Finally, for each subject (elections, parties, communication, etc.) there are specialized journals which include comparative work. Examples are: *Party Politics, Electoral Studies, European Journal of Public Policy, Local Government Studies, Publius: The Journal of Federalism, Journal of Common Market Studies, Journal of Democracy, Democratization, Journal of European Social Policy, Media, Culture and Society*, and *Political Communication*.

online resource centre

For additional material and resources, please visit the Online Resource Centre at:
http://www.oxfordtextbooks.co.uk/orc/caramani3e/

Theories and methods

CHAPTER 1

The evolution of comparative politics

Klaus von Beyme

Chapter contents

Reader's guide

The history of comparative politics shows that the discipline as a scientific enterprise is fairly recent. Machiavelli in the pre-modern era came closest to a modern social science approach. In the nineteenth century the predominance of historicism was not favourable to comparison. John Stuart Mill was the first to differentiate between Methods of Agreement and Difference. In the period of modern comparative politics there were two approaches to comparison: one, ranging from Durkheim to systems theory, thought that all social sciences are comparative; the other school, in the wake of Max Weber, developed a comparative method based on a hermeneutic approach of 'understanding'. The value-free approach to comparison was challenged when policies, the result of political decision-making, were analysed and considered as more important than the institutional setting which favoured certain decisions. The chapter also shows that comparative politics has been shaped by many influences from historical events.

Introduction

The evolution of comparative politics has been classified in stages, such as the 'pre-paradigmatic phase' which was not dominated by a single theoretical approach in the scientific community, and the 'paradigmatic phase', in which the scientific community adhered to a dominant theory. According to this classification (Chilcote 1994: 58) the paradigmatic phase is followed by a 'crisis phase' and finally ends up in a 'phase of scientific revolution', which occurs when the scientific community shifts to different paradigms. More important, perhaps, are the three approaches to comparative political theory which have developed since the early modern times.

However, Kuhn's frequently abused term 'paradigm' is hardly applicable in this context. Most phases in the evolution of political science have been 'pre-paradigmatic' in the sense that no single approach predominated completely. Chilcote is aware that his subdivision into 'traditional', 'behavioural', and 'post-behavioural' approaches does not precisely fit Kuhn's definition of paradigms. Only the dominance of the 'behavioural revolution' came close to the idea of a paradigm which conquered the community and tolerated deviant approaches only in marginal positions. But the typology is ethnocentric in so far as it generalizes American development. The behavioural approach was never dominant in Europe. In this chapter, I prefer a threefold classification for the evolution of comparative politics, with stages such as 'pre-modern' (or 'early modern'), 'modern', and 'post-modern'.

Table 1.1 shows the three main traditions of comparative theory in politics: two are actor-oriented, and one is systems-oriented. The three approaches correspond to the general categories of *macro-theories*, *meso-theories*—which represent the mainstream of theories in political science—and *micro-theories*.

> ### KEY POINTS
>
> - It is difficult to describe the evolution of comparative politics as a sequence of paradigms (even in the case of the behavioural revolution; see the Introduction to this volume).
> - The evolution of comparative politics follows the pre-modern, modern, and post-modern sequence.

Comparative politics in pre-modern times

The pre-modern stage, or the traditional approach to comparison since Aristotle, was highly speculative and normative; mostly ethnocentric, it used comparison in an anecdotal way, but hardly ever attempted a systematic comparison over time. Political science is the youngest social science in terms of modern professional performance. Comparative political science owes a lot to other sciences: philosophy since Aristotle, legal constitutionalism from Bodin to Bryce, and political economy from Smith, Ricardo, Bentham, Marx, and Mill. Mill was especially fruitful in methodology. In the nineteenth century 'sociology'—a term coined by Auguste Comte—was added and soon became important in helping political science liberate itself from jurisprudence and be transformed into a 'social science'.

During the Renaissance Machiavelli came close to a social science approach, minimizing the philosophical normativism of former times. Later comparisons were sometimes used to criticize one's regime, disguised under the description of distant systems, as in Montesquieu's *Lettres Persanes* (1721), or even utopian constructions of systems such as in the *Oceana* (1656) of James Harrington. One of the earliest and most complete comparisons was the work of Traiano Boccalini (1614: 1), a follower of Machiavelli. In his *Ragguagli di Parnaso* a 'university of politicians' was summoned by Apollo on Mount Parnassus and had to give responsible answers concerning their various political systems. Despite many insights, this work was distorted by a blind hatred of the 'imperialist power' of that time, the Spanish monarchy, which according to Boccalini interfered too much in Italian affairs.

Many historical comparisons in early modern times—from Machiavelli's *Discourses on the First Ten Books of Titus Livius* (1513) to Montesquieu's *Considérations sur les Causes de la Grandeur des Romains et de leur Décadence* (1734)—were rather ahistorical confrontations of Roman experiences and the life of modern states. Reasons for the decay of the Roman Empire were popular as a kind of normative warning for modern states. The diachronic comparisons treated various systems like contemporary societies, but they did not help to develop a critical methodology of comparison.

The evolutionist counter-reaction to the French Revolution was also unfavourable for a scientific theory of comparison. History in the nineteenth century turned increasingly to historicism, and the discipline developed more reservations to the comparative method than former political theories in the age of Enlightenment. Every historical event and development was declared 'unique'. Indeed, Goethe said 'only blockheads compare'—but he had only works of art and literature in mind. Goethe was afraid that mediocre connoisseurs might avoid a value judgement about works of art. This was indeed a permanent danger of the comparative sciences in many fields: relativism describing various historical solutions led neither to a conclusion nor even to a prediction about possible future historical developments.

Table 1.1 Approaches to comparative political theories

	Teleological historical theories	Actor-oriented institutionalism	Behaviour-oriented theories
	Macro-level	**Meso-level**	**Micro-level**
Early modern periods	Hegel Comt Spencer Marx	Machiavelli Montesquieu Constant Tocqueville *Legalistic institututionalism* Mohl Bryce Duguit Jellinek Burdeau	*Economic theories* Adam Smith Ricardo Turgot *Utilitarianism* Bentham Mill

Classical modernity	*Systems theories*
	
	Durkheim
	Parsons
	
	Functionalism
	Easton
	
	Historical sociology
	Eisenstadt
	Linz
	Rokkan
	Bendix
	Apter
		Institutions *groups*
		           Bentley
		           Truman
		Weber *elites*
		Friedrich Pareto
		Finer Mosca
		Duverger Michels
		Theories of democracies
		Theories of totalitarianism
		
		Transition theories
			Behaviouralism
			
			Almond
			Verba
			Eulau
			
			Public choice
			
			Downs
			Buchanan
			Riker
			Olson

Post-modern approaches	*Autopoietic systems theories* Maturana Luhmann Foucault	*Governance theories* *Network theories*	

Otto Hintze, with his comparative typologies, was an outsider in his discipline of German history. Troeltsch (1922 [1961]: 191), another social-science-oriented historian, accepted comparisons only when they kept their 'methodological and heuristic character' at the level of building of hypotheses. This was consistent with older pioneers of the historical method, such as Droysen (1858 [1969]: 163), who knew already that without implied comparisons no meaningful hypothesis could be found in an ocean of facts and motivations among historical actors. American history in the twentieth century, with Barrington Moore, Charles Tilly, Theda Skocpol, and many others, led the anti-historicist counter-reaction and gave up the anti-comparative bias of historicist historiography.

Since Tocqueville (1961: 5, 12) there had been a widespread assumption that a new world under conditions of modernization needs a 'new political science', able to work on certain social developments which were likely to spread in all modern societies. The US was only a pretext to denounce the threats of equalization and democratization which were likely to spread also in Europe. Even a pioneer of comparative methods such as John Stuart Mill (1840, 1859: 62) in the *Edinburgh Review* resented that his friend Tocqueville in his seminal book 'has bound up in one abstract idea the whole of tendencies of modern commercial society, and given them one name—democracy'. This was an important precedent in the history of book reviews, criticizing the remains of a teleological approach to the evolution of comparative politics.

In pre-modern political theories certain features of the decision-making process in polities were mostly deducted as constant types, but hardly ever scientifically analysed as politics. The policies were still more rarely investigated. Some utopias, such as Harrington's *Oceana* (1656), represented a notable exception. The theory of the 'reason of state' of Machiavellians like Giovanni Botero (1589 [1948]: 58ff.)—which represented a kind of 'Jesuit welfare-Machiavellism'—went far beyond Machiavelli's obsession with foreign and military policies in so far as he developed the elements of domestic welfare policies in different states as the main criterion for political stability.

Pre-modern comparisons mostly aimed at classifications of whole political orders (**polity**). Only in modern times was **politics** compared when the techniques of ruling in theories of 'reason of the state' or 'sovereignty' were discussed after Machiavelli. Comparisons were rather simple typologies, such as those counting the number of rulers. Many of them contained normative assumptions. The characteristic features were not always logically consistent, such as Montesquieu's classification of monarchy, republic, and despotism. Voltaire mocked this typology, which appeared to him as logical as the categories of a 'church registration of births', containing the elements: 'male', 'female', and 'illegitimate'.

Pre-modern approaches in the nineteenth century 'modernized' by turning away from static ontological classifications to historical theories of evolution. The most influential models were the evolutionary model of Darwin and the historical materialism of Marx, with his historical stages. In comparative social science the two extremes were sometimes synthesized as in the evolutionary model of Herbert Spencer. The three authors presented approaches to theory-building: Darwin's was a kind of early 'functionalism', Marx adopted the dialectical method from Hegel, and Spencer established himself as a precursor of systems theory. Since John Stuart Mill (1843 [1959]: 253) the logic of social science implied two methods, the Method of Agreement and the Method of Difference. The first method was a kind of 'artificial experiment' and the second method was to be applied in situations where experiments were unfeasible. Early comparisons in the pre-modern era were obsessed with finding similarities. Only in the twentieth century was the primacy of the Method of Difference increasingly developed.

KEY POINTS

- Pre-modern comparative politics was speculative, normative, and anecdotal. The boundaries with philosophy, jurisprudence, and history were not clearly defined.

- Machiavelli, Montesquieu, and Tocqueville come close to founding a modern comparative political science. This was acknowledged by John Stuart Mill when establishing his Methods of Agreement and Difference.

- Polities, rather than politics and policies, were described. The main goal of these analyses was to establish classifications and typologies. Very often these classifications concerned evolutionary models (derived from Darwinism), as in the cases of Spencer and Marx.

Comparative politics in modern times

Scientific comparison as controlled experiment

There is no agreement as to when modernity starts. In art and literature it is often located earlier in the nineteenth century. In the social sciences modernity is scheduled later. The criteria of definition—a truly scientific theory which can be controlled empirically—offer a more precise proof for modernity than works of art. In order to avoid quarrels of definition we should use the term *classical modernity* for the new social sciences in the twentieth century.

Classical modernity coincides largely with the establishment of separate disciplines in the social sciences, such as sociology and political science. In the nineteenth century the neighbouring social sciences, such as public law, political economy, or general history, still claimed to deal with politics in the evolution of modernization and specialization. In the twentieth century they withdrew from comparative politics. 'Comparative economics' continued to exist as a subfield, but it never played the dominant role of comparative politics in political science because of the mathematical character of the most influential economic models.

The German *Staatslehre* (theory of state), located in law departments, had a certain influence among the founding fathers of American political science, such as Francis Lieber, a Prussian refugee who taught at Columbia University. But the second generation of American scholars, including Woodrow Wilson, already abhorred general theories of the state. A pioneer of group theory, such as Arthur F. Bentley (1908, 1949: xix), after studies in Berlin and Freiburg, turned away from the 'spooks in the grain fields' which he discovered in the metaphysical-minded *Staatslehre*. On the basis of American pragmatism he developed in Chicago an extremely anti-state theory of politics. Groups, instead of states, were now the basic concept of comparative analysis. Former deductive elements of comparison were substituted by inductive observations. In Europe, British guild socialism and Harold Laski created an equivalent of an empirical political theory directed against the 'statism' of continental political theory.

Among the 'evolutionists' of the nineteenth century, Spencer was the most influential thinker for empirical comparative politics. But, despite his variation of a systems theory, the founder of structural–functional systems theory, Talcott Parsons (1968: 3), opened his theory of action with an attack: 'Spencer is dead, but who killed him and how?' Spencer was not killed, but increasingly forgotten—as were most of the theories of historical stages in the nineteenth century, especially Auguste Comte. Parsons tried to smooth down his verdict in a footnote: 'Not, of course, that nothing in his thought will last. It is his social theory as a total structure that is dead.' Critical rationalism of the neopositivist school of Karl Popper was later keen on 'hunting' what it called 'historicism'. Charles Merriam and other founders of political science in the US were more tolerant and recognized at least a certain progress because this kind of historicism was 'historical–comparative' and no longer normative and purely deductive like the traditional, mainly anecdotal, comparisons in the classical political literature.

The various approaches had some assumptions in common, even if Durkheim, Weber, and Pareto, for Parsons (1968) the champions of modern social science, differed in many ways. Oddly enough they did not relate to each other—though all three were able to read the language of the two others. Historical factors, which Darwin (biological struggle for life) or Marx (class conflict grounded on the contradiction between the economic base and the political superstructure) saw as the driving force behind the evolution, were no longer accepted. But nevertheless a 'dominant variable' was behind the modern evolution: for Weber it was occidental rationalism and bureaucracy, for Durkheim it was the division of labour, leading to a kind of 'organic solidarity', and for Pareto it was the cycles of rise and decay of elites.

Despite these differences there are four principles common to all thinkers of classical modernism.

1. *History is not identical with evolution.* There is no longer a telos, a final point towards which the evolution is aiming. In so far as political theory has to give up the old normative idea, *historia magistra vitae*, history can no longer serve as a teacher for later generations.

2. *Theory and practice are divided.* The scholar is not obliged to take political action, as was still the case in the theories of Marx and Engels. This did not prevent Pareto and Weber from standing as candidates for parliamentary election. Fortunately for the progress of social science, they failed. Anti-normative value-free science was discovered as a protection against the interference of the state as well as against the demands of political groups which consider scholars close to their ideologies. There is no longer the hope for a 'philosopher king' who combines knowledge and political action.

3. *Subsystems are autonomous* The spheres of life and subsystems of the social system are separate and autonomous. There is no hope that the political system—as in the times of absolutism—will be able to steer the subsystems of the whole society. With totalitarian ideologies this kind of hope was renewed, until the dictatorships collapsed between 1949 and 1989. Carl Schmitt was probably the most influential political theoretician who tried, in a heroic turn back to 'revolutionary conservatism', to re-install 'political decision' in its primordial rights in society. The driving force behind this was that Schmitt was afraid of a lasting dominance of the economy in society. Especially after the failures of dictatorship, political theory reduced its claims and renounced the primacy of the political subsystem.

4. *Science is guided by theory.* Value-free science should be comparative and theory-guided, not just an enumeration and typology of institutions as in the works of some pioneers of 'comparative government'—as the new discipline was initially called by scholars from James Bryce to Carl J. Friedrich.

Typologies are the initial stage of theory-building in order to develop a hypothesis for empirical work. Some typologies claimed to be a theory. Theories contain generalizations about political reality; typologies are abstractions about political reality according to some formal criteria. Some theories were close to one approach, such as functionalism (see Chapter 2). In other cases a methodology such as the behaviouralist approach tried to gain the status of a monopolistic theory. In recent times rational choice showed similar tendencies. Some typologies were comparative only in an indirect way. Even Max Weber's typology of types of legitimate rule—traditional, charismatic, and rational or legal–bureaucratic rule—are not free of remainders of the old debate on 'uniqueness vs. comparability' because the ideal types contained elements of uniqueness as 'individual totalities'. The ideal types served to elaborate the special features of social institutions. Only in the time of classical modernity were typologies of dynamic processes offered. However, historical research continued to suspect such taxonomies as they were developed in Crane Brinton's *Anatomy of Revolutions* (1937).

We should not identify the modern breakthrough to scientific comparisons with behaviourism, as sometimes occurs in American literature. Even the broader and less rigid form of 'behaviouralism'—which dominated for a while the torchbearers of modern political science in the 1950s and 1960s—was soon combined with other approaches, such as functionalist system theories. Functional considerations were not completely compatible with the strictly individualistic assumptions of behaviourism.

This contradiction can be shown in the seminal research on *The Civic Culture* by Almond and Verba (1963: 52, 68). The authors had some misgivings as to whether the uses of comparative survey studies would allow the 'uniformity of a psychological type' to be discovered in a whole country. In order not to distort the results, a concentration was recommended on the behaviour or attitudes that are least determined by the structure of the situation. Behaviouralism started from a rather mechanistic stimulus-response model of behaviour; functionalism was closer to organic models. Systems theory is holistic and presupposes 'purposes' of a system which was speculative for many behaviouralists. But, in practice, neither systems theory nor behaviouralism stayed completely dogmatic, so that a cooperation of various methodological tenets was possible.

Beyond the general meta-theoretical consensus of all empirical scholars in political science, behaviouralism developed major tenets, as David Easton classified them in his *Framework for Political Analysis* (1965a: 7).

- Regularities or uniformities in political behaviour should be expressed in generalizations or theory.
- The validity of these generalizations has to be tested. Contrary to Popper's orthodoxy, which admitted only falsification, verification was possible.
- Techniques of seeking and interpreting data have to be developed.
- Quantification and measurement in the recording of data.
- Values as distinguished between propositions relating to ethical evaluation and those relating to empirical explanation.
- 'Pure science', or the seeking of understanding and explanation of behaviour before utilization of knowledge for solution of societal problems.
- Integration of political research with that of other social sciences.

Only when political science was well established in American universities did 'comparative politics' develop its dominant position, in theory-building of the discipline as well as in the evaluation of the ranks of individual scholars in the scientific community. American and German rankings since Somit and Tanenhaus (1964: 66) and Falter and Klingemann (1998) have shown that comparative scholars had the highest reputations among their colleagues. In American political science after 1945, seven scholars among the top ten were in comparative politics, two in theory, and one in international politics. In the German case there was only one scholar in the field

of international relations among the top ten in political science. All the rest—mostly Americans, one Italian, one Dutch, and one German—were scholars in comparative politics (see Table 1.2).

Thanks to a new world situation, the development of the 'Third World' and modernization theories which dealt with the transition from traditional societies to modern democracy, the main theoretical innovations in political science were developed by comparative scholars. Only political science has accommodated the comparative aspects in a special subfield. However, the existence of a subdiscipline, 'comparative politics', was not uncontested in the organized discipline. There was never a dominant behavioural stage of comparative politics as postulated by Chilcote (1994: 56).

From *sociology*—in methodological questions far more sophisticated—political science inherited two traditions.

1. The historical–institutional tradition of Max Weber was comparative. Weber almost excessively looked in all the great cultures of the world for comparable elements, especially in his sociology of religions.

2. The opposite school was initiated by Herbert Spencer and led by Emile Durkheim (1950: 137). He opposed a subdiscipline of 'comparative sociology' because comparison for him was *la sociologie même* (sociology itself). Systems theory joined this opinion with various degrees of intensity, most vehemently the autopoietic variant of Niklas Luhmann (1970: 25, 46) who tried to go beyond Talcott Parsons' structural–functional theory.

From *economics*—in mathematical questions far more sophisticated—political science inherited formal modelling. In economics the former historical orientations were increasingly substituted by mathematical models. One branch of political science took over this kind of approach. Anthony Downs gave the prediction abilities of political theory priority over its capacity to describe the political reality: 'Theoretical models should be tested primarily by the accuracy of their predictions rather than by the reality of their assumptions' (Downs 1957: 21).

Comparative politics has been particularly embarrassed by its failure to predict any major political events since 1945. The student rebellions of the 1960s, the oil crisis, the rise of new fundamentalism, the collapse of communism of 1989—all these events came as a surprise to comparative political scientists. Some forecasts were correct, such as the possible end of the Soviet Union, but the prediction was based on the wrong reasons, such as a Chinese–Soviet war in the bestseller by Amalrik (1970). Forecasting had to lower its ambitions. In forecasting short-term electoral results the discipline boasts of only 5 per cent margins of error. Many political scientists came to accept that macro-theoretical predictions are little more than informed guesswork. The evolution can only be reconstructed *ex post facto* (post-diction).

Table 1.2 Ranking of influential political scientists

US ranking by Somit and Tanenhaus (1964)			German ranking by Falter and Klingemann (1998)		
Rank	Author	Discipline	Rank	Author	Discipline
1	Key	CP	1	Huntington	CP and IR
2	Truman	PT	2	Lipset	CP
3	Morgentau	IR	3	Lijphart	CP
4	Dahl	CP and PT	4	Keohane	IR
5	Lasswell	CP and PT	5	Dahl	CP and PT
6	Simon	CP	6	Almond	CP
7	Almond	CP	7	Schmitter	CP
8	Easton	CP and PT	8	Linz	CP and PT
9	Strauss	CP	9	Sartori	CP and PT
10	Friedrich	CP	10	von Beyme	CP and PT

CP = comparative politics; IR = international relations; PT = political theory.

The 'most similar design' of comparison was still widespread, but some researchers preferred a 'most different system design' (Przeworski and Teune 1970: 31ff.; see also Chapter 3). In historical perspective the similarities were mostly demonstrated by the diffusion of institutions, a method widely applied in anthropology. Systems theory, on the contrary, looked for dissimilarities which were able to serve as 'functional equivalents' in various systems with sometimes 'similar results'. Only the post-modernist Luhmann went as far as to claim that the one-party state in communist systems was a functional equivalent of the pluralist democratic party regimes in the West.

Typologies and classifications: the first step to comparison

There is a large consensus that the main purpose of comparative research is not comparing but explaining. Comparison is a tool for building empirically falsifiable explanatory theories. A first step is a rigid classification. 'Miscomparing' starts from 'misclassification', 'concept stretching', and what Sartori (1991: 248) called 'degreeism'. This neologism meant the replacement of dichotomous treatment by continuous notions. According to Sartori, classification by degrees leads to logical messiness. Premodern and some modern typologies do not live up to these rigid criteria. The predicaments of typological work as a base for comparison show that systems theories are frequently characterized by geometrical obsessions of order, while institutional typologies follow arithmetic intentions. Religious remainders invade typologies: trinities are discovered everywhere (see Table 1.3).

These trinities do not violate Sartori's verdict against 'degreeism', but logically we would prefer dual typologies,

Table 1.3 Typologies in comparative social sciences

Authors	Types
Historical types	
Comte	Theological era
	Metaphysical era
	Positive era
Morgan	Wildness
	Barbarianism
	Civilization
Engels	Communist original society
	Exploiting society (slavery, feudalism, capitalism)
	Communism
Theoretical types	
Weber	Traditional rule
	Charismatic rule
	Rational rule
Almond	Absolute value orientation
	Traditional style
	Pragmatic bargaining style
	Subject political culture
Almond and Verba	Parochial political culture
	Participant political culture
Duverger	Party cells and militia
	Traditional electoral committee of notables
	Mobilized party organized in sections
Apter	Mobilization developing regime
	Consociational developing regime
	Modernizing developing regime

such as those of Spencer (society of warriors/industrial society), Durkheim (mechanical/organic solidarity), Tönnies (community/society), and Bagehot (dignified/efficient parts of the constitution). If more than three elements are put into one taxonomy, the danger that the theoretical value is reduced to a kind of checklist cannot be excluded. Remainders of a teleological typology are frequently found in trinitarian classifications. The third element is quite often hailed as the normatively desired type in the development.

The problem of different criteria in classifications of types of regime was not always solved—not even in modern typologies. Probably the last scholar who tried to classify all the regimes in history—from anarchy and tribal rule to totalitarian dictatorships—was Carl J. Friedrich (1963: 188–9). He listed thirteen types of rule, but they lacked a common criterion of classification. Some regimes were characteristic of early societies; others were only minor institutional variations of representative government such as presidential or parliamentary systems. Some regimes, such as types of dictatorship, were classified not by their institutional characteristics, but by the extent of control over the citizens. For a while in formal sociology there was a tendency to classify outrageously, as in the treatises of Georges Gurvitch in France or Leopold von Wiese in Germany. In political science this happened only occasionally in the classification of regimes. Classifications of regime types should not reinvent Greek notions, as Küchenhoff (1967) did, but rather try to find a common-sense solution in terms which are accepted by scholars as well as by the public debate.

Excessive preoccupation with terminological clarity revealed a predicament: neologisms, mostly in Greek or Latin, reduced terminological ambiguities, but they had no chance of entering the public debate. Political science terminology is imbued with traditional perceptions of politics and can hardly proceed like chemistry or medicine in preserving purely scientific jargon. As an example of this predicament we might consider the type of a 'semi-presidential system' (see Chapter 5). The term is not quite correct, because a system with a popularly elected president remains a variation of a parliamentary system: parliament can topple the government by votes of non-confidence and the president can dissolve the chambers. But Duverger's (1988) expression was accepted in the scientific community. In popular debates, however, 'presidial' or even 'presidential government' still occurs for this type of representative government. A survey has shown that as many as 6 per cent of German deputies wrongly classified the German parliamentary system.

The problem of miscomparing by misclassification has been overcome by the construction of fourfold matrices which allow at least two classificatory elements (close to a typology of Arend Lijphart (1984)) to be put into relation to each other and to subsume various countries in four fields (Figure 1.1).

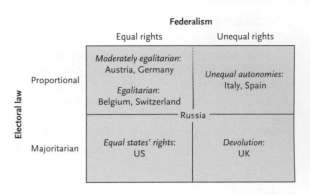

Figure 1.1 Institutional mix for the mitigation of territorial conflicts

The more complex such a matrix, the more comparative scholars have to be aware that such instant pictures can change quickly. For instance, since the institutionalization of parliaments for Scotland and Wales, British devolution has developed in the direction of Spain—with the exception of electoral law. If a proportional electoral system is one day accepted even for British elections—under pressure from the European Union—the whole type might shift to a top quarter of the matrix. Russia, with its mixed type of an electoral law and with different levels of equality of the rights of the federal units lies somewhere in between the four fields of the matrix.

From the comparisons of 'polities' and 'politics' to the comparisons of 'policies'

Comparative politics overcame the remaining institutional typologies in the 1970s and 1980s when it turned from politics to policies. Input–output comparisons were clearly inspired by the economic sciences. The main question was 'does politics matter?' (For a development of this question, see Chapter 3.) Comparative politics, influenced by political economy, even suggested that the difference between capitalist and communist systems in the light of modernization theory was exaggerated by the propaganda of both systems in a bipolar world of confrontation. Socio-economic determinism of Western theories of convergence of the systems since the 1970s had some traits in common with economy-centred Marxism which, for reasons of methodology, was not accepted.

By the early 1970s *comparative public policy* had emerged as a recognized subdiscipline within political science (see Chapter 20). The timing was not a surprise. Worldwide intellectual unrest from Berkeley to Berlin had mobilized scholars to support an activist image of the state. Most of the scholars—except Huntington who wrote from a neoconservative point of view—were liberal leftists. Though many of these comparativists had some 'social-democratic bias' and admired the Scandinavian welfare state, they were tired of ideological discussions. The grand debates between neo-Marxism and critical rationalism were abandoned. Scholars from different meta-theoretical schools agreed to stop discussing abstract constructs and study instead the needs of groups in the society. 'The state is better described by its policies than by its principles and alleged norms of individual choice and preference' (Ashford 1977: 572) was a widely shared assumption, especially in American political science, though less so in Europe where the remains of ideological debates were still strong.

The behaviouralist approach in the 1950s and 1960s frequently started with survey studies of individuals. Therefore it was normally less open to transnational comparisons. The predicament of the small number of cases for comparison drove research into studies of cities or parts of cities in the Californian Bay area or in New York (Sharpe and Newton 1984: 218). Przeworski and Teune (1970) pleaded for concentration on the sub-units of a political system for comparison. But the result sometimes came close to a new parochialism which could be dubbed 'The West Side story' of comparative politics, because research concentrated on comparisons of hospitals or school districts in West Side New York.

One further result of this kind of evolution was the abandonment of theories in comparative research. The new policy orientation in the 1970s again concentrated on transnational comparisons. A model was created when Heidenheimer, Heclo, and Adams received an award for the best political science publication. Their definition was as follows: 'Comparative public policy is the cross-national study of how, why, and to what effect government policies are developed' (Heidenheimer *et al.* 1975: v). The two schools which initiated comparative research also continued to fight each other in the subfield of 'comparative public policy'. The Heidenheimer–Heclo school was criticized for its descriptions without theories.

The 'Quasi-Eastonians' in the school of Dye (1966) and Hofferbert, on the other hand, overcame the lack of theory by abundant adoption of the terminology of structural–functional systems theory. On the grounds of a modernization theory, this approach had one assumption in common with the neo-Marxists: levels of economic development were more important than the political characteristics of individual states. In the US this assumption was mainly tested by comparisons among the policy performance of states. Harold Wilensky (1975: xiii) upheld the hypothesis of the centrality of economic development for the provision of social services: 'Economic growth and its demographic and bureaucratic outcomes are the root causes of the general emergence of the welfare state'. Only European-born scholars, such as Anthony King (1973: 423), challenged this widespread consensus on the priority of economic development by asserting that ideas constitute a sufficient condition for

explaining the variance in policy performance. Most scholars combined the importance of ideas with the focus on elite groups or answered positively the question 'do parties matter?'. The discovery of corporatism in the 1970s linked the elite approach with an emphasis on interest groups rather than on parties alone.

The Heidenheimer–Heclo school, based on historical and institutional studies, had the virtue of not neglecting 'politics' and the actors of decision, or reducing them to a kind of 'black box' for the production of a policy outcome which had little causal linkage to the decision-making process. Parties and interest groups were considered as analytically important. Increasingly, the role of the administrators was discovered. These were the main actors in an intermediary stage of decision. They operated between input and output of the political system and their contribution has been called *within-put*. The variance in the output of the systems compared was frequently explained in terms of rather vague special institutions, such as corporatism in Scandinavia or consensus democracy in Switzerland and the Benelux countries. Only the enlightened neo-institutionalism of the 1980s stopped to look for unilateral causal relationships between two variables in the polity system and the policy output. But the inclination of comparative public policy for historical determination of policy outputs was mostly preserved.

The concept of path dependence was introduced to explain why so many rising expectations for reform had failed in the 1970s. Restrictions, generated by historical developments and institutional barriers, left only 'narrow corridors' and windows of opportunity for policy action (on path dependence, see Chapter 21). To avoid a new kind of historicism it was important for comparative research to grow in order to avoid 'culture-bound generalizations' as a danger of one-country studies. The hopes for reform proved to be dependent on the type of decision which has been classified. Different types of conflict give rise to different types of legislative response and measures. *Policy determines politics* was an exaggerated slogan proposed by Theodore Lowi (1964) which was frequently tested in comparative politics. Lowi's typology initially showed a trinitarian design (regulative, distributive, and redistributive). Later, he added a fourth type: constituent policy (see Chapter 20). However, the elements of the typology were not all on the same logical level. If we differentiate between regulative (restrictive limitation of rights, regulative laws, neutral to the question of gain and loss, extensive measures aiming at an enlargement of rights) and distributive (protective, distributive, and redistributive measures) levels of decision, we end up with a sixfold typology (Beyme 1998: 5–6).

The typologies of policy fields and instruments of politics were soon connected by the network approach. A new slogan, *network determines policy*, was launched, but the differences between network theory and Lowi's assumptions were slight. Both predominantly saw a determination of the policy output by interest groups and other actors in the 'cosy triangles' of the decision-making process (deputies, interest groups, and administrators who prepare implementation) even if they start from policies as an 'independent variable'.

Comparative politics in post-modern times

Post-modernism in comparative political theory is not conceived as a completely new paradigm. Most reasonable post-modernists accept post-modernism only as a stage of modernity which implements its basic principles in a more consequential and systematic way than classical modernity. It cannot be equated with post-materialism or with certain processes of further differentiation and individualization which may lead to more decline of the old class social stratification and end up in theories of 'lifestyle'. Post-modernity is a set of theoretical assumptions rather than a clearly discernible new structure of society. The hopes which were widespread in those European countries where ecological parties were strong—that a new 'society of movements' might develop—failed to materialize. The new social movements in most systems were strong in the phase of agenda setting (see Chapter 16), but decision and implementation were predominantly directed by traditional organizations.

Post-modernism strengthened thinking in terms of constructivism. Durkheim's assumption that sociology is, by definition, comparative was most eagerly adopted in post-modern autopoietic theories of systems. But Durkheim was still a realist and not yet a constructivist. 'Le fait social', the social fact, was his basic assumption but, despite his realistic way of thinking, it was a kind of 'construct'. Post-modernist theories sometimes referred to Durkheim's approach to comparative social science.

The comparative method was not a special approach for Luhmann, because he suspected that it aimed at a 'normative ontological framework'. He emphasized instead that comparative aspects had to be kept 'variable'. In autopoietic systems theory comparisons were not concerned with facts. In a society without a steering centre only the 'codes' which determined the development of the subsystems could be compared. But radically different codes (government–opposition in politics, true–false in science, legal–illegal in law, beautiful–ugly in the arts) can hardly be compared since they function according to radically different logics. Systems and subsystems which evolve according to different codes can only 'observe' but not 'influence' each other. Adaptations from one system in another are hardly feasible. Thus, the main impetus for comparative politics was given up.

Post-modern theories, such as Foucault's *Archaeology of Knowledge* (1969), looked for variety. The 'summing up notions' in the 'archaeological comparisons' aimed at further pluralization of discourses. The critical approach to comparative politics in post-modern thinking was overdue. But 'thinking in fragments' finally leads to '*ad absurdum*' because a controlled comparison is no longer feasible. In autopoietic theories of systems comparisons are close to pathology in biology, where degenerated cells are compared with sound elements of an organism.

The evolution of comparative politics is not, as has sometimes been presented in the literature, a clear evolution of subsequent paradigms. There is permanent change in the perception of the needs of scientific comparisons, but a dominant mainstream which deserves Kuhn's mostly overstretched term of a 'paradigm' can hardly ever be traced. However, there are phases in the relationship of political theory with comparisons. The eras of 'pre-modernity', 'classical modernity', and 'post-modernism' show differences in the application of comparative methods. Pre-modern scholars mostly used comparison in an anecdotal way or deduced characteristics from human nature or certain forms of rule (e.g. the Roman Empire vs. the Greek states). From the nineteenth century a historicist approach, believing in a teleological development of the political systems, began to spread. Comparisons had to show the influence of a dominant factor, such as demography or economy, on political systems. Comparison was predominantly applied to 'polities', rarely to 'politics', and seldom to 'policies' in the respective systems.

The era of classical modernity developed rigorous criteria for scientific comparison for the first time, no longer confounding evolution and history, or theory and practice, and accepting that the political subsystem was no longer steering a whole society. Post-modern theories aimed even more strongly at variety and doing away with the remains of 'reification' of phenomena in classical modernity. 'Communication' as a key concept, and the assumption of constructed mutual perceptions changed the mood of comparative scholars. The authors of classical modernity also tried for the first time to develop logically consistent typologies as a tool for developing hypotheses.

Two traditions, which can be traced back to Max Weber's historical institutional comparisons or to Emile Durkheim's early systems approach, starting from the assumption that there is no special field of comparative social science, dominated comparative research. Sociology and political science were considered as comparative *per se.* The second line of development—under the impact of economic theory—was more interested in forecasting future developments than in a realistic description of facts.

KEY POINTS

- Post-modernism contests the idea that there are 'social facts' and is based more on the idea that social facts are constructs. However, this does not represent a total rupture with the past, but rather a different set of ontological assumptions.

Political influences on comparative politics

Theories and methodological approaches do not arise out of a blue sky. Methods of comparative politics proved to be influenced by political events. After 1945, American interest in foreign countries called for a new interest in foreign institutions. Soon, however, the behavioural revolution was distinguished from the old institutionalism in the tradition of Herman Finer or Carl J. Friedrich.

The counter-movement emphasized the comparison of dynamics of politics and political behaviour. The emphasis shifted towards interest groups and political movements. As a consequence of worldwide unrest and disobedience among young people in the late 1960s, new critical–dialectical and sometimes Marxist theories challenged the alleged conservatism of the behaviouralist mainstream which was blamed for only duplicating the alienated political world by its surveys. Political science discovered that the institutions were ill adapted but remained unchallenged by behaviouralists and functionalists. The scientific revolt started under the label of 'critique of parliamentarianism' and soon ended up in a dogmatic new political economy of revolution.

When the revolt petered out, neo-institutionalism and policy analysis became a minimal common denominator of leftists and mainstream scholars. The decline of communist regimes facilitated the change in theories and methods of comparative politics. New democracies were founded. In the era of the behavioural revolution nobody would have dared talk about *constitutional engineering.* The breakdown of dictatorship in the 1970s and 1980s created the need to discuss old and new institutions. Even *rational choice institutionalism* was applied to the study of who took which option when creating a new constitutional order. Some former leftist scholars, such as Jon Elster, Claus Offe, and Adam Przeworski, developed an approach, dubbed 'rational choice Marxism' which no longer accepted a 'telos of history' but worked out alternative options for the new elites in a post-communist world.

The breakdown of communism re-encouraged most distant systems designs. Transitions to democracy were compared in different areas and at different times. The theories of modernization and transition to democracy were mostly modelled on developments in Southern Europe and South America in the 1970s. With the simultaneous transformation of both economic and political systems which had no precedent in recent history, old assumptions of modernization theories about the economic prerequisites of successful democratization were no longer applicable. New approaches were applied to the unique character of the peaceful revolutions in 1989, such as the testing of chaos theories from recent developments in biology and physics, although most of the applications remained metaphorical (Marks 1992).

Theories of various feasible roads to modernity in the tradition of Barrington Moore (1966) suddenly became outdated. On the other hand, typologies of transitions, such as 'liberalization', democratization, and 'consolidation', were prematurely generalized (see Chapter 5). They were difficult to find in many areas of the world and proved to be a generalization of those former dictatorships in Southern Europe which consolidated quickly because they were soon integrated into the European Union (O'Donnell and Schmitter 1986). They might apply only to the Western tier of states in East-Central Europe which had recently become members in the EU. *Consolidology* as a subfield of *transitology* became a new branch of comparative politics. The normative equation—communism was a perversion of modernity, whereas post-communism is enlightened modernity—was quickly seen to be an untenable simplification. Soon comparativists discovered the 'defective democracies' which created another busy growth sector of comparativism (Merkel *et al.* 2003).

The acceptance of three worlds—the capitalist West, the communist world, and the Third World—until 1989 included the acceptance of a plurality of systems. Since the breakdown of communism, convergences have been increasing throughout the world (see the Introduction to this volume). The concept of a 'world society', emphasized by post-modern variations of systems theory, seems to be more plausible than before 1989. When, in the early 1980s, the biologist Maturana developed the hypothesis that no country in the world was able to develop its communism fully because the world system was predominantly capitalist, this was taken as an abstract oddity from a non-social scientist. Nevertheless, the hypothesis proved to be true. Oddly enough, theories of post-modernity which emphasize plurality face an increasing streamlining of the world.

The consequences of this development for the methodology of comparative politics are not yet fully recognized. Political science mostly ignored the 'grand debates' on the level of macro-systems (see Chapter 24). Business as usual continued. Political science stuck to the middle level of mainly actor-oriented approaches. Recent revivals such as neo-institutionalism or rational choice had more impact on political science than the abstract peaks of a general theory in sociology. The status of institutionalism in comparative politics changed dramatically over the years. Institutionalism used to be an invective. At the turn of the century a new exaggeration was offered: 'we are all institutionalists now' (Pierson and Skocpol 2002: 706).

The rational choice approach initially served as a counterbalance to the dominance of behavioural studies in the 1960s. It was easily combined with a multilevel analysis and with an enlightened neo-institutionalism which spread in the 1980s. It was linked with new attempts to reach the scientific level of neighbouring social sciences, such as economics: 'Rational choice institutionalism began as pure theft, lifting analytical tools from mathematics, operations research, and economics' (Shepsle 2006: 55). Rational choice approaches had the virtue of being applicable to any behaviour, from the most egotistic rationality to the most altruistic behaviour of saints. Against the assumptions of macro-theories about autopoietic systems, the analysis of political actors remained meaningful. The strictly individualistic origin of the new approach was soon abandoned. Rational choice was applied to collective entities and even to whole states. The research programme of rational choice institutionalism conquered many departments in American universities, but never dominated in Europe. It was not unchallenged, because of its abstractions, its simplifications, its analytical rigour, and neglecting context. 'Context' was a new catchword of comparative studies which turned back to individual cases or to comparisons in a middle-range historical perspective.

KEY POINTS

- Theories, contents, and methods of comparative politics were influenced by political events. Especially after the Second World War there was a new interest in foreign institutions, groups, and movements.

- Modernization, decolonization, transitions to, and consolidation of, democracies influenced comparative politics and the practical application of its theories. Also the development after the Second World War of social welfare states had an impact on the move away from institutions towards policies and their impact on society.

Conclusion

The evolution of comparative politics was not a self-steering development, but one that proved to be deeply influenced by political events. The predicament of political science was that its capacity to forecast major events was limited. There was little anticipation of the student rebellion, the 'third-worldism', the technological and ecological revolutions, or the breakdown of communism. After 1945 the scope of American political science broadened to worldwide interests in area and systems studies.

For a while the 'behavioural revolution' seemed to develop into a kind of dominant paradigm—but only in the US. The events after 1968 challenged the naive trust in democratic institutions, and an 'enlightened neo-institutionalism' had a revival. In combination with rational choice approaches, the two traditions merged in many ways. The crisis of policy-making under the impact of the oil crisis in 1973 strengthened interest in transnational comparisons of public policies. The breakdown of communism renewed fields of comparisons which had formerly been treated under the auspices of modernization theories with a simplified analysis of dominant factors. Democratization and consolidation of the new democracies was one major interest. But soon the failure of consolidation ended in a new boom of studying defective democracy all over the world. If democracy was the final normative target of comparative studies, the scientific community had to face the fact that there are many defective democracies but nowhere a perfect democracy—not even in the world of consolidated states and representative governments in North America and Europe.

Questions

1. Why can the evolution of comparative politics not be described as a sequence of paradigms?

2. What characterized comparative politics in pre-modern times? Who were the most important thinkers?

3. What characterizes comparative politics in modern times?

4. What was the contribution of the 'behavioural revolution' to the development of a scientific comparative political science?

5. Can experiments in comparative politics lead to a true scientific discipline?

6. Why are classifications and typologies important but problematic at the same time?

7. Why did comparative politics progressively shift its attention from polities to politics and policies?

8. Does politics determine policies or the other way round?

9. What is the influence of rational choice theory on comparative politics?

10. In what ways have political events influenced the evolution of comparative politics?

Further reading

For a more extensive treatment of the evolution of comparative politics see:

Almond, G. A. (1997) *A Discipline Divided: Schools and Sects in Political Science* (Newbury Park, CA: Sage).

Apter, D. E. (1996) 'Comparative Politics, Old and New', in R. Goodin and H.-D. Klingemann (eds), *The New Handbook of Political Science* (Oxford: Oxford University Press), 372–97.

Blondel, J. (1999) 'Then and Now: Comparative Politics', *Political Studies*, 47(1): 152–60.

Institutional theories

Chilcote, R. H. (1994) *Theories of Comparative Politics* (2nd edn) (Boulder, CO: Westview).

Daalder, H. (1993) 'The Development of the Study of Comparative Politics', in H. Keman (ed.), *Comparative Politics: New*

Directions in Theory and Method (Amsterdam: VU University Press), 11–30.

Daalder, H. (ed.) (1997) *Comparative European Politics: The Story of a Profession* (London: Pinter).

Laitin, D. D. (2002) 'Comparative Politics: The State of the Subdiscipline', in I. Katznelson and H. V. Milner (eds), *Political Science: The State of the Discipline* (Washington, DC: W. W. Norton and American Political Science Association), 630–59.

Munck, G. and Snyder, R. (2007) *Passion, Craft and Method in Comparative Politics* (Baltimore, MD: Johns Hopkins University Press).

Schmitter, P. C. (2009) 'The Nature and Future of Comparative Politics', *European Political Science Review* 1(1): 33–61.

Wiarda, H. J. (ed.) (2002) *New Directions in Comparative Politics* (3rd edn) (Boulder, CO: Westview Press).

Web links

www.politicalthought.com
Webpage called politicalthought.com. Particularly useful is the link to 'theorists'.

www.keele.ac.uk/depts/por/ptbase.htm
The Keele Guide to Political Thought and Ideology on the internet.

www.political-theory.org/
Foundations of political theory (an organized section of the American Political Science Association).

For additional material and resources, please visit the Online Resource Centre at:
www.oxfordtextbooks.co.uk/orc/caramani3e/

online
resource
centre

CHAPTER 2

Approaches in comparative politics

B. Guy Peters

Chapter contents

Reader's guide

Theories and approaches are crucial in guiding research and the awareness of what specific perspectives imply is important to make sense of scientific results. The chapter discusses five main approaches in comparative politics that represent important contributions (the five I's): old and new institutional analysis, interests and actors' strategies to pursue them through political action, ideas (political culture and social capital), individuals, and the influence of the international environment. The role of 'interaction' is also stressed. The chapter concludes by discussing the importance of looking at political processes as well as of defining what the 'dependent variables' are.

Introduction

The political world is complex, involving a range of institutions, actors, and ideas that interact continuously to provide governance for society. The complexity of politics and government is compounded when we attempt to understand several different political systems, and to compare how these systems function. As comparative politics has moved beyond simple descriptions of individual countries or a few institutions, scholars have required substantial guidance to sort through the huge amount of evidence available, and to focus on the most relevant information. Thus, we need alternative approaches to politics, and particularly to develop approaches that are useful across a range of political systems.

Political theories are the source of these approaches to comparison. At the broadest level, there is the difference between **positivist** and **constructivist** approaches to politics (see Box 2.1). At less general levels a number of different theories enable comparative political scientists to impose some analytical meanings on the political phenomena being observed, and to relate that evidence to more comprehensive understandings of politics. This chapter will first discuss some general questions about using theory in comparative political analysis, and then discuss alternative approaches to politics. Each approach discussed provides some important information about politics, but few if any are sufficient to capture the underlying complexity. Therefore the chapter will also discuss using multiple approaches and assess the ways in which the approaches mentioned interact for more complex explanations.

KEY POINTS

● Given the high complexity of political systems and the wide range of variation between them across the world, it is important to develop approaches that are useful across them all and not simply in single countries.

● Political theories are the main source of such approaches—the division between positivism and constructivism being the more general distinction.

Uses of theory in comparison

Although there is an important interaction between theory and empirical research in all areas of the discipline, that interaction is especially important in comparative politics. Even with an increasing amount of statistical research in political science, a still significant amount of case research, and a limited amount of experimental research, comparison remains the fundamental laboratory for political science.[1] Without the capacity to compare across political systems, it is almost impossible to understand the scientific importance of findings made in a single country (see Lee 2007), even one as large as the US.[2]

Without empirical political theory effective research might be impossible, or it certainly would be less interesting. Some questions that are almost purely empirical can and should be researched. It is interesting to know variations in cabinet sizes in European countries, for example, but if the scientific study of politics is to progress, research needs to be related to theory. The information

Box 2.1　Positivism and constructivism

Most of contemporary political science, and comparative politics, is founded on positivist assumptions. The most basic assumption of positivism is a fact value distinction, implying that there are real facts that are observable and verifiable in the same way by different individuals. Further, it is assumed that social phenomena can be studied in much the same way as phenomena in the natural sciences, through quantitative measurement, hypothesis testing, and theory formation. For example, the study of political attitudes across political cultures (beginning with work such as *The Civic Culture* (Almond and Verba 1963) and extending to contemporary work) has assumed that there are dimensions of individual political thought than can be measured and understood through surveys and rigorous statistical analysis.

Constructivism, on the other hand, does not assume such a wide gulf between facts and values, and considers facts to be socially embedded and socially *constructed* (see Finnemore and Sikkink 2001). Thus, the individual researcher cannot stand outside political phenomena as an objective observer but rather to some extent imposes his/her own social and

cultural understandings on the observed phenomena. While most positivist research assumes that the individual is the source of social action (methodological individualism), constructivism asserts the importance of collective understandings and values, so that phenomena may not be understood readily in the absence of context. Rather than relying on variables to define the objects of research, constructive approaches focus more on dimensions such as scripts or discourses to promote understanding.

Each of these approaches to comparative politics can make major contributions to understanding. The use of the variable-oriented research associated with positivism has added greatly to the comparative understanding of individual-level behaviour, as well as to the understanding of political parties and other mass-based organizations. On the other hand, much of the analysis of formal political institutions and processes of governing still relies on methods that, if not explicitly constructivist, do share many of the assumptions concerning collective understandings and the importance of ideas (see Bevir and Rhodes 2010).

on cabinets can be related to the capacity of those cabinets to make decisions through understanding the number of 'veto players' in the system (Tsebelis 2002).

Therefore comparative political theory is the source of questions and puzzles for researchers. For example, once we understand the concept of **consociationalism**, why is it that some societies have been able to implement this form of conflict resolution and others have not, even with relatively similar social divisions (see Lijphart 1996; Bogaards 2000)? And why have some countries in Africa been successful in implementing elite pacts after civil conflicts (a strategy like consociationalism) while other have not (LeVan 2011)? Likewise, political systems that appear relatively similar along a number of dimensions may have very different experiences maintaining effective coalition governments (Müller and Strøm 2000). Why? We have theories that help explain how cabinets are formed and why they persist, but the anomalies in and exceptions to these theories are crucial for elaborating the models and enhancing our understanding of parliamentary democracies.

One crucial function of theory in comparative politics is to link micro- and macro-behaviour. Much of contemporary political theory functions at the micro-level, attempting to understand individual choice. The most obvious example is rational choice which assumes utility maximization by individuals, and uses that assumption about individuals to interpret and explain political phenomena.[3] Likewise, cognitive political psychology is central in contemporary political science. However, in both cases the individual behaviours are channelled through institutions. Further, there is some reciprocal influence as institutions shape the behaviour of individuals and individuals shape institutions. For example, the institution of the presidency in the US was different after the personal indiscretions of Bill Clinton, and varies in practice under different presidents.

The link between the micro and the macro is crucial for comparative politics, given that one primary concern is explaining the behaviour of political systems and institutions rather than individuals. Variations in individual behaviour and the influence of cultural and social factors on that behaviour are important, but the logic of comparison is primarily about larger structures, and thinking about how individuals interact within parliaments, parties, or bureaucracies. Indeed, one could argue that if a researcher went too far down the individualist route, comparison would become irrelevant and all the researcher would care about would be the individual's behaviour. This problem is perhaps especially relevant for rational choice approaches that tend to posit relatively common motivations for individuals (but see Bates *et al.* 2002).

Theory is at once the best friend and the worst enemy of the comparative researcher. On the one hand, theory is necessary for interpreting findings, as well as providing questions that motivate new research. Without having political theory, research would simply be a collection of useful information and, although the information would be interesting, it would not advance the analytical understanding of politics. Further, theory provides scholars with the puzzles to be solved, or at least addressed, through comparative research. Theory predicts certain behaviours, and if individuals or organizations do not behave in that manner we need to probe more deeply. We should never underestimate the role that simple empirical observation can play in setting puzzles, but theory is a powerful source for ideas that add to the comparative storehouse of knowledge.

As important as theory is for interpreting findings and structuring initial research questions, theory is also a set of blinders for the researcher. After choosing our theoretical approach and developing a research design based on that theory, most people find it all too easy to find support for that approach. This tendency to find support for a theory is not necessarily the result of dishonesty or poor scholarship, but generally reflects a sincere commitment by the researcher to the approach and a consequent inability to identify any disconfirming evidence. Most research published in political science tends to find support for the theory or model being investigated, although in many ways negative findings would be more useful.[4]

Given the tendency to find support for theories, comparative research could be improved by greater use of triangulation.[5] If we explore the same data with several alternative theories, or go into the field with alternative approaches in mind, we become more open to findings that do not confirm one or another approach. Likewise, if we could collect several forms of data—substantiating the findings of quantitative research with those from qualitative methods—then we could have a better idea whether the findings were valid.[6] This type of research can be expensive, involves a range of skills that many researchers may not possess, and may result in findings that are inconclusive and perhaps confusing.

When we discuss comparative political theory, we have to differentiate between *grand theories* and *middle-range theories*, or even analytical perspectives. At one stage of the development of comparative politics the emphasis was on all-encompassing theories such as structural functionalism (Almond and Powell 1966) and systems theory (Easton 1965b) (see Box 2.2). These theories became popular as comparative politics had to confront newly independent countries in Africa and Asia, and find ways of including these countries in the same models as industrialized democracies. Those grand theories fulfilled their purpose of expanding the geographical concerns, as well as including less formal actors in the political process, but it became evident that by explaining everything they actually explained nothing. The functions of the political system and their internal dynamics discussed were so general that they could not produce meaningful predictions. Since that time there has been a tendency to rely

Box 2.2 Major approaches to comparative politics

Structural functionalism

The purpose of this approach was to identify the necessary activities (functions) of all political systems and then to compare the manner in which these functions were performed. As it was elaborated, it had developmental assumptions about the manner in which governing could best be performed that were closely related to the Western democratic model.

Systems theory

This approach considered the structures of the public sector as an open system that had extensive input (supports and demands) and output (policies) interaction with its environment.

Marxism

Class conflict is an interest-based explanation of differences among political systems. While offering some empirical predictions about those differences, Marxist analysis also posits a developmental pattern that would lead through revolution to a 'dictatorship of the proletariat'.

Corporatism

This approach stresses the central role of state and society interactions in governing, and especially the legitimate role of social interests in influencing policy. Even in societies such as Japan or the US which have not met the criteria of being corporate states, the identification of the criteria provides a means of understanding politics.

Institutionalism

Although there are several approaches to institutitionalism, they all focus on the central role of structures in shaping politics and also in shaping individual behaviour. As well as formal institutional patterns, institutions may be defined in terms of their rules and their routines, and thus emphasize their normative structure.

Governance

As an approach to comparative politics governance has some similarities to structural functional analysis. It argues that certain tasks must be performed in order to govern a society and then posits that these can be accomplished in a number of ways. In particular, scholars of governance are interested in the roles that social actors may play in the process of making and implementing decisions.

---

more on mid-range theories and analysis, although contemporary governance theories have some of the generality of functional theories.

Finally, as we attempt to develop theory using multiple approaches, we need to be cognizant of their linkages with methodologies, and the possibilities for both qualitative and quantitative evidence. Comparative politics is both an area of inquiry and a method that emphasizes case selection as much as statistical controls to attempt to test its theories. Each approach discussed below has been linked with particular ways of collecting data, and we must be careful about what evidence is used to support an approach, and what evidence is being excluded from the analysis.

KEY POINTS

- Theory is necessary to guide empirical research in comparative politics. It is also necessary to interpret the findings. It provides the puzzles and the questions that motivate new research.

- Without theory, comparative politics would be a mere collection of information. There would be no analytical perspective attempting to answering important questions. However, theories and approaches should never become blinders for the researcher. Ideally, we should investigate the same question from different angles.

- An important distinction concerns grand theories and middle-range theories. With the behavioural revolution there was a great emphasis on all-encompassing theories. At present, there is a tendency to develop 'grounded theories' or middle-range theories that apply to more specific geographical, political, and historical contexts.

Alternative perspectives: the five 'I's

Institutions

The roots of comparative political analysis are in institutional analysis. As far back as Aristotle, scholars interested in understanding government performance, and seeking to improve that performance, concentrated on constitutional structures and the institutions created by those constitutions. Scholars documented differences in constitutions, laws, and formal structures of government, and assumed that, if those structures were understood, the actual performance of governments could be predicted. Somewhat later, scholars in political sociology also began to examine political parties as organizations, or institutions, and to understand them in those terms (Michels 1915).

The behavioural revolution in political science, followed by the increasing interest in rational choice, shifted the paradigm in a more individualistic direction. The governing assumption, often referred to as *methodological individualism,* became that individual choices, rather than institutional constraints, produced observed differences in governments. It was difficult to avoid the obvious existence of institutions such as legislatures, but the rules of those organizations were less important, it was argued, than the nature of the individual legislators. Further, it was argued that decisions emerging from institutions were to a great extent the product of members' preferences, and those preferences were exogenous to the institutions.

While other areas of political science became almost totally absorbed with individual behaviour, comparative politics remained more true to its institutional roots. Even though some conceptualizations of behaviour within institutions were shaped by individualistic assumptions, understanding structures is still crucial for comparative politics. With the return to greater concern with institutions in political science, the central role of institutions in comparative politics has at once been strengthened and made more analytical.

The 'new institutionalism' in political science (Peters 2011) now provides an alternative paradigm for comparative politics. In fact, contemporary institutional theory provides at least three alternative conceptions of institutions, all having relevance for comparative analysis. *Normative* **institutionalism**, associated with James March and Johan P. Olsen, conceptualizes institutions as composed of norms and rules that shape individual behaviour. **Rational choice** *institutionalism*, on the other hand, sees institutions as aggregations of incentives and disincentives that influence individual choice. *Historical institutionalism* focuses on the role of ideas and the persistence of institutional choices over long periods of time, even in the face of potential dysfunctionality. Each approach to institutions provides a view of how individuals and structures interact in producing collective choices for society.

Thus, merely saying that institutional analysis is crucial for comparative politics is insufficient. We need to specify how institutions are conceptualized, and what sort of analytical role they play. At one level the concept of institutions appears formal, and not so different from some traditional thinking. That said, however, contemporary work on formal structures does examine their impact more empirically and conceptually than the traditional work did. Also, the range of institutions covered has expanded to include elements such as electoral laws and their effects on party systems and electoral outcomes (Taagapera and Shugart 1989).

Take, for example, studies of the difference between presidential and parliamentary institutions. This difference is as old as the formation of the first truly democratic political systems, but has taken on new life. First, the conceptualization of the terms has been strengthened for both parliamentary and presidential (Elgie 1999) systems, and the concept of divided government provides a general means of understanding how executives and legislatures interact in governing.[7] Further, scholars have become more interested in understanding the effects of constitutional choice on presidential or parliamentary institutions. Some scholars (Linz 1990a; Colomer and Negretto 2005) have been concerned with the effects of presidential institutions on political stability, especially in less developed political systems. Others (Weaver and Rockman 1993b) have been concerned with the effects of presidential and parliamentary institutions on policy choices and public sector performance.

The distinction between presidential and parliamentary regimes is one of the most important institutional variables in comparative politics, but other institutional variables are also useful for comparison, such as the distinction between federal and unitary states (and among types of federalism (Schain and Menon 2006)). Further, we can conceptualize the mechanisms by which social actors such as interest groups interact with the public sector in institutional terms (Peters 2011: Chapter 5). The extensive literature on corporatism has demonstrated the consequences of the structure of those interactions. Likewise, the more recent literature on networks in governance also demonstrates the structural interactions of public and private sector actors (Sørenson and Torfing 2007).

The preceding discussion concentrated on rather familiar institutional forms and their influence on government performance, but the development of institutional theory in political science has also focused greater attention on the centrality of institutions. Of the forms of institutional theory in political science, historical institutionalism has had perhaps the greatest influence in comparative politics. The basic argument of historical institutionalism is that initial choices shape policies and institutional attributes of structures in the public sector (Steinmo *et al.* 1992). For example, differences made in the initial choices about welfare state policies have persisted for decades and continue to resist change (Pierson 2001b). In addition to the observation about the persistence of programmes—usually referred to as path dependence—historical institutionalism has begun to develop theory about the political logic of that persistence (see Peters *et al.* 2005).

Institutional theory has been important for comparative politics, and for political science generally, but tends to be better at explaining persistence than explaining change (but see Mahoney and Thelen 2010). For some aspects of comparative politics we may be content with understanding static differences among systems, but dynamic elements are also important. As political systems change, especially democratizing and transitional regimes, political theory needs to provide an understanding of this as well as predicting change. While some efforts are being made to add more dynamic elements to institutional analysis—for example, the 'actor-centered institutionalism' of Fritz Scharpf (1997c)—institutional explanations remain somewhat constrained by the dominance of stability in the approach.

Historical institutionalism also can be related to important ideas about political change such as 'critical junctures' (Collier and Collier 1991; Cortell and Peterson 1999), and the need to understand significant punctuations in the equilibrium that characterizes most institutionalist perspectives on governing (see also True *et al.* 2007). In this approach change occurs through significant interruptions of the existing order, rather than through more incremental transformations. Much the same has been true of most models of transformation in democratization and transition, albeit with a strong concern about consolidation of the transformations (Alexander 2002). This view contrasts with the familiar idea of incremental change that has tended to dominate much of political science.

Interests

A second approach to explaining politics in comparative perspective is to consider the interests that actors pursue through political action. Some years ago Harold Lasswell (1936) argued that politics is about 'who gets what', and that central concern with the capacity of politics to distribute and redistribute benefits remains. In political theory, interest-based explanations have become more prominent, with the domination of rational choice explanations in much of the discipline (Lustick 1997; for a critique see Green and Shapiro 1994). At its most basic, rational choice theory assumes that individuals are self-interested utility maximizers and engage in political action to receive benefits, usually material benefits, or to avoid costs (see Box 2.3). Thus, individual behaviour is assumed to be motivated by self-interest and collective

behaviour is the *aggregation of the individual behaviours* through bargaining, formal institutions, or conflict.

Rational choice theory provides a set of strong assumptions about behaviour, but less deterministic uses of the idea of interests can produce more useful comparative results. In particular, the ways in which societal interests are represented to the public sector and affect policy choices are crucial components of comparative analysis. The concept of corporatism was central to comparative analysis in the 1970s and 1980s (Schmitter 1974, 1989). The close linkage between social interests and the state that existed in many European and Latin American corporatist societies provided an important comparison for the pluralist systems of the Anglo-American countries, and produced a huge literature on the consequences of patterns of interest intermediation for policy choices and political legitimacy.

The argument of corporatism was that many political systems legitimated the role of interest groups and provided those groups with direct access to public decision-making. In particular, labour and management were given the right to participate in making economic policy, but in return had to be reliable partners, with their membership accepting the agreements (e.g. not striking). These institutionalized arrangements enabled many European and some Latin American countries to manage their economies with less conflict than in pluralist systems such as the United Kingdom.

The interest in corporatism also spawned a number of alternative means of conceptualizing both corporatism itself and the role of interests. For example, Stein Rokkan (1966) described the Scandinavian countries, especially Norway, as being 'corporate pluralist', with the tightly defined participation of most corporatist arrangements extended to a wide range of actors. Other scholars have

Box 2.3 Rational choice and comparative politics

Rational choice models have made significant contributions to the study of politics and government. By employing a set of simplifying assumptions, such as utility maximization and full information, rational choice models have enabled scholars to construct explanatory and predictive models with greater precision than would be possible without those assumptions. For example, if we assume that individuals act rationally to enhance their own self-interest, then we can understand how they will act when they have the position of a 'veto player' in a political process (Tsebelis 2002). Likewise, if we assume that voters engage in utility maximization, then their choice of candidates becomes more predictable than in other models that depend more on a mixture of sociological and psychological factors (e.g. partisan identification).

By positing these common motivations for behaviour, however, rational choice adds less to comparative politics

than to other parts of the discipline of political science. Comparative politics tends to be more concerned with differences among political systems and their members than with similarities. Comparative politics, as a method of inquiry (Lijphart 1971) rather than a subject matter, relies on selecting cases based on their characteristics and then determining the impact of a small number of differences on observed behaviours. However, if everyone is behaving in the same way, important factors in comparative politics such as political culture, individual leadership, and ideologies become irrelevant. Differences in institutions remain important, or perhaps even more important, in comparison because their structures can be analysed through veto points or formal rules that create incentives and disincentives for behaviours.

discussed 'meso-corporatism' and 'micro-corporatism', and have attempted to apply the concept of corporatism to countries where it is perhaps inappropriate (Siaroff 1999).

The institutionalized pattern of linkage between social interests and the state implied in corporatism has been eroding and is being replaced by more loosely defined relationships such as networks (Sørenson and Torfing 2007; Koppenjan and Klijn 2005). The shift in thinking about interest intermediation to some degree reflects a real shift in these patterns, and also represents changes in academic theorizing. As the limits of the corporatist model became apparent, the concept of networks has had significant appeal to scholars. This idea is that surrounding almost all policy areas there is a constellation of groups and actors seeking to influence that policy, who are increasingly connected formally to one another and to policy-making institutions. The tendency of this approach has been to modify the self-interested assumption somewhat in favour of a mixture of individual (group) and collective (network or society) interests.

Network theory has been developed with different levels of claims about the importance of the networks in contemporary governance. At one end, some scholars have argued that governments are no longer capable of effective governance and that self-organizing networks now provide governance (Rhodes 1997; for a less extreme view see Kooiman 2003). For other scholars, networks are forms of interest involvement in governing, with formal institutions retaining the capacity to make effective decisions about governance. Further, the extent of democratic claims about networks varies among authors, with some arguing that these are fundamental extensions of democratic opportunities, and others concerned that their openness is exaggerated and that networks may become simply another form of exclusion for the less well-organized elements in society.

Finally, although we tend to think of interests almost entirely in material terms, there are other important interests as well. Increasingly, individuals and social groups define their interests in terms of identity and ethnicity, and seek to have those interests accommodated within the political system along with their material demands.[8] This concern with the accommodation of socially defined interests can be seen in the literature on consociationalism (Lijphart 1968a). Consociationalism is a mode of governing in which political elites representing different communities coalesce around the need to govern, even in the face of intense social divisions. For example, this concept was devised originally to explain how religious groups in the Netherlands were able to coalesce and govern despite deep historical divisions.

Like corporatism, consociationalism has been extended to apply to a wide range of political systems, including Belgium, Canada, Malaysia, Colombia, and India, but has been rejected as a solution for the problems of Northern Ireland and Iraq. The concept is interesting for comparative political analysis, but like corporatism may reflect only one variation of a more common issue. Almost all societies have some forms of internal cleavage (Posner 2004) and find different means of coping with those cleavages. In addition to strictly consociational solutions, elite pacts (Higley and Gunther 1992) have become another means of coping with difference and with the need to govern.

Approaches to comparative politics built on the basis of interest tend to assume that those interests are a basis for conflict, and that institutions must be devised to manage that conflict. Politics is inherently conflictual, as different interests vie for a larger share of the resources available to government, but conflict can go only so far if the political system is to remain viable. Thus, while interests may provide some of the driving force for change, institutions are required to focus that political energy in mechanisms for making and implementing policy.

Ideas

Although ideas are amorphous and seemingly not closely connected to the choices made by government, they can have some independent effect on outcomes. That said, the mechanisms through which ideas exert that influence must be specified and their independent effect on choices must be identified. In particular, we need to understand the consequences of mass culture, political ideologies, and specific ideas about policy. All these versions of ideas are significant, but each functions differently within the political process.

At the most general possible level, political culture influences politics, but that influence is often extremely vague. Political culture can be the residual explanation in comparative politics—when everything else fails to explain observed behaviours, then it must be political culture (Elkins and Simeon 1979). Therefore the real issue in comparative analysis is to identify means of specifying those influences with greater accuracy. As comparative politics, along with political science in general, has moved away from behavioural explanations and interpretative understandings of politics, there has been less analytical emphasis on understanding culture and this important element of political analysis has been devalued.[9]

How can we measure political culture and link this somewhat amorphous concept to other aspects of governing? The most common means of measuring the concept has been surveys asking the mass public how they think about politics. For example, in a classic of political science research, *The Civic Culture* (Almond and Verba 1963), the public in five countries were asked about their attitudes towards politics and particularly their attitudes to political participation. More recent examples of this approach to measurement include Ronald Inglehart's (1990, 1997) numerous studies using the World Values

Table 2.1 Patterns of political culture

Grid	Group	
	High	Low
High	Fatalist	Hierarchical
Low	Egalitarian	Individualist

Source: Douglas (1978).

Survey, as well as studies that explore values in public and private organizations (Hofstede 2001).

Of course, before surveys for measuring political culture can be devised, scholars must have some ideas about the dimensions that should be measured. Therefore conceptual development must go along with, or precede, measurement. Lucien Pye (1968) provided one interesting attempt at defining the dimensions of comparative political culture. He discussed culture as the tension between opposite values such as *hierarchy and equality, liberty and coercion, loyalty and commitment,* and *trust and distrust.* Although these are expressed as dichotomies, political systems tend to have complex mixtures of these attributes that need to be understood to grasp how politics is interpreted within that society.

The anthropologist Mary Douglas (1978) (see also Table 2.1) provided another set of dimensions for understanding political culture that continues to be used (Hood 2000). She has discussed culture in terms of the concepts of *grid* and *group,* both of which describe how individuals are constrained by their society and its culture. Grid is analogous to the dimension of hierarchy in Pye's framework, while group reflects constraints derived from membership in social groups. As shown in Table 2.1, bringing together these two dimensions creates four cultural patterns that are argued to influence the government performance and the lives of individuals. These patterns are perhaps rather vague, but they do provide means of approaching the complexities of political culture.

The trust and distrust dimension mentioned by Pye can be related to the explosion of the literature on social capital and the impact of trust on politics. The concept of social capital was initially developed in sociology (Coleman 1990), but gained greater prominence with Robert Putnam's work on Italy and the US (Putnam 1993, 2000). This concept was measured through surveys as well as through less obtrusive measures. What is perhaps most significant in the social capital literature is that the cultural elements are linked directly with political behaviour, of both individuals and systems.

As well as the general ideas contained in political culture, political ideas also are important in the form of *ideologies.* In the twentieth century, politics in a number of countries was shaped by ideologies such as communism and fascism. Towards the end of the last century and into the current one an ideology of neoliberalism came to dominate economic policy in the industrialized democracies and was diffused through less-developed systems by donor organizations such as the World Bank. Within the developing world, ideologies about development, such as Pancasila in Indonesia, reflect the important role of ideas in government, and a number of developing countries continue to use socialist ideologies to justify interventionist states.

Although ideologies have been important in comparative politics, there has been a continuing discussion of the decline, or end, of ideology in political life. First, with the acceptance of the mixed economy welfare state in most industrialized democracies the argument was that the debate over the role of the state was over (Bell 1965). More recently, after the collapse of the Soviet Union, a similar argument was made concerning the exhaustion of political ideas and the end of political conflicts based on ideas (Fukuyama 1992). However, this presumed end of the role of ideas could be contrasted with the increased importance of conservative ideologies and the increased significance of religion as a source of political conflicts.

A final way in which ideas influence outcomes in comparative politics is through specific policy ideas. For example, while at one time economic performance was considered largely uncontrollable, after the intellectual revolution in the 1930s governments had tools for that control (Hall 1989). Keynesian economic management dominated for almost half a century, but then was supplanted by monetarism and to a lesser extent by supply-side economics. Likewise, different versions of the welfare state, for example the Bismarckian model of continental Europe and the Beveridge model in the United Kingdom (see Esping-Andersen 1990), have been supported by a number of ideas about the appropriate ways in which to provide social support.

In summary, ideas do matter in politics, even though their effects may be subtle. This subtlety is especially evident for political culture, but tracing the impact of ideas is in general difficult. Even for policy ideas that appear closely related to policy choices, it may be difficult to trace how the ideas are adopted and implemented (Braun and Busch 1999). Further, policy learning (Sabatier and Jenkins-Smith 1993) and the social construction of agendas and political frames can shape behaviour.

Individuals

I have already discussed the methodological individualism that has become central to political theory. Although I was arguing that an excessive concern with individual behaviour, especially when based on an assumption that individual motivations are largely similar, may make understanding differences among political systems more difficult, it is still impossible to discount the importance of individuals when understanding how politics and government work. The importance of political biography and

Table 2.2 Styles of political leaders

Orientation to politics	Activity	
	Active	Passive
Positive	Bill Clinton;	George H. W. Bush;
	Tony Blair	Jim Callaghan
Negative	Richard Nixon;	Calvin Coolidge;
	Margaret Thatcher	John Major

Source: Based on Barber (1992). The role of political elites can also be seen in studies of political leadership (Helms 2013).

political diaries as sources of understanding is but one of many indications of how important individual-level explanations can be in understanding governing.

Many individual level explanations are naturally focused on political elites and their role in the political process. One of the more interesting, and perhaps most suspect, ways of understanding elite behaviour is through their personality. There have been a number of psychological studies, usually done from secondary sources, of major political figures (Freud and Bullitt 1967; Berman 2006). Most of these studies have focused on pathological elements of personality, and have tended to be less than flattering to the elites. Less psychological studies of leaders, e.g. James David Barber's typology of presidential styles (Barber 1992; see also Simonton 1993), have also helped to illuminate the role of individual leaders (see Table 2.2). Barber classifies political leaders in terms of their positive or negative orientations toward politics and their levels of activity, and uses the emerging types to understand how these individuals have behaved in office.

A more sociological approach to political leaders has stressed the importance of background and recruitment, with the assumption that the social roots of leaders will explain their behaviour. Putnam (1976) remarked several decades ago that this hypothesis was plausible, but unproven, and that assessment remains largely true. Despite the absence of strong links there is an extensive body of research using this approach. The largest is the research on 'representative bureaucracy' and the question of whether public bureaucracies are characteristic of the societies they administer, and whether this makes any difference (Seldon 1997; Meier and Bohte 2001). While the representativeness of the bureaucracy is usually discussed at the higher, 'decision-making' levels, it may actually be more crucial where 'street level bureaucrats' meet citizens (Meyers and Vorsanger 2005).

The ordinary citizen should not be excluded when considering individuals in comparative politics. The citizen as voter, participant in interest groups, or merely as the consumer of political media plays a significant role in democratic politics, and less obviously in non-democratic systems. The huge body of literature on cross-national voting behaviour has generated insights about comparative political behavior. Further, the survey-based evidence on political culture already mentioned uses individual-level data to make some (tentative) statements about the system level.

In those portions of political science that deal with government activities the role of the individual has become more apparent. Citizens are consumers of public services, and the New Public Management has placed individual citizens at the centre of public sector activity (see Chapter 8). This central role is true for the style of management now being pursued in the public sector. It is also true for a range of instruments that have been developed to involve the public in the programmes that serve them, and also for a range of instruments designed to hold public programmes accountable.

International environment

Much of the discussion of comparative politics is based on analysing individual countries, or components of countries. This approach remains valuable and important. That said, it is increasingly evident that individual countries are functioning in a globalized environment and it is difficult, if not impossible, to understand any one system in isolation. To some extent the shifts in national patterns are mimetic, with one system copying patterns in another that appear effective and efficient (see DiMaggio and Powell 1991; see also Chapter 24). In other cases the shifts may be coercive, as when the European Union has established political as well as economic criteria for membership.

International influences on individual countries, although ubiquitous, also vary across countries. Some, such as the US or Japan, have sufficient economic resources and lack direct attachments to strong supranational political organizations, and hence maintain much of their exceptionalism. Poorer countries lack economic autonomy and their economic dependence may produce political dependence as well, so that their political systems may be influenced by other nations and by international organizations such as the World Bank and the United Nations.

The countries of the European Union present a particularly interesting challenge for comparative politics. While most of these countries have long histories as independent states, and have distinct political systems and political styles, their membership of the Union has created substantial convergence and homogenization. The growing literature on Europeanization (Knill 2001; Schimmelfennig and Sedelmeier 2005; see also Chapter 23) has been attempting to understand these changing patterns of national politics in Europe and the increasingly common patterns of governance. This is not to say that British parliamentary democracy and the presidentialism of Poland will merge entirely, but there is reciprocal influence and some difficulties in sorting out sources of change.

The case of the European Union also points out the extent to which interactions among all levels of government are important for shaping behaviours in any one level. The concept of 'multilevel governance' has been popular for analysing policy-making in the European Union (Hooghe and Marks 2001; Bache and Flinders 2004). For individuals coming from federal regimes this interaction is a rather familiar feature of governing, and in many cases the sub-national governments have been the principal policy and political innovators. For many European countries, however, multilevel governance is a more distinctive phenomenon that links both internationalization and the increasing political power of sub-national governments to the national government.

The interaction among countries, and across levels of government, raises an analytical question. When we observe a particular political pattern in a country, is that pattern a product of indigenous forces and national patterns, or is it a product of diffusion? The so-called 'Galton problem' has been present for as long as there have been comparative studies, but its importance has increased as interactions have increased, and as the power of international organizations has increased (Seeliger 1996). Unfortunately, we may never really be able to differentiate all the various influences on any set of observed patterns in the public sector, despite the numerous answers that have been proposed to the problem (Braun and Gilardi 2006).

While diffusion among countries can be conceived as an analytical problem for social sciences, it can be a boon for governments and citizens. If we conceptualize the international environment as a laboratory of innovations in both political action and policy, then learning from innovations in other settings becomes a valuable source for improving governing. A number of governments have attempted to institutionalize these practices through evidence-based policy-making.

Add a sixth 'I': interactions

Up to this point I have been dealing with five possible types of explanation independently. That strategy is useful as a beginning and for clarifying our thoughts about the issue in question, but it vastly understates the complexity of the real world of politics. In reality these five sources of explanation interact with one another, so that to understand decisions made in the political process we need to have a broader and more comprehensive understanding. Given that much of contemporary political science is phrased in terms of testing hypotheses derived from specific theories, this search for complexity may not be welcomed by some scholars, but it does reflect political realities.

Let me provide some examples. Institutions are a powerful source of explanations and are generally our first choice for those explanations. However, institutions do not act—the individuals within them act, and so we need to understand how institutions and individuals interact in making decisions. Some individuals who may be very successful in some political settings would not be in others. Margaret Thatcher was a successful prime minister in the majoritarian British system, but her directive leadership style might have been totally unsuccessful in consensual Scandinavian countries, or even perhaps more consensual Westminster systems such as Canada. And these interactions can also vary across time, with a bargainer such as Lyndon Johnson being likely to have been unsuccessful in the more partisan Congresses of the early twenty-first century.

Another example of interaction among possible explanations can occur between the international environment and institutions. Many of the states in Asia and Latin America have adopted a 'developmental state' model to cope with their relatively weak position in the international market place and to use the power of the state for fundamental economic change (Evans 1995; Minns 2006). On the other hand, the more affluent states of Europe and North America have opted for a more liberal approach to economic growth—a model that better fits their position in the international political economy.

The literature on social movements provides a clear case for the interaction of multiple streams of explanation (see Chapter 16). On the one hand, social movements can be conceptualized as institutions, albeit ones with relatively low levels of institutionalization. These organizations can also be understood as reflecting an ideological basis, and as public manifestations of ideas such as environmentalism and women's rights. Finally, some social movements reflect underlying social and economic interests, although again in somewhat different ways than would conventional interest groups. Again, by using all these approaches to triangulate these organizations, the researcher gains a more complete understanding of the phenomenon.

Multiple streams of explanation and their interaction help to emphasize the point made at the outset of this chapter. The quality of research in comparative politics can be enhanced by the use of multiple theories and multiple methodologies when examining the same 'dependent variable'. Any single analytical approach provides a partial picture of the phenomenon in question, but only through a more extensive array of theory and evidence can researchers gain an accurate picture of the complex phenomena with which comparative politics is concerned. This research strategy is expensive, and may yield contradictory results, but it may be one means of coping with complexity.

What more is needed?

The preceding discussion gives an idea of major approaches to comparative political analysis. These five broad approaches provide the means of understanding almost any political issues (whether within a single country or comparatively), yet they do not address the full range of political issues as well as they might. Indeed, there are at least two comparative questions that have not been explored as completely as they might have been. We can gain some information about these issues utilizing the five I's already advanced, but it would be useful to explore the two questions more fully.

Process

Perhaps the most glaring omission in comparative analysis is an understanding of the **political process**. If we look back over the five I's, much of their contribution to understanding is premised on rather static conceptions of politics and governing, and thus issues of process are ignored. This emphasis on static elements in politics is unfortunate, given that politics and governing are inherently dynamic and it would be very useful to understand better how the underlying processes function. For example, while we know a great deal about legislatures as institutions, as well as about individual legislators, comparative politics has tended to abandon concern about the legislative process.

Institutions provide the most useful avenue for approaching issues of process. If we adopt the common-sense idea about institutions, then each major formal institution in the political system has a particular set of processes that can be more or less readily comparable across systems. Further, various aspects of process may come together and might constitute a policy process that, at a relatively high analytical level, has common features. Even if we do have good understanding of the processes within each institution, as yet we do not have an adequate comparative understanding of the process taken more generally.

Outcomes

Having all these explanations for political behaviour, we should also attempt to specify what these explanations actually explain—the dependent variable for comparative politics? For behavioural approaches to politics the dependent variables will be individual-level behaviour, such as voting or decisions made by legislators. For institutionalist perspectives the dependent variable is the behaviour of individuals within institutions, with the behaviour shaped by either institutional values or the rule and incentives provided by those institutions. Institutionalists tend to be more concerned about the impact of structures on public sector decisions, while behavioural models focus on the individual decision-maker and attributes that might affect his/her choices.

As implied in several places earlier, one of the most important things that scholars need to understand in comparative politics is what governments actually do. If, as Harold Lasswell argued, politics is about 'who gets what', then public policy is the essence of political action and we need to focus more on policy. As Chapter 1 shows, this was indeed the case. However, policy outcomes are not just the product of politics and government action, but rather reflect the impact of economic and social conditions. Therefore understanding comparative policy requires linking political decisions with other social, economic, and cultural factors. Unfortunately, after having been a central feature of comparative politics for some time, comparative policy studies appear to be out of fashion. True, some of those concerns appear as comparative political economy (Pontusson 1995), or perhaps as studies of the welfare state (Myles and Pierson 2001), but the more general concern with comparing policies and performance has disappeared in the contemporary literature in comparative politics.

If we look even more broadly at comparative politics, then the *ultimate dependent variable is governance,* or the capacity of governments to provide direction to their societies. Governance involves *establishing goals for society, finding the means for reaching those goals, and then learning from the successes or failures of their decisions* (Pierre and Peters 2000). All other activities in the public sector can be put together within this general concept of governance. The very generality of the concept of governance poses problems for comparison, as did the structural–functionalist and systems theories (Almond and Powell 1966) popular earlier in comparative politics. Still, by linking a range of government activities and demonstrating their cumulative effects, an interest in governance helps counteract attempts to overly compartmentalize comparative analysis. To some extent, it returns to examining whole systems and how the constituent parts fit together, rather than focusing on each individual institution or actor.

Governance comes as close to the grand functionalist theories of the 1960s and 1970s as almost anything else in recent developments in comparative political analysis (see Box 2.2). Like those earlier approaches to comparative politics, governance is essentially functionalist, positing that there are certain crucial functions that any system of governance must perform, and then attempting to determine which actors perform those tasks, regardless of the formal assignment of tasks by law. While some governance scholars have emphasized the role of social actors rather than government actors in delivering governance, this remains an empirical question that needs to be investigated rather than merely inferred from the theoretical presumptions of the author.

Governance also goes somewhat beyond the comparative study of public policy to examine not only the outputs of the system but also its capacity to adapt. One of the more important elements of studying contemporary governance is the role of accountability and feedback, and the role of monitoring previous actions of the public sector. This emphasis is similar to feedback in systems theory (see Figure I.1 in the Introduction to this volume), but does not have the equilibrium assumptions of the earlier approach. Rather, governance models tend to assume some continuing development of policy capacity as well as institutional development to meet the developing needs.

KEY POINTS

- One weak point of comparative politics is its focus on the static elements of the political system and a neglect of dynamic political processes. The field of comparative politics with greater attention to processes is comparative public policy analysis.

- The dependent variable in comparative politics varies according to approaches: but, perhaps, the ultimate dependent variable is 'governance', i.e. establishing goals for society, finding means to reach those goals, and then learning from the successes or failures of their decisions.

Conclusion

Understanding politics in a comparative perspective is far from easy, but having some form of theoretical or analytical guidance is crucial to that understanding. The discussion in this chapter devotes little time on grand theory but rather has focused on analytical perspectives that provide researchers with a set of variables that can be used to approach comparative research questions. These five I's were phrased in rather ordinary language, but underneath each is a strong theoretical core. For example, if we take the role of individuals in politics, we can draw from political psychology, elite theory, and role theory for explanations.

Comparative politics should be at the centre of theory-building in political science, but that central position is threatened by the emphasis on individual-level behaviour. Further, the domination of American political scientists in the marketplace of ideas has tended to produce a somewhat unbalanced conception of the relevance of comparative research in contemporary political science. I would still argue that the world provides a natural laboratory for understanding political phenomena. We cannot, as experimenters, manipulate the elements in that environment, but we can use the evidence available from natural experiments to test and to build theory.

Questions

1. What is the purpose of theory in comparative politics?

2. What is a functionalist theory?

3. What is meant by triangulation in social research?

4. What forms of institutional theory are used in comparative politics, and what contributions do they make?

5. Do institutions make a difference?

6. Both behavioural and rational choice approaches focus on the individual. Where do they differ?

7. Does political culture help to understand political behaviour in different countries?

8. Do people always act out of self-interest in politics?

9. Will globalization make comparative politics obsolete?

10. Are the policy choices made by political systems a better way of understanding them than factors such as formal institutions or voting behaviour?

Further reading

Basic discussions

Bates, R., Greif, A., Levi, M., Rosenthal, J.-L., and Weingast, B. (2002) *Analytic Narratives* (Princeton, NJ: Princeton University Press).

Geddes, B. (2002) *Paradigms and Sand Castles: Theory Building and Research Design in Comparative Politics* (Ann Arbor, MI: University of Michigan Press).

Peters, B. G. (2013) *Strategies for Comparative Political Research* (Basingstoke: Palgrave).

Institutional theories

March, J. G., and Olsen, J. P. (1989) *Rediscovering Institutions* (New York: Free Press).

Steinmo, S., Thelen, K. A., and Longstreth, F. (1992) *Structuring Politics* (Cambridge: Cambridge University Press).

Interest-based theories

Sørenson, E. and Torfing, J. (2007) *Theories of Democratic Network Governance* (Basingstoke: Palgrave).

Tsebelis, G. (2002) *Veto Players* (Princeton, NJ: Princeton University Press).

The role of ideas

Hall, P. A. (1989) *The Political Power of Economic Ideas* (Princeton, NJ: Princeton University Press).

Putnam, R. D. (1993) *Making Democracy Work: Civic Traditions in Modern Italy* (Princeton, NJ: Princeton University Press).

Individual theories

Greenstein, F. I. (1987) *Personality and Politics* (Princeton, NJ: Princeton University Press).

Helms, L. (2013) *Oxford Handbook of Political Leadership* (Oxford: Oxford University Press).

The role of the international environment

Keohane, R. O. and Milner, H. (1997) *Internationalization and Domestic Politics* (Cambridge: Cambridge University Press).

Cowles, M. G. and Caporaso, J. A. (2002) *Europeanization and Domestic Change* (Ithaca, NY: Cornell University Press).

Governance

Pierre, J. (2003) *Debating Governance* (Oxford: Oxford University Press).

Web links

www.nd.edu/~apsacp
Website of the Comparative Politics Section, American Political Science Association.

www.asu.edu/clas/polisci/cqrm
Website of the Arizona State University Institute for Qualitative Methods.

http://upslinks.net
Ultimate Political Science Links Page.

www.politicalresources.net
Political Resources on the Net.

online resource centre

For additional material and resources, please visit the Online Resource Centre at:
www.oxfordtextbooks.co.uk/orc/caramani3e/

CHAPTER 3

Comparative research methods

Hans Keman

Chapter contents

Reader's guide

In this chapter the 'art of comparing' is elaborated by demonstrating how to relate a theoretically guided research question to a properly founded research answer by developing an adequate research design. First, the role of variables in comparative research will be highlighted. Second, the meaning of 'cases' and their selection will be discussed. These are important steps in any comparative research design. Third, the focus will turn to the 'core' of comparative method: the use of the logic of comparative inquiry to analyse the relationships between variables—representing theory—and the information contained in the cases—the data. Finally, some problems common to the use of comparative methods will be discussed.

Introduction

As the Introduction to this volume stresses, both its substance and its method characterize comparative politics. The method is the 'toolkit' of what, when, and how to compare political systems. In this chapter the focus is on research methods used in comparative political science: what rules and standards should we adopt to develop a comparative research design?[1] A research design is a crucial step for developing and testing theories and for the verification of rival theories. Hence, as Peters emphasizes, '[t]he only thing that should be universal in studying comparative politics ... is a conscious attention to explanation and research design' (Peters 1998: 26). Theory development and research design are closely interlinked in comparative politics.

Contrary to everyday practice, where most people are often *implicitly* comparing situations, in comparative politics the issue of what and how to observe reality is *explicitly* part of the comparative method. Dogan and Pelassy (1990: 3), for example, remark '[t]o compare is a common way of thinking. Nothing is more natural than to consider people, ideas, or institutions in relation to other people, ideas and institutions. We gain knowledge through reference.' Yet, as we have seen in Chapter 1, the evolution of comparative politics has moved on from implicit comparisons in pre-modern times to explicit ways of comparing political systems and related processes. The major modern development in comparative political science is on linking theory to evidence by means of comparative methods. The particular method to be used depends on the research question (RQ) asked and the research answer (RA) to be given (see also Box 3.1). The actual method chosen is what we label research design (RD), and this is what this chapter is about.

A theory in its simplest form is a meaningful statement about the relationship between two real-world phenomena: X, the independent variable, and Y, the dependent variable. According to theory, it is expected that change in one variable will be related to change in the other. The conceptual and explanatory understanding of such a relationship is the point of departure for conducting research by comparing empirical evidence across systems (see also Brady and Collier 2004: 309; Burnham *et al.* 2004: 57). In more formal terms a theory posits the *dependent variable* in the analysis—what is to be explained? Additionally the researcher wishes to know: what are the most likely 'causes' of the phenomenon under investigation? Again, in formal terms: which *independent variables,* or explanatory factors, can account for the variation of the dependent variable across different systems (e.g. countries) or features of political systems (e.g., parties)? The answer to this question rests heavily on the development of a 'correct' research design. therefore comparative methods can be considered as a 'bridge' between the research question asked and the research answer proposed. This is what we label the 'triad' RQ → RD → RA.

Box 3.1   The triad RQ → RD → RA

The point of departure is that all research questions are theory guided. The *theoretical* guidance is expressed in relating research questions (RQs) to research answers (RAs) in the shape of *logical* relationships between a dependent variable (Y: what is to be explained) and the independent variables (X: the most likely causes, i.e. factors serving as an explanation). The 'bridge' between RQ and RA is called a research design (RD). Therefore the comparative method is a *means to an end:* to make choices as to which of the potentially vast mass of relevant empirical data (the evidence) and possible cause (X) explaining variations in Y are valid and reliable in arriving at a research answer.

Developing a research design in comparative politics requires careful elaboration. First, the research design should enable the researcher to *answer the question* under examination. Second, the given answer(s) ought to meet the *'standards' set in the social sciences:* are the results valid (authoritative), reliable (irrefutable), and generalizable (postulated) knowledge (Sartori 1994)? Third, are the research design and the methods used indeed *suitable for the research goals* set? This chapter will elaborate these issues and attempt to guide the student towards linking research questions to research answers.

KEY POINTS

● The proper use and correct application of methods is essential in comparative politics.

● A correct application implies that the comparative method meets the 'standards' set in terms of validity, reliability, and its use in a wider sense, i.e. generalizability.

● The relationship between variables and cases in comparative research is crucial in order to reach empirically founded conclusions that will further knowledge in political science.

The role of variables in linking theory to evidence

Since the 1960s the comparative approach in political science has been considered highly relevant to theory development (see also Almond (1996) and the Introduction to this volume). Therefore a research question should always either be guided by theory or itself constitute a potential answer to an existing theoretical argument. The comparative method is about observing and comparing carefully selected information (across space or time, or both) on the basis of a meaningful, if not causal, relationship between variables. A variable is a concept that can be systematically observed (and measured) in various situations (such as in countries or over time). It allows us to understand the similarities and differences between observed phenomena. For example, we can make a difference between democracies and non-democracies or between different types of democracies (e.g. presidential, semi-presidential, and parliamentary). The extent to which the similarities and differences across systems are more or less systematic can tell us more about the plausibility of a theoretical relationship under review. For example, Linz and Stepan (1996), discussing the pros and cons of presidentialism, argued that parliamentary democracies are more enduring than presidential ones. They found that the independent variable, parliamentary vs. presidential systems (a dichotomy), differed considerably in terms of political stability measured in years.

Typologies are often used as a first step in examining the theoretical association between two variables without explicitly arguing a causal relationship. The first step towards a typology is to decide what is to be classified on the basis of a research question. Let us take Figure 1.1 as an example. In it, von Beyme shows an association between Federalism and Electoral Laws. This allows classifying different systems and discussing the significance of territorial conflict within a nation in relation to both variables. The major problem of this type of analysis is that miscomparing can lead to misclassification and therefore to wrongly informed conclusions. However, this can be avoided by checking that all (in this case four) cells validly include at least a case (inclusiveness) and further that one case cannot be placed in more than one cell (exclusiveness). This is called an 'in-between' or hybrid case. Other examples can be found elsewhere in this book (see Tables 1.3, 5.7, and 21.1, and Figures 5.1 and 7.2).

In sum, the comparative method allows us to investigate hypothesized relationships among variables systematically and empirically. In contrast with the methodology of the 'exact sciences', however, the conclusions are drawn from comparisons *not* experiments. Therefore the real world of comparative politics provides a *quasi-experimental* workplace for political scientists to examine how the complex world of politics 'turns' by demonstrating in a systematic and rigorous fashion *theoretical relationships among variables*.

An example of how the triad (recall Box 3.1) works and helps to answer a contested issue is the debate 'does politics matter?' (see Chapter 21). The dependent variable or the outcome (Y) in this example is welfare state development, i.e. what the researcher seeks to explain. It is called dependent because we expect that the variation in welfare state provisions across systems also depends on one or more independent variables.[2] As a tentative *answer* the researcher comes up with a *hypothesis.* In this example the variation in welfare state development (Y) is dependent on the relative strength of left-wing parties and trade unions in a country (X). This research answer, or hypothesis, is a

conjecture about the relationship between the dependent variable and the independent variable and is supposed to explain the outcome, i.e. the development of the welfare state. In a comparative research design a theoretical relationship is elaborated to account for the differences and similarities in welfare state development (Figure 3.1).

Obviously, any type of 'X–Y' relationship in social science is an abstraction from the complexities of the real world. This is deliberate. By means of hypotheses or explanations (X) those factors are included that can account for the variation in Y. This procedure allows us to establish whether or not a meaningful relationship indeed exists, and whether or not this relationship can be qualified as 'causal' or not (i.e. it is noted as $X \rightarrow Y$).

Causality is a fraught concept in the social sciences and in strict terms is hard to establish. Yet, it is now accepted that if the variation in the dependent variable (Y—here: more or less expansion of the welfare state) is evidently and systematically related to the variation in (one of) the independent variable(s) and a theory as to why this is the case (X_1—socio-economic and X_2—political indicators), then we can assume causality—at least for the cases included in the analysis.[3] This refers to the idea of 'internal validity' (see Box 3.2).

Our ability to establish causal relationships by means of comparative research design is considered as major advantage. As I have already stated, comparative analysis is often labelled 'quasi-experimental', meaning that, to a certain extent, we can manipulate reality, enabling the researcher to conduct *descriptive inference* (King *et al.* 1994: 34ff). This implies that the empirically founded relationship

Box 3.2 Internal and external validity in comparative methods

Internal validity refers to the degree to which descriptive or causal inferences from a given set of cases are indeed correct for most, if not all, the cases under inspection. *External* validity concerns the extent to which the results of the comparative research can be considered to be valid for other more or less similar cases but not included in the research.

Both types of validity are equally important, but it should be noted that there is a trade-off (Peters 1998: 48; Pennings *et al.* 2006: 5–6). The more the cases are included in the analysis can be considered as representative, the more 'robust' the overall result will be *(external validity)*. Conversely, however, the analysis of fewer cases may well be conducive to a more coherent and solid conclusion for the set of cases that is included *(internal validity)*.

It should be noted that the concepts of internal and external validity are *ideal-typical* in nature: in a perfect world with complete information the standards of both internal and external validity may well be met, but in practice this is hard to achieve.

between the independent and dependent variables, based on a number of observations, allows generalization over and beyond the cases under review. Hence, the results of the analysis are considered to be relevant for all political systems where a welfare state is present or emerging (for instance, in Southern and Eastern Europe since the 1990s). In these circumstances the researcher claims that his/her results are 'externally valid' (see Box 3.2). It is obvious that this 'leap' from the empirical evidence to a more general explanation (the 'theory') is open to criticism and drives contesting theories—in this example, politics does *not* matter but socio-economic developments do—that are developed to disprove or to enhance the theory.

Hence, socio-economic development (represented as X_1 in Figure 3.1) is considered as an important 'cause' explaining the variation in the development and level of welfare statism across OECD countries (e.g. Wilensky 1975). Political variables, such as differences between left- and right-wing parties with respect to how much welfare state is sufficient or the relative strength of these parties in government and the strength of trade unions (X_2 in Figure 3.1), were considered as less relevant (or merely coincidental) to explaining the growth of a welfare state. In other words, the research conducted appeared to prove that 'politics did *not* matter'.

Yet, a major objection concerned the finding that the *non*-political variables (X_1 in Figure 3.1) were insufficiently capable of explaining *why* cross-system differences in welfare statism *differed*, although in many instances the non-political variables X_1 were quite *similar*. The descriptive inference was not homogeneous (i.e. the assumption that a given set of variables produces always the same outcome). This criticism was supported by empirical observations. It appeared that levels of welfare statism tended to become more *divergent* (i.e. more different) whereas the explanatory variables (X_1) would predict otherwise: a *convergent* (i.e. more similar) development would be expected to occur. Another criticism concerned the operationalization of the dependent variable. By examining the

various policy components of 'welfare statism' (like expenditure on social security, education, and health care), it could be demonstrated that the *design* of the welfare state showed a large cross-system variation in the distribution of what was spent on education, health care, and social security within the different countries. Table 22.2 (Chapter 22) shows that change in social expenditures differed considerably between 1980 and 2003. In short, the dependent variable 'welfare statism' could neither exclusively nor causally be linked to non-political factors alone, and nor could political factors could be ignored. The comparative analysis conducted demonstrated that political variables appeared to have a considerable (and statistically significant) impact as well. Hence, the 'new' research answer became: 'yes, politics does matter'!

Note that the research design not only concerns establishing the $X_2 \rightarrow Y$ relationship, proving that political variables played their role, but is also controlling for the relative impact of 'politics' by including the original explanatory relationship $X_1 \rightarrow Y$ as a rival explanation. The message conveyed here is that research in comparative politics requires a precise and detailed elaboration of a research design—in terms of relationships examined by means of variables and developing corroborating evidence across the cases under review—connecting research questions to research answers that are conducive to causal interpretation by means of descriptive inferences.[4] In the next section I turn to selecting the cases suited for comparison. This will direct the 'logic' of comparison implied in the research design to be used.

KEY POINTS

- Theory comes *before* method and is expressed in its simplest form as the relationship between dependent (Y) and independent (X) variables. The research method follows the research question in order to find the proper research answer.

- Research answers are (tentative) hypotheses that are interpreted by means of descriptive inference on the basis of *comparative* evidence, possibly allowing for causal interpretation.

- The research design is the toolkit to systematically *link* empirical evidence to theoretical relationships by means of comparative methods *enhancing* the internal and external validity of the results.

Comparing cases and case selection

Recall that linking theory to evidence always entails the reduction of real-world complexities so as to analyse the (logical) relationship between the X and Y variables. Hence, the researchers must make decisions about *what*

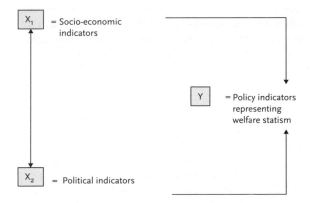

Figure 3.1 Investigating 'does politics matter?'

Source: Adapted from Pennings *et al.* (2006: 34).

to compare, i.e. select the cases (the carriers of relevant information), and about *how* this information can be transformed into variables. The key to the development of a proper comparative research design is to decide *which* cases are useful for comparing and *how many* can be selected (see Figure 3.2). The answer to this question has led to many views and debates (see Brady and Collier 2004). The thrust of this concerns the apparent trade-off between selecting many cases, but with few variables available for analysis, or a few cases available but many variables for use. I shall first clarify what a 'case' is.

Cases

The term 'case' has a general meaning in social science methodology, but in comparative methods it is used in a specific manner and is to some extent confusing (Pennings *et al.* 2006: 34ff). In comparative politics, cases denote the units of observation to be compared, such as countries. Yet the level of measurement may be different. Take, for instance, individual voters in several countries: the country is the case compared and determines the level of *analysis,* whereas the voter is the unit of observation (within the case). Conversely, if one compares party governments within a country, both the case and the unit of observation, governments, are at the same level of observation. For clarity, I propose to reserve the term 'case' in comparative methods for any type of *system* included in the analysis (recall Note 1). In addition I refer to *observations* as the values (or scores) of a variable under investigation. For example, if one compares party behaviour of regional parties, then the 'case' is the regional party *within* a system. Conversely, if the welfare state is the focus of comparison, then this concerns the systems to be compared. Public expenditures on social security are the empirical value for each system (see for instance Table 22.4). In Box 3.3 cases and variables are discussed in terms of a data matrix (i.e. the organization of the empirical observations by case and by variable). It is important to be precise in this matter because the *number* of observations—large- or small-N—determines what type of (statistical) analysis is feasible in terms of descriptive inference, given the available variation across the systems, or cases, under review (Pennings *et al.* 2006: 11).

The relationship between the cases selected and the variables employed to analyse the research question is a crucial concern. As can be seen from Figure 3.2, the process of case selection is structured as a kind of scale: from one case (often including many variables) to maximizing the number of cases (often with few(er) variables). In addition, it is sometimes suggested that this choice between few or many cases is related to the type of data—quantitative or qualitative—used. This is debatable (see also Brady and Collier 2004: 246–7).[5] For example, the study of welfare states often combines qualitative elements with statistical data (e.g. van Kersbergen 1995). Or take the study on 'social capital' by Putnam (1993) who combines survey data (reporting attitudes across the population) with a historical analysis of the development of politics and society in Italy since medieval times. Hence, comparative historical analysis is useful as a cross-sectional quantitative approach.

Comparative historical analysis has returned to the comparative method of late. Its point of departure is that the 'comparative historical analysis aims at the explanation of substantively important outcomes by describing processes over time using systematic and contextualized comparisons' (Mahoney and Rueschemeyer 2003: 6). Thus this type of historical analysis is thus meant to be explanatory and its mode of analysis is to use time (i.e. process and sequences) as the major variable. Second, processes have to be studied within the context of historical developments not in isolation. Third, historical sequences can be employed to explain the meaning of change. Karl Marx's theory of social and economic change, from feudalism through capitalism to socialism if not communism, is an example. Likewise, some students employ so-called 'critical junctures' (e.g. the World Wars or the End of the Cold War) that have transformed the relationship between state and society. Finally, there is the notion of 'path dependence', meaning that certain political choices made in the past can explain certain policy outcomes at present (see Chapter 22). The explanation rests then on the idea that alternative options for choice were not open any more, or given the time a policy exists the 'point of no return' has been definitively passed (Pierson 2000). In short, comparative historical analysis has a lot to offer to the comparative student, either in combination with other approaches or on its own (Keman 2013).

Box 3.3 **Cases and variables in a comparative data set**

In comparative research the term 'case' is reserved for *units of observation* that are comparable at a certain *level of measurement* be it micro (e.g. individual attitudes), meso (e.g. regional parties), or macro (e.g. national government). The information in a data set is a two-dimensional rectangular matrix: *variables* in columns (vertical) and *cases* in rows (horizontal). Each cell contains values for each variable, i.e. observations (e.g. levels of GDP, types of governments, or votes for parties), for each case (e.g. countries, regions, or parties). Likewise, variables may represent information *over time* (e.g. points in time, such as years, and are then cases (see Tables 22.1 and 22.2).

In sum, the selection of cases and variables depends on a deliberate *choice* in relation to the research question and on consideration of the type of approach chosen in view of the explanatory goals set (see also Ragin 2008). Therefore case selection is a crucial step.

Case selection

Cases are the building blocks for the theoretical argument underlying the research design. The number of cases selected in the research design directs the type and format of comparison. This is illustrated in Figure 3.2.

Figure 3.2 shows that there are different possible options for selection depending on how many cases and how many variables are involved. *Intensive strategies* are those with many variables and few cases. An example is the analysis of the few consociational democracies that exist. *Extensive strategies* are those with few variables and many cases. An example is the analysis of welfare states as discussed in Chapters 21 and 22. Here, many cases, if not all (e.g. all established democracies) are selected, whereas only a few variables are included. If N (number of cases included) is less than ten to fifteen, the strategy is intense. In addition, whether or not 'time' is a relevant factor needs to be taken into account (Pennings *et al.* 2006: 40–1). This is often the case, in particular when change (or a process development) is a crucial element of the research question (e.g. explaining welfare state developments). This is called *longitudinal* analysis if it is quantitatively organized or historical analysis if it is based on qualitative sources. Finally, if statistical analysis is used, as many cases as feasible are required to allow for tests of significance (King *et al.* 1994: 24; Burnham *et al.* 2004: 74). Five options for case selection are presented in Figure 3.2.

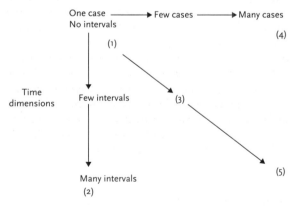

(1) Case study (at one time point);
(2) Time series (one case over time);
(3) Closed universe (relevant cases in relevant periods);
(4) Cross-section (all cases at one time point);
(5) Pooled analysis (maximizing cases across time and space).

Figure 3.2 Types of research design

Source: Adapted from Pennings *et al.* (2006: 21).

The single-case study

A single-case study may be part of a comparative research design. But as it stands alone it is at best implicitly comparative and its external validity is low or absent (see Landman 2003: 34–5). However, it can be used for post hoc validation to inspect whether or not the general findings hold up in a more detailed analysis or to study a *deviant* case (i.e. a case that appears to be an 'exception to the rule') and is also used as a *critical* or *crucial* case study (e.g. Rueschemeyer *et al.* 1992). Another use of a single-case study is as a pilot for generating hypotheses, or confirming or invalidating extant theories (Lijphart 1971: 691).

Time series

Time series or longitudinal analysis can be useful in two ways: first, to compare a specific configuration within a few cases in order to inspect comparative change; second, to analyse which factors are (or have become) relevant over time as causes. An example is the analysis of new parties that were electorally more successful after the 1990s than before (see Table 12.2). Another use is to replicate a cross-sectional study by time series analysis to observe differences in the outcomes (King *et al.* 1994: 223).

Closed universe

The third option in Figure 3.2 concerns the 'few' cases for comparison at different points of time, taking into account change by defining periodic intervals based on external events (or 'critical junctures'), for instance after a discrete event like war or an economic crisis. A good example is the developments during the inter-war period when in some European countries democracy gave way to dictatorship, whereas in other countries democracy was maintained (see Berg-Schlosser and de Meur 1996). A few(er) cases research design is often called a 'focused comparison' derived from the research question under review.

Cross-section

The fourth option in Figure 3.2 implies that several cases are compared simultaneously. This research design is frequently used. It is based on a selection of those cases that resemble each other more than they differ and thereby reduce variance caused by other (unmeasured) variables. It implies that the 'circumstances' of the cases under review are assumed to be constant, whereas the included variables vary. This enhances the internal validity of the analytical results. For example, if the focus is on formation of coalition governments, then it follows that we only take into account those democracies where multiparty systems exist.

Pooled analysis

The final option is disputed among comparativists. Although the number of cases can be maximized by pooling cases across time and systems (e.g. 20 rows and 20 columns taken together implies that the N of cases is 400 instead of 20), whereas in a time series data set the years (or other points in time, e.g. periods) are exclusively the cases and in a cross-sectional data set the cases are exclusively the political systems to be compared, the pitfall is that the impact of time is held constant across all cases (or, at least, changes across cases do not vary (Kittel 1999)). A possible fallacy is that comparative analysis suffers from the fact that the cases are 'too much' alike and therefore there are no meaningful differences from which to draw conclusions (see King *et al.* 1994: 202–3). To avoid this, one can include control cases (e.g. analysing EU members in conjunction with non-member states). Another remedy would be to include a 'rival' explanatory variable (as we showed in Figure 3.1: politics vs. economics). Pooled analysis is mainly used in sophisticated quantitative approaches and it requires skills in statistical methods at a more advanced level.

All in all, the message is that the range of choice with regard to case selection is larger than is often thought. First, the options available (in Figure 3.2, options 3 and 5 are in fact combinations). Second, the options in developing a research design can be used sequentially. For instance, one could follow up a cross-sectional analysis (option 4) with a critical or a crucial case study (option 1) as an in-depth elaboration. However, it should be noted that the options for choice as depicted in Figure 3.2 are not completely free. For instance, if industrialization is seen as a *process*, it must be investigated *over time* in order to answer the research question of whether or not this results in a change towards welfare statism.

A good example of such a research design is Peter Flora's analysis (1974) of West European welfare states. Various European societies were analysed from the time point in which they slowly developed into more or less liberal democracies (1850–1970). In this research design the issue was not the actual number of cases or systems, but the information available for the whole period (i.e. option 2 in Figure 3.2). By comparing the development of the welfare state in Europe with the rate of democratization, it was possible to demonstrate how political parties, organized interest, and governments played their distinctive roles.

The main point of this section is not only that case selection is important for how many cases can or should be included in the analysis, but also that the choice is neither (completely) free nor (completely) determined. First, the choice of cases depends on the theoretical relationship under review (X–Y) which defines what type of political system can be selected. Obviously, if one researches the working of democracies, non-democratic systems cannot

be included. Second, the type of empirical data available can limit the choice of cases.

Relating the cases and concomitant information (i.e. data) is the next step in performing comparative analysis. This stage of the research design concerns establishing and assessing the relationship between the evidence (data) collected across the selected cases for the independent and dependent variables in search of a (causal) relationship.

KEY POINTS

- In comparative research case selection is a central concern for the research design. It is important to keep in mind that the level of inquiry as derived from the research question is related to the type of system under investigation. The comparative variation across systems is empirically observed by means of indicators representing the variables that are in use.

- The balance between (many or fewer) cases and variables is an important option for case selection and the organization of the data set (see Box 3.3).

- Figure 3.2 shows the options for case selection. The selection of cases depends on the research question and the hypotheses that direct the research design. The choice of cases can be limited due to lack of data and therefore can impair the chosen research design.

The logic of comparison: relating cases to variables

In comparative methods there are two well-known research designs that employ a different type of logic: the *Most Different Systems Design* (MDSD) and the *Most Similar Systems Design* (MSSD). These designs relate directly to the type and number of cases under review and to the selection of variables by the researcher in view of the research question and the related (hypothetical) answers. Both have been developed following John Stuart Mill's dictum: *maximize experimental variance—minimize error variance—control extraneous variance* (Peters 1998: 30). In fact they are 'ideal types'—something to strive for.

Experimental variance

This points to the observed differences or changes in the dependent variable (Y) of the research question, which is supposed to be a function of the independent variable (X). Figure 3.1 is an example of the basic structure of modelling the relationship between a research question and a research answer. The question at stake was whether or not 'politics matters'. A crucial requirement for answering this question and attempting to settle this debate is that the dependent variable (Y = 'welfare statism') indeed varies across cases or over time (or both). Where there is *no* experimental variance we cannot tell whether or not the independent variables make a difference or not. Hence, the research design would lead to insignificant results because we cannot tell whether the effect-producing variables (X) account for the observed outcomes (in Y).

Error variance

This is the occurrence of random effects of unmeasured variables. These effects are almost impossible to avoid in the social sciences, given its quasi-experimental nature which always implies a reduction of 'real-life' circumstances. Even in a single-case study or comparing a few cases, a 'thick' descriptive analysis cannot provide full information. However, error variance should be minimized as much as is feasible (in statistical terms, the error term in the equation is then constant or close to zero). One way to minimize error variance would be to increase the number of cases. However, this is not always feasible, as mentioned earlier in the discussion on case selection (see also 'Conceptual stretching').

Extraneous variance

The final requirement in Mill's dictum is controlling for extraneous variance. If there is no control for other possible influences, the hypothetical relation X–Y may in part be produced by another (unknown) cause. This is often due to omitted variables and can lead to a *spurious relationship* (a third variable affects both the independent and dependent variables under investigation). There is no 'best' remedy to prevent extraneous variance exercising an influence other than by having formulated a fully specified theory or statistical significance tests and control variables.[6] The best approach is to apply the principles of the Methods of Agreement and Difference. Using these methods we are in a position to draw causal conclusions by means of logically ordering the *differences* and *similarities* between the dependent and independent variables, based on the empirical evidence available.

The use of Methods of Agreement and Difference in comparative analysis

The logic of comparative enquiry is obviously meant to assess the relationship between the independent variables and the dependent variable in light of the number of cases (many, few, or one) selected for comparison. As we have already seen, case selection has implications

for the use of the logics of comparison. Two logics are distinguished:

- Method of Difference;
- Method of Agreement.

The Methods of Difference and Agreement originate from John Stuart Mill's *A System of Logic* (1843). The basic idea is that comparing cases is used to interpret commonalities and differences between cases and variables. Hence, these 'logics' refer to the type of descriptive inference used to examine whether or not there is indeed a causal relationship between X and Y. This assessment is inferred from the empirical evidence (data) collected.

The **Method of Difference** focuses on comparing cases that *differ* with respect to either the dependent variable (Y) or the independent variable (X) but do *not* differ across comparable cases with respect to other variables (the *ceteris paribus* clause). Hence, covariation between the dependent and independent variables is considered crucial under the assumption that the context remains constant. This is the MSSD: locating variables, in particular the dependent variable, that differ across similar systems and accounting for the observed outcomes. An example is the debate on the role of 'politics' as regards the welfare state. We look at the political differences between systems that are similar in terms of their institutional design and examine the extent to which party differences (X) match differences in welfare state provisions (Y). The stronger the match between, for instance, the strength of the left in parliament and government and the 'generosity' of welfare entitlements, on the one hand, and its absence in cases where parties of the right are dominant, the more likely it is that 'politics matters'. Alternatively, the **Method of Agreement** consists of comparing cases (systems) in order to detect those relationships between X and Y that remain *similar* notwithstanding the differences in other features of the cases compared. Hence, other variables may be different across the cases except for those relationships that are considered to be causal (or effect-productive). This is the so-called MDSD. An example is Luebbert's analysis investigating the possible causes of regime types during the inter-war period (1919–39). He distinguishes three regime types: liberalism, social democracy, and fascism (Luebbert 1991). The explanatory variable (X) is 'class cooperation' (between middle class, farmers, and the working class) and regime type is the dependent variable (Y). Luebbert finds that only specific patterns of class cooperation consistently match the same regime type across twelve European countries. Most other variables considered (as possible causes) in the comparative analysis do not match the outcome (regime type) in the same way.

This distinction between 'most similar' and 'most different' is elaborated by Przeworski and Teune (1970) for use in research in comparative politics in order to interpret hypothetical relations in terms of causality given the similarities or differences between the cases taken into consideration. However, it should be noted that neither approach implies a choice like a 'zero-sum game': they offer *guidance* to elaborate a proper research design. Therefore it is important to note the limitations of these rules of comparison. First, Mill's logic presupposes that we have a list of potential causes to consider. But the logic itself does *not* produce this list. This depends on our theory about likely causes of the effects. Second, another assumption is that among the list of factors under consideration, *only* one factor is the unique cause of the effect. But there is no guarantee that this assumption always holds. Instead the cause might be a combination of various factors (Ducheyne 2008).

Second, recall the triad introduced earlier. The crux is in how the relationship between Research Question and Research Answer(s) is formulated in terms of X–Y. Table 3.1 summarizes both logics of comparative inquiry and illustrates each logic and system design through examples based on published research.

In practice, this 'logic of comparison' runs as follows. In an MSSD, where the cases have more circumstances in common (similar) than not, we interpret the research outcomes by concentrating on the *variation across the cases*, meaning 'cross-system *co*variation' and this forms the basis for explanation. An MDSD approach involves a comparison made on the basis of dissimilarity in many respects by concentrating on the *commonalities across the cases*. This procedure eliminates many other circumstances as possible explanations and one emerges

on which most cases are in agreement. In Table 3.1 both logics of comparison are presented in conjunction with, respectively, the MDSD and MSSD. The last two columns at the right-hand side concern the way conclusions are drawn by means of the 'method' and the descriptive inferences allow for *verifying the hypothesis* by eliminating irrelevant and non-causal variables. Table 3.1 demonstrates that, depending on the hypothetical relationship under review, the researcher must deliberate what cases and variables should be included in the comparative analysis if applying the Methods of Agreement or Difference. This will enable him/her to apply a logic of comparison in accordance with the data.

Recently, an alternative approach—*Qualitative Comparative Analysis* (QCA)— has been developed which attempts to cater for 'multiple causalities' (one of the limits of Mill's logic of comparison). This type of analysis allows for the handling of many variables in combination with a relatively high number of cases simultaneously (recall option 3 in Figure 3.2). Ragin (2008) claims that this type of research design is a way of circumventing the trade-off between many cases/few variables vs. few cases/many variables. The logic of comparison employed is based on Boolean algebra in which qualitative and quantitative information is ordered in terms of *necessary and sufficient* conditions as regards the relationship under investigation.[7] This approach also appears to be well suited to focusing on the variation of comparative variables within cases. Instead of aiming at detecting one (at best) effect-producing circumstance (X) by

Table 3.1 Features of the Most Similar and Most Different Systems Design

Type of design	Case selection	Variables included	Logic of comparison	Descriptive inference
MSSD	Similar on features *not* part of X → Y relation: *ceteris paribus* clause	Dependent and independent variables: X and Y vary across the cases included	Method of Difference	X → Y relation shows covariance (+ or −)
Example of research question: Does politics matter?	Democracies that are members of the OECD assuming that these countries have more *in common* than differences	Relative strength of left- and right-wing parties in government (X) influences level and growth of public expenditures on welfare (Y)	• Positive correlation between the left in government and level of welfare state expenditures • Correlation may disappear over time: convergence	
MDSD	Dissimilar on many features *not* part of X → Y relation	The relation between the dependent and independent variable does *not* vary across the cases	Method of Agreement	Specific X → Y relation remains constant across the cases
Example of research question: Do different forms of class cooperation produce different regimes?	European political systems: selecting cases that are different in *most* features, in particular regarding regime types	Different configurations of class cooperation between classes (X) and a specific regime type (Y) remain *constant*	• If X and Y co-vary, the form of class cooperation is considered as effect-producing as regards the regime type occurring	

Sources of examples: Schmidt 2002; Keman 2002a; Luebbert 1991.

means of a variable-oriented approach, the *homogeneity* of comparable cases directs the process of descriptive inference. An example is the search for the conditions under which economic development is more or less promoted by public policy (Vis *et al.* 2007). Instead of searching for the strongest or single relationship, the researcher attempts to find out which *combination* of factors is connected with cases in view of their economic development. This procedure and concomitant logic of comparison has been developed into a 'fuzzy-set logic' (Ragin 2008) and is a promising development.

> **KEY POINTS**
>
> - The point of departure is a hypothesis concerning the relationship between two or more variables (X–Y) whose empirical validity is to be verified by means of real world data across a number of cases.
>
> - The Method of Agreement uses MDSD to allow descriptive causal inference. Conversely, the Method of Difference derives its explanatory capacity from MSSD. The shared goal is to eliminate those variables that exemplify no systematic association between X and Y across the cases selected.
>
> - An alternative logic of comparison has recently been developed: QCA/fuzzy-set logic. This approach allows scrutiny of multiple causality across various cases and variables.

Constraints and limitations of the comparative method

Although the comparative approach in political science is considered to be advantageous in linking theory to evidence, enhancing it as a 'scientific' discipline, there are a number of constraints that limit its possibilities and can impair its usefulness. In this section we discuss some of these and offer possible solutions. While it is important to be aware of them, it is often difficult for starting students to find appropriate solutions. Hence, it is wise to seek advice from an experienced researcher or lecturer.

One major concern is that we often have too many different theories that fit the same data. This means that collecting *valid and reliable* data for the cases we have selected to test theoretical relations can turn out to be a daunting task. If this problem is insufficiently solved, it will undermine the quality of the results. More often than not we are forced to stretch our *concepts* so that they can *travel* to other contexts and increase the number of observations across more cases. However, this may create too large a distance between the stretched

concept and the original theoretical concept (Sartori 1970, 1994). If this problem occurs (and it often does), it may well affect the internal *and* external validity of the results (see Box 3.2). In conjunction with this hazard, it has been noted that reliability problems may arise as a result of including (functional) *equivalents* that are used to widen the case selection (and thus increase the number of cases). An example is the concept of the 'federal state'. What defines a federation and how can such a concept be transformed into measurable entities? Thus the problem is to what extent a concept transformed into an empirical indicator has the same meaning across different settings or cultures (Van Deth 1998). Finally, some caveats need to be taken into account when interpreting the comparative data available: (1) Galton's problem, (2) individual and ecological fallacies, and (3) over-determination.

Conceptual stretching

Conceptual stretching is the distortion that occurs when a concept developed for one set of cases is extended to additional cases to which the features of the concept do not apply in the same manner. Sartori (1970) illustrated this problem by means of the 'ladder of generality'. Enhancing a wider use of a theoretical concept by extension (of its initial meaning, i.e. moving from A to B in Figure 3.3) involves a loss of intension (where the observations reflect the original features of the concept, i.e. remain close to B). Intension will obviously reduce the applicability of a concept in comparative research across more cases, but it enhances the internal validity of the cases compared. Extension will have the opposite effect, and the question is then whether or not the wider use (i.e. in a higher number

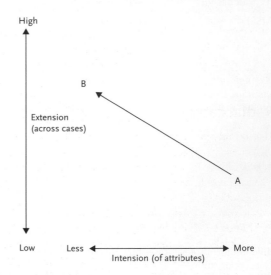

Figure 3.3 Sartori's ladder of generality

Source: Pennings et al. (2006: 49).

of cases to be compared) impairs the claim for external validity of the analytical results. In Figure 3.3 this choice is visualized: the more the meaning of a concept moves due to the process of operationalization from position A to B, the less equivalent the information collected for each case may be and therefore the validity of the results is negatively affected.

The choice to be made and the matter of dispute among comparativists is how broadly or extensively (i.e. from A to B) we can define and measure variables without a serious loss of meaning. There are different opinions on the degree of flexibility that is allowed when 'stretching' concepts to make variables 'travel' across (more) cases. Sartori remarks that *over*stretching is dangerous and not all concepts can travel all over the world and through all time, like a political party, whereas constitutional design may (Sartori 1994). However, attempts have been made to develop methods to cope with the problem of over-stretching and travelling.

Family resemblance

Some comparativists have suggested another solution by means of 'family resemblance' (Collier and Mahon 1993: 846–8). In its simplest fashion this method extends the initial concept by adding features which share some of the attributes of the original concept. How far this type of extension can go depends on what the research question is. For example, if we are investigating the behaviour of political parties and define these as any actor that is vote-seeking (= A), office-seeking (= B), and policy-seeking (= C), then the concept of a party can be used in a wider sense. Instead of requiring that all three characteristics are present *simultaneously*, we allow the inclusion of parties that have fewer in common. Examples are electoral democracies, where people can vote (= A), but parties are not allowed to govern (= B), let alone to make policy decisions (= C). This latter type of party often occurs in emerging democracies (see Vanhanen 1997).

Radial categories

The second option of going up the 'ladder of generality' is the use of *radial* categories. Here the underlying idea is that each step of extension, thus including new comparable cases, is defined by a *hierarchy* of attributes belonging to the initial concept. In Figure 3.4 this is made visible by defining A as the essential attribute, whereas B and C are considered as secondary. Figure 3.4 demonstrates these two strategies for extension through which the number of cases is to be increased. Family resemblance requires a degree of commonality and this produces three cases in comparison, instead of one under the initial categorization, by sharing two out of the three defining features

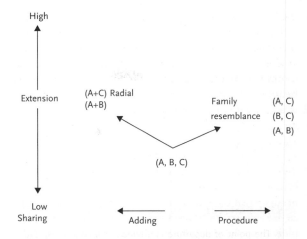

Figure 3.4 Radial categorization and family resemblance
Source: Pennings *et al.* (2006: 50).

(AC, AB, BC). The radial method requires that the primary attribute (A) is always included. In Figure 3.4, this means two cases instead of the original single case (A + B and A + C). It is advisable to develop a *typology* first to see empirically how this transformation of a concept may work out.

Equivalence

A related problem of transforming concepts into empirically based indicators concerns the question of whether or not the meaning of a concept stays constant across time and space. Landman (2003: 43–6) argues that this problem is less a matter of whether or not a concept is measured with *identical* results (which is a matter of reliability regarding the measurement). Whatever solution is chosen, at the end of the day it is up to the researcher to convince us whether or not the degree of equivalence between measured phenomena is acceptable.

Interpreting results

Galton's problem, ecological and individual fallacies, and over-determination are all hazards that are related to the *interpretation* of the results of the comparative analysis.

Galton's problem

Galton's problem refers to the situation where the observed differences and similarities may well be caused by an exogenous factor that is common to all the cases selected for comparison, such as comparing fiscal policy-making across states in Europe after the introduction of the EMU requirements, or the choice for a Westminster-style of parliamentary governance in former British colonies (Burnham *et al.* 2004: 74). Another example is the process of 'globalization' (see Chapter 24). Obviously, diffusion will affect the process of descriptive inference because the explanation is corrupted by a common cause (Lijphart 1975: 17).

Individual and ecological fallacies

These fallacies are likewise problematic *vis-à-vis* the causal interpretation of evidence. An ecological fallacy occurs when data measured on an aggregated level (e.g. at the country level) are used to make inferences about individual- or group-level behaviour. Conversely, individual fallacy is the result of interpreting data measured at the individual or group level as if they represent the 'whole' (e.g. using electoral surveys for party behaviour or national attitudes; see also the Introduction to this volume). This type of fallacy occurs regularly in comparative politics and shows the need for developing a proper level of measurement.

Over-determination and selection biases

Over-determination and selection biases are risks that emanate from case selection. In particular, when MSSD is used, the chances are high that the dependent variable is over-determined by another difference that is not actually catered for in the research design (Przeworski and Teune 1970: 34). Conversely, if the cases included in the analysis are fairly homogeneous there is a chance that a selection bias will go unnoticed. As King *et al.* (1994: 141–2) note, if the similarities among the cases affect the degree of comparative variation of the independent and dependent variables we cannot draw valid conclusions.

To conclude this section, these constraints and limitations of the comparative method need permanent attention. However, it would be wrong to conclude that—given the complexities discussed in this chapter—the comparative approach to politics is therefore misdirected or fallacious. If we accept the fact that most political science is comparative, even if not explicitly so, then it is one of the *strengths* of the comparative method that both the advantages and disadvantages are recognized and discussed in terms of its methodology.

Conclusion

Some time ago, Gabriel Almond lamented the lack of progress in political science at large (Almond 1990). His main complaint concerned the lack of constructive collaboration among the practitioners. However, he made an exception as regards the field of comparative politics:

> Mainstream comparative studies, rather than being in a crisis, are richly and variedly productive ... In the four decades after World War II, the level of rigor has been significantly increased in quantitative, analytical, and historical-sociological work.
>
> (Almond 1990: 253)

Much of the credit should go to those involved in the further development of the methodology of comparative politics by means of debates on difficult issues in the comparative method. However, new developments, like QCA and the re-emergence of comparative historical analysis, take place and are welcome. This chapter has attempted to demonstrate this. Throughout I have maintained that comparative politics is a (sub)discipline of political science where theory development is explicitly linked to empirical evidence by means of a rigorous application of the comparative method. Even if not all the problems—and they do exist—can be solved at this stage, I hold the view that the comparative method is the best way to go forward to further comparative politics within political science at large.

Questions

1. Why is the 'art of comparing' not only useful for *explicit* comparison, but also a *implicit* part of the toolkit of any political scientist?

2. Can you explain why the comparative method is often called '*quasi*-experimental'? Can you argue *why* this would justify the use of statistics in comparative politics?

3. What exactly is the difference between internal and external validity? Why is this distinction important? Can you give an example of each type of validity?

4. If you examine the debate on 'does politics matter?' can you describe the research design used? Are you able to develop an alternative one—in terms of variables and cases—to test the same issue of this debate?

5. What is a comparative variable and what is the relation between a concept and an indicator?

6. What is a case? Can you elaborate what the case is in terms of unit of observation and level of measurement if it concerns a comparative investigation of party government.

7. There are different options as regards the type and number of cases needed to develop a research design. Can you think of a research question that would justify the choice of a single-

case study where 'time' is relevant and 'inter'-system references are necessary?

8. The distinction between 'many cases and few variables' and 'few cases and many variables' is frequently debated in comparative politics in relation to the choice between an MSSD and an MDSD research design. List the pros and cons of the choice involved.

9. Describe the basic differences between the Methods of Agreement and Difference. Give an example of each, demonstrating this difference.

10. A constraint of the comparative method is 'conceptual stretching' and the solution may lie in extending the number of cases by means of 'family resemblance' or 'radial categories'. Can you think of an example of each to extend the number of valid cases?

Further reading

General literature on methods in political science

Brady, H. D., and Collier, D. (2004) *Rethinking Social Enquiry: Diverse Tools, Shared Standards* (Lanham, MD: Rowman & Littlefield). This edited volume discusses a wide variety of methodological concerns that are relevant for comparative methods.

King, G., Keohane, R. D., and Verba, S. (1994) *Designing Social Inquiry* (Princeton, NJ: Princeton University Press). This is a contemporary classic in social science methods written by three political scientists. It is an introduction and uses much material taken from comparative politics.

Landman, T. (2003) *Issues and Methods in Comparative Politics: An Introduction* (2nd edn) (London: Routledge). This introductory text discusses various fields within comparative politics, focusing on different research designs by means of one, few, and many cases.

Specific literature on comparative methods

Mahoney, J., and Rueschemeyer, D. (eds) (2003) *Comparative Historical Analysis in the Social Sciences* (Cambridge: Cambridge University Press). This reader contains many different views on developing qualitative types of comparative research with an emphasis on history and the use of case studies.

Pennings, P., Keman, H., and Kleinnijenhuis, J. (2006) *Doing Research in Political Science: An Introduction to Comparative Methods and Statistics* (2nd edn) (London: Sage). This is a course book intended for students. It is an introduction to the use of statistics in comparative research and contains many examples of published research.

Ragin, C. (2008) *Redesigning Social Inquiry. Fuzzy Sets and Beyond* (Chicago, IL: University of Chicago Press). The book centres on the 'fuzzy-set' approach as an alternative to other comparative methods as discussed in this chapter (see also Box 3.3) and discusses the advantages of this approach in comparison with extant practices.

Web links

The historical context

CHAPTER 4

The nation-state

Gianfranco Poggi

Chapter contents

Reader's guide

The most significant political units of the modern world are generally referred to as 'states' or 'nation-states'. It is within and between states that contemporary political business is carried out. This chapter explains where, when, why, and how this particular kind of political unit came into being and how it became dominant. It provides the conceptual and historical background knowledge necessary for the study of many other themes of comparative politics. We suggest that this chapter is read in combination with Chapter 24 on 'Globalization and the nation-state' which discusses some recent challenges to the dominance of this political unit.

Introduction

The comparative analysis of the arrangements under which political activity is carried out refers chiefly to a multiplicity of interdependent but separate, more or less autonomous, units—let us call them polities. Polities differ among themselves in numerous significant respects, and entertain with one another relations—friendly or antagonistic—which reflect those differences. These exist against the background of considerable similarities. The most important of these qualify the polities making up the modern political environment for being called states.

The expression 'state' has been applied by scholars to polities which have existed in pre-modern contexts— say, to ancient Egypt, or imperial China. This is legitimate, but here we propose that 'state' is more appropriately used to designate the polities characteristic of the *modern political environment*, which came into being in Western Europe at the end of the Middle Ages, roughly between the thirteenth and the fifteenth centuries.

First, this chapter offers a general and streamlined portrait of the state—a concept that sociologists inspired by Max Weber (whose work will be a prime source for much that follows) might call an ideal type. Such a concept points up which features most states share to a greater or lesser extent. Such a conceptual portrait of the state may appear out of date on various counts, since a number of contemporary developments within the modern political environment have made some of the portrait's features, for instance the notion of state sovereignty, less plausible (see Chapter 24).

To present this conceptual portrait, first I consider the most fundamental aspects of the state, and then amplify and qualify the portrait by adding other aspects, which generally have developed over the last two or three centuries. After this, assuming that we now know what states *are like*, I will ask how they came into being and through what processes.

> **KEY POINTS**
>
> - Most contemporary political units (polities) share aspects which justify calling them 'states'.
> - To that extent, they all constitute present-day embodiments of a kind of polity which first developed in the modern West.
> - A sustained scholarly engagement with 'comparative politics' should consider both the constitutive features of that kind of polity and the major steps in its development.

A portrait of the state

Monopoly of legitimate violence

States are in the first place polities where a single centre of rule has established its exclusive entitlement to control and employ the ultimate medium of political activity—organized violence—over a definite territory. Individuals and bodies operating within that territory may occasionally exercise violence, but if they do so without mandate or permission from the centre of rule, the latter considers that exercise illegitimate and seeks to suppress it. Typically, it mobilizes its own potential for violence to overwhelm that wielded by those individuals or bodies, and compels them to 'cease and desist'. If it *cannot* do so, and if in the territory alternative seats of power can act with impunity on the assumption that it cannot, you no longer have a state proper, but some other kind of polity.[1]

Territoriality

The territory itself is a most significant element of the state. To qualify as a state the polity must be able not only to 'police' a given portion of the Earth by overwhelming any internal challenges that may arise to its own monopoly of legitimate violence, but also to claim that portion, against all comers, as exclusively its own, be able and disposed to defend it, patrol its boundaries, confront and push back any encroachment by other states upon its territory's integrity, and prevent any undue exploitation of its resources. Once more, the ultimate medium of such activities is organized violence.

The relation between state and territory is an intimate one. The territory is not simply a locale of the state's activities (violent or other), or its cherished possession. Rather, it represents the physical aspect of the state's own identity, the very *ground* (this expression is itself a significant metaphor) of its existence and of its historical continuity. The state does not so much *have* a territory, rather it *is* a territory (Romano 1947: 56).

Sovereignty

It is with reference to its territory, furthermore, that the state establishes and practises its sovereignty. Being sovereign signifies, for each state, that it recognizes no power superior to itself. It engages in political activity on nobody's mandate but its own, commits resources of its own, operates under its own steam, at its own risk. It is the sole judge of its own interests and bears the sole responsibility for pursuing those interests, beginning with its own security. A sovereign, the state holds within the territory (and thus over the people residing in it) the ultimate authority. Sovereignty also means that each state accepts no interference from others in its own domestic affairs.

Plurality

Thus the modern political environment consists in a plurality of territorially discrete, self-empowering, self-activating, self-securing states. Each of these presupposes the existence of all others, and each is in principle their equal, since it shares with them (and acknowledges in them) its own characteristics—sovereignty in particular. Since there does not exist a higher layer of authority over the states—a superior unit endowed with its own resources for violence, entitled to oversee and control the states—these necessarily tend to regard each other as potentially hostile, as constituting impending threats to their own security, and enter into relations with one another aimed in the first instance either to neutralize or to confront and defeat those threats.

Relation with the population

States exercise rule over people, issue commands to and expect obedience from people, pursue policies binding over people. But states, though they sometimes project themselves as self-standing personified entities, are themselves *made of* people and operate exclusively within and through the activities of individuals. On this account the existence itself of states involves a form of social inequality, a more or less stable and pronounced asymmetry between people exercising rule (a minority) and people subject to it (the great majority).

Asymmetry is to an extent bounded and justified by a sense in which both parts to it belong together, and jointly make up a collective entity. Together with the ruling minority, the ruled-over people constitute a *political community*. For this community the activities of rule constitute a medium for coming into being, for achieving and maintaining a shared identity, for pursuing putatively common interests. As is the case for the territory, the relationship between the state and its population is not purely factual; the population is not perceived as a mere demographic entity but as a people (or, as we shall see, as a nation). As such it entertains a more significant, more intimate, one might say *constitutive*, relation with the state itself.

All this, of course, lends itself to much ideological mystification, and induces Marx to speak of the nation as an 'illusiory' community, and deride the view of the people or the nation as the source and/or carrier of the state's sovereignty. But how illusory can you call a commonality in the name of which feats of great magnitude and significance have been accomplished (for good or for evil) throughout modern history?

KEY POINTS

- Internally, states possess a single centre of power that reserves for itself the faculty of exercising or threatening legitimate violence.
- A state does not respond to any other power for the uses to which it puts that faculty and others.
- The state uses the faculty of violence to protect one portion of the Earth which it considers its own territory. It claims exclusive jurisdiction over the population inhabiting that territory and at the same time considers itself the guardian of its interests.
- Externally, each state exists side by side with other states, all endowed with the same characteristics, and treats them as contenders, allies, or neutral parties.

A more expansive concept

A definition of the state in Weber's *Economy and Society* is both retrospective of what I have said so far and prospective of the points to be made in this section.

> The primary formal characteristics of the modern state are as follows: it possesses an administrative and legal order subject to change by legislation, to which the organised activities of the administrative staff, which are also controlled by regulations, are oriented. This system of order claims authority, not only over the members of the state, the citizens, most of whom have obtained membership by birth, but also to a very large extent over all action taking place in the area of its jurisdiction. It is thus a compulsory organisation with a territorial basis. Furthermore, today, the use of force is regarded as legitimate only so far as it is permitted by the state or prescribed by it. (Weber 1978: 56)

This definition points to additional features of states active in the nineteenth and twentieth centuries—though of course individual states display them to a different extent and in different ways. This *diversity* is the main theme of the study of comparative politics.

The role of law

We begin by noting that *law*, understood as a set of general enforceable commands and prohibitions, has played a significant role in the construction and management of states. In all societies, law so understood has chiefly performed two functions: first, to repress antisocial behaviour; second, to allocate between groups or individuals access to and disposition over material resources. In the West, however, law has been put to a third use: *establishing polities, deciding issues of policy, instituting public agencies and offices, and activating and controlling their operations.*

These uses of law developed first in the Greek *polis*, and then in the Roman Republic and Empire. Subsequently, European polities maintained a connection with the realm of law: rulers were expected to serve **justice,** observe it in their own conduct, and enforce it in adjudicating disputes and punishing crimes. But for a long time the commandments in question were understood to express folkways and the moral values of religion. Local judges and juries were said to *find* the law, and were not meant to *make* it. Much less did the rulers do so. Instead, they mostly enforced the verdicts of judges and juries.

This arrangement subsequently changed. Rulers undertook to play a more active legal role. Increasingly assisted by trained officials, they began to codify local vernacular sets of customs and usages and to enforce them uniformly over the territory. Above all, they asserted themselves as the source of a new kind of law—*public* law. This regulated the relations on the one hand between the organs and offices of the state itself and on the other between the state and various categories of individuals and groups, generally asserting the supremacy of the former's interests over those of the latter.

Two later developments counterbalanced one another. On the one hand, it was increasingly asserted that *all law was such only in so far as it was produced by the state*, through special organs and procedures. Law had become, so to speak, the exclusive speech of the state. On the other hand, *the state declared itself bound by its own laws.* The activities of its organs and the commands of state officials were considered valid only if their content or, more often, the ways in which they were produced, conformed with some express legal principles, such as those contained in constitutions.

Particularly on the European continent, academic credentials in law became the standard qualification for those aspiring to enter the state's administrative apparatus. To an extent that varied in time and from region to region, the state—without ceasing to assert its own grounding in sheer might—became involved in producing and implementing (and, by the same token, complying with) arrangements expressed in legal instruments of diverse kinds: constitutions, statutes, decrees, judgements, ordinances, and by-laws.

Centralized organization

These instruments do not stand on the same plane, but make up a more or less explicit and binding hierarchy of legal sources. Typically, the constitution lies at the top, by-laws stand lower than statutes, and so on. This is so in three closely related senses.

1. Higher sources authorize and place boundaries upon lower ones.
2. The products of lower sources can change without altering the content of higher ones, but articulate and specify them in different and variable ways.
3. The verified contrast between the content of a higher source and that of a lower one invalidates the lower one. Different judicial organs are empowered to issue judgements of different scope or gravity. Higher ones may review and nullify or revise the judgements of lower ones.

This hierarchical arrangement is intended to bring unity and coherence to a variety of legal instruments and related organs. But other aspects of the state reveal the same preoccupation with unity and coherence, and express it through hierarchy. For instance, the monopoly in the exercise of violence has a legal aspect (Weber speaks of 'legitimate force'). But much more significant are its organizational components, summarized in the contemporary expression 'command, communication, and control', without which that monopoly cannot be secured. Those components have sometimes a very loose relationship (if any) to legal constraints. The organizational blueprint of the state mostly reveals a *managerial rather than a legal* rationality. It is chiefly intended to make the operations of all state agencies as responsive as possible to the directives of the political centre, and to render them uniform, prompt, predictable, and economical. Together, two rather different but equally common and persistent images of the state—the pyramid and the machine—convey a preoccupation with unity and coherence.

The distinction between state and society

The distinction between 'state' and '(civil) society', theorized by Hegel among others, is more or less expressly reflected in the constitution of several Western states. The state, in principle, is an ensemble of institutional arrangements and practices which address *all and only* the political aspects of the management of a territorially bounded society. It represents and justifies itself as a realm of expressly political activities (legislation, jurisdiction, police, military action, public policy) complementary to a different realm—society—comprising diverse social activities not considered political in nature, which the state's organs do not expressly promote and control. Individuals undertake those activities in their private capacities, pursuing values and interests of their own, and establishing among themselves relations which are not the concern of public policy. At the centre of the realm of society stand two sets of concerns which for a long time the state saw very much as its own, but subsequently, via lengthy and complex processes, released to that realm.

Religion and the market

First, the state becomes increasingly secular. That is, it progressively dismisses any concern with the spiritual welfare of individuals, which previously it had fostered, mostly by privileging (and professing) one religion and associating itself with one church. (A critical reason for this development was the breakdown of the religious unity of the West caused by the Reformation.)

Second, the state progressively entrusts to the two central institutions of private law—property and contract—the legal discipline of the activities which relate to the production and distribution of wealth, and which increasingly take place via the market. Rule, religion, and the economy, thus differentiated, can each affirm its own autonomy and develop its rationality. These domains do not stand on the same plane. One meaning of sovereignty is that the state's specific concern with external security and public order may override those of private individuals, especially in confronting emergencies. Furthermore, private activities are carried out within frameworks of public rules which the state is responsible for enacting and enforcing.

In the same way, it is the state's prerogative to fund its own activities by extracting resources from the economy. But typically the modern state is a 'taxation state': it extracts resources from the society's economic system chiefly by regularly levying moneys from stocks and flows of private wealth. Such levies, authorized by law and carried out by public officials, are compatible with the security of private property and with the autonomous operations of the market. The name itself of another subsidiary form of extraction, the *public debt,* again suggests that compatibility: private individuals become creditors of the state. Furthermore, the state plays an indispensable role in issuing and guaranteeing money, but is not supposed to allocate the wealth stored and vehicled by state-backed money.

With modernization, the distinction between state and society is deepened by further processes of differentiation taking place within both realms. For instance, within the civil society there emerges a domain—science—which attends expressly and exclusively to the production and distribution of secular knowledge about nature, autonomously from religious authorities. Within the state itself, the so-called 'separation of powers' between the legislature, the judiciary, and the executive constitutes the outcome of a process of differentiation. Differentiation also produces its effects in the context of the executive, with the development of bureaucratic systems of administration—a phenomenon to which I shall return (see also Chapter 8). As a result, the state increasingly presents itself as a complex of purposely differentiated and coordinated parts, each designed to perform a specific task. The image of *the state as a machine* and the growing significance of the expression *organization,* and related expressions, convey this.

The public sphere

Behind these processes lies a further phenomenon—the formation of the 'public sphere' as a kind of hinge between state and society. As if to balance and complement the extent to which the state monitors and assists the processes of the civil society, the subjects active in it acquire a capacity first to observe the activities of the state,

then to communicate with one another about them, to criticize them, and finally to make significant inputs into them. This is only possible, at first, for a narrow minority within the population who possess the leisure and the necessary material and cultural resources. But over time that minority grows.

The public sphere comprises institutions such as the freedom of speech, of the press, of assembly, of association; rules that require some state organs to conduct their activities in public to expose them to legitimate debate and criticism; and above all, the institutions of 'representative' government.

Liberal and democratic arrangements for participation

Thanks to these institutions, the selection of the small minorities who directly and continuously operate some state organs comes to depend on registering the preferences periodically expressed by the much larger numbers of people making up the electorate. Again, at first only a narrow minority within the population can form and express such preferences, and even as that minority grows, with the progress of liberalism, for a long time it remains bounded by two qualifications: (1) material possessions (*census voting*) and (2) cultural attainments (*capacity voting*) (see also Chapter 5). We can characterize the progress of *democracy* as the progressive lowering and then elimination of these barriers. In the long run, the great majority of the adult population (for a long time, excluding women in many countries) acquires, through suffrage, an equal (though minimal) capacity to express preferences and to make them affect the selection of political elites and, via these, the formation of public policy.

The new 'entrants into politics' are mobilized by expressly formed organizations—political parties (see Chapter 12)—which compete to determine directly who at a given time has the decisive say in legislative and executive organs, and indirectly the content of their activities. In other words, the formation of public policy is made to depend on 'adversary politics', involving the periodic contest between parties for electoral support, but also the right of the party which has failed in a given contest to criticize the policies of the successful party, propose alternative policies, and seek success in the next contest.

The burden of conflict

Although we generally think of political participation chiefly as a *vertical* flow of influence from the society at large towards its political summit, we should not forget the etymological meaning of 'participation'—*taking sides.* This meaning points instead to a *horizontal* split, a division within the society itself. Put otherwise, through the public sphere the contrasts of opinion on political matters formed within the society map themselves onto the state, affecting the operations of its legislative organs and of those charged with the initiation and implementation of policy. Such contrasts, though generally they do not express themselves through organized violence (given the state's monopoly of that), can be bitter and divisive, for expressly *political* alignments such as parties often derive their conflicting policy orientations from deep and long-standing *social* cleavages within the population (see Chapter 13).

Such cleavages do not just represent different orientations of opinion concerning individual issues, but sometimes reflect serious cultural differences (say, between religious or linguistic groups), tensions between a country's centre and its periphery, ethnic differences, or sharp class antagonisms. In the modern political vocabulary, the significance of such a threat is particularly evident in negative expressions like 'sectionalism', 'factionalism', 'partisanship', or 'interest', and in the contrasting emphasis on the necessity of protecting the state's 'unity' from such phenomena, appealing instead to 'loyalty', 'discipline', and 'spirit of sacrifice'.

Citizenship and nation

In most modern states, this threat is countered by two different and to an extent complementary strategies: citizenship and the nation.

Citizenship

The first strategy consists in the institution of citizenship, which finds its primordial expression in the dictum *all citizens are equal before the law*. Eventually, the principle came to signify the progressive inclusion of all individuals making up the people into a formally equal relationship to the state itself.

Individuals who found themselves placed under the same obligations and enjoyed the same entitlement vis-à-vis the state were made to feel more equal to one another. Furthermore, their entitlements relating to the public sphere were put at the service of a new principle of equality, associated with the progress of democracy, and originally phrased as *one man, one vote*. Under this principle, as we have seen, broader and broader masses of individuals entered the political process and made inputs into the state's activities via the electoral competition between parties. Those supported chiefly by economically disadvantaged strata promoted public policies—those we generally associate with the welfare state—that added to citizenship new entitlements toward the state. These, to an extent, reduced or compensated for inequalities generated among individuals by the market economy and the resultant class cleavage.

As a consequence, as one argument goes (which is not uncontested), those cleavages lost much of their power to threaten the state's unity. However, this happened by mobilizing class contrasts, by making the processes of creation and distribution of wealth an object of public contention and of policy, no longer shielded from the state by the separateness of the social realm. The state acknowledges the significance of socio-economic cleavages and expressly works to reduce it via the growing structures of the welfare state. To this end it extracts from the economy greater and greater resources, and entrusts them to expressly created public organs, mandating them both to redistribute those resources and to assist the economy in producing further resources. Nonetheless, it presents problems of various kinds, at any rate from the standpoint of the elites who control those economies, although often they also benefit amply from the growing involvement of the state in economic affairs.

Nationhood

The second strategy seeks to generate in the whole society, across the classes, a shared sense of solidarity grounded on nationhood. The political community typical of modern states is supposed to constitute a **nation**. Most of the polities with which this book deals define themselves as nation-states; the relations of states with one another make up international politics; the pursuit of the national interest by each state is supposed to be the key rationale of those relations; finally, the largest international organization in the contemporary political environment is called the United *Nations*. Furthermore, nationalism is widely seen (for better or for worse) as a most significant determinant of political activity.

For all this, the concept of nation is notoriously hard to define. The etymology of the expression hints at a nation's origins in a shared biological heritage, for it has the same root as 'nature' and *nasci* (Latin for 'to be born'). And indeed some contemporary accounts of the concept can be called 'ethnic', for they emphasize similarity (and continuity) of blood, suggesting a very remote origin for the phenomenon of nationhood. Although this emphasis is echoed in the ideologies of many political movements, it does not accord well with the fact that the appeal to nationhood as a political value and the corresponding 'consciousness of kind' are by and large modern phenomena—often brought about in the context and in the interest of a previously existing state.

Reflecting this, most contemporary scholarly constructions of nationhood treat it as a response or component of other modern phenomena, such as industrialization, the diffusion of literacy, the emergence of media of communication addressing broader and broader publics, and—indeed—a state's need to generate at large a sense of identification with itself and of commitment to its interests. In this understanding, nations appear as *imagined and socially constructed*

Box 4.1 Imagined communities

The nation is an 'imagined' political community.

- It is *imagined* because the members of even the smallest nation will never know most of their fellow-members, meet them, or even hear of them, yet in the minds of each lives the image of their communion.

- It is imagined as *limited* because even the largest of them, encompassing perhaps a billion human beings, has finite, if elastic, boundaries, beyond which lie other nations.

- It is imagined as *sovereign* because the concept was born when Enlightenment and Revolution were destroying the legitimacy of the divinely ordained hierarchical dynastic realm.

- It is imagined as a *community* because, regardless of the actual inequality and exploitation that may prevail in each, the nation is always conceived of as a deep horizontal comradeship.

Source: Adapted from Anderson (1983: 6–7).

communities (Anderson 1983) (see Box 4.1). That is, most nations have been brought into being by protracted, intense, diffuse communication processes, mostly activated by the state and carried out on its behalf, funded from the public purse, and carried out by modern intellectuals (historians, journalists, poets, musicians, teachers, political leaders). Their products are diffused by the compulsory public education system and vehicled by various symbolic practices (such as monuments, street names, public festivities, commemorations, and military parades). In so far as this operation is successful, it sustains in the members of the public a sense of trust, mutual belonging, pride, and solidarity.

As a result of such socialization processes, a people who generally had already lived for generations within the same framework of rule may come to share a value-laden emotionally compelling image of its history and its destiny, a sense of its own uniqueness and superior value. It comes to perceive itself as a distinctively significant, binding, active, collective entity. It generally identifies closely with the territory of the state, which it considers its own cradle and its prime possession; or it aspires to make the territory on which it resides the seat of a new self-standing state, intended to give political expression to its unity, to redeem its population from its painful and demeaning subjection to a state governed by foreign people. It may then happen that the emergence of a nation as a cultural entity *precedes* the formation of a state, intended to become the nation's own institutional container and give it political expression.

The emphasis on nationhood counteracts the tendency of the public sphere to project into the political realm divisions arising from the diverse, often conflicting, interests which motivate the activities of private individuals in the civil society. But the appeal to nationhood also has a more positive significance, which relates it to citizenship and the trend towards widening and enriching its significance.

Earlier in this chapter, I have attributed this trend to the attempt by underprivileged social groups to reduce their disadvantage with respect to privileged groups. But a search for greater socio-economic equality can also impart more significance to nationhood itself. In the historical career of citizenship the rhetoric of 'one nation' has played at least as great a role as that of 'social justice'. In fact, the earliest modern statewide 'welfare' policies, initiated by Bismarck in nineteenth-century Germany, were probably inspired more by the first concern than by the second. And one may detect a connection between the burden and suffering that the state's military ventures imposed on a people, supposedly on behalf of the national interest, and the state's attempt to ease those burdens or compensate for those sufferings through *welfare* initiatives.

This awkward expression refers to a complex development which progressively affects political practice in established states. Although, I would argue, political power maintains its ultimate grounding in the exercise or the threat of organized violence, the latter ceases to manifest itself openly and harshly in everyday experience. Most of the people professionally involved in (so to speak) the business of politics no longer differ markedly (as they did in earlier stages of state development) in their attire, their posture, their speech, the ways they relate to one another and to other people, from individuals involved in commerce, management, or the liberal professions.

Most kinds of political and administrative activity are carried out in peaceable and orderly sites (legislative bodies, courts, public agencies of various kinds), where people generally talk politely to one another, consult and refer to documents, argue about solutions to problems, negotiate arrangements, express reasons for their preferences, put forward proposals and suggestions. Even when superiors expressly give orders to their subordinates in the expectation of being obeyed, they refer at most in an implicit covert manner to the sanctions which would follow from disobedience, and those sanctions rarely entail the exercise or the threat of violence. The highest and most general legal commands—say, statutes—are expressed in highly codified sophisticated language. Lower-level commands (say, a fine or an order to pay tax) are only valid and binding if they refer to higher-level ones.

This does not mean that political activity has lost its ability to threaten or exercise violence. However, the personnel routinely involved in it are generally (not in times of war) a minority among the multitude of people carrying out the manifold political activities characteristic of a developed state.

Significantly, that minority also operates within distinctive components of the state's political and administrative machinery. Generally, only people serving in the police and the armed forces are authorized and expected to bear arms, to wear uniforms. They belong to bodies where an imperious chain of command obtains; harsh sanctions may be promptly inflicted on those members who disobey or disregard orders. Thus the threat or exercise of violence is entrusted to specialized personnel and separated from the normal practices of political authority, both materially (for instance, soldiers reside in specially designed buildings) and symbolically (see again the uniforms military people wear, with their markers of rank).

Punishment is no longer inflicted on miscreants in public places, in a particularly dramatic, cruel, visible manner. The most common among serious punishments—imprisonment—is mostly carried out in a routinized, silent, invisible manner, in separate buildings, often out of the public eye. And the decision to bring to bear the means of violence on criminals or on enemies belongs in principle to political personnel not themselves directly involved in practising violence—judges, members of representative bodies, and top political officials.

This kind of 'civilianized' arrangement typically does not diminish the state's capacity for organized violence but increases it. Paradoxically, this increase in the *potential* for violence may be accompanied by a decrease in the *actual* exercise of violence. As they go about the ordinary business of their lives, individuals may be spared the experience of fear by the very fact that the potential violence monopolized by the state becomes more, not less, fearsome.

The conceptual portrait recapped

The modern political environment is composed of a plurality of states sharing some formal characteristics. Thanks to its monopoly of legitimate organized violence, each state exercises sovereign power over a population which inhabits a delimited territory, and constitutes a political community, often referred to as a nation. The interactions between states are normally peaceable, but since they are not overseen and regulated by a superior power capable of imposing sanctions, they ultimately depend on the might that each state can bring to bear to oppose or overwhelm other states pursuing interests opposed to its own. Thus those interactions are highly contingent and may periodically be adjusted by the threat or exercise of military action between the states involved.

Over the course of the last two or three centuries, many states have, to a greater or lesser degree, acquired additional traits. Their internal structure is generally designed and controlled by laws which each state produces and enforces, but which in turn regulate its own activities. These are very diverse, and are generally carried out by a number of organs and specialized agencies. They deal directly with matters the state considers to be of public significance, leaving other matters making up the concerns of (civil) society to the initiative of individual subjects.

However, some state activities, including the making of laws and their enforcement, lay down frameworks for the pursuit by individuals of their own private concerns. Furthermore, the institutions of the public sphere may empower individuals to form and exchange opinions on state policies, and to organize themselves in parties which represent the diverse (and often contrasting) interests within the society, select the personnel of various state organs, and mandate their policies.

In the course of the last two centuries, most states have conferred on the individuals within their populations a variable set of citizenship entitlements, beginning with those relating to the public sphere, and comprising claims to various benefits and services provided by the state, but ultimately funded from the proceeds of the state's fiscal activities. The advance of citizenship has often entailed making a public issue of socio-economic differences between individuals, and committing state policy to their moderation. For this reason it has often been contested. One may consider the appeal to nationhood, and the state's positive efforts to 'push' that appeal, as a way of curbing the divisive effects of the contests over the reach and content of citizenship entitlements.

Box 4.2 Citizenship

So far my aim has been to trace in outline the development of citizenship in England to the end of the nineteenth century. For this purpose I have divided citizenship into three elements, civil, political, and social. I have tried to show that civil rights came first, and were established in something like their modern form before the first Reform Act was passed in 1832. Political rights came next, and their extension was one of the main features of the nineteenth century, although the principle of universal political citizenship was not recognised until 1918. Social rights, on the other hand, sank to vanishing point in the eighteenth and early nineteenth century. Their revival began with the establishment of public elementary education, but it was not until the twentieth century that they attained to equal partnership with the other two elements of citizenship.

Source: Marshall 1950: 27–8.

KEY POINTS

- States differentiate between their political activities and those of the civil society (the pursuit of private economic interests and the expression of personal beliefs and values). They articulate themselves through legal instruments (constitutions, statutes, decrees, various kinds of rulings) into units operated by distinct bodies of personnel. In particular, they have entrusted practices involving internal order and external defence to the police and the military.

- In the democratic state decisions over state policies are the products of the peaceable competition between parties seeking to maximize their electoral support in order to occupy the top positions in various state bodies and to promote the interests of their supporters.

- Policies pursued by states since the middle of the nineteenth century have sought to moderate inequalities by assigning individual members of the population civil, political, and social rights—citizenship (see Box 4.2).

- To counter divisive tendencies between groups, states have undertaken policies intended to generate a sense of commonality—chiefly, a sense of national belonging.

Box 4.3 Patterns of state formation

We can distinguish at least five paths in state formation.

1. Through *absolutist kingship* which obtained independent power by building up armies and bureaucracies solely responsible to monarchs (e.g. France, Prussia).

2. Through *kingship-facing judges and representative bodies* (and, within them, eventually political parties) which developed sufficient strength to become independent powers (e.g. England, Sweden).

3. State formation from below through *confederation or federation*, due to the maintenance of effective autonomy for the constituent 'states' and a general emphasis on the division of power within the centre through 'checks and balances' (e.g. Switzerland, US).

4. State formation through *conquest and/or unification* (e.g. Germany, Italy).

5. State formation through *independence* (e.g. Ireland, Norway, and cases of break-up of empires: Habsburg and Ottoman empires).

Source: Adapted from Daalder (1991: 14).

State development

The features of the state presented in the preceding section are the outcomes of numerous complex historical events (see Box 4.3). These differed not just in their location in space and time, but also in (1) the sequence in which they occurred, (2) the degree to which their protagonists expressly sought to produce those outcomes, (3) the extent to which the features agreed or conflicted with one another, and (4) the impact they had on the patterns of political activity of each state, its relations to the civil society, and its capacity to respond to new challenges.

Furthermore, as we have seen, all states-in-the-making operated in the presence of one another. This led some states to imitate some aspects of others, or on the contrary to emphasize their differences. This further complicated the historical processes. For instance, some states previously unified by the successful efforts of royal dynasties sought to strengthen their unity by promoting a sense of nationhood in the populations over which they ruled. Later, other states imitated such a nation-building project. Furthermore, populations which, despite being ruled over by foreign powers, had somehow acquired a sense of themselves as 'nations without states' sought to build states of their own. Thus, in some cases state-building preceded nation-building; in other cases it was the opposite.

The study of comparative politics necessarily simplifies these complex phenomena, for instance by stressing either differences or similarities between units. It contrasts states built early, in late medieval or early modern Europe (for instance, England or France), with others built during later stages of modernization (for instance, in the second half of the nineteenth century, as in the case of Germany or Italy). It distinguishes states built upon successful conquest (for instance, England) from those owing their existence to the breakdown of larger polities (for instance, contemporary Serbia or Ukraine).

This section of the chapter distinguishes three main phases within the story of state formation and development, which unfolded first in Europe, then extended to polities built elsewhere by European powers (for instance, North America), and later encompassed other parts of the world. However, the way in which it is narrated here chiefly reflects the European experience. Even in this context the succession of phases suggested purposely abstracts from a huge variety of events, incidents, and episodes which a properly historical treatment would have to account for.

Consolidation of rule

We can label the first phase, which takes place, largely, between the twelfth and the seventeenth centuries, 'consolidation of rule'. During this phase, with different timings in different countries, a decreasing number of political centres each extend their control over a larger and larger portion of Europe. Each, typically, broadens the territorial reach of its own monopoly of legitimate violence and imposes it on other centres. The political map of the continent becomes simpler and simpler, since each centre now practises rule, in an increasingly uniform manner, over larger territories. Furthermore, these tend to become geographically more continuous and historically more stable—unless, of course, they become themselves objects of further processes of consolidation.

Sometimes these are peaceful. For instance, the scions of two dynasties ruling over different parts of Europe marry, and the territorial holdings of one spouse become welded to those of the other. However, consolidation is mostly the outcome of open conflicts between two centres over which one will control which territory. Such conflicts are mostly settled by war, followed by the winner conquering and forcibly annexing all or part of the loser's territory. 'States make war', as someone memorably put it, 'and wars make states' (Tilly 1990: 42).

Thus, a decisive role in the consolidation of rule is played by military resources. But these in turn require the 'sinews of war', that is the financial capacity to muster those resources—troops, officers, *matériel*—and deploy them against opponents, making them prevail in the clash of arms against the resources wielded by the enemy. Very often military innovation confers an advantage to larger armies and fleets, which can wage war over more than one front, and become internally differentiated into 'services' performing distinct complementary military tasks. But such armies and fleets can only be afforded by rulers who marshal larger resources, and in turn this requires raising troops from larger populations, tapping the wealth produced by larger territories. This premium on size is a strong inducement to consolidation.

But the recourse to war, however frequent throughout European history, is intermittent. When weapons are silent, however temporarily, resources of a different nature come into play. Often, political centres intent on consolidating rule do this in response to an appeal for peace, which recurs most frequently in European history, often voiced by religious leaders. Each centre argues (and seeks to prove) that by establishing its control over a larger territory it can put an end to rivalries between lesser powers which would otherwise occasion war. This does not always involve prevailing over those powers in battle. Diplomatic action, alliances and coalitions, the ability to isolate opponents or to make them accept a degree of subordination, sometimes the recourse to arbitration by the empire or the papacy, also play a role.

Besides, military activity itself requires and produces rules of its own, the very core of an emerging body of law seeking, more or less successfully, to regulate aspects of the relations between states. Another significant part of such law makes conflict over territory less likely by laying down clear principles for succession into vacant seats of power, which generally make the exclusive entitlement to rule depend on legitimate descent. Other developments contribute to the same effect, which we might call

'pacification'. In particular, advances in geography, in the measurement of terrain, and in cartography allow the physical reach of each centre of rule to be clearly delimited by geographical borders, in turn often determined by features of the terrain. It remains true, as Hobbes put it, that states maintain towards one another, even when they are not fighting, 'a posture of warre'. But they partition the continent of Europe, and later other continents, in a clear and potentially stable manner.[2]

Rationalization of rule

There is often an overlap between the processes of consolidation of the first phase of state formation and development, and the processes of a second phase, which I label the rationalization of rule. Consolidation, we have seen, produces larger, more visible, and stable containers of state power; rationalization bears chiefly on the ways in which such power is exercised. We can characterize such ways by distinguishing in turn three aspects of it: (1) centralization, (2) hierarchy, and (3) function. Let us take them in turn.

Centralization

In consolidating and then exercising rule, rulers largely availed themselves of the cooperation of various subordinate but privileged power holders—chiefly, aristocratic dynasties, towns and other local or regional bodies, bishops and other ecclesiastical officials. Often that cooperation was granted only after the subordinate powers had been forced to renounce some of their privileges—in particular, especially as concerns aristocrats, that of waging private wars.

All the same, their later cooperation generally had to be negotiated, for the privileged powers maintained a degree of autonomous control over various resources, and managed them in the first instance on their own behalf. They could be induced to do so on the ruler's behalf only under certain conditions, sanctioned by tradition or by express agreements between themselves and the ruler. For instance, the cooperating lesser powers would extract economic resources from the local population under their jurisdiction in order to convey them to the ruler. But they would do so only if they had given their consent to the purpose to which the ruler intended to commit those resources. They often kept a fairly large part of those resources for themselves, and controlled locally the ways in which the remainder of them were managed and expended in their respective part of the territory.

Obviously, such arrangements considerably limit the rulers' freedom of action, their ability to lay down policy for the state as a whole and have it promptly, reliably, and uniformly implemented over the whole territory. They make the conduct of political and administrative business discontinuous and sometimes erratic, since who is charged with it at a given time—in particular, qua head of an aristocratic lineage—depends on the vagaries of hereditary succession, and often has no particular inclination or capacity for that business. Even the cooperation granted, as we have seen, by constituted collective bodies (the so-called 'estates') tends to give priority to their particular interests, and thus to preserve traditional arrangements, beginning with their autonomy. This makes it difficult for the ruler to coordinate and render predictable the practices of the several powers interposed between himself at the top and, at the bottom, a territory made larger by consolidation and its population.

To remedy this situation, rulers progressively dispossess the existent individuals and bodies of their faculties and facilities they had employed in their political and administrative tasks.[3] They put in place alternative arrangements for performing both those tasks and those required by new circumstances. Instead of relying on their former cooperators, they choose to avail themselves of **agents** and *agencies*, i.e. individuals and bodies which the rulers themselves select, empower, activate, control, fund, discipline, and reward. In other terms, rulers build *bureaucracies* (see Box 4.4).

In principle, this process could greatly increase the hold upon social life at large of the political centre, enable the ruler to exercise power in an unbounded, arbitrary, and despotic fashion, and expose all those subject to it to extreme insecurity. In fact, the previous cooperators who objected to the ruler's new arrangements often raised complaints to that effect, sometimes rightly so. But more often their objections simply reflected their attachment to their previous privileges. We would not characterize this phase as 'rationalization of rule' if its chief import had been solely to unbind rule.

It is an aspect of 'the European miracle'—the title of the book by Jones (1981)—that this phase of state-building has two apparently contrasting aspects. Rulers do come to oversee, control, and to an extent manage social life at large in a more and more intense, continuous, systematic, purposive, and pervasive manner. However, to be legitimate, rule must appear to be oriented to interests acknowledged as general, and be exercised in a more and more impersonal and formal manner. The notion of *raison d'état* conveys both aspects. It asserts that the might and security of the polity are a general and paramount interest whose pursuit may occasionally override all others. But that interest is to be sought through self-conscious deliberation, grounded on an assiduous, careful, detached monitoring of circumstances.

In fact, the rationalization of rule itself is part of a broader process of rationalization of social existence at large. Each major sphere of society (beginning with the three already mentioned: politics, economy, and religion) becomes the exclusive concern of a different institutional complex—an ensemble of arrangements, personnel, resources, principles, and patterns of activity. This allows (and perhaps demands) each concern to be pursued in such a way as to maximize a distinctive goal: respectively the might and security of the state, the profitability of economic operations, and the individual's prospects of spiritual salvation.

Hierarchy

In the political context, rationalization changes the basis of the routine exercise of power: the public understanding of its nature, its objective, its boundaries. As we have seen, that basis was traditionally constituted by the *rights and perquisites* of a number of privileged individuals and bodies (see Chapter 8). The new basis consists in the *duties and obligations* of individuals (we may label them 'bureaucrats' or 'officials') appointed purposefully to established offices. Their political and administrative activities can be programmed from above by means of express commands. Those issuing such commands can reward those to whom they are issued if they comply with them, and punish them if they do not. The commands themselves have two critical characteristics: (1) they tend to be general, i.e. they refer in abstract terms to a variety of concrete circumstances; (2) their content can legitimately change, and thus respond to new circumstances (see Box 4.4).

Box 4.4 The bureaucratic state

Where the rule of law prevails, a bureaucratic organization is governed by the following principles.

1. Official business is conducted on a continuous basis.

2. There are rules in an administrative agency such that (1) the duty of each official to do certain types of work is delimited in terms of impersonal criteria, (2) the official is given the authority necessary to carry out his/her assigned functions, and (3) the means of compulsion at his/her disposal are strictly limited.

3. Official responsibilities and authority are part of a hierarchy.

4. Officials do not own the resources necessary for the performance of their functions but are accountable for their use. Official and private affairs are strictly separated.

5. Offices cannot be appropriated by their incumbents in the sense of private property that can be sold or inherited.

6. Official business is conducted on the basis of written documents.

Source: Bendix (1960: 418–19).

For this to happen, the new ensembles of individuals who carry out political and administrative activities—the bureaucratic units—must be hierarchically structured. At the bottom of the structure, even lowly officials are empowered to give orders (issue verdicts, collect taxes, conscript military recruits, deny or give permissions) to those lying below the structure itself. However, those officials themselves are supposed to do so in compliance with directives communicated to them by superiors. These monitor the activity of their direct subordinates, verify their conformity with directives, and if necessary override or correct their orders. This arrangement, replicated at various levels within the whole structure, establishes an ordered array where higher offices supervise, activate, and direct lower ones. In a related hierarchical arrangement, lower offices *inform* higher ones—make suggestions on how to deal with situations—and higher ones *make decisions* and transmit them downwards to lower ones for implementation.

As already indicated, law plays a significant role in structuring these arrangements for rule. First, as we have seen law itself is a hierarchically structured set of authoritative commands. Second, law can be taught and learned, and the knowledge of it (at its various levels) can determine, to a greater or lesser extent, the content of the agents' political and administrative operations.

This second aspect of the law points to a broader aspect of the rationalization of rule—the growing role of *knowledge* in the government and administration of the state. As rulers increasingly dispense with the cooperation of privileged individuals and bodies, the agents who replace them are largely chosen on account of what they know, or are presumed to know, and by their having earned academic degrees and passed selective tests. Agents are expected to orient their practices of rule less and less to their own individual preferences or to local particular tradition and lore, but instead more and more to expressly imparted and learned systematic knowledge. Legal knowledge is the prototype of this, especially on the European continent, but it is increasingly complemented and supplemented by different kinds of knowledge—those relevant to, say, waging war, building roads and bridges, charting the country, collecting statistical data, keeping financial accounts, minting money, policing cities, and safeguarding public health.

Function

Another principle structuring the centralized system of offices is *function*: the system is internally differentiated to have each part deal optimally with a specific task. To this end, the system parts must possess materially different resources—not only various bodies of knowledge, acquired and brought to bear by appropriately trained and selected personnel, but artefacts as diverse as weapons at one end and printing machines at the other.

For all its diversity, the whole structure is activated and controlled not only by knowledge but by *money*, another public reality distinctly connected with rationality, chiefly acquired through *taxation*. Traditional power-holders had usually engaged in collaborating with rulers' material and other resources from their own patrimony; their collaboration was self-financed and unavoidably self-interested. Now, agencies operate by spending public funds allocated to them on the basis of express periodic decisions (budgets) and are held accountable for how those funds are spent. Office-holders are typically salaried, manage resources that do not belong to them but to their offices, and as they comply with their duties are not expected to seek personal gain, except through career advancement.[4]

To the extent that it is rationalized, the exercise of rule becomes more compatible with the individuals' pursuit of their interests within the civil society. From the perspective of those individuals, rule, as exercised by officials, appears more regular and predictable, and occasional deviations from rules can be redressed. Rulers are interested in increasing the resources available to the society as a whole, if only to draw upon them in funding their political and administrative activities. But to this effect they must at least recognize the requirements of the country's economic system, at best protect or indeed foster its productive dynamic, which rests increasingly on the market. To this end, again, the extraction from the economy of private resources increasingly takes place chiefly by means of taxation.

The security of those resources and of their employment must be sustained by guaranteeing, through appropriate legislation and the machinery of law enforcement, the institutions of private property and contract. But other social interests and cultural concerns, not just economic ones, also benefit from the limits that rationalized rule sets on its own scope and from the arrangements it makes in order to recognize and protect the autonomy of civil society.

The expansion of rule

In the third phase, states display a dynamic which we may label the 'expansion of rule'. For centuries, the activities of each state had been oriented to two main concerns.

1. On the international scene, it sought chiefly to secure itself from encroachments on its territory by other states and on its ability to define and pursue its own interests autonomously.

2. Within its territory, it was committed to maintaining public order and the effectiveness of its laws.

In the second half of the nineteenth and through much of the twentieth century, however, states brought their activities of rule to bear on an increasingly diverse range of social interests.

Essentially, the state no longer simply *ordains* through legislation the autonomous undertakings of individuals and groups or *sanctions* their private arrangements through its judicial system. Increasingly, it *intervenes* in private concerns by modifying those arrangements or by collecting greater resources and then redistributing them more to some parties than to others. Also, it seeks to *manage* social activities according to its own judgements and preferences, for it considers the outcome of those activities as a legitimate public concern, which should reflect a broader and higher interest (for example, the promotion of industrial development, social equity, or national solidarity).

The expansion of rule modifies deeply the relationship between state and society of the previous phase. On this account, we can classify most of its explanations according to whether they locate the main source of the drive to expand in the state itself or in society.

The former accounts occur in various versions.

1. First, they may impute to the state's administrative machinery an inherent tendency to grow, to avail itself of more resources, to take charge of more tasks, and to address more numerous and diverse social interests, instead of leaving them to the market or to the autonomous pursuits of individuals and groups (see Box 4.5).

Box 4.5 Wagner's law

Consider the following scattered indication of the validity of 'Wagner's Law', which states that government spending tends to rise faster than the growth of the national economy as a whole. In the UK, government spending accounted for the following percentages:

Year	%
1890	8.9
1920	20.2
1938	30.0
1960	36.4
1970	43.0
1981	50.3
1983	53.5

Similarly, in the US the amount of government (federal, state, and local) spending as a proportion of the net national product almost tripled between 1926 and 1979. For all OECD countries over the period 1953–73 the average of the national product accounted for by government spending rose from 34 to 39 per cent.

Source: Poggi (1999: 109).

2. Or, second, they may see the main reason for state expansion in the dynamics of representative democracy and of adversary politics. Putting it simply, it pays for a party out of power to increase its support by promising, if voted into power, to devote more public resources to this or that new state activity, and thus advance the interests of social groups responding to its appeal. Typically, it is parties of the left which have successfully played this card, and made new use of state activity and state expenditure to reduce the disadvantages inflicted on their supporters by market processes.

3. This interpretation fits closely with a third one, which imputes the expansion of the state chiefly to phenomena located in the society side of the state–society divide. Here, underprivileged groups stand to gain most by state expansion, and thus invoke it and favour it, through their suffrage or by other forms of mobilization.

4. However, according to a fourth interpretation, many aspects of state expansion support directly or indirectly, rather than correct and counteract, the workings of the market economy in the interest primarily of firms and employers. For instance, some colonial ventures of European states favoured major economic forces seeking privileged access to the raw materials, manpower, and market opportunities that they saw in foreign lands, or seeking profit in supplying the state with military and naval hardware. Furthermore, for over a century now, many public resources have been committed to educational activities, which deliver to the labour market employees equipped with the diverse qualifications and skills the economy needs. In the second half of the twentieth century the state often underwrote, on behalf of firms and thus primarily of employers, substantial research and development costs to sustain more advanced and profitable production processes.

More widely, this fourth interpretation attributes much state expansion to the fact that, left to itself, the market often does not generate enough demand for industrial products to sustain capital investment, a reasonable level of employment, and thus domestic demand for industrial products. From this perspective, the main beneficiaries of state expansion are, in the end, the more established and privileged social groups.

In fact, the frequently evoked imagery of states expanding by claiming as their own social tasks previously performed by autonomous social forces, and usurping society, is sometimes misleading. Many of the activities carried out, well or otherwise, by the expanding state, respond to *novel* needs, potentialities, and opportunities generated by ongoing social developments, such as the demographic explosion, urbanization, increasing literacy, mass motorization, further industrialization, and the increasing complexity of society itself. Already at the end of the nineteenth century, Durkheim had argued, in opposition to Spencer, that in the process of modernization the development of the private realm also requires the development of the public one.

Whatever the reasons for it, state expansion entails a growth in three interdependent aspects:

- the *fiscal take*, i.e. the portion of a country's yearly product extracted and managed by the state;
- the degree of *internal differentiation* of the organizational machinery of the state;
- the *total number of individuals* whom those units employ, and who possess increasingly varied qualifications and skills.

The last two phenomena not only displace the line between state and society, but also affect deeply the state itself, which increasingly resembles an ever-growing ill-coordinated ensemble of increasingly diverse units. The ordinary political processes—the articulation of collective interests via the parties and their periodic electoral competition, the determination of the executive by majorities, and the formation of policies through the interplay between the executive and parliaments—can less and less effectively activate and steer an administrative machinery so vast, expensive, complex, and diverse.

Much in political decision-making and in the subsequent administrative activity responds to the interests of the units themselves, or those of the specific, often narrow, sections of society they cater to, rather than expressing a political project reflecting a comprehensive view of the society as a whole. Thus, the administrative machinery becomes *overloaded* by multiple, ever-changing, conflicting demands. Furthermore, components of it are 'captured' by powerful and demanding social forces, and serve their needs rather than those of the public at large. All these phenomena make it more and more difficult for the political elites themselves to design and put into effect the policies for which the electorate has expressed a preference.

These phenomena manifest themselves in most contemporary states, but they do so to a different extent and in diverse ways. As the subsequent chapters show, one of the major tasks of the study of comparative politics is to establish empirically, and to account for, the variations present in the contemporary political environment, both in those manifestations and in the responses they find in the political authorities, the parties, and the social movements.

KEY POINTS

- One can distinguish, within the historical career of the modern state, three main phases which different European states have followed in somewhat varying sequences.

- *Consolidation of rule*: within each larger part of the continent (beginning with its Western parts) one particular centre of rule asserted its own superiority, generally by defeating others in war, subjecting the respective lands to its control, and turning them into a unified territory.

- *Rationalization of rule*: each centre of rule increasingly relied on functionaries selected and empowered by itself, expressly qualified for their offices, and forming hierarchically structured units, their careers within which would depend on the reliability and effectiveness of their actions.

- *Expansion of rule*: states progressively took on broader sets of functions, in order both to confront social needs generated by ongoing processes of economic modernization, and to respond to demands for public regulation and intervention originating from various sectors of society. They added new specialized administrative units and funded their activities by increasing their 'fiscal take' from the economy.

Conclusion

It can safely be assumed that the vast majority of this book's readers live in a political environment which resembles more or less closely the portrait of 'the state' given in this chapter, and whose institutions and practices bear traces of the developments sketched in the last section. For this reason, those readers—whatever their feelings about the state of which they are citizens, and however they position themselves vis-à-vis the particular government which runs it—may take for granted its main features, including the fact that they are able, among other things, to study scientifically that state itself and to compare it with others. However, this chapter, and others in this book, is intended to challenge the assumption that such matters can indeed be taken for granted.

The following statement by a notable German social theorist, Heinrich Popitz (1925–2002), entails such a challenge.

> The history of society shows only rare instances where the question 'how can one lay boundaries around institutionalized violence?' has been confronted in a positive and viable manner. Essentially, this has happened only in the Greek *polis*, in the Roman republic and a few other city states, and in the history of the modern constitutional state. And the answers given to that question have been astonishingly similar. The principle of the supremacy of the law and of the equality of all before the law (the Greeks named it *isonomia*). The notion that the making of norms by the state encounters limitations (fundamental rights). Norms assigning different

competences to various political organs (division of powers, federalism). Procedural norms (decisions by collective bodies, their public nature, appeals to and review by higher organs). Norms on the occupancy of offices (turn-taking, elections). Finally, norms concerning the public sphere (freedom of opinion, freedom of association and assembly). The similarity, or indeed the commonality among such answers suggests that there are systematic solutions of the problem, how to limit institutionalized power and violence, and that these solutions, although they presuppose certain premises if they are to hold, can to an extent hold across different contexts—as different, say, as city states and those ruling over extensive territories. (Popitz 1992: 65)

Popitz's statement suggests some comments.

1. Although I have treated 'the state' as essentially a modern phenomenon (and its development as the chief political dimension of the broader phenomenon of modernization), some of its distinctive institutional arrangements had already manifested themselves in antiquity, as well as in the Middle Ages.

2. Both the earlier and the later (modern) arrangements appear at first as part of a distinctive Western story, for they originated in Europe and were subsequently transposed to parts of the rest of the world conquered and settled by European powers, especially in North America and Australia. (However, the US was the first place where a peculiar arrangement, federalism, was more expressly and successfully experimented with, and it served as a model for further experiments—see Chapter 11.) Since then, some such arrangements have become common to polities operating across the globe, although in different modes of interpretation and implementation.

3. The arrangements mentioned by Popitz, singly and together, succeed in an intrinsically difficult job—limiting, constraining, and 'taming' institutionalized political power.

This last point suggests a further consideration, left implicit in Popitz's statement. Such success cannot be taken for granted. It is a matter of degree, for it requires overcoming a built-in tendency of political power to grow upon itself, to escape limits and constraints, to 'go wild' as it were—a tendency that can manifest itself in many circumstances and in many ways. In fact, some states which shared the characteristics mentioned in the first section of this chapter have not presented all those mentioned in the second section, which have appeared in later phases of political modernization and which (in the author's personal judgement) go a long way towards 'civilizing' the state itself.

For instance, the Tsarist Empire refused to endorse many characteristic institutions of the constitutional, liberal, democratic states of Western Europe. Worse, even states which at a given point exhibited all those characteristics subsequently veered away from constitutionalism, liberalism, and democracy, and underwent institutional changes generally associated with the notion of 'totalitarianism'—as happened in the twentieth century in Italy and Germany (see Chapter 6). And even some of the constitutive features of states listed in the first section, such as 'sovereignty', are currently put under stress by a number of developments—for example, those associated with 'globalization' or with the formation of transnational polities (see Chapter 24).

Even apart from such dramatic developments, the liberal–democratic states themselves differ from one another in many relevant respects. For instance, some impart a centralized and some a federal structure to the relations between the state's political centre and its political periphery. States differ in the extent to which they have broadened and enriched the entitlements of citizenship, or in the extent to which and the manner in which a given state seeks through its policies to support and plan the development of its national economy, as against leaving such development entirely to the workings of the market. The size of the so-called 'public sector' of the economy, and the way in which it has been managed, again have differed from state to state, as have their respective taxation policies.

These and other issues have often been fought over in significant lasting confrontations between parties and between sectors of opinion, and their settlement has been more or less stable, creating affinities or contrasts between states. Besides being the themes of public life, those issues constitute the main topics of the scholarly study of politics, whether focused on a particular state or on the diversity and similarity between states. The latter, of course, is the main concern of this book as a whole.

Questions

1. What is meant by 'civilianization'?
2. How can one explain the fact that members of a state's population progressively acquired rights vis-à-vis the state?
3. What is civil society?
4. Do nations create states or vice versa?
5. What part did law play in the development of the modern state?

6. For what reasons did rulers establish bodies of officials appointed and empowered by themselves?
7. What is meant by 'consolidation of rule'?
8. What is meant by 'sovereignty'?
9. What part did military force play in the making of European states?
10. How do states, typically, acquire the economic resources they use?

 ## Further reading

Elias, N. (2000) The *Civilizing Process: Sociogenetic and Psychogenetic Investigations* (Oxford: Blackwell 1st edn 1938). The second large volume of this impressive deals with the 'sociogenesis of the state'.

Lachmann, R. (2010) *States and Power* (Cambridge: Polity Press) A valuable interpretation of many phenomena considered in this chapter, mostly from a perspective at some variance from that adopted here.

Poggi, G. (1978) *The Development of the Modern State: A Sociological Introduction* (Stanford,: Stanford University Press). A compact and accessible statement, ranging from the Middle Ages to the contemporary era.

Tilly, C. (ed.) (1975) *The Formation of National States in Western Europe* (Princeton, :Princeton University Press). A very influential collection of major contributions to its theme, including its military, fiscal, and economic aspects.

Weber, M. (1994) 'Politics as a Profession and Vocation' (1919), in *Weber: Political Writings*, ed. P. Lassman and R. Speirs (Cambridge: Cambridge University Press) 309–69. A compact but most illuminating and provocative discussion of the nature of politics and the modern state by one of the most significant modern social theorists.

 ## Web links

www.pipeline.com/~cwa/TYWHome.htm
Webpage about the Thirty Years' War which gave rise to the modern states after the Peace of Westphalia (1648).

www.arcaini.com/ITALY/ItalyHistory/ItalianUnification.htm
Webpage about Italian unification, independence, and democratization.

http://americancivilwar.com
Webpage about the American Civil War.

 For additional material and resources, please visit the Online Resource Centre at:
www.oxfordtextbooks.co.uk/orc/caramani3e/

CHAPTER 5

Democracies

Peter Mair

Reader's guide

Since the fall of the Berlin Wall in 1989, scholars and institutional designers have become much more interested in understanding how democracies differ from one another. This chapter compares democracies, and looks at the different types and definitions of democracy, paying particular attention to procedural definitions. Following a brief assessment of the milestones that were reached on the path towards developing democracy, the chapter reviews the attempts to model democracies as holistic systems and argues that most efforts in this direction are almost bound to be frustrated. The chapter concludes by looking at the notion of audience democracy as well as at the growing levels of popular dissatisfaction with democracy.

Introduction

Prior to the 1970s the democracies of the world constituted a small and homogeneous group of regimes. Figures published in a retrospective review by Freedom House suggest that fewer than one in four of the world's polities were democratic in 1950, with most of these being in the West or having developed under the influence of Western models; therefore three-quarters of the polities could be defined as one or other of the then many varieties of non-democracy.[1] As late as 1974, when Portugal launched the so-called 'third wave of democratization', just 27 per cent of the independent states in the world were democratic, including just 22 per cent of those states with populations greater than one million (Diamond 1999: 24).

For most of the early post-war decades, in short, more than 70 per cent of states could be counted in the non-democracy category, and it was the variation within this larger group that proved of greater interest to comparative political research (see Chapter 6). Non-democracy was seen to take many forms, whereas democracy was simply democracy. That is, the differences which were analysed were not those of the regime as a whole but those which operated across particular institutions within the polity (Keman 2002b; see also Chapter 1).

To be sure, an ambitious and comprehensive country-by-country comparison of democratic development was organized by Dahl in the 1960s in his famous and still unrivalled volume *Political Oppositions* (Dahl 1966). But even here the burden of the analysis tended to focus on political parties, their support bases, and their patterns of competition both inside and outside parliament. Almond's (1956) classic categorization of democracies into Anglo-American, continental European, and what were later defined as 'working' multiparty systems (the Benelux countries, Switzerland, Scandinavia) was also heavily influenced by an interpretation of the prevailing patterns of party competition, with the primary distinction revolving around the question of whether the parties represented closed and conflictual 'subcultures' or were more likely to engage in competition within shared electoral markets (see also Lijphart 1968b).

In other words, while particular institutions *within* democracies have always been compared and evaluated, little attention was paid to the comparison of models of democratic regimes (e.g. Beer and Ulam 1958; Finer 1970). Today, however, there is an increasing concern to specify more clearly what is entailed by the notion of democracy as well as to compare different forms of democratic regime in terms of their policy performance, legitimacy, and stability. Within comparative politics, as well as in real-world discussions, variations *among* democracies have become much more important. What had once been a small and homogeneous group of regimes has now become large and heterogeneous—hence the various attempts in the contemporary scholarly literature to establish new classifications and typologies of democracy.

> **KEY POINTS**
>
> - Having constituted fewer than one in four of world regimes in the 1950s and 1960s, democracies now count for almost three in four.
>
> - What had once been a small and homogeneous group of democratic regimes has now become large and heterogeneous. Therefore typologies and classifications are important in understanding how democracies function.

Comparing democracies

There are at least four important and related factors which have contributed to this new interest in comparing democracies.

The comparison of regimes

The first factor came from scholarship itself, with two important studies in the early 1980s by Powell (1982) and Lijphart (1984) which sought to characterize and compare democratic regimes and institutional structures as a whole.

In Lijphart's case, this led him to elaborate the more all-embracing distinction between majoritarian and consensus models of democracy (see Table 5.1), which was to prove a highly influential contribution to the literature on comparative democracy both in the first version in 1984 and in the revised and extended version which was published later (Lijphart 1999). This study encouraged other scholars to think of democracies in more comprehensive terms, and to attempt to measure their survival and impact in terms of the entire complex of institutions that were involved.

The 'third wave' of democratization

The second major impetus came from the 'third wave' of democratization, and particularly from the explosion in transitions to democracy that occurred with, and in the immediate aftermath of, the fall of the Berlin Wall in 1989.

In a very influential study published soon after the fall of the wall, Samuel Huntington (1991) argued that democratization has developed in a series of bursts or 'waves', with a wave being defined as 'a group of transitions from democratic to nondemocratic regimes that occurs within a specified period of time and that significantly outnumbers transitions in the opposite direction' (Huntington 1991: 15). Much as a wave breaks on the beach, democratization has come in ebbs and flows, with the many transitions to democracy being followed by a smaller number of transitions back to non-democratic alternatives.

Table 5.1 Majoritarian and consensus models of democracy

Institutional feature	Majoritarian model	Consensus model
Executive	Concentration of executive power in single-party majority cabinets or minimum winning coalitions	Executive power-sharing in broad multiparty coalitions
Executive–legislative relations	Executive dominates legislature	Balance of power in executive–legislative relations
Party system	Two-party system	Multiparty system
Electoral system	Majoritarian and disproportional electoral system	Proportional representation (PR)
Interest group system	Pluralist	Corporatist
Type of government	Unitary and centralized government	Federal and decentralized government
Legislature	Unicameralism	Strong and incongruent bicameralism
Constitution	Flexible and easily amended	Rigid and difficult to amend
Judicial review	Parliamentary sovereignty	Constitutional court
Central bank	Dependent on executive	Independent of executive

Note: In the updated and extended version of a typology originally introduced in 1984 with eight key features, Lijphart (1999) identified ten features that distinguished between Westminster and consociational models of democracy.

Table 5.2 Democracies in the world

Year	Number of democracies*	Number of countries	Democracies as % of all countries
2005	123	192	64.1
2000	120	192	62.5
1995	117	191	61.3
1990	76	165	46.1
1974	39	142	27.5

* These are 'electoral democracies' as defined by Freedom House based exclusively on a judgement of the electoral process and ignores possible limits on civil liberties.

Source: Freedom House, *Democracy's Century* (LeDuc *et al.* 2002: 211).

For Huntington, the first 'long' wave lasted from 1826 to 1926, and was then reversed in part by the rise of fascism and authoritarianism in the 1920s and 1930s; the second wave came after the Second World War and was reversed in the 1960s and 1970s; the third wave was initiated in Portugal in 1974 and reached explosive levels after 1989. Thus far, there have been no serious reversals (Huntington 1991) (for a corrective on the counting of cases by Huntington, see Doorenspleet (2000)). Therefore by the end of the twentieth century the number of democracies had rapidly increased, and had come to constitute almost 75 per cent of the world's polities (Table 5.2). Since then this process has continued, not least with the Arab Spring in 2011. Within this expanded universe, democracies inevitably reflected an immense variety of institutional structures and forms.

With more cases and more variety, it became more important to classify democracies and to distinguish their variations. As Linz argued, '[t]he fact that there is currently no alternative to democracy as a principle of legitimacy, and that so many countries have undergone a transition to democracy, compels us to look more closely at the variety of democracies and the ways they function' (Linz 1992: 182). By becoming 'the only game in town,'[2] democracy developed into a new focus for inquiry as the alternatives to democracy faded from relevance.

Institutional engineering

The third major impetus was related to the lack of democratic experience in many of the polities making this transition, leading to a resurgence in practical interest in the question of 'institutional engineering' (Sartori 1994). In building democracies from scratch, it became an imperative for constitution-builders to gather advice about the likely implications of particular institutional choices, while the process also offered a new and unprecedented laboratory in which scholars could test theories concerning the causes and consequences of democratic design (e.g. Lijphart and Waisman 1996). The issue became one of evaluating the different models of democracy in terms of their effectiveness, stability, and legitimacy. It was in this context, for example, that comparative political science witnessed the recrudescence of the debates between advocates of presidential and parliamentary models (e.g. Linz and Valenzuela 1994; see also Chapter 7).

The debates surrounding the merits of these alternative systems were of crucial importance to many post-1989 constitutional engineers (Lijphart 1992; Sartori 1994).

Neo-institutionalism

The fourth impetus came again from developments within comparative politics, and was prompted by the so-called neo-institutional turn (March and Olsen 1984; see also Chapter 2). Institutions had often tended to be seen as primarily dependent variables which could be explained by social, economic, or cultural factors. Democracy itself, most crucially, was believed to have its 'social requisites' (Lipset 1959). Within the emerging neo-institutional approach, by contrast, institutions came to be seen as independent variables which impacted upon outcomes and behaviour, almost regardless of the social and economic context. This encouraged scholars to begin to inquire systematically into the effects of democracy rather than simply the sources of democracy, and to explore the way in which different forms of democracy exerted a differential impact on economic growth, social stability, democratic satisfaction, and so on. This encouraged new modes of classifying democratic polities, and new ways of comparing the varied institutional architecture. By the late 1980s, it was the form and quality of democracy rather than its existence as such that were seen to matter (e.g. Diamond and Morlino 2005).

> **KEY POINTS**
>
> - Democracy has developed in waves, with the 'third wave' coming in 1974 and reaching explosive proportions after 1989.
> - Since the onset of the 'third wave', constitutional engineers have become especially interested in why some systems appear to perform 'better' than others.
> - Since democracy has become 'the only game in town', scholarly research has tended to focus on the quality rather than the quantity of democracy.

Defining democracy

This explosion of interest also led to a huge variety of suggestions about how to approach the comparison of democracies.[3]

As Collier and Levitsky (1997: 430–1) noted in a valuable early assessment of the emerging literature on the topic, the challenge of dealing with the sudden variety of post-authoritarian regimes provoked wide-ranging conceptual confusion, leading to a proliferation of alternative classifications and denominations, and an almost inevitable resort to the analysis of democracy 'with adjectives'.

Democracy was no longer just democracy; now there was *electoral* democracy, *illiberal* democracy, *delegative* democracy, *deliberative* democracy, *reflective* democracy, and so on. But not only was there a large-scale variation in how democracy was beginning to be defined and qualified, there was also a great range of terms of reference through which such definitions were approached.

Procedural vs. substantive democracy

There are two distinct approaches to defining democracy. On the one hand, there are the many *procedural definitions* of democracy, which focus on how the regime is organized and the processes by which representation, accountability, and legitimacy are assured. On the other hand, there are the various *substantive definitions* of democracy, which deal also with the goals and effectiveness of the regime, and the extent to which the will of the people might be served in a more purposive sense.

Schumpeter, most famously, offered a strictly procedural definition of democracy: 'the democratic method is that institutional arrangement for arriving at political decisions in which individuals acquire the power to decide by means of a competitive struggle for the people's vote' (Schumpeter 1947: 269). This has become one of the most widely used definitions of democracy, and Schumpeter went on to simplify it even further by stating that democracy entails 'free competition for a free vote' (Schumpeter 1947: 271).

With substantive definitions, by contrast, particular goals are also envisaged, such that real democracy cannot be defined by process alone, but also entails efforts to promote equality, fairness, and inclusion. It was precisely this approach that Schumpeter sought to leave behind, in that he explicitly rejected an earlier and more normative eighteenth-century sense of democracy which viewed 'the democratic method [as] that institutional arrangement for arriving at political decisions which *realises the common good* by making the people itself decide issues through the election of individuals who are to assemble in order to carry out its will' (Schumpeter 1947: 250, emphasis added).

Polyarchy

In practice, procedural definitions are usually preferred in comparisons of democratic regimes. Indeed, the employment of substantive definitions of democracy has become very rare in contemporary scholarly debates, despite Dahl's insistence that process and substance cannot really be separated: 'the democratic process is not only essential to one of the most important of all political goods—the right of people to govern themselves—but is itself a rich bundle of substantive goods' (Dahl 1989: 175).

It is perhaps for this reason that Dahl prefers not to refer to 'democracies' when addressing real-world cases, since that rich bundle of substantive goods is not always on offer, but instead to 'polyarchies' (Dahl 1971: 8), which he then goes on to define in primarily procedural terms. However, with Dahl, in contrast to Schumpeter, the procedural definition is maximalist rather than minimalist. That is, polyarchies are defined by more than simply an electoral process, but also by a more or less inclusive citizenship, and by the right of these citizens to oppose and vote out their governing officials. The definition of polyarchy goes beyond the free competition for the free vote to include the provision of complete rights of participation and contestation.

In his classic *Polyarchy* (Dahl 1971: 3), Dahl specified eight institutional guarantees which were required in order that citizens (1) might formulate their preferences, (2) signify these preferences, and (3) have these preferences weighted equally in the conduct of government—the three elements that he deemed necessary if government is to be democratically responsive to its citizens. Later, in *Democracy and its Critics* (Dahl 1989: 221), he specified the seven institutions 'which must exist for a government to be classified as a polyarchy' and which included elected officials, free and fair elections, inclusive suffrage, the right to run for office, freedom of expression, alternative sources of information, and associational autonomy.

These conditions extend far beyond Schumpeter's earlier definition, even when that earlier definition is qualified by Schumpeter's own references to the need for free elections and institutional pluralism, and since then they have been expanded even further by other scholars. In an assessment of the developing democracies of Latin America, for example, O'Donnell (1996) has emphasized that the comparison of polyarchies also needs to take account of the degree of governmental accountability and the acceptance of the rule of law, suggesting an even weightier definition of democracy than that used by Dahl.[4] This is also the key element highlighted in an earlier and admirably clear definition proposed by Schmitter and Karl: democracy is 'a regime or system of governance in which rulers are held accountable for their actions in the public domain by citizens acting indirectly through the competition and cooperation of their elected representatives' (Schmitter and Karl 1991: 76).

Therefore in the *thin* procedural version, mainly associated with Schumpeter, democracy is about elections and little more than elections;[5] in the *thick* procedural definition, mainly associated with Dahl, democracy (or polyarchy) also entails the provision of constitutional guarantees and controls on the exercise of executive power. This distinction also overlaps considerably with that sketched in Dahl's (1956) early contrast between *populistic democracy* (thin) and *Madisonian democracy* (thick), as well as that developed by Riker (1982) in his much-cited contrast between *populism* (thin) and

liberalism (thick). In a more recent essay, Dahl (2000) also comes back to these versions when he distinguishes two 'dimensions of democracy'.

1. The first of these is characterized by an *enforceable set of rights and opportunities* on which citizens may choose to act if they wish, and which includes the rights of *association, belief, freedom of expression*, and so on: 'A country without these necessary rights and opportunities', notes Dahl (2000: 38), echoing his earlier arguments in *Polyarchy*, 'would as a consequence also lack the fundamental political institutions required for democracy'. This, then, is part of the 'thick' procedural version.

2. The second of Dahl's dimensions is where the 'thin' version comes in, and refers to *actual participation in political life:* 'The continuing existence of a democratic order would seem to require that citizens, or at least some of them, sometimes do actually participate in political life by exercising their rights and act on the opportunities guaranteed to them' (Dahl 2000: 38). However, to view democracy only in the light of this second dimension would be wrong, he adds, since the presence of fundamental rights and opportunities is also an intrinsic element of the definition.

In a similar vein, Mény and Surel (2002: 7–11) draw a distinction between *popular democracy* and *constitutional democracy* as two pillars which together determine the legitimacy and effectiveness of democratic regimes (see also Mair 2002: 81–4). The popular democracy pillar encompasses the role of the demos— the free association of citizens, the maintenance of free elections, the freedom of political expression, and government 'by' the people. The constitutional pillar encompasses the institutional requirements of good government, such as limits on executive autonomy, the guarantee of individual and collective rights, and the more generalized Madisonian system of checks and balances. This is government 'for' the people and for the public good and, following Mény and Surel, an ideal democracy needs to reflect an equilibrium between the two pillars.

Liberal and illiberal democracy

In one version or another, this distinction between what might be termed political participation and civil rights recurs throughout the debate on democracy. However, this is not the only reason to highlight it here. Rather, the distinction has now also become of immediate empirical importance in the comparison and evaluation of real-world democracies—particularly since the post-1989 explosion of 'third-wave' transitions.

Among these new democracies a new categorization has been suggested which distinguishes those democracies which conventionally foster both pillars, and which continue to be defined as liberal democracies or polyarchies; and those in which an acceptance of popular democracy and of government 'by' the people is combined with the persistence or even reintroduction of restrictions and limits on individual freedoms and rights. These latter regimes have been defined as *electoral democracies* or *illiberal democracies* (see Diamond 1999; Zakaria 1997).

This new category of democracy, essentially unknown prior to the late 1980s, is characterized by the formal establishment of a democratic electoral process but with major shortcomings in terms of the provision of constitutional liberties and the establishment of any limits on the arbitrary exercise of executive power. For O'Donnell, for example, who underlines very clearly how this form of democracy differs from those established in the past:

> [this new] delegative democracy [is] more democratic, but less liberal than representative democracy ... is strongly majoritarian ... and consists in constituting, through clean elections, a majority that empowers someone to become, for a given number of years, the embodiment and interpreter of the high interests of the nation. ... After the election, voters/delegators are expected to become a passive but cheering audience of what the president does. (O'Donnell 1994: 60)

Having studied the Latin American democracies, he also adds that these new democracies 'exhibit a rather remarkable capacity for endurance' (O'Donnell 1994: 67).

Oversloot and Verheul (2006) identify a similar pattern in Russia, and suspect that it is becoming institutionalized. Here, democracy has become something which is managed by 'the party of power'—not an autonomous organization which has won power through elections as such, but rather a body constituted by 'the actual group whose members wield power in and through the executive branch of government, and which creates an 'electoral branch' in order to hold on to power' (Oversloot and Verheul 2006: 394; see also Cammack 1997). In other words, power flows from the executive downwards, rather than from the citizens upwards, unhindered by any serious constitutional curbs, and helped along by the lavish use of state resources.[6] For Zakaria, surveying the developing patterns of democracy in the world in the mid-1990s, 'illiberal democracy is a growth industry ... And to date few illiberal democracies have matured into liberal democracies; if anything they are moving towards heightened illiberalism' (Zakaria 1997: 24).

With these real-world cases, we see a separation between the two pillars of democracy in practice. Many new democracies are seen to have democratized only in terms of the elections, and to have neglected the building of corresponding constitutional guarantees and liberties. This is also seen to relate to the conditions of democracy and the overall path of political development.

Zakaria (1997) suggests that polities which establish constitutional liberties prior to full electoral enfranchisement are more likely to establish and maintain a stable liberal democratic order than those which open up the electoral process before—if at all—they seek to establish liberal constitutionalism: '[c]onstitutional liberalism has led to democracy, but democracy does not seem to bring constitutional liberalism', he argues (Zakaria 1997: 28; see also Chua 2003). In this reading, the path towards democratization taken by many of the Western European states—in which the civil or constitutional rights of contestation were established *prior* to the political rights of participation (Dahl 1971: 1–9, 33–47; see also section on 'Paths of democratization')—is seen as being much more benign than that in which the political rights of participation are established first.

In the event, however, as Møller (2007) clearly shows, the evidence of a growing divide between the liberal and illiberal worlds of democracy has ceased to be convincing, in that this specific and rather novel combination of electoral freedoms and constitutional restrictions is now beginning to prove thin on the ground. Møller's more recent evidence, as well as that adduced by Diamond and Zakaria for the mid-1990s, is based on Freedom House data.

The composite Freedom House scores in terms of both sets of freedoms range from 1 (completely free) to 7 (completely unfree). These are aggregated and averaged into an overall freedom score, in which the threshold for free polities (liberal democracies) is 2.5 (for example, the average of 2 on the political liberties scale, indicating some minimal restrictions; and 3 on the civil liberties scale, indicating restrictions but also something that is substantially removed from repression). Averages higher than this push the polity out of the 'free' category and into the category of 'partly free' or 'unfree'. The illiberal democracies are those in which acceptable levels of freedom on the political scale are combined with strong restrictions of freedom on the civil liberties scale, and it is this category which various observers believe to be increasing in frequency.

But while this category appeared common in the mid-1990s, it has now begun to fall back, with the proportion of electoral or illiberal democracies in relation to the total number of democracies dropping from over 27 per cent in 1998 to just 8 per cent in 2005. More specifically, if we take recent Freedom House data, and assume that a score of 1 or 2 on each of the two scales measures effective freedom, then some 40 per cent of the world's polities now score at the top of both scales at the same time; that is, they score at more or less the conventional liberal democratic and Western standard of democracy.

In effect, therefore, this new category of democracy—combining free elections with limited constitutional freedoms—scarcely seems to exist any more. As in the long-standing Western democracies, the right to participate is increasingly found in combination with rights of association, free speech, and so on, and this appears to be true even when the rights of participation are established before those of the constitutional liberties. Conversely, when civil liberties are curtailed, as in contemporary Russia for example, political freedoms also tend to be restricted. Increasingly, therefore, as was the case prior to the 1990s, both dimensions of democracy are tending to coincide rather than diverge, and to cumulate rather than conflict. Democracies tend to be liberal and democratic, or not liberal and not democratic. Other combinations are simply hard to find (Møller 2007).

KEY POINTS

- Democracies have a popular participatory pillar and a liberal constitutional pillar.

- Procedural definitions of democracy have become much more common than substantive definitions. The definition of democracy by Schumpeter specifies very minimal electoral criteria, whereas the 'thicker' definition of polyarchy by Dahl identifies a long list of conditions.

- Since 1989, scholars and policy-makers have warned of the emergence of 'illiberal democracy', in which popular elections are combined with limits on individual rights and freedoms.

- Recent evidence suggests that most democracies tend to be liberal and democratic, or not liberal and not democratic.

Developing democracy

According to Dahl (1966: xi), there have been three great milestones in the development of democracies: First, that of *incorporation*, when the mass of the citizenry was gradually admitted into political society; second, that of *representation*, when the right to organize parties was accepted; and third, that of *organized opposition*, when citizens won the right to appeal for votes against the government. Dahl was referring here primarily to the stages that were reached during Huntington's long first wave of democratization, in which these milestones were passed one by one, and often over an extended period of time. During the third-wave transitions, by contrast, the milestones were reached more or less simultaneously.[7]

Incorporation

The first milestone was reached when citizens won the right to participate in governmental decisions by casting a vote, which implied a widening of political society and the opening up of the polity to the involvement of—eventually—all adult citizens. Among the older and more long-standing democracies, this milestone began to be passed in the mid-nineteenth century—France, Germany, and then Switzerland effectively introduced universal male suffrage for the first time in 1848, followed by the US in 1870, when former slaves were first enfranchised. By the end of the First World War, most of these political systems had accorded voting rights to their male citizens regardless of property or other status qualifications (see Box 5.1 and Table 5.3).

Box 5.1 The extension of voting rights

The right to vote was extended progressively until suffrage became universal. The percentage of males above voting age increased during the second half of the nineteenth century from around 3–5 to nearly 100 per cent around the First World War (people who are imprisoned, some mentally ill people, and those supported by poor relief have been excluded from the right to vote for longer).

Besides gender and age the main restrictions on the right to vote were:

- *Census voting* The right to vote was granted only to wealthy people (above a certain level of income or taxation, as well as property of real estate or land).

- *Capacity voting* The right to vote was restricted to educated people (those with a given level of education, being able to read and write, as well as those who served in the army or were civil servants).

- *Race* The non-white population was excluded from the right to vote, as for example in the US, in a number of Latin American countries, and in South Africa until 1994 when the apartheid regime was abolished and the first multiracial elections took place.

Sometimes, instead of restrictions in the right to vote, *plural voting systems* were used in which, based on wealth, different voters had the right to more or fewer votes. In Belgium between 1893 and 1918 voters had one, two, or three votes—depending on their wealth and profession (and whether or not they had a family). In Prussia between 1848 and 1870 there were three classes of taxation. Those who paid more taxes also had more votes. In the UK until 1950 university graduates had an additional vote in the so-called 'university constituencies', a practice that is still maintained for Senate (upper house) elections in the Irish Republic. Plural voting systems run counter to the principle of 'one person, one vote'.

Table 5.3 Voting rights

Country	Universal male suffrage first introduced	Universal female suffrage first introduced
Australia	1902	1902
Austria	1897	1919
Belgium	1894	1949
Canada	1918	1918
Denmark	1918	1918
Finland	1907	1907
France	1848	1945
Germany	1848	1919
Iceland	1916	1916
Ireland	1918	1923
Italy	1913	1946
Japan	1947	1947
Netherlands	1918	1922
New Zealand	1893	1893
Norway	1900	1915
Sweden	1911	1921
Switzerland	1848	1971
UK	1918	1928
US	1870	1920

Sources: Caramani (2000: 53); Therborn (1977); Inter-Parliamentary Union.

Female suffrage was slower to develop. The first countries to introduce universal female suffrage, and hence universal suffrage as such, were New Zealand in 1883, Australia in 1902, and Finland in 1907. A number of the other European democracies and the US followed in the wake of the First World War, often under pressure from militant women's suffrage organizations. Some were even later. The UK accorded women equal voting rights with men in 1928, France in 1945, Italy, after fascism and the Second World War, in 1946, and Belgium in 1949. Switzerland accorded women equal voting rights in 1971, thus finally becoming a full-fledged democracy, but it was not until 1989 that one recalcitrant canton, under pressure from the Swiss federal government, adopted gender equality in voting at local level as well. However, in most of these democracies foreign residents are still denied voting rights, except at the local level. Suffrage is universal only among the national citizenry.

During the long first wave democratization was signalled by the gradual abolition of the various restrictions on the right to vote—restrictions that had been defined by gender, status, capacity, and so on—such that the population incorporated as full participants in the political society was substantially expanded. Among the democracies of the first and even the second waves, the only important subsequent change in voting rights came with the lowering of the age threshold, from twenty-five to twenty-one and eventually to eighteen in most countries by the end of the 1970s. In the Austrian general election of 2007, in what is the first experiment for national-level elections, the age threshold was reduced to sixteen years.

Representation

The second of Dahl's milestones was the right to be represented, i.e. the right to organize parties and have these participate in parliament on equal terms with other parties. The organization of parties as such was never a very major obstacle, even in more restrictive polities, but their formal registration and recognition, and the ease with which they could participate in parliament, varied substantially from system to system. One useful, if not wholly accurate, indication of the passing of this milestone was the shift from the conventional majoritarian voting systems that characterized more exclusive regimes in the nineteenth century to more open and proportional voting formulae (PR).

As Rokkan (1970) and later Boix (1999) have argued, a large part of the impetus to adopt more proportional voting was because of the threat posed by the mobilization of new political parties to the dominance of the established alternatives. In other words, voting systems became more proportional as new opposition parties began to make significant inroads. Had the systems remained majoritarian, the new parties, often emerging with a strong base in the new and previously disenfranchised mass electorate, would possibly have enjoyed a massive advantage with respect to the more elite-based parties that were already in parliament.

Therefore it is not surprising to see PR systems being adopted in many of the European countries at the same time as the franchise was universalized—1907 in Finland, 1918 in the Netherlands, 1919 in Germany (Table 5.4). The same logic applied later to the electoral system reforms that were introduced in South Africa in the lead-up to the abolition of apartheid. In a small number of countries, notably the UK, the US, and Canada, the new parties were not seen as especially threatening, and the systems remained majoritarian and eventually also less fragmented.

Organized opposition

Dahl's third milestone was marked by the right of an organized opposition to appeal for votes against the government in elections and in parliament, a right which has been more crudely summarized as one that affords the citizens the democratic means to 'throw the rascals out'.[8] In parliamentary systems, this milestone is reached

Table 5.4 The adoption of proportional voting formulae

Country	PR first introduced
Australia	1918/19*
Austria	1919
Belgium	1900
Canada	–
Denmark	1920
Finland	1907
France	1945
Germany	1919
Iceland	1959
Ireland	1922
Italy	1919
Japan	1947
Luxembourg	1919
Netherlands	1918
New Zealand	1993
Norway	1921
Sweden	1911
Switzerland	1919
UK	–
US	–

* Alternative vote in single-member districts.

Source: Caramani (2000: 60); Mackie and Rose (1991).

Table 5.5 Socialist parties enter cabinets

Country	First socialist party presence in cabinet
Australia	1904
Austria	1919
Belgium	1917
Canada	–
Denmark	1918
Finland	1926
France	1936
Germany	1919
Iceland	1947
Ireland	1948
Italy	1945
Japan	1993
Luxembourg	–
Netherlands	1939
New Zealand	1935
Norway	1928
Sweden	1917
Switzerland	1943
UK	1924
US	–

Sources: Bartolini (2000: 360); various party websites.

when the executive becomes fully responsible to the legislature, and hence when it can be dismissed by a majority in parliament.

One rough indicator of when this milestone was first reached among the more long-standing democracies can be seen in the timing of the first acceptance of socialist or social democratic parties into government (Table 5.5). This has varied quite considerably among the older democracies, especially beyond Europe, beginning in Australia in 1904 and coming finally in Japan in 1993. As yet, a party that might be defined as socialist or social democratic has failed to win executive office at the national level in either Canada or the US, while in most of the European polities access was achieved either in the inter-war years (Austria, Finland, France, Norway, the UK) or immediately following the Second World War (Iceland, Ireland, Italy). Given that these parties constituted the last major opposition to develop in most democracies prior to 1989, their acceptance into executive office marked a crucial watershed in democratic development.

But although the right of opposition has now been established in all liberal democracies, there remains significant variation in the everyday *capacity* of parliaments to

effect full executive turnover. In particular, the fragmentation of the party system and the need for parliamentary majorities sometimes encourage a reliance on multiparty coalitions that cannot be displaced in their entirety. That is, given certain types of coalition, and given a multiplicity of parties, full-scale alternation becomes difficult, and hence only some of the rascals can be thrown out at any one time.

In two-party systems, by contrast, as well as in the various bipolar systems that are characteristic of contemporary France and also in a number of the newer democracies, wholesale alternation in government is a normal expectation and a relatively frequent occurrence (Mair 2006b). In this case, opposition is clearly defined and effectively mobilized. It is also increasingly visible; as can be seen from Table 5.6, which reports the patterns that prevail among the long-standing European democracies, the traditional home of coalition government, bipolarism has become more common in recent decades. During the 1950s and 1960s, the majority of polities changed governments by means of shifting and overlapping centrist coalitions; during the 1990s, by contrast, almost two-thirds of these older polities had experienced at least some two-party or bipolar competition involving

Table 5.6 Growing bipolarism among the long-standing European democracies

Bipolar competition	1950s–60s	1990s–2000s
Present	43.8% (*n* = 7)	62.5% (*n* = 10)
	Denmark	Austria
	France	Denmark
	Ireland	France
	Malta	Germany
	Norway	Ireland
	Sweden	Italy
	UK	Malta
		Norway
		Sweden
		UK
Absent	56.2 % (*n* = 9)	37.5 % (*n* = 6)
	Austria	Belgium
	Belgium	Finland
	Finland	Iceland
	Germany	Luxembourg
	Iceland	Netherlands
	Italy	Switzerland
	Luxembourg	
	Netherlands	
	Switzerland	

Note: Table entries refer to countries that have experienced bipolar competition for government at either some or all elections in the given period.

wholesale alternation in government. This has already been the prevailing pattern in the older Commonwealth democracies—Australia, Canada, New Zealand—and it is rapidly becoming the norm in many of the newer democracies in Southern and post-communist Europe.

Paths of democratization

In a more schematic presentation, Dahl (1971: 6–9, 33–47) also charted the transformation of non-democratic regimes towards democracy along two dimensions—that of *liberalization,* or public contestation (the right to be represented and to mobilize opposition), and that of *inclusiveness,* or participation and voting—to compare paths towards mass democracy. Non-democratic regimes (in most cases absolute monarchies) that liberalized without becoming more inclusive were classified by Dahl as *competitive oligarchies.* These included the parliamentary regimes with restricted suffrage in the UK and France prior to the First World War. Non-democratic regimes that became more inclusive without liberalizing were classified as *inclusive hegemonies.* These included the totalitarian fascist and communist regimes in Nazi Germany and the Soviet bloc that regularly resorted to non-competitive mass electoral processes. The polities that became effectively democratic (the polyarchies) did so by *both* liberalizing *and* becoming more inclusive, whether simultaneously or in stages (Figure 5.1).

This is similar to the variation that was later highlighted by Zakaria (1997; see previous section) in his discussion of more recent paths towards democracy. For Zakaria, the most likely path towards liberal democracy was one in which *constitutionalism preceded participation*; when participation comes first, he argued, the process can become stalled and may lead to the consolidation of illiberal democracy. Dahl had voiced similar concerns, warning of the risks that are involved 'when the suffrage is extended *before* the arts of competitive politics have been mastered and accepted as legitimate among the elites', adding that 'the liberalization of near-hegemonies will run a serious risk of failure because of the difficulty, under conditions of universal suffrage and mass politics, of working out a system of mutual security' (Dahl 1971: 38–9).

In the analysis of the development of party organizations in Southern and Eastern Europe, van Biezen (2003: 15–27) has returned to Dahl's initial distinction, contrasting the cases of Portugal and Spain, which moved from an authoritarian past and democratized on both dimensions at more or less the same time, with those of the Czech Republic and Hungary, which moved from a totalitarian but inclusive past (marked by the use of uncontested popular elections) and which then democratized on the dimension of public contestation. The latter is a seemingly risky scenario, and while the regimes in question and others in the similar post-communist circumstances have not usually

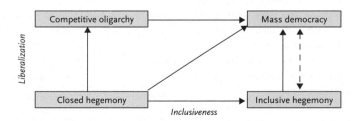

Figure 5.1 Robert Dahl's typology of democratization processes (1971)

failed, or fallen back from democracy, there is increasing concern about the quality of the democracies they maintain (Mungiu-Pippidi 2005). Moreover, they have also proved substantially less stable than Spain or Portugal in electoral and governmental terms (e.g. Gallagher *et al.* 2005: 298–303).

In other words, while Zakaria's concern about the rise of illiberal democracy may have come to nothing, it does appear that the character of the path towards democracy, and the particular sequencing of particular rights and freedoms, may well have consequences for the stability and quality of the regimes concerned. The pace of democratization also marks a crucial distinction between the older and the newer democracies. Whereas the three milestones identified by Dahl were reached over a relatively extended period in the case of the older democracies (see Tables 5.3, 5.4, and 5.6), they were reached more or less simultaneously in the case of many of the newer democracies. That is, the right to vote, to be represented, and to organize opposition was won at one and the same time in many of the third-wave polities, leaving little room for the party system, and the institutional order more generally, to settle.

KEY POINTS

- The three great milestones on the path to developing democracy have been those of incorporation, representation, and opposition.
- The older and more established democracies reached these milestones one by one, and over a long period of time.
- The newer democracies have reached these milestones simultaneously.

Typologies of democracy

Majoritarian vs. consensus democracies

There have been only a handful of attempts by scholars to devise typologies of democracies as whole systems, and the most comprehensive of these has been the influential distinction between majoritarian and consensus democracies that was elaborated by Arend Lijphart in a series of key publications in the 1980s and 1990s (Lijphart 1984, 1999). This was in fact a development of an earlier approach that Lijphart had first developed in 1968 when he proposed a new typology of democratic systems as a corrective to the models then being developed by Gabriel Almond.

Almond's initial goal had been to build a classification of political systems throughout the world, including the many non-democracies, and within the democratic

universe he had drawn a key distinction between what he called the Anglo-American democracies, on the one hand, and the continental European democracies, on the other. The former model was characterized by a secular homogeneous political culture in which bargaining actors and associations were interdependent but autonomous, while the latter was characterized by a fragmented political culture with separate and non-overlapping political subcultures, in which independent actors came to politics not without bargainable differences but with 'conflicting and mutually exclusive designs for the political culture and the political system' (Almond 1956: 406). In the one case, the political system is likely to be centripetal, moderate, and stable; in the other, it is likely to be conflictual, polarized, and unstable.

Lijphart's (1968*b*; 1977: 104–41) corrective to this basic model involved taking account of a second crosscutting and quasi-institutional dimension, in which he distinguished two types of political elite behaviour, *coalescent* and *adversarial,* and through which he suggested that the choices and strategies pursued by political leaders could offset some of the problems posed by conflicts at the level of the political culture. In other words, divisions at the level of the society and culture could be tempered by certain types of political institutions and political behaviour.

Setting this new classification against that of Almond yielded a simple fourfold typology of democratic regimes (see Table 5.7), in which Lijphart's particular attention was devoted to what he deemed 'consociational democracies', i.e. those systems in which coalescent elites sought to defuse the worst effects of social fragmentation and conflict.[9] Lijphart applied this model in particular to a number of the smaller European democracies that had been effectively passed over by Almond's typology—the so-called 'working' multiparty systems of Austria, Switzerland, the Netherlands, and Belgium—in which deep and potentially highly conflictual cleavages were controlled and accommodated by consensus-seeking political elites.

Although much of Lijphart's later comparative work was devoted to developing and refining the theory of consociational democracy, the model remained necessarily

Table 5.7 Lijphart's 1968 typology of democracies

Elite behaviour	Structure of society	
	Homogeneous	*Plural*
Coalescent	Depoliticized democracy	Consociational democracy
Adversarial	Centripetal democracy	Centrifugal democracy

Source: Lijphart (1968*b*; 1977: 106).

tied to the original classification developed by Almond, and hence was seen as relevant only to those particular societies that were marked by so-called fragmented political cultures. Therefore, though highly insightful and very influential among constitutional engineers, it enjoyed a relatively limited geographic application.

The new typology of democracies which Lijphart developed in the 1980s was more broad-ranging, and given that it was defined in almost exclusively political and institutional (rather than political cultural) terms, it also enjoyed almost limitless geographic application.[10] This was the distinction between majoritarian and consensus democracies, which was built on a broad-ranging and quite exhaustive set of political and institutional indicators (see Table 5.1), particularly in the 1999 version when the interest group system and the degree of independence of the central bank were added to the list of distinguishing criteria. In the original consociational model, by contrast, just four institutional characteristics were considered: proportionality, minority veto, segmental autonomy, and grand coalition.

However, the two approaches were closely related, and in work published in the late 1970s and early 1980s, Lijphart actually referred to the contrast as one between consociational and majoritarian models (Lijphart 2000: 228–30; Blondel 1988: 5–8). In brief, **majoritarian democracies** were regarded as those in which a winning party or coalition of parties could exercise virtually limitless power within a political system, in that executive authority was scarcely constrained. Among these democracies, in other words, there was a great difference between winning and losing, and power was exclusive—the losers had no voice—rather than inclusive. In **consensus democracies**, by contrast, developing on the earlier notion of consociationalism, power was more likely to be shared than contested, minorities were formally included in decision-making processes, and executive power was limited by constitutional courts, powerful second chambers, and a decentralized system of territorial governance.

Lijphart developed his new framework by first identifying the various political and institutional features that could be associated with majoritarian democracy—which were originally typified by the cases of the UK and New Zealand—and then by defining each of the features of consensus democracy as the opposite of that which prevailed in the majoritarian case. It was, to all intents and purposes, an inductive framework for the comparison of democracies, building out from two real-world cases and positing two extreme models at opposite ends of a notional continuum. Moreover, it represented one of the first serious attempts to construct a holistic model of democracy, taking into account not only the patterns of behaviour of the political elites, but also the institutional structures that defined the polity in which the elites operated and that constrained their behaviour.

However, it was also a problematic approach, and it was not always internally consistent. The eight features associated with the majoritarian model in the 1984 version, and the ten adopted in 1999, fitted together very coherently in the particular political system from which they were inductively derived—the British system. Similarly, although with more careful adaptation, the eight (and then ten) features of consensus democracy also fitted together quite well at the opposite end of the spectrum—in the cases of Belgium and Switzerland. However, in between these two extremes, most other real-world systems reflected a sometimes confusing mix of both majoritarian and consensus features.

Lijphart tried to deal with this problem by separating what had been designed as a one-dimensional model into two dimensions, which were also derived inductively (through factor analysis): a federal–unitary dimension, on which, for example, the US scored strongly on the consensus side, and an executive–parties dimension, on which the same US scored strongly on the majoritarian side. In other words, not all systems could be defined as consensus or majoritarian democracies: some were consensual and inclusive on both dimensions, and some were majoritarian and exclusive on both dimensions, but quite a number were mixed, being consensual on one and majoritarian on the other, while yet others were grouped in a poorly specified middle range.

Therefore what had begun as a comparison of distinct types or categories of democracies—majoritarian vs. consensus—fell foul of a complex reality in which more-or-less values along each of a group of not necessarily congruent dimensions led to a host of equivocal cases. Indeed, typical of the problems involved in this approach is the treatment of party systems, which are included in the initial framework in terms of the familiar categoric distinction of two-party vs. multiparty, but which are then operationalized as the more-or-less 'effective number of parties' variable in a way that inevitably clouds the initial definitional clarity (Lijphart 1999: 62–9; see also the comments in Mair 2006a: 63–4).

Decentralist vs. centripetal democracies

Similar problems can be seen in the recent attempt by Gerring *et al.* (2005) to go beyond Lijphart and develop an alternative whole-system categorization of democracies. This approach, which with Lijphart is one of the very few to attempt a holistic comparison of democracies, incorporates a more detailed range of institutional and political variables than does Lijphart, and proposes a categoric distinction between so-called 'decentralist' and 'centripetal' models of democracy. The **decentralist** model emphasizes several core features, including 'diffusion of power, broad political participation, and limits on governmental action' (Gerring *et al.* 2005: 568). It is also marked by the fragmentation of both popular and political power; single-member districts and weak party cohesion are combined with Madisonian features such as a pronounced separation of powers and strong limits on executive authority. The **centripetal** model, by contrast, emphasizes the importance of inclusive but authoritative institutions, and builds strongly on the model of 'responsible party government' (Gerring *et al.* 2005: 569; Ranney 1962). It is marked by strong and unified government, along majoritarian lines, which combines with PR, centralized interest groups, and well-organized and strongly bounded political parties (Gerring *et al.* 2005: Table 1).

Decentralized democracies are typified by the US case; centripetal democracies by the cases of Norway and Sweden, or by what Almond had formerly seen as the 'working multiparty systems' (see section on 'Majoritarian vs. consensus democracies'). In fact, despite their different starting point, what Gerring and his colleagues offer here is almost the mirror image of the Lijphart distinction. That is, the categories of decentralized and centripetal fall almost squarely within the mixed categories created by Lijphart's crossing of the federal–unitary and executive–parties dimensions of his consensus and majoritarian models. What for Lijphart are mixed cases—combining federal (consensus) institutions with majoritarian cabinets, or unitary (majoritarian) institutions with consensus cabinets—are, for Gerring *et al.*, the new models of decentralized and centripetal democracy, respectively.

Inevitably, then, these alternative models run into the same problems as those of Lijphart, although these prove more acute in the case of the centralist–centripetal distinction since more variables are involved (the authors list twenty-one possible features of each model) and the models of democracy themselves are applied to more than 120 countries. Here too, but more evidently so, a relatively simple categoric distinction between models of democracy is diffused across a host of potentially incongruent institutional dimensions, with the result that we remain unsure whether any real-world examples of these types of democracy actually exist.

The problems of holistic models

The work of Gerring *et al.* and Lijphart is unusual in that in both cases an attempt is made to model democracies as whole systems. That said, these authors also tap into older and longer-term concerns in comparative politics (Daalder 2002) in that they address the question of what makes for a 'better' democracy, a question that also links them to the more recent concerns with the quality of democracy.

For Lijphart, for example, the key choice is between a majoritarian system that is responsive, accountable, and often efficient, but in which the representative channel may deny a voice to large proportions of the citizenry, and a consensus system which is inclusive and more

representative, but that may prove less efficient in the longer term. However, despite all the potential decision-making problems and veto points in Lijphart's consensus democracy, it remains for him a 'kinder, gentler' and hence more valued model of democracy (Lijphart 1999: 275–300). For Gerring *et al.*, it is the centripetal democracies that are superior: 'good governance arises from institutions that pull towards the center, offering incentives to participate and disincentives to defect' (Gerring *et al.* 2005: 580).

But this is by the way. What is more relevant to this present discussion is that both studies reach their conclusions having examined a large variety of institutional dimensions along which different individual polities could be placed, and it is here that the problems arise. For example, in neither approach is any single one of the various dimensions of comparison prioritized. Although Gerring *et al.* (2005: 571) refer to four dimensions in particular as being of 'primary interest' to their analysis—territorial sovereignty, legislative structure, the form of executive, and the electoral system—each of their twenty-one defining features weighs equally in their definition.

The same is true for the ten defining features specified by Lijphart (1999). And the principal difficulty in applying these models to the comparison of real-world democracies arises when these different dimensions prove incongruent, such as when a polity is majoritarian in terms of, say, its interest group system, but consensual in terms of its electoral system; or when, in the model proposed by Gerring *et al.*, a system is decentralized with respect to its legislative branch, but centripetal in terms of its use of referendums. Nor are these incongruities uncommon or exceptional. Gerring *et al.*'s misfits are Lijphart's ideal types, and vice versa.

But why should ostensibly coherent models of democracy prove so difficult to apply to real-world comparisons? Why should comparative politics face these problems when it seeks to model democracies *tout court*? After all, both sets of categories discussed above are strongly grounded in theory as well as in logic. Gerring *et al.* draw their models from reasoning associated with the founders of American democracy, for example, and from classic work in the history of political thought, while Lijphart infers his models from the standard-setting majoritarian system, as well as from his own exhaustive work on consociationalism.

In practice, however, and this is the most important lesson to draw from this discussion, real-world democracies rarely prove as sharply bounded or as internally coherent as the various theoretically informed whole-system models might suggest. Indeed, there are few, if any, democracies which have been first constructed in the abstract in such a way that the different institutional elements knit together in forms that are both predictable and make sense. Even in the American case, as Dahl (2002: 66–7) emphasized, institutional design not only followed high-minded republican theories but was also strongly influenced by the exigencies of day-to-day bargaining in the Convention. However persuasive the arguments of the *Federalist* in promoting the need for a separation of powers, for example, what proved decisive in the end was 'a group of baffled and confused men who finally settle on a solution more out of desperation than confidence [and who] had little understanding of how their solution would work out in practice' (Dahl 2002: 67; see also Rakove 1996).

Two centuries later, in the context of the extensive wave of post-communist constitution-making, and at a time when the institutional designers could call on a great deal more historical experience of democracy than was ever available to the Convention in Philadelphia, contingency also often proved decisive. As Grzymala-Busse (2006) has shown in the case of the oversight institutions that were established in the wake of the transition in East-Central Europe, for example, much of the real cross-national variation in what might have been theoretically expected to be a relatively uniform set of procedures came about as a result of the specifics of party competition as it developed in the different polities: 'Postcommunist political parties attempted both to build the state and to ensure their own survival', she concludes (Grzymala-Busse 2006: 297). And the result of this double-headed strategy was the collage or even mishmash of different institutional arrangements that are now to be found among the post-communist polities.

Holistic models are also increasingly undermined by cross-national learning processes, and by the diffusion of particular institutional arrangements and solutions (Jahn 2006; see also Galton's problem in Chapters 22 and 23). As national borders become more porous, and cross-national communication and lesson-drawing become more commonplace, this process of diffusion becomes all the more pronounced. Diffusion across neighbouring territories was one of the few structural factors highlighted by Doorenspleet (2005: 143–61), for example, in her comprehensive analysis of the factors that might explain the explosion of transitions to democracy in the early 1990s: 'States surrounded by democratic neighbors were generally more likely to make a transition to democracy states with nondemocratic neighbors' (Doorenspleet 2005: 168).

Diffusion also marks the cross-national learning processes that are increasingly noticeable among the long-standing democracies. One of the reasons why the Dutch held a referendum on the European constitution in 2005, the very first use of such a constitutional device in modern Dutch history, was because of Danish, French, and British examples; one of the reasons why the British government began to experiment with directly electing city mayors was because of the Canadian, US, and French examples; and one of the reasons

why many polities have opted to free their central banks from direct political control is because of German and American examples.

Democracies, in short, are less and less likely to be closed or self-contained systems (as Chapter 24 shows), and in this sense they are also less and less likely to reflect totally consistent patterns when subject to comparative whole-system analysis. As Streeck and Thelen have argued:

> [T]he institutional frameworks that exist in any particular society are never completely coherent. While some institutional arrangements may impose a dominant logic of action, these typically coexist with other arrangements, created at different points in time and under different historical circumstances, that embody conflicting and even contradictory logics. (Streeck and Thelen 2005: 19–20)

The problem in comparing democracies in this sense is not so much the problem of comparing apples and pears—something which can always be solved with the help of the ladder of abstraction (Sartori 1970; see also Chapter 3); rather it is one of comparing apples which have become part pear with pears which have become part apple. Therefore the lack of progress made by comparative politics in developing whole-system models of democratic regimes owes less to any intrinsic weaknesses in the discipline, and rather more to the increasing problems of complexity and exogeneity in the set of variables with which this sort of inquiry is concerned.[11]

KEY POINTS

- Developing typologies of democracy as whole systems has always proved very difficult.

- The most important attempt to develop a comprehensive typology is seen in Arend Lijphart's distinction between majoritarian and consensus democracy.

- The increasing transnational diffusion of institutions and ideas tends to make models of democracy less internally coherent and consistent.

Audience democracy?

Although democracy has now become the most common regime type across the world, there is a growing concern that its foundations are less robust than before. One symptom of this emerging problem is the widespread evidence of citizen dissatisfaction with aspects of democracy, as well as that of declining levels of participation and engagement. These signs of citizen withdrawal from conventional political involvement are increasingly pervasive, and seem to stretch across many of the advanced industrial and post-industrial democracies as well as across many of the new democracies (e.g. Dalton 2004). Turnout at elections has fallen, particularly since the end of the 1980s; levels of party membership have often sunk to record lows; and both the stability and strength of levels of partisan identity have become considerably weakened.[12] More generally, popular confidence in politics and politicians has dropped almost to the bottom of the scale, with a recent assessment of the data from across the EU showing that political parties are trusted less than any comparable social or political institution, including large companies, trade unions, the press, and the police (Dalton and Weldon 2005).

During the early post-war years, and probably through to at least the 1970s, conventional politics was seen to belong to the citizen, and was seen as something in which the citizen could, and often did, engage. By the beginning of the new century, on the other hand, conventional politics appears to have become part of an external world that people prefer to observe from the outside. There is a world of the parties, and a world of political leaders, that is increasingly separated from the world of the citizenry, and hence also one in which popular participation is becoming less relevant. As Bernard Manin (1997: 218–35) put it, what we are now witnessing is the replacement of representative democracy or party democracy by audience democracy.

Although the democratic audience is occasionally taken with or moved by the spectacle that plays out before it, it is usually indifferent and passive. As Hibbing and Theiss-Morse put it in a discussion of the US case, '[a] vigorous democracy is the last thing people want, and forgetting entirely about politics is precisely what they do want' (Hibbing and Theiss-Morse 2002: 232). It is this growing indifference to politics that has helped to encourage support for more 'non-majoritarian' decision-making, and for a greater role to be accorded to various non-partisan and non-political agencies—judges, regulatory bodies, central banks, international organizations, and the EU itself (Thatcher and Stone Sweet 2002). In other words, as citizens withdraw from politics, decision-making becomes more depoliticized.

At worst, the audience can be dissatisfied and somewhat angry, and it is this latter response which sometimes fuels the sort of populist anti-political protest that is now being experienced in many democracies, both old and new (Mény and Surel 2002; Mudde 2004). In other words, largely because of growing citizen dissatisfaction, the functioning of democracy and the status of the political class itself have become issues of contention in political debates in many democratic polities, and have in turn encouraged more frequent institutional experiments with alternatives to representative democracy, including the use of referendums, citizens' juries, and other forms of participatory politics (Schmitter and Trechsel 2004).

In other words, in contemporary democracies there is an increasing tendency to pass decisions back down to the citizens for their final approval, or to pass them up to non-political agencies and institutions, where they are subject to expert judgement and more technocratic evaluations. In neither of these circumstances is there much emphasis on the importance of conventional political mediation—elections, parties, or political competition more generally. Therefore this is a challenge not only to Dahl's criteria for an effective polyarchy, and to his emphasis on the capacity to organize opposition, but also to Schumpeter's thinner definition of democracy. As citizens are offered more opportunities for direct participation, and as non-political agencies and 'guardian institutions' take on a more decisive role, it makes less sense to speak of power being acquired through a competitive struggle for the people's vote.

KEY POINTS

- In recent years, audience democracy has tended to replace representative democracy and party democracy.
- Citizens have often withdrawn from political life and are now more likely to distrust their democratically chosen leaders.
- Decision-making procedures are now often depoliticized.

Conclusion

Since the fall of the Berlin Wall in 1989, and the explosion of transitions to democracy in the 1990s, scholars and policy-makers have become increasingly attentive to the differences among democratic systems. Treating democracy itself as the default option among political regimes, concern has shifted from focusing on the question of the quantity of democracy, in the sense of an older concern with explaining why some countries become democratic while others do not, to the question of the quality of democracy, which reflects a newer concern with explaining why some democracies seem 'better' than others.

At the same time, the capacity to compare democracies systematically has become undermined as democratic regimes themselves become subject to global and transnational influences, and as institutions are reformed or transplanted without much heed for coherence and consistency. What had been once a small and homogeneous group of democratic regimes has now become large and heterogeneous, and much less amenable to classification and modelling.

Democracies have also proved more troubled in recent years. Citizen disengagement from elections and other conventional modes of political participation, as well as the growing popular distrust of and dissatisfaction with political leadership, has tended to create a more passive audience-oriented democracy. The electoral process, once seen as the defining feature of a democratic polity, has often become discredited and subject to challenge, with the result that decision-making rests increasingly in the hands of the judiciary and other non-majoritarian agencies. In an effort to encourage greater links to the citizenry, political leaders lay increasing emphasis on the use of referendums and primaries, diverting decision-making power away from the increasingly tarnished political parties which once epitomized democracy.

In these circumstances, the role of the constitutional pillar of democracy acquires a new resonance, while that of the popular pillar seems less and less relevant. In other words, democracy, whether at the national or transnational level, now seems to be more about protecting people's rights, and less about ensuring that they still have a voice.

 Questions

1. Why did authors increasingly feel that typologies of democracies are necessary?

2. When have the three 'waves' of democratization taken place, and where?

3. What do we mean by 'thin' and 'thick' definitions of democracy?

4. What do we mean by an electoral or illiberal democracy?.

5. What are the main milestones in the development of democracy?

6. What are the alternative 'paths' toward democratizations distinguished by Dahl?

7. What differentiates majoritarian from consensus democracies? Give real-world examples of both types.

8. What differentiates decentralized from centripetal democracies? Give real-world examples of both types.

9. Why is it difficult to compare democracies as whole systems?

10. Are representative democracies turning into audience democracies and, if so, why?

 Further reading

Definitions and typologies of democracies

Dahl, R. A. (ed.) (1966) *Political Oppositions in Western Democracies* (New Haven, CT: Yale University Press).

Dahl, R. A. (1971) *Polyarchy* (New Haven, CT: Yale University Press).

Dahl, R. A. (1984) *Democracies* (New Haven, CT: Yale University Press).

Dahl, R. A. (1999) *Patterns of Democracy* (New Haven, CT: Yale University Press).

Lijphart, A. (1977) *Democracy in Plural Societies* (New Haven, CT: Yale University Press).

Mény, Y. and Surel, Y. (eds) (2002) *Democracies and the Populist Challenge* (Basingstoke: Palgrave).

Schumpeter, J. A. (1947) *Capitalism, Socialism, and Democracy* (2nd edn) (New York: Harper & Brothers).

Overviews of contemporary democracies

Keman, H. (ed.) (2002) *Comparative Democratic Politics* (London: Sage).

LeDuc, L., Niemi, R. G., and Norris, P. (eds) (2010) *Comparing Democracies 3* (London: Sage).

Powell, G. B. (1982) *Contemporary Democracies* (Cambridge, MA: Harvard University Press).

Recent developments and topics

Diamond, L. (1999) *Developing Democracy* (Baltimore, MD: Johns Hopkins University Press).

Diamond, L. and Morlino, L. (eds) (2005) *Assessing the Quality of Democracy* (Baltimore, MD: Johns Hopkins University Press).

Huntington, S. P. (1991) *The Third Wave: Democratization in the Late Twentieth Century* (Norman, OK: University of Oklahoma Press).

Manin, B. (1997) *The Principles of Representative Government* (Cambridge: Cambridge University Press).

Pharr, S. and Putnam, R. (eds) (2000) *Disaffected Democracies: What's Troubling the Trilateral Countries?* (Princeton, NJ: Princeton University Press).

Zakaria, F. (2003) *The Future of Freedom: Illiberal Democracy at Home and Abroad* (New York: Norton).

Web links

www.freedomhouse.org
Website of Freedom House.

https://www.cia.gov/library/publications/the-world-factbook/index.html
Website managed by the CIA and detailing information about countries around the world.

www.electionworld.org/election/indexfrm.htm
Website on elections and election outcomes.

www.psr.keele.ac.uk/election.htm
Hugely comprehensive website detailing links and sources on elections and electoral systems.

www.idea.int
Website of an intergovernmental organization promoting democracy around the world and an excellent source of data on voting and elections.

www.cses.org
Website of the collaborative programme of research among election study teams from around the world.

www.ipu.org/english/home.htm
Website of the Inter-Parliamentary Union.

www.constitution.org/cons/natlcons.htm
Website giving details of constitutions around the world.

www.tol.cz
Website offering coverage of events in the twenty-eight post-communist countries.

online resource centre

For additional material and resources, please visit the Online Resource Centre at:
www.oxfordtextbooks.co.uk/orc/caramani3e/

CHAPTER 6
Authoritarian regimes

Paul Brooker

Chapter contents

Reader's guide

The concept of an authoritarian regime is a residual one that throws all the non-democratic political systems in together. Apart from the fact that they are *not* democracies, these regimes have little in common and, in fact, display a bewildering diversity: from monarchies to military regimes, from clergy-dominated regimes to communist regimes, and from seeking a totalitarian control of thought through indoctrination to seeking recognition as a multiparty democracy through using semi-competitive elections. The chapter begins with an introduction to the historical evolution of authoritarian regimes, especially the three-phase modernization of dictatorship in the nineteenth and twentieth centuries. Then the chapter examines the key questions of who rules an authoritarian regime, why they rule (their claim to legitimacy), and how they rule (their mechanisms of control). Finally, the conclusion discusses whether these regimes are becoming extinct or will come up with some evolutionary surprises.

Introduction

Until modern times states were normally ruled by authoritarian regimes and most of these were hereditary *monarchies*. These monarchical authoritarian regimes were based on a traditional form of inherited personal rule that was restrained to varying degrees by traditional customs and institutions. However, the notion that rule over a state and its people could be inherited like private property—like a family business concern—would seem very primitive once democracy began to compete with the monarchies. In order to survive, let alone flourish, the authoritarian regime had to modernize by introducing a new and modern form of *dictatorship* rather than monarchy. The notion of dictatorship could be traced back to ancient Rome's invention of the post of 'Dictator', which enabled the Roman republic in an emergency to appoint someone to act as a temporary monarch-like ruler with extraordinary powers but without the ceremonial trappings of royalty (see Box: The Roman connection, in the Online Resource Centre). Since then the notion of dictatorship had acquired a broader meaning that included 'self-appointed' dictators who had taken power and did not intend to relinquish it. But the modernization of dictatorship went much further in terms of organization and legitimation during the three phases of modernization that occurred in the nineteenth and twentieth centuries (see Brooker 2009: 4–6).

The first phase of modernization was not very innovative organizationally, for dictatorship by a military organization or its leader had actually appeared as long ago as Julius Caesar and other politically ambitious commanders of ancient Rome's professional army (see Box 6.1). But when General Napoleon Bonaparte pioneered first-phase modernization after his military coup in 1799 in post-revolutionary France, he took the very innovative step of using a plebiscite, or referendum, to claim a form of *democratic* legitimacy for his seizure of power. Thus the first phase in the modernization of dictatorship involved (1) rule by a military organization *or* its leader and (2) 'democratic' legitimation through a plebiscite or one-candidate presidential election *or* by claiming that it was a temporary dictatorship aimed at democratizing or 'cleansing' the political system. During the nineteenth century, such modernized dictatorships often appeared in Latin America, but in the twentieth century they spread to other parts of what became known as the Third World. In fact, they were the most common form of authoritarian regime in the twentieth century and therefore numerically overshadowed the new form—the *ideological one-party state*—that appeared with the *second* phase of modernization of dictatorship (Brooker 2009: 81).

Second-phase modernization created the ideological one-party state by two radical innovations. First, it adopted democracy's key organization, the *political party*, but as a single-party rather than a multiparty system (see

online resource centre

Box 6.1 Military seizures of power

Historical background

The seizure of power by a military organization or its leader is historically the oldest way of setting up a modern form of authoritarian regime. Napoleon's 1799 coup and the later seizures of power by armies or military leaders in Latin America starkly revealed how the private ownership of public offices can occur in other ways than through ownership by a royal family. Clearly public offices could be 'stolen' by an organization or its leader that uses force to take power from an old monarchy or a young democracy.

The seizure of power

This seizure of the country's public offices is carried out by means of an actual or threatened *coup d'état*, which means literally a blow by/of the state, but in practice is an often bloodless attack by the military arm of the state against its own government.

Types of coup

- The *corporate coup*, which is carried out by the military as a corporate body and under the command of its most senior officers.

- The *factional coup*, which is carried out by only a faction of the military and often under the command of only middle-ranking officers (and so is often described as a colonels' coup).

- The *counter coup*, which is launched against a *military* government by a disaffected or ambitious faction of officers.

Practical implications

Such distinctions are important in practice as well as theory. For example, most coups are factional and most factional coups fail, so any democratic government faced with a military coup has a good chance of defeating it unless the coup happens to be one of the relatively rare cases of a corporate type of coup.

Chapter 13). Second, it claimed legitimacy through an *ideology* of some kind, such as communism or fascism. This new and distinctively twentieth-century form of authoritarian regime first appeared after the October 1917 socialist revolution in the former Russian Empire, which was later renamed the Union of Soviet Socialist Republics or 'Soviet Union'. The post-revolutionary dictatorship established by the Communist Party espoused a Marxist–Leninist ideology that legitimated a one-party state in which the party ruled over state and society. By the 1930s a new party leader, Stalin, had established a personal dictatorship that was rivalled for 'totalitarian' thoroughness (see later section) only by the two *fascist* ideological one-party states established by Mussolini in Fascist Italy and by Hitler in Nazi Germany. The Second World War destroyed these two fascist regimes but also led, directly or indirectly, to a huge expansion in the number of communist regimes, which were established throughout Eastern Europe, in North Korea, and, most importantly, in *China*. There were occasional additions to the number of communist regimes during the 1950s, 1960s, and 1970s, such as Cuba and Vietnam (see Box: Revolutionary seizures of power, in the Online Resource Centre). However, these additions were numerically overshadowed by the swathe of non-communist ideological one-party states that emerged in the 1950s–70s as decolonization greatly increased the number of states in what became known as the 'Third World'.

**online
resource
centre**

The dissolution of the British, French, and Portuguese colonial empires in the 1950s–70s created dozens of new states in Asia and Africa and also led to a surprisingly large number of second-phase dictatorships (Brooker 2009: 106). Some developed innovative ideologies or versions of the one-party state, notably what became known as 'African socialism' and then 'the African one-party state'.[1] And several arose from military dictatorships developing military versions of the second-phase format by claiming legitimacy through some kind of ideology and acquiring an official political party, which in these cases was subordinate in some way to the military. In addition, the *first-phase* military dictatorship found a new niche in decolonized Asia and Africa and also began a new cycle of 'popularity' in Latin America in the 1960s. So by the mid-1970s it seemed that the authoritarian regime was dominating the globe not only numerically but also politically.

However, the mid-1970s also saw the beginning of a *global wave of democratization* (see Chapter 5). Although it 'missed' the Middle East, it 'swept through the other regions of the world in an almost sequential manner: southern Europe in the mid-1970s, Latin America and Asia in the later 1970s and the 1980s, Eastern Europe in 1989 and Africa in the early 1990s', not to mention the 1991 disintegration of the Soviet Union into more than a dozen new and non-communist states (Brooker 2009: 200). The global triumph of democracy seemed assured with this collapse of communism in the Soviet Union and Eastern Europe, the end of the African one-party state, and the demise of most military regimes. But there now appeared a *third* phase in the modernization of dictatorship, the *democratically disguised* dictatorship, which involved (1) replacing the one-party state with a supposedly 'democratic' multiparty system and (2) replacing ideological legitimation with a claim to democratic legitimation based on having supposedly 'competitive' multiparty elections. The third phase of modernized dictatorship further increased the already amazing diversity of authoritarian regimes in present times as well as throughout history. Such a huge variety of regimes is best categorized and described by applying the formula of who rules, why do they rule, and how do they rule.

KEY POINTS

- Until the nineteenth century most of the world's states were ruled by authoritarian regimes which were mostly hereditary monarchies.

- During the nineteenth century an important new form of authoritarian regime emerged, namely modernized dictatorship by a military organization or a military leader with some—however spurious—claim to democratic legitimacy.

- In the twentieth century there was a second phase in the modernization of dictatorship, with the emergence of the ideological one-party state, such as the communist and fascist regimes.

- In the third quarter of the twentieth century the majority of the world's states were ruled by first-phase and second-phase modernized dictatorships—including such new varieties as the African one-party state.

- The final quarter of the twentieth century saw a global wave of democratization but also saw a third phase in the modernization of dictatorship, with the appearance of democratically disguised dictatorships claiming the democratic legitimacy of having 'competitive' multiparty elections.

Who rules?

The question 'who rules?' has long been used—since the time of ancient Greece—to categorize regimes. But the three-phase modernization of authoritarianism has created a complex categorization of 'who rules?' that distinguishes between (1) the *organizational* rule of a dictatorial military or party and (2) the *personal* rule of (a) the *leader* of a dictatorial organization or (b) a *democratically disguised* dictator who is typically a 'populist presidential monarch', as will be described in a later section. Furthermore, the category of personal rule has to be extended to include the pre-modernization era's typical form of personal rule, the *ruling monarchy*, because there are still some surviving examples and those in the Arab world, notably the kingdom of Saudi Arabia, are still internationally significant.

Dictatorial monarchs

Although all monarchs are clothed in the ceremonial trappings of royalty, only *ruling* monarchies exercise the same kind and/or degree of power as a dictatorship. In contrast, *reigning* monarchies are typically found in democracies, where the monarch is a hereditary but largely ceremonial head of state with constitutionally very limited powers. Of course, throughout history even *ruling* monarchies have had their power limited by traditions, religions, constitutions or just the power of other players in the political game, as King John discovered in 1215 when his barons forced him to accept Magna Carta as written confirmation of the traditional limits on a feudal monarch's power. The absolutist monarch exercising unlimited powers in a discretionary or even arbitrary manner is very much the historical exception rather than the rule. None of the world's surviving monarchies are absolutist and some are merely reigning rather than ruling, such as the reigning monarchies to be found in several Western European democracies. The surviving *ruling* monarchies are to be found predominantly in the Arab world and notably in the Arabian Gulf, where there are such important examples as the Kingdom of Saudi Arabia, the United Arab Emirates, and the Sultanate of Oman.

The survival of these Arab monarchies cannot be explained by the hold of tradition, as most of them originated in the nineteenth or even twentieth century. For example, the kingdom of Saudi Arabia was founded in 1932 as the culmination of decades of political and military endeavours by a great Arab tribal leader, Ibn Saud. In contrast, it was British imperialism that established the Gulf emirates' monarchical rule in the nineteenth century, through treaties that recognized some prominent families as royal and ruling families (Anderson 1991). The British also created Arab monarchies in other parts of the Middle East, notably the still surviving Hashemite kingdom of Jordan, when Britain and France carved out a group of new states—including Iraq, Syria, and Lebanon—from the Arab territories of the defeated Ottoman Empire after the First World War.

It is tempting to explain the survival of the Saudi and other Arab monarchies by pointing to their oil wealth. And indeed 'rentier state' theories argue that oil-rich authoritarian regimes survive by exploiting the 'rent' revenues from the oil industry. These revenues allow a regime to provide its subjects with substantial material benefits without the need for heavy taxation and therefore without the need for democratic representation: in other words, 'no representation without taxation'. But, as Herb (1999) points out, oil wealth has proved neither a necessary nor a sufficient condition for the survival of a ruling monarchy in the Middle East. For example, it has not been necessary for the survival of Jordan's monarchy and it was not sufficient to prevent the Iranian monarchy being toppled by the 1979 Islamic Revolution.

Herb suggests that a better explanation for the survival of the Arab ruling monarchies is that they are often *dynastic monarchies.* Their royal families do not have to follow the rule of primogeniture (where the eldest son of the monarch automatically succeeds him) that is characteristic of the Western monarchies. The dynastic royal family can prevent an incompetent or unreliable person

from succeeding to the throne, and can also remove a monarch who has become incompetent or unreliable. Furthermore, these dynastic royal families have ensured that any intra-family rivalries about succeeding to the throne have not torn the family apart and left them vulnerable to outsiders, such as military officers, seeking to dispossess the family of their power.

Another distinctive feature of these dynastic monarchies is that their royal families are very large and have shown willingness to 'engage in public service' in government, the civil service, and the military. The numerous members of these royal families not only occupy key posts in the government but are also widely employed in the civil service and the military—in fact there is a 'profusion' of royals in the military (Herb 1999: 35). Such an extensive presence in government and the state machinery can give the dynastic royal families the sort of control over the state that is characteristic of a ruling communist party in a second-phase modernized dictatorship.

Furthermore, the subjects of some Arab monarchies have the right to present in person their grievances and requests to the monarch—a practice that has been trumpeted as 'desert democracy' (see Herb 1999: 41–2). The rulers' democratic-like accessibility may be intended to compensate for a lack of democratic institutions but the *non*-dynastic Arab monarchies of Jordan and Morocco have gone further by establishing supposedly democratic parliamentary institutions and even sharing power with elected politicians. That both these successful monarchies lack oil but not political skill is another indication of the 'primacy of politics' in the survival of such a primeval anachronistic form of authoritarian regime.

Monarchical dictators

Just as it is crucial to distinguish between monarchs who rule and those who only reign, it is crucial to distinguish between dictators who are personal rulers and those who are only agents of the ruling organization. For example, the president and prime minister of communist China are more comparable in power to a ruling than a reigning monarch, but they are still merely *agents* of the communist party that they lead and that is the organizational ruler of China. (To use the language of the 'new institutionalism', there is a principal–agent relationship between the party as the organizational principal and the public officials as its two individual agents.) In contrast, the communist party leader Mao Zedong was the *personal ruler* of China in the 1960s–70s and in fact his power was comparable to that of an *absolutist* ruling monarch. Like the three classic totalitarian dictators described in a later section, Mao had actually *reversed* the principal–agent relationship with his party and had converted this supposedly 'ruling' party into merely an agent or instrument of his personal rule.[2] Although relatively few personal dictators have been absolutist rulers, they have achieved varying degrees of *autonomy* from the party or military that they have led to power or have led during the organization's consolidation of power. To use the language of the 'new institutionalism', the principal–agent relationship between him and his party or military has become so weak (or even non-existent) that he is able to 'shirk' his responsibilities to this organizational principal (Brooker 2009: 40–1, 126–9).

An indication of this autonomy is the tendency to become monarchical rulers 'for life' and even to be succeeded in hereditary fashion by a son or brother—they have established what political scientists in the 1960s termed a *presidential monarchy* (e.g. Apter 1965). By then it was apparent that Third World personal dictators were institutionalizing their personal rule through the monarchical post and extensive powers of a president of the republic (Apter 1965: 307, 309). The presidential monarchy was becoming prevalent in Africa and would soon become prominent in other parts of the Third World, as in the case of President Suharto of Indonesia and President Hafiz Assad of Syria, and it even appeared in the communist world, with such presidential monarchies as those of Kim Il Sung in North Korea and Fidel Castro in Cuba. Although most presidential monarchies were overthrown by the global wave of democratization in the 1980s–90s, Hafiz Assad was succeeded by his son Bashir in 2000, Kim Il Sung was succeeded by his son Kim Jong Il in 1994 (who in turn was succeeded by his son in 2012), and Fidel Castro was succeeded by his younger brother Raul in 2005 when the president retired for health reasons.

The global wave of democratization that removed most of the presidential monarchies also produced a political climate in which an unusual form of presidential monarchy has now become the standard form and should be distinguished as a separate category of personal rule—the *populist* presidential monarchy. It is a historically old form of personal dictatorship that dates back to the middle of the nineteenth century and occasionally thereafter appeared in Latin America (see Box 6.2). However, the 'mainstream' personal dictatorships of the first and second phases of modernization were much more numerous and historically momentous; it was only with the recent third-phase shift to democratically disguised dictatorship that the populist presidential monarchy came into its own. This is partly because it is so well suited to being a democratically disguised personal dictatorship, but it is also because the way in which a populist presidential monarchy is established is so well suited to the world's democratic political climate.

Since at least the 1990s it has no longer been acceptable to take power by military coup or by revolution unless these seizures of power are aimed at democratization and are quickly followed by democratic elections. But the populist presidential monarchy emerges through an *elected* president's personal *misappropriation* of power, which Latin America long ago labelled an *autogolpe* or

Box 6.2 Louis-Napoleon as a 'chip off the old block'

Louis-Napoleon Bonaparte, the nephew of Napoleon Bonaparte, proved himself as politically innovative as his uncle by pioneering a new type of personal dictatorship—the 'populist' presidential monarchy. Louis-Napoleon was elected president of France after the 1848 revolution and three years later followed in his late uncle's footsteps by establishing a personal dictatorship. But this was a populist rather than a military personal dictatorship and was established by misappropriating power through an *autogolpe* (self-coup) rather than by seizing power through a military coup (see Box: Misappropriation of power, in the Online Resource Centre). After his presidential *autogolpe* Louis-Napoleon presented the country with a new constitution to be approved by plebiscite/referendum, and during the short period that he retained the republican title of president he created the prototype of the populist form of presidential monarchy (see McMillan 1991: 43–54). This type of personal dictatorship would be much rarer than the military type pioneered by his uncle but would occasionally be found in Latin America, with the most notable case being the *autogolpe* of President Vargas of Brazil and his innovative period of populist presidential monarchy in the 1930s–40s (see Box: The Latin American connection, in the Online Resource Centre).

online resource centre

online resource centre

online resource centre

'self-coup' (see Box: Misappropriation of power, in the Online Resource Centre). This misappropriation has tended to occur during or soon after **democratization** and has been very rare among older democracies, but that pattern may not continue in the democratic political climate of the twenty-first century.

Like other forms of personal dictatorship, the populist presidential monarchy can be analysed in principal–agent terms, but in this case there is a reversal of the relationship between the *electorate* as the principal and the elected president as its agent. By reversing that relationship the president makes the electorate the instrument of his personal rule in the sense of providing him with a claim to democratic legitimacy, which he usually confirms by having himself re-elected. These new elections will be undemocratic, but the populist presidential monarch may be genuinely popular with a wide section of the people and, what is more, the third-phase cases of populist presidential monarchy are using *semi-competitive* elections rather than non-competitive one-candidate elections in order to make their re-elections appear more democratically credible (see semi-competitive and non-competitive elections in section on 'Democratic claims to legitimacy').

During the third-phase modernization of dictatorship there was also a regional shift in the prevalence of populist presidential monarchy. The Latin American tradition of *autogolpe* and populist presidential monarch was maintained in the 1990s by Fujimori in Peru and, his opponents might say, by Chavez in Venezuela (see Box: The Latin American connection, in the Online Resource Centre). By then, however, the populist presidential monarchy was becoming more commonly found among the fifteen new states that were created by the 1991 disintegration of the Soviet Union, especially those created in Central Asia (Brooker 2009: 243–9). Several of these countries have evolved a new and more sophisticated version based upon a more gradual or 'creeping' *autogolpe* misappropriation of power and upon a new variant of semi-competitive elections that includes puppet parties offering phony opposition to the regime (see section on 'Democratic claims to legitimacy').

online resource centre

However, it is time to shift attention from the various and varied examples of personal rule to the almost as diverse examples of *organizational* rule and dictatorship, which can be categorized into two basic types: *military* rule and *one-party* rule. Before doing so, though, it is important to emphasize that there is often some *overlap* with cases of *personal* dictatorship by an organization's leader because in these cases his personal rule has emerged *from* or *with* the rule of the military or party that he leads. Therefore overlapping cases are normally described in terms of both the leader's organization *and* his personal rule, such as Nazi Germany being described as 'Hitler's regime' as well as 'a fascist regime' or, more fully, 'an example of the fascist subtype of one-party rule'. And this overlap is just one of the many complications involved in analysing the two different types of organizational rule: the military and the one-party.

Military rule

The *military dictatorship* is a very obvious case of rule by a 'distinctive' organization, which in this case has its own uniforms, barracks, career structure, and even legal system. There was a time in the mid-1970s when it appeared that the military was well on the way to ruling every country in the Third World; during the previous thirty years the military had intervened in more than two-thirds of these countries and was exerting some form of rule over a third of them (Nordlinger 1977: 6). On the other hand, the military had often relinquished power to civilians by holding democratic elections, whether because it never intended to hold power for long or because it discovered that the institutional costs of holding power outweighed the benefits. Therefore it was not surprising that military rule had an average lifespan of several *years* rather than decades (Nordlinger 1977: 139). And the global wave of democratization that began in the mid-1970s not only removed most of the existing military dictatorships but also drastically reduced the number of countries prone to military intervention in their politics.

Military intervention in politics has produced several different structural forms of military rule. As Finer (1976) pointed out, these structural forms include:

1. *open forms* of military rule and
2. *disguised forms* of military rule, including
   (a) civilianized rule or
   (b) indirect rule through a civilian government.

Open military rule

Undisguised **open military rule** occurs when a military coup leads to officers forming a **junta** (council) to act as the country's *de facto* supreme government (see Box: Military juntas, in the Online Resource Centre) *and/or* appointing themselves to key positions in the country's legal government, whether a presidency or a cabinet of ministers. The junta can become a highly institutionalized means of representing the military and of preventing any senior officer from becoming a personal dictator, as in the recent case of the Supreme Council of the Armed Forces that ruled Egypt in 2011–12 during the transition to democratic elections. But juntas have often failed to prevent the emergence of personal rule by a military leader, while some of the military dictatorships that did *not* use a junta still succeeded in remaining cases of organizational rather than personal rule.

online resource centre

Disguised military rule (civilianized or indirect rule)

Disguised military rule occurs when the military's rule has either been civilianized or operates indirectly through behind-the-scenes influence over a civilian government.[3] The *civilianization* of a military dictatorship involves a highly publicized ending of such obvious features of military rule as a junta or a military officer holding the post of president (though often the supposed civilianization of the presidency involves no more than the military incumbent resigning or retiring from the military). Civilianization has usually included a supposed democratization through some form of elections to the legislature and/or presidency.

The military's *indirect* rule disguises its dictatorship by controlling a civilian government from behind the scenes and even perhaps as a puppet-master pulling the strings of a puppet government. As Finer (1976: 151–7) pointed out, indirect rule can take the form of continuous control of the government or of exerting control only intermittently and over a limited range of policies, such as military budgets and national security policy. For example, there was concern that after the 2012 elections that the Egyptian military might shift to *continuous* indirect rule rather than merely controlling a *limited* range of policies related to national security and the military's privileges.

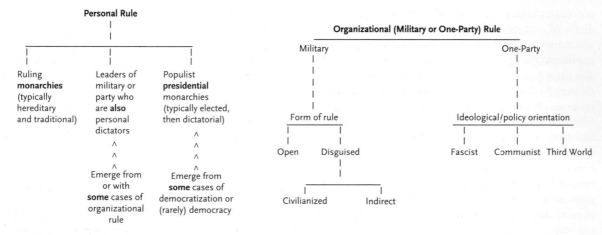

Figure 6.1 Types of authoritarian regime

online
resource
centre

One-party rule

The other type of organizational dictatorship, one-party rule, has not been as common as military rule but has tended to produce longer-lasting dictatorships. They come about through a dictatorial party either seizing power through a revolution or misappropriating power after it has won key government positions through democratic elections (see Box 6.2 and Box: Misappropriation of power, in the Online Resource Centre). The party then establishes one of the three structural forms of one-party state: (1) the openly and literally *one*-party state in which all other parties are banned either in law or in practice, (2) the partly disguised and *virtually* one-party state in which the regime's official party 'leads' some form of coalition with one or more puppet parties, and (3) the disguised and *effectively* one-party state in which all other parties are prevented from competing properly against the official party (on single-party systems, see Chapter 13).

However, a one-party state is not necessarily a case of one-party *rule*. The various structural forms of the one-party state have sometimes been established by military dictatorships, military personal dictators and even a few ruling monarchs as merely an instrument of their rule. There are also many occasions when the party's own leader has converted his party into merely an instrument of his personal rule, but at least this personal dictatorship has emerged *from* or *with* rule by his party. Furthermore, the dictator usually continues to display some of the characteristic features of his party, especially its ideological and/or policy orientation.

The subtypes of one-party rule have usually been categorized by political scientists according to variations in this ideological/policy orientation rather than variations in the structural form of the one-party state. The two obvious ideological/policy categories are the communist and fascist subtypes, but there is also a large residual grouping that is difficult to categorize in ideological/

policy terms and will be labelled simply the 'Third World' subtype because it emerged in Africa and other parts of the Third World. Of these three subtypes the fascist has been historically the rarest—Fascist Italy and Nazi Germany were the only examples—and has been extinct since Germany was militarily defeated in 1945. In contrast, the communist and the Third World subtypes have been relatively numerous historically and the communist subtype has managed to avoid extinction.

Communist

The communist regime is historically the most important as well as the most numerous subtype. It produced one of the twentieth century's superpowers, the now defunct Soviet Union, and seems set to produce another superpower in the twenty-first century if China maintains its rate of economic progress—and its communist one-party rule. At their numerical peak in the 1980s there were nearly two dozen regimes that espoused the basic communist ideology of Marxism–Leninism (Holmes 1986: viii). However, about a third of these regimes were actually military leaders' personal dictatorships and/or were using Marxism–Leninism only as an ideological facade and symbolic claim to legitimacy. Even amongst the core examples of communist regime there were some cases of personal rule by the party leader, notably Fidel Castro in Cuba and Kim Il-Sung in North Korea, which left less than a dozen 'true' cases of organizational rule by the communist party. And so many communist regimes collapsed in the late 1980s and early 1990s that now only three of these organizational dictatorships still survive—China, Vietnam, and Laos.

Third World

The 'Third World' subtype is a residual category with a diverse collection of examples. Its most significant subgrouping is the series of about a dozen 'African one-party states' that emerged from the decolonization of the British and French Empires in Africa from the 1940s to the 1960s (Brooker 2009: 106, 114–15). Each ruling party had won elections during the transitional period of decolonization and went on to misappropriate power after the country became independent, establishing an openly *one*-party state in law or in practice. But these African examples of one-party rule were soon either overthrown by military coups or saw their party leader become a personal dictator, usually in the form of a presidential monarch. The majority of these personal dictatorships survived for a generation before being removed by the wave of democratization that swept through Africa in the 1990s.

There have also been some cases of Third World one-party rule outside Africa, such as the Baathist party's rule in Iraq under the leadership of Saddam Hussein. The Baathist regimes in both Iraq and Syria were established by the military in the 1960s as one-party states, but in the Iraqi case a civilian party administrator, Saddam Hussein, gradually took over power from the military in the 1970s and shifted the regime to one-party *rule* before in turn establishing a personal dictatorship that survived until the US-led invasion in 2003. (In contrast, the Baath party in Syria was transformed into an instrument of personal rule by the military leader, General Hafiz Assad, and was later inherited and used by his son Bashir until the 2011–12 reshaping of the regime.) In Latin America three notable examples of one-party rule were those of the Party of Institutionalized Revolution (PRI) in Mexico from the 1940s to the 1990s, the National Revolutionary Movement (MNR) in Bolivia in the 1950s, and the Sandinistas in Nicaragua in the 1980s—the most ideologically leftist of these three revolutionary regimes. They preferred the disguised, effectively rather than virtually or literally, one-party form of rule and they were also less vulnerable than other Third World cases to being converted into personal dictatorships. In fact the Mexican PRI developed the unique system of installing temporary presidential monarchs, with each president being allowed a degree of personal rule but only for a single six-year term of office.

KEY POINTS

- A ruling monarch is a personal ruler, but a merely reigning monarch is typically a democracy's constitutional head of state.

- Dictatorship by an organization, such as the military or a party, is often transformed into personal rule by the organization's leader.

- Dictatorship can result from a military or revolutionary seizure of power or from a misappropriation of power by an elected party or an elected president through an *autogolpe* (self-coup).

Why do they rule?

Authoritarian regimes do not claim that 'might is right' or that those they rule should be obedient solely out of fear of the punishments inflicted for disobedience. Even the most tyrannical and brutal of regimes will claim to exercise a *legitimate authority* that gives it a right to rule and gives its subjects a *duty*—a moral obligation—to obey. When authoritarian regimes ask themselves the rhetorical question 'why do we rule?' they have an answer ready, no matter how spurious or self-serving, that proclaims their right to rule and therefore the duty of the ruled to obey. For example, authoritarian regimes typically make some claim to *legal* legitimacy by claiming a legal justification and basis for their rule. In fact, apart from 'emergency' or 'temporary' versions of military rule through a junta and martial law, authoritarian regimes typically have some sort of constitution, legislature, and judiciary that can provide an impressive formal claim to legal legitimacy even if the substance or practice falls far short of being 'the rule of law'. In addition to this claim to legal legitimacy, there will be (1) a claim to religious or ideological legitimacy and/or (2) some claim to democratic legitimacy. So the ruled can have no cause for complaint, according to the regime, if their obedience is also enforced by fear and through an authoritarian regime's various control mechanisms (see the section on 'How do they rule?').

Religious and ideological claims to legitimacy

Religion

Religious claims to legitimate authority have historically been the most common but are now relatively rare and found only in the Middle East and the Vatican City. Religious claims to legitimacy have been associated with monarchies for more than a thousand years, perhaps most famously with the European monarchs' coronation anointing and their claims to rule by 'the grace of God' or 'the divine right of kings'. And religion is still used by contemporary ruling monarchies to bolster their legitimacy, as in the case of the Saudi monarchy's alliance with the Islamic Wahhabi movement (Anderson 1991).

However, religious claims to legitimacy re-emerged in a new guise with the 1979 revolution in Iran that established a self-proclaimed Islamic Republic (Brooker 1997: Chapter 9). The new constitution included several religious elements and also a new public office had been designed for the religious and political leader of the 1979 revolution, Ayatollah Khomeini. This unique public office not only included religious as well as political responsibilities but also constitutionally 'outranked' the president and therefore is often described in the West as the post of 'supreme leader' rather than 'spiritual leader'. After

Khomeini's death in 1989 it was conferred on another politically active member of the Shiite clergy, Ayatollah Khamenei, in what appears to be another lifetime appointment.

Ideology

online
resource
centre

During the twentieth century, claims to legitimacy based on religion were largely 'replaced' by claims based on ideology. These ideologies ranged from the communists' systematic and comprehensive Marxism–Leninism to the grievances and aspirations of Latin American populism (see Box: the Latin American connection, in the Online Resource Centre). But all ideologies are similar to religion in holding certain things to be sacred, even if ideologies are more concerned with 'this worldly' than 'other worldly' matters and with ideas, goals, and principles rather than rituals and symbols. An ideology usually lacks the social presence and influence of such long-established religions as Christianity or Islam, which also have a network of churches or mosques staffed by professional clergy who are expert in maintaining and propagating the religion. So if an ideology is to be as effective as these religions in providing a basis for an authoritarian regime's legitimacy, it will have to be given a similar social presence and influence by 'its' regime—through use of mass media, the education system, and mass-mobilizing organizations, such as the regime's official party, youth movement, and labour unions.

This investment of time and energy may be acceptable to an ideologically driven dictatorship, such as Hitler's Nazi regime, that already has a usable ideology and political party. But a dictatorship that is not ideologically driven may well baulk at the cost of this investment (and also perhaps at the possibility of having to take ideological matters into account in its policy-making). It may well prefer instead to avoid ideological claims to legitimacy, as many military regimes have done, or to adopt a merely token ideology that provides a symbolic claim to legitimacy. Therefore the ideological diversity of authoritarian regimes includes not only the content of their ideologies but also the fact that many of these ideologies are not taken seriously and that many military regimes have never bothered with even a token ideology.

Another source of diversity is that ideological claims to legitimate authority take different (but often overlapping) *forms*. There have been ideological claims to legitimacy in:

- the personal sense of leaders claiming a prophetic legitimacy as ideologists;
- the organizational sense of parties or militaries claiming an ideological right to rule;
- the visionary or programmatic sense of a regime claiming that the goals and principles enshrined in its ideology give it a right to rule.

The communist ideology has been the most widely used ideological claim to legitimacy, with its core of Marxism–Leninism providing both a Leninist organizational form and a Marxist visionary form (see Box 6.3 on

Box 6.3 Communist ideological vision and Chinese economic practice

Communist ideology

The communist ideology has provided the most widely used *visionary* or programmatic form of legitimacy. It views rapid economic growth as a sacred goal because this will produce the material abundance required for the envisioned shift to a fully communist, classless society.

Stalin's influence

In the late 1920s Stalin initiated an economic Five Year Plan in the Soviet Union that also produced a new economic doctrine for orthodox communists to believe in. This Stalinist economic doctrine declared that a state-planned and largely state-owned economy was needed to progress through the transitional 'socialism' stage that would eventually lead to full communism. During this socialist stage the urban economy of industry and commerce would be owned as well as planned by the state, while agriculture would be state-planned but owned by huge 'collective' farms that would each be owned and worked cooperatively by thousands of peasants.

The new pragmatism

In the 1980s the post-Mao Chinese communist regime introduced a pragmatic reinterpretation of the communist economic approach. The new economic doctrine, 'Socialism with Chinese Characteristics', argued that capitalist economic methods were a more effective way of attaining the rapid economic growth required in the transitional socialist stage of progressing towards full communism. In fact the regime had already begun to shift to an increasingly market economy with an increasing amount of private enterprise and private ownership (except of land, which could only be leased). Furthermore, the economic emphasis had shifted from the Stalinist focus on heavy industry towards first agriculture and then increasingly the consumer and export sectors of the economy.

A long transition to full communism?

The notion of a specifically 'Chinese way' was supplemented in 1987 with the new theory of a 'primary' stage of socialism. The main medium-term goal was to raise living standards and develop productive forces—through capitalist methods. And later it was suggested that China would remain in this primary capitalist-like stage of socialism for a hundred years!

the visionary form). Its organizational form of claim to legitimacy is based on Lenin's theory of the communist party as the 'vanguard party of the proletariat [working class]' that leads the proletariat not only *to* revolution but also *after* a revolution, when the post-revolutionary regime is seeking to achieve Marx's visionary goal of a classless, communist society. All the many communist regimes that arose during the twentieth century adopted this ideological justification of one-party rule as part of their commitment to Marxism–Leninism. The communist regime in China may well abandon Mao Zedong's ideological additions to Marxism–Leninism, and may even abandon the visionary, Marxist component of the ideology, but would the regime ever abandon the Leninist legitimation of one-party rule?

There has been no equivalent of Leninism among the rare attempts to justify *military* rule ideologically. The leader of the 1952 military coup against Egypt's monarchy, Colonel Nasser, claimed in somewhat Leninist fashion that the Egyptian military was acting as the temporary and transitional 'vanguard of the revolution'.[4] But Nasser's ideological justification of military rule was not adopted by coup-makers in other countries, except by the Nasser-emulating Colonel Gadhafi when he overthrew Libya's monarchy in 1969. An even less influential military equivalent of Leninism was the Indonesian military's 'dual function' ideology of the 1960s–90s, which claimed that the army had a permanent political–social as well as military function. Armies have, in fact, tended to be wary of any ideology and have preferred to express an ideological commitment only to introducing or restoring democracy.

'Democratic' claims to legitimacy

Since the time of Napoleon Bonaparte's plebiscites most dictatorships have claimed a form of democratic legitimacy. Sometimes it has taken the ideological form of claiming to be a special or superior type of democracy, as with a communist regime's claim to be a 'proletarian democracy' and an African one-party state's claim to be an 'African democracy'. Even the Fascist and Nazi regimes claimed to be, respectively, an 'authoritative democracy' and a 'German democracy'.

But always the claim to democratic legitimacy has also or instead taken an institutional form. There has been a claim either to be *using democratic institutions*, such as an elected parliament or presidency, or to be *preparing to introduce/reintroduce them*. The latter case typically arises after the military has seized power from what it claims to be an undemocratic, corrupt, or incompetent government. Usually the military then quickly reassures international and domestic audiences that military rule is only temporary and is preparing the way for the (re)introduction of democracy. But it

may take a long time to 'deliver' on its promises, as in the case of the Burmese military waiting until 2011 to dissolve the military junta that had ruled since the 1988 'democratizing' coup.

In contrast, the claim to be *using* democratic institutions is based on the 'delivery' of an elected parliament and/or president, but they have been elected *undemocratically*. For example, a parliament may be elected in the plebiscitary manner pioneered by the first phase of modernization, whereby voters are given the 'choice' of either approving or rejecting the official candidate or list of candidates (if proportional representation elections) that is the *only* candidate or list appearing on the ballot paper. An early example of a second-phase dictatorship electing a legislature in this plebiscitary manner arose in 1938 in Nazi Germany—five years after it had become literally and legally a one-party state. Hitler held new elections to the Reichstag (parliament) that appeared to use a proportional representation list system (see Chapter 10) but with just the *one* list of candidates to approve or reject. And it was not a Nazi *party* list but instead 'the list of the Fuehrer [Leader]', i.e. Hitler's personal list of candidates that he wanted elected to the Reichstag. Thanks to vote-rigging and other undemocratic methods, the election result was a more than 99 per cent vote in favour of the list. 'Goebbels's Propaganda Ministry congratulated itself. "Such an almost 100 per cent election result is at the same time a badge of honour for all election propagandists" it concluded' (Kershaw 2001: 82).

Although such elections have been termed one-list or one-candidate elections, a broader and better description is 'non-competitive' elections. They were taken to a higher level of sophistication by the communist regimes established in Eastern Europe and Asia after the Second World War. These virtually one-party states included one or more puppet parties in a communist-dominated combined or coalitional list of candidates that would produce a 'multiparty' election and legislature while retaining the simplicity of a non-competitive election. China's communist regime differed from the other virtual one-party states in using indirect elections to its NPC legislature but it also had no fewer than *eight* puppet parties, with a total membership in recent years of more than 700,000, and has officially described its system as 'multiparty cooperation' rather than a one-party state (Saich 2011: 213).

However, even when including puppet parties, non-competitive elections cannot match the sophistication of the *semi*-competitive election, which was invented long ago in Latin America and has become the standard method of the third phase of modernization and its democratically disguised dictatorships. Semi-competitive elections provide a more credible claim to democratic legitimacy than any non-competitive election because they allow some electoral competition between parties, even if the official party or candidate cannot lose—if necessary, the regime will resort to vote-rigging or even annulling the election in some manner. The third-phase modernization has already produced new variants of semi-competitive elections, notably adding puppet parties or candidates to provide phony competition and 'opposition' to the government or regime. This variant emerged in Kazakhstan and other parts of Central Asia as early as the 1990s, and more sophisticated mixtures of phony and genuine competition or opposition soon appeared in Azerbaijan and Belarus in the 2000s (Brooker 2009: 244–9).

The increased sophistication of third-phase dictatorships' electoral methods has aggravated the problem of distinguishing between them and *hybrid* regimes that are to be found in the grey area between authoritarianism and democracy. A recent large-scale study of a hybrid category labelled 'competitive authoritarianism' used a sample of more than thirty cases and acknowledged that it was covering a broad range of hybridity that extended 'from "soft," near-democratic cases' at one extreme 'to "hard," or near-full authoritarian cases', such as Putin's Russia in the mid-2000s, at the other extreme (Levitksy and Way 2010: 34). Distinguishing between the near-full-authoritarian extreme and third-phase dictatorship can be problematic. And even the experts agreed that there were borderline cases, such as Azerbaijan and Singapore, which 'arguably could be included' in their category of competitive authoritarianism but which they had judged 'insufficiently competitive' and therefore presumably had classified as *fully* authoritarian rather than near-full authoritarian (Levitsky and Way: 2010: 34).

A second, related problem is distinguishing when a near-full-authoritarian hybrid has *changed* into a fully authoritarian regime by becoming a third-phase modernized form of authoritarian regime, i.e. a democratically disguised dictatorship. Considering the sheer number of authoritarian hybrids and the prevalence of third-phase modernization, the problem seems likely to plague political scientists' categorizing and coding for a long time to come.

KEY POINTS

- Authoritarian regimes claim that they have *legitimate* authority, i.e. a *right* to rule.

- Dictatorships claim to be a form of democracy or to be preparing the way for democracy.

- Holding elections is a sign of shrewd dictatorship rather than real democracy if these elections are non-competitive or semi-competitive.

How do they rule?

This section describes how authoritarian regimes have used various mechanisms to exert *control* over state and society. It also describes the most extreme way in which dictatorships have ruled—what political scientists have termed *totalitarianism*. Few authoritarian regimes have attempted to be so extreme, but the very concept of a 'totalitarian' regime has led political scientists to develop a concept of 'authoritarianism' that describes the less extreme and standard way of authoritarian rule.

Totalitarianism and authoritarianism

Totalitarianism

The term 'totalitarian' was first popularized in the 1920s–30s, when Mussolini described the fascist state as totalitarian. The term was adopted by political scientists after the Second World War, but they gave it a wider application which included Hitler's Nazi regime and even Stalin's communist regime in the Soviet Union. Occasionally, it was also applied to the new communist regimes that had emerged in China, North Korea, and Eastern Europe. Political science's theorists of totalitarianism depicted it as a new and very ambitious type of dictatorship that readers of George Orwell's futuristic novel *1984* (written in 1948) would describe as 'Orwellian' (Brooker 2009: 17–24). Unlike previous types of dictatorship, it sought to transform human nature through a 'totalitarian' organization of all aspects of life and an official ideology that not only justified and guided this transformation of human nature but also provided a psychological means of carrying it out—assisted of course by external controls produced by the regime's party and other organizations, especially the 'terror' produced by the secret police.

The early theorists of totalitarianism paid special attention to the role of ideologically inspired *leadership* by the Hitler or Stalin leader figure who prophetically interprets and is driven by the ideology (see Box 6.4). But this and other aspects of the concept of totalitarianism had to be reappraised after Stalin's death in 1953 because the post-Stalin leadership of the Soviet Union ended the secret police's reign of terror and criticized Stalin's personal rule by accusing him of having established a 'cult of personality'. What is more, by the 1960s historical research was beginning to show that Hitler's and Stalin's regimes had failed to achieve a total control of actions, let alone thought, and that the concept of totalitarianism could only be applied to the aspirations or goals of these regimes rather than their actual 'achievements'. In fact it seems that a few later dictatorships, such as the communist regime in North Korea, have been better examples of totalitarianism and its extremist way of ruling.

Box 6.4 Fascist totalitarian leaders

Fascist Italy

Origins

In 1922 Mussolini led the militaristic, radically rightist Fascist party in an attempted 'revolutionary' coup, the March on Rome, which led to the king of Italy appointing Mussolini as his constitutionally legitimate prime minister.

Consolidation

Mussolini took several years to convert what remained of Italy's democracy into a one-party state. He also converted the post of prime minister into the more powerful post of 'Chief of the Government' and reversed the principal–agent relationship between himself and the Fascist party, which was relegated to the subordinate role of assisting the new 'Fascist State'.

Personal rule

By the 1930s Mussolini was clearly the personal dictator as well as *Duce* (leader) of Italy. For example, his personal propaganda cult had become so prominent that *mussolinismo* seemed to overshadow Fascist ideology and such ideologically inspired innovations as the 'Corporative State' economic policy. But Mussolini never replaced the king as head of state, and was sacked by him in 1943 when the Allies invaded Italy and seemed certain to win the war.

Nazi Germany

Origins

The fascist Nazi party came to power in Germany after a series of increasingly successful *election* performances in the early 1930s, when the country was suffering from the social and economic effects of the Great Depression.

Consolidation

As the Nazis had become the largest party in parliament, the president appointed Hitler to the post of head of government in early 1933. Hitler took only a few months to take over the parliament's legislative powers and establish a one-party state.

Personal rule

Hitler's personal rule became absolutist in 1934 under his new legal title of *Führer* (leader), which combined the powers of head of state and government. This was accompanied by a personal oath of allegiance from all members of the military as well as from civil servants, police, and even the judiciary. Like Mussolini, he had the power to take his country into an ideologically driven, unwinnable war which would bring an end to his regime.

Authoritarianism

The difference between the totalitarian way of ruling and the authoritarian regimes' standard way was highlighted by a sophisticated concept of authoritarianism developed by Linz in the 1960s (Linz 1970). He described four defining elements or features of authoritarianism that delineated something that was more than monarchy but less extreme than totalitarianism:

- the presence of some limited political pluralism;
- the absence of an ideology that is elaborate and/or used to guide the regime;
- the absence of intensive or extensive political mobilization;
- a predictably limited rather than arbitrary or discretionary leadership by a small group or an individual.

These four features have been present in the great majority of dictatorships, regardless of whether the dictatorship was personal, military, or one-party. In fact Linz suggested that even totalitarian regimes might eventually develop into something that looked more like an authoritarian regime. He later coined the term 'post-totalitarian' to describe this development and to provide more differentiation and categorization within the very broadly applicable concept

of authoritarianism (Linz and Stepan 1996). Later, he also coined the term 'modern sultanism' to describe absolutist personal dictators who not only lacked the ideological motivation and legitimation of totalitarian leaders but also used *greed* as well as fear to motivate key subordinates (see Chehabi and Linz (1998) for an extension of the concept of sultanist dictatorship to mean a tendency that appears in different varieties of regime, to varying degrees, and in different stages of a personal dictator's career).

Exercising control

Both totalitarianism and authoritarianism deploy a range of control mechanisms to ensure that the regime will be obeyed even if its claims to legitimacy are not effective. The control is exercised by monitoring and enforcing political loyalty as well as by implementation of the regime's policies.

The most effective control mechanism is a force of competent political or 'secret' police. Depending upon the regime and its circumstances, the political police's methods (1) of information-gathering range from using torture and informers to merely electronic surveillance and (2) of punishment range from execution or 'disappearance' to merely ending a person's career prospects.

Totalitarianism is more likely than authoritarianism to involve extreme methods of political policing, but any dictatorship may use them in a peak period of repression. In these periods of extreme repression the political police may be so concerned with *potential* as well as *actual* disloyalty or disobedience that even politically reliable sectors of the population are 'terrorized' by the repression's scope and apparent arbitrariness.

A military regime has some distinctive control mechanisms, notably the junta and the declaration of martial law. The latter bestows policing and judicial powers upon the military, which can then use its soldiers to police and control society at street and village level. The junta can be used to control the military regime's presidential or ministerial government and counterbalance the civilian influence upon and *within* the government, especially that of the civilians used to fill technical posts such as minister of finance (see Box: Military juntas, in the Online Resource Centre). A few military regimes have further extended their control over the state by appointing military officers to important positions in the civil service and regional or local government. And one of the reasons why the military have occasionally adopted a military version of the one-party state is in order to use a political party as a means of extending control over state and society.[5]

online resource centre

One-party rule's distinctive control mechanisms have been based on using a political party to control state and society. The communist regimes have led the way since 1917 in seeking strong and extensive party control of the state from the top downwards. The party's Politburo or Standing Committee of the Politburo (in the case of China) is the equivalent of a junta and acts as the country's *de facto* government, with its decisions being passed on to the state's legal government—the council of ministers—for implementation. The party also uses its extensive membership in the civil service and the military to ensure that these policies are carried out. Party members monitor policy implementation as well as political loyalty, while party officials may actually provide 'guidance' to civil servants about how to implement party policy—indeed regional and district party leaders have often been the *de facto* governors of their areas. Considering that even a generation ago the Chinese regime had some 600,000 party officials and administrators, the extent and range of this party control mechanism is very impressive (Hamrin 1992: 96). On the other hand, the fascist and Third World cases of one-party rule have seldom adopted the communist practice of strong and extensive party control; for example, a party committee has not often acted as a junta-like *de facto* government of the country. This may be at least partly because of their tendency to be transformed into personal dictatorships by their party's leader, who is unlikely to favour institutions that represent 'collective leadership' and organizational rule by the party.

Conclusion

The safest way to draw conclusions about the past and future of authoritarian regimes is to present two differing perspectives: (1) the extinction interpretation and (2) the evolution interpretation. The *extinction* interpretation would argue that authoritarian regimes are political dinosaurs in a world whose political climate clearly favours democracy. It would back up this argument by citing such large-scale theories as Fukuyama's 'end of history' claim that liberal democracy was the end of humanity's ideological evolution and its final form of government (Fukuyama 1992: xi). An older and larger-scale theory is Weber's early twentieth century interpretation of modern history as the tendency towards formal rationalization and its emphasis on rules-and-numbers calculability; the *economy* will be rationalized through the development and spread of market capitalism, *administration* will be rationalized through the development and spread of bureaucracy, and therefore, by implication, *politics* will be rationalized through the development and spread of representative *democracy* (Brooker 2014).

The *evolution interpretation* uses the biological analogy to emphasize the proven ability of of authoritarian regimes to adapt to change in their political environment. After all, they are now engaged in a *third* phase of modernization that may well be as successful as the nineteenth-century first phase and twentieth-century second phase. Furthermore, the third-phase modernization has adapted to the democratic political climate by evolving democratically disguised dictatorships that use democratically credible semi-competitive elections. And this evolution interpretation becomes very plausible if the biological analogy is used to argue that competitive–authoritarian *hybrid* regimes should be classified as part of 'modern authoritarianism'. Then the recent history of authoritarian regimes can be interpreted as a very successful adaptation to the democratizing change in the political climate that was explained by Fukuyama and predicted by Weber. In other words, there has been what Polanyi described long ago as a 'double movement' (2001[1944]: 136–8), which in the present case meant a global movement away from the outdated forms of authoritarian regime and then a global movement towards the more modern democratized forms of authoritarianism.

Questions

1. Why have authoritarian regimes been more diverse and innovative than democracies?

2. Why did democracy take so long to win?

3. Can an authoritarian regime be popular? If so, how?

4. Why are there so many authoritarian regimes in the Middle East?

5. Why is the military more willing than a dictatorial political party to relinquish power?

6. Why is China still categorized as a communist state despite its apparently capitalist economy?

7. How would a dictatorial politician set about misappropriating power?

8. How would you know if your country's elections were only semi-competitive?

9. What does the future hold for authoritarian regimes?

10. Why have authoritarian regimes been allocated only one chapter in this book?

Further reading

Brooker, P. (2014) *Non-Democratic Regimes* (3rd edn) (Basingstoke: Palgrave Macmillan).

Finer, S. E. (1988) *The Man on Horseback: The Role of the Military in Politics* (2nd rev. edn) (Boulder, CO: Westview).

Herb, M. (1999) *All in the Family: Absolutism, Revolution, and Democratic Prospects in the Middle Eastern Monarchies* (Albany, NY: State University of New York Press).

Holmes, L. (1986) *Politics in the Communist World* (Oxford: Oxford University Press).

Linz, J. J. (2000) *Totalitarian and Authoritarian Regimes* (Boulder, CO: Lynne Rienner).

Saich, T. (2011) *Governance and Politics of China* (Basingstoke: Palgrave).

Web links

www.freedomhouse.org
Website of Freedom House with assessments of global trends in democracy that also highlight cases of dictatorship.

www.amnesty.org
Website of the worldwide movement Amnesty International that campaigns for human rights and, therefore, also highlights cases of repression.

www.hrw.org
Website of Human Rights Watch that seeks to protect human rights around the world and, therefore, also highlights cases of repression.

www.wmd.org
Website of World Movement for Democracy that seeks to promote and advance democracy and, therefore, to help challenge dictatorships and democratize semi-authoritarian systems.

online resource centre

For additional material and resources, please visit the Online Resource Centre at:
www.oxfordtextbooks.co.uk/orc/caramani3e/

Structures and institutions

CHAPTER 7
Legislatures

Amie Kreppel

Chapter contents

Reader's guide

This chapter addresses the political roles and powers of legislatures. The first step is to define different types of legislature on the basis of their functions and relationship with the executive branch. The analysis then turns to examination of the roles of legislatures within the political system as a whole, as well as several critical aspects of the internal organizational structures of legislatures. Finally, the relationship between the political power and influence of a legislature and the structure of the broader political and party system is discussed. Throughout the chapter the focus is on legislatures within modern democratic political systems, although many points apply to all legislatures regardless of regime.

Introduction

The role of legislatures within the political environment in which they exist is far from straightforward. Different scholars have come to very different conclusions about the political power and policy influence of legislatures. General evaluations vary depending on the cases that are studied, the theoretical framework employed, the historical period under examination, and the precise understanding of 'power' and 'influence' invoked.

This chapter examines the influence and importance of legislatures across a variety of different 'core' tasks including representing and linking citizens and government, overseeing the executive, and, of course, policy-making. The importance of these tasks and the variation between legislatures in their performance make the understanding of legislatures a critical component of any attempt to comprehend politics more generally. Legislatures exist in nearly every country on the planet, and have the potential to play an important political role even in non-democratic systems.[1]

> ## Box 7.1 Definitions
>
> Assembly: a legislative body; specifically, the lower house of a legislature.
>
> Legislature: a body of persons having the power to legislate; specifically, an organized body having the authority to make laws for a political unit.
>
> Parliament: the supreme legislative body of a usually major political unit that is a continuing institution comprising a series of individual assemblages.
>
> Congress: the supreme legislative body of a nation and especially of a republic.
>
> *Source:* Merriam-Webster online (www.m-w.com).

KEY POINTS

- Legislatures are present throughout the world and play a central role in almost all political systems.
- However, variations in their powers and structures are large.

What is a legislature?

The variety of terms such as 'assembly', 'congress', or 'parliament' that are often used interchangeably with the term 'legislature' increases uncertainty about the roles and powers of legislatures. Before we can examine the types of legislature that exist it is necessary to define what a legislature is. The exact meaning of these terms is not as clear as one might expect. Definitions of assembly, legislature, parliament, and congress provided in dictionaries do not always differentiate between these terms (see Box 7.1). All four are defined as 'a legislative body' or 'a body of persons having the power to legislate', making efforts to clearly distinguish between them difficult. Yet most would agree that the terms are not interchangeable.

Of these four terms 'assembly' is the most general. Additional definitions of the word (uncapitalized) refer simply to the coming together of a group of people for some purpose—for example, a school assembly. It is only when we add the qualifier 'political' or 'legislative' that we think of assemblies in the same context as legislatures, parliaments, and congresses. Parliaments and congresses, generically, can best be understood as specific types of legislature. This interpretation of these four terms creates a hierarchy of institutions from the most general (an

assembly) to the most specific (congresses and parliaments) which are types of the mid-level category of 'legislatures' (see Figure: A hierarchy of institutions, in the Online Resource Centre).

online resource centre

Assemblies and legislatures

If we begin with the broadest definition of an assembly as 'a group of persons gathered together, usually for a particular purpose, whether religious, political, educational, or social', we can then designate legislatures as those assemblies for which the 'particular purpose' in question is political and legislative (*American Heritage Dictionary*, 4th edn). This definition of legislatures is expansive enough to include a wide array of very different institutions, while still distinguishing between legislatures and other types of assemblies organized for religious, educational, or social purposes.

Precisely because of its inclusiveness, the term 'legislature' is too broad to help us distinguish between different types of legislative institutions. To accomplish this task we must move beyond dictionary definitions and concentrate on the structural characteristics of the political system in which legislatures are located. Regardless of whether or not a political system can be categorized as democratic, *if there is a legislature in addition to an executive branch the relationship between the two will determine the core characteristics of the legislature.* The central characteristic is the relative level of interdependence between the two branches.

Parliaments

In what are commonly referred to as 'parliamentary systems' the executive branch is selected by the legislature, usually from among its own members. The executive branch or 'government' is formally responsible to the legislature throughout its tenure. This means that it can be removed from office at any time should a majority of the legislature oppose it, regardless of the electoral cycle. In turn, removal of the executive by the legislature may be accompanied by early legislative elections. Because there is a high degree of mutual dependence between them, these types of system are known generically as fused-powers systems.

Legislatures in parliamentary systems are generally referred to as 'parliaments', regardless of their formal title. This name reflects not only the type of system in which the legislature resides, but also its central task. The word parliament is derived from the French verb *parler*, to speak.[2] The name is well chosen as the institutional and political constraints on parliaments generally serves to focus their activities on debate and discussion.

Congresses

A different type of legislature is called 'congress', within what are popularly referred to as presidential systems. Presidential systems are a type of separation-of-powers (SoP) system. The legislative and executive branches are selected independently, and neither has the ability to dissolve or remove the other from office (except in the case of incapacity or significant legal wrongdoing). The best-known SoP system is that of the US. The fact that the official name of the legislature of the US is 'the Congress' is neither an accident, nor a reason to avoid using the term congress to refer to a type of legislature more generally.

The word 'congress' is derived from the Latin *congressus,* 'a meeting or [hostile] encounter; to contend or engage' (Harper 2001). This is focused on the potentially conflict-ridden interactions between individuals. The use of congress to denote legislatures within SoP systems in general is justified by the policy-making focus of their activities, as well as the likelihood of a more conflictual relationship with the executive branch when compared with fused-power systems. Examples of both types of system can be found in Table 7.1 .

KEY POINTS

- The words 'assembly', 'legislature', 'parliament', and 'congress' are not interchangeable and care should be taken to use the right one to avoid confusion and/or a lack of precision.
- Parliaments exist in fused-powers (usually parliamentary) systems.
- Congresses exist in separation-of-powers (usually presidential) systems.
- Both parliaments and congresses are types of legislature, meaning that they are political assemblies with some legislative tasks.

Table 7.1 'Parliament' and 'Congress' type legislatures (a selection)

Country	Lower chamber	Legislature type	Regime
Argentina	Chamber of Deputies	Congress	SoP
Austria	National Council (Nationalrat)	Parliament	Fused
Belarus	Chamber of Representatives		Non-democratic
Belgium	House of Representatives	Parliament	Fused
Bhutan	Tsgogdu		Non-democratic
Bolivia	Chamber of Deputies	Congress	SoP
Brazil	Chamber of Deputies	Congress	SoP
Canada	House of Commons	Parliament	Fused
Chile	Chamber of Deputies	Congress	SoP
China	National People's Congress		Non-democratic
Colombia	Chamber of Representatives	Congress	SoP
Czech Republic	Chamber of Deputies	Parliament	Fused
Denmark	Folketing	Parliament	Fused
Finland	Eduskunta	Parliament	Fused
France	National Assembly	Parliament	Fused
Germany	Federal Council	Parliament	Fused
Greece	Vouli	Parliament	Fused
Guyana	National Assembly	Parliament	Fused

Table 7.1 'Parliament' and 'Congress' type legislatures (a selection) (*continued*)

Country	Lower chamber	Legislature type	Regime
India	Lok Sabha	Parliament	Fused
Iran	Islamic Consultative Assembly		Non-democratic
Israel	Knesset	Parliament	Fused
Italy	Chamber of Deputies	Parliament	Fused
Japan	House of Representatives	Parliament	Fused
Korea, South	Kukhoe	Congress	SoP
Mexico	Chamber of Deputies	Congress	SoP
New Zealand	House of Representatives	Parliament	Fused
Pakistan	National Assembly	Parliament	Fused
Peru	Congress	Congress	SoP
Poland	Sejm	Parliament	Fused
Romania	Chamber of Deputies	Parliament	Fused
Russia	State Duma	Parliament	Fused
Singapore	Parliament		Non-democratic
Slovakia	National Council	Parliament	Fused
Spain	Congress of Deputies	Parliament	Fused
Switzerland	National Council	Congress	SoP[a]
Taiwan	Legislative Yuan	Congress	SoP
Tanzania	Bunge	Parliamentary	Fused
Turkey	Grand National Assembly	Parliamentary	Fused
UK	House of Commons	Parliament	Fused
US	House of Representatives	Congress	SoP
Venezuela	Chamber of Deputies	Congress	SoP

[a] The executive in Switzerland is unique in that it is collegial (seven members) and indirectly elected by the legislature, but it is not responsible to the legislature, nor can it dissolve the legislature.

Source: Kurian *et al.* (1998).

The role of legislatures

Although the activities and roles that legislatures perform will vary significantly according to the political environment in which they exist, they can be loosely organized into three categories: (1) linkage and representation, (2) oversight and control, and (3) policy-making.

When fulfilling the first task legislatures serve as the 'agents' of the citizens they represent and are expected to act in their interests. In the second case legislatures become the 'principals' and are tasked with the monitoring and collective oversight of the executive branch (including the bureaucracy). Finally, when pursuing the third type of activity, legislatures engage in legislating and may be acting as agent, principal, or both, but the task is specifically focused on the policy process. What differentiates legislatures is not which of these roles they play, but the degree to which their activities emphasize some roles over others.

An 'agent' is an actor who performs a set of activities and functions on behalf of someone else (the principal). The standard 'principal–agent problem' revolves around the fact that agents are likely to have both incentives and opportunities to shirk their duties and still receive the benefits associated with having done them. Thus the principal has an incentive to devise some form of oversight to ensure that the agent is performing its tasks.

In the political realm legislatures serve as agents and principals in relation to the electorate and the executive respectively. Thus the electorate (citizens) must act to control the legislature and the legislature must seek to control the executive branch.

Legislature as agent: linkage, representation, and legitimation

Linkage

Linking citizens to the government is one of the most fundamental tasks that legislatures perform. It serves 'as an intermediary between the constituency and the central government' (Olson 1980: 135). In this context, legislatures act as a conduit of information allowing local-level demands to be heard by the central government and the policies and actions of the central government to be explained to citizens. The ability of legislatures to serve as *effective* tools of communication as well as the *relative importance* of this role varies.

The degree to which a legislature is able to serve as an effective means of communication between citizens and government depends critically on the level of regularized interaction between the members of the legislature and their constituencies, as well as the type and frequency of opportunities to convey information to the executive branch. In general, individual legislators will spend more time and be more actively engaged with their constituents when they are elected in single-member districts as opposed to multi-member districts (see Chapter 10). This is because they are the sole representative of the citizens in their constituency (the citizens within their district) at the national level.

The linkage role will be more important in political systems in which citizens do not elect the executive directly. Thus, in parliamentary systems the linkage function of the parliament-type legislature is likely to be more important because it may be the only mechanism of communication between citizens and the central government.

Representation

The individual members of a legislature are also expected to *represent* their constituents and work to protect their interests. Legislators are responsible for advocating for their constituents in their stead, ensuring that the opinions, perspectives, and values of citizens are present in the policy-making process (Pitkin 1967).

However, there are different interpretations of the representative responsibility of legislators depending on whether they are understood to be *delegates* or *trustees*. In the former case members of legislatures are expected to act as mechanistic agents of their constituents, unquestioningly carrying messages and initiatives from them to the central government. In contrast, if members of the legislature are viewed as trustees, the expectation is that they will serve as an interpreter of their constituents' interests and incorporate the needs of the country as a whole, as well as their own moral and intellectual judgement, when acting within the political, and especially policy, realm.

Debating

The plural characteristic of legislatures also enables them to serve as public forums of debate, in which diverse opinions and opposing views can directly engage with one another with the goal of influencing public opinion and policy outcomes. In general the debate function will be a more central and important activity in those legislatures with limited direct control over the policy-making process, which includes most non-democratic systems.

By fostering debate and discussion legislatures can serve as important tools of compromise between opposing groups and interests within the society. The capacity of a legislature to effectively serve as a public forum of debate will be more important in heterogeneous societies in which there are significant policy-related conflicts between groups. Even when compromises are not achieved, the opportunity for minority or oppositional groups to openly and publicly express their views within the legislature may serve to limit conflict to the political realm, avoiding the much more detrimental effects of social unrest and instability.

Legitimation

Ultimately, the ability of a legislature to create links between citizens and government by providing adequate representation to critical groups and minority interests and fostering public debate will determine both its institutional legitimacy and its ability to provide legitimacy for the political system as a whole. The ability to mobilize public support for the government as a whole is an important aspect of a legislature's performance. In fact, even if legislatures 'are not independently active in the development of law, and even if they do not extensively supervise the executive branch, they can still help obtain public support for the government and its policies' (Olson 1980: 13). This legitimizing function of legislatures is fundamentally a reflection of their linkage and representational activities (Mezey 1979).

Legislature as principal: control and oversight

Control

The ability of the governed to control the government is one of the foundational tenets of representative democracy. The primary tool used to achieve this goal is regularly scheduled free and fair elections. The type of executive oversight and control practised by the legislature is directly linked to the nature of the relationship between voters and the executive branch *and* between the legislature and the executive branch.

Democratic political systems have two different 'principals' monitoring the executive branch, each of which has a different set of tasks. Voters directly or indirectly select the executive during elections. However, citizens often lack sufficient time, information, and the technical skills needed to effectively oversee the details of the political activity of the executive branch. It is the task of the legislature to fill this lacuna. In this context there is a greater degree of difference between presidential (SoP) and parliamentary (fused-powers) political systems.

1. The control functions of congress type legislatures in SoP systems are more limited than those in fused-powers systems. The critical difference is the extent to which policy initiatives are a legitimate subject of control and oversight by the legislature. In SoP systems the policy agenda of the executive branch is not subject to legislative control or oversight. The executive cannot be removed from office because a majority in the legislature disapproves of its policies. In fact, the legislature's ability to remove an executive from office in SoP systems is usually restricted to cases of illegal activity and/or physical or mental incapacity. This type of formal *impeachment* of the executive is a rare and generally complex legal process.

2. Parliament-type legislatures in fused-powers systems are explicitly tasked with policy-related control of the executive branch. Executives are responsible to the legislature for their policy agenda and can be removed from office if their policy goals are deemed unacceptable by a majority in the legislature. Removal of the executive in fused-powers systems is accomplished through a *motion of censure* or a *vote of no confidence*. This does not imply any legal wrongdoing. As a result, in most fused-powers systems the removal of the sitting executive by the legislature does not result in a crisis or systemic instability.[3]

The significant difference between fused-powers and SoP systems in the policy-related control activities of legislatures is a function of the broader political system. More specifically, it is a result of the character of the legislative–executive relationship. In SoP systems voters select their legislature and executive independently from one another. In fused-powers systems voters cast votes only for the legislative branch. Selection of the executive occurs indirectly through the legislature. This difference is significant for two reasons.

First, the independent election of the executive and legislative branches makes it far more likely that there will be *substantial differences in their respective ideological or partisan identities.* For example, in the US the election of a president from one party and a congressional majority from the other is a relatively common occurrence (**divided government**). In fused-powers systems, however, it is impossible for the majority in the parliament and the executive branch to be from wholly distinct

and opposing parties or coalitions. All governments in fused-powers systems *must* have the implicit or explicit support of a majority of the legislature to remain in office. The executive branch (prime minister and the cabinet ministers) are elected by the legislature. This process reduces the likelihood of policy-related conflict between the legislature and the executive.

The second reason for the difference in the control function is tied to the requirements of the democratic process. Representative democracy requires that elected officials be responsible to those who elected them. In SoP systems voters elect the executive, and therefore only voters have the power to change or remove the executive. If a congress could remove a popularly elected president though a vote of censure or a similar mechanism on the basis of policy disagreement it could easily undermine the democratic process as a whole.

Oversight

Legislatures in both SoP and fused-powers systems play a critical role in ensuring proper oversight of both the budgetary implications of policies and their implementation. Legislatures may be able to exercise oversight and control functions in non-democratic systems, even if they are unable to effectively control the executive branch as a whole.

Legislative oversight of the executive branch is generally quite broad, entailing the development and passage of policies as well as the monitoring of executive agencies tasked with the implementation of those policy decisions. Although most legislatures engage in both types of oversight, in general the former task is of greater significance in fused-powers systems, while the latter takes precedence in SoP systems.

Question time, inquiries, hearings, and investigative committees are frequently used by legislatures to gather information and, if necessary, hold various actors and agencies within the executive branch accountable. Legislatures have increased their executive oversight activities over time, largely in response to the growing complexity of government and the need to delegate activities to other agencies.

1. *Question time* is used in parliaments and provides a regularly scheduled opportunity for members of the legislature to present oral and written questions to members of the government, including the prime minister.

2. In contrast, *special inquiries* and *hearings* are organized on an ad hoc basis to investigate specific topics or issues that are considered important by some legislators.

3. *Investigative committees* are similar, but are more formalized, tend to address higher-order issues, and often have a longer duration.

4. In addition, legislatures may request or require that the executive and/or its bureaucratic agencies provide it with *reports on specific issues* of concern, make presentations to the full legislature or relevant committees, or respond to specific inquiries in hearings.

Budget control

Legislatures may also engage in indirect oversight of executive policy initiatives through their control over the budgetary process. The earliest forms of legislatures were little more than groups of aristocratic lords called together by the king to approve new taxes and levies. Although monarchs had access to vast resources, they were often in need of additional funds to pay for the armies necessary to wage war and quell uprisings (see Chapter 4). This practice established the nearly ubiquitous norm of legislative control over the *power of the purse*. The result is that most political systems require legislative approval of national budgets and tax policies.

Control and oversight of expenditure, even if limited by entitlements and other political artifices, is a powerful tool that can provide even the weakest of legislatures the opportunity to influence policy decisions.[4] There are few policy goals that can be achieved without some level of funding. As a result, the ability of the legislature to withhold or decrease funding for initiatives supported by the executive branch can become a useful bargaining tool. In fact, the need to obtain legislative approval for spending initiatives can even provide legislatures with the potential to influence decision-making in policy arenas traditionally reserved for the executive branch, such as foreign and security policy.

Legislature as legislator: policy-making vs. policy-influencing

There are a number of ways that legislatures can be directly involved in the policy-making process, ranging from simply giving opinions to making significant amendments, and from initiating independent proposals to vetoing the proposals of the executive branch. However, as already discussed, there are a broad variety of tasks regularly accomplished by legislatures, and in many cases legislating is not one of the most important (see Table: Legislative powers of legislatures, in the Online Resource Centre).

online
esource
centre

Consultation

The most basic, and generally least influential, type of legislative action is consultation. This power grants the legislature the authority to present an opinion on legislation, general plan of action, or broad policy programme. Consultation in no way guarantees that the executive branch will abide by the opinion of the legislature. Yet, the ability to present an opinion and to differentiate the views of the legislature from that of the executive can be important in many contexts. In particular, legislative opinions that are in conflict with the proposals put forward by the executive branch and are public in nature may serve as a tool of linkage and representation.

Delay and veto

A common ability among even comparatively weak legislatures is the power to delay legislation. This is a 'negative power' in that the legislature can only slow down the process, not provide positive input or substantive change directly. Despite this, the ability to delay passage of a proposal can be an effective bargaining tool when the executive branch prefers rapid action.

In its most extreme incarnation the power of delay becomes the power of veto. Legislatures with veto power can definitively and unilaterally block policies from being adopted. Like the power of delay, veto power is negative. As a result it will only be an effective bargaining tool for the legislature when the executive branch has a strong interest in changing the status quo.

Amendment and initiation

The most important positive legislative tools are the power to amend and initiate proposals. The ability to amend bills allows the legislature to change aspects of the executive branch's proposal to achieve an outcome in line with the preferences of a majority of its members. Frequent restrictions to amendment power include limitations on the stage in the process at which amendments can be introduced (Spain), the number of amendments that can be introduced (Austria), or the ability of the legislature to make changes that would incur additional costs (Israel).

An independent power of initiative grants individuals or groups within the legislature the right to introduce their own policy proposals independent of the executive branch. In some legislatures all proposals must formally be initiated by the legislature (the US), while in others the legislature has no formal ability to initiate proposals independently (the European Union). Most political systems fall somewhere between these two extremes.

In most fused-powers systems independent member initiatives are rarely adopted. In West European countries, for example, 80–90 per cent of successful proposals are initiated by the executive branch. In some cases, such as Israel, private-member bills are estimated to account for less than 9 per cent of adopted proposals (Mahler 1998). In Belgium between 1971 and 1990 a total of 4,548 private-member bills were initiated, but just 7.3 per cent were ultimately adopted (Mattson 1995).

The centrality of the policy-making function of government has led to the development of a number of different attempts to categorize legislatures on the basis of their policy influence (see Table: Major classification of legislatures, in the Online Resource Centre). Thus, we can differentiate in a dichotomous way between *transformative legislatures* that have a high degree of direct policy-making influence and *arena type legislatures* that are more engaged in the linkage and oversight functions with little direct policy influence (Polsby 1975). Alternatively, legislatures can be understood in terms of their 'viscosity' or capacity to slow down and even block the executive in its attempts to make policy decisions (Blondel 1970).

KEY POINTS

- Legislatures engage in a variety of tasks including providing a link between citizens and the central government, representing citizen interests, executive oversight, and participating in the policy-making process.

- While most legislatures in democratic systems perform all of these roles to some extent, the emphasis placed on the various roles and tasks will vary between legislatures.

- The very different character of the relationship between the executive branch and the legislature in fused-powers and separation-of-powers systems influences which roles and tasks are emphasized by a legislature.

- There are a number of different tools that a legislature may employ within the policy-making process, including consultation, delay, veto, amendment, and initiation. While the powers of delay and veto are 'negative' in that they delay or block policies, amendment and initiation are 'positive' powers.

The internal organizational structures of legislatures

Legislatures are likely to be ineffective if they do not have an internal structure that allows for an effective division of labour, specialized expertise, access to independent sources of information, and other basic organizational and operational resources. An analysis of the internal structures and resources of a legislature can provide a more accurate assessment of its general level of activity and influence than a review of the formal powers granted to it in the constitution.

Number and type of chambers

In most cases legislatures have either one chamber (unicameral) or two (bicameral). Multi-chamber legislatures are generally created to ensure adequate representation for different groups within the political system. The lower (and usually larger) chamber provides representation for the population as a whole, while the upper chamber represents specific socially or territorially defined groups.

These can be the political subunits such as states (US), *Länder* (Germany), or cantons (Switzerland), or different groups of citizens such as aristocrats (UK) or ethnicities (South Africa under apartheid).[5] Unicameral legislatures are more likely to be found in unitary political systems with comparatively homogeneous populations (such as Scandinavia).

More important than the actual number of legislative chambers is the relationship between them. In unicameral systems all the powers of the legislative branch are contained within the single chamber. However, in bicameral systems these powers may be (1) *equally shared* (both chambers can exercise all legislative powers), (2) *equally divided* (each chamber has specific, but more or less equally important, powers), or (3) *unequally distributed* (one chamber has significantly greater powers than the other). The first two cases are considered to be *symmetric bicameral* systems, while the latter are *asymmetric bicameral* systems. Table 7.2 provides some examples.

Knowing how many chambers a legislature has and understanding the relationship between them (symmetric or asymmetric) is important because it can impact the broader policy-making process. For example, if the chambers within a symmetric bicameral legislature have significantly different or opposing ideological majorities it may delay the legislative process as a proposal acceptable to the majority of both chambers must be developed. Such a situation may also force increased political compromise and ensure a higher level of representation for minorities or territorial groups. However, failure to reach a compromise, can block the policy process as a whole, or force the executive branch to attempt to govern without the legislature (through decrees for example). In the worst-case scenario, such a blockage might even threaten the stability of the political system if necessary policies cannot be adopted.

Number, quality, and consistency of members

By their nature legislatures bring together a comparatively large number of people. The legislature is usually the most numerous and most diverse of the primary branches of government. Thus, the tools and structures it uses to organize itself are particularly critical and often quite informative in assessing the effective roles of the legislature within the broader system.

Size

A few basic descriptive statistics can reveal a good deal about the character and political role of a legislature. For example, the number of members relative to the size of the general population, the number of days per year the legislature is in session, the extent to which members are

Table 7.2 Representation and role/asymmetry of upper chambers

Country	Federal (Y/N)	Upper chamber	Size	Basis of representation	Mode of selection	Symmetric (Y/N)
Argentina	Y	Senate	72	Provincial	Directly elected	Y
Austria	Y	Bundesrat	64	Lander	Indirect election by provincial legislature by PR	N
Belarus	N	Council of the Republic	64	Regions	Indirectly elected, 8 appointed by President	Y
Belgium	Y	Senate	71	Regions	Direct elections (40)—proportional and indirect selection (31)	N
Bolivia	N	Senate	27	Departments	Directly elected—top 2 parties (2/1) 3 seats per Admin. Dept.	Y
Brazil	Y	Senate	81	States	Directly elected—simple majority, 3 seats per state	Y
Canada	Y	Senate	104	Regions	Appointed—by government	Y
Chile	N	Senate	47	Regions	Directly elected—majority (38), appointed (9)	Y
Colombia	N	Senate	102	National	Directly elected in a single national constituency—PR	Y
Czech Republic	N	Senate	81	National	Directly elected—simple majority 1/3 every 2 years	N
France	N	Senate	321	Departments	Indirect election by electoral colleges in each Department	N
Germany	Y	Bundesrat	68	*Länder*	Indirectly selected by *Länder* governments	N
Grenada	N	Senate	13	National	Appointed—by governor general (on advice of prime minister)	N
India	Y	Rajya Sabha	245	States/ Territories	Indirectly elected (233), appointed by president (12)	N
Italy	N	Senate	315	Regions	Directly elected—PR and majority bonus within regions	Y
Japan	N	House of Councillors	252	National and Prefecture	Directly elected—nationally (100) and within prefectures (152)	N
Mexico	Y	Senate	128	States	Directly elected—modified majority (1 per state to second party)	Y
Pakistan	Y	Senate	87	Provincial and Tribal Areas	Indirectly elected (4/province + 8/ tribal areas + 3/Capital Territory)	N
Poland	N	Senate	100	Districts	Directly elected—simple majority 2 or 3 per district	N
Romania	N	Senate	143	National	Directly elected—two-ballots majority	Y
Russia	Y	Council of Federation	178	Federal Units	Indirectly selected (2/Republic, Oblast, Krais, Okrug, and Federal City)	N
St Lucia	N	Senate	11	National	Appointed by governor general, prime minister selects 6 and opposition 3	N
Spain	N	Senate	257	Regional	Directly elected (208)—majority indirectly elected (49)	N
Switzerland	Y	Council of States	46	Cantons	Directly elected—simple majority	Y
UK	N	House of Lords	731	Class	Hereditary and by appointment	N
US	Y	Senate	100	Federal Units	Directly elected—simple majority	Y

Source: Compiled by the author from Kurian *et al.* (1998). Updated from official national legislative websites.

'professional' legislators or maintain additional external employment, the rate of member turnover from one election to the next, and the general 'quality' of members can all provide information on the likely level of political influence that a legislature has within the political system and the policy-making process (see Table: The impact of general characteristics on legislative influence, in the Online Resource Centre).

The relationship between these characteristics and the roles of the legislature is relatively straightforward in most cases. The size of the legislature is telling because of the difficulty that large diverse groups generally have in reaching coherent decisions. The more members a legislature has, the more time each decision is likely to require (as a result of the need to allocate speaking time to all members, for example). More members are likely to lead to more complex mechanisms of internal organization and more thinly spread institutional resources. However, membership numbers must be interpreted in context, as very small countries will naturally tend to have much smaller legislatures while more populous countries will on average have larger legislatures (see Table 7.3).

Time

The amount of time that legislators spend attending to legislative tasks is also a useful indicator of the broader role of the legislature. At one extreme are legislatures that are formally or functionally 'in session' year-round. On the other end of the spectrum are 'part-time' legislatures that meet for only a few days (see Table 7.4).

The length of the annual session of a legislature is often directly tied to the type of members it attracts. Part-time legislatures that are in session only for short periods of the year not only provide the opportunity for their members to engage in other professional activities, but they often make it a functional requirement. The average annual salary of a legislator is more likely to constitute a 'liveable' wage when the task performed constitutes a full-time job. Of course there are also legislatures that are formally 'full-time' that nonetheless fail to provide members with a sustainable salary.[6]

The need for legislators to maintain additional external employment reduces the amount of time and effort they can dedicate to their legislative tasks. In some cases the role of the legislature is so limited that this is not a concern. In others, however, it will not only reduce the effectiveness of legislators, but will also impact the type of individuals who join the legislature. This impacts both the quality of members and the rate of membership turnover from one election to the next. When legislative wages are low it can serve to restrict membership to those with alternative sources of wealth and keep the most qualified individuals from considering the legislature as a career option.

Committees

Almost without exception legislatures organize internally on the basis of committees. However, the variations that exist between these committees can be enormous. Legislatures may have few or many committees and they may be created on an ad hoc basis or permanently established. In addition, there may be highly specialized subcommittees and/or temporary committees of inquiry created to address specific crises or questions. In some cases committees are responsible for reviewing and amending proposals before the full plenary discusses them; in others they are in charge of implementing the changes decided by the plenary. These relationships are outlined in the Table: The impact of committee characteristics on legislative influence, in the Online Resource Centre.

Permanency and expertise

One of the most important aspects of committees is their permanency. Committees that are created on an ad hoc basis not only tend to be less efficiently organized, but their members lack the opportunity to develop area-specific expertise or the contacts with external actors that facilitate independent and informed decision-making. Given the size of most legislatures, committees often serve as the forum for most legislative activity, including bargaining and coalition-building between political parties. The smaller size and less public nature of committees increase their utility as a forum for these types of activity. However, if the committees are not permanent they are unlikely to provide the necessary level of stability and expertise.

Specialization

Committees within influential legislatures also mirror the organization of the executive branch, with distinct committees for each cabinet portfolio. The association of specific committees with cabinet ministries can foster relationships between the members and staff of the legislature and the executive branch, which can improve inter-institutional cooperation.

Subcommittees and temporary committees

The potential for additional flexibility and specificity can be added through the incorporation of subcommittees and temporary investigative committees (sometimes referred to as committees of inquiry). These allow for still greater levels of specialization and permit the legislature to react to significant events or crises in a timely fashion.

One of the surest indicators of the role of committees, and through them the policy influence of the legislature, is the order in which proposals move between the plenary

Table 7.3 Population and size of lower chamber in forty-one countries

Country	Lower chamber	Population	Size	Reps/citizens
Argentina	Chamber of Deputies	40,117,096	257	156,098
Austria	National Council (Nationalrat)	8,458,023	183	46,219
Belarus	Chamber of Representatives	9,460,700	110	86,006
Belgium	House of Representatives	10,170,000	150	67,800
Bhutan	Tsgogdu	720,679	150	4,805
Bolivia	Chamber of Deputies	10,426,155	130	80,201
Brazil	Chamber of Deputies	193,946,886	513	378,064
Canada	House of Commons	35,002,447	301	116,287
Chad	National Assembly	11,274,106	125	90,193
Chile	Chamber of Deputies	16,572,475	120	138,104
China	National People's Congress	1,347,350,000	2978	452,435
Colombia	Chamber of Representatives	46,882,000	163	287,620
Czech Republic	Chamber of Deputies	10,513,209	200	52,566
Denmark	Folketing	5,599,665	179	31,283
Egypt	People's Assembly	83,780,000	454	184,537
Finland	Eduskunta	5,428,830	200	27,144
France	National Assembly	65,635,000	577	113,752
Germany	Federal Diet (Bundestag)	81,923,000	598	136,995
Greece	Vouli	10,815,197	300	36,051
India	House of the People (Lok Sabha)	1,210,193,422	545	2,220,538
Iran	Islamic Consultative Assembly	77,082,000	270	285,489
Israel	Knesset	7,968,300	120	66,403
Italy	Chamber of Deputies	60,870,745	630	96,620
Japan	House of Representatives	127,520,000	500	255,040
Korea, South	Kukhoe	50,004,441	299	167,239
Mexico	Chamber of Deputies	112,336,538	500	224,673
New Zealand	House of Representatives	4,453,000	120	37,108
Pakistan	National Assembly	181,819,000	217	837,876
Peru	Congress	30,135,875	120	251,132
Poland	Sejm	38,538,447	460	83,779
Romania	Chamber of Deputies	19,043,767	341	55,847
Russia	State Duma	143,300,000	450	318,444
Singapore	Parliament	5,312,400	83	64,005
Slovakia	National Council	5,445,324	150	36,302
Spain	Congress of Deputies	46,815,916	350	133,760
Switzerland	National Council	8,014,000	200	40,070
Taiwan	Legislative Yuan	23,305,021	164	142,104
Tanzania	Bunge	44,929,002	275	163,378
Turkey	Grand National Assembly	74,724,269	550	135,862
UK	House of Commons	63,181,775	659	95,875
Venezuela	Chamber of Deputies	28,946,101	165	175,431

Source: Compiled by the author from Kurian *et al.* (1998), national websites, and the CIA *World Fact Book* (2011).

Table 7.4 Comparison of annual session duration

Country	Lower chamber	Annual session(s)	Meeting days (sittings)
Argentina	Chamber of Deputies	Annual session from 1 March to 30 November	
Austria	National Council (Bundesrat)	Annual session from mid-September to mid-July	
Belarus	Chamber of Representatives	Variable	170 days
Belgium	House of Representatives	Annual session from second Tuesday in October to 20 July	Minimum of 40 days per session
Bhutan	Tsgogdu	Must meet at least once per year (May–June or October–November)	
Bolivia	Chamber of Deputies		90 days (possible to extend to 120)
Brazil	Chamber of Deputies	Two sessions annually: 1 March–30 June and 1 August–5 December	
Canada	House of Commons		
Chad	National Assembly	Two sessions annually in April and October	90 days in session
Chile	Chamber of Deputies	One annual session 21 May–18 September	
China	National People's Congress	Once per year (usually in March)	14 days
Colombia	Chamber of Representatives	Two sessions annually: 20 July–16 December and 16 March–20 June	
Denmark	Folketing	Annual session, October–October (no meetings in July, August, and September)	Approximately 100 plenary meetings per year
Finland	Eduskunta	Spring and autumn sessions (recess December–January and summer)	
France	National Assembly	Annual session, October–June	
Greece	Vouli	Annual session from first Monday in October (for not less than 5 months)	
India	House of the People (Lok Sabha)	Three sessions per year: February–May, July–August, November–December	
Italy	Chamber of Deputies	Year-round (official vacations: 1 week for Easter, 2 weeks for Christmas, and August)	
Japan	House of Representatives	Ordinary session January–May (extraordinary sessions summer–autumn)	150 days/ordinary session (extraordinary ones vary)
Korea, South	Kukhoe	Regular session may not exceed 100 days (special session not to exceed 30 days)	Average of 45 days per year in plenary session
Mexico	Chamber of Deputies	Two sessions annually: 1 September–15 December and 15 March–30 April	
New Zealand	House of Representatives	Session runs for full calendar year generally no sittings in January	
Pakistan	National Assembly	2 annual sessions. Must not remain in recess for more than 120 days at a time	
Poland	Sejm	Continuous, sittings determined by Presidium	26 sittings per year (1–4 days each) October 2001–October 2005
Romania	Chamber of Deputies	2 sessions annually: February–June and September–December	
Russia	State Duma	2 sessions annually: mid-January–mid July and beg. October–end of December	Generally 2 days per week 3 weeks per month in session

Singapore	Parliament	No set calendar, one sitting per month 6 months maximum between sessions	
Slovakia	National Council	Two annual sessions (spring and autumn)	
Spain	Congress of Deputies	Two sessions annually: February–June and September–December	
Switzerland	National Council	Four times per year (every 3 months), extraordinary sessions are allowed	3 weeks/ordinary session, 1 week/ extraordinary session
Taiwan	Legislative Yuan	Two sessions annually: February–May and September–December	2 sittings per week while in session
Tanzania	Bunge	Variable number of sessions lasting between 4 days and 2 weeks	25–30 days per year on average
Turkey	Grand National Assembly	Annual session: 1 October–30 September may recess for a maximum of 3 months	Meets Tuesday–Thursday in session
UK	House of Commons	Full year, adjourns for Christmas (3 weeks), Easter (1 week), and summer (10 weeks)	4–5 days per week while in session
Venezuela	Chamber of Deputies	Ordinary sessions: early March–early July and early October–late November	

Source: Based on Kurian *et al.* (1998), updated from official national government and legislative websites.

and the committees. If legislation is fully vetted in plenary *prior* to being sent to committee, committees are unlikely to play a substantial role in policy-making. Given the hurdles to engaging in a thorough analysis of policy proposals in plenary, this process of vetting bills indicates a comparatively small policy role for the legislature. In contrast, when bills are reviewed and amended within the committees first, the legislature is more likely to have a substantial influence on policy outcomes.

Hierarchical structures and internal decision-making

Within every legislature there are a variety of internal positions of authority and power, even if the institution itself is relatively weak. At the level of the legislature there is generally a president, one or more vice-presidents, and in some cases questors or other secretarial/administrative positions. In addition, most legislatures will also have leadership positions within organized subunits—for example, chairs of committees, subcommittees, and/or specialized delegations and/or working groups.

The most fundamental difference between legislatures occurs between those that distribute internal positions of authority proportionally amongst all the groups (usually political parties) represented, and those that use a 'winner-take-all' system, assigning positions only to members of the majority (party or coalition). In the former case cooperation and compromise between government and opposition groups is facilitated by the requirements of working within an institution with clear power-sharing structures. In contrast, winner-take-all systems are more likely to foster polarization.

Majoritarian or winner-take-all systems discourage compromise. As a result, these types of legislature will function well only when the majority in charge is reliable, either because of a high degree of party discipline or because of significant numerical superiority over the opposition. When parties are weak or undisciplined, and/or majorities are slim, individual member defections can lead to the defeat of majority proposals. On the other hand, when majorities are large and/or parties are disciplined, decision-making is likely to be more efficient and policy innovation easier to achieve.

In contrast, legislatures that distribute leadership positions among the parties and groups of both the majority and the opposition are more likely to witness cross-party agreements and compromises, and in some cases this may even be a requirement, given the proportional distribution of positions of power. This type of policy process is less likely to suffer significant negative consequences from individual member defections on particular issues. At the same time, however, this approach to policy-making is likely to be more time-consuming and to lead to incremental policy reform based on compromises between opposing groups rather than sweeping ideologically informed policy innovations.

These are the two most extreme scenarios and there are, of course, a number of intermediate alternatives. For example, the majoritarian system is used to distribute internal positions of power in the US legislature; however, there is also a comparatively low level of party discipline. As a result, a number of different outcomes are possible depending on the size of the majority held by the largest party and the level of bipartisan cooperation possible on a given issue. In general, however, legislatures that share internal positions of authority proportionally *tend* to be more consensual in character than those that use a winner-take-all system.

Assessing a legislature's power

All legislatures, democratic or not, claim to fulfil the central representative/linkage, oversight, and legislative roles discussed above. Yet, there are vast differences between legislatures in terms of the emphasis and centrality they ascribe to these roles and, as a result, to the function they perform within the political system. There are legislatures for which the linkage and oversight functions are clearly pre-eminent (as in the UK, Greece, and Chile), while others place more emphasis on their legislative function (the US, Italy, and the Netherlands). The next task is to understand the systemic characteristics that lead to these variations.

The underlying cause of the differences between legislatures is surprisingly simple, at least conceptually. Fundamentally, the extent to which a legislature is an active and effective participant in the legislative process versus assuming a more passive legislative role (focusing instead on oversight and linkage) is directly tied to the *degree of autonomy* it enjoys. More specifically, there are two aspects of a legislature's relative autonomy that are important:

- the independence of the institution as a whole;

- the independence of its members individually.

Institutional independence: executive–legislative relations

The institutional autonomy of a legislature is a function of its formal structural interaction with the executive branch. As seen above, fused-powers systems centralize legislative authority in the executive; while SoP systems tend towards decentralized legislative decision-making, increasing the role of the legislature (see also Chapter 8).[7]

Fused-powers systems are structured hierarchically in so far as voters elect the members of the legislature and the members of the legislature, in turn, select the executive branch. In contrast, in SoP systems both the leader of the executive branch and the members of the legislature are elected by citizens (see Figure 7.1). The difference in

Fused-powers systems

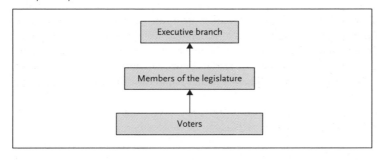

- Voters elect and may choose not to re-elect members of the legislature.
- Members of the legislature elect and may dismiss the executive branch through a vote of censure or no-confidence vote (restrictions may apply).
- The executive branch can dissolve the legislature (restrictions generally apply) and call for new elections. This results in dissolution of the executive branch as well)

Separation-of-powers systems

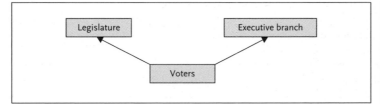

- Voters elect, and may choose not to re-elect, members of the legislature.
- Voters elect, and may choose not to re-elect, the executive branch (president).
- The executive *cannot* dissolve the legislature. The legislature can remove the executive *only* in case of legal wrongdoing.

Figure 7.1 Powers systems

the method of choosing the executive branch is of critical importance. The selection of the executive branch by the legislature has significant implications for the latter's relative institutional autonomy. Perhaps counterintuitively, the power to elect and dismiss the executive branch serves to *reduce* the autonomy and independent policy influence of a legislature.

In a SoP system, elections for the legislative and executive branches are not necessarily linked to each other in timing or, more importantly, outcome. This means that there is no guarantee that the result will be a similar partisan distribution. In contrast, in a fused-powers system the elections of the two branches are integrally connected because following each legislative election the new legislature must select the executive branch. In fused-powers systems the need for the executive to be selected by and maintain the support of a majority within the legislature requires a partisan link between the two branches. Even in systems with frequent minority governments, the implicit support (or lack of opposition) of a majority of the legislature is necessary to maintain the government in office.

In contrast, in SoP systems the executive and legislative branches are selected independently, even when election occurs simultaneously. Citizens are given the opportunity to cast separate and distinct votes for each branch, despite the fact that these votes are often cast on a single ballot. By decoupling the two votes, SoP systems impose no restrictions on the partisan or ideological relationship between the two branches and any partisan distribution of majorities is possible. The absence of a partisan link between the executive and legislative branches, in combination with their structural independence, is essential in ensuring that the legislature has the potential to play an influential role in the policy-making process.

The impact of the interdependent relationship that exists between the executive and legislature in fused-powers systems is particularly important. The responsibility of the legislature for both installing and maintaining the executive branch severely constrains its ability to pursue independent legislative action. Majorities must

remain comparatively stable in their support for the executive and, by extension, the executive's policy initiatives. In many cases the defeat of an executive initiative of even moderate significance is considered a *de facto* vote of 'no confidence' with the potential to force the resignation of the government. The resulting instability, including the potential for new legislative elections, makes such actions risky for legislatures in fused-powers systems.

SoP systems do not place any of these restrictions on the legislature. Because the executive branch is wholly distinct there is no need for the legislature to maintain any form of support for it. The defeat of a policy proposal from the executive branch in the legislature has no capacity to impact the tenure of the executive branch or the timing of legislative elections. The fixed terms of office for both the legislative and the executive branches frees the legislature from the burden of maintaining the executive in office. At the same time it liberates both branches from any need for ideological affinity or policy consensus.

Member independence: the role of political parties

The ability of legislatures to take full advantage of the possibilities offered by a SoP system, as well as the degree to which those in fused-powers systems are able to make the most of their more limited legislative prospects, also depends on a less formal aspect of the political system. The character of the party system, and in particular the relative level of autonomy individual members of the legislature enjoy *vis-à-vis* their parties, can significantly affect the ability of the legislature as a whole to influence policy outcomes.

Unlike institutional independence, which is a function of the constitutionally defined structures of the political system, partisan autonomy depends on the characteristics of the party system. There are some elements of the party system that are especially important. These can be divided into two categories: (1) party-specific characteristics and (2) systemic attributes of the party

Table 7.5 Party and system characteristics related to member autonomy

Party characteristics	
Candidate selection	Centralized vs. decentralized selection by local units and/or activists, existence of leadership veto, self-nomination, etc.
Internal organization of political party	Hierarchical vs. decentralized party structures, role of legislative leadership in party structures (sharing of leaders)
Party system characteristics	
Electoral system	Party centred (i.e. party lists with or without preference votes), candidate centred (usually single-member districts)
Sources of party and campaign funding	Existence of and rules regulating state financing, presence of fixed donor groups (labour), private resources, etc.

system. Examples of each type of variable are provided in Table 7.5. The underlying question addressed by each of these variables is fundamentally the same in all cases: to what extent is the political future of an individual member of the legislature controlled by his/her political party?

For most legislators there are two primary concerns or goals: (1) election/re-election and (2) the achievement of some set of policy outcomes (Fiorina 1996; Kreppel 2001). Both are intrinsically related to each other and central in determining legislator behaviour, regardless of the broader political system.[8] Secondary concerns often include the attainment of internal party or institutional positions of power such as a committee chairmanship or a party leadership role. Both the candidate selection mechanisms and the internal organizational structure of political parties deeply impact the ability of members to achieve these goals if they lose the support of their party leadership.

Party organization

If re-election is important to legislators then their autonomy is reduced to the extent that their re-election is controlled by their party leaders. If candidate selection (or the ordering of the party lists) is controlled by the party elite, those wishing to be re-elected must maintain their support (on electoral systems see Chapter 10). On the other hand, in parties that allow local party organizations to select candidates or in which the ordering of the party lists is predetermined or decided by party members, individual legislators will enjoy a comparatively high level of partisan independence. In other words, the greater the party leadership's control over a member's re-election, the lower is the member's autonomy.

The impact of the centralization of a political party on member autonomy is less direct, but equally important. The more centralized a political party, the fewer opportunities there are for independent decision-making by members. In decentralized parties there may be multiple centres of decision-making offering individual members both more opportunities to influence decisions and a broader array of policy outcomes supported by some portion of the party. Decentralized parties are also less likely to issue vote instructions, freeing members to vote in accordance with their personal preferences.

The relationship between organized party leadership within the legislature and the leadership structures that govern the 'electoral party' is also important. Although ostensibly the party in the legislature is simply a subset of the larger electoral party, there are many cases in which the two-party organizations clash, creating opportunities for members to act independently. It is not an uncommon phenomenon for the compromises required by the policy-making process within the legislature to cause alarm amongst party activists and leaders outside the legislature. Parties that employ a single unified leadership structure within and outside the legislature are less likely to face this type of intra-party strife, effectively decreasing opportunities for members to act independently.

Electoral laws

While the different scenarios discussed above can vary between political parties within a political system, there are other elements that will generally affect all parties equally (and thus all individual members of a legislature) in a similar manner. Two of the most important systemic variables are (1) the electoral system and (2) the rules regulating campaign funding.

Electoral systems influence member independence directly and profoundly by determining the nature of the voters' choices. In single-member districts voters are asked to select between individual candidates, while in PR systems the choice is between political parties. The latter method highlights the importance of parties and reinforces their primacy in mediating the citizen–government relationship. In contrast, in candidate-centred elections the political and personal attributes of the individual candidate are primary and in some cases may even overshadow the significance of party affiliation.

Thus, the relative autonomy of individual members of a legislature will increase as the electoral system offers opportunities for them to win re-election as a result of a high level of personal voter support. Elections that focus exclusively or even primarily on political parties significantly reduce the capacity of members to compete in the face of opposition or even indifference from their party's leadership. As important as electoral opportunity is, however, without access to sufficient financial resources no candidate will be competitive.

The most important aspect regarding finance is the presence (or absence) of state funding and the rules that govern access to these funds (on party finances, see Chapter 12). Where state funding for electoral campaigns is the primary source of funds, easily accessible state-financing for parties and campaigns increases the possibilities for new parties to form, and/or independent candidates to compete. As a result, the costs to members of leaving their party to run for election independently or to form a new party are reduced and political independence is increased. Even if members rarely choose to pursue either of these opportunities, the fact that they exist is enough to diminish the capacity of the party to take action against members for failing to follow the party line.

Summing up, the combination of individual and institutional autonomy defines the extent to which a legislature can effectively shape the policy process and help to determine legislative outcomes. These underlying relationships between the executive and the legislature and between the political parties and their members within the legislature create the broad structural constraints within which all the other elements we have discussed operate. At one extreme are legislatures that are dominated

	Centralized party system	Decentralized party system
Fused-powers system	**PARLIAMENT** UK Greece	**STRONG PARLIAMENT** Italy Poland
Separation-of-powers system	**WEAK CONGRESS** Colombia Argentina Bolivia South Korea	**CONGRESS** US

Figure 7.2 Types of legislature

by the executive branch (parliaments) with individual members largely controlled by their political parties. At the other extreme are legislatures that are formally independent from the executive branch (congresses) within political systems in which political parties are weak or decentralized and unable to effectively control the members of the legislature. These variables can be condensed into a simple 2 × 2 table such as Figure 7.2.

KEY POINTS

- The institutional autonomy of the legislature (from the executive branch) and the individual autonomy of its members (from political parties) are the most fundamental variables affecting the policy influence of a legislature.

- Institutional autonomy is largely dependent on the formal political structures. In fused-powers systems in which the legislature selects the executive the two branches are mutually dependent and the institutional autonomy of the legislature is reduced. In separation-of-powers systems the legislature and the executive are both selected by the voters and the institutional autonomy of the legislature is increased.

- The autonomy of individual members of the legislature is a function of their dependence on political parties to achieve their electoral and policy goals. Individual members will have less autonomy in party-centred PR electoral systems.

- Additional factors influencing the relative independence of individual members include the availability of state funding for electoral campaigns.

Conclusion

In the end, what difference does it make if a legislature is powerful or not? Why does it matter if the legislature has the capacity to independently affect policy outcomes? Is a strong legislature better or worse than a weak one?

Ultimately, there is no 'best' type of legislature, nor is there any reason that a more powerful legislature should be considered 'better' than one that is less influential. However, it is important to understand what type of legislature exists, particularly if there are concerns about key aspects of the political process, such as its representativeness, efficiency, or the quality of the policy outputs it produces.

The primary difference between the two general types of legislatures (parliamentary or congressional) and the variations of each presented in Table 7.1 is the relative importance of the core tasks performed by all legislatures—representation, linkage, oversight, and policy-making—in terms of the legislature's workload.

That said, the ability of the legislature to independently affect policy outcomes does have the potential to change the character of the political system by shifting the balance of power between the executive and legislative branches, and this carries with it significant repercussions. For example, political systems with parliament-type legislatures that are focused primarily on their linkage and oversight functions will tend to have a more hierarchically structured policy-making process in which power is concentrated within the executive branch (and often within the political party hierarchy). This will generally lead to more *efficient* decision-making because fewer actors are involved in the process. However, the restricted level of access may result in the exclusion of key social groups from the policy-making process or may lead to large policy swings when a new government enters office.

In contrast, political systems that disperse power and facilitate the participation of a strong congressional-type legislature in the policy process are likely to be less efficient in terms of decision-making speed, but more *inclusive*. Because both the executive and the legislature participate in the policy process more coordination and compromise is necessary. This will certainly be the case when these institutions are controlled by different political parties (and/or when party control over individual members is weak). The likely result is a slower decision-making process with outcomes that represent broad compromises. Large policy swings are less likely and incremental change more common. However, because of this there is less likelihood that significant minority groups in society will be wholly excluded from the policy-making process or violently opposed to the resulting policy outcomes.

Understanding the type of legislature that exists within a given political system, including both its formal relationship to the executive and less formal links to the political parties, can provide a good deal of information about the political system itself. Additional information about the legislature's internal organizational structures, the strength of its committee system, the quality of its members, and its access to resources will all provide significant additional clues about the type and relative policy influence of the institution as a whole.

Questions

1. What are the differences between an assembly, a legislature, a parliament, and a congress?

2. What are the core tasks of a legislature in a democratic society?

3. Why are legislatures generally better able to represent the interests of citizens than the executive branch?

4. What are separation-of-power systems and fused-power systems?

5. How are the oversight and control functions of legislatures different in fused powers and separation-of-powers systems?

6. What are the five possible tools that legislatures may have at their disposal to influence the policy-making process? Which are 'negative' and which are 'positive'?

7. What is the difference between a symmetric and an asymmetric bicameral legislature? Why is it important?

8. Why are the structure and role of the committee system a good indicator of the policy-making influence of the legislature?

9. Why are political parties influential in determining the autonomy of a legislature?

10. What are the broader implications of having a strong legislature that is able to independently influence policy outcomes?

Further reading

Döring, H. (ed.) (1995) *Parliaments and Majority Rule in Western Europe* (New York: Palgrave Macmillan).

Döring, H. and Halleberg, M. (eds) (2004) *Patterns of Parliamentary Behaviour: Passage of Legislation Across Western Europe* (Aldershot: Ashgate).

Kurian, G.T., Longley, L.D., and Melia, T.O. (1998) *World Encyclopedia of Parliaments and Legislatures* (Washington, DC: Congressional Quarterly).

Inter-Parliamentary Union (1986) *Parliaments of the World: A Comparative Reference Compendium* (2nd edn) (Aldershot: Gower House).

Loewenberg, G. and Patterson, S. (1979) *Comparing Legislatures* (Boston, MA: Little, Brown).

Loewenberg, G., Patterson, S., and Jewell, M. (1985) *Handbook of Legislative Research* (Cambridge, MA: Harvard University Press).

Norton, P. (1999) *Parliaments in Asia* (London: Routledge).

Web links

http://www.ipu.org/english/parlweb.htm
The Inter-Parliamentary Union's websites of national parliaments.

www.electionworld.org/parliaments.htm
Electionworld.org's Parliaments Around the World website.

www.c-span.org
C-span.org's clearing house of televised legislatures and legislature websites from around the world.

http://library.cqpress.com/phw/
Congressional Quarterly Press electronic version of the *Political Handbook of the World*.

For additional material and resources, please visit the Online Resource Centre at:

online resource centre www.oxfordtextbooks.co.uk/orc/caramani3e/

CHAPTER 8

Governments and bureaucracies

Wolfgang C. Müller

Chapter contents

Reader's guide

This chapter looks at decision-making modes of governments and their capacities to govern. Special attention is given to the relationship between the political and administrative parts of government. The chapter begins by addressing definitions and distinguishing what constitutes government under different regimes. The chapter presents different modes of government that reflect the internal balance of power: presidential, cabinet, prime ministerial, and ministerial government. Then it addresses the autonomy of government, in particular from political parties and the permanent bureaucracy. Next, the chapter discusses the political capacity of governments, the relevance of unified vs. divided government, majority vs. minority government, and single-party vs. coalition government. Finally, the chapter highlights the bureaucratic capacities of government, addressing issues such as classic bureaucracy, the politicization of bureaucracies, and the New Public Management.

Introduction

The term 'government' has several meanings. In the broadest sense it refers to a hierarchical structure in any organized setting, including private clubs, business firms, and political institutions. Within politics a broad definition of government includes all public institutions that make or implement political decisions and that can be spread over several tiers, which are called federal, state, and local government. That general understanding of government includes the executive, legislative, and judicial branches. Most common, however, is to refer to a country's *central political executive* as 'the government', and this is how this term will be used in this chapter.[1]

The job of the government is to govern the country. Governing means ruling. It is not, as the term 'executive' might suggest, just implementing laws passed by the legislature. Rather, governing means the government having a strong imprint on the laws passed during its reign and more generally exercising overall control over a country and determining its direction. As we shall see, governments are not always able to live up to very strong expectations about their ability to dominate political decision-making. Yet, even weak governments tend to be the political system's most important single political actor. This is a major reason why individuals and political parties mostly want to be in government. And because government is so important, positions in the central political executive tend to come with other goods that make them even more attractive: social prestige, decent income, public recognition, and privileged access to other powerful and/or famous people. The chance to govern the country and to enjoy these privileges is meant to motivate the best people to compete for government office. In democracies, such competition for government office is ultimately tied to elections. Either the government is directly elected or it is responsible to a parliament that results from general elections.

A few men and (increasingly also) women, distinguished and carefully selected as they may be, cannot run a country. Therefore governments have bureaucracies to support them in their tasks of ruling and administrating the country. Thus, in functional terms, governing is not the exclusive task of the government. This has given rise to the notion of the *core executive*, which comprises 'all those organizations and procedures which coordinate central government policies, and act as the final arbiters of conflict between different parts of the government machine' (Rhodes 1995: 12). This implies that it is difficult to pin down the precise composition of the core executive. While the government in the narrow sense constitutes its centre, the core executive also comprises top civil servants, the key members of ministers' private cabinets, and a list of actors which varies over time and space. Realistically, the demarcation line between what constitutes the core and what belongs to the remaining parts of the executive also depends on the analyst's perspective and judgement. At the same time the core executive focus emphasizes coordination and negotiation rather than hierarchical relations among the units that constitute the core executive (Rhodes and Dunleavy 1995; Smith 1999).

> **KEY POINTS**
>
> ● The term 'government' has several meanings. The most common refers to the country's central political executive.
>
> ● Governing means ruling, exercising overall control over a country, and determining the course it will take.

Types of government
Government and the separation of powers

Today's governments emerged through the piecemeal splitting-off of state functions from a traditionally undivided central government (usually a monarch) (King 1975; Finer 1997). In order to limit the government's power, judicial functions were transferred to courts and legislative functions to parliaments. This process began in twelfth- and thirteenth-century England. It had many national variations and, in Europe, was not completed before the twentieth century. The constitutional doctrine of the separation of powers—as developed first and foremost by the political philosophers Locke, Montesquieu, and Madison—provides a normative justification for the separation of institutions (Vile 1967; see also Chapters 7 and 9).

In practice, state functions were never as neatly separated as envisaged by political philosophers. The executive has retained important legislative functions, in particular drafting legislation and issuing government decrees and ordinances (Carey and Shugart 1998). With political parties establishing themselves as the main mechanism to structure elections and to coordinate incumbents, executives have gained an almost *de facto* monopoly in law-making in parliamentary systems. In presidential systems this is not true to the same extent, but executives also exercise a large influence on legislation.

The normative foundations of democratic government rest on two premises: the government must be connected to the electoral process and must work under constitutional constraints. Within these confines government can be organized in many ways. Three are quite common: *parliamentarism*, *presidentialism*, and *semi-presidentialism*. Another is connected with the successful Swiss model

Box 8.1 Government creation and accountability under different regime types

Presidentialism

- Direct or quasi-direct popular election of the president for a fixed period.
- The head of state is identical with the head of government.
- The president is not politically accountable to the legislature.
- Appointment of government members by the president (mostly with the consent of the legislature).

Parliamentarism

- The head of government (prime minister, chancellor, etc.) is different from the head of state (monarch or president).
- Most parliamentary systems allow for parliamentary dissolution by the head of state (typically on the prime minister's or government's proposal).
- Election of the prime minister by parliament in some countries (e.g. Germany, Spain), appointment by the head of state (e.g. Italy, Ireland) or speaker of parliament (Sweden) with subsequent vote of confidence in other countries, and appointment by the head of state without an obligatory vote of confidence in another set of countries (e.g. UK, the Netherlands).
- The prime minister and the cabinet are politically accountable to the parliament, i.e. they can be removed from office by a vote of no confidence at any time for no other reason than that the parliament no longer trusts the government. Some countries (Germany, Spain, Belgium, Hungary) require a *constructive* no-confidence vote, i.e. parliament must replace the sitting government by an alternative government with the same vote.

Directorial government

- Currently, only Switzerland works with directorial government. The *Bundesrat* or *Conseil Fédéral* (Federal Council) consists of seven individuals who are elected individually by parliament (the joint meeting of both chambers) for the entire term of parliament.
- The federal president is head of government and head of state. This is inspired by US presidentialism, but the country's linguistic and religious diversity have required collegial government—the cabinet members rotate the presidency between them on an annual basis.
- The government is not politically accountable to parliament.

Directly elected prime minister

- Only Israel practised this system from the elections between 1996 and 2003. The prime minister was popularly elected with absolute majority (in two rounds, if necessary) at the date of each parliamentary election and when the office of prime minister was vacant.
- The cabinet was nominated by the prime minister but required a parliamentary vote of confidence to take office.
- The prime minister was politically accountable to parliament. However, a successful vote of no confidence also triggered the dissolution of parliament and hence led to new elections.

Semi-presidentialism

- The president is directly (or quasi-directly) elected.
- The president appoints the cabinet.
- The cabinet is politically accountable to parliament.
- The president can dismiss the cabinet and/or dissolve parliament.

---

and deserves a mention: the *directorial* form of cabinet government. Finally, government with a directly elected prime minister, which may appear as a 'natural' democratic improvement on parliamentarism, has failed in its only real-world test in Israel. Box 8.1 and Figure 8.1 show how these regime types can be distinguished.

In presidential systems the executives are not politically accountable to the legislatures, but the legislatures do play a significant role in holding presidents accountable for judicial offences such as treason or bribery. However, often the decision to investigate such offences and to proceed with the impeachment of the president is primarily political (Pérez-Liñán 2010). Typically, it involves actors from both chambers of the legislature and qualified majorities to do so.

The government under different democratic regime types

What constitutes the government depends on the regime type. Presidentialism constitutionally provides for a one-person executive, but including his cabinet under the label of 'government' may be a useful working definition. Although the relations between the president and the cabinet are fundamentally different under fully fledged semi-presidentialism, both can be considered as constituting the government. Yet, semi-presidential regimes offer a wide range of different working modes (Elgie 1999). Sometimes the president acts as the real head of government, relegating the prime minister to a mere assistant and occasionally the scapegoat for things that do

Head of government's taking office rests on support of	Fixed term	
	Yes	No
Electorate	Presidential (US)	Parliamentary with directly elected PM (Israel)
		Semi-presidentialism (F)
Parliament	Directorial government (Switzerland)	Parliamentary (UK)

Figure 8.1 Regime types

Note: Only one example is included for each type.

not go well, sometimes the holders of these two offices work together or against each other in complex power-sharing arrangements, and sometimes the president is little more than a powerful head of state in reserve for crisis situations. The archetypical case of semi-presidentialism, France, has seen the two former variants, while other countries (e.g. Austria) resemble the latter and combine a semi-presidential constitution with a parliamentary working of the system.

Parliamentarism in many ways is a simple form of government: the cabinet is the government (Strøm *et al.* 2003). And although the mechanisms of creation and accountability are fundamentally different, the cabinet also constitutes the government in systems with a directly elected prime minister (Israel) and in systems with directorial government (Switzerland).

KEY POINTS

- Today's governments constitute what remains of absolute monarchs, after splitting-off of judicial and legislative functions.

- Notwithstanding the separation-of-powers doctrine, state functions are not fully separated. The government has retained important legislative powers, although differences exist between different regime types.

- Different regime types also distinguish themselves by the definition of government. Constitutionally, one-person executives and collective bodies can be distinguished. Some governments include the head of state while others have a separate head.

The internal working of government

Constitutional texts are typically silent about the internal working and decision-making of government and much is left to the political actors. Over time conventions

may establish themselves. Conventions are normative rules that are generally respected. Although they are not backed up by law, breaking conventions typically is not cost-free for the breaker. Nevertheless, the more a mode of governing rests on formal rules, the more difficult it is to introduce change.

Political science has established a number of descriptive models of government. These models are partly derived from the constitutional order, but try to highlight how government actually works and arrives at decisions. Models capture which actors are typically able to leave their imprint on the outcome of the government decision-making process to a greater extent than other participants. They were developed with the background of the archetypal cases of presidential and parliamentary government—the US and the UK—and subsequently applied to other cases.

Presidential government

The principle of presidential government is to vest all executive power in a single, directly elected politician for a fixed term (i.e. the president is not politically accountable to the legislature). As Article II of the US Constitution puts it, 'The executive Power shall be vested in a President of the United States of America.' Lijphart (1992) lists 'a one-person executive' among the defining principles of presidentialism. More realistically, the 'elected executive names and directs the composition of the government' (Shugart and Carey 1992: 19). Thus, within the executive domain, the president is sovereign. Different US presidents have developed their own styles. Some have used their cabinet members mainly for executing their orders while others have used them as advisers, but a collective decision-making system has never been established (Warshaw 1996).

Cabinet government

Cabinet government represents the operating mode of the parliamentary system as it emerged in Britain in the first half of the nineteenth century. Then the cabinet discussed and decided the important issues collectively. The prime minister was a first among equals (*primus inter pares*), not the boss of the other ministers. The background to that was the limited role of the state and the fact that initially the cabinet was the monarch's creation. A slim state kept the cabinet agenda manageable. The cabinet being the monarch's creation had three implications.

1. In many ways the monarch was his own 'prime minister', dealing with his ministers on an individual basis.
2. The ministers objected to a strong prime minister undermining their direct link to the monarch.

3. So did parliament which was keen to avoid individual ministers' accountability being obscured by cabinet hierarchy (Mackintosh 1977: 56). Cabinet government continued to prevail when electoral reform gradually loosened the cabinet's tie with the monarch while strengthening that with the House of Commons (Mackintosh 1977: 155–8, 257–343).

However, with the gradual increase of government tasks, more and more issues needed to be handled and decided. While their number clearly exceeded what a cabinet could handle as a collective body, at the same time many issues became too technical to allow a meaningful discussion between non-specialists. This had two consequences. First, the proportion of government decisions going though cabinet declined. Second, many cabinet decisions became formal, only ratifying what was 'precooked' before the cabinet meeting within and between the ministries (Burch and Holliday 1996; S. James 1999; Smith 1999). Thus, classical cabinet government is a thing of the past. Yet this has not made the cabinet an empty vessel, making decisions only in name but not in substance. A number of authors have identified important issues that are still decided by the cabinet in substance and have stressed the role of the cabinet 'as court of appeal for *both* ministers radically out of sympathy with a general line, *and* for a premier confronted by a ministerial colleague who insists on ploughing her or his furrow' (Dunleavy and Rhodes 1990: 11). If a cabinet fulfils these functions, i.e. deliberates and decides important issues and also functions as court of appeal, then we can speak of *post-classical cabinet government*.

Prime ministerial government

Since the early 1960s, a transformation of the operating mode of British cabinets has been noted. Richard Crossman coined the term **prime ministerial government** (Crossman 1963, 1972). In this model, collective deliberation and effective decision-making in and by the cabinet have been replaced by monocratic decision-making by the prime minister. Authors writing about other European states that experienced long stretches of single-party government, in particular Greece and Spain, have echoed the British diagnosis: cabinet government has given way to prime ministerial government.

There are three different modes of prime ministerial government: (1) a generalized ability to decide policy *across all issue areas* in which the prime minister takes an interest; (2) by *deciding key issues* which subsequently determine most remaining areas of government policy; (3) by defining a *governing ethos*, 'atmosphere', or ideology which generates predictable solutions to most policy problems, and hence constrains other ministers' freedom of manoeuvre so as to make them simple agents of the premier's will (Dunleavy and Rhodes 1990: 8).

Prime ministerial government suggests monocratic decision-making and hence resembles presidential government. The difference is that presidents have a constitutional right to do so while prime ministers need to go beyond their constitutional role. Also, presidents are unassailable, as their term is fixed, while in principle prime ministers can be forced out of office. Such involuntary departure from office is not just a hypothetical possibility, as the most powerful British post-war prime minister, Margaret Thatcher, experienced in 1990 when she was ousted by her party.

Ministerial government

Finally, the transformation of cabinet government is seen to have occurred in the opposite direction. Rather than concentrating power in the prime minister, it has dispersed among the individual cabinet members. This is **ministerial government** or, in Andeweg's (1997) terminology, 'fragmented government'. Decisions ending up in the cabinet typically are ratified only. Ministers are overworked and primarily concerned about getting their own act together. They are inclined to interfere in the business of other ministers only if the decisions concerned would produce negative fallout for their own department. Otherwise ministers respect a tacit rule of mutual non-intervention. As non-intervention is mutual, this rule helps them to get cabinet support for their own policies, and it is the success or failure in directing their respective ministry that is crucial for the conduct of their careers. Recognizing this development, Laver and Shepsle (1990, 1996) have described ministers as 'policy dictators' within their own domain as the founding assumption for their coalition theory.

Models of government and cabinet coalitions in parliamentary systems

Thus far, party has been absent from the government modes presented here. The implicit assumption is that no party line of division runs through government, though party-bonds may be important to overcoming other centrifugal forces (such as conflicting departmental interests). Indeed, cabinets consisting of more than a single party are unlikely to approach either full-blown prime ministerial or ministerial government.

To begin with, in the former the prime minister's dominance is partly due to his/her role as electoral leader and indeed victor when coming to office. The ministers' submission to the prime minster partly rests on his role as a party asset that is not to be damaged by internal challenges. Coalition governments can come close to prime ministerial government when one party is dominant and the coalition builds on an electoral alliance which ties together the cabinet parties. Yet, in most cases the analogy to prime ministerial government in coalition governments is the establishment of an oligarchic leadership, consisting of the leaders of the coalition parties, with each party leader being on the one hand a 'prime minister' of his/her party team in government, and on the other hand deciding critical issues together with the other party leader(s). Note, however, that there are limits to collective leadership and 'sharing' the prime minister's powers. Party leaders cannot attend international summits—which are often the place where important decisions are made (e.g. on the managment of the recent Euro crisis)—in tandem. Nor can constitutional powers be formally shared. Thus, in the case of conflict, the prime minister can always invoke whatever powers the constitution has endowed the office.

In strict terms, ministerial government in coalition regimes would mean that 'the cabinet is not simply a *collection* of coalition partners, but instead it is a *distribution* of specific powers over policy formulation and implementation among those partners' (Laver and Shepsle 1996: 282). In other words, each government party would implement its own policy in its departments and exercise no influence on the departments held by its partner or partners. This assumption underlies the coalition theory of Laver and Shepsle (1990, 1996; for a critique see Dunleavy and Bastow 2001) that predicts the formation of the government that allows each of the government parties full control over its most preferred policy dimension.

Coalition government works nowhere strictly according to the ministerial government model (see the contributions in Laver and Shepsle (1994)). At least some policies are agreed between the parties before the coalition is set up. These deals are often fixed in coalition agreements. Moreover, coalition governance mechanisms such as coalition committees, watchdog junior ministers, and other scrutiny mechanisms are established to guarantee that the deals are being observed by the coalition partners (Müller and Strøm 2000; Thies 2001; Timmermans 2003, 2006; Martin and Vanberg 2004, 2011; Strøm, Müller, and Bergman 2008; Strøm, Müller and Smith 2010). Yet, within these important confines even coalition governments can display a tendency to work according to the ministerial government mode.

Variability of government modes

Government modes are not fixed once and for all. The preceding discussion of the transformation of cabinet government into prime ministerial government and/or ministerial government already suggests some long-term change. Yet, government modes also vary according to political conditions and issues (Andeweg 1997). Thus

single-party governments are more likely to become prime ministerial than coalition cabinets. At the same time, each cabinet is likely to handle issues differently, depending on their relevance and potential of causing damage to the government.

The autonomy of government

In the previous section when political parties were mentioned the assumption was that there is no difference whatsoever between government members and their parties. Yet political parties are complex entities. They consist of (1) the mass organization (the 'party on the ground'), (2) the parliamentary party, and (3) the party team in government (both the latter are also referred to as 'party in public office'). To make it more complicated, the 'party in the electorate' also exists. Although this layer lacks organization, and therefore the quality of a political actor, it is a highly relevant reference point for politicians.

Thus, understanding governments requires exploring the autonomy these layers have from other actors or providers of essential resources without which they would not be able to govern. This section discusses political parties and, more briefly, the bureaucracy (following section). Parties are essential for getting a government into office and maintaining it there, and without the permanent bureaucracy the government could not govern.

Government autonomy: the party dimension

It is the electoral connection which makes government democratic, and it is political parties which play a crucial role in structuring elections even when the electoral system allows the choice of individual candidates (Katz 1997). Modern democracies, therefore, have party government in a general sense (Müller and Narud 2013). Yet, this understanding of party government can be contrasted with a more specific one. According to Richard Rose:

> … party government exists only in so far as the actions of office-holders are influenced by values and policies derived from the party. Where the life of party politics does not affect government policy, the accession of a new party to office is little more significant than the accession of a new monarch; the party reigns but does not rule. (Rose 1976: 371)

What role parties have after the elections is subject to normative and empirical discussions. It is sufficient here to say that conflicting normative theories suggest both the full autonomy of elected officials from their party and, conversely, a strong role of the party in determining the course steered by the government. The former position can be associated with constitutional theory and liberal and conservative thinkers, and the latter one with much of constitutional practice and mostly socialist ideas (Birch 1967). The remainder of this section explores the issue empirically.

Thus, the key question is to what extent political parties can control the behaviour of their government teams. Three means of control are of particular importance (Rose 1976; Katz 1986; Müller 1994; Blondel and Cotta 2000).

Party programmes

Party control of the cabinet will be enhanced in situations where party programmes not only clearly state the intentions of the party, but also specify appropriate means to the desired ends. In such circumstances, ministers will have clear targets, whilst the party will have a yardstick for measurement of their performance.

Selection of cabinet members

Party control of the cabinet will be enhanced where cabinet ministers have internalized and acted upon party values. The internalization of party values is hard to measure, but holding high party office is certainly a plausible indicator. Note that ministers who have good intentions of serving their party still need to be skilled executives in order to succeed.

Permanent control of the party over the cabinet

While the above conditions increase the likelihood of 'partyness of government' (Katz 1986), they do not guarantee the implementation of party policies. Therefore parties may want to exercise permanent control over their ministers. Naturally, the less these two conditions

are fulfilled—for instance, because of the need to appoint technical experts rather than party leaders—and the more changed circumstances (such as international crises und unexpected economic developments) have dated the party programmes, the more important such control can be considered.

Empirical studies of party programmes and their relevance to government policy have a long tradition, though most of them confine themselves to single countries and cabinets. In one of the few comparative and comprehensive studies, McDonald and Budge (2005) took a highly aggregated approach and compared party ambitions (programmes) in twenty-one countries with government ambitions (government declarations) and actual outputs in terms of budget priorities. This study did not find relevant party impact on government in a short-term perspective. The inertia of public policy is simply too strong. In the words of McDonald and Budge (2005: 180): 'The reason is not that changes are not made but that they are slow, because of preexisting budgets, contracts, commitments, and entitlements in the field of expenditures; time constraints, due process, legislative and social opposition, and administrative bottlenecks in the field of legislation.'

Only when a party manages to hold on to government for a long time—McDonald and Budge list the New Deal Democrats in the US, the Thatcher–Major Conservatives in the UK, and the Scandinavian Social Democrats—will a party imprint on public policy be clearly visible.

Blondel, Cotta, and associates chose a less aggregated approach (Blondel and Cotta 1996, 2000). Conceptually, they considered both directions of influence: party on government and government on party. Three ideal types of party–government relations can be distinguished:

- dominance—one of the two dominates the other;
- autonomy—government and government parties coexist without exercising influence on each other;
- fusion—party and government become politically indistinguishable.

Empirically, this research was concerned with appointments (to the cabinet and the party executive), government patronage, and fifty policy decisions in a set of West European countries. Unlike the Budge and McDonald (2005) study, which extracted general policy concerns of parties from their manifestos and the general direction of government policies from budget domains, this research was concerned with specific pledges and specific government policies. The aim was to establish to what extent government behaviour has a party origin and in what direction, if any, top-level recruitment takes place—from the party to the government (as the party government model suggests) or in the opposite direction.

The more exploratory study by Blondel and Cotta (1996, 2000) suggests that the ideal-typical picture of party government—with the party taking over government—needs correction. Specifically, following an initial period of *fusion* after a party enters government, new government appointments lead to increasing *autonomy* of the two, though 'fast-track' appointments of government members to high party office suggest even a tendency towards *dependence* of the party. With regard to policy, the government is not just the technocratic executor of party policy. Rather, the government plays a significant role in shaping policies originating from the party and initiating its own ones. Patronage, it seems, is used to compensate the party for its desired policies which the government cannot deliver or does not want to deliver.

Presidentialization?

One recent attempt to capture the strengthening of the executive *vis-à-vis* political parties is the concept of presidentialization. Specifically, it means the strengthening of the chief executive. Although the term 'presidentialization' has been used earlier in studies of the British prime minister (Foley 1993, 2000; Pryce 1997), the most systematic comparative attempt has been made by Poguntke, Webb, and collaborators (Poguntke and Webb 2005). They associate presidentialization—in all regime types—with '(1) increasing leadership power resources and autonomy within the party and the political executive respectively, and (2) increasingly leadership-centred electoral processes' (Poguntke and Webb 2005: 5). In their analysis this process affects the internal working of the executive, the running of political parties, and the functioning of the electoral process.

Presidentialized government represents one ideal type of government. The 'partyfied' type of government occupies the opposite end of the continuum. The key question then is what is the role of individual leaders and of collective actors? Poguntke and Webb note that different regime types—parliamentarism, semi-presidentialism, and presidentialism—provide the actors with different power resources and hence constrain the place a specific government can take on the continuum. Thus a parliamentary system under a strong prime minister can be more 'presidentialized' than a presidential system under a weak president, but never more so when the president is strong.

In their fourteen-country empirical analyses Poguntke, Webb, and associates identify an almost uniform trend towards presidentialism. Specifically, they recognize shifts in intra-executive power to the leader, increasing autonomy of the executive leader from the party, shifts of intra-party power to the leader, the leader's increasing autonomy from other party heavyweights, a growth of the leader's media coverage, increasing focus on the leader in electoral campaigns, and growing leader effects on voting behaviour. In combination, these developments

indeed suggest a major shift away from the 'partyfied' type of democracy.

Government autonomy: bureaucratic government?

The number of people who enter or leave government after elections (i.e. elected leaders and political appointees) differs from system to system. Yet, in most systems their numbers are tiny compared with those of bureaucrats, even when lower-rank civil servants are not considered. In many parliamentary systems in the first post-war decades little more than two dozen posts changed hands when a wholesale government turnover occurred.

The idea of bureaucratic government (Rose 1969) rests on the assumption that a small group cannot run the whole show and critically depends on the permanent bureaucracy. Bureaucrats can set the agenda of their political masters by identifying problems that need to be addressed; they can limit political choices by presenting a narrow set of alternatives and by undermining the viability of ideas that run counter to the department's common wisdom. Such ideas are labelled, for instance, as not workable, too expensive, having huge undesirable side effects, conflicting with higher-level rules (such as the Constitution or EU rules), having already failed in earlier attempts, etc. More so than any other mode of government, bureaucratic government remains and needs to remain invisible. Thus politicians continue to dominate the public stage. They may even make consequential decisions (according to one of the above modes). Yet these decisions can be compared to choosing the flag to fly on a ship sailing on the ocean, while it is bureaucrats who determine its course. Moreover, most administrative decisions escape the politicians' attention altogether.

KEY POINTS

- Party government means that government actions are strongly influenced by the values and policies of the government party or parties.
- Political parties control their teams in government by the means of party programmes, the recruitment of party leaders into government office, and permanent oversight over and control of the government.
- Empirical studies mostly demonstrate that parties have only a limited impact on government. Initial fusion of party and government often gives way to government autonomy and occasionally party dependence on the government.
- Individual leaders tend to gain weight relative to the parties ('presidentialization').

The political capacity of government

Modern governments of rich nations can achieve much. They can maintain law and order, provide essential services to their citizens, strengthen the economy, and send men and women into orbit or to explore outer space. Yet, whether governments can indeed do what is in the capacity of modern states depends largely on the political conditions that prevail during their reign. This section can discuss only a few selected topics. It leaves aside much of the often very consequential nitty-gritty details of institutional rules (see e.g. Weaver and Rockman 1993*b*; Strøm *et al.* 2003). Nor does it discuss systematically the reactions of citizens, interest groups, and the economy to government policy that at times have brought governments to their knees. It is sufficient here to refer to a few examples: the 2006 riots in the French *banlieues* (suburban housing complexes) which led the government to partly reverse its reform of the labour law; the mass strikes of the British trade unions that brought down the Heath government in 1974; and the less visible but much more common influence exercised by the investment decisions of firms in a globalized economy that have considerably constrained national governments' freedom of manoeuvre.

Unified vs. divided government

The concepts of unified and divided government were invented in the US. **Divided government** means that the presidency is held by one party and at least one chamber of Congress is controlled by the other party; **unified government** is when all three are under the control of the same party (see also Chapter 7). The concepts of unified and divided government transfer easily to other presidential systems, although the multiparty nature of some of them requires some modification. Leaving aside non-partisan presidents, the (one-person) presidency by necessity must be under the control of one party and one party only. In contrast, no single party may control a majority in the legislature.

Yet a legislature passing a great number of detailed laws could make the president its mere servant. This could indeed be the case if no further provision were added to the definition of presidential government—some law-making authority of the president (Shugart and Carey 1992).

The US presidency represents the archetypal case of presidentialism. The formal law-making capacity of the president is negative: the president can veto any law passed by Congress. As long as no vote in both the House of Representatives and the Senate overrides the veto with a two-thirds majority, the law is rejected and the status quo prevails. The US has seen divided government for most of the post-war period. Yet empirical studies suggest that this was not very consequential, as open battles between the Congress and the president resulting in vetoes and occasional overrides have been very limited (Mayhew 1991; Binder 2003). Note, however, that actors anticipating defeat may avoid such battles. While many studies of the US highlight the factors that prevent legislative immobilism, a comparative perspective can be particularly useful as it brings out many of the same factors more sharply and adds additional ones.

In Latin America the most powerful presidents enjoy a much richer set of legislative instruments than their US counterpart. Veto power can take the form of the line veto, enabling the president to veto specific clauses in legislation but accepting the rest, and most presidents also enjoy decree power, the right of legislative initiative, and some procedural power in Congress (Mainwaring and Shugart 1997; Morgenstern and Nacif 2002). At the same time these systems are multiparty. Hence, the chances of a president finding his party endowed with a legislative majority are often modest or non-existent. One influential study (Linz 1990*a*, 1994) has seen here the main reason for the frequent breakdowns of democracy in Latin America. The institutional 'rigidity' of presidentialism—with fixed terms of both the president and the legislature—causes long periods of legislative gridlock followed by short periods of legislative overproduction. Both encourage frustrated political actors to resort to non-democratic means. Yet the specific assumptions about the behaviour of actors underlying Linz's theory have not withstood empirical scrutiny (Cheibub 2007). While it is true that democracy has had a rough life in Latin America, this is not just down to divided government. Presidents have found ways to cope with it, as Cox and Morgenstern (2002) demonstrate (see Table 8.1).

Depending on their own strength in terms of institutional empowerment and party support in the legislature, presidents employ four different strategies. I consider first the two extreme categories. The president uses unilateral powers if the legislature is hostile (*recalcitrant*). He uses presidential decrees to push forward his own policies (rather than making legislative proposals to the assembly) and vetoes laws passed by the legislature that run counter to his policy ambitions. In Cox and Morgenstern's typology this is the *imperial* president. This was the behavioural pattern of Chile's President Allende before General Pinochet's tragic military coup in 1973.

At the opposite end of the spectrum, if the president is sure that the assembly will follow his lead, he dictates his terms in the form of legislative initiative. Such a *dominant* president could be found in Mexico in the years of the Party of the Institutionalized Revolution (PRI) single-party dominance.

The two intermediate cases require the president to engage in give-and-take relations with the assembly. For the president this is more rewarding than unilateral action, as he does not need to push his powers to the very limits

Table 8.1 President–assembly relations under presidentialism

Presidential strategy	Assembly strategy			
	Reject	Bargain	Demand payments	Acquiesce
Undertake unilateral action	Imperial president, *recalcitrant assembly*			
Bargain		Coalitional president, *workable assembly*		
Pay-off			Nationally oriented president, *parochial assembly*	
Dictate				Dominant president, *subservient assembly*

Source: Cox and Morgenstern (2002: 455).

of constitutionality (or beyond) and because legislation is harder to overturn than presidential decrees. If the president meets a legislature that is *workable* he engages in legislative coalition-building. This requires policy deals (substantive compromises) and perhaps appointments from the coalitional parties to cabinet office. According to Cox and Morgenstern (2002), presidents in post-dictatorial Chile have followed that strategy.

Finally, if the president meets a legislature that largely consists of constituency-bound representatives who need to bring home immediate benefits for the purpose of their re-election, the president offers pork and large-scale patronage rather than policy concessions. Elected representatives then sell their policy-making powers for goods and services that, in turn, they can allocate in their districts to secure their re-election. Probably much of Brazil's recent history provides a good example of the relevance of a *parochial* strategy (Ames 2002).

As Cox and Morgenstern (2002) make clear, the same forces are at work in the US as in the two intermediary cases. Clearly, the office of the US president is not endowed with the institutional powers of imperial presidents in Latin America and elsewhere. But different presidents were in different situations with respect to party support in Congress and other resources and chose their strategies accordingly. The record suggests that they were quite successful, although less so in more recent situations of divided government (Mayhew 1991; Binder 2003).

Attempts have been made to apply the concepts of unified and divided government to other regime types than presidentialism (Laver and Shepsle 1991; Elgie 2001). Accordingly, semi-presidential systems are treated as a close analogy to presidential ones. The only difference is that the division line does not run between the executive and the legislature but between the legislature plus the cabinet on one side and the president on the other. With regard to parliamentary systems, the authors identify minority governments as cases of 'divided government'.

Here, the division line runs between the cabinet (supported by a parliamentary minority) and the parliamentary majority. Without doubt these situations replicate some characteristics of divided government as it has emerged in presidential systems. Yet the very fact that the survival of government is not at stake in the latter while it is in the two former makes the analogy less than perfect and perhaps a case of 'conceptual stretching' (Sartori 1970; see also Chapter 3).

Majority vs. minority government

Governments that enjoy majority support—at least 50 per cent of the seats plus one—in parliament can not only survive in office but also enact their political programme. For a long time **minority governments**—governments comprising parties that collectively miss that mark—were considered an anomaly. They were considered as unwanted crisis symptoms, coming to power when no **majority government** could be formed. Such situations are also referred to as *immobiliste,* as they will be unable to produce political decisions (Laver and Schofield 1990: 72). Yet, as Strøm (1990) demonstrated, and more recent studies confirmed, minority governments are neither rare nor particularly unstable. This result is not driven by governments that have a *formal* minority status but can rely on a legislative (rather than government) majority coalition.

What is the rationale of minority governments? Laver and Schofield (1990: 77–81) suggest that minority governments occupying the ideological centre or, more technically, that hold the median legislator, are 'policy viable'. This means that they can divide the opposition by policy proposals at the centre of the policy space. Although the left opposition will consider them too much to the right and the right opposition will find them too much to the left, these parties cannot join forces to bring down the government and enact alternative policies.

Of course, effective government by minority cabinets suggests that policy is the only or overwhelming motive that drives political parties. If office were dominant, parties left and right of the government would join forces to bring down any minority cabinet, as any new government would at least increase their chances for government office. In practice, most parties are indeed interested in government office in its own right (Müller and Strøm 2000). Yet, their behaviour is constrained by the anticipated reaction of their voters. The bringing down of a social democratic minority cabinet by parties further to the left in alliance with right-wing parties may not be well received by left voters, particularly when it results in a new government more to the right than the one replaced. Anticipated voter reactions also matter in another sense: governing often results in electoral costs which some parties have good reasons to avoid (Strøm 1990). Indeed, as Narud and Valen (2008) show, there has been a monotonic and strong trend for government parties to lose votes since the 1980s. More dramatically, most European governments have not been returned to office in the years since the outbreak of the current financial crisis.

Table 8.2 provides a broad overview of the frequency of government types in democracies worldwide. The upper part of the table shows that minority situations—situations where no single party commands a parliamentary majority—are frequent, though more so in parliamentary than in presidential systems. The lower part suggests that about 45 per cent of these situations produce minority government in parliamentary systems and close to 78 per cent in presidential systems. More recently, the post-war or post-democratization record of 28 European countries shows a similar picture: the breakdown of 610 cabinets

is 12 per cent majority and 30 per cent minority single-party and 54 per cent majority and 15 per cent minority coalition cabinets (Bergman *et al.* 2013).

Overall majority cabinets enjoy a longer life than minority cabinets. Yet minority governments have a similar or even longer duration in some Western countries, particularly in those where they are a regular outcome of government formation. Thus in most cases minority cabinets are clearly more than temporary solutions between two 'regular' majority governments.

As we have seen, minority governments can be helped by their central location in the policy space. Institutional mechanisms such as presidential powers (already discussed in the context of divided government) can also increase their capacity. The French government is particularly lucky as the prime minister can draw on an arsenal of procedural rules which help to force through government policy. The strongest instrument is Article 49.3 of the constitution. It allows the government to turn any decision about legislation into a confidence issue, shifting the burden of proof to its opponents. Legislative proposals introduced under Article 49.3 are automatically adopted—without a vote on the proposal itself—as long as no no-confidence vote (requiring a majority of *all* MPs) unseats the government (Huber 1996). While this instrument is used frequently in France, most governments lack such strong instruments. Therefore in order to survive and get policies passed, minority cabinets need to engage in negotiations with the opposition. This limits their capacities, as is also reflected in government durations (Table 8.3). Overall, majority cabinets enjoy a longer life. In aggregate they outlive minority cabinets by eight months. Yet, this is not true in every case.

Table 8.2 Coalitional status of governments under parliamentarism and presidentialism (1945–2002)

	Parliamentary regimes		Presidential regimes	
	N	%	N	%
Majority situations	215	43.2	121	55.5
Minority situations	283	56.8	97	44.5
Total	498	100.0	218	100.0
Government types in minority situations				
Majority coalitions	175	54.2	31	22.3
Single-party minority governments	83	25.7	49	47.6
Minority coalitions	65	20.1	31	30.1

Notes: The upper part of the table identifies government formation situations by counting the number of legislative seat distributions. Changes in the seat distribution are triggered by elections and by splits and mergers of parties. The lower part records the government *type* that was formed in minority situations. Changes in the composition of government that did not affect its type (e.g. the switch from one majority coalition to another in a sitting parliament) are not registered. The number of government types exceeds that of minority situations because different government types were subsequently formed under the same seat distribution.

Source: Cheibub *et al.* (2004: 573–5).

Table 8.3 Absolute and relative cabinet duration in twenty-eight European democracies, 1945–2011

Country	Period	Absolute duration			Relative duration		
		Mean	Standard deviation	No. of cabinets	Mean	Standard deviation	No. of cabinets
Austria	1945–2011	911	401.35	25	0.71	0.26	24
Belgium	1946–2011	544	519.28	40	0.45	0.36	40
Bulgaria	1990–2011	728	556.58	10	0.54	0.38	9
Czech Rep.	1992–2011	605	462.64	11	0.61	0.37	10
Denmark	1945–2011	680	337.83	35	0.55	0.26	35
Estonia	1992–2011	536	296.45	12	0.58	0.36	12
Finland	1945–2011	457	415.36	50	0.53	0.34	50
France	1959–2011	660	466.76	29	0.58	0.29	28
Germany	1949–2011	762	505.48	29	0.65	0.37	28
Greece	1977–2011	822	517.38	15	0.62	0.36	14
Hungary	1990–2011	760	456.04	10	0.83	0.24	9
Iceland	1944–2011	747	487.06	32	0.61	0.35	31
Ireland	1944–2011	958	450.60	25	0.59	0.25	25
Italy	1945–2011	390	347.46	55	0.34	0.31	54
Latvia	1993–2011	323	179.44	19	0.43	0.31	18
Lithuania	1992–2011	559	431.16	12	0.58	0.40	11
Luxembourg	1945–2011	1239	652.71	19	0.86	0.24	18
Malta	1987–2011	1279	552.48	7	0.75	0.37	6
Netherlands	1945–2011	773	541.73	28	0.65	0.34	27
Norway	1945–2011	793	409.17	30	0.76	0.31	29
Poland	1991–2011	429	354.09	16	0.45	0.37	16
Portugal	1976–2011	629	530.17	19	0.50	0.34	19
Romania	1990–2011	446	275.95	17	0.53	0.36	16
Slovakia	1992–2011	686	593.49	10	0.59	0.37	10
Slovenia	1992–2011	614	408.32	12	0.74	0.27	12
Spain	1977–2011	1111	330.45	11	0.82	0.21	11
Sweden	1945–2011	829	434.47	29	0.82	0.29	28
UK	1945–2011	997	509.99	24	0.66	0.30	23
All 28		687	490.54	631	0.59	0.34	613

Note: Absolute duration is in days, relative duration in percentage of the time until the end of the constitutional inter-election period (CIEP).

Sources: Saalfeld 2013 (calculated from S. Andersson and S. Ersson (2012) 'The European Representative Democracy Data Archive'. Principal Investigator T. Bergman (www.erdda.se)).

Single-party vs. coalition government

Single-party governments have the distinctive advantage that no party line of division runs through the government. This implies that the government goals will be relatively uncontroversial internally. Any remaining differences are likely to be suppressed, given the common goal of survival in office. Parties holding government office as a result of their strong position—commanding a parliamentary majority or occupying a strategic position in the party system—are also likely to have strong leadership that can overcome internal difficulties. Hence, with everything else equal, governments consisting of a single party can be considered homogeneous. This implies that they can make decisions quickly, avoid disagreeable compromises, and maintain a common front.

Coalition governments, in turn, need to satisfy at least some of the ambitions of each of the government parties. Even in the unlikely case of (almost) complete *a priori* agreement between the coalition partners about government goals, the fact remains that office-sharing means that the personal ambitions of some would-be ministers in the parties must be frustrated. This, in turn, may result in only half-hearted support of the government (Sartori 1997). In most cases some of the party's policy ambitions will be compromised. This typically lengthens the internal decision-making process and often exposes internal divisions to the public, with the consequence that the government appears divided and therefore weak. The alternative of one party quietly submitting would allocate the costs of coalition one-sidedly; that party would be considered by its activists and voters to be selling out to its coalition partner. These problems tend to remain modest in ideologically homogeneous coalitions but accelerate in heterogeneous ones. And they tend to be particularly tricky when they are fuelled not only by party policy ambition but also by office ambition. Whenever the most prestigious office—that of prime minister—is at stake *between* the coalition partners, coalitions tend to be seriously hampered by internal rivalry and conflict.

According to Table 8.2, in minority situations coalition governments are the dominant outcome in parliamentary regimes and still result in more than half of such situations in presidential regimes. A wealth of research shows that the overall picture is remarkably balanced between single-party and coalition cabinets. In the aggregate, single-party governments do not last significantly longer than coalition governments. Yet, this similarity should not prevent us from seeing that very different forces are at work here. Coalition governments that do not reach the maximum possible duration generally terminate over internal conflict and unbridgeable differences between the partners. In contrast, single-party governments tend to shorten their term because they feel strong and early elections are likely to return them to government (Strøm and Swindle 2002). In East-Central Europe the picture is remarkably similar, particularly given the lack of consolidation of both parties and party systems in most of the countries (Nikolenyi 2004; Conrad and Golder 2010).

KEY POINTS

- The political capacities of governments differ widely, depending on the government's support base in the political institutions and the society.
- In presidential regimes, 'unified government' suggests greater capacities. 'Divided government' requires the president to use institutional prerogatives, bribe members of the legislature, or compromise with legislative parties.
- In parliamentary regimes single-party majority governments normally have the greatest political capacity.

Bureaucratic capacities

No government can achieve its goals, limited as they may be, without many helping hands. The modern state has developed the permanent bureaucracy as the prime instrument for that purpose (see Chapter 4). In order to fulfil the bureaucracy's mission, its members—the bureaucrats—need to be able and willing to do their job. In addition, the internal organization of tasks and processes can exercise a major influence on bureaucratic capacities.

Working from an idealization of the Prussian bureaucracy, Max Weber (1947) outlined the key characteristics of bureaucratic organization.

- *Personnel*: formal lifelong employment of bureaucrats who receive a fixed salary and earn pension rights in return for their service and who are promoted largely on the basis of their seniority (the length of their service).
- *Organization*: specialization, training, functional division of labour, well-defined areas of jurisdiction, and a clear hierarchy among the bureaucrats.
- *Procedure*: impersonal application of general rules (mostly laws and government decrees); business is conducted on the basis of written documents, bureaucratic decisions are recorded, and the relevant documents carefully stored.

Each of these features has a specific function in making the bureaucratic organization an effective instrument. Indeed, Weber suggested that it is not only *effective* (i.e. getting things done) but, indeed, 'capable of attaining the highest degree of *efficiency* (i.e. getting things done with a minimum of cost) (1947: 337). Lifelong employment and career perspectives allow the administration to attract and retain qualified staff. Personnel stability, in turn, is one condition for a smooth working of the administrative machine that builds on division of labour and specialization. Well-trained bureaucrats who work on clearly defined issues and who are part and parcel of an unambiguous command chain are able to produce 'standardized' decisions. This means that, when confronted with the same case, different bureaucrats would arrive at identical decisions derived from the general rules. Paying the bureaucrats a fixed salary and having strong rules of incompatibility aim at preventing personal interest intervening in their decisions. Finally, the requirement that decisions are fully documented and hence can be checked at any time helps to keep bureaucrats on track.

A cornerstone of the bureaucratic system is **merit system** recruitment. Accordingly, access to the administration is not restricted to particular segments of society; selection and promotion aim at appointing the best-qualified individuals. With regard to promotion, in the case of equal qualifications seniority is decisive. Clearly, in such a system political affiliation and attitudes of job applicants and members of the bureaucracy do not play any role. Such considerations would not only be inappropriate but also unnecessary, as the bureaucracy is considered a neutral instrument. Within the confines of laws and regulations the merit bureaucrats serve every government loyally.

Problems of bureaucracy

To be sure, Max Weber's appraisal of bureaucracy rested on its comparison with pre-modern types of organization (including patrimonial systems where offices were sold and, in turn, generated income for their holders). He was quick to add that real-life bureaucracies become inefficient when decisions need to take into consideration the individual characteristics of the cases to be decided. Indeed, the term 'bureaucracy', and even more so the adjective 'bureaucratic', in ordinary language implies excessive rules and complicated procedures, formalism, and rigidity in their application—hence delay and inefficiency in making decisions and consequently the waste of public money. It is true that each of the principles of bureaucratic organization can be overdone. The rule of law then degenerates to rigidity and inertia in procedures and over-regulation, specialization of bureaucrats leads to civil servants who perform acts without understanding their consequences, and personnel stability and arcane internal rules create a closed system out of touch with its environment. One possible consequence of the latter is groupthink. Groupthink means the unconscious minimizing of intra-organizational conflict in making decisions at the price of their quality, which can lead to disaster (Janis 1972; 't Hart 1990). A famous case of groupthink was the Kennedy administration's Bay of Pigs invasion, and perhaps the same can be said about the more recent Iraq war planning of the Bush administration.

Theories of bureaucracy have been concerned with such phenomena but more often with less spectacular developments. Parkinson's Law is a famous formula for the creeping but consequential growth of the bureaucracy. Parkinson (1958) suggested that in a bureaucratic organization 'work expands to fill the time allotted'. Consequently, the development of bureaucratic organizations, such as the British Colonial Office, does not reflect its objective function. Indeed, that office increased its staff size considerably as the British Empire declined.

As we have seen, the principles of bureaucratic organization aim at separating the private interest of bureaucrats from the decisions they have to make. Yet to assume that human beings will ever be able and willing to separate completely their private preferences from their behaviour as officials would be naive. Bureaucrats do have private interests and political preferences. They want to boost their income and prestige by climbing up the career ladder and will probably take account of their own political preferences when preparing or making decisions.

Let us consider first the growth of bureaucracy. Parkinson (1958) noted that officials want to 'multiply subordinates, not rivals'. The Public Choice School made the private interests of bureaucrats their starting point. Within this approach, the work of Niskanen (1971) has been the most influential. His theory builds on the simple assumption that bureaucrats have the goal of increasing their budgets. This is because most of the bureaucrats' personal incentives—salary, reputation, power, policy-making capacity—are positively related to the size of their organization's budget. The push of the bureaucrats is met by the pull from societal groups and their representatives who make increasing demands on government. Two reasons make it difficult to keep the growth of government at bay.

1. It is often hard or impossible to measure objectively the 'final outputs' of bureaucracies. With regard to many outputs it is hard to say when an optimal level is reached and to avoid over-production. The many times overkill capacity built up by the superpowers during the Cold War is a case in point.

2. Specific bureaucracies tend to be the only suppliers of particular (public) goods (e.g. defence or public health). This avoids wasteful duplication but also frees the bureaucracies from competitive pressure (which has negative effects on efficiency) and deprives the politicians of alternative sources of information. All this contributes strongly to the growth of government.

Niskanan's theory is difficult to test. When confronted with empirical data, the evidence has been mixed. While some have found very little evidence conforming to the theory (Blais and Dion 1991), other studies remain sceptical about the power of bureaucrats to set the agenda in a way that results in ever-increasing budgets, but marshal impressive empirical evidence that production of services by private sector firms is considerably cheaper than that by bureaucrats (Mueller 2003: 371–80). In any case, with Niskanan serving on the Board of Economic Advisers under President Reagan and having inspired this president's thinking, his theory has been quite important for the efforts at rolling back the state since the 1980s.

I now turn to the effort that bureaucrats bring to their job and to the question of whether they diverge from the directions given by political officials. In recent years several studies have employed the principal–agent framework of micro-economics to address these issues (see also Chapters 7 and 9). Brehm and Gates (1997: 50) have nicely summarized the set of options that bureaucratic agents have.

1. They may either work in the interest of their principal (no agency problem) or engage in leisure-shirking, dissent-shirking, or sabotage.

2. In the case of *leisure-shirking*, bureaucrats simply do not work as much as they are expected to do (and are paid for). They may have a late start in the morning, enjoy an extended lunch break, and 'compensate' for this by leaving their office early, as a widespread stereotype of civil servants suggests (for an empirical example see Putnam (1993: 5)).

3. *Dissent-shirking* means that bureaucrats do not do their best to implement the policies desired by their principals because they themselves have different preferences. This either means that the status quo is preserved or that the incumbent minister experiences an improvement from the status quo, but not enough to satisfy his/her ambitions.

4. While shirking leads to insufficient or no policies, *political sabotage* means the production of negative outputs. In this case, civil servants actively work against the interests of their principal.

Note, however, that it is not necessarily the fault of bureaucrats if politicians are not satisfied with their services. Simply, sometimes politicians demand more than a Weberian (neutral) bureaucrat can give: privilege the minister's constituency, help acquaintances of the minister obtain government permits to which they are not entitled, twist a public tender to benefit a sponsor of the minister's party, help mislead the opposition when preparing answers to parliamentary questions, and obstruct investigations of the Audit Court, parliamentary investigation committee, or public prosecutor. Indeed, there are plenty of cases where members of government have suggested such behaviour to their civil servants. Of course, we know only those that eventually were exposed to the public, mostly ending with ministerial resignation. Yet it may be safe to assume that these cases constitute only the tip of the iceberg.

Politicians have responded in two ways to their uneasiness with the bureaucracy: (1) establishing spoils systems and (2) introducing New Public Management.

Spoils systems

In a spoils system the victorious party is free to appoint large layers of the administration after each election, with the jobs going to the party faithful. Thereby the party rewards them for their work towards victory, either by providing their labour or by making important financial contributions. An open spoils system was practised in the US in the nineteenth century, with President Andrew Jackson (1829–37) being crucial in its introduction. The claim was that the spoils system would be democratic in two ways.

1. It would allow the victor of the democratic contest to work with an administration that shares his political philosophy and hence would help him to live up to the promises made in the campaign.

2. It was radically democratic as it entrusted ordinary Americans rather than a closed elite of professional bureaucrats with the business of government.

In the second half of the nineteenth century the spoils system came under attack. Eventually, the Pendleton Civil Service Act (1883) established a merit system that was gradually introduced for the bulk of government positions. Only senior government jobs remained up for grabs

for the victor. Yet, compared with most other systems, the US maintained a large degree of open politicization. Each change in the office of president is accompanied by the replacement of thousands of government employees by people more akin to the new incumbent and his party.

The major advantage of open spoils systems is that they provide the politicians with administrators who are committed to the government goals. Hence, if political faith would suffice to move mountains, the government would be enabled to achieve its goals. The disadvantage of bringing in cohorts of new people, often with little prior experience in public administration, is that the appointees do not know enough about their organization and its environment. Nor do they know each other, resulting in a 'government of strangers' (Heclo 1977). Moreover, political appointees often do not stay long enough to compensate for these disadvantages by learning 'on the job'.

While open spoils systems are rare, covert ones are more frequent. These are merit systems only in name, with the jobs in the civil service and more broadly in the public sector being allocated among party candidates. To provide just a few examples, such practices were widely applied in Austria, Belgium, and Italy for much of the post-war period, they have been reinvented in some of the post-communist systems, including Slovakia and Poland (O'Dwyer 2006: Chapter 3), and they are endemic in Latin America and in the Third World in general. Party politicization affecting exclusively the top layers of the bureaucracy has been practised even more widely, for example in France, Germany, and Spain (Page and Wright 1999, 2007; Suleiman 2003).

As bureaucracies are formally merit systems, bureaucrats appointed as political trustees of a specific party stay on even when the government changes. The disadvantages are obvious: elected leaders have to work with bureaucrats who are not politically neutral but oppose the goals of the government and may indeed engage in dissent-shirking or political sabotage. Thus, while the problem of the bureaucrats' willingness can be resolved for those politicians who make the appointments, it may make things worse for their successors from different parties. One possible 'way out' for them is to strip the alien partisans of their most important functions, cut them off from politically critical communication, and hence make them 'white elephants', and hire another layer of partisans. The consequence will be an oversized bureaucracy for which the taxpayer will have to settle the bill.

New Public Management systems

New Public Management (NPM) systems represent a more fundamental challenge to the classic bureaucratic system than the undermining of merit recruitment. They aim at resolving the problems of both the willingness and efficiency of bureaucrats. Moreover, the proponents of NPM systems claim that establishing these systems can reverse the growth of the state.

NPM systems were first introduced in the US under the Reagan presidency in the 1980s. They were soon imported by the UK and New Zealand, and later diffused throughout the Western world. NPM builds on transferring methods from the market economy to the public sector.

Personnel

Top positions in the public sector are open to outside candidates who are hired on a fixed-term basis (rather than lifelong employment). Consequently, salaries for public sector managers match those of the private sector and payment is tied to performance.

Organization

NPM methods aim at creating 'internal markets' in the public sector. This implies splitting large bureaucratic units into smaller ones and allowing for—indeed encouraging—competition between different public sector units (e.g. schools) and, where possible, between public and private sector units (e.g. agencies and firms). In other words, NPM aims at creating an environment that makes profit-seeking the survival strategy.

Procedure

According to NPM doctrine, it is no longer sufficient for a civil servant to observe administrative regulations in every detail, to follow the specific instruction of his/her superiors, and not to steal public money. Rather, accountability is based on the civil servant's performance in attaining the agency's goals. Thus, public sector managers are expected to engage in managerialism and entrepreneurship (Suleimann 2003; Peters and Pierre 2001).

NPM schemes greatly enhance the potential for political control over the bureaucracy. Politicians (i.e. people whose positions are ultimately tied to the electoral process) control more financial and career incentives and can—by tying rewards to outcomes—more effectively align the preferences of civil servants with their own. Interestingly, the parliamentary accountability of ministers has not been enhanced in the sense of making them more directly responsible for the acts of their civil servants. Thus, one of the side effects of NPM schemes is the shoring up of politicians against scrutiny (Strøm *et al.* 2003). Critics of the NPM revolution focus on the deprofessionalization and politicization of the bureaucracy. As Suleiman (2003: 17–18) has put it: 'Political affiliation has once again become a determining criterion in appointments to top-level positions', with the tendency to view the bureaucracy 'as the instrument of the government *of the day* rather than of the government *of the state*.' Critics also suggest that the goal of the state organized along NPM lines 'is no longer to protect society from the market's demands but to protect the market from society's demands' (Daniel Cohen, quoted in Suleiman 2003: 16).

The quality of governance

Finally, let us take a look at the performance of the bureaucracy. Table 8.4 reports the World Bank's government effectiveness index for selected countries for the earliest and most recent years available. With regard to the developments outlined previously, 1996 is the year when most Western administrations had been affected by some NPM reforms, while they had already had a profound impact on the administrations of the pioneer countries—the US, the UK, and New Zealand. As noted earlier, the performance of bureaucracies is difficult to measure, and this index is the most ambitious attempt to do so to date. It draws on a wealth of cross-country data, mostly measures of the perceptions of the clients of government agencies and professional observers, such as rating agencies. Governance is conceptualized as an overall measure of the quality of the public services and civil service, the degree of the civil service's independence from political pressure, the quality of policy formulation and implementation, and the credibility of the government's commitment to such policies. The data employed and the index construction is carefully documented in the paper cited at the bottom of Table 8.4 and a number of earlier papers that are available on the World Bank's webpage.

Table 8.4 shows that the quality of governance differs considerably between regions and countries (higher scores indicate better outcomes). Given that the more recent data include more variables, not too much should be made out of small changes in the absolute values. What is more reliable is the relative placement of countries. Comparing the regions, we see that the Anglo-Saxon settler democracies and the countries of Western Europe can pride themselves on good governance, while the other established democracies (Israel, Japan, and India), the more recent democracies in Latin American and the Central and East European post-Soviet systems are clearly lagging behind. In Western Europe we observe a clear North–South decline of good governance. In Latin America Chile, the country with the longest democratic tradition, also provides the best governance. The positive development in the post-Soviet states is that the quality of governance has improved considerably over the last decade.

KEY POINTS

- A government's capacity to implement its decisions depends critically on the ability and willingness of bureaucrats and the structures and processes of the public administration.

- Classic bureaucracy aims at making the civil service a neutral instrument. In practice, the inclusion of individual political preferences by bureaucrats can lead to agency loss; bureaucratic career concerns foster the growth of the state.

- The establishment of spoils systems and New Public Management methods can provide governments with greater grip on their bureaucrats. Yet both methods have their own problems.

Table 8.4 Government effectiveness index (1996–2011)

	1996	2005	2011
Non-European democracies			
Australia	2.00	1.88	1.74
Canada	2.03	1.92	1.85
India	−0.45	−0.11	−0.03
Israel	1.49	0.95	1.20
Japan	1.33	1.16	1.35
New Zealand	2.46	1.90	1.93
US	2.06	1.59	1.41
Western Europe			
Austria	1.99	1.60	1.66
Belgium	1.93	1.65	1.67
Denmark	2.09	2.12	2.17
Finland	2.04	2.07	2.12
France	1.94	1.46	1.36
Germany	2.01	1.51	1.53
Iceland	1.56	2.20	1.57
Ireland	1.70	1.63	1.42
Italy	0.93	0.60	0.45
Luxembourg	2.34	1.94	1.73
Netherlands	2.44	1.95	1.79
Norway	2.13	1.99	1.76
Portugal	1.03	1.03	0.97
Spain	1.70	1.40	1.02
Sweden	2.05	1.93	1.96
Switzerland	2.53	2.03	1.89
UK	2.33	1.70	1.55
Post-Soviet systems			
Bulgaria	−0.64	0.23	0.01
Czech Republic	0.52	0.94	1.06
Estonia	0.53	1.03	1.20
Hungary	0.39	0.79	0.71
Latvia	−0.34	0.68	0.68
Lithuania	−0.16	0.85	0.68
Poland	0.50	0.58	0.68
Romania	−0.88	−0.03	−0.22
Slovak Republic	0.17	0.95	0.86
Slovenia	0.52	0.99	0.99
Russia	−0.79	−0.45	−0.40
Latin America			
Argentina	0.65	−0.27	−0.16
Brazil	−0.25	−0.09	−0.01
Chile	1.20	1.26	1.17
Mexico	−0.20	−0.01	0.32

Note: The World Bank's government effectiveness index includes measures of the quality of the public services and civil service, the degree of the civil service's independence from political pressure, the quality of policy formulation and implementation, and the credibility of the government's commitment to such policies. The mean of 213 countries is zero, and virtually all scores lie between −2.5 and 2.5. Higher scores indicate better outcomes.

Source: Kaufmann *et al.* (2006). Updated from: http://info.worldbank.org/governance/wgi/index.asp.

Conclusion

Governments are key institutions in democratic states. Who occupies government normally determines the direction a country will take. This is particularly true where cohesive political parties allow the fusion of executive and legislative power. This chapter has been concerned with three important and interrelated questions: (1) how government decisions are made, (2) how autonomous governments are from the providers of key resources, and (3) what capacities governments have to rule the country.

Government decision-making depends on basic regime characteristics but within such confines can take different forms such as cabinet, prime ministerial, and ministerial government under parliamentarism. The modes of government change with functional requirements and according to the prevailing political conditions (e.g. single-party vs. coalition government).

Government autonomy vis-à-vis the parties that bring governments to office is controversial from a normative point of view. The party government model denies autonomy, while constitutional theory prescribes it. Empirically, government autonomy from parties has enormously increased. Part and parcel of that process is the tendency towards presidentialization—the vesting of more power in the chief executive.

Government capacities are high in situations of unified or majority single-party government, and they are considerably constrained in situations of divided or minority government and when the government is a coalition. Institutional rules can partly compensate for the lack of party support. Governments depend critically on support from their bureaucracies. The classic model of a neutral bureaucracy, which serves any government equally well, has come under attack from two sides: one focuses on the self-interest of bureaucrats, and one denies the bureaucracy's neutrality or demands its 'democratization' so that politicians have an instrument in tune with their preferences.

 Questions

1. Which different meanings does the term 'government' carry?
2. What distinguishes prime ministerial government from cabinet government?
3. How can parties provide party government?
4. What distinguishes divided and unified government?
5. Why can minority governments survive?
6. What are the problems of coalition governance?
7. What are the problems of bureaucracy?
8. What are spoils systems and which forms exist?
9. What distinguishes classic bureaucracy from New Public Management bureaucracy?
10. What is the presidentialization of politics?

 Further reading

Important texts on government not cited in this chapter

Baylis, T. T. (1989) *Governing by Committee: Collegial Leadership in Advanced Societies* (Albany, NY: State University of New York Press).

Edwards, G. C. and Howell, W. C. (eds) (2011) *The Oxford Handbook of the American Presidency* (Oxford: Oxford University Press).

Hayward, J. and Wright, V. (2002) *Governing from the Centre: Core Executive Coordination in France* (Oxford: Oxford University Press).

Jones, G. W. (ed.) (1991) *West European Prime Ministers* (London: Cass).

Peters, B. G., Rhodes, R. A. W., and Wright, V. (eds) (2000) *Administering the Summit: Administration of the Core Executive in Developed Countries* (Basingstoke: Macmillan).

Rhodes, R. A. W., Wanna, J., and Weller, P. (2009) *Comparing Westminster* (Oxford: Oxford University Press).

Rose, R. (2001) *The Prime Minister in a Shrinking World* (Cambridge: Polity).

Rose, R. and Suleiman, E. N. (eds) (1980) *Presidents and Prime Ministers* (Washington, DC: American Enterprise Institute).

Rothstein, B. (2011) *The Quality of Government: Corruption, Social Trust, and Inequality in International Perspective* (Chicago, IL: University of Chicago Press).

Scartascini, C., Stein, E., and Tommasi, M. (eds) (2010) *How Democracy Works*. New York: Inter-American Development Bank.

Weller, P. (1985) *First Among Equals: Prime Ministers in Westminster Systems* (Sydney: Allen & Unwin).

Web links

www.psr.keele.ac.uk
Richard Kimber's website on Political Science Resources
(University of Keele).

http://www.parlgov.org/
Holger Döring and Philip Manow's website devoted to parties
and governments in Europe (University of Bremen).

www.gksoft.com/govt/en/parties.html
Webpage of Government on the WWW devoted to political
parties and party systems around the world. The main page
includes additional information on heads of state, parliaments,
executives, courts, and other institutions.

http://pdba.georgetown.edu/
Website of the Political Database of the Americas.

**https://www.cia.gov/library/publications/the-world-factbook/
index.html**
Website of CIA's *The World Factbook* with information on
institutions, social structures, economic data, and party
systems for most countries of the world.

www.eiu.com
Country Reports and Country Profiles published by the
Economist Intelligence Unit are very useful for an overview and
recent data.

**online
resource
centre**

For additional material and resources, please visit the Online Resource Centre at:
www.oxfordtextbooks.co.uk/orc/caramani3e/

CHAPTER 9

Constitutions and judicial power

Alec Stone Sweet

Chapter contents

Reader's guide

This chapter compares the evolution of different national systems of constitutional justice since 1787. After introducing and defining key terms, it surveys types of constitutions, rights, models of constitutional review, and the main precepts of 'new constitutionalism'. Thus the chapter presents a simple theory of delegation and judicial power, focusing on why political elites would delegate power to constitutional judges, and how to measure the extent of power, or discretion, delegated. The evolution of constitutional forms is then presented comparatively. Beginning in the 1980s new constitutionalism took off and today has no rival as a model of democratic state legitimacy. As constitutional rights and review have diffused around the world, so has the capacity of constitutional judges to control policy outcomes.

Introduction

This chapter provides an overview of the emergence, diffusion, and political impact of systems of constitutional justice. Systems of constitutional justice are the institutions and procedures, established by a constitution, for the judicial (third-party) protection of fundamental rights. In 1787, when the fully codified written constitution was just emerging, no such system existed anywhere in the world. In the twenty-first century, one finds that virtually all new constitutions include a charter of rights that is enforceable by a constitutional or Supreme Court, even against legislation. With very few exceptions, legislative sovereignty has formally disappeared. The new constitutionalism killed it, paradoxically perhaps, in the name of democracy.

Until recently, comparative political scientists paid almost no attention to law, courts, and constitutions. The two major American journals in the field—*Comparative Politics* and *Comparative Political Studies* (both founded in 1968)—failed to publish a single article relating to courts or constitutions in their first twenty-five years of existence. In American political science 'judicial politics' is a subfield of American politics. Outside the US, no equivalent field exists. Around the globe, academic discourse on courts is dominated by law. In this discourse, the fact that courts are political actors, and that they interact with other institutions to make policy, is ignored or even actively resisted.

As noted in Section 1 of this book, in the 1950s comparative politics began to turn away from the approaches that Roy Macridis (1955) derided as 'formal–legal', in favour of research into how actors actually behaved or took decisions. Courts and constitutions are arguably the most 'formal' and 'legal' of state institutions. To take seriously what courts do—they produce a 'jurisprudence' or 'case law'—one has little choice but to immerse oneself in the formalism of legal reasoning and the rhetoric of justification. The neglect of judicial institutions may also be a consequence of the inherent difficulties of doing comparative research (language problems, for example), compounded by the professional–technical nature of legal discourse.

However, there are important indicators of change. Over the past twenty years, political scientists have gradually rediscovered law, courts, and constitutions, for various reasons. First, a broad interest in how rule systems and organizations structure political life took hold across the social sciences (Hall and Taylor 1996; see also the Introduction to this volume, as well as Chapters 1 and 2). New institutionalists studied the state and so they could not help but encounter law and courts.

Second, the concern for rules and organizations intersects with the emergence of rational choice and game theory approaches, which emphasize how the 'rules of the game' shape the strategies of the actors and thus help to determine outcomes. It is almost always legal rules (constitutions, standing orders, electoral laws, and so on) that constitute the 'rules of the game'. Thus, many political scientists began to deal with law routinely, though they did not adopt traditional methods of legal scholarship.

Third, the huge wave of constitution-making in Central and Eastern Europe following the collapse of the Soviet Empire drew the attention of a field that had also become interested in democratization (see Chapters 5 and 25). New systems of constitutional justice began to emerge outside North America and Europe. Law and courts have also become a significant component of international politics (Volcansek 1997), led by courts of the European Union (EU) and the World Trade Organization (WTO). Today, a growing field devoted to comparative judicial politics can be identified.

The chapter proceeds as follows. The first section presents basic concepts and defines key terms. Then a simple theory of judicial power is presented, focusing on the potential for constitutional judges to build and exercise authority over other state actors. The chapter charts the diffusion of written constitutions, charters of rights, and constitutional review since 1787. Finally, research on the impact of rights adjudication on the greater political system is discussed.

Concepts and types

Definitions

There is no consensus on how to define constitutions, constitutionalism, and rights. The aim is to provide useful definitions of these and other terms to students of comparative politics, not to fix authoritative meanings. Students should note the discussion of alternative views and debate them, and they should remember that virtually any attempt to define concepts carefully will be controversial.

Let us start with the word **constitution**. A constitution is a body of meta-norms, higher-order legal rules, and principles that specify how all other legal norms are to be produced, applied, enforced, and interpreted (Stone Sweet 2000: Chapter 1). Meta-norms constitute political systems, as written constitutions do for the modern nation-state. In England (later the United Kingdom), whose constitution has evolved over centuries, meta-norms provide a model of how the political system has been institutionalized and is expected to function.

In today's world, written constitutions are the ultimate formal source of state authority: they establish governmental institutions (**legislatures**, executives, courts), and grant them the power to make, apply, enforce, and interpret laws. Constitutions tell us how lower-order legal norms are to be made, especially statutes. They lay down legislative procedures; and they tell us how legislative authority is constituted (through elections, for example), and what the legislature can do (through enumerating powers). Constitutions also indicate how the various institutions are expected, if only ideally, to interact with one another (through separation of powers). New constitutions written over the last sixty years typically contain a catalogue of rights which are, by definition, substantive constraints on government. These constitutions also establish an institutional means of protecting rights against governmental incursion, typically in the form of a supreme or constitutional court.

First, **constitutionalism** refers to the commitment, on the part of any given political community, to accept the legitimacy of, and to be governed by, constitutional rules and principles. Therefore constitutionalism is a variable. The commitment to live under a constitution varies across countries. In any specific country, it can be strong or weak, and its character can change over time. Second, constitutionalism refers to those practices and understandings of government that are derivable from, or in, any constitutional order. For example, an American would focus on federalism and checks and balances between the branches of government, while a Canadian would add an emphasis on the value of multiculturalism.

It is worth noting other definitions. For the political scientist Carl Friedrich (1950: 25–8, 123), constitutionalism refers to 'limited government'—situations wherein the constitution 'effectively restrains' those who control the coercive instruments of the state. Lenaerts (1990: 205), a legal scholar and an EU judge, defines it as 'limited government operating under the rule of law'. Rosenfeld (1994: 3) notes that 'there appears to be no accepted definition of constitutionalism', and that 'modern constitutionalism requires imposing limits on the powers of government, adherence to the rule of law, and the protection of fundamental rights'. Thus, constitutions do not just limit state power, they constitute and enable it.

Others conceive of constitutionalism in wider terms (second definition in this section), i.e. as the whole of a community's practices and understandings about the nature of law, politics, citizenship, and the state. 'Constitutionalism is the set of beliefs associated with constitutional practice', Walker (1996: 267) suggests; another constitutional theorist, Preuß (1996: 1113), defines it as 'the basic ideas, principles, and values of a polity [that] aspires to give its members a share in government'. In this view, constitutionalism encapsulates the fundamental notions of how, 'in our political system', 'we' organize the state (federal or unitary, republican or monarchical), constitute our government (separation of powers, checks and balances), provide for representation and participation (elections, referendums), protect minorities (rights and judicial review), promote equality (social welfare regimes), and so on. Here again, constitutionalism will vary. Institutional arrangements and public policies that are viewed as legitimate, and even required, in country X, for example, may be considered unacceptable in country Y.

Still others take an even broader cultural view,[1] conceiving it as an overarching ideology of politics, community, citizenship, and the state. In this tradition, constitutions are analysed in terms of their capacity to express the collective identity of the people—their values, aspirations, and idealized essence (Post 2000; Shaw 1999; Wolin 1989). A robust constitutionalism is a wellspring of legitimizing resources for the *demos*, the body politic. In contrast, a weak constitutionalism fails to represent collective identity, and fails to reconstruct the legitimacy of the state in times of crisis.

A typology of constitutional forms and the 'new constitutionalism'

Many notions of constitutionalism emphasize the good or proper functions that a constitution is supposed to perform: to limit government, to embody political ideals, to express collective identity. Constitutionalism refers to the commitment of a polity to govern itself in conformity with meta-norms, but this commitment may be absent in some places, at some times. A constitution can be 'bad' for democracy, establish dictatorship, and deny the people any say in their own governance; a polity's 'constitutionalism' could help to legitimize authoritarianism. In world history, there are far more examples of constitutional regimes that have failed to sustain limited government and participatory democracy than there are examples of success.

Empirically, constitutions have differed a great deal, not least, in their capacity to constrain legislative power. Consider the following simple typology of constitutional models.

Type 1: the absolutist constitution

In this model, the authority to produce and change legal norms, including the constitution, is centralized and absolute. The controlling meta-norm is the fact that the rulers are 'above the law'. In such systems, the meta-norms reflect, rather than restrict, the absolute power of those who govern. The type 1 constitution typically rejects popular sovereignty, rights, and separation of powers. The archetype of the type 1 constitution in Europe is the French Charter of 1814, which was widely imitated by other monarchies, especially in the Germanic regions (Dippel 2005: 162). In the twentieth century, examples include the USSR and many Central European states under communist party control, and situations resulting after military coups in Asia, Africa, and Central and South America. Although less prevalent in recent decades (see Chapters 5 and 6), there have been a few constitutions since 1980 that expressly enshrined one-person or one-party rule (Sri Lanka, Togo, and Niger, among others).

Type 2: the legislative supremacy constitution

In this form, the constitution provides for (1) a stable set of governmental institutions and (2) elections to the legislature. Elections legitimize legislative authority, and legislative majorities legitimize statutory authority. Once adopted by the legislature, statutes are commands, until abrogated by subsequent legislative commands. The crucial meta-norm is the rule of legislative sovereignty, which has a number of important consequences. The first is that the constitution is not entrenched, i.e. there are no special (non-legislative) procedures for revising it. Instead, the constitution can be changed through a majority vote of the parliament. In 1912, for example, the British House of Commons abolished the veto of the House of Lords, removing the last important constraint on its own law-making powers. The second consequence is that any act that conflicts with a statute is itself invalid. Judicial acts are also subject to this rule, so the judicial review of statutes is prohibited. The third is that there is no layer of substantive constraints—rights—in the constitution. Rights are, in effect, granted by parliament, in statutes. The British and New Zealand parliamentary systems, and the French Third Republic (1875–1940) and Fourth Republic (1946–58), are almost pure examples of type 2 systems.

Type 3: the 'higher law' constitution

Type 2 and 3 constitutions share a common attribute: the constitution establishes (or recognizes the status of) state institutions and links these institutions to society, via elections. However, the type 3 form adds substantive constraints on the exercise of public authority—in the form of constitutional rights—and establishes an independent judicial means of enforcing rights, even against the legislature. Legislative sovereignty is expressly rejected. Type 3 constitutions are entrenched: they specify amendment procedures.

One of the most remarkable developments in global politics over the past fifty years has been the consolidation of the type 3 constitution as a standard without rival. The point is not that all type 3 constitutions are the same; it is a fact that no two constitutions are exactly alike. What is important is the *broad global convergence around beliefs that only type 3 constitutions are considered to be 'good' constitutions.* This convergence has been called the **new constitutionalism** (Shapiro and Stone Sweet 1994).

The precepts of this new constitutionalism include the following.

- Institutions of the state are established by, and derive their authority exclusively from, a written constitution.
- This constitution assigns ultimate power to the people by way of elections or referendums.

- The use of public authority, including legislative authority, is lawful only in so far as it conforms to the constitutional law.
- The constitution provides for a catalogue of rights, and a system of constitutional justice to defend those rights.
- The constitution itself specifies how it may be revised.

Rights

Constitutions establish the procedures for producing various forms of law. These are procedural constraints: if the procedure is not followed, then the legal norm produced (statute, administrative determination, judicial decision) is not constitutionally valid. Rights are a different type of meta-norm, in that *they impose substantive constraints on the exercise of public authority.* When state officials make, interpret, and enforce law, they must respect rights, or their acts may be invalidated as law.

The nature of rights varies along a number of dimensions, two of which deserve special attention.

1. The first concerns the *hierarchical relationship* between a rights provision, on the one hand, and the purposes for which public authority is exercised, on the other. A right might be conceived as more or less absolute: when an act of government violates the right, that act is unconstitutional. The right, being hierarchically superior, trumps any norm in conflict with it. Rights might also be conceived as relative values, to be balanced against other constitutional values, including state purposes. Because the constitution grants powers to state institutions to do certain things—to provide for the country's defence, roads and utilities, social security, and welfare, for example—these purposes rise to constitutional status. In this conception, such purposes are not, *a priori*, hierarchically inferior to rights. Balancing is a basic technique that judges use to resolve tensions between a right and a state purpose, once judges have determined that a right is not absolute. The balancing judge weighs the cost of infringement of the right against the social benefits of the state action in question, and then decides which value will prevail, in light of the facts of the case. When the state decides to build a new airport on existing farmland, for example, the property rights of the farmers whose land is to be expropriated may be outweighed by the 'public' or 'general' interest in the project.

2. The second dimension of variation concerns the *scope of the obligation* imposed on public authority by rights provisions. A right may impose a negative obligation: (1) the state may not infringe upon the right (an absolute version of rights), or (2) the state may not infringe upon the right more than is necessary to achieve a legitimate public purpose (a balancing version of

rights). In some countries, rights provisions may impose a duty on the part of government, for example, to take measures to facilitate the enjoyment of a particular right. Or a right might entitle citizens to certain benefits—such as adequate health care, employment, and housing. One classic typology categorizes *rights as negative or positive*: the former constrain government not to do certain things; the latter encourage (or requires) government to act to accomplish certain goals. Older constitutions rarely contain positive rights; newer constitutions all do (see Chapter 4 for a description of the increasingly numerous activities of states and bureaucracies over time).

Constitutional review

Once a polity decides to live under a type 3 constitution, the problem of how to guarantee the constitution's normative supremacy over other law arises. The type 3 constitution solves this problem by establishing a system of 'constitutional review'—a 'judicialized' (third-party) mechanism for assessing the constitutional legality of all other legal norms.

Two modes of constitutional review are dominant in the world today (see Box 9.1).

1. The first is **judicial review**, the archetype of which is found in the US. American review is 'judicial' in that it is performed by the judiciary in the course of resolving litigation.

2. The second mode has its origins in Austria and Germany: the powers of constitutional review are exercised by a special court—a *constitutional court*— while the ordinary (non-constitutional) courts are denied the authority to void legal norms, like statutes, when they conflict with the constitution.

At this point, we confront radically different notions of separation of powers, which are constitutional conceptions of how the various state institutions, or branches of government, should function. Simplifying, in judicial review systems, the courts are understood to comprise a separate but co-equal branch of government, within a system of 'checks and balances'. The duty of American courts (their judicial function) is to resolve legal disputes: cases or controversies that arise under the laws of the US. The constitution is one of the laws. If litigants can plead the constitutional law before the courts, American judges will need to possess the power of judicial review in order to resolve the dispute, that is, in order to do their jobs. Such is the logic of *Marbury* v. *Madison* (1803), the Supreme Court decision that established constitutional review authority in the US. The American model of judicial review is also called the 'decentralized model', since review powers are held by all courts, not just the Supreme Court.

As we shall soon see, giving review powers to all courts is not as popular as concentrating review authority in a

Box 9.1 The American vs. the European models of judicial review

American judicial review	European constitutional review
Constitutional judicial review authority is decentralized: all judges possess the power to void or refuse to apply a statute on the grounds that it violates the constitution law.	Constitutional review authority is centralized: only the constitutional court may annul a statute as unconstitutional. Judicial review of statute is prohibited.
The Supreme Court is a court of general jurisdiction: it is the highest court of appeal in the legal order, for all issues of law, not just constitutional issues.	The constitutional court's jurisdiction is restricted to resolving constitutional disputes. The ordinary courts handle civil suits and criminal matters.
Judicial review is defensible under prevailing separation-of-powers doctrines to the extent that it is a 'case or controversy' review. Judges possess review authority because they resolve legal 'cases', some of which have a constitutional dimension.	Review powers are defensible under separation-of-powers doctrines to the extent that it is not exercised by the judiciary, but by a specialized 'constitutional' organ, the constitutional court.
Judicial review is understood to be 'concrete', in that it is exercised pursuant to ordinary litigation. Abstract review decisions look suspiciously like 'advisory opinions', which are prohibited under American separation of powers.	Constitutional review is typically 'abstract': the review court does not resolve concrete cases between two litigating parties, but answers constitutional questions referred to it by judges or elected officials.

specialized jurisdiction. Constitutional courts are favoured in countries where judicial review has traditionally been prohibited. Those who wrote new constitutions wished to enable rights protection while, at the same time, preserving legislative sovereignty as much as possible. In such polities (most of Europe and Latin America, for example), separation-of-powers doctrines take great pains to distinguish the *political function* (to legislate, to make law) from the *judicial function* (to resolve legal disputes according to legislation). The American checks and balances system appears to create a 'confusion of powers', since it permits the courts to participate in the work of the legislature. Because this system of review emerged in Europe and later spread globally, it is often called the 'European model' or the 'centralized model'.

We can break down the centralized model of constitutional review into four constituent components.

1. Constitutional courts enjoy *exclusive and final constitutional jurisdiction.* Constitutional judges alone may invalidate a law or an act of public authority as unconstitutional, while the 'ordinary' courts (i.e. the judiciary, the non-constitutional courts) remain prohibited from doing so.

2. Constitutional courts *only settle constitutional disputes.* The US Supreme Court is a court of 'general jurisdiction'—it is the highest court of appeal for almost all disputes about rights in the American legal order. In contrast, constitutional courts do not preside over litigation, which remains the function of the ordinary judges.

3. Constitutional courts are *formally detached from the judiciary and legislature* although they have links with these institutions. They occupy their own constitutional space, a space neither clearly judicial nor political in traditional separation-of-powers terms.

4. Some constitutional courts are empowered to *review legislation before it has been enforced,* i.e. before it has actually affected any person negatively, as a means of eliminating unconstitutional legislation and practices before they can do harm. Thus, in the centralized model of review, the judges who staff the ordinary courts remain bound by the supremacy of statute, while constitutional judges are charged with preserving the supremacy of the constitution.

Modes of review: abstract and concrete

The American and the European models of review differ with respect to the pathways through which cases come to the judges. In the US, rights review is activated when a litigant pleads a right before a judge—any judge. In countries with constitutional courts, there are three main procedures that activate review, although not all constitutions establish all three procedures.

1. Abstract review is the pre-enforcement review of statutes. Some systems enable the statute to be reviewed before it enters into force (*a priori review*), others after promulgation but before application (*a posteriori review*). Abstract review is also called 'preventive review', since its purpose is to filter out unconstitutional laws before they can harm anyone. Abstract review is politically initiated. Typically, executives, parliamentary minorities, and regions or federated entities in federal states possess the power to refer laws to the court.

2. Concrete review is initiated by the judiciary in the course of litigation in the courts. Ordinary judges activate review by sending a constitutional question—is a given law, legal rule, judicial decision, or administrative act constitutional?—to the constitutional court. The general rule is that a presiding judge will go to the constitutional court if two conditions are met: (1) that the constitutional question is material to litigation at bar (who wins or loses will depend on the answer to the question); and (2) there is reasonable doubt in the judge's mind about the constitutionality of the act or rule in question. Referrals suspend proceedings pending a review by the constitutional court. Once rendered, the constitutional court's judgement is sent back to the referring judge, who then decides the case on the basis of the ruling. In such systems, ordinary judges are not permitted to determine the constitutionality of statutes on their own. Instead, aided by private litigants, they help to detect unconstitutional laws and send them to the constitutional court for review.

3. The *constitutional complaint* brings individuals into the mix. Individuals or an ombudsman are authorized to appeal directly to the constitutional court when they believe that their rights have been violated, usually after judicial remedies have been exhausted.

Abstract review is 'abstract' because the review of legislation takes place in the absence of litigation—in American parlance, in the absence of a concrete 'case or controversy'. Concrete review is 'concrete' because the review of legislation, or other public act, constitutes a stage in ongoing litigation in the ordinary courts. In individual complaints, a private individual alleges the violation of a constitutional right by a public act or governmental official, and requests redress from the court for this violation. In American judicial review, all review is (at least formally) 'concrete', in that it is embedded in a concrete 'case'.

KEY POINTS

- A constitution is a body of legal norms—meta-norms—that govern the production and application of all other legal norms. Constitutionalism refers to a polity's commitment to abide by the constitution, and to the main principles found in any polity's constitution.

- A system of constitutional justice is a central component of the type 3 constitution and of the new constitutionalism. Such systems combine a written, entrenched constitutional text, rights, and a third-party mechanism—constitutional review—for the protection of rights.

- There are two main models of constitutional review today: the American model of judicial review, and the European model of review performed by a constitutional court. The models rest on different notions of separation of powers. American judicial review is expected to be concrete, whereas European constitutional review is often abstract.

Delegation and judicial power

The power of constitutional judges is delegated power (Stone Sweet and Thatcher 2002): a written constitution expressly confers upon the judges review authority and indicates how it may be used. Why would political elites, those who draft a constitution and will live under it, choose to grant review authority to constitutional judges? Why should they choose to constrain themselves? This section discusses some of the consequences of this choice from the perspective of delegation theory, focusing on issues of agency and control (see Box 9.2). In doing so, it responds to a further question: to what extent can we expect political elites to remain 'in charge' of the evolution of the polity after delegating review powers?

The constitution as incomplete contract

Modern democratic constitutions can be conceived as contracts. They are negotiated by political elites—representatives of political parties—seeking to establish rules, procedures, and institutions that will enable them to govern under the cloak of constitutional legitimacy. In establishing a democracy, each contracting party knows that it will be competing with others for political power through elections. Constitutional contracting also yields another crucial benefit—to constrain one's opponents when they are in power. Thus the constitution produces two important common goods for the parties, in the form of a set of enabling institutions and a set of constraints.

Constitutional contracting, like all contracting, generates a demand for third-party dispute resolution and enforcement. Indeed, the social logic of contracts provides a logic of courts. Third-party enforcement of contracts is an institutional solution to a classic commitment problem (the prisoner's dilemma of game theory), which is one reason why we find it everywhere, at all times, in one form or another. The move to constitutional review is one way of dealing with commitment problems associated with constitutional contracting. If the polity is federal, review will provide a means of resolving disputes between the federal government and the federated states, and among the federated states themselves. It is an old truism that federalism needs an umpire, which helps to explain why all federal constitutions provide for review. Contracting rights also heavily favour the delegation of review authority to a constitutional judge.

Take the following scenario, which is a simplified version of what in fact has occurred in many places since 1945. Once the contracting parties (political elites) decide to include a charter of rights in their constitution, not least to constrain their future opponents when the latter are in power, they face two tough problems. First, they disagree about the nature and content of rights, which threatens to paralyse the drafting process. The left-wing parties favour positive social rights and limits on the rights to property. The right-wing parties prefer to privilege negative rights and do not want to restrict strong property rights. They compromise, drafting an extensive charter of rights that (1) lists most of the rights that each side wants, (2) implies that no right is absolute or more important than another, and (3) is vague about how any future conflict between two rights, or a right and a legitimate governmental purpose, will be resolved. Second, they have to decide how rights will be enforced. Delegating rights review authority to a constitutional court helps them to deal with both problems.

Box 9.2 A normative debate: is rights review democratic?

Con	Pro
Rights review subverts majority rule, by allowing constitutional judges to substitute their policy choices for those of legislators.	Democracy does not simply mean the domination of the majority over everyone else. It also means basic standards of good governance which must include the protection of rights.
Rights provisions are vague and ill-defined. In a good democracy, elected officials will determine how rights should be protected in law.	It is precisely because rights provisions are not expressed as clear rules that we need judges to interpret them. Good constitutional rulings will lead legislators to care more about rights.
Judges can interpret rights in any way they wish, without being held democratically accountable. We can expect an effective system of constitutional review to subvert the will of the elected representatives of the people.	Rights are too important to be left to the protection of elected politicians. Judges are relatively more insulated from short-term political calculation, and thus are more likely to protect rights.
The judicialization of politics through rights adjudication reduces the centrality of legislative debate, and therefore reduces the political responsibility of legislative majorities for their policy decisions. Such responsibility is basic to democratic legitimacy.	Judicialization means that legislatures govern, in dialogue with judges, in order to make rights protection effective. The legitimacy of the regime depends, in part, on how legislators and judges interact with one another to protect rights.

In this account, courts are an institutional response to the fact that most constitutions are 'incomplete' contracts to the extent that there exists meaningful uncertainty as to the precise nature of the rights and obligations of the parties under the contract over time. Because of the impossibility of negotiating specific rules for all possible contingencies, and given that, as time passes, conditions will change and the interests of the parties to the agreement will evolve, all contracts are incomplete in some significant way.[2]

Type 3 constitutions—complex instruments of governance designed to last indefinitely, if not forever—are paradigmatic examples of relational contracts. Much is left general, even ill-defined and vague, as in the case of rights. Generalities and vagueness may facilitate agreement at the bargaining stage. But vagueness is legal uncertainty, which threatens to undermine the reason for contracting in the first place. The establishment of constitutional review is an institutional response to the problems of uncertainty and enforcement. Each party has an interest in seeing that the other parties obey their obligations, and that they will be punished for non-compliance.

Principals, agents, trustees

Across the social sciences, as well as in the law and economics tradition, scholars use the 'principal–agent' framework to depict or model authority relations constituted by delegation (see Chapter 7). The framework focuses on the relationship between those who delegate, the 'principals', and those to whom power is delegated, the 'agents'. Let us assume that the principals are those who govern a political system, and that they create institutions—agents—when they believe that doing so helps them govern more efficiently and effectively. Assume now that the political system is one of legislative sovereignty. The principals are therefore the legislators who produce the statutes that are meant to govern the polity. They decide, for good reasons, that it is too difficult to perform two governance functions at once, both making the laws, and enforcing and resolving disputes under the laws.[3] They therefore decide to delegate to agents—courts—to help them with the second set of governance functions.

Here is a stylized account of the ordinary courts as agents of the legislature in a system of parliamentary sovereignty—a type 2 constitutional system. Judges are bound to enforce parliamentary statutes because they express the sovereign's will. The judge's principal is the parliament, and the norm the principal controls—the statute—constitutes the substantive terms of the judge's mandate to govern. The judge's formal governance function is to enforce the parliament's law. However, statutes can only be enforced once they have been interpreted; and, because statutory interpretation is a form of law-making, the law often comes to mean what the courts have said they mean. Even where this is true, the principal still remains in charge. If the legislators notice that a judge has applied a statutory provision in a way that they did not intend and do not like, the law can be changed. The principals may overturn judicial decisions by amending the statute to preclude the offending judicial interpretation. The decision rule governing the principal–agent relationship—a majority vote of the parliament—favours the principal's control.

The traditional principal–agent framework loses much of its relevance when it comes to systems of constitutional justice. It is more appropriate to apply a model of 'constitutional trusteeship' to situations wherein the founders of new constitutions confer expansive open-ended 'fiduciary' powers on a review court (Stone Sweet 2002). The constitutional court exercises fiduciary responsibilities with respect to the constitution. In most settings, they do so in the name of a fictitious entity: the sovereign people.

In systems of constitutional trusteeship, political elites—the political parties, the executive, members of parliament—are never principals in their relationship with constitutional judges. These officials may seek to overturn constitutional decisions or restrict the powers of the constitutional court, but they can do so only by amending the constitution. But, as we have seen, the decision rules governing constitutional revision processes are typically more restrictive than those governing the revision of legislation; in many countries, amendment is a practical impossibility, especially when it comes to rights provisions (see Box 9.3).

Elected officials typically perform some of the functions usually associated with principals, as when they appoint members of the supreme or constitutional courts. Politicians influence constitutional and Supreme Courts through appointments.[4] Nonetheless, by establishing (1) the normative superiority of the constitution, (2) a review organ, and (3) specific procedures for constitutional revision, they shifted the power to control constitutional development away from themselves and to constitutional judges. They compete with each other in order to be in the position to govern and, once in power, they legislate—but under the control of the constitutional judge.

Mapping a zone of discretion cannot tell us what constitutional courts will actually do with their powers. The best we can do is to predict that, given a steady case load, constitutional judges operating in a relatively large zone will come to exercise more influence over the evolution of the polity than those operating in relatively small zones. The prediction, of course, can be tested in comparative case studies.

Other logics

To this point, the discussion presupposes that the elites want to establish constitutional democracy, and that they have decided that a mechanism of third-party rights protection is a good thing for them, in the future. Such an

Box 9.3 The structural determinants of judicial power

The zone of discretion

The zone of discretion is a theoretical understanding of the strategic environment in which any court operates. The size of the zone is determined by (1) the sum of powers delegated to the court, and possessed by the court as a result of its past rulings, minus (2) the sum of control instruments available to overrule or otherwise constrain the court by, for example, political elites who do not like the court's decisions. The zone varies across countries, and it will vary across time in the same country, depending upon how the court interprets the constitution and its role in enforcing it.

France and Germany

The German Federal Constitutional Court enjoys one of the largest zones of discretion of any court. It possesses wide jurisdiction over all constitutional issues, defends both rights and federal arrangements, exercises abstract and concrete review, and receives constitutional complaints. In its case law, the court has made it clear that the German legislative authority must be exercised to enhance rights protection, wherever possible, given other constitutional values. Control instruments are extraordinarily weak. The German constitution does not allow an amendment to weaken rights provisions which, in practice, means that the court's decisions on rights are irreversible, except by the court itself. Because most important political issues make it to the court through one procedure or another, German politics has become highly judicialized.

The French Constitutional Council exercises the abstract review of statutes adopted by parliament, prior to their entry into force. The council radically expanded its own zone of discretion in the 1970s when it incorporated, against the founder's wishes, a charter of rights into the constitution. Compared with the German case, however, the council's zone is quite restricted. It does not handle referrals from the courts or individuals, thus reducing its capacity to control policy outcomes beyond legislative space. As important, the decision rules governing constitutional revision are more permissive than in the German situation: the constitution can be revised by a 3/5 vote of deputies and senators in a special session. Two council decisions have been overruled in order (1) to permit the right-wing majority to tighten immigration policy (amendment of 1993), and (2) to allow the left-wing majority to develop affirmative action policies for women (amendment of 1999).

European countries with Kelsenian courts operate in large zones of discretion, given that (1) the courts possess broad powers to protect charters of rights, most of which are more extensive than in the German situation, and (2) it is almost impossible to amend constitutional rights provisions.

The US and Canada

In the US and Canada, all courts may exercise the judicial review of statutes.

The US Federal Constitution provides for a short list of negative rights, although the Supreme Court has 'discovered' a longer list of rights, such as privacy, thereby expanding its own zone of discretion. It is difficult to amend the US Constitution—readers should check out Article V! In practice, this means that the Court's case law on constitutional rights can only be changed if the Supreme Court changes its mind.

In 1982, Canada became fully independent from the UK, when it 'repatriated' its constitution and supplemented it with an extensive Charter of Rights and Freedoms. Repatriation radically expanded the judiciary's zone of discretion. The 'Notwithstanding Clause' of the charter permits the federal and provincial parliaments to 'override' a right for a period of five years, renewable thereafter. Thus there is no *de facto* judicial supremacy when it comes to rights, as there is in much of Europe and the US. Canadian legislators can choose to violate a right, but their responsibility for doing so is complete. The Canadian Parliament has never chosen to do so, although some provincial legislatures have voted overrides.

Students should consider this question, to which there may not be a clear answer: is the zone of discretion of the US Supreme Court greater or smaller than that of the Canadian Supreme Court? On the one hand, the Canadian Constitution gives a privileged place for the Charter of Rights and Freedoms, which is a richer text than the American Bill of Rights. On the other hand, a Canadian Supreme Court's ruling on rights can be more easily set aside. But as this chapter emphasizes, the zone of discretion does not tell us what a court will actually do with its discretionary authority. Might a 'Notwithstanding Clause' encourage a court to be a more aggressive rights protector if it knows that it does not have the last word on a statute's constitutional legality?

explanation does not work very well in understanding why autocrats and dictators also write constitutions with rights and review (see Ginsburg 2003). In general, courts can be useful to those who run authoritarian states as a relatively cheap means of monitoring what is going on in the country (Moustafa 2007: Chapter 2). Courts may also help the ruler enforce new national policies in the face of regional resistance. But logics such as these do not apply to constitutional courts and rights review, which can directly challenge the ruler's power at its source. It is likely that rulers institute review for other reasons—to achieve a measure of international respectability, for example—never doubting their capacity to control the review courts.

The evolution of constitutional review

In 1789, no system of constitutional justice existed anywhere on Earth. After 1950 'the new constitutionalism' emerged and then, in the 1990s, exploded into prominence. Between 1789 and 1950, the institutional materials that would solidify into the current 'models' of review were beginning to take shape, in the US, France, Austria–Germany, and in Scandinavia.

1789–1950

In America, the Federal Constitution of the US (1787) replaced the Articles of Confederation (1781), one of the first written constitutions. The new constitution established a Supreme Court and the judiciary as a separate branch of government, but the document neither contained a charter of rights nor expressly provided for the judicial review. The court's main purpose was to manage federalism, in particular to secure national supremacy with regard to interstate commerce and finance. In 1791, the Bill of Rights was added to the text, as amendments, and constitutional review was added in 1803 through the Marbury decision. Only in the 1880s did rights review begin to emerge. In its most important decisions during this period, the court defended the property rights of merchants and firms against state laws designed to regulate their commercial activities. During the First World War, the court began to deal with civil and political rights, but it did very little to protect them. In 1937, the court abandoned its opposition to market regulation of economic rights, after successive elections had cemented the power of New Deal Democrats and in the face of President Roosevelt's threat to 'pack the Court' (Balkin 2005).

By the end of the Second World War, it would have been difficult to argue that constitutional experience in the US provided a respectable example of an effective 'system of constitutional justice', at least by today's standards. The constitution, after all, had formally sanctioned slavery. The Civil War led to slavery's abolition, and to the adoption of the 13th, 14th, and 15th Amendments (1865–70). Prior to 1950, the court made little of the 14th Amendment, which guarantees 'equal protection under the laws', for the purposes for which it was designed—to combat institutionalized racism and other forms of discrimination. Instead, the court, and therefore the constitution, was complicit in systematic rights abuses of the worst kind. In 1883 the court struck down as unconstitutional a Congressional statute banning discrimination against former slaves in hotels, the railroads, theatres, and so on; and in 1896 it bestowed constitutional legitimacy on the official apartheid that many Southern states had instituted after Reconstruction.[5] Apartheid would remain an important element of American constitutional law until well after the Second World War.

The US produced a model of judicial review that has been adopted by other polities. Further, the Supreme Court demonstrated to the world that constitutional review could survive and even prosper, not only through supervising federalism, but also through protecting rights. In the 1950s, the court gradually moved to protect civil rights, especially freedom of speech and assembly, voting rights, 14th Amendment protections, and the rights of defendants in criminal cases. Indeed, by the end of the 1960s, the court had transformed itself into a formidable rights protector. This posture helped to create and sustain a rights-based litigation-oriented politics in the US (Epp 1998), a politics that remains vibrant today. As important, Americans occupied post-Second World War Germany and Italy, and they insisted that these countries write constitutions that included a charter of rights and a review mechanism, thus helping to provoke the move to the 'new constitutionalism' in Europe.

In 1803, when *Marbury* v. *Madison* was rendered, the French were completing the destruction of independent judicial authority. That process began with the Great Revolution of 1789. In 1790, the legislature prohibited judicial review of legislation, and that statute remains in force today. By 1804, a new legal system had emerged. It was constructed on the principle—a corollary of legislative sovereignty—that courts must not participate in the law-making function. The judge was cast as a 'slave' of the legislature, more precisely of the code system. The codes are statutes which purport to regulate society in a comprehensive way, not least in order to reduce judicial discretion to nil. Through imitation, revolution, and war, the code system and the prohibition of judicial review spread across Europe during the nineteenth century (the British Isles and the Nordic region being the most important exceptions). Constitutions could be revised at the discretion of the lawmaker, separation-of-powers doctrines subjugated judicial to legislative authority, and constraints on the lawmaker's authority, such as rights, either did not exist or could not be enforced by courts.

Curiously, the French Revolution did produce the first modern charter of rights. In 1789, the Constituent Assembly adopted the Declaration of the Rights of Man and of the Citizen before it completed its task of drafting the constitution of 1791. Since 1791, the French have lived under fifteen different written constitutions, but none provided for rights review, and none made the Declaration judicially enforceable. Constitutional review powers were periodically conferred on specialized state organs (never courts) in order to police the boundaries between executive and legislative authority, not to protect rights from legislative infringement. In the 1970s, the Constitutional Council incorporated the Declaration into the Constitution of the Fifth Republic (1959 to the present), against the express wishes of the founders (Stone 1990: Chapters 3, 4).

The founders of the Fifth Republic established the Constitutional Council to help ensure the dominance of the executive (the government, named by the president) over the parliament in legislative processes. Its role was transformed by two constitutional changes. First, as mentioned, the council incorporated a bill of rights into the constitution, a process completed by 1979. The decision expanded the council's zone of discretion considerably. Second, in 1974 the power to refer statutes adopted by parliament before their entry into force was given to any sixty National Assembly deputies or sixty senators—that is, to opposition parties. The council exercises only politically initiated, pre-enforcement, abstract review of statutes. Once a statute has entered into force, it is no longer subject to constitutional review of any kind; thus legislative sovereignty remains formally intact.

The French experience is important for two main reasons. First, its code system and its conception of legislative sovereignty and separation of powers spread across Europe, and would later take hold in Africa and Latin America through the influence of French and Spanish colonialism. Second, like the Germans, the French experimented with models of non-judicial, politically activated, constitutional review in the form of specialized state organs. These experiments are cousins of the modern constitutional court, and a number of states use the 'constitutional council' model today.

In the area now comprised of Austria, Germany, and Switzerland, specialized state organs became a common feature of government in various federal polities during the nineteenth century. These bodies dealt primarily with jurisdictional disputes between state institutions, or among levels of government. The modern constitutional court is the invention of the Austrian legal theorist, Hans Kelsen, who developed the European model of constitutional review partly from these experiences. Kelsen drafted the constitution of the Austrian First Republic (1920–34), and he included a constitutional court among its most important state institutions. He was also a legal theorist whose writings and teachings turned out to be extraordinarily influential after the Second World War. The Kelsenian court, which is at the heart of the European model, is now the most popular institutional form of review in the world.

Some scholars speak of a Scandinavian model of review, and note that it is one of the world's oldest (Husa 2000). In Norway, the power of the judiciary to invalidate law as unconstitutional has been asserted since at least the 1860s, although the question of whether this power extended to judicial review of statutes was not definitively resolved until a Supreme Court decision of 1976 suggested that the answer was yes. Simplifying, the Danish Constitution of 1849 expressly provides for rights but not for review, and the Swedish Constitution (elements of which have been in place since 1809) provided for review but not for rights (until 1974). None of the courts in the region ever used review authority to any noticeable effect. Indeed, even today, these courts do almost no constitutional judicial review of any political consequence, and deference to the legislature is the rule (Husa 2000; Scheinin 2001).

The diffusion of higher law constitutionalism

During the inter-war period (roughly 1918–38), constitutional review was established in Czechoslovakia (1920), Liechtenstein (1925), Greece (1927), Spain (1931), and Ireland (1937); further, the German Supreme Court of the Weimar Republic also flirted with review (Stolleis 2003). Of these, only the Irish Supreme Court actually did much review, and only the Irish Court survived the Second World War. Today, it is one of the world's most effective review courts.

Review courts were established in Europe in successive waves of constitution-making, following the war, the end of fascism in Greece, Spain, and Portugal in the 1970s, and the fall of communism in Central and Eastern Europe after 1989. Apart from the Greek and Estonian mixed system, every country adopted the Kelsenian constitutional court. Kelsenian courts were established in Austria (1945), Italy (1948), the Federal Republic of Germany (1949), France (1958), Portugal (1976), Spain (1978), Belgium (1985), and, after 1989, in the post-communist Czech Republic, Hungary, Poland, Romania, Russia and other post-Soviet states, Slovakia, and the Baltics, as well as in the states of the former Yugoslavia (see Box 9.4).

The American model is found in Africa, Asia, and the Caribbean, especially in those countries that had been colonized by Great Britain, or are part of the

Box 9.4 Modes of constitutional review

The American model and judicial review

A legal 'case'—defined as a legal dispute brought to a court as litigation between two parties who have opposed interests—activates review, once one of the parties pleads the constitution, such as a right. Any court can, at the behest of either party, void a law as unconstitutional if that court determines that the statute violates the constitution.

The European model and abstract review

Abstract review is initiated when elected officials—typically the parliamentary opposition, the executive, or the government of a regional or federated state—refer a law for review after the law has been adopted by the legislature, but before it has been enforced. This mode of review is called 'abstract' because it proceeds in the absence of a concrete judicial case, since the law has yet to be applied. The review court compares the constitutional text and the statute, in the abstract, to determine if the latter conforms to the former. Abstract review is also called 'preventive review', since it allows the system to filter out unconstitutional laws before they can harm people.

The European model and concrete review

Concrete review is initiated when an ordinary judge, presiding over litigation in the courts, refers a constitutional question—for example, is law X, which is normally applicable to the dispute at bar, unconstitutional?—that the constitutional court must answer. The referring judge then resolves the dispute with reference to the constitutional court's ruling. This mode of review is called 'concrete' since it is related to a concrete case already under way in the ordinary courts. However, in comparison with American judicial review, concrete review still looks more 'abstract' in that the constitutional court does not preside over or settle the case, which remains the responsibility of the referring judge.

The European model and the constitutional complaint

Individuals may activate the constitutional court directly by sending to the judges a constitutional complaint, which alleges that their rights have been violated by a public authority, after judicial remedies have been exhausted or are not available. Most constitutional complaints are, in effect, appeals of judicial decisions.

Commonwealth. In moving to rights and review, these systems, in effect, 'constitutionalize' the basic common law legal order. Judicial review is also found in countries that were under American occupation or influence after 1950, such as Japan and parts of Central and South America.

With decolonization, the number of states in the world expanded steadily throughout the 1950s and 1960s. Beginning in the 1970s, many post-colonial states in the developing world began to experiment with different constitutional forms. Written constitutions proliferated, most of which did not last, but they were almost always replaced with new written constitutions. By the 1990s, the basic formula of the new constitutionalism—(1) a written, entrenched constitution, (2) a charter of rights, and (3) a review mechanism to protect rights—had become standard, even in authoritarian states.

Systems of constitutional justice in the twenty-first century

The written constitution is the norm. There are 194 states in a recent data set compiled on constitutional forms,[6] 190 of which have written constitutions. Bhutan, Israel, New Zealand, and the UK do not have fully codified constitutions. Nonetheless, Israel possesses a powerful Supreme Court that protects rights as part of the higher law (Gross 1998), and the Kingdom of Bhutan has drafted a constitution which includes both rights and review. New Zealand (1990) and the UK (1998) adopted charters of rights in the form of statutes, but courts may not enforce these rights against the will of Parliament (Gardbaum 2001).

Out of the 194 states, 183 contain a charter of rights. Most constitutions written in the past three decades contain an extensive catalogue of rights which includes not only traditional civil and political rights, but positive or social rights. At present, few new constitutions omit rights. There have been 114 constitutions written since 1985 (not all of which have lasted), and we have reliable information on 106 of these. All 106 of these constitutions contain a catalogue of rights. It seems that the last constitution to leave rights out was the racist 1983 South African constitution, hardly a model to emulate.

Of the 106 constitutions written since 1985 on which we can reliably report, all but five—those of North Korea, Vietnam, Saudi Arabia, Laos, and Iraq (in its 1990 constitution)—established constitutional review.

Table 9.1 presents data on the regional distribution of the various review mechanisms. The European model is clearly ascendant. Moreover, the most powerful review courts in the world are Kelsenian courts. The spread of the European model has also meant the diffusion of abstract review. Mavčič (www.concourts.net) examined modes of review in 125 constitutions currently in force, and determined that 70 of them conferred abstract review authority on judges. Most of these also provide for individual constitutional complaints. The American 'case or controversy' model is moribund, with little chance of being revived.

Table 9.1 Regional distribution of models of constitutional review

Region	Constitutional judicial review (American model)	Constitutional court (European model)	Mixed[a]	Other[b]	None
Europe	5	31	3 (1)	1	2
Africa	12	29	1	6	3
Middle East	2	5	0	3	1
Asia and South East Asia	18	13	2	11	0
North America	2	0	0	0	0
Central America	3	3	3 (1)	0	0
South America	3	4	5 (3)	0	0
Caribbean	8	0	0	1	0
Total	53	85	14	22	6

[a]The number in parentheses refers to systems with European model constitutional courts, such as Portugal, but which also give review authority to ordinary judges.

[b]Review mechanisms, often unique, that are unclassifiable.

Source: Data compiled by Dr Arne Mavčič, available online at www.concourts.net. French council-based systems were counted under the 'Constitutional court (European model)' column, and Saudi Arabia, which is not included the Mavčič dataset, was counted under the 'None' column.

KEY POINTS

- Prior to 1950, there was little effective constitutional review outside the US, where it functioned more in favour of powerful economic interests and institutionalized racism than it did to protect minority rights.

- After 1950, the European model of review spread from Austria and Germany throughout Europe and beyond.

- Today, nearly every country has a written constitution that provides for rights and rights review. The American model is found primarily in Commonwealth countries and in areas that have been under American influence. However, the European model is far more popular.

Effectiveness

Comparative political scientists will not be interested in these developments if systems of constitutional justice do not influence broader political processes: the development of the constitution; the making of public policy; competition among political elites. To the extent that constitutional review is effective, it will be central to these and other processes.

Constitutional review can be said to be effective to the extent that important constitutional disputes arising in the polity are brought to the review authority on a regular basis, that the judges who resolve these disputes give reasons for their rulings, and that those who are governed by the constitutional law accept that the court's rulings have

some effect as precedents. Effectiveness varies across countries and over time.

Most review systems throughout world history have been relatively ineffective, even irrelevant. In weak systems, important political disputes may not be sent to constitutional judges for resolution, and decisions that constitutional judges do render may be ignored. Political actors may seek to settle their disputes by force, sometimes with fatal consequences for the regime. Put simply, elites may care much more about staying in power, enriching themselves, rewarding their friends and punishing their foes, or achieving ethnic dominance, than they care about building constitutional democracy. Constitutional regimes may also be overthrown by force. Since 1950, over 100 examples can be found in Africa, Central and South America, and Asia. In some countries, the military *coup d'état* remains a constant threat. In the most recent decade (1997–2006), at least twenty-five coups were attempted in these areas, and at least fourteen were successful, including in Ecuador, Fiji, Guinée-Bissau, the Ivory Coast, Mauritania, Pakistan, Thailand, and Turkey. Nonetheless, despite the odds, some courts and constitutions have operated as constraints even on military dictatorship, as in Pinochet's Chile (Barros 2002).

There are several necessary conditions for the emergence of effective review systems. First, constitutional judges must have a case load. If actors, private and public, conspire not to activate review, judges will accrete no influence over the polity. Second, once activated, judges must resolve these disputes and give defensible reasons in justification of their decisions. If they do, one output of constitutional adjudication will be the production of a constitutional case law, or jurisprudence, which is a record of how the judges have interpreted the constitution. Third, those who are governed by the constitutional law must accept that constitutional meaning is (at least partly) constructed through the judges' interpretation and rule-making, and use or refer to relevant case law in future disputes.

Why only some countries are able to fulfil these conditions is an important question that scholars have not been able to answer. The achievement of stable type 3 constitutionalism depends strongly on the same macropolitical factors that are related to the achievement of stable democracy, and we know that democracy is difficult to create and sustain. Among other factors, the new constitutionalism rests on a polity's commitment to elections, a competitive party system, protecting rights, including those of minorities, practices associated with the 'rule of law', and a system of advanced legal education. Each of these factors is also associated with other important sociocultural phenomena, including attributes of political culture.

Therefore it is not surprising that one finds relatively effective review mechanisms in areas where one finds relatively stable democracy, which now include the post-communist countries of Central Europe. Ranked in terms of effectiveness, I would place the systems of (1) Canada and the US in the Americas, (2) Germany, Ireland, and Spain in Western Europe, and (3) the Czech Republic, Hungary, Poland, and Slovenia in Central Europe at the top of the list. Outside these regions, there are probably only three courts that would make this list, those of India (Verma and Kumar 2003), Israel (Hirschl 2001), and South Africa (Klug 2000).

The impact of constitutional review

There has been no systematic research or data collection on constitutions, rights, and rights protection, or on the politics of constitutional review. However, since 1990, scholars have produced single-case studies, and a handful of small-N comparative studies. I will focus on the impact of new review systems on politics in the two areas that have attracted the most attention.

Transitions to constitutional democracy

Since 1950, type 3 constitutions, rights, and review have been crucial to nearly all successful transitions from authoritarian regimes to constitutional democracy. Indeed, it appears that the more successful any transition has been, the more one is likely to find an effective constitutional or Supreme Court at the heart of it (Japan may be the most important exception). Review performs several functions that facilitate the transition to democracy. It provides a system of peaceful dispute resolution, under the constitution, for those who have contracted a new beginning in light of illiberal or violent pasts. It provides a mechanism for purging the laws of authoritarian elements that have built up over many years, given that the new legislature may be overloaded with work. And a review court can provide a focal point for a new rhetoric of state legitimacy, one based on respect for rights and other values of the new constitution, and on the rejection of old authoritarian rhetoric.

Today, constitutional democracy is defined in terms of the new constitutionalism, which assumes that constraining majority rule with rights and review is a good thing. Thus, it is hardly shocking that a new generation of scholars claim that constitutional courts have been—or simply are—more democratic than parliaments, and that they have cajoled or persuaded political elites to be more democratic than they would otherwise have been (e.g. Scheppele 2005). Moreover, many of today's newer and more successful review courts do not conceive of constitutionalism in restricted national terms, but in terms of an emerging 'global constitutionalism' with human rights at its core. The courts of Hungary, Poland, Slovenia, and South Africa do not hesitate to cite sources of law outside their constitutions, including the decisions of other constitutional courts (Klug 2000).

The 'judicialization' of politics

A second important strain of research focuses on the impact of review on policy processes and outcomes (see Box 9.5). Most studies of judicialization proceed by conceptualizing constitutional review and rights adjudication as an extension of the policy process, and then observing and evaluating the impact of review on final outcomes and subsequent policy-making in the same area. The classic work is Martin Shapiro's *Law and Politics in the Supreme Court* (1964), but the basic approach has been applied to Europe (Shapiro and Stone Sweet 1994) and Latin America (Sieder *et al.* 2005), as well as many other specific countries.

Charles Epp (1998) has analysed the 'rights revolution' in four countries whose review systems would be classified under the American judicial review model. He shows that effective rights review does not just emerge spontaneously or naturally, but is the product of a constellation of structures and agency. Effective rights review depends on building a network of 'rights advocates' who are able to mobilize the resources necessary to litigate in the courts, often for causes that will benefit people who do not have such resources. Epp argues that the rights revolution has gone furthest in the US and Canada, but his book also helps to explain development in India, and more recent changes in the UK and other Commonwealth countries.

It is easier to study the impact of rights review on legislative activity in centralized review systems than in decentralized systems, because constitutional judges and

Box 9.5 The judicialization of politics through rights adjudication

The phrase 'judicialization of politics' refers to the process through which the influence of courts on legislative and administrative power develops over time. In some places, in some sectors, policy is highly judicialized; in others, it may not be judicialized at all.

Rights review leads to the judicialization of legislative politics to the extent that (1) constitutional rights provisions have a legal status superior to statutes, (2) the review court receives important cases in which statutes are alleged to have violated rights, and (3) the court sometimes annuls statutes on the basis of rights, and gives reasons for doing so. In judicialized settings, legislators worry about and debate the constitutionality of bills during the legislative process, and they will draft and amend their bills in order to insulate them from constitutional censure. In judicialized settings, constitutional courts routinely take decisions that serve both to construct the constitutional law and to amend legislation under review.

Some of the more controversial examples of highly judicialized politics around the world concern attempt to combat racial and gender discrimination, to liberalize and regulate abortion, and to criminalize 'hate speech', obscenity, and pornography.

In policy domains that are highly judicialized, courts and judicial process are part of the greater policy process. If political scientists do not pay close attention to courts, they will miss a large part of the action.

have become highly 'judicialized'. The web of constitutional constraints facing legislators has grown and become denser as constitutional courts have processed a steady stream of cases and built a policy-relevant jurisprudence. This orientation is also applicable to Central Europe (Sadurski 2005).

KEY POINTS

- Systems of constitutional review are effective in so far as constitutional judges are able to influence the development of the constitutional law and public policy through their interpretations of rights and other constitutional provisions. We do not find much effectiveness in countries that are not relatively stable democracies.

- In some places, including South Africa and Central and Eastern Europe, constitutional courts have been important to processes of democratization.

- In countries where review is highly effective, constitutional judges have become powerful policy-makers. Examples are mainly found in North America and Western Europe, although the courts of Colombia, Israel, and South Africa deserve mention.

Conclusion

Constitutional law is political law: it is the law that constitutes the state and governs acts of authority made in the name of the polity. Since the 1950s, new constitutionalism—which combines (1) written entrenched constitutions, (2) rights, and (3) constitutional review—has been consolidated as an unrivalled standard. Though we find provision for rights review virtually everywhere today, not all systems of constitutional justice are equally effective. Indeed, in many places they are irrelevant.

Where such systems are effective, constitutional judges govern. They do so through two linked processes. First, given a steady case load, they will adapt the constitution to changing circumstances, on an ongoing basis, through interpretation. Second, in applying their constitutional interpretations to resolve rights disputes, the judges will make policy, including legislative policy. The more effective any system of review is, the more judges will, inevitably, become powerful policy-makers. Both outcomes inhere in a simple legal fact, made real through effective review: the constitution is higher law and therefore binds the exercise of all public authority.

legislators interact with one another directly, through abstract review referrals and decisions. I have developed a theory of the constitutional judicialization of politics in Western Europe (Stone Sweet 2000), showing that the impact of rights and the court on legislative activity will vary as a function of three factors: (1) the existence of abstract review, (2) the number of veto points in the policy process, and (3) the content of the court's case law. The more centralized the policy process—the greater the parliamentary majority, the more that majority is under the control of a unified executive, and the fewer veto points there are in legislative procedures—the more the opposition will go to the constitutional court to block important policy initiatives. Abstract review referrals are the most straightforward means of doing this. In many policy domains, legislative politics

Questions

1. In what ways does a constitution constitute the state and the political system?

2. What are the main differences between a type 2 and a type 3 constitution?

3. What is 'the new constitutionalism' and what does it have to do with politics?

4. What is the difference between a court that is 'an agent of the legislature' and a court that is a 'trustee of the constitution'?

5. How does the American model of review differ from the European model?

6. Why is the zone of discretion, in part, determined by constitutional provisions that specify how the constitution is to be revised?

7. Do you think that it is good for a country to have a large catalogue of rights and an effective system of review?

8. Would you rather live in a country whose politics are relatively more, or relatively less, constitutionally 'judicialized'?

9. Why do you think that an authoritarian dictator might draft a constitution with rights and review?

10. Which are the most effective courts?

Further reading

Recent comparative treatments of judicial politics and constitutional review

Epp, C. (1998) *The Rights Revolution: Lawyers, Activists, and Supreme Courts in Comparative Perspective* (Chicago, IL: University of Chicago Press).

Ginsburg, T. (2003) *Judicial Review in New Democracies: Constitutional Courts in Asian Cases* (Cambridge: Cambridge University Press).

Hirschl, R. (2004) *Towards Juristocracy: The Origins and Consequences of the New Constitutionalism* (Cambridge, MA: Harvard University Press).

Schwartz, H. (2000) *The Struggle for Constitutional Justice in Post-Communist Europe* (Chicago, IL: University of Chicago Press).

Sieder, R., Schjolden, L., and Angell, A. (2005) *The Judicialization of Politics in Latin America* (New York: Palgrave Macmillan).

Stone Sweet, A. (2000) *Governing with Judges: Constitutional Politics in Western Europe* (Oxford: Oxford University Press).

Tate, C. N. and Vallinder, T. (eds) (1995) *The Global Expansion of Judicial Power* (New York: New York University Press).

See also the works cited throughout this chapter. *The International Journal of Constitutional Law* is the leading journal devoted to research on constitutional law and courts.

Web links

http://www.comparativeconstitutionsproject.org/
The Comparative Constitutions Project.

www2.lib.uchicago.edu/~llou/conlaw.html
University of Chicago's 'Research Constitutional Law on the Internet'.

www.concourts.net
Data, data analysis, and commentary on constitutional courts and review around the world.

www.jurist.law.pitt.edu/countries/
University of Pittsburgh School of Law's website for 'legal news and research', country by country.

www.glin.gov/
Global Legal Information Network, maintained by the US Library of Congress.

http://confinder.richmond.edu/
'Constitution Finder', University of Richmond.

www.findlaw.com/01topics/06constitutional/03forconst/index.html
Find Law, constitutions.

online
resource
centre

For additional material and resources, please visit the Online Resource Centre at:
www.oxfordtextbooks.co.uk/orc/caramani3e/

CHAPTER 10

Elections and referendums

Michael Gallagher

Chapter contents

Reader's guide

This chapter covers the two main opportunities that people have to vote in most societies: elections and referendums. Elections are held to fill seats in parliaments or to choose a president, while at referendums citizens decide directly on some issue of policy. Elections are the cornerstone of representative democracy, in that the people elect others to make decisions. Referendums are sometimes perceived as the equivalent of 'direct democracy', but in practice they are deployed only as a kind of optional extra in systems of representative democracy, with hardly anyone suggesting that all decisions should be made by referendum. The chapter explores the variety of rules under which elections are held, and examines the consequences of this variation. It then looks at the use of the referendum and assesses its potential impact on a country's politics.

Introduction

We saw in Chapters 7 and 8 that parliaments and governments have the potential to be important actors. In this chapter we look at how governments and parliaments come into being in the first place. The process of election is an essential requirement of any political system that hopes to be regarded as possessing democratic credentials. The election is the main mechanism by which the people are able to express their views about how their country should be governed.

However, not all elections are quite the same. Elections are governed by rules that determine what kind of choices people can make when they turn out to vote and how those choices are converted into seats in parliament or the election of a president. Identical sets of voter preferences in two adjacent countries might have to be expressed differently if the electoral rules are different or, even if the ballot papers capture their preferences in the same way, the counting rules might deliver different results. Hence, it is important to understand what kinds of rules are used and what consequences different rules have.

Governments and parliaments, produced by elections, make most of the political decisions facing a country, albeit within the constraints imposed by some of the other actors studied in this book, such as courts and interest groups (see Chapters 9 and 14, respectively). However, some decisions are taken not by these elected authorities but, rather, by the people themselves in referendums on specific issues. Whereas the use of elections is universal among democracies, the use of referendums varies enormously.

This variation is itself intriguing, as is the question of why some issues are put to referendums while others are not. The chapter examines the different kinds of referendums that are held or are provided for in countries' constitutions, and the kinds of issues that tend to be the subject of referendums. It looks at the reasons advanced for their use and at the concerns expressed by critics. There has been some dispute as to whether voters in referendums take much notice of the question supposedly at issue, and the chapter reviews the evidence before assessing the impact of referendums.

KEY POINTS

- Elections and referendums are the two main opportunities that people have to vote.
- Elections are held to fill seats (representatives) in a parliament or some other institution.
- Referendums are votes on a specific issue to be approved or rejected.

Elections and electoral systems

Elections are a virtually universal feature of modern politics. Even regimes that cannot be considered democracies in any sense of the word, and which provide voters with little or no freedom of choice when they arrive at the polling station, have felt there might be some kind of legitimacy to be derived from holding elections.

In modern liberal democracies, elections are the central representative institution that forms a link between the people and their representatives. For the most part, the decisions that affect us all are taken by a tiny handful of individuals, such as members of parliament, government ministers, or presidents, sometimes known collectively as the 'political class'. The reason why we regard this state of affairs as legitimate rather than as an appalling usurpation of our rights is that the members of the political class are not simply imposed upon us but, rather, are elected by us to be our political representatives. Moreover, they face re-election and therefore can be voted out at the next election if they fail to satisfy us. This mechanism of achieving representation and accountability is central to the concept of modern democracy (see Chapter 5). A regime whose leaders are not elected and are not subject to the requirement of regular re-election cannot be considered democratic.

By an electoral system we mean the set of rules that structure how votes are cast at elections and how these votes are then converted into the allocation of offices. We look first at electoral regulations (the rules governing the breadth of the franchise, ease of ballot access, and so on) and then specifically at electoral systems.

Electoral regulations

Among modern democracies, variations in the extent of the franchise are matters of detail rather than of principle (for an overview see Caramani 2000: 49–57). Generalizing somewhat, in the first half of the nineteenth century the male landed gentry constituted the bulk of the *electorate* (those who are entitled to vote), but from the middle of the century the franchise was gradually extended to the male section of the growing middle class. Around the turn of the century further advances meant that the male working class had the vote by the time of the First World War (1914). The struggle to secure the same rights for women took longer and, particularly in some mainly Catholic countries such as France and Italy, women did not get the vote on the same basis as men until after the Second World War (1945). The voting age was reduced steadily throughout the twentieth century, and in most countries these days stands at 18 (Caramani 2000: 56–7). There are pressure groups in many countries seeking further reduction, achieving some success in Argentina and Austria (voting age of 16), Brazil (16), and Indonesia

Box 10.1 Should voting be compulsory?

Arguments for compulsory voting	Arguments against compulsory voting
Our forebears struggled and died in order to win the right to vote, so people today have a duty to vote.	It is perfectly legitimate to take no interest in politics, or not to vote for whatever reason.
Politicians have a strong incentive to skew their policies towards those who will punish or reward them, depending on their record in office, and to neglect those who are unlikely to vote. When voting is optional, the better off are much more likely to vote than the poor, so policy outputs will favour the better off.	If everyone is compelled to vote, the votes of those who actually care about the outcome of an election are diluted by the votes of those with no interest in the outcome and who may be voting on a virtually random basis.
The role of money in politics is reduced since parties no longer need to motivate their supporters to turn out.	The onus should be on parties and candidates to persuade citizens that there is some reason why they should vote rather than being able to rely on the state to compel them to do so.
All citizens have an incentive to inform themselves about the issues and about the performance of politicians, making for a better informed electorate.	Even those with no real interest in the election have to vote, so politicians have even more of an incentive than under optional voting to engage in attention-catching stunts to try to impress those who know nothing about the issues
Compulsion is not a breach of principle; for example, everyone has to pay taxes whether they want to or not.	Freedom of choice implies the right not to turn out if you don't wish to, and this would be infringed by compelling people to turn out.

(17). Voting is generally voluntary, though in a few countries such as Australia and Belgium it is compulsory. Given that turnout in most countries is related to socio-economic status (SES), it has been argued that making voting compulsory would help eliminate the 'yawning SES voting gap' (L. Hill 2006) (see Box 10.1).

The ease of access to the ballot varies across countries and can be an important factor in determining whether new candidates or parties take the plunge and stand at an election. Most states impose some kind of requirement, such as a financial deposit, demonstrated support from a number of voters, or the endorsement of a recognized party. The requirements are typically more demanding in candidate-oriented systems than in party-oriented ones (see Katz 1997: 255–61). Onerous access requirements can be a significant deterrent for small parties or independent candidates.

Generally, the term of presidents is fixed, while for parliaments constitutions specify a maximum period but not a minimum. The president of the US has a four-year term, while the French president has five years. The term of some parliaments is fixed: for example, those of Norway, Sweden, and Switzerland have a four-year lifespan, while members of the US House of Representatives serve terms of only two years, which means that they operate all the time in election campaign mode. Senators in the US, by contrast, have six years to savour the fruits of election. However, most parliaments do not have a fixed term; instead, the government (or prime minister, or in some cases the head of state) of the day has the power to dissolve parliament, and characteristically uses this power to call the election at the time most advantageous to itself. The maximum time between elections is usually four years, though in a few countries (including Canada, France, Italy, and the UK) it is five years, while in Australia and New Zealand it is an exceptionally short three years.

Electoral systems

The precise rules governing the conversion of votes into seats may seem a rather technical matter, yet electoral systems matter. They can have a major impact upon whether a country has a two-party or a multiparty system, whether government is by one party or a coalition of parties, whether voters feel personally represented in a parliament, and whether women and minorities are heavily under-represented in parliament.

This is not the place to supply a complete account of how the entire world's electoral systems work (see Farrell 2010; Gallagher and Mitchell 2008: appendix A; Reynolds *et al.* 2005). However, we can sketch the main categories and the dimensions of variation, before moving on to examine the consequences of different configurations.

The main categories of electoral systems

There are many ways in which to categorize electoral systems, the most straightforward of which relates to the magnitude of the constituencies in which seats are allocated (a **constituency** is the geographic area into which the country is divided for electoral purposes). We may begin with the distinction between systems based on *multi-member constituencies,* in which the seats are shared among the parties in proportion to their vote shares, and those based on *single-member constituencies,* in which the strongest party in each constituency wins the seat. The former are often termed **proportional representation** (PR) systems, while the latter are termed **majoritarian** systems.

Single-member plurality

The simplest system of all is single-member plurality (SMP), also known sometimes as 'first-past-the-post' (FPTP). Voters simply make a mark, such as placing a cross, beside their choice of candidate, and the seat is then awarded to the candidate who receives most votes (i.e. a plurality). This is used in some of the world's largest democracies, such as India, the US, the UK, and Canada; over 40 per cent of the world's population, and over 70 per cent of those in an established democracy, live in a country employing this system (Reynolds *et al.* 2005: 30; Heath *et al.* 2008; Mitchell 2008; Massicotte 2008).

Alternative vote

Under the alternative vote (AV), voters are able to rank order the candidates, placing a '1' beside their first choice, '2' beside their second, and so on (Farrell and McAllister 2008). The counting process is a little more complicated. If one candidate's votes amount to a majority of all votes cast, that person is deemed elected. If not, then the lowest-placed candidate is eliminated from the count and his/her ballots are redistributed according to the second preference expressed on them. Supporters of this candidate are in effect asked 'given that your first choice lacked sufficient support to be elected, which candidate would you like to benefit from your vote instead?' The counting process continues, with successive eliminations of the bottom-placed candidate and transfers of their votes to the remaining candidates, until one candidate does have an overall majority of the votes. In consequence, AV is regarded as a majority system, given that the winner requires an absolute majority of the votes at the final stage, whereas under SMP a plurality suffices. AV is employed in Australia but scarcely anywhere else; in May 2011 the people of the UK voted heavily (68% to 32%) against adopting it for elections to the House of Commons (Whiteley *et al.* 2012).

Two-round system

Another way of filling a single seat is by the two-round system (2RS): if no candidate wins a majority of votes in the first round, a second round takes place in which only certain candidates (perhaps the top two, or those who exceeded a certain percentage of the votes) are permitted to proceed to the second round, where whoever wins the most votes is the winner. This is employed to elect parliaments in over twenty countries, including France, Iran, and several former French colonies, and is widely used to elect presidents (Elgie 2008; Blais *et al.* 1997).

These three systems—SMP, AV, and 2RS—thus differ, yet they have much more in common than differentiates them, as we shall see later, because they are all based on single-seat constituencies.

Proportional representation

PR is a principle, which can be achieved by any number of different methods, all of which have the aim, with some qualifications as we shall see, of awarding to each group of voters its 'fair share' of representation—or, putting it another way, of allocating to each party the same share of the seats as it won of the votes. The simplest way of achieving this is to treat the whole country as one large constituency, as happens in Israel, the Netherlands, and Slovakia; then it is a straightforward matter to award, for example, twenty-four seats in a 150-member parliament to a party that receives 16 per cent of the votes (Rahat and Hazan 2008; Andeweg 2008). That guarantees a high level of **proportionality**, by which term we mean the closeness with which the distribution of seats in parliament reflects the distribution of votes ('disproportionality' refers to the degree of difference between these two distributions). At the same time, it might leave voters feeling disengaged from the political system as they do not have a local MP. More commonly, then, the country is divided into a number of smaller constituencies, each returning on average perhaps five, ten, or twenty MPs. Now the seats are awarded proportionally within each constituency, but it cannot be guaranteed that the overall level of proportionality will be quite as high as when there is just one national constituency. Brazil, Finland, Indonesia, and Spain all exemplify this approach (Raunio 2008; Hopkin 2008).

There are different methods of awarding seats proportionally within each constituency, which are based on slightly different conceptions of what constitutes 'perfect proportionality'. Some methods are even-handed between large and small parties, while others, such as the widely used D'Hondt method, give the benefit of any doubt to larger parties. (For an explanation of the technical details, see Gallagher and Mitchell (2008: appendix A); see also Chapter 13.)

The systems outlined above are known as list systems, because each party presents a list of candidates to the voters. While list systems are still the most common form of electoral system in the world (Reynolds *et al.* 2005: 30), in recent years a number of countries have adopted what are usually termed mixed systems. Here the voter casts two votes: one for a local constituency MP and one for a party list. A certain proportion of MPs are elected from local (usually single-member) constituencies and the rest from party lists; in Germany, the archetype of this category, the proportions are half and half, though in other countries the balance might tilt this way or that. The constituency seat is usually allocated under SMP rules.

The allocation of the list seats depends on whether the constituency part and the list part of the election are integrated or separate (on mixed systems see Shugart and Wattenberg 2003). In the first case, the system is known as a *compensatory* **mixed system** (sometimes the word compensatory is replaced by corrective or linked, and the system is also known as mixed-member proportional (MMP)). The list seats are awarded in such a way as to rectify the under-representations and over-representations created in the constituencies, ensuring that a party's overall number of seats (not just its list seats) is proportional to its vote share. Typically, small parties fare badly in the single-member constituencies, winning hardly any seats, but are brought up to their 'fair share' overall by receiving the appropriate number of list seats, while the larger parties, which usually win more than their 'fair share' in the constituencies, are awarded few or none of the list seats because their constituency seats alone bring them up to or close to the total number to which they are entitled. Compensatory mixed systems can thus result in highly proportional outcomes, though they are easy for parties to manipulate so as to produce distorted outcomes. Germany, New Zealand, and Venezuela are examples of this system (Saalfeld 2008; Vowles 2008).

If the list part and the constituency part of the election are separate, though, we have a *parallel mixed system* (sometimes termed mixed-member majoritarian (MMM)). Now, the list seats are awarded to parties purely on the basis of their list votes, without taking any account of what happened in the constituencies. This benefits large parties, which retain the over-representation they typically achieve in the constituencies, and offers less comfort to smaller ones than a compensatory system would. Parallel mixed systems are more widely employed than compensatory ones, with Japan and Mexico among the users (Reed 2008).

While virtually all PR systems use party lists somewhere along the line, the *single transferable vote* (STV) in multi-member constituencies (PR-STV) dispenses with them. This takes the logic of the alternative vote and applies it to multi-member constituencies. That is, as under AV, voters are able to rank all (or as many as they wish) of the candidates in order of their choice and yet, as under a PR system, the results will reflect a high degree of correspondence between the votes cast for a party's candidates and its share of the seats. Any explanation of how the votes are counted under PR-STV tends to make the system sound more complicated than it actually is, and examining a specific example is the best way to understand the mechanics (examples are given in Gallagher and Mitchell 2008: 594–6; Sinnott 2010: 117–24). In brief, if a voter's top-ranked candidate is so popular that he/she does not need the vote, or so unpopular that he/she cannot benefit from the vote, the vote is transferred to the candidate ranked second by the voter. Typically, because voters are party-oriented, they give their second preference to another candidate from the same party as their first-choice candidate.

PR-STV differs from list systems not only in voters' power to rank but also in that it does not presuppose the existence of parties or their salience in voters' minds: voters may rank candidates on the basis of whatever factor is most important to them, which might be (and in parliamentary elections usually is) party affiliation but could also be views on a particular issue, perceived parliamentary or ministerial ability, gender, locality, and so on. Thus voters can convey a lot of information about their attitudes towards the candidates, rather than having, in effect, to say 'yes' to one and 'no' to the rest as under most systems. The 'discreet charm' of PR-STV lies in the paradoxical combination of its popularity among students of electoral systems (see below) but its far from widespread use; only Ireland and Malta employ it to elect their national parliaments (Gallagher 2008*b*).

Dimensions of variation

There are many different electoral systems, but they vary in a limited number of dimensions. Three are particularly important. The first is *district magnitude*, by which is meant the number of MPs elected from each constituency. A second is the degree of *intra-party choice*, the extent to which voters are able to decide which of their party's candidates take the seats that the party wins. A third concerns the difficulty of winning seats, expressed through the idea of *thresholds*.

District magnitude

District magnitude varies from one in countries that employ single-member constituencies up to the size of the parliament when the whole country constitutes a single large constituency. The higher the average district magnitude, the more proportional we can expect the election result to be. When there are more seats to share out it is easier to achieve a 'fair' distribution, whereas when there is only one seat the largest party in the constituency takes it and the other parties receive nothing.

Intra-party choice

Much of the discussion so far has been about how seats are shared among parties, but some voters may be at least as interested in which particular individuals fill those seats. How much intra-party choice among candidates is provided by the electoral system? Under single-member constituency systems there is no intra-party choice for the simple reason that no party runs more than one candidate; if a voter likes a party but not its candidate, or likes a candidate but not her party, he simply has to grit his teeth and accept an unpalatable option.

Under PR systems, the degree of choice varies. Some list systems offer no intra-party choice; these are based on what are termed *closed lists*, where the party determines the order of its candidates' names on the list and the voters cannot overturn this. Under such a system, if a party wins, say, five seats in a constituency, those seats go to the first five names on its list, as decided by the party, whatever the voters think of those individuals. Closed lists are used in Israel, Italy, South Africa, and Spain, and in the overwhelming majority of countries that have mixed systems.

Other list systems, though, use **preferential** or open lists, in which the voters can indicate a preference for an individual candidate on their chosen party's list. In some cases the voters' preference votes alone determine which candidates win the seats; in others, it needs the preference votes of a certain number of voters to earn a candidate a seat ahead of someone whom the party placed higher on the list (Shugart 2008: 36–50). Belgium, Brazil, Chile, and Poland are examples of countries where the voters have an effective voice in determining which of their party's candidates become MPs (De Winter 2008; Siavelis 2008). In PR-STV, the voters have complete freedom to award rank-ordered preferences for any candidate, not just within parties but also across party lines.

Thus, under closed-list systems the key intra-party battle takes place at the candidate selection stage, since, in order to have a chance of election, aspiring MPs must ensure that the party gives them a high position on the list. Under preferential list systems and PR-STV, candidate selection is important but not all-important, because the voters decide which of the selected candidates are elected.

Thresholds

Usually, electoral systems contain some inbuilt feature designed to prevent very small parties from winning seats; this may be justified on the grounds that it is desirable to prevent undue fragmentation of parliamentary strength and to facilitate the formation of stable governments, though of course it can also be motivated simply by the desire of larger parties to discriminate against smaller ones.

A good example of a threshold is that employed in Slovakia, which as mentioned earlier has just one, national, constituency. This would make possible a very high degree of proportionality—except that the country also applies a 5 per cent threshold, meaning that no party that receives fewer votes than this wins any seats at all. At Slovakia's 2010 election, 16 per cent of voters cast a

ballot for a party that did not reach the threshold, and so they were unrepresented in parliament. Thresholds in the range of 3–5 per cent are common; that of the Netherlands is unusually low (0.67 per cent) and Russia's threshold, at 7 per cent, is unusually high.

Origins of electoral systems

Despite parties' obvious vested interest in electoral system choice, not all the electoral systems that countries use today result from a partisan battle. Some were, of course. For example, Australia's alternative vote electoral system was chosen in 1918 by the two centre-right parties, since it enabled them to continue as separate entities without splitting the centre-right vote and allowing the Labor party to win. In other countries, such as France, Greece and Italy, the electoral system is periodically changed by the party in power in order to benefit itself and damage its opponents.

In other countries, though, there was a degree of consensus behind the initial selection of an electoral system, and partisan motives alone do not always determine the stances taken by parties on adoption or reform of the electoral system (Rahat 2011; Renwick 2010). This is true of Denmark and Finland, for example, and helps to explain why the electoral systems of both countries have lasted since the early twentieth century. In other countries again, the electoral system was never consciously 'chosen'; in the US and the UK, for example, it evolved and became the electoral system at a time when there was no awareness of the options that could have been considered. If there is a long-term trend, it is in the direction of a move away from majoritarian systems and towards PR, which is especially pronounced in Europe (Caramani 2000: 48, 58–63).

Consequences of electoral systems

The most widely studied aspect lies in the impact of electoral systems upon party systems (Lijphart 1994). In the 1950s the French political scientist Maurice Duverger coined what has become known as 'Duverger's law'. In essence, he argued that the single-member plurality system was associated with a two-party system and that PR was associated with multiparty systems (for fuller discussion see Box 13.3); of course, any impact may be visible only over the course of several elections (Best 2012). As many people, including Duverger, have observed, the causal relationship also runs the other way round; that is, the parties in a two-party system may retain the existing SMP system in order to pre-empt the growth of rivals, while if a multiparty system emerges under SMP, as happened in several European countries in the early twentieth century, they may agree to move to PR in order to produce mutually assured survival.

The impact upon party systems has a knock-on effect upon government formation. When disproportionality is low and parliamentary strength is fragmented, as typically occurs under PR systems, the likelihood of any one party winning an overall majority is lower than under a non-PR system. Consequently, under archetypal PR systems, such as those in Belgium or Finland, the prospect of single-party government, let alone single-party majority government, is unthinkable.

Other consequences of electoral systems are not so easy to quantify. Proponents of PR argue that it tends to produce parliaments that are more representative socio-demographically, as well as politically, than other parliaments. This is partly because under PR parties need to nominate a 'ticket' or list containing a number of candidates, and they normally take good care to ensure that this is a balanced ticket so as to ensure its wide appeal. Gender representativeness is the easiest aspect to measure, and on average there are more female MPs in PR countries than in non-PR countries (Norris 2004). However, there can be wide variation among countries with similar electoral systems, highlighting the role of other factors.

Electoral systems might also have an impact on the way in which MPs behave, as was discussed in Chapter 7. Here, we can expect the main variation to be not between PR and non-PR systems, but between those systems under which voters do and do not have a choice of candidate from their preferred party. In the former (open-list PR or PR-STV) candidates of each party are, in effect, competing with each other for preference votes from the electorate. In the latter (closed-list or single-member constituency systems) voters are unable to express a view on individual candidates but simply have to take the list (a one-person list in single-member constituency systems) as the party offers it to them. Thus, we would expect MPs in the first category to pay more attention to constituency service than those in the second. There is some evidence of this and, in addition, the proportion of locally born and presumably locally oriented MPs is higher in open-list and PR-STV countries than in closed-list countries (Gallagher 2008*a*: 557–62; Shugart *et al.* 2005). At the same time, though, political culture also plays a part in determining the behaviour of MPs; for example, MPs in Britain and France, as well as their voters, see constituency work as an important part of the MP's role and accordingly engage in it extensively, even though they are not subject to competition with running mates for votes.

Which system is best depends, of course, on what we want from an electoral system (Gallagher 2008*a*: 566–75; Katz 1997: 278–310). The main choice any electoral system designer has to make is between a PR and a non-PR system. PR systems are usually supported on the grounds that they produce a parliament that accurately represents the people's preferences: can elections really be considered democratic unless the distribution of seats among parties closely reflects the way people voted? PR ensures that no party will be hugely over-represented and that no significant group of voters will be left under-represented. Any danger of excessive fragmentation can be averted by adjusting variables such as the threshold or the district magnitude.

Supporters of non-PR systems stress the greater likelihood that these will lead to a two-party system and argue the merits of this (see Box 13.2), such as stable effective government rather than multiparty coalition and the opportunity for voters to eject a government from office. Those who study electoral systems tend to prefer mixed systems or PR-STV (Bowler *et al.* 2005)—but the political actors who choose electoral systems may not seek advice from academics.

KEY POINTS

- The most basic distinction among electoral systems is between those based on single-member constituencies (non-PR systems) and those based on PR in multi-member constituencies.

- Single-member constituency systems all give an advantage to the strongest party in the constituency and leave supporters of other parties unrepresented.

- The main categories of PR systems are list systems, mixed systems, and the single transferable vote. PR systems can be made more proportional by using constituencies of larger district magnitude and by lowering or removing the threshold.

- PR systems vary in the degree of choice that they give voters to express a choice among their party's candidates. Non-PR systems do not give voters any intra-party choice.

- Non-PR electoral systems are more likely to engender a two-party system, especially as regards the distribution of seats, while PR systems are more likely to lead to a multiparty system, though the shape of the party system also depends on other factors such as the nature of the politicized cleavages in society.

Referendums

Government today is representative government, meaning that the great majority of political decisions in all countries are taken by elected officials rather than directly by the people themselves. Nonetheless, some countries employ the device of the referendum, in which the people are able to vote on some issue.

We should be clear that this does not amount to 'direct democracy', a much-used but vague term. Rather, it is simply a question of whether a given country's system of basically representative government does or does not include provision for the referendum. The term 'direct democracy' has its roots in the idea that, under the institutions of representative government, the people's role in decision-making is only indirect, in that they elect representatives who then make the decisions. When the referendum is used, it seems that the people are making the decisions themselves. However, 'direct democracy' has many connotations, both positive and negative, so scholars tend to give the phrase a wide berth and instead analyse the referendum as an institution within the framework of representative democracy.

Types of referendum

In a referendum, as Butler and Ranney (1994: 1) usefully define the term, 'a mass electorate votes on some public issue'. The most useful typology designed to impose some order upon the potential chaos of a large number of referendums is that of Uleri (1996*a*; 2003: 85–109). While we do not have space to elaborate the full typology, three of the dimensions it identifies are particularly important.

First, a referendum might be mandatory in the circumstances, or optional. For example, the referendums in Denmark and Ireland in 1972 on whether to join the European Community were mandatory because both countries' constitutions specified the necessity for a referendum on an issue with such major implications for sovereignty, whereas the French and Dutch referendums of 2005 on the proposed EU constitution were optional in that it was not legally or constitutionally necessary that a referendum be held. When referendums are optional, the device is open to partisan manipulation, for example by a government that decides to put an issue to a referendum in the hope of boosting its position or dividing the opposition.

Second, the referendum may take place at the request of either a number of voters, in which case we term it the **initiative**, or a political institution. The distinctive feature of a people's initiative is clear: it enables a set number of voters to bring about a popular vote. The initiative is conspicuous by its rarity in the world's constitutions, though those few states that employ it do so on a large scale. Switzerland leads the way here, with most of its popular votes being initiated by voters; if a prescribed number (which varies from 50,000 to 100,000 depending on the nature of the proposal) signs a petition calling for a vote on amending the constitution or rejecting a bill recently passed by parliament, such a vote must take place. Italy is the only other West European country to allow the initiative, and while the engaged citizenry brought about many popular votes in the 1980s and 1990s, the use of this weapon against the political class—for that was how many of these initiatives were perceived—has since declined. A number of post-communist countries have provision for the initiative in their constitutions, but the difficulty of mobilizing the population in most of these countries means that the initiative has not become significant. The initiative is also a prominent feature of state-level politics in parts of the US, especially the south-west.

Third, there is a distinction between *decision-promoting* and *decision-controlling* referendums. Provision for the former is rare; so-called 'plebiscitarian' referendums, where an authoritarian leader makes a proposal and then calls a popular vote to endorse this, belong in this category, examples being the referendums held in France by Napoleon and Louis Napoleon, or more recently in some post-communist countries such as Belarus and Turkmenistan on extending the rule of the incumbent president. Decision-controlling referendums, where an actor opposed to some proposal may invoke the people as a potential veto player, are more common. Here we may distinguish between abrogative referendums or initiatives (which aim to strike down an existing law or constitutional provision) and rejective ones (which aim to prevent some proposal from passing into law or the constitution). Switzerland has a widely used provision for the rejective initiative, under which, within ninety days of parliament's approval of a bill, 50,000 citizens may launch a challenge to it by calling a popular vote. Italy provides for the abrogative initiative, allowing citizens to call a vote on any existing law. In some other countries a minority of parliamentarians (as in Denmark or Spain) or a number of regional councils (as in Italy) may call a rejective referendum on certain proposals.

The rationale of the referendum

Why use referendums? There are, of course, cases for and against, yet on the whole the evidence is strangely inconclusive and suggests that neither supporters nor sceptics are on secure ground when they try to make a general case about referendums. We can categorize the arguments as related to process or to outcome. Process-related arguments suggest that, regardless of the decisions reached, the very fact that they have been reached through a referendum is important in itself, while outcome-related arguments suggest that the quality of decisions may be affected by the direct involvement of the voters (see Box 10.2). On the whole, supporters of referendums are more likely to invoke process-related arguments while opponents tend to emphasize the impact on outcomes.

Process-related arguments

The two main process arguments are, first, that certain policies can be fully legitimated only by their endorsement in a referendum and, second, that participation in a referendum is good in itself and also educates voters about issues.

The legitimation argument rests on the fact that at elections individual voters are influenced by many factors. Simply because a party includes a particular policy promise in its manifesto, we cannot conclude that anyone who votes for a candidate of this party necessarily wants to see that policy implemented. The policy may not have

Box 10.2 Referendums: arguments for and against

Arguments for the referendum	Arguments against the referendum
The referendum enhances democracy by enabling more people to become directly involved in decision-making.	Elected politicians have an expertise in policy-making that ordinary people do not, so taking decision-making out of the hands of political representatives is likely to lead to lower-quality decisions.
Because of the way policies are bundled together at elections, only by holding a referendum on an issue is it possible to get a clear verdict from the people on that issue.	In practice, many people decide how to vote in a referendum on the basis of extraneous factors, so we cannot draw inferences about policy preferences from voting behaviour in a referendum.
A decision made by the people directly has more legitimacy than one made by the political class alone, especially if the issue is a fundamental one for the future of society.	Referendums give insensitive or prejudiced majorities an opportunity to ride roughshod over minority rights
The referendum process creates a more informed electorate as people are exposed to arguments on either side of the issue.	Those most likely to vote in a referendum are those who feel most strongly on an issue and the better off, so referendums work against the interests of moderates and the less well off.
All the evidence suggests that the referendum, sensibly used, can enhance representative democracy.	The use of referendums opens the door to the prospect of a 'direct democracy' in which people cast votes on the 'issue of the day' without taking the trouble to inform themselves, thus trivializing the decision-making process.

affected their vote at all, or they may have voted for the party despite rather than because of this particular policy. Consequently, opponents of a policy might claim that the government has no explicit mandate for it.

Hence, it is argued, we can only be sure that the people are in favour of a particular policy if they have actually endorsed it in a referendum. While no one except a referendum fanatic would suggest that this kind of validation process is needed for every piece of legislation or government decision, the argument has special force in the case of major choices facing a society: whether to join a transnational body such as the European Union (EU), whether to secede from an existing state and become independent, or whether to make a significant change to the political institutional regime or to the moral ethos of society. In these cases many voters may feel that elites do not have the right to make such decisions on their behalf. The case for a referendum is even stronger if the proposal is one that did not feature prominently in the preceding election or that, if implemented, would be more or less irreversible.

For example, fourteen of the nineteen countries that joined the EU between 1973 and 2004 held a referendum to decide whether to join, while Norway's people decided against joining in two referendums. The secessions of Norway from Sweden in 1905, Iceland from Denmark in 1944, East Timor from Indonesia in 1999, and Montenegro from Serbia in 2006 were all put to, and approved in, referendums. The proposed adoption or fundamental alteration of a new constitution is sometimes decided by referendum, as in Egypt (both 2011 and 2012), France (1958), Kenya (2010), and Spain (1978).

The second process-related argument is that the opportunity to vote in referendums increases political participation, which is inherently a good thing. The use of referendums might be able to reduce feelings of disengagement from the political process by involving people directly in decision-making. Citizens may respond to this empowerment by educating and informing themselves about the subject, thus raising the level of political knowledge in society. Yet, it would be facile to imagine that unleashing a tranche of referendums on an indifferent populace will somehow create an engaged citizenry. Unless electors regard the issues at stake as important, they are unlikely to make the effort to vote.

Outcome-related arguments

Giving people more chances to take part in decision-making is cited as an argument in favour of referendums, but there is also a counter-argument. As Papadopoulos puts it, increasing the number of opportunities to participate also increases the opportunities for exclusion, and hence the use of referendums may lead to worse outcomes than purely representative democracy (quoted in Uleri 1996*a*: 17). If those of lower socio-economic status are the least likely to vote in referendums— as some data suggest, though the pattern is not universal (Qvortrup

2005: 31–5)—then the use of referendums could work against the interests of the less well off.

Another outcome-related related argument is the claim that, because the referendum is an inherently majoritarian device, it might result in infringement of the rights of minorities. Legislators, it is argued, are aware of the need for balance and for toleration even of groups whose behaviour they personally disapprove of. In contrast, the mass public, which bases its opinions on information fed to it by partisan sources or gleaned via the simplistic coverage of the tabloid press and their broadcasting equivalents, has no inhibitions about giving free rein to its prejudices in the privacy of the ballot box. As James Bryce summed up this line of thought, parliamentarians 'may be ignorant, but not so ignorant as the masses' (quoted in Gallagher 1996: 241). The Swiss referendum of November 2009, when the people voted by 57 to 43 per cent to ban the building of any more minarets in Switzerland, might be cited as an example by proponents of this view.

However, empirical evidence from the US suggests that the key factor is not the mode of decision-making but the size of the unit making the decision: minority rights receive less protection in small local units than at state level (because the former are more likely to be homogeneous) regardless of whether the decision is made by referendum or by elected representatives, but there is no sign that referendums *per se* discriminate against minorities (Donovan and Bowler 1998: 264–70).

Moreover, there is often room for normative debate as to whether a particular decision amounts to unfair and discriminatory treatment of a minority or whether it is simply a perfectly legitimate choice by a majority of the voters. As defenders of the latter position are wont to say, majorities have rights too. Representative government is often criticized for being unduly responsive to pressure from well-organized and sometimes well-resourced minorities, who secure concessions at the expense of the public weal, and referendums could help to counter this. Still, unbridled use of the referendum does have the potential to upset what may be a delicate balance within society, and consequently, in most states employing it, there are devices to curb the danger of majoritarianism.

1. In most countries access to the referendum is highly restricted. Usually, it is the legislature that decides whether, and on what proposal(s), a vote is to take place, so it has control over the items that get onto the referendum agenda in the first place.

2. In countries that provide for the initiative, where a certain number of voters themselves can trigger a public vote without needing the consent of parliament, a judicial body such as a constitutional court frequently has a veto role. Such bodies have been active in Italy and in a number of post-communist countries. Courts also play an important role in the US, possessing the power (regularly used) to strike proposals from the ballot paper or, *post hoc*, to nullify the outcome of a vote on the basis that its implementation would be contrary to the state or federal constitution (Tolbert *et al.* 1998: 50–3; Magleby 1994: 235–6).

3. In federal countries, a 'double majority' is a common requirement: a proposal requires the support of a majority of voters and also a majority within at least half of the federal units (Australia, Switzerland).

The outcome-related arguments, then, are largely critical of the referendum, but for the most part they are not convincing. The process-related arguments tend to be cited primarily by advocates of the referendum, but here too there is plenty of room for debate. The fact that it is impossible to point to clinching arguments on one side or the other helps to explain why there is such variation across the world in the use of the referendum, as we shall now see.

Empirical patterns

The use of referendums is widespread, albeit uneven. Legal and constitutional provision increased somewhat in the last three decades of the twentieth century (Scarrow 2003: 48) and the frequency of referendums is also increasing over time (LeDuc 2003: 21). Even so, we should not exaggerate their use. Of the forty-four countries included in Table 10.1, eighteen have held two or fewer referendums since 1945. Switzerland is responsible for nearly half of the total number, and leaving it and its tiny neighbour Liechtenstein aside, the other countries have held on average only nine popular votes each over this period.

The variation in the frequency of referendums is striking. Some established democracies have held no national referendums at all (post-war Germany, India, Japan, the US) or very few (Netherlands, Spain, the UK). In some others, such as Australia, Denmark, France, Ireland, and New Zealand, the referendum has become established as a means by which the country reaches decisions on major questions. In others again, a large and disparate range of issues, some major and some more or less trivial, have been put to a vote of the public; Switzerland and, to a lesser extent, Italy and Liechtenstein epitomize this pattern.

Explaining the variations is not easy. Worldwide, the largest countries make little use of the referendum, but within Europe large countries such as France and Italy are regular users. Some federal countries eschew the referendum, while others such as Australia and Switzerland embrace it. There are apparent cases of diffusion, or common roots, of patterns between neighbouring countries, such as Switzerland and Liechtenstein, yet there is significant variation among the Scandinavian countries, which generally keep a close eye on each other's experiences.

Table 10.1 National referendums 1945–2012 in selected countries

Country	Number of referendums	Country	Number of referendums
Australia	29	Latvia	10
Austria	2	Liechtenstein	80
Argentina	1	Lithuania	20
Belgium	1	Luxembourg	1
Brazil	9	Malta	3
Canada	1	Mexico	0
Chile	6	Netherlands	1
Cyprus	2	New Zealand	36
Czech Republic	1	Norway	2
Denmark	18	Poland	7
Estonia	4	Portugal	4
Finland	1	Russia	6
France	14	Slovakia	15
Germany	0	Slovenia	23
Greece	4	South Africa	0
Hungary	12	Spain	4
Iceland	8	Sweden	5
India	0	Switzerland	432
Ireland	34	Turkey	6
Israel	0	UK	2
Italy	73	US	0
Japan	0	Uruguay	21
		Total	898

Notes: In cases of countries that have not been continuous democracies since 1945, the period covered is the time during which they were democracies. All figures refer to national-level referendums only.

Source: Website of the Research Centre on Direct Democracy (C2D); see web links at the end of the chapter.

The dramatic contrast between Switzerland and every other country represents a qualitative as well as a quantitative difference. Elsewhere, democracy is fundamentally representative in nature, and the referendum is a kind of 'optional extra' that modifies, to a greater or lesser degree, the way in which the political process functions. In Switzerland, in contrast, the referendum is woven deep into the fabric of democracy, and far from constituting an occasional 'shock to the system' it is an inherent part of that system.

Referendum subjects, outside Switzerland, do not usually cover the full range of political issues. In particular, conventional left–right issues such as the familiar tax-versus-spending trade-off, which usually underlie the party system, rarely feature on referendum ballots. More characteristically, as already mentioned, referendum votes concern sovereignty-related questions such as independence, secession, or closer integration within the EU. The rationale is that these are non-partisan issues that transcend the day-to-day political warfare between parties and that the parties do not have the right to decide on the people's behalf.

Voting behaviour at referendums

A central argument in favour of referendums is that they allow the people to decide directly on the resolution of some important issue. This argument would be weakened if it transpired that, in practice, many people's voting behaviour is determined not by their views on the issue at stake but by peripheral or extraneous questions. Allegations to this effect were heard in the summer of 2005, when the people of France and the Netherlands rejected the proposed EU constitutional treaty. Critics of the referendum suggested that many of the 'No' voters had not been voting on the substantive issue at all but had allowed themselves to be swayed by irrelevancies. Some, it was said, had voted against because of a fear of the 'Polish plumber' who stood for the threat supposedly posed by low-cost Eastern European labour, while others had taken the opportunity to strike a blow at the unpopular political establishment by rejecting one of its most cherished proposals.

More broadly, the academic literature in this area has implied two 'ideal-type' interpretations of referendum voting behaviour. According to one point of view, sometimes termed the *issue-voting perspective*, voters decide mainly on the basis of the issue on the ballot paper. According to the other, sometimes termed the *second-order election perspective*, voters take little notice of that issue and instead cast a vote according to what really matters to them, i.e. their evaluation of the actors on each side, especially the government; if they dislike the government of the day they will vote against pretty much any proposition that it puts to a referendum.

The reality, as most people would expect, is somewhere between the two ideal-type interpretations. That is to say, voters take into account a range of factors: they do assign a lot of importance to the substantive issue itself, but they are also interested in knowing about who its proponents and opponents are. Other things being equal, a proposal advocated by a popular government will of course fare better than one advanced by an unpopular one, but that is not to say that voters do not give primacy to the question on the ballot paper. It may be that the more intense the campaign, the greater is the voters' focus on the substantive issue (Marsh 2007; Binzer Hobolt 2009: 107). The role of campaign finance is also uncertain, and there is surprising variation in the extent to which this is regulated cross-nationally (Gilland Lutz and Hug 2010). The combination of attitudes towards the substantive issue, and the influence of other factors such as discontent with the domestic socio-economic situation, was seen clearly in the French and Dutch referendums on the proposed EU constitution (Hainsworth 2006; Nijeboer 2005).

Whether this adds up to an argument for holding more referendums on the EU, or for holding none at all, is a question that divides students of the EU. It is difficult to answer many of the questions to which we would like to know the answers, such as whether the pace of European integration would have been more rapid if there had been fewer referendums on the subject (Hobolt 2009: 242–8)—and if we did know the answer to that, it would simply raise the normative question of whether this should be seen as an argument for or against the use of referendums on European integration.

Referendum turnout is usually lower than in parliamentary elections, but it varies quite markedly depending mainly on how important the issue is (Kobach 2001; LeDuc 2003: 169–72). For example, in New Zealand 83 per cent of voters turned out in a 1993 referendum on changing the electoral system, whereas two years later only 28 per cent voted on a question concerning the number of firefighters who should be employed. General election turnout, in contrast, is much more stable.

Similarly, campaign effects can be much greater in referendums than in general elections. If the issue is of low salience for most voters and has not been extensively politicized before the campaign begins, the campaign has scope to make a major impact and we may see large shifts of opinion as it proceeds. When the reverse applies, there is typically no more volatility than during an election campaign. If a large swing occurs, it is likely to be in a negative direction. Characteristically, the process is one whereby voters initially incline to a 'soft Yes' (in other words, they like the sound of the proposal in principle), but opponents are able to conjure up the 'fear of the abyss' (Darcy and Laver 1990). They raise a host of objections and doubts, so even if voters are by no means sure that the dire warnings really are valid, they still feel it would be safer to maintain the status quo.

The impact of referendums

Referendums might make a significant difference to politics in a number of ways, most obviously to policy outcomes. Here we could expect it to have a conservative impact, in that the people are brought into the decision-making process as an additional 'veto player'. A policy change agreed by the elite can potentially be prevented unless the people also approve it. Therefore critics warn of the danger of policy immobilism if the referendum is too readily available as a blocking mechanism, asking

whether any of the main advances of the past, such as extending the franchise to those with little property and to women, or the establishment of religious freedom, would have occurred had the eligible voters of the day been able to prevent it by a direct vote on the issue. Defenders argue that this is exaggerated, and that the endorsement of the voters is 'a powerful legitimiser of political decisions', depriving the outvoted minority of any sense that they have a valid grievance (Setälä 1999: 161). Major decisions involving sovereignty, or the allocation of values within a society, might not be regarded as fully legitimate by opponents if they are taken solely by the political class. Testing these propositions empirically—that policy innovation is slower in countries that employ the referendum, and that decisions made by a referendum enjoy greater legitimacy than those made by representative institutions alone—would of course be a challenge.

Where the initiative is available, the danger is of too much rather than too little policy innovation. Minorities might be able to get their superficially attractive but essentially populist schemes approved by a public that does not take the trouble to scrutinize them thoroughly or to ask how they will be funded, whereas elected parliamentarians would not be so gullible. This is a particular concern of elite theorists of democracy such as Giovanni Sartori, who refers to the 'cognitive incompetence' of most citizens, and of others who attribute great power to those who control the media and see referendums as merely 'devices for the political mobilization of opinion-fed masses by the elite' (Sartori 1987: 120; Hirst 1990: 33). However, some of the arguments against allowing ordinary people to make decisions through referendums virtually amount to arguments against allowing people to vote at all. Moreover, the picture of voter incompetence can be disputed; even if voters do not possess comprehensive information about the case for and against the referendum issue, they may have acquired as much information as they actually need (Lupia and Johnston 2001). In addition, contrary to the claims that the media can exert power over easily led voters, overt attempts by the media to sway opinion may prove counterproductive (Aboura 2005).

Finally, what about the impact of referendums on the quality of democracy? As indicated earlier, it is possible to construct plausible arguments to the effect that the use of the referendum will greatly enhance, or greatly damage, the functioning of democracy. Yet the final verdict is that the quality of democracy seems to be little affected one way or the other by the incidence of referendums. The standard of democracy does not seem to differ so very much between Denmark (with eighteen post-war referendums) and Finland (one), or between France (fourteen) and Germany (zero). It is difficult to find countries whose people feel their quality of democracy has been ruined by either the existence or the non-existence of referendums. Public attitudes, as far as we can tell, are broadly supportive (Dalton 2004: 182–4; Donovan and Karp 2006).

The referendum, then, is entirely compatible with the institutions of representative government. It is not an essential feature of a system of representative democracy but is, rather, an 'optional extra'. In the minds of some of its more fervent proponents and opponents, it might become the cornerstone of governance, transforming representative democracy into direct democracy, with citizens texting in their votes on the 'issue of the day' as they might for the winner of a TV talent show. This is not a realistic vision. Representative government has established itself across the developed world, and the evidence suggests that the referendum can play a significant role within it.

KEY POINTS

- Referendums take many forms, depending on whether or not the people themselves can initiate a popular vote, on whether parliament has discretion as to whether to decide a matter itself or put the issue to a referendum, and on whether the verdict of the people is binding or merely advisory.

- Supporters argue that referendums give the people the chance to make important decisions themselves and that being exposed to a referendum campaign increases people's information about the issue. Opponents maintain that referendums may discriminate against minorities and can result in incoherent policy choices.

- The frequency of referendums is rising over time, though they are still rare events in most countries.

- When people decide which way to vote in a referendum, their views on the issue at stake are usually the most important factor, but they also take some account of cues from parties and politicians.

- Despite the fears of opponents and the hopes of proponents, there is little firm evidence to show that policy outcomes are affected greatly by the availability of referendums.

Conclusion

In this chapter we have looked at the two main voting opportunities in modern democracies: elections and referendums. Elections are central to any political system that claims to be democratic, while referendums, in contrast, are used extensively in some countries yet rarely or never in others.

Electoral regulations, the set of rules governing the holding of elections, tend to be quite similar among democracies, though there are some variations when it comes to the age at which one can vote or be a candidate, the ease of

access to the ballot, and the term of office of elected representatives. The franchise was broadened steadily during the nineteenth and twentieth centuries, and the main debate now concerns not whether certain categories of citizens should be allowed to vote but, rather, whether people should be compelled to vote. Some argue that compulsory voting leads to more equitable policy outputs; others see it as an infringement of personal rights.

Electoral systems, the set of rules that structure how votes are cast at elections and how these votes are then converted into the allocation of offices, have the potential to play a significant role in influencing a country's political system. While there is a good deal of variation across countries, we have seen that electoral systems can be grouped into two main categories, PR and non-PR. Proportional representation systems provide a closer relationship between the distributions of votes and of seats, and are associated with multiparty systems; non-PR systems are more likely to produce single-party governments and something approaching a two-party system.

When we look at referendums we find a good deal of variation, not only in the frequency of use but in the kind of referendum. Some are initiated by the voters themselves, others by governments or parliaments. Some are held because the country's constitution prescribes that a referendum is necessary before a particular step can be taken; others are held at the whim of a government that hopes to derive some partisan advantage from the vote. Some are decisive, others merely advisory. While referendum issues can also cover a wide range, certain issues do seem to be regarded as especially suitable for popular votes: those concerning sovereignty, for example, or moral issues that cut across party lines.

The merits and demerits of referendums have been vigorously argued for many decades. One line of criticism casts doubt on voters' competence to reach a conclusion on the issues placed before them, suggesting that they are easily manipulated and tend to vote primarily on the basis of their attitude to the government of the day. The evidence does not support this, though undoubtedly voters' behaviour is affected by their evaluations of those arguing the case for and against the referendum issue. Referendums undoubtedly increase participation in the decision-making process, though proponents and opponents disagree as to whether this a good thing; for the former, it results in a more informed electorate, while for the latter it places decisions in the hands of those ill-equipped to make them. Proponents argue that a vote by the people legitimizes a decision in a way that a vote by parliament never could; opponents are concerned about the dangers of intolerant majorities trampling over the rights of minorities. The available evidence suggests that the hopes of proponents and the fears of opponents may both be exaggerated.

The two institutions are linked in that the significance of elections may be reduced when referendums are available to opponents of government measures. When there are no referendums, elections have a greater potential to be a decisive arena, since they produce governments whose proposals cannot be blocked by a popular vote. In a country where major issues must be put to the people in a referendum, in contrast, elections settle less; the people retain veto power in certain areas regardless of the wishes of the government or parliament. If the opposition has the power to trigger a rejective referendum, the government has a strong incentive to make whatever concessions are necessary to prevent this from happening. Where there is provision for the initiative, the opposition has a further weapon to block the government, and the link between 'winning' an election and being able to impose one's policy preferences becomes even weaker.

Questions

1. Should voting be made compulsory in modern democracies? What would be the main consequences of compulsory voting?

2. Do electoral systems shape party systems, or do party systems choose the electoral system that suits them?

3. What are the main consequences of electoral systems?

4. Taking any country as an example, what difference would we expect to see in its politics if it changed from a PR electoral system to a non-PR system, or vice versa?

5. Should the power of a sufficient number of ordinary citizens to initiate public votes, which at present is confined to a few countries, be given to people in every country?

6. Are there certain subjects that are especially suitable, and certain subjects that are especially unsuitable, to be put to the people for decision by referendum?

7. Why is the referendum widely used in some democracies and rarely or never used in others?

8. How real is the danger that referendums will result in majorities infringing the rights of minorities?

9. Does the use of the referendum result in better policies than would be made without it?

10. Does the use of referendums threaten representative democracy, enhance it, or have little impact either way?

Further reading

Auer, A. and Bützer, M. (eds) (2001) *Direct Democracy: The Eastern and Central European Experience* (Aldershot: Ashgate). Overview of the post-communist experience.

Bowler, S. and Donovan, T. (1998) *Demanding Choices: Opinion, Voting, and Direct Democracy* (Ann Arbor, MI: University of Michigan Press). Overview of the US experience.

Colomer, J. (ed.) (2004) *Handbook of Electoral System Choice* (Basingstoke: Palgrave Macmillan). Comparative analysis of the origins of electoral systems.

Farrell, D. M. (2010) *Electoral Systems: A Comparative Introduction* (2nd edn) (Basingstoke: Palgrave Macmillan).

Gallagher, M. and Mitchell, P. (eds) (2008) *The Politics of Electoral Systems* (Oxford: Oxford University Press).

Gallagher, M. and Uleri, P. V. (eds) (1996) *The Referendum Experience in Europe* (Basingstoke: Macmillan).

LeDuc, L. (2003) *The Politics of Direct Democracy: Referendums in Global Perspective* (Peterborough, Ontario: Broadview Press).

Lijphart, A. (1994) *Electoral Systems and Party Systems: A Study of Twenty-Seven Democracies, 1945–1990* (Oxford: Oxford University Press).

Qvortrup, M. (2005) *A Comparative Study of Referendums: Government by the People* (2nd edn) (Manchester: Manchester University Press).

Setälä, M. (1999) *Referendums and Democratic Government: Normative Theory and the Analysis of Institutions* (Basingstoke: Macmillan).

Shugart, M. S. and Wattenberg, M. P. (eds) (2003) *Mixed-Member Electoral Systems: The Best of Both Worlds?* (Oxford: Oxford University Press).

Web links

www.electiondataarchive.org
This is the most complete archive of electoral results since the development of democratic systems worldwide with data at the level of single constituencies and a thorough documentation.

psephos.adam-carr.net/
Adam Carr's site, based in Melbourne, describing itself as 'the largest, most comprehensive and most up-to-date archive of electoral information in the world, with election statistics from 182 countries'.

aceproject.org/
Site of the 'Electoral Knowledge Network' with information on every country's electoral system.

http://www.ipu.org/parline-e/parlinesearch.asp
Site of Inter-Parliamentary Union's Parline database, with information on each member country's electoral system and electoral rules, plus links to national parliaments.

www.unc.edu/~asreynol/ballots.html
Andrew Reynolds's site at University of North Carolina, with ballot papers from over 100 countries, showing the choices and constraints facing voters in different countries.

www.tcd.ie/Political_Science/staff/michael.gallagher/ ElSystems/index.php
Site with data on indices of disproportionality and party system fragmentation at elections in over 120 countries, plus information on electoral systems and downloadable files for calculation of indices.

www.c2d.ch/
Site of the Research Centre on Direct Democracy (C2D), with data on past referendums worldwide and news about forthcoming ones.

www.iandrinstitute.org
Site of Initiative and Referendum Institute at the University of Southern California, Los Angeles: news and information about referendums (and research on them) across the US.

online resource centre

For additional material and resources, please visit the Online Resource Centre at:
www.oxfordtextbooks.co.uk/orc/caramani3e/

CHAPTER 11

Federal and local government institutions

John Loughlin

Chapter contents

Reader's guide

The nation-state is the quintessentially modern form of political organization in which nations are meant to be coterminous with states. The territorial organization of nation-states may be either federal or unitary, although each of these categories may be further categorized as being either more or less decentralized. Therefore comparing territorial governance across states means constructing elaborate typologies. The welfare states of the post-war period represent the culmination of the nation-state-building process and tended to emphasize central control over sub-national levels of government. However, this has been changing since the 1980s, and sub-national authorities are today much less centrally regulated even if they still largely operate within the legal and constitutional structures of their national states. Nevertheless, the current period is characterized by a much greater complexity than was the case during the old welfare state period.

Introduction

Contemporary territorial governance means the territorial organization of the nation-state, the quintessentially 'modern' form of political organization. Before the nation-state, there existed other forms of political organization: the Holy Roman Empire, city-states like Florence and Venice, city-leagues the Hanseatic League, and various types of ecclesiastical organization—bishoprics and abbeys and, indeed, the papacy itself (Spruyt 1994).

The nation-state has not gone unchallenged, and in recent years there have been predictions of its demise (Ohmae 1995; Guéhenno 1995) because of pressures from above—globalization and, in Europe, the growth of the European Union (see Chapters 24 and 23, respectively)—and from below— the rise of regions and local authorities as political actors. The importance of these factors may have been exaggerated and it is premature to write the obituary of the nation-state, but there is little doubt that it has changed significantly. One could speak of its 'transformation' in several important ways (Loughlin 2004a). If the nation-state has meant a certain form of territorial governance, then its transformation will have important consequences for the latter.

This chapter will explore the ways in which territorial governance has been understood and implemented within the nation-state model as well as how it may be affected by these transformations. The classical distinction has been between 'federal' and 'unitary' states but, as we shall see, the realities today are much more complex.

KEY POINTS

- The nation-state is the quintessentially modern form of political organization with distinctive features of territorial organization.
- Claims that it is disappearing have been exaggerated.
- The classical distinction between 'federal' and 'uitary' states is giving way to more complex forms of the nation-state.

The modern nation-state and territorial governance

The modern nation-state

The modern international state system originated with the Treaty of Westphalia in 1648, but the territorial forms of the modern state came about as a result of a series of revolutions in the eighteenth century. From the English constitutional and industrial revolutions emerged the United Kingdom of Great Britain and Ireland, built on a series of Acts of Union between England and the other three nations—the multinational 'Union' state. The American Revolution created the United States, first as a 'confederal' then as a 'federal' state, the first in the modern world. The French Revolution which began in 1789 produced the 'unitary' state *par excellence,* characterized by 'unity and indivisibility' (Hayward 1983; Loughlin 2007b). Each of these state forms—union, federal, and unitary—would be imitated by almost all other modern nation-states. The French Revolution left another legacy to political thought and practice: nationalism, an ideology built on the assumption that nations ought to have states and states ought to be coterminous with nations (Alter 1994; Guibernau 1996).

Unitary states and nationalism

The French model of the unitary state was imposed by Napoleon I in the Netherlands, Spain, and Portugal. However, the French Revolution also produced nationalism in reaction to these conequests. Nationalism was the driving force behind the unification of politically fragmented territories such as Germany and Italy, as well as the break-up of empires such as the Austro-Hungarian, Ottoman, British, and French. Liberalism, especially in Catholic southern Europe, was associated with both nationalism and a strong centralized state capable of wresting control over education and social welfare from the church.

The much diversified states of the Italian peninsula were unified between 1860 and 1870 in a movement known as the *Risorgimento,* under the leadership of the Piedmontese Camillo Cavour, who became the first prime minister of a unified Italy. Although there were voices in favour of a decentralized federalist model, in the end the new unified monarchy chose the French model precisely in order to overcome this diversity.

Germany, for its part, was no less fragmented than Italy, but German nationalists were divided between those who followed Herder in defining nationhood in linguistic and cultural terms, and therefore wished to see a *Großdeutschland* (Greater Germany) and those liberals who were influenced by the French concept of civic nationalism, who were more in favour of a *Kleindeutschland* (Smaller Germany). The German-speaking lands, made up of many political entities from kingdoms to bishoprics, were also religiously divided between a Protestant north dominated by Prussia and a Catholic south dominated by Austria. This complexity led to ambiguities about what a German nation-state might look like and whether it should be federalist or unitary. The federalist tradition is probably the older one but, during the democratic Weimar Republic and the Nazi Third Reich, the model of the unitary nation-state was adopted, which, under the Nazis, evolved into a totalitarian state under the control of the Führer and the Nazi Party. This eventually led to the catastrophe of the Second World War.

Other states which opted for the French model were Albania, which became independent in 1912 (Bogdani and Loughlin 2007), Finland (1918), and many of the states of East and Central Europe (e.g. Moldova, Romania, and Bulgaria). Turkey also became, and remains, a French-style unitary state, with Atatürk's secularist state replacing the Ottoman Empire in 1921.

Federal states and nationalism

This does not mean that all modern nation-states adopted the French model. Some chose a federal system. The US and Switzerland are the two oldest modern federal states. After the Second World War, Germany and Austria reverted to their federal roots. Switzerland provides a much older model dating from the 'Old Confederacy', which existed between 1291 and 1523, and later confederal models before it became, in 1848, the Helvetic Confederation which, despite its name, is a federation rather than a confederation. The UK was neither a unitary state like France nor a federal state like the US but what is sometimes called a 'union' state, i.e. a state which has been formed by a series of Acts of Union (Rokkan and Urwin 1982).

In all these cases of federal and union states, the nation-state model is retained. The 'national' dimension is represented at the federal or union level, where the representative assembly and government are responsible for those affairs which concern the nation as a whole—war, diplomacy, internal security, and national economic development. The component entities are responsible for affairs dealt appropriately to that level—education, health, social welfare, local government, etc. With regard to the unity of the nation, both unitary and federal states agree that this should not be compromised.

Not all unitary, federal, or union states have succeeded in maintaining this unity, and there are numerous examples of failure or at least of incomplete unification. The 'first' 1801 United Kingdom of Great Britain and Ireland, was replaced by the current United Kingdom when the southern part of Ireland seceded in 1921. Several federations established by colonial powers after the Second World War also failed: the Malayan Union (1946–8); the Federation of Malaya (1948–63); the Federation of Rhodesia and Nyasaland (1953–63); the West Indies Federation (1958–62); the Mali Federation (1959–60); and the Federal Republic of Cameroon (1961–72).

More recently, two former communist federations collapsed, one peacefully (Czechoslovakia) and the other with great bloodshed (Yugoslavia). At least one of the principal reasons for the collapse of these federations, which aimed to unite a number of disparate states and nations, was their failure to construct an overarching and common *national* identity. Instead, the constituent units adopted individual nation-state-building projects, with some of the constituents, for example, the Czechs and the Serbs, dominating the federation, which led to a great deal of resentment among the others and undermined the unity of the whole. The Union of Soviet Socialist Republics (USSR) changed its federal structures (which in any case existed largely on paper as it was a system under the strict control of the Communist Party of the Soviet Union) to form a looser Commonwealth of Independent States (CIS).

Unitary states also face difficulties. Belgium was established in 1830 as a unitary state but in the 1980s, because of Flemish resentment at Francophone domination, it became a highly decentralized federation in an attempt to hold the state together. Other unitary states have experienced difficulties because of internal nationalisms which challenge the legitimacy of the dominant nation-state. In Spain, state unity is challenged by powerful Catalan and Basque nationalist movements (Moreno 2001; Requejo 2005). In France there have been similar challenges from Breton and Corsican nationalist movements (Loughlin 1989). Thus, even in countries with a strong unitary tradition, unification may still be incomplete. However, the majority of nation-states have succeeded in constructing a sense of national identity and of belonging to a particular nation for the majority of their populations. This 'nation' is identifiable with a 'state', whether federal or unitary, with clearly differentiated borders and where the principal source of political legitimacy lies with the core political institutions at the national level.

> ### KEY POINTS
>
> - The different kinds of modern state resulted from three distinctive historical 'moments' in the seventeenth and eighteenth centuries: the parliamentary and industrial revolutions in England (seventeenth century), the American Revolution in the US (1776), and the French Revolution (1789).
>
> - Each of these revolutions produced distinctive kinds of modern states: the union state in the UK; the federal state in the US; the 'one and indivisible' Jacobin state in France.
>
> - The modern nation-state gave rise to the ideology and political movement of nationalism.
>
> - In the nineteenth and twentieth centuries, nationalism has shaped the territorial organization of modern states—breaking up the older empires and uniting disparate territories into single states. Nationalism affected both federal and unitary states.

Territorial governance in welfare states

The establishment of welfare states, which began before the Second World War but reached its peak in the postwar period, may be seen as the final stage of nation-state building. This had consequences for the organization of the central state and administration as well as for territorial governance (Loughlin 2004a).

The crisis and reconfiguration of the welfare state (1970s–90s)

In the 1970s, the welfare state, and the old industrial capitalism which underlay it, went through a series of crises which led to important transformations. The state was reconceptualized less as a top-down directive agency capable of bringing about the common good and realizing extensive welfare policy goals and more as a stimulator from below of the forces of society and the economy that can achieve these themselves. The old-style welfare state encouraged uniformity and standardization across the national territory in order to ensure that there would be no deviation in the standards of services available to citizens of the nation. The most extreme forms of this approach were in the unitary states of the Nordic countries and the Napoleonic states of southern Europe. But these general trends could also be found in other states, including the Austrian and German federations and in the UK.

Asymmetrical diversity vs. symmetrical uniformity

We can distinguish political, administrative, and fiscal symmetry and/or asymmetry. There is today a general tendency to increase asymmetrical diversity of all three kinds, although the combinations vary in different countries. Even the Scandinavian countries which, as remarked previously, were marked by high levels of homogeneity, uniformity, and symmetry despite the vast areas they cover (with the exception of Denmark), have been willing to accept some degree of diversity since the 1990s (Loughlin *et al.* 2005). The UK, a state with a high degree of administrative diversity, has also increased its political asymmetry by setting up devolved elected assemblies in Scotland, Wales, and Northern Ireland, and each new institution is quite different from the others.

From the 'principal–agent' to the 'choice' model and the right to experiment

Central–local relations during the welfare state period were characterized by the 'principal–agent' model. This changed in the 1980s as central governments either reduced welfare services or even terminated some programmes of resource redistribution. In response to these challenges, many regional and local authorities made a virtue of necessity and began to mobilize their resources and to form alliances with other local authorities both inside and outside their national states (Keating 1998*b*).

To some extent, these shifts have reflected the recognition that regional and local democracy are essential elements of democracy itself and that local autonomy implies some diversity and freedom from central government control (Council of Europe 1985). For the most part, however, the 'choice' model is also an expression of the neoliberal approach which predominated in Western states during the 1980s and 1990s. Local autonomy, in application of the principle of subsidiarity (see Box 11.1), means deciding local policies at the appropriate level. From a neoliberal perspective, it also means adopting a competitive approach to local policy and politics. Without going as far as adopting the fiscal federalism of the US, where society functions quite differently from European countries, from

Box 11.1 Subsidiarity

The term 'subsidiarity' comes from Catholic social teaching and is based on the principle that decisions should be taken as close to the citizen as possible, and should be taken by a higher level when the lower level is unable to perform a function or task.

It was first enunciated in an official document by Pius XI in his encyclical *Quadregismo Anno* (1931), which was a statement against the centralized states of the Fascist, Nazi, and Communist regimes of that period.

But the idea is older and may be found in the Tenth Amendment of the United States Constitution: 'The powers not delegated to the United States by the Constitution, nor prohibited by it to the States, are reserved for the States respectively, or to the people'.

It was also implicit in the 1985 European Charter of Local Self-Government of the Council of Europe. Article 4, paragraph 3, states: 'This paragraph articulates the general principle that the exercise of public responsibilities should be decentralised'.

Its most famous contemporary formulation is in Article 9 of the Treaty on European Union (Maastricht 1992):

> The Community shall act within the limits of the powers conferred upon it by this Treaty and of the objectives assigned to it therein.
>
> In areas which do not fall within its exclusive competence, the Community shall take action, in accordance with the principle of subsidiarity, only if and in so far as the objectives of the proposed action cannot be sufficiently achieved by the Member States and can therefore, by reason of the scale or effects of the proposed action, be better achieved by the Community.
>
> Any action by the Community shall not go beyond what is necessary to achieve the objectives of this Treaty.

However, the Maastricht definition has been interpreted to mean devolving functions back to national governments, and not in its original meaning of devolving them from national to sub-national levels of government.

the 1990s onwards there has been a significant increase in competition among regional and local authorities, both within their own states and with regional and local authorities more widely as they try to create the conditions necessary to attract inward investment. The acceptance of 'diversity' might also mean the acceptance of disparities in wealth and levels of socio-economic development at the territorial level in the same way that neoliberalism accepts these at the level of individuals and social classes. As national governments have become less involved in developing explicit policies to reduce these disparities, the European Union has stepped in with its own structural action and cohesion policies. Even if these are conditional on matched funding from central governments, the latter are relieved of important functions which they had exercised during the heyday of the welfare state.

Changing patterns of fiscal relations

Local autonomy is viable only if it is accompanied by fiscal autonomy, i.e. the right and capacity of local authorities to raise their own revenues or to have a degree of discretion over those fiscal resources they receive from central governments. Two opposing arguments are found in the academic literature with regard to the **decentralization** of control over local funding. The first was made in the 1950s in a situation of (national) welfare economics. It contends that 'only central governments could achieve local economic efficiency through policies of fiscal equalization and redistribution' (Caulfield 2000).

The counter-argument, known as fiscal federalism or fiscal decentralization, stresses that local fiscal autonomy is necessary as a way of increasing the accountability and responsiveness of sub-national governments. Fiscal federalism was the application of this notion to local authorities and was based on the idea that citizens could choose from among a variety of services offered by different local authorities by simply moving residence from one authority to another. This was meant to lead to the optimal allocation of resources in a market situation and to local authorities adapting services to local circumstances. It implied high levels of local political, policy, and fiscal autonomy, and high levels of mobility among the citizenry. Of course, these conditions are more characteristic of the US than they are of most European countries. Nevertheless, there has been some attempt to apply principles of fiscal federalism within Europe (e.g. Switzerland).

These two approaches to fiscal policy reflect the difference between choice and agency models of local–central government relations already discussed. In the choice model, local authorities are seen as being best placed to make decisions that reflect the needs and preferences of their local communities. In the agency model, local authorities are seen first and foremost as agents carrying out policies on behalf of the principal, which is central government. Under the principal–agent model, local authorities had a low degree of discretion and the majority of grants received from central government were earmarked for specific purposes. But one of the underlying causes of the crisis of the welfare state model was, precisely, the 'fiscal crisis of the state', or the inability of the state itself to fund the ever-increasing demands of its own policy programmes (O'Connor 1973). Thus, among the first casualties of the crisis were the local authorities. In the UK, under Mrs Thatcher's premiership, funding for local authorities was drastically reduced and one of their most important 'own resources', the business tax, was transferred to the national government.

More generally, what has occurred in Europe is the application of a market-type approach, even if this is not full-blown fiscal federalism. The situation is complex in that most countries today *combine* the 'agency' and 'choice' models, though most tend to emphasize one or the other as the dominant tendency (Caulfield 2000). This combination of models leads to a great deal of variety in the fiscal arrangements of European states, but one overall trend has been an increase in grants from central governments and a decrease in 'own resources', such as local taxes and fees. This might suggest less local autonomy but it is also the case that central grants are becoming less earmarked and more general (Council of Europe 2000). This means that, despite losing some of their fiscal resources, local authorities may still retain a certain amount of fiscal autonomy if they have discretion over how the grants are used.

From hierarchy to 'equality of levels'

A final trend to note in this survey of changes in territorial governance from the welfare state to a more pluralistic state model is the abandonment in a number of states of a hierarchical relationship among different levels of government. In Sweden, the counties and municipalities are on the same level, and the two experimental regions do not have a hierarchical relationship with the municipalities found within them. In France, too, there is equality among the three sub-national levels of government: the region, the department, and the municipality. This was a deliberate choice made when the regions were established, as the 'departmentalist' lobby in France feared that the regions might be in a superior position (as the departments had been over the communes). To avoid this, *all* hierarchy was abolished. In the UK, there are no regions in England so the issue does not arise, but it does in the case of Scotland and Wales. In the Netherlands, the provinces are relatively weak levels of government which do not dominate the municipalities (*gemeente*), while the latter have a kind of corporatist relationship with the central state. In Italy and Spain, the regions and autonomous communities are in a relationship of superiority over the provinces and municipalities but the general trend is towards non-hierarchical relations. The development of 'non-hierarchical systems of governance' reflects the wider shifts from 'principal–agent ' to 'choice' models

Table 11.1 Changes in territorial governance from the old-style to the new-style welfare state

Old-style welfare state	New-style welfare state	Examples
Political, policy, and functional centralization in the name of national unity	Political and functional decentralization	France, Spain, Italy, Netherlands, Sweden, UK
Fiscal centralization	Fiscal decentralization but also some recentralization	Sweden, France
Administrative deconcentration rather than political decentralization	Political decentralization accompanied by administrative deconcentration	France, Spain, Belgium
Institutional and policy standardization: 'one size fits all'	'Customization', heterogeneity, and the right to experiment	Sweden, France, UK
Territorial symmetry	Territorial asymmetry	Spain, Italy, UK, Belgium
Hierarchical central–local relations	Non-hierarchical relations among regional and local governments	France, Sweden, UK
Principal–agent relations between central and sub-national government	The 'choice' model	Sweden, UK, France

and has meant that relations among levels of government now exist in new and varying configurations.

The shift from the old-style welfare state model to a more hybrid model meant significant shifts in territorial governance. These changes are summarized in Table 11.1

KEY POINTS

- The post-war welfare state was the final stage of the process of nation-state building which began at the French Revolution.

- In both federal and unitary states, it implied a certain form of territorial organization, which emphasized centralization and central regulation of sub-national authorities.

- This has been termed the 'principal–agent' relationship whereby sub-national authorities were given responsibility for the delivery of social welfare services but highly regulated by the central state.

- This began to change in the 1980s with the arrival of neoliberalism, leading to the freeing up to some extent of these central constraints and greater freedom for sub-national authorities.

- Territorial organization has been reconfigured with trends towards asymmetry and diversity, greater choice, experimentation, greater local fiscal autonomy (albeit with some contradictory tendencies as well), and fewer hierarchical relations among sub-national authorities.

Federal vs. unitary states

The classical distinction

Given these shifts, one may wonder whether the classical distinction between federal and unitary states is still useful. What are the differences between federal and unitary states?

It will be easier to begin with attempted definitions of a federal state. Kenneth Wheare claimed that most who use the term 'have in mind an association of states, which has been formed for certain common purposes, but in which the member states retain a large measure of their original independence' (Wheare 1963: 1). However, as the author points out, this definition may cover a wide variety of different types of associations of states, including entities such as the present-day United Nations but also previously existing political entities such as the German Empire or the Austro-Hungarian Empire which he denies were federations.

Wheare chooses the US as the prototype of a federation and judges other federations, such as the Australian, the Canadian, or the South African (as it existed before the transition to democracy), according to criteria derived from the US system. What distinguishes the US from other political systems and makes it a federation is that '[t]he principle of organization upon which [it] is based is that of the division of powers between distinct and co-ordinate governments' (Wheare 1963: 2). This means that certain powers are exercised by the federal or 'general' government and other powers by the 'regional' governments of the constituent states. Each government is supreme in its own sphere. In this model of 'coordinate federalism' the powers of the federal government are circumscribed by the constitution and the remaining 'residuary' powers may be exercised by the regional governments. In theory, neither level of government may intervene in the sphere of the other. Both the general and the regional governments act directly on all the citizens, depending on the issue and which level of government is responsible for this issue.

The use of the US as the template against which other political systems may be evaluated as federal or not has been challenged by more recent scholarship (Karmis and Norman 2005). Hueglin (2003) points out that the US

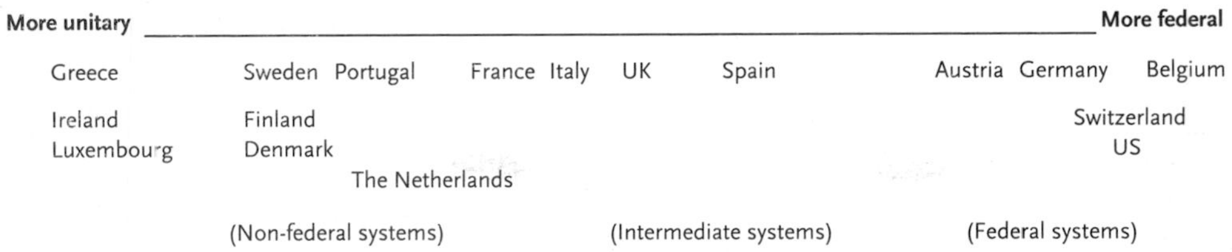

More unitary						More federal
Greece	Sweden Portugal	France Italy	UK	Spain	Austria Germany	Belgium
Ireland	Finland					Switzerland
Luxembourg	Denmark					US
	The Netherlands					
(Non-federal systems)		(Intermediate systems)		(Federal systems)		

Figure 11.1 A spectrum of unitary and federal states

federalist tradition itself evolved out of an older confederal tradition, so that two competing traditions of federalism emerged. Watts (1996) argues further that, although the US was the first modern federation and a reference point for subsequent federations, it is but one example of a wider phenomenon and needs itself to be placed in a comparative perspective.

Watts accepts 'the basic notion of involving the combination of shared-rule for some purposes and regional self-rule for others within a single political system so that neither is subordinate to the other' but argues that '[t]here is no single pure model of federation that is applicable everywhere' (Watts 1996: 1). Besides the US model of 'co-ordinate' federalism, there is also the example of German 'cooperative' federalism. Furthermore, some scholars (Elazar 1991; Watts 1996) classify the 'Autonomic State' of post-Franco Spain as a federation, although this would not be accepted by the majority of Spanish scholars nor, indeed, is it recognized as such by the Spanish Constitution (Moreno 2001; Requejo 2005).

This is an important insight as it suggests that there may be a spectrum ranging from complete unitary states, such as France or Portugal, to fully federal states, such as the US or Germany, with a range of options (e.g. Spain) in between. A useful starting point to situating states on this spectrum is to employ the distinction between 'federalism' and 'federations' developed by King (1982), and further developed by Burgess (1986) and Burgess and Gagnon (1993). 'Federalism' is a normative political ideology and movement which advocates the application of federalist principles in state organization. A 'federation' is a state which fully applies these principles, albeit in different forms, and leads to a variety of types of federation.

Federalism as a political movement may be found in unitary states such as France, Italy, or the UK which are not federations and where the dominant state ideology, as in France, may in fact be hostile to federalism (Loughlin 1986). On the other hand, even unitary states may have some 'federal characteristics' in their state organization. The examples which spring to mind are Spain after 1978 and the UK, especially following the devolution reforms of 1998. In Spain, there are strong federalist currents, for example, in the Spanish Socialist Party (PSOE), while in the UK there is less expression of federalist ideology but the configuration of the state following devolution has a 'quasi-federal' look.

Thus, our spectrum might have at one end the more completely unitary states such as Portugal, Ireland, and Greece, with France a little further on, and, at the other end, Belgium, the US, and Germany. Spain, Italy, and the UK would be placed somewhere in the middle (Figure 11.1). Of course, it is extremely difficult to find a method of measuring the degree of federation, just as it is difficult to measure degrees of centralization and decentralization.

It is clear from this discussion that the simple division into unitary and federal states is inadequate to capture the complexities of modern state organization and that there is a variety of arrangements in between the two extremes. In order to capture this complexity, Watts (1996) adds the term 'federal political systems' to those of federalism and federation. This new term describes a broad genus encompassing various kinds of non-unitary political systems, including federations. 'Federal political systems' differ from unitary systems in that they have two or more levels of government 'which combine elements of *shared-rule* through common institutions and *regional self-rule* for the governments of the constituent units' (Watts 1996: 6–7). They include 'federations', 'quasi-federations', and 'confederations'.

The 'basic notion' of federalism—'the combination of shared-rule for some purposes and regional self-rule for others within a single political system so that neither is subordinate to the other' (Watts 1996: 1–2)—has been applied in different ways to fit very different circumstances. This author provides a useful checklist of the dimensions along which there may be variation:

- the character and significance of the underlying economic and social diversities;
- the number of constituent units and the degree of symmetry or asymmetry in their size, resources, and constitutional status;
- the scope of the allocation of legislative, executive, and expenditure responsibilities;
- the allocation of taxing power and resources;
- the character of federal government institutions and the degree of regional input to federal policy-making;
- procedures for resolving conflicts and facilitating collaboration between interdependent governments;
- procedures for formal and informal adaptation and change.

The complexity of non-unitary states

Elazar (1995) lays out a list of 'federal-type' arrangements, which include constitutionally decentralized unions, federations, confederations, federacies, associated statehood, condominiums, leagues, and joint functional arrangements. Watts (1996) provides a useful explanation of these categories and a number of examples (Table 11.2).

Table 11.2 The variety of federal political systems

Type	Description	Examples
Unions	Polities compounded in such a way that the constituent units preserve their respective integrities primarily or exclusively through the common organs of the general government rather than through dual government structures	New Zealand Lebanon Belgium (pre-1993)
Constitutionally decentralized unions	Unitary in form in the sense that ultimate authority rests with the central government but incorporates constitutionally protected sub-national units of government which have functional autonomy	China Italy Netherlands UK
Federations	Compound polities, combining strong constituent units and a strong general government, each possessing powers delegated to it by the people through a constitution, and each empowered to deal directly with the citizens in the exercise of its legislative, administrative, and taxing powers, and each directly elected by the citizens	Argentina Australia Austria Belgium (post-1993) Brazil Canada Germany Nigeria Switzerland US
Confederations	Where pre-existing polities join together to form a common government for certain limited purpose (foreign affairs, defence, or economic affairs), but the common government is dependent upon the constituent governments	Commonwealth of Independent States (former USSR) Benelux (Belgium, the Netherlands, Luxembourg) European Union (but with some features of a federation) Switzerland (1291–1847) US (1776–89)
Federacies	Political arrangements where a large unit is linked to a smaller unit or units, but the smaller unit retains considerable autonomy and has a minimum role in the government of the larger one, and where the relationship can be dissolved only by mutual agreement	Azores (Portugal) Puerto Rico (US) Aaland Islands (Finland) Faroe Islands (Denmark) Isle of Man (UK)
Associated states	Similar to federacies, but can be dissolved by either of the units acting alone on prearranged terms	Bhutan (India) Cook Islands (New Zealand) Liechtenstein (Switzerland) Marshall Islands (US) Monaco (France)
Condominiums	Political units which function under joint rule of two or more external states in such a way that the inhabitants have substantial internal self-rule	Andorra (1278–1993) (France and Spain)
Leagues	Linkages of politically independent polities for specific purposes that function through a common secretariat rather than a government and from which members may unilaterally withdraw	Arab League ASEAN Commonwealth of Nations NATO Nordic Council
Joint functional authorities	An agency established by two or more polities for joint implementation of a particular task or tasks	International Atomic Energy Agency International Labour Organization
Hybrids	Political systems which combine characteristics of different kinds of political system	Canada in 1867 South Africa after 1996 European Union after Maastricht

Source: Watts (1996: 8–13).

Table 11.3 Degrees of federalism and decentralization in thirty-six democracies*

Federal and decentralized [5.0]		
Australia	Switzerland	
Belgium (after 1993)	US	
Canada		
Germany		
Federal and centralized [4.0]		
Venezuela		
Austria [4.5]		
India [4.5]		
Semi-federal [3.0]		
Israel	Papua New Guinea	
Netherlands	Spain	Belgium before 1993 [3.1]
Unitary and decentralized [2.0]		
Denmark	Norway	
Finland	Sweden	
Japan		
Unitary and centralized [1.0]		
Bahamas	Jamaica	France [1.2]
Barbados	Luxembourg	Italy [1.3]
Botswana	Malta	Trinidad [1.2]
Colombia	Mauritius	
Costa Rica	New Zealand	
Greece	Portugal	
Iceland	UK	
Ireland		

*The indexes of federalism are in square brackets with 5 being the most federal and 1 the least.

Source: Lijphart (1999: 189).

Although some categorizations of particular states could be debated, this approach is useful since it highlights the complexity of contemporary territorial arrangements both within states and between them. Perhaps the greater conceptual danger, however, is that it interprets all political systems, whether unitary or federal, through the lens of federalism and may find 'federal arrangements' where they do not really exist. This is especially true of the categories 'unions' and 'constitutionally decentralized states', which are in fact unitary states with varying degrees of regionalization and decentralization (see Table 11.3).

Lijphart (1999: 189) has provided a more refined analysis of the degrees of centralization and decentralization in federal and unitary states as part of a wider analysis of democracy and government performance in thirty-six countries (Table 11.3). This illustrates that there is not a direct relationship between federalism/decentralization on the one hand, and 'unitariness'/centralization on the other, but that both federal and unitary states can be more or less centralized or decentralized. Lijphart's scheme also recognizes a difficult to categorize intermediate category which he calls 'semi-federal' (which is also 'semi-unitary'). Some of his allocations are questionable—for example, placing of France, Italy, and the UK in the unitary/centralized box. But these may simply reflect the fact that the original research for this book was carried out in the 1980s and the table does not take into account recent developments such as the 'federal' constitutional reforms in Italy, the second phase of French decentralization culminating in the French constitution to describe France as a *République avec une organisation décentralisée,* or the 1998 devolution reforms in the UK.

Trends towards regionalization and decentralization in unitary states

A general trend towards decentralization

As with federal states, unitary states exist along a spectrum that goes from highly decentralized to highly centralized and a range of possibilities in between (see Figure 11.1).

Decentralization, 'deconcentration', regionalism, and regionalization

It is necessary to clarify the concept of decentralization, which is used to cover a variety of phenomena. *Political* decentralization means the transfer of decision-making powers from the central state to any of the sub-national levels of government. This differs from *administrative* decentralization (called *déconcentration* in French). We need further to distinguish political and/or administrative decentralization from *regionalism* and *regionalization*. *Regionalism* refers to an ideology and political movement that advocates the control of regional affairs by regional populations through setting up regional governments of some kind. It is generally a bottom-up movement. *Regionalization*, on the other hand, tends to be top-down in the sense that it consists of policies developed by central governments (or the EU) *for* regional territories and may involve establishing regional administrations to implement those policies. This does not always involve the regional populations themselves and, indeed, may provoke the emergence of regional movements. However, there is usually an attempt to combine both regionalization and regionalism.

Administrative decentralization ('deconcentration') means the transfer of some administrative functions to sub-national levels of administration. It is not identical with political decentralization since the central administration may remain in control of policy-making and administrative behaviour. In France, *déconcentration* was used as a substitute for political decentralization at least until the 1982 decentralization reforms when there was an attempt to make it a tool of the latter (Loughlin 2007*a*).

Occupying the 'meso'-level: the emergence of the region as a political 'actor'

The regional question is concerned with the 'meso'-level of territorial governance—the level between the national and the local levels (Sharpe 1993*b*). In federal states, the component units of the federation are *ex officio* the 'meso' level and their position defines the nature of the federation. It is less clear cut in unitary states which vary in how they organize their 'meso' space. Larger unitary states, such as France, Italy, Spain, and the UK, have set up meso-level governments.

Italy adopted the regionalized model in its 1948 constitution, which distinguished between five 'special' regions (Sicily, Sardinia, Val d'Aosta, Friuli Venezia Giulia, and Trentino Alto Adige (South Tyrol)) and fifteen 'ordinary' regions. In its 1978 constitution, Spain also distinguished between special regions—Andalusia and three regions (the Basque Country, Catalonia, and Galicia) which are called 'nationalities' but not 'nations'—and seventeen regions which covered the rest of Spain. To some extent, the Spanish were influenced by the Italian example although the regional governments, known as autonomous communities, possess far greater powers than their Italian counterparts.

In the 1970s, France set up administrative regions to promote economic development. The 1982 decentralization reforms transformed them into fully fledged regional governments on a par with the departments and communes. The first regional elections were held in 1986 and they have slowly emerged as an important level of French territorial governance (Loughlin and Mazey 1995). In Italy and Spain, the regional reforms were more a result of regionalism than simple regionalization, while in France they were initially more a form of regionalization, although, after 1982, there was an element of regionalism as well. Setting up the regions was largely a result of factors found within their respective states: in Italy and Spain as responses to the excessive centralization of the Fascist and Francoist regimes respectively, and as part of a desire to accommodate the cultural and geographical diversity of each country; in France as part of the Socialists' programme of modernizing the French state and also in line with their acknowledgement of some of the regionalists' demands (Loughlin 1989). The UK was the last of the large states in Western Europe to follow this trend when, after the election of Tony Blair and the New Labour government in 1997, devolution was launched in 1998. Like the other large unitary states, there were internal factors behind these reforms, mainly the demand of the Scots for the 'return' of their parliament, but also as part of a perception that regions were necessary in the new Europe.

The acceleration of European integration from the mid-1980s encouraged regionalism when EU Regional Policy was upgraded to the Structural and Cohesion Funds (Hooghe 1996). This provoked a vast mobilization of regional and local authorities who hoped to obtain some of these funds. It also placed the 'Europe of the Regions' idea high on the agenda within both the EU and its member states. In the large unitary states it encouraged those who argued that regionalism and regionalization should be key dimensions of contemporary European governance. Some of the more extreme interpretations of this postulated that we are witnessing the disappearance of the nation-state. But in the end it was little more than the setting up of the Committee of the Regions by the Maastricht Treaty (Jeffery 1997).

The idea that regional government is an important element of the new model of European governance has been influential in both the smaller unitary states of Western Europe and the new democracies of East and Central Europe. In the former, with the encouragement of the European Commission, it led to the setting up of administrative regions in Greece, Portugal, and Ireland in order to absorb the EU funds coming into these countries. In Denmark, Finland, and Sweden, it meant setting up both political and administrative regions, not so much to receive funds but in order that these regions might be stronger competitors in what was then perceived as the emerging 'Europe of competitive regions'. This trend has also been followed in the new democracies, with Poland and Hungary also setting up regional levels of government.

Other former communist states such as Bulgaria, Romania, and Albania have programmes of decentralization aimed at strengthening local government, but have hesitated about setting up elected regional governments. Among the reasons for this is the desire of national governments to retain control over the sub-national level but also the connivance of the European Commission which quietly discouraged setting up political regions as it felt that this would endanger the effective and efficient administration of its funds. Table 11.4 illustrates the variety of situations existing with regard to regional government prior to enlargement. In order to assist comparison with federal states, these are also included in the table. The table shows what kind of region—political or administrative—exists in each state and how the regions relate to the central level.

KEY POINTS

- Unitary states, like federal states, vary according to their degree of regionalization and decentralization.

- It is useful to distinguish between regionalization (top-down approaches to regions by central states), regionalism (bottom-up political movements from the regions themselves), and various kinds of decentralization (political, administrative, fiscal) as these describe different processes which may not coincide.

- There are also different kinds of regions (political, administrative, economic, cultural) which do not always coincide with each other.

- In recent decades, there have been tendencies towards strengthening regionalism as well as political decentralization.

- The European Union has encouraged these tendencies, although its regional policies are more akin to regionalization than regionalism.

The local level

Local government and local autonomy

All states, with the exception of the Vatican, possess a level of local government, but there is a great deal of variation in its position within the overall system of government. One important difference is between federal and unitary states. In federal states, as a general rule, local government does not have a direct relationship with the federal government but with the sub-federal meso-government. In unitary states, there is usually a direct relationship between the central and local levels. However, in some cases (Italy, Belgium, Spain) the body occupying the 'meso' space—the region or the autonomous community—is the hierarchical superior of the local authorities. This has sometimes led, as in Catalonia and Flanders, to a kind of 'regional Jacobinism' or 'regionalist centralism', which may infringe local autonomy.

Political decentralization here means the strengthening of local government autonomy, which is exercised both *vis-à-vis* the central state and *vis-à-vis* other sub-national entities such as regions or provinces. The Congress of Local and Regional Authorities of Europe (CLRAE), a body of the Strasbourg-based Council of Europe, has been one of the main organizations encouraging greater political decentralization to the local level. The Council promotes democracy and human rights and, in line with the former, has developed regional and local democracy. These are considered essential elements of democracy itself, which had hitherto been primarily national democracy expressed in, and exercised through, national representative institutions. The main legal instrument in promoting local democracy is the European Charter of Local Self-Government promulgated

Table 11.4 A typology of the pre-enlargement fifteen EU member states

Type of state	State	Political regiona	Administrative/ planning regionsb	Right of regions to participate in national policy-making	Right of regions to conclude foreign treatiesc	Political/ legislative control over sub-regional authorities
Federal	Austria	*Länder* (10)		Yes	Yes (but limited)	Yes (not absolute)
	Belgium	Communities[d] (3)		Yes	Yes (but limited)	No
		Regions (3)		Yes	Yes (but limited)	Yes (not absolute)
	Germany	*Länder* (16)			Yes (but limited)	Yes (not absolute)
Region-alized unitary	Italy[e]	*Regioni*[f] (20)		Consultative	No	Yes
	France	*Régions*[g] (21)		Consultative	No	No
	Spain	*Comunidades autonomas* (17)		No	No	Yes
	UK[h]	Scottish Parliament Welsh National Assembly Northern Ireland Assembly	English standard regions	No with regard to English regions; through informal 'concordats'	No at present, but may evolve	Yes in Scotland and Northern Ireland No in Wales (so far)
Decen-tralized unitary	Denmark	Faroe Islands	Groups of *Amter*	No	No	No
	Finland	Aaland Islands	Counties have a regional planning function	No	No (but has a seat in the Nordic Council)	Yes No
	Netherlands	Rijnmond region[i]	*Landsdelen*	Consultative	No	
	Sweden		Regional administrative bodies	No	No	No
Central-ized unitary	Greece		Development regions (13)	No	No	No
	Ireland		Regional authorities (8)	No	No	No
	Luxembourg					
	Portugal	Island regions[j]	Potential planning regions	No	No	No

[a] This refers to regions and nations (as in Scotland, Wales, Catalonia, the Basque Country, and Galicia) with a directly elected assembly to which a regional executive is accountable.

[b] This refers to regions without a directly elected assembly, which exist primarily for administrative/planning purposes.

[c] There is a sharp distinction between the federal and non-federal states in this regard; however, the majority of non-federal states may engage in international activities with the approval of, and under the control of, the national governments.

[d]The Flemish linguistic community and the Flanders economic region have decided to form one body; the French-speaking community and the Walloon region remain separate.

[e]Italy in the 1990s underwent reforms that were meant to create a state with some federal features. However, although the position of the regions was strengthened, this was not a federal state such as Germany or Belgium.

[f]In Italy there are seventeen 'ordinary' regions and five regions with a special statute because of their linguistic or geographical peculiarities: Sicily, Sardinia, Trentino-Alto Adige (South Tyrol with a large German-speaking population), Val d'Aosta, and Friuli-Venezia Giulia.

[g]There are twenty-one regions on mainland France. However, to this one must add Corsica and the overseas departments and territories (the DOM and TOM). Since 1991 Corsica has a special statute and is officially a *collectivité territoriale* rather than a region. The TOM too have special statutes, and in May 1998 one of them, New Caledonia, was permitted to accede to independence within a period of twenty years.

[h]Until the referendums in Scotland and Wales in September 1997, the UK was a highly centralized 'union' state. However, the positive outcome of the referendums meant that there was a Scottish Parliament and a Welsh National Assembly by 1999. A referendum in 1998 on a Greater London Authority with an elected mayor was also successful, and this is seen as a precursor to possible regional assemblies in England. The successful outcome of the Northern Ireland peace process means there is a Northern Ireland Assembly as well as other new institutions linking together the different nations and peoples of the islands.

[i]In 1991 it was decided to set up a new metropolitan region with an elected government in the Rotterdam area to replace the *Gemeente* of Rotterdam and the Province of South Holland. However, this was rejected by a referendum held in Rotterdam.

[j]Portugal, while making provision in its constitution for regionalization, has so far granted autonomy only to the island groups of the Azores and Madeira. The mainland remains highly centralized.

Source: Loughlin 2004b.

in 1985 and now signed and ratified by almost all of the current forty-seven member-states. There is a draft European Charter of Regional Autonomy which has still not been accepted by all the member-states of the Council. Other bodies have also promoted political decentralization (the World Bank and UN-Habitat;) and regional and local democracy (the EU's Committee of the Regions (CoR)).

Comparing and typologizing local government

The trends outlined above simply deal with 'local governments' in general without specifying whether there are different kinds of local government. However, it is clear that there is a wide variety of arrangements in different states and a range of ways of categorizing these arrangements.

In an influential comparative analysis of European local government, Page and Goldsmith (1987) use a combination of institutionalist and functionalist approaches. They first categorize the kinds of institutional relationships by distinguishing between 'political localism', characteristic of southern European countries, and 'legal localism' which is found in northern European countries. They then explore the functional relationships within these two broad categories: the functions that central governments allocate to local governments; the degree of discretion (what we have called above 'autonomy') allowed to local governments; and the access that local political actors have to the centre. In a system characterized by legal localism (the northern group), there is a high degree of administrative regulation from above (functions are determined by the

centre) and a high degree of discretion, and local political actors have limited access to the centre. Where there is political localism (the southern group), local governments have a general competence over local affairs and a low degree of discretion, and local actors have easier access to the centre through informal relationships such as Italian clientelism or more formal arrangements such as the French *cumul des mandats* (Table 11.5).

The Page–Goldsmith typology, while useful in drawing attention to the different legal or political bases of local government in Europe, has been criticized for being too 'broad brush' to be capable of analysing with any degree of finesse the variety of situations (John 2001). John's analysis suggests that, while there are important differences between local governments in Northern and Southern Europe, the situation is more complex than this simple division would suggest.

There are important differences within each group and even within a single country such as Germany. It may be that an Anglo group (the UK and Ireland) should be separate from the Northern European group. Furthermore, the Scandinavian countries might be distinguished

Table 11.5 Functional allocation, discretion, and access in the local government systems of Western Europe

	Functions	Discretion	Access
North	High	High	Low
South	Low	Low	High

Source: John (2001).

from both the UK and Ireland on the one hand, and from Germany and the Netherlands on the other. Hesse and Sharpe (1991) try to capture this complexity by distinguishing three types of state:

- an Anglo group (UK, Ireland, North America);
- a Franco group (France, Italy, Spain, Belgium, Portugal, and, to some extent, Greece);
- a northern and middle European group (Scandinavian countries, the Netherlands, and Germany).

Similarly, Loughlin and Peters (1997), drawing on Dyson (1980), have used the concept of 'state tradition' to suggest four state traditions: the Anglo-Saxon, the Germanic, the Napoleonic, and the Scandinavian. Each conceives territorial organization in a distinctive manner based on a fundamental set of concepts related to the nature and functions of the state, its internal organization, and its relationship with civil society (Table 11.6).

Financial and fiscal trends

Fiscal local autonomy is the basis of political autonomy and it is important to examine recent trends in this regard (Loughlin and Martin 2003). A first important distinction is between two principal sources of local revenue:

- 'own resources' generated by local authorities themselves;
- 'transfers' paid to sub-national governments by central government.

There are a variety of 'own resources' including local taxes of various kinds, fees, loans, and rent from property. 'Transfers' usually take the form of grants, but some forms of shared taxation may also be transfers. The key issue in terms of local autonomy is the extent to which local authorities participate in the determination of such taxes and can influence both their base and their rate. In the vast majority of cases, local authorities have little control over these. However, there are regimes with relatively high levels of 'own resources' and low levels of transfers (e.g. Germany, Switzerland, the Nordic countries, and France) as well as others with low local resources and high degree of transfers (e.g. Austria, the Netherlands, and the UK).

Second, it is important to consider degrees of (1) political decentralization and (2) fiscal decentralization, since it is the combination of the two that determines the level of discretion that local authorities actually have over fundraising and expenditure. There are a number of countries in which there has been quite extensive political/administrative decentralization in the last ten to fifteen years, but this has not always been accompanied by fiscal decentralization.

Third, it is important to take account of the extent to which resources may be (1) 'earmarked' for specific purposes or (2) 'non-earmarked' or general. Both 'own resources' and 'transfers' may be ring-fenced. A key determinant of the level of local fiscal autonomy is therefore which tier of government determines the uses to which funding can be put. Thus, 'own resources' that are ring-fenced for specific purposes by a central government may allow less local control than transfers that are not ring-fenced.

Table 11.6 State traditions and their features

	Anglo-Saxon	Germanic	French	Scandinavian
Is there a legal basis for the state?	No	Yes	Yes	Yes
State–society relations	Pluralistic	Organicist	Antagonistic	Organicist
Form of political organization	Union state/ limited federalist	Integral/organic federalist	Jacobin	Decentralized unitary
Basis of policy style	Incrementalist 'muddling through'	Legal corporatist	Legal technocratic	Consensual
Form of decentralization	State power (US) Devolution/local government (UK)	Cooperative federalism	Regionalized unitary state	Strong local autonomy
Dominant approach to discipline of public administration	Political science/ sociology	Public law	Public law	Public law (Sweden) Organization theory (Norway)
Countries	UK, US, Canada (but not Quebec), Ireland	Germany, Austria, Netherlands, Spain (after 1978), Belgium (after 1988)	France, Italy, Spain (until 1978), Portugal, Quebec, Greece, Belgium (until 1988)	Sweden, Norway, Denmark

Source: Loughlin and Peters (1997).

Underlying these distinctions are the two contrasting models of central–local relationships referred to above: (1) a principal–agent model and (2) a 'choice' model (Caulfield 2000). The study by Loughlin and Martin (2003) suggests that there appears to be a general tendency towards the increasing use of 'transfers' and decreasing reliance on 'own resources'. Accompanying this trend, and apparently contradicting it, is a general move in favour of 'block' ('non-earmarked') rather than 'ring-fenced' grants. The result has been that, in general terms, the level of local fiscal control has increased in recent years and the 'choice model' seems to have become more important, though most states continue to embody elements of the 'principal–agent' approach. The explanation of this apparent contradiction may be that the choice model is served by the element of fiscal control over transferred resources rather than by 'own resources'. At the same time, from the point of view of strengthening local democracy, there are concerns about the decline in the level of 'own resources' and in most EU countries there have been attempts to keep down the overall level of local authority spending in order to meet the convergence criteria laid down in the Maastricht Treaty. The financial crisis of 2007–8 has also undoubtedly had an important effect on these fiscal relations, but more research needs to be carried out to ascertain exactly what this has been.

KEY POINTS

- There are a great variety of systems of local government, which makes it difficult to classify.
- A classical way of typologizing local government in Europe is to distinguish between systems in Northern Europe (legal localism) and in Southern Europe (political localism).
- This simple division needs to be complemented by more complex typologies which take into account the differences within the two broad categories: the Anglo-Saxon, Germanic, French–Napoleonic, and Scandinavian systems.
- There are trends towards greater local fiscal autonomy, but this has recently been somewhat tempered by the new fiscal orthodoxy which makes central governments responsible for their countries' fiscal rectitude (thus constraining local authorities).

Conclusion

Three points emerge from the above analysis.

1. The territorial dimension of governance is as important as ever and is growing in importance.
2. There are general trends which affect all political systems, whether unitary or federal or those in between.
3. These general trends are expressed in terms of the distinctive histories, political and administrative cultures, and traditions of the different states. In other words, there are patterns of convergence and divergence, thus making the territorial dimension a highly complex phenomenon which is difficult to grasp and analyse empirically.

This is in line with the notion of the emergence of a new system of governance which does not abolish the traditional forms of governance of the classical nation-state, whether this is a federation or a unitary state, but does introduce new configurations and sets of relationships alongside them. This means that the rigid division between federal and unitary states is less relevant than in the past, and that today we should think more of a spectrum with strong federal and unitary states at each end of the spectrum and, in between, a variety of types of state.

The classical organization of the nation-state, which culminated in the welfare states of the *Trente Glorieuses* (1945–75), implied a certain type of territorial organization but has been transformed from a hierarchical, symmetrical, and standardized model to one that is more non-hierarchical, asymmetrical, and diversified. This has led to the emergence of regions and local authorities as political actors in their own right. Their position has been strengthened by the various decentralization and regionalization reforms that have taken place in all states since the 1980s. These processes and the new status of subnational governments have, in turn, been strengthened by European bodies such as the EU and the Council of Europe as well as by the United Nations. These trends have important consequences for the nation-state itself and its forms of political representation, as well as its political and administrative organization. These political and institutional changes are also reflected in shifts in fiscal and financial relationships, where local authorities have greater discretion in the use of local finances but, at the same time, may be held more accountable by central governments and by the electorate for the use they make of these.

 Questions

1. How has the nation-state determined modern territorial organization?
2. Is the distinction between federal and unitary states still valid?
3. What are the different kinds of federal arrangements?
4. Is there an intermediate group of states that are neither federal nor unitary?
5. How has the post-war welfare state affected the territorial organization of nation-states?

6. What is the difference between regionalization and regionalism?

7. Does political decentralization lead to the establishment of political regions?

8. Are we seeing the emergence of a 'Europe of the Regions'?

9. How useful is the distinction between northern European 'legal localism' and southern European 'legal localism'?

10. Is there a contradiction between increased political decentralization and growing fiscal central control?

 Further reading

Starting point for discussion of federalism

Burgess, M. (2006) *Comparative Federalism: Theory and Practice* (London: Routledge).

Wheare, K. (1963) *Federal Government* (4th edn) (Oxford: Oxford University Press).

Useful contemporary analyses of federalism

Elazar, D. (1995) *Federalism: An Overview* (Pretoria: HSRC Publishers).

Karmis, D. and Norman, W. (eds) (2005) *Theories of Federalism: A Reader* (Basingstoke and New York: Palgrave). This is a useful collection of publications ranging from the classical early texts to more contemporary theoretical debates.

Watts, R. (1996) *Comparing Federal Systems in the 1990s* (Kingston, Ontario: Institute of Intergovernmental Relations, Queen's University).

Regions and regionalism

Keating, M. (1998) *The New Regionalism in Western Europe: Territorial Restructuring and Political Change* (Cheltenham: Edward Elgar).

Keating, M. (ed.) (2004) *Regions and Regionalism in Europe* (Cheltenham: Edward Elgar).

Keating, M. and Loughlin, J. (eds) (1997) *The Political Economy of Regionalism* (London: Routledge).

Swenden, W. (2006) *Federalism and Regionalism in Western Europe: A Comparative and Thematic Analysis* (Basingstoke: Palgrave). This is a useful reader.

For more literature on regionalism, see Chapter 15.

Multi-level governance

Bache, I. and Flinders, M. (eds) (2004) *Multi-Level Governance* (Oxford: Oxford University Press).

Hooghe, L. and Marks, G. (2001) *Multi-Level Governance and European Integration* (Lanham, MD.: Rowman & Littlefield).

Overviews of local and regional government in the EU

Delcamp, A. and Loughlin, J. (eds) (2003) *La Décentralisation dans les États de l'Union européenne* (Paris: La Documentation Française).

John, P. (1991) *Subnational Governance in Western Europe* (London: Sage).

Loughlin, J. (2004) *Subnational Democracy in the European Union* (Oxford: Oxford University Press).

Page, E. and Goldsmith, M. (eds) (1987) *Central and Local Government Relations: A Comparative Analysis of West European Unitary States* (London: Sage).

 Web links

Federalism

www.indiana.edu/~speaweb/IPSA/article11.html
International Political Science Association Comparative Federalism and Federation Research Committee.

Organizations

www.coe.int/T/Congress/Default_en.asp
Congress of Local and Regional Authorities of the Council of Europe.

http://cor.europa.eu/Pages/welcome.html
Committee of the Regions (of the European Union)

Local government

http://www.ecpr.eu/StandingGroups/StandingGroupsList.aspx
Consortium of Political Research Standing Group on Local Government and Politics. This Standing Group has an electronic newsletter LOGOPOL which provides news of activities of the Group. To subscribe send a message to LOGOPOL-L@LISTS.UTWENTE.NL.

Regionalism

www.essex.ac.uk/ecpr/standinggroups/regionalism/index.aspx
European Consortium of Political Research Standing Group on Regionalism.

 For additional material and resources, please visit the Online Resource Centre at:
www.oxfordtextbooks.co.uk/orc/caramani3e/
online resource centre

Actors and processes

CHAPTER 12

Political parties

Richard S. Katz

Reader's guide

Political parties are among the central institutions of modern democracy. But what is a political party? Why are parties central to democracy, and how are they organized? This chapter considers the definition, origins, and functions of parties. What role do parties play in the working of democracy? And what benefits do parties provide for those who organize them? The chapter then considers the ways in which parties are organized, regulated, and financed. It concludes with brief discussions of the role of parties in the stabilization of democracy in the late twentieth and early twenty-first centuries, and of challenges confronting parties in the new millennium.

Introduction

Organizations that identify themselves as 'political parties' are among the central actors in politics. Whether or not in power as the result of victory in free and fair elections, the governments of most countries have effectively been in the hands of party leaders: Winston Churchill as leader of the British Conservative Party; Indira Gandhi as leader of the Indian National Congress; Adolf Hitler as the leader of the German Nazi Party; Mikhail Gorbachev as leader of the Communist Party of the Soviet Union; Ahmed Sékou Touré as leader of the Parti Démocratique de Guinée-Rassemblement Démocratique Africain.

When governments were not in the hands of party leaders, most often because party government was interrupted by a military takeover, the resulting juntas (see Chapter 6) usually announced that their rule would be only temporary—until a regime of legitimate or honest or effective parties can be restored. And if, at the beginning of the twenty-first century, there are occasional suggestions that social movements and governance networks might supplant parties as the leading institutions channelling political participation and structuring government, experience to date offers little reason to suspect (or hope) that this will happen any time soon.

KEY POINTS

- Political parties are the central actors in democratic politics, as well as in many authoritarian and totalitarian regimes.

- It is unlikely that social movements or governance networks will replace the parties' many roles.

Definitions of party

Given their ubiquity, one might think that the definition of political party would be straightforward, but quite the reverse is true. Parties like the American Democrats, the Italian Fascists, or the Kenyan African National Union (KANU)—not to mention the myriad smaller parties like the Polish Beer Lovers or the British Official Monster Raving Loony Party—are so different in motivation, organization, behaviour, and relevance as to raise the question of whether a single umbrella category can encompass them all. Indeed, there are many scholars who would argue that some of these 'parties' should not be included.

Although it is only one among many possible definitions of party (see Box 12.1 for more examples), it is instructive to unpack Huckshorn's (1984: 10) definition—'a political party is an autonomous group of citizens having the purpose of making nominations and contesting elections in the hope of gaining control over governmental power through the capture of public offices and the organization of the government'—in order to highlight the issues involved. Huckshorn explicitly combines four elements, common to many definitions, and implicitly adds another.

The first explicit element concerns the *objective of parties*: 'gaining control over governmental power through the capture of public offices and the organization of the government'. However, there has been considerable disagreement concerning the underlying motivation for this pursuit of power. For some (Lasswell 1960), the pursuit of power reflects psychopathology; others (Downs 1957; Schumpeter 1962; Schlesinger 1991) emphasize the pursuit of office essentially as an employment opportunity. From a more public regarding perspective, one finds Edmund Burke's (1770) classic definition quoted in Box 12.1.

The second explicit element concerns *methods*: 'making nominations and contesting elections ... and the organization of the government'. This points to two separable arenas in which parties operate, the electoral and the governmental; as will be noted below, one significant question is: which came first?

The third explicit element of Huckshorn's definition is *competition,* expressed in the 'contesting' of elections and the 'hope [as opposed to the certainty] of gaining control'. But does the contesting of elections require free and fair competition among independent competitors or merely that the form of elections is observed? This is related to the fourth element, that the group of citizens be *autonomous.* At the extreme, these criteria appear to disqualify the parties of 'one-party' states, although on the other side these parties may claim to be facing real, if clandestine and illegal, opposition from 'counter-revolutionary forces'. Moreover, these parties' structures may also play a significant role in the organization and control of the government, more conventionally understood.

The implicit element of Huckshorn's definition is that the group of citizens has some level of coherence that allows them to coordinate their actions and to maintain an identity over time. While this does not require a formal organization, it certainly is facilitated by one, so that both some minimal level of organization and some minimal level of unity have become part of the definition of party.

KEY POINTS

- Parties are ubiquitous in modern political systems.

- The definition of 'party' is contentious because it specifies which cases provide appropriate evidence for confirming or discontinuing empirical theories.

- Definitions centring on the objectives and methods of party, and emphasizing their role in political competition, reflect value-laden assumptions about the proper functioning of politics.

Box 12.1 Definition of party

David Hume (1741)	Factions may be divided into personal and real; that is, into factions, founded on personal friendship or animosity among such as compose the contending parties, and into those founded on some real difference of sentiment or interest … though … parties are seldom found pure and unmixed, either of one kind or the other.
Edmund Burke (1770)	[A] party is a body of men united, for promoting by their joint endeavours the national interest, upon some particular principle in which they are all agreed.
Walter Bagehot (1889)	The moment, indeed, that we distinctly conceive that the House of Commons is mainly and above all things an elective assembly, we at once perceive that party is of its essence: there never was an election without a party.
Max Weber (1922)	'[P]arties' live in a house of 'power'. Their action is oriented toward the acquisition of social 'power', that is to say toward influencing communal action no matter what its content may be.
Robert Michels (1911)	The modern party is a fighting organization in the political sense of the term, and must as such conform to the laws of tactics.
Joseph Schumpeter (1950)	A party is not … a group of men who intend to promote the public welfare 'upon some particular principle on which they are all agreed'. A party is a group whose members propose to act in concert in the competitive struggle for political power.
Anthony Downs (1957)	In the broadest sense, a political party is a coalition of men seeking to control the governing apparatus by legal means. By coalition, we mean a group of individuals who have certain ends in common and cooperate with each other to achieve them. By governing apparatus, we mean the physical, legal, and institutional equipment which the government uses to carry out its specialized role in the division of labor. By legal means, we mean either duly constituted or legitimate influence.
V. O. Key Jr (1964)	A political party, at least on the American scene, tends to be a 'group' of a peculiar sort. … Within the body of voters as a whole, groups are formed of persons who regard themselves as party members. … In another sense the term 'party' may refer to the group of more or less professional workers.… At times party denotes groups within the government. … Often it refers to an entity which rolls into one the party-in-the-electorate, the professional political group, the party-in-the-legislature, and the party-in-the-government.
William Nisbet Chambers (1967)	[A] political party in the modern sense may be thought of as a relatively durable social formation which seeks offices or power in government, exhibits a structure or organization which links leaders at the centers of government to a significant popular following in the political arena and its local enclaves, and generates in-group perspectives or at least symbols of identification or loyalty.
Ronald Reagan (1984)	A political party isn't a fraternity. It isn't something like the old school tie you wear. You band together in a political party because of certain beliefs of what government should be. (quoted in *Time Magazine*, 3 September)
Joseph Schlesinger (1991)	A political party is a group organized to gain control of government in the name of the group by winning election to public office.
John Aldrich (1995)	Political parties can be seen as coalitions of elites to capture and use political office. [But] a political party is more than a coalition. A political party is an institutionalized coalition, one that has adopted rules, norms, and procedures.

Origins of parties

The origins of modern parties lie first in the representative assemblies of the sixteenth to nineteenth centuries, and second in the efforts of those who were excluded from those assemblies to gain a voice in them. In both cases, parties arose in response to the fact that coordinated action is likely to be more effective than action taken by isolated individuals, even if they are in perfect agreement.

The earlier parties were *parties of intra-parliamentary origin*, evident, for example, in the British parliament in the seventeenth century—and even then the novelty was not the existence of factions but rather acceptance of the ideas that disagreement was not synonymous with disloyalty and that organization was not synonymous with conspiracy. Over time, these parties developed recognizable leadership cadres and became active in electoral campaigns. Their most significant contribution to the development of modern politics, as well as the greatest reinforcement of their own strength, was to wrest control of the executive from the hands of the monarch and replace that control with responsibility to parliament, which ultimately meant that ministers would in fact be chosen by, and be responsible to, the parties (and especially their leaders) that controlled a majority of the parliamentary seats.

The rise of parliamentary government was far from equivalent to democratization, because well into the nineteenth century, and generally into the twentieth, the right to participate in political life, including the right to vote, was highly constrained by a variety of economic, religious, and gender restrictions. The need to mobilize and organize large numbers of those excluded from legitimate participation to support leaders advocating for reforms—generally including the extension of political rights—gave rise to development of *parties of extra-parliamentary origin.* The ultimate success of these parties in inducing the parties of the *régimes censitaires* to broaden the suffrage was instrumental in converting the liberal regimes of the nineteenth century into the liberal democracies of the twenty-first century. Indeed, as Schattschneider (1942: 1) famously remarked, 'the political parties created democracy, and modern democracy is unthinkable save in terms of the parties'.

The distinction between parties of intra- and extra-parliamentary origin (Duverger 1954) is not only a matter of timing, with parties of internal origin generally coming earlier. Especially at their origins, they often differ quite substantially in their organizations as well, and these 'genetic' differences tend to persist for many decades after parties of external origin win parliamentary representation, or parties of internal origin build membership organizations 'on the ground' (see Panebianco 1988).

Parties of internal and external origin have also tended to differ with respect to their social bases, with those originating in parliament representing the 'establishment' of the upper and upper middle classes (or earlier, the nobility and gentry, and more recently, particularly in 'pacted' transitions to democracy in the former Soviet bloc, the clientele of the old regime), while those of external origin represent the middle, lower middle, and working classes, sometimes the adherents of dissenting religions, speakers of marginalized languages, opponents of the old regime, etc.

In the late twentieth century, a new type of externally originating party has appeared in a number of countries—most notably and successfully in Italy. In these cases, a rich entrepreneur used his wealth in effect to create (or 'buy') a party in much the same way as he might create a chain of retail stores (Hopkin and Paolucci 1999). Although created outside parliament, these parties tend to look more like older parties of internal origin, both in their balance of power between the central party organization (dominated by the entrepreneur through party officials who are in reality his employees) and ordinary members (if any), and in their conservative, or at least pro-business, policy profile. In particular, they are created to be 'cheerleaders' and supporters of an already established leader, who has little interest in or need for input of ideas or resources from below. Like the earlier parties of internal origin, and unlike most leader-centred parties of external origin, they depend on the material resources that the leader can mobilize, rather than on his/her personal charisma.

> **KEY POINTS**
>
> ● Some parties originated within parliaments, while others originated outside parliaments with the objective of getting in.
>
> ● The subsequent power relations of a party generally favour leaders whose positions in public office, or in an external party organization, are analogous to the positions of the leaders who originally built the party.

The functions of parties

Political parties perform a number of functions (see Box 12.2) that are central to the operation of modern democracies. Indeed, as already observed, parties are often defined at least in part by the performance of these functions. At the same time, however, it should be recognized that these are not the only things that parties do (for example, parties may serve as social outlets for their members), nor do all parties effectively perform (or even attempt to perform) all of these functions.

Coordination

Historically, the first function of political parties, and still one of the most important, is that of coordination within government, within society, and between government and society at large.

Coordination within government

Coordination within government (the 'party in public office') takes place in many venues. Most obviously, the coordination function is manifested in party caucuses (or groups, clubs, or *Fraktionen*) in parliaments, with their leaders, whips (party officials in charge of maintaining discipline and communication within the party's parliamentary membership, and 'newsletters' informing members of the expectations of their leaders), policy committees, etc. Parliamentary party groups also structure the selection of committee members and the organization of the parliamentary agenda. Whether in a system of formal separation of powers, like the US, or more pure parliamentary government, like New Zealand, parties provide the bridge between the legislative and executive

Box 12.2 Functions of parties

Coordination	Maintaining discipline and communication within the parliamentary caucus.
	Coordinating action of the parliamentary caucus in support of, or opposition to, the cabinet.
	Organizing the political activity of like-minded citizens.
	Patterning linkage between representatives in public office and organized supporters among the citizenry.
Conducting electoral campaigns and structuring competition	Providing candidates, and linking individual candidates to recognizable symbols, histories, and expectations of team-like behaviour.
	Developing policy programmes.
	Recruiting and coordinating campaign workers.
Selection and recruitment of personnel	Selection of candidates for elections.
	Recruitment and/or selection of candidates for appointed office.
	Recruitment and socialization of political activists and potential officeholders.
Representation	Speaking for their members and supporters within or in front of government agencies.
	Being the organizational embodiment in the political sphere of demographically or ideologically defined categories of citizens.

branches. They also structure coordination between different levels (national, regional, etc.) of government. To the extent that parties perform this function comprehensively and effectively, it becomes reasonable to regard parties, rather than the individual politicians who hold office in their name, as central political actors.

Coordination within society

Political parties are among the institutions (along with interest groups, NGOs, and the like) that organize and channel the political activity of citizens. Even in the absence of a formally organized 'party on the ground', party names and histories serve as points of reference and identification for citizens. Where there are more formal organizations, these provide venues for political education, discussion, and the coordination of collective action.

Coordination between government and society

Parties also link the party on the ground as a group of active citizens supporting a particular political tendency and the party in public office as a group of officials claiming to represent the same tendency. Within party organizations, this function is often performed by a party central office. Whether this linkage takes, or is supposed to take, the form of control over the party in public office on behalf of the party on the ground, or direction of the party on the ground as an organization of supporters of the party in public office, varies among parties, as indeed does the effectiveness of the linkage whichever way it runs, and the level of coordination and discipline within either the party on the ground or the party in public office.

Contesting elections

A second major defining function of political parties is the conduct of electoral campaigns, and of political competition more generally. Parties provide most of the candidates in elections, and an even larger share of those with any real chance of being elected. In many political systems, parties are the formal contestants of elections—the ballot clearly identifies parties as the things among which the citizen is asked to choose—but even when the object of choice formally is individual candidates, the most relevant characteristic of those candidates is usually their political party affiliation. Ordinarily (the US, in which the organization and funding of campaigns is based primarily on individual candidates, being a notable exception), most of the funds required for a political campaign are raised and spent by parties, whether nationally or at the constituency level, and campaign workers are recruited and directed by parties. The policy positions advocated in a campaign are generally those that were formulated and agreed to within parties. Between elections as well, parties generally act as the primary protagonists in political debates.

Recruitment

A third major function of parties is the recruitment and selection of personnel, with the balance between recruitment (finding someone willing to do the job) and selection (choosing among multiple aspirants) depending both on the party and the nature of the position to be filled. The selection function is most significant with regard to candidacies for important offices, such as the presidency, membership in the national parliament, or a regional governorship, and within parties whose candidates have a high probability of success. For minor offices (especially those that are unpaid), hopeless constituencies, or positions at the bottom of a party list of candidates, the primary function often is recruitment—avoiding the embarrassment of not being able to fill the position (Sundberg 1987).

Taken together, these three functions of coordination (especially within the party in public office), conducting electoral campaigns (especially the formulation and presentation of policy programmes, platforms, or manifestoes), and recruitment of candidates for both elective and appointive office, to the extent that they are performed in a coordinated way, and to the extent that party elected officials effectively control the state, make the parties the effective governors, and give rise to the idea of 'democratic party government' (Rose 1976; Castles and Wildenmann 1986). Of course, not all democratic governments are democratic in this way. In the US, for example, the coherence of parties is much lower than in most other democracies, making individual politicians rather than their parties the real governors. In Switzerland, the referendum makes the citizens, and the variety of groups (including but by no means limited to parties) that can organize petitions demanding a referendum, the ultimate deciders of individual questions at the expense of party government.[1]

Representation

Finally, parties perform a variety of functions that may be classified as representation. First, parties speak and act for their supporters, in electoral campaigns, in the corridors of power, and in the media and other public fora of discussion. Parties serve as agents of the people, doing things that the people do not have the time, the training and ability, or the inclination to do for themselves. Parties also represent citizens in the sense of being the organizational embodiment in the political sphere of categories of citizens, as with a labour party, a Catholic party, the party of a language group or region, or even possibly a women's party.[2] Parties may, by analogy, represent the organizational embodiment of ideologies.

KEY POINTS

- Political parties play a central role in coordinating among public officials, among citizens with common political preferences, and between citizens and officials.

- Political parties are generally the central participants in elections, responsible for both the candidates and the issues among which voters will choose.

- Political parties are central participants in the recruitment of political personnel, both for the elective and appointive office.

- Political parties serve as representatives of both social groupings and ideological positions.

Models of party organization

Types of party

Models of parties are summarized in Table 12.1.

Cadre or elite parties

The earliest 'modern' parties were the **cadre** (or elite or caucus) parties that developed in European parliaments. Because, particularly in an era of highly restricted suffrage, each of the MPs who made up these parties generally owed his election to the mobilization of his own personal clientele or the clientele of his patron, there was little need for a party on the ground, and certainly not one organized beyond the boundaries of individual constituencies. Hence, there was also no need for a party central office. Within parliament, however, the advantages of working in concert both to pursue policy objectives and to secure access to ministerial office led to the evolution of parliamentary party organizations, frequently cemented by the exchange of patronage.

As electorates expanded, elite parties in some places developed more elaborate local organizations—most famously the 'Birmingham caucus' of Joseph Chamberlain—and some greater coordination (frequently taking the form of centrally prepared 'talking points' and centrally organized campaign tours by nationally known personalities) by a central office, but the heart of the organization remained the individual MP and his/her personal campaign and support organization. At the level of the electorate, the concept of 'party membership' remained ill-defined. In the twenty-first century, parties that approximate the caucus format remain significant in the US and to a certain extent in Japan (the Liberal Democratic Party) and on the right in France.

Mass parties

The **mass party** developed from the second half of the nineteenth century. In contrast with the intra-parliamentary origins of the caucus party, the 'genetic myth' of the mass party identifies it as a party of extra-parliamentary origin.[3] In the initial absence of either elected officials (a party in public office) or a network of local organizations (a party on the ground), the mass party begins with a core of leaders who organize a party central office with the aim of developing a party so as to be able to win elections and ultimately gain public office.

In contrast with the cadre party, which generally claimed to be speaking for the 'national interest' (although often based on a highly truncated view of who constituted 'the nation'), mass parties claimed to represent the interest only of a particular group (most often a social class),[4] and frequently built on the pre-existing organizations of that group (e.g. trade unions). Their primary

Table 12.1 Models of parties

	Elite, caucus, or cadre party	Mass party	Catch-all party	Cartel party	Business firm party
Period of dominance	Rise of parliamentary government to mass suffrage	Drive for mass suffrage to 1950s	1950s to present	1970s to present	1990s to present
Locus of origination	Parliamentary origin	Extra-parliamentary origin	Evolution of pre-existing parties	Evolution of existing parties	Extra-parliamentary initiative of political entrepreneurs
Organizational structure	Minimal and local Party central office subordinate to party in public office	Members organized in local branches Central office responsible to an elected party congress	Members organized in branches, but marginalized in decision-making Central office subordinate to party in public office	Central office dominated by party in public office, and largely replaced by hired consultants Decisions ratified by plebiscite of members and supporters	Minimal formal organization, with hierarchical control by the autonomous entrepreneur and his/her employees
Nature and role of membership	Elites are the only 'members'	Large and homogeneous membership Leadership formally accountable to members	Heterogeneous membership organized primarily as cheerleaders for elites	Distinction between member and supporter blurred Members seen as individuals rather than as an organized body	Membership minimal and irrelevant
Primary resource base	Personal wealth and connections	Fees from members and ancillary organizations	Contributions from interest groups and individuals	State subsidies	Corporate resources

Source: Adapted in part from Katz and Mair (1995) and Krouwel (2006).

political resource was numbers, with many small contributions of labour and money substituting for the few, but large, contributions available to elite parties. Both as a reflection of their subcultural roots and as a way of mobilizing their supporters, mass parties often pursued a strategy of 'encapsulation', providing a range of ancillary organizations (women's groups, after-work clubs, trade unions) and services (a party press, party-sponsored insurance schemes) which both helped isolate supporters from countervailing influences and made party support a part of the citizen's enduring personal identity rather than a choice to be made at each election.

Naturally, all of this required extensive organization. The archetypal mass party is organized on the ground in branches composed of people who have applied for membership, have been accepted (and potentially are liable to expulsion), and have certain obligations to the organization (most commonly including the payment of a subscription or fee) in exchange for which they acquire rights to participate in the organization's governance, especially by electing delegates to the party's national congress (or convention or conference).

In principle, the national congress is the highest decision-making body of a mass party, but as a practical matter it can only meet for a few days every year (if that often), and therefore elects a party executive committee and/or chairman or president or secretary who is effectively at the top of the party hierarchy. The executive also manages the staff of the party central office. Again in principle, the representatives elected to public office under the party's banner are agents of the party, on the presumption that voters were choosing among parties and not individual candidates, and so are subject to the direction of the party congress and executive, which are also responsible for formulating the party's political programme.

In reality, of course, things are often rather different with, as indicated by Michels' 'iron law of oligarchy' (Michels 1915), the very structures of internal party democracy leading to the domination of the party by its elite—a result that is less surprising when one remembers that the extra-parliamentary elite were initially the creators of the party. Moreover, in many parties that approximate the ideal type of mass party, ancillary organizations as well as the parliamentary party and the central office staff are guaranteed representation in the national congress and/or the national executive, increasingly making the question of whether authority in the mass party flows from the bottom up, or from the top down, an open one.

Catch-all parties

The mass party originated primarily as the vehicle of those groups that were excluded from power under the *régimes censitaires.* However, it proved highly effective, first in securing broader rights of participation for its clientele groups and then in winning elections under

conditions of broadly expanded suffrage, and in many cases this forced the cadre parties to adapt or risk electoral annihilation.[5] Simply to become mass parties was not appealing, however. In general, the social groups that they would represent were not large enough to be competitive on their own under mass suffrage and thus they had to be able to appeal across group boundaries. Moreover, the party in public office did not find the idea of ceding ultimate authority to a party congress and executive, even if in name only, attractive. The result was to create a new party model, with much of the form of the mass party (members, branches, congress, executive), but organized as the *supporters* of the party in public office rather than as its masters.

At the same time, many mass parties were forced to change, both by pressure from a party in public office increasingly able to claim responsibilities and legitimacy based on a direct relationship with the electorate rather than one mediated by the external party organization, and by changes in society (e.g. breakdown of social divisions, spread of mass media) that made the strategy of encapsulation less effective and the resources provided by the parties' *classes gardées* less reliable and less adequate.

The result was (1) a reduction in the role of members relative to professionals, (2) a shedding of ideological baggage, (3) a loosening and ultimate abandonment of the interconnection of party and a privileged set of interest organizations (again, particularly unions), and (4) a strategy that reached across group boundaries for votes and resources. Particularly looking at these changes in mass parties of the left, Kirchheimer (1966) identified this new type as the **catch-all party**. In fact, however, in both strategy and organization, Kirchheimer's catch-all party looks very much like that just described as the adaptation of the old cadre parties. As the catch-all party developed, it became increasingly reliant on political professionals—pollsters, media consultants, etc. (see Chapter 19)—leading to the idea of the electoral-professional party as an alternative to, or simply a variant of, the catch-all model (Panebianco 1988). Although most electoral-professional parties have formal membership organizations, the emphasis has shifted so much towards the party in public office and the central office (or hired consultants) that the membership is effectively superfluous, or maintained primarily for cosmetic reasons (i.e. the belief that having a membership organization will make the party look less elitist or oligarchic).

Cartel parties

By the last quarter of the twentieth century, even the catch-all model was under considerable pressure. Increasing public debts confronted ruling parties with a choice between dramatic increases in taxes and dramatic cuts in welfare spending. Globalization reduced the ability of governments to control their economies. All this was exacerbated by the financial crises beginning around 2007. Increases in education and leisure time, along with the growth of interest groups, NGOs, etc., gave citizens both the abilities and opportunities to bring pressure to bear on the parties themselves, and on the state without requiring the intermediation of the parties. Party loyalties, and memberships, began obviously to erode. Shifts in campaign technology increased the cost of electoral competitiveness beyond the willingness of members and other private contributors to provide—at least without the appearance, and often the reality, of corruption which, when revealed, made parties even less popular.

These developments have inspired a number of adaptations and other initiatives. Katz and Mair (1995) have suggested that in many countries catch-all parties have been moving in the direction of what they call the 'cartel party'. This involves at least four major changes in the relationships among the parties, the citizenry, and the state, and between parties and their members.

1. The mainstream parties, i.e. those that are in power, or are generally perceived to have a high probability of coming to power in the medium term, in effect form a *cartel to protect themselves both from electoral risks* (e.g. by shifting responsibility away from politically accountable agencies so that they will not be held to account for them or by minimizing the difference in rewards to electoral winners and electoral losers) *and to supplement their decreasingly adequate resources with subventions from the state* (justified in terms of the parties' centrality to democratic government or of insulating parties from corrupt economic pressure).

2. The parties reduce the relevance of their role of representation, in favour of a part of their role as governors, defending policies of the state (including those made by bureaucrats, 'non-political' agencies like central banks, and even previous governments made up of other parties), in effect becoming *agencies of the state rather than of society*.

3. Cartel parties tend to increase the formal powers of party members, and indeed in some cases to allow increased participation by supporters who are not formal members. However, they do this as a way of *preserving the form of internal democracy while disempowering party activists*, who are perceived to be more doctrinaire and policy-oriented, and hence less willing to accept the limitations implicit in a cartel. For example, leadership selection might be moved from the party congress, which allows a forum for internal opposition to be organized and expressed, to a direct mail ballot of the full membership, although generally with central control over who can be a candidate.

4. In part, simply extending the trends evident in the catch-all party, cartel parties also tend to replace the staff of the party central office with hired consultants, both *further privileging professional expertise over political experience and activism*, and *removing another possible source of challenge* to the leaders of the party in public office.

Anti-cartel parties

Although both Duverger (the principal elaborator of the idea of the mass party) and Kirchheimer (the elaborator of the idea of the catch-all party) presented their models as somehow representing an end-state of party development, each of the models has generated its own challenger. In the case of the cartel party, Katz and Mair (attributing the idea to Lars Bille), identify what they call the anti-party-system party as the cartel party's challenger. Parties of this type have also been identified as 'left-libertarian' or 'new right' parties, or as 'movement parties'. They tend to expect a much deeper commitment from their members than either catch-all or cartel parties, and in this way are similar to the mass party, but they are organized around an idea rather than a social grouping (although the idea may be differentially attractive/popular among different groups). However, two of their primary appeals are simply to a sense of frustration that substantive outcomes appear to change little, if at all, regardless of which of the mainstream parties wins an election, and to a sense that all the mainstream parties are more interested in protecting their own privileges than in advancing the interests of ordinary citizens.

Particularly in their early days (before they faced the temptations of joining the cartel and enjoying public office), both Green Parties on the left and Scandinavian Progress Parties on the right exemplified anti-cartel parties.

Business-firm parties

An alternative form of challenger to established parties is represented by what Hopkin and Paolucci (1999) have called the 'business-firm party'. The prototypical example is Forza Italia, a 'party' created by Silvio Berlusconi—a businessman who became prime minister in Italy—essentially as a wholly owned subsidiary of his corporate empire and staffed largely by its employees. While there may be an organization on the ground to mobilize supporters, it is only 'a lightweight organisation with the sole basic function of mobilising short-term support at election time' (Hopkin and Paolucci 1999: 315). Although Forza Italia developed from a previously existing firm, Hopkin and Paolucci argue that essentially the same model will typify 'purpose-built' parties in the future.

Parties in the US

Parties in the US present yet another model. From a European perspective, they appear to have much in common

Box 12.3 Types of American primary

Closed primary	Only those who have registered in advance as 'members' of the party may participate.
Modified primary	Those who have registered as 'members' of the party, and—at the party's discretion—those who are registered as 'independent' or 'non-affiliated' voters may participate.
Open primary	All registered voters may participate in the primary election of the one party of their choice.
Blanket primary	All registered voters may participate, choosing if they wish among the candidates of a different party for each office. The candidates of each party with the most votes become the nominees.
Louisiana 'primary'	All registered voters may participate, choosing among all of the candidates for each office. If a candidate receives an absolute majority of the votes, that person is elected, and the 'primary' in effect becomes the election for that office. Otherwise, the two candidates with the most votes, regardless of party, become the candidates for the (run-off) general election.
Top Two Primary	All registered voters may participate and all candidates are listed together. The two candidates with the most votes, regardless of party, compete in the general election.

with the nineteenth-century cadre party, and Duverger famously identified them as a historical throwback or case of 'arrested development'. What they have in common with the cadre party is (1) a weak central organization, (2) a focus on individual candidates rather than enduring institutions, and (3) the absence of a formal membership organization. Where they differ profoundly, however, is in being extensively regulated by law, to the extent that Epstein (1986) could reasonably characterize them as 'public utilities', and in allowing the mass 'membership' (see later for an explanation of the quotation marks) to make the most important decision, that of candidate selection.

Reflecting the federal nature of the country, the basic unit of party organization is the state party. The national committees of the two parties, which control the national party central offices and elect the national chairmen, are made up of representatives of the state parties. The national conventions are not policy-makers, even in form; they are called for the purpose of selecting—and effectively since the 1950s merely confirming the selection of—presidential candidates. Moreover, reflecting the separation of powers in the American constitution, both parties have separate organizations in each house of the Congress, which not only serve as the equivalent of parliamentary party caucuses but also maintain their own independent fundraising and campaign-mounting capacity, almost as if they were separate parties.

The three key features of the American legal system of party regulation are (1) the use of primary elections, (2) the vacuous definition of party membership, and (3) the candidate-centred nature of party regulation. In the decades around the turn of the twentieth century, reformers intent on breaking what they saw as the corrupt and excessive power of party bosses, 'democratized' the parties by putting power into the hands of ordinary party members (whom they identified as party voters) through the use of primary elections (see Box 12.3).

Virtually all of the party's candidates for public office, as well as the vast majority of delegates to its national nominating convention, are also chosen in primary elections. Unlike so-called primaries in other countries, these are public elections, run by the state and structured by public law rather than party rules. The second element of these reforms was to deny the parties the right to define or control their own memberships. Rather than having formal members, American parties only have 'registrants', i.e. voters who have chosen to affiliate with one of the parties in the process of registering to vote.

American law generally treats registrants as if they were members in a more substantive sense, but the party has no control over who registers as a 'member', and the member takes on no obligation by enrolling. Moreover, some states do not have partisan registration, and even in some states that do have partisan registration any voter can claim the right to participate in a party's primary elections (open primary) without even the pretence of prior registration in it. Generally, the choice between open and closed (only party registrants may participate) primaries is determined by state law, although the parties have won (in court) the right for each party to determine for itself whether to allow voters who are not registered as 'members' of any party to participate in its own primary. Finally, even when ostensibly dealing with parties, American legal regulations focus on candidates as individuals. The overwhelming majority of the money spent in American campaigns is controlled by the candidates' own committees or by ostensibly non-partisan groups, and in general the parties are regarded merely as a privileged class of 'contributor'.

Even though eligibility for the public support given to finance presidential campaigns is based on the vote shares of their parties' candidates in the previous election, the money itself is given to the campaign committees of the candidates, not to the party organizations. The right to call oneself the candidate of a party is won in its primary election, with the party organization unable to bar any qualified voter who presents the requisite number of petition signatures and/or fee from competing.

Membership

Although the original parties of intra-parliamentary origin had no members other than the MPs who aligned themselves with a party caucus, most modern parties claim to have a membership organization. However, the modes of acquiring membership, the role played by members both in rhetoric and in practice, and the size of the membership organization vary widely among parties.

As suggested previously, the prototypical membership-based party is the mass party. In its simplest form, the members of a mass party are individuals who have applied and been accepted as members of local branches or sections. In some parties, this form of direct individual membership is, or was, supplemented by indirect membership acquired as part of membership in an affiliated organization. Most commonly these were trade unions affiliated to social democratic parties, such as the British Labour Party.

Affiliated membership might come automatically and inescapably as part of union (or other group) membership, or it might require an explicit choice by the potential member either to acquire party membership ('contracting in') or to decline party membership ('contracting out'); membership rights, such as voting for members of the party executive, might be exercised by the individual or indirectly through representatives of the affiliated organization. With the development of the catch-all party model and the weakening of social class as the basis of party politics, affiliated memberships have been dropped by some parties (e.g. the Swedish Social Democrats), leaving only individual membership.

Membership remains important to the self-understanding of many parties, and the idea that party leaders should be responsible to a membership organization has been widely embraced as a necessary element of democratic governance, although there are prominent dissenters from this view (e.g. Sartori 1965: 124).

Despite its perceived importance, party membership has generally been declining, often in absolute terms but almost always relative to the size of the electorate (see Table 12.2 for examples). Although some scholars (e.g. Katz 1990) argue that members may cost a party more than they are worth—and that the value to a citizen of being a party member may also exceed its cost—this has

Table 12.2 Party membership

Country	Membership/electorate (%)			
	Time 1	%	Time 2	%
Austria	1980	28.48	2008	17.27
Belgium	1980	8.97	2008	5.52
Czech Republic	1993	7.04	2008	1.99
Denmark	1980	7.30	2008	4.13
Finland	1980	15.74	2006	8.08
France	1978	5.05	2009	1.85
Germany	1980 (West only)	4.52	2007 (whole)	2.30
Greece	1980	3.19	2008	6.59
Hungary	1990	2.11	2008	1.54
Ireland	1980	5.00	2008	2.03
Italy	1980	9.66	2007	5.57
Netherlands	1980	4.29	2009	2.48
Norway	1980	15.35	2008	5.04
Portugal	1980	4.28	2008	3.82
Slovakia	1994	3.29	2007	2.02
Spain	1980	1.20	2008	4.36
Switzerland	1977	10.66	2008	4.76
UK	1980	4.12	2008	1.21

Sources: Mair and Biezen (2001); Biezen *et al.* (2012).

commonly been regarded as a problem, for which, however, no real solution has yet been found.

Regulation

Whether or not they reflect the merging of parties with the state, an increasing number of countries have enacted special 'party laws', either supplementing or replacing legal regimes that treated parties as simply one more category of private association. In some cases, these party laws are embedded in the national constitution, while in others they are ordinary statutes or bodies of regulations.

Justifications of special party laws can generally be categorized into three groups. The first is the *centrality of parties to democracy*. In several cases (Germany, France, Spain, Portugal, Greece, Italy), this is specifically acknowledged in the national constitution, while in others it has been acknowledged either in the law or in the parliamentary debates when the law was enacted. In general, the importance of parties to democracy has been a justification for giving parties special rights, protections, or privileges beyond those that would normally be granted to an 'ordinary' private association.

The second, albeit closely related, justification is the *power of parties*. Because of their central position in democratic government, a party that is anti-democratic or corrupt may pose a particularly serious threat to democracy. Hence, if their importance justifies special privileges, the dangers they pose justify special oversight and restrictions.

Third, a party law may be justified as a matter of administrative convenience or necessity. Most commonly, this justification has revolved around the twin problems of ballot access (the right to place candidates on the ballot) and control over the party's name or symbols (particularly on the ballot), although the related question of the right to form a parliamentary group may also be involved. (Alternatively, this may be regulated by the parliament's own Rules of Procedure—see Chapter 7.)

Where there is a party law, one of the first issues to be dealt with is the definition of party—to determine whether a group is entitled to the privileges and subject to the regulations of the law. Unlike the definitions discussed earlier, legal definitions are generally procedural and organizational, and may indeed distinguish between parties in general and parties that are entitled to special treatment. For example, while the Canada Elections Act defines a party simply as 'an organization one of whose fundamental purposes is to participate in public affairs by endorsing one or more of its members as candidates and supporting their election', the 'real' definition is that of a 'registered party'. To be a registered party, an organization must file an application declaring that it meets the definition of a party just quoted, but also declaring its full name, a short-form name or abbreviation (that will appear on the ballot), its logo (if any), and the names,

addresses, and signed consent of the party's leader, officers, auditor, chief agent, and 250 electors. Finally, it must endorse at least one candidate.[6] In other countries, official recognition may require that the party 'offer sufficient guarantee of the sincerity of their aims' (German Law on Political Parties of 1967, Section 2(1)), and/or adhere to prescribed norms of internal democracy.

Continuing with the Canadian example, once a party is registered it acquires a number of privileges including the following: (1) contributions to the party become eligible for tax credits; (2) the party's name appears on the ballot; (3) if it has received at least 2 per cent of the valid votes nationally or 5 per cent of the valid votes in the districts in which it had candidates, half of its election expenses can be reimbursed by the federal treasury and the party can receive a quarterly subvention based on its vote at the previous election. The requirements for ballot access in Canada are the same for party and non-party candidates (except that a candidate wishing to have a party designation on the ballot must submit a letter of endorsement from the party leader in addition to the required signatures and deposit), but in some countries the candidates of a registered party, or a party that already has some level of representation in parliament, may be given a place on the ballot without having to satisfy the requirements imposed on non-party or new party or very minor party candidates.

On the other hand, acquiring official status often also subjects a party to a number of obligations. Canadian registered parties, for example, are required to submit frequent, and audited, financial reports. German law requires membership participation in the selection of party leaders and that candidates be selected by secret ballot, requirements that are not imposed in equivalent detail on other private associations.

Finance

As is implicit in the preceding section, one field in which state involvement in the affairs of parties has been particularly prominent is that of finance. Traditionally, this has taken the form of regulation, and most specifically of prohibitions—against taking money from certain sources, or using it for certain purposes. Although they were directed at candidates rather than parties *per se* (which the law did not explicitly recognize), the British Corrupt Practice Prevention Act of 1854 and the Corrupt and Illegal Practices Prevention Act of 1883 were early examples. Often these were supplemented by requirements of public disclosure of sources of income, objects of expenditure, or both. In recent decades, these regulatory regimes have been supplemented in many countries by programmes of state support for parties. Some of these take the form of 'tax expenditures', while in other cases parties receive either partial reimbursement of expenses or subventions directly from the state, frequently accompanied by even more invasive regulations justified as monitoring the use of public money.

Regulation of spending

Regulation of party spending has been more or less synonymous with regulation of *campaign* spending—although, of course, parties spend money on many things that are at best indirectly related to campaigns (e.g. social events that help cement member commitment but have no overt connection to a campaign). These regulations take three general forms: bans on particular forms of spending, limitations on total spending, and required disclosure of spending.

Aside from bans on such obviously corrupt practices as vote buying or bribery, the most significant prohibition (or limitation) of a specific form of expenditure concerns the buying of advertising time in the broadcast media. Limitations on total spending are generally based on the size of the electorate and the type of office involved. Expenditure reports are frequently required, and provide some element of transparency, but differ widely among countries with regard to the categories of expenditure that are reported, the degree of detail (e.g. specific recipients or only category totals), the frequency and currency of reports, and the degree to which reports are audited or otherwise subject to independent verification.

Beyond these questions of reporting, all forms of regulation of party spending confront a number of interrelated problems concerning exactly whose spending is to be controlled. Is it parties as organizations, or candidates as individuals, or everyone, including those without formal ties to either candidates or party organizations? To exclude parties (or to include national party organizations but not their local affiliates) is likely to make regulation nugatory, but to include them requires a level of official recognition that until recently was rare in countries with single-member district electoral systems. To include everyone may be seen as an unacceptable limitation on the political speech rights of citizens, but to include only formal party organizations and their candidates risks the explosion of spending by organizations that are simply the party in another guise, but now unregulated or less regulated.

Once party and campaign spending are equated, a further problem becomes the definition of the campaign. This involves two questions. First, when does the campaign begin? If the regulated campaign period is too short, its regulation may be of little consequence. Japan, for example, has a very short formal campaign period during which virtually everything is prohibited, but it is preceded by a real campaign subject to very little regulation. Second, what activity is campaign activity? As with the question of regulating non-party spending, an excessively broad definition of campaigning may subject all political speech to burdensome regulation, but

an excessively narrow definition, such as the American 'magic words' doctrine (only messages containing words or phrases like 'vote for', 'elect', 'Smith for Congress', 'vote against', and 'defeat', and referring to a specific candidate, count as campaigning) may defeat the purpose of the regulations.

Regulation of fundraising

Contribution limits are designed to prevent wealthy individuals or groups from exercising undue influence over parties (although, of course, the meaning of 'undue' is often in the eye of the beholder). In various places, foreigners, corporations (sometimes only public corporations or only firms in heavily regulated industries; in other cases all businesses), or trade unions are barred from making, and parties from accepting, political contributions. Anonymous contributions are also generally barred, perhaps from fear that the anonymity will be in name only.

Regardless of who is allowed to make contributions, there may also be limits on the size of contributions from an individual donor to an individual recipient, in aggregate, or both. However, both kinds of limits are relatively easy to evade: rather than making a corporate contribution, a corporation can 'bundle' (collect centrally and then deliver together) what appear to be individual donations from its officers or employees; an individual can give many times the individual legal limit by 'arranging' to have donations made in the name of his/her spouse, children, and other close relatives. Moreover, the definition of 'contribution' itself is problematic. Money is obvious, but should in-kind contributions be included (and how should they be valued)? What about the donation of services? And perhaps most vexing of all, if a person or group independently advocates the election of a party or candidate (what in the US are called 'independent expenditures'), does that count as a contribution subject to limitation, or free speech that must be protected? Finally, whether or not contributions are restricted, their subversive (of democracy) effect may be limited by requirements of public disclosure.

Public subventions

A growing number of countries provide support for parties through their tax systems, through the direct provision of goods and services, or through direct financial subventions. In some cases, these supports are specifically tied to election campaigns (or alternatively limited to non-campaign-related research institutes) while in others they are unrestricted grants for general party activities (see Chapter 7).

The earliest and most common public subventions are the provision of staff to parliamentary parties or their members, ostensibly to support their official functions but often convertible to more general political purposes. Particularly in countries in which broadcasting is a public monopoly, parties are generally given an allocation of free air time; other examples of free provision of services include the mailing of candidates' election addresses (e.g. UK), free space for billboards (e.g. Spain, Israel, and Germany), free use of halls in public buildings for rallies (e.g. UK, Spain, Japan), and reduced rates for office space (e.g. Italy). Although these raise some problems, the more contentious question is the direct provision of money, which is nonetheless becoming nearly universal.

Public support for parties raises two questions (beyond the somewhat specious question of whether people should be compelled through their taxes to subsidize causes with which they do not agree). First, is the primary effect of state subventions to allow parties to perform better their functions of policy formulation, public education, and linkage between society and the government? Or is it to further the separation between parties and those they are supposed to represent by making parties less dependent on voluntary support? Second, do systems of public support (in which the levels of support are almost always tied to electoral support at the previous election),[7] as well as rules limiting individual contributions, further fairness and equality, or do they unfairly privilege those parties that already are dominant?

KEY POINTS

- Party organizational types have evolved over time as suffrage was expanded and societies changed.

- Rather than reaching an endpoint, organizations continue to evolve and new types continue to develop.

- Party membership, and involvement of citizens in party politics more generally, appears to be declining virtually throughout the democratic world.

- Parties are increasingly the subject of legal regulation which, while justified in the name of fairness, may also contribute to the entrenchment of the parties that currently are strong.

Parties and the stabilization of democracy

Parties were central to the transition from traditional monarchy to liberal democracy in the first wave of democratization (primarily in the late nineteenth and early twentieth centuries), but they have also been central actors in the third wave (see Chapter 5). In the older democracies, where the liberal rights of contestation were established before suffrage was expanded to the majority of citizens, parties helped to integrate newly enfranchised citizens into the established patterns of competition. While enfranchisement generally led to the rapid growth of parties (most often socialist) appealing specifically to the new voters, even what are now identified as 'bourgeois parties' found it in their interest to appeal to the new voters—for example, as citizens, or Christians, or members of a peripheral culture rather than as workers.

In immigrant societies, such as the US, Canada, Australia, or those in South America, the parties also contributed to the integration of arrivals into their new country. The degree to which parties (and other institutions) could perform this function successfully was strongly influenced by the magnitude of the load placed upon them by the rapidity of suffrage expansion. Where the franchise was broadened in several steps spaced over decades, as in the UK, the existing parties were generally able to adapt, with the result that would-be demagogues or revolutionaries found a very limited market. When franchise expansion was more abrupt, as in France in 1848 or Italy in 1913, the twin dangers that masses of new voters would be mobilized by radicals, and that this possibility would be perceived by others to be a threat requiring drastic measures, often led to the collapse of democracy.

This function of integration and stabilization is also potentially important in the new democracies of the late twentieth century. Particularly in the formerly communist bloc (but not only there), the process of democratization has differed from that in the earlier waves in that political mobilization of the citizenry preceded the development of public contestation (Enyedi 2006: 228). Moreover, the levels of literacy, general education, access to mass media, and international involvement far exceed those of earlier waves. Coupled with this has been a deep distrust of the whole idea of political parties, rooted in the unhappy experience of the communist party state. Among the results have been extremely low rates of party membership (giving rise to the idea of a 'couch party'— one whose membership is so small that they could all sit on a single couch) and quite high electoral volatility. Not only has the attachment of voters to particular parties been problematic, so too has the attachment of elected politicians, with parliamentary party groups showing such low levels of stability that in some cases parliamentary rules have been changed specifically to discourage party splits or defections.

A second major area in which the role of parties in stabilizing democracy is in doubt is the Islamic world, where the question is whether the electoral success of Islamist parties helps to integrate their followers into democratic politics, or alternatively threatens to undermine democracy altogether (Tepe 2006). The underlying conflict of values—the will of God as articulated by clerics versus the will of the people as articulated at the ballot box—is hardly unique to the Islamic world (and indeed was important throughout the nineteenth century in Europe), but now appears particularly pressing there.

Conclusion

Political parties remain central to democratic government in the twenty-first century. It is still parties that contest elections and identify most of the candidates. It is still parties that structure the coalitions required to enact legislation and support governments. Nonetheless, parties face a number of potentially serious challenges.

As already suggested, party membership is declining almost everywhere (van Biezen *et al.* 2012). One result has been to force parties to become more dependent on financial contributions and other forms of support from corporations and organizations of special interests, and more recently to 'feed at the public trough' through direct public subventions. This decline in party involvement has not been limited to formal members, but is also reflected in declining party identification, and perhaps most significantly in the growth of hostility not just to the particular parties in a given country at a given time, but to the whole idea of parties and of partisanship. One manifestation of this is the growth of anti-party-system parties; another is the number of new parties that eschew the use of that word in their names and even of existing parties that try to 'rebrand' themselves without the party denomination (e.g. 'New Labour' instead of 'Labour Party').

The growing popularity of such ideas as 'consensus democracy' (Lijphart 1999) and 'deliberative democracy' (e.g. Guttmann and Thompson 2004; Budge 2000), like the complaint of former President Carter that the 2004 US presidential election campaign was 'too partisan', are reflective of a desire for amicable agreement that denies the existence of real conflicts of interest. But if one accepts Finer's (1970: 8) definition of politics as what happens when 'a given set of persons ... require a *common* policy; and ... its members advocate, for this common status, policies that are *mutually exclusive*', this is in effect to want to take the politics out of democracy.

Although rarely put overtly in these terms, the alternative to contentious and partisan politics is generally some form of government by experts or technocrats. Often these 'reforms' have been advocated and enacted by parties themselves as a way of avoiding responsibility for unpopular but unavoidable decisions or for outcomes that are beyond their control. Even when the parties remain centrally involved in policy, increasingly their role (and the basis upon which they compete) is defined in terms of management rather than direction. However, by reducing the policy stakes of elections, parties have also decreased the incentives for citizens to become active in them (Katz 2003) and given ammunition to those who ask why the state should provide subsidies and other special privileges (Mair 1995).

The role of parties as representatives of the people, or as links between the people and the state, has also been challenged by the increasing range of organizations that compete with them as 'articulators of interest'. Rather than being forced to choose among a limited number of packages of policy stances across a range of issues—some of which may be of little interest, and others which he/she may actually oppose—the modern citizen can mix and match among any number of groups, each of which will reflect his/her preferences more accurately on a single issue than any party could hope to do. With improved communications skills, and especially with the rise of the internet, citizens may feel less need for intermediaries—they can communicate directly with those in power themselves.

Many parties have themselves tried to adapt to more sophisticated electorates and new technologies, giving rise to the possibility of 'cyber parties' (Margetts 2006; see also Chapter 19). In its initial stages, this may be little more than the use of mass e-mailings to 'members' (now of mailing lists rather than of real organizations) and the use of the mechanisms of e-commerce to facilitate fundraising from individuals. In a more developed form, exemplified by Barack Obama's 2008 campaign in the US, it is likely to include chat-rooms, discussion list-servers, and extensive fund-raising facilities. In theory, the technology might allow what would amount to a party meeting that is always in session. To date, however, there has been more evidence of people at the grass roots using the internet to send messages to those in positions of authority rather than evidence of those in authority actually listening. And as with the party congresses of the last century, even if the internet (or simply the regular mail) is used to allow party members or supporters to make decisions, real power will continue to rest with those who frame the questions. It remains unlikely that the internet will somehow lead to the repeal of the iron law of oligarchy.

Overall, then, there are two challenges facing parties at the beginning of the twenty-first century. One is the increasing complexity of problems, the increasing speed of social and economic developments, and increasing globalization—all making the problems facing parties as governors less tractable. The other is the increasing political capacity of citizens (cognitive mobilization) running into the ineluctable limitations of individual influence in societies of the size of modern states—expectations of effective individual involvement, even if restricted to the minority who are politically interested, are often unrealistic. Both challenge widely held views of how democratic party government should work. How parties adapt to these changing circumstances, whether by redefining their roles or by altering public expectations, will shape the future of democracy.

Questions

1. Is a group that nominates candidates in order to put pressure on other parties, but with no real hope of winning an election itself, properly called a political party?

2. Is 'political party' better understood as a category, into which each case either does or does not fit, or as an ideal type, which each case can more or less closely approximate?

3. Is democracy conceivable without political parties?

4. What is the 'iron law of oligarchy'?

5. How do cartel parties differ from catch-all parties?

6. Does the US have 'real' political parties?

7. Is the regulation of political parties' finance compatible with political freedom?

8. What is the meaning of 'left' in political terms?

9. Do political parties play the same role in new democracies as in the established democracies?

10. Must a democratic political party be internally democratic?

Further reading

Katz, R. S. and Crotty, W. (eds) (2006) *Handbook of Party Politics* (London: Sage). Extensive discussions of many of the topics raised.

Katz, R. S. and Mair, P. (1992) *Party Organizations: A Data Handbook on Party Organizations in Western Democracies, 1960–90* (London: Sage). Extensive, but somewhat dated, data concerning party organizations.

Classics on political parties

Duverger, M. (1954) *Political Parties* (New York: John Wiley).

Hershey, M. R. (2006) *Party Politics in America* (12th edn) (New York: Longman).

LaPalombara, J. and Weiner, M. (eds) (1966) *Political Parties and Political Development* (Princeton, NJ: Princeton University Press).

Panebianco, A. (1988) *Political Parties: Organization and Power* (Cambridge: Cambridge University Press).

Sartori, G. (1976) *Parties and Party Systems: A Framework for Analysis* (Cambridge: Cambridge University Press).

Annual reports (from 1991) on party politics in most established democracies are available in the *Political Data Yearbook*, published as the last issue each year of the *European Journal of Political Research*. In addition, the *European Journal of Political Research*, *West European Politics*, and *Party Politics* focus heavily on issues concerning political parties.

Web links

www.electionresources.org
Manuel Álvarez-Rivera's Election Resources in the Internet.

www.psr.keele.ac.uk
Richard Kimber's website on Political Science Resources (University of Keele).

www.electionworld.org
Website includes information on political parties around the world with up-to-date election results and other information on the party system and the main institutions.

www.gksoft.com/govt/en/parties.html
Webpage of Government on the WWW devoted to political parties and party systems around the world. The main page includes additional information on heads of state, parliaments, executives, courts, and other institutions.

http://pdba.georgetown.edu/
Website of the Political Database of the Americas including information on parties and party systems.

http://libraries.ucsd.edu/locations/sshl/data-gov-info-gis/ssds/guides/lij/
Website of the Lijphart Election Archive with information on party systems, electoral systems, and recent election results around the world.

https://www.cia.gov/library/publications/the-world-factbook/index.html
Website of CIA's The World Factbook with information on institutions, social structures, economic data, and party systems for most countries of the world.

www.idea.int
Website of the International Institute for Democracy and
Electoral Assistance (IDEA).

www2.essex.ac.uk/elect/database/aboutProject.asp
Website of the project on Political Transformation and the
Electoral Process in Post-Communist Europe (University of
Essex).

www.partylaw.leidenuniv.nl/
Website of the Party Law in Modern Europe project.

www.eiu.com
Country Reports and Country Profiles published by the
Economist Intelligence Unit are very useful for an overview and
recent data.

**online
resource
centre**

For additional material and resources, please visit the Online Resource Centre at:
www.oxfordtextbooks.co.uk/orc/caramani3e/

CHAPTER 13

Party systems

Daniele Caramani

Chapter contents

Reader's guide

This chapter looks at the competition between parties and how it leads to different party systems. First, the chapter looks at the *origins* of party systems. Historical cleavages between left and right, the liberal state and religious values or ethno-regional identities, agrarian and industrial sectors of the economy, led to socialist, liberal, religious, regionalist, and other party families. Why are they still the main actors today? Second, the chapter looks at the *format* of party systems, some of which include two large parties (two-party systems) while others are more fragmented (multiparty systems). What is the influence of the electoral system, and what are the consequences for governmental stability? Third, the chapter analyses the *dynamics* of party systems. To maximize votes parties tailor their programmes to voters' preferences and converge towards the centre of the left–right axis. Is this why parties propose increasingly similar policies and programmes?

Introduction

This chapter views parties in their connections within a system. As in planetary systems, the focus is not on single planets but on the constellations they form: their number, the balance of size between them, and the distance that separates them. Parties can be ideologically near or distant, there are systems with many small parties or few large ones or even—to pursue the analogy further—one large party with 'satellites' (as in some authoritarian systems). Over time some systems change while others remain stable. Thus the variety of party 'constellations' is very large.

Whereas the dynamic principle of planets is gravity, the motor of political interactions is competition for power. In liberal democracies this competition is based on popular votes. The shape and dynamics of **party systems** are determined by the electoral game in which parties are the main actors. Therefore a party system is first and foremost the result of *competitive interactions* between parties. As in all 'games' there is a goal: the maximization of votes to control government. In this sense, party systems are much more changeable than planetary systems. However, the set of interactions between parties is not exclusively composed of competition, but also of *cooperation* (for instance, when they build a coalition).

Three main elements of party systems are important.

1. *Which parties exist?* Why do some parties exist in all party systems (e.g. socialists) whereas others only in some (e.g. regionalists or religious parties)? This relates to the origin, or genealogy, of party systems.

2. *How many parties exist and how big are they?* Why are some systems composed of two large parties and others of many small ones? This relates to the format, or morphology, of party systems.

3. *How do parties behave?* Why in some systems do parties converge towards the centre whereas in others they diverge to the extremes of the ideological 'space'? This relates to the dynamics of party systems.

An obvious but important point is that party systems must be composed of several parties. There is no 'system' with one unit only. The competitive interaction between parties requires pluralism. If the goal is to get the most votes, there must be free elections and pluralism without which competition cannot exist. Therfore this chapter focuses on democratic systems and excludes authoritarian regimes such as China with single parties.

KEY POINTS

- Party systems are sets of parties that compete and cooperate with the aim of increasing their power in controlling government.
- Interactions are determined by (1) which parties exist, (2) how many parties compose a system and how large they are, (3) the way in which they maximize votes.
- It is appropriate to speak of a party system only in democratic contexts in which several parties compete for votes in open and plural elections.

The genealogy of party systems

The 'national' and 'industrial' revolutions

Most contemporary parties and party families originated from the socio-economic and political changes between the mid-nineteenth century and the first two decades of the twentieth. Lipset and Rokkan (1967) distinguish two aspects of this transformation: (1) the *Industrial Revolution* refers to changes produced by industrialization and urbanization; (2) the *National Revolution* refers to the formation of nation-states (culturally homogeneous and centralized political units) and liberal democracy (parliamentarism, individual civil and voting rights, rule of law, and secular institutions).

The Industrial and National Revolutions created socio-economic and cultural divisions opposing different social groups, values, and interests. Lipset and Rokkan called these conflicts cleavages (see Box: What is a cleavage?, in the Online Resource Centre). With the birth of modern parliaments and free elections, and with the extension of franchise, political parties developed and mirrored the socio-economic and cultural divisions created by the two 'revolutions'. Modern party families appeared as the 'political translation' of social divisions in systems in which conflict is settled through vote.

online resource centre

Cleavages and their political translation

Lipset and Rokkan distinguish four main cleavages created by the two 'revolutions' (see Table 13.1). These revolutions have each produced two main cleavages. Subsequent transformations have produced additional cleavages, namely the 'International Revolution',

Table 13.1 Stein Rokkan's cleavages and their partisan expression

Revolution	Timing	Cleavage	Divisive issue(s)	Party families	Examples
National	Early 19th century (restricted electorates)	Centre–periphery	Liberals face resistance to state centralization and cultural standardization (language/religion)	Regionalists, ethnic parties, linguistic parties, minorities	Scottish National Party, Bloc Québéquois, Partido Nacionalista Vasco
		State–church	Conflict between liberal and secularized state against clerical and aristocratic privilege, and over religious education, influence of church in politics	Conservative and religious parties (Catholic mainly), Christian democracy	Austrian People's Party, Christian-Democratic Union, Swiss Catholic Party, Partido Popular
Industrial	Late 19th century (suffrage extension)	Rural–urban	Conflict between industrial and agricultural sectors on trade policies: agrarian protectionism vs. industrial liberalism (free trade vs. tariffs)	Agrarian and peasant parties	Finnish Centre Party, Australian Country Party, Polish Peasant People's Party
		Workers–employers	Employers vs. the working class on job security, pensions, social protection, degree of state intervention in economy	Workers' parties, socialists and social democrats, labour parties	British Labour Party, Argentinian Socialist Party, Swedish Social-Democratic Workers' Party, Spanish PSOE
International	Early 20th century (mass electorates)	Communists–socialists	Division within the 'left' (workers' movement) over centrality of the Soviet Union Communist Party and its international leadership, and over reformism vs. revolution	Communists	Partito Comunista Italiano, Izquierda Unida, Parti Communiste Français, Japan's Communist Party
Post-industrial	Late 20th century (demobilized electorates)	Materialist–post-materialist values	Generational cleavage over policy priorities: new values of civic rights, pacifism, feminism, environment	Green parties, libertarians	Die Grünen, Pirates Party, Austrian Grünen/ Grüne Alternative, Democrats '66, Women's Party
		Open–closed societies	Globalization of the economy, opening up of labour markets, competition from cheap Asian labour, fiscal and monetary integration in Europe, and against Americanization of culture	Protest parties, extreme right-wing parties, neopopulist parties	FPÖ, Front National, Danish Progress Party, Fifth Republic Movement (Hugo Chávez), Movement for Socialism (Evo Morales)

triggered by the Soviet Revolution of 1917, and the 'Post-Industrial Revolution' in the 1960s–70s, which led to a value cleavage between generations and **globalization** since the late 1990s.

In the nineteenth century, socio-economic and cultural conflicts emerged simultaneously with democratic reforms: the creation of modern parliaments, free elections, and the extension of civil and political rights. Conflicts of that time were expressed in organizations that were typical of this new regime. Political parties are the product of the parliamentary and electoral game, and party systems reflect the social oppositions that characterized society when parties first appeared. The fundamental features of today's party systems were set during the early phases of mobilization of, at first, restricted electorates (only very few people had the right to vote when liberals and conservatives dominated in the nineteenth century) and, later, of 'massifying' electorates when socialist parties mobilized the vast working class that emerged from the Industrial Revolution.

The National Revolution produced two cleavages.

Centre–periphery cleavage

This conflict emerged when nation-states formed in the nineteenth century, and political power, administrative structures, and taxation systems were centralized. This process also brought about national languages and sometimes religions. Most national territories were heterogeneous with different ethnicities and languages, and administration was fragmented. Nationalist and liberal elites carried out state formation and nation-building, facing resistance from subject populations in peripheral territories in two aspects.

1. *Administrative:* peripheries were incorporated in the bureaucratic and fiscal system of the new state (e.g. with the creation of provinces or departments through which the central state controlled the territory of and extracted taxes), implying a loss of autonomy for regions.

2. *Cultural:* religious, ethnic, and linguistic identities in peripheral regions were replaced by the allegiance to the new nation-state fostered through compulsory schooling, military conscription, and other means of national socialization. As the first Italian prime minister said in 1870 after Italy unified, 'We have made Italy, let us make Italians'. Nation-building also took place in old-established states. In France in 1863, according to official figures, only 22 per cent of the communes spoke French, all located around the Paris region (Weber 1976: 67).

Resistance to administrative centralization and cultural standardization was and still is expressed in regionalist parties, such as the Scottish National Party, the Swedish Party in Finland, the various Basque and Catalan parties in Spain, the Bloc Québéquois in Canada, and so on, opposing nationalist/liberal parties.

State–church cleavage

Nation-states in the nineteenth century were not only centralized and homogeneous, but also based on liberal ideology and secular institutions (no church influence), individualism, and democracy (sometimes republicanism). Liberal reforms and the abolition of estates (clergy, aristocracy, bourgeoisie, peasantry) of pre-modern parliaments, as well as the individual vote and free elections, put an end to clerical and aristocratic privilege. In this, liberals were opposed by conservatives in a conflict between the rising industrial bourgeoisie and the corporate privilege of clergy and aristocracy.

The new liberal secular state fought against the long-established role of the church in education. Compulsory education by the state was used to 'forge' new *citizens*. Especially in Catholic countries this led to conflicts, whereas in Protestant countries—where churches belong to the state—the cleavage focused on moral principles. The church was also expropriated of real estate and, in Italy, it lost its temporal power and state (about a fourth of the Italian peninsula) when Italy unified as a nation-state in 1860–70.

Conservatives wanted the return to the old pre-democratic regime. In some countries, Catholics took the place of conservatives, as in Belgium, Switzerland, and Germany. In other countries, Catholics were banned from being candidates and voting by papal decree (for this reason, Catholic parties did not appear in Italy and France until the early 1920s). In fact, it was not until after the breakdown of democracy and the inter-war fascist period that the Catholic Church fully accepted democracy. 'Christian democracy'—in Italy, France, Germany, Austria—appears from this evolution after the Second World War.

An interesting case is that of countries with mixed religious structures. In the Netherlands there was one unified Catholic party and a number of Reformed and Calvinist parties reflecting the fragmentation of Protestantism. In 1972 the religious parties merged into the Christian Democratic Appeal. An inter-confessional party also developed in Germany (the Christian Democratic Union). In Switzerland a major Catholic party emerged from the opposition to the Protestant Radicals/Liberals.

The Industrial Revolution produced two additional cleavages.

Rural–urban cleavage

The first was the contrast between landed interests (agriculture) and the rising class of industrial and trading entrepreneurs. This cleavage focused on trade policies, with agrarians favouring trade barriers on agricultural products (protectionism) and industrialists favouring free market and trade with low tariffs (liberalism). This cleavage was reinforced by cultural differences between the countryside and urban centres where industries concentrated.

Weak sectors of the economy tend to be protectionist because of the threat of imports, whereas strong sectors favour the opening up of economic borders to increase exports (Rogowski 1989). Agriculture was threatened by technological progress and growth of productivity. The defence of agrarian interests—when peasant populations received the right to vote—was expressed through agrarian parties (also called peasants' or farmers' parties). Large or small agrarian parties existed everywhere in Europe, but were particularly strong in Eastern Europe and in Scandinavia. They also existed in Latin America.

The period after the Second World War witnessed both the decline and transformation of these parties. On the one hand, in most countries peasants' parties disappeared. On the other, the large agrarian parties of the north and east abandoned the agrarian platform and changed into centre parties. The recent reawakening of this cleavage is most notable in Latin America where opposition to multinational companies, defence of raw materials and resources, and the threat of globalization has led to protectionist policies (e.g. gas and oil nationalization in Bolivia and Venezuela). In the 1990s a number of peasant upheavals took place in the Chapas region in Mexico. This cleavage is also present in the European Union where farmers' pressure groups lobby for protectionist trade agreements and state subsidies.

Workers–employers cleavage

This is the cleavage between the industrial entrepreneurial bourgeoisie who started the Industrial Revolution and the working class that resulted from it. It is the opposition between 'capital' and 'labour' which, up to the present, characterizes the left–right alignment. In so far as this split is present in all countries, it is the most important one. Left–right is the most common ideological dimension along which parties are placed, even in the US where a socialist party never developed (see Box 13.1).

Industrialization had a very deep impact on Western societies. It radically changed the production mode, caused unprecedented levels of geographical mobility through urbanization (the dislocation of people from countryside to urban industrial centres), and transformed family structures. Living conditions in industrial centres were extremely poor. Therefore workers were easy to mobilize through trade unions, with socialism providing a unifying ideology. With the extension of voting rights, social democratic and labour parties gained parliamentary representation.

Socialist parties campaigned for labour protection against the capitalist economy. They promoted *social rights* and *welfare state* provisions on top of civil and political rights, and a substantial equalization of living conditions in addition to formal legal equality (Marshall 1950; Kitschelt 1994). These claims concerned under-age and female labour, wages, working hours, contract security, protection in the workplace and during unemployment or illness, progressive taxation, accident insurance, and pension schemes. Socialists favoured economic policies with a strong intervention of the state in steering the economy and public investments (later Keynesianism) against the liberal free-market ideology. They looked for

---

Box 13.1 Why is there no socialism in the US?

A number of classical studies have addressed this question. The main factors explaining the absence of a socialist ideology and workers' party in the most advanced capitalist country are as follows.

- *Open frontier* Geographical and social mobility gave American workers the possibility to move on in search of better conditions.

- *Party machines* Dominance of Democrats and Republicans since the nineteenth century made the rise of third parties difficult.

- *The free gift of the vote* Working-class white men all had the right to vote, were integrated in the political system, and had a say in government's actions.

- *Roast beef and apple pie* The American working class was more affluent than the European and all socialist utopias come to grief with a satisfied working class.

- *No feudalism* The absence of aristocracy in America made the working class very similar to the European bourgeoisie.

Read:

- Lipset, S. M. (1977) 'Why No Socialism in the United States?', in S. Bialer and S. Sluzar (eds), *Sources of Contemporary Radicalism* (Boulder, CO: Westview Press), 131–49.

- ___ and Marks, G. (2000) *It Didn't Happen Here: Why Socialism Failed in the United States* (New York: Norton).

- Sombart, W. (1976) *Why is there No Socialism in the United States?* (London: Macmillan), translated from the German 1906 text.

state ownership of infrastructure (transportation, energy), industries, and sometimes finance.

Many socialist and labour parties originate from previously existing trade unions, the main organizations of the working class before universal suffrage. With restricted franchise most workers did not have the right to vote. Therefore, for most of the nineteenth century, the state was controlled by liberals and conservatives. Unions responded to a number of needs of the working class, increased solidarity and cooperation within it, and provided a wide range of 'services'. With enfranchisement, workers' parties developed as an 'electoral branch' of trade unions.

The Soviet Revolution of 1917 produced a cleavage within the workers' movement.

Communism–socialism cleavage

In the aftermath of the First World War and the Russian Revolution that led to the Soviet Union and the single-party regime controlled by the Communist Party, communist parties in all countries formed as splinters from the socialists. The main issue was the acceptance of the lead of the Soviet Communist Party in the international revolutionary movement and also ideological differences, namely whether a revolution would be necessary to take the proletariat to power, or if this goal could be achieved through elections.

As a reaction against the radicalization of the working class and its powerful action through a new type of **mass party** organization, fascist parties emerged in a number of European countries and, more or less directly, dominated government during the 1930s. These parties favoured the nation over class and 'internationalism', and private property over communism. Fascist parties were the product of the radicalization of the industrial bourgeoisie threatened by socialist policies, and of the aristocracy threatened by redistribution through land reforms.

Finally, the 'Post-Industrial Revolution' (Bell 1973) created two more recent cleavages.

Materialism–post-materialism cleavage

A cleavage between generations over sets of values emerged in the 1960s and 1970s as a consequence of the protracted period of international peace, economic wealth, and domestic security since the Second World War (Inglehart 1977). The younger cohort developed 'post-materialist values' focused on tolerance, equality, participation, expression, emancipation, respect for the environment, fair trade, peace, and Third World solidarity, as opposed to the 'materialist' values of the war generation centred around themes of national security, law and order, full employment, protection of private property, tradition, and authority (within the family and the state).

These new values were primarily expressed in a number of new social movements (see Chapter 16): the civil rights movement in the US in the 1950s, pacifism from the Vietnam War in the 1960s, feminism in the 1970s claiming equality in the labour market and family, and environmentalism in the 1980s. In the 1990s, new anti-globalization movements developed against the globalization of the economy and the Americanization of culture (Della Porta *et al.* 1999). From a party politics perspective, however, there are only a few examples of a significant impact of these 'new left' movements, the main one being green parties (Müller-Rommel and Poguntke 2002). A more pervasive impact of the Post-Industrial Revolution is on the 'new right'.

The globalization cleavage

Economic globalization has created a cleavage between sectors of the economy that profit from the blurring of national boundaries, and sectors that suffer from the competition from new markets and cheap labour from the East and Asia. 'Losers' of globalization and integration (Betz 1994) have reinforced support for neopopulist protest parties who favour trade barriers to protect local manufacture and 'locals-first' policies in the labour market. These groups are the small and medium enterprises, unskilled workers, craftsmen, and agricultural producers.

The economic defensive attitude of these groups is reinforced by cultural, anti-immigration, and xenophobic prejudice, stressing religious and national values against multiethnic society and cosmopolitanism. Many of these parties rely upon an extreme right-wing heritage, such as the Austrian Liberal Party and the French and Belgian National Fronts (Kitschelt 1995). New parties include the British National Party, the UK Independence Party, and the Scandinavian Progress Parties (Kriesi 2013). Others are sporadic parties, such as the One-Nation Party in Australia. In Latin America neopopulist tendencies have a left-wing 'Bolivarian' character as in Bolivia, Ecuador, and Venezuela (Burgess and Levitsky 2003). Neopopulism is also a reaction to changing security conditions which, since the terrorist attacks in the early 2000s, have created a resurgence of law-and-order values.

Variations in cleavage constellations

Cleavage constellations change through space (from country to country) and over time.

Space

Not all cleavages exist in all countries. There are a variety of constellations, and thus of party systems. Why do some cleavages exist in specific countries while not in others? It is difficult to summarize the explicative part of the Lipset–Rokkan model here. Whereas the left–right cleavage exists everywhere and is a source of similarity, the state–church cleavage developed particularly in Catholic countries in Europe and Latin America. The rural–urban cleavage was strong in regions with small farming and independent units, where farmers were not under the control of landlords. The centre–periphery cleavage appears where there are ethno-linguistic minorities.

Therefore country-specific cleavage constellations are determined by the following.

- Differences in objective factors such as diverse social structures: multiple ethnicities or religious groups, structure of the peasantry, class relations.

- The extent to which socio-economic and cultural divisions have been politicized by parties, i.e. by the action of elites (Rose 1976; Lijphart 1968*b*).

- The relationship between cleavages: their existence and strength can prevent the development of new ones (agrarian claims have been incorporated by Catholic parties or by conservative parties where, as in England, agriculture had been commercialized early).

There are *homogeneous constellations* where there is one predominant cleavage, namely the left–right cleavage (e.g. the US) and *heterogeneous constellations* in which various cleavages—economic, ethno-linguistic, religious, territorial—overlap or cut across one other in plural democracies such as Belgium, Canada, India, the Netherlands, and Switzerland (Lijphart 1984).

Time

Party systems have remained extraordinarily stable since the 1920s. Up to the present even party labels have not changed (liberal, socialist, conservative), as a sort of political *imprint*. Lipset and Rokkan have formulated the so-called freezing hypothesis:

> [T]he party systems of the 1960s reflect, with few but significant exceptions, the cleavage structures of the 1920s... [T]he party alternatives, and in remarkably many cases, the party organizations, are older than the majorities of the national electorates. (Lipset and Rokkan 1967: 50; italics omitted)

online resource centre

Today's party systems reflect the original conflicts from which they emerged (see Box: Party families, in the Online Resource Centre) despite a decline in cleavage politics with the blurring of social divisions (Franklin *et al.* 1992). In the 1920s the full mobilization of the electoral market through universal suffrage and PR caused its saturation. Voters acquired strong political identities through partisan identification and socialization processes that proved stable over time. As in all markets, there are entry barriers in the electoral market. Little room was left for new parties. Thus existing parties were able to maintain their control over electorates over generations.

Empirical research debates the basic stability of electorates over time, with theses of *dealignment and realignment* of Western electorates (Dalton *et al.* 1985) based on survey data, or *stabilization* in a long-term perspective (Bartolini and Mair 1990) based on electoral volatility data (the change of votes from one election to the next).

KEY POINTS

- Party families originate from socio-economic and cultural cleavages created by industrialization, urbanization, and the formation of liberal states.

- The centralized and liberal state creates conflicts with the church and with peripheral regions, leading to religious and regionalist parties. Industrialization opposes liberal economic interests to the rural world as well as to the working class, leading to agrarian and labour parties.

- Party constellations 'froze' and have remained stable until the present.

- Examples of recent realignment are the generational cleavage over (post-)materialist values and globalization that led to new party families: greens and neopopulist parties.

The morphology of party systems

The competitive interaction between parties depends on the shape of party systems. The two main elements of their morphology are: (1) the *number* of competing units, i.e. parties, and (2) the *size* of these units. How many players are there and how strong are they? The number and strength of actors can be observed at two levels: the *votes* parties get in elections and the *seats* in parliament. therefore a 'variable' that must be considered is the **electoral system** through which votes are translated into parliamentary seats.

Two types of party systems are not considered in this section because they do not fulfil the democratic conditions that allow competition.

1. Single-party systems with only one legal party: the authoritarian experiences of the Communist Party in the Soviet Union and today in China, the National Socialist Party in Germany in the 1930s, and the Baathist Party in Iraq until 1993 and in Syria until last year.

2. Hegemonic party systems in which other parties are legal but as 'satellites', under the control of the hegemonic party: these are also totalitarian or authoritarian systems which existed in Egypt and Tunisia until the Arab Spring, and in many communist regimes in Central and Eastern Europe before 1989.

The other four types are dominant-party systems, two-party systems, multiparty systems, and bipolar systems.

Dominant-party systems

Dominant-party systems are characterized by one large party with a majority *above the absolute majority* of 50 per cent of seats for *protracted periods of time* (several decades). In these systems all parties are allowed to compete in free elections to challenge the dominant party. However, no other party receives enough votes to come close to 50 per cent. Therefore there is no alternation in power and the dominant party does not need to enter coalitions to form a government.

An example is India between 1947 and 1975. After Independence, the Congress Party received over 50 per cent of votes and was able to rule unchallenged until 1975–77 when the 'state of emergency' was declared. Over the long period of uncontested rule forms of patronage developed, and in 1977 the Congress Party was eventually defeated. A more recent example of a dominant-party system is South Africa since the end of apartheid in the early 1990s. The African National Congress, initially led by Nelson Mandela, has been able to secure an absolute majority of votes because of the role it had in enfranchising the black population. In Europe, a case of a dominant-party system is Sweden. The Social Democratic Workers' Party formed almost all governments from 1945 until 1998, with around 45 per cent of the votes on average. In Mexico, the Institutional Revolutionary Party was in power from the revolution of 1917 until 2000, when it was defeated for the first time.

Two-party systems

A two-party system is one in which two equally balanced large parties dominate the party system and alternate in power. The two parties have comparable sizes and equal chances of winning elections. Even a small amount of votes changing from one party to the other (electoral swing) can cause a change of majority. Therefore alternation in power is frequent. These are very competitive systems. Because both parties are large, the winning party is likely to receive an absolute majority of seats and form single-party governments without the need for partners.

The features of two-party systems are listed in Table 13.2. The two large parties have similar sizes (around 35–45 per cent of the votes each) which plurality electoral systems transform into absolute majorities of seats for the largest party. A number of other smaller parties compete in the elections. However, they are marginal as they are not necessary to form a government. In the UK, the Liberal Democratic Party was needed to support a government together with the Conservatives for the first time after the 2010 election.

In two-party systems single-party governments tend to alternate from one legislature to the next. This is, to a large extent, an effect of plurality electoral systems. Because the threshold in first-past-the-post (FPTP) systems is very high, the two main parties propose policies and programmes that are acceptable to a large part of the

Table 13.2 Types of party system in democracies

Type of party system	Features	Cases
Dominant-party	One large party with more than absolute majority of votes and seats No other party approaching 50% No alternation One-party government	India until 1975, Japan between 1955 and 1993, Mexico until 2000, South Africa since 1994
Two-party	Two large parties sharing together around 80% of votes and seats Balanced (35–45% each) with one of the two reaching 50% of seats Alternation between parties One-party government	Austria, UK, Costa Rica, Malta, New Zealand until 1998, Spain, South Africa until 1989, Turkey, US
Multiparty	Several or many parties, with none approaching 50% of votes and seats Parties of different sizes Parties run for elections individually and form coalitions after elections Alternation through coalition changes Coalition government	Belgium, Canada, Colombia, Czech Republic, Denmark, Finland, Germany until 1989, Hungary, Italy before 1994, Netherlands, Poland, Russia, Switzerland
Bipolar	Two large coalitions composed of several parties sharing together around 80% of votes and seats Coalitions are balanced (40–50% each) Coalitions are stable over time and run elections as electoral alliances Alternation between coalitions Coalition government	France in the Fifth Republic, Germany since 1990, Italy since 1994, Portugal

electorate. Plurality leads to ideological moderation and similarity of programmes. In turn, this similarity makes it easier for voters to switch from one party to the other, creating alternation.

These systems are typical of the Anglo-Saxon world where plurality in single-member districts has been maintained, unlike continental Europe where around the First World War countries changed from majoritarian to PR systems. Today, only the US provides a 'perfect' example of a two-party system where Republicans and Democrats have dominated since 1860.[1] Australia maintains a strong two-party system with the Australian Labour Party and the Liberals. Other examples include Costa Rica (National Liberation Party and Citizens' Action Party) and Malta (where the Labour Party and the Nationalist Party receive together close to 100 per cent of the votes). In Canada, Conservatives and Liberals dominated until 1993 (with a strong New Democratic Party), when the Bloc Québécois and the Reform Party increased their support.

Two-party systems can also be found in countries with PR electoral systems. Until recently, Austria has been dominated by two parties—the Austrian People's Party and the Austrian Socialist Party. After the end of Franco's regime in 1977, Spain moved towards a two-party system. Despite many (but small) regionalist parties, the party system in Spain presents two large parties of a similar size: the Spanish Socialist Workers' Party and the People's Party. Germany was close to a two-party system and was named a 'two-and-a-half system', with two large parties together (the Christian-Democratic Union and the Social Democratic Party) collecting more than 80 per cent of the votes and a smaller Liberal Party (around 5 per cent) with a pivotal position which enabled it to decide—through alliance—which of the larger parties would be in charge of government. With the rise of the Greens the system turned towards a bipolar system. Israel has used a PR electoral system since the creation of the state in 1948, but until 2000 the system was structured around two main parties: Likud and Labour Party.

Multiparty systems

Multiparty systems are the most frequent and also the most complex type of party system. The number of parties ranges from three to double-digit figures. Three to five parties exist in Canada, Ireland, Japan, and Norway. Party systems in which the number of parties is about ten are Belgium, the Netherlands, and Switzerland. None of the parties in a multiparty system is majoritarian (with 50 per cent of the votes or seats). Furthermore, parties that compose a multiparty system are of different sizes: some are large (say, 30 per cent of the votes) and some are small (less than 5 per cent).

Because no single party has an overall majority in multiparty systems the result is that parties form coalitions to support a government. In parliamentary systems (see Chapters 5 and 7) the vote of confidence requires a 50 per cent majority of seats. Parties run individually in elections (contrary to bipolar systems) and governmental coalitions are negotiated after elections.

Unlike plurality in single-member constituencies, PR does not hinder small parties from addressing small segments of the electorate, sometimes through extreme ideologies. Therefore PR does not lead to ideological moderation, which, in turn, makes it more difficult for voters to switch from one party to the other and cause a government change. In addition, PR does not provide the 'amplification' effect of electoral swings as under plurality. As a consequence, government change rarely takes place through electoral change but rather by swaps of coalition partners.

While multiparty systems are considered to represent better pluralism in countries with religious, territorial, and ethno-linguistic cleavages, their negative aspects have been at the forefront since the Second World War. Multiparty systems are considered less stable, subject to frequent coalition 'crises', with no single party clearly accountable. PR and multiparty systems are also blamed for lack of ideological moderation at the same time as they score high on the dimension of representativeness (Powell 2000).

Other positive aspects of multiparty systems have been stressed since analyses in the 1960s and 1970s included small countries such as Belgium, the Netherlands, Switzerland, and the Scandinavian countries. Studies of 'consensus democracies' showed that multiparty systems are stable, functioning, and peaceful. In plural societies, PR and multiparty systems are a viable way to involve minorities in decision-making processes and reach consensus.[2] As Chapter 5 shows, consociational or consensus democracies represent a different model of democracy from the majoritarian or 'Westminster' model. Both have advantages and disadvantages (see Box 13.2).

The way in which multiparty systems function largely depends on the degree to which parties are ideologically polarized. Sartori (1976) has distinguished two main types of multiparty systems.

Moderate multiparty systems

The dynamic is similar to that of two-party systems. The number of parties is small and the direction of the competition is centripetal, i.e. the main parties tend to converge towards the centre of the left–right scale to attract the support of the moderate electorate. At the centre are one or more small parties with whom the two large ones on either side may form a coalition. The role of these small parties is 'pivotal' in that they can decide whether the coalition is going to be centre-left or centre-right. The ideological distance between parties is limited so that all coalitions are possible.[3]

Polarized multiparty systems

These have three main features. First, there is a large ideological distance between parties with a strong dose

Box 13.2 A normative debate: advantages and disadvantages of party systems

Two-party systems	Multiparty systems
Historically positive connotation	*Historically negative connotation*
Two-party systems are the main cases that resisted the breakdown of democracy between the First and Second World Wars: UK and US.	After the First World War in Italy, Weimar Germany, the Spanish Second Republic, and the French Fourth Republic (1946–56) instability led to a crisis of democracy.
Effective	*Ineffective*
Produces governments immediately after elections. Governments are stable because they are formed by a single party.	Governments take a long time to form after elections because of negotiations between parties. Coalitions lead to unstable governments.
Accountable	*Non-accountable*
Because there is only one party in government responsibility is clearly identifiable by the electorate.	Because governments are formed by many parties, responsibility is obfuscated.
Alternation	*No alternation*
Two main parties alternate in power. Voters directly influence the formation of goverment, and a small shift can cause government change.	Coalition negotiations are out of the reach of voters' influence and shifts of votes are not necessarily followed by changes of government.
Distortive	*Representative*
FPTP under-represents minorities and over-represents large mainstream parties of left–right.	PR fairly represents minorities in societies with ethno-linguistic and religious minorities.
Moderation	*Radicalization*
All main parties have a chance to govern and thus avoid extreme claims. Need to gather votes from large moderate segments of the electorate.	Multiparty systems allow representation of extreme parties. Some do not have any government prospect and do not hesitate to radicalize their claims.
Discontinuity	*Continuity*
Decisions are made by majority with a clear strategy, but subsequent cabinets often reverse legislation.	Decisions are made by consensus through consultation. More difficult to find a clear strategy but more continuity in legislation.

of radicalism. *Anti-system parties* aim to change not only government but also the *system of* government (the regime). These parties do not share the principles of the political system and aim to change its institutions (Capoccia 2002). Thus not all coalitions are viable, with some parties continuously excluded and in constant opposition. They become irresponsible and radicalize their discourse with promises that they know they will never be called to put into practice. Second, there is one main party placed at the *centre of the left–right axis* which represents the 'system' against which extreme anti-system parties are opposed. Being always in power it also becomes irresponsible and unaccountable. This party is not punished electorally because of the absence of viable alternatives. Third, the occupied centre discourages a centripetal move on the part of other parties. As a consequence, there is divergence and *competition is centrifugal*. Examples of polarized systems are the Weimar Republic in Germany from 1919 until 1933, and Italy between 1946 and 1992.

Bipolar systems

Bipolar party systems combine elements of both multi- and two-party systems. As in multiparty systems there are many parties, none of which has a majority. Again, coalition governments are the rule. However, coalitions—rather than single parties—are the important players. These form before elections and run as electoral alliances. They remain stable over time. There are usually two large parties of evenly balanced size alternating in power. Therefore competition resembles that of two-party systems.

In France left and right have alternated in power since 1958.[4] The left includes Socialists, Radicals, Communists, and Greens, whereas the right includes Gaullists and Liberals (they merged in 2003 as the Union for a Popular Movement). In Italy since 1994 the centre-left coalition is composed of Social Democrats, Communists, Greens, and Catholics, whereas the centre-right coalition includes Silvio Berlusconi's party (which merged with the post-fascist party) and the Northern League. The coalitions have alternated in power in 1996, 2001, 2006, 2008, and partly in 2013. Finally, in Germany two coalitions oppose each other: Social Democrats and Greens on the one hand, and Christian-Democratic Union, Christian-Social Union, and Liberals on the other.

The number of parties

As we have seen, the number of parties is important. But how, exactly, should parties be *counted?* If all parties that run in an election are counted (or even only those that get some votes) the number would be extremely large and useless for building a typology. In every election there are dozens of parties and candidates that get no votes or very few. Therefore it is necessary to have reasonable rules to decide how to count. There are two ways to count parties: (1) *numerical* with indices based on the *size* of parties; (2) *qualitative* with rules based on the *role* of parties in the system.

Numerical rules

These rules represent quantitative attempts to classify party systems on the basis of the number and size of parties that compose them. Various indices have been devised to summarize this basic information: are there many small parties (a *fragmented* party system) or a few large parties (a *concentrated* party system)?

The most frequently used indices are Rae's *fractionalization index* (Rae 1971) and the *effective number of parties* (Laakso and Taagepera 1979). The fractionalization index (F) varies from zero (full concentration of seats or votes in one party) to one (total fragmentation with each seat going to a different party). The effective number of parties (E) indicates the number of parties in a system and does not have an upper limit.

The two formulas are as follows:

$$F = 1 - \sum p_i^2 \qquad E = 1/\sum p_i^2$$

where p is the percentage of votes or seats for party i and Σ represents the sum for all parties. The percentages for all parties are squared to weight parties by their size. If there are two parties A and B, each receiving 50 per cent of the seats, first calculate the squares for party A (0.50 × 0.50 = 0.25) and party B (0.50 × 0.50 = 0.25) and then add them together (0.25 + 0.25 = 0.50). Thus

$$F = 1 - 0.50 = 0.50 \qquad E = 1/0.50 = 2$$

In this example, F is exactly mid-way between zero and one (0.50) and E counts perfectly that there are two parties.

Table 13.3 lists the effective number of parties (based on seat distributions) contesting recent elections in a number of countries.[5] As can be seen there is a wide variation between countries. The less fragmented countries are those using plurality/majoritarian or transferable vote systems in single-member districts (Australia, France, UK, Hungary, Malta, the US), whereas the most fragmented countries are those with PR and many religious and ethno-linguistic parties (Belgium, Finland, the Netherlands, New Zealand, Norway, Switzerland).

Qualitative rules

In many cases it is not appropriate to consider numerical criteria only to decide whether or not a party is relevant. Often small parties—which quantitative rules would weight lightly—have far-reaching consequences for coalitions, influencing important decisions, mobilizing people, and so on. Sometimes small parties are much more important than what their sheer size would suggest. Sartori (1976) has developed two criteria to decide which parties really 'count' and should be 'counted'.

1. *Coalition potential*: a small party is irrelevant if over a period of time it is not necessary for any type of governmental coalition. On the contrary, a party must be counted if, disregarding its size, it is pivotal and determines whether or not a coalition is going to exist and which.

2. *Blackmail potential*: a small party must be considered relevant when it is able to exercise pressure on governmental decisions through threats or veto power.

The influence of electoral laws on the format of party systems

Given the impact of party system fragmentation on stability, accountability, and representativeness, research in comparative politics has been concerned with the causes for varying numbers and size of parties. Apart from the number of cleavages in the society seen above, the main cause is the electoral system.

Electoral systems are mechanisms for the translation of preferences into votes, and votes into parliamentary seats. Chapter 10 shows that there are two main 'families' of electoral systems: (1) majoritarian systems in single-member constituencies; (2) PR systems in multi-member constituencies. The first and best-known formulation of the causal relationship between electoral and party systems is Duverger's laws from his classic book *Les Partis Politiques* (1951, translated in 1954). As can be seen in Box 13.3, the two laws are simple: plurality or majoritarian electoral systems favour two-party systems, whereas PR leads to multiparty systems. This causal relationship between electoral and party systems is due to two types of effect.

Table 13.3 Rae's parliamentary fractionalization index (F), effective number of parliamentary parties (E), and Gallagher's index of disproportionality (LSq)

Country	Election	F	E	LSq
Australia	2010	0.53	2.1	11.3
Austria	2008	0.79	4.3	3.3
Argentina	2009	0.86	7.1	9.6
Belgium	2010	0.90	8.4	4.9
Brazil	2010	0.90	10.3	2.6
Canada	2011	0.58	2.4	12.6
Chile	2009	0.82	5.6	6.8
Czech Republic	2010	0.85	4.5	9.1
Finland	2011	0.85	5.8	3.1
France	2012	0.80	2.8	17.8
Germany	2009	0.78	4.1	2.7
Greece	2012 (June)	0.80	3.7	10.7
Hungary	2010	0.65	2.0	12.1
India	2009	0.86	7.1	3.9
Ireland	2011	0.77	3.5	8.7
Israel	2013	0.88	7.3	3.6
Italy	2013	0.81	3.5	17.7
Japan	2012	0.59	2.5	25.7
Malta	2008	0.52	2.0	1.5
Mexico	2009	0.67	3.0	6.4
Netherlands	2010	0.86	6.7	1.0
New Zealand	2011	0.67	3.0	2.4
Norway	2009	0.78	4.1	3.4
Poland	2011	0.73	3.0	6.3
Portugal	2009	0.74	2.6	5.9
Russia	2011	0.64	2.8	3.5
Spain	2011	0.70	2.6	7.3
Sweden	2010	0.79	4.5	1.7
Switzerland	2011	0.84	4.6	4.1
Turkey	2011	0.57	2.4	7.8
UK	2010	0.73	2.6	15.1
US	2012	0.50	2.0	4.83

Notes: For calculations parties rather than alliances have been considered (France, Chile, Italy). For mixed electoral systems, PR votes have been taken (Japan, Mexico, Hungary). For Germany *Zweitstimmen* have been used and in France first-ballot figures for votes. As a general rule for including parties in the calculation, all parties polling at least 1 per cent, or securing at least one seat, have been taken into account.

Source: See sources in 'Country Profiles' (see also the Online Resource Centre).

online resource centre

Mechanical effects refer to the formula used to translate votes into seats. In single-member constituencies winning the seat is difficult. Only the party with the most votes gets the single seat. The second, third, fourth, etc. do not get any seat (first-past-the-post). If in a constituency Party A receives 29.4 per cent of votes, Party B 29.3 per cent, and all other parties even less, only Party A is represented. This means that the threshold is high and

Box 13.3 The influence of electoral systems on party systems

Duverger's 'laws' (1954)

First Law

'The majority [plurality] single-ballot system tends to party dualism.'

Second Law

'The second ballot [majority] system or proportional representation tend to multipartyism.'

Rae/Riker's 'proposition' (1971, 1982)

'Plurality formulae are always associated with two-party competition exept where strong local minority parties exist.'

Sartori's 'tendency laws' (1986)

Law 1

'Given systemic structuring and cross-constituency dispersion (as joint necessary conditions), plurality systems cause (are a sufficient condition of) a two-party format.'

Law 2

'PR formulas facilitate multipartyism and are, conversely, hardly conducive to two-partyism.'

Cox's 'coordination argument' (1997)

'Why ... would the same two parties necessarily compete in all districts [cross-constituency coordination or nationalization]?' Local candidates link together to compete more effectively for (1) seats to implement policies, (2) support presidential candidates, (3) elect the prime minister, (4) obtain more upper-tier seats, and (5) obtain more campain finances.

'If a system (1) elects legislators by plurality rule in single-member districts; (2) elects its chief executive by something like nationwide plurality rule; and (3) holds executive and legislative elections concurrently, then it will tend to ... have a national two-party or one-party-dominant system.'

---

all parties but the first one are eliminated. With PR, on the contrary, in each multi-member constituency many seats are allocated in proportion to the votes. If Party A receives 32.4 per cent of votes, it has a right—more or less—to a third of the seats allocated in that constituency. Small parties are not excluded (a party with 5 per cent of votes gets roughly 5 per cent of seats) and therefore the overall number of parties making it into parliament is high.

Psychological effects refer to the behaviour of voters and parties.

1. On the *demand side* (voters), in electoral systems in which only large parties have a chance to win seats, voters tend to vote *strategically* (not necessarily their first party preference) to avoid wasting votes on small parties with no chance of getting seats. Converging votes on large parties reduces their overall number. On the contrary, with PR in which small parties can win seats, voters vote *sincerely* (their first preference) because their vote is not wasted. This increases the vote for small parties and thus their overall number.

2. On the *supply* side (parties), with plurality small parties have an incentive to merge with others to increase their chances of passing the threshold, thus reducing the number of parties. On the contrary, with PR parties have no incentive to merge: they can survive on their own and small splinter parties are not penalized. This increases the overall number of parties.

Rae (1971), Riker (1982), and Sartori (1986) have questioned these laws by asking whether the reductive effect of majoritarian electoral systems works at *the constituency level or at the national level*. At the constituency level the high threshold reduces the number of parties. But does this always translate into a reduction at the national level?

Suppose that a parliament has 100 seats from 100 single-member constituencies. If in each constituency a different party wins the seat, we would end up with a fragmented parliament. Thus the question is: under what conditions does the reductive effect of FPTP at the constituency level also reduce the number of parties at the national level? The answer is: majoritarian systems produce two-party systems at the national level only if parties are 'nationalized', i.e. receive homogeneous support in all constituencies (see Cox's argument in Box 13.3). If there are many parties with territorially concentrated support, this leads to fragmentation in the national party system. A party which is small nationwide can nonetheless be strong in specific regions and thus win seats and create fragmentation in the national parliament. If many parties are territorially concentrated, the national fragmentation is larger.

In most countries party systems nationalized at the beginning of competitive elections in the mid-nineteenth century, so the support parties receive is increasingly homogeneous across regions and territorialized support has declined. This can be observed not only in Europe and North America, but also in India and Latin America (Caramani 2004; Chhibber and Kollman 2004; Jones and

Table 13.4 Results of the 2005 New Zealand election and Gallagher's LSq index of disproportionality

Party	Votes (%)	Seats (N)	Seats (%)	Difference (% seats −% votes)	Squared
Labour Party	27.4	34	28.1	0.7	0.49
National Party	47.2	59	48.8	1.6	2.56
Green Party	11.0	14	11.6	0.6	0.36
New Zealand First	6.5	8	6.6	0.1	0.01
Mana Party	1.7	1	0.8	−0.9	0.81
Māori Party	1.3	3	2.5	1.2	1.44
ACT New Zealand	1.1	1	0.8	−0.3	0.09
United Future	0.5	1	0.8	0.3	0.09
Others	3.3	1	0.8	−2.5	6.25
Total	100.0	122	100.0		12.10

Note: Votes refer to party list votes whereas seats include both party list seats and electorate seats.

Mainwaring 2003) due to the development of national party organizations and increasing candidate coordination (Cox 1997). Therefore where plurality systems exist, reduction of the number of parties has taken place. Plurality systems *distort* party votes when they translate them into seats.

- They *over*-represent large parties (the share of seats for big parties is larger than their share of votes).

- They *under*-represent small parties.

How can we measure the (dis)proportionality between votes and seats? Various indices have been devised: the one most frequently used is the least squares index of disproportionality (LSq) (Gallagher 1991; Gallagher and Mitchell 2008: appendix B):

$$LSq = \sqrt{1/2\Sigma(v_i - s_i)^2}$$

where v is the percentage of votes for party i, s is the percentage of seats for party i, and Σ represents the sum for all parties. This index varies between zero (full proportionality) and 100 (total disproportionality). Take, as an example, the results of the 2011 New Zealand election in Table 13.4. If the total of the squared differences is halved (12.1/2 = 6.05) and then the square root is taken, the result is 2.4, i.e. an almost perfect proportionality between votes and seats.

The values of the LSq index are given in the last column of Table 13.3. In countries with plurality systems (Canada, the UK, India) there is a stronger distortion of the popular vote. The same applies for other systems based on single-member constituencies such as France with a two-ballot majoritarian system. On the contrary, disproportionality is lower for countries with PR systems.

However, PR systems also have a reductive effect on the number of parties if the *magnitude of constituencies* is small, as in Spain. The magnitude refers to the number of seats allocated in a given constituency. The larger the magnitude, the higher the proportionality between votes and seats. If the magnitude is small, the few seats go to the few largest parties.[6]

KEY POINTS

- The morphology of party systems is important for the competition between parties: it concerns the number of players and their size. The main types are dominant-party, two-party, multiparty, and bipolar systems.

- In two-party systems, moderate multiparty systems, and bipolar systems competition is centripetal and there is alternation in power. In dominant-party systems and polarized multiparty systems there is no alternation and competition is centrifugal.

- Measures of fragmentation are based on the number and size of parties. However, small parties can also be important if they have coalition or blackmail potential.

- The format of party systems is influenced by electoral systems. Through mechanical and psychological effects plurality tends towards two-party systems (large parties are over-represented) and PR tends towards multiparty systems.

The dynamics of party systems

In the wake of Joseph Schumpeter's (1943) definition of democracy—a set of rules for selecting political leaders and making decisions by means of competition for

Table 13.5 The analogy between economic and electoral competition

Dimensions	Economy	Elections
Market	Economic	Electoral
Actors	Firms	Parties
	Consumers	Voters
Profit	Money	Votes
Supply	Goods, services	Programmes, policies
Demand	Product preferences	Policy preferences
Communication	Advertising	Campaigns

votes—authors have developed analogies between *electoral competition* and *market competition*. In the electoral market, parties and candidates compete for 'shares' of the electorate, as happens in the economic world where firms compete for shares of the market. Parties are organizations whose main motive is the *maximization of votes*, and the exchange between represented and representatives is similar to that between demand and supply in the economy (see Table 13.5).

The market analogy

Anthony Downs's *An Economic Theory of Democracy* (1957) is a pioneering book in which the basic elements of these models were spelled out for the first time. In this model, actors (parties and voters) are *rational*.

Parties calculate their strategies by formulating platforms with the goal of maximizing votes and being elected or re-elected. Parties are coalitions of individuals seeking to control institutions rather than implement programmes. Parties act self-interestedly to gain office. Like firms in the economic market, they are interested in making profit (money in the economic market, votes in the electoral market). To maximize votes parties offer programmes that appeal to many voters.

Voters, like consumers, face alternatives which they order from most to least preferred and choose the alternative that ranks highest. Voters make a rational choice by voting for parties whose programmes are closest to their policy preferences, because they are close to their interests or to their values and moral orientations. Voters vote on the basis of the *proximity* between parties'

positions and their preferences. For that they must know what the alternative proposals by different parties are, i.e. they are *informed* about their choices.

On the one hand, citizens vote on the basis of a self-interested calculation, like consumers who calculate the benefit between products. On the other hand, parties are like businesses competing for customers. They establish what people like so that they can 'sell' more. Following *supply and demand* rules, parties offer policies that voters can either choose to 'buy' or not. Once elected, parties seek re-election through policies appealing to large segments of the electorate. The goal of parties is to *maximize utility* in terms of votes; the voters' goal is to maximize utility through policies satisfying their interests and values. As in economic theory, the search for individual advantages produces *common goods*, namely responsiveness and accountability.

Rational choice competition models were first devised for two-party systems—mainly the US. However, maximization of votes is also the main motive in systems in which governments are coalitions. The more votes the better the chances to enter a coalition, control governmental institutions, and place individuals in key official positions.

The spatial analogy

The idea of proximity/distance between individual preferences and parties' policies indicates that players move within a space. The second element that Downs 'imported' from economic models of competition is their spatial representation. In particular, Downs adapted models of the dynamics of competition between firms, i.e. where firms locate premises according to the physical distribution of the population.

Let us take the simple case of a village in which there is only one street (the example is from Hotelling (1929)). On each side of the street there are evenly spaced houses (the square dots in Figure 13.1). What are the dynamics between two competitors, say two bakeries A and B? Assuming that both bakers offer the same quality of bread for the same price and that consumers will rationally try to reduce their 'costs' by buying bread in the nearest shop (proximity), if A and B are located as they are in Figure 13.1, B will have a larger share of the market. The share of B's market goes from the right-side end of the street to the M-point, which is the mid-point between the locations of A and B. Residents on the right of the M-point will buy bread in bakery B and residents on the left of the M-point

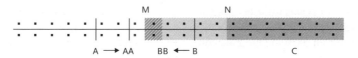

Figure 13.1 Hotelling's model (1929)

will buy bread in bakery A. The dynamic element in this model consists of A's move to increase its share of the market. By relocating the bakery at AA, the baker is able to gain the share of the market indicated by the dashed area. Obviously, B can also move towards the centre (BB) and win back part of the lost share of the market. Both bakers seek to *optimize their location*.

An additional element introduced by Smithies (1941) concerns the elasticity of demand. The further away they are from the bakery, the higher the 'costs' for buyers. To what extent is relocation towards the centre tolerated by residents of the extremes? Incentives for a new bakery at the edges of the village increase as people feel that AA and BB are too distant. The risk of strategies of relocation towards the centre is that a new bakery C appears, taking away part of B's share of the market (the dark shaded area). Therefore there are two dynamic elements in these models: (1) the movement caused by the search for the optimal location and (2) the appearance of new competitors in spaces left uncovered. Equilibrium is reached when no competitor has an interest in changing its position along the axis.

Downs's model

Through the spatial analogy between physical and ideological space, Downs imports these elements into the analysis of the dynamics of party systems. Most elements are maintained: (1) the one-dimensionality of the space, (2) the principle according to which costs are reduced by choosing the closest option (proximity), and (3) competitors' search for the optimal location through a convergence towards the centre.

Downs represented the ideological space by a zero to 100 scale ranging from left to right. As will be seen, one-dimensionality is maintained, even if it is not always a realistic assumption, because it summarizes other dimensions and is the most important one (in terms of size of parties that define themselves according to this dimension), and because it is present in all party systems (as seen earlier in the discussion on cleavages).

Both Hotelling and Smithies had previously applied spatial models to politics through analogies with the ideological space and were able to predict that parties tend to converge towards one another in the effort to win the middle-of-the-road voters, and to present increasingly similar programmes and policies. Downs adds one crucial element to the models: the *variable distribution of voters* along the left–right continuum. Voters are not distributed regularly along the scale but concentrate in particular ideological positions, namely around the centre. For Downs this is the crucial explanatory and predictive element of the dynamics of party systems: 'if we know something about the distribution of voters' preferences, we can make specific predictions about how ideologies change in content as parties maneuver to gain power'

(Downs 1957: 114). If one assumes a normal (or 'bell-shaped') distribution of the electorate with many voters at the centre of the scale and fewer at the extremes (see type A in Figure 13.2), the prediction of the model is again that parties will converge towards the centre.[7]

The first dynamic element of these models is that they predict the convergence towards the centre and the increasing similarity of platforms and policy actions. This centripetal competition is determined by the parties' aim to win the *median voter* (see Box 13.4). Examples are the progressive convergence of previously radical left-wing workers' parties towards the centre to attract moderate voters (the German Social Democrats in 1959, the French Socialists in the 1970s, the New Labour Party under Tony Blair, or the US Democrats under Bill Clinton).

The second dynamic element consists of centripetal competition arising not only because of the proximity principle, but also because there are more voters in the centre. Party strategy does not depend only on the logic of the model (the assumption of proximity voting) but also on the *empirical distribution of the electorate*. The potential loss of voters at the extremes does not deter parties from converging because there are few voters at the extremes. This is not the case if the distribution of the electorate is different, a two-model distribution as depicted in type B in Figure 13.2. This is a case of ideological polarization within a political system (for example, the Weimar Republic and Italy during the 'first republic'). Therefore the distribution of the electorate determines the *direction* of competition (centrifugal or centripetal).

The third element of the dynamics of party systems is that in voters the middle of the left–right axis are more *flexible* than at the extremes where they are firmly encapsulated in strict ideologies and/or party organizations. 'Available' voters (Bartolini and Mair 1990), located in the middle, are less ideologized and have weak party identifications. These voters are ready to change their minds and therefore are very appealing to parties seeking to 'seduce' them.

The broader application of rational choice models

What are the links of these models with other aspects of parties and party systems?

First, rational choice models help to interpret the transformation of *party organizations* from mass parties to **catch-all parties** (see Chapter 12). This transformation can be seen as organizational and ideological adaptation to competition.

Second, they also help to interpret patterns of *dealignment*, i.e. the loosening of the relationship between parties and specific segments of society (workers for social democrats, for example). Centripetal competition and the maximization of votes lead parties to make their programmes and ideologies more vague to attract support from other groups. This blurs the connection between groups and parties, and causes a higher propensity to change vote from one election to the next.

Third, these models can be applied historically to processes of *enfranchisement and democratization*. In both type A and type B the distributions are symmetrical. In type C, on the contrary, we have a *skewed distribution*. The solid curve represents an electorate that is skewed towards the

Box 13.4 The median voter

The median voter is the voter who divides a distribution of voters placed on a left–right scale into two equal halves. In a distribution from zero to 100 in which for each point there is a voter (including position zero), the median voter is on position 50 (with fifty voters on each side). Suppose, however, that there are fifty voters on position 100, and the remaining voters are distributed regularly between positions 49 and 99 (one voter on each position). In this case the median voter is on position 99.

right of the axis. Here the median voter is around position 65 rather than 50, and accordingly parties A and B would converge towards this point. This is typical of restricted electorates in the nineteenth century when lower classes were excluded from the franchise. Accordingly, A and B would be the parties of the periods of restricted electorates, namely liberals and conservatives as the parties of 'internal origin' (Duverger 1954). Enfranchisement and democratization processes changed the shape of voters' distribution as represented by the dashed curve. This new distribution explains the emergence of new parties C and/or D of 'external origin' (such as social democrats and agrarians).[8]

The dream of reformists (as opposed to revolutionary socialists) was that socialism and the proletariat could come to power through votes ('paper stones') and the extension of the franchise, rather than through revolution (real stones!). For analytical Marxists the development of the industrial society would naturally lead workers to power through sheer numbers. Yet the numbers of industrial workers did not grow—in fact, they declined—and socialist parties faced a dilemma between moving towards the centre to maximize their appeal to the middle classes—thus relaxing their programme—and losing voters from workers (Przeworski and Sprague 1986).

Type A: Downs's basic model (1957): the bell-shape (or normal) distribution of the electorate: centripetal competition

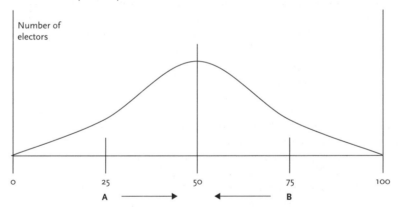

Type B: A two-modal distribution of electors: centrifugal competition

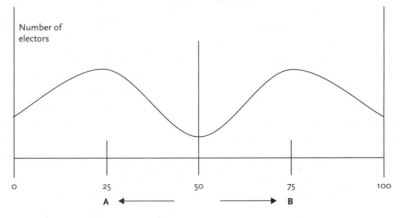

Figure 13.2 Types of voter distribution

Type C: A skewed distribution of electors: enfranchisement in the nineteenth century and new parties

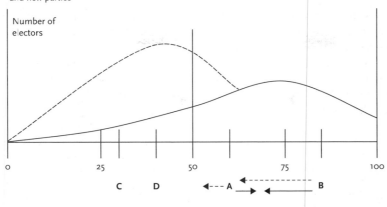

Type D: Polymodal distribution in multi-party systems

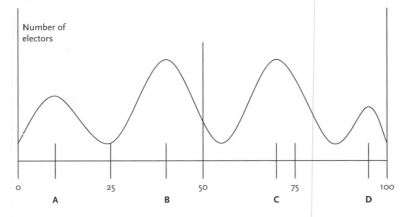

Figure 13.2 Types of voter distribution (Continued)

Fourth, one needs to consider these models under *PR and multiparty systems*. Convergence is likely under FPTP because the threat of other parties appearing at the extremes is low, given the high threshold required to win a seat. Rather than new parties, under these systems, the model predicts *high abstention levels* as is the case in the US.

Multiparty systems, on the other hand, develop when the distribution of the electorate is polymodal, with more than one or two peaks (type D). With this type of distribution of electors, the dynamics of the competition is not centripetal. PR is no hindrance to new parties. Existing parties have no incentive to converge towards the centre. Therefore it is less likely that parties in two-party systems will look like each other ideologically. On the contrary, Sartori (1976) shows that *ideological spaces are elastic*, i.e. they can stretch, with extremes becoming even more extreme and an increasing ideological distance between parties. Parties may adopt the strategy of becoming more extreme to distinguish themselves from moderate parties. This leads to radicalization to maintain a distinctive character.

Empirical spatial analysis

The crucial determinant is the distribution of the electorate. If we know the shape of the curve we can predict the behaviour of parties. However, to know what the voters' distribution looks like and to know where parties are located is a matter of **empirical research**. How can one measure these two aspects?

First, the *distribution of voters* can be measured empirically through surveys in which, through questions and scales, respondents to questionnaires are asked to position themselves, for example, along the left-right axis. Examples are the World Value Survey, Eurobarometers, European Social Survey, Latinobarometers, etc.

Second, the *position of parties* can be measured empirically through two main instruments. The most important one is based on *text data* whereby party manifestos are analysed using special software able to identify favourable or unfavourable mentions of a large number of issues, from taxation and the free market to development aid and the environment. Such items are often combined to build a more general scale such as the left–right

Table 13.6 Manifesto items used to build economic and cultural dimensions of the left–right scale

Dimensions	Left-wing items	Right-wing items
Economic	Economic planning Corporatism Keynesian management Controlled economy Nationalization Marxist analysis Welfare expansion Labour groups	Free enterprise Incentives Economic orthodoxy Welfare limitation Against labour groups Middle class and professional groups
Cultural	Anti-imperialism Internationalism Social justice Anti-nationalism Against tradition Multiculturalism	Anti-internationalism Political authority Nationalism Tradition Law and order Against multiculturalism

Source: Camia and Caramani (2011) with data from Comparative Manifesto Project.

scale, with an economic and cultural dimensions (see Table 13.6 for an example). The most important data are those of the Comparative Manifesto Project (Budge *et al.* 2001; Klingemann *et al.* 2006). The alternative possibility is *expert surveys* whereby the position of parties on various issues is established by asking a sample of scholars. The problem with these data is that they rarely allow an estimation of parties' past positioning. Two main projects exist: the Benoit, Hunt, and Laver project (Benoit and Laver 2006) and the Chapel Hill project (Steenbergen and Marks 2007).

Despite critiques (see Box 13.5) spatial models are extremely useful. In all countries a number of voters are ready to change their vote. This is an available electorate around which competition turns and on which these models focus. The electorate is composed of *opinion voters* or 'pocket-book voting', i.e. based on particular interests, values, and opinions, rather than *identity voters* based on socio-economic and identification factors. Rational choice models apply less to segments that are encapsulated through identification (ethno-linguistic and religious dimensions with strong identities and non-available voters) and primarily to the left–right dimension along which voters are available. Even if applicable to parts of the electorate only, they are crucial as they determine the direction of competition.[9]

A more fundamental question, however, is how to interpret the convergence of parties and the increasing similarity of their programmes. It is difficult to separate

Box 13.5 Critiques of rational choice models

Assumption	Critique
Rationality	The relationship between parties and voters is determined by a number of 'non-rational' factors: socio-economic conditions, party identification, political socialization, influence of the media.
Full information	Voters are not fully informed about platforms and programmes, and are unable to evaluate the extent to which they correspond to their own preferences. With technical issues this often proves unlikely.
Vote maximization	First, parties as office seekers do not require to maximize votes but to get just enough. Second, parties may just seek to influence public policy rather than aim for office. Third, vote maximization faces resistances within parties to keep a less 'cynical' attitude and more coherent ideology. Müller and Strøm (2000) find that only half of the parties they examine follow a strategy of vote maximization.
One-dimensionality	Not all parties compete along the left–right dimension. This may be true in two-party systems but in multiparty systems the number of dimensions is larger. In most cases the space of competition is multidimensional.

the impact of competition from other factors, such as the development of a large and homogeneous middle class and the disappearance of class distinctions through the reduction of social inequalities and the secularization of society, the integration of societies, and the disappearance of ethno-linguistic particularities through nationalization and globalization. Is convergence a result of this evolution rather than a product of competition?

KEY POINTS

- In the electoral market parties (the supply side) present platforms to appeal to many voters whose vote is determined by the proximity of their preferences (the demand side) to the parties' offer. Voters are assumed to be rational, informed about alternative proposals, and able to choose the alternative closest to their top preferences.

- The dynamics of party systems is determined by parties' search for the optimal location on the left–right axis. Depending on the distribution of the electorate along the scale, parties move to a position where the support is largest.

- The prediction of competition models is that parties converge towards the centre of the left–right axis, as the point where most votes concentrate, and as the point where voters are less rigidly ideologized.

Conclusion

Understanding party systems requires the combination of the various perspectives presented in this chapter.

The *macro-sociological* approach must be combined with *institutional* and *actor-oriented* models. They complement each other and are not mutually exclusive. We cannot understand party systems without reference to the social cleavages from which parties have emerged. However, we must also take into account parties' capacity to act independently from social conditions—in fact, to shape them through ideology and policy. The motivations of parties are not entirely determined by their origins. Parties' strategies, in turn, must take into account the rules of the game—electoral laws being the most important ones—influencing the number and size of players.

Both *descriptive* and *explanatory research* is needed. The ultimate goal is to account for the shape and dynamics of party systems. However, before searching for causes, party systems should be described carefully. As seen with counting parties, this is often more complicated than appears at first sight.

Finally, we cannot understand party systems in isolation. We need *comparison* to assess whether or not they are fragmented or unstable, as well as a *long-term* perspective rather than a myopic focus on just the most recent elections. This is the only way of assessing how exceptional a given party system or a given change really is.

 ## Questions

1. What are the National and Industrial Revolutions?

2. What are Stein Rokkan's four main social cleavages and which party families emerged from them?

3. How should the number of parties in a system be counted?

4. What are the characteristic features of a two-party system?

5. What does 'effective number of parties' mean?

6. What is the effect of electoral systems on the shape of party systems?

7. What does it mean when we say that parties are 'vote-maximizers'?

8. Describe centripetal and centrifugal party competition in Downs's model.

9. Are voters really rational?

10. Can the space of competition be reduced to one left–right dimension?

 ## Further reading

Classical texts on party systems

Cox, G. W. (1997), *Making Votes Count: Strategic Coordination in the World's Electoral Systems*. Cambridge: Cambridge University Press.

Downs, A. (1957) *An Economic Theory of Democracy* (New York: Harper Collins).

Duverger, M. (1954) *Political Parties* (New York: John Wiley).

Lipset, S. M., and Rokkan, S. (1967) 'Cleavage Structures, Party Systems, and Voter Alignments: An Introduction', in S.M. Lipset and S. Rokkan (eds), *Party Systems and Voter Alignments* (New York: Free Press), 1–64.

Sartori, G. (1976) *Parties and Party Systems: A Framework for Analysis* (Cambridge: Cambridge University Press).

For a more recent bibliography see the works cited throughout in this chapter.

Up-to-date reports on party systems can be found in journals. Detailed country-by-country developments from 1991 onwards are reported in the *Political Data Yearbook*. Students may also find useful material in journals such as the *American Political Science Review*, *Comparative Politics*, *Comparative Political Studies*, *Electoral Studies*, *Party Politics*, and *West European Politics*.

 ## Web links

www.electiondataarchive.org
The Constituency-Level Elections Archive (CLEA) is the largest databank on elections at the level of single constituencies since the beginning of competitive elections covering the entire world.

http://manifesto-project.wzb.eu
Website of the Manifesto Project Database hosted by the WZB in Berlin with data on ideological and programmatic position of political parties.

http://psephos.adam-carr.net
Adam Carr's website with election results for 182 countries for legislative and presidential elections.

www.nsd.uib.no/european_election_database
Searchable database of the Norwegian Social Science Data Services (NSD) with results for national legislatures in Europe and for the elections of the European Parliament. Includes information on parties and party systems.

www.electionguide.org
Information on elections and electoral systems from the Consortium for Elections and Political Process Strengthening (CEPPS). Includes information on parties and party systems world-wide.

en.wikipedia.org/wiki/List_of_political_parties_by_country
Information about names, ideologies, mergers, and splits of political parties worldwide, and results for legislative and presidential elections with different levels of quality depending on countries.

www.gksoft.com/govt/en/parties.html
Webpage of Government on the WWW devoted to political parties and party systems around the world. The main page includes additional information on heads of state, parliaments, executives, courts, and other institutions.

http://dodgson.ucsd.edu
Website of the Lijphart Election Archive with information on party systems, electoral systems, and recent election results around the world.

www.idea.int
Website of the International Institute for Democracy and Electoral Assistance (IDEA).

online resource centre

For additional material and resources, please visit the Online Resource Centre at:
www.oxfordtextbooks.co.uk/orc/caramani3e/

CHAPTER 14

Interest groups

Roland Erne

Chapter contents

Reader's guide

Political scientist should not just compare political institutions, but also assess the role of associations that seek to advance particular socio-economic and political interests. Interest groups play a crucial role in all political systems. But the forms in which interests are articulated depend on the particular context. Accordingly, this chapter begins with a review of different definitions of interest groups that have been used across time and space. Scholars of interest politics have also been inspired by different theoretical paradigms. Hence, the chapter discusses the legacies of competing theoretical traditions in the field, namely republicanism, pluralism, and neocorporatism. The final sections of the chapter assess the role of interest associations in practice, distinguishing different types of action that are available to different interest associations, namely direct lobbying, political exchange, contentious politics, and private interest government.

Introduction

Arthur Bentley captured the focus of interest politics when he argued that it is necessary 'in considering representative government, or democracy, not only past or present, but future as well, to consider it in terms of the various group pressures that form its substance' (Bentley 1908: 452). Therefore we should not just compare political institutions, but also assess the role of associations that seek to advance particular interests in the political process. The term *interest group* is often used interchangeably with interest association or pressure group; but before reviewing different definitions of the term, I will go back to its origins.

It is no coincidence that the study of interest politics can be traced back to the United States of the early twentieth century. The establishment of this academic field is closely related to the socio-economic and political conjunctures of the time. When Bentley published his pioneering *The Process of Government* in 1908, the interventions of ever larger corporations in US politics caused widespread popular alarm. At the same time, the rise of large-scale industrial capitalism triggered counter-reactions, namely industrial conflict and movements that sought to eliminate corruption, improve working conditions, and give citizens more control over the political process. Yet, it would be wrong to associate the origins of comparative interest politics exclusively with the rise of big business. The *behavioural revolution* in the social sciences, which changed the analytical focus from formal institutions to social processes, was equally important (see Introduction to this volume). The consequent broadening of perspectives made it possible to analyse tensions between pluralistic democratic theory and practice.

In post-1945 America, the steady rise of professional lobbyists provided political scientists not only with a new subject area and a new occupational domain for their graduate students, but also with a topic for heated debate (Dahl 1982): can a pluralistic democratic state regulate interest groups without questioning the right of association? The broader analytical focus also enabled scholars to capture alternative types of association–state relations, such as neocorporatism, which did not follow the Anglo-American model.

> **KEY POINTS**
>
> ● Comparativists should not only analyse formal political institutions but should also assess interest group pressures that shape the substance of politics.
>
> ● Interest groups play important, but also different, roles in political systems across time and space, even if the rise of interest politics is closely related to the rise of capitalist modes of production.

What are interest groups?

Interest groups are not easy to define. The American pioneers in the field proposed very encompassing definitions: Bentley (1908) and Truman (1971 [1951]) defined interest groups as associations that make claims to other groups in society. But is this definition still useful today? Many contemporary scholars disagree because such a broad definition makes it impossible to distinguish interest associations from political parties (see Chapter 12). Instead, interest groups are usually defined as membership organizations that appeal to government but do not participate in elections (Wilson 1990). However, this definition also raises questions. Whereas parties and interest groups are sharply differentiated in North America, this differentiation is much less evident in other parts of the world where cross-organizational interactions blur the lines between interest groups and political parties. Therefore, Gabriel Almond (1958) did not use formal definitions when he was studying interest groups comparatively. Instead, he focused on the *function of interest representation* because the institutions by means of which interests are articulated would depend on the political and socio-economic context of the particular political system.

Functionalist approaches

Students of interest politics should indeed be cautious of comparisons based on context-free measures. Identical measures, such as the union density rate (i.e. the number of trade union members as a proportion all workers in employment), mean different things in different countries. Given the high number of workers covered by collective agreements and the capacity of the French unions to instigate strike action, French unions are hardly the least influential labour organizations in the industrialized world (Goetschy and Jobert 2011). However, there is almost no industrialized country in the world where fewer people are union members as a percentage of the entire labour force (see Table 14.1). In turn, China displays the highest union density in Table 14.1, but China's official unions function rather as a transmission belt of the ruling party than as an effective tool of labour representation (Cooke 2011; Kuruvilla *et al.* 2011). Obviously, unions play different roles in different political systems. In the English-speaking world, union influence is related to membership levels. However, in other parts of the world other factors are as important, such as close political party–trade union connections, co-determination rights of worker representatives enshrined in corporate governance, institutionalized access to policy-making, collective bargaining and trade union laws, and the ability of union activist to inspire social movements (Bamber *et al.* 2011). The same observation also applies to employers' organizations.

Table 14.1 Trade union and employer organization density, and collective bargaining coverage[a]

Country	Union density (%)	Employer organization density (%)	Collective bargaining coverage (%)[2]
Brazil	29[b]	–	35
Canada	30	–	32
China	79	–	22[b]
Denmark	69	65[b]	80[c]
France	8[b]	75[b]	90[b]
Germany	19	60[b]	62
Italy	35	58[b]	80
Japan	19	–	16[b]
South Africa	28[c]	–	43[c]
Sweden	70[b]	83[b]	91[b]
UK	28	35[b]	33
US	11	–	13

[a]2009 except where indicated otherwise.

[b]2008

[c]2007

Source: ICTWSS database (Amsterdam Institute for Advanced Labour Studies 2011).

For this reason, functionalists argue that studying interest associations comparatively may require using different measures for the same function (e.g. interest representation) in different cases to reflect differences in context across political systems. This approach allows us to broaden the comparative analysis of interest politics beyond the boundaries of Anglo-American systems. However, functionalists also face a tricky analytical problem. Is it accurate to assume a universal interest representation function, as suggested by Almond? Or should we distinguish between different types of interest representation, as suggested by scholars who differentiate between private and public interest associations?

Private vs. public interests

Most scholars use all-embracing definitions of interest groups (Cigler and Loomis 2011). These definitions are typically based on formal properties, namely 'voluntary membership, a more or less bureaucratic structure of decision-making, dependence upon material and motivational resources, efforts to change the respective environments into more favourable ones, and so forth' (Offe and Wiesenthal 1985: 175). However, this view has not precluded some scholars from introducing different subcategories. For instance, Jeffrey Berry (1977) proposed distinguishing *public* and *private* interest groups on the

basis of whether an association pursues public interests or only sectional interests of its members. Similar distinctions have been used by scholars around the world (Young and Wallace 2000; della Porta and Caiani 2009). But does it make sense to use the same label for associations that seek private profit and associations that advance public good? This question is not only of academic interest. The scope of the definition also predetermines the scope of laws that regulate the rights and obligations of associations.

Yet, however popular this distinction is, it is also analytically problematic, as all interest associations usually present their claims as measures that enhance the public good. For instance, business organizations frequently argue, invoking the theories of neoclassical economists, that the pursuit of private profit serves the public good. Claims that an action is consistent or not with the public interest are certainly influential in political debates. Analytically, however, the phrase 'public interest' is 'meaningless if it is taken to refer to an interest so persuasive that everyone in the system is agreed upon it' (Truman 1971: xiv). Does this mean that there is no way of distinguishing between types of interest associations in an analytically meaningful manner? Not necessarily, as we shall see in the section on interest associations in practice.

KEY POINTS

- Many scholars define interest groups as voluntary organizations that appeal to government but do not participate in elections. In a comparative context, however, this formal definition is problematic as the form of interest representation varies across countries.

- It has also been proposed to distinguish 'public' and 'private interest groups'. Claims that a group's action is in the 'public interest' are politically influential. Analytically, however, the term 'public interest' is problematic because of its contentious nature. Indeed, there is hardly a claim that is so persuasive that everyone can agree upon it.

Interest associations in theory

Republican (unitarist) traditions

Although the radical-democratic Swiss–French philosopher Jean-Jacques Rousseau (1712–1778) recognized that every political body includes interest associations, he perceived them as a threat to the rule of the people. He feared that 'there are no longer as many votes as there are men, but only as many as there are associations ... Lastly, when one of these associations is so great as to prevail over all the rest ... there is no longer a general will, and the opinion which prevails is purely particular'. Therefore,

Rousseau argued, 'there should be no partial society in a state and each citizen should express only his own opinion'. Yet, he also proposed a pragmatic solution to the interest group problem: 'But if there are partial societies, it is best to have as many as possible and to prevent them from being unequal' (Rousseau 1973 [1762] Book 2: 204).

Nonetheless, the leaders of the French Revolution clearly adopted a *unitarist* view of democracy, according to which interest associations would undermine the general will of the people. Accordingly, the French constitution of 24 June 1793 succinctly stated in its first sentence: 'The French Republic is one and indivisible'. This sentence still delineates the republican approach to interest groups today, despite the suspension of the constitution on 10 October 1793 because of the state of war.

Whereas the French Revolution established the right to hold popular assemblies and even a constitutional duty to rebel when the government violates the right of the people, the notion of a one and indivisible republic also justified banning associations that were assumed to interfere with the general will of the people. Incidentally, the French revolutionaries not only dissolved the guilds and congregations of the *Ancien Régime*, but also adopted a law that outlawed workers' associations. In 1791, the French constituent assembly adopted the *loi Le Chapelier*, which prohibited trade unions until the law's abrogation in 1884. With this law the assembly responded to reports of alarmed employers: 'The workers, by an absurd parody of the government, regard their work as their property, the building site as a Republic of which they are jointly the citizens, and believe, as a consequence, that it is for them to name their own bosses, their inspectors and at their discretion to share out work amongst themselves'. Thus, the *Le Chapelier* law was designed to 'put an end to such potential industrial anarchy' (Magraw 1992: 24ff).

The fact that employers convinced the constituent assembly to suspend the freedom of association of French workers highlights a contradiction within the unitarist republican tradition of thought. If particular interests aim to become dominant in order to prevail over the rest, as argued by Rousseau, how can one be sure that any restriction of freedom of association 'in the name of the general will of the people' does not simply serve the particular interests of a group that has acquired a dominant position in the political process?

As noted by Robert Dahl (1982), democratic republics face a major dilemma when dealing with interest associations. On the one hand, the larger a democratic political system becomes the more likely interest associations are to play an important role in the political process. On the other hand, as with individuals, so with organizations: the ability to act autonomously also includes the ability to do harm. Whereas republicans try to solve the classical dilemma between control and autonomy in political life through the introduction of the democratic principle of popular sovereignty, liberals typically fear a tyranny of the majority and emphasize instead the liberty of individuals to act and to associate freely.

Liberal (pluralist) traditions

Liberal scholars do not perceive interest associations as a potential threat to the sovereignty of the democratic state, but as an essential source of liberty. This view is pertinently outlined by the French political thinker Alexis de Tocqueville (1805–1859). In 1831, Tocqueville was charged by the French monarchy under King Louis-Philippe to examine the penitentiary system in America. Ironically, however, Tocqueville's travels in America also inspired him to write *Democracy in America* (Tocqueville 2006*a* [1835], 2006*b* [1840]), which became a crucial study within the pluralist tradition of interest politics.

Tocqueville, as an offspring of an ancient aristocratic dynasty which narrowly escaped the guillotine during the French Revolution, had very good reasons to be wary of the general will of the people. However, in contrast with many of his aristocratic contemporaries, he was also convinced that democracy was unavoidable. Whereas politics was a privilege of the few in pre-modern times, the changing social conditions caused by the modernization of the economy and society would affect more and more people. The scope of politics would increase, which in turn would also require a new source of legitimacy for politics—namely democracy. For this reason, Tocqueville studied democracy in America in search of social factors that would prevent it from turning into a tyranny of the majority.

Two strands of Tocqueville's analysis relate to this chapter, namely his observations regarding the role of interests and the role of associations in American politics. In relation to the former, Tocqueville found that Americans were fond of explaining almost all their actions by the 'principle of interest rightly understood'. In Europe, however, claims were justified in absolute moral terms, even if the principle of interest played a 'much grosser' role in Europe than in America (Tocqueville 2006*b* [1840]: Chapter VIII). For Tocqueville, the consequences of this distinction were obvious. On the one hand, absolute moral claims represented a danger to liberty, even if they were meant to advance the general will of the people. On the other hand, the mutual acknowledgment of conflicting interests, as observed in the US of the early nineteenth century, enabled the accommodation of conflict within democratic procedures.

With regard to the role of associations in democratic societies, Tocqueville made the following argument: as the rise of the modern state would make individual citizens weaker, they would need to learn to unite with fellow citizens to defend themselves against the despotic influence of the majority or the aggressions of regal power. Therefore, all kinds of associations, even those formed in civil life without reference to political objects, are important because they cultivate the habits and virtues that are necessary for self-rule.

> Nothing, in my opinion, is more deserving of our attention than the intellectual and moral associations of America. ... In democratic countries the science of association is the mother of science; the progress of all the rest depends upon the progress it has made. Amongst the laws which rule human societies there is one which seems to be more precise and clear than all others. If men are to remain civilized, or to become so, the art of associating together must grow and improve in the same ratio in which the equality of conditions is increased. (Tocqueville 2006b [1840]: Chapter V)

This quotation highlights Tocqueville's views. Associations represent the lifeblood of civic life. Therefore, the state should guarantee its citizens' right of association. At the same time, however, it should not interfere with the associative life of its citizens. Nevertheless, contemporary pluralists are not against political regulation of associations. State involvement is especially warranted to guarantee the freedom of association of its citizens (Dahl 1982). This qualification is of particular importance in relation to workers' rights to organize. Until January 2013, more than 150 nation states had ratified the two core *International Labour Organization* conventions regarding workers' freedom of association. However, important states, including the US, failed to do so (see Table 14.2), reflecting the rise of a new truncated view of liberalism called neoliberalism. Following the world economic crisis of 1973, General Pinochet in Chile, UK Prime Minister Margaret Thatcher, and US President Ronald Reagan initiated a radical 'neoliberal' policy shift that curtailed workers' freedom of association in order to increase the profitability of enterprises (Harvey 2005; Milne 2004).

Nevertheless, Tocqueville's classical liberal views on interests and associations still influence contemporary beliefs about the role of interest associations in democratic societies, as highlighted by the vast literature that treats interest associations as 'schools of democracy' (Sinyai 2006). Certainly, several contemporary studies also deplore a decline in associative practices in the US, such as Robert Putnam's *Bowling Alone* (2000) or Theda Skocpol's *Diminishing Democracy* (2003), but it is equally noteworthy that these critical accounts of American civic and political life did not trigger a fundamental break with the pluralist paradigm. Whereas the classical pluralist approach to interest politics has repeatedly been criticized for its implicit assumptions—notably the assumption that all people enjoy the same capacity to associate and the resulting claim that interest associations are equally distributed across the entire political spectrum (Connolly 1969; Barach and Baratz 1969; Lowi 1969a, 1969b; Lukes 1974; Lindblom 1977, Offe and Wiesenthal 1985)—most students of democracy, explicitly or tacitly,

Table 14.2 Ratification of the core ILO conventions on workers' 'freedom of association'

Country	Freedom of Association and Protection of Right to Organise Convention (n. 87)	Right to Organise and Collective Bargaining Convention (no. 98)
Argentina	1960	1956
Australia	1973	1973
Brazil	Not ratified	1952
Canada	1972	Not ratified
Chile	1999	1999
China	Not ratified	Not ratified
France	1951	1951
Germany	1957	1956
India	Not ratified	Not ratified
Indonesia	1998	1957
Italy	1958	1958
Japan	1965	1953
Nigeria	1960	1960
South Africa	1996	1996
South Korea	Not ratified	Not ratified
Spain	1977	1977
Sweden	1949	1950
Turkey	1993	1952
UK	1949	1950
US	Not ratified	Not ratified

Source: NORMLEX Information System (ILO 2013).

continued to use the pluralist paradigm as a normative yardstick. However, there were exceptions, as shown by the growing interest in neocorporatism that emerged in the late 1970s.

Corporatist traditions

In the 1970s, European social scientists and American scholars of Latin America and Western Europe became increasingly aware of political systems that did not fit into the pluralist Anglo-American model. Some scholars established the concept of neocorporatism as an alternative to pluralist theory in the area of interest politics (Schmitter 1974; Goldthorpe 1984; Katzenstein 1984). Others used concepts like *consensus democracy* or *consociational democracy* for political systems in which parties that represent different sections of society share power (Lijphart 2008; Armingeon 2002). Although the discovery of a *second tier of government,* composed of a complex system of intermediary associations, was nothing new (Rokkan 1966; Gruner 1956), Philippe Schmitter's (1974) article 'Still the century of corporatism?' inspired a generation of comparativists: 'All of a sudden, a research field that to many had seemed hopelessly empiricist and American-centred, began to open up exciting perspectives on vast landscapes of democratic theory, political sociology and social theory in general' (Streeck 2006: 10).

Schmitter's concept of neocorporatism not only enabled comparativists to capture the particular role that the organizations of capital and labour play in many countries, but also challenged republican and pluralist notions of interest politics. Like republicans, neocorporatists perceive the political system as a *body politic* (Rousseau 1973 [1762] Book 2: 260) and not as an aggregation of particular interests, as pluralists would argue. Fittingly, the term **corporatism** had been derived from *corpus* (body). However, unlike republicans, neocorporatists argue that the body politic is constituted not only by individual cells, but also by organs that perform different, but complementary, functions. Hence, the life and death of the body politic depends on the *organic solidarity* (Durkheim 1964 [1893]) between its organs as much as on the vitality of its individual cells. As with human bodies, so with the body politic—the uncontrolled growth of individual cells or organs could threaten the functioning of the entire system.

Unlike republicans, neocorporatists argue that interests and interest associations cannot be excluded from the political process. Contrary to pluralists, however, neocorporatists question the notion of free competition between different interests. Free competition would simply lead to the strongest interests prevailing over weaker interests. This would challenge governability, undermine social justice, and hamper the economic performance of modern mass democracies. Therefore the state should not only guarantee freedom of association. Public policies should also include measures that guarantee a balance of power between the opposing social interests, notably between the organizations of capital and labour. Only in this case can the outcome of the policy-making process reflect the best arguments, rather than mere power relations between social interests.

The last point is of particular interest in relation to Western Europe, where both the political left and right agreed on the desirability of institutionalizing social interests. On the left, Social Democrats were the direct offspring of the organized labour movement. Moreover, labour parties favoured shifting the conflict between employers and employees from the market place to the political arena, where the number of workers tends to be higher than the number of capitalists. This explains why the labour movement fought for centuries for the extension of the franchise. On the right, Christian Democrats were closely related to the Catholic Church which also doubted the ability of liberal individualism to provide social integration (Pope Leo XIII 2010 [1891]). Similarly, European and Latin American fascist and peronist movements were intrigued by an authoritarian variant of corporatism, namely the pre-modern *Ständestaat* (corporate state) where power relied, at least on paper, on functional constituencies (*estates*). Incidentally, Schmitter introduced the term *neocorporatism* in order to distinguish it from the fascist corporate state. Arguably, the post-1945 neocorporatist class compromises have little in common with the authoritarian corporatism of the past. But despite the elective affinity between state traditions, Social Democrats, and Christian Democrats, neocorporatist arrangements have always remained controversial. Whereas Marxists criticized neocorporatist pacts as attempts to contain socialist labour activism (Panitch 1980; Hyman 1975), capitalists were never really enthusiastic about sharing power with trade unions. Therefore it is not surprising that business elites actively supported the shift towards neoliberal politics in the 1970s (Harvey 2005).

However, neocorporatism is not only a politically contentious subject; it has also been questioned methodologically. Whereas it is easy to define neocorporatism in theory, neocorporatist scholars have not been able to agree on a set of unambiguous measures of corporatism in practice (Schmitter 1981; Traxler *et al.* 2001). In Germany, for example, effective corporatist arrangements, both formal and informal, have been reached between the employers' associations and unions of a particular sector, whereas the national peak organizations of capital and labour have not signed national social pacts (see Table 14.3). In contrast, the Maastricht Treaty established the *European Social Dialogue* between the peak organizations of capital and labour as far back as 1993, but the fact that the European social partners can negotiate legally binding agreements has not led to a neocorporatist European Union (Erne 2008). Likewise, Hong Kong can hardly be described as a neocorporatist political system, even if half of its Legislative Council is composed of interest group representatives selected by functional constituencies, representing, however, predominately business interests (Goodstadt 2005). For this reason, any comparative analysis of interest politics systems, it has to be reiterated, must be very aware of the particular context of the different interest politics systems in place in different regions of the world.

Nevertheless, the theoretical divide between pluralist and neocorporatist systems of interest articulation has been very productive for **empirical research**, especially in comparisons of Anglo-American and European socio-economic and political systems. During the last two decades, the neocorporatism vs. pluralism frame has inspired several studies, comparing the legitimacy and performance of the coordinated systems of Scandinavia, the Low Countries, Austria, Germany, and Switzerland

Table 14.3 Evolution of labour relations regimes (1985–2010)

	Labour relation regimes[a]		Corporatist legacy[b]	Corporatist crisis agreements[c]
	1973	1996	1998-2007	2008–2010
Finland	Classic corporatism	(Neoliberalism)	1	1[d]
Norway	Classic corporatism	Lean corporatism	1	1[d]
Denmark	Classic corporatism	Lean corporatism	1	1[d]
Germany	Lean corporatism	Lean corporatism	1	1[d]
Netherlands	Other corporatism	Lean corporatism	1	1
France	Statism	Statism	0	0[d]
Italy	(Other corporatism)	Lean corporatism	1	1[e]
Ireland	(Other corporatism)	Lean corporatism	1	0
Spain	*Military dictatorship*	(Lean corporatism)	1	0
Japan	(Lean corporatism)	(Lean corporatism)	0	1
Canada	Pluralism	Neoliberalism	0	0
UK	(Pluralism)	Neoliberalism	0	0
US	Pluralism	Neoliberalism	0	0

[a]Traxler *et al*. 2001. Borderline cases in parenthesis.

[b,c]Baccaro and Heeb (2012), except for Denmark, Finland, and Norway (Rehfeldt 2009). Social partners signed a social pact or were otherwise involved in corporatist policy making arrangements = 1.

[d]No encompassing national social pacts, but agreements in several sectors.

[e]Crisis agreements signed only by minoritarian trade union confederations.

Source: Adapted from Traxler *et al*. (2001), Rehfeldt (2009), and Baccaro and Heeb (2012).

with the liberal systems of interest politics in the English-speaking world (Crouch 1999; Hall and Soskice 2001; Traxler *et al*. 2001; Pontusson 2005; Block 2007).

Interest associations in practice

Interest group formation

In 1965, US economist Mancur Olson challenged the pluralist assumption that group formation was equally available to everybody. Assuming that individual action is determined by individual cost–benefit calculations, his book *The Logic of Collective Action* concluded that *selective incentives* motivate rational individuals to join interest groups (Olson 1965). According to the *logic of rational choice*, only associations that provide private benefits will prosper, whereas associations that provide public goods, i.e. general benefits without regard to a person's membership status, will find it almost impossible to attract members.

Why should rational individuals pay union subscriptions when collectively agreed wage increases or improvements in social benefits will be applied to everybody whether they are union members or not? Union organizers might respond by saying that the strength of a union, and therefore its capacity to improve working and living conditions, is directly related to the number of its adherents. But how decisive is this argument? The power of a union does not increase noticeably if its membership increases by one individual. Therefore, from Olson's perspective, it would be more rational for a potential union member to take a free ride, relying on the contributions of the existing union members, than to bear the cost of union membership. Consequently, Olson concluded that the formation of interest associations is biased in favour of those associations that are able to offer special advantages, such as automobile clubs that offer insurance cover to their members.

At first sight, a comparative assessment of trade union membership figures across countries seems to confirm Olson's arguments; in almost all countries union membership density figures are considerably lower than in Denmark, Finland, Sweden, and Belgium (the so-called Ghent system countries) where union membership includes unemployment insurance cover (see Table 14.1 and Scruggs (2002); see also Chapters 21 and 22). In turn, however, Olson cannot explain why rational people voluntarily join unions in countries where union membership does not include selective benefits. Olson's (1965) claim to have indentified *the* logic of collective action has also been proved wrong by the events of 1968, which triggered an unexpected resurgence of civic activism and social movements across the world (see Chapter 16). Whereas Olson's model can explain why some groups have more members than others, it cannot explain the formation of interest associations generally.

Olson's individualistic logic of the *homo economicus* is not the only logic at play when people decide to join interest associations. Collective experiences and moral concerns can also trigger a feeling of an identity of interests between people, as shown in E. P. Thompson's seminal history *The Making of the English Working Class* (1963). Olson's logic has also been qualified by European social scientists who studied *The Resurgence of Class Conflict in Western Europe since 1968* (Crouch and Pizzorno 1978) and by scholars who emphasized the role of entrepreneurial organizers (Salisbury 1969) or external sponsors in the formation of interest groups. For instance, Jeffrey Berry emphasized that at least a third of the eighty-three American public interest organizations received at least 50 per cent of their funding from private foundations (Berry 1977: 72). Similarly, Greenwood quoted the 2010 records of the *European Transparency Register* which indicate that EU grants represented on average 64 per cent of the total income of the EU's major 'citizen interest groups', such as the *European Environmental Bureau* or the *European Anti-Poverty Network* (Greenwood 2011: 139). But even if external support somewhat mitigates the disadvantages of public interest groups, a review of Olson's legacy suggested that groups that offer selective incentives to their members still have an advantage. However, the advantage may be declining, as insurance companies have started to undercut groups, such as the British *Automobile Association*, by offering insurance cover at a lower cost (McLean 2000).

The pluralist notion of equality between interest associations has also been losing ground among scholars of interest politics who did not follow Olson's rational choice paradigm. In the 1970s, several studies appeared which suggested that group formation and membership were biased in favour of particular social categories with particular resources, notably wealth and time. And in 1985, Offe and Wiesenthal (1985: 175) even challenged the entire 'interest group stereotype', arguing that it would make little sense to use the same label for business associations and trade unions, given the distinct logics of collective action used in the two cases.

Offe and Wiesenthal's two logics of collective action

In their influential work, Offe and Wiesenthal (1985) assessed the associational practices of labour and capital. They proposed distinguishing between *two logics of collective action* in terms of the individual *or* collective ability of an interest to affect the policy-making capacity of the political system. Offe and Wiesenthal did not argue that business organizations have an advantage because they tend to spend more money on lobbying than other organizations. Instead, they highlighted the structural dependence of politicians in capitalist societies on the holders of capital. As any *individual* investment decision has an impact on the economic performance of a territory, politicians must consider the views of capitalists whether they are well organized or not. This simplifies the task of business interest representation enormously. Business interests do not face the difficult collective action problems that labour unions and other organizations face. Whereas investment strikes by capital holders do not require collective organization, the withdrawal of labour requires *collective organization* and the willingness of workers to act together despite the availability of individual exit options.

Certainly, at times, business associations also fail, for instance due to competition between different firms for government support, such as government contracts, government bailouts, or privatization bids. Accordingly, Traxler and colleagues have argued that 'it is problematic to translate the pre-associational power asymmetry between businesses and labour into corresponding differentials in terms of associational capacities' (Traxler *et al.* 2001: 37). Even so, the collective action problem facing workers is much more difficult to solve than that facing corporations. Trade unions rely on their members' willingness to act collectively. In contrast, business associations only have to tell policy-makers that individual firms will act in an undesirable way if politicians fail to accommodate their interests. In this vein, even the imminent ruin of an organization can turn out to be an effective political tool, as demonstrated in 2008 when business interests successfully lobbied governments around the world to bail out failing banks (Stiglitz 2010).

A new typology of interest associations

Offe and Wiesenthal's analysis allows us to introduce a new typology of interest associations in action which does not distinguish groups on the basis of their subject matter or the private or public nature of the interests represented. Instead, I propose a two-by-two table based on two analytical distinctions that relate to two dimensions of collective action. First, I distinguish interest groups on the basis of the nature of their members' ability to act: to what degree does the representation of an interest rely on collective action by the members of an interest group beyond the simple payment of membership fees? Second, I distinguish interest groups on the basis of their relation to the political system: to what degree can they shape public policy-making through autonomous action outside the formal democratic policy-making process? In other words, to what degree are interest groups capable of creating facts outside the formal parliamentary system that governments and parliaments cannot ignore? At the outset, this leads us to a typology that enables us to distinguish business interests (which are not obliged to act collectively) from other interest groups, such as trade unions and other organizations which must act collectively in order to have a political impact (Figure 14.1). In addition, our typology also enables us to distinguish both business groups and trade unions from other non-governmental organizations that do not have the power to affect policy-making through autonomous action in the economic sphere. In contrast with these organizations, business interests—especially global firms—are able to determine rules and regulations without having to go through government (Crouch 2010, 2011; Graz and Nölke 2008). In turn, globalization seems to be curbing workers' capacity to exercise political power through industrial action. Nevertheless, even transnational supply and production chains contain weak links which can be exploited by trade union action (Erne 2008: 36). Therefore trade unions retain more power compared to other non-governmental organizations that play no role in the economic production process.

Figure 14.1 enables us not only to distinguish business associations, trade unions, and other non-governmental organizations analytically, but also to distinguish different repertoires of action that go beyond the *lobbying* activities that are available to all interest groups. Reflecting contributions to the study of interest politics from cognate disciplines, such as industrial and labour relations and political sociology, our typology also captures alternative action repertoires that are available only to specific types of interest associations.

- The capacity to conclude *political exchanges* with the government (Pizzorno 1978), available to organizations with a high degree of autonomy *vis-à-vis* the political system (e.g. business associations and trade unions).
- The capacity to engage in *contentious politics* (Tilly and Tarrow 2007), available to organizations with a high capacity to engage in collective action (e.g. trade unions and other social movement organizations).
- The capacity to set up *private interest government* structures (Streeck and Schmitter 1985), available to organizations with a high degree of autonomy *vis-à-vis* the political system (e.g. business associations).

		Necessity of collective action	
		Low	**High**
Autonomy from the political system	**High**	**Private interest government** *Global firms* *Business associations* **Political exchanges** *Global firms* *Business associations*	**Private interest government** *Employer associations and trade unions* **Political exchanges** *Trade unions* **Contentious politics** *Trade unions*
	Low	**Direct lobbying** *Global firms* *Business associations*	**Contentious politics** *New social movements* **Direct lobbying** *Non-business interest associations*

Figure 14.1 Action repertoires of interest groups

Direct lobbying

Although the term 'lobbying' was originally used to describe attempts to influence lawmakers in the lobbies of the British Houses of Parliament, the lobbying literature usually refers to all activities that aim to influence any branch of government at any level of decision-making. However, in order to distinguish lobbying from other repertoires of action of interest associations, I am reserving this term for activities that are based on personal access to decision-makers in line with the concept of *direct* or *inside lobbying*.

The American lobbying literature, which still influences the agenda of lobbying researchers across the world, has been particularly concerned with practical questions. What factors explain the success of lobbyists? Whom to lobby to be effective? Truman (1971 [1951]) and numerous scholars who came after him described and compared the lobbying strategies of interest groups *vis-á-vis* the branches of government: the executive, the state bureaucracy, the legislature, and even the courts. Predictably, most scholars concluded that the more an interest group is endowed with resources, such as money, legitimacy, and expertise, the higher is its capacity to influence decision-makers and policy outcomes. Lobbying specialists also came to the conclusion that the accessibility of institutions affects the degree of interest group influence on policy outputs. And finally, there also seems to be a consensus among lobbying specialists that the nature of an issue influences the efficacy of lobbying.

In addition, growing popular concerns about the impact of interest group money in US elections triggered not only several studies (Currinder *et al.* 2007; Rozell *et al.* 2006) but also political reform. However, these reforms did not aim to balance power inequalities within the interest group system, in line with neocorporatist thought, but rather mirrored a shift from a pluralist to a republican understanding of interest group politics. Fittingly, in 2002 the US Congress passed the bipartisan McCain–Feingold Act which restricted the ability of corporations—but also trade unions—to advertise on behalf of, or in opposition to, a political candidate. However, on 21 January 2010, the Supreme Court of the United States ruled that the McCain–Feingold Act violated the Constitution, stating that its free-speech provisions should apply to corporations and unions as well as to individuals. It goes without saying that the ruling, which was determined by the Supreme Court's conservative majority, caused widespread dismay among commentators, who argued that elections should be won—not bought (Streisand 2010).

Be that as it may, a comparative assessment of European state traditions suggests that there are alternative ways to contain the influence of corporate money in the political process. European states do not limit the free-speech rights of interest groups; however, they do balance the power of competing interest associations through public policy measures that strengthen weaker interest associations, namely through financial assistance as well as institutionalized consultation, co-determination, and veto rights. Consequently, it seems implausible to suggest converging perspectives on interest group research in Europe and America, as has been argued recently (Mahoney and Baumgartner 2008; Dür 2008).

Perhaps the application of American questions and paradigms in European interest politics research can be justified by the presence of a plethora of professional lobbyists in Brussels (Corporate Europe Observatory 2010, Greenwood 2011) or the EU's mode of multi-level governance, which resembles the federal US system at least to some extent (see Chapter 23). However, interest groups must play a particular lobbying game in Brussels. For example, European business lobbyists do not set up US-style political action committees in order to campaign for or against political candidates or legislation (Coen 2010). Given the much more technocratic and consensual nature of the EU policy-making process, they try instead to establish themselves as trusted actors in EU-level policy networks that 'seek some kind of "negotiated order" out of conflict and uncertainty' (Coen and Richardson 2009: 348). This is leading to a system of interest intermediation called 'elite pluralism' (Coen 1997) in which only those players who can prove their presence to be politically advisable gain political access to a particular EU policy network. In social policy, however, the automatic participation of employer associations and unions still reflects neocorporatist rather than pluralist patterns of interest intermediations (Léonard *et al.* 2007), although the unilateral EU labour market and social policy reforms that have been imposed in the EU's periphery after 2010 may suggest a different conclusion in the future (Erne 2012*a*, 2012*b*). Nevertheless, policy-making processes and the regulatory regimes that govern interest group–government relations vary across countries and different varieties of capitalism to such a degree (Grant 2005, McMenamin 2013) that any analysis that fails to go beyond US paradigms of lobbying must lead to flawed results.

Political exchange

As shown in Figure 14.1, direct lobbying is not the only mechanism through which interest associations influence political power. Associations that operate in the economic sphere, namely business associations and trade unions, are also able to conclude *political exchanges* with political leaders (Pizzorno 1978). Governments have frequently traded goods with unions or employers in exchange for social consent. In such cases, political exchange power is paradoxically linked to the (partial) renunciation of economic power, namely the capacity to withdraw capital or labour from the production process. In addition, political institutions are dependent on expert knowledge which might not be available within an increasingly restricted and residual public service (Crouch 2004: 89). Accordingly, even corporate lobbying can be conceptualized as political exchange, namely as an exchange of information that is crucial in the policy-making process as against access to the policy-making process (Bouwen 2002).

Sometimes, exchange power even takes on a symbolic form, in which neither politicians nor interest groups exchange any material goods but only legitimacy (Crouch 2000). For example, trade unions have shared the burden of legitimizing contested *political* decisions in exchange for more or less favourable public policies, as in the case of past EU referendums (Hyman 2010; Wyler 2012). Unions have also offered employers their collaboration to persuade workers to use controversial technologies, to respect safety regulations, or to retrain. In addition, unions and employers have made joint submissions in favour of their industries, which political decision-makers usually find very hard to deny.

As capital depends on labour in the production process, and vice versa, the organizations of capital and labour may also decide to enter into tripartite agreements with the government in exchange for economic performance and social peace. In such agreements during the 1970s unions often accepted wage moderation in exchange for legislation that strengthened workplace co-determination rights, and more recently simply to make a country more competitive. In this context, interest associations can no longer be perceived as a counter-power to the state. Instead, they become actors within a policy network that also assumes governmental functions. However, given the increasing exit options introduced by neoliberal politics and the internationalization of capital, even the proponents of neocorporatism had doubts about whether the political exchanges that characterized neocorporatism could be sustained (Streeck and Schmitter 1991).

But, surprisingly, in the 1990s social pacts were concluded even in countries, such as Ireland, Italy, and Spain (Molina and Rhodes 2002), where the structural preconditions of neocorporatism—namely a strong policy co-ordination and enforcement capacity on the part of the participating 'social partners' and a balance of class forces between capital and labour—were missing (Schmitter and Lehmbruch 1979). Accordingly, Traxler *et al.* (2001) used the term *lean corporatism* with reference to the unexpected reappearance of the 'corporatist Sisyphus' in the 1990s (Schmitter and Grote 1997). But in 2008 and 2009, social partnership collapsed again in Ireland, Italy, and Spain, whereas the peak associations of capital and labour continue to play a major role in the face of the economic crisis in established neocorporatist countries (see Table 14.3).

The collapse of social pacting in Ireland highlights a particular problem related to 'competitive corporatism' (Rhodes 1998). Workers accepted wage moderation, i.e. a smaller share of the national income, in exchange for an overall higher growth rate that would follow from higher profits of Irish businesses. During the booming Celtic Tiger years, it seemed that capital, labour, and the state had found an arrangement that triggered a spectacular period of economic and employment growth (Roche and Cradden 2003). But when growth rates collapsed, the Irish government and employers' associations abandoned partnership and imposed unilateral wage cuts. Whereas Irish workers accepted a smaller share of the national income when it was growing, they found it very difficult to accept getting a smaller slice of a shrinking cake. It follows that corporatist deals can be very risky, especially for labour. How can unions be sure that employers do not take advantage of unions' concessions within social pacts in boom years when unions are strong, and then abandon corporatist arrangements in crisis years when unions are weak?

The major difficulty with the exchange power of a union, however, is its dependence on the capacity to threaten social stability (Offe and Wiesenthal 1985). In contrast to the exchange power of capitalists, labour's exchange power depends entirely on its collective mobilization power. Hence, exchange power uses—but does not reproduce—mobilization power (Erne 2008). The use of exchange power might even cause a decline in union membership that would finally undermine the very capacity to conclude exchanges. This explains why unions that univocally support social partnership need to demonstrate occasionally that their consent cannot be taken for granted, as shown by Hyman (2001) with regard to the German case.

Contentious politics

Interest associations also engage at times in *contentious politics* (Tilly and Tarrow 2007; see Chapter 16)—or *outside lobbying* (Schattschneider 1975 [1960]) in the language of the American lobbying literature. Whereas business associations very rarely see the need to engage in contentious collective action (e.g. public demonstrations or lockouts), strike action is often seen as the constitutive power of labour. In contrast with other social movements, unions engage in contentious politics mainly to compel institutions to compromise. In contrast with Rosa Luxemburg (2008 [1906]), most unions understand contentious politics not as tool to achieve a different society, but rather as an action of last resort to remind corporations and governments of labour's price for cooperation. However, the more the unions' capacity to wage collective action declined, the more difficult it became to defend the achievements of the mid-twentieth-century class compromise that led to the formation of the modern welfare state (see Chapter 21).

The growing cross-border mobility of capital provides employers with a wider range of possibilities to counter collective action on the part of labour. Ongoing restructuring processes and threats to delocalize enterprises have considerably weakened union power in industrialized countries, even if capital is not as footloose as is often alleged. Nevertheless, it would be wrong to say that strikes have disappeared in the new world of global capitalism (Silver 2003; van der Velden *et al.* 2007; Bieler and Lindberg 2010). Yet, industrial conflicts often involve relatively small groups of core workers, especially in the public sector, and fail to include the marginalized peripheral workforce. Although the European peak organizations of employers and workers signed a legally binding *European Social Dialogue* agreement that stated that employees on fixed-term contracts cannot be treated less favourably than permanent staff (European Industrial Relations Dictionary 2010), Hyman (1999) observed a growing polarization between different sections of the working class. This obviously undermines working class solidarity, and thus the capacity of unions to conclude general political exchanges.

Although the contemporary orthodoxy that social class no longer exists can be contested with sociological analysis, the increasing difficulty of subordinate groups to unite as a class entails major consequences for interest politics and democracy alike (Crouch 2004: 53): How is it possible to reconcile democracy and interest politics, if the latter seem to be increasingly dominated by a self-confident global shareholding and business executive class? In the wake of the financial crisis of 2008, Crouch gave a pessimistic answer to this question: whereas democratic politics would continue to play a role in some areas, the democratic state would be vacating its 'former heartland of basic economic strategy'. Instead, economic policy would be shaped by 'the great corporations, particularly those in the financial sector' (Crouch 2009: 398), because of the decline of the manual working class and the failure of new social movements to constitute a new class that stands for a general social interest. Consequently, economic policy would become a private matter of business interests, even if corporations might, at times, be held accountable by public appeals to *corporate social responsibility* (Crouch 2011).

Private interest government

In neocorporatist systems, the state integrates associations into policy networks. In the case of *private interest government*, however, the state goes even further and delegates its authority to make binding decisions to interest groups (Streeck and Schmitter 1985). As far back as the Middle Ages, producer associations established private interest government structures, namely the guilds, in order to police the markets. However, after the French Revolution the regulation of markets became a domain of the nation-state, mainly to suit the needs of modern industry. When the working class entered as a compelling social force in politics, it seemed that the days of self-regulation of economic affairs by business would definitely be numbered. Yet, in a particular economic sector, guild-like patterns of private interest government remained crucially important.

In the agriculture sector, self-governing producer associations continued to police the production and distribution of goods throughout the twentieth century (Streeck and Schmitter 1985; Farago 1985; Traxler and Unger 1994; Stan 2005). Although agriculture policy became an important pillar of the European common market project, states continued to support the self-governing bodies of the sector by public policy and laws. Even in countries with no corporatist traditions, farmers' associations were co-opted into public policy networks that governed agricultural policy (Smith 1993; Muller 1984). However, the more the agricultural sector internationalized, the more evident conflicts between local farmers and international agribusiness corporations became. In several countries, small farmers left the once all-encompassing farmers' associations and founded autonomous farmers' groups (della Porta and Caiani 2009). In this context, it became increasingly difficult, but not impossible, to sustain private interest governing structures in this sector. Traditional private interest governments such as the *Swiss Cheese Union* collapsed. However, in some cases new self-governing private interest government systems also emerged, for instance around *Appellations d'Origine Contrôlée* (AOC) food certification, production control, and marketing regimes (Wagemann 2012). In other sectors, however, powerful interest groups were even able to establish *transnational private governance* structures to regulate, for example, the internet, international accountancy standards, and banking regulation in a way that suited their interests (Graz and Nölke 2008).

The shift in policy-making from partisan politics to autonomous agencies has also been the focus of scholars who studied the rise of *regulatory governance* (Majone 1994). According to Majone, regulatory governance is meant to keep interest groups out of policy-making process by relieving the process of the 'negative consequences' of electoral pressures on the quality of regulation. In other words, advocates of regulatory governance aim to reduce interest group influence by the exclusion of elected politicians from the policy-making process. Policy-making would be better if it was left to independent agencies—for example, to independent central banks in relation to monetary policy, or independent competition authorities in relation to competition policy. However, the exclusion of interests and interest intermediation from the policy-making process is at variance with both pluralist and neocorporatist paradigms of interest politics. To some extent, the theory of regulatory governance comes closest to the unitarist republican paradigm, but without its democratic rhetoric. Like republican theory, however, regulatory governance faces a major problem: how can one be sure that regulatory agencies do not serve the interest that was able to capture a dominant position in the agency's decision-making process? Regulative agencies tend to be shaped by powerful political actors and ideologies, as confirmed by the exclusion of social and labour interests from the frames of references that govern the monetary policy of the European Central Bank and the competition policy of the Directorate General for Competition of the European Commission (Erne 2008). For that reason regulatory governance structure 'often masks ideological choices which are not debated and subject to public scrutiny beyond the immediate interests related to the regulatory management area' (Weiler *et al.* 1995: 33). In this vein, regulatory governance might be more properly understood if it were conceptualized as disguised private interest government.

KEY POINTS

- Selective incentives motivate individuals to join interest groups. But collective experiences and moral concerns can also trigger collective action. Finally, organizers or external sponsors may also play a role in the formation of interest groups.

- Whereas business groups do not need to engage in collective action, as each individual investment decision has a political impact, trade unions and other citizens' organizations must organize collective action to have an impact.

- The power of interest groups depends on their ability to affect the policy-making capacity of a political system. Hence, powerful interest groups not only engage in direct lobbying, but also pressurize the government by other means, notably through actions in the economic sphere (business relocation threats, workers' industrial action, etc.).

- The different action repertoires (direct lobbying, political exchange, contentious politics, and private interest government) are not available to all interest groups to the same extent.

- Government–interest group relations reflect not only the power resources of interest groups but also the institutional context of the particular political and socio-economic system.

Conclusion

Comparativists agree that interest associations play a crucial role in the political process. However, this chapter has also shown that there is no agreement on whether interest groups represent a danger or a 'school for democracy' (Sinyai 2006). Therefore it is not surprising that government–interest group relations, which preoccupied

Rousseau and Tocqueville centuries ago, still engage contemporary scholars. Some analysts note that corporate interests are increasingly determining socio-economic policy (Crouch 2004, 2011), whereas others detect twin processes of popular and elite withdrawal from politics (Mair 2006). To this, Tocqueville might have responded: the weaker individual citizens become, the more they need to learn to combine with fellow citizens to defend themselves against the despotic influence of corporate power. Accordingly, many studies ask what contribution interest associations make to the democratic involvement of citizens in the current era (Jordan and Maloney 2007; Cohen and Rogers 1995). This democracy–interest association nexus is also of particular importance in studies that assess EU politics (Horn 2012; Kohler-Koch and Quittkat 2011; Erne 2008; Balme and Chabanet 2008; Kohler-Koch *et al.* 2008; Smismans 2006).

Comparative studies of interest politics are also crucial in order to explain variations in capitalisms and welfare states across the developed world (Hancké 2009). Why did companies in Germany lay off fewer workers in 2009 than corporations in the US, although the global economic crisis hit both countries equally? Arguably, the difference can be explained by the different systems of interest intermediation that are in place in the two countries.

Given the impact of interest group politics on both democracy and the social and economic well-being of people, it is no exaggeration to claim that the study of politics and society cannot forego the contributions of comparativists in this field. However, there remains one caveat. Students of interest politics should remain sceptical of studies that seek to increase the field's coherence by reducing its scope to the narrowness and parochialism that dominated some sections of the lobbying and pressure group literature in the past.

KEY POINTS

- Interest associations play a crucial role in the political process. But there is no agreement on whether interest associations sustain or undermine democracy, especially in the current context of a growing internationalization of interest politics. For this reason, the relationship between democracy and interest politics is of particular importance in studies that assess the democratic legitimacy of supra-national organizations, such as the European Union.

- Interest associations—and the particular rules and regulations that govern them—also affect the socio-economic and political outcomes of a particular country. Therefore comparative studies of interest politics have been crucial in order to explain variations in capitalisms and welfare states across the world.

Questions

1. What is an interest group?

2. Why are interest groups so difficult to define in a comparative context?

3. Does it make sense to distinguish 'public' and 'private' interest groups?

4. On which assumptions are republican and pluralist paradigms of interest politics based?

5. What advantages do neocorporatist systems of interest intermediation offer governments?

6. To what extent do US and EU lobbying activities differ from each other, and why?

7. Why do business interest groups retain a privileged position in capitalist democracies?

8. What repertoires of interest group action are available to farmers' and women's associations?

9. Are neocorporatist systems of interest intermediation in the workers' interest?

10. Why aren't we witnessing a greater convergence of interest politics across the globe?

 ## Further reading

Cigler, A. J., and Loomis, B. A. (eds) (2011) *Interest Group Politics* (8th edn) (Washington, DC: CQ Press). A contemporary review of US interest politics.

Coen, D., Grant, W., and Wilson, G. (2010) *The Oxford Handbook of Business and Government* (Oxford: Oxford University Press). A fine collection on business-government relations.

Crouch, C. and Streeck, W. (eds) (2006) *The Diversity of Democracy: Corporatism, Social Order and Political Conflict* (Cheltenham: Edward Elgar). A lucid reassessment of the neocorporatist argument by major protagonists in the field.

Dahl, R. A. (1982) *Dilemmas of Pluralist Democracy: Autonomy vs. Control* (New Haven, CT: Yale University Press). A self-reflective reassessment of the pluralist argument.

Erne, R. (2008) *European Unions: Labor's Quest for a Transnational Democracy* (Ithaca, NY: Cornell University Press). A comparative study of transnational trade union action that challenges the assertion that no realistic prospect exists for remedying the EU's democratic deficit.

Greenwood, J. (2011) *Interest Representation in the European Union* (3rd edn) (Basingstoke: Palgrave). A comprehensive textbook on the role of interest associations in the EU.

Harvey, D. (2005) *A Brief History of Neoliberalism* (Oxford: Oxford University Press). A very readable book on the rise of business interests in politics since the 1970s.

McMenamin, I. (2013) *If Money Talks, What Does it Say? Corruption and Business Financing of Political Parties* (Oxford: Oxford University Press). A very intelligent study of the role of business money across a variety of countries and capitalisms.

Offe, Claus (1980) *Disorganized Capitalism: Contemporary Transformations of Work and Politics* (Cambridge: Polity). This book includes Offe and Wiesenthal's seminal chapter on 'Two Logics of Collective Action'.

Olson, M. (1965) *The Logic of Collective Action; Public Goods and the Theory of Groups* (Cambridge, MA: Harvard University Press). A seminal book on interest group formation written from a rational choice perspective.

Smismans, S. (ed.) (2012) *The European Union and Industrial Relations. New Procedures, New Context* (Manchester: Manchester University Press). A book on changing European economic governance and industrial relations after the global crisis.

 ## Web links

http://ebooks.adelaide.edu.au/r/rousseau/jean_jacques/r864s/
Rousseau's *The Social Contract: and Discourses* as a free e-book.

http://europa.eu/transparency-register/index_en.htm
The *European Transparency Register* provides information about who is engaged in EU lobbying activities.

http://www.corporateeurope.org/
The Corporate Europe Observatory is a campaign group that challenges privileged access enjoyed by business lobby groups in European policy making.

http://www.eurofound.europa.eu/areas/industrialrelations/dictionary/
The European Industrial Relations Dictionary of *Eurofound* which is the tripartite EU agency that provides expertise on living and working conditions and industrial relations in Europe.

http://www.fec.gov/
The Federal Election Commission is the US agency which discloses campaign finance information and oversees the funding of Presidential elections.

http://www.gutenberg.org/etext/815 and http://www.
gutenberg.org/etext/816
Tocqueville's *Democracy in America* as a free e-book.

http://www.ilo.org/
The ILO is the tripartite UN agency that is promoting decent
working conditions throughout the world.

http://www.oecd.org/gov/ethics/lobbying
The OECD provides guidance on how to promote 'good
governance principles in lobbying'.

www.labourstart.org/
A comprehensive collection of links to trade union news in 28
languages.

http://www.uva-aias.net/207
A comprehensive database on institutional characteristics of
trade unions, wage setting, state intervention, and social pacts
in 34 countries.

www.businesseurope.eu
European confederation of business and employers' associations.

www.etuc.org
European Trade Union Confederation.

www.ioe-emp.org
International Organization of Employers.

www.ituc-csi.org
International Trade Union Confederation.

**online
resource
centre**

For additional material and resources, please visit the Online Resource Centre at:
www.oxfordtextbooks.co.uk/orc/caramani3e/

CHAPTER 15

Regions

James Bickerton and Alain-G. Gagnon

Chapter contents

Reader's guide

This chapter examines the concept of region and starts by reviewing the main theories and approaches that are used to understand the political role and importance of regions. It then discusses the various dimensions and aspects of regions and regionalism. Regionalism from below concerns the political mobilization of regional identities, whether by movements or political parties. Looking at regional institutions involves an examination of how regions have been constituted, recognized, and accommodated. Sometimes regions have been created by states through a process of regionalization 'from above', undertaken by central governments with administrative and governance purposes in mind; at other times it happens through a process of institution building from within, initiated and pursued primarily by regional actors. Finally, the chapter focuses on the political economy of regions, tracing the changing economic role and place of regions within the national and global economy. Of particular note is the emergence of a new regionalism tied to the economic, technological, and political changes associated with increasing integration and globalization.

Introduction

What is a region? It is a geographical space. But beyond that, many meanings are attached to it, and many approaches are used to understand it. According to Michael Keating, it may relate to an identity; it often has a cultural element; it may sustain a distinct society and a range of social institutions. It can be an economic unit or a unit of government and administration. And all these meanings may coincide, to a greater or lesser degree (Keating 2004: xi).

The idea of region is both simple and highly ambiguous. We are reminded that:

> In most states, the region is a contested area, both territorially and functionally. Spatially, it exists between the national and the local and is the scene of intervention by actors from all levels, national, local, regional and now supranational. Functionally, it is a space in which different types of agency interact and, since it is often weakly institutionalized itself, a terrain of competition among them. (Keating 1997: 17)

Sometimes used when referring to intermediate levels of political representation or governance (provinces, states, Länder, counties, supra-urban areas), region also has been employed to refer to a spatial area within a state encompassing more than one political unit (New England), or a supra-national area stretching across state boundaries (e.g. the Great Lakes or Cascadia regions of North America). It may not be demarcated by political boundaries at all but by particular cultural or economic characteristics (such as the Acadian region in Eastern Canada or Silicon Valley in California). The latter use of the term denotes 'a territorial entity having some natural and organic unity or community of interest that is independent of political and administrative boundaries' (Stevenson 1980: 17).

Not surprisingly, then, geographers, economists, sociologists, and political scientists all define region using different criteria, leading Richard Simeon to argue that 'regions are simply containers … and how we draw the boundaries around them depends entirely on what our purposes are: it is an a *priori* question, determined by theoretical needs or political purposes' (Simeon 1977: 293). With such a malleable nature, 'political entrepreneurs themselves seek to shape the definition of region to reflect their values and interests' (Keating 1997: 17). So, while the concept of region must always be associated with territorial space (as it traditionally has been), it must also be understood as a social, economic, and political construction, i.e. the historical work of human actors and actions. Regions and **regionalism** are not static, unchanging, and geographically determined; they are the continuous creation of human history, the product of complex interactions. This makes the task of delineating regions—their number, shape, and character, and the identities associated with them—dependent upon a host of factors.

Following from this, a region can be defined as a territorial entity distinct from either the local or the **nation-state** level that constitutes an economic, political, administrative, and/or cultural space, within which different types of human agency interact, and towards which individuals and communities may develop attachments and identities. Regionalism is the manifestation of values, attitudes, opinions, preferences, claims, behaviours, interests, attachments, and identities that can be associated with a particular region. As we intuitively know, not all regions are equally 'regional' in their manifestations of regionalism. Following Michael Burgess, who uses the concept of 'federality' to gauge the federal quality of the diverse practices of federalism that he finds in different settings (Burgess 2011: 200), 'regionality' can be used to refer to the intensity, distinctiveness, and cohesiveness that distinguishes the regionalist behaviours and practices of a particular regional community, including the possibility of a different degree of regionality at the societal level as opposed to its expression in terms of regional political institutions.

The continuum of regionalism suggested by the concept of regionality can be attributed to the interaction of three factors. First, the extent of a region's organic unity and community of interest is significant. This is a compound factor with territorial, historical, sociocultural, and economic dimensions. A second factor is the degree of institutionalization a region enjoys. This is both a matter of whether regional institutions exist, the quantity and quality of these institutions, and how congruent they are with the 'organic regions' mentioned above. However, it should be stressed that institutions can and will exert their own independent effect on regionalism—shaping, reinforcing, and legitimizing particular conceptions and representations of the region and the constellation of interests associated with it. A third factor, in close relationship and tending to vary in accordance with the previous two, is regional identity. Like institutions, however, a regional identity once established can be mobilized by regional actors in diverse ways—politically, culturally, and economically—endowing it with the potential to exert a reciprocal effect on the other factors, augmenting and transforming the region and its associated regionalism in important ways.

Whether strong or weak, with a high or low degree of regionality, regions are never completely autonomous or sovereign entities. They are nested within other regions, nations, and supra-national collectivities. These various levels of territorial affiliation and identity are often benignly complementary or mutually reinforcing, but they may also be competitive, or even antagonistic and confrontational. The character of these relationships depends on the region's specific context: historical legacies, institutional and fiscal arrangements (including policies of inter-regional redistribution), cultural factors, economic constraints and opportunities, and so on—factors which are subject to change over time.

Owing to the constraints of space and the parameters of our expertise, the examples and references employed in this chapter are drawn predominantly from Europe and Canada. However, regions and regionalism are an irrefutable fact of political life in almost all states (exclusive of micro-states), making their study an important part of the collective effort to understand politics in all its complexity. In Europe, the Americas, and around the world, regions have influenced the composition and practices of political party systems, set political agendas, shaped constitutions, legislatures, and administrative structures, contested national identities, and been the cause of or stimulus for a wide range of public policies and governance mechanisms. Their impact on both government structures and political processes has been significant. Yet, their pervasive character and their sometimes elusive and intangible quality make their study a challenging and often imprecise exercise. Nonetheless, the manifestations and complicated dynamics of regions and regionalism have perhaps never been as important an aspect of global politics as they are today.

KEY POINTS

- Region is a concept with multiple meanings, though always referring to a territorial space. Its exact meaning in any particular instance is determined by the theoretical needs or political purposes for which it is being used.

- Regions exist as territorial entities distinct from the nation-state and local level that constitute political, economic, cultural, and/or administrative spaces within which different types of human agency interact. Regionalism is understood primarily as the political mobilization of individuals based on their regional interests, attachments, and/or identities.

- The political strength and cohesiveness of a region will vary according to (1) its 'organic unity' and community of interest, (2) its degree of institutionalization, and (3) the salience of its regional identity.

- Regions are nested within other regions as well as nations and supra-national collectivities, and can have an effect on and interact with all the various structures and processes that define and shape the political system.

Theories and approaches

The modernization paradigm

Until the 1960s, the study of regions in social science was dominated by the modernization paradigm and development theory. Industrialization, bureaucratization, and the emergence of the nation-state had generated a scholarly focus on functionalism and national integration as the hallmarks of modern societies. These concepts were theorized and applied by a long line of social scientists, including Smelser (1966), Deutsch (1966a), Shils (1975), and many others. Regions and regionalism were seen as remnants of pre-industrial, pre-modern societies, fated to be eclipsed by the inexorable march of progress in the form of the homogeneous, functionally organized, nationally integrated nation-state (Caramani 2004).

For modernization theorists, cultural homogenization is a key process in the inevitable decline of regionalism and territorially based conflict. Regional peripheries are seen as isolated, distant from the centre, and oppressively traditional in their cultural values. The challenge for elites is to diffuse their 'modern' values to the peripheries, thereby securing adherence to a core value system. Ruling in this model consists of the universalization within society of the values and the rules inherent in the ordering of modern societies (Tarrow 1977: 20). (For data on national communication networks see Comparative table 1 at the end of this volume.)

In conjunction with this approach, a behaviouralist regional science emerged that increasingly emptied region of its historical and social content, substituting an abstract notion of space defined by one or more criteria, such as population density or income, as the delineators of region. This allowed economists to apply micro-economic models to these spatial units unfettered by concerns such as regional history, culture, or social conflict. Reduced to economic development units, regions could be subjected to technocratic forms of planning. Out of this grew such notions as 'stepping down' the economic dynamism of the core to peripheral regions, first elaborated by François Perroux (1950) and Gunnar Myrdal (1957), leading to the spread of growth centre strategies as the leitmotiv of regional planning. With the critique of the modernization perspective, scholarly interest in regions and regionalism was reinvigorated. In the 1960s, Stein Rokkan and others began to challenge the idea that territorial **cleavages** were of declining significance by demonstrating the persistence of territorial cleavages into modern times. Indeed, since the 1970s these cleavages have spawned peripheral protest movements and the political mobilization of territorial–cultural opposition to ruling elites in many societies. Seeking more autonomy, recognition, and accommodation of their distinctive interests and identities, these regional movements, parties, and authorities have sometimes been successful in enticing central governments to adopt decentralist, devolutionist, or *federalizing* strategies in response (Rokkan 1980).

Regional cultures and minority nations

One way that scholars have understood the persistence of regionalism is to view it from a cultural perspective.

Distinct regional cultures can sustain a sense of regional community and provide the basis for values, attitudes, and policy preferences that differ from other regions or the larger national community. This cultural approach has long informed the historical treatment of regions and the phenomenon of regionalism.

Almond and Verba (1963), Hartz (1955, 1964), Lipset (1990), and others have used a culturalist approach to explain cross-national variations in political life based on differences in national values (see Chapter 17). Widely shared identities and values are thought to structure a society's political behaviour. This general approach has also been used to explain regionalism *within* countries, whether through reference to regional differences in political attitudes or initial settlement patterns (in Hartzian terms, 'founding fragments'). This is argued to have produced spatially distinct value systems capable of supporting different regional outlooks and policy preferences (for Canada, see McRae 1964; Wiseman 1981).

However, regions as cultural spaces are difficult to definitively locate or pin down to a single spatial context. Cultural sensibilities, outlooks, or identities can be nested within particular geographies, economies, and institutions, as well as social characteristics such as class, religion, language, ethnicity, and community heritage (Soja 1989). However, to the extent that regional identities exist, they can be mobilized politically, giving voice to a particular territorial identity and the interests and concerns that political actors link to it. In this way a region's history, mythologies, and cultural symbols become a discursive and ideological resource that can be used to advance a particular conception of the region and any political strategies or development projects that may be associated with it.

When ethnolinguistic minorities with claims to historic nation status are present, the role of culture in shaping the distinctiveness, if not the singularity, of the regional experience is magnified. In such circumstances, the congruence of nation and state is countered by the assertion of the existence of competing national identities within state boundaries. The political claims of these regions tend to be greater (Gagnon and Tully 2001). At the same time, given appropriate institutional arrangements, cultural convergence (the increasing commonality of values) can expand the basis for people with distinct national identities to share institutions; it can increase their potential for living together and living apart at the same time.

Marxism and uneven economic development

Marxism has provided yet another theoretical jumping off point for the study of regions, one critical of both the modernization paradigm and cultural approaches.

A variety of class and dependency theorists share in common the premise that the unfettered market does not operate in a spatially impartial way, and that political power has been a key factor in structuring unequal relations in the market place. Initially developed to explain continuing conditions of underdevelopment in the Third World, Marxist-inspired regional theories have also been applied to explain the situation of less-developed regions within industrialized countries. Generally, Marxist theorists have argued that regions can only be understood in terms of their relationship with the national and global political economy, and in particular the dynamics inherent in the process of capitalist development.

However, there are contending approaches to regions within Marxism. What might be termed the 'logic of accumulation' approach sees regional underdevelopment as a necessary condition of accelerated **capital accumulation**. In short, regional disparities and inequalities are a structural consequence of the internal development logic of capitalism (Carney 1980; Clark 1980). Other scholars have contested this approach as too abstract and mechanistic, and instead advocate detailed analysis on a case-by-case basis, stressing the historical specificity of each region's experience (Vilar 1977). Yet another variation of dependency theory argues that areas of the world that are lagging in terms of the transition to a capitalist mode of production are locked into this underdeveloped condition through a process of imperialist exploitation by advanced capitalist countries (Wallerstein 1979), an interpretation contested by scholars who contend instead that it is the persistence of pre-capitalist class relations within underdeveloped regions that constitutes the main barrier to their economic and social development (Brenner 1977).

These disagreements over how to interpret regional inequalities parallel Marxism's theoretical disagreements regarding the significance of emergent regionalist and nationalist movements. The Hobsbawm–Nairn debate over the meaning of such movements is instructive here. Hobsbawm links them to the gradual disintegration of national economies due to changes within global capitalism. This creates a situation of greater vulnerability and exploitability for the smaller and more economically dependent states that are the outcome of movements pursuing separatist agendas (Hobsbawm 1977). Nairn agrees that the sociopolitical fragmentation occasioned by minority nationalist movements is a response to the increasingly uneven development of regions in the era of global capitalism. He argues that in the case of Britain this will eventually lead to the country's break-up, a prospect which (unlike Hobsbawm) he views as both positive and inevitable (Nairn 1977).

Certainly, these debates over how to understand regionalist and ethno-territorial nationalist movements illustrate the benefits of historical specificity for students of regionalism, as well as how an understanding of the dynamics of global capitalism can inform the study of territorial movements (Markusen 1987).

Institutionalism

Despite prognostications of imminent political fragmentation emanating from a number of sources, Derek Urwin has shown the limited success of regionalist and ethno-national movements pursuing secessionist agendas within Western liberal democratic states. Certainly there are instances where greater regional autonomy has been won, such as Belgium, Spain, and the UK, and the nationalist movement within Quebec has clearly altered both the structure and processes of Canadian federalism. But, as yet, no Western liberal democratic state has broken apart due to such movements; indeed, over time some have actually become less threatening to the stability of these states (Urwin 1998). They have successfully contained regionalist and minority nationalist sentiment, their resilience borne of institutional inertia and a willingness to bend if necessary, 'prepared to accommodate either symbolically or in limited ways the demands of minorities' (Urwin 1998: 226). Urwin claims that this experience shows that the interplay of state, territory, and ethno-national identity is constrained by some basic facts: 'powerful and influential structures and institutions; broad and positive acceptance of pluralism and difference; tolerance as an integral element of democratic practice; and the ability of many people to live reasonably comfortably with dual identities' (Urwin 1998: 240).

Urwin's observations suggest the need for a corrective to the societal focus of various cultural and economic approaches to the study of regions. This is supplied in the form of neo-institutional and new institutional theorists who argue that political analysis is best conducted through a focus on the design and workings of state institutions. In terms of the study of regions, institutionalists proclaim the central importance of a range of institutions—constitutions, bureaucratic and governance structures, courts, party and electoral systems—not only for providing the basic framework for regions, but for explaining the extent and form of regionalism in a society. In short, institutional design can entrench and strengthen territorial politics and regional identities in a society, or undermine and weaken this base of identity.

Take, for example, the US and Canada. Both are geographically and demographically diverse federations. However, Canada is a country in which regionalism is strong and pervasive, whereas its existence in American politics is muted at best. This can be explained in part by differences in the constitutional frameworks, party systems, and social movements of the two countries. In Canada, the federal division of the country has been into fewer and larger provinces and territories, with significantly more powers than their American counterparts. Just as important is that the Canadian constitutional order *inadvertently* encourages regionalism through the impairment of regional representation within national parliamentary institutions by national politicians. In Canada this function is sacrificed for responsible government which comes with cabinet solidarity, tight party discipline, and *de facto* unicameralism (since the Canadian Senate is largely an empty shell in terms of power, representation, and effectiveness). As a result, Canadian federalism, unlike its American counterpart, is of the *inter-state* variety, where regional conflict is externalized to the realm of intergovernmental relations, with provinces assuming the role of defenders of the regional interest (Gibbins 2004). This is reinforced by a regionalized and fragmented party system and an electoral system that rather perversely disfavours smaller parties with diffuse national support, while conversely rewarding any party with regionally concentrated support (Cairns 1968; Gibbins 2005).

In the 1990s, an institutionalist perspective on regional economic development was developed to explain the 'new regionalism' then emerging, particularly in Europe. Building on the insights of endogenous growth pole theory and institutional economics, and sensitive to local path dependencies, this perspective uncovers the key role within regions of local networks of association and stresses the importance to the success of regions in the current global economy of 'intermediate forms of governance [regions] to build up broad-based, local "institutional thickness" that could include political institutions and social citizenship' (Amin 1999: 313).

KEY POINTS

- The modernization paradigm defined regions as spatial units to be integrated into the mainstream, but regions have resisted homogenizing and centralizing pressures.

- Regions can also be understood as cultural spaces, with distinct meaning systems and identities.

- Regions have been shaped and reshaped by the dynamics of capitalist development and global capitalism. Attention to the political economy of regions can inform the study of regionalism.

- Western liberal democratic states have proved highly resilient in the face of demands for greater political autonomy (or even secession) by regionalist and nationalist movements.

- Institutions, once established, exercise an independent influence on political processes and behaviour. Institutional design has an impact on territorial politics and regional identities.

Regionalism from below: cultures, identities, and parties

Regional identities and political parties constitute the main focus of this section. First we discuss the notion of regional political cultures and examine a variety of examples drawn from different national contexts and political systems. While feeling some attachment to a particular place or territory is an almost universal phenomenon, this takes different forms and is embedded in different social, cultural, and historical experiences worldwide. We next study the political mobilization of these identities through movements and political parties, and examine how and why these identities become politicized.

Cultures and identities

Regional political cultures were initially studied in terms of their differential intensity with respect to political behaviour as it pertains to trust, efficacy, and modes of political participation, an approach formulated by Almond and Verba in their classic 'civic culture' studies (Almond and Verba 1963) and replicated by others investigating the contours of regional cultures in various national contexts (Elkins and Simeon 1980; Henderson 2007). The civic culture approach has been extensively critiqued, and subsequent studies of national and regional cultures have both broadened and deepened their focus, providing evidence of a long-term trend towards cultural convergence both within and across the Western industrialized countries (Ornstein 1986; Nevitte 1996; Adams

2003). Also, some scholars have differentiated between various kinds of cultural and identity difference which may not only distinguish but also 'encode' (Bannerji 2000: 131–3), or that represent an expression of 'deep diversity' (Taylor 1993). Where 'distinct societies' have been constructed on this basis, the political repercussions will tend to be more far-reaching.

In multinational societies, such as Belgium, Canada, Spain, and the UK, political leaders, key social actors, and institutions in both the majority and minority nations are all involved in the processes of socialization, cultural differentiation, and political education. This is made manifest by the extent to which citizens acquire dual or even multiple political identities. In such cases, we see some overlap between sub-national (ethno-territorial) and state (national) identities. At times, it is the state identity that prevails, at other times the ethno-territorial. Maintaining some semblance of a balance between these two allegiances, even if asymmetrically held by majority and minority communities, is a key variable in determining the stability of multinational states. Table 15.1 conveys the potential tensions that exist between ethno-territorial and state identities in Catalonia, Quebec, and Scotland.

Explaining the rise of regional parties

A general trend concerning regionalist parties can be identified all over Europe. They have been gaining prominence due to three processes: (1) the democratization of state structures and political practices, (2) the resurgence of regional interests in the wake of the retrenchment of the welfare state, and (3) the politicization of minority nations (see previous section).

Table 15.1 Dual identity in Catalonia, Quebec, and Scotland (1997–2010) (%)

	Catalonia 1998	Catalonia 2010	Quebec 1998	Quebec 2010	Scotland 1997	Scotland 2010
Only (1)	11.5	8.2	12.0	25.7	23.0	30.0
More (1) than (2)	23.4	9.0	31.0	34.4	38.0	33.0
As (1) as (2)	43.1	41.3	32.0	20.4	27.0	28.0
More (2) than (1)	7.6	25.6	17.0	12.1	4.0	4.0
Only (2)	13.0	13.6	5.0	4.1	4.0	5.0
Did not know or refused to answer	1.4	2,3	3.0	3.3	4.0	0

(1) = Catalan, Québécois, Scots.

(2) = Spanish, Canadian, British.

Sources: Moreno, L., Arriba, A., and Serrano, A. *Multiple Identities in Decentralized Spain: The Case of Catalonia*, Working Paper 97–06, Instituto de Estudios Sociales Avanzados (CSIC), Madrid; Spanish Center for Sociological Research (CSI Studies), Barometro Autonomico; Wells, P. 'Quebecers? Canadians? We're Proud to be Both', *The Gazette*, 4 April 1998; Sondage Léger Marketing, *The Globe and Mail, Le Devoir, Sondage Québécois*, Press release available at: http://legermarketing.com/documents/spclm/050427fr.pdf; Jedwab, J. 'Quebec Identity in 2011: Attachments, Identity and Diversity' available at: http://www.acs-aec.ca/; Scottish Social Attitudes Surveys (National Centre for Social Research: http://www.natcen.ac.uk/natcen/pages/or_socialattitudes.htm#ssa).

Democratization

Let us first address the process of democratization as an explanatory variable. In the case of Spain, the emergence of regionalist parties is the result of the claims for regional autonomy that accompanied the democratization process in the post-Franco era and the adoption of the 1978 constitution (Gunther *et al.* 1986). This is especially so within the historic nations of Catalonia, Galicia, and the Basque Country where demands for autonomy have been fed by a strong sentiment of shared identity and culture. In the Canadian case, it is worth noting that, although the Bloc Québécois (BQ) has as its principal goal the secession of Quebec from Canada, other federal parties have not contested the legitimacy of their elected representatives within the House of Commons. In turn, the BQ, though promoting an independentist stance, has made a valuable contribution to the overall performance of the parliament in its day-to-day work (Gagnon and Hérivault 2007).

Neoliberalism

Second, country-wide parties of national integration have been challenged by regional forces with renewed vigour since the early 1980s (Smith 1985: 1–68; Wilson 1983; Bickerton 2007: 412). During the heyday of the welfare state, stretching from 1945 to 1975, political parties pursuing national objectives tended to be more successful with voters (see Chapter 11). With the advance of globalization and the widespread implementation of a neoliberal agenda, regionalist political parties have gained in popularity, especially in countries characterized by deep divisions along ethnic, religious, cultural, or economic lines. A case in point is the Lega Nord that advocates the establishment of an autonomous region, known as Padania, in Northern Italy (Brouillaud 2005: 119–46).

Scots, who were generally very critical of Westminster's neoconservative policies during the Thatcher years, became more receptive to nationalist arguments for secession as a means to establish a more progressive regime. The same arguments were used by Quebec independentists during the 1995 referendum in Quebec (Gagnon and Lachapelle 1996). The situation in Belgium—where there are no longer any country-wide parties—is unique, leaving the national parliament in the hands of regionalist parties (Peeters 2007: 38).

Minority nations

Third, we have witnessed the politicization of minority nations which have used various democratic instruments to advance their cause. Election campaigns and referendums have been key means by which regional party leaders have given democratic legitimacy to their claims. In Spain, setting-up of autonomous communities has led to the development of nationalist parties at the regional level in Catalonia and the Basque country. Other autonomous regions, with the notable exception of Galicia, have generally adhered to the national party system.

The role of regionalist parties in national party systems

Beyond the minority nationalism that so marks politics in Catalonia, Quebec, and Scotland, regionalism has played a key role as a marker of political identity in Canada, the UK, and Spain. Canada has long experienced distinct regional patterns of voting behaviour (Bickerton *et al.* 1999). The classic works of Lipset (1968) and Macpherson (1953) on the emergence of regional parties in the Canadian West during the first half of the twentieth century were influential in accounting for the sources and impact of regionalism on Canadian politics. Their conclusions were that class structure and economic conditions were central to the emergence and persistence of right-wing and left-wing agrarian parties on the Canadian prairies. These initial studies have since been joined by many others (Simeon 1977; Forbes 1979; Brym 1986; Bickerton 1990; Young and Archer 2002), all of whom highlight the continuing importance of regionalism in Canadian politics.

Political parties are known to exercise a variety of functions, including aggregation of interests, elaboration and dissemination of political ideas, electoral campaigning, and ultimately assuming power (see Chapter 12). In federal or federalizing countries such as Belgium, Canada, Spain, and the UK, political parties are involved at multiple levels of governance, and electoral success at one level is not necessarily replicated at other levels; indeed, parties may compete exclusively at one or other level.

The tension between centralist parties and regionalist parties has too often been neglected by students of party politics. Pierre Trudeau, Canada's Liberal prime minister for virtually the whole period from 1968 to 1984, clashed repeatedly with Quebec-centred parties in the federal Parliament (Ralliement Créditiste and Bloc Québécois), as well as the exclusively provincial parties that have governed Quebec since 1944 (the Union Nationale, Parti Libéral, and Parti Québécois) (Bickerton *et al.* 1999: 164–92). During the last two decades, the Bloc Québécois and the Reform (later Canadian Alliance) Party are two regionalist parties that have championed regional issues and interests within the federal parliament, whereas the previous period had been marked by the domination of political parties with an almost exclusively national focus (Bickerton 2007: 412).

Similar behaviour has been witnessed in Spain where both the Partido Socialista Obrero de España (PSOE) and the Partido Popular (PP) have taken a centralist stand, as a result alienating large segments of voters in the Basque Country, Catalonia, and Galicia. Concomitant with the democratization process, numerous regionally based political parties emerged, but most studies of political parties in

Spain have explored the 'national' party system *per se* rather than investigating regional parties. As a result, issues at the regional level tend to be neglected, although 'regional parties are part of the Spanish party system and yet are also distinct, competitively pitting themselves against the national parties' (Lancaster and Lewis-Beck 1989: 29–43).

In fact, regional parties can play a key role in the political stability of their host political system. During several years of minority governments in Canada, the Bloc Québécois often sided with the governing party in order to avoid triggering a snap election. In Spain, Convergencia i Unió (CiU) was doing the same, while negotiating more accommodating measures from Madrid. And regional parties have demonstrated their relevance and usefulness in other ways over time. They have addressed issues of regional representation in the case of fragmented societies. They have influenced the policy process, making governing parties accountable to a larger population by forcing them to address issues of redistribution, social security, political rights, and environmentalism.

Pascal Delwitt, in a thorough account of regional parties within eight European countries, found that of the thirty-two regional parties that have obtained at least 4 per cent of the vote at a national election, twenty-two have assumed responsibilities within the executive branch of government, either at the regional or the national level. Four of those parties have assumed political leadership at both the regional and the national levels, while three others have been part of the executive at the national level only. The remaining sixteen were involved at the executive level within the regions (Delwitt 2005: 51–84).

The emergence and strengthening of regional parties can be connected to the mobilization of ethnic and nationalist movements or else it is due to the sense of alienation within regional electorates in countries as varied as Belgium, Canada, the UK, Italy, and Spain. This suggests the utility of a more sophisticated analysis of party dynamics that can account for the emergence and continuing salience of this regionalist pattern (Johnston 2005).

KEY POINTS

- 'Regionalism from below' has its roots in distinctive cultures and identities, which can be described in terms of differences in values, beliefs, attitudes, orientations, and patterns of participation. Ethno-territorial minorities often have dual identities which coexist.

- The rise of regionalist parties can be explained by three general factors or trends: the democratization of societies, the crisis of the welfare state and the turn towards neoliberalism, and the political mobilization of minority nations.

- Regional parties in multinational countries tend to be integral parts of their respective national party systems, and can constitute an element of stability or disruption.

Regionalism from below and above: institutions

Corresponding to the variety of regionalisms that exist are different modes of regional government and governance, with the institutionalization of regions varying widely from country to country. The relations between regional and central institutions within any given political system (unitary, federalizing, or federal) can be seen as a complex interplay of **centrifugal** and **centripetal** pressures. Particular governmental and societal arrangements can be understood as different strategies of regional representation and the management of territorially based conflicts and tensions.

Regionalism and federalism

Regional government, meaning regionally autonomous legislative and executive institutions, is most advanced in federal countries like Canada, the US, Germany, Australia, Austria, Belgium, and Switzerland, as well as in federalizing countries like Spain or 'devolved unions' like the UK. In federal countries, regions are constituted as autonomous political entities with constitutionally protected powers and the right to participate in national politics through a second legislative chamber at the national level, or through mechanisms of institutionalized cooperation between governments. In unitary systems, regional administrative institutions are simply decentralized arms of the state. In France and Italy, there are regions with limited powers and without significant autonomy, created through processes of *de-concentration* and existing alongside more traditional administrative units (large cities, departments, communes, provinces). However, some of these regions (Sicily, Sardinia, Valle d'Aosta, Trentino-Alto Adige, Friuli-Venezia-Giulia, Corsica) have been granted a special status and forms of asymmetric regionalization in response to their specific territorial claims (see Chapter 11).

Canada stands out as an interesting case because of its combination of federalism and Westminster-style parliamentarism (a situation replicated in Australia). As in Belgium and Spain, Canada has used its system of intergovernmental relations to strike deals pertaining to national issues through a variety of mechanisms including constitutional conferences, regular meetings of federal–provincial committees, joint initiatives, intergovernmental accords, and the periodic revamping of relations between the central state and the provinces to address fiscal imbalances (Burgess 2011). It is worth remembering that '[f]ederalism is not only a *response* to regionalism, but also ensures that it will continue. … it provides an institutional focus for loyalty and identity' (Simeon 1977: 508). As a result, economic, social, and political interests can be mobilized behind a given set of institutions, challenging at times the stability of political regimes, especially when sought after recognition for national communities is being denied.

Clearly, regions take on a multiplicity of forms in different historical contexts. Quebec has seen its frontiers evolve over the centuries, as have other historic regions such as the Basque Country or Catalonia. Nor is there universal agreement on the meaning and status of these ethno-territorial regions. For instance, Quebec has been portrayed by some as an autonomous political entity best understood as a region-state, if not nation-state in waiting, while others prefer to see it as the *foyer* of the French–Canadian culture in a bilingual Canada. The same pattern of contestation applies to Catalonia. In some cases what matters are the political institutions through which an ethno-territorial community can mobilize and assert itself; in other cases it is a region's cultural role and influence within the overarching political community that matters most.

With regional differences such an essential characteristic of Canada, regionalist movements in English-speaking Canada (outside the dominant central Canadian province of Ontario) have tended to pursue the goal of increasing their influence over the central government, and their perceived failure to do so has fuelled sentiments of inadequate representation, unfair treatment, and regional alienation. Quebecers, who couch their demands in terms of national affirmation, for the most part have pursued an alternative course of demanding increased autonomy and enhanced forms of self-rule. These differences in regionalist strategies are ultimately linked to differences in political identities. The national vision that tends to dominate among the majority of English-speaking Canadians is that Canada constitutes a single national political community or *demos*. This creates ongoing tensions in Quebec since it tends to undermine the notion of dualism (equality of founding peoples and dual national identities), considered by Quebecers to be a founding pillar of the Canadian federation.

Federalizing processes in unitary states

Devolutionist and federalizing strategies in some states have made it more difficult to clearly distinguish the patterns of territorial management and power-sharing arrangements that exist within unitary states versus federal systems. Spain is probably the best example of this, considering that it remains a unitary system that has acquired many of the features of a multinational federation (Moreno 2001). The Spanish case is one in which a variety of federalizing measures were implemented after a transition to democracy in the late 1970s. In the process, the central state has recognized the existence within Spain of several historic nations (Catalonia,

Galicia, Basque Country, and more recently Andalusia, Aragon, Valencia, and the Balearic Islands). The main objective pursued by Madrid has been to try to provide each autonomous community with identical powers (an idea that is best conveyed by the expression *café para todos*) so as to avoid granting even more distinct status to the historical nations. This has led to major conflicts between central and regional authorities over the years and has encouraged historic nations to ask for an asymmetrical devolution of powers to their respective regions, or more simply a demand for greater autonomy (Maiz and Losada 2011).

Varying self-definitions stimulate regions to make distinct political claims. Catalonia, the Basque Country, and Galicia make regional claims as historic nations and on this basis call for the further devolution of powers from the central government in Madrid, prompting other regional communities to seek similar status. Madrid's decision to grant these regions nationality status can be explained in part by its desire to encourage other political communities to make similar claims, thereby reducing the extent of asymmetry. Central government attempts to water down the implications of such recognition is an example of the territorial management strategies employed by central authorities, which not surprisingly has produced some backlash from the three originally recognized historic nations.

More recent developments suggest that further reforms to the Spanish State of Autonomies will be difficult to achieve. Thirty years after its return to democracy, the Spanish state entered into a political impasse with Catalonia following the rejection by its Highest Court in 2010 of several key clauses of the 2006 Statute of Autonomy for Catalonia (earlier ratified by the Catalan Parliament, revised by the Spanish Parliament to comply with the Constitution, and approved by referendum in Catalonia). Among the key provisions rejected by the Court was the recognition of Catalonia as a nation, the acceptance of its national symbols, preferential status for the Catalan language, and the possibility for the region to levy its own taxes. Political reaction in Catalonia to the Court's negative decision included large demonstrations and the election to the Catalan Parliament of a majority comprised of independentist candidates. The state's governing coalition then made known its intention to hold a referendum on independence (Guibernau 2012; Muñoz and Guinjoan 2013).

It is noteworthy that these developments in Spain coincided with an agreement between the Scottish and Westminster governments to hold a referendum on Scotland's secession from the UK in 2014. The historical context for this referendum is far removed from either the Quebec or Catalonia situations. In the UK, Scottish, English, Welsh, and Irish national identities have always coexisted, with each acknowledging the presence and legitimacy of the others. Political interactions in this case take place within the constitutional and political context of a state union (Forsyth 1981). Over the years tensions have appeared at different historical junctures, based on the political attitudes of Westminster towards regional claims emanating from the periphery. The work of Colley (1992), Hechter (1975), and Nairn (1977) is particularly revealing on this question. It should be underlined that, until the late 1990s:

> The United Kingdom was alone among the larger European Union states in lacking elected regional governments. The development here is highly asymmetrical: inevitably so, given the very different histories of the four countries [England, Scotland, Wales, Northern Ireland] of the Union. (Rawlings 2001: 481)

To attenuate these tensions, in 1997 the Labour government of Tony Blair launched a major devolution project with a view to responding to different needs by providing varying forms of power within Britain to different representative assemblies. After a Scottish Referendum which approved Blair's plan for Devolution, he declared: 'This is a good day for Scotland, and a good day for Britain and the United Kingdom; the era of big centralized government is over!' (Leeke *et al.* 2003: 18). The process of devolution in the UK has continued ever since, though without any overarching design (Jeffrey 2011).

This brief survey suggests a competition for ascendancy between two approaches to defining the political community. On the one side, there are those who envisage one national *demos*, despite the presence of minority nations (Canada and Spain). These majority populations cling to political arrangements based on territorial and symmetrical federalism. In contrast, political leaders of minority nations or *demoi* wish to move towards different arrangements based on a multinational and asymmetrical model of federalism (Kymlicka 1998).

Nor should the role of federalism be neglected in accounting for the international activities of regions. It is worthwhile referring to the Belgian case here. As Article 1 of the Constitution stipulates: 'Belgium is a federal state, composed of communities and regions'. Federalizing constitutional reforms were instrumental in allowing each layer of the Belgian state apparatus (central, regional, community) a legitimate role at the international level, within their own spheres of jurisdiction (Paquin 2003: 625–6).

But what matters most is definitely 'the importance of nationalism in explaining the breadth, scope and intensity of a region's international activity in the former [multinational states] and its absence, or lesser prominence, in the latter [nation-states]' (Lecours and Moreno 2003: 268). This understanding helps to explain the presence of region-states (such as Bavaria, Catalonia, Scotland, Flanders, and Quebec) in various international forums.

KEY POINTS

- In general, regions have attained the greatest degree of autonomy where they are constitutionally protected through federal institutions.

- Asymmetric regionalization has occurred in some unitary states, and an institutional 'blending' is under way that blurs the difference between multinational unitary states and federal systems in terms of the power-sharing arrangements instituted for regions.

- Regional autonomy and asymmetry for regions has proceeded furthest where minority nations are present and concentrated, whether or not the countries are federations.

Political economy of regions

A central theme in the study of the political economy of regions is the degree to which regional inequality and dependence have been internally determined—related to some indigenous characteristic of the region or its people—or alternatively ordained by structures and conditions that have been externally imposed on those regions that are less economically advantaged. The next section will introduce the reader to this theme and survey the range of research and opinion to which it has given rise.

Regional differentiation: causes and repercussions

From the mid-nineteenth to the mid-twentieth centuries, the industrializing states of the Western world were transformed by processes of political, social, and economic integration associated with the consolidation of nation-states, bureaucratic modernization, and capitalist development focused for the most part on protected national economies (with or without attached colonial empires). Diverse regions at uneven levels of development were incorporated into these emergent national political economies, though not on equal terms. Location, initial resource endowments, transportation links, population base, previous rounds of investment in productive capacity, and various forms of infrastructure were all relevant factors in determining the advantages accruing to regions in subsequent phases of economic growth and development. The migration of labour to expanding urban and industrial centres, and the stimulus this gave to new rounds of investment, produced agglomeration effects that reinforced the initial advantages of some regions, while draining capital and human resources from others, leading to their further differentiation (Massey 1978).

The role that politics and state policy played in all this was not negligible. It was national politicians who initiated, planned, and supervised the incorporation of lands and peoples into consolidated nation-states; it was through politics that the policy frameworks that supported and directed national development were created, installed, and maintained. These multi-generational state and nation-building projects were sustained and legitimized with nationalist visions, symbols, and rhetoric, and the political promise of security and economic prosperity. Regionalist resistance was sometimes violent and dramatic (as with the nineteenth-century wars of unification in Europe, the American Civil War and Indian Wars, the Métis-led rebellions in Canada, or the Spanish Civil War), but more often was limited to periodic episodes of political protest through social movements or regional political parties (re. discussion of regional movements and parties).

In the post-war era of economic expansion and relatively full employment (1945–75), regional concerns about inequality and fair representation tended to be subsumed, if not completely submerged, under class politics and the social policy agenda associated with the construction of national welfare states. The problem of regional inequalities was dealt with primarily, if at all, as a residual matter for state managers focused on the 'main game' of full employment and price stability, which they pursued in good Keynesian fashion through the use of the fiscal levers of centralized taxation and spending. Like other citizens, the residents of less developed regions generally benefited from the redistribution of income enabled by progressive tax systems and the public provision of pensions, healthcare, and social services. Economic growth and government social spending did alleviate poverty, while equalization schemes in most federal states (based on inter-governmental transfers) contributed to the standardization of public services across regions. But none of these mechanisms succeeded in eliminating regional disparities in economic growth, per capita income, and unemployment rates.

The rise and decline of regional development policy

In the 1950s and 1960s, regional planning, described by Friedmann as 'the process of formulating and clarifying social objectives in the ordering of activities in supra-urban space—that is, in any area larger than a single city' (Wannop 1997: 154), became common in most Western industrialized countries. Initiated as part of post-war reconstruction and often focused on the development of satellite communities to relieve urban congestion, in the 1960s priorities shifted towards the development of growth centres in peripheral regions. These initiatives, supported by emerging economic theories such as variants of Perroux's strategy of 'growth poles', were meant to foster more decentralized industrial growth to redress

regional disparities. Such decentralization was made palatable by the growing diseconomies of metropolitan locations for industry, and the benefits of diverting some of the growth from the often overheated economies of industrial core areas. Throughout Europe—in France, Italy, Germany, the UK—regions were viewed primarily as units for spatial planning to be managed by central states (Keating 2004: xii). In the US, sub-state regional councils became eligible for federal planning and economic development funds, as well as other conditional grants. By 1980, almost the entire US was covered by regional planning organizations, though only weakly empowered and with no popular base (Wannop 1997). In Canada, a spate of development agencies and programmes was consolidated in 1969 in a new Department of Regional Economic Expansion, focused initially on reducing economic disparities between the Atlantic region (inclusive of eastern Quebec) and the rest of Canada (Savoie 1986).

The economic logic of regional development policies was to make regions self-sustaining, whereupon transitional regional policies would no longer be necessary and regions could positively contribute to national economic growth. In the meantime, the costs of congestion and stress in booming areas could be relieved. However, there were also separate political and social logics at work in the creation of these policies. The political weight of poorer regions was used to counter their economic weakness, and their demands to bring work to the workers rather than vice versa could not always or easily be ignored, especially during periods when their political importance to national governing coalitions was significant, or when they harboured the potential for political disruption. Also, citizenship in advanced industrial countries was undergoing a 'thickening' process, with the state assuming responsibility for the social integration of all its citizens by seeking to equalize opportunities and living standards, thereby preventing or reversing the marginalization of groups or regions (Keating 1997: 18–20).

In its early phases this form of **regional policy** being pursued by central states was largely depoliticized and technocratic, for the most part left in the hands of bureaucrats. However, it soon became more interventionist, with more far-reaching policies covering larger areas. As local political and economic elites were inevitably brought into the process of policy-making and implementation, it quickly became apparent 'that regional preferences and priorities were not always consistent with those of central governments' (Keating 1997: 22–3).

Regional policy went into decline with the widespread onset of stagflation (low growth, simultaneously rising unemployment, and inflation), growing international competitive pressures from the mid-1970s onwards, and eventually the government's adoption of neoliberal policies. These developments first disrupted and then gradually brought to an end the national systems of mass production and welfarist politics of the post-war era. As governments of Western industrialized countries began to shift their attention and concern to shoring up their national competitiveness, the post-war model of territorial management broke down. Reducing regional disparities suddenly became much less of a priority.

As Keating has noted, this growing policy and political vacuum was filled by three types of regionalist politics: first, a *defensive regionalism* committed to resisting change, which was tied to traditional economic sectors and the threatened communities that depended on them; second, an *integrating* or *modernizing regionalism* aimed at adapting to change and reinserting lagging regions into their national economies; third, an *autonomist regionalism,* particularly in regions with historic claims to nation status, seeking a distinctive path to modernization by combining political autonomy, cultural promotion, and economic modernization (Keating 1997: 24). Since the 1970s these three modes of regionalism have coexisted within many countries, often disharmoniously because of the basic contradictions between them at the level of public policies.

Globalization and the new regionalism

There is now a new international context for regions, creating for them opportunities but also dangers, and providing the conditions for the incubation of a new regionalism. A number of interrelated changes have contributed to this altered context: falling international trade barriers, the adoption of a neoliberal policy framework with its agenda of tax-cutting, deregulation, and free markets, the creation of free trade and economic union agreements (e.g. the North American Free Trade Agreement (NAFTA) and the EU), and in general the sweeping economic, technological, political, and cultural changes associated with globalization. In many ways these changes have undermined or threatened to destroy the traditional employment base of peripheral regions, as well as the established programme supports for these regions.

The Janus-faced nature of globalization for regions, however, is that it has opened up new vistas that, practically speaking, were not previously available. This has occurred because of the changing character of international economic competition, itself a function of changes in technology, production methods, corporate organizations, and the removal of restrictions on international trade and investment. This has made accessible to regions global markets that absorb an increasingly diverse range of products and services. As a result, the determinants of regional competitiveness in the contemporary global economy have shifted. Traditional factors of comparative advantage—such as economies of scale, plentiful supplies of labour, access to cheap raw materials, and proximity to markets—still matter, but these are now joined and sometimes superseded by the entrepreneurial, technological, social, and cultural strengths of a region (Piore and Sabel 1984; Porter 1990).

In response to these changes, regional policies in many jurisdictions have been revamped. To be more specific, governments have recognized that the competitive imperative is now not only greater and more immediate for all economies (because of their greater exposure to international economic forces and markets), but also different in terms of the structure of constraints and opportunities which it presents for regions, as well as the factors and resources that are directly relevant to long-term regional competitiveness. This means that governments have found it expedient, if not necessary, to adapt to the new context by supporting new forms of regionalization of policy-making and implementation. This usually involves partnerships between various levels of government (supra-national, national, provincial/regional, local), as well as the private sector and key actors in civil society, in order to create regional policy frameworks that are both flexible and collaborative.

The phenomenon of 'devolved governance' and 'regionalization' varies greatly in practice. Certainly, the EU has been very active in this area, insisting on the creation of regional partnerships in the management of EU funds made available for regional development purposes. As a result, regionalization has become a contentious issue in many EU states, especially in the accession countries admitted to the Union since 1990 (Trigilia 1991; Sharpe 1993a; Keating 1998a; Brusis 2002).

This trend to regionalization has been accompanied by a reprioritization of the key factors in regional development, with much greater significance now being accorded to so-called *endogenous* factors based on the region's human, social, and cultural capital, what some have called a **socially embedded growth model** (Amin 1999). This revalues the development significance of high-quality health and education services, cultural amenities, entrepreneurial and managerial training, and information and innovation networks, as well as supports for marketing, technology transfer, and business start-ups. Selective financial and industrial incentives and physical infrastructure are still an important part of the regional development 'toolbox' that governments use, but both the dynamics of regional development and the policy focus of governments is changing. In general terms, this seems to be the consensus reached by many regional development researchers in Europe and beyond (Stohr 1990; Putnam 1993; Storper 1995; Amin 1999; Florida 2003).

In summary, the contemporary understanding of regional development has four aspects: economic development, social integration and redistribution, cultural development and identity, and environmental considerations (Keating 1997: 31). The new approach is to involve a broader range of actors and policies than previously, and to create more region-specific strategies tailored to local needs, circumstances, and potentials. This in turn requires a higher degree of regionalization of governance than previously, involving cooperation at the regional/local level between various levels of government, as well as private sector and civil society actors. Creating this new nexus for regional development requires all levels of government to acknowledge that the policies and decisions most likely to nurture sustainable regions will emerge from a strong network of regional actors brought together on the basis of a shared territorial and cultural identity, and a direct interest in the economic fate of the community and its residents. If regions can cohere socially and culturally, and if they are actively supported by government, they will be more capable of adapting to and taking advantage of the new economic challenges and opportunities. Alternatively, they will be better equipped to adapt to a managed process of downsizing and transformation due to long-term economic and demographic trends.

> **KEY POINTS**
>
> - The differentiation of regions within nation-states occurred over an extended period of time. Ongoing state and nation-building projects were met by regional resistance in the form of military conflict, minority/majority nationalism, territorial movements, and party-based politics.
>
> - The construction of welfare states in the post-war era included a regional dimension. At first largely submerged by class-based and redistributive politics, persistent regional economic disparities led to the introduction of regional development policies as a complement to national social programmes. Changes in the international political economy in the 1970s led to the decline of regional development policy, giving rise to defensive, modernizing, and autonomist modes of regionalism.
>
> - A new regionalism emerged in the 1990s in the context of globalization. The traditional determinants of regional economic competitiveness based on comparative advantage are now supplemented by an endogenous 'socially-embedded' growth model that requires regionalized governance to nurture collaborative regional policy frameworks. This adds social, cultural, and environmental factors to the traditional economic aspects of regional development.

Conclusion

Region as a social science concept can be pliable and abstract, as well as mundane. This quality is due primarily to its multiple potential meanings. Political, economic, social, and cultural actors will define it to reflect their values and their particular interests and needs. In this sense,

though region is always associated with geographic space, it is a socially constructed entity or outcome.

A number of different theories and approaches have been used to explain and inquire into the meaning of regions as economic, social, cultural, and, last but not least, political phenomena. Mainstream modernization and development theory ascribed diminishing significance to regions, since the differences they represented were inevitably fated to fade as the integration processes linked to modernity and capitalism proceeded apace. Other approaches and perspectives remained sceptical of this outcome. Culturalists described the persistence of spatially distinct meaning systems that continued to define regions as cultural spaces, a persistence that was especially notable for regions populated by minority nations. In these cases, individuals frequently espouse multiple political identities, which continue to be available to political elites for mobilization purposes, despite a lessening over time in culturally inscribed differences between regions. Marxists are less sanguine than modernization theorists about the convergence of regions undergoing development within a global capitalist system, though there remains some disagreement on this point. What is shared within this approach is certainty about the necessity to understand the past, present, and future of regions within the broader national and international contexts, particularly as this pertains to the economic forces acting on and within regions. Institutional theorists of various persuasions bring to the study of regions their insights into the independent shaping effect on regions and regionalism exerted by the design and workings of political and social institutions.

'Regionalism from below' refers to the societal forces that have given cultural and identity content to regions and regionalism. These are located within regional political cultures, the political alienation of regionally identifying electorates, or the multiple identities nurtured within individuals who are members of minority nations. This helps to explain the rise and role of regionalist parties in Western liberal democratic states, especially those that feature ethno-territorial minorities or regions with claims to historic nation status, such as Spain, Canada, Belgium, and the UK.

The degree of institutionalization of regions, and the extent of their autonomy from central governments, is directly related to two broad factors:

- whether the country in question is a federal state with a constitutionally protected division of powers between central and regional governments and autonomous democratically elected representative assemblies;

- whether the state in question is multinational, in the sense of having one or more clearly defined ethno-territorial minorities with claims to historic nation status.

Either or both of these conditions within liberal democratic states virtually ensures the gradual development over time of power-sharing arrangements between central and regional authorities, as democratically supported elites seek to accommodate regionalist sentiment. In those states with minority nationalist movements or parties, the tendency will be for this accommodation to take the form or evolve in the direction of asymmetrical power-sharing arrangements, as illustrated in the cases of Catalonia, Quebec, and Scotland.

Finally, the economic differentiation of space conjointly produced by the processes of capitalist development and the state policies put in place to provide the framework for this development can be seen to have had a determinant effect not only on the formation of regions, but also on the timing and forms of regionalism which subsequently emerged. The rise, decline, and revival of regional development policy, despite some variations between countries, can be related to changes in the macropolitical economy of states, most recently the economic, political, cultural, and technological changes associated with globalization. While this has generated a more complex understanding of regional development, one which has initiated movement towards more devolved or regionalized forms of governance, it has neither 'resolved' the challenge of region from the perspective of territorial management, nor ensured the success of complex projects of regional economic development.

Questions

1. Why is the concept of region so difficult to define? What are the factors giving rise to a continuum of regionalism based on differing degrees of regionality?

2. What are some of the different theoretical approaches that can be used to understand the meaning and significance of regions?

3. What is the relationship between regional political identities and distinct regional cultures?

4. Can it be argued that the nation-state is becoming a thing of the past?

5. How are changes brought about by national minorities influencing the prospects for democracy in the Western world and beyond?

6. Do strong regions produce federalism, or does federalism produce strong regions?

7. Unitary and federal states have more in common than it seems at first glance. What accounts for this?

8. What are the contributions of minority nations in Canada, the UK, and Spain to the development of federal and regional practices in their respective context?

9. How has the process of capitalist development affected the formation and uneven development of regions?

10. What is the 'new regionalism' and how does it reflect the changing role of regions and the economic challenges they face?

Further reading

Brodie, J. (1990) *The Political Economy of Canadian Regionalism* (Toronto: Harcourt Brace Jovanovitch).

Gagnon, A.-G., and Tully, J. (eds) (2001) *Multinational Democracies* (Cambridge: Cambridge University Press).

Gagnon, A-G. and Keating, M. (2012) *Political Autonomy and Divided Societies* (Basingstoke: Palgrave Macmillan).

Gibbins, R. (1982) *Regionalism: Territorial Politics in Canada and the United States* (Toronto: Butterworths).

Keating, M. (2001) *Plurinational Democracy: Stateless Nations in a Post-Sovereignty Era* (Oxford: Oxford University Press).

Keating, M. (ed.) (2004) *Regions and Regionalism in Europe* (Cheltenham: Edward Elgar).

Keating, M. and Loughlin, J. (eds) (1997) *The Political Economy of Regionalism* (London: Frank Cass).

Keating, M. and McGarry, J. (eds) (2001) *Minority Nationalism in the Changing State Order* (Oxford: Oxford University Press).

Loughlin, J., Kincaid. J., and Swenden W. (eds) (2013) *Routledge Handbook of Regionalism and Federalism* (London: Routledge).

Maiz, R. and A. Losada (2011) 'The Erosion of Regional Powers in the Spanish "State of Autonomies"', F. Requejo and K.-J. Nagel (eds), *Federalism beyond Federations: Asymmetry and Processes of Resymmetrisation in Europe* (Farnham: Ashgate), 81–107.

Markusen, A. (1987) *Regions: The Economics and Politics of Territory* (Totowa, NJ: Rowman & Littlefield).

Scott, A. J. (2001) *Global City-Regions: Trends, Theory, Policy* (Oxford: Oxford University Press).

Web links

www.essex.ac.uk/ecpr/standinggroups/regionalism/index.aspx
The website of the Standing Group on Regionalism, which
organizes conferences, seminars, and workshops on various
aspects of regionalism. The group's publishing outlets are the
journal *Regional and Federal Studies* and the Frank Cass series of
books on regionalism.

http://eur.sagepub.com/
The website of the journal *European Urban and Regional Studies*.
The journal's mandate is to provide a means of dialogue
between different European traditions of intellectual inquiry
on urban and regional development issues, highlighting
the connections between theoretical analysis and policy
development.

www.curs.bham.ac.uk
The website of the Centre for Urban and Regional Studies
(CURS), at the University of Birmingham, an international
centre for research and teaching in regional and local
economic development, urban policy, and regional and urban
regeneration.

www.wiley.com/bw/journal.asp?ref=0309-1317
The website of the *International Journal of Urban and Regional
Research* encompasses material from a range of critical,
comparative, and geographic perspectives. Embracing a
multidisciplinary approach, *IJURR* is essential reading for
social scientists with a concern for the changing roles of cities
and regions.

online resource centre

For additional material and resources, please visit the Online Resource Centre at:
www.oxfordtextbooks.co.uk/orc/caramani3e/

CHAPTER 16

Social movements

Hanspeter Kriesi

Chapter contents

Reader's guide

This chapter looks at a phenomenon which is not usually part of the core business of comparative political scientists, but deserves to be taken seriously in a world that is increasingly shaped by non-state actors, such as **social movements**. The chapter begins with a discussion of what we mean when we speak of social movements and a conceptualization of key terms. It then moves on with the presentation of three theoretical ap≠proaches which have successively shaped the debates of the specialists: the classical model, the **resource mobilization** model, and the political process model. It pays particular attention to the political process approach, which is the most promising from the comparativist's point of view. This approach is elaborated in the third section. The final section presents some results about the emergence, the level of **mobilization**, and the success of social movements.

Introduction

Starting on 17 September 1991, right-wing thugs violently attacked asylum seekers' hostels in Hoyerswerda, Northern Saxony, and initiated a wave of right-wing violence against asylum seekers and other ethnic minority groups across Germany in which several dozen immigrants were killed. These events, in turn, provoked one of the largest mass movements in German history, involving millions of citizens in rallies, nightly candlelit marches, and vigils in front of asylum seekers' hostels to protect them against attacks. On 8 November 1992, more than 300,000 people gathered in Berlin to demonstrate against extreme right violence (Koopmans 2001).

On 15 February 2003, two and a half million Italians marched past the Coliseum in Rome in protest at the impending war in Iraq. On the same day in Paris, 250,000 people protested against the war, and half a million people walked past the Brandenburg gate in Berlin. In Madrid, there were a million marchers, in Barcelona 1.3 million; in London, 1.7 million people—the largest demonstration in the city's history. Even in New York, more than 500,000 people assembled on the east side of Manhattan. 'On that day in February, starting from New Zealand and Australia and following the sun around the world, an estimated 16 million people marched, demonstrated, sang songs of peace, and occasionally—despite the strenuous efforts of organizers—clashed with police (Tarrow 2005: 15).

On 17 September 2011, hundreds of demonstrators took to the streets of Manhattan's financial district under the slogan 'We are the 99%', in a largely peaceful protest against the financial industry. Modelled on the Arab Spring uprisings that swept through Egypt, Tunisia, Libya, and other Arab countries earlier in the same year, Occupy Wall Street occupied Zuccotti Park in Manhattan, where some 100–200 protesters camped for several weeks to draw attention to the plight of the large parts of the population that were suffering the consequences of the financial and economic crisis.

These are examples of protest events organized by social movements of various stripes—movements of the extreme right and anti-racist movements in the first example, the transnational peace movement in the second, and the movement aimed against powerful financial interests and orchestrated through Twitter, Facebook, and other social media tools in the third. Traditionally, social movements have not been considered part of comparative politics. The study of social movements has been the preserve of sociologists dealing with collective behaviour such as panics, crazes, fads, or crowds. As we shall see, social movements are specific forms of collective behaviour. They have action repertoires of their own which distinguish them from established political actors, but they cannot be reduced to their particular action repertoires. To the extent that political scientists paid attention to

movements at all, they considered them as public interest groups, i.e. as interest groups defending the collective interests of the general public, and proceeded to analyse them as if they were nothing more than interest groups. Social movements have organizations which often closely resemble interest groups or, for that matter, political parties, but they cannot be reduced to their organizational component.

Comparativists have disregarded social movements for too long. As pointed out in Chapter 24, the current master process of globalization, among other things, widens the resources available to non-state actors, including social movement organizations. Local, regional, national, and transnational social movements have become regular participants in the political process at all levels of polities.

According to some scholars (Meyer and Tarrow 1998b), our society has become a 'social movement society': social protest has become a perpetual element of modern life, protest behaviour is employed with greater frequency, by more diverse constituencies, and is used to represent a wider range of claims than ever before, and professionalization and institutionalization may transform the social movement into an instrument within the realm of 'conventional' politics. Even if somewhat exaggerated, this idea reflects well the current tendencies in the political process of democratic polities.

> **KEY POINTS**
>
> ● Social movements constitute an integral part of the contemporary political process in democratic polities.
>
> ● Social movements are not simply another type of interest group.
>
> ● Social movements have action repertoires of their own that distinguish them from established political actors.

Social movements as regular participants in political processes

Defining social movements

Although everybody seems to have a fairly good idea of what a social movement is, the concept is not easy to define. By a social movement, we often mean a group of people involved in a conflict with clearly identified opponents, sharing a common identity, a unifying belief, or a common programme, and acting collectively. In other words, the concept of social movement includes at least three component elements: (1) a group of people with a conflictual orientation towards an opponent, (2) a collective identity and a set of common beliefs and goals, and (3) a repertoire of **collective actions**.

The various definitions of social movements (Box: What is a social movement? in the Online Resource Centre provides three examples) all emphasize that *movements are engaged in conflicts with some opponents,* but scholars are not of one mind when it comes to specifying the character of the conflicts involved. Some leave the question open-ended; others narrow the range of opponents primarily to those within the political arena, as reflected in the recent conceptualization of movements as a variant of 'contentious politics' (McAdam *et al.* 2001; Tilly and Tarrow 2007). This narrower view excludes movements within established institutions, such as religious movements within established churches that attempt to reform the church or to block such reforms (e.g. Tarrow 1988), or challengers of cultural authorities. Snow *et al.* (2004) propose a more inclusive, yet not entirely open-ended definition by considering as social movements challengers or defenders of 'existing institutional authority—whether it is located in the political, corporate, religious, or educational realm—or patterns of cultural authority, such as systems of beliefs or practices reflective of those beliefs' (Snow *et al.* 2004: 9).

However, since most conflicts involve some aspect of politics, the narrower view may not be so narrow after all. For example, the women's movement challenges cultural authorities—patriarchal values and beliefs—but it also mobilizes women as women 'to demand equal rights from Fiji to Finland … to confront authoritarian rule (e.g. Mothers of the Disappeared in Argentina and El Salvador), to demand peace (e.g. Women in Black in Serbia and Israel), to call for handgun control (e.g. the Million Moms March in the US), and to address a variety of social problems across their communities' (Ferree and McClurg Mueller 2004: 578). In any case, in comparative politics we are primarily interested in movements which target the political process in one way or another.

Movements vs. organizations

As to the group of people constituting the social movement, the question of how to define its boundaries proves to be particularly difficult (see also Chapter 18). The boundaries of social movements are inherently disputed, unstable, and ultimately dependent on mutual recognition by the members of the group involved. The people participating in a movement must somehow be connected to one another and they must share a common goal. Diani and Bison (2004) propose that we speak of a social movement only in cases of conflictual collective action which is based on dense informal inter-organizational networks. No single actor can claim to represent a movement as a whole. Instead, a social movement is constituted by a network of multiple individual and organized actors who, while keeping their autonomy and independence, engage in a sustained coordinated effort to achieve collective goals.

This distinguishes social movements from organizations such as political parties or interest groups, who are more formally constituted. Parties and interest groups may be part of the network that constitutes a social movement, but movements may not be reduced to them. In addition, for a social movement to exist, Diani and Bison require that all participants in the dense informal network share a strong common identity. Collective identities take shape on the basis of the informal networks and, in turn, reinforce them. Organizational and individual actors with a common identity no longer merely pursue specific goals, but come to regard themselves as elements of much larger and encompassing processes of change—or resistance to change.

This element distinguishes social movements from coalitions, which are formed for specific campaigns and do not have the sustained character of social movements. We do not speak of social movements in the case of 'episodic' events of protest or single campaigns that do not have certain duration in time. Social movements involve a protracted series of protest events produced by more or less stable networks of organizational actors. Clearly, there is a considerable variability in their careers and trajectories, as some movements do indeed last for a comparatively short time only, as with most neighbourhood NIMBY oppositions ('Not In My BackYard'), while others endure for decades, as with the labour movement or the women's movement. However, the kind of changes movements pursue, whatever their degree or level, typically require some measure of sustained organized activity.

The most distinctive of the three defining elements of the social movement is probably the collective action component. At its most elementary level, collective action consists of any goal-directed activity engaged in jointly by two or more individuals. It entails the pursuit of a common objective through joint action. To identify the specificity of social movements, it is useful to distinguish those collective actions that are institutionalized from those that are not and that fall outside institutional channels (Snow *et al.* 2004: 6). In pursuing their collective political objectives, social movements typically engage in *non-institutionalized* collective action because they do not have regular access to the decision-making arenas in parliament and the state administration. Social movements are forced to draw attention to their cause by mobilizing in the public sphere and addressing themselves to the general public.

Social movements and media

Very generally, the public sphere can be defined as the arena where the political communication between decision-makers and citizens takes place (Neidhardt 1994). Although no decisions are taken in the public sphere, the public debate is part and parcel of the political process. The political contest in the public sphere focuses on the attention of the public to specific political issues, on its support for specific political actors, and their issue-specific positions (public opinion).

As Schattschneider argued a long time ago, the 'expansion of conflict' beyond those immediately concerned plays a crucial role in democratic polities. Conflicts are 'frequently won or lost by the success that the contestants have in getting the audience involved in the fight or in excluding it, as the case may be' (Schattschneider 1988: 4). The agenda-setting approach has adopted and developed this basic idea. It considers the struggle for the attention of the public as the central element of democratic representation, and attention shifts as key mechanisms for the development of (political) conflicts. Under contemporary conditions, where the media plays a key role in politics, the struggle for public attention involves all political actors. However, those who do not have regular access to the decision-making arenas—such as social movements—are particularly dependent on it.

In general, social movements use two types of strategy to draw attention to their cause (Keck and Sikkink 1998b: 226–30):

- *protest politics*—mobilizing for protest events in the public sphere;
- *information politics*—collecting credible information and deploying it strategically at carefully selected sites.

Protest events sometimes directly challenge the movement's opponent, such as in a strike. More often, however, they address the public more generally. The publicity created by protest events pursues two objectives (Gamson *et al.* 1992: 383): it is intended to create a public debate and to increase the 'standing' and 'legitimacy' of the social movement in the conflict in question. To be able to have some impact on the political process, or on any other decision-makers, social movements must draw the attention and support of the public, i.e. they need to become visible in the media and their ideas have to obtain resonance and legitimacy in the citizen public. The challengers need to gain 'standing', i.e. a voice in the media, and they need to do the right 'framing', i.e. develop central organizing ideas (frames) that some part of the citizen public understands and supports (Ferree *et al.* 2002: 86, 105). However, public debate is not the ultimate goal. In the final analysis, the social movement seeks, via public support, to have an impact on the decision-makers in the conflict in question. Creating controversy is a way of increasing opportunity by opening media access to movement spokespersons and allies (Gamson and Meyer 1996: 288).

While non-institutionalized 'protest politics' have the distinctive characteristics of social movements, they do not engage only in these forms of collective action. They typically combine *protest politics* with *information politics* and the two elements tend to support each other. On the one hand, protest provides the opportunity for 'information politics'; only when a movement has obtained a certain public visibility can it successfully employ an 'information strategy'. As Meyer and Tarrow (1998a: 18) point out, the organizational and technical requirements for the 'information strategy' today are less restrictive than they have been in the past, which means that resource-poor organizations can pursue efficient information strategies.

Given the media's fascination with controversy and conflict, providing controversial information about a given issue—in addition to protest politics—often constitutes a promising strategy for social movements. Efficient protests, in turn, often presuppose a credible information policy. For example, Greenpeace—an organization of the environmental movement—before mobilizing does its own research, acquires the necessary expertise, and searches for alternative solutions. In the course of the subsequent campaign, this background information is offered to the public and decision-makers. However, the action repertoire of social movements is typically skewed in the direction of non-institutional lines of action.

KEY POINTS

- The concept of the social movement includes three constitutive components: (1) a group of people with a conflictual orientation towards an opponent, (2) a collective identity and a set of common beliefs and goals, and (3) a repertoire of collective actions.
- The conflicts may be of a cultural or political nature. We are focusing here on movements that target the political process.
- The group of people constituting a social movement are connected by a dense informal inter-organizational network and share a strong common identity.
- They engage in a sustained series of non-institutionalized collective action, since they do not have regular access to the decision-making arenas in parliament and state administration.
- To be able to have some impact on the political process, social movements have to attract the attention and gain the support of the public. They do so by a combination of protest politics and information politics.

Theoretical approaches

The theoretical approaches to social movements have been conveniently divided into three models (McAdam 1982)—the classical model, the resource mobilization model, and the political process model.

Classical model

The classical model, in fact, refers to a *set of theories* with a common denominator: they all start from the notions of 'structural strain' or 'breakdown'. These notions imply a social order whose normal condition is one of integration. If the social order remains sufficiently integrated, strain and breakdown may be avoided and collective behaviour—the classical model speaks of collective behaviour rather than collective action—may not take place. In this logic, as observed by Buechler (2004: 48), 'all roads lead to Durkheim's overriding concern with social integration and the problematic consequences of insufficient integration in modern societies' (Durkheim 1964). Durkheim's analysis of anomie and egoism identified breaches in the social order that could lead to chronic strains or acute breakdown.

Subsequent theories of strain and breakdown as explanations for collective behaviour all presume that structural strain and breakdown of standard routines of everyday life have a disruptive psychological effect on individuals, which triggers some form of collective behaviour (Figure 16.1). The motivation for movement participation is held to be based not so much on the desire to attain political goals as on the need to manage the psychological tensions of a stressful social situation.

The most general of all the classical models is the theory of collective behaviour, which is associated with authors such as Smelser (1962) and Turner and Killian (1987). Other variants include the theory of mass society (Kornhauser 1959) and theories of relative deprivation (Gurr 1970). All variants have in common the belief that collective behaviour is sharply set off from conventional behaviour, with elements of contagion, excitability, spontaneity, and emotionality being prevalent. In some versions of the theory, collective behaviour is seen as irrational, disruptive, dangerous, and excessive.

As McAdam (1982: 11–19) points out, social strain is a necessary, but insufficient, cause of social movements. The classical model is too deterministic and leaves no room for political actors and it does not take into account the larger political context. Moreover, the atomistic focus of this model on the individual is problematic. It ignores the fact that social movements are collective phenomena. It is not isolated individuals who become movement participants; rather, social movements develop within established interaction networks.

Resource mobilization model

In sharp contrast with the classical model, the resource mobilization theory views social movements as normal, rational, political challenges by aggrieved groups. The predecessors of this approach are John Stuart Mill and the utilitarians, Weber and Marx, rather than Durkheim.

The new approach implies a shift from a deterministic to an agency-oriented paradigm. Attention turns from the social forces and conditions that produce movements to the question of how movements mobilize and produce their success. Students of social movements are no longer preoccupied by the question of social order, but adopt the point of view of those engaged in purposeful efforts at social change. This theory claims that discontent is more or less constant over time and thus inadequate as a full explanation of social movements. The entrepreneurial–organizational variant of this approach even allows for the possibility that grievances and discontent may be defined, created, and manipulated by political entrepreneurs and organizations. At the most fundamental level, social movements develop not from an aggregate rise in discontent, but from a significant increase in the level of resources available to support collective protest activities. Solidarity and organization, as well as external support, are treated as key resources for social movements and receive central places in the theory—the more organization, the better the prospects for mobilization and success.

Tilly's explanation focuses on *group solidarity* as the key factor accounting for collective action (Tilly *et al.* 1975). He seeks to undermine any sharp distinction between routine political struggle and violence by arguing that the same political dynamics and solidarity processes underlie both. Oberschall (1973), Gamson (1975), and McCarthy and Zald (1977) all stress the fundamental importance of organization or, more generally, of mobilization structures for the transformation of grievances into successful collective action. In insisting on the importance of organizations, proponents of the resource mobilization model reject the classical theorists' exclusive focus on the movement's mass base in favour of an analysis of the crucial role played by segments of the elite in the generation of the challenge.

Tilly (1978: 62–4) casts the organizational preconditions for the mobilization of social movements in a neat formula based on Harrison White's concept of a 'catnet'—a set of individuals comprising *both a category* (such as 'women' or 'blacks') *and a network*: the more extensive the 'groupness' of the category, i.e. the greater the

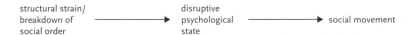

Figure 16.1 Classical model

Source: McAdam (1982: 7).

group's inclusiveness and the more pronounced its common identity, and the denser its internal network, the more organized it is:

$$\text{CATNESS} \times \text{NETNESS} = \text{ORGANIZATION}$$

Note that this formula includes not only formal organizations, but also the range of everyday life social locations that are not aimed primarily at movement mobilization, where micro-mobilization may take place: friendship networks, voluntary associations, family and work units, and elements of the state structure itself. It is not a particular form of organization that is emphasized by resource mobilization theory, but the overall structure of the discontented group (Figure 16.2).

In addition to organization, the resource mobilization perspective also puts the emphasis on the tactical and standardized action repertoires of social movements. Protest politics can take different forms, but the repertoire at a given moment in a given context proves to be highly standardized. McAdam's (1982) critique of the resource mobilization approach points to the failure of its proponents to adequately differentiate organized change efforts by excluded groups from those of established interest groups. By emphasizing the similarities between conventional action and protest politics, the resource mobilization perspective normalized protest too much. While this was a salutary corrective against the tendency to assimilate protest and deviant behaviour, the distinction between **conventional** and **unconventional** forms of protest was seriously blurred and the role of *organizations* in protest was exaggerated.

McAdam (1982: 29) also criticizes the 'consistent failure by many of its proponents of resource mobilization to acknowledge the political capabilities of the movement's mass base'. In particular, resource mobilization theorists fail to acknowledge the power inherent in the disruptive tactics of the truly powerless. They tend to overlook the crucial importance of the indigenous resources of the aggrieved population and to put the emphasis on the external resources of allies and other external supporters. Finally, the approach has to some extent failed in its own terms, because it has tended to neglect the role of leadership in social movements (Ganz 2000).

Political process model

Based on his critique of the resource mobilization model, McAdam (1982) formulates a third perspective on social movements—the political process model. This model shares the basic assumptions of the resource mobilization approach but it also considers the level of organization within the aggrieved population as a crucial element for its mobilization. Therefore, it is often treated as just another variant of the resource mobilization approach. However, it adds two elements to the previous model.

1. First, the political process model puts the group into its *political context* and focuses on the *political opportunities and constraints* structuring the way that it interacts with its adversaries. The political process model is based on the idea that the social processes of the classical model do not directly promote the mobilization of social movements, but do so only indirectly through a restructuring of existing power relations.

2. The second element added by the political process models refers to the *subjective meaning* people attribute to their situation. The emergence of a social movement implies a transformation of consciousness within a significant segment of the aggrieved population. Before collective action becomes possible, people must collectively define their situations as unjust and subject to change through collective action. McAdam (1982: 51) refers to this condition as a *cognitive liberation,* which is facilitated by expanding political opportunities, by the internal solidarity and organization of the aggrieved group, and by strategic attempts by political entrepreneurs.

This model has subsequently been elaborated into a more encompassing 'social movement paradigm' which attempts to integrate the various models. Political opportunities, mobilizing structures, cultural framings, and repertories of contention became integral parts of this more encompassing perspective—the 'social movement paradigm' (McAdam *et al.* 1996).

The political process model and its successor have also met with criticism. Thus the concept of 'political opportunity structure' has been criticized for its all-inclusive character (Gamson and Meyer 1996). Critics have also pointed

Figure 16.2 Resource mobilization model

Source: Adapted from Tilly *et al.* (1975) and Tilly (1978).

out (Goodwin and Jasper 1999: 34) that not all social movements are equally focused on the political process, and therefore are not dependent to the same degree on political opportunities for their mobilization and success. Finally, it has been suggested that the concept of opportunity often serves as a substitute for breakdown (Buechler 2004: 61). What constitutes opportunities from the perspective of the movement actors represents a *breakdown of social control mechanisms* from the point of view of the established authorities and the defenders of the status quo.

KEY POINTS

- There are three basic theoretical approaches to social movements: (1) the classical model, (2) the resource mobilization model, and (3) the political process model.

- Classical theories presume that structural strain and breakdown of standard routines of everyday life cause discontent among the individual members of the group to trigger collective behaviour.

- According to the resource mobilization theory, social movements develop not from an aggregate rise in discontent but from a significant increase in the level of resources available to support collective protest activities of the aggrieved group. Solidarity, organization, and external support are key resources for social movements.

- The political process model builds on the resource mobilization approach, but with two additional elements. First, it puts the aggrieved group into its political context and focuses on the political opportunities and constraints structuring the way it interacts with its adversaries. Second, it recognizes that the emergence of a social movement implies a transformation of consciousness within the aggrieved population.

- Although the political process model has, like the other two models, met with serious criticism, it holds out the greatest promise for comparative politics.

The comparative analysis of social movements

For comparative politics, the political process model holds considerable promise. By putting social movements into their political context, it brings the study of social movements into the mainstream of political science. This section discusses the specific ways of how social movements are determined by and interact with their political context. Figure 16.3 provides a framework for the comparative political analysis of social movements. This framework distinguishes between three sets of variables—political opportunity structures, configurations of power, and interaction contexts. Let us look at the different elements of each set.

Political opportunity structure

The political opportunity structure constitutes what we could call the hard core of the political process framework. The basic idea of the framework is that 'political opportunity structures influence the choice of protest strategies and the impact of social movements on their environment' (Kitschelt 1986: 58). Since Eisinger (1973) first introduced the notion of political opportunity structures, students of social movements have distinguished between 'open' and 'closed' structures, i.e. structures which allow for easy access to the political system or which make access more difficult. Kitschelt (1986) introduced the additional distinction between *input* and *output* structures, i.e. structures referring specifically to either the openness of the political system in the input phase of the policy cycle or its capacity to impose itself in the output phase. In practice, it proved to be difficult to clearly separate these two types of structures from one another. At the same time, open systems tend to have only a limited capacity to act, whereas closed systems tend to have such a capacity.

The core of the structures, in turn, is made up of formal political institutions. The degree of openness of the political system is a function of its (territorial) centralization and the degree of its (functional) separation of power. The greater the degree of decentralization, the wider the formal access and the smaller the capacity of any one part of the system to act. Decentralization implies a multiplication of state actors and, therefore, of points of access and decision-making. In federal states, such as those of Germany, Switzerland, or the US, there are multiple entry points at the national, regional, and local level. In centralized states, such as those of France, the Netherlands, the UK, or Sweden, regional and local entry points are rather insignificant. In addition, the system's openness is closely related to the (functional) separation of power. The greater the separation of power between the legislature (parliamentary arena), the executive (government and public administration), and the judiciary, and the greater the division of power within each of these branches of government (e.g. between partners in the governing coalition as a result of the electoral system), the greater the degree of formal access for movement actors and the more limited the capacity of the state to act. The overall accessibility of the political institutions can be summarized by the usual models in comparative politics (see Section 3 of this volume).

Given the key importance of the media, the political process approach has paid surprisingly little attention to the structure of the media system in a given country. Hallin and Mancini (2004) provide a comparative framework for the study of the impact of media systems on the political process (see Chapter 19).

The extent to which social movement actors obtain access to the decision-making arenas depends not only on

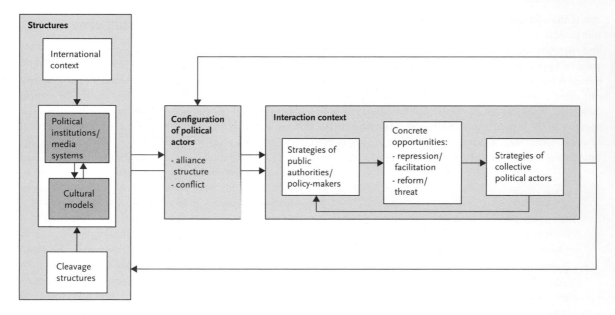

Figure 16.3 A framework for the study of the impact of the political context

Source: Adapted from Kriesi (2004: 70).

the formal institutional structure, but also on more informal preconditions, which I propose to call *cultural models*.

A first example of such cultural models refers to the prevailing strategies of the authorities with regard to social movements, i.e. to the procedures typically employed by members of the political system when they are dealing with challengers. We may distinguish between *exclusive* (repressive, confrontational, polarizing) and *integrative* (facilitative, cooperative, assimilative) strategies. These prevailing strategies have a long tradition in a given country and they are related to its institutional structure. Thus political authorities in consensus democracies are rather more likely to rely on integrative strategies than their colleagues in majoritarian democracies (for the distinction between these two types of democracy, see Chapter 5).

In consensus democracies, the tendency to rely on integrative strategies is the result of a collective learning experience that reaches back to the resolution of the religious conflicts which had torn these countries apart for centuries. The resolution of these conflicts provided the models for dealing with political challenges for centuries to come. Similarly, the tendency to rely on repressive strategies is a result of historical experiences, as is argued by Gallie (1983), who traces the repressive reactions of the French ruling elites to the challenge by labour movement protest after the First World War back to the earlier experience of repressing the Parisian Commune in 1870.

A second major category of cultural models concerns the political–cultural or symbolic opportunities that determine what kind of ideas become visible for the public, resonate with public opinion, and are held to be 'legitimate' by the audience. Koopmans and Statham (1999: 228)

proposed the term *discursive opportunity structure* to denote this second type of cultural model. They apply the concept to the mobilization by the extreme right—a social movement that uses an ethnic–cultural model of citizenship and national identity to mobilize against immigration in Western Europe. Ethnic–cultural models of national identity assert that people belong to a nation because of their ethnic or cultural (e.g. linguistic or religious) origin. This kind of model contrasts with civic–political models of citizenship, which conceive of the nation as a political community of equal citizens to which everybody who has been born into the community in question belongs. Comparing the differential success of the extreme right in postwar Italy and Germany, Koopmans and Statham (1999: 229) test and confirm the hypothesis that the resonance of the extreme-right frame, and consequently its chances of mobilization and success in a given country, depends on the dominant model of national identity and citizenship. Its mobilization and success turn out to be greater (1) the more the dominant discourse on national identity and citizenship corresponds to and legitimates the ethnic–cultural ideal type of national identity, and (2) the less the dominant conception of the nation is grounded in and legitimized by civic–political elements.

Cultural models can be combined with political institutional structures in order to arrive at more complex and more focused opportunity sets. Table 16.1 provides an example of a typology of context conditions based on institutional structures and prevailing strategies.

Both institutional structures and cultural models are influenced by even more fundamental structures, which we should include in our conceptualization of the structural

Table 16.1 The general settings for the mobilization of social movements

Dominant strategy	Formal institutional structure	
	Weak state	**Strong state**
Exclusive	*Formalistic inclusion*: formal, but no informal, facilitation of access; strong repression; possibility of veto, but no substantive concessions (Germany, Brazil, US)	*Full exclusion*: neither formal nor informal facilitation of access; strong repression; possibility of neither veto nor substantive concessions (France, Japan, Argentina)
Inclusive	*Full procedural integration*: formal and informal facilitation of access; weak repression; possibility of veto, but no substantive concessions (Switzerland, Canada)	*Informal cooptation*: no formal, but informal, facilitation of access; weak repression; no possibility of veto, but substantive concessions (Netherlands, Sweden)

Source: Kriesi (1995: 177).

political context in the broader sense of the term. Thus, political institutions and cultural models are influenced by the country-specific political cleavage structures and by the country's international context. As discussed in Chapter 13, the specific political cleavage structure of a country, in turn, is rooted in the history of social and cultural conflicts. Traditional social and cultural cleavages constitute the basis of the political cleavage structure even today. To the extent that traditional conflicts are still salient and segment the population into mutually exclusive adversarial groups, there is little manoeuvring space for new types of challenger who attempt to articulate a new kind of social or cultural conflict. A comparison of the mobilization of new social movements (see Box 16.1) in four Western European countries in the 1970s and 1980s shows evidence for the existence of such a 'zero-sum' relationship between traditional and new political cleavages (Kriesi *et al.* 1995).

Moreover, even if the national political context today is still the most significant one for the mobilization of social movements, it is important that we do not lose sight of sub-national as well as international contexts. On the one hand, nation-states are subdivided into regional and local levels of governance. The variance of the opportunity structure between regions or member-states is of great importance, above all in federal states, but the significance of the variations in local contexts for the mobilization of social movement is highly relevant everywhere. On the other hand, nation-states are increasingly inserted into supra- or international systems of governance that impose constraints and open opportunities for social movement actors. Internationalism offers a wide range of venues for conflict.

According to Tarrow (2005), the unusual character of the contemporary period is not that it has detached

Box 16.1 New social movements

The so-called 'new social movements' have been responsible for the bulk of the mobilization that took place in Western Europe from the 1970s up to the 1990s. Most authors would probably agree that this family of movements includes *the ecology movement* (with its anti-nuclear energy branch), the *peace movement, the solidarity movement (solidarity with developing countries), the women's movement, the human rights movement, the anti-racist movement, and the squatters' movement*, as well as various other movements mobilizing for the rights of minorities which are discriminated against (such as the gay movement).

These movements were called 'new' at the time in order to distinguish them from the 'old' labour movement, which had dominated the mobilization for collective action in Western Europe up to the 1960s.

On the one hand, these movements go back to the new left—the new generation of radicals who were the protagonists of the anti-authoritarian revolt of the late 1960s. On the other hand, they are an offspring of the citizens' action committees which had started to articulate more specific grievances of local or regional populations in the early 1970s. These citizens' action committees were much more pragmatic and at the same time much broader in scope than the new left proper. Thanks to their dual political roots, the new social movements have managed to achieve what the new left has never been able to do on its own—namely, the political mobilization of masses of citizens on behalf of their emancipatory goals.

Source: Kriesi *et al.* (1995).

individuals from their societies or created transnational citizens, but that it has created what he calls 'rooted cosmopolitans' and 'transnational activists'. This is a stratum of people who are able to combine the resources and opportunities of their own societies into transnational networks, leading to an 'activism beyond borders' (Tarrow 2005: 43). Transnational activism and transnational movement organizations are, as Tarrow shows, a growing phenomenon even if, as I would add, the bulk of social movement campaigns still take place in a national context and address domestic targets. Examples of transnational movements include the resistance to the war in Iraq, which was mentioned at the outset of this chapter, and the global justice movement which mobilizes against the World Trade Organization (WTO), the World Economic Forum (WEF), or the G8 meetings and organizes its own yearly Social Forums (originally in Porto Alegre, Brazil, and more recently in different locations across the world).

Configuration of power

The next set of variables refers to the configurations of actors. From the point of view of a mobilizing social movement, this configuration has three major components.

- *Protagonists:* the configuration of allies (policy-makers, public authorities, political parties, interest groups, the media, and related movements).
- *Antagonists:* the configuration of adversaries (public authorities, repressive agents, and counter-movements).
- *Bystanders:* the not directly involved, but nevertheless attentive, audience.

Actor configurations represent what we know of the set of actors at a given point in time—their capabilities, perceptions, and evaluations of the outcomes obtainable (their 'pay-offs' in terms of game theory), and the degree to which their interests are compatible or incompatible with each other. The configuration describes the level of potential conflict, the 'logic of the situation' at that point in time, but it does not specify how the situation is going to evolve, nor does it say how it has been created.

The configuration of political actors at any given point in time is partly determined by the *structures of the political context*. Thus the new social movements in Western Europe faced a very different alliance structure depending on the configuration of the left, their natural ally (the new social movements were essentially 'movements of the left'; see Box 16.1), which was, in turn, decisively shaped by the *heritage of the prevailing strategies* to deal with challengers in a given country (Kriesi *et al.* 1995).

The heritage of exclusive strategies in a country like France caused the radicalization and eventual split of the labour movement into a moderate social democratic left and a radical communist left. This split in the labour movement, in turn, contributed to the continued salience of the class conflict which, at the time of the emergence of the French new social movements in the latter part of the 1970s, limited the availability of the left for the mobilization of the new social movements. In the French situation, where the left was dominated by the Communist Party up to the late 1970s, the Socialists could not become unconditional allies of the new social movements. They had to continue to appeal to the working class in traditional class terms to ward off Communist competition, and both the Socialists and the Communists tended to instrumentalize the new social movements—especially the peace movement and the solidarity movement—for their own electoral purposes.

However, the configuration of political actors is less stable than the structural component of the political context. For example, the alliance structure of a given movement may change decisively at any election, depending on whether the political party which constitutes a natural ally for the social movement in question is elected into power or loses its government position. Thus the social democrats tended to support the new social movements in Western Europe when they were in opposition, but were much less reliable allies when in government. Moreover, it is also much easier for social movements to modify the configuration of political actors than to modify the structural context.

While authors who analyse the mobilization of social movements in a comparative (cross-national, cross-regional, or cross-local) perspective rely heavily on explanations involving structural elements, authors who perform case studies within national contexts tend to put the accent more on configurations of political actors. Most importantly, they tend to adopt a longitudinal perspective involving comparisons across time and important shifts in the configurations of political actors. In their view, it is the shifts in the configurations of political actors—the instability of political alignments— which create the opportunity for successful mobilization (Tarrow 1994: 87–8). Such instability may relate to the changing electoral fortunes of major parties.

The civil rights movement in the US provides a well-known example of the leverage created by electoral realignments; both the decline of their Southern white vote and the movement of African American voters to the Northern cities increased the incentive for the Democrats to seek black support. With its 'razor-thin electoral margin, the Kennedy administration was forced to move from cautious foot-dragging to seizing the initiative for civil rights, a strategy that was extended by the Johnson administration to the landmark Voting Rights Act of 1965' (Tarrow 1994: 87).

The instability of political alignments may also refer to a policy-specific situation. In other words, shifting opportunities for mobilization and success may be policy-domain specific. Some exogenous shock, such as changes in socio-economic conditions, natural catastrophes, system-wide governing coalitions, or policy outputs from other subsystems, may destabilize the domain-specific equilibrium. Social and cultural shifts and unpredictable catastrophic events may cause policy failures in the domain in question, system-wide power shifts may cause corresponding domain-specific shifts, and policy outputs of other subsystems may cause disarray in the traditional problem-solving routines in the domain in question.

American nuclear power is an example of the construction and collapse of a policy monopoly. Baumgartner and Jones (1993: 70) maintain that the opponents of nuclear energy in the US won primarily by getting their vision of the issue accepted and altering the nature of the decision-making process by expanding the range of participants involved. When the venue had been expanded by opponents to include licensing, oversight, and rate-making, the industry lost control of the issue and the future was determined. Whatever the ultimate reason for the breakdown of the nuclear power coalition in the US (see next section), the case of US nuclear power illustrates the opportunities that open up for social movements as the hold of dominant coalitions over a policy domain loosens up.

Interaction contexts

The third level of analysis concerns the interaction context. This is the level of the mechanisms linking structures and configurations to agency and action, and it is at this level that the *strategies of the social movements and*

their opponents come into view. 'Strategy' is the conceptual link actors make between the places, the times, and the ways they mobilize and deploy their resources and the goals they hope to achieve. Strategy is a way of 'framing' specific choices about targeting, timing, and tactics. Movement actors will make their strategic choices on the basis of their appreciation of the specific chances of reform and threat, and the specific risks of repression and facilitation they face. Box 16.2 defines these mechanisms and describes how they are expected to operate with regard to the level of mobilization.

A striking illustration of how repression operates and how social movements may use its anticipated effects in their own strategic choices is again provided by the civil rights movement. This movement deliberately chose a strategy of demonstrating in cities in the South of the US, where an unmistakably repressive reaction to peaceful demonstrations could be expected. The violent clashes that followed brought the movement more media attention than it would otherwise have received, and conveyed the movement's message in a most powerful way, which consequently led to increased external support. Although, at least in democratic regimes, repression may not reduce the level of movement mobilization, it can be expected to have a considerable effect on the action repertoire. It will increase the amount of radical mobilization.

As Gamson and Meyer (1996: 283) argue, the definition of opportunity, i.e. the appreciation of the concrete situation, is typically highly contentious within a social

---

Box 16.2 Four mechanisms involved in linking the general structural setting to the mobilization of social movements

Four mechanisms involved in linking the general structural setting to the mobilization of social movements

- *Facilitation:* any action by other actors that lowers the costs of mobilization.
- *Repression:* any external action that increases such costs.
- *Chances of success:* the likelihood that collective action will contribute to the realization of a movement's goals.
- *Threat/reform:* a situation where collective benefits are expected even if no collective action is undertaken/where collective 'bads' are expected if the movement does not act.

Impact on the volume of mobilization

Facilitation
This will generally lead to an increase in the level of mobilization.

Repression
Extremely high levels of repression will make collective action unattractive for the large majority of potential activists.

At lower levels, increased repression may not be able to reduce the amount of mobilization; several examples of movements that were actually stimulated by repression in can be found the literature.

Chances of success:
The level of mobilization is likely to increase with the chances of success. There are two types of success.

- *Proactive success:* implies the introduction of new advantages; it is difficult to achieve under any kind of circumstances.
- *Reactive success:* implies the avoidance of new disadvantages; may be more easily achieved, which is why defensive mobilization is more likely to occur than proactive mobilization.

Threat/reform
The level of mobilization is likely to increase with the intensity of threat; the level of mobilization is likely to decrease with the chances of reform; threat contributes to the likelihood of 'defensive' mobilization.

Source: Adapted from Tilly (1978) and Koopmans (1992).

movement, and they suggest that 'we focus on the process of defining opportunity and how it works'. The debates within movements typically turn around questions of 'relative opportunity' for different courses of action. Opportunity may shift in favour of some specific part of the movement, the radicals for example, and may result in a radicalization of the movement as a whole. However, according to the political process approach, the 'relative opportunities' are to a large extent determined by the configuration of actors and the structural context. In other words, the outcome of the internal debates of the movements is constrained by the larger political context, which the strategically oriented movement actors will not fail to take into account in their deliberations.

Ganz (2000) adds the important notion of *strategic capacity*, i.e. the movement's capability of developing effective strategy, which is a function of *leadership* and *organization*. Box 16.3 provides excerpts from a famous speech by Martin Luther King Jr, which may serve as an illustration of the strategic capacity of this great leader of the American civil rights movement.

Differences in strategic capacity may explain why some new organizations fail while others survive, and they may at the same time account for less adaptive behaviour among older organizations. The Spanish 'Indignados', who burst onto the public scene with their demonstration all over Spain on 15 May 2011 expressing outrage against politicians and bankers and claiming social justice, and more participation, transparency, and accountability, illustrate how a contemporary movement can develop a strategic capacity. Instead of relying on coverage by established media, they innovated by relying mainly on internet-based informal organizations, without formal membership. They mobilized via alternative online media, online social networks, and via personal networks of friends and acquaintances. This allowed them to reach beyond the usual political activists and mobilize the discontented who are not organized by traditional groups such as unions or civic organizations (Anduiza *et al.* 2012).

An array of specific mechanisms links the general structural setting to the mobilization of social movements. They constitute what we could call 'concrete opportunities'. Tilly (1978) introduced the pair of mechanisms 'facilitation and repression', and Koopmans (1992) added 'success chances and reform/threat'. McAdam *et al.* (2001) pursued this line of reasoning further and introduced several additional mechanisms, which allowed the structural context to be linked to the concrete episodes of mobilization (see Box 16.2).

Box 16.3 Excerpts from the speech delivered by Martin Luther King Jr on the steps at the Lincoln Memorial in Washington DC on 28 August 1963

Five score years ago, a great American [Abraham Lincoln], in whose symbolic shadow we stand, signed the Emancipation Proclamation. This momentous decree came as a great beacon light of hope to millions of Negro slaves who had been seared in the flames of withering injustice. It came as a joyous daybreak to end the long night of captivity.

But one hundred years later, we must face the tragic fact that the Negro is still not free. One hundred years later, the life of the Negro is still sadly crippled by the manacles of segregation and the chains of discrimination. One hundred years later, the Negro lives on a lonely island of poverty in the midst of a vast ocean of material prosperity. One hundred years later, the Negro is still languishing in the corners of American society and finds himself an exile in his own land. So we have come here today to dramatize an appalling condition.

...

I am not unmindful that some of you have come here out of great trials and tribulations. Some of you have come fresh from narrow cells. Some of you have come from areas where your quest for freedom left you battered by the storms of persecution and staggered by the winds of police brutality. You have been the veterans of creative suffering. Continue to work with the faith that unearned suffering is redemptive.

Go back to Mississippi, go back to Alabama, go back to Georgia, go back to Louisiana, go back to the slums and ghettos of our northern cities, knowing that somehow this situation can and will be changed. Let us not wallow in the valley of despair.

I say to you today, my friends, that in spite of the difficulties and frustrations of the moment, I still have a dream. It is a dream deeply rooted in the American dream. I have a dream that one day this nation will rise up and live out the true meaning of its creed: 'We hold these truths to be self-evident: that all men are created equal.'

I have a dream that one day on the red hills of Georgia the sons of former slaves and the sons of former slave-owners will be able to sit down together at a table of brotherhood. I have a dream that one day even the state of Mississippi, a desert state, sweltering with the heat of injustice and oppression, will be transformed into an oasis of freedom and justice. I have a dream that my four children will one day live in a nation where they will not be judged by the color of their skin but by the content of their character.

I have a dream today. I have a dream that one day the state of Alabama, whose governor's lips are presently dripping with the words of interposition and nullification, will be transformed into a situation where little black boys and black girls will be able to join hands with little white boys and white girls and walk together as sisters and brothers. I have a dream today.

KEY POINTS

● The political context for the mobilization of social movements can be broken down into political opportunity structures, configuration of actors, and interaction contexts.

● The formal institutional political structures and the cultural models, such as prevailing strategies, combine to define the overall structural context.

● The configuration of power refers to the shifting configurations of allies, adversaries, and bystanders who exist at the level of authorities and policy-makers in the policy-specific context or in the polity at large, and who constitute the alliance and conflict structures facing the movement.

● The overall context is linked by specific mechanisms to the strategic choices made by the social movements in the interaction context: facilitation vs. repression, and success chances vs. reform/threat are examples of such mechanisms.

Emergence, mobilization, and success of social movements

Social movement studies intend to explain three aspects of social movements—their emergence, mobilization, and eventual success.

Emergence

The political context has above all been used to account for the emergence of social movements. A famous example of the kind of reasoning involved is Skocpol's book, *States and Social Revolutions* (1979). At the origin of the three social revolutions she studied—the French, Russian, and Chinese Revolutions—Skocpol finds a conjunction of two key factors: (1) a political crisis and (2) agrarian socio-political structures (i.e. a given form of national cleavage structures) which gave rise to widespread peasant discontent and facilitated insurrections against landlords. The political crisis is brought about by the intensification of international pressure (shifts in the geopolitical context structure) which leads to a military and fiscal crisis of the state (institutional strain and even breakdown), which in turn gives rise to profound divisions in the ruling elites over how to respond to the state's declining effectiveness and fiscal problems (realignments in the configuration of actors). The peasant revolts become uncontrollable at the moment when regime defections become widespread and when the elite loses its cohesion and is no longer capable of exercising its social control (by repressive measures).

Skocpol (1979: 154) claims to have identified the sufficient causes of social revolutionary situations. However, the various elements of the political context define only a set of necessary conditions for the emergence of contention—its 'opportunity set'. The transformation of a potentially explosive situation into the unfolding of events within the interaction context is historically contingent and therefore quite unpredictable. Precipitating factors, exogenous shocks, contingent or catalysing events, and suddenly imposed grievances play a crucial role in such a transformation. In addition to the 'opportunity set', the unfolding of events crucially depends on the choices made by actors on the basis of their preferences.

Thus the events leading up to the French Revolution were set in motion by the king's move to invite the population to submit its grievances to the authorities *(cahiers de doléances)*—a 'window of opportunity' with quite unanticipated consequences. The death of Franco set off the transition to democracy in Spain—a somewhat more predictable outcome. The incident with Rosa Parks launched the Montgomery Bus Boycott, which marked the beginning of the civil rights movement. The declaration of the state of emergency in Kenya in 1952 resulted in the arrest of nationalist leader Jomo Kenyatta and 145 other Kenyan political figures, which unleashed the Mau Mau revolt. The assassination of opposition leader Benigno Aquino was the origin of the Philippines Yellow Revolution. The accidents at Three Mile Island and Chernobyl were crucial for the mobilization of the anti-nuclear movement.

The contingency of the precipitating event may vary from one occasion to another. As McAdam *et al.* (2001: 147) observe, the catalytic event is often neither accidental, nor the primordial starting point of the episode, but the culmination of a long-standing conflict. To the extent that the build-up of a political conflict systematically increases the opportunity for mobilization, we are more likely to be able to account for the unfolding of subsequent contentious episodes.

Mobilization

The political opportunity structures are ideally suited to the explanation of the volume and form of a movement's mobilization. In a cross-national study of four Western European countries, we have shown that the level and form of collective action vary quite closely as a function of the openness of the political system of the respective countries (Kriesi *et al.* 1995). We found that the openness of the Swiss system facilitates the mobilization for collective action. The existence of direct democracy institutions, in particular, invites citizens to mobilize collectively. At the same time, the openness of the system and the availability of conventional channels of protest, such as the direct democratic channels, have a strong moderating effect on the strategic choices of the Swiss movement actors. They have learned to use the available direct democracy instruments, and they continue to use them even if they are not very successful in doing so. In contrast, the

Table 16.2 Action repertory of social movements per country (% of total number of protest events)

Action form	Switzerland	Netherlands	Germany	France
Direct democracy	8.1	–	–	–
Petitions	8.1	2.8	2.7	1.2
Festivals	5.5	1.4	2.2	1.4
Demonstrations	52.5	49.7	60.6	41.7
Confrontations	13.4	35.0	19.3	24.5
Light violence	7.7	5.1	6.2	5.8
Heavy violence	4.7	6.0	9.0	25.4
All	100.0	100.0	100.0	100.0
N	1,322	1,319	2,343	2,132

Source: Kriesi *et al.* (1995: 50).

relative closure of the French system provides little facilitation for mobilization by collective actors, which not only dampens the level of mobilization, but also contributes to the radicalization of the movement's action repertoires. These results are presented in Table 16.2.

The example of the Arab Spring in 2011 illustrates the importance of the media for the level of mobilization of social movements today. Many observers have attributed an important role to the media in explaining the sudden mobilization of long-standing grievances of the Arab public in early 2011. On the one hand, cross-national political communication (such as the influence of Al-Jazeera) are likely to have undermined the control of domestic media by authoritarian regimes. The Qatar-based satellite channel Al-Jazeera continued to air reports on Egypt and Tunisia despite the pleas of these regimes to the Qatari government to stop it (Dalacoura 2012: 68). On the other hand, social media such as Facebook and Twitter, and of course mobile phones, were widely used to organize the revolts and link the protesters to each other and the outside world. Perhaps even more crucially, the media played a role in preparing for the rebellions over a number of years, and even decades, by facilitating the circulation of ideas in national and global spaces and challenging state monopolies of information.

Overall, a preliminary analysis by Wilson and Dunn (2011: 1269) suggests that, while digital media use was not dominant in Egyptian protest activity, 'digital media use—and social media especially—were nevertheless an integral and driving component in the media landscape'. This is particularly obvious in the role that Twitter played in actively and successfully engaging an international audience in the Egyptian revolution.

Success

Social movements do not only intend to mobilize successfully. Ultimately, they want to have an impact on political decision-making or on society at large. In comparative politics, where we primarily deal with instrumental movements that seek to influence politics, their impact on policy decisions is of key importance. Outcomes are still studied less often than the emergence and mobilization of social movements. However, the field is not as empty as many observers have claimed (Giugni 1998).

There is one movement in particular whose success has been the object of several studies with a comparative political process perspective—the anti-nuclear movement. It provides an excellent illustration of how the different aspects of the political context have been used to explain a movement's outcomes. Kitschelt's (1986) influential analysis put the accent on the structural element and compared the movement's impact in four countries with quite distinct political opportunity structures: Germany, France, Sweden, and the US. He made the general point that there is *no one-to-one correspondence between the level of mobilization and the success of social movements*: strong mobilization does not necessarily lead to profound impact if the political opportunity structures are not conducive to change. Conversely, weak mobilization may have a disproportionate impact owing to properties of the political opportunity structure.

More specifically, Kitschelt argued that in Germany, Sweden, and the US, where political opportunity structures were conducive to popular participation, greater responsiveness to the anti-nuclear opposition invariably led to extremely tight and often changing safety regulations. Once formulated, these new safety standards allowed opponents to intervene and insist that they be complied with. Construction delays were the result, especially in the US and Germany—the two countries with fragmented implementation structures. Much shorter delays were typical in France and Sweden, where tight implementation procedures offered few opportunities for outside intervention in the construction process. In Sweden, nuclear policy was also ultimately changed, not by disrupting the policy implementation process, but by the shifting electoral fortunes of major parties and changes in government. In the open Swedish system, the anti-nuclear movement finally prevailed because it was largely supported by the institutional structure, the prevailing cultural models, and the configuration of power in the Swedish system.

KEY POINTS

- The emergence of a social movement or radical transformations such as revolutions can be explained by the combination of structural preconditions and contingent events (precipitating factors, suddenly imposed grievances, exogenous shocks).

- The volume and form of social movement mobilization is heavily conditioned by the relative openness of the political context and by the congruence between media frames and movement frames, which in turn is conditioned by the political context in which it is embedded.

- There is no one-to-one correspondence between the level of mobilization and the success of social movements. Strong mobilization does not necessarily lead to profound impact if the political opportunity structures are not conducive to change. Conversely, weak mobilization may have a disproportionate impact owing to properties of the political opportunity structure.

Conclusion

There are very good reasons not to treat social movements as a distinct set of phenomena to be dealt with by a specific subfield of social sciences. It is fruitful to include them in the comparative analysis of the political process,

as they have become regular participants in policy-making in democratic societies.

Among the specialists of social movements, there is currently a tendency to enlarge the perspective beyond social movements to *contentious politics* (or protest politics, as I have called it here) and to focus less on social movements as such and more on the mechanisms and processes through which contentious politics operates (McAdam *et al.* 2001; Tilly and Tarrow 2007). In this perspective, social movements are only one version of contentious politics, which ranges from small-scale protest events to large-scale revolutions. This is a promising perspective as long as we do not lose sight of the fact that social movements constitute distinctive social processes in their own right.

The political process approach is of particular interest for the integration of these distinctive processes into the mainstream of comparative politics. A number of mechanisms contribute to integrate contemporary social movements into the political process of liberal democracies, i.e. to institutionalize them (Meyer and Tarrow 1998*a*: 23–4): social movement activists have learned to employ conventional and unconventional collective actions; police practices increasingly encourage the routinization of contention; the tactics used by movement organizations and those used by more institutionalized groups increasingly overlap.

At the same time, such mechanisms contribute to the increasing integration of social movement actors into the policy-making process and to the adoption of social movement strategies by routine participants in policy-making. Moreover, the attention that social movement scholars increasingly pay to the outcomes produced by popular claims-making and contention (Giugni 1998; Giugni *et al.* 1999) also brings them closer to the analysis of public policy-making which, in turn, enhances the usefulness of the political process approach.

 Questions

1. What is a social movement? What is its relation to interest groups, political parties, and the media?

2. What is the difference between a movement challenging political authorities and a movement challenging cultural authorities? Discuss this question on the basis of the feminist movement.

3. Describe the three major models for the analysis of social movements and discuss the weaknesses of each.

4. What are political opportunity structures and cultural models?

5. What are configurations of power and how do they change?

6. In which countries does the peace movement face favourable context conditions, and in which countries are these context conditions rather unfavourable?

7. Describe some aspects of the interaction context.

8. Under which conditions do movements emerge?

9. What kind of conditions favour the mobilization capacity of social movements and under what kind of conditions do they radicalize?

10. When do social movements have success, i.e. under what conditions are they able to reach their goals?

Further reading

Classical texts on social movements

Della Porta, D. and Rucht, D. (eds) (2013) *Meeting Democracy. Power and Deliberation in Global Justice Movement* (Cambridge: Cambridge University Press).

Gamson, W. A. (1975) *The Strategy of Social Protest* (Homewood, IL: Dorsey).

McAdam, D. (1982) *Political Process and the Development of Black Insurgency, 1930–1970* (Chicago, IL: University of Chicago Press).

McAdam, D. and Boudet, H. S. (2012) *Putting Social Movements in Their Place. Explaining Opposition to Energy Projects in the United States, 2000–2005* (Cambridge: Cambridge University Press).

Tarrow, S. (2012) *Strangers at the Gates. Movements and States in Contentious Politics.* (Cambridge: Cambridge University Press).

Tarrow, S. (1994) *Power in Movement: Social Movements, Collective Action and Politics* (Cambridge: Cambridge University Press).

Tilly, C. (2008). *Contentious Performances* (Cambridge: Cambridge University Press).

Turner, R. A., and Killian, L. (1987) *Collective Behavior* (3rd edn) (Englewood Cliffs, NJ: Prentice Hall).

Useful collections of articles

McAdam, D., McCarthy, J. D., and Zald, M. N. (eds) (1996) *Comparative Perspectives on Social Movements: Political Opportunities, Mobilizing Structures, and Cultural Framings* (Cambridge: Cambridge University Press).

Snow, D. A., Soule, S. A., and Kriesi, H. (eds) (2004) *The Blackwell Companion to Social Movements* (Oxford: Blackwell).

For a more extended bibliography see the works cited throughout this chapter.

In addition, up-to-date reports on social movements can be found in specialized journals such as *Mobilization* (published in the US), *Social Movement Studies* (published in the UK), and *Forschungsjournal Neue Soziale Bewegungen* (published in Germany). Students may also find useful material in the major journals in American sociology: *American Sociological Review*, *American Journal of Sociology*, *Social Forces*, and *Social Problems*.

 Web links

http://www.bc.edu/bc_org/avp/cas/soc/mrap/
Website of the Boston College Media Research and Action Project (directed by William Gamson).

www.amnesty.org
Website of Amnesty International, a worldwide campaigning movement that works to promote all the human rights enshrined in the Universal Declaration of Human Rights and other international standards.

http://www.wzb.eu/en/research/completed-research-programs/civil-society-and-political-mobilization
Website of the research group on Civil Society, Citizenship, and Political Mobilization in Europe.

www.greenpeace.org/international/
Website of Greenpeace International.

www.globalfundforwomen.org
Website of the Global Fund for Women. Makes grants to seed, support, and strengthen women's rights groups around the world, envisioning a just and democratic world where women and men can participate equally in all aspects of social, political, and economic life.

http://asp6new.alexanderstreet.com/wam2/wam2.index.map.aspx
Website of Women and Social Movements in the United States, 1600 to 2000, from Alexander Street Press and the Center for the Historical Study of Women and Gender at SUNY Binghamton.

www.wcml.org.uk
Website of the Working Class Movement Library.

http://www.troy.edu/rosa-parks-museum/montgomery-rosa-parks-museum.html
Website of Rosa Parks Library and Museum.

http://depts.washington.edu/civilr/index.htm
Website of the Seattle Civil Rights and Labor History Project.

www.usm.edu/crdp
Website of the Civil Rights Documentation Project.

http://culturalpolitics.net/social_movements
Website of Social Movements and Culture—A Resource Website.

www.globaljusticemovement.org
Website of the Global Justice Movement.

www.psr.keele.ac.uk/parties.htm
Political parties, interest groups, and other social movements. Contains many links to parties and social movements.

www.nathannewman.org/EDIN/
Economic Democracy Information Network. Contains links to social movements, sorted by issue area.

www.vcn.bc.ca/citizens-handbook
The Citizen's Handbook: 'As far as we know, this is the best quick guide to community organizing on the web' (quoted from website).

www.mobilization.sdsu.edu/index.html
The Mobilization homepage: *'Mobilization* is an international
journal of research and theory specializing in social
movements, protests and collective behavior. *Mobilization* was
created to fill the void that there was no scholarly journal of
research and theory with an interdisciplinary and international
scope that dealt exclusively with social movements, protest and
collective action.'

www.igc.org/index.html
Institute for Global Communications. Network of several social
movements.

https://www.theengineroom.org/projects/tds/
Tahrir Data Project: data on the large demonstrations on Tahrir
Square in Cairo Egypt in 2011 (see also Wilson and Dunn 2011).

online resource centre

For additional material and resources, please visit the Online Resource Centre at:
www.oxfordtextbooks.co.uk/orc/caramani3e/

CHAPTER 17

Political culture

Christian Welzel and Ronald Inglehart

Chapter contents

A stable and effective democratic government ... depends upon the orientations that people have to the political process ... upon the political culture.

(Almond and Verba 1963: 498)

Reader's guide

This chapter describes what role the concept of **political culture** plays in comparative politics. We outline the concept's premises, insights, and recent progress. Our chapter places special emphasis on what we see as the major contribution of the political culture field: increasing our understanding of the social roots of democracy and how these roots are transformed through cultural change. In examining the inspirational forces of democracy, we compare key propositions of the political culture approach with the political economy approach. The chapter concludes with some suggestions regarding the rise of democratic values in non-Western cultures.

Introduction

The term 'culture' covers a broad set of phenomena. It includes traditions, habits, and patterns of behaviour shaped by a society's prevailing beliefs, norms, and values (Nolan and Lenski 1999). 'Political culture', then, denotes the subset of these phenomena that is shaped specifically by *political* beliefs, norms, and values.

A society's dominant beliefs, norms, and values are often described as if they constitute an inherited 'national character'. Such descriptions are at times unscientific. In the *Clash of Civilizations*, for example, Huntington (1996) provides descriptions of the typical beliefs, norms, and values of entire 'families of nations' without any reference to systematic data.

To avoid such unscientific tendencies, political culture research must be based on systematic evidence. A description of the typical beliefs, norms, and values of a society (see Box 17.1) can be accepted as scientific only if it is derived from representative survey data. For this reason, this chapter is limited to a tradition of political culture research that is committed to this premise and derives its descriptions from cross-nationally representative survey data. Table 17.1 provides a selection of milestone studies in this tradition of empirical, cross-nationally comparative studies of political culture.

The foundation of the comparative study of cross-national survey data is the *Civic Culture* study by Almond and Verba (1963). These authors define the term *political culture* 'as the particular distribution of patterns of orientation towards political objects among the members of a nation' (Almond and Verba 1963: 13). This is still the most widely accepted definition of the term 'political culture'. According to this definition, political culture concerns the psychological dimension of political systems; it includes all politically relevant beliefs, values, and attitudes. Focusing on different reference populations, one can examine elite cultures and mass cultures as well as local, regional, and national cultures, or the subcultures of specific groups. Yet, in every case the concept refers to some *collective* unit of which people are aware and to which they have some feeling of belonging.

To what extent actual political behaviour is included in the notion of political culture is not always clear, but in so far as certain patterns of political behaviour are ritualized, they can be considered to be behavioural manifestations of political culture.

Because political orientations exist in individuals, political culture research gathers data from individuals. But the unit of interest is usually some population, so individual-level data are aggregated to describe entire populations or subgroups within them. Since these descriptions should be representative, the political culture approach focuses on population surveys as its main source of evidence.

The comparative study of political culture covers manifold themes. Since it is impossible to describe each of them in this chapter, we have limited ourselves to those themes that loom largest in the discussion of democracy's cultural foundations—arguably the normative lead concept in comparative politics. This limitation implies, for instance, that in this chapter we ignore, among others, the themes of national pride, ethnic identities, and left–right orientations.

Box 17.1 Norms, values, and beliefs

Beliefs are understood here as what people think is *factually* right or wrong. Values, by contrast, mean what people think is *morally* good or bad. Values are internalized and hence guide people's behaviour without social sanctions that enforce them. In contrast with values, norms are behavioural guidelines that are socially sanctioned, either informally or formally, whether people have internalized these guidelines or not.

KEY POINTS

- A scientific approach to studying political culture requires the reliance on systematic evidence based on representative data.

Cultural differences around the world

Over several decades, comparative researchers have identified various sets of questions that can be used in standardized surveys to measure cultural differences between societies in valid ways. Arguably, the largest of these surveys in both spatial and temporal scope is the World Values Survey (WVS). Since the early 1980s, the WVS has been conducted at least once in more than ninety societies worldwide, including countries from all inhabited continents.

Repeated analyses of WVS data over more than two decades have found a robust pattern of cross-national cultural differences (Inglehart 1990, 1997). On a global scale, much of the cultural differences between nations boil down to just two major dimensions: '*sacred* versus *secular* values' and '*survival* versus *emancipative* values' (for simplicity, henceforth secular values and emancipative values). *Inter*-societal differences on these two value dimensions are usually larger, and often much larger, than *intra*-societal differences (Inglehart

Table 17.1 An overview of some milestone studies in the cross-national comparative tradition of political culture studies

Recent		Inglehart & Norris (2003): traditional–secular/rational values	Inglehart & Welzel (2005): human empowerment		Dalton (2008): engaged citizenship
2000s			Bratton & Mattes (2000): intrinsic and instrumental support for democracy	Rose & Shin (2000): idealistic and realistic support for democracy	Putnam (2000): social capital decline
Late 1990s	Huntington (1996): clash of civilizations	Inglehart (1997): world cultural map	Verba *et al.* (1995): civic voluntarism	Klingemann (1999): dissatisfied democrats	Norris (1999): critical citizens
Late 1980s/ early 1990s		Flanagan (1987): authoritarian–libertarian values	Dalton et al. (1987): old and new politics	Inglehart (1990): elite-challenging publics	Putnam (1992): civic community, civic trust, social capital
1970s			Sniderman (1975): personality and democracy	Inglehart (1977): materialist–post-materialist values	Barnes & Kaase (1979): unconventional political participation
1960s		Almond & Verba (1963): the civic culture	Easton (1965): specific and diffuse support	Inkeles (1965): individual modernity	Eckstein (1966): authority orientations, congruence theory
Modern classics		Adorno *et al.* (1950): authoritarian personality	Lasswell (1951): democratic character	Stouffer (1955): political (in) tolerance	Rokeach (1960): the open and closed mind
					Weber (1920): legitimacy beliefs
Classical classics					Tocqueville (1835): *De la Démocratie en Amérique*
					Montesquieu (1756): *De l'Esprit des Lois*
					Aristotle (350 bc): *The Politics*, Book IV

and Welzel 2010; Welzel 2013). Mean national positions on secular values and on emancipative values are highly indicative of the typical state of mind that comes to dominance in a population at certain stages of its socio-economic and socio-political modernization. These values are mental representations of the development of given populations. For this reason, nations cluster on these values into relatively coherent culture zones, reflecting historically similar paths of development (Inglehart and Baker 2000).

In Figure 17.1 each national population's mean position on these two sets of values is plotted including evidence from the most recent WVS and using the most up-to-date measures of secular values[1] and emancipative values.[2] The theoretical range on both dimensions is from zero to 1.0.

The mean national positions on secular values and emancipative values shown in the global cultural map of Figure 17.1 hide considerable intra-national differences along the lines of social class, religion, and ethnicity. In fact, in almost any sample one can find at least some individuals at each corner of the cultural map. Still, it is also true for each national sample that individual respondents cluster in increasing density the closer one comes to the national mean position. These mean positions represent a given nation's cultural gravity centre.

The 'revised theory of modernization' proposed by Inglehart and Welzel (2005) can explain to a considerable

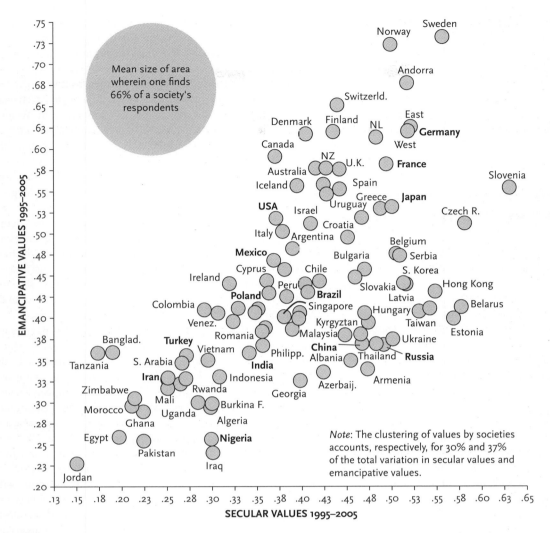

Figure 17.1 A cultural map of the world

extent why national populations take which mean position in both secular and emancipative values. By and large, the process of modernization has brought rising levels of existential security for most of the people in a society. But so far, modernization has favoured two different versions of existential security in two different phases. The industrial phase of modernization has standardized people's life courses through the advancement of bureaucratization. Bureaucracies nurtured a rationalistic world view, which in turn favoured secular values. Secular values are compatible with liberal democracy as well as with industrial forms of authoritarianism. In contrast, the post-industrial phase of modernization has pluralized people's life courses through the advancement of individualization. Individualization nurtures an independent world view, which in turn favours emancipative values. These values are only compatible with liberal democracy (see Box 17.2). As the rise of these values is most fundamental for the

cultural basis of democracy, we will turn to this topic later in this chapter.

Box 17.2 Liberal democracy

The term liberal democracy is not to be misunderstood in an economic sense as a 'market-liberal' democracy that only has a minimal welfare state. Liberal democracy can certainly be a 'market-liberal' democracy but it can also be a 'social-liberal' democracy with an extended welfare state. Hence, the extension of the welfare state is not a definitional criterion of liberal democracy. Instead, the term liberal democracy is to be seen in contrast with electoral democracy. In an electoral democracy, citizens are beneficiaries of political rights but not necessarily of basic civil liberties. In a liberal democracy, in contrast, political rights rest on a solid fundament of civil liberties.

Historical roots of the political culture concept

A basic assumption of the political culture paradigm is that a population's prevailing orientations, beliefs, and values determine the type of political system by which a given population is likely to be governed. This assumption was formulated more than 2300 years ago by Aristotle (c. 350 bc) in Book IV of *The Politics*. In this book, Aristotle argued that democracies emerge from middle-class-dominated societies where an egalitarian ethos is predominant among the citizens.

Here we find the classical formulation of a three-fold causal process in which (1) the social structures characterizing a given population make (2) certain beliefs predominant among its members, which then make (3) specific types of political systems more widely accepted. Thus there is a sequence from social structures to subjective beliefs to the legitimacy of political institutions. This sequence provides an early theory explaining the origins of dictatorship and democracy: hierarchical social structures lead to authoritarian beliefs under which dictatorship becomes the legitimate form of government; horizontal social structures lead to egalitarian beliefs under which democracy becomes the legitimate form of government.

Aristotle's idea that the citizens' beliefs shape political systems seemed realistic in the world of the Greek city-states. In the history of the Greek *polis*, the citizenry itself appeared several times as an 'agent' in engineering political institutions, for instance when popular movements expelled rulers who were considered tyrants (Finer 1999: Vol. II). But the idea of 'civic agency' became unrealistic in the subsequent eras of Roman imperialism and medieval feudalism, falling into oblivion for centuries. Emphasis on the importance of civic agency became widespread again only when the liberal revolutions of early modern times and the first political mass movements brought the people back in as agents of change. Thus, some 2000 years after Aristotle, Montesquieu (1748) argued in *De l'Esprit des Lois* that whether a nation is constituted as a tyranny, a monarchy, or a republic depends on the prevalence of servile, honest, or egalitarian orientations among the people. Likewise, Tocqueville (1835) reasoned in *De la Démocratie en Amérique* that the flourishing of democracy in the US reflects the prevalence of liberal, egalitarian, and participatory orientations among the American people.

In modern times, a disastrous illustration of the fact that people's orientations influence a regime's chances of survival was the failure of democracy in Weimar Germany. Although the Weimar Republic had adopted what was considered a model constitution at its time, the constitutional order lacked legitimacy among much of the public as well as among the conservative elites, who viewed the authoritarian era of the Kaiser as 'the good old days'. In the wake of the Great Depression, the Nazi Party, supported by a plurality of the German electorate, came to power, with catastrophic consequences for the world. For decades, social scientists and intellectuals sought to understand the causes of the Holocaust and the Second World War, and many of them came to the conclusion that a 'democracy without democrats' is unlikely to survive.

In this vein, Lasswell (1951) claimed that democratic regimes emerge and survive where a majority of the people share orientations that are compatible with the operation of democracy. In Lasswell's eyes these orientations are rooted in 'freedom from anxiety', which he saw as nurturing a general 'belief in human potentialities' and a sense of 'self-esteem', as well as a sense of 'respect for others'. Similarly, when Lipset (1959: 85–9) asked why modernization is conducive to democracy, he concluded that modernization changes mass orientations in ways that make them more compatible with the operation of democracy by increasing people's tolerance for opposition, criticism, and political pluralism. In philosophical terms, Popper (1962 [1971]) described these characteristics as the prevailing mindset of *The Open Society*.

In **empirical research** Almond and Verba (1963) and Eckstein (1966) introduced the term 'congruence', arguing that in order to be stable political institutions must accord with people's legitimacy beliefs. This is particularly true of democratic institutions, which cannot survive by repressing mass preferences without corrupting their own principles. The congruence theorem has become the most axiomatic assumption of the political culture school.

The question of citizens' democratic maturity

Almond and Verba's *Civic Culture* study (1963) had an immense influence on subsequent political culture research. Comparing two old democracies (UK and US), two then young democracies (Italy and Germany), and a developing nation (Mexico), this study aimed to identify the psychological attributes of a culture that sustains democracy. In identifying these attributes, the authors emphasized two concepts: civic competence and civic allegiance.

Like most scholars, Almond and Verba assumed that democracies put higher demands on the citizens than authoritarian forms of government. For democracy requires voluntary participation in the political process, at least in elections, to fill positions of power. Even in a limited democracy that restricts mass participation to elections, citizens must understand the electoral process. They must be capable of evaluating what the governing parties have done, and what the alternatives are, in order to make reasonable choices in an election. If these conditions are not met, the electoral process will be irrational and democracy itself is a flawed idea. Thus civic competence is a fundamental precondition for democracy to be meaningful.

Since then the field has explored citizens' political competence. To examine cognitive competence, researchers have developed survey questions asking people about their political knowledge (Zaller 1992). Inspired by an influential study by Converse (1964), scores of researchers demonstrated low levels of political knowledge even among the electorates of the most advanced democracies (McClosky and Brill 1983). Quite often, it was concluded from such studies that one should not burden democracy with too high expectations because the democratic process easily overwhelms most people's capacities. These conclusions then served as a justification for elite-guided, strictly representative versions of democracy. This position rejected any attempt at extending democracy into a more mass-participative version. Indeed, mass apathy was considered a stabilizing feature of democracy (Crozier *et al.* 1975; Dye and Ziegler 1970).

The description of modern mass publics as insufficiently competent has not remained unquestioned (Delli Carpini and Keeter 1996; Lupia and McCubbins 1998). Invoking the theory of informational shortcuts, scholars argue that the demands for voter competence are more modest than the critics of voter sophistication suggest. Politics is a remote area that ranks low in most people's daily priorities, so people economize the time they invest to obtain the information needed to make reasonable judgements. Instead of studying given policy proposals in detail, most people pay attention to how the representatives of various groups position themselves. From this positioning, they draw conclusions about whether or not the proposal is in their own interest. What is important for people to make reasonable choices, then, is to have ready access to reliable clues.

The theory of informational shortcuts shifts the burden of democratic rationality from the expertise of the citizens to the quality of the intermediary system. To be capable of making reasonable choices, the citizens do not themselves need to become political experts. All that is needed is political pluralism, which involves easily identifiable group clues that work as reliable informational shortcuts (Dalton 2006: 20–31).

Another phenomenon that weakens the criticism of incompetent citizens in post-industrial societies is what came to be known as 'cognitive mobilization' (Inglehart 1977; Dalton 2004: 20–31). Scholars argue that rising levels of education, the expansion of intellectual tasks in the growing knowledge sector, and the increasing exposure to informational diversity have all contributed to expand people's ability to arrive at independent judgements of given matters. People's factual political knowledge might not have significantly increased in post-industrial societies (Wattenberg 2006), but their skills in acquiring information and processing it have certainly grown through cognitive mobilization. Thus ordinary people have become more capable of making independent judgements. One piece of evidence that clearly supports this interpretation is the so-called 'Flynn effect': in all populations among whom IQ tests have been carried out repeatedly for many years, one finds a significant, continuous, and in many cases remarkable increase in test scores over recent decades (Flynn 2007).

Civic competence has not only an objective cognitive component, but also a subjective perceptual component. Subjective political competence was defined by Almond and Verba (1963: Chapter 8) as people feeling that they understand the political process and the belief that they can participate in meaningful ways, and—when they do so—that it helps to change things for the better. Certainly citizens can grossly misperceive their political competence. But, whether misperceived or not, subjective competence is a political orientation that has significant consequences: people who feel competent and efficacious about what they can contribute are more likely to participate in politics. They have a stronger sense of agency, which generally motivates action (Verba *et al.* 1995).

KEY POINTS

- Democracies put a higher burden on citizens' information-processing capacities than other regimes.

- Cognitive mobilization and other processes related to the rise of knowledge societies seem to have improved citizens' information-processing abilities.

The allegiance model of the democratic citizen

As much as Almond and Verba's (1963) *Civic Culture* study emphasized civic competence, it also emphasized the importance of civic allegiance. In contrast with competence, allegiance is an affective mode of orientation. A minimum of civic competence is thought to be necessary to make the democratic process rational. But the democratic process not only needs to be rational; in order to survive, democracy also needs to be widely accepted and to be seen as the most desirable way to organize politics. Accordingly, Almond and Verba considered a basic sense of allegiance to the norms, institutions, and actors of democracy as an attribute of the ideal democratic citizen.

The emphasis on allegiance was inspired by Easton's (1965b) concept of political support. Easton thought that, because modern polities mobilize the masses into politics, these polities need mass support. This is particularly true of democracies, which allow collective actors to compete for power—which involves the possibility of voting anti-democratic actors into office who might then abandon democracy. To minimize this possibility, mass support for democracy must be sufficiently widespread, so that anti-democratic forces have little chance of winning elections. In a stable democracy, citizen disaffection must be limited to particular policies and specific actors; it must not turn into dissatisfaction with the democratic process and the basic principles of democracy, especially representation. Democracy can cope with low levels of 'specific' support for concrete policies and particular actors, but it cannot cope with the absence of 'diffuse' support for its basic norms, principles, and institutions.

Among scholars concerned with political support, the ideal democratic citizen is usually seen as a person who takes part in elections and other forms of *elite-mandating* participation that are necessary to make representation work. But the ideal citizen is not supposed to become active in non-institutionalized ways that challenge representatives. This is because representation is the constitutive principle of modern democracies. To retain legitimacy, this principle needs reliable party–voter alignments. This requires voters to be loyal to representatives once they have been voted into office. Allegiant democratic citizens do not disobey or oppose decisions made by democratically elected representatives. They accept the leadership role of their representatives and when they are not in line with their policies, they respond by changing their political alignment. The allegiance model holds that allegiant democratic citizens must operate within party–voter alignments. They can change their alignment but not operate in a free-floating space outside alignments. In the allegiant model, specific support for particular actors and parties is allowed to erode but it must be compensated by realignments to new actors and parties, if the principle of representation is to continue to work.

As a consequence, the allegiance model holds that democracy is in danger when party–voter alignments decrease in general. Three decades of growing evidence from cross-national survey data seem to suggest that exactly this has been happening throughout post-industrial societies (Dalton and Wattenberg 2000).

> **KEY POINTS**
>
> - The allegiance model of the ideal democratic citizen favours the limitation of citizen political activity to elite-mandating forms of participation.

Party–voter dealignment

The allegiance model of citizenship came under strain with the emergence of protest politics and new social movements in the late 1960s. Scholars who believed that democracy suffers from mass mobilization outside institutionalized channels viewed this development with alarm, fearing that government would be overloaded with excessive demands by publics who were too highly mobilized. It was argued that civic mobilization outside the channels of representative institutions will render governments unable to fulfil increasingly inflated mass demands. This will disappoint the citizens and democratic institutions will fall into disfavour. Thus the emergence of a legitimacy crisis and a governability crisis were predicted as the consequence of increasingly elite-challenging masses (Crozier *et al.* 1975).

However, the first comparative empirical study of protest politics reached different conclusions (Barnes and Kaase 1979). Based on surveys of representative samples in the US, Great Britain, Germany, the Netherlands, Austria, and other countries, the study found that:

(1) protest participants had higher levels of formal education and greater political skills, and felt more efficacious than non-participants;

(2) protest participants emphasized democratic norms *more* strongly, not less strongly, than non-participants;

(3) protest participants were in general more engaged and active than non-participants.

Parallel studies on new social movements in the fields of environmental protection, gender equality, human rights, fair trade, and equal opportunities obtained similar findings (Tarrow 1998; McAdam *et al.* 2001; Dalton, van Sickle, and Weldon 2009). This line of research has helped reshape our understanding of protest behaviour and its role in democratic politics.

For a long time the predominant explanation of elite-challenging mass activities was influenced by deprivation theories designed to explain violent mass upheavals (Gurr 1970). But collective violence is a way of expressing dissent that differs fundamentally from the peaceful forms of mass protest observed in post-industrial societies since the late 1960s. Still, the assumption of deprivation theories that some sense of grievance and frustration motivates protest behaviour strongly influenced the initial views on the rising protest movements in post-industrial societies. But what is true for the supporters of violent activities—that frustration about social marginalization is a prime motivation—is not true for peaceful forms of dissent in advanced post-industrial societies. It is not marginalized parts of the population and the people who are most deprived of basic resources who constitute the mass base for elite-challenging activities. Rather, it is those who have relatively high levels of participatory resources, including the skills, education, and networks that enable them to launch or join in various campaign activities (Dalton and Kuechler 1990; Verba *et al.* 1995; Dalton, van Sickle, and Weldon 2009).

Post-industrial society (Bell 1973) has been linked with rising levels of formal education, more easily accessible information, improved means of communication and mobility, and wider opportunities to connect people across the boundaries of locality, ethnicity, religion, or class (Inkeles and Smith 1975). These processes have increased the part of the population possessing the participatory resources that are key to the campaign activities nurturing social movements and mass pressures on elites. Surprising as it may seem, societies that are most advanced in providing their populations with long, secure, prosperous, and entertaining lives show the highest rates of protest activity. In other words, people are more likely to initiate and sustain civic forms of protest activity when their objective living conditions are more comfortable, not more miserable (Welzel *et al.* 2005).

This is surprising only if one believes that raising one's voice results from suffering. This can and does happen, of course, but then it is often an eruptive and violent outbreak of collective frustration that implodes as quickly as it surfaced. Suburban riots illustrate this pattern. Misery-induced types of protest are more radical in form but usually not sustainable over time because the most deprived lack in many ways the resources needed to express dissent repeatedly and continuously. Moderate, yet continuous, forms of protest activity are more prevalent where people have the capability to mount and sustain pressures and where they have adopted the critical attitudes that motivate the expression of dissent. As Inglehart (1977, 1990, 1997) has argued, the transition from industrial to post-industrial societies increases both factors, enabling as well as motivating citizens to put elites under increasingly effective mass pressures.

KEY POINTS

- Party–voter dealignment and other processes of group dealignment linked to post-industrial individualization trends have eroded the allegiance model of democratic citizenship.

The assertive model of the democratic citizen

Rising emancipative values

The rise of post-industrial societies nurtures elite-challenging mass activities in two ways. On one hand, it increases the participatory resources that *enable* people to initiate and sustain the kinds of activities that put pressure on elites. On the other hand, it is conducive to value changes that bring increasing emphasis on emancipatory attitudes that *motivate* people to make their voices heard. Both objectively and subjectively, post-industrial mass publics are more likely to keep elites under sustained pressure to respond to their demands.

This process was described in Inglehart's *Silent Revolution* (1977). The author argues that post-industrial society brings 'existential security', which is conducive to a rising emphasis on post-materialist values. These values give high priority to participation and freedom of expression. At the same time, post-industrial society advances the process of cognitive mobilization that makes people increasingly skilled in expressing their preferences and making themselves heard.

In his subsequent work, Inglehart (1990, 1997) argues that post-materialist priorities are part of a broader syndrome of 'self-expression values' whose components are held together by an emphasis on freedom of choice and equality of opportunities. Since self-expression values are a broad phenomenon that permeates a wide range of life domains, it can be measured by various combinations of attitudes. Inglehart and his collaborators have continued to improve the measurement of these values using data from the World Values Survey (www.worldvaluessurvey.org). The most refined and updated measurement of these values has recently been presented by Welzel (2013) under the label 'emancipative values'. These values focus on the four emancipatory goals outlined in endnote 2:

(1) an emphasis on *voice* reflected in post-materialist priorities that give people more say in important government decisions and how things are done at their jobs and in their communities, and for protecting freedom of speech;

(2) an emphasis on *choice* reflected in the acceptance of divorce, abortion, and homosexuality;

(3) an emphasis on *equality* reflected in support for women having equal access to education, work, and power;

(4) an emphasis on *autonomy* reflected in support for independence and imagination, but not obedience, as important qualities for children to learn.

The average position of national populations on the index of emancipative values varies between a score of 0.22 for Iraq and 0.75 for Sweden. All ninety-five populations included in the WVS show single-peaked and mean-centred distributions on this index of emancipative values.

As Flanagan and Lee (2003) show, modern values such as these grow stronger with the rise of post-industrial societies. This type of society satisfies most people's fundamental survival needs and expands their capacities to exercise freedoms. Thus, freedoms gain in utility in a very objective sense. As people become aware of this they emphasize freedoms more, which is reflected in stronger emancipative values. With growing emancipative values, democratic institutions that allow people to exercise freedoms obtain an increasing impact on people's life satisfaction (Inglehart *et al.* 2008; Welzel and Inglehart 2010).

Based on prior work by Inglehart and Welzel (2005), Welzel (2013) argues that the close connection that ties emancipative values to socio-economic development, on the one hand, and effective democracy, on the other hand, reflects a broader process of 'human empowerment'. In this framework (see Figure 17.2), socio-economic development empowers people on the level of *abilities* by widening the means, skills, and opportunities that enable them to exercise democratic freedoms. Emancipative values empower people on the level of *motivations* by increasing the priority they give to exercising democratic freedoms. Finally, effective democracy empowers people on the level of *entitlements* by giving them the rights to exercise democratic freedoms. Emerging from a broad process of human empowerment, democracy becomes increasingly effective in response to people's growing motivation to exercise freedoms, which in turn reflects their growing ability to do so.

In line with the human empowerment model, emancipative values have been on the rise throughout the post-industrial world, as Figure 17.3 illustrates. And, increasingly emancipative publics emphasize new citizenship norms (Dalton 2008). As Dalton and Welzel (Welzel 2013) note, rising emancipative values turn allegiant citizens into assertive citizens for whom the role of a loyal and obedient follower of elected elites loses appeal. This is a major reason why Putnam (2000) observes in *Bowling Alone* a decline in various types of civic activities, including participation in elections and voluntary work in a number of formal associations. Most of these activities are linked with the allegiance model of citizenship in which citizens are supposed to mandate elites to make

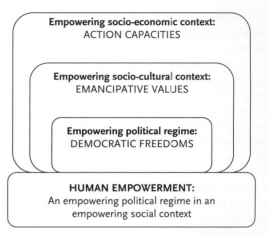

Figure 17.2 The human empowerment concept

choices for them. But this decline in elite-mandating activities is only one side of the coin. The other side is an *increase* in activities linked to the new assertive model of citizenship. Citizens are less attracted by those parts of the democratic process that are designed to mandate elites. They are more attracted to activities in which they express themselves and challenge elites. This is part of the explanation why Norris (2002) in *Democratic Phoenix* finds various forms of self-initiated and elite-challenging activities to be on a long-term rise.

The assertive model of citizenship has far-reaching consequences, some of which are outlined below. These consequences are strikingly evident from the temporally and spatially widest exploration into political culture ever carried out, the WVS.

KEY POINTS

- As part of a broader process of human empowerment, emancipative values have been on the rise throughout post-industrial societies during the past decades.

Criticality and disaffection

As outlined by Nevitte (1996) in *Decline of Deference* and by Norris (1999) in *Critical Citizens*, the value changes that accompany the post-industrial transformation of modern societies make people increasingly critical of institutionalized authority over them. Indeed, all societies for which survey data are available over a considerable time series show a decline of people's confidence in hierarchically structured mass organizations and in institutions that exert authority over people, as Dalton (2004) demonstrates in *Democratic Choices—Democratic Challenges*.

This tendency affects representative institutions directly, because the principle of representation is designed to transfer authority from the people to institutions.

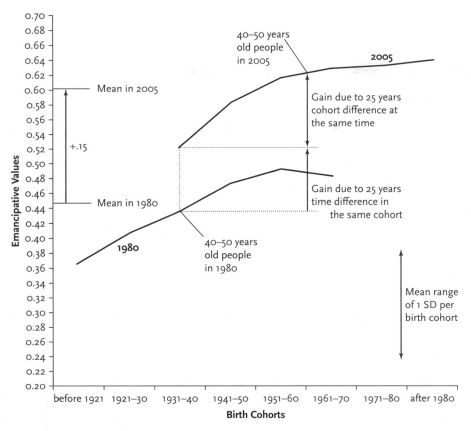

Figure 17.3 The rise of emancipative values in post-industrial societies

Note: Evidence based on samples from Australia, Canada, France, West Germany, Italy, Japan, Netherlands, Norway, Sweden, US, and UK. Each sample weighted to a size of *N* = 1000.

Source: WVS I (1981–3) and WVS V (2005–7).

Accordingly, rates of confidence in parliaments and identification with political parties have shown a long-term decline (Dalton and Wattenberg 2000). These tendencies seem to be most pronounced in societies where emancipative values have become strongest.

In keeping with these findings, the evidence in Figure 17.4 shows that individuals with stronger emancipative values have lower 'vertical' trust in institutions of order (i.e. the police and the military) but higher 'horizontal' trust in their fellow citizens. This tendency is most pronounced in 'strongly emancipative' societies in which emancipative values are most widespread: individuals with the same scores on these values show lower levels of vertical trust and higher levels of horizontal trust when they live in societies where emancipative values are more widespread.

Efficacious and elite-challenging publics

These trends are reshaping political life. Parallel to people's growing dissatisfaction with politics in representative channels, they are gaining a growing sense of efficacy about their ability to shape their lives. This rising sense of 'civic agency' seems to be a consequence of the activating tendencies linked with rising emancipative values. As Inglehart *et al.* (2008) demonstrate, throughout post-industrial societies, people have been developing a rising sense of efficacy.

This has important implications for a society's capacity to initiate and sustain elite-challenging actions, and thus for democratic mass power. It is known from protest mobilization research that some sort of grievance provides an important motivation for the mass actions that challenge elites (Klandermans 1997). But grievance is only a necessary but not sufficient condition to motivate people to elite-challenging actions. When grievance goes together with low feelings of efficacy, it results in resignation and passivity. Only when grievance goes together with strong feelings of efficacy do people feel encouraged to actively express their concerns in public. Hence, the combination of grievance with a growing sense of agency has a powerful effect on a public's tendency to initiate and sustain elite-challenging activities.

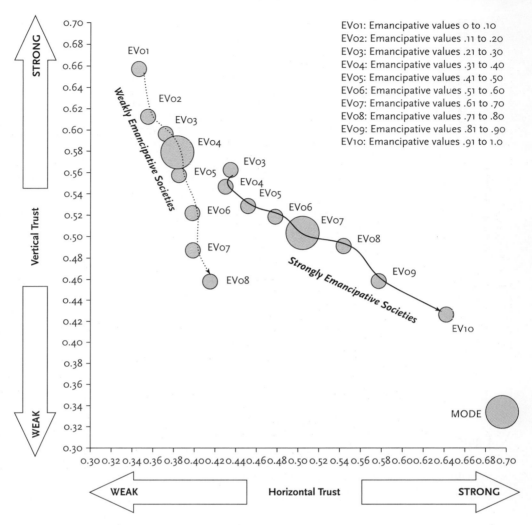

Figure 17.4 Emancipative values, vertical trust, and horizontal trust

Notes: 'Weakly emancipative societies' score below 0.33 scale points; they include Burkina Faso, China, Egypt, Ghana, India, Indonesia, Iran, Iraq, Jordan, Mali, Morocco, Russia, Rwanda, Thailand, Turkey, Ukraine, and Vietnam. 'Strongly emancipative societies' score above 0.5 scale points; they include Andorra, Argentina, Australia, Canada, Finland, Germany (West and East), Italy, Japan, Netherlands, New Zealand, Norway, Slovenia, Spain, Sweden, Switzerland, UK, US, and Uruguay. All national samples are weighted to equal size (*N* = 1000).

Horizontal axis ranges from a theoretical minimum of zero when no respondent in a society reports trust in other people to a theoretical maximum of 1.0 when each respondent reports trust.

Vertical axis ranges from a theoretical minimum of zero when each respondent in a society reports no confidence at all in the police, the army, and the civil service to a theoretical maximum of 1.0 when each respondent in a society reports a great deal of confidence in each of these institutions.

Indeed, as the evidence in Figure 17.5 indicates, individuals with stronger emancipative values have a stronger sense of agency and a stronger affinity to elite-challenging actions. Again, this tendency is more pronounced in societies where emancipative values are more widespread.

KEY POINTS

Emancipative values make citizens:
- more critical of and disloyal to representative institutions;
- more efficacious and elite-challenging in their political actions.

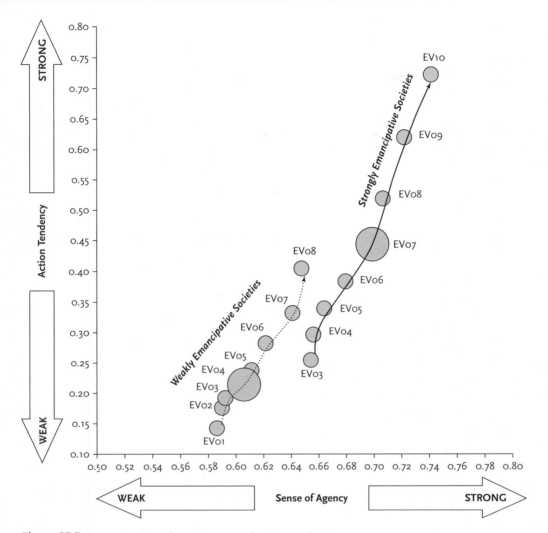

Figure 17.5 Emancipative values, agency, and action tendencies

Notes: Horizontal axis ranges from a theoretical minimum of zero when each respondent in a society reports having no choice at all about how his/her life turns out to a theoretical maximum of 1.0 when each respondent of a society reports having a great deal of choice about how his/her life turns out.

Vertical axis ranges from a theoretical minimum of zero when each respondent of a society reports not having participated in a petition, boycott, or demonstration to a theoretical maximum of 1.0 when each respondent in a society reports having participated in each of these activities.

Democracy: more liberal understanding, more critical assessment

With rising emancipative values, the democratic idea that power belongs to the people resonates more strongly in a society. This has two consequences. First, people's understanding of democracy becomes more liberal: people base their definition of democracy more on the freedoms that empower people and less on strong leadership and popular policy outcomes such as order and prosperity. This is demonstrated by the results from a battery of questions fielded for the first time in the most recent round of the WVS. These questions ask people to indicate, among ten different characteristics, whether they consider them essential characteristics of democracy, using a scale from 1 ('not at all a defining element of democracy') to 10 ('absolutely a defining element of democracy'). These items include liberal characteristics, such as free elections, civil liberties, and equal rights. However, they also include populist issues, such as punishing criminals harshly or having economic prosperity, and outright anti-liberal items, such as military takeovers. When one examines how people define democracy, it is clear that emphasis on 'liberal' characteristics is linked with stronger emphasis on emancipative values (see Figure 17.7).

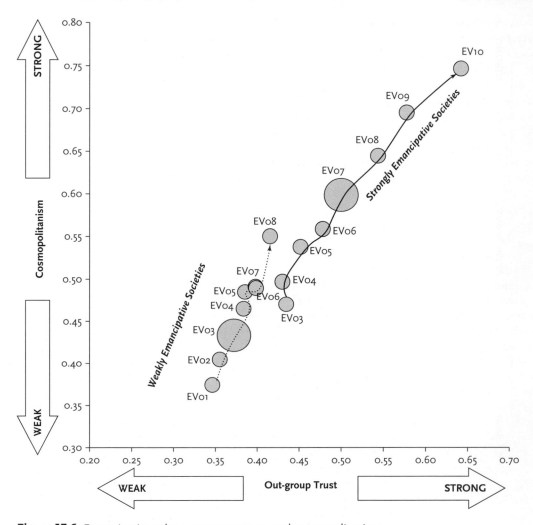

Figure 17.6 Emancipative values, out-group trust, and cosmopolitanism

Notes: Horizontal axis ranges from a theoretical minimum of zero, when each respondent in a society reports no trust at all in people one meets for the first time, people of a different nationality, and people of a different religion, to a theoretical maximum of 1.0, when each respondent in a society reports complete trust in each of these three groups of people.

Vertical axis has a theoretical minimum of zero when each respondent in a society supports an ethnocentric form of citizenship ('having ancestors from my country'), rejects ethnic diversity, and emphasizes identity categories that establish group boundaries (locality, nation) at the expense of categories that defy such boundaries (individual, world). The theoretical maximum is 1.0 when each respondent in a society holds opposite attitudes on each of these three accounts.

It is also true that people who emphasize emancipative values assess their society's actual level of democracy more critically than others. This becomes evident when one uses Freedom House's expert ratings of democracy as an indicator. The 2007 round of the WVS asked people to rate their country's level of democracy on a scale from 1 ('not at all democratic') to 10 ('fully democratic'). If one compares people's democracy ratings of their country with the ratings that Freedom House assigns it, one finds that their 'subjective' personal ratings often deviate from the 'objective' expert ratings that Freedom House assigns that country. One can interpret these discrepancies as indications of an uncritical versus critical assessment of democracy. The more a respondent overrates his/her country's level of democracy relative to the expert ratings, the more 'uncritical' is the democracy assessment. Vice versa, the more a respondent underrates his/her country's level of democracy relative to the expert ratings, the more critically he/she assesses democracy.

Comparing these ratings, it becomes clear that people with stronger emancipative values assess their country's state of democracy more critically than people with other values (see Figure 17.7). Objectively, people who emphasize emancipative values are more likely to live in democracies than those who do not. Subjectively, however, people with emancipative values assess their own society's level of democracy more critically than others. Again, the tendency is more pronounced—in this case, much more pronounced—in strongly emancipative than in weakly emancipative societies.

Wider circles of solidarity and trust

One of the most surprising findings from this body of research is that rising emphasis on emancipative values is not linked with greater selfishness, as Flanagan and Lee (2003) assume. On the contrary, the evidence is clear that stronger emphasis on emancipative values widens the circle of others with whom people build up a sense of solidarity (Welzel 2010).

Emancipative values are weak when pressing existential conditions force people into bonding behaviour, in which case people ally with members of their in-group while discriminating against members of out-groups (Tajfel 1970). When more favourable existential conditions give rise to emancipative values, group boundaries become more variegated, porous, and permeable (Simmel 1908 [1984]). This diminishes both the forcefulness of intra-group harmony and the fierceness of inter-group conflict, allowing people to overcome bonding behaviour and to engage in bridging behaviour. This process places human solidarity on a different basis. Familiarity, belongingness, and alikeness with others become less important, while mutually agreed interests and empathy with the situation of others become more important factors in creating a sense of solidarity. Group affinity becomes more intrinsically chosen and less externally enforced.

Evidence supporting these claims is provided by the 2005–7 round of the WVS which uses a battery of items to distinguish between 'in-group' trust (towards related and familiar others) and 'out-group' trust (towards unrelated and dissimilar others).Another set of questions makes it possible to measure cosmopolitanism based on the extent to which people (1) reject a xenophobic notion of citizenship, (2) tolerate ethnic diversity, and (3) define themselves by identity categories that transcend rather than establish group boundaries. Analysing the responses to these questions, Figure 17.6 demonstrates that people with strong emancipative values have stronger out-group trust and a more cosmopolitan orientation. Once again, these tendencies are most pronounced in societies with a strong emphasis on emancipative values.

Similarly, Welzel (2010) finds that stronger emancipative values not only go together with stronger individualistic values (which is not surprising) but also with

stronger altruistic values. Apparently, emancipative values merge individualism and altruism into what one might call humanism.

These findings seem paradoxical if one equates individualism with selfishness, which is a widespread misconception. Scholars often think of collectivism as the basis of human solidarity and of individualism as its antipode (Triandis 2001). In fact, however, individualism does not destroy solidarity but places it on a different basis. This was recognized early on by sociologists such as Durkheim (1893/1988) and Tonnies (1887/1955). They described the individualization trend of modernity as bringing a transition from 'mechanical' solidarity to 'organic' solidarity or from 'community' to 'association'. Both descriptions refer to a transition from externally imposed solidarity to internally chosen forms of solidarity. Beck (2002) describes the solidarity effects of individualization in similar terms, speaking of a transition from 'communities of necessity' to 'elective affinities'. Empirical research of interpersonal networks supports the view that modern individualized societies integrate people into more widespread and more diverse solidarity networks.

Collectivism means that people see others not as autonomous individuals but as group members by birth (Triandis 2001). When group categorization dominates people's views of others, people tend to privilege members of their own group and discriminate against members of other groups (Tajfel 1970). Collectivism in this sense is a form of group-egoism that hinders the creation of solidarities beyond group boundaries. Individualism, by contrast, means that one does not consider others as members of groups in the first place but as autonomous individuals. This orientation provides a common ground—personhood—on which one can place all people equally. Consequently, individualism and altruism go together with emphasis on emancipative values (Welzel 2010).

> **KEY POINTS**
>
> Emancipative values make citizens:
> - more liberal in their understanding of democracy and more critical in the assessment of its operation,
> - more open and tolerant in their attitude towards out-groups.

Emancipative values as a democratizing motivational force

If one examines the aggregate levels of emancipative values across societies, these values appear to be a good indicator of overall life quality on various dimensions.

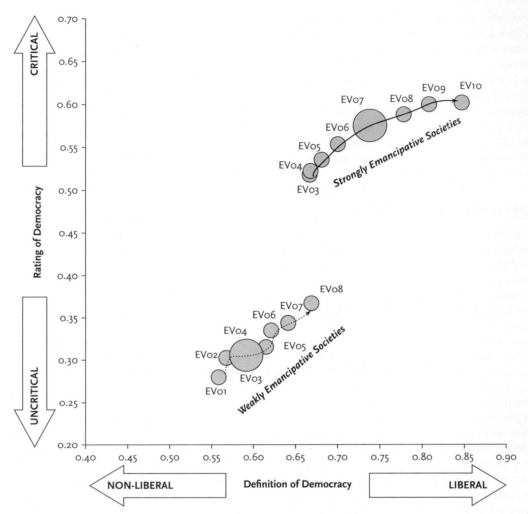

Figure 17.7 Emancipative values, understandings of democracy, and assessments of democracy

Notes: Horizontal axis has a theoretical minimum of zero when each respondent in a society considers free elections, civil liberties, equal rights, and referendums not at all an essential characteristic of democracy, while considering military takeovers, religious authority, punishing criminals, and prosperity absolutely essential characteristics of democracy. The theoretical maximum is at 1.0 when each respondent of a society takes the exact opposite position.

Vertical axis has a theoretical minimum of zero when each respondent in a society rates his/her country as absolutely democratic while Freedom House gives it the lowest political rights and civil liberties rating in the year of the survey. The theoretical maximum is at 1.0 when each respondent in a society rates his/her country not at all democratic while Freedom House gives it the highest political rights and civil liberties rating in the year of the survey.

On the one hand, this is evident from the fact that these values are closely associated with almost any indicator of socio-economic development, as Inglehart and Welzel (2005: 150) have demonstrated. As they argue, this relationship exists because the fading of existential threats on a mass level tends to give rise to emancipative values.

An equally strong relationship exists between emancipative values and indicators of the quality of a society's institutions. Measures of democracy and of 'good governance', including rule of law, absence of corruption, and accountable governance, all correlate strongly positively with emancipative values at the mass level (Inglehart and Welzel 2005: 151). Here the causal relationship seems to operate in a different direction. Emancipative values do not primarily result from democratic and accountable governance; instead, the true causal connection is that increasing emphasis on emancipative values motivates elite-challenging mass actions, which help to remove authoritarian elites from power and to make democratic elites behave in a more responsive manner (Welzel 2007: 417–18). Thus emancipative mass values constitute an important motivational force in bringing about democracy where it does not yet exist and in strengthening it where it is already in place.

Implicit regime affinities and explicit regime preferences

Emancipative values are inherently conducive to democratic institutions because they emphasize autonomous choice in all domains of life, including the political. This implies a rejection of unlimited authority over people, making authoritarian systems illegitimate. Because of this, emancipative values imply an inherently pro-democratic regime affinity. The civil and political freedoms that define democracy intuitively resonate with these values.

Because they are anchored in people's values, regime affinities have strong motivational power, even though these affinities are only implicit. Regime preferences, by contrast, are explicit but their motivational effects are uncertain. In surveys, people express a preference for democracy for many reasons. It might be that they are influenced by the current social desirability of the term or that they prefer democracy simply because they associate it with other desirable things, such as prosperity, peace, and low corruption (Inglehart 2003). In these cases the motivation to prefer democracy is not based on an intrinsic valuation of the freedoms that define democracy, making it unlikely that these preferences strongly motivate people to struggle for democratic freedoms. However, when people value freedoms intrinsically, as they do when they emphasize emancipation, there is a strong motivation to struggle for democratic freedoms as something good in itself. In this case the emergence of effective mass pressures in support of these freedoms is more likely.

Accordingly, Welzel (2013) finds that the implicit affinities to democracy inherent in emancipative values provide a stronger force in sustaining and attaining democracy than do explicit preferences for democracy. Emancipative values motivate people to initiate and sustain elite-challenging actions that mount effective pressure on power-holders, even if the political system is undemocratic and confronts people with the risk of suppression (Welzel 2007).

From the perspective of this research, the mainstream in political culture research has been misguided in focusing on measuring explicit regime preferences (asking if people prefer democratic institutions) rather than intrinsic regime affinities based on moral values.

KEY POINTS

- Emancipative values are a more valid indicator of true mass demands for democracy than explicit regime preferences for democracy.

Trust, confidence, and social capital

Putnam's *Making Democracy Work* (1993) paid renewed attention to the political culture approach in comparative politics. In stark contrast with neo-institutional approaches, his study seemed to demonstrate that differences in the design of institutions are of secondary relevance and that civic traditions account for most of the differences in explaining a community's political performance.

For good reasons, Putnam's understanding of social capital emphasizes psychological orientations that facilitate human interaction. The orientation supposed to be most instrumental in this respect is interpersonal trust. Trust is understood to overcome collective action dilemmas, for people who trust others do not see themselves in the prisoner's dilemma when interacting with people (Uslaner 2001). Hence, interpersonal trust shapes the collective action capacity of a society. It enables the masses to initiate and sustain the actions that put elites under popular pressure and make them responsive.

Interpersonal trust certainly increases a society's collective action capacity. But it does not tell us for which ends this capacity will be used because purely by itself trust is not directed towards a particular end, such as democratic freedoms. This is often overlooked in theories of trust. However, research based on the WVS shows that trust matters mostly in conjunction with emancipative values, not in isolation from them. In isolation from orientations that give trust a direction, trust does not show a strongly pro-democratic effect, neither in helping to attain democracy nor in sustaining it (Welzel 2007: 405).

Another aspect of trust that has been considered important for democracy is political trust, usually measured as confidence in a set of basic societal institutions, such as the national parliament or the civil service. Inspired by the allegiance model of democratic citizenship, scholars assume that in order to flourish, democracy needs people who place trust in basic institutions. However, evidence that a society's democratic performance depends on the amount of the citizens' political trust is non-existent. On the contrary, Welzel (2007: 405) finds that higher political trust affects a society's democratic performance negatively, even after controlling for a society's democratic tradition and various other factors. Accordingly, low levels, not high levels, of political trust are conducive to democracy.

From the viewpoint of Norris's *Critical Citizens* (1999), this finding is not surprising. From this perspective, low political trust can be interpreted as a widespread critical attitude towards authorities and such a critical attitude can be a source of the mass pressures that help to keep the elites responsive.

When social capital is understood to include orientations that motivate people to initiate and sustain collective actions, emancipative values should certainly be included in the notion of social capital. For these values motivate people to undertake collective actions, especially the elite-challenging actions that have been found to help in bringing about and strengthening democracy. In that sense, emancipative values constitute a particularly pro-democratic form of social capital.

Conclusion

Declining social capital or growing human *empowerment*?

Two main approaches exist for interpreting ongoing cultural changes in post-industrial societies. Both of them view individualization as a key trend in post-industrial societies, but they interpret this trend in opposite ways. Influenced by Putnam's *Bowling Alone* (2000), the declining social capital approach views individualization as a process that erodes trust between people, brings growing selfishness, and diminishes collective action. This interpretation sees individualization as a threat to democracy.

In contrast, the progressing human empowerment approach proposed by Welzel (2013) interprets individualization as a positive trend that empowers people to shape their commitments, solidarities, and actions as they prefer. This author sees individualization as conducive to democracy.

In our view, progressing human empowerment offers an explanation that accounts for a wider range of phenomena than declining social capital. Some types of association are indeed declining, and some types of collective action are decreasing—but others are increasing. Declining social capital can only account for the decreasing part. Progressing human empowerment, in contrast, explains both trends as opposite sides of the same coin. Modernization transforms life from something dictated by needs into a source of opportunities. This process makes people agents in shaping their lives. Accordingly, all kinds of commitments and activities that are imposed by external needs tend to decrease. But, by the same token, all kinds of commitments and activities that are nurtured by intrinsic choices tend to increase. The two are flip sides of the same coin.

KEY POINTS

- With declining social capital, one can only explain the downward trends in some political culture variables but not the upward trends in other political culture variables.

- With progressing human empowerment, one can explain both the downward and upward trends in different political culture variables.

Political economy or political culture?

Both the political economy approach and the political culture approach argue that modernization works in favour of democracy, but their claims contradict each other. From the point of view of Acemoglu and Robinson (2006), modernization favours democracy because it brings growing income equality and capital mobility that make democracy more acceptable to elites. From the political culture viewpoint (Inglehart and Welzel 2005), modernization favours democracy because the masses become increasingly effective in struggling for democracy, and increasingly motivated to demand democratization from the elites.

These opposing views reflect different understandings of democracy and its motivating forces. In political economy it is thought that the driving force behind democracy is the demand of the impoverished masses for universal suffrage in order to obtain economic redistribution. It is assumed that the masses profit from universal suffrage because it enables them to impose redistributive policies, and so their demand for democracy is a constant. The privileged elites, in contrast, fear it for exactly the same reason. Thus authoritarian regimes do not survive because the majority of the public does not prefer democracy—the majority always prefers democracy. Instead, authoritarian regimes survive because elites are able to repress the majority. Consequently, the only way democracy can be established is to make elites accept it and concede it to the masses. Modernization tends to equalize the income distribution so that mass demands for redistribution become less radical. As a consequence, democracy becomes less threatening to the elites. Eventually, elites may come to see continuing repression of mass demands for democracy as more costly than conceding democracy.

From a historical perspective, these assumptions seem doubtful. Throughout history, most authoritarian regimes did not survive mainly because of their ability to suppress dissenting majorities, but because until recently they were not confronted with well-organized and motivated dissenting majorities. This reflects the fact that throughout most of pre-modern history the masses had neither the capabilities nor the motivation to express and organize political dissent (Gat 2006: 570–661; Nolan and Lenski 1999: 233–55). The major effect of modernization is not that it makes democracy more acceptable to elites, but that it confronts elites with increasingly articulate, capable, and motivated masses. When the masses become able and motivated to struggle for democratic freedoms, the elites are left with little choice in the matter.

Moreover, it is not true that the masses invariably prefer democracy. Throughout most of history, vast numbers of people accepted such legitimating myths as the divine right of kings. How strongly people take action in demanding democracy depends on their values—and mass demands for democracy become stronger as people place increasing emphasis on human freedom and emancipation. The strength of mass demands for democracy is definitely not a constant, as the political economy model assumes. Furthermore, it seems evident that the most recent wave of democratization was not simply motivated by mass desires for greater income equality. In the ex-communist countries, regimes that provided high levels of economic equality but low levels of freedom were replaced by regimes that provide much less economic equality but much higher levels of freedom.

While political economists assume that the motivating force behind democracy is a mass desire for universal suffrage in order to obtain economic redistribution, from the political culture point of view it is largely a struggle for freedom on the part of increasingly articulate, organized, and motivated masses. Future research should clarify to what extent these opposing emphases can be reconciled.

KEY POINTS

- The political economy approach argues that modernization favours democracy because it makes democracy more acceptable in the eyes of the elites.

- The political culture approach argues that modernization favours democracy because it confronts elites with more capable and ambitious mass publics.

Questions

1. Is culture or the economy more important for understanding political modernization?

2. What is the difference between norms, values, and beliefs?

3. Can one say that there are distinct national cultures?

4. What is the difference between secular and emancipative values?

5. Do civilizations matter for politics? How compact are world religions and major cultures?

6. What is stated by the allegiance model of the democratic citizen?

7. How can one define social capital and trust?

8. How important are secular values in the modern world?

9. Does political culture affect the functioning of political institutions and how?

10. Are all cultures compatible with or conducive to democracy?

Further reading

Almond, G. A. and Verba, S. (1963) *The Civic Culture: Political Attitudes and Democracy in Five Nations* (Princeton, NJ: Princeton University Press).

Dalton, R. J. and Welzel, C. (2013) *The Civic Culture Transformed: From Allegiant to Assertive Citizenship* (New York: Cambridge University Press).

Huntington, S. P. (1995) *The Clash of Civilizations and the Remaking of World Order* (New York: Simon & Schuster).

Inglehart, R. (1977) *The Silent Revolution: Changing Values and Political Styles Among Western Publics* (Princeton, NJ: Princeton University Press).

Inglehart, R. (1997) *Modernization and Postmodernization: Cultural, Economic and Political Change in 43 Societies* (Princeton, NJ: Princeton University Press).

Inglehart, R. and Norris, P. (2003) *Rising Tide: Gender Equality and Cultural Change Around the World* (Cambridge: Cambridge University Press).

Putnam, R. D. (1993) *Making Democracy Work: Civic Traditions in Modern Italy* (Princeton, NJ: Princeton University Press).

Putnam, R. D. (2000) *Bowling Alone: The Collapse and Revival of American Community* (New York: Simon & Schuster).

Welzel, C. (2013) *Freedom Rising: Human Empowerment and the Quest for Emancipation* (New York: Cambridge University Press).

Web links

www.cses.org
Comparative Study of Electoral Systems.

www.issp.org
International Social Survey Program.

www.globalbarometer.org
Global Barometers Project.

www.worldvaluessurvey.org
World Values Surveys.

For additional material and resources, please visit the Online Resource Centre at:

online resource centre

www.oxfordtextbooks.co.uk/orc/caramani3e/

CHAPTER 18

Political participation

Herbert Kitschelt and Philipp Rehm

Chapter contents

Reader's guide

This chapter tackles one of the most ubiquitous, *yet also* least understood phenomena in political science. Political participation covers a wide range of activities, from turning out to vote, to giving money to a campaign, to outright violence in the streets. This chapter addresses four fundamental questions. First, it explores different modes of political participation. How does it happen? How intense and how risky is political participation? Second, the chapter sheds some light on the motivation for political participation. Why do people engage in participation? If they do, why are they choosing one way of participation over another? Third, we want to know under which contextual conditions participation is more likely. What is the role of economic affluence? Are there systematic differences between democracies and autocracies? Finally, the chapter turns to the motivations of individuals to engage in participation. Who participates and why are some people more likely to become involved in politics than others?

Introduction

Political participation establishes links from the mass public to the political elites. The term refers to a wide range of activities, including voting in elections, donating time or money to political campaigns, running for office, writing petitions, boycotting, organizing in unions, demonstrating, carrying out illegal sit-ins or occupations, blockades, and even physical assault on the forces of order.

Democracy does not work without the (voluntary and legal) political participation of its citizens. Consider, for example, the following famous definition of democracy as 'a system in which parties lose elections' (Przeworski 1991: 10; see also Chapter 5). There is political participation all over the place! Parties have to be founded, financed, and run. People need to run for office, organize campaigns, collect money, and manage staff. Elections need the involvement of citizens, most obviously by the act of voting. But even many authoritarian regimes may tolerate some modes of political participation, if for no other reason than to gather information about grievances among their subjects to quell pent-up frustration. Totalitarian regimes also institute compulsory participation to maintain the existing political order, while repressing autonomous bottom-up participation of subjects. While these types of involuntary acts of political polarization may be included in a definition (see Box: Definitions of political participation, in the Online Resource Centre), this chapter restricts its focus to *voluntary participation*, and puts an emphasis on *democracies*.

online resource centre

Voluntary political participation has attracted the attention of many scholars, and it raises fascinating puzzles. First, scholars are still trying to find out why people engage in political participation at all. After all, most of the acts of political participation are somewhat costly (in terms of time or money), and many of them are not effective. For example, the chance of a voter's vote being decisive in a mass democracy is (almost) zero, while casting the vote is costly. Yet millions of people go to the voting booths. Second, scholars also try to understand why some people engage in political participation, while others do not. Finally, why do people choose certain types of political participation over others?

As these examples suggest, political participation addressed to a central authority is costly and difficult to achieve. Thus political participation is an activity that occurs *despite all kinds of obstacles and preferences for more spontaneous self-reliant action*. In a sense, it is a 'miracle' that political participation, as a voluntary and deliberate engagement with collective decision-making and authoritative decision-makers, occurs at all.

KEY POINTS

- The object of analysis is voluntary, not coerced, political participation.
- Participation manifests itself in a wide variety of forms that need to be explained.
- Political participation is a costly undertaking and rarely occurs spontaneously.

How? Modes of political participation

There is no unanimously agreed upon typology of participatory practices, but the political science literature has established some rather widely accepted conventions which we try to capture in Tables 18.1 and 18.2. First, political participation may take place in *different arenas or political contexts*. Second, the *intensity* of participation (time and resources) varies greatly. Third, participatory activities can be distinguished in terms of their *riskiness* to the freedom, life, and limb of the participants.

Sites of participation

Table 18.1 distinguishes sites and intensities of participation. As in the online box already mentioned, (1) people can become involved in a public arena to advertise and communicate demands to anyone willing to listen, (2) they may target policy-makers in legislatures or the executive branch as addressees of their communications, or (3) they may get involved in the selection process of those who aspire to legislative or executive office. Each of these sites involves its own ladder of personal effort and commitment, as people move from intermittent to continuous participation and leadership in organized efforts. Unless actors are independently wealthy, high involvement is ultimately associated with monetary compensation once they allocate so much time to their political involvement that they cannot pursue regular jobs or professions as well.

The **riskiness of participation** obviously depends on the legal and political regime in which it occurs. The less tolerant a regime is of the free expression and organization of citizens' political opinions, the more risky and costly are even restrained forms of political interest articulation. In democracies, activities expressed in two sites of participation—communication with governmental personnel and participation in the nomination and choice of elected politicians—are low risk. In contrast, in democracies 'unconventional' participation in the public forum tends to run from low-risk activities to those that

Table 18.1 Sites of political participation and intensity of involvement

Intensity of involvement	Sites of participation		
	Community, street, and media politics: public expression of demands ('forum politics')	Communicating preferences to policy-makers in legislature and executive branch	Choosing legislative and executive policy-makers
1	Persuasive rhetoric: public advocacy	Persuasive rhetoric: contacting elected or administrative officials	Voting for candidates/parties
2	Participation in collective events	Contributions to sustain communication with political officials/associational membership	Contributions to sustain contenders for political office and coalitions of such contenders (parties)
3	Activist/mobilizer for collective events	Volunteer activism, unpaid functionary	Volunteer activism, unpaid party functionary, or unpaid electoral office holder
4	Spokesperson, public leader	Paid officer, associational executive	Party executive leader or elected career politician

are legally prohibited because they inflict physical harm on human beings and property (Table 18.2).

Because our entries in Table 18.2 focus on the personal riskiness of political participation in different regimes, the division of categories is slightly at odds with common distinctions between 'conventional' and 'unconventional' participation or participation through institutionalized channels and extra-institutional protest politics. In democracies at least, some unconventional activities are low risk (for example, lobbying or licensed street demonstrations). In all political regimes, protest politics that harms people or property rights is subject to criminal sanctions. In non-democratic regimes, more activities are 'unconventional' and punished.

Modes of participation

Most popular participation is organized and regular. While in some instances people may decide to become involved in a particular participatory event on a single-shot basis, most of the time actors contribute to a specific site of political interest articulation where claims

Table 18.2 Riskiness of political participation

Riskiness of participation	Democratic civic and political liberties	Mildly repressive authoritarianism (A) and severely repressive despotism (D)
Legally codified and permitted venues	Voting; contacting policy-makers (lobbying/petitioning); associational memberships; lawful industrial action (strikes, walkouts); lawful street politics (demonstrations)	Voting/often compulsory (D, some A); some state-directed associational memberships/often compulsory (D); some state-directed public manifestations/often compulsory (D)
Not legally codified, but tolerated forms	Boycotts; some unlicensed public manifestations; unofficial strikes	Lobbying/petitioning public officials (A); some voluntary associational memberships (A); some voluntary public manifestations (A)
Legally prohibited activities: breaking political–institutional and property laws (mild punishment)	Legally unregistered demonstrations; site occupations, sit-ins	Petitions (most D); strikes (some A); spontaneous public manifestations (some A; all D)
Legally prohibited activities: breaking laws, severe punishment (detention or capital punishment)	Destruction of property, political vandalism, sabotage; physical assault on the forces of order; assassinations, bombings, hijackings, kidnappings (terrorism)	Strikes (most A, all D); boycotts (all A and D); site occupations, sit-ins (all A and D); destruction of property, political vandalism, sabotage (all A and D); physical assault on the forces of order (all A and D); assassinations, bombings, hijackings, kidnappings

are advanced and specific organizational practices evolve over some extended period of time.

Social movements

Streams of activities that target demands at policy-makers through community, street, and media events as their primary sites of articulation are **social movements** (see Chapter 16). Social movements may involve large numbers of people, but they have generally *small* formal organizational cores. Typically, there is no formal membership and many participants are not interested in that. Likewise, movement leaders do not make major investments in the construction of an organizational infrastructure of coordination among activists.

Interest groups

Activities where participants mainly rely on communicating preferences, demands, and threats to policy-makers situated in legislative and executive arenas tends to create durable interest groups (see Chapter 14). They are typically formally organized, with explicit membership roles and internal statutes. This is one source of their influence (*encompassingness* of interest organization).

Membership is one indicator of an interest group's threat capacity *vis-à-vis* policy-makers, but it may be insufficient as such. In part, the power of an interest group derives from the **centralization** of its internal organization (the capacity of the association to make decisions that bind all members). Centralized interest groups can make *credible commitments* to holding their end of a bargain and therefore are attractive for policy-makers willing to craft compromises among contending interests.

Political parties

Activities in which participants cooperate in order to nominate legislative candidates, help them attract voters, and organize voter turnout in favour of such candidates amount to the formation of political parties (see Chapters 12 and 13). In mass democracy, most candidates face obstacles to getting their message out, and parties help in overcoming these. From the voter's perspective, the decision to participate in an election is made easier if there are only a few alternative candidates under identifiable labels. Parties' reputations and promises play a crucial role in the competition for votes. Parties develop reputations and can credibly make promises only if they rally a large number of politicians for a long time period and make them agree on roughly similar demands.

Obviously, political activists using the same organizational label may at one point in time act more like a social movement, while at another more like a party. Nevertheless, almost all political associations focus on one 'core competence' and site of participatory **mobilization** at any given time.

> **KEY POINTS**
>
> - Participation occurs at different sites: in public places, in communication with political decision-makers, and by involvement in the electoral process.
> - At each site of participation, actors decide about the depth and extent of their involvement.
> - Participants face greater or lesser risks to their personal welfare as a consequence of their choice of political involvements. Political regimes shape the riskiness of different participatory acts.
> - Participatory acts typically are not disjointed events, but happen around social movements, interest groups, or political parties.

Why? Determinants of political participation

Why do people engage in political participation? What types of actor become involved in certain types of political activity, but not others? And how do citizens and politicians choose their portfolio of political involvements between social movements, interest groups, and political parties?

Political vs. other types of participation

Political participation is only one of several ways for members of a society to further their life chances. Alternatively, they may rely on *markets* or *families and communal associations*. This gives a first answer to the question of why people participate in politics. It is a *choice of last resort*. When simpler problem-solving techniques fail to deliver, people participate. People become political when contractual exchange or generalized communal reciprocity does not deliver what they expect.[1]

The paradox of collective action

People participate in politics to bring about authoritative decisions allocating goods and bads to large groups. These have the character of *collective goods*. Once produced, no individual belonging to a polity can be excluded from enjoying (or suffering) the consequences of having such goods, regardless of whether or not that individual has contributed to their production. This generates a seeming **collective action paradox** (Olson 1965). If individuals are self-regarding and try to minimize their effort in producing some benefit, they may not contribute to produce collective goods. Instead, people behave as free-riders. We would expect this in most large group situations where the personal costs of fighting for the political provision of the good ('participation') far outweigh the personal benefits of enjoying the good. Therefore if *each* individual reasons that *others* should bear the costs of producing the collective good, no good will ever be produced at all.

Olson submits that, nevertheless, political participation occurs because selective incentives overcome the free-rider problem. Participants in a mobilizational effort to produce collective goods receive additional 'private' benefits that only accrue to participants. If such selective incentives are sufficiently valuable to *outweigh the costs* of participation, then political mobilization will occur.

But Olson's theory runs into an empirical challenge: political participation appears to happen much more frequently than the theory would permit. A particularly prominent example is the so-called 'paradox of voting' (Aldrich 1993). Millions of citizens regularly show up at the voting booth without obvious selective incentives. Much research since the appearance of Olson's book has focused on reasons why Olson's paradox of political participation may be less stark in practice than in theory (see Box: Internal solutions to the problem of collective action, in the Online Resource Centre). One line of research suggests external solutions to the collective action problem. Solutions are 'external' if they deviate from Olson's original assumptions when setting up the paradox of collective action (see Box: Assumptions of the free-rider problem, in the Online Resource Centre. An extensive review of such solutions can be found in Hardin (1982) and Lichbach (1995)). Some solutions to the 'paradox of collective action' are as follows.

online resource centre

online resource centre

- There may be some political entrepreneurs who do not consider political involvement costly. They may disregard the costs of political action for reasons of moral passion or a striving for glory and be willing to supply the bread-and-butter selective incentives that make more economically rational self-regarding people join in.

- The premise of Olson's set-up is that people treat political participation as a cost. But what if it is a benefit or the benefit itself? Some may value the experience of enjoying solidarity with a large number of other human beings in collective action, all the way to building barricades and throwing Molotov cocktails at the forces of order, as an intrinsically gratifying experience. On a more mundane level, many people may derive satisfaction from the experience of communal deliberation over the value of collective pursuits and over the strategies to obtain them. In all these instances, the process of participation itself is a most powerful benefit.

- Actors may be motivated to underrate the costs of participation. This may be a simple matter of misperception, or political entrepreneurs may have persuaded them to discount the costs of action, or such leaders may have made them believe that a major pay-off resulting from collective action is within reach with only a little more involvement, turning the cost–benefit balance of involvement positive.

- Social networks may serve as a monitoring device. This may motivate some individuals to join in the collective effort. Such mechanisms may amount to a dynamic of information cascades and tipping points in collective action (Kuran 1991; Chwe 2001). As more individuals signal willingness to participate, effective repression becomes harder to achieve and more costly for the forces of order. A spiral may unfold in which people observe a given level of collective action at a time t that, contrary to their prior expectations, triggers little repression. This signal, in turn, boosts greater participation in the next round at time $t + 1$ which makes it even more costly for the forces of order to deploy repressive measures. The catalyst of expanding participation and faltering repression emboldens even more participants to join in collective actions in subsequent rounds (Lohmann 1994).

Olson's work has stimulated a tremendous amount of research on political participation. But starting from an elegant simple theorem (free-riding and selective incentives), it has ultimately added a level of complexity that makes straightforward predictions of collective action impossible to achieve.

KEY POINTS

- Political participation as an appeal to a public authority to make a binding decision is a last-resort strategy to resolve social conflicts when other, more direct, approaches fail.

- Much political participation aims at the provision of collective goods, from whose benefits those who did not contribute to their production cannot be excluded. This poses a free-rider problem.

- Selective incentives that provide benefits targeted only at those who contribute to the production of a collective good provide a partial, incomplete solution to the free-rider problem.

- Sometimes actors may contribute to collective action because participation itself is experienced as a reward or the costs of participation are deemed to be minimal.

When and where? Explaining political participation at the macro-level

Political demands are a necessary, but not a sufficient, condition for political mobilization (see also Chapter 16 on this point). The answer to why people engage in political participation comes in two parts: (1) because they are in a certain place at a certain time (the role of context and opportunity) and because political entrepreneurs devise appropriate organizations of political action (this section), and (2) because they have resources and dispositions that facilitate participation (individual or micro-level factors which are dealt with in the next section).

Differences in participation across regime types

The range of organizational vehicles that citizens and political leaders can employ to pursue political objectives varies by systemic context (see Table 18.3).

1. In *democracies* with elections for legislative and executive office through universal suffrage and institutions to protect civil and political rights of citizens there exists a very wide range of participatory acts that crystallize in time and space around movements with small core organizations, large interest associations, and political parties.

2. In *authoritarian regimes,* such as nineteenth-century constitutional monarchies or many twentieth-century military and civilian dictatorships, the executive is beyond democratic accountability, but tolerates some activities of spontaneously emerging social movements, interest groups, and even political parties that may compete for legislative seats.

3. In *harshly repressive despotic regimes* opportunities are substantially more restricted, particularly those with far-flung organizations to control and mobilize subjects from above. They do not simply thwart and repress any sort of organized sustained participatory coordination among actors from below, but impose compulsory political participation through state-run mass organizations from above (see Chapter 6).

Differences in participation within democracies

Participation varies not only across but also within regime types. When we analyse participation and its organizational modes comparing democracies, there is considerable diversity in time and space. It appears that *levels of economic development* are somewhat related to participation. Figure 18.1 reports the percentage of respondents in thirty-three countries indicating participation in at least one of three low-risk modes of political participation (signing a petition; joining a boycott; attending a lawful demonstration) as well as two high-risk modes (joining unofficial strikes; occupying buildings or factories). The figure distinguishes countries by geographical areas which also reflect levels of affluence. A simple conclusion that can be drawn from the figure is that, clearly, the most affluent tier of countries shows much greater participatory experience than post-communist or other developing countries.

These differences may have to do with the political opportunity structure potential that entrepreneurs of a new political cause are facing.[2] If existing parties and interest groups are willing and able to incorporate new demands without alienating elements of their existing support coalitions, a new salient cause may have little impact on a polity's profile of participation. However, if existing vehicles of interest aggregation resist incorporation of new

Table 18.3 Political regimes and venues of political participation

Voluntary action	Liberal democracy	Authoritarian polity	Despotic polity
Repertoire of collective action	Wide range of legally permitted and tolerated modes of participation; severe sanctions against violence	Narrow range of legally licensed, but broader range of tolerated modes of participation; severe sanctions against participation using violence and some non-violent acts	Some legally compulsory participation; no tolerated spontaneous participation; severe sanctions against most forms of political participation, whether violent or non-violent
Social movements	Yes	Yes	No
Interest groups	Yes	Yes	No
Political parties	Yes	(Yes/no)(Semi-competitive elections to legislatures, but no legislative choice of the executive or direct democratic election of the executive)	(No)(Parties from above: single-party or single-list united front party ballots; no strategic deliberation in parties)

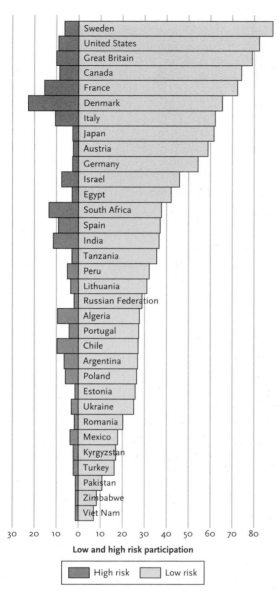

Figure 18.1 Low- and high-risk participation in selected countries

Notes: In the World Values Survey (WVS, wave 4: 1999–2004) (see web links) respondents were asked the following question: 'I'm going to read out some different forms of political action that people can take, and I'd like you to tell me, for each one, whether you have actually done any of these things, whether you might do it or would never, under any circumstances, do it.' 'Low-risk political participation' refers to the following three items covered by this survey question: signing a petition (E025), joining in boycotts (E026), and attending lawful demonstrations (E027). 'High-risk political participation' refers to the following two items: joining unofficial strikes (E028), or occupying buildings or factories (E029).

Source: World Value Surveys (www.worldvaluessurvey.org), wave 4.

and salient demands in the polity, outside political entrepreneurs might decide to begin independent political mobilization.

Fragmented **multiparty systems** with a differentiated menu of party labels tend to make it more likely that established vehicles of interest aggregation pick up new demands. Counterbalancing this, however, is the easier entry in electoral systems with **proportional representation** (PR) that prevail among fragmented multiparty systems (see Chapter 13). Such rules make it possible for political entrepreneurs to organize an effective independent electoral partisan challenge around a newly salient demand. However, in **two-party systems** a lack of internal party cohesion (such as within the two US parties) may create access points for new demands within established politics which make it unnecessary for such interests to follow the route of sustained protest and construction of new rival political associations. Let us look at two examples where contextual effects in democracies can be reasonably expected to affect political participation. The first relates to the 'paradox of voting' mentioned earlier (see Box: The paradox of voting, in the Online Resource Centre) and relates a country's context to its level of turnout. The second example relates to different levels of union membership.

online resource centre

Voter turnout

Figure 18.2 shows average voter turnout rates in recent parliamentary or presidential elections in several dozen countries. The figure shows that countries with compulsory voting laws tend to have much higher turnouts. Beyond that, the figure does not reveal strong cross-national patterns. However, there is a sophisticated cross-national comparative literature on voting turnout.[3] Beyond such broad forces as development, political regime, and the timing of the enfranchisement of new voters (women, youths) who reach turnout levels of established voter groups only with a delay of a generation, there are several important institutional mechanisms that influence aggregate electoral turnout. In the following, we focus on four of them.

- *Compulsory voting* is linked to turnout. It is critical to know whether and how non-voting is punished. However, regardless of enforcement, it can be observed that, across Western democracies, countries with compulsory voting systems tend to have higher turnout rates; the difference in turnout is usually about 10–15 percentage points (see Blais 2006: 112–13; see also box in the Online Resource Centre).

- *Electoral rules* are linked to turnout. One usually distinguishes between PR systems (every vote counts) and **majoritarian** or single-member districts (winner takes all). Under conditions of PR and low thresholds of representation, most voters can choose their preferred

online resource centre

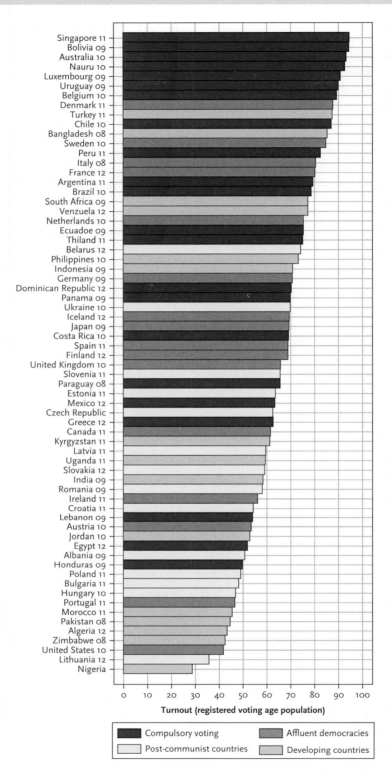

Figure 18.2 Voter turnout in selected countries

Note: Turnout data are from http://www.idea.int/vt (8-Dec-12); only selected countries and most recent elections are displayed. Information on compulsory voting comes from https://www.cia.gov/library/publications/the-world-factbook/fields/2123.html#le.

party and expect it to gain seats in the legislature. This is different in systems with single-member or a small number of member districts or other stipulations generating high electoral thresholds of representation. In all of these systems rational voters who find that their favourite party or candidate has no chance of winning a seat and who dislike all second-best options intensely tend to stay home. Inspecting Figure 18.2, it can be seen that, among affluent OECD countries, with the exception of Switzerland, all countries with a long-term voter turnout of less than 75 per cent of the voting-age population have some other electoral system than multimember district PR (see also Chapters 10 and 13).

- *Registration requirements* are linked to turnout. In many democracies, registration is automatic and therefore is not a constraint on voting. In the US, however, citizens have to seek out registration actively and many, particularly the young and mobile and the very old and infirm, as well as poorer citizens, are seriously under-represented in the registered electorate. Not surprisingly, turnout levels among registered voters in the US are low. In fact, Powell (1986) calculates that if European democracies were operating under the same institutional rules as the US (single-member districts, registration requirements, work-day voting, frequency of elections, and the number of offices on which people vote), voter turnout in Europe would be even lower than in the US.

- The *timing of elections* is linked to turnout outside parliamentary democracies. Turnout tends to be greater if *legislative and presidential elections take place on the same day*. In these so-called 'concurrent' elections voters award the big prizes for the executive and the legislature in one single go rather than in staggered contests.

Beyond these and other more minor institutional rules, there are important strategic and political–economic conditions that affect turnout, such as the closeness of an election (Aldrich 1993; Franklin 2004) or income and educational inequality (Anderson and Beramendi 2008).

Labour union membership

In democracies, labour unions tend to have more members than other organized interest groups. Yet, membership varies dramatically in time and space. Four points can be made about the cross-national variance of labour union membership.

1. The transition from agriculture to urban manufacturing and service industries, particularly if they concentrate labour in large factories or offices, enables wage earners to overcome collective action problems

and organize interest associations. This is one important reason why labour union membership tends to be higher in affluent polities than in developing countries.

2. Political regime also matters. Voluntary interest associations, such as unions, thrive in democratic polities. In the early European democratic transitions unions promoted democratization (Collier 1999), but in highly repressive regimes government-sponsored labour unions may serve as organizational techniques to mobilize actors into the established order. An example is communist China. Also, in Latin America authoritarian regimes set up unions and business associations and deployed them as transmission belts of corporatist authoritarian governance, such as under Getulio Vargas in Brazil from the mid-1930s.

3. In both communist and corporatist authoritarian regimes, economic development policy comes into play as a catalyst of interest group participation. Both types of regime pursued strategies of nurturing domestic industries by protecting them from foreign competitors behind high tariff walls and by cheapening the factor inputs that could not be supplied domestically by overvalued currencies combined with discretionary import licenses. This development strategy was promoted by the political mobilization of relatively scarce and expensive domestic industrial capital and labour seeking protection from foreign competitive pressure. But, conversely, it also reinforced such interest organization: as domestic industries grew, but remained relatively inefficient behind the protective walls of regulated international trade and capital flows, the mobilization of political influence became vital for its survival.

4. Beyond economic development and regime, however, there are also dramatic differences even within a set of 17 relatively similar democracies, as can be seen from Figure 18.3. Not only are there huge differences in terms of levels (compare France and Sweden), but there are also interesting differences in terms of trends: unionization remained high or *increased* in countries where it was strong to begin with, but it almost invariably *decreased* in countries where unions had only median strength or were already weak. Structural change away from large offices and workshops and towards post-industrial jobs and professions is fairly similar across all affluent OECD countries, but unionization clearly diverges. How can we make sense of this pattern?

We want to highlight just one factor that provides a powerful institutional explanation of the observed variance: the **Ghent system** (named after the city where it was first introduced). Under the Ghent system, initiated in countries where socialists had become a highly

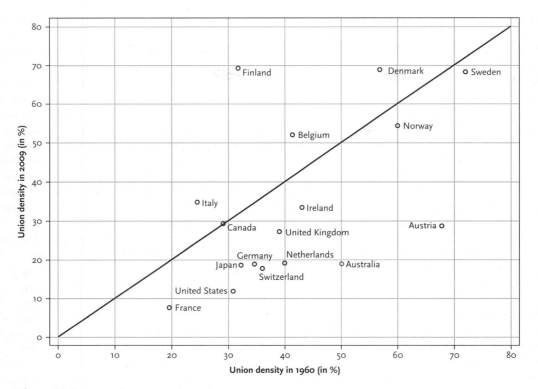

Figure 18.3 Union density in selected countries, 1960 vs. 2009

Notes: Trade union density is defined as the number of wage and salary earners that are trade union members divided by the total number of wage and salary earners.

Source: OECD (http://stats.oecd.org).

competitive party to win executive control, governments delegated the task of organizing and administering unemployment insurance to labour unions, thus providing a very powerful selective incentive, in Olson's sense, for wage earners to join unions and pay their dues in order to gain the private benefit of prompt unemployment pay compensation in case of job loss in the market economy. In Belgium, Denmark, Finland, and Sweden the Ghent system prevailed, and these countries are among the most unionized countries in the world.

The presence of the Ghent system also makes itself felt in change over time. Technological change, de-industrialization, and other shocks that increased the risk of unemployment for typical union members led to different reactions in countries with and without the Ghent system (see Figure 18.4). In countries with the Ghent system, the increasing risk of unemployment prompted wage earners to rally to labour unions even more vigorously than in the past (see Chapter 22). In contrast, in countries without the Ghent system the value of unions in maintaining wages and job security appeared ever more marginal, a perception further reinforced where socialist parties were weak and in opposition. In most of these countries we see a contraction of union density throughout the 1980s and 1990s.

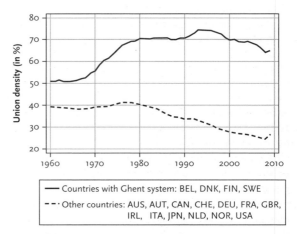

Figure 18.4 Union density by unemployment insurance scheme (Ghent)

Notes: Trade union density is defined as the number of wage and salary earners that are trade union members divided by the total number of wage and salary earners. Four countries are classified as Ghent system (following Western 1997: Table 4.1, p. 54): Belgium, Denmark, Finland, and Sweden. The remaining countries are Australia, Austria, Canada, France, Germany, Ireland, Italy, Japan, Netherlands, Norway, Switzerland, the UK, and the US.

Source: OECD (http://stats.oecd.org).

Political organizations and mobilization

Why is it that some forms of participation lead to the mobilization of social movements, while others gravitate towards interest group association or the rise of political parties? And why are political entrepreneurs across polities more successful in organizing parties and interest groups around some causes—such as social class or religion—whereas other demands routinely fail at the level of party mobilization, such as demands of women, retirees, taxpayers, or consumers, all of which have generated considerable efforts to build parties over the past fifty years?

To sketch an answer to these questions, let us assume that actors will invest in collective action only if future benefits justify current expenses. Two types of investment at the meso-level of participatory mobilization are particularly prevalent.

1. Mobilization may build on an *organizational infrastructure that facilitates coordination* among large numbers of people and disseminates political messages. This may require office space, communication equipment, and a full-time staff of specialists continuously processing information about 'who does what' and 'where' and attending to the maintenance of the organizational structure.
2. The goals of the mobilizational effort are not given exogenously, but undergo constant review and reinterpretation by leaders and followers. Leaders and participants might invest in the *process of redefining or expanding the objectives driving the mobilizational effort* in order to attract new allies and supporters.

The broader the range of political objectives over which participants try to coordinate collective action, the more they will have to invest time and procedural energies in either associational techniques of conflict deliberation and resolution or capabilities to punish deviators and enforce collective compliance.

What are the conditions under which incipient political entrepreneurs make investments in organizational infrastructure and modes of interest aggregation to establish the domain of objectives over which a collective mobilization claims jurisdiction? The answer is that this depends on a *learning process* among participants in a mobilizational effort to establish how durable and how broadly interdependent their original demands are with other causes pursued in the polity.

At one extreme, political objectives are *temporally discrete* single-shot demands that some authoritative policy should be granted, denied, or reversed. If political goals can be reached one-off and participants discover that they are pretty disconnected from other salient struggles in the polity, participants and their entrepreneurs may not find it worthwhile to invest in an elaborate associational structure and confine themselves to protest events.

At the other extreme, actors must envision open-ended and permanent struggles around certain objectives. This encourages activists to invest in organizational structures that increase capabilities for operational coordination through associational statutes detailing internal governance and material resource acquisition. They scale up from social movement organizations to interest associations that incorporate a considerable share of their constituencies as members who pay dues, and many of whom are ready to participate in internal and external organizational activities when called upon by the associational functionaries.

Political interest associations, however, confine themselves to a *limited issue domain* and therefore are not compelled to make large investments in procedures of goal-finding, refinement, and generalization. In fact, in order to minimize internal disagreements and to maximize the external strategic capabilities of their association, political entrepreneurs may vigilantly police the boundaries of the issue domain over which they claim jurisdiction. Extending the claims of the organization to new issues may only inject dissent and create paralysis in the organization.[4]

Political interest groups, however, are not making authoritative political decisions in democracies, even if they may have the ear of political decision-makers and may even participate in procedures of deliberation. The formal authoritative decisions lie with legislatures, parties in legislatures, and political executives. Can interest groups challenge unresponsive legislatures and executives by forming their own parties and joining the competitive fray? There is a large literature on party formation which typically emphasizes as preconditions for entry that (1) institutional thresholds of entry are not formidable and (2) the party appeals to a salient issue demand that is not represented by existing parties. We would like to add a third stipulation that leads to a consideration of investments into procedures of strategic deliberation and generalization of political objectives.

Parties that strive to win representative legislative offices can never succeed and sustain themselves over many rounds of electoral contest if they appeal to a single issue, no matter how salient it may be.[5] Parties cannot restrict the agenda of legislatures to their favourite issues. As representatives of territorial constituencies, legislators participate in decisions over an uncertain and potentially infinite range of policies. Even if a party's constituencies rally around a single issue, the daily need for its legislators to make decisions on many other issues may generate internal divisions. Voters cannot perceive what parties stand for. Even on core issues, divided parties may become incapable of advancing their agenda. Therefore political entrepreneurs have to find ways of overcoming the confines of single-issue appeals (see Box:

online
resource
centre

Ways to overcome single issue appeals, in the Online Resource Centre).

At the meso-level of mobilization, then, political entrepreneurs are not entirely free to choose their mode of action. Their differential capabilities to sustain the struggle over political objectives through time and generalize it across an encompassing issue space leads them to opt for different modes of mobilization, even if they face rather similar institutional and strategic contexts within a framework of liberal democracy.

KEY POINTS

- Actors participate only if they are motivated, and if they have the capacities and opportunities to act on their aspirations.

- More affluent societies provide more resources to stimulate political participation.

- Political regime—democracy and dictatorship—regulates the opportunities actors encounter to participate in politics.

- The nature of political stakes shapes the organization of political participation. Single-issue causes that aim for a one-off discrete decision typically result in *social movements* with little organizational structure. Efforts mobilizing around a narrowly specialized range of issues that persist over time facilitate the construction of *interest groups*. Where political causes pursue complex agendas of interdependent issues, they are likely to form *political parties* and enter the arena of electoral competition.

Who? Explaining political participation at the micro-level

As a last step, we would like to know what sorts of individual select what sorts of participatory activity. The choice of participatory practices may be governed by both *individual traits* (resources, capabilities, attitudes, dispositions) and *contextual cues* that actors glean from the strategic political situation and basic regime conditions, as discussed in the previous section. However, in what follows we will only consider individual traits.

Individual traits

We have already mentioned that people engage in political participation if they have resources and dispositions that facilitate participation. The most important individual-level factors can be further distinguished into four different sets (following Schlozman 2002: 439; Verba *et al.* 1995): (1) resources, (2) recruitment, (3) orientations

towards politics, and (4) contextual cues. In other words, '[i]ndividuals are more likely to take part when they can, when they want to, ... when they are asked to' (Schlozman 2002: 439) and when they are in certain contexts.

Resources

Probably the most generally and consistently confirmed influence on participation comes from socio-economic skills and endowments.[6] A simple baseline condition for political participation, especially more involved modes of participation, is the *availability of time.* People who do not work, or do not work full-time, tend to display higher levels of political participation. Young retirees or high school and university students, for example, provide great reservoirs for intensive political participation.

Once we move beyond this simple endowment, *schooling/education* is clearly a key variable. Better education enables citizens to process more information about ongoing political decisions and sort out what does or does not affect one's life chances in ways that might prompt political action. Better education also fosters a stronger self-confidence and sense of individual capacity to govern one's own life rather than to let external authorities make decisions on one's behalf. Thus education cuts down on paternalist deference. Furthermore, the capacity to process information enables actors to identify more efficient strategies to pursue their objectives through political action. Finally, better education enables people to participate in deliberative processes to determine desirable objectives of political action and to discover ways to pursue them.

Beyond these direct effects, education indirectly enhances participation through its impact on *income* and *occupational time* sovereignty. Better educated people tend to earn higher incomes which enable them to divert part of their finances to discretionary activities, such as politics. Better educated people also tend to have jobs in which they enjoy more time sovereignty (but not more free time) which makes them available for complex time-consuming political activities.[7]

Education, income, and professional or occupational life also promote involvement in a variety of *civic activities,* such as professional and cultural associations. These, in turn, serve as intermediate relays that facilitate interpersonal communication of beliefs and political preferences (i.e. *orientations*). Enhanced communication among like-minded actors thus fosters a readiness for political participation and even the coordination of collective action through mutual monitoring, if not sanctioning, of those individuals in the network who become free-riders.

Recruitment

This brings us to recruitment as an important explanation for participation. *Associational involvement* is a proximate mechanism that explains political participation not only for those who have favourable personal endowments to become involved in politics (education, time, money). Associational involvement may be an even greater and more important enhancer of participation precisely for individuals who lack such resources, but nevertheless reach levels of political activism not foreseen by a naive socio-economic resource model of political participation. Under which conditions does exposure to civic associations and networks of communication lead to increased participation? Parameters of both occupational and residential life might be influential in this regard.

Occupations that do not require high human capital and that do not grant their practitioners great time sovereignty may stimulate political participation, if the *organization of the work process* affords actors plenty of exposure to others living under very similar social conditions. This tends to be particularly the case where people converge on large workplaces with many hundreds or even thousands of employees operating under exactly the same work conditions. Examples are manufacturing plants or mines, dockyards before the advent of containerized shipping, or newspaper printing factories before electronic text-editing. In the great factory interpersonal communication can easily reach large numbers of people. Moreover, people can observe and monitor each other's behaviour to sanction free-riders. The resulting high capacity for collective action is further enhanced by the residential family life of employees being concentrated in neighbourhoods close to the work facilities. Chances are that occasional interactions, but also cultural, regional, or social civic associations, spring up that organize social communications.

The resulting *class and group milieux* foster and sustain a high capacity for collective action. Historically, the peak of milieu-based social organization and political participation was probably reached in the first half of the twentieth century when factory size reached its zenith and urbanization was far advanced but had not yet given way to sprawling suburbanization. Going back to the late nineteenth and early twentieth century in Europe or the US up to the 1940s or 1950s, civic associations such as occupational and cultural organizations (e.g. churches or trade unions) served as 'quasi-schools', creating readiness for political participation among those who had acquired few educational skills and had low incomes.

Thus the presence of encompassing associations draws into political life people who would otherwise linger at the margins of the polity. The shrinking size of workplaces, the increasing separation of work and residential life, and the dispersal of residential patterns that has come with the advent of the automobile as a relatively cheap mode of transportation since the Second World War have progressively undercut the capacity of the workplace and surrounding neighbourhoods to organize political participation. Thus this process has reduced some of the social capital of civil society ties built up independently of, or even in compensation for, the lack of high personal socio-economic endowments that enable individuals to engage in political participation.

Somewhere at the intersection between socio-economic resources (education, income, occupational time sovereignty) and civic associational memberships we can consider the *role of the family* in political participation. The family unit bundles the experiences of work and residential life for members of the next generation. The family is the critical site at which youngsters acquire a taste for, or a dislike of, political participation. Parents introduce their children to political practices that shape their future dispositions towards politics and transmit essential skills of participation in collective action. An early exposure to political involvement often spawns lifelong political activism. The personalistic nature of political competition may create 'family dynasties' of political involvement at all levels of politics, particularly in countries with weak formal party structures. The US and Japan are good examples.

In relation to the connection between family and political participation, it is finally also necessary to bring up the demographic traits of *age and gender*. Many of the effects of age and gender are mediated by the resource and social network endowments that affect political participation. Nevertheless, they may have a net effect on political participation, once all these other factors are held constant. Young people and women tend to be less active in politics than older people and men, for reasons that have to do with political experience and cultural upbringing. And if they are active, their profile of activities tends to differ between age and gender groups, contingent upon the nature of participatory activities at stake.

Orientations

As another proximate determinant of political participation that is at least in part conditioned by all the elements of the picture we have already assembled, let us add *political interest and ideology*. Political participation results from, and stimulates, political knowledge formation. Individuals may organize their political knowledge in complex ideologies that combine descriptive and analytical propositions of how politics and social organizations work with normative images of desirable end states of a reformed or rebuilt social and political order and strategic prescriptions about how to move from the status quo to the desirable end state. While political ideologies may display some empirical association with individuals' socio-economic and occupational background, more immediate causal mechanisms that shape ideology are civic involvement and engagement in political participation itself. The level of ideological organization in actors' belief systems, in turn, is a good predictor of political participation (Marsh 1990).

Contextual cues

Comparing levels of participation among countries—voting, campaigning, membership in unions or parties, protest activities—reveals that the distribution of citizens' resources and dispositions—education, income, interest in politics—explains only a small share of the cross-national differences: Swedes are not that much more likely to vote in national elections because they are, on average, so much more educated than Americans. Belgians, on average, are not that much more interested in politics to explain why they are so much more likely to be affiliated with unions than French citizens.

With regard to citizens' willingness to join and contribute to political associations in affluent post-industrial countries, Morales (2009) postulates three clusters. First, in Northern European countries, associational memberships are very strong, yet participation in associational activities is extremely weak. Second, in Anglo-Saxon and some continental countries, political group membership is moderate, but activism is stronger. Finally, in Mediterranean countries few people join political associations, but those who do show a greater willingness to participate. Overall, the proportion of the population that is active in political associations is smaller than in Scandinavia, but not as much smaller as differentials in organizational membership would make one expect.

Large differences in citizens' average propensities to participate in politics, such as joining interest groups, result from contextual factors. We have already indicated some of them, such as the impact of electoral rules on voter turnout or the role of the Ghent system for differential levels and change rates of labour unionization. More generally, we can distinguish at least four different levels of contextual effects that leave their imprint on individual and aggregate profiles of political participation (see Morales 2009).

- At the micro-level networks of family and friends influence participation. Where one's personal social networks are heavily politicized, chances are high that one also will become politically active.

- At the meso-level, the existence of large encompassing associations and densely organized parties makes a difference. The presence of such networks is likely to render it less costly and more attractive for citizens to join and get involved. As a legacy effect, where associational affiliations were always a widespread phenomenon in the past, say as early as the post-Second World War decades, chances are that later generations of citizens will also join political associations in great numbers, even as mobilization spreads from one type of political cause to another.

- At the macro-level, not only democratic institutions (such as electoral laws), but also strategic alignments among political forces, may encourage or discourage involvement. Thus, where large hierarchically organized encompassing national interest groups, such as unions and employers' associations, dominate wage bargaining and have great clout in policy-making ('corporatism'), more people may join such interest groups, but also more activists might become involved in spontaneous disruptive grassroots movements when their voices on salient issues are simply not listened to by the leaders of large centralized associations.

- The nature of the party system also shapes participation. Where people choose among a wide variety of political parties rather than only two major parties, chances are greater that one of them has a political programme very close to exactly what the individual citizen would like to see realized in policy-making. This may encourage him/her to contribute to that party by becoming a member. Hence, greater party system fragmentation may translate into greater partisan membership (Morales 2009: Chapter 6).

Political involvement may even be shaped by interaction effects between citizens' individual resources and the broader context in which they operate. Thus, where labour unions involved in corporatist interest intermediation make the voice of less educated and less well-off citizens heard, they are likely to attract the affiliation of constituencies that would stay unorganized elsewhere. Conversely, highly educated and affluent citizens may seek out other ways to protect their interest than through political involvement.

Finally, contextual conditions can bring about complex causal chains that reinforce differentials of participation. In highly inegalitarian polities in which a large share of citizens has poor general education and little political information, even the politically interested members of this constituency may refrain from politics. They expect that low turnout among their own constituency will lead to under-representation of constituency interests in legislatures and executives. This expectation itself may generate cynicism and alienation from politics and reinforce the low turnout among poor uneducated people. Then the effective median voter who elects legislatures and parties that govern shifts further towards the affluent and educated who have little inclination to redistribute life chances to the worse off. Their political representatives choose policies that reinforce educational and income inequality, further reducing political participation of the ill-endowed, and thus once again exacerbating the under-representation of interests of disadvantaged groups in legislatures and political executives.

Conclusion

Democracy without political participation is like *Hamlet* without the prince: it just does not work. Political participation covers such a broad set of phenomena—inside and outside democracies—that it is difficult to offer a concise definition, *let alone* detailed explanations for particular types of participation.

This chapter has illustrated that scholars have amassed a great deal of knowledge about political participation over the past half century. But large open questions remain.

1. We need to understand better the interaction between the capacities and motivations of individuals to engage in political participation and the socio-economic, institutional, and political–strategic context in which such actors are embedded. Political behaviour cannot be explained merely in terms of individual-level traits or macro-level conditions and rules. We also need to consider contextual factors. For example, the correlation between education and turnout seems to be systematically higher in more unequal societies. Rather, we have to understand the contingent interaction between micro- and macro-level.

2. We need to understand more clearly why everyday political actors and political entrepreneurs who produce selective incentives for others to participate in politics opt for different modes of political participation in different circumstances and in light of different demands. To be sure, there are grey zones between social movements, interest groups, and political parties that make it hard to discern distinctive modes of political participation. Nevertheless, it is a fascinating and by and large under-studied question why political actors sometimes invest in trajectories of political involvement that crystallize more around volatile social movements, or durable interest groups, or programmatically complex parties.

3. The differentiation between modes of political action appears to grow in post-industrial democratic polities. Consider the contrast with labour movements in the early twentieth century. The same actors who were activists in socialist parties also tended to lead labour unions—regardless of whether these were the 'transmission belt' of parties or whether parties were the electoral mouthpieces of labour unions. Furthermore, these core cadres also organized disruptive extra-institutional street politics that sustained labour mobilization as a social movement. However, by the late twentieth century socialist parties and unions rarely ever engage in protest events. And even the relationship between labour mobilization as a functional interest group and as an electoral undertaking has become an arm's length affair where all sides struggle to preserve their mutual autonomy.

Not only the causes, but also the consequences, of increasing differentiation between modes of political action deserve more attention. What takes place is a 'de-centring' of democratic politics across diverse sites and modes of action—a pluralization of political democracy and political involvement. Why is there so much and such diverse political activism? This is a real and unresolved puzzle when thinking about political participation. Perhaps the best answer we can give is: because they don't want to see *Hamlet* without the prince.

 Questions

1. Why do people participate in politics?

2. What are the three principal sites of participation and what are the three principal modes of participation?

3. What is the 'paradox of collective action'?

4. What are the solutions to the paradox of collective action?

5. Why is union membership higher in Ghent systems?

6. Which factors are known to increase levels of turnout?

7. Do you think that low turnout rates are a threat to democracy?

8. Why do political entrepreneurs sometimes initiate social movements, sometimes build interest organizations, and sometimes found parties?

9. What are the four different types of micro-level factors for participation? Give examples for each.

10. Should theories of collective action start from the premise that participation is a 'cost' or should theories reverse the premise and treat participation as a 'benefit'?

Further reading

Barnes, S. H. and Kaase, M. (1979) *Political Action: Mass Participation in Five Western Democracies* (Newbury Park, CA: Sage).

Dalton, R. J. (2013) *Citizen Politics: Public Opinion and Political Parties in Advanced Industrial Democracies* (6th edn) (Chatham, NJ: Chatham House Publishers/Seven Bridges Press).

Franklin, M. N. (2004) *Voter Turnout and the Dynamics of Electoral Competition in Established Democracies since 1945* (Cambridge: Cambridge University Press).

Hardin, R. (1982) *Collective Action* (Baltimore, MD: Johns Hopkins University Press).

Jackman, R. W. (1987) 'Political Institutions and Voter Turnout in the Industrial Democracies', *American Political Science Review*, 81(2): 405–24.

Lichbach, M. I. (1995) *The Rebel's Dilemma: Economics, Cognition, and Society* (Ann Arbor, MI: University of Michigan Press).

Lijphart, A. (1997) 'Unequal Participation: Democracy's Unresolved Dilemma', *American Political Science Review*, 91(1): 1–14.

Olson, M. (1965) *The Logic of Collective Action: Public Goods and the Theory of Groups* (Cambridge, MA: Harvard University Press).

Powell, G. B., Jr (1986) 'American Voter Turnout in Comparative Perspective', *American Political Science Review*, 80(1): 17–43.

Verba, S., Nie, N. H., and Kim, J. (1978) *Participation and Political Equality: A Seven-Nation Comparison* (Cambridge, MA: Cambridge University Press).

 Web links

Parties, unions, social movements

www.janda.org/ICPP/index.htm
International Comparative Political Parties Project. Comprehensive data collection on parties around the world.

http://eurofound.europa.eu/eiro/
European Industrial Relations Observatory. Offers news and analysis on European industrial relations.

www.dol.gov/ILAB/media/reports/flt/main.htm
Foreign Labor Trends (ILAB). Website maintained by the US Department of Labor, with information from about twenty countries around the world.

www.ilo.org
The International Labour Organization. A UN specialized agency which seeks the promotion of social justice and internationally recognized human and labour rights. Contains a wealth of data on union-related matters; see especially www.ilo.org/public/english/bureau/stat/portal/index.htmData

www.idea.int/vt/survey/voter_turnout_pop2-2.cfm
Website of International IDEA. Comprehensive set of data on turnout.

www.worldvaluessurvey.org
Website of the World Value Survey.

http://stats.oecd.org/
OECD Statistics. Contains, besides many other data, information on union membership.

www.parlgov.org
The Parliament and Government Composition database (ParlGov) contains comprehensive information on parties and election results.

 online resource centre For additional material and resources, please visit the Online Resource Centre at: **www.oxfordtextbooks.co.uk/orc/caramani3e/**

CHAPTER 19
Political communication

Pippa Norris

Chapter contents

Reader's guide

Political communication focuses on the transmission of information among politicians, the media, and the public. This chapter starts by outlining the logic of the comparative study of political communications. Two distinct approaches are identified. First, some accounts emphasize typologies of **media systems**, reflecting the enduring features of the media landscape, exemplified by contrasts among state-owned, public service, or commercial broadcasting systems. This approach was useful during the modern era of communications, but it has proved increasingly limited given the fragmentation and multidimensionality of contemporary channels during the third age of **digital communications** in the twenty-first century. Second, others use *disaggregated* indices to compare multiple dimensions of political communication, such as measures of press freedom, audience access, and media ownership and pluralism. This chapter proposes a sequential model of political communications and then uses multidimensional disaggregated indices to compare some key features of political communications worldwide.

Introduction

The role of the mass media in democracy and development remains contested. There is no agreement about the most appropriate normative standards which the media are supposed to meet, nor a consensus about how far these standards are achieved in practice. Should the news media serve as an agenda-setter, calling attention to urgent social needs and global problems? Or should they instead prioritize their role in providing entertainment and soft news for the broadest possible audience, allowing the free market to determine coverage? Should journalists strive to maintain neutrality and balance across diverse partisan viewpoints, or should they be passionate and committed advocates crusading for causes? In fragile states, should reporters be watchdogs critical of powerful interests, or consensus builders strengthening support for the government authorities and building national unity?

Political communication is an interactive process concerning the transmission of information among politicians, the media, and the public. The process operates downwards from governing institutions towards citizens, horizontally through linkages among political actors, and also upwards from public opinion towards the authorities. Newer technologies have merged diverse platforms, but a conventional distinction can still be drawn concerning *interpersonal communication* (such as one-to-one discussions, say on doorsteps, by email, or by phone bank connecting election workers and party supporters, or by constituents contacting elected representatives), *within group networks* (exemplified by local meetings, newsletters, weblogs, Tweets, YouTube uploads, and Facebook postings), and *mass communications* through the media (typified by regional and national newspapers, radio, and television broadcasts).

The earliest *classical era* of political communication evolved as representative democracies developed and the franchise expanded in Western Europe during the eighteenth and nineteenth centuries. Face-to-face interpersonal interactions connected citizens and politicians directly through election canvassing, town hall meetings, printed handbills and posters, and local rallies and candidate hustings. These channels were supplemented among the European elite by the printed word, including publication of occasional political pamphlets, newsletters, periodicals, journals, and newspapers. Railways expanded the opportunities for party leadership whistle-stop tours and facilitated the cheaper and faster distribution of daily newspapers among a growing literate population, with commercial advertising reducing the price of mass-circulation papers and magazines. Telegraphs connected distant reporters with newsrooms, and news wire agencies, first established by Associated Press in the mid-nineteenth century, provided international news feeds from worldwide locations. The early twentieth century saw the growth of wireless radios, used for leadership fireside chats and the first party political broadcasts (aired by the British Broadcasting Corporation (BBC) in 1924). This era also saw technological advances in photography and wire transmissions which facilitated publication of realistic visual images, replacing engravings. During the interwar years, film documentaries and cinema sound newsreels covered events and breaking developments around the world.

The *modern era* of political communications, following the end of the Second World War, saw the rapidly expanding role of terrestrial television broadcasting, carrying both TV party political broadcasts on public service channels and commercial advertising on privately owned TV networks. Interpersonal communications between local candidates, party workers, and citizens continued to play a vital role in doorstep campaigns, while the mass-circulation national and regional newspapers and magazines reached more educated and literate populations. By the mid-twentieth century these resources were supplemented in post-industrial societies by the golden age of national and regional television and radio broadcasts carrying news and current affairs, with later decades experiencing the expansion of satellite and cable transmissions and channels.

The rise of the internet is widely regarded as demarcating the *third age* of political communication, focused on a wide range of digital technologies. Email services and networked computers had been available in scientific research networks for decades, but technological advances, leading to the development of the first visual browser in the mid-1990s and the World Wide Web, have transformed political communication during recent years. The developments include a fragmentation and proliferation of information sources available from the rapid expansion of interpersonal and group email and text messaging, search engines, the blogosphere and the wealth of websites maintained by candidates, parties, government agencies, and advocacy groups, the easy availability 24/7 of online newspapers and TV video news, and the popularity of social networking sites such as Facebook. Newspapers, radio, and television are in the process of adapting to the evolving digital landscape, taking advantage of opportunities such as smart mobile phones to diversify their means of transmission and their audience, although many are also facing serious financial challenges through the loss of traditional sources of subscription and advertising revenues.

The third age of communications is part of a continuously evolving process. Many of the most popular political functions of the internet return to some of the key features of interpersonal and group communications characteristic of the classical age of political communications, eroding the more centralized role of televised mass communications which predominated in the mid-twentieth century during the modern age. The newer forms of digital political communications usually supplement, but do not automatically replace, older forms; hence in contemporary election campaigns, personal canvassing by party workers continues alongside television broadcasts and party websites, widening sources of information and thus citizen choice. Moreover, as discussed later in this chapter, lack of access to newer information and communication technologies persist in many developing nations worldwide.

KEY POINTS

- Political communication is an interactive process concerning the transmission of information among politicians, the media, and the public.
- The evolution of political communication can be distinguished into a classical era, a modern era, and a third age.

The logic of comparative political communications

There are two distinct approaches to the comparative study of political communication. The older tradition focused on developing and comparing categorical typologies of *media systems*, analogous to distinguishing and classifying types of regimes. This approach was most common during the modern era, and it proved useful for delineating contrasts in the global landscape of radio and television broadcasting. However, it has proved to be problematic, given the fragmentation and multidimensionality of contemporary channels occurring in the third age of digital communication. Existing typologies are normative and culturally specific. Classification schemas remain descriptive and difficult to operationalize. Instead, this chapter proposes that a more satisfactory research strategy uses *disaggregated indices* to compare multiple dimensions of contemporary political communication, such as measures of press freedom, audience access, and media ownership and pluralism.

All empirical analysis of political communication is comparative, if this is understood to mean contrasting different units, including types of media channels (such as TV versus the internet), programme genres (e.g. news or soaps), or media effects (such as framing and agenda-setting). However, the heart of the comparative study of political communication is conventionally understood to focus more narrowly upon contrasting spatial units, usually comparing nation-states but also local communities, media markets, or global regions. Indeed, given the rapid expansion of cosmopolitan communications and transborder information flows, focusing upon comparison of single countries as the unit of analysis is problematic.

A further distinction can be drawn between cross-national studies that use other places as a convenient way of testing propositions that would otherwise have been examined at home (for example, examining whether individual-level patterns of internet use in America are also apparent in Sweden or Germany), and more ambitious comparative research, seeking to understand how varying institutional contexts (such as those generated by different types of state regimes and political institutions, cultural regions, levels of development, or media systems) shape processes of political communications. Through systematic comparison, scientific research about political communication aims to make descriptive or explanatory inferences based on empirical observations.

To do this, comparative studies of political communications can either adopt what John Stuart Mill identified as the logic of the '*most similar* strategy', seeking to analyse the mass media while 'controlling' for certain shared cultural, social, or regime characteristics, such as studies comparing election campaigns among member states within the European Union. Alternatively, research can follow the '*most different* strategy', seeking to maximize contextual variations when identifying regularities in the phenomenon under examination, such as comparing press freedom among electoral autocracies and electoral democracies. Comparative research designs can also choose to focus in depth upon a few selected case studies, examining historical processes within a specific context, ideally illustrating broader theoretical frameworks and conceptual typologies. Contrasts can also involve a limited number of units. Or else studies can adopt large-N comparisons, using econometric techniques to identify regularities over space and time around the world. Research designs with a limited number of cases, such as studies of the culture of journalism comparing only a handful of countries, are problematic if the findings are interpreted, implicitly or explicitly, as representing the larger universe of, say, post-industrial societies.

The advantages of comparative research designs are many (Esser and Pfetsch 2004). This approach expands the contextual environments for observations, allowing reliable generalizations to be established. This process reveals parochialism and highlights the underlying causal factors taken for granted within any particular environment. Individual-level social psychological behavioural studies conducted within specific societies (such as the US) commonly assume that certain general empirical relationships exist—for example concerning the impact of negative news on voter turnout, or agenda-setting effects on policy priorities. Cross-national research is also invaluable for communications policy by highlighting the impact of alternative interventions, strategies, and programmatic reforms that can inform the decision-making process, adapting best practices to local needs.

The older tradition of comparative political communications focused upon developing and comparing typologies of media systems. But what should be included as an effective conceptual typology? In the modern era, the classification was relatively straightforward, based primarily upon patterns of state, public, or private sector ownership of newspapers and radio and television broadcasting within each nation. One major challenge to this approach arising in the digital era is to define which units should be compared, since the media now includes multiple outlets. If one reads online newspapers and watches TV programmes through Hulu or its equivalent, for example, is this equivalent to experiencing these activities in the non-online world? Even the simple concept of 'mass' communication, which used to be exemplified by terrestrial broadcasts, has dissolved more recently with the expansion of interpersonal and group-to-group networks (are 'blogs' a form of mass communications or social networks?).

Moreover, the concept of a media 'system' implies a relatively stable and enduring institutional arrangement. This notion becomes confusing where political communications are defined by several separate components, such as the predominance of public sector or commercial broadcasting, the degree of journalistic professionalism, or the existence of strong links between parties and newspapers, which may, in fact, be unconnected. Other concepts which are used in the political communications literature, such as 'personalization', 'professionalization', 'game frames', or 'media logics', are often also poorly defined and operationalized. Misleading conceptual classifications provide blinkers that hinder rather than help by obscuring the real commonalities and contrasts in the countries under study.

KEY POINTS

- There are two distinct approaches to the comparative study of political communication: typologies of media systems and disaggregated indices.
- Comparative research designs provide a number of advantages for analysing political communication.
- Classical typologies are challenged today by the fragmentation and multidimensionality of the media systems.

Conceptual typologies of media systems

Visitors to countries such as the US or the UK, Qatar or Syria, and Burma or the Philippines are quickly struck by the major contrasts in processes of political communication, whether comparing the capacity of the independent media to criticize the state, the structure of ownership and control of the broadcasting system, new information and communication technologies (ICTs) in everyday life, or the society's degree of openness. The study of political communication has long been interested in making sense of media environments across diverse societies and regimes, yet no consensus has developed about the most appropriate typologies useful for comparison. The absence of standard conceptual frameworks for understanding media systems in this subfield is in sharp contrast with those which have become established elsewhere in comparative politics, discussed in other chapters in this volume.

Classic classifications of media systems: the Cold War models

The origins of comparative work on media systems can be traced to the seminal *Four Theories of the Press* (Siebert *et al.* 1956). This was an early attempt to develop conceptual models describing how media systems functioned worldwide, and the framework was heavily influenced by the Cold War era. The authors theorized that media systems are embedded within their broader social and political context, although in practice they focused mainly upon the relationship between the state and the mass media. They suggested that media systems around the world could be classified into four main categories, each reflecting different normative values.

Libertarian media systems emphasize the importance of the press as a free marketplace of ideas without state interference or regulation, exemplified by privately owned newspaper and commercial television networks in the US. Ideally, the legal and policy regulatory framework should be conducive to freedom of expression, pluralism, and diversity of the media. In this perspective, independence of broadcasting should be guaranteed by law, and the state should not censor or place unwarranted legal restrictions on the media.

Socially responsible media systems reflect many of the core values embodied in public service broadcasting predominant during this era in Western Europe. The BBC played a major role in shaping this perspective, where radio and television broadcasters are seen to have a mission, in the words of Lord Reith, 'to educate and inform, as well as entertain' when serving the broader public interest. Moreover, public service broadcasters also emphasize the need for programmes designed to reach audiences with special needs, including children and young people, ethnic, national, and linguistic minorities, the disabled, and rural communities. Thus, freedom of expression remains central to public service journalism but nevertheless in this tradition the state is acknowledged to play an important role by appointing independent broadcasting authorities to regulate and issue transmission licenses, with broadcasting revenues derived from television and radio licence fees.

Authoritarian media systems are those where journalists are subservient to the state, in the interests of maintaining social stability and national cohesion. For Siebert *et al.*, this category was found in many developing countries where a more direct form of state control over radio and television broadcasting remained common, the commercial and non-profit sectors were underdeveloped, and the audience share of the independent media was limited.

Lastly, the authors identified a distinct *Soviet Communist* model, where the role of the press was to serve as a collective agitator on behalf of the party (and thus the working class), although in many other respects this category overlapped with authoritarian systems.

In subsequent decades, the fourfold Siebert *et al.* typology has come in for growing criticism, but no consensus has emerged about the most useful alternative classification to replace this framework (McQuail 1994). The original typology was heavily ideological, strongly favouring the libertarian model exemplified by the US rather than providing a more neutral categorization, and thus it was highly contested. The era of *glasnost*, and the eventual fall of the Berlin Wall, drove another nail into the coffin of the 'Soviet' model (De Smaele 1999). The absence of theorizing about the wide range of media systems found in the developing world became increasingly apparent (McQuail 2010).

Commercial vs. public service broadcasting

One alternative approach collapsed the fourfold Siebert *et al.* typology into two categories of broadcasting systems found in post-industrial societies. One was focused on the more market-oriented *commercial* broadcasting industry, which developed in the US and throughout much of Latin America (following the libertarian ideal). This can be contrasted with the alternative *public service* model of broadcasting (following the social responsibility ideal), which traditionally dominated contemporary Western Europe and Scandinavia (Blumler and Gurevitch 1995). Increasingly, however, following the deregulation and privatization of telecommunications in the 1980s, many European countries have evolved towards a *mixed* or dual system of broadcasting, such as that long used in the UK, which combines both public service and commercial channels (Norris 2000). Moreover, the simple conceptual distinction between market-oriented and state-oriented media systems, as well as between commercial and public service broadcasting, conceals important differences within each category. Even the core notion of 'the press' or 'broadcasting' is now becoming dated, given the great diversity of mass media outlets and the merger of alternative information platforms, such as the expansion of online newspaper websites and journalistic blogs, social media such as Facebook and Twitter, and YouTube news videos.

Modern classifications of media systems: comparing established democracies

One of the most ambitious recent attempts to replace the Siebert *et al.* framework, which attracted widespread attention, was developed by Hallin and Mancini (2004). The authors restrict the focus to conceptualizing and classifying 'media systems' in eighteen established democracies and post-industrial economies within North America and Western Europe, emphasizing that this universe facilitates comparison of like with like. Thus they do not claim that these ideal types apply to developing countries and newer democracies elsewhere in the world.

The Hallin and Mancini classification focuses upon four major dimensions of media systems.

- The degree of *state intervention in the media system*, especially via public service broadcasting, as well as by legal regulation and subsidies.
- The extent of *political parallelism*, referring to how far news media outlets are partisan or more neutral, and how far media systems reflect party systems.
- The *historical development of media markets*, especially the legacy of this process for contemporary newspaper circulation rates.
- The extent of *journalistic professionalism*.

The authors argue that these criteria cluster together, at least loosely, into distinct types, suggesting a threefold classification of media systems. They identify three models.

- A *liberal* model, which they suggest prevails in Anglo-American countries (the UK, the US, Canada, and Ireland), is seen as characterized by commercial media and market mechanisms.
- The *democratic corporatist* model, which is thought to prevail across the consensus democracies in Northern Europe (Austria, Belgium, Denmark, Finland, Germany, Netherlands, Norway, Sweden, and Switzerland), is regarded as emphasizing the links between commercial media and organized social and political groups, within the context of an active but limited role of the state.
- Lastly the polarized pluralist model, which they suggest typifies Mediterranean Europe (France, Greece, Italy, Portugal, and Spain), integrates media into party politics, with a weaker commercial broadcasting sector and a stronger role for the state.

Hallin and Mancini conclude that, although the liberal model has dominated Anglo-American media studies, in fact the polarized pluralist model probably provides a more accurate description of journalism in many democracies. The typology has been adopted by other scholars to understand and explain contrasts within the post-industrial societies included in the original study, such as when analysing the media landscape for journalistic cultures and election coverage. Researchers have also applied the ideas when analysing the function of the media in other global regions and types of regime, such as Russia and China.

Nevertheless, the Hallin and Mancini framework also suffers from several major shortcomings that limit the value of the conceptual typology. Perhaps most importantly, it is not apparent whether the four dimensions identified by Hallin and Mancini—state ownership, political parallelism, media markets and journalistic professionalism—form a cohesive syndrome that defines the major contrasts found today among contemporary media systems in established democracies, still less in other countries. Two major challenges arising from any conceptual framework include the problem of excluding certain important dimensions of political communications and difficulties of empirical measurement, leading to the misclassification of cases.

First, certain essential dimensions of contemporary digital era communications are not incorporated into these models. Hence the framework emphasizes the importance of the historical development of mass circulation newspapers, which influences the contemporary structure of the news industry in different nations. Similarly, the historical role of public broadcasting corporations, established during the early decades of radio broadcasting, continues to shape modern television. Even among affluent post-industrial societies, major contrasts are evident in the adoption of these technologies, from the general level of access and use of computers and the internet to the diffusion of mobile (cell) phones, text messaging, online social networks, blogging, and TV teletext. Hence, Eurostat (http://epp.eurostat.ec.europa.eu) estimates that in 2008 more than eight out of ten households had internet access in Sweden and the Netherlands, for example, compared with just four out of ten in Italy and one out of ten in Greece. The digital divide worldwide is, of course, even broader.

Similarly, although the roles of the state ownership and public subsidy of the media are regarded as important, there is little explicit acknowledgement of the importance of press freedom and minimal comparison of the legal regulatory framework guaranteeing freedom of expression, press pluralism, and journalistic diversity. Even within the European Union there are significant differences in legal regulations, such as the stringency of libel and defamation laws, protection of journalistic independence, freedom of information rights, regulations designed to prevent ownership concentration, and the use of media subsidies.

Lastly, the classification remains impressionistic, allowing room for alternative judgements about specific cases. For example, the British dual commercial–public service media system is classified by the authors as Anglo-American, but McQuail (2005) points out that the UK may have far more in common with the North European model, given the strong role of BBC public service broadcasting, rather than with the more commercially dominant American television market. Since the 1950s, the UK has had a dual system of broadcasting, dominated by the standards and ethos established by the BBC, with the commercial sector heavily regulated to maintain high standards of public broadcasting. American television, aside from PBS and C-Span, is predominately commercial. As Scammell and Semetko note, 'It [Britain] shares with the U.S. a commitment to free markets, freedom of speech, and self-regulation as the guiding principles for newspapers. It shares with northern Europe a history of highly partisan newspapers and regulated television markets, dominated by well-funded public service broadcasters' (Strömbäck and Lee Kaid 2008). Thus, arguably, media systems in the UK and the US have little in common. And if it is accepted that the conceptual logic is faulty in these particular cases, this raises broader doubts about other classifications, for example whether there are indeed closer similarities between Germany and Norway, or between Germany and France, Italy, or Spain. In general, without any rigorous process for testing the classification independently, whether by establishing certain standardized indicators or a set of explicit decision rules, typologies remain fuzzy, impressionistic, and unscientific. To resolve these issues, it is important to operationalize and measure the core concepts in any classificatory schema of media systems to test how far the different dimensions actually cluster together in meaningful ways— and to examine the systematic consequences arising from any differences.

KEY POINTS

- Concept and typologies used to compare media systems across countries are less developed than those of other subfields of comparative politics.

- Cold War classifications distinguished four types of media systems: libertarian, socially responsible, authoritarian, and Soviet communist systems. Later typologies distinguish commercial, public service, and mixed models.

- Hallin and Mancini provide a useful typology. They distinguish liberal, democratic corporatist, and polarized pluralist media systems.

Disaggregated indices of political communications

Disaggregated indices capture several specific features of political communications and facilitate global comparisons. But which indices are most relevant? The selection still requires a normative and conceptual framework. During the 1970s and 1980s, heated debate surrounded claims about the ideal roles and normative standards which are appropriate for evaluating the performance of the media in the public interest (McQuail 2009). Libertarians have argued for minimal state interference in the media as a necessary condition for an environment that can support democracy. Others have emphasized that the construction of a media environment requires a more pro-active role by the state—in providing infrastructure, funding public and community broadcasting, and ensuring the most appropriate regulatory environment. Arguments came to a head in international debates surrounding publication of the McBride Commission report, *Many Voices One World* (McBride 1980), triggering a major rift within UNESCO. During this debate, some representatives argued that the media needed to assist in the task of nation-building and supporting government authorities in developing societies and fragile states (see also Chapter 25). The Commission called for democratization of communication and strengthening of national media to avoid dependence on external sources, such as a handful of international wire services. In contrast, other countries emphasized that the proposals conflicted with the need for media independence and freedom of expression. The rift eventually led the US and the UK to withdraw official membership and resources from UNESCO during the mid-1980s, deeply damaging the organization. In recent years, however, a broader international consensus has emerged about the role of the media in both development and democratic governance.[1] This new agreement, led by UNESCO, has helped to encourage common normative standards for evaluating media development, strengthening integration among multiple initiatives designed to strengthen the media among many donor agencies, international organizations, NGOs, and national stakeholders. The agreement also spurred the need for more adequate empirical indices and data to compare patterns of media development and to diagnose needs.

To understand and compare the roles and functions of the media in different societies worldwide, and the shared normative standards, the process of political communication can be divided into six major components: the communications infrastructure, the regulatory environment, the structure of media ownership, the skills and capacities of the journalism profession, the contents of political communications, and the effects of communications (see Figure 19.1). Each of these dimensions can be understood separately, but they can also be organized analytically as a sequential process which ranges from the most general context (relating to the technological infrastructure available for communication in each society, such as the availability of broadband and wireless connectivity) to the most specific (concerning the diversity of contents available through the press and broadcasting and the impact of media messages on citizens).

Communications infrastructure

The first component of the process concerns whether the communications infrastructure in any society has the capacity to support diverse, independent, and pluralistic media. Ideally, the technological infrastructure should

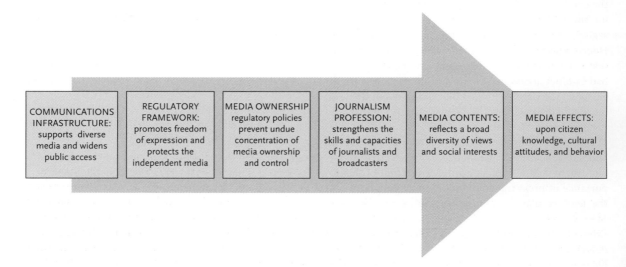

COMMUNICATIONS INFRASTRUCTURE: supports diverse media and widens public access

REGULATORY FRAMEWORK: promotes freedom of expression and protects the independent media

MEDIA OWNERSHIP regulatory policies prevent undue concentration of media ownership and control

JOURNALISM PROFESSION: strengthens the skills and capacities of journalists and broadcasters

MEDIA CONTENTS: reflects a broad diversity of views and social interests

MEDIA EFFECTS: upon citizen knowledge, cultural attitudes, and behavior

Figure 19.1 Nested model of steps in the political communication process and normative standards for media development

maximize opportunities for media distribution and public access, including for marginalized communities. This includes public access both to traditional media, including local, regional, and national radio, television, and newspapers, and to newer information and communication technologies, including mobile telephones, computers, and the internet. Where substantial sections of the population are excluded from universal access, this generates social inequalities, for example where the internet does not reach rural areas, where radio broadcasts fail to serve minority linguistic communities, or where illiterate groups lack access to information from the printed press. Basic lack of essential public utilities can greatly hinder development of the media sector, for example in societies lacking a reliable continuous supply of electricity, let alone the investment in broadband connectivity, WiFi, and computers.

Access to the internet

Has access to the new and old media gradually widened to include most of the population in developing societies or do deep-rooted inequalities persist? During the 1990s, many interpretations of the digital divide envisaged the necessity of distributing personal computers and wired broadband connections (DSL, cable) to access the internet and email—and thus the need for reliable electricity sources, keyboard skills and computer literacy, landline telephone infrastructure, and the like. But recent years have witnessed important technological innovations in this field that have reduced some of the hurdles to information access in poorer societies. This includes the availability of wind-up radios, solar power batteries, wireless connectivity, $100 rugged laptops, internet cafes, community telephone and internet centres, and mobile phones with social media, data services, email, and text messaging. All these developments will probably help to close the global digital divide. At the same time, however, some observers suggest that the core inequalities in information poverty have persisted and may even have deepened (James 2008). Post-industrial societies and emerging economies that invested heavily in advanced digital technologies have reaped substantial gains in productivity. This may encourage them to build on their success and expand this sector of the economy still further. Moreover, it still remains the case that, beyond isolated pockets of innovation and mobile phones, many of the poorest societies in the world continue to lack the basic infrastructure and resources to connect their rural populations fully to global communication networks and markets.

Despite a substantial surge in access to mobile cell phones with data services, the available evidence on the distribution of internet users in Comparative table 1 suggests that the relative size of the gap between rich and poor societies worldwide has widened, rather than narrowed, in recent years. Evidence from the International Telecommunications Union (ITU) suggests that the online population suddenly accelerated in high-income nations during the early 1990s, so that the majority of the population living in these countries became connected. Nevertheless, substantial variations remain even among these nations; for example, within the European Union today around one-fifth of all households in Bulgaria and Romania are connected to the internet, compared with more than three-quarters of all households in such countries as the Netherlands, Sweden, and Denmark.[2] The diffusion of the internet among middle-income economies accelerated later than in richer nations, and most of these societies continue to lag far behind in internet connectivity. In rapidly growing emerging markets that are large consumers and producers of ICT goods and services, such as Brazil, China, Russia, South Africa, and India, internet access and email has spread most widely among the professional urban middle classes, often via smart mobile phones rather than traditional laptops.

In contrast, despite these trends, the populations living in the least developed societies around the world, such as Mali, continue to lack internet access, including connectivity via computers with fast broadband connections as well as data service cell phones. The starkest contrasts are in Africa and Asia. According to ITU estimates, internet access is gradually growing in most poor nations; places such as Mali, Benin, and Burkina Faso are not untouched by these developments, but they lag far behind the rapid rate of diffusion of PCs, laptops, and smart phones with fast wireless and broadband connections that is common in most affluent post-industrial nations.

Access to landline and cellular telephones

Access to the internet used to be limited by the availability of personal computers and the need for dial-up connections through landline telephones. This represented a major bottleneck; in particular, state-controlled telecommunication monopolies in Central and Eastern Europe, Africa, and Asia often failed to provide universal services to many remote rural areas, and the demand for landlines lagged far behind supply (Barnett and Choi 1995; Barnett et al. 1996, 1999; Barnett 2001). Today WiFi connections have reduced the need for landline broadband connections for internet access, and the surge in the use of mobile cell phones, many of which provide data services, has been dramatic. Nevertheless, although mobile cell phones have greatly reduced the barriers to social media, and although they represent a cheaper technology, they have not totally eliminated global inequalities in internet access. Disparities between rich and poor societies show a familiar pattern, with affluent countries expanding connectivity at the fastest rate.

Access to radio, television, and newspapers

How do these trends compare with the diffusion of radio and TV sets (whether connected via terrestrial, cable, or satellite signals), as well as the circulation and sales of newspapers? Today TV penetration has reached saturation levels in advanced industrialized societies; almost all households in these countries have a TV set. Emerging economies and middle-income societies rapidly gained access, but the absolute global gap (the difference between the proportion of households with TV sets in low- and high-income societies) remains. UNESCO estimates that in 2005 about a quarter of all households worldwide had a TV set, but less than 5 per cent of homes in countries such as Uganda, Burma, Rwanda, and Ethiopia had access to TV sets.[3]

Radios are one of the most important ways that people in developing societies learn about the world, particularly through coverage of news and current affairs, talk shows, and popular music transmitted locally by non-profit community radio stations. However, according to the latest available figures, on a per capita basis almost five times as many radios are available in rich societies as in poorer societies.

Access to newspapers

UNESCO also gathers statistics on the number of outlets and the distribution, circulation, and sales of printed daily newspapers and periodicals. When standardized on a per capita basis, the trends suggest that this is the only medium with growing convergence between high- and low-income societies. However, this is not due to a significant expansion of readership or circulation figures in the low- or medium-income countries, but reflects an erosion of newspaper circulation figures in the high-income countries since the mid-1980s (predating the rise of online newspapers on the internet). Even with this closure, the gap in newspaper circulation between rich and poor nations remains substantial. Multiple readers may compensate somewhat for the contrasts in sales and circulation, but on a per capita basis one newspaper per 100 people is sold in low-income countries compared with twenty-six per 100 in rich countries. Rising levels of literacy in developing societies have not substantially increased sales of daily papers. Evidence comparing the distribution of published books and periodicals show similar disparities.

Therefore we can conclude that recent years have seen the dramatic growth of digital information and communication technologies associated with the rise of computers and the internet, facilitating the use of text messaging, email, and websites, and spread even farther through smart cellular mobile phones and communal technology kiosks. Despite these developments, the gap *between* rich and poor nations in access to all major forms of information and communication resources remains substantial, as does the digital divide *within* societies (Haywood 1995; Saur and Wresch 1996; Norris 2001; Yu 2006). The World Bank estimates that in 2005 there were more than ten times as many mobile telephone subscribers in high-income countries as in low-income countries. While TV sets are present in almost all households in Europe and the US, only one in seven households have a TV in low-income nations.[4] In 2006, fewer than five out of every 100 Africans used the internet, compared with an average of one in two inhabitants of the G8 countries.[5] In developing societies, access to printed media (daily newspapers, magazines, and books) is limited by enduring problems of illiteracy and the cost of these products, as well as by language barriers. All these factors combine to generate severe information poverty in poor nations, making these societies, and especially their rural populations, increasingly marginalized at the periphery of communication networks (Wang *et al.* 2000). The least developed and poorest countries are often the ones that are most isolated from modern communication and information technologies, and thus cut off from the knowledge economy, without the telecommunications infrastructure needed for landline telephones in many homes and businesses. Many rural areas in these societies also lack a regular supply of electricity and, where reliable power is available, limited access to TV sets and computers restricts connectivity via television and the internet.

The regulatory environment

Beyond infrastructure, the second sequential component of communications processes concerns the *regulatory environment*, based on the policies, laws, and administrative decisions regulating political communications within each country, including how far journalists and the general public are free to express criticism of those in authority, whether in the public or private sectors. This understanding is based on a classical liberal and human rights based understanding of the role of the media. Thus, freedom of expression was recognized as a core component of the UN Universal Declaration of Human Rights in 1948:

> Everyone has the right to freedom of opinion and expression; this right includes freedom to hold opinions without interference and to seek, receive and impart information and ideas through any media and regardless of frontiers (Article 19)

Freedom of expression is widely seen as underpinning other fundamental freedoms, such as the right to vote, to form political parties, to exchange political ideas, and to scrutinize public officials. The mass media are crucial to freedom of expression as they provide the public platform through which this right is effectively exercised within any community.

One approach to assessing the degree of freedom of expression has compared rights contained in written constitutions, and whether countries have passed Freedom of Information laws (Banisar 2006; Ackerman and Sandoval-Ballesteros 2006). These measures are an important part of an open society, but they remain limited because what matters for the actual degree of press freedom is the implementation of such rights or legislation more than their existence as a legal formality. For example, the Kyrgyz Republic, Russia, and Colombia have Freedom of Information laws, and Uzbekistan's constitution guarantees freedom of speech and the press, but this does not mean that in practice journalists are safe from imprisonment or intimidation in these countries or that these regulations have proved effective in promoting partisan balance in the news, freedom of expression and publication, or transparency in government.

Broader comparisons outside Europe suggest that legal regulations are a critical dimension for comparing and understanding political communications. The regulatory environment can best be compared using detailed national reports provided by human rights watch organizations, the detailed comparisons produced by the International Research and Exchanges Board (IREX) for eighty countries in Africa, Europe, Eurasia, and the Middle East in the Media Sustainability Index, and global composite indices, including the annual Freedom of the Press index provided by Freedom House and the Worldwide Press Freedom Index by Reporters sans Frontières (Reporters without Borders).

The Worldwide Press Freedom Index is constructed to reflect the degree of freedom that journalists and news organizations enjoy in each country, and the efforts made by the state to respect and to ensure respect for this freedom. The organization compiles a questionnaire with fifty-two criteria used for assessing the state of press freedom in each country every year. It includes every kind of violation directly affecting journalists (such as murder, imprisonment, physical attacks, and threats) and news media (censorship, confiscation issues, searches, and harassment). It registers the degree of impunity enjoyed by those responsible for such violations. It also takes account of the legal situation affecting the news media (such as penalties for press offences, the existence of a state monopoly in certain areas, and the existence of a regulatory body), the behaviour of the authorities towards the state-owned news media and the foreign press, and the main obstacles to the free flow of information on the internet. The Worldwide Press Freedom Index reflects not only abuses attributable to the state, but also those by armed militias, clandestine organizations, or pressure groups that can pose a real threat to press freedom. The survey questionnaire was sent to partner organizations of Reporters sans Frontières, including fourteen freedom of expression groups in five continents, and to the organization's 130 correspondents around the world, as well as to journalists, researchers, jurists, and human rights activists. A 100-point country score can be estimated for each country.

This index can be compared with the results of Freedom House's annual index of Press Freedom.[6] This measures how much diversity of news content is influenced by the structure of the news industry, legal and administrative decisions, the degree of political influence or control, the economic influences exerted by the government or private entrepreneurs, and actual incidents violating press autonomy including censorship, harassment, and physical threats to journalists. The assessment of press freedom by Freedom House distinguishes between the broadcast and print media, and the resulting ratings are expressed as a 100-point scale for each country under comparison.

The estimates provided by the global indices show strong correlations across both measures, despite differences in their construction and measurement. Thus, long-standing autocracies, including North Korea, Cuba, and Libya, score exceptionally poorly on freedom of expression. In Burma, for example, in late September 2007 thousands of monks and civilians took to the streets of Rangoon in a week-long uprising against the Burmese government. In response, the military junta shut down the internet, arrested or intimidated Burmese journalists, and severed mobile and landline phone links to the outside world. A Japanese video journalist from AFP news was shot dead. Cameras and video cell phones were confiscated by soldiers. The official Division for Press Scrutiny and Registration pressured local editors to publish stories claiming that the unrest was organized by 'saboteurs'. In the immediate aftermath of these events, thousands of monks were said to have been arrested, but after the media clampdown no images of these events were published in either the domestic or the international news.[7] Even in less turbulent times, critical coverage of the Burmese junta is restricted in domestic news media, silencing negative stories about the military leadership. Citizens are punished for listening to overseas radio broadcasts. Nor are these isolated instances of state control of the airwaves. Although Burma is an extreme case, regularly ranking near the bottom of worldwide annual assessments of press freedom produced by Reporters sans Frontières and Freedom House, human rights observers report that many other states routinely deploy techniques designed to suppress independent journalism, manipulate and slant news selectively in their favour, and limit critical coverage of the regime. Thus, for example, China has liberalized the newspaper industry and yet it still exerts strict censorship in access to search engines and websites such as Google (Kalathil and Boas 2001; Palfrey et al. 2008). A more comprehensive classification needs to include contemporary autocracies with severe limits on freedom of expression, independent journalism, and human rights, exemplified by the diverse cases of Zimbabwe, Syria, and North Korea, as well as examining whether journalists play a distinctive function in electoral autocracies and electoral democracies (Hyden *et al.* 2002; Voltmer 2006). In contrast, many countries with moderate experience of democracy have a mixed record of freedom of the press, with considerable variations among countries such as the Philippines, Mexico, El Salvador, and Turkey. Finally, countries with the longest historical experience of democracy, such as Denmark, Belgium, Australia, and Ireland, also have the greatest media freedom, in the top right-hand quadrant, according to both indices.

The structure of media ownership

The regulatory environment is closely related to the next step in the sequential communication process, the *structure* of media ownership, which includes the direct and mediated channels of communication available in each society, including traditional mass media and new ICTs. To maintain media pluralism and diversity of media suppliers, ideally the legal and policy regulatory framework should prevent monopoly ownership and control. Regulations should also promote and encourage diversity in the availability of alternative *technologies of transmission* (radio and television broadcasts, newspapers, and the internet); *ownership sectors* (public, private, and community media); *media outlets* within each sector; *levels of dissemination* (supra-national, national, and sub-national); *information sources* (such as news agencies); *content* (such as news and cultural programmes); and *target audiences* (such as by income, gender, age, language, and cultural identities).

Monitoring the degree of media pluralism and diversity is a challenging task with the available data, not least because overlapping patterns of commercial ownership and control often lack transparency. The most comprehensive study comparing the degree of state intervention in major media firms, covering almost 100 nations, was estimated by Simeon Djankov and colleagues at the World Bank. The study focused on the five largest daily newspapers in each country, as measured by share of the total circulation of all dailies, and the five largest television stations, as measured by share of viewing. They found that most newspapers are privately owned; only a few countries, such as Belarus, Chad, Cameroon, and Egypt, have a large share of state-owned papers. In contrast, the audience share for state or public service television channels varies substantially worldwide, including among established democracies. Hence the US and many Latin American countries, with a tradition of commercial broadcasting, have a minimal audience share for public broadcasters, but the audience for public service television remains strong in many other countries which have

deregulated telecommunications, such as South Africa, Switzerland, India, and Denmark, as well as the UK.

The main danger to pluralism and diversity arising from media ownership patterns is where citizen access is restricted to one or two television channels, constituting monopolies or oligopolies, thereby limiting consumer choice. The case of Syria prior to the Arab uprising illustrates the role of the state in limited freedom and pluralism. In Syria, the government own and control much of the media, including the daily newspapers, *Al-Thawra* (The Revolution), *Tishrin,* and the English-language *Syria Times,* while the Baath party publishes *Al-Baath.* There was a brief flowering of press freedom after Bashar al-Assad became president in 2000. The normally staid government newspapers cautiously started to discuss reform and democracy. For the first time in nearly forty years, private publications were licensed. The new titles included the political party papers *Sawt al-Shaab* and *Al-Wahdawi,* and a satirical journal. However, within a year, under pressure from the old guard, the president cautioned against over-zealous reform, a subsequent press law imposed a new range of restrictions, and publications could be suspended for violating content rules. Criticism of President Bashar al-Assad and his family is banned, and the domestic and foreign press is censored over material which is deemed to be threatening or embarrassing. Journalists practice self-censorship and foreign reporters rarely get accreditation. Reporters sans Frontières documents common abuses:

> Journalists and political activists risk arrest at any time for any reason and are up against a whimsical and vengeful state apparatus which continually adds to the list of things banned or forbidden to be mentioned. Several journalists were arrested in 2006 for interviewing exiled regime opponents, taking part in conferences abroad and for criticizing government policies. They were subjected to lengthy legal proceedings before the Damascus military court that, under a 1963 law, tries anyone considered to have undermined state security.[8]

Critical journalists outside the country write for the Lebanese or pan-Arab press, such as the Beirut daily *Al-Nahar,* and the influential London daily *Al-Hayat,* as well as contributing to Al-Jazeera and other regional satellite channels.[9]

Syrian TV, operated by the Ministry of Information, operates two terrestrial channels and one satellite channel. It has cautiously begun carrying political programmes and debates featuring formerly 'taboo' issues, as well as occasionally airing interviews with opposition figures. Syria also launched some privately owned radio stations in 2004, but these were restricted from airing any news or political content. With an estimated 1.5 million internet users in Syria by 2007, the web has emerged as a vehicle for dissent. However, in the view of Reporters sans Frontières, Syria is one of the worst offenders against internet freedom as the state censors opposition bloggers and independent news websites. Human Rights Watch notes that the government of Syria regularly restricts the flow of information on the internet and arrests individuals who post comments that the government deems too critical.[10] Overall, Syria ranks 154 out of 166 countries in the Reporters sans Frontières 2007 Worldwide Press Freedom index. Similarly, in terms of press freedom, Freedom House ranks the country 179 out of 195 states worldwide.[11]

The capacity and skills of the journalistic profession

Beyond diversity of media ownership, an effective independent press also depends on the skills and capacities of the journalistic workforce, such as whether professional training is widely available, whether independent press councils protect journalists and monitor professional ethical standards, and whether media monitoring organizations and human rights watch groups based in civil society help to protect freedom of expression, pluralism, and diversity. Professional training strengthens the skills and expands the capacities of journalists and broadcasters, and it is particularly important to provide equal opportunities for women and marginalized groups in both training and employment. Nevertheless, although widely recognized as important for media development, and a major focus of donor aid and technical cooperation, the extent of journalistic professionalism is challenging to monitor and measure cross-nationally with any degree of reliability. Some comparative surveys of news professionals are gradually expanding to fill the gap here, monitoring journalists' attitudes, role orientations, background, and experience (Weaver 1998). These supplement some proxy aggregate indicators, for example concerning the number of journalism training departments and the accreditation processes used in tertiary education in different countries.

The contents of the news media

Diversity of media ownership is important in part because this is seen to underpin diversity of contents, although the two are far from synonymous. Ideally, the media should serve as a platform for democratic discourse, with the contents reflecting and representing the diversity of views and interests in society, including those of marginalized groups. Of course, the media are widely recognized as an essential constituent of the democratic process and as one of the guarantors of free and fair competitive elections (Voltmer 2006). But the idea of the mass media as a platform for democratic debate embraces a wide variety of overlapping functions (Gunther and Mughan 2000). Principally, the media can be seen as a watchdog over the powerful, expanding transparency in both the public and private sectors. Journalists and reporters can strengthen good governance by promoting public scrutiny of those with power, exposing corruption, maladministration, and corporate wrongdoing. The media can also serve as an agenda-setter for policy issues, strengthening government responsiveness, for example by highlighting social needs in complex humanitarian disasters and calling international attention to emergency relief (James 2006; Besley and Burgess 2002). Journalists and commentators can function as advocates for certain issues or causes—as social actors in their own right. The media can also function as gatekeepers, providing balanced coverage of politics and elections (Norris 2009). Beyond this, media outlets are channels through which citizens can communicate with each other, acting as a facilitator of informed debate between diverse social actors and encouraging the non-violent resolution of disputes. The media can also serve as a national forum, a means by which a society can learn about itself and build a sense of community and shared values—a vehicle for cultural expression and cultural cohesion. The media disseminates stories, ideas, and information and acts as a corrective to the 'natural asymmetry of information' between governors and governed and between competing private agents.

Understanding how far media coverage of politics reflects these different functions is a major challenge for researchers, and unfortunately systematic and rigorous cross-national data, based on content analysis of a representative range of media outlets and a random sample of stories, is extremely scarce. As a recent comparative study of campaign coverage by Strömbäck and Lee Kaid (2008) notes, 'There do not seem to be any standardized instruments and coding instructions. The unfortunate end result is that it is often difficult to compare the election news coverage across borders, and although the terminology used is often similar, the extent to which the empirical results are comparable is often uncertain' (Strömbäck and Lee Kaid 2008). More cross-national content analysis is gradually becoming available, for example, concerning media coverage of elections to the European Parliament and party messages embodied in election manifestoes, but nevertheless the communications subfield lacks far behind the availability of standard cross-national datasets available for decades in electoral studies and voting behaviour.

The effects of media coverage of politics

The last step in the sequential communication process focuses upon understanding effects, particularly a wealth of research analysing the primary impact of political communications upon political knowledge and cognition, cultural attitudes and values, and political behaviour. This literature draws upon many theoretical perspectives, but three approaches, in particular, have attracted widespread attention. Thus, *agenda-setting* theories suggest that the news headlines inform us about which issues deserve attention on the policy agenda. *Framing* theories emphasize that reporting shapes the context and background used to comprehend and interpret the workings of government authorities, political institutions, and the policy process. Moreover the process of *priming* is thought to influence which standards are used to evaluate these actions. Each of these processes has been extensively studied to understand how citizens respond to political communications and, in turn, how they seek to influence the political process. Most of the research has been based upon single countries, especially the US, but a growing comparative literature is also emerging, for example, comparing the role of agenda-setting of specific events, such as natural or humanitarian disasters, on public opinion about salient issues in different countries. Others have compared the effects of exposure to commercial vs. public service television in different societies on political knowledge, and the impact of cosmopolitan communication across national borders on cultural values.

In general, however, the comparative study of the effects arising from the communication process remains underdeveloped. In 1975, for example, a review of the literature could only identify a few cross-national studies on comparative political communications. Blumler and Gurevitch (1975) concluded that the subfield was 'in its infancy', lacking a shared consensus about the core theoretical focus, as well as an accumulated body of empirical studies. Two decades later, they observed that work continued to remain patchy, although the study was progressing to 'late adolescence' (Blumler and Gurevitch 1995). Since then, the comparative literature has undoubtedly grown substantially, including cross-national studies of the structure, contents, and effects of the mass media, especially within the European Union and among younger democracies. Despite these encouraging signs, many books continue to follow the older Grand Tour travelogue tradition ('if it's chapter 4, it's Belgium') by presenting national case studies in separate chapters, loosely integrated around some common organizational subheadings (e.g. Lee Kaid and Holtz-Bacha 1994, 2004; Kelly *et al.* 2004; Shoemaker and Cohen 2006). In contrast with equivalent subfields in comparative political science—and more than three decades after Blumler and Gurevitch's original plea—arguably comparative political communications has still not reached mature adulthood. It has not yet established a range of theoretically sophisticated analytical frameworks, buttressed by rigorously tested scientific generalizations, a common lingua franca and shared concepts, standardized instruments, and archival datasets, with the capacity to identify common regularities that prove robust across widely varied contexts (Esser and Pfetsch 2004).

KEY POINTS

- Communication systems are composed of many elements, from the infrastructure (landlines, access to internet points, etc.) to the legal regulatory environment, and the structure of media ownership.

- Democracy requires an effective independent press and depends upon the skills and capacities of the journalistic workforce, such as whether professional training is widely available, whether independent press councils protect journalists and monitor professional ethical standards, and whether media monitoring organizations and human rights watch groups based in civil society help to protect freedom of expression, pluralism, and diversity.

- *Agenda-setting* theories state that news headlines inform us about which issues deserve attention on the policy agenda. *Framing* theories emphasize that reporting shapes the context and background used to comprehend and interpret the workings of government authorities, political institutions, and the policy process.

Conclusion

Comparative studies of political communication are a growing subfield, but in general much previous work has often been hampered by poor conceptualization and measurement, with the main categories used to classify media systems reflecting the modern era characteristic of post-industrial societies during the mid-twentieth century, but far from adequate to compare the complex, fragmented, and multi-platform digital environment of the third age. The traditional distinction between commercial and public service broadcasting has become diluted today, with convergence caused by the deregulation, commercialization, and proliferation of channels now available in European societies, as well as the spread of transnational media conglomerates (Gunther and Mughan 2000; Kelly *et al.* 2004; Esser and Pfetsch 2004). A broader lens that goes beyond the role of mass media in post-industrial societies and in established democracies is necessary to compare political communications around the world.

KEY POINTS

- Political communication is an essential part of the political system and the political process. Structures and processes vary greatly across countries and systematic data are essential for their analysis.

- The quality of political communication is a central element of the quality of democracy.

Questions

1. In what ways does political communication matter for the quality of democracy?

2. What is meant by 'global gap' in the access to telephone, television, radio, and internet?

3. What are the characteristics of the 'third age' of political communication?

4. What are the main types of media system?

5. Discuss the two main approaches of communication studies: typologies of media systems and disaggregated indices.

6. How did campaigning evolve over time since the birth of democracy in the nineteenth century?

7. What are the main elements of a communication system?

8. How can one measure the freedom of political communication comparatively?

9. How does media coverage affect politics?

10. In what ways did the internet affect political communication?

Further reading

Ackerman, J. M. and Sandoval-Ballesteros, I. E. (2006) 'The Global Explosion of Freedom of Information Laws', *Administrative Law Review*, 58(1): 85–130.

Esser, F. and Pfetsch, B. (eds) (2004) *Comparing Political Communication: Theories, Cases, and Challenges* (New York: Cambridge University Press).

Gunther, R. and Mughan, A. (eds) (2000) *Democracy and the Media: A Comparative Perspective* (New York: Cambridge University Press).

Hallin, D. C. and Mancini, P. (2004) *Comparing Media Systems* (Cambridge: Cambridge University Press).

McQuail, D. (1994) *Mass Communication Theory* (3rd edn) (London: Sage).

Norris, P. (2000) *A Virtuous Circle* (New York: Cambridge University Press).

Norris, P. (2001) *Digital Divide* (New York: Cambridge University Press).

Norris, P. (ed.) (2009) *Public Sentinel: News Media and Governance Reform* (Washington, DC: World Bank).

Norris, P. and Inglehart, R. (2009) *Cosmopolitan Communications: Cultural Diversity in a Globalized World* (New York: Cambridge University Press).

Strömbäck, J. and Lee Kaid, L. (2008) *The Handbook of Election News Coverage* (London: Routledge).

Voltmer, K. (ed.) (2006) *Mass Media and Political Communication in New Democracies* (London: Routledge).

Web links

www.cpj.org
Committee to Protect Journalists.

www.freedomhouse.org
Freedom House.

www.indexoncensorship.org
Index on Censorship.

www.ifj.org
International Federation of Journalists.

www.itu.int
International Telecommunications Union, including cross-national statistics on technological diffusion.

www.unesco.org
UNESCO: The official website of the United Nations Educational, Scientific and Cultural Organization.

www.freedominfo.org
Freedom of Information Around the World: A Global Survey of Access to Government Records and Laws.

For additional material and resources, please visit the Online Resource Centre at:
www.oxfordtextbooks.co.uk/orc/caramani3e/

online resource centre

Public policies

CHAPTER 20
Policy-making

Christoph Knill and Jale Tosun

Chapter contents

Reader's guide

The process related to policy-making touches the core function of democratic politics namely the elaboration and discussion of policy solutions to societal problems. This chapter provides a theoretical entree to the analysis of policy-making and identifies potential determinants of **policy** choices. It pursues two core objectives. First it intends to familiarize the reader with the general concept of the policy cycle which helps to focus more specifically on the relevant actors and institutions. Second, it outlines the most crucial domestic and international factors shaping the design of policies. To demonstrate the relevance of the introduced theoretical arguments and analytical concepts, the chapter further presents some empirical findings

Introduction

Policies follow a particular purpose: they are designed to achieve defined goals and present solutions to societal problems. More precisely, policies are government statements of what it intends to do or not to do, including laws, regulations, decisions, or orders. Public policy, on the other hand, is a more specific term, which refers to a long series of actions carried out to solve societal problems (Newton and van Deth 2010: 282). Hence, (public) policies can be conceived of as the main output of political systems (see Figure I.1 in the Introduction to this volume). But how are public policies actually made? Which factors determine their shape?

The classic policy analysis literature approaches these questions by using policy typologies as 'analytical shortcuts' for the underlying process (cf. Anderson 2003; Howlett *et al.* 2009; Knill and Tosun 2012). The most influential typology has been developed by Theodor J. Lowi (1964), who distinguishes between (1) *distributive policies* relating to measures which affect the distribution of resources from the government to particular recipients, (2) *redistributive policies* which are based on the transfer of resources from one societal group to another, (3) *regulatory policies* which specify conditions and constraints for individual or collective behaviour, and (4) *constituent policies* which create or modify the states' institutions. The typology's main objective is to offer scholars support in building more specific theories since each of these four policy types is related to a varying degree of costs and potential opposition when the governments seek to modify the *status quo*.

These considerations about costs and benefits are even more systematically addressed by James Q. Wilson's (1973, 1989, 1995) typology. The author distinguishes between policies on the basis of whether the related costs and benefits are either widely distributed or narrowly concentrated. Each of the four possible combinations yields different implications for policy-making. When both costs and benefits of a certain policy are widely distributed, a government may encounter no or only minor opposition, indicating **majoritarian politics** as the likely outcome. When, by contrast, both costs and benefits of a certain policy are concentrated, a government may be confronted with opposition of rivalling interest groups, which signals **interest group politics**. If costs are, however, concentrated and benefits diffused, a government may encounter opposition from dominant interest groups. In this case, **entrepreneurial politics** are the probable outcome. This implies that policy change requires the presence of 'political entrepreneurs' who are willing to develop and put through political proposals despite strong societal resistance. The fourth and final scenario consists of a situation in which costs are diffuse and benefits concentrated. In such a case, governments are likely to be confronted with a relevant interest group that is favourable to its reform endeavour, indicating that **clientelistic politics** is the likely outcome.

The addressees' opposition or consent to policy options surely represents a central aspect in the analysis of policy-making. Furthermore, both typologies deserve credit for having introduced the notions of costs and benefits related to policy alternatives. Yet, we argue that we can raise the analytical leverage of policy analysis by

Box 20.1 Types of policies

Lowi's typology (1964)

Type of policy	Definition	Examples
Regulatory policies	Policies specifying conditions and constraints for individual or collective behaviour	Environmental protection; migration policy; consumer protection
Distributive policies	Policies distributing new resources	Agriculture; social issues; public works; subsidies; taxes
Redistributive policies	Policies modifying the distribution of existing resources	Land reform; progressive taxation; welfare policy
Constituent policies	Policies creating or modifying the states' institutions	Changes of procedural rules of parliaments

Wilson's typology (1973, 1989, 1995)

Costs	Benefits	
	Concentrated	Diffuse
Concentrated	Interest group politics	Entrepreneurial politics
Diffuse	Clientelistic politics	Majoritarian politics

focusing more explicitly on the political processes. This **politics perspective** involves scrutinizing the roles of the executive and legislative branches of government. Moreover, it implies the employment of sophisticated theories of decision-making and the exploration of policy-making structures for understanding how besides political and institutional forces, social and economic interests shape the content of policies. From this it follows, that the politics perspective enables a more refined definition of the costs and benefits related to a given policy option. Consequently, studying policy-making in terms of comparative politics can significantly enhance our scientific understanding (see Chapter 22). Additionally, by providing the possibility of disaggregating of the policy-making process along various politics stages, this perspective allows for analysing the effects of new political developments, such as internationalization.

KEY POINTS

- Policies are the outputs of the political system; they come along in different forms, including laws, regulations, or rules.

- The policy analysis literature relies on policy typologies as 'analytical shortcuts' for grasping the costs and benefits related to a certain policy option. Based on the respective magnitude of these two parameters, expectations about the likelihood of promulgating new policies and changing existing policies are formulated.

- By studying the policy-making process from a comparative politics perspective, we gain a fuller understanding of the causes and consequences of policy decisions.

Conceptual models of policy-making

What would an ideal policy look like? What is the best policy design that can be achieved? Both questions are crucial to policy-making. The first one refers to the functionality of a policy to be formulated, i.e. which design a particular policy should have in order to meet an *ex ante* defined goal. The second one touches upon the constraints that appear when policies are actually made. These are principally given by politics, i.e. the process by which the actors involved make decisions. Therefore, it is essential for our purpose to examine **how politics shapes policies**.

A number of conceptual models help to clarify our understanding of the relationship between politics and policies. The major models that can be found in the literature are (1) the institutional model, (2) the rational model, (3) the incremental model, (4) the group model, (5) the elite model, and (6) the process model. These models are not

competitive but rather complementary as they focus on different aspects of political life, and hence concentrate on separate characteristics of policies (Dye 2005: 12).

The main implication of these models is that they make different assumptions about the importance of the actors involved—institutions, politicians, bureaucrats, interest groups, and the public—and their rationality. We now shortly explain these models—except the process model, which we address in the next section—to provide an initial theoretical access to policy-making.

Institutional model

For a long time, the central interest of political science was on how institutional arrangements influence the content of policies (cf. March and Olsen 1984, 2008; Weaver and Rockman 1993b). The analytical focus of the institutional model is hence primarily on the balance between executives and legislatives, which show notable variation across political systems (cf. Lijphart 1999). From the institutional perspective, policies are formulated and implemented exclusively by these institutions. In consequence, policy-making is seen as a smooth and largely technical process in which all relevant institutions participate. All the intra-institutional processes, however, remain a 'black box'.

Rational model

First developed in the field of economic analysis, the rational model of decision-making formulates guidance on how to secure 'optimal' policy decisions, implying that no other alternative is better according to the decision-makers' preferences (Shepsle and Bonchek 1997: 25). The rational model is also associated with a particular mode of learning, namely the concept of Bayesian learning. According to this perspective, governments update their beliefs on the consequences of policies with all available information about policy outcomes in the past and elsewhere and choose the policy that is expected to yield the best results (Meseguer Yebra 2009).

Rational policy-making involves a number of demanding assumptions. For example, policy-makers are expected to have perfect information, which has provoked strong criticism (Simon 1955, 1957). Despite this central point of criticism, the rational model remains important for analytical purposes as it helps to contrast ideal policy decisions with actual ones. By assuming that all political actors behave rationally, i.e. reduce costs and maximize benefits, it also provides the starting point for public choice approaches to policy-making. Public choice theory examines the logic and foundation of actions of individuals and groups that are involved in the policy-making process. In this regard, the main objects of analysis are voting behaviour and party competition, coalition and government formation, the involvement of interest groups and bureaucracy in policy-making (cf. Mueller 2003 for an overview).

Along the same lines, the rational model is related to game theory, which serves for analysing decisions in situations in which two or more rational players interact, and where the outcome depends on the choices made by each (cf. McCarthy and Meirowitz 2007). Since game theory allows for systematically modelling the interaction of policy actors, it represents an instructive way of examining the outcomes of policy-making in areas that are affected by externalities, such as trade or environmental policy (cf. Lusztig *et al.* 2003; Bechtel and Tosun 2009; König *et al.* 2010).

Incremental model

Incrementalism emerged as a response to the rational model. Rather than an ideal, it purports to be a realistic description of how policy-makers arrive at their decisions (Lindblom 1959, 1977; Wildavsky 1964). This is related to its foundation on 'bounded rationality', i.e. an alternative concept to rational choice that takes into account the limitations of both knowledge and cognitive capacities of decision-makers. Generally, incremental decisions involve limited changes to existing policies (Anderson 2003: 123).

Similar to rational learning, there is also a concept of bounded learning. In that case, governments likewise engage in information-gathering activity but do not scan all available experience. Instead, they use analytical shortcuts and cognitive heuristics to process the information (cf. Weyland 2006). An example of such heuristics is the adoption of policies from countries that are considered to be particularly successful (cf. Pierson 2003; Braun and Gilardi 2006).

The Achilles heel of the incremental model is that it does not explain how decision-makers arrive at these incremental adjustments. In response to this central shortcoming, Jones and Baumgartner (2005) propose a model of choice that combines incrementalism and punctuated equilibrium theory. This approach states that political processes are generally characterized by stability and incremental-ism, but occasionally produce large-scale departures from the past. By employing data on governmental processes in the US, Belgium, and Denmark, Baumgartner *et al.* (2009) show that incrementalism is an empirical reality.

Group model

Group theory hypothesizes that policies are the result of an equilibrium reached in group struggle, which is determined by the relative strength of each interest group (Truman 1951; Latham 1965). Groups can be distinguished concerning several aspects, such as income, membership size, membership density

and recruitment, organizational aspects, sanctioning mechanisms, and aspects of leadership (Newton and van Deth 2010: 170). Consequently, changes in the relative strength of the individual interest groups involved may trigger policy change.

More generally, group theory presupposes that policy-makers are constantly responding to group pressures, which motivates politicians to form majority coalitions for which they have the competence to define what groups are to be included (Dye 2005: 21). The potential effect of groups for policy-making depends on the particular political structures. In (neo-)corporatist systems, for instance, economic interests are strongly integrated in policy-making (Schmitter and Lehmbruch 1979). Pluralist systems, by contrast, are a market place in which individuals, political parties, and interest groups compete for influence over policy domains.

Elite model

Related to group theory is the view that policy-making is determined by the preferences of governing elites (Mills 1956). The elite model is more specific in a sense as it claims that the electorate is generally poorly informed about policies and that the elites shape the public opinion on policy questions. In this way, the elite model mainly highlights the potential source of bias in policy-making in terms of the adoption of policy alternatives that correspond to the preferences of the elite rather than of the general public.

KEY POINTS

- The conceptual models represent starting points for the analysis of policy-making.
- The models vary regarding their perception of policy-actors as either fully or partly rational.
- The models also differ concerning their focus on either political institutions, actors, or both.

Analysing policy-making as a process: the policy cycle

What are the main characteristics of policy-making? Basically, three features can be identified. First, policy-making occurs in presence of *multiple constraints,* e.g. shortage of time and resources, public opinion, and of course the constitution. Secondly, policy-making involves the existence of *various policy processes.* Governments are not unitary actors but consist of different departments that overlap and compete with each other. Thirdly, these policy processes form an *infinite cycle of decisions and policies.* Current policy decisions are not independent of decisions taken before, and policies under discussion today may have 'knock-on effects' leading to further policies tomorrow (Newton and van Deth 2010: 266).

Given these characteristics, it is convenient to conceive of policy-making as a process model, which is also often labelled *policy cycle* (Lasswell 1956). The policy cycle is a useful heuristic that breaks policy-making into different units to illustrate how policies are actually made and implemented. It models the policy process as a series of political activities, consisting of (1) **agenda setting**, (2) **policy formulation**, (3) **policy adoption**, (4) **implementation**, and (5) **evaluation**. Each policy cycle begins with the identification of a societal problem and its placement on the policy agenda. Subsequently, policy proposals are formulated, from which one will be adopted. In the next stage, the adopted policy is taken to action. Finally, the impacts of the policy are evaluated. This last stage leads straight back to the first, indicating that the policy cycle is continuous and unending.

Agenda setting

The first stage in policy-making refers to the identification of a societal problem requiring the state to intervene. There are many societal problems, but only a small number will be given official attention by legislators and executives. Those that are chosen by the decision-makers constitute the policy agenda. Setting the agenda is therefore an important source of power as it is policy consequential, i.e. legislative institutions grant an advantage to the first movers as compared to the second movers (Shepsle and Weingast 1987). The factors determining whether an issue reaches the agenda may be cultural, political, social, economic, or ideological (cf. Schattschneider 1960; King 1973; Howlett *et al.* 2009). Further, the ability to exclude societal problems from the policy agenda and to realize the occurrence of 'non-decisions' is an important source of policy-shaping power (Bachrach and Baratz 1962).

Cobb *et al.* (1976) distinguish between three basic policy initiation models:

1. The *outside-initiative model* refers to a situation where citizen groups gain broad public support and get an issue onto the formal agenda.

2. The *mobilization model* describes a situation in which initiatives of governments need to be placed on the public agenda for successful implementation.

3. In the *inside-initiation model,* influential groups with access to decision-makers present policy proposals, which are broadly supported by particular interest groups but only marginally by the public.

On the basis of these considerations, Kingdon (2003) defines agenda setting as 'three process streams flowing

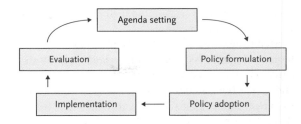

Figure 20.1 The policy cycle

through the system—streams of problems, policies, and politics. They are largely independent of one another, and each develops according to its own dynamics and rules. But at some critical junctures the three streams are joined, and the greatest policy changes grow out of that coupling of problems, policies, and solutions.'

The result of the convergence of the three streams is the opening of a 'policy window', which allows advocates of a certain issue to put it on the policy agenda. Similar to the *garbage can model* (Cohen *et al.* 1972), Kingdon's conception of agenda setting emphasizes the relevance of chance, and therefore qualifies the view that agenda setting represents rational behaviour.

Baumgartner and Jones (2009) modified Kingdon's model by extending it to the notion of 'policy monopolies', in which particular subsystems control the interpretation of a problem. These subsystems comprise both governmental and societal actors. The members of specific subsystems seek to change policy images in order to weaken the stability of existing policy arrangements. In doing so, the subsystem members can either publicize a problem and encourage the public to demand its resolution by government ('Downsian strategy'), or they can modify the institutional arrangements within which the subsystem operates ('Schattschneider strategy').

In most cases, the policy agenda is set by four types of *actors:* (1) public officials, (2) bureaucracy, (3) mass media, and (4) interest groups (Gerston 2004: 52). Elected public officials, e.g. the president, the parliament, the ministries and courts, are the most obvious agendasetters. However, actual agenda setting is related to the larger political game in terms of power and the intensity of ideological conflict both within and between the (coalition) government and parliament. Consequently, there exists a considerable variation in the rules and practices of agenda setting—even in the relatively similar Western European polities (Döring 1995: 224).

Originally, the potential impact of the bureaucracy on agenda setting was proposed by William A. Niskanen (1971). His economic model of bureaucratic behaviour assumes that bureaucrats impose upon a passive legislature their most preferred policy alternative from among the set of alternatives that dominate the status quo. While theoretically plausible, empirical studies (cf. Hammond 1986) reveal that bureaucrats can influence the policy agenda but certainly not impose their most preferred alternative on the voting bodies.

Mass media can influence agenda setting through priming and framing. Priming is about modifying the standards people use to evaluate policy-making through news coverage. Framing concerns the characterization of an issue by the mass media and how this influences people's feelings about it (Scheufele and Tewksbury 2006: 11).

The fourth source of agenda-setting power is interest groups. That interest groups place issues on the public agenda seems to be indisputable (cf. Cobb and Elder 1972; Jones and Baumgartner 2005; and Jones 2009). However, the question emerges whether and to what extent their interests are compatible with public needs.

Over the years, research on agenda setting has become increasingly sophisticated and now addresses a wide range of questions. Various scholars ask, for instance, how political representation affects agenda setting (cf. Jones and Baumgartner 2005; Penner *et al.* 2006). Another aspect is about the role of political parties for agenda setting (cf. Walgrave *et al.* 2006; Green-Pedersen 2007). A further fashionable perspective on agenda setting scrutinizes the effects of experts and the scientific community (Scholten and Timmermans 2010).

Policy formulation

The second stage in the policy cycle—policy formulation—involves the definition, discussion, acceptance, or rejection of feasible courses of action for coping with

Box 20.2 Formulating policy

Thomas R. Dye (2005: 42)

Policy formulation occurs in government bureaucracies; interest group offices; legislative committee rooms, meetings of special commissions; and policy-planning organizations otherwise known as 'think tanks'. The details of policy proposals are usually formulated by staff members rather than their bosses, but staffs are guided by what they know their leaders want.

policy problems. Policy formulation is strongly related to policy adoption—the subsequent stage here. Generally speaking, policy formulation deals with the *elaboration of alternatives of action,* whereas policy adoption refers to the *formal acceptance* of a policy.

Policy formulation takes place within the broader context of technical and political constraints of state action. The political constraints can be either substantive (i.e. related to the nature of the societal problem to be solved) or procedural (i.e. related to institutional and tactical issues) (cf. Howlett *et al.* 2009).

This phase brings the relationship between executives and legislatures to the forefront. The literature generally argues that executives dominate over legislatures since they can rely on more resources (cf. Bräuniner and Debus 2009 for qualifications). Also the ministerial bureaucracy

Table 20.1 Legislative bills by initiator and country

Country	Government	Government parties	Opposition parties	Government and opposition parties	Total
Belgium	1,010	1,700	2,089	297	5,096
	(19.8%)	(33.4%)	(41.0%)	(5.8%)	(100%)
	[90.9%]	[8.7%]	[4.2%]	[36.7%]	
France	1,444	1,867	2,150	5	5,466
	(26.4.1%)	(34.2%)	(39.3%)	(0.1%)	(100%)
	[67.9°%]	[5.7%]	[0.7%]	[10.0%]	
Germany	1,573	426	658	110	2,767
	(56.9%)	(15.4%)	(23.8%)	(4.0%)	(100%)
	[90.2%]	[79.6%]	[2.0%]	[84.6%]	
UK	519	705	785	16	2,025
	(25.6%)	(34.8%)	(38.8%)	(0.8%)	(100%)
	[95.0%]	[12.6%]	[4.2%]	[93.8%]	

Notes: N = 15,634. Figures are numbers of bills introduced by government or (groups of) members of lower chambers of parliament. Share of bills by initiator in parentheses; share of successful bills in brackets.

Source: Bräuninger and Debus (2009).

plays a role in policy formulation. Jann and Wegrich (2006), for instance, argue policy formulation is a rather informal process of negotiations between ministerial departments and interest groups. Interest groups may especially play a big part in formulating legislation about complex and technical issues, and when elected officials and bureaucrats lack time, staff, and expertise to cope with such matters (Anderson 2003: 105–7). Furthermore, scientific experts and policy advisors can inform the design of policies (cf. Stone 2005; Knill and Tosun 2012).

Policy adoption

In contrast to preliminary stages of decision-making, the final adoption of a particular policy alternative is determined by government institutions and predominantly depends on two sets of factors. Firstly, the set of feasible policies can be reduced by the necessity to build majorities for their approval implying considerations about values, party affiliation, constituency interests, public opinion, deference, and decision rules (Anderson 2003: 126).

In this context, party loyalty is an important decision-making criterion for most members of parliament (cf. Benedetto and Hix 2007 for qualifications). Therefore, party affiliation is a central predictor for the likelihood of a member of parliament to approve a policy draft. Another important decision criterion is given by the expected costs and benefits of a policy proposal for the constituency. As a rule, a member of parliament is expected to adopt a policy option if the benefits for the constituency prevail, although considerations about re-election might lead to suboptimal policy projects (Weingast et al. 1981). Further, considerations about the public opinion also affect policy choices as well as decision rules, values, and perception of deference.

The second set of factors refers to the allocation of competencies between the actors involved in policy-making. Cross-national research concludes that the type of state organization, whether federal or unitary, affects the success, speed and nature of governmental policy-making (cf. Lijphart 1999; Braun 2000). An adequate theoretical underpinning for this aspect offers the concept of 'veto players' (Tsebelis's 1995, 2000, 2002; König et al. 2010). For example, in the French presidential system, 'divided government' can impede policy adoption as there are generally insufficient incentives for political parties to cooperate and build policy-making coalitions. Another illustration is provided by Germany's bicameral legislature, which limits governmental policy-making to the consent of a set of institutional veto players (Tsebelis and Money 1997; Bräuninger and König 1999).

Implementation

Implementation represents the conversion of new laws and programmes into practice. At the first glance,

implementation appears as an automatic continuation of the policy-making process. Yet there often exists a substantial gap between the passage of new legislation and its application (Pressman and Wildavsky 1973). It is the explicit objective of implementation research to open the 'black box' between policy formation and policy outcomes. To this end, various theoretical approaches were elaborated which Pülzl and Treib (2006) divide into three generic categories:

- Top-down models (cf. Pressman and Wildavsky 1973; Bardach 1977; Mazmanian and Sabatier 1983) primarily emphasize the ability of policy-makers to produce unequivocal policy objectives and control the implementation process.
- Bottom-up models (cf. Lipsky 1971, 1980) regard local bureaucrats as the central actors in policy delivery and view implementation as negotiation processes within networks.
- Hybrid models (cf. Mayntz 1979; Windhoff-Héritier 1980) integrate elements of both previously mentioned models and other theoretical models.

For successful implementation, there must be an entity that is able to translate the policy objectives into an operational framework and that is accountable for its actions (Gerston 2004: 98). Often bureaucracies emerge as principal actors during implementation. In his study of the US bureaucracy, Meier (2000) finds that implementation depends on the policy types proposed by Lowi (1964). When implementing regulatory policies, most agencies are responsive to the communities over which they preside, while distributive policies are implemented with some bureaucratic discretion, with congressional subcommittees and organized interest groups exercising continuous oversight. With redistributive policy, by contrast, little discretion is left to bureaucracy since US Congress puts in a lot of effort when designing these policies.

Related to this perspective is the choice of policy instruments, which are perceived to be vulnerable to specific kinds of implementation problems (Mayntz 1979). Yet it is not only the policy type and the instrument choice that determines the likelihood of proper implementation. In federal systems, for instance, implementation efforts may move between and within levels of government (Gerston 2004: 103). If implementation is a matter of horizontal implementation, in which a national legal act must be applied solely by an agency in the executive branch, the number of actors remains low and implementation can be attained smoothly. The opposite scenario is likely, if vertical implementation is concerned, implying that various segments of the national government must interact with different sub-national levels.

The relevance of bureaucracy during implementation reveals a contradictory picture of great interest. On the one hand, bureaucracies are essential for making policies work. On the other hand, senior bureaucrats are often more experienced and better trained than their political masters, which paves the way for 'bureaucratic drift' (cf. Grossman and Hart 1983). Hence, a policy might drift towards the liking of bureaucracy and away from what was originally intended by legislation (cf. Hammond and Knott 1996).

Evaluation

After a policy is passed by the legislature and implemented by the bureaucracy, it becomes a subject of evaluation. The main question at this stage is whether the output of the decision-making process—a given public policy—has attained the intended goals. Evaluation is often a formal component of policy-making and is commonly carried out by experts who have some knowledge about the processes and objectives pertaining to the issue undergoing review.

Evaluation can be carried out in different ways. In this context, Munger (2000: 20) differentiates between (1) purely *formal* evaluations (monitoring routine tasks), (2) *client satisfaction* evaluation (performance of primary functions), (3) *outcome* evaluation (satisfaction of a list of measurable intended outcomes), (4) *cost-benefit* evaluation (comparison of costs and impacts of a policy), and (5) evaluation of *long-term consequences* (impact on the core societal problem, rather than symptoms alone).

Policy evaluation provides a feedback loop, which enables decision-makers to draw lessons from each particular policy in operation. This feedback loop identifies new problems and sets in motion the policy-making process once again, creating an endless policy cycle. This turns policy evaluation into a powerful tool of the policy-making process: it possesses the potential to reframe an issue once thought to be resolved by policy-makers.

In practice, policy evaluation presents numerous challenges to the evaluators (cf. Knill and Tosun 2012). Citizens and governments alike tend to interpret the actual effects of a policy so as to serve their own intentions. Often governments avoid the precise definition of policy objectives because otherwise politicians would risk taking the blame for obvious failure (Jann and Wegrich 2006). Further, policy decisions cannot be limited to intended effects only. An additional problem stems from the time horizon: 'Program circumstances and activities may change during the course of an evaluation, an appropriate balance must be found between scientific and pragmatic considerations in the evaluation design, and the wide diversity of perspectives and approaches in the evaluation field provide little firm guidance about how best to proceed with an evaluation' (Rossi *et al.* 2004: 29).

The results of the evaluation procedure can also lead to the termination of a certain policy. In theoretical terms, policy termination should be likely when a policy problem has been solved, or if evaluation studies reveal the dysfunctionality of a policy. Nonetheless, the empirical findings show that, once a policy is institutionalized within a government, it is hard to terminate it (Bardach 1976; Jann and Wegrich 2006). This immortality of policies stems from various sources. The most rampant view is that inefficient programmes continue because their benefits are concentrated in a small, well-organized constituency, while their greater costs are dispersed over a large, unorganized group. Additionally, legislative and bureaucratic interests may impede termination. This is related to the concept of incrementalism, which implies that attention to proposed changes focuses on parts of existing policies and not on their entirety (Dye 2005: 344–5).

From this it follows that termination should become more likely if a government experiences some kind of 'external shock', justifying drastic measures, such as economic crises (cf. Geva-May 2004). Another stimulus can be given by supra-national policy harmonization for the creation of a common market such as in the case of the EU (cf. Knill *et al.* 2009).

> **KEY POINTS**
>
> - In analytical terms, it is helpful to view policy-making as a series of political activities encompassing agenda setting, policy formulation, policy adoption, implementation, and evaluation.
> - The number of actors involved decreases when we move from agenda setting to implementation.
> - The evaluation findings may lead to the modification of existing policies, which may entail adjustments of varying degrees as well as complete policy termination.

Institutions, frames, and policy styles

While we scrutinized rather generally the different stages of policy-making in the first section, we now refine our analytical focus and examine how certain structures in different countries can impact policy decisions. In doing so, we concentrate on institutions, cognitive and normative determinants, and national policy styles.

The role of institutions

In a broader sense, we can interpret policy-making as a strategy for resolving societal problems by using institutions. From a rationalist perspective, institutions can structure the interaction of actors and avoid the suboptimal solutions they are given by the prisoner's dilemma.

From a sociological point of view, institutions can support cooperation through the provision of moral or cognitive templates (Hall and Taylor 1996).

As policy interventions in democratic systems originate in electoral systems, it is the most essential formal institution when scrutinizing policy-making. Electoral competition is largely party competition, turning political parties into important actors (see Chapter 13). One of their main functions is to structure and articulate public opinion. Most frequently, political parties are described by a left-right dichotomy, implying that they have diametrically opposed policy preferences. In fact various studies—based on expert judgements as well as content analysis of party manifestoes—found a level of consistency with this dichotomy (Laver and Hunt 1992; Budge and Klingemann 2001; Laver *et al.* 2003; Debus 2007).

Strongly related to this is the relevance of the voting systems, of which we can distinguish between three main types:

- **Plurality-majority systems**, in which the elected candidates get more votes than any other (e.g. UK).
- **Proportional representation**, in which seats are allocated according to a formula that seeks to ensure proportionality (e.g. Germany).
- **Mixed systems** that combine plurality-majority with proportional representation aspects (e.g. Japan).

Each system has strengths and weaknesses (see Chapters 5, 10, and 13 for further discussions of these models). While the proportional system ensures the representation of all societal groups, including small parties, plurality-majority systems are usually associated with stable and effective governments. These aspects have strong repercussions on the quality of policy-making.

The relationship between legislative and executive is also of crucial importance. In parliamentary models, the executive is a group of ministers elected from the very parliament, while in pure presidential systems the two branches of government are separate. In this context, Lijphart (1999) claims that, despite strong variations among countries, democratic systems tend to fall into two categories: majoritarian and consensus democracies. The majoritarian system—which is generally associated with the UK, and hence is also known as the 'Westminster model'—concentrates power and fuses executive and legislative powers in the classic parliamentary manner (e.g. Colombia, Costa Rica, France, Greece, New Zealand (before 1996)). By contrast, the consensus model focuses on sharing power by separating and balancing executive and legislative power (e.g. Austria, Germany, India, Japan, the Netherlands, and Switzerland). Remarkably, consensus democracies score higher in terms of democratic quality as well as the state's generosity in social welfare, environmental policy, criminal justice, and foreign aid than majoritarian democracies.

Role of cognitive and normative frames

The concepts of normative and cognitive frames are crucial for explaining how actors understand and interpret policy-making situations. Cognitive frames refer to the schemes through which actors view and interpret the world (Campbell 1998: 382). Normative frames are about values and attitudes that shape the actors' view of the world (Fischer 2003). Both cognitive and normative frames can enable but also constrain policy action.

Thus, to gain a more comprehensive understanding of policy-making, we need to supplement our analytical framework by normative and cognitive determinants. Although rational motivation may explain the adoption of new policies, cognitive and normative factors may be essential for understanding better the decision-making at each stage of the policy-process (Miller and Banaszak-Holl 2005: 214).

In this context, Surel (2000) discusses three concepts, i.e. those on policy paradigms (Hall 1993), *advocacy coalitions* (Sabatier and Jenkins-Smith 1993; Sabatier 1998), and *referential*. According to Hall (1993), there are certain paradigms present in the real world that imply distinct policy goals. These goals—that are intertwined with the paradigm—then define the choice and specification of instruments. The advocacy coalition framework, by contrast, assumes a similar construct to affect the entire society, which is the 'deep core'. Subordinated to it is the 'policy core', which refers to the belief systems within a subsystem of public policy. From this perspective, 'secondary aspects' are the instrumental decisions that are necessary to implement the policy core. Finally, the *référentiel* equals a paradigm as it comprises values and norms (Surel 2000: 496).

Cognitive and normative frames produce a sense of specific identity. Yet certain actors have a privileged role in policy-making as they generate and diffuse cognitive frames. Since elites and other privileged actors frame policy ideas to convince each other as well as the public, they are important for the adoption of policies (Campbell 1998: 380). This category of actors are 'policy-brokers' (Sabatier 1998). Furthermore, frames help to reduce tension and conflict by marking out 'the terrain for social exchanges and disagreements, rather than simply supporting an unlikely consensus' (Surel 2000: 502). The relevance of these considerations is, for instance, illustrated by Dobbin (1994), who shows that the differences in how decision-makers promoted railway development in the late nineteenth century can be explained by variations in cognitive frameworks.

National policy styles

The concept of policy styles—or also regulatory styles—is another heuristic tool and refers to the routines and choices of actors involved in policy-making and implementation. To a certain extent, this concept takes up the discussion about institutional characteristics (Lijphart 1999) as well as Dyson's (1980) elaboration on 'strong' and 'weak' states. Further, it is related to the ideas of 'policy communities' and 'administrative culture' (van Thiel 2006: 118). The objective of this section is therefore to elucidate that for the analysis of policy-making nations matter.

The influential volume by Richardson (1982) distinguishes policy styles along two dimensions. The first dimension is about how policy-makers respond to the issues on the policy agenda. Do decision-makers anticipate societal problems (technocratic approach), or do they merely react to them (diplomatic approach)? The first notion presupposes that the government is perfectly informed and able to foresee and forestall policy problems before they become critical. By contrast, the second notion about the government's approach is built around the concept of imperfect information and hence seems to be more realistic. The second dimension is about the relative autonomy of the state *vis-à-vis* other actors involved in policy-making and implementation. Here, the question is whether decision-makers seek to ensure consensus among the parties involved, or whether they simply impose their decisions on the executing actors.

The above mentioned dimensions correspond to Van Waarden's (1995) typology of regulatory styles, which comprises six sub-dimensions that refer to the 'what', 'how', and 'who' questions of policy-making:

1. Liberal-pluralist versus étatist versus corporatist style: the first style prefers 'market' solutions to policy problems, while étatism implies a preference for 'state solutions'. **Corporatism**, by contrast, favours 'associational' solutions to policy problems.

2. Active versus reactive styles: active styles are higher in their degree of intensity, radicalism, and innovation as compared to reactive ones.

3. Comprehensive versus fragmented or incremental styles: comprehensive policies are integrated into larger plans, while the latter are not.

4. Adversarial versus consensual paternalistic styles: the first type strongly relies on coercion and imposition, while the latter is based on consultation.

5. Legalistic versus pragmatic styles: legalistic styles are characterized by formalism, detailed regulation, and rigid rule application. The pragmatic style, on the other hand, is informal and flexible in both policy formulation and implementation.

6. Formal versus informal network relations between state agencies and organizations of state agencies.

Altogether, policy styles provide an analytically useful concept for determining the design of policies (Howlett

	Anticipatory	Reactive
Consensus-seeking	Netherlands, Spain	Germany, Sweden
Imposing	United Kingdom	France*

Figure 20.2 Richardson's (1982) typology of policy styles

*Concerning financial regulations, the French style is anticipatory.

Source: Based on Bovens *et al.* (2001: 645–7).

1991; Arentsen 2003) and the mode of implementation (Freeman 1985). Yet, assessing the extent of impact of national policy styles augers for systematic comparative analysis. Richardson's (1982) volume itself, however, could not deliver empirical evidence for existence of national policy styles. By contrast, Bovens *et al.* (2001) present evidence that different national policy styles affect how policies are formulated. Most importantly, policy styles in some countries tend to be more stable and clearly defined than are those of others, even though very much also seems to depend on the policy sector.

KEY POINTS

- Policy-making can be thought of as a strategy for resolving societal problems by using institutions.
- Cognitive and normative frames fulfil important functions during the policy-making process and therefore complement the politics perspective.
- Similar to the policy cycle, the concept of national policy styles serves as a useful heuristic tool for elaborating more specific theoretical explanations.

International factors for domestic policy-making

In this section, we concentrate on the impact of international factors on domestic policy-making. The notion that countries do not constitute independent observations has been known for a long time in comparative politics, and became discussed as 'Galton's problem' (Braun and Gilardi 2006; Jahn 2006; Chapter 3). This recognition has led researchers to scrutinize more carefully the link between domestic processes and the international arena (Risse-Kappen 1995). The concepts of policy diffusion and transfer and the analysis of cross-national policy convergence provide an ideal basis for shedding light on the role of international factors (see also Chapter 22 on these concepts).

Theories of policy diffusion, policy transfer, and cross-national policy convergence

Diffusion is generally defined as the socially mediated spread of policies across and within political systems, including communication and influence processes which operate both on and within populations of adopters (Rogers 1995: 13). Diffusion studies typically start out from the description of adoption patterns for certain policy innovations over time. Subsequently, they analyse the factors that account for the empirically observed spreading process (cf. Gilardi 2008).

Regarding domestic politics, diffusion mainly affects the stages of agenda setting, and to a lesser degree policy formulation. The likelihood of adopting a diffusion policy increases if the proposal originates from a country that is culturally similar to the receiving country (Strang and Meyer 1993; Strang and Soule 1998). This, however, does not reduce the relevance of domestic factors, such as considerations about values, party affiliation, constituency interests, public opinion, and decision rules. Along these lines, Lenschow *et al.* (2005), for instance, argue that the extent to which a policy innovation is accommodated by a given country can be explained by three aspects: institutional, cultural, and socio-economic factors.

Transfer can best be described as 'processes by which knowledge about policies, administrative arrangements, institutions and ideas in one political system (past or present) is used in the development of policies, administrative arrangements, institutions and ideas in another political system' (Dolowitz and Marsh 2000: 5). It is not restricted to merely imitating policies of other countries, but can also include profound changes in the content of the exchanged policies, leading to four forms (Rose 1991, 1993; Dolowitz 1997; Dolowitz and Marsh 2000: 13):

- Copying (direct and complete transfer).
- Emulation (transfer of the ideas behind the programme).
- Combinations (mixture of different policies).
- Inspiration (final policy does not draw upon the original).

The focus of transfer studies is on the analysis of the specific processes and factors that influence the way and degree to which one country learns from other countries with regard to policy-making in a certain area. Here again domestic factors come into play—it is important which actors engage in transfer, which negotiation power they possess, and whether they can build a supportive coalition. Another aspect for the success of a policy import might be its regulatory legitimacy (Majone 1996: ch. 13). It is indeed reasonable to hypothesize that some countries have more problems in regarding external policy proposals as legitimate than others.

Diffusion and transfer share a number of assumptions, for example, that governments do not learn about policy practices randomly, but rather through common affiliations, negotiations, and institutional membership (Simmons and Elkins 2004). They hence require that actors are informed about the policy choices of others (Strang and Meyer 1993: 488). Furthermore, transfer and diffusion might result in policy convergence, which can be defined as 'any increase in the similarity between one or more characteristics of a certain policy (e.g. policy objectives, policy instruments, policy settings) across a given set of political jurisdictions (supra-national institutions, states, regions, local authorities) over a given period of time' (Knill 2005: 768). It has close proximity to the concept of isomorphism which has been developed in organization sociology and is defined as a process of homogenization that 'forces one unit in a population to resemble other units that face the same set of environmental conditions' (DiMaggio and Powell 1991: 66).

International sources that affect domestic policy-making

Internationalization does not only affect policy sectors that are generally associated with externalities, e.g. environmental policy (cf. Holzinger *et al.* 2008; Tosun 2013) or tax policy (cf. Genschel and Schwarz 2011), but also policy fields with no immediate international connection, e.g. social policy (cf. Brooks; Jahn 2006; Starke et al. 2008; Jensen 2011). Yet, internationalization is a highly complex phenomenon with varying effects on different policy sectors and states. To disentangle the mechanisms behind internationalization, we rely on the concepts introduced by Holzinger and Knill (2005), who distinguish between (1) imposition, (2) international harmonization, (3) regulatory competition, and (4) transnational communication.

Imposition—sometimes also labelled 'coercive isomorphism' (DiMaggio and Powell 1991) or 'penetration' (Bennett 1991)—occurs whenever an external political actor forces a government to adopt a certain policy. This presupposes asymmetry of power, and often policy adoption is accompanied by an exchange of economic resources. Policies can either be unilaterally imposed on a country by another, or imposition can occur as a condition of being part of an international institution (Dolowitz and Marsh 2000: 9). Unilateral imposition happens rarely and only in extreme situations, such as wars. Conditionality, on the other hand, can be observed more frequently, as where applicant countries for membership in the European Union have to adopt the entire *acquis communautaire*, i.e. the total body of European law accumulated thus far (cf. Lavenex 2002). Imposition implies that the country forced to adopt a certain model has not much choice in modifying the policy. In such cases, domestic politics are mainly bypassed.

International harmonization refers to a situation in which member states voluntarily engage in international cooperation, and hence corresponds to 'negotiated transfer' (Dolowitz and Marsh 2000: 15). This mechanism implies that countries comply with uniform legal obligations defined in international or supra-national law. International harmonization presupposes the existence of interdependencies or externalities which push governments to resolve common problems through cooperation within international institutions, thus sacrificing some independence for the good of the community (Drezner 2001: 60). Once established, institutional arrangements will constrain and shape domestic policy choices (Martin and Simmons 1998: 743).

The mechanism of regulatory competition is closely related to the notion of internationalization as economic globalization. It is expected to homogenize the countries' policies when these are mutually faced with competitive pressures. The competitive pressure arises from (potential) threats of economic actors to shift their activities elsewhere, inducing governments to lower their regulatory standards. In this way, regulatory competition among governments may lead to a race to the bottom in policies (Drezner 2001: 57–9; Simmons and Elkins 2004).

Theoretical work, however, suggests that there are a number of conditions that may drive policy in both directions (Vogel 1995; Scharpf 1997d; Holzinger 2002, 2003). In this context, often a distinction is made between product and production process standards (Vogel 1995; Scharpf 1997d; Holzinger 2008). In the case of production standards, we find a widely shared expectation that states will gravitate towards the policies of the most *laissez-faire* country (Drezner 2001). If the regulation of production processes implies an increase in the costs of production, potentially endangering the international competitiveness of an industry, regulatory competition will generally exert downward pressures on economic regulations (Hahn 1990; Scharpf 1997d: 524).

Expectations are yet less homogeneous for product standards. While industries in both low-regulating and high-regulating countries have a common interest in harmonization of product standards to avoid market segmentation, the level of harmonization can hardly be predicted without the examination of additional factors. Most important in this context is the extent to which high-regulating countries are able to factually enforce stricter standards, e.g. through the erection of exceptional trade barriers (Vogel 1995; Scharpf 1997d).

So far, most empirical findings for different policy sectors, such as environmental and social policy, do not support the race to the bottom scenario but rather give hints for the occurrence of a race to the top, i.e. upward ratcheting of regulatory standards (cf. Holzinger et al. 2008; Tosun 2013; see Chapter 21 on the welfare state and Chapter 22 on the impact of public policies).

Box 20.3 International harmonization and domestic politics

Bernstein and Cashore (2000: 79–80)

The importance of domestic politics is largely limited along this path to the stage of rule creation/ratification and to the decision of whether to comply or not in specific circumstances. In the two-level game of international negotiations, governments balance, and sometimes play off, the interests of their negotiating partners and domestic constituencies. Domestic policy-making structures are also important when states require domestic ratification of international agreements or implementing legislation.

However, once rules are in place, assuming states view them as legitimate, they create a 'pull toward compliance' regardless of domestic political factors. Contravening the rule could result in costly disputes in international adjudication bodies or domestic courts or sanctions of various sorts. It could also erode the legitimacy of other related rules that a state may want others to obey or, in utilitarian terms, erode general reciprocity that creates a broad incentive to obey international rules in the long run. The rule also becomes a resource on which transnational and/or coalitions of domestic actors can draw when governments do not comply. For example, they can publicize non-compliance, pressure governments to live up to their commitments or press governments to launch disputes against other countries which do not fulfil their obligations.

Transnational communication consists of a number of mechanisms, which are purely based on communication among countries, namely lesson-drawing, transnational problem-solving, emulation, and the transnational promotion of policy models. Lesson-drawing refers to constellations of policy transfer in which governments rationally utilize available experience from elsewhere in order to solve domestic problems (Rose 1991, 1993). Transnational problem-solving is also based on rational learning. It is driven by the joint development of common problem perceptions and solutions to similar domestic problems as well as their subsequent adoption at the domestic level. In doing so, transnational elite networks or epistemic communities, international institutions, and common educational and normative backgrounds play an important role in forging and promulgating transnational problem-solving (DiMaggio and Powell 1991; Haas 1992; Elkins and Simmons 2005).

Emulation, on the other hand, is motivated by the desire for conformity with other countries rather than the search for effective solutions to given problems. States might sometimes copy the policies of other states simply to legitimate conclusions already reached (Bennett 1991; Powell and DiMaggio 1991). Finally, policy adoption can be driven by the active role of international institutions, for example, the EU, that are promoting the spread of distinctive policy approaches they consider particularly promising (Keck and Sikkink 1998).

Similar to all the other mechanisms, the effects of transnational communication strongly depend on mediation by domestic politics (Radaelli 2005). Thus, as concerns the national effect of these mechanisms of internationalization, we must conclude that the political context matters (Steinmo *et al.* 1992). As already argued for policy diffusion, it can be expected that if the cultural, institutional, or socio-economic similarity between communicating countries and international institutions is high, the adoption of the corresponding policy proposals should become more likely.

KEY POINTS

- As internationalization is a complex phenomenon, it is useful to approach its underlying mechanisms via the concepts of policy diffusion, policy transfer, and cross-national policy convergence.

- There are four main mechanisms: imposition, harmonization, regulatory competition, and transnational communication.

Conclusion

Policy-making is complex. Therefore, the first approaches to understanding how policies come about were the so-called conceptual models. They focus on differential aspects of the policy-making process and primarily deal with issues about the actors' power resources and rationality. While these models certainly draw attention to crucial aspects of policy-making, they fall short of providing complete explanations.

More promising is the analysis of policy-making by focusing on the process. Since the number, nature, and interactions of actors change across the single stages, this theoretical disaggregation allows for deriving more clear-cut theoretical expectations. Agenda setting ensures important strategic advantages, turning this stage into a highly competitive one. Many actors participate in the selection of suitable items from an undefined universe of societal problems. Power fragmentation also affects policy formulation and adoption. If the political system is a rather cooperative one, decision-making in the political process remains unchallenging. Otherwise, there can be harmful delays in policy-making.

Once we move to implementation, the number of involved actors notably decreases. This stage is associated with the dominance of bureaucratic actors over political ones. In the subsequent evaluation stage, the floor is opened to experts and their appraisal of whether a policy performs well or poorly. In some—rare—instances, an evaluation can entail policy termination.

There are, however, also structures present in the political sphere that help to reduce the complexity of policy-making. Institutions, for instance, possess such a function. In a similar vein, cognitive and normative framing mechanisms serve to structure politics. Finally, the development of routines and particular national policy styles help to establish a stable negotiation framework and therewith ensure the continuity of the policy-making process.

In the final section we learnt that a policy is not exclusively the outcome of domestic bargaining processes. Policy-making is also affected by internationalization, implying a variety of stimuli and corresponding reaction patterns. Generally speaking, internationalization can either enable or constrain policy-making. How these effects are translated into policy outcomes depends on domestic policy-making processes.

 Questions

1. How can we think of policy-making in terms of theory?

2. In which ways are policy typologies related to the policy-making process?

3. What are the main stages of the policy cycle, and how does this concept enhance our understanding of policy-making?

4. Which actors—societal and political—participate in the single stages?

5. What is the role of political institutions in policy-making?

6. How can we define normative and cognitive frames?

7. What are national policy styles?

8. Which theoretical concepts cope with the effects of internationalization on domestic policy-making?

9. What are the mechanisms behind these concepts? And how do they interact with domestic policy-making?

10. Does internationalization matter empirically?

Further reading

Bauer, Michael W., Andrew Jordan, Christoffer Green-Pedersen and Adrienne Heritier (eds) (2012) *Dismantling Public Policy: Preferences, Strategies, and Effects* (Oxford: Oxford University Press). This edited volume brings together stimulating case studies of policy dismantling in the fields of environmental and social policy.

Engeli, Isabelle, Christoffer Green-Pedersen and Lars Thorup LarsenMorality (eds) (2012) *Politics in Western Europe: Parties, Agendas and Policy Choices* (Basingstoke: Palgrave Macmillan). A carefully edited collection of studies on how morality policies are made.

Knill, Christoph and Jale Tosun (2012). *Public Policy – A New Introduction* (Basingstoke: Palgrave Macmillan). This book covers the topics presented in this chapter in greater length.

Moran, Michael, Martin Rein and Robert E. Goodin (eds) (2008). *The Oxford Handbook of Public Policy* (Oxford: Oxford University Press). An encompassing and stimulating overview of the key topics in the study of public policy.

Wallace, Helen, Mark A. Pollack and Alistair Young (eds) (2010). *Policy-Making in the European Union* (Oxford: Oxford University Press). Gives an intuitive and compelling overview of policy-making in the EU's multi-level polity.

Web links

www.policyagendas.org
The Policy Agendas Project.

www.fp7-consensus.eu
Confronting Social and Environmental Sustainability with Economic Pressure.

http://www.polver.uni-konstanz.de/knill/forschung-projekte/comparative-analysis-of-moral-policy-change/
Comparative Analysis of Moral Policy Change

www.defendingscience.org
Project on Scientific Knowledge and Public Policy.

polidoc.net
Political Documents Archive.

online resource centre

For additional material and resources, please visit the Online Resource Centre at:
www.oxfordtextbooks.co.uk/orc/caramani3e/

CHAPTER 21

The welfare state

Kees van Kersbergen and Philip Manow

Chapter contents

Reader's guide

The **welfare state** is important for comprehending democratic politics in modern societies, just as knowing about modern politics is crucial for understanding the causes, sources of variation, and consequences of the state's social interventions into markets and families. The chapter focuses on the key issues of the emergence, expansion, variation, and transformation of the welfare state. It explains that studying the welfare state necessarily means engaging in debates about some of the most fundamental and enduring questions of comparative political science and political economy.

Introduction

Why is the welfare state interesting for comparative political science? Because it represents the single most important transformation of advanced capitalist democracies in the post-Second World War period. Understanding the welfare state is key to understanding modern politics, just as an understanding of modern politics is key to understanding the causes of welfare state formation and growth, as well as its various social and economic effects. Moreover, studying the welfare state confronts us with some of the most fundamental and enduring questions of political science.

From different normative perspectives, classical political economy (John Stuart Mill as well as Karl Marx) was convinced that capitalism and democracy were incompatible. But the welfare states of the West prove that capitalism and democracy can indeed go together—even with beneficial consequences for both. High social spending does not need to have detrimental effects on economic competitiveness, as the combination of a generous welfare state and a competitive market economy in a country like Sweden demonstrates. Apparently, the 'democratic class struggle' (see Lipset 1960: 220; Korpi 1983) can allow for a beneficial class compromise, and the welfare state seems to be its most prominent embodiment.

Comparative politics has studied the origins, growth, and crises of the welfare state, testing various theories of political **mobilization** and development. What and who were pivotal in this process—social classes, the workers' movement, historical legacies of state structures, wars, economic development, demographic pressures, employers' interests? Are the various political structures, actors, and struggles responsible for differences in size, type, and quality among welfare states? Comparative political scientists have also looked at the impact of the welfare state (its performance) to see to what extent politics matters for society and economy. Does politics (e.g. the strength of political movements and parties or the composition of a government) matter for the type of social and economic policies (output) carried out in a country? And do these policies influence social and economic variables (outcome) such as economic growth, unemployment, inequality, and poverty (see Chapter 22)?

Finally, there is also a practical interest in the study of the welfare state. Many people care whether they live in a society in which the ratio between the highest and the lowest income decile is around 5.7 (US) or around 2.5 (Germany) (Smeeding and Gottschalk 1999). Also, many people care whether they live in a society in which taxation and welfare state transfers reduce poverty by 13 per cent (US) or by 82 per cent (Sweden) (see Iversen 2006; see also Comparative tables 5 and 6 at the end of this volume). The study of the welfare state addresses fundamental questions of social fairness, basic notions of a good society, and non-tolerable degrees of inequality and social exclusion. This also has its technical side: given certain political aims (like full employment), we would like to know how best to achieve these goals. Thorough comparative studies of the working of social protection programmes promise to provide us with this kind of practical 'how to' knowledge.

KEY POINTS

- The welfare state is the product of the interplay between political equality (democracy) and economic inequality (capitalism).

- The welfare state represents a fundamental transformation of advanced capitalist democracies in the post-1945 period.

- Comparative politics tries to explain the emergence, growth, and consequences of welfare states, but also addresses fundamental issues of social justice and the good society.

What is the welfare state?

What do we mean when we talk about the welfare state? Harold L. Wilensky described 'the essence of the welfare state' as 'government-protected minimum standards of income, nutrition, health, housing and education, assured to every citizen as a political right, not charity' (Wilensky 1975: 1). Here, the welfare state is first and foremost a democratic state that—in addition to civil and political rights (see Marshall 1950 and Box 21.1)—guarantees social protection as a right attached to **citizenship**. Most political scientists tend to think along the state-centric lines that Wilensky advocated and agree that social policy must be seen as 'lines of state action to reduce income insecurity and to provide minimum standards of income and services and thus to reduce inequalities' (Amenta 2003: 92). Other definitions of the welfare state stress protection against social risks and distribution of life chances rather than income security and equality.

The advantage of state-centred definitions is that they are clear-cut and provide straightforward operationalizations for **empirical research**: the welfare state, its growth and expansion, are measured in terms of public social spending expressed as a proportion of total state spending or of the gross domestic product (GDP). However, there are many drawbacks to this approach. An exclusive focus on social policy tends to overlook the fact that although the state is an important

Box 21.1 Marshall's three elements of citizenship

I propose to divide citizenship into three parts. I shall call these three parts, or elements, civil, political and social.

The civil element is composed of the rights necessary for individual freedom—liberty of the person, freedom of speech, thought and faith, the right to own property and to conclude valid contracts, and the right to justice. ...

By the political element I mean the right to participate in the exercise of political power, as a member of a body invested with political authority or as an elector of the members of such a body. ...

By the social element I mean the whole range from the right to a modicum of economic welfare and security to the right to share to the full in the social heritage and to live the life of a civilized being according to the standards prevailing in a society. ...

It is possible, without doing too much violence to historical accuracy, to assign the formative period in the life of each to a different century—civil rights to the eighteenth, political to the nineteenth and social to the twentieth.

Marshall 1965: 78, 81

institution providing welfare it is not the only one. Moreover, it is not easy to draw a clear line between social policies and other types of policies promoting welfare. Finally, not all social policies actually promote welfare, even though their intention may be to do so (M. Hill 2006: Chapter 1).

Esping-Andersen (1990) has criticized the exclusive focus on the state and public social spending, arguing that the welfare state 'cannot be understood just in terms of the rights it grants' and the amount of money it spends. It is hardly conceivable that 'anybody fought for spending per se'. What we need to know instead is for which purpose the money is used. Moreover, we have to avoid studying welfare state activity in isolation, because 'we must also take into account how state activities are interlocked with the market's and the family's role in social provision' (Esping-Andersen 1990: 21). It is the specific institutional mixture of market, state, and family that characterizes how a nation provides work and welfare to its citizens, and various nations do this in very different ways. The question of how much a state spends (welfare effort) is much less relevant than the questions that ask (1) *on what* it spends its public resources, (2) *how it influences the distribution of resources and life chances* in other ways than through spending (e.g. via tax expenditures or through the 'hidden welfare' state (Howard 1993; Hacker 2002)), and (3) *what other social institutions* play a role in social provision.

Scharpf and Schmidt have argued that all welfare states:

> provide free primary and secondary education, and all provide social assistance to avoid extreme poverty. Beyond that, the 'golden age' models differ fundamentally from one another along two dimensions: the extent to which welfare goals are pursued through the regulation of labour markets and employment relations or through the 'formal welfare state' of publicly financed transfers and services, and the extent to which 'caring' services are expected to be provided informally in the family or through professional services. (Scharpf and Schmidt 2000: 7)

The market, the state, and the family can all be the main welfare providers (Esping-Andersen 1990, 1999, 2002). The interaction between these institutions in the provision of work and welfare is called a **welfare regime**. It is a *complex system of managing social risks,* where each institution represents a radically different principle of doing this: 'Within the family, the dominant method of allocation is, presumably, one of reciprocity ... Markets are governed by distribution via the cash-nexus, and the dominant principle of allocation in the state takes the form of authoritative redistribution' (Esping-Andersen 1999: 35–6). What one institution does, affects what the others can, will, or must do. Esping-Andersen gives a succinct example:

> [A] traditional male bread-winner's family will have less demand for private or public social services than a two-career household. But when families service themselves, the market is directly affected because there will be less labour supply and fewer service outlets [for data on labour markets see Comparative table 13 at the end of this volume]. In turn, if the state provides cheap daycare, both families and the market will change: there will be fewer housewives, more labour force participation, and a new demand multiplier caused by double-earner households' greater propensity to purchase services. (Esping-Andersen 1999: 36)

Certain risks of life potentially become **social risks** and subject to political struggles, (1) because they are shared by many people and therefore affect the welfare of society as a whole (say loss of income because of disability and/or old age), (2) because they are interpreted as a threat to certain strata of society (say poverty that causes protest and uprisings against the ruling elite), (3) because the risks are beyond the control of any individual (say mass unemployment in a market society), or (4) because shared values of fairness and social justice seem to be violated. Why and how risks become social risks has been the topic of several decades of research.

Box 21.2 The emergence of the welfare state

The modern welfare state is a European invention—in the same way as the nation state, mass democracy, and industrial capitalism. It was born as an answer to problems created by capitalist industrialization; it was driven by the democratic class struggle; and it followed in the footsteps of the nation state.

Flora 1986: xii

The emergence of the welfare state

What drives the emergence and development of the welfare state? Three theoretical perspectives can be identified: (1) a functionalist approach, (2) a class mobilization explanation, and (3) a literature emphasizing the impact of state institutions and the relative autonomy of bureaucratic elites.

Functionalist approach

'The welfare state is an answer to problems created by capitalist industrialization': functionalist theories see the welfare state as an answer to new citizen needs that emerge with the disappearance of traditional means of subsistence and traditional bonds of mutual assistance (in families, through guilds, or charities) and with the new risks of modern, urbanized, and industrialized society: industrial accidents, cyclical unemployment, the inability to gain one's own living due to sickness or old age, the health risks in the new urban agglomerations. With pressing demands for protection against these modern risks, the scope of state intervention increased tremendously and the nature of the state was transformed (Flora and Heidenheimer 1981: 23).

The increased demand for socio-economic security came primarily from a system of industrial capitalism that dislodged masses of people and made them dependent on the whims of the labour market, thus destroying traditional forms of social protection. Industrialization involved rapidly changing working conditions, the emergence of the free labour contract, and the loss of income security. Welfare state development was related to the problem of social disorder and disintegration caused by capitalist industrial development (Flora and Alber 1981: 38). Modernization was seen as causing social disintegration. The welfare state steps in to solve problems of social integration (see Box 21.2).

This theory expected policy *convergence*—different nations adopting similar social and economic policies. If welfare states differed with respect to the coverage they provided and the benefits they granted, the causes of variation were assumed to be 'chronological', namely explained by the *different timing of industrialization and modernization* in the various countries. These differences would disappear in the long run.

Class mobilization

'Welfare state growth was driven by the democratic class struggle': class mobilization and interest group theories emphasized that collective political actors, such as labour movements, special interest groups, and political parties, demand and fight for social policies in the interest of their clientele. The welfare state is then seen as the outcome of a struggle between social classes and their political organizations, each with their own power base.

In a market economy, in which income stems from selling one's labour power, anything which hinders labour from being 'marketable' turns into an existential threat for the worker: unemployment, sickness, invalidity due to accidents or old age, etc. The market could neither cope with this new type of social risk directly (e.g. through private insurance) nor provide the collective goods needed to solve these problems. therefore if many of the new risks stemmed from treating *labour as a commodity,* the main task of the welfare state seemed to lie in *decommodifying labour,* i.e. in granting labour temporal relief from the pressure to sell itself in the labour market (Esping-Andersen 1990). Such a decommodifying effect of welfare state intervention lay in the interest of workers, and so it seems straightforward to identify the labour movement as the main political driving force behind welfare state formation and growth (Stephens 1979; Korpi 1983).

Not convergence, but *variation* among welfare states was emphasized by these approaches: the more powerful labour was, the more elaborate the welfare state tended to be. The causes for variation are 'synchronic', i.e. they are expected to persist in the longer run—or at least as long the power differentials persist.

However, the feminist critique of the class-mobilization literature has stressed that in order to be decommodified, you have to be commodified first (Pedersen 1990; Lewis 1992; Orloff 1993; Sainsbury 1994, 1996; O'Connor *et al.* 1999; Morgan 2002, 2003, 2006). Decommodification as an analytical concept ignored the fact that many women remained excluded from the labour market in the first place. It is in this context that concepts like 'de-familialization' were introduced, which discussed how and to what extent state provision of welfare could substitute those social services traditionally provided in the family (Esping-Andersen 1999).

State institutions and bureaucracy

'The welfare state followed in the footsteps of the nation state': finally, institutionalist theories point to those rules and regulations of policy-making and state structures, such as federalism (cf. Obinger *et al.* 2005), that operate relatively autonomously from social and political pressures as the main determinants of the emergence and growth of the welfare state.

This approach emphasized the 'state building' aspect in welfare states (Skocpol 1985, 1992; Skocpol and Orloff 1986). When countries were confronted with the social problems generated by modern society for the first time, it mattered whether their bureaucratic elite was relatively autonomous, as in Japan (Garon 1987) or Sweden (Heclo 1974), or whether the lack of bureaucratic autonomy led to a 'politicization' of early welfare state formation and to welfare clientelism. For instance, the harsh critique that the US progressive movement voiced against political clientelism in US veteran pensions delegitimized and delayed state social protection in the US for a long time (Skocpol 1992). If one focuses on how the state took over social responsibility for its citizens, it is easier to recognize that early welfare state programmes were not always exclusively targeted at workers, but often at other social categories whose risks did not coincide with class—such as soldiers or mothers (Skocpol 1992; see also Pedersen 1990, 1993). A perspective on how the state responded to the perils of modern society also helps us to understand the diffusion of policies, international policy learning, and the travel of concepts across the Atlantic or Pacific (cf. Rodgers 2000) and to account for the important role that war (both hot and cold) played in modern welfare state development (Obinger and Schmitt 2011). Finally, it points to the emergence of an international social policy, with international organizations like the World Health Organization or the International Labour Office and declarations such as the Universal Declaration of Human Rights (UDHR) (Paris 1948) or the International Covenant on Economic, Social and Cultural Rights (adopted by the United Nations in 1966), in which labour rights, the right to health and education, and the right to an adequate standard of living were declared.

The insights of the institutionalist school nicely squared with earlier observations in the modernization literature, namely that often it was the *least* democratic countries where suffrage was *not* yet extended which had actually pioneered building the modern welfare state. Also, it was not always the most economically advanced countries which took the lead in the introduction of state social protection programmes. Rather, it is the early pre-emptive strategy of state elites who anticipate workers' unrest that explains much of the pioneering role of not yet fully democratic and economically less advanced nations like Germany and Austria in the late nineteenth century. Here social rights were not granted because of the extended political participatory rights of workers, but as a kind of *compensation* for the lack of such participatory rights (Flora and Alber 1981; Alber 1982).

The power resources approach and the institutionalist literature reacted to the fact that the causal link between industrialization (or modernization more generally) and welfare state development was not always elaborated well theoretically and not often confirmed empirically (see Wilensky and Lebeaux 1965; Kerr *et al.* 1973; Cutright 1965; Pryor 1968; Rimlinger 1971; Jackman 1975; Wilensky 1975). In order to demonstrate the great variety among Western welfare states Figure 21.1 locates countries in two dimensions: first, according to the *chronological* point in time when they have introduced the first major social insurance programme and, second, according to the *economic* point in time, i.e. according to the level of economic development and prosperity when they introduced such a programme.

As Figure 21.1 shows, there is no clear relationship between the level of modernity, industrialization, or GDP per capita, and the relative 'earliness' or 'lateness' of welfare state formation. The Anglo-Saxon countries (UK, US, Canada) introduced social protection programmes relatively late and at a relatively high level of economic development. They are joined by Protestant liberal countries like the Netherlands or Switzerland which also qualify as welfare latecomers (Manow 2004). Countries like Germany or Austria were welfare pioneers in a chronological sense, but several countries (e.g. Japan, Portugal, Finland, Italy) introduced their first social insurance programmes at much lower levels of economic development than those two countries. A look at Latin America also reveals the interplay of economic development, political freedom and working class strength to explain the emergence of the welfare state (Segura-Ubiergo 2007). But do the political and social forces which can be held responsible for early or late welfare state building also explain the different paths of further welfare state development? This is the question for the following section.

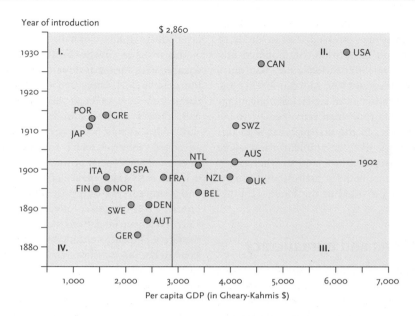

Figure 21.1 Level of economic development at the time of introduction of the first major social protection programme

Sources: Schmidt 1998: 180; Maddison 1995: 194–201; cf. Wagschal (2000: 49).

KEY POINTS

- The welfare state has been understood as the (functional) response to the social problems generated by modernization, as the result of the political conflicts between capital and labour in modern capitalist societies, and as a central element in modern nation-state building.

- There is no obvious connection between the level of economic development or democratization of a society and the development of its welfare state.

- Different approaches have different explanatory goals or problems: the functionalist approach tries to explain the convergence of modern welfare states; the power resources and institutionalist approaches attempt to account for the enduring variation among welfare states.

The expansion of the welfare state

The impact of social democracy

In the 1980s and 1990s a new approach criticized the logic of industrialism thesis and the median voter view that democratic politics as such can explain the expansion of the welfare state (Jackman 1975, 1986). The theoretical goal was to demonstrate how politics mattered for the different welfare state paths that countries had followed in the post-war period, focusing particularly on how differences in party political government composition explain differences in welfare state expansion. Hewitt (1977), for instance, argued that social democratic rule was a necessary condition for expansion and egalitarian outcomes. The explanatory importance of party politics was also underlined by the failure of economic models which predicted that welfare state redistribution should increase with increases in income inequality (Meltzer and Richard 1981). It was not the highly unequal societies which redistributed the most. On the contrary, countries like Sweden or Norway have both a highly compressed wage and income structure *and* a generous welfare state, and countries like the US combine an unequal pre-tax income distribution with a rather residual welfare state.

A large number of studies corroborated the causal effect of social democratic power on welfare state performance and discovered the conditions under which these movements were actually capable of refracting the working of the market through social protection programmes. Decommodification was found to be strongest if the *left was strong* (Stephens 1979) and the *right was divided* (Castles 1978). Moreover, social democratic attempts to expand the welfare state were most effective if the party was supported by a strong and coherent union movement (Stephens 1979; Higgins and Apple 1981).

Cross-national quantitative studies extensively tested the thesis that politically organized labour (social democracy) was primarily responsible for the social transformation of capitalism (Hewitt 1977; Korpi 1983, 1989; Stephens 1979; Hicks and Swank 1984; Esping-Andersen

1985*a*; Alvarez *et al.* 1991; Griffin *et al.* 1989; Hicks 1999; see also Huber and Stephens 2001). The main finding of this literature was that the more the mass of the population is organized as wage-earners within the social democratic movement, the higher the quality (universalism, solidarity, redistribution) of the welfare arrangements tended to be and, as a result, the higher the extent of equality. Therefore a developed welfare state was interpreted as evidence for a decisive *shift in the balance of power in favour of the working class* and social democracy (see Shalev 1983).

Indeed, there was considerable evidence in favour of a social democratic effect on income distribution (Hewitt 1977; Björn 1979; Stephens 1979; Hicks and Swank 1984; Swank and Hicks 1985; Muller 1989; Hage *et al.* 1989). However, for several reasons income distribution was still a problematic variable. On technical grounds, aggregate data available until the publication of the Luxembourg Income Study (Smeeding *et al.* 1990; Mitchell 1990) were not truly comparable. On theoretical grounds, income distribution was problematic to the extent that the kinds of universalistic and generous welfare programmes associated with successful social democratic politics tended to lose their redistributive effect because they increasingly favoured the middle classes (LeGrand 1982; Goodin and LeGrand 1987; Esping-Andersen 1990; Korpi and Palme 1998).

There was some evidence to suggest that the social democratic effect was more evident when measured against institutional characteristics of welfare states (Myles 1989; Korpi 1989; Kangas 1991; Esping-Andersen 1990). Yet, as research moved in the direction of studying the institutional and qualitative properties of welfare states it also moved away from the kind of linear 'more or less' or 'the bigger, the better' social democratization conception. Thus, Kangas's study of social expenditure and social rights concludes that 'the biggest are not necessarily the best, but the best are rarely the smallest' (Kangas 1991: 52).

Neocorporatism and the international economy

Others argued that the political efficacy of left-wing parties to decommodify labour and promote welfare state expansion depended structurally on centralized neocorporatist industrial relations systems (Cameron 1978, 1984; Schmidt 1983; Scharpf 1984, 1987; Hicks *et al.* 1989).

Cameron (1978, 1984) suggested that the association between strong social democracy and welfare states was linked to a country's position in the international economy. The vulnerability that small open economies faced favoured the expansion of the public economy so as to reduce uncertainty via social guarantees, full employment, and more active government management of

the economy. Katzenstein (1985) argued that *small open nations developed democratic corporatist structures as a way to enhance domestic consensus, facilitate economic adjustments, and maintain international competitiveness.* While democratic corporatism was promoted by the presence of strong social democratic labour movements, Katzenstein pointed to Switzerland and the Netherlands to suggest that they did not constitute a necessary condition (see Keman 1990; Garrett 1998).

Social democracy was most likely to promote the expansion of the welfare state if its parliamentary power was matched by *strong consensus-building mechanisms* in both the polity and economy (Schmidt 1983; Keman 1988; Hicks *et al.* 1989). Neocorporatist intermediation came to play an important role in maintaining welfare policies during economic crisis periods; the distributive battles that erupt when growth declines were better managed with 'all-encompassing' interest organizations. Hicks and Swank (1984) and Muller (1989) suggested that the strength of left-wing parties (and economic openness) influenced the income distribution directly, while trade unionization and **centralization** of wage bargaining had decisive indirect effects by providing the electoral basis for social democracy.

By the end of the 1980s the literature came to agree that parties or unions alone had little effect and that successful social democratization required a configuration of strong left-wing parties in government supported by an encompassing and centralized trade union movement (Alvarez *et al.* 1991; Garrett 1998). Only in the 'coherently' liberal political economies, in which a weak labour movement met with a political dominance of conservative parties, or in the coherently social democratic political economies, where a strong labour movement went hand in hand with left-wing governments, were macro-economic policies, wage bargaining, and welfare expenditures expected to complement each other. 'Incoherent political economies', on the other hand, were expected to perform much less well, when right-wing governments that pursued neoliberal economic policies met with strong union resistance, causing industrial strife, or when the attempt at macro-economic management by left-wing governments was counteracted by fragmented and particularistic unions which proved unable to engage in concerted wage restraint. Today's debate about the impact of **globalization** on the sustainability of generous welfare state programmes in many respects reflects this earlier corporatist debate about economic vulnerabilities in open economies and the concomitant need for welfare compensation (see later in this chapter and Chapter 24).

Risk redistribution

In one of the more fundamental challenges to the literature, Baldwin (1990) rejected the causal link between social democracy and solidaristic social policies altogether.

While growing equality may have been a characteristic feature of modern welfare states, it has not been its goal. The welfare state was more about reapportioning risks than about the redistribution of wealth. Baldwin rejected what he called the labourist (i.e. class mobilization) account for its narrow focus on the working class as the only risk category. The critical insight was that class is neither the only risk category nor always a risk category. The labourist view mistakenly assumed that welfare policies were explained in terms of a victory of the working class over the bourgeoisie.

What had historically determined the solidarity of social policy was not working-class strength but, in contrast, the fact that 'otherwise privileged groups discovered that they shared a common interest in reallocating risk with the disadvantaged' (Baldwin 1990: 292). Similarly, Heclo and Madsen (1986) and Therborn (1989) argued that the principles of solidarity and equality that characterize Swedish social democracy had less to do with socialism than with the Swedish historical tradition. The implication was that the Swedish model was inapplicable elsewhere (Milner 1989).

Christian democracy and Catholic social doctrine

One of the major problems of the social democratic model was that several countries (e.g. the Netherlands or France) pursued equality and had a large welfare state without the advocacy of a strong social democratic labour movement (Castles 1978, 1985; Stephens 1979; Wilensky 1981; Skocpol and Amenta 1986). Both the incapacity to explain early reforms of capitalism by liberal and conservative state elites and the fact that other political parties also behaved as pro-welfare actors made it clear that the political process of welfare state construction and expansion needed to be reconsidered. One answer came from those who showed that Christian democracy (or political Catholicism) constituted a functional equivalent or alternative to social democracy for expanding the welfare state (Wilensky 1981; Schmidt 1982). Consequently, the power of labour could not be equalled with the power of social democracy. Christian democratic parties operating in the centre enjoyed considerable working-class support and were commonly backed by powerful Catholic unions (see van Kersbergen 1995). This political constellation was highly favourable to welfare state development.

Secular trends

Emphasizing political agency against the functionalist approaches has the danger of falling into the other extreme of neglecting how much the growth of the welfare state is influenced by secular processes beyond the control of single political actors. Some of them are as follows.

1. Demographic ageing: longer life expectancy and lower birth rates lead to demographic ageing and increase the demand for social spending on health, pensions, and care. Medical progress is costly and puts an increasing strain on healthcare spending.

2. Baumol's disease: productivity increases more slowly in services than in manufacturing, which means that (social) services will increase in economic importance. At the same time, economies with a larger service sector will grow at a slower pace (Pierson 2001a).

3. Structural change: job losses in agriculture and industry increases the demand for welfare state compensation (job protection, retraining; active labour market policies) (Iversen and Cusack 2000; Wren 2013).

4. Wagner's law predicts an ever-increasing share of public expenditures in developed industrial economies, causing a secular trend towards higher public spending in all developed economies.

5. 'Politics for profit' (e.g. Buchanan 1977): politicians aim at expanding public spending to maximize their 'political income' and to increase their re-election prospects.

6. Programme maturity, 'positive feedback', and ratchet effects—each welfare programme breeds its own supporters. Once introduced, it proves very hard to abandon a welfare scheme later (Pierson 1994, 1998; Huber and Stephens 2001).

While all advanced welfare states have to cope with these secular challenges, their vulnerabilities and opportunities in coping with them vary according to their institutional set-up.

KEY POINTS

- The political impact of left-wing parties on the welfare state depended on a centralized neocorporatist industrial relations system that helped to enhance domestic consensus, facilitate economic adjustments, and maintain international competitiveness.

- Important criticisms of the social democratic or labourist model are: (1) the welfare state is about reapportioning social risks and the working class is only one risk category; (2) there are countries that pursued equality and a developed welfare state, but did not have a strong social democratic labour movement.

- There are other pro-welfare state actors (e.g. Christian democracy) and important non-political processes (e.g. demographic ageing) that promote expansion and development.

Variations among developed welfare states

Each welfare state is a 'unique' combination of regulations and institutions. However, in comparative politics we are not interested in uniqueness, but in comparability and systematic variation. In order to compare welfare states, some simple dimensions of variation can be distinguished. They comprise the following.

1. Is the welfare state tax-financed or contribution-financed?
2. Is every *citizen* protected or is every *worker* (and his or her dependants) insured?
3. Are benefits a right, gained either through previous contributions to social insurance programmes or attached to the status of citizenship, or do benefits depend on proven need, i.e. are they conditional on means testing?
4. Are benefits uniform (flat rate) or do they reflect prior income, i.e. are pension or unemployment payments temporary substitutes for wages or do they aim at securing some 'minimum' standard of living?

That welfare states come in a limited variety can be partly explained by the fact that choosing a particular institutional solution in one dimension simultaneously narrows the choice set in others. The advanced welfare states represent packages or bundles of institutional and regulatory answers to the social problems of modern society.

For example, take welfare state financing. If the welfare state is tax-financed, eligibility should be linked to the citizen status (with or without means testing), but not to the employment relation. But this would also mean that benefits are unlikely to reflect prior income but rather a social notion of a socially fair and accepted (minimum) standard of living. In a contribution-financed welfare state, in contrast, proportional deductions from the payroll justify differentiated benefits that reflect the length of the previous contribution period and the level of the contributions paid. If social protection is primarily linked to the employment relation, it seems to be a 'natural' solution to insure those who are not in dependent employment (e.g. spouse, children) via the family member who is dependently employed.

Welfare states as bundles of institutional or regulatory solutions to social problems can be analysed as *models or regimes*. In the late 1950s Richard M. Titmuss (1958) suggested distinguishing the following.

- The *residual welfare model,* in which social protection 'comes into play only after the breakdown of the private market and the family as the "natural" channels for the fulfilment of social needs' (Flora 1986: xxi).
- The *industrial achievement performance model,* in which welfare rights and benefits are linked to the

Box 21.3 Esping-Andersen's three welfare state regimes

[In the liberal welfare state,] means tested assistance, modest universalist transfers, or modest social insurance plans predominate. Benefits cater mainly to a clientele of low-income, usually working-class, state dependents. ... In turn, the state encourages the market, either passively—by guaranteeing only a minimum—or actively—by subsidizing private welfare schemes. In conservative and strongly 'corporatist' welfare states, the liberal obsession with market efficiency and commodification was never pre-eminent and, as such, the granting of social rights was hardly ever a contested issue. What predominated was the preservation of status differentials; rights, therefore, were attached to class and status. This corporatism was subsumed under a state edifice perfectly ready to displace the market as a provider of welfare; hence, private insurance and occupational fringe benefits play a truly marginal role. ... The third ... regime-cluster is composed of those countries in which the principles of universalism and decommodification of social rights were extended also to the new middle classes. We may call it the 'social democratic' regime-type since, in these nations, social democracy was clearly the dominant force behind social reform. ... [and] pursued a welfare state that would promote an equality of the highest standards. ... This model crowds out the market, and consequently constructs an essentially universal solidarity in favour of the welfare state. All benefit, all are dependent; and all will presumably feel obliged to pay.

Esping-Andersen 1990: 26–8

employment relation and reflect 'merit, work performance and productivity' (Flora 1986: xxi).
- An *institutional redistributive model,* in which social welfare institutions are an integral part of society, providing 'universalist services outside the market' (Flora 1986: xxi) based on citizenship.

There is obviously considerable overlap between Titmuss's welfare state typology and Gosta Esping-Andersen's *Three Worlds of Welfare Capitalism* (1990). In his book, Esping-Andersen distinguished three regimes (see Box 21.3).

Anglo-Saxon liberal regime

In a liberal regime, benefits tend to be low and flat rate. They are means-tested or targeted at clearly delineated groups in society. The welfare state is predominantly tax-financed. More encompassing social protection has to be purchased individually on the market (e.g. life insurance or private pension plans), because the welfare state

Table 21.1 Esping-Andersen's three worlds of welfare capitalism

Esping-Andersen's welfare regimes (Titmuss's welfare models)	'Liberal' (residual model)	'Conservative' (achievement-performance model)	'Social democratic' (institutional redistributive model)
Prime example	US, UK	Germany	Sweden
Decommodification	Low	Medium	High
Social rights	Needs-based	Employment-related	Universal
Welfare provision	Mixed services	Transfer payments	Public services
Benefits	Flat benefits	Contribution-related	Redistributive

Source: Ebbinghaus and Manow (2001: 9).

only protects the most needy. Public spending on social protection is comparatively low. This welfare regime is to be found where conservative parties are often in government, in the US and the UK and to some extent also in Australia and New Zealand (see section on Australia and New Zealand).

Scandinavian social democratic regime

The social democratic regime is also predominantly tax-financed, but in contrast with the liberal model, benefits are granted without means testing. They are a citizen's right and benefits tend to be much more generous. Subsequently, levels of public spending tend to be much higher. Social democratic regimes also provide many welfare services in care, health, and education, and the welfare state itself becomes a major employer especially of women (Huber and Stephens 2000). This regime is found mainly in Scandinavian countries in which social democratic parties are strong and often participate in government, where levels of unionization are high, and where the political right is divided.

Continental conservative regime

The continental conservative regime comes close to Titmuss's 'performance achievement' model. Here, social rights are not based on citizen status, but on the employment relation. The welfare state is contribution-financed rather than tax-financed. Those not employed are covered via their employed spouse or relatives. Welfare benefits are differentiated according to income and to the record of contributions to the social insurance fund. The conservative welfare state is transfer heavy and service lean. Based on occupational principles, conservative welfare states display a high degree of programme fragmentation. The major occupational groups (white collar and blue collar workers, civil servants, free professions, self-employed, etc.) all have their own social insurance

schemes (see Table 21.1). This welfare state is mainly to be found in continental European countries in which Christian Democratic parties occupy a central position in the party system.

Esping-Andersen's welfare state typology has become extremely influential and is successfully orienting research to the present day. Whether studying employment growth in the service economy (Scharpf 1997*b*), or different political choices between full employment, balanced budgets, and income equality (Iversen and Wren 1998), or patterns of income inequality among the OECD countries (Korpi and Palme 1998), the 'three worlds' heuristic has been confirmed time and again.

However, the voluminous literature on Esping-Andersen's welfare state typology (see Arts and Gelissen 2002) has debated whether additional regime types should be added. Some add a distinct *Southern European welfare regime* (Italy, Spain, Portugal, Greece, sometimes including France), and some treat the two antipodean welfare states (Australia and New Zealand) as special cases (Castles 1989; Castles and Mitchell 1992; Ferrera 1996, 1997).

Southern Europe

The Southern European welfare regime distinguishes itself from the rest of continental conservative welfare states as follows.

- The long-time absence of a nationwide uniform social assistance scheme.
- The dominance of pension spending among total social spending.
- Highly segmented labour market with the highest protection standards for the 'happy few' in the state sector and in state enterprises, combined with large segments of low protection in the private sector, plus unregulated employment in the large shadow economy. This leads to low female employment and high youth unemployment.
- Finally, national health systems which are rather untypical of the conservative welfare regimes on Europe's continent.

Australia and New Zealand

The welfare states of New Zealand and Australia represent a type of their own (Castles 1989, 1996; Castles and Mitchell 1992). While targeting plays a prominent role, eligibility rules are not particularly restrictive. Moreover, state social protection in both countries often works 'through the market', especially via state arbitration of industrial conflicts, high employment protection, and compressed wages, which makes post hoc welfare intervention and redistribution often unnecessary.

Esping-Andersen's typology was based on his *index of decommodification* and used 1980 data. From the beginning, controversy arose over the categorization of single countries and over the clusters per se: for an overview see Arts and Gelissen (2002), for a recent replication see Scruggs and Allan (2006a), and see Table 21.2 and the web links at the end of the chapter. Despite all criticism, Esping-Andersen's typology has remained the single most important contribution to the comparative welfare state literature of the last three decades.

Table 21.2 Decommodification scores in the three worlds of welfare capitalism

Benefit generosity index results								
	UE	Sick	Pension	Total decom		UE	Sick	Pension	Total decom
Australia	4.0	4.0	5.0	13.0	US	7.4	0	11.3	18.7
US[a]	7.2	0	7.0	13.8	Japan	4.5	6.2	9.4	20.0
New Zealand	4	4.0	9.1	17.1	Australia	5.0	5.0	10.1	20.1
Canada	8	6.3	7.7	22.0	Italy	3.2	7.3	10.0	20.5
Ireland	8.3	8.3	6.7	23.3	Ireland	6.9	6.2	8.3	21.4
UK	7.2	7.7	8.5	23.4	UK	7.2	7.2	8.5	22.9
Italy	5.1	9.4	9.6	24.1	New Zealand	5.0	5.0	13.3	23.3
Japan[a]	5.0	6.8	10.5	27.3	Canada	7.2	6.4	11.4	25.0
France	6.3	9.2	12.0	27.5	Austria	6.9	9.7	11.2	27.8
Germany	7.9	11.3	8.5	27.7	France	6.3	9.5	12.0	27.8
Finland	5.2	10.0	14.0	29.2	Finland	4.9	10.0	13.0	27.9
Switzerland	8.8	12.0	9.0	29.8	Germany	7.5	12.6	8.7	28.8
Austria	6.7	12.5	11.9	31.1	Netherlands	10.6	9.7	11.5	31.8
Belgium	8.6	8.8	15.0	32.4	Switzerland	9.2	11.0	12.0	32.2
Netherlands	11.1	10.5	10.8	32.4	Belgium	10.2	8.6	14.0	32.9
Denmark	8.1	15.0	15.0	38.1	Denmark	8.6	12.6	11.8	32.9
Norway	9.4	14.0	14.9	38.3	Norway	8.5	13.0	11.9	33.4
Sweden	7.1	15.0	17.0	39.1	Sweden	9.4	14.0	15.0	38.4
Mean	7.1	9.2	10.7	27.2		7.1	8.6	11.3	27.0
Standard deviation	1.9	4.0	3.4	7.7		2.1	3.5	1.9	5.8
Coefficient of variation	0.27	0.44	0.32	0.28		0.29	0.41	0.17	0.21
					Correlation with original scores	0.87	0.95	0.70	0.87
Correlation between programmes					Correlation between programmes				
UE – Sick *r* = 0.44					UK – Sick *r* = 0.45				
UE – Pension *r* = 0.23					UE – Pension *r* = 0.36				
Sick – Pension *r* = 0.72					Sick – Pension *r* = 0.30				
Cronbach's α = 0.72					Cronbach's α = 0.59				

Note[a] 'Total decom' score is amount in Table 2.2 of Esping-Andersen (1990), not the sum of programme scores.

Source: Adapted from Scruggs and Allan (2006b: 68).

KEY POINTS

- The advanced welfare states represent packages or bundles of institutional and regulatory answers to the social problems and risks of modern society, such as unemployment, sickness, and inability to work due to old age or invalidity.

- The literature distinguishes three to five different welfare regimes: (1) an Anglo-Saxon liberal regime; (2) a social democratic regime found in Scandinavia; (3) a conservative model that is typical for continental Europe; (4) a Southern European regime; (5) a 'radical' type found in Australia and New Zealand.

The effects of the welfare state

Comparative political science research has tended to take a broad approach to the study of the effects of social policies. Theoretically, they have been inspired by T. H. Marshall (1950) (see Box 21.1). His concept of social citizenship not only stresses social *rights,* but also how the granting of such rights structures and restructures *status* relations in society. The main questions were whether the welfare state (1) modifies social inequality, (2) alleviates poverty, and (3) reduces social risks, and (4) whether different welfare states have varying consequences for social stratification.

(In)equality and redistribution

The relevant social stratification in our societies concerns status or occupational groups, social classes, gender, and ethnicity. Social policies, their design and content, are likely to be affected by the prevailing differentiation in society and may or may not influence the unequal distribution of social risks. Research deals with the question of whether social policies structure, cause, reproduce, reinforce, or moderate social inequality.

Class, gender, and ethnicity as concepts are supposed to capture systematically how society is structured in such a way that certain groups of people are privileged or disadvantaged in terms of their occupational position, income, wealth, status, skills, education, and above all power. These structural characteristics are expected to determine to a large extent the life chances of the individuals within these groups and they are affiliated with many other things, including health, happiness, death rates, lifestyle, culture, political preference, etc.

With respect to class, the debate is whether and to what extent it is possible to 'escape' one's own class. Is social mobility, both within a generation and between generations, rare? Are social policies capable of decreasing class closure? Do social policies reduce or reproduce social inequalities? And do different welfare regimes (re)structure social divisions differently?

Universalism vs. targeting

It is important to realize that redistribution does not always imply more equality. For instance, saving money during periods of relative prosperity (e.g. when in a job) for periods of need (e.g. when old and retired) is a form of redistribution, but does not lead to more equality. Redistribution is not necessarily from the rich to the poor. With respect to equality, the issue is whether social policies *targeted at specific groups* (e.g. the working class, women, migrants) reduce inequalities or whether *universalism* in social policy, i.e. 'the provision of a single, relatively uniform service or benefit for all citizens regardless of income or class' (M. Hill 2006: 192), actually does a better job.

Different welfare regimes vary precisely in this respect, with the *social democratic model being a universal system and the liberal regimes the most strongly targeting.* Moreover, in the conservative regime, social inequalities and status differentials are intentionally reproduced in the welfare system through occupational and earnings-related social insurance schemes. Inequalities are also reproduced, but to a lesser extent, in the universalist schemes because the better-off and highly educated people with higher skills and competences are much more capable of taking advantage of universal services (healthcare, education) than poorer and less educated people.

At face value, it seems that targeting is ultimately better for the poor or the less well-off, primarily because social policies are designed exclusively for those who need it most. Moreover, redistribution via targeting is fair and efficient because it does not waste resources by transferring money to people who do not need aid. However, targeting is a kind of 'Robin Hood strategy' ('stealing' from the rich, giving to the poor) that antagonizes the rich and provokes them to defect from the system. As Korpi and Palme (1998: 672) explain: 'By discriminating in favour of the poor, the targeted model creates a zero-sum conflict of interests between the poor and the better-off workers and the middle classes who must pay for the benefits of the poor without receiving any benefits'.

An alternative is a *simple egalitarian system* with flat-rate benefits for all, giving relatively more to the poor than to the better-off. However, this system (known as the Beveridge system) also has incentives for the middle classes to opt out and look for private insurance. Finally, there is the evangelical *Matthew strategy* ('For unto every one that hath shall be given, and he shall have abundance: but from him that hath not shall be taken away even that which he hath') of earnings-related provision that gives relatively more to the rich than to the poor. The Matthew effect is most pronounced in services, for instance in (higher) education from which the rich profit much more than the poor, not only because they receive the service, but also because education greatly advances earnings capacity.

When empirically comparing welfare state regimes, we find the *paradox of distribution:* 'The more we target benefits at the poor only and the more concerned we are with creating equality via equal public transfers to all, the less likely we are to reduce poverty and equality' (Korpi and Palme 1998: 681–2). Encompassing models that combine a simple egalitarian system with the Matthew strategy are the most redistributive systems which also have a high level of political support and legitimacy. How is this to be explained? Korpi and Palme provide an answer:

> By giving basic security to everybody and by offering clearly earnings-related benefits to all economically active individuals, ... the encompassing model brings low-income groups and the better-off citizens into the same institutional structures. Because of its earnings-related benefits, it is likely to reduce the demand for private insurance. Thus the encompassing model can be expected to have the most favourable outcomes in terms of the formation of cross-class coalitions that include manual workers as well as the middle classes. By providing sufficiently high benefits for high-income groups so as not to push them to exit, in encompassing institutions the voice of the better-off citizens helps not only themselves but low-income income groups as well. (Korpi and Palme 1998: 672)

Similarly, Smeeding (2005) shows that the targeting welfare state regimes, especially the US, have the highest levels of poverty and inequality. Smeeding also argues that when the distance between the rich and the less well-off becomes too great, the rich opt out and cater for themselves: they get private insurance, receive the best healthcare, and make sure that their children have the best education available. This reproduces and even reinforces social divisions. Therefore in a comparative politics perspective, we must look not only at the economic consequences, but also at the political preconditions of social protection.

Empirical research (e.g. Kenworthy 1999; Korpi and Palme 2003; Brady 2005; Scruggs and Allen 2006a) underscores the differential impact of various welfare state regimes on equality and poverty. Although some (e.g. Brady 2005: 1354) find that the welfare state, regardless of the period or the type one studies, strongly reduces poverty, there seems to be a consensus that *universalism in particular produces the most pronounced effects*.

The issue of inequality is predominantly phrased in terms of income and market position, and especially addresses the class issue. Feminist critiques pointed out that this perspective had great difficulty in dealing with the class position of women, particularly those not active in the labour market. In order to understand the working of the regimes in terms of market, state, *and* family, one also needs to develop theoretical tools that can make sense of the gender dimension of social stratification and how social policies presuppose and affect the

relations between men and women (see Bussemaker and van Kersbergen 1994).

Social policies often took the distribution of labour between men and women for granted and tended to reinforce it. For the position of women, it is crucial whether they are entitled to benefits as individuals or whether rights are tied to families in which men are often the sole income earner. Also, women have different types of risks and needs (e.g. think of single parenthood). As a result, the outcomes of welfare state interventions in terms of equality and poverty and in terms of labour market behaviour are markedly different for men and women. For instance, in the European Union (except in Finland and Sweden) the poverty risk for women is considerably larger than for men, although the welfare state reduces the risk of poverty everywhere (European Commission 2004: 188).

In the golden age of the welfare state (the 1960s and 1970s), income security and redistribution were considered to be a matter not simply of social justice, but also of macro-economic efficiency. Welfare state expenditures could be viewed as part of Keynesian demand management that helped maximize economic performance, particularly economic growth and the prevention of mass unemployment. Also, a neocorporatist exchange between the expansion of social programmes and wage moderation was often part of the management of the macro-economy. Moreover, many of the welfare state's programmes contribute to the supply of labour. The welfare state's jobs and programmes (such as child care, parental leave, sickness benefits) have played a crucial role in increasing the supply of female labour. Or, to put it differently, the welfare state has helped women to enter the labour market on a scale that would have been impossible without it. The welfare state also facilitated economic reconstruction and adaptation by offering 'easy' exit routes for redundant workers in non-competitive industries via disability schemes and early retirement.

KEY POINTS

- The welfare state is itself a system of social stratification: it can counter, reproduce, or reinforce social (class, gender, ethnic) inequalities.

- The impact of social policies on poverty and inequality varies enormously among regimes, with the universalist social democratic regime the most and the liberal targeting regime the least redistributive.

- Paradoxically, the more benefits are targeted exclusively at the poor and the more public policies are devised to create equality via equal transfers to all, the less likely it is that poverty and equality are reduced.

- Men profit more than women from welfare state interventions to reduce equality and poverty and to improve their chances in the labour market.

The challenges and dynamics of contemporary welfare states

Today, the welfare state is under pressure from many sides: population ageing, sluggish economic growth, mass unemployment, changing family structures and life-cycle patterns, post-industrial labour markets that generate new risks and needs, the erosion of systems of interest intermediation and collective bargaining, and international pressures from globalization and global financial crises (see Schwartz 2001). In particular, the globalization literature started from the assumption that an increasingly internationalized market would force the generous welfare states of the Western world into a common downward movement (see Chapter 24).

Globalization: efficiency vs. compensation

However, it seems that the advanced OECD economies have maintained their ability to 'tax and spend' to a surprising degree, even under conditions of crisis. What is most remarkable from the viewpoint of the early pessimistic predictions is that the welfare state basically survived (Kuhnle 2000). This has led to an as yet unresolved debate between, on the one hand, those researchers who think that globalization is indeed a major challenge that is potentially undermining the economic foundations of social policies and, on the other hand, those scholars who argue that the challenges and threats to the welfare state, such as ageing, are essentially endogenous and have little to do with globalization.

In the debate one side holds that the internationalized market and its intensified economic competition have rendered high levels of welfare spending unsustainable (the *efficiency hypothesis*); others argue that welfare state compensation of those who lose from economic openness has historically been a social and political precondition for the liberal post-war trade regime (the *compensation hypothesis*) (Rodrik 1996; Rieger and Leibfried 1998, 2001; Glatzer and Rueschemeyer 2005).

Adherents of the compensation hypothesis argue that economic openness and a liberal trade regime rested on the domestic political promise to compensate the losers of economic integration. With downward pressures on the advanced welfare states, economic openness is endangering the very social and political preconditions on which it rests. As of yet, the 'race to the bottom', commonly attributed to globalization, has failed to materialize. Also, the link between economic openness and domestic social protection has not yet been convincingly established, neither theoretically nor empirically (Iversen and Cusack 2000).

Moreover, it seems still possible to implement social and economic policies that redistribute wealth and risk in such a manner that the potential victims of the global market are protected. Such policies can be beneficial to economic growth, because they yield collective goods that the market cannot produce. These especially concern investments in human capital and the infrastructure. It was especially the 'varieties of capitalism' literature which highlighted this important contribution of the welfare state to skill-intensive production regimes (Hall and Soskice 2001*a*; Iversen and Soskice 2001). Workers invest in those special skills on which skill-intensive production regimes in coordinated market economies depend only when they have a guarantee that their investment will pay off in the long run. Generous unemployment payments that take into account the previous wage level and that can be drawn for relatively long periods of time, as well as generous early retirement rules, make sure that investments in special skills will not be lost even in the case of unemployment (Estevez-Abe *et al.* 2001). Employers may also value the welfare state's contribution to the stability of centralized wage bargaining and to the prevention of cut-throat price competition (Swenson 2004) by clearing the market of firms that underbid wages and working conditions. It also turns out that a nation's economic, political, and social stability is increasingly important for investment decisions, particularly for those investors who are forced to take their decisions under conditions of uncertainty and high risk. Certainty and predictability are highly valued in an increasingly uncertain and volatile global economy (but see Huber and Stephens 2001; Stephens 2005: 63).

After more than ten years of debate on the effects of globalization on the generous welfare states of the West, the competing hypotheses can now clearly be distinguished (Glatzer and Rueschemeyer 2005).

1. The *compensation hypothesis* holds that open markets create a need for new compensatory policies that (democratic) governments may supply. Moreover, social policies can also be productive assets as they foster a better educated, better trained, and healthier workforce, provide coordinated market economies with specific skill profiles and contribute to the development of a more equal and less conflictual society.

2. The *efficiency hypothesis* states that globalization hampers social policy. International competition forces national governments to reduce costs by scaling down taxes and social policies. At the same time, open capital markets critically reduce the nation-state's taxing capacity, thereby undermining the welfare state's financial basis.

The literature seems to have reached a 'politics matters' conclusion (see Garrett and Nickerson 2005: 48; Huber and Stephens 2001; Stephens 2005). Trade openness leads to the expansion of the welfare state only under social democratic or Christian democratic leadership, but not when secular right parties are in power. Generous welfare states were not only compatible with competition on the world market, but 'to the extent that they enabled wage restraint and provided collective goods valued by employers, such as labor training, the generous social policies actually contributed to competitiveness' (Stephens 2005: 70). It is soaring unemployment and budget deficits that cause public spending cuts. Welfare state retrenchment is caused by globalization only to the extent that rising unemployment is an effect of globalization. But these effects are mediated by politics.

Most recent studies indicate that domestic politics and institutions are of great consequence for how the pressures of globalization make themselves felt in social policy and the welfare state. Globalization does not *always* undermine the welfare state. Under favourable political conditions, increasing openness can imply welfare state development, but if such conditions are absent, the compensation hypothesis also fails to convince. This makes social policy outcomes more dependent on raw political struggles. Welfare state outcomes are predominantly the result of the complex *interplay* of international economic forces and domestic politics and institutions (Glatzer and Rueschemeyer 2005: 215).

Welfare defence: the politics of retrenchment and transformation

Critics of the globalization argument emphasize that welfare states have been remarkably resilient, notwithstanding the mounting challenges they face. So, an interesting new puzzle was formulated: how is it possible that the major institutions of the welfare state persist in the light of all the pressure for change (see Green-Pedersen and Haverland 2002)?

Paul Pierson (1996: 178) has argued that 'frontal assaults on the welfare state carry tremendous electoral risks' and that our current times of austerity should not be misunderstood as the simple mirror image of the former times of growth. Welfare expansion usually generates a popular politics of credit claiming for extending social rights and raising benefits to an increasing number of citizens, while austerity policies affront voters and networks of organized interests. In other words, *welfare state reform* tends to induce *political backlash*, and this has been taken to explain the striking inertia of social programmes.

The post-1945 welfare state has also produced an entirely novel *institutional context*. Once welfare programmes, like social housing and healthcare, were solidly established, they created their own programme-specific constituencies of clients and professional interests. This may have made the welfare state 'less dependent on the political parties, social movements, and labour organizations that expanded social programs in the first place' (Pierson 1996: 147). Therefore, a general weakening of

social democratic and Christian democratic parties and the trade union movement—the main political supporters of welfare state expansion—need not translate into a commensurate weakening of social policy. The programme-specific constituencies of clients and professional interests have developed into powerful defenders of the status quo.

Supported by strong popular attachments to specific policies, professional policy networks are able to muster substantial veto powers against reform efforts. Moreover, given the political salience and popularity of social policy, it is not easy to turn a programme of welfare state retrenchment into an electorally attractive proposition, although instances of popular welfare cutbacks have also been observed (Armingeon and Giger 2008). In his later work, Pierson (2001a: 428) stresses that different welfare regimes constitute different settings for the 'new politics' of welfare state reform, and acknowledges that he may have underestimated the continuing political salience for welfare state politics of organized labour in some regimes.

One of the major challenges to the welfare state is posed by the transition to a service economy (see Wren 2013). In Esping-Andersen's (1999) analyses, post-industrialism leads to serious trade-offs, particularly between protecting labour market insiders and creating opportunities for outsiders (Rueda 2005) and, more generally, between employment and equality. Iversen and Wren (1998) even identify a post-industrial *tri*lemma between (1) budgetary restraint, (2) wage equality, and (3) employment growth, where only two of these three policy goals can be successfully pursued simultaneously.

> Because budgetary restraint precludes any rapid expansion of public sector employment, governments wedded to such discipline must either accept low earnings equality in order to spur growth in private service employment or face low growth in overall employment. Alternatively, governments may pursue earnings equality and high employment, but they can do so only at the expense of budgetary restraint. (Iversen and Wren 1998: 513)

The changing welfare state

How best can we conceptualize and operationalize welfare state change, reform, and retrenchment? This 'dependent variable problem' (see Green-Pedersen 2004; Kühner 2007) needs to be clarified before we can answer the question of how much welfare states have actually changed since the 1980s. Some (e.g. Pierson 1996) have concluded on the basis of aggregate expenditure data, particularly transfer payments, that there has been no radical dismantling of welfare state arrangements. But looking at the organization of the public sector, particularly the delivery of social services and the development of public employment, Clayton and Pontusson (1998) observed that current reforms tended to have an anti-service bias which was not picked up when studying transfer payments.

Pierson (2001a) argued that welfare state change cannot be measured along a single scale. This would reduce the problem of welfare state retrenchment and reform to a dichotomy of 'less' versus 'more' and 'intact' versus 'dismantled', which is an unwarranted theoretical simplification. Pierson proposed looking at three dimensions of welfare state change.

- Recommodification: the attempt 'to restrict the alternatives to participation in the labour market by either tightening eligibility or cutting benefits' (Pierson 2001: 422), i.e. strengthening the whip of the labour market.

- Cost containment: the attempt to keep balanced budgets through austerity policies, including deficit reduction and tax moderation.

- Recalibration: 'reforms which seek to make contemporary welfare states more consistent with contemporary goals and demands for social provision' (Pierson 2001: 425).

In his view each regime—social democratic, liberal, or conservative—is characterized by its own specific 'new politics' of welfare state reform. In the liberal regime voters are least likely to be attached to the welfare state. Recommodification is here the pivotal feature of welfare state reform. In the social democratic welfare regime, voters are highly attached to, and dependent on, the welfare state. Recommodification is not so much on the political agenda of reform, but—if only because of the sheer size of the public sector—cost containment is. The conservative regime is the most ill-adapted model of the three worlds of welfare capitalism, as a result of which recalibration and cost containment are the two dimensions of reform that dominate. Here the issues are how to stimulate job growth in the underdeveloped service sector and how to contain the exploding costs of pensions, disability, and health.

Most recently, the debate has shifted to the analysis of the impact of the financial and economic crises since 2008. Are these crises inducing a fundamental overhaul of the welfare state and are harsh retrenchment and austerity as a means to consolidate the public budget the only options available? Or are welfare states, at least those that had their public finances in good shape before the crises hit, capable of continuing to provide education and protection against poverty and the risks of sickness, invalidity, unemployment, and old age?

KEY POINTS

- All welfare state regimes face various internal and external challenges and threats, but they have shown a remarkable capacity to survive.

- The argument that globalization forces welfare states to scale down seems compelling, but empirical evidence is not conclusive.

- Domestic politics and institutions still matter in how the pressures on the welfare state are translated and refracted; unemployment is a major threat, while ageing puts the greatest pressure on financial viability.

- Welfare state reform seems to be regime-specific: the liberal regime prioritizes recommodification, the conservative regime focuses on recalibration, and the social democratic regime is preoccupied with cost containment.

Conclusion

Institutional and electoral analyses have come a long way in explaining why welfare states have been capable of resisting (radical) change or reform. However, there are many empirical examples of substantial changes that seem momentous in the light of mainstream institutional theory. So, how and under what conditions is it possible to override the mechanisms of sclerosis and resilience? Some have offered answers by describing specific institutional mechanisms or political conditions under which substantial reform is possible (e.g. Kitschelt et al. 1999; Levy 1999; Ross 2000; Bonoli 2000, 2001; Green-Pedersen 2001; Kitschelt 2001; Swank 2001; Vis and van Kersbergen 2007), and others suggest that ideational factors, discourse (e.g. framing), and policy learning can prevail over electoral and institutional resistance against major policy reform (Cox 2001; Schmidt 2002; see also Green-Pedersen and Haverland 2002; van Kersbergen 2002; Starke 2006). Most recently, researchers have documented how welfare states change in various dimensions, what their causes are, and what effects or consequences follow from such changes (e.g. Palier 2010; Emmenegger et al. 2012; Hemerijck 2013). In the coming years, research will certainly focus on the impact of the financial and economic crises (see e.g. the special issue on the crisis and the welfare state of *Social Policy & Administration* (2011: Vol. 45, Issue 4)).

The welfare state will remain interesting for comparative political science, because it continues to have a profound influence on the quality of life of citizens. Welfare state reform is a political process in which power struggles are crucial, not only for understanding why and how reform occurs, but also for grasping what politics is all about: who gets what, when, and how. In this sense, the study of the welfare state will continue to offer us essential and never-ending questions in comparative political science and political economy.

Questions

1. Why is the welfare state an important topic for comparative political science?

2. Why is an exclusive focus on the welfare *state* misleading if one tries to understand how a nation provides work and welfare?

3. What makes a risk a social risk?

4. Are left-wing parties that promoted the expansion of the welfare state also the main defenders of the welfare state?

5. What non-political processes have stimulated the growth of the welfare state?

6. Why is it that the more we target benefits at the poor only and the more concerned we are with creating equality via equal public transfers to all, the less likely we are to reduce poverty and equality?

7. Does the welfare state reduce poverty and inequality?

8. Why does globalization not necessarily lead to the downsizing of the welfare state?

9. Why are welfare states so resilient?

10. Which are the three worlds of welfare capitalism?

Further reading

Baldwin, P. (1990) *The Politics of Social Solidarity: Class Bases of the European Welfare State 1875–1975* (Cambridge: Cambridge University Press). A beautifully written historical analysis of how solidarity was produced 'through the backdoor' and the major challenger of the social democratic model of welfare state development.

Esping-Andersen, G. (1990) *The Three Worlds of Welfare Capitalism* (Oxford: Polity Press). The classic work that introduced the welfare regime typology and a central work of reference.

Flora, P. and Heidenheimer, A. J. (eds) (1981) *The Development of Welfare States in Europe and America* (Piscataway, NJ: Transaction Books). An early but still highly relevant work in the tradition of modernization theory that is very rich in historical data.

Hacker, J. S. (2002) *The Divided Welfare State: The Battle over Public and Private Social Benefits in the United States* (New York: Cambridge University Press). A highly informative analysis of US social policy.

Huber, E., and Stephens, J. D. (2001) *Development and Crisis of the Welfare State: Parties and Politics in Global Markets* (Chicago, IL: University of Chicago Press). An encompassing book that combines quantitative comparisons and detailed case analyses and gives the best overview of welfare state development currently available.

Korpi, W. (1983) *The Democratic Class Struggle* (London: Routledge & Kegan Paul). The study that firmly founded the social democratic/power resources approach to welfare state development.

O'Connor, J., Orloff, A., and Shaver, S. (1999) *States, Markets, and Families: Gender, Liberalism and Social Policy in Australia, Canada, Great Britain and the United States* (New York: Cambridge University Press). An analysis of the liberal regime from a gender perspective.

Pierson, P. (1994) *Dismantling the Welfare State? Reagan, Thatcher, and the Politics of Retrenchment* (Cambridge: Cambridge University Press). Why was it impossible, even for those who really tried, to dismantle the welfare state? The classic statement on the new politics of the welfare state.

Rimlinger, G. V. (1971) *Welfare Policy and Industrialization in Europe, America and Russia* (New York: John Wiley). A still relevant historical study of how industrialization is linked to the emergence of the welfare state.

Scharpf, F. W. and Schmidt, V. A. (eds) (2000) *Welfare and Work in the Open Economy*: (i) *From Vulnerability to Competitiveness*, (ii) *Diverse Responses to Common Challenges* (Oxford: Oxford University Press). An impressive book that collects theoretically sophisticated essays and valuable country studies of how welfare states adjust to their changing economic and social environments.

Web links

http://sp.uconn.edu/~scruggs/
Scruggs welfare state entitlement data set.

http://www.lisdatacenter.org/
Luxembourg Income Study.

www.ssa.gov/international/links.html
Social Security in Other Countries, social security online.

www.ilo.org/
International Labour Organization.

www.oecd.org
CECD webpage.

www.bertelsmann-stiftung.de
Bertelsmannstiftung on social policy reform.

For additional material and resources, please visit the Online Resource Centre at:
www.oxfordtextbooks.co.uk/orc/caramani3e/

online
resource
centre

CHAPTER 22

The impact of public policies

Jørgen Goul Andersen

Chapter contents

Reader's guide

This chapter looks at the effects of public policies. It analyses different policies of regulation of the economy and the welfare system, and their impact on economic performance and social equality. The chapter discusses not only the impact of concrete policies, but also the impact of broader patterns and principles of policies. First, the chapter describes the overriding historical change in approaches to the economy, from Keynesian ideas of macro-economic steering to more market-oriented economic perspectives. Second, the chapter presents the main typologies of welfare regimes, varieties of capitalism, and flexicurity. Third, the chapter addresses some of the empirical analyses of the effects of welfare policies and the tension between welfare and economic efficiency. Finally, the chapter discusses the feedback mechanisms from policy effects to new demands for policy change.

Introduction

Whereas political decisions (also called **policy** or output) were traditionally taken as the final result of the political process, comparative political science has increasingly turned attention towards 'outcomes' or the impact of policies (see Chapter 1). This change in focus has entailed a great interest in the **implementation** of political decisions, on the one hand, and in the relationship between **politics** and the economy—the economic and social effects of public policies—on the other. This chapter deals with the latter question (on implementation see Chapter 20).

Many of these issues are on the borderline between politics and economics. The so-called 'new political economy' approach seeks to combine insights from both disciplines. To some extent, this also holds for comparative welfare state research (see Chapter 21). Many of these discussions revolve around the theme of reconciliation between welfare and economic efficiency in the broadest sense. In the so-called 'golden age' of the welfare state, governments applied Keynesian macro-economic steering to secure economic growth, full employment, and social welfare (see Chapter 21). However, after the widespread failure to combat unemployment by such measures in the 1970s, economists began searching for alternative diagnoses and solutions. In the fields of welfare, labour market, and tax policies, economists became increasingly concerned with the impact on economic incentives. The 1980s saw a revival of neoclassical thinking, with a focus on distortions of the smooth functioning of the market and the corresponding loss of economic efficiency. When Ronald Reagan was elected president of the US, and Margaret Thatcher became prime minister of the UK, this sort of criticism of the welfare state moved from the margins to the mainstream of politics.

This turn in policies set the stage for many subsequent debates about the impact of public policy. What is the *impact of various public policies?* How should it be measured? Are equality and efficiency compatible, or is there a trade-off? Some researchers have claimed that **globalization** aggravates negative economic side effects and enforces a harmonization towards more market conformity. Others have questioned whether welfare policies have the intended welfare effects for those in need.

Addressing such questions, researchers have constructed various conceptualizations of clusters of policies that tend to go together because they are mutually connected. Such configurations of policies that are *complementary* can also be labelled *regimes*. In one branch of research, scholars have formulated conceptions of **welfare regimes**, emphasizing (re)distribution and taking their point of departure from a 'politics against markets' way of thinking. Others have focused on the positive interplay between the state and different types of market economies, arguing that there are different types of regulation or coordination that work equally well—but differently. Still others have discussed various

conceptualizations of flexicurity, i.e. combinations of economic flexibility and social security, in labour market policies.

Policies also impact on politics, and on future policies. In the final section, we discuss such feedback effects on policy actors, and on the paths of public policy development. In addition, we briefly discuss policy transfer and policy diffusion from one national context to another, and finally we return to the issue of convergence between welfare states amid common exogenous pressures such as ageing and globalization.

KEY POINTS

- The impact of welfare policies on the economy is one of the most important—and one of the most controversial—issues in modern social science.
- Policies/institutions tend to cluster in characteristic configurations because they are complementary. This means that they can be viewed as policy regimes.
- Political decisions also have political effects. Past decisions are a major determinant of future decisions, sometimes also extending across policy areas or across countries.

Economic paradigms and approaches to welfare

The long-term expansion of the public sector after 1945, in particular social protection and services, took place in a climate of rapid economic growth. After the protectionist policies during the crisis of the 1930s which dramatically lowered international trade and economic growth, in 1944 the Western capitalist countries decided on the Bretton Woods system which linked the American dollar to gold at a fixed price, and other currencies to the dollar at (in principle) fixed exchange rates.

This system, alongside a gradual lowering of tariffs, contributed to long-term uninterrupted economic growth, almost full employment, and relatively stable prices. For the twelve European countries for which statistics are available for the entire period, average annual growth in GDP between 1950 and 1973 was 4.6 per cent, compared with 1.6 per cent for 1890–1913 and 1.4 per cent for 1913–50. In the period 1973–92 growth rates slowed down—but only to 2.0 per cent (Table 22.1).

Until the 1970s, increasing public and social expenditure (see Table 22.2) was generally regarded as a 'natural' concomitant of industrialization and modernization, including population ageing (Wilensky 1975: 47). Political scientists, taking a more conflictual and less functionalist view, also emphasized the political mobilization of the lower social classes and the strength of socialist parties (Korpi 1983)—the 'power resources explanation'. Cameron (1978) described this as a sufficient but not necessary

Table 22.1 Economic growth in Europe, 1890–1992

Periods	Average annual growth in real GDP		
	Total	Per capita	Per person-hour
1890–1913	1.6	1.7	1.6
1913–1950	1.4	1.0	1.9
1950–1973	4.6	3.8	4.7
1973–1992	2.0	1.7	2.7[a]
1890–1992	2.5	1.9	2.6[a]

Notes: Countries: Germany, France, Italy, Austria, Belgium, Netherlands, Switzerland, UK, Sweden, Finland, Denmark, and Norway. For 1992–2005, real annual growth rate for the EU-15 was 2.1 per cent (as against 3.2 per cent in the US); per capita growth rate in the EU-15 was 1.7 per cent (as against 2.1 per cent in the US) (OECD 2007: Tables A3 and A.9). It is mainly low growth in Germany, Italy, and France that accounts for the lower per capita growth rate in EU-15.

[a]Last year for the calculation of GDP per person-hour is 1987.

Source: Maddison (1991), quoted in Crafts and Toniolo (1996: 2).

Table 22.2 Social expenditure as a percentage of GDP

Countries	Historical calculations[a]		OECD old series[a]			OECD social expenditure database (2013)[b]				
	1900	1930	1960	1970	1980	1980	1990	2000	2005	2010
Germany	0.6	4.8	18.1	19.5	25.7	22.1	21.7	26.6	27.3	27.1
Austria	0.0	1.2	15.9	18.9	23.3	22.4	23.8	26.6	27.1	28.8
France	0.6	1.1	13.4	16.7	22.6	20.8	25.1	28.6	30.1	32.2
Belgium	0.3	0.6	13.1	19.3	30.4	23.5	24.9	25.3	26.5	29.5
Netherlands	0.4	1.0	11.7	22.5	28.3	24.8	25.6	19.8	20.7	23.5
Sweden	0.9	2.6	10.8	16.8	25.9	27.1	30.2	28.4	29.1	28.3
Finland	0.8	3.0	8.8	13.6	19.2	18.1	24.1	24.2	26.2	29.4
Denmark	1.4	3.1	12.3	19.1	27.5	24.8	25.1	26.4	27.7	30.1
Norway	1.2	2.4	7.9	16.1	21.0	16.9	22.3	21.3	21.6	23.0
Italy	0.0	0.1	13.1	16.9	21.2	18.0	19.9	23.1	24.9	27.8
Spain	0.0	0.1	–	–	–	15.5	19.9	20.2	21.1	26.5
Portugal	0.0	0.0	–	–	–	9.9	12.5	18.9	23.0	25.6
Greece	0.0	0.1	10.4	9.0	11.1	10.3	16.6	19.3	21.1	23.3
Czech Rep.	–	–	–	–	–	–	15.3	19.1	18.7	20.8
Poland	–	–	–	–	–	–	14.9	20.5	21.0	21.8
Switzerland	–	1.2	4.9	8.5	14.3	13.8	13.5	17.8	20.2	20.0
UK	1.0	2.2	10.2	13.2	16.4	16.5	16.7	18.6	20.5	23.7
Ireland	–	3.7	8.7	11.9	19.2	–	13.7	15.2	16.3	18.0
Australia	0.0	2.1	7.4	7.4	12.8	10.3	13.2	17.3	16.5	17.9
NZ	1.1	2.4	10.4	9.2	15.2	17.0	21.5	19	18.1	21.2
Canada	0.0	0.3	9.1	11.8	15.0	13.7	18.1	16.5	16.9	18.6
US	0.6	0.6	7.3	10.4	15.0	13.2	13.6	14.5	16.0	19.9
Japan	0.2	0.2	4.1	5.7	11.9	10.2	11.1	16.3	18.5	22.4[c]
Turkey	–	–	–	–	–	3.2	5.7	–	9.9	–
OECD total	–	–	–	–	–	15.5	17.6	18.9	19.7	22.0

[a]From Lindert (2004a: 12–13).
[b]Entries are public expenditures excluding administration (see also Adema and Ladaique 2009).
[c]2009.

condition; economic openness and corporatist coordination were decisive. However, there was strong optimism about politics prevailing over markets (Ringen 2006). Few questioned the impacts on welfare and employment, and few were concerned about negative side effects.

This changed after the breakdown of the Bretton Woods system in 1971 when the US suspended the convertibility of dollars to gold (which eventually made currencies free-floating), and after the first oil crisis in 1973–4 which resulted in mass unemployment in most countries. In the first place, the largely unsuccessful attempts to combat unemployment by traditional Keynesian policies (stimulation of aggregate demand) and the anomaly of stagflation (stagnation combined with inflation)[1] paved the way for theories of rational expectations (Lucas 1972, 1973). These theories implied that economic actors would anticipate the inflationary effects of fiscal and monetary policies and adjust their behaviour accordingly. Thus the negative effects of stimulating demand would, so to speak, come before the positive ones.

Further, economists began questioning the assumption of the economic neutrality of redistribution (Sandmo 1991). Previously, economic redistribution via taxes and cash transfers to households had been described in textbooks as a matter of transferring a bucket of water from one person to another. This was challenged by Okun (1975) who argued that the 'bucket is leaking', i.e. there was an inevitable loss in economic efficiency associated with this redistribution as it distorted the market mechanisms.

This was the beginning of a paradigmatic change in economic theory, away from macro-economic steering and towards a more 'neoclassical' focus on the micro-level. Economists and governments came to focus on the supply side of the economy, not least on the economic incentives that could stimulate labour supply and growth. Unemployment in Europe was increasingly seen as 'structural' or 'natural' unemployment, i.e. as unemployment that would *not* disappear even if demand for labour power increased. Only structural changes towards more market conformity in social policies, tax policies, labour market regulation, and wage formation could help.

The *OECD Jobs Study* report (OECD 1994) summarized the new approaches and underlined the constraints of globalization which would make it difficult for governments to avoid the necessary labour market reforms. However, this was disputed. Rather than seeing this policy change as an instance of social learning, Korpi (2002) maintained that it was more a matter of political choice, reflecting changing power balances between capital and labour.

At any rate, the policy impacts of the welfare state more frequently came to be seen as adverse: unintentionally, social protection could aggravate the very problems which it was supposed to solve. Owing to the phenomenon called 'hysteresis' (Blanchard and Summers 1986)—loss of skills during long-term unemployment—persistent unemployment could generate large-scale *unemployability* which,

in turn, according to neoliberal scholars, might lead to the development of an underclass characterized by a dependency culture (Murray 1984). Even researchers known as proponents of the welfare state could question whether the price of equality might sometimes be less wealth *plus* less equality if some groups were chronically marginalized from the labour market (Esping-Andersen 1996; Esping-Andersen 2002).

This diagnosis could be convincingly illustrated by the different employment/unemployment records of the EU and the US. In the 1960s and 1970s, the US seemed to suffer from a 'structural' unemployment problem which Europeans used to explain by poverty and the under-developed American welfare state (see Figure 22.1). However, from the 1980s onwards it was the other way around: unemployment in Europe was chronically higher than in the US. Employment rates looked even worse, revealing a steady increase in the US, but equally steady decline in Europe. Europe had tried to combat unemployment by early retirement and other arrangements aimed at reducing labour supply, but the long-term dynamic effect seemed to be fewer jobs rather than lower unemployment. Declining employment rates only aggravated the future ageing crisis, which for purely demographic reasons was also more threatening in Europe because of lower fertility and immigration rates (see Comparative tables 4 and 14 at the end of this volume).

In short, during the 1980s and 1990s the US was often praised for market conformity whereas Europe was pictured as a victim of self-inflicted stagnation. The European welfare states were considered less sustainable (OECD 1994; Nickell 1997; Jackman 1998), or even described as 'virtual "time bombs" waiting to explode' (Ljungkvist and Sargent 1998: 546). The price for equality and security was persistent unemployment and long-term unsustainability of the welfare state. Under intensified global competition, it was argued, the effects were increasingly adverse.

However, even though wage differentials increased (Förster and d'Ercole 2005; OECD 2008*b*) and incentives were strengthened, European countries were reluctant to lower minimum wages or give up substantial elements of social protection. As can be seen from Table 22.2, the growth of social expenditure as a percentage of GDP slowed down, but there were few examples of genuine cuts in aggregated budgets. At the 2000 Lisbon summit, the European Union (EU) confirmed its devotion to pursuing a different employment strategy with more emphasis on education and training, (state-supported) innovation, and social cohesion.

The question of reconciliation between regulation, welfare, and equality on the one hand, and employment or economic growth on the other, has been a core theme of discussion in comparative research on the impact of public policies. However, modern economics has been accused of putting too much emphasis on theoretical arguments and modelling, and too little on empirical

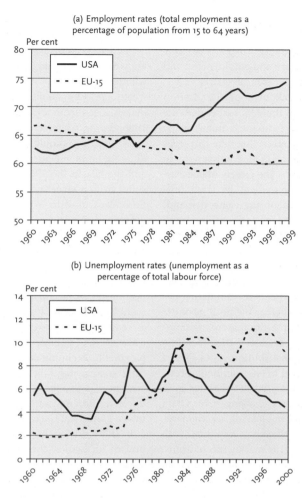

(a) Employment rates (total employment as a
percentage of population from 15 to 64 years)

(b) Unemployment rates (unemployment as a
percentage of total labour force)

Figure 22.1 Employment rates and unemployment rates: EU-15 and USA (1960–99)

Source: OECD (*Historical Statistics*, 1999 CD-ROM) and OECD (2000) *Economic Outlook.*

evidence. As argued by Lindert against key findings of neoclassical economics:

> such findings ... are not really findings. Contrary to the words offered ... none of these authors actually 'found' or 'showed' their results. Rather, they chose to imagine the results' as they are based on 'a theoretical model laden with assumptions. It is educated, intelligent, plausible fiction—but fiction nonetheless. (Lindert 2004*b*: 82)

KEY POINTS

- The failure of Keynesian policies to combat unemployment after 1973 paved the way for new economic perspectives focusing on the negative economic side effects of welfare/tax policies.

- European governments have been reluctant to reduce social expenditures; at best, they have managed to reduce the growth in expenditures to the growth in GDP.

Welfare regimes, varieties of capitalism, and flexicurity

More than economists, political scientists often address analyses of the impact of policies or institutions from a 'regime' perspective. That is, they take their point of departure in ideal types of welfare states or political economies that build on a combination of variables that are seen as interdependent or complementary. The two best known are the concepts of **welfare regimes** (Esping-Andersen 1990, 1999) and **varieties of capitalism** (Hall and Soskice 2001*b*). In addition, there is a variety of concepts at a somewhat lower level of abstraction, among which the notion of **flexicurity** has been much debated. As far as causes are concerned, welfare regime theory puts the main emphasis on politics (interest conflicts) whereas varieties of capitalism theory is more 'functionalist' (with emphasis on what is beneficial for the economy). However, it is impact rather than causes that is our main concern here.

The concept of welfare regimes

The concept of welfare regimes builds on the observations that (1) welfare state characteristics tend to cluster, and (2) there is a strong relationship between *labour markets, the family,* and *the welfare state?*.[2] 'Welfare regimes' refers to the interaction, or the unison, between these three elements (Esping-Andersen 1999: 4). What differs between welfare states is not just the level of expenditure (Table 22.2) but even more the division of tasks and the ways entitlements and expenditures are structured.

Inspired by Titmuss (1974), Esping-Andersen (1990) distinguished between three ideal types of welfare regime (described in detail in Chapter 21).

Conservative welfare regimes

In the *conservative* model, benefits are mostly financed by mandatory social contributions by employers and workers, paid to social insurance funds (often jointly controlled by the unions, employers, and the state). In principle, eligibility depends on contributions, and entitlements depend on contribution record. For instance, pensions are more or less proportionally (actuarially) related to contributions. The rationale is to secure income replacement, i.e. security rather than equality. However, principles have frequently been modified (decommodified).

The conservative model was designed to support a single-breadwinner family. Male breadwinners should be able to provide for their family even in the event of income loss due to unemployment, disability, etc. Women should be responsible for family care. As care was seen mainly as a family duty, this welfare regime traditionally had an underdeveloped public service sector.

As to labour market regulation, this model logically corresponds to uninterrupted careers and employment protection of core workers (Esping-Andersen 1999: 18). This 'inflexible' employment protection has come under pressure. Even more, the male breadwinner model became obsolete and economically counterproductive, and inadequate provision of social services, not least 'social investments' in childcare, was highlighted. This left the conservative model in need of reform (Esping-Andersen *et al.* 2002).

Liberal welfare regimes

The liberal model is based on selective support for those who cannot provide for themselves. Benefits are usually tax-financed and, even though benefits are targeted, coverage is in principle universal for all citizens, men and women alike. By its very residual nature, this model is aimed at alleviating poverty rather than large-scale redistribution, let alone decommodification. But it does involve a higher degree of de-familialization and less gender segregation than the conservative model.

When it comes to labour market regulation, the liberal model is intrinsically linked to weak unionization and weak wage coordination. The labour market is allowed to function as a market with a minimum of public regulation.

A transitional stage between the liberal and the social democratic welfare model (described below) is the Beveridgean model (in 1942 Lord Beveridge issued a report about the future of social security in the UK). The core element is *basic security*—universal but rather low flat-rate benefits which prevent poverty but encourage people to sign up for supplementary insurance.

Social democratic welfare regimes

This model went further, typically by providing a certain income replacement as an alternative to or on top of the basic protection, typically based on citizenship and financed through general taxes. The model aims at covering the entire population, enabling everybody to maintain a decent standard of living regardless of employment record (decommodification). The social democratic regime enables the middle classes to gain adequate protection from public arrangements in order to avoid 'crowding in' of privately financed welfare. De-familialization is manifested by the expansion of the public care sector in response to—and with the deliberate aim of facilitating—women's labour force participation. A dual-earner model based on two lifelong (almost) full-time incomes is the standard.

As to labour market regulation, this model goes together with coordinated wage bargaining. However, employment protection legislation remained liberal in Denmark, whereas the other Nordic countries moved towards stronger employment protection. Danish trade unions were heading in the Nordic direction, but eventually decided on what came to be labelled 'flexicurity'(see below).

According to the 'power resources model', the welfare model hinges on the political mobilization of the working class and its ability to forge alliances with the middle classes (Korpi 1983; Esping-Andersen 1990). However, some scholars have objected to this idea of 'politics against markets' (Esping-Andersen 1985*b*).

Varieties of capitalism

Varieties of capitalism theory claims that large welfare states, as well as being redistributive, also have highly beneficial economic impacts. According to this theory, highly regulated economies with large welfare states develop competitive advantages of their own which can make for equal or even superior economic performance. The attraction of this approach is that it provides explicit theoretical arguments for this claim which seems to be in accordance with real-world observations.

Rather than decommodification, the point of departure for varieties of capitalism theory is companies' interests in using the market as the main instance of coordination, vis-à-vis using other forms of coordination (Hall and Soskice 2001*b*). These mechanisms tend to be self-reinforcing and create a permanent divide between liberal market economies (LMEs) and coordinated market economies (CMEs). The propensity of institutional traits to cluster or reinforce each other because they work together well (as is the case with welfare regimes) is called *institutional complementarity*.

The *small state theory* proposed by Katzenstein (1985) argues that small open economies, being vulnerable to international competition, are in extra need of coordination. Such states tend to develop consensual corporatist structures which serve to stabilize the economy and enhance competitiveness. This argument is equivalent to the varieties of capitalism theory, only it spells out why some countries have been particularly inclined to develop those kinds of structure.

Trying to bridge the gap between varieties of capitalism and welfare regime theory, Iversen (2005) underlined the common insurance interests of workers and employers in different types of economies. According to this theory, a key variable is the nature of skills needed in production. Where companies demand specialized skills that are not transferable between branches, they are highly dependent on workers' willingness to invest in these skills. In turn, the willingness among workers to do so depends on insurance against the risk of losing jobs. Therefore employers are as dependent on protection as workers. In contrast, companies that demand general skills are not interested in such protection, but prefer simple market regulation. Even workers may have less interest in social protection in this instance. In short, the level and composition of human capital is seen as a core determinant of welfare state characteristics (Iversen 2005: 13; Estevez-Abe *et al.* 2001). However, as a side effect, insurance almost inevitably involves redistribution.

Accordingly, theorists in this tradition have criticized power resources theories for their notion of 'politics against markets'. Social protection, according to Iversen (2005: 8), 'can improve the operation of markets as well as undermine them'. Some researchers claim that, historically, employers have been just as supportive of social protection as workers (Baldwin 1990; Swenson 2002).

Needless to say, protagonists of the power resources theory are critical. Korpi (2006) claims that historical accounts are flawed and points out that, even if the arguments were correct, they concern a much narrower range than the entire welfare state.

However, Korpi is far less critical of the arguments about *impact*. At this point the varieties of capitalism theory has quite a lot to add, arguing plausibly that institutional differences constitute *comparative institutional advantages* (Hall and Soskice 2001*a*: 36–44). LMEs, where skills tend to be general, develop competitive advantages in 'radical innovation'. In contrast, CMEs, with emphasis on co-specific skills, including, not least, skilled work (like the German *Facharbeitertradition*), find themselves being particularly competitive in 'specialized quality production'—in what the Volkswagen car company has sometimes marketed as *Bessermachen*.

This theory also provides an explanation of why LMEs and CMEs have reacted differently to globalization—in fact, key indicators such as government outlays as a proportion of GDP reveal little convergence except for EU countries that are catching up (Table 22.3). Rather, data show an increasing *difference* between the US and Europe from the 1970s until the outbreak of the 2008 economic crisis. Apparently, LMEs had found one way of adapting to globalization, and CMEs another (Swank 2002).

Welfare regime theory could provide similar arguments, but is less developed at this point. However, the varieties of capitalism theory is silent on the relationship between family structure, the state, and the labour market. The approach also differs from the welfare regime approach by operating with only two worlds of capitalism. The conceptual scheme does not leave room for distinguishing between universal and corporatist/conservative welfare institutions.

Flexicurity

The concept of flexicurity simply refers to the combination of flexibility and security (Bredgaard *et al.* 2005). It was developed as political discourse after the 1995 Dutch labour market reform, as a kind of *post hoc* rationalization. In academic theory, it was introduced by Wilthagen (1998) and continued by Auer (2000) and Madsen (2002) for example.

Theories of flexicurity are narrower in scope. Moreover, they contain no grand theory of the origin of various arrangements—but they add the observation that welfare and labour market institutions are seldom deliberately designed. For example, until the concept of flexicurity emerged, few experts in Denmark had noticed the country's particular institutional complementarity of flexibility and security. Rather, the country was typically considered a 'laggard' in the development from 'numerical' to 'functional' flexibility (Piore and Sabel 1984; Porter 1990).

Theories of flexicurity emphasize 'politics for markets' but may complement the varieties of capitalism approach by introducing new divisions among the CMEs. However, the theories have been formulated in both a narrow and a much broader version. The narrow concept of flexicurity refers to a specific combination of (1) liberal employment protection legislation ('flexibility'), (2) generous employment protection such as high compensation levels or long duration ('security'), and (3) active labour market policies aimed at bringing people back to work (by solving matching problems between supply and demand of

Table 22.3 Total outlays as a percentage of GDP

	OECD old series[a]				OECD *Economic Outlook*[b]				
	1960	1968	1980	1990	1990	1995	2000	2005	2010
Germany	32.4	39.1	48.8	45.8	44.5	48.3	45.1	47.0	47.8
Austria	35.7	40.6	48.9	49.3	51.5	56.2	51.9	50.0	52.5
France	34.6	40.3	47.0	49.9	49.6	54.4	51.6	53.6	56.6
Belgium	34.5	41.7	50.7	53.2	52.3	52.1	49.1	51.9	52.5
Netherlands	33.7	43.9	56.9	57.5	54.9	56.3	44.1	44.8	51.2
Sweden	31.0	42.8	61.9	60.8	59.8	64.9	55.1	53.9	52.3
Finland	26.6	32.8	36.4	46.8	48.2	61.6	48.4	50.4	55.8
Denmark	24.8	36.3	56.9	58.6	55.4	59.3	53.7	52.8	57.7
Norway	29.9	37.9	50.7	51.3	54.0	50.9	42.3	41.8	45.5
Italy	30.1	34.7	42.0	53.9	52.6	52.2	45.8	47.9	50.4
Greece	17.4	23.5	30.5	49.6	–	45.8	46.7	44.6	51.5
Spain	13.7	21.3	33.1	43.0	42.9	44.5	39.2	38.4	46.3
Portugal	17.0	20.9	39.5	40.6	38.9	41.9	41.6	46.6	51.3
Czech Rep.	–	–	–	–	–	53.0	41.6	43.0	43.7
Poland	–	–	–	–	–	47.7	41.1	43.5	45.5
Switzerland	17.2	20.7	–	28.8	29.7	34.8	35.6	35.2	33.8
UK	32.2	39.3	45.2	42.3	41.2	43.5	36.6	43.7	50.2
Ireland	28.0	35.2	–	40.9	42.3	41.0	31.2	33.8	48.7[c]
Australia	21.2	24.1	–	37.5	33.4	35.8	33.9	33.3	36.3
NZ	–	–	–	–	52.6	41.9	38.3	38.3	42.9
Canada	28.6	34.2	–	49.3	48.0	47.5	40.3	38.3	43.0
USA	26.8	30.3	34.1	36.2	37.2	37.1	33.9	36.3	42.7
Japan	17.5	19.2	33.0	31.9	31.2	35.6	38.6	36.4	40.8

[a]*OECD Historical Statistics* (1999); Andersen and Christensen (1991).
[b]*OECD Economic Outlook* 79 (June 2006).
[c]2009 (extraordinary accounting of financial losses 2010)

qualifications). This is sometimes described as a 'golden triangle'. Key countries are Denmark and to some extent the Netherlands (Auer 2000; Madsen 2002). The notion of flexicurity acknowledges the economic need for flexibility. When employers are free to fire, they are less reluctant to hire. And when workers can rely on solid protection, they are more inclined to change jobs—and more willing to accept restructuring and change.

However, there is also a broader concept of flexicurity which is in the spirit of the varieties of capitalism approach by identifying varieties of flexicurity (e.g. numerical vs. functional). Wilthagen *et al.* (2003) distinguish between four types of flexibility:

- external numerical flexibility (as described in the previous paragraph);
- internal numerical flexibility (working time, overtime, etc.);

- functional flexibility (workers move between tasks in the organization);
- wage flexibility (wage dispersion according to productivity).

They also add different aspects of security:

- job security (as described in the previous paragraph);
- employment security;
- income security (as described in the previous paragraph);
- combination security (combination of work, family, etc.).

According to this concept, there is a 4 × 4 matrix of various flexicurity arrangements, and countries which appear 'inflexible' on some combinations may be flexible on others. Whereas Denmark and, to a lesser extent, the Netherlands, have tended to substitute job security by employment security and income security, other countries have maintained job security but sought to enhance functional flexibility and/or internal numerical flexibility. As it recognizes the existence of some kind of flexicurity in most European countries and makes no *a priori* assumptions that any model is superior, Wilthagen's concept of flexicurity is complementary to the varieties of capitalism theory.

KEY POINTS

● Welfare regimes refer to particular combinations of the welfare state, the family, and the labour market.

● Varieties of capitalism refers to different methods of coordination in the economy—via the market, or via negotiations and regulation. A key variable is the types of skill (general vs. specific) and, accordingly, the need for protection in order to secure willingness to invest in those skills.

● Welfare regime theory emphasizes conflict, whereas varieties of capitalism is more functionalist and emphasizes common interests between employers and workers and beneficial impacts on the economy.

● Flexicurity in the narrow sense refers to a particular hybrid between liberal and coordinated market economies.

Tensions between welfare and economic efficiency

As already mentioned, much research about the impact of policy—including the theories referred to in the preceding section—is concerned with what can in broad terms be described as the tension between equality/welfare and economic growth/employment/efficiency. What is the impact of public welfare policies (taxation, cash benefit systems, and public services) and labour market policies/institutions on various aspects of economic performance? I first describe some findings from the literature comparing welfare regimes or varieties of capitalism. Next, I address the issues of welfare/tax expenditure, equality, and economic growth. Finally, I discuss the impact of labour market policies.

Comparing social and economic impact of regimes

In an exploratory study that was consistent with a subsequent more detailed literature, Goodin *et al.* (1999) compared the social and economic accomplishments of three welfare states (US, Germany, and the Netherlands), representing three welfare regimes (liberal, conservative, and social democratic, respectively).[3] As regards equality

and reduction of poverty, the authors found significant differences, confirming the predicted rank order, with the social democratic regime being the most redistributive and the liberal the least. Moreover, the American welfare state, despite being targeted to the poor, is extremely inefficient in redistributing income and alleviating poverty (Goodin *et al.* 1999: 152–86; see also Korpi and Palme 1998; Kenworthy 2004: 102–5; and Box: The distributional impact of welfare regimes, in the Online Resource Centre). This corresponds to OECD studies showing an almost linear association between non-health social spending (towards working age population) and poverty rates (Förster and d'Ercole 2005: 29).

online resource centre

Goodin *et al.* (1999) also found that the social democratic regime had the highest score on social integration, stability in life, and securing autonomy in life, whereas the liberal model failed in most of these respects as well. The economic performance of the liberal model was better as regards labour market integration (see also section on 'Impact of labour market policies and institutions'), but they found little difference as regards economic growth and prosperity, confirming the classical statement that 'incentives are not behaviours' (Marmor *et al.* 1990: 219).

In their book about European unemployment regimes, Gallie and Paugam (2000*a*) examined the impact of welfare policies on the social conditions of the unemployed. The regime clustering was distinguished from Esping-Andersen's (1990) by singling out the 'sub-protective' Southern European model from the 'ordinary' conservative model (Gallie and Paugam 2000*b*: 17). Almost regardless of indicator—poverty, financial hardship, subjective well-being—they found the best conditions for the unemployed in social democratic regimes followed by the conservative regimes. However, in several respects the long-term unemployed were worse off in the 'sub-protective' regimes than in the liberal ones.

Whereas the findings regarding the social impact of welfare regimes are extremely robust, the reported impacts on economic performance are sensitive to the delineation of time periods, data sources, and methods. This is even more significant when we come to the distinction between LMEs and CMEs in the varieties of capitalism literature (Hall and Soskice 2001*b*). The prediction that CMEs are not economically inferior is largely confirmed in empirical analyses, for example, in Pontusson's (2005) study of 'Social Europe' vs. 'Liberal America'. On average, GDP growth rates were roughly similar over the long term (Pontusson 2005: 5–9), and the two regime types also performed equally well regarding unemployment. In the 1990s, LMEs were the most successful in reducing unemployment (Pontusson 2005: 71, 81–2). It may be added that, regarding the crisis from 2008–9 onwards, intra-regime differences appear to be more significant than regime differences because of variations in credit and housing bubbles and crisis strategies.

Tax/welfare system, equality, and economic efficiency

To what extent do taxes and transfers harm economic efficiency, as claimed by Okun (1975) and by many others since then? Theoretically, there are several arguments that welfare spending could have beneficial effects on economic performance. Everybody seems to agree that welfare expenditure has positive effects up to a certain limit, and that some welfare expenditure, for instance in childcare, not to mention education, should be seen as social investment in human capital (Morel *et al.* 2012). Social security also helps to avoid child poverty and the transmission of poverty from one generation to the next. Further, unemployment insurance may boost 'good jobs' and make workers more willing to take risks (Andersen *et al.* 2007). Korpi (1985) protested against Okun's metaphor of a leaking bucket and stated that, rather, it should be seen as an irrigation system. At any rate, effects must be assessed empirically. I now address a sample of **empirical** studies.

Among the most thorough studies is Peter Lindert's two-volume book *Growing Public* (Lindert 2004*a,b*) which treats the economic impact of welfare state growth over more than a century and the technically more simple book by Pontusson (2005) referred to in the previous section. An earlier overview of findings and arguments is provided in *The Economic Consequences of Rolling back the Welfare State* (Atkinson 1999). In *Egalitarian Capitalism*, Kenworthy (2004) addressed the issue of compatibility of equality and economic efficiency.

As can be seen from the overview in Table 22.2, there is a large variation in social expenditure between countries. However, there are many pitfalls in such statistics, as benefits are paid as taxable incomes in some countries, but as net benefits in others. When these differences are corrected (Adema and Ladaique 2005; 2009; Adema *et al.* 2011) the ranking looks somewhat different (see Table 22.4). Further, if we include private welfare expenditure, the ranking changes completely. In particular, the US moves from the low-spending to the high-spending countries. Welfare is simply more privately financed than in Europe. However, the impact on distribution is very different. In private insurance people pay the same amount per head, or even according to risk (which is typically highest among the poor). Taxes, in contrast, are much higher on high incomes than on low incomes, and this holds even for regressive taxes such as taxes on consumption.

By avoiding disincentives and distortions of high taxes, countries with high private financing of welfare should theoretically be more efficient. However, no significant correlations are found between public expenditures on the one hand and level or growth of GDP on the other (see Table 22.5). In their survey of empirical findings, Atkinson (1999: 32–3) and Lindert (2004*b*: 86–8)

conclude that most studies have found no significant associations. In his own, rather more accurate test, Lindert (2004*b*: 172–93) found no significant associations either.

These findings only cover the period until the 1990s, and one may ask whether they are contradicted by the fact that American growth rates were significantly higher than those in Europe, at least from 1992 to 2005 (3.2 per cent compared with 2.1 per cent). However, when population growth is discounted, the difference in per capita growth was small: 2.1 per cent compared with 1.7 per cent (Table 22.1). Moreover, as noted by Pontusson (2005), the US was more over-consuming than Europe in this period. Further, comparisons on productivity are sensitive to measurement. Pontusson (2005) has argued that measures should be discounted by the long working hours in the US; in contrast, Europeans have enjoyed reduction of weekly working hours as well as longer holidays. As can be seen from Table 22.1, measuring GDP per working hour also gives a more optimistic picture of economic growth after 1973 more generally. There are few signs in these data that emerging new pressures, such as globalization, force welfare regimes to converge.

Why is the bumblebee flying? In line with findings regarding public expenditure, Kenworthy (2004) demonstrated that there is no obvious tension between equality and economic performance. Adjusting for catch-up effects, Kenworthy actually found the highest growth rate in the period 1980–2000 in countries with low inequality. The same association is found in comparisons between American states (Kenworthy 2004: 56). For extended comparisons of the impact of inequality across nations and across American states, see Wilkinson and Pickett (2009).

Impact of labour market policies and institutions

The reinterpretation of unemployment was a core issue in the paradigmatic change from Keynesianism to what has been called supply-side economics. However, it should be added that many economists emphasize that their preoccupation with disincentives and distortions does not imply that Keynesian insights are scrapped. It can be an add-on policy rather than a replacement (Nickell *et al.* 2004). In Europe, mainstream economists tend to be Keynesian in the short run, but focus on the supply side in long-term analyses.

In many countries, in accordance with *The OECD Jobs Study* (OECD 1994), the focus in economic policies and employment policies was shifted to the issue of structural unemployment. In economic terms, structural unemployment is defined as the non-accelerating inflation (or wage) rate of unemployment, i.e. the lowest level of unemployment compatible with stable price or wage increases (Elmeskov and MacFarland 1993). Structural

Table 22.4 Net social expenditure as a percentage of GDP (2007)

Countries	Gross public expenditure	Net publicly mandated expenditure	Net social expenditure including private expenditure on welfare	Rank of net social expenditure
Germany	28.4	27.2	28.4	3
Austria	29.6	24.8	25.8	8
France	32.8	29.9	32.7	1
Belgium	29.6	26.2	30.5	2
Netherlands	22.7	20.4	25.3	9
Sweden	32.1	25.9	27.8	4
Finland	28.2	22.6	23.4	13
Denmark	30.8	23.9	25.3	9
Norway	23.3	20.0	20.5	17
Iceland	18.6	16.8	18.0	21
Italy	28.8	25.8	26.4	7
Greece	21.3	–	–	
Spain	24.1	21.6	21.8	15
Portugal	25.6	23.6	25.0	11
Czech Republic	20.7	19.2	19.3	18
Poland	22.8	18.6	18.6	20
Switzerland	18.5	–	–	
UK	23.3	22.7	26.9	6
Ireland	18.6	16.8	18.0	21
Australia	17.9	18.3	21.0	16
NZ	20.9	18.4	18.8	19
Canada	18.9	19.4	24.0	12
USA	17.4	18.9	27.5	5
Japan	20.3	20.3	23.4	13

Source: Adema ET AL. (2011).

Table 22.5 Correlations between social expenditure as a proportion of GDP and economic performance

Periods	Correlation between social expenditure and Growth of GDP per capita	Level of GDP per capita
1880s	0.10	−0.18
1890s	0.34	−0.05
1900s	−0.23	0.09
1910s	0.12	0.31
1920s	−0.24	0.49
1960s	−0.17	−0.07
1970s	0.14	0.00
1980s	−0.07	0.12
1990s	0.01	0.12
Simple average	0.00	0.09

Note: Social expenditure (1880–1930: welfare, employment, pensions, health, and housing subsidies) as percentage of GDP, initial year in decade.
Source: Lindert (2004a: 17).

unemployment will always be above zero because of 'frictional unemployment', i.e. the fact that people switch between jobs. Workers are involuntarily dismissed and cannot always find a new job immediately. Indeed, in a flexible labour market the absolute minimum level of structural unemployment is bound to be slightly higher than in an inflexible labour market because there is more job exchange.

However, in most countries, structural unemployment is assumed to be far above that minimum level. In the mid-1990s structural unemployment estimates were usually very close to the actual level of unemployment (OECD 1997), indicating that only structural reforms could bring about significant improvement (see Table: Calculated structural unemployment in 1996 and subsequent development of unemployment (1996–2002), in the Online Resource Centre).

Theoretically, there may be several causes of structural unemployment.

- High minimum wages, which mean that labourers with low productivity will not be hired
- Insufficient incentives—too generous levels and too long a duration of unemployment benefits, social assistance, etc.
- Employment protection legislation preventing employers from hiring when they cannot fire, and enabling the core labour force to demand high wage increases without meeting competition from those who are unemployed and would be willing to work for less (the 'insider–outsider' problem) (see Lindbeck and Snower 1988).
- (Other) 'matching problems', such as insufficient mobility between geographical areas, or across trade borders, creating coexistence of unemployment and demand for labour power.

Most recommendations from the OECD and others since the mid-1990s have generally focused on flexibility: more wage flexibility, more flexible employment protection legislation (i.e. less protection), more mobility across regions, trades, and occupations, and stronger work incentives or control/sanctions to make workers more flexible. This has also been the general trend of reforms in Europe. However, empirical research has come up with somewhat more nuanced answers.

In the first place, estimations of structural unemployment can be quite uncertain. As can be seen from Table: Calculated structural unemployment in 1996 and subsequent development of unemployment (1996–2002), in the Online Resource Centre, some countries have experienced unexpectedly rapid decline in unemployment.

Next, systematic studies of the impact of the labour market and social policies give somewhat mixed results. As far as policy impact on unemployment is concerned, many studies have focused on the following effects (Nickell and Layard 1999; Nickell et al. 2004; OECD 2006).

Unemployment protection

There is consensus from most comparative studies that duration of unemployment benefits tends to have adverse effects; in particular, it tends to increase duration of unemployment spells and the proportion of long-term unemployed (OECD 2006: 61). Evidence regarding the effects of replacement rates is more mixed but overwhelmingly confirms the conventional wisdom (Nickell 1997; Blanchard and Katz 1996; Holmlund 1998; Nickell and Layard 1999; Nickell et al. 2004; OECD 2006: 61). However, it is also emphasized by the OECD (2006: 190–1) that some countries have achieved low unemployment despite generous benefits, in particular if they are combined with a strict work test. Lindert (2004b: 119) adds that high replacement rates may harm employment, but tend to boost productivity, so that economic growth impact is small.

Minimum wages

Minimum wages were a main concern in *The OECD Jobs Study* (1994). However, no studies indicate that high minimum wages are associated with higher unemployment rates (Holmlund 1998; Galbraith et al. 1999), and the OECD eventually de-emphasized this factor (OECD 2006: 88). In addition, there is increasing awareness of dangers of entrapment in low-paid work (e.g. OECD 2006: 174–9).

Employment protection

In actual practice, employment protection does not, on average, seem to have any impact on the *level* of unemployment (OECD 2006: 95–6), but it has a strong impact on the *structure* of unemployment. Long-term unemployment is most widespread in countries with strict employment protection (e.g. Bertola et al. 1999; Nickell and Layard 1999; Esping-Andersen 2000). This does not question theories of flexicurity, but it does mean that these systems should be analysed in relation to specific national contexts.

Taxation

Some evidence indicates that targeted tax cuts may have effects on unemployment—and perhaps even more on employment—but this remains a highly contested issue (Jackman et al. 1996; Blanchard and Katz 1996: 67; Disney 2000; Davieri and Tabellini 2000). The OECD (2006: 95) was reluctant to give any strong advice on this issue, or on the appropriate balance between social contributions and income taxes. However, it was emphasized that the negative effects of taxes may depend on corporatism and a feeling of responsibility among union leaders.

Activation

Activation was pointed out by the OECD (1994) as a good second-best solution and was advocated by the EU. However, both micro- and macro-level evaluations of the impact of activation have been disappointing (Martin 2000; OECD 2006: 68). It is far from being a panacea, and effects often seem small in relation to costs. However, some activation measures work in some contexts and, for whatever reason, countries that put emphasis on activation generally tend to perform better. At least it is well documented that the test of availability in activation works (Kohnle-Seidl and Eichhorst 2008).

Corporatism

Probably the most robust finding in the literature is that corporatism and wage coordination have beneficial impacts on employment. The OECD (1994) used to be sceptical about corporatism because it tended to entail high minimum wages. But facing quite unambiguous empirical evidence, it modified its view (OECD 2006: 82). Some studies indicate that *unionization* as such has a negative impact on employment (OECD 2006). But it is the *coverage and centralization* of bargaining that count, probably because they inflict a sense of responsibility for the economy on union leaders. This leads to wage moderation in periods with a high demand for labour power. It is also important to emphasize that unionization is not straightforwardly related to collective bargaining coverage. In several countries, collective bargaining results among the minority of organized workers are extended to most of the labour market by so-called *erga omnes* arrangements. Collective bargaining coverage is often more than 80 per cent, even if unionization is only 30, 20, or even 10 per cent.

It is often found that the relationship is U-shaped or 'hump-shaped' (OECD 2006: 84–5; Calmfors and Driffill 1988; Scarpetta 1996; Elmeskov *et al.* 1998; see also Hemerijck and Schludi 2000; Nickell and Layard 1999; Scharpf 2000). Both completely unorganized (market-determined) and centralized/coordinated bargaining have beneficial impact, whereas bargaining at the company or sectoral level is detrimental. The ability of trade unions to moderate wage demands even has a positive effect on the level of structural unemployment. This is basically in accordance with the varieties of capitalism predictions.

The preferred type of analysis in this kind of research is analysis of aggregate data on country variations and time series—and increasingly on both. But one can also choose a very different point of departure in micro-level survey-based studies. This is what we find in search theory which examines the impact of various types of incentives (possibly including non-economic incentives) on job search and transition to job. As such studies are generally conducted within individual countries, it may be impossible to find any direct policy variations, at least in cross-section studies. However, even if the unemployment benefit system has to be treated as a constant, there may still be individual variations in compensation rates. Such studies serve to bring out some of the micro-level mechanisms that mediate macro-level associations, and they also present an additional way of testing hypotheses (Clement and Andersen 2007). Another possible design is to compare two or more otherwise seminal countries in order to bring out the effects of macro-level policy variations.

> **KEY POINTS**
>
> - Generous welfare policies have a very strong impact on the level of poverty.
> - Universal or social democratic welfare regimes have lower poverty rates and more equality, whereas the opposite is typically found in liberal regimes.
> - There are few indications that generous welfare policies have adverse effects on economic growth.
> - The incentive effects of social protection on unemployment are generally quite uncertain, but duration of unemployment does seem to have negative effects and, on average, this also holds for compensation levels.
> - Centralized and coordinated wage bargaining has a strong positive impact on employment.
> - There is not one single equilibrium but different combinations of policies that may have the same impact.

Policy feedback and path dependence

So far, we have only looked at policy feedback on welfare or on economic measures. However, policies also have impacts on future politics and policy. This is also labelled *policy feedback* (Pierson 1994: 39–50; see also Figure I.1 in the Introduction). This section briefly elucidates how policy change affects politics, how policy learning takes place, and how feedback mechanisms may often mean that policy changes follow a particular course determined by pre-existing policy programmes. This is what has become known as *path dependence*. Finally, policies are *diffused* and *transferred* or *translated* from one country to another, or from one policy field to another.

Policy feedback on politics

The most obvious feedback effect of policies is the impact on the constellation of interests in society and thereby on future inputs to the political process. This may happen in several ways.

- Policies generate 'vested interests' in maintaining particular programmes.

- Policies create entirely new interest groups (see Chapter 14).
- Policies change distribution of power resources between interest groups.
- Policies create divisions of interests as well as unity of interests.
- Policies open or close access opportunities to influence future policies and shape actors' perceptions of interests.

These effects may be intentional or unintentional. All welfare programmes generate interest groups, many of which become organized. An example of unintentional generation of vested interests is found in early retirement policies in Europe in the 1980s. At that time, it became a popular strategy to combat unemployment by means of various programmes giving older workers an incentive to retire before pension age. Very soon, however, most such arrangements came to be seen as vested interests, so that it could involve substantial political costs to change them. This is one of the main reasons why policy change has been considered nearly irreversible (Pierson 1994), even though the most recent reforms have demonstrated this claim to be exaggerated (e.g. Palier 2010; Clasen and Clegg 2011; Ebbinghaus 2006, 2011; Bonoli and Natali 2012).

Sometimes policy change involves the creation of entirely new interests which may contribute to new dynamics. A case in point is outsourcing of public services to private providers. Almost instantly, such policies create a new interest group of private service providers who will lobby for further increases in outsourcing. If these service providers manage to capture a substantial proportion of the market, there may also be a division of interest between privately and publicly employed service workers in such services.

Power distribution between interest groups is also strongly related to policy. For instance, trade unions have remained much stronger in countries with voluntary state-subsidized unemployment insurance organized by trade unions—the **Ghent system** (see Chapter 18 and Figure 18.4). Another key example is universal vs. targeted welfare arrangements. Targeting is usually legitimized by the intention to improve conditions for those who are 'really in need'. But in the long run, those who are 'really in need' often find themselves worse off. In the first place, if welfare arrangements are universal, their numerical basis of support is broader. Further, they enjoy greater legitimacy as people find benefit recipients resembling themselves more 'deserving' (van Oorschot 2006). But perhaps most importantly, as noted by Titmuss (1974), if the middle classes are enrolled in a programme, they will not only make larger demands but will also have more resources to have such demands heard.

Policy learning, social learning

Another important instance of policy feedback is 'policy learning' or 'social learning'. The notion of learning is based on Hugh Heclo's classical remark that '[g]overnments not only "power" ... they also puzzle' (Heclo 1974: 305). They try to find out how policies work and which policies can produce the intended effects. Sometimes the terms 'policy learning' and 'social learning' are used interchangeably, as describing 'the process by which civil servants, policy experts, and elected officials evaluate the performance of previously enacted policies' (Béland 2006: 361).

The broad definition may include learning that is relatively 'detached and technocratic in nature' (Béland 2006) and is aimed at narrower adjustments of policies after evaluation of their impact. However, comparative research has been more concerned with broader changes in sentiments among entire policy networks (Sabatier 1988), with changes of the basic ideas and paradigms that define problems and possible solutions (Hall 1993), or with development of 'epistemic communities' of people coming to share the same general framework of ideas (Haas 1992). Bennett and Howlett (1992) distinguished between 'government learning', 'lesson drawing', and 'social learning' on the basis of a classification of who learns what. They reserve the label 'social learning' for a paradigm shift in an entire policy community.

A paradigm shift may have several sources. A standard source is some sort of crisis for the old paradigm which includes its particular set of problem definitions and possible solutions, i.e. policy instruments. When these instruments successively fail, the old paradigm reaches a crisis. For instance, in Denmark, any imaginable Keynesian policy instrument was adopted between 1975 and 1986 to combat unemployment (Andersen 2002). When all these instruments had failed, this paved the way for a rapid paradigm shift which redefined unemployment not as a matter of insufficient demand for labour power or excessive supply, but as a matter of 'structural' problems such as discrepancies between minimum wages and qualifications, insufficient mobility, incentives to work, and so on. This interpretation gave meaning to unexpected phenomena such as wage inflation beginning at a high level of unemployment. This could be interpreted as evidence that the 'structural' level of unemployment had been reached. In Denmark, this paradigm shift was accepted by all major political actors in a surprisingly short time, probably because a variety of policy options could be derived, some of which were also very acceptable to social democrats, not least 'active' labour market policy with its emphasis on enhancing qualifications and facilitating mobility for those who were unemployed.

It is important to emphasize that such policy learning is not always rational. As pointed out by Weyland (2005) and Béland (2006), the search for alternative paradigms is often steered by a 'logic of availability' where political actors make cognitive shortcuts because they *need* new ideas that can give meaning to anomalies, 'reduce uncertainty [and] propose a particular solution to a moment of crisis' (Blyth 2002: 11). Following the crisis in 2008, Keynesianism had a revival, at least as a short-run practical measure, simply because there was nothing else to do. It remains to be seen whether the crisis will leave a permanent impact on economic philosophies.

Once accepted, a new policy paradigm also installs its own standards of evaluating policy impact. This is by no means just an 'objective' assessment. The crucial premises are seldom questioned. If the expected results appear, nobody asks whether they may have been caused by other factors. And even if a certain policy *does not* work, this rarely leads to a questioning of the underlying causal assumptions, but rather towards a focus on implementation problems, on problems of giving the medicine in sufficient doses, etc. In short, a paradigm carries its own learning and mislearning from observed policy impacts (Larsen 2002).

Path dependence

Policy learning in relation to paradigm shift is one among several mechanisms that tend to make policies path-dependent. Path dependence in the very broadest sense means that policies at one point of time tend to impact on, or indeed determine, policies at a later point of time because of high switching costs. This also implies that initial policy choices are often very crucial as they determine or at least constrain later policy choices (Powell 1991: 192–3). Thus it is no accident that current variations in European welfare systems to a large extent reflect initial differences in choices that were made more than 100 years ago.

The theory of path dependence is borrowed from institutional economics where it was developed with the aim of explaining, for example, why inferior technologies survived in competition with superior ones. For instance, if a particular type of software obtains a dominant position in the market, compatibility with this software itself becomes a survival criterion for other products, and this in turn becomes an argument for adhering to this software. Or take the instance of a computer keyboard where the position of letters is determined by their previous position on the QWERTY typewriter. Allegedly, the position of the letters on the typewriter was deliberately developed with the aim of *slowing down* the speed of typing because a mechanical typewriter cannot function beyond a certain speed—the keys will simply jam (Pierson 1994: 43). Thus, it would seem rational to change the position of letters on the computer keyboard as this could increase the speed of typing. But once everybody has learned this system, the switching costs are too high.

In politics too, there are switching costs. Quite a few of these costs may be mainly practical/administrative, but the most important switching costs are political: switching policies involves losses and gains. For instance, incumbent governments will almost certainly be punished by those voters who suffer significant losses, whereas they are far less likely to be rewarded by those who experience gains.

There are four main lines of interpretation of path dependence in comparative social research.

1. The first one emphasizes 'lock-in' effects and the 'stickiness' of policies—not least welfare policies—analogous with the example of the keyboard. Policies rarely change, except in extraordinary situations where external pressures and/or political conjunctures enable ground-breaking reforms. In particular, vested interests tend to block major reforms.

2. Decisions at one point in time tend to impact strongly on decisions at a later point in time. This is why comparative policy analysis should be extremely sensitive to history. However, this notion of path dependence has been criticized for being too indiscriminate and too vague; certainly, it does not run any risk of falsification.

3. More in line with economic institutionalism, Pierson (2000) has attempted to develop path dependence into a theory. Here the concept refers to a model of 'positive feedback' which is basically analogous to the example of competing technologies. What we should do is to look systematically for those *mechanisms* which produce path dependence, i.e. positive feedback where each new policy step reinforces the current path.

4. Still others acknowledge the importance of identifying mechanisms but adhere more to the notion of path dependence as a *perspective* which draws attention to such mechanisms whereby previous policies determine later policy choices. As such, it cannot be falsified, but it is a useful perspective.

To take a classic example, universal flat-rate pensions have the disadvantage that they do not cover the pension needs of the new middle classes sufficiently. As a consequence, a pension system of purely flat-rate pensions tends to 'crowd in' private pension arrangements if it is not supplemented by some kind of earnings-related scheme (Esping-Andersen 1990; Myles and Pierson 2001). The predictable consequence is that countries seeking to maintain universal flat-rate state pensions will eventually find themselves ending up with a 'multi-pillar' pensions system with a large private component. However, by the same token, countries introducing a supplement will find themselves under pressures to switch to a purely contribution-defined system. In short, because of the mechanisms of path dependence, universal tax-financed flat-rate pensions as we knew them tend to eliminate themselves.

Sometimes such changes take place in major reforms, but there is increasing awareness that small changes may also lead to large transformations in the long run

(Thelen 2004; Hacker 2004; Streeck and Thelen 2005; Mahoney and Thelen 2010). New layers may be inserted with faster growth rates; for instance pensions savings in the pensions system. Or policies may not be adjusted to deal with new problems and may drift apart. Often path dependence is more about changing interest constellations and power resources. It should be added that within comparative welfare state research, an overly static view of path dependence was previously widespread, resembling more a negative than a positive feedback model.

Alongside differences in interest constellations and in exposure to problem pressures, path dependence is the main explanation of continuing cross-national differences in policies, in particular welfare policies. However, there may also be instances of policy feedback that lead to convergence.

Policy transfer and policy diffusion

Policy transfer and policy diffusion are examples of such policy feedback mechanisms that may lead to convergence between policies in different countries. The two concepts are often used interchangeably (see Chapter 20).

We should probably reserve *policy transfer* or *policy translation* for the use of knowledge about policies and their impact in one system (or in one policy field) to deliberately change policies in another country (or in another policy field). Thus, policy transfer is about processes which do not always involve imitation or emulation, but may indeed occasionally involve substantial change while implanting policies from one institutional and cultural context to another (Knill 2005). It is a matter of deliberate cross-national or cross-sectoral policy learning.

Policy diffusion is a broader concept that refers to all conceivable channels of influence between countries (or between policy fields). The major emphasis is on studying various mechanisms of diffusion, from imposition to voluntary adoption of policy models that are communicated across borders or across policy fields in one way or another (Knill 2005; Rogers 1995).

Since the 1990s, there have been waves of welfare and tax reforms across Europe, sometimes stimulated by the OECD or the EU, and sometimes just adopted by inspiration from neighbours and being implemented country by country. An interesting European framework is the open method of coordination (OMC) which is an instance of 'soft law' regulation based on recommendations rather than sanctioned rules. The OMC, which was given this label at the EU summit in Lisbon in 2000, is a deliberate attempt to encourage policy transfer by bringing actors together to formulate common goals on the basis of recognition of institutional differences. The OMC builds on policy learning and policy transfer (de la Porte *et al.* 2001).

Policy convergence

Policy diffusion constitutes a sort of 'disturbance' in some cross-national research aiming to explain policy as an effect of structural, institutional, or political forces (Knill 2005). For instance, country variations in policy could be interpreted as an effect of variations in economic pressures, variations in institutions, or variations in strength of political parties. But then comes the problem that countries may simply have learned from each other. In purely quantitative analyses, this constitutes a serious 'disturbance' that is almost impossible to control.

However, there are some important problems relating to the issue of policy convergence itself. In the first place, should convergence be measured by policy or institutions on the one hand, or by the *impact* of policies—policy outcomes—on the other? What is the 'dependent variable' (Clasen and Siegel 2007; Andersen 2007b)? Secondly, four different patterns are conceivable (Kautto and Kvist 2002).

- *Convergence:* policies or policy outcomes become increasingly similar.
- *Divergence:* policies or policy outcomes become increasingly different.
- *Persistent difference:* policies or policy outcomes remain as they are.
- *Parallel trends, persistent differences:* policies or policy outcomes change in the same direction, but differences are maintained.

The last of these patterns is often conflated with convergence. For instance, Gilbert (2002: 138) noted a common trend towards more targeting (means testing) of social benefits in nearly all welfare states. However, according to his indicators, this common trend is combined with persistent differences between Anglo-Saxon countries that generally target, and Scandinavian countries where targeting remains the exception.

Regarding outcomes in terms of equality, we also find a parallel trend towards higher inequality (OECD 2008a, 2011), but regime differences remain. At a meta-level, however, we find stronger signs of convergence. As mentioned earlier, we find striking similarities across countries when we aggregate public and private social expenditures. Total expenditures follow modernization, public expenditures much less so. Also if we look at the profile of the entire pensions system, nearly all countries have developed some kind of earnings-related system, either within state arrangements or as a private proliferation of the welfare state. Moreover, by different means, the costs of ageing are increasingly imposed on future pensioners themselves. Such highly different policies may often be described as *functionally equivalent* in the sense that they produce similar outcomes.

KEY POINTS

- Policies shape politics and future policies.

- Policies affect power resources and generate vested interests, or even new interest groups.

- Policies are path dependent, at least in the broad sense that past decisions structure and constrain new ones, and often also in the more narrow sense that precise mechanisms can be identified.

- Policy learning often takes place within a paradigm, but even paradigm shifts can be ascribed to learning.

- Policy convergence may derive not only from 'functional necessity', but also from policy transfer.

Conclusion

The study of the impact of policy is a relatively novel branch of comparative politics. It is also a difficult one because it is complicated to disentangle effects of policies from all sorts of other effects. Furthermore, it is difficult in the sense that it often involves cross-disciplinary insights in both politics and economics. Nonetheless, it is also a very important field of research. To determine what the outcomes are of different types of policy and how policies should be designed to obtain desired outcomes is one of the most challenging fields of research in political science. It is also a field where economists begin to learn from comparative politics, not least from the insights in 'institutional complementarity'.

When it comes to the *political* impact of policies, this is also a rapidly expanding field of research that helps us to understand policy change in general, and not least policy change across nations. It helps to illuminate why countries exposed to the same external pressures often pursue quite different roads, as the theory of path dependence teaches us. It helps to understand some of the *political* forces behind policy convergence across programmes or across nations. And it helps to understand the *dynamics* of policy change.

  Questions

1. What does institutional complementarity mean?

2. What is the difference between welfare regimes and the regimes of varieties of capitalism theory?

3. What is understood by flexicurity?

4. How does corporatism impact on unemployment, and why?

5. How do different welfare models impact on equality, and why?

6. What is structural unemployment?

7. What generated a paradigm shift in the interpretation of unemployment?

8. How can policy changes affect the mobilization of interests?

9. What does path dependence mean, and are policies always path-dependent?

10. What contributes to policy transfer between countries, and between policy fields?

  Further reading

Classical texts on policy regimes

Esping-Andersen, G. (1990) *The Three Worlds of Welfare Capitalism* (Cambridge: Polity Press).

Hall, P. A., and Soskice, D. (eds) (2001) *Varieties of Capitalism: The Institutional Foundations of Comparative Advantage* (Oxford: Oxford University Press).

Titmuss, R. (1974) *Social Policy: An Introduction* (edited by B. Abel-Smith and K. Titmuss) (New York: Pantheon).

Useful guides to impact of policies

Iversen, T. (2005) *Capitalism, Democracy, and Welfare* (Cambridge: Cambridge University Press).

Lindert, P. A. (2004) *Growing Public: Social Spending and Growth since the Eighteenth Century* (Cambridge: Cambridge University Press).

OECD (1994) The OECD *Jobs Study* (Paris: OECD).

OECD (2006) *Employment Outlook 2006: Boosting Jobs and Incomes* (Paris: OECD).

Classical texts on policy feedback

Heclo, H. (1974) *Modern Social Politics in Britain and Sweden: From Relief to Income Maintenance* (New Haven, CT: Yale University Press).

Pierson, P. (1993) 'When Effect Becomes Cause: "Policy Feedback" and Political Change', *World Politics*, 45(3): 595–628.

Web links

http://www.lisdatacenter.org/resources/other-databases/
Luxembourg Income Study (LIS) Comparative Welfare States Data Set.

http://sp.uconn.edu/~scruggs/
Comparative Welfare Entitlements Dataset (Lyle Scruggs).

http://www.europeansocialsurvey.org/
European Social Survey (ESS): free downloadable data from 2002, 2004, 2006, and subsequent years.

www.issp.org/
International Social Survey Programme (ISSP).

www.worldvaluessurvey.org/
World Values Survey (WVS).

http://www.edac.eu/
General data guide to more than 500 comparative data sources with macro- and micro-level data on work, welfare, attitudes, and other issues. Links are provided alongside short descriptions.

online
resource
centre

For additional material and resources, please visit the Online Resource Centre at:
www.oxfordtextbooks.co.uk/orc/caramani3e/

Beyond the nation-state

CHAPTER 23

The EU as a new political system

Simon Hix

Reader's guide

This chapter analyses the development and operation of the European Union (EU) from a comparative politics perspective. It starts by looking at the evolution of the EU and the process of European integration. The chapter then discusses what it means to think of the EU as a political system. There are two basic dimensions of the EU system: (1) the vertical dimension—policy-making power between the EU and the member-states; (2) the horizontal dimension—the design and operation of EU decision-making. These two dimensions are considered separately before we turn to the 'missing link' in the EU system—the lack of genuine democratic politics.

Introduction

In the twentieth century, Europe suffered the two most destructive wars in history as the pinnacle of bitter political and economic rivalries between the states of Europe. At the beginning of the twenty-first century the states of Eastern and Western Europe are united in a continental-scale political system, where certain executive, legislative, and judicial powers are collectively pooled. Despite its problems, the EU remains one of the most remarkable political achievements of modern times. The EU single market guarantees the economic prosperity of almost half a billion people, and most EU citizens take for granted the investment, consumption, educational, travel, and lifestyle opportunities that exist because of the EU. Above all, for the first time in history, a war between the major states of Europe is almost unimaginable.

How did this happen? When six European states decided in the 1950s to place their coal and steel industries under collective supra-national control, few would have expected that this would have led to a new continental-scale political system (see Box 23.1). In the

Box 23.1 Key dates in the development of the European Union

18 February 1951	Belgium, France, Germany, Italy, Luxembourg, and the Netherlands sign the Treaty of Paris, launching the European Coal and Steel Community (ECSC)
23 July 1952	Treaty of Paris enters into force
1 January 1958	Treaties of Rome enter into force, establishing the EEC and Euratom
30 July 1962	Common Agricultural Policy starts
5 February 1963	Van Gend en Loos ruling of the European Court of Justice (ECJ) establishes the 'direct effect' of EEC law
15 July 1964	*Costa v. ENEL* ruling of the ECJ establishes the 'supremacy' of EEC law
29 January 1966	Luxembourg compromise, which effectively means that the Council must decide unanimously
1 July 1967	Merger Treaty, establishing a single set of institutions for the three communities
1–2 December 1969	Hague Summit: governments agree to push for further economic and political integration
27 October 1970	Governments start foreign policy cooperation (European Political Cooperation)
1 January 1973	Denmark, Ireland, and the UK join
10 February 1979	Cassis de Dijon ruling of the ECJ establishes 'mutual recognition' in the provision of goods and services in the common market
13 March 1979	European Monetary System begins
7–10 June 1979	First 'direct' elections of the European Parliament
1 January 1981	Greece joins
26 June 1984	Margaret Thatcher negotiates the 'British rebate' from the annual budget
1 January 1985	First 'European Communities' passports are issued
1 January 1986	Portugal and Spain join
19 May 1986	European flag used for the first time
1 July 1987	Single European Act enters into force, launching the single-market programme
13 February 1988	First multi-annual framework for the EC budget agreed
9 November 1989	Berlin Wall falls
1 January 1993	Single European Market starts
1 November 1993	Maastricht Treaty enters into force, launching the EU and the plan for Economic and Monetary Union (EMU)
21 July 1994	European Parliament rejects a piece of EU legislation for the first time
1 January 1995	Austria, Finland, and Sweden join
1 January 1999	EMU starts

15 March 1999	Santer Commission resigns before a censure vote is held in the European Parliament
1 May 1999	Amsterdam Treaty enters into force, starting the 'area of freedom, security and justice'
24 March 2000	European Council agrees the 'Lisbon strategy' to promote growth and productivity.
1 January 2002	Euro notes and coins replace national notes and coins for ten member-states
1 February 2003	Nice Treaty enters into force, launching defence cooperation and reforming the institutions in preparation for enlargement
1 May 2004	Cyprus, Czech Republic, Estonia, Hungary, Latvia, Lithuania, Malta, Poland, Slovakia, and Slovenia join
26 October 2004	European Parliament blocks the election of a new Commission
29 October 2004	Treaty establishing a Constitution for Europe signed
29 May/1 June 2005	'No' votes in referendums in France and the Netherlands on the Constitutional Treaty
1 January 2007	Bulgaria and Romania join
1 December 2009	Lisbon Treaty enters into force
27 September 2012	European Stability Mechanism becomes effective
1 January 2013	'Fiscal Compact' Treaty between 25 member-states (EU27 minus UK and Czech Republic) enters into force
1 July 2013	Croatia joins

1960s, Western Europe became the first region in the world to establish a customs union, with an internal free trade area and a common external tariff. Added to this 'common market' was the first genuinely supranational public expenditure programme: the Common Agricultural Policy (CAP). European integration then took a major step forward in the 1980s. The so far unique continental-scale 'single market' was created by the 1990s, with the removal of internal barriers to the cross-border flow of goods, services, capital, and labour, a single competition policy, and a single currency (the euro). Partly as a consequence of the single market, the EU began to coordinate national macroeconomic, justice and policing, and foreign and security policies.

Many aspects of the EU are unique. Yet, from the point of view of comparative politics, there are many things the EU shares with other multilevel polities. For example, the division of powers between the lower (national) and higher (European) levels of government determines how policy-making works. Moreover, at the European level, the design of agenda-setting and veto powers in the decision-making process determines which actors are likely to secure the policies they most prefer and how easy or difficult it is to change existing policies. The field of comparative politics has developed analytical tools to understand aspects of multilevel political systems which are increasingly applicable to the EU.

KEY POINTS

- In half a century the EU has evolved from an organization governing coal and steel production and a common market to a continental-scale political system, with extensive executive, legislative, and judicial powers.

- The process of European integration began with six member-states; the EU now has twenty-eight members and may enlarge to thirty or even thirty-five in the next decade or so.

- The EU shares many characteristics of other multilevel political systems, which enables the tools of comparative politics to be applied to it.

Explanations of European integration

In the 1950s and 1960s several scholars expected that 'regional integration' would happen in many parts of the world. However, by the mid-1960s, the extent of institution-building and the intensity of political and economic cooperation were far greater in Western Europe than in any other region. As a result, an explanatory framework developed for the sole purpose of understanding 'European integration'. Simplifying, explanations fall into two main camps: (1) *intergovernmental approaches*, which see preferences and decisions of national governments as primary; (2) *supranational approaches*, which see supranational political, social, and economic forces as primary.

Intergovernmental approaches

The basic assumption of these approaches is that the main actors in the EU are the governments of the member-states (e.g. Hoffmann 1966, 1982; Taylor 1982; Moravcsik 1991). National governments have a clear set of preferences about what policies they would like to see allocated to the European level. For example, British governments have traditionally preferred economic to political integration, while German governments have wanted both. British governments have wanted the EU to adopt a free-market approach to economic integration, while German governments have looked to adopt a 'social market' approach, with harmonized social and labour market regulations. Governments usually 'bargain hard' with each other on the basis of these preferences, and only agree to outcomes at the European level if these outcomes promote their preferences.

One might expect that, if governments are self-interested and are determined not to lose any ground when bargaining at the European level, nothing will ever be done in the EU. Indeed, this was one of the conclusions of some of the early intergovernmental theorists, who assumed that European integration could not progress beyond a very minimal level (e.g. Hoffmann 1966). However, more recent intergovernmental approaches argue that there are good collective reasons for member-state governments to hand over significant powers to the EU institutions (Moravcsik 1993, 1998; Pollack 1997). For example, it is often in the governments' interests to have a common policy for the single market, yet agreement cannot be reached as each government has their own particular policy preference which they are reluctant to give up. This 'coordination problem' can be resolved by delegating agenda-setting power to the European Commission, where the Commission works out which is the best policy option for the EU as a whole.

The intergovernmental approaches explain well why the process of integration stalled in the 1970s, as governments preferred national to European solutions to the economic problems in that period. These approaches also explain how a convergence of governments' preferences in favour of a continental-scale market, and the careful design of a set of new decision-making rules, enabled European integration to be re-launched in the 1980s and 1990s.

Nevertheless, there are several aspects of European integration that these approaches have not been able to explain so well. They cannot explain the increase in the powers of the European Parliament (EP) since the mid-1980s. In addition, if the governments are in control of European integration, it is hard to explain why there is declining support for this process. Indeed, from an inter-governmental perspective, since the governments run the EU, and the governments are elected by the citizens, there is no 'democratic deficit' in the EU (Moravcsik 2002). Finally, although inter-governmental approaches may be very useful for understanding the 'grand bargains' such as the Single European Act or the Maastricht Treaty, they seem less useful for understanding day-to-day decision-making, where there are multiple actors and interests and more complex sets of preferences.

To understand how the EU works on a day-to-day basis, it is more useful to think of it as a political system, and apply approaches from comparative politics.

Supranational approaches

The basic assumption of these approaches is that European integration is a deterministic process driven by underlying political, economic, and social forces. In the early period of European integration, Ernst Haas proposed what he called a 'neofunctionalist' theory of economic and political integration (Haas 1958, 1961; cf. Lindberg 1963). At the heart of this theory was the concept of 'spillover', whereby 'a given action, related to a specific goal, creates a situation in which the original goal can be assured only by taking further actions, which in turn create a further condition and a need for more, and so forth' (Lindberg 1963: 9). For example, a common market in coal and steel would work much more efficiently if there was a common market in other goods and services used in the production and distribution of coal and steel. Similarly, once the free movement of labour was established, there was pressure on the member-state governments to agree common justice and home affairs policies.

One variant of this approach was Béla Balassa's (1961) theory of economic integration. Balassa argued that, once a customs union had been established, the potential economies of scale from such a union could not be met unless all barriers to the free movement of goods and services had been removed (in other words, a single market). Then, once a single market had been established, it would function more effectively if a single currency could be established, which would allow for greater price transparency and reduced transaction costs of doing business. Then, if a single currency were established, economic shocks to the currency union could no longer be addressed through monetary policies, so there would need to be fiscal transfers from high-growth regions to low-growth regions. These fiscal transfers would need to be legitimized somehow, which would require the establishment of genuine political union, with democratic elections for the central institutions. In other words, Balassa predicted a logical teleological development from a customs union to a political union.

Most scholars within the supranationalist approach were not as economically determinist as Balassa, in that integration would not proceed without the input of actors. Economic forces are insufficient on their own to force states to take major integrationist steps. However, in contrast with the intergovernmental view, the supranational framework emphasizes the role of 'non-state' actors, such as interest groups and the institutions of the EU themselves (Marks *et al.* 1996; Pierson 1996; Sandholtz and Stone Sweet 1997; Pollack 2003). For example, transnational businesses in the early 1980s put pressure on the governments to create a single market in Europe (Sandholtz and Zysman 1989).

Meanwhile, the Commission, led by Jacques Delors, played an important role in shaping the single market, the reform of the EU budget in the late 1980s, and the plan for economic and monetary union (Pollack 2003). Similarly, by establishing the doctrines of the 'direct effect' and 'supremacy' of EC law in the early 1960s, the ECJ has fashioned a quasi-federal legal framework, beyond the intentions of the signatories of the early treaties (Weiler 1991). And the EP has interpreted the decision-making rules of the EU in a way that has maximized its influence (Hix 2002).

Overall, supranationalism does well in capturing the remarkable, and perhaps teleological, evolution of the EU from a customs union in the 1960s to a full-blown political system by the end of the twentieth century. Nevertheless, the inherent determinism of the supra-nationalist approaches means that they are less able to explain why the process of European integration slowed between the late 1960s and the mid-1980s, or why some member-states decided to join the EU at different times or indeed remain largely outside (such as Norway and Switzerland). These approaches are also less able to explain why the EU is more able to adopt common policies in some areas, such as environmental policy, than in other areas, such as social policy.

Again, thinking of the EU as a political system helps us to understand its internal workings in detail.

KEY POINTS

- For most of its history, the EEC/EU has been understood by social scientists as a unique case of political and economic 'integration' between sovereign nation-states.

- Intergovernmentalism focuses on how the policy preferences and actions of the governments, in particular Germany, France, and Britain, shape the design of the EU at the various stages of integration.

- Supranationalism focuses on how the underlying economic, political, and social factors and the behaviour of interest groups and EU institutions constrain the choices of governments and hence further integration.

Understanding the EU as a political system

A political system but not a state

In the 1950s comparative political scientists tried to develop a common framework for analysing the complex array of political systems throughout the world (e.g. Almond 1956; Easton 1957; see also the Introduction to this volume). There are four essential characteristics of all democratic political systems.

1. There is a clearly defined set of institutions for collective decision-making and rules governing relations between these institutions.

2. Citizens seek to achieve their political desires through the political system, either directly or through intermediary organizations such as interest groups and political parties.

3. Collective decisions have an impact on the distribution of economic resources and the allocation of values across the whole system.

4. There is a continuous interaction between these political outputs, new demands on the system, new decisions, and so on.

The EU possesses all these characteristics. First, the level of institutional development in the EU is far greater than in any other international organization. Second, a large number of public and private groups, from multinational corporations and global environmental groups to individual citizens, are involved and influence the EU policy process. Third, EU policy outcomes are highly significant and are felt throughout the EU. Fourth, the EU political system is a permanent feature of political life in Europe. The quarterly meetings of the heads of government of the member-states in the European Council may be the only feature that many citizens and media outlets notice. Nevertheless, EU politics is a continuous process, within and between the EU institutions in Brussels, national governments and Brussels, national public administrations, private interests and governmental officials in Brussels and at the national level, and private groups involved in EU affairs at the national and European levels.

Conceptualizing the EU as a political system rather than a unique example of regional integration enabled social scientists in the late 1980s and early 1990s to start to apply tools and methods from the comparative study of political systems to the EU (Scharpf 1988; Streeck and Schmitter 1991; Sbragia 1992; Tsebelis 1994; van der Eijk and Franklin 1996; Majone 1996; McKay 1996; Hix 2005). These tools helped provide answers to a new set of generalizable questions, such as which actors are most influential in the EU legislative process, how independent from political control is the ECJ, why do some citizens support the EU while others oppose it, and why does the EU produce some policy outcomes but not others?

The constitutional architecture of the EU

The Treaty establishing a Constitution for Europe, which was signed by the member-states in 2004, was an effort to simplify and codify the rules of the EU. The proposed 'EU Constitution' was rejected by voters in France and the Netherlands in 2005. The resulting Lisbon Treaty, which entered into force in December 2009, stripped away many of the symbolic elements from the original 'Constitution' but kept almost all the provisions relating to the simplification of the competences of the EU relative to the member-states and the changes to the powers of the EU institutions. But even before the proposed EU Constitution and the resulting Lisbon Treaty, the EU already had a basic 'constitutional architecture'. Indeed, one of the remarkable things about the new treaty is how little of the established policy and institutional architecture it actually changed.

As far as policies are concerned (Box 23.2), the EU level has exclusive responsibility for the regulation of the single market, and for managing the competition, customs, and trade policies that derive from this task. The EU level is also responsible for the monetary policies of the member-states whose currency is the euro, and for the common agricultural and fisheries policies.

A wide array of policy competences are 'shared' between the EU and the member-states. The European-level policies aim to supplement existing national policies. This is the case, for example, in the areas of labour market regulation, regional spending, and immigration (such as a common visa policy) and asylum. The third area of policies can be described as 'coordinated competences'. Action remains primarily at the member-state level, but the governments accept that they need to coordinate their policies because there are effects on each other. For example, with the freedom of movement of persons inside the EU there is a need to coordinate some policing and criminal justice policies. Similarly, following the sovereign debt crisis of 2010–12, the states who share the single currency decided to undertake much deeper coordination of their macro-economic policies, such as requiring national governments to run 'balanced budgets' (in the new Fiscal Compact Treaty). Finally, all the major areas of public spending, such as education, healthcare, transport, housing, welfare provision, and pensions, remain the exclusive preserve of the member-states.

Turning to the institutions, Box 23.3 describes the basic institutional architecture of the EU. Executive powers are shared between the Council and the Commission. Whereas the Council sets the medium- and long-term policy agendas (particularly via the heads of state and government in the European Council), the Commission has a formal monopoly on legislative initiative. The Commission and the member-states are also

---

Box 23.2 The basic policy architecture of the EU

Exclusive EU competences

Regulation of the single market, including removing barriers and competition policy

Customs union and external trade policies

Monetary policy for the member-states whose currency is the euro

Price-setting and subsidy of production under the Common Agricultural Policy

Common fisheries policy

Shared competences (where action is taken at both national and European levels)

Social regulation, such as health and safety at work, gender equality, and non-discrimination

Environmental regulation

Consumer protection and common public health concerns, such as food safety

Economic, social, and territorial cohesion

Free movement of persons, including policies towards third-country nationals

Transport

Energy

Coordinated competences (where national actions are coordinated at the EU level)

Macro-economic policies

Foreign and defence policies

Policing and criminal justice policies

Health, cultural, education, tourism, youth, sport, and vocational training policies

Exclusive member-state competences

All other policies (e.g. most areas of public spending)

Box 23.3 The basic institutional architecture of the EU

Council of the European Union (Brussels)

The Council is a legislative and an executive body composed of ministers from the governments of the member-states. On the legislative side, the Council adopts EU legislation and the budget. On the executive side, the Council coordinates the broad economic policies of the member-states, concludes international agreements of the EU, develops the common foreign and security policy, coordinates cooperation between national courts and police forces, and reforms EU treaties. The Council meets in ten configurations: general affairs; foreign affairs; economic and financial affairs; justice and home affairs; employment, social policy, health, and consumer affairs; competitiveness; transport, telecommunications, and energy; agriculture and fisheries; environment; and education, youth, culture, and sport. The overall agenda of the Council is set by a separate institution—the European Council—which brings together the heads of state and government of the EU four times a year. The current president of the Council is Herman Van Rompuy. The presidency of the other meetings of the Council rotates between the member-states every six months.

The Council is aided by the Committee of Permanent Representatives of the EU (COREPER), which is composed of the ambassadors of the member-states to the EU.

European Parliament (Brussels, Strasbourg, and Luxembourg)

There are 754 MEPs (766 from 2014), who are elected every five years by the EU citizens, and organize together in transnational political groups. The Parliament is half of the EU's legislative authority (jointly with the Council). The Parliament amends and adopts EU legislation and the budget, and monitors the work of the other EU institutions. The Parliament has the power to approve or reject the nominated Commission president and the team of Commissioners, and also has the right to censure the Commission as a whole (by a two-thirds majority vote).

European Commission (Brussels)

The Commission is composed of one member from each member-state and is the main executive body of the EU. The Commission is responsible for proposing EU legislation,

managing and implementing EU policies and the budget, enforcing EU law (jointly with the ECJ), and representing the EU on the international stage (e.g. in the WTO). The Commission is divided into Directorates-General (DGs), each of which is responsible for a different area of policy. Following each European Parliament election, the Commission president is nominated by a qualified majority vote in the European Council and accepted or rejected by a simple majority vote in the EP. José Manuel Barroso, the conservative former prime minister of Portugal, was re-elected as Commission president in 2009.

European Court of Justice (Luxembourg)

The ECJ is the judicial authority of the EU. The ECJ ensures that EU legislation is interpreted and applied in the same way in all member-states and undertakes judicial review of the Treaties, the secondary legislation, and the tertiary instruments of the EU. The ECJ is composed of one judge per member-state. The Court is assisted by eight advocates-general. Vassilios Skouris (from Greece) was elected president of the ECJ in 2003. To help the ECJ with the large number of cases, the ECJ is assisted by the Court of First Instance.

Other Institutions

The *European Central Bank* (Frankfurt) is responsible for monetary policy, including setting interest rates for the European single currency (the euro).

The *European Court of Auditors* (Luxembourg) checks that EU funds are properly collected and spent legally, economically, and for their intended purpose.

The *Committee of the Regions* (Brussels) represents regions and local authorities in the member-states in the EU policy-making process.

The *European Investment Bank* (Luxembourg) finances EU investment projects.

There are thirty-two other EU Agencies, such as European Environment Agency (Copenhagen), European Food Safety Authority (Parma), European Medicines Agency (London), European Monitoring Centre on Racism and Xenophobia (Vienna), European Defence Agency (Brussels), and European Police Office (the Hague).

jointly responsible for the implementation of EU policies. Legislative power is also shared between two institutions: the legislative meetings of the Council and the EP. The EP has equal power with the Council under the main legislative procedure, the *co-decision procedure* (formally called the 'ordinary legislative procedure'). However, some highly sensitive areas of policy, such as

tax harmonization, are passed under the *consultation procedure,* under which the Council is only required to consult the EP before passing legislation. Finally, judicial power in the EU is shared between the ECJ and national courts, where national courts are primarily responsible for enforcing EU law and refer cases to the ECJ if a domestic case raises a significant point of EU law.

KEY POINTS

- The EU is not a 'state' in that powers are shared between the EU and the member-states, the EU is based on voluntary cooperation between the member-states, there is no direct EU taxation, the EU budget is small, and the EU relies on the forces of coercion of its member-states.

- Nevertheless, the EU can be understood as a political system, in that it possesses a constitutional architecture which determines the balance between the EU and the member-states and between the institutions at the European level, and the policies of the EU have significant implications on the economy and society in Europe.

- Conceptualizing the EU as a political system allows application of tools and methods from the comparative study of political systems.

Vertical dimension: the EU as a 'regulatory state'

The dominant policy goal of the EU is the creation and regulation of a market on a continental scale. Other policies are in many respects 'flanking' policies of this goal. These policies make Europe's continental-scale market work more effectively (the single currency), or correct potential market failures (environmental and social policies), or compensate potential losers from market integration (budgetary policies), or address potential social and security externalities from market integration (justice and interior policies). Given the primacy of the single market and the centrality of EU market regulation policies, the EU is often described as a 'regulatory state' (Majone 1996). This concept nicely captures the contrast between the EU and the national level in Europe, where the main policy instruments are taxation and public spending.

Creation and regulation of the single market

The single market notionally started on 1 January 1993, after the passage of almost 300 pieces of legislation. However, in practice the single market is an ongoing project, as major areas of the economy (such as the provision of services and the professions) still operate in separate national markets.

The creation of the single market has both deregulatory and re-regulatory elements. On the *deregulatory* side, creating the single market involves the removal of barriers to the free movement of goods, services, capital, and labour between the EU member-states. Three types of barriers had to be removed.

1. *Fiscal barriers,* such as the harmonization of value-added tax and excise duties (on goods like alcohol and tobacco).

2. *Physical barriers* on the movement of goods and persons, such as the abolition of customs formalities. Removing border controls on the movement of persons was also an original aim of the single-market programme. However, several member-states (including the UK, Ireland, and Denmark) refused to accept that it was necessary to remove border controls in order for the free movement of persons to function effectively—all that was needed, they contended, was the right to move, reside, and work anywhere in the EU. In response, the other member-states agreed to remove their border controls as part of the Schengen Accord, which was initially outside the formal framework of the EU.

3. *Technical barriers* to the free movement of goods and services, such as separate national product standards that could be used as 'non-tariff barriers'. The EU had tried to establish common standards via harmonized rules throughout the EU. However, in the landmark *Cassis de Dijon* judgement in 1979, the ECJ established the principle of 'mutual recognition', whereby any product meeting the standards of one member-state can be legally sold in all other member-states. Another key area of removal of technical barriers was in public procurement, where rules were established preventing governments from favouring home companies in public contracts. A host of directives have also been passed to liberalize air, water, and road transport, and to open up national energy, telecoms, and television markets. Regarding the movement of capital, controls on the free flow of capital between the member-states were abolished, and the European Company Statute, which enables multinational companies to be registered as single European-wide entities, was adopted in 2001.

On the *re-regulatory* side, as part of the single-market programme, the EU replaced existing national regulations. The three clearest examples of this are EU competition policies, environmental policies, and social policies. On *competition policies*, the EU has anti-trust regulations (which outlaw a variety of agreements between companies such as price-fixing or predatory pricing) and prohibits government subsidies to industry that threaten competition between the member-states, and the Commission is required to review mergers between companies of a certain size. On *environmental policy*, common EU regulations cover, among other things, air and noise pollution, waste disposal, water pollution, chemicals, biodiversity, environmental impact assessments, eco-labelling and eco-audits, and natural and technological hazards. The European Environment Agency was set up in 1994 in Copenhagen to collect data and develop environmental forecasts. On *social policy*, EU legislation covers the rights of workers to free movement, health and safety at work, working conditions, worker consultation, gender equality, anti-discrimination (race, ethnic origin, religion, disability, age, and sexual orientation), and rights of part-time and temporary workers.

Re-regulatory policies are usually regarded as benefiting all EU citizens rather than particular groups by correcting certain 'market failures' that might arise in a continental-scale market. For example, harmonized consumer protection standards enable consumers to gain information about the quality of products that would otherwise not be publicly available. Health and safety standards and environmental standards reduce the adverse effects ('negative externalities') of market transactions on individuals not participating in the transactions. Competition policies prevent monopolistic markets from emerging, market distortions, and anti-competitive practices. Put this way, EU 'social regulations' are very different from national 'social policies', in that while the latter are usually geared towards providing benefits to particular social groups, the former aim to allow the labour market to function more efficiently (Majone 1993).

Nevertheless, there are significant indirect redistributive consequences (Leibfried and Pierson 1995; Streeck 1996; Scharpf 1997*a*; Kleinman 2001). The EU does not have the direct redistributive capacity of national welfare states (see Chapter 21), but the regulatory regime reflects a particular 'welfare compromise' at the European level that constrains existing welfare compromises and choices at the domestic level. For example, the single market places downward pressure on states with higher labour market standards (such as Germany and Scandinavia). In addition, the redistributive capacities of the national welfare states are further constrained by the restrictions on national fiscal policies as a result of economic and monetary union.

Economic and Monetary Union and the European Central Bank

The Maastricht Treaty (1993) established a three-point plan for Economic and Monetary Union (EMU).

1. It involved a timetable, with the launch of EMU on 1 January 1999 and the introduction of euro notes and coins on 1 January 2002.

2. It established four 'convergence criteria', which member-states have to meet to be able to join the single currency: (1) a stable currency, (2) a convergent economic cycle with the EU average cycle, (3) an annual government deficit of less than 3 per cent of GDP, and (4) a gross public debt of less than 60 per cent of GDP.

3. It established an institutional design of EMU.

The European Central Bank (ECB) has the sole responsibility of defining and implementing monetary policy (including setting interest rates) for the member-states whose currency is the euro, with the sole aim of maintaining price stability. The ECB comprises a six-member executive board, appointed by the European Council, and a governing council, comprising the executive board members and the governors of the national central banks of the EMU member-states. However, the governments, meeting in the Council of Economic and Finance Ministers, have the final say over interventions in foreign exchange markets, adopt common economic policy guidelines for the EU as a whole, and monitor the national economic policies of the EU member-states.

Not all EU member-states are members of EMU. Eleven of the then fifteen EU states launched EMU in 1999—Austria, Belgium, Finland, France, Germany, Ireland, Italy, Luxembourg, the Netherlands, Portugal, and Spain. Greece became the twelfth EMU member in 2001. Of the 'old fifteen' states, the UK, Denmark, and Sweden chose to stay outside EMU, and none of the 'new ten' joined the EMU when they became members of the EU in 2004. Slovenia joined in 2007, Malta in 2008, Slovakia in 2009, and Estonia in 2011. Today, seventeen of the twenty-seven EU states are in the Eurozone, while ten remain outside.

A key element of the EMU is the Stability and Growth Pact (SGP). The German government, in particular, was concerned that once states had met the initial convergence criteria and entered EMU they might then be tempted to run large public deficits, which would undermine the stability of the euro and so negatively affect the more fiscally responsible states. Hence the SGP was agreed in 1997 as a way to limit this problem by requiring that member-states must maintain an annual budget deficit of less than 3 per cent of GDP, or otherwise face a fine (established as a percentage of national GDP). However, one problem with the pact was that a fine could only be imposed by collective agreement. When France and Germany were the first major breakers of the SGP rules, no fine was imposed, which brought its credibility into question.

However, a decade after the launch of the Euro it became clear that the convergence criteria and the SGP rules were insufficient to guarantee economic convergence among the Eurozone member-states. In 2009, the banking liquidity crisis spilled over into a sovereign debt crisis. The interest rates charged on Greek government bonds rose to unprecedented levels. Member states feared that if the Greek government defaulted on its debts it would have to leave the euro. Hence, the other member-states—particularly those countries (such as Germany) whose banks were lending money to Greek, Irish, and Portuguese governments and banks—had to prevent the potential collapse of the Eurozone. The Eurozone member-states pieced together a plan to ensure stability in the Eurozone.

There are three main elements to the emerging new architecture of the Eurozone. First, the European Stability Mechanism (ESM), which entered into force in 2012, is a financial instrument backed by national tax-payers. Second, in return for this 'emergency bailout fund', the creditor states (such as Germany, the Netherlands, and Finland) insisted that measures should be taken by debtor states to ensure economic stability. These measures include 'austerity' agreements in return for loans, a new Fiscal Compact Treaty under which states must introduce a 'balanced budget' clause in their national constitutions, and more extensive oversight of national macro-economic policies (including pensions, unemployment benefits, labour-market rules). Third, to reduce the likelihood of future banking crises, and to guarantee banking liquidity, a 'banking union' was set up, under which all banks would be governed by a single set of rules and regulated by the European Central Bank. Only time will tell whether these measures are sufficient to guarantee stability in the Eurozone.

The main theoretical framework for understanding economic and monetary integration is the 'optimal currency area' (OCA) theory, developed by Robert Mundell (1961). According to this theory, independent states will form a monetary union if the benefits of joining exceed the costs. The main cost of a monetary union is the loss of an independent exchange rate. With a 'one size fits all' monetary policy, differential economic cycles between states have to be tackled by other policies, such as labour mobility (from states in recession to states growing more quickly), wage flexibility (where workers in the state where there is low demand reduce their wages), or fiscal transfers (from high-growth to low-growth states). If labour mobility is low, if there is limited wage flexibility, and if fiscal transfers are small, a group of states do not form an OCA. Put this way, the EU is clearly not an OCA.

However, for some states, the economic benefits of EMU might outweigh some of these potential costs. A single currency lowers transactions costs in the economy (by removing the need to change money), produces a more efficient market, leads to greater economic certainty, and in general creates lower interest rates and higher growth rates. In general, for states with high levels of trade integration with the Eurozone, the benefits of joining EMU outweigh the costs, since higher trade integration means higher economic convergence and the greater transaction costs benefits of a single currency (e.g. Krugman 1990). In contrast, for states with lower trade integration and less convergent economic cycles, the costs of joining EMU are likely to outweigh the benefits—which is broadly speaking the current situation of the UK.

EU expenditure policies

Compared with the powerful effects of the single market and EMU on the lives of EU citizens, and in contrast with the huge public spending programmes of the national governments, the spending power of the EU is small, since the EU budget represents only about 1 per cent of the total GDP of the EU member-states. Spread across all EU citizens, the costs of the EU budget are absolutely tiny. However, for those who receive money out of the EU budget—namely poorer states, farmers, backward economic regions, and scientists—the sums can be huge.

The EU adopts multi-annual budgets (see the Table: Size and main expenditure categories of the EU budget, 2007–13, in the Online Resource Centre). The main EU spending policy is the CAP, which is a system of price support for a wide range of agricultural products and other subsidies to farmers. The CAP represents more than 30 per cent of total EU spending. The second main area of EU spending is on regional policy, covered under the heading 'economic and social cohesion', which is targeted at economically backward regions, regions with high levels of unemployment, and regions undergoing major industrial restructuring. EU regional funds are mainly spent on infrastructure projects, such as roads, schools, airports, and telecommunications systems. The third main area of EU spending is on scientific research. Most of the EU's research and development funds are distributed to networks of researchers working in the natural sciences, such as biotechnology and telecommunications.

online resource centre

Figure 23.1 shows 'who got what' under the EU budget in 1995 and 2005 as a proportion of each member-state's gross national income (GNI). In general, there are six main net contributor states: Austria, Germany, Luxembourg, the Netherlands, Sweden, and the UK. Prior to the 2004 enlargement there were four main net beneficiary states: Greece, Ireland, Portugal, and Spain. Nevertheless, after the 2004 enlargement, the benefits to these countries fell considerably, as the funds began to be targeted towards the poorer regions in many of the new member-states. Also, after enlargement, the Netherlands replaced Germany as the largest net contributor to the EU budget as a percentage of its GNI and as a percentage of the Dutch population, which played a significant role in the anti-Europe campaign in the 2005 referendum in the Netherlands on the EU Constitution.

EU spending policies are a combination of 'solidarity' and 'side payments'. On the *solidarity* side, transfers through the EU budget have generally passed from the

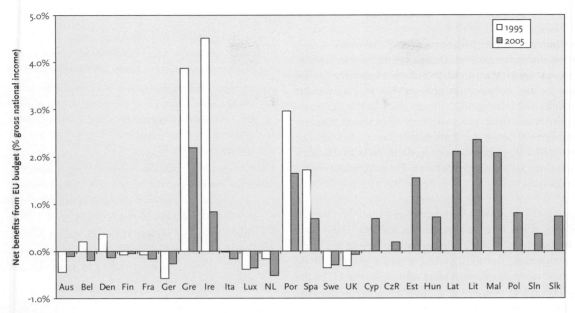

Figure 23.1 Net benefits from the EU budget, 1995 and 2005

Source: Calculated from data in European Commission (2006).

richer states to the poorer states, on the grounds that the EU is more than simply an economic union, and so there should be some mechanism for redistributing wealth. On the *side-payments* side, however, most EU spending policies are the result of specific inter-governmental bargains, where member-states who expect to 'lose' from major policy changes in the EU demand some compensation. For example, in the Treaty of Rome negotiations, France proposed the CAP, as a subsidy regime mainly for French farmers, because the common market was expected to benefit Germany's manufacturing-based economy. Similarly, in return for agreeing to the single-market programme, which was expected to benefit the main exporting economies of central and northern Europe, Spain, Italy, Portugal, Ireland, and Greece requested a doubling of EU spending under the regional funds.

Once spending policies have been set up they are very difficult to change, even if the original policy aims are no longer justified. This is because any change to the EU budget requires unanimous agreement among the governments.

Interior policies and external relations

Finally, there are two main areas of EU policy-making that are not strictly related to the EU's main economic policies.

- The array of justice and interior affairs policies, which include immigration, asylum, and other policies on the free movement of persons, as well as police and judicial cooperation.

- The EU's external relations policies, which include trade policies, development and humanitarian aid, the Common Foreign and Security Policy (CFSP), and European Security and Defence Cooperation (ESDP).

While in economic terms the EU is more a 'regulatory state' than a 'welfare state', where the EU's interior and external relations policies are concerned, the EU is developing some elements of a 'security state' managing the *internal and external* political rights, responsibilities, and security of their citizens.

Internal side

On the internal side, the Maastricht Treaty established the Justice and Home Affairs pillar of the EU, which brought into the legal framework of the EU a number of existing inter-governmental cooperation arrangements between the interior ministries of the EU member-states. These provisions covered the removal of border controls between the member-states, immigration and asylum policies and common policies towards 'third-country nationals', and police and judicial cooperation to combat drug-trafficking, terrorist activities, cross-border crime, and illegal immigration.

The Amsterdam Treaty separated the policies covering the movement of persons (immigration, asylum, internal and external borders, etc.) from the police and judicial cooperation policies. The free-movement policies were set up in the main body of the EU treaty in the framework of a new 'area of freedom, security and justice'. Since the Amsterdam Treaty, the EU has adopted a large number of legislative acts in this area covering common rules for non-EU nationals working in the EU.

External side

On the external side, since the establishment of a common market, the EU has had a single external trade policy, where the Commission represents the EU in the WTO and in bilateral and multilateral trade negotiations. The EU has also developed an array of external economic policy instruments that it uses to project 'soft power' on the world stage (see Chapter 25). These include direct humanitarian and economic assistance as well as various preferential trade agreements, such as the European Economic Area (EEA), association agreements, free-trade agreements, partnership agreements (e.g. with the EU member-states' former colonies in Africa, the Caribbean, and the Pacific), inter-regional association agreements with other regional trade blocs, and mutual recognition agreements (mainly with the US).

External security and defence policies developed more slowly. However, the Maastricht Treaty formally established the CFSP pillar of the EU, to which the Nice Treaty added the ESDP—as the 'European pillar' of the NATO transatlantic defence alliance. Under CFSP, the EU member-states adopt, by unanimity, 'common strategies' and 'common positions' which set out the EU's position on a key foreign policy issue. Then, the EU member-states only require a qualified majority vote to adopt a 'joint action' implementing a common position. This combination has allowed the EU to act in a wide variety of areas. For example, the EU adopted a common strategy towards Russia in 1999 and the Mediterranean in 2000, the EU took an active collective role in the conflict in the former Yugoslavia, and in 2003 the EU adopted a common European Security Strategy which sets out how and why EU security policies differ from the US administration's 'pre-emptive strike' doctrine. Nevertheless, a genuinely 'common' EU foreign policy is inevitably hampered by the conflicting security and foreign policy preferences of the key EU member-states, as was so clearly demonstrated in the internal rift in the EU over whether to support the US in the second Iraq war.

KEY POINTS

- Regulation of the free movement of goods, services, capital, and labour is the main policy instrument, as part of the creation and organization of the single market.

- Economic and monetary union is a complement to the single market, in that a single market functions more effectively with a single currency, and a single currency governed by an interdependent central bank ensures economic stability.

- EU expenditure policies, in contrast, are a secondary policy instrument of the EU, and have mainly been used to enable major steps in the process of economic integration by consensus.

- The EU has begun to expand beyond economic policies, into justice and interior affairs policies and foreign and security policies, but policy-making in these areas has developed much more slowly.

- The basic policy architecture of the EU, where a continental-scale market is created and regulated at the European level while spending and security policies remain largely at the national level, means that the EU is more a 'regulatory state' than a welfare state or security state.

Horizontal dimension: a hyper-consensus system of government

The main determinant of how policies are made by the central institutions in a political system is how far the power to set the agenda and the power to veto decisions are centralized in a single actor or dispersed between multiple actors. At one extreme, a political system can have a single 'agenda-setter' and 'veto-player', for example where there is single-party government. At the other extreme, multiple actors could potentially veto any change to existing policies, for example where there is coalition government or where there is a separation of powers between the executive (the president) and the legislature (Tsebelis 2002). In the EU multiple actors have the ability to block policy changes in its legislative process. As a result, the EU has an extremely consensual model of government.

Executive politics: competing agenda-setters

First of all, agenda-setting power is split between the heads of government in the European Council and the Commission. The heads of government, meeting in the European Council, decide on treaty reforms, which determine the allocation of powers between the EU institutions, and set the medium-term policy agenda. The European Commission, meanwhile, has a formal monopoly on the initiative of most EU legislation.

In the European Council, political leadership is shared between the permanent president of the European Council (often mislabelled the 'EU president') and the government of the member-state who holds the six-monthly rotating presidency of the other meetings of the Council (Hayes-Renshaw and Wallace 2006; Tallberg 2006). Because the president of the European Council, who is appointed for a period of two-and-a-half years, renewable once, is a new position created by the Lisbon Treaty, it is not yet clear how powerful the person holding this position is. Regarding the rotating presidency of the Council, some member-states are clearly better at this role than others. For example, larger member-states generally have more administrative capacity. However, the largest member-states also tend to try to place their domestic political issues on the EU agenda, and are less concerned about coordinating the overall policy agenda with the Commission. Furthermore, the powers of the rotating Council presidency are actually quite limited. This is because the member-state holding the rotating Council presidency cannot initiate legislation, and must deal with legislation that has already been initiated by the Commission and may already have been through several stages of negotiations.

The Commission, on the other hand, has traditionally been regarded as being politically and institutionally committed to the process of European integration, and so is often assumed to have policy preferences that are more 'integrationist' than most member-states. For example, in the process of creating the single market, the Commission generally wans legislation that promoted further market integration or a high level of EU-wide regulation. Nevertheless, this view of the Commission as an 'integrationist preference outlier' may be unfounded. The commissioners are appointed by national governments, and most commissioners have strong ties to the political parties who chose them and seek to return to domestic politics after their careers in the Commission. Hence, commissioners are unlikely to be very much more pro-integrationist than the governments that appoint them. Also, below the level of the commissioners, research has shown that the senior officials in the Commission bureaucracy have policy preferences that are typical of politicians from the member-states from which they come and from the national political parties they support (Hooghe 2001).

In addition, since the college of commissioners formally decides by a majority vote, the Commission generally initiates policies that are close to the policy preferences of the median member of the Commission (Crombez 1997; Hug 2003). Nevertheless, the left-right policy location of the Commission has changed dramatically in recent years.

Whereas the Prodi Commission was relatively evenly balanced between left and right, a clear majority of the members of both the first and second Barroso Commissions were on the centre-right. This change is partly explained by the shifting make-up of the governments who appoint the commissioners—from a centre-left majority in the late 1990s to a centre-right majority since the early 2000s. The shift is also explained by a change introduced by the Nice Treaty, whereby the larger member-states no longer have two commissioners each. Now that each member-state has only one commissioner, the make-up of the Commission mirrors the political make-up of the Council at the time that the commissioners are appointed.

Bicameral legislative politics: rising power of the European Parliament

The most significant change over the last twenty years in the way that the EU institutions work has been the steady increase in the powers of the EP. Originally, the EP had a limited right to be consulted. However, with the programme to establish the single market, which required the adoption of over 300 pieces of legislation, the EP was granted two readings of most major pieces of legislation and was able to have a significant impact on how the single market was designed (Tsebelis 1994). The Maastricht Treaty then established the co-decision procedure, extended by the Amsterdam Treaty. As a result, today the EP and the Council have equal power in most EU legislation.

Figure 23.2 illustrates the main stages in the co-decision procedure. The Commission is responsible for proposing legislation to the Parliament and Council. The Parliament then adopts an 'opinion', in the form of a series of amendments. These amendments are prepared in one of the Parliament's committees, where one of the members of the EP (the 'rapporteur'), is responsible for writing the Parliament's report on the bill and shepherding the legislation through the committee and the plenary. Once the plenary of the Parliament has adopted the report, the Council takes a 'common position' on the bill. If the texts adopted by the Council and Parliament are identical after the first readings, the legislation is adopted and becomes law. If the texts are not identical, the legislation passes back to the EP for a second reading and back to the Council for a second reading. If the two institutions still cannot agree, a Conciliation Committee is convened. If the Conciliation Committee reaches an agreement on a 'joint text', this is put to the Parliament and the Council for a final reading. This may sound complicated; however, the procedure is remarkably efficient, in that the EU adopts approximately 100 pieces of legislation a year, about 50 of which pass through the co-decision procedure. Also, about half the bills that pass

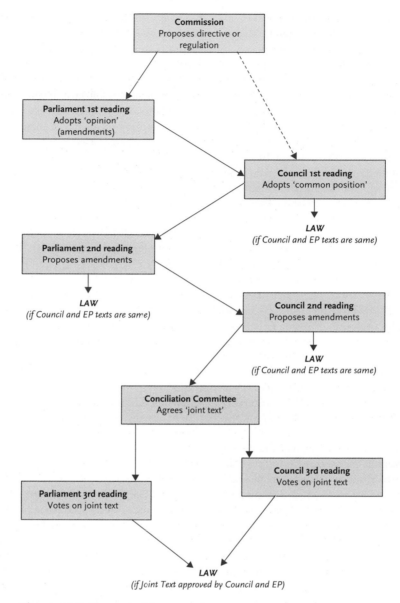

Figure 23.2 The co-decision procedure

through the co-decision procedure are adopted after just the first reading.

When voting on legislation the Council usually acts by a system of weighted voting known as qualified majority voting (QMV). Unanimous voting is kept for some highly sensitive policy issues, such as tax harmonization. (Table: Qualified-majority voting in the Council, in the Online Resource Centre, shows how the QMV system works.) In general, larger states have more votes than smaller states, which translates into a greater chance of being on the winning side in a vote—as represented by the 'power' column. The system was reformed by the Nice Treaty, where the larger member-states gave up one of their two commissioners in return for more influence under QMV in the

Council. The voting rules were then reformed again by the Lisbon Treaty, which introduced a 'double-majority' system, where to adopt a measure a qualified majority must be composed of 55 per cent of the member-states (fifteen out of the current twenty-eight) as well as 65 per cent of total EU population. As the table shows, the four largest states (particularly Germany) as well as the six smallest states, are more influential in the Council under this double-majority voting system than either of these groups of states were under the Nice Treaty voting rules.

Nevertheless, this measure of the 'power' of the member-states in the Council is only one way of understanding how the Council works. Voting rarely takes place in the Council, as there are strong incentives for the governments to decide by 'consensus' (Hayes-Renshaw and Wallace 2006). And, when votes do take place, coalitions form between the governments in the Council along geopolitical, economic, and ideological lines—for example, north vs. south, east vs. west, net contributors vs. net beneficiaries, and left governments vs. right governments (e.g. Mattila 2004).

Table 23.1 shows the number of seats per member-state in the EP. The size of the Parliament has increased tenfold since it was first established in the early 1950s, and has almost doubled in size since it was first elected in June 1979. The number of seats per member-state has also been changed with successive enlargements.

However, these numbers are misleading, in that the MEPs do not sit or vote along national lines. Ever since the first session of the Parliament in September 1952, the MEPs have formed transnational political groups, and sat in the Parliament along left-right lines. The European People's Party (EPP), which brings together all the main Christian Democratic and conservative parties, was the largest group in the 2004–9 and 2009–14 Parliaments, with the Alliance of Socialists and Democrats (S&D), which brings together all the socialist, social democratic, and labour parties, the second largest. Between these two groups is a coalition of centrist and liberal parties: the Alliance of Liberals and Democrats for Europe. There are two smaller parties who sit to the left of the socialists: a coalition of green and left-regionalist parties (the Greens/European Free Alliance), and a group of left-socialist and ex-communist parties (the European United Left/Nordic Green Left). A group of more Eurosceptic conservative parties (the European Conservatives and Reformists Group) sits just to the right of the EPP, and a group of anti-European parties (Europe of Freedom and Democracy) sits even further to the right. Finally, almost 30 'non-attached' MEPs sit on the furthest right, since most of these members come from extreme right parties.

Judicial politics: a powerful and independent court

The ECJ, together with national courts, provides a powerful check on the EU's executive and legislative institutions. The ECJ played a significant role in the development of the legal basis of the EU political system, in particular by developing *the doctrines of the direct-effect and supremacy of EU law.* On several occasions the ECJ has struck down legislation adopted by the Council and Parliament on the grounds that the treaties did not give the EU the right to adopt legislation in a particular area. Like all supreme courts, the ECJ is not completely isolated from external pressures, since it knows that if it strays too far from the meaning of the treaties, the governments can act collectively to rein in its powers. The ECJ is also aware that national courts, particularly the

German Constitutional Court, are protective of their right to interpret whether EU law is in breach of fundamental human rights as set out in national constitutions (see Chapter 9). The EU's Charter of Fundamental Rights is an attempt to provide a set of basic rights for the ECJ to apply, although until the EU Constitution is implemented the Charter is not binding.

KEY POINTS

- With multiple actors and checks and balances, the EU has a hyper-consensus system of government.

- On the positive side, the checks and balances mean that legislation cannot be adopted without overwhelming support in the Commission, amongst the governments in the Council, and the parties in the EP, and with the approval of the ECJ.

- On the negative side, the checks and balances mean that the EU is prone to 'gridlock' and lowest common denominator policy outcomes, and these problems are likely to increase with the enlargement of the EU from fifteen to twenty-eight or more states.

Democratic politics: the missing link?

Procedurally, the EU is 'democratic', in that the governments in the Council and the MEPs are elected by EU citizens, the EU's decision-making procedures are fair and transparent, and the checks and balances in the EU system ensure that policy outcomes from the EU are inevitably close to some notional EU-wide median voter (Moravcsik 2002). In a substantive sense, however, the EU does not have real 'democratic politics', meaning that there is competition between political elites for political office and in the policy process, there are identifiable winners and losers of this competition, and there is participation and identification of the public with one side or another in the political process (Føllesdal and Hix 2006).

Low public support for the EU

One of the key problems facing the EU is the relatively low and declining support for the project. Since the early 1970s, Eurobarometer polls of public attitudes towards the EU have been conducted every six months in every member-state. Public support for the EU rose in the late 1980s, with the widespread enthusiasm for the single-market project, but then declined rapidly until the mid-1990s and has remained at a relatively low level ever since. These days, only about one in two EU citizens think that their country's membership of the EU is a good thing. There is a widespread belief that the EU is an elitist

Table 23.1 Member-states' seats in the European Parliament

	September 1952	March 1957	January 1973	June 1979	January 1981	January 1986	June 1994	January 1995	May 2004	June 2004	January 2007	June 2009	December 2009	June 2014
Germany	18	36	36	81	81	81	99	99	99	99	99	99	99	96
France	18	36	36	81	81	81	87	87	87	78	78	72	74	74
Italy	18	36	36	81	81	81	87	87	87	78	78	72	73	73
Netherlands	10	14	14	25	25	25	31	31	31	27	27	25	26	26
Belgium	10	14	14	24	24	24	25	25	25	24	24	22	22	22
Luxembourg	4	6	6	6	6	6	6	6	6	6	6	6	6	6
UK			36	81	81	81	87	87	87	78	78	72	73	73
Denmark			10	16	16	16	16	16	16	14	14	13	13	13
Ireland			10	15	15	15	15	15	15	13	13	12	12	12
Greece					24	24	25	25	25	24	24	22	22	22
Spain						60	64	64	64	54	54	50	54	54
Portugal						24	25	25	25	24	24	22	22	22
Sweden								22	22	19	19	18	20	20
Austria								21	21	18	18	17	19	19
Finland								16	16	14	14	13	13	13
Poland									54	54	54	50	51	51
Czech Republic									24	24	24	22	22	22
Hungary									24	24	24	22	22	22
Slovakia									14	14	14	13	13	13
Lithuania									13	13	13	12	12	12
Latvia									9	9	9	8	9	9
Slovenia									7	7	7	7	8	8
Cyprus									6	6	6	6	6	6
Estonia									6	6	6	6	6	6
Malta									5	5	5	5	6	6
Romania											35	33	33	33
Bulgaria											18	17	18	18
Croatia														15
Total	78	142	198	410	434	518	567	626	788	732	786	736	754	766

Note: The number of seats in June 2014 assumes that there will be no new EU member-states between now and the June 2014 election.

project and European citizens no longer trust their political leaders to 'go off to Brussels' and negotiate on their behalf, as was starkly shown by the rejection of the EU Constitution in the French and Dutch referendums.

Part of the pattern in support for the EU can be explained by economics: the EU is popular when the European economy is booming and is blamed when the EU economy is performing badly. However, the economy does not tell the whole story. At an individual level, research has shown that those with higher incomes and higher levels of education (who benefit most from the single market) are more likely to support the EU than those on lower incomes and with lower levels of education (Gabel 1998). Also, political extremists tend to be more anti-EU than political centrists. However, political parties and domestic institutions can influence which people like the EU. For example, the political party a person supports, and the position that party takes towards the EU, has a strong influence of whether that person is 'pro' or 'anti' EU (Anderson 1998). Also, concerns about a 'democratic deficit' in the EU have a significant impact on attitudes towards it in countries that have strong domestic democratic institutions (Rohrschneider 2002). Nevertheless, public support for the EU has declined in all EU member-states and across all groups in society since its peak in the early 1990s.

A competitive party system in the European Parliament

Democratic politics has begun to emerge inside the EU institutions. As discussed, the policy direction of the Commission is influenced by whether it is dominated by left-wing or right-wing politics. Also, votes in the Council split along ideological as well as national-interest lines. However, it is in the EP that a genuine 'party system' has emerged. As discussed, the MEPs have always sat in transnational, rather than national, political groups. Over the last twenty years, these groups have gradually become more powerful and more competitive. For example, votes in the Parliament increasingly split along left-right lines, and the two largest groups now vote against each other as often as they vote together, which places the Liberals in the centre of the Parliament in a powerful position since they determine whether a centre-left or a centre-right majority wins in a particular vote (e.g. Hix *et al.* 2007).

The party groups in the Parliament have also become highly 'cohesive'. Figure 23.3 shows how cohesive the three main political groups were in recorded ('roll-call') votes in the first six directly elected EPs, where a score of one means that all the MEPs in a particular group voted the same way in every single vote in a parliament and a score of zero means that the MEPs in a particular group were split down the middle in every vote in a parliament. Voting along party lines was already relatively high in the first directly elected Parliament, but rose dramatically between the third and fifth Parliaments. As a comparison, the main political groups in the EP are now more cohesive in votes than the Democrats and Republicans in the US Congress, and are almost as cohesive as party factions in national parliaments in Europe.

The 'failure' of European Parliament elections

Despite the growing levels of party competition and cohesion in the EP, elections do not provide a very effective link between the citizens and the behaviour of the MEPs and the transnational political parties. This is because EP elections are less important than national parliamentary elections and so are generally regarded by political parties, the media, and the voters as 'second-order' contests (see especially van der Eijk and Franklin 1996). Because they are second-order

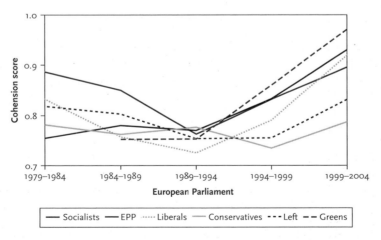

Figure 23.3 Levels of cohesion in parliamentary federations in the European Parliament

national contests, like regional or local elections, EP elections are fought by national parties and on the performance of national party leaders and national governments, rather than by European parties and on the performance of the European Commission or the political groups in the EP.

This has two significant implications:

1. Turnout in EP elections is approximately 20 per cent lower than in national parliament elections and has fallen steadily, to about 40 per cent of EU citizens in the June 2009 elections.

2. Voters use EP elections to express their views on national rather than European political issues, and so vote to punish unpopular governments or to express their views on particular issues, thus voting for smaller single-issue parties.

online resource centre

As a result, throughout the EU, governing parties tend to lose votes in EP elections, while opposition parties tend to gain votes (see Table: Governing party performance in European Parliament elections, 1979–2004, in the Online Resource Centre). For example, the UK Labour government received 21 per cent fewer votes in the 2009 EP elections than it received in the 2005 UK general election. Moreover, despite the dramatic increase in the powers of the EP over the past twenty years, the evidence suggests that EP elections have become increasingly rather than decreasingly second-order (in terms of the proportion of votes lost by governing parties across the EU in each set of European elections).

Interest groups in Brussels: an EU civil society

One aspect of democratic politics which is highly developed in the EU is interest group organization and mobilization. In terms of the number of interest groups trying to influence government and policy-making, Brussels is more like Washington, DC than any national capital in Europe (see Chapter 14). This is partly because many groups in society have stakes in how the single market is regulated, and so have an incentive to try to shape EU legislation in their preferred direction. It is also because there are multiple points of access in EU decision-making for interest groups, whereas policy-making at the national level in Europe tends to be dominated by governmental and party political elites, with only limited access for particular interest groups.

Researchers estimate that over 2,000 interest groups are represented in Brussels, and together these groups employ more than 10,000 people (e.g. Greenwood 2011). In other words, there are as many people on the outside in Brussels trying to influence the EU institutions as there are on the inside involved in drafting and negotiating EU policies. These numbers might suggest that business

interests dominate Brussels. However, this is misleading, as many groups representing 'public interests', such as the environmental lobby, the consumer lobby, and the trade unions, are part-funded directly from the EU budget and also have direct access to many governments and the party groups in the EP. As a result, the EU has a very vibrant civil society, with more or less equal access for every major group in society.

KEY POINTS

- There are growing concerns about a 'democratic deficit' in the EU, in that many citizens feel that they have little influence over the direction of EU policies.

- Public support for the EU has declined since widespread enthusiasm for the single-market programme in the late 1980s, and the EU is widely perceived as an elitist project which benefits highly educated and highly skilled citizens.

- Although EP elections do not provide an effective link between EU citizens and EU policy-making, there is growing political contestation inside the EU institutions, particularly in the EP, where the political groups compete and coalesce along left-right lines.

- There is a vibrant and representative civil society in Brussels in terms of the number and extent of interest groups involved in the EU policy process.

Conclusion

The EU was established by sovereign nation-states primarily to create and govern a Europe-wide market and to tackle the policy questions that arise at both the European and national levels from the free movement of goods, services, capital, and persons on a continental scale. As such, the EU is a remarkable and unique achievement: the only genuinely supra-national polity that is the result of voluntary choices of citizens and democratic governments. However, the EU possesses many of the features and processes of other democratic political systems. As in other multilevel polities, policy powers are divided between the European and national levels. Also, how policies are made by the EU institutions is similar to that in other political systems which have a separation of powers between the executive and the legislature and where large coalitions are required for legislation to pass. Multiple checks and balances guarantee broad consensus, but also make it difficult for policies to be changed. Nonetheless, compared with other democratic political systems, the connection between citizens' policy preferences and policy outcomes from the EU is extremely indirect. Citizens elect national governments and the EP, but in no sense do citizens have a choice about who governs them at the European level and the direction of the EU policy agenda.

Questions

1. Is the EU a political system?
2. Why is regulation the main policy instrument of the EU?
3. Why have some member-states joined the euro, but not others?
4. Who are the winners and losers from the EU budget, and why?
5. Who is the main agenda-setter in the EU—the Council or the Commission?

6. How powerful is the European Parliament?
7. Is the European Court of Justice beyond political influence?
8. Why has public support for the EU declined since the early 1990s?
9. Why do European parties vote cohesively in the European Parliament?
10. Why are European elections 'second-order national elections'?

 Further reading

Classics in European integration and EU politics

Haas, E. B. (1958) [2004] *The Uniting of Europe: Political, Social, and Economic Forces, 1950–1957* (South Bend, IN: University of Notre Dame Press).

Majone, G. (1996) *Regulating Europe* (London: Routledge).

Milward, A. S. (2000) *European Rescue of the Nation-State* (2nd edn) (London: Routledge).

Moravcsik, A. (1998) *The Choice for Europe: Social Purpose and State Power from Messina to Maastricht* (Ithaca, NY: Cornell University Press).

Pollack, M. A. (2003) *The Engines of European Integration: Delegation, Agency, and Agenda Setting in the EU* (Oxford: Oxford University Press).

Weiler, J. H. H. (1999) *The Constitution of Europe: 'Do the New Clothes have an Emperor?' and Other Essays on European Integration* (Cambridge: Cambridge University Press).

General reference books

Corbett, R., Jacobs, F., and Shackleton, M. (2007) *The European Parliament* (7th edn) (London: John Harper).

Dinan, D. (2004) *Europe Recast: A History of European Union* (Basingstoke: Palgrave).

Hix, S. and Høyland, B. (2011) *The Political System of the European Union* (3rd edn) (Basingstoke: Palgrave).

Rosamond, B. (2000) *Theories of European Integration* (Basingstoke: Palgrave).

Wallace, H., Wallace, W., and Pollack, M. A. (eds) (2010) *Policy-Making in the European Union* (6th edn) (Oxford: Oxford University Press).

Books on specific aspects of the EU system

Alter, K. J. (2001) *Establishing the Supremacy of EU Law: Making of an International Rule of Law in Europe* (Oxford: Oxford University Press).

De Grauwe, P. (2009) *Economics of Monetary Union* (8th edn) (Oxford: Oxford University Press).

van der Eijk, C. and Franklin, M. (eds) (1996) *Choosing Europe? The European Electorate and National Politics in the Face of Union* (Ann Arbor, MI: University of Michigan Press).

Franchino, F. (2007) *The Powers of the Union: Delegation in the EU* (Cambridge: Cambridge University Press).

Gabel, M. J. (1998) *Interests and Integration: Market Liberalization, Public Opinion, and European Union* (Ann Arbor, MI: University of Michigan Press).

Greenwood, J. (2011) *Interest Representation in the European Union* (3rd edn) (Basingstoke: Palgrave).

Hayes-Renshaw, F. and Wallace, H. (2006) *The Council of Ministers* (2nd edn) (Basingstoke: Palgrave).

Hix, S., Noury, A., and Roland, G. (2007) *Democratic Politics in the European Parliament* (Cambridge: Cambridge University Press).

Hooghe, L. (2001) *The European Commission and the Integration of Europe* (Cambridge: Cambridge University Press).

Hug, S. (2002) *Voices of Europe: Citizens, Referendums, and European Integration* (Atlanta, GA: Rowman & Littlefield).

Thomson, R., Stockman, F. N., Achen, C. H., and Konig, T. (eds) (2006) *The European Union Decides* (Cambridge: Cambridge University Press.

 Web links

EU institutions

http://europa.eu
Web portal of the European Union.

http://ec.europa.eu
European Commission.

www.consilium.europa.eu
Council of the European Union.

www.europarl.europa.eu
European Parliament.

www.curia.europa.eu
European Court of Justice.

www.ecb.eu
European Central Bank.

EU data, legislative tracking, and documents

http://epp.eurostat.ec.europa.eu
Statistical office of the EU (Eurostat).

http://ec.europa.eu/public_opinion/index_en.htm
Eurobarometer opinion polls.

http://eur-lex.europa.eu
Portal to EU law and the Official Journal of the EU (Eurlex).

http://www.europarl.europa.eu/oeil/home/home.do
EP's legislative observatory (Oeil).

www.votewatch.eu
Tracking the voting behaviour of the MEPs.

Research groups and datasets

www.eu-newgov.org
New modes of governance project (NewGov).

http://www2.sowi.uni-mannheim.de/lspol2/dosei/
Domestic Structures and European Integration project (DOSEI).

http://www.lse.ac.uk/government/research/resgroups/EPRG/MEPsurveyData.aspx
European Parliament Research Group (EPRG).

http://personal.lse.ac.uk/hix/HixNouryRolandEPdata.htm
Hix–Noury–Roland data set of roll-call votes in the European Parliament.

online resource centre

For additional material and resources, please visit the Online Resource Centre at:
www.oxfordtextbooks.co.uk/orc/caramani3e/

CHAPTER 24

Globalization and the nation-state

Georg Sørensen

Chapter contents

Reader's guide

Processes of globalization and other forces significantly increase connections and exchanges between nation-states at all levels: social, economic political, and cultural. As a result, states become much more dependent on their surroundings. The old distinction between a First, a Second, and a Third World is being replaced by a new typology of states: the *advanced capitalist state* is today post-modern rather than modern, and a group of *weak post-colonial states* in the South are increasingly marginalized, fragile, and unable to stand on their own feet. Between these two groups are a number of *modernizing states* in Asia, Eastern Europe, Latin America, and elsewhere. These changes are critical to the study of comparative politics. First, the state units that comparativists compare have changed significantly. Second, 'international' and 'domestic' politics are now intimately related. This calls for an approach which emphasizes both; therefore the disciplines of comparative politics and international relations need to work much more closely together or maybe even merge.

Introduction

The standard image of the sovereign **nation-state** is that of an entity within well-defined territorial borders: a national polity, a national economy, and a national community of citizens. The focus of **comparative politics** is on politics *within* countries; the focus of *international relations* is on politics *across* countries. Each discipline has developed a specific set of approaches and theories (see the Introduction to this volume). Many of these approaches and theories rest on the premise 'other things being equal' (Riggs 1994: 1); that is to say, comparative politics researchers can safely ignore what takes place outside the borders of the countries they are studying and international relations researchers can equally ignore what takes place inside countries. This in turn is predicated on the idea that domestic politics and international politics are two qualitatively different things. The former takes place in an environment where there is an ultimate locus of final authority (see Chapter 4), and the latter takes place in an environment where there is no such authority—'anarchy' is the label that international relations scholars use for that situation.

A number of questions related to comparative politics can possibly be studied without considering the international context (and vice versa for international relations), also in the future. But many of the most interesting research questions, including the core issue of the fate of the state itself, can only be studied if the relationship between 'domestic' and 'international' is given serious consideration. That is because the standard image of a sovereign nation-state does not apply any more; the national polity, the national economy, and the national community are no longer neatly separated from the outside in the way that the traditional approaches and theories would have us believe. Even **sovereignty** is changing in ways that indicate the decreasing significance of borders.

The focus in this chapter is on **globalization** and the changes in sovereign statehood that it has helped to bring about. The next section briefly introduces the debate that is taking place about the consequence for states of globalization; in that connection we must look closer at the core concepts for analysis—globalization and the sovereign state. The following three sections trace the modalities of statehood as they have developed over the last several decades.

First, the **advanced capitalist** states are transforming from modern into post-modern states. This involves changes at the levels of economics, politics, and nationhood (i.e. the transformation of community). It also involves changes in the institution of sovereignty; a new 'sovereignty game' is in the making.

Second, the *weak post-colonial* states were created out of special circumstances—the globalization of the institution of sovereignty in the context of decolonization. The core features of weak statehood will be identified below. Weak states also play a special sovereignty game which reflects their fragility; they remain highly dependent on the international community.

Third, the *modernizing states*, such as China, India, Russia, and Brazil, amalgamate features of modern, post-modern, and weak post-colonial statehood in different combinations. In economic terms, the international context is increasingly important for them, but in broader political terms their relationship to international society is more unstable. Finally, against the background of this new typology of states, the last section speculates about the pursuit of comparative politics in a new setting.

> **KEY POINTS**
>
> - Globalization has made a considerable contribution to the change in sovereign statehood.
> - The fate of the state can only be assessed if the relationship between 'domestic' and 'international' is taken into consideration.
> - As a result of state transformation due to globalization, a new typology of states is proposed: (1) post-modern, (2) weak post-colonial, and (3) modernizing states.

The debate about globalization and states

There are three major positions in the debate about globalization and states. First, there are scholars who think that states are losing power and influence as a result of globalization. There is a *retreat of the state* because 'globalization erodes the power of states' (Julius 1997: 454). Second, there are *state-centric* scholars who believe that states remain in charge of globalization and have even managed to expand their capacities for regulation and control (Hirst and Thompson 2000; Weiss 1998). At the same time, very few 'retreat' scholars would claim that the state is 'losing out' to the extent that states are withering away or becoming entirely powerless. And very few 'state-centric' scholars would maintain that states are always 'winning' and are all-powerful. (See Box 24.1.)

Therefore most scholars support some version of a third pragmatist middle position; instead of a zero-sum view of either 'winning' or 'losing', it is accepted that both can take place at the same time. As a result of globalization, states are becoming stronger in some respects and weaker in others. A process of state *transformation* is taking place and it plays out differently in different states (Held and McGrew 2002; Jessop 2002; Brenner *et al.* 2003). The 'transformationalist' position is more open than the 'retreat' and 'state-centric' views, but it is not very precise. If states are indeed changing, what exactly is going on and what are the larger implications? That is the central question in what follows.[1]

Box 24.1 'Retreat' vs. 'state-centric' scholars

Three 'retreat' scholars	Three 'state-centric' scholars
The nation-state has become an unnatural, even dysfunctional unit for organizing human activity and managing economic endeavour in a borderless world. It represents no genuine, shared community of economic interest. It defines no meaningful flows of economic activity. (Ohmae 1993: 78)	There are now sufficient grounds to suggest that globalization tendencies have been exaggerated, and that we need to employ the language of internationalization to understand better the changes taking place in the world economy. In this kind of economy, the nation-state retains its importance as a political and economic actor. (Weiss 1998: 212)
The nation-state is dead. Not because states were subsumed by super-states, but because they are breaking up into smaller, more efficient parts— just like big companies … We are moving toward a world of 1,000 countries because many people of the new tribalism want self-rule and every day they see others getting self-rule, or moving toward it. (Naisbitt 1994: 43)	[M]ost of the social, economic, and other problems ascribed to globalization are actually due to technological and other developments that have little or nothing to do with globalization. Even though its role may have diminished somewhat, the nation-state remains prominent in both domestic and international economic affairs. To borrow a phrase from the American humorist Mark Twain, I would like to report that the rumours of the death of the state 'have been greatly exaggerated'. (Gilpin 2002: 350)
[T]he domain of state authority in society and economy is shrinking … what were once domains of authority exclusive to state authority are now being shared with other loci of sources of authority. (Strange 1996: 82)	Economic actors look to states in order to gain market access and to level the playing field of international competition. (Kapstein 1994: 6) [S]tates continue to adapt to ongoing changes in the world economy … and firms continue to value their national identity … (Kapstein 1993: 503)

Globalization is a contested concept (see Box 24.2). There is general agreement about what it means in the broadest sense, namely the expansion and intensification of all kinds of social relations across borders—economic, political, cultural, and so on (Holm and Sørensen 1995: 1). Globalization is uneven in terms of cross-national intensity, geographical scope, and national and local depth. It is driven by various forces, including governments, corporations, popular groups, and many others; they help shape what globalization is and what it does. In other words, globalization is both a cause and a consequence. It is not an anonymous entity that has suddenly taken control of peoples and states. At the same time, globalization increasingly shapes the context for inter-state relations as well as for the everyday lives of ordinary citizens.

Here I want to concentrate on the consequences of globalization for salient aspects of sovereign statehood. What is a state? It is a *sovereign territorial entity with a population and a government.* For the present purposes, it is relevant to focus on four aspects of statehood.

1. All states have *political–administrative* (including military) *institutions of government*, but there are huge differences between them in terms of efficiency, capacity, and legitimacy. It cannot be taken for granted, for example, that all states enjoy a monopoly on the legitimate use of force.

2. The *economic basis of the state* comprises the ability to design, construct, produce, finance, and distribute economic goods. Some states have well-defined national economies; others do not. Weak states are highly dependent on the world market and have extremely heterogeneous economies.

3. The definition of *nationhood and identity* must be examined. Nationhood means that people within a territory make up a community. The community is based on nationality or 'sentiment' (meaning a common language and a common cultural and historical

Box 24.2 Definitions of globalization

Globalization refers to all those processes by which the peoples of the world are incorporated into a single world society, global society. (Albrow 1996)

The world is becoming a global shopping mall in which ideas and products are available everywhere at the same time. (Kanter 1995)

Globalization can be defined as the intensification of world-wide social relations which link distant localities in such a way that local happenings are shaped by events occurring many miles away and vice versa. (Giddens 1990)

identity) as well as on citizenship (including political, social, and economic rights and obligations).

4. *Sovereignty* is an institution which defines the rules that, in turn, define the locus of political authority and set the context for relations between states. We must trace the major changes in sovereignty related to processes of globalization.

KEY POINTS

- Globalization is a contested concept. In the broadest sense, it means the expansion and intensification of all kinds of social relations across borders.

- As a result of globalization, a process of state transformation is taking place. States are becoming stronger in some respects and weaker in others.

- Four aspects of statehood are in focus when discussing the transformation of the state: (1) the political–administrative institutions of government; (2) the economic basis of the state; (3) nationhood and identity; (4) the institution of sovereignty.

Advanced capitalist states

From modern to post-modern

Since the debate about globalization and state transformation has primarily concerned the advanced capitalist states, it is appropriate to begin with them. In order to be precise about how these states have been transformed, it is necessary to have an idea about how they looked in the past. It is common to focus on the Peace of Westphalia at the end of the Thirty Years War in 1648 as the birthplace of the modern sovereign state. That peace accord undermined the power of the church and strengthened secular power. The power and authority of kings was further strengthened in a context of fierce competition and violent conflict with rivals. The build-up of state power changed the relationship between the state and the people. A large group of individuals within a defined territory, subject to one supreme authority, became 'the people'. They are subjects and citizens of a particular state, and at the same time they have a shared idea of themselves as a cultural and historical entity; they are an 'imagined community' (Anderson 1991), or a nation. A modern state is a nation-state in the sense that the population shares the characteristics of **citizenship** and *nationhood*. A nation-state is not necessarily based on a homogeneous ethno-national group of people. Very few modern states are nation-states in this more narrow sense.

The modern state is based on a national economy. The state rulers helped create a national space for economic development by removing local barriers to exchange and supporting both industry and infrastructure. The modern national economy is characterized by the combined presence within its territory of the major economic sectors, i.e. means of production and distribution as well as means of consumption. What particularly defines a national economy is the fact that the most important inter- and intra-sectoral links are domestic. There is external trade, of course, but the economic structure is introvert rather than extrovert (for data on trade see Comparative table 16 at the end of this volume).

The political–administrative institutions of government were considerably strengthened in the course of major wars, in particular the world wars of the twentieth century. State intervention in the economy was pushed by a need to mitigate social tensions via redistribution and to procure the necessary means for the war effort. That had to be combined with great increases in the level of taxation (Zürn 1998; Porter 1994).

The core characteristics of the modern Westphalian state, as it had developed mainly in Western Europe and North America around 1950, are summarized in Table 24.1. This ideal type provides an image of the previous shape of the state against which later changes can be assessed.

How do these characteristics transform in the context of globalization? Let us begin with the economy. Technological changes in transport, communication, and production, together with a more liberalized world economy, mean that 'shallow integration', manifested as arm's length trade between independent firms, is being replaced by 'deep integration' where production chains (i.e. the various stages in the production of goods and services, from procurement of inputs to sales and service) are globally organized within the framework of a single transnational corporation (UNCTAD 1993: 113). As a result, trade increasingly takes place within the context of the same company or network of companies. Such intra-firm trade now accounts for roughly one-third of world trade.

The real world is probably a mixture of old and new in the terms described here, uneven across countries and economic sectors. On the one hand, a unified, homogeneous, and fully integrated global economy has not emerged. On the other hand, 'national' economies are less self-sustained than they used to be because of the processes of 'deep integration' which have been combined with more intense integration in other economic sectors, not least the financial sector (Dicken 2011).

A financial and economic crisis has engulfed the post-modern states and much of the rest of the world since 2008. It began with a burst housing bubble in the US; opaque derivative markets, labelled 'financial weapons of mass destruction' by Warren Buffett, aggravated the crisis. The financial system is deeply integrated on a global scale, but regulation and control remains almost purely national. Thus it was left to national governments to respond to the crisis with different national 'packages',

Table 24.1 Four types of state

State dimensions	Modern state	Post-modern state	Weak post-colonial state	Modernizing state
Government	A centralized system of democratic rule based on a set of administrative, policing, and military organizations, sanctioned by a legal order, claiming a monopoly of the legitimate use of force, all within a defined territory.	Multilevel governance in several interlocked arenas overlapping each other. Governance in the context of supra-national, international, transgovernmental, and transnational relations.	Inefficient and corrupt administrative and institutional structures. Rule based on coercion rather than the rule of law. Monopoly on the legitimate use of violence not established.	The modernizing states combine features of the modern, the post-modern, and the weak post-colonial state.
Nationhood	A people within a territory making up a community of citizens (with political, social, and economic rights) and a community of sentiment based on cultural and historical bonds. Nationhood involves a high level of cohesion, binding nation and state together.	Identities less exclusively national. Collective identities 'above' and 'below' the nation reinforced. Transformation of citizenship. Less coherent 'community of citizens'.	Predominance of local/ethnic community. Weak bonds of loyalty to state and low level of state legitimacy. Local community more important than national community.	Brazil, China, India, and Russia are major examples of modernizing states.
Economy	A segregated national economy, self-sustained in the sense that it comprises the main sectors needed for its reproduction. The major part of economic activity takes place at home.	National economies much less self-sustained than earlier because of 'deep integration'. Major part of economic activity embedded in cross-border networks.	Heterogeneous combination of traditional agriculture, an informal petty urban sector, and some fragments of modern industry. Strong dependence on the global economy.	Additional examples include Argentina, Mexico, and Venezuela in Latin America, as well as Indonesia, Malaysia, and Thailand in Asia.
Sovereignty	National authority in the form of constitutional independence. The state has supreme political authority within the territory. Non-intervention: right to decide without outside interference.	From non-intervention towards mutual intervention. Regulation by supra-national authority increasingly important.	Constitutional independence combined with 'negotiated intervention' (donor control of aid, supervision by international society). 'Non-reciprocity' (special treatment of weak states because they cannot reciprocate).	Each of these countries contains a unique mixture of different types of statehood.

only thinly coordinated. The crisis has not led to de-globalization; markets remain open. But there are no indications of impending institutional reform that will prevent a new crisis. The international financial institutions continue to place their confidence in perfect markets; the task is to 'restore confidence' in those markets. That might not be sufficient in the longer term; in any case, the crisis has re-emphasized the role of states in the regulation of the globalized economy.

We now turn to the political level. What has happened to national government? Economic globalization tends to increase the demand for political cooperation across borders because states are increasingly dependent on activities outside their territory. More cooperation is a way of gaining influence outside the state's jurisdiction (Zürn 1998). At the same time, political initiatives, such as the creation of the single market in the European Union (EU), or liberalizations in context of the World Trade

Organization (WTO), also significantly push economic globalization.

Several observers point to the combined growth of transnational, transgovernmental, international, and **supra-national** relations. Transnational relations are cross-border relations between individuals, groups, and organizations from civil society. Transgovernmental relations are relations between governments at different levels. External relations are no longer the prerogative of foreign ministries and heads of state. Sector ministries, regulatory agencies, officials responsible for corporate supervision, and so on are connected with their counterparts in other countries (Slaughter 1997). The growth of conventional inter-state relations is evidenced in the growth of International Governmental Organizations (IGOs) from 123 in 1951 to 260 by the mid-1990s (Table 24.2). The most far-reaching form of political cooperation across borders is supra-national **governance**. Governance, in contrast with government, refers to activities everywhere (local, national, regional, global) involving regulation and control. Supra-national refers to the fact that some institutions, such as the EU, have the powers to write the rules for member-states in some areas. For example, rulings by the European Court of Justice take priority over rulings by national courts.

The EU, then, is the clearest example of what could be called multilevel governance (see Chapter 23), i.e. a situation where political power is diffused and decentralized. Instead of a purely national political regulation, a complex network of supra-national, national, and sub-national regulation has developed. The EU is in a class by itself in terms of the intensity and extensity of regional cooperation among member-states. Other regional initiatives are primarily based on conventional forms of inter-state cooperation. At the global level, supra-national elements can be found in some places—for example, the dispute settlement system in the WTO (see Box 24.3) or in the International Criminal Court (jurisdiction over persons for the most serious crimes of international concern)—but the bulk of global governance continues to be of a more conventional kind.

Table 24.2 Number of international governmental organizations (IGOs) and international non-governmental organizations (INGOs)

Year	IGOs	INGOs
1909	37	176
1951	123	832
2006	246	7,306

Source: Zacher (1992: 65); Held *et al.* (1999: 53); Union of International Associations. (http://www.uia.org/statistics/organizations/types-2004.pdf (accessed 11 March 2010).

Box 24.3 Settlement system of the WTO

By reinforcing the rule of law, the dispute settlement system makes the trading system more secure and predictable. Where non-compliance with a WTO agreement has been alleged by a WTO member, the dispute settlement system provides for a relatively rapid resolution of the matter through an independent ruling that must be implemented promptly, or the non-implementing member will face trade sanctions.

Source: http://www.wto.org/

In any case, there appears to be a general trend away from national government within a defined territory towards multilevel governance in several interlocked arenas overlapping each other. Some of that governance reflects a more intense conventional cooperation between independent states. Some of it reflects a more profound transformation towards supra-national governance in a context of highly interconnected societies. There are also sceptical voices who want to preserve national autonomy, as can be seen currently (2013) among Conservatives in the UK.

National identity

As regards nationhood and identity, the modern state is based on two kinds of community: (1) a *community of citizenship* concerning the relations between citizens and the state, including political, social, and economic rights and obligations; (2) a *community of sentiment*, based on a common language and a common cultural and historical identity.

What happens to these two types of communities in the context of globalization? The community of citizens transforms in the sense that civil and other rights are no longer being granted solely by the sovereign state. At the global level, a set of universal human rights has been defined. In some regional contexts, common rights for citizens of different countries have emerged. The EU has established a common citizenship which grants a number of rights to EU citizens in all member-states (Soysal 1994: 148). The process is not confined to Europe. According to one scholar, the increasing adherence to universal human rights means that national citizenship is in the process of being replaced by 'post-national membership' based on these universal rights. This indicates a transformation of citizenship 'from a more particularistic one based on nationhood to a more universalistic one based on personhood' (Soysal 1994: 137). It goes together with a much increased forging of transnational links among people that practice 'citizenship without moorings' (Rosenau 1993: 282) in order to address issues of common concern (e.g. environment, equality, or security problems).

In sum, there is no breakdown of national citizenship, but there are different forces at work to transform the coherent community of citizens as it existed in context of the modern state.

What about the community of sentiment—the cultural and emotional attachment to the nation? According to Anthony Giddens (1990), the creation of identity is increasingly becoming an individual project. Religious and other beliefs, for example, are not simply taken over from previous generations. Rather, they are reflected upon, evaluated, and then actively accepted or rejected. When identity is something that has to be actively created and sustained by individuals, the result may be less commitment to the national community of sentiment. At the same time, new collective identities 'above' the nation could be in the process of emerging. One analysis speaks of a 'Western civic identity' that is an 'essential component of the Western political order'; at its core is a 'consensus around a set of norms and principles, most importantly political democracy, constitutional government, individual rights, private property-based economic systems, and toleration of diversity' (Deudney and Ikenberry 1999: 193).

It is indicated in this analysis that the emergence of a Western civic identity is concentrated among the elite groups of Western societies because they are the ones who have engaged in circulation and educational exchange. Possibly the creation of self-identities analysed by Giddens, taking place in sophisticated processes of reflexive endeavour, is also primarily an elite phenomenon. If so, what happens with collective identities among those for whom economic globalization is more of a threat than an opportunity? According to Manuel Castells, such groups frequently develop a 'resistance identity' (Castells 1998: 60). They might be nationalistic groups turning against immigration and seeking to emphasize a narrow understanding of national identity, such as the Front National in France or the Alleanza Nazionale in Italy. They might also be regional community organizations, or religious or ethnic movements (see also Chapter 13 on neopopulist parties).

In sum, globalization would appear to reinforce collective identities both 'above' and 'below' the nation. Identities are less exclusively national, and the emergence of a Western civic identity is an indicator of that. However, more defensive 'resistance identities' are also gaining importance, among them nationalistic and local identities.

Sovereignty

Finally, there is the issue of sovereignty. The juridical core of sovereignty is constitutional independence. The sovereign state stands apart from all other sovereign entities. There is no final political authority outside or above the state (James 1999: 461). Even in the face of globalization, the international system continues to be organized in this

manner: it consists of sovereign states that have final political authority within their territory.

However, this does not mean that the institution of sovereignty has remained completely unchanged (Sørensen 2001). Sovereignty can be seen as a special kind of game played by states that have it. Constitutional independence defines what the game is all about (i.e. political authority and its appropriate distribution among the players). The rules regulating the game stipulate how the players should behave towards each other in various situations. There are many such rules (Jackson 1990: 35), the most important one being *non-intervention*, i.e. the right for states to choose their own path and to conduct their affairs without outside interference. The rule of non-intervention has been changed, or at least strongly modified, because of the more intense political cooperation across borders that globalization has stimulated.

The EU is a good example in this respect. Instead of non-intervention, the EU member-states undertake comprehensive intervention in each other's affairs. During the past decade, institutions at the European level have gained considerable influence over areas that were traditionally thought to be prerogatives of national politics: currency, social policies, border controls, law and order. A key player in this development is the European Court of Justice which has helped push supra-national governance by establishing the supremacy of European law in several important areas (Caldeira *et al.* 1995).

This does not mean that we approach the 'twilight of sovereignty' (Wriston 1992) as some 'retreat' scholars have implied. States can withdraw from this kind of cooperation if they want to—they do retain constitutional independence. But because of the demand for more cooperation spurred by globalization, it is unlikely that they would wish to do so.

Having gone through changes in salient aspects of changes of sovereign statehood among the advanced capitalist states, we can summarize the results and compare them with the characteristic features of modern statehood as they were presented above. The modern state was first and foremost a national entity, with national government, national community, national economy, and national sovereignty. The emerging entity is less 'national' on all counts. At the same time, it is not certain where the processes of change will eventually lead. Together with several others, I prefer to speak of 'post-modern' states (Holm and Sørensen 1995: 187) in order to indicate these processes of transformation. The 'post-' terminology indicates that the traditional picture of the modern state needs revision, but we remain unsure about what exactly is taking its place.

Some state-centric scholars will argue that the image of the post-modern state is merely applicable to the members of the EU. It is a regional phenomenon not very relevant for larger advanced states outside Europe, such as the US and Japan (Waltz 1999). The counter-argument is that these latter states are deeply involved in economic and other processes of globalization (*Foreign Policy*/Kearney 2006) and that even super-powers cannot 'go it alone' (Nye 2002) in an increasingly integrated world. These views reflect the ongoing debate about globalization and state transformation.

Weak post-colonial states

The lack of 'stateness'

The debate between 'state-centric' and 'retreat' scholars about the consequences of globalization for sovereign states is focused on the advanced states in Western Europe, North America, and Japan. As discussed in the previous section, that debate concentrates on the extent to which there has been a transformation away from the traditional modern state towards a type of state that is less 'national' in basic respects. This is not a relevant debate for weak post-colonial states in the Third World. They were never 'modern states' in the first place and they are not on the way to becoming 'post-modern'. The weak states display a different trajectory of state formation. Since most of these states are in Sub-Saharan Africa, I shall focus on that region. But the ideal type of the weak state defined here is relevant for other areas as well.

Before colonization, these areas were not states with distinct territories. They were tribal and other communities with no clearly defined jurisdictions. Therefore borders were created from the outside and the surprisingly straight lines on the map were drawn by the colonizers. The colonial powers took no particular interest in the political and economic development of the areas they took into possession. They were more interested in maximizing profits, so the focus was on the extraction and export of natural resources, combined with an effort to curtail the cost of controlling the colonies. In some places, colonial rule involved building some infrastructure, together with some political as well as social and economic institutions; in the worst cases, such as the Belgian King Leopold's rule in Congo, the colonizers left nothing in terms of development.

After the Second World War, the prevailing view on colonies changed dramatically. Before the war, colonial rule was considered legitimate and even necessary, given the backward condition of the colonized areas. After the war, colonialism came to be considered fundamentally wrong, even 'a crime' (UN General Assembly Resolution 3103, quoted in Jackson 1990: 107). That normative change led to decolonization, which in turn meant the globalization of the institution of sovereignty. For the first time, sovereign statehood became the only form of political authority worldwide.

The modern states introduced in the previous section were, in a manner of speaking, *created from the inside*. The struggle between various state-seeking groups ended with victory for one group or coalition of groups that went on to achieve—in Max Weber's expression—a monopoly of the legitimate use of force within a defined territory. At the same time, states were constantly at each other's throats. War between states was an important aspect of state-building, as emphasized in Charles Tilly's well-known phrase: 'states make wars and wars make states' (Tilly 1990: 20–8; see also Chapter 4). An important ingredient in war was the conquest of enemy territory: the stronger swallowed the weaker.

Fundamentally, this kind of competition was a basic driving force in European state-making and development. The preparation for war forced power-holders into a series of compromises with their subject populations which constrained their power and paved the way for rights of citizenship. Citizenship, in turn, meant material benefits for the population. Combined with the creation of domestic order and the promotion of capital accumulation, these processes furthered the building of bonds of loyalty and legitimacy between kings and people.

In contrast, in the case of weak states in the Third World, decolonization gave independence (i.e. recognition as a sovereign state) to entities which had very little in terms of substantial statehood (Jackson 1990). In that sense these states were *created from the outside* when the international society rejected colonialism. Power-holders in weak states faced no serious external threat. Both states and regimes were protected from outside threat by the strong international norms created in the context of decolonization and strengthened during the Cold War.

Recolonization, annexation, or any other format of strong states in the North taking over weak states in the South is not on the agenda. For most post-colonial leaders, the situation at independence was one of no severe external threats against the state and the regime, combined with few domestic institutional constraints. It was under those circumstances that a large number of leaders chose the path that led to the formation of weak states. Why?

After the successful anti-colonial struggle, there was little left to create unity. It was a huge task to bring together diverse ethnic groups with different languages and traditions. The state elites quickly gave up trying. At the same time, institutional structures were generally weak, lacking capacity, competence, and resources. In this context, a system of 'personal rule' emerged (Jackson and Rosberg 1982) where key positions in the state apparatus are manned by loyal followers of the leader. State elites do not primarily seek to provide public or collective goods. The state apparatus is rather a source of income for those clever enough to control it. The spoils of office are shared by a group of followers making up a network of patron–client relationships.

Lack of 'nationness'

Ethnic identities connected to tribal, religious, and similar characteristics continue to dominate over the national identity in weak states. Because the state does not deliver on political, social, and legal rights, it creates no bonds of loyalty leading to state legitimacy. When the ethnic community becomes the primary focus for the satisfaction of people's needs, loyalties are projected in that direction, and ethnic identities are reinforced; the national 'community of citizens' fails to develop. Similarly, the national 'community of sentiment' is in trouble because local (ethnic, tribal, religious) communities are primary. They provide sources of identification via rituals and myths. Patron–client relationships serve to reinforce ethnic loyalties (Ndegwa 1997: 602).

The weakness of the economy

The economy in weak post-colonial states is a heterogeneous amalgamation of traditional agriculture, an informal petty urban sector, and some elements of modern industry, frequently controlled by external interests. In both urban and rural areas large parts of the population are outside the formal sectors, living in localized subsistence economies. Exports consist of few primary products, and the economies are strongly dependent on imports of manufactured and technology-intensive products.

Weak states are not attractive sites for foreign investment. There is no dynamic domestic market, no adequate supply of skilled or semi-skilled labour, and no developed physical infrastructure, and they do not offer stable market-friendly conditions of operation. A little more than 2 per cent of total foreign direct investment (FDI) goes to Sub-Saharan Africa (World Bank 2006). In other words, the circuits of global capital—often thought to be the spearheads of globalization—do not include the weak states in any major way. In that sense, they are marginalized bystanders in the process of economic globalization. At the same time, they remain strongly dependent on the global economy. On the one hand, export earnings from primary products are of great importance for the economies. On the other hand, economic aid makes up an increasing share of the means they have at their disposal. Official development assistance (ODA) increased from 12 to 18.6 per cent of GDP in Sub-Saharan Africa between 1990 and 2003 (UNDP 2005). In some countries, more than half the state budget is financed by ODA.

The weakness of sovereignty

Weak states have formal sovereignty, understood as constitutional independence granted in the context of decolonization. Formal sovereignty is of great importance for weak states because sovereignty offers access to international institutions, including the UN system where states are legally equal (e.g. every country has one vote in the General Assembly). It also provides access to economic, military, and other forms of aid. In formal terms, sovereignty leaves supreme legitimate power in domestic affairs to the government. Therefore rulers of weak states seek to emphasize and confirm the principles and rules of sovereignty (Ayoob 1995: 3). This emphasis amounts to a demand to be treated as *equals* in the international society of states—to have their sovereignty respected and count on par with every other country in the international system—irrespective of the fact that these states are terribly weak and able to do very little on their own.

But rulers of weak states also seek to be considered *unequal* as they are at the losing end of the international system. To compensate for that situation, weak states demand special treatment in terms of economic aid, market access, compensation for natural resources and colonialism, and so on, i.e. weak states want to be allowed to receive extra resources from the developed world. The demand is that economic aid, for example, should be a clear international obligation for the developed countries and not something that the weak states have to respectfully apply for.

So even if weak states have sovereignty in the form of constitutional independence, they cannot play the classical game of sovereignty based on non-intervention. Aid flows mean that donors will want to make sure that the resources they provide are used according to plan. This creates a pressure in the direction of 'negotiated intervention' for that kind of supervision to take place. Weak states can refuse, of course, but that might cut them off from significant funding. The most obvious cases of external intervention are the 'humanitarian interventions' in 'failed states' such as Somalia, Liberia, Rwanda, or Sierra Leone. International society steps in primarily for humanitarian reasons when domestic conflict has got out of hand.

There is another respect in which the fragility of weak states influences their sovereignty game. The classical sovereignty game is based on reciprocity: states are equals and deal with each other on an equal *quid pro quo* basis. Weak states cannot do that because they are not in a position to reciprocate. They want something (e.g. economic aid) but are unable to give anything in return. Sovereignty is built on the assumption that states that have it *can basically take care of themselves.* Weak states fail to meet that requirement; they cannot play a game of self-help. They play a different game of 'non-reciprocity' and 'negotiated intervention', and that is a source of tension in the international society of states.

It is the combined presence of the elements summarized in Table 24.1 that amounts to a 'lack of stateness'. Even if the ideal type is inspired mainly by the weak states in Sub-Saharan Africa, lack of stateness is also a problem elsewhere—for example, in such countries as Afghanistan, Colombia, Burma, Haiti, Nepal, Kyrgyzstan, Uzbekistan, and Yemen.

The larger question is whether weak states are also developing countries, i.e. are they really on the road to development? The idea that every country can achieve development is an ideology created in context of decolonization. We only have to go back to the 1930s to find an entirely different ideology, which was especially dominant in the colonial motherlands. On that view, only some, maybe even rather few, colonies would ever be able to stand on their own feet and thus achieve development. Most peoples in the colonies were seen to require 'an indefinite period of European tutelage' and some were likely to 'remain wards of the states-system for centuries, if not forever' (Jackson 1990: 73). That outlook was sustained by a Western belief in its own superiority which was rejected with decolonization. But the adoption of a new outlook does not alter the empirical conditions for development which continue to be almost absent in the weakest states. These conditions are behind the processes of state breakdown or the emergence of 'failed states', a notion indicating the breakdown of states in various ways (Brock *et al.* 2011).

Modernizing states

Between post-colonialism and post-modernism

The previous sections argue that in the current international system there are two radically different modalities of sovereign statehood. On the one hand, the advanced capitalist states are transforming from modern to post-modern. On the other hand, the weak post-colonial states display a particular set of features that amount to a lack of 'stateness'. Between these ends of the spectrum is a large group of states that will be called 'modernizing' states. They combine features of the three ideal types of state presented so far: the modern, the post-modern, and the weak post-colonial state. The term 'modernizing' is meant to indicate that such states are in a general process of transition. It is not meant to indicate that they will certainly discard every aspect of weak statehood, and graduate to modern and then to post-modern. No such teleology is implied, as transitions can move in different directions and change may not mean change for the better.

Brazil, China, India, and Russia are major examples of modernizing states; additional examples include Argentina, Mexico, and Venezuela in Latin America, as well as Indonesia, Malaysia, and Thailand in Asia, and also South Africa. Each of them contains a unique mixture of different types of statehood. Many parts of India, for example, display the economic characteristics of weak statehood (i.e. a heterogeneous combination of traditional agriculture, an informal petty urban sector, and some fragments of modern industry), but the country also has larger elements of a modern industrial structure. It even has advanced economic sectors that are now seeking active integration in cross-border networks via direct investment and much more involvement in economic globalization. A similar mixture can be found in China, but this country is already a highly active participant in economic globalization. Russia may have modernized even more, but its relationship to the global economy remains more like that of a member of the Organization of Petroleum Exporting Countries (OPEC), in that it exports energy and raw materials and imports more sophisticated products.

The mixture of state types also applies to the political level. Massive corruption and weak state structures remain a serious problem in all four states, but in other areas there is a higher degree of effective national government. The countries are all seeking closer integration into the global economy and also to some extent into the international organizations and networks of multilevel governance. The question then is what the consequences will be of this economic and political globalization for their trajectories of development.

New global competitors: India and China

Compared with the weak states discussed earlier, modernizing states are better positioned to benefit from economic globalization. They possess companies of their own that are able to participate in strategic alliances and economic networks, and that increases their prospects for gaining from economic globalization in terms of technology transfers, market access, product upgrading, and competence development. The host states possess sufficient regulatory capacity for establishing the necessary frameworks concerning relations to foreign operators.

The liberalizing measures that have widely opened the doors to comprehensive participation in economic globalization have certainly boosted economic growth in both India and China. India began liberalization in 1991. India's opening up to globalization represents a crucial breakthrough for its development (Singh and Srinivasan 2003). Yet serious problems remain. There have not been significantly positive effects on employment because the traditional sectors are being squeezed while the modern sector provides only a limited increase in the workforce. With 41.6 per cent of the population living on less than $1.25 a day (UNDP 2011), poverty continues to be widespread.

China began liberalizing much earlier and has been able to attract a much higher level of foreign investment. Economic growth has averaged more than 9 per cent annually over the last twenty-five years, an unparalleled achievement; and the number of extreme poor (less than $1.25 a day) has dropped to 15.9 percent of the population (UNDP 2011). But even in China, economic globalization is a mixed blessing. Inequality has risen sharply: 'by 2005, the top 10 percent earned 45 percent of the income, while the bottom 10 percent earned only 1.4 percent' (Wen 2005: 2). The Gini ratio rose from 0.20 in 1980 to 0.45 in 2005 (see Comparative tables 5 and 6 at the end of this volume).

Another aspect of globalization in both China and India are sweatshop factories with poor working conditions, low job security, low wages, and long hours of work. In the Pearl River and Yangtze River delta regions in China, for example, 'migrant workers routinely work 12 hours a day, 7 days a week; during the busy season, a 13- to 15-hour day is not uncommon' (Wen 2005: 3). In other words, even in relatively successful modernizing states, a significant part of their participation in economic globalization has nothing to do with upgrading and sophisticated production. It might better be called 'downgrading', with deteriorating conditions for labour. Some will argue that there is improvement in the sense that previously unproductive work in stagnant and inefficient public enterprises is being replaced by more productive work in a competitive world market, but from the point of view of the labour force it is hardly a great leap forward.

Economic globalization in China has led to serious environmental problems because rapid economic growth has taken place with little or no attention to the environment. Some 60 per cent of China's major rivers are classified as being 'unsuitable for human contact'. China's Deputy Minister of the Environment recently stated that 'cities are growing, but desert areas are expanding at the same time; habitable and usable land has been halved over the past 50 years' (Wen 2005: 10). Seven of the ten most polluted cities in the world are in China. More than one-third of industrial wastewater enters waterways without any treatment.

The economic changes in China have pushed some political change. For example, private entrepreneurs, i.e. 'capitalists', have been allowed to become members of the Communist Party since 2002. There is less direct party control of people's daily lives. But independent trade unions are still not permitted, and freedom of assembly and association is highly restricted. The judiciary is not independent; it is controlled by the party. Human rights abuse remains widespread (Freedom House 2012). This might help explain why a strong increase in social unrest is combined with a new popularity of Maoism, especially in the poorest sections of society.

The international community, meanwhile, demands in principle that China should pay more respect to civil and political rights in order to become a fully legitimate member of international society. But because of China's economic importance, such demands are formulated in a low voice and are not backed by strong political or economic pressure. In sum, even if modernizing states are able to benefit from globalization, the process of participating in it is no panacea. It does not open a smooth course to economic and political change. Involvement in globalization increases several tensions in the process of development that present new challenges to both the modernizing states and the international community.

> **KEY POINTS**
>
> - Modernizing states combine features of the three ideal types of state: the modern, the post-modern, and the weak post-colonial state.
>
> - The term 'modernizing' is meant to indicate that such states are in a general process of transition; transitions can move in different directions and change may not mean change for the better.
>
> - Brazil, China, India, and Russia are examples of modernizing states.
>
> - Modernizing states are in a better position than weak states to benefit from participation in globalization. But such participation is not a cure-all; it can also increase tensions in their process of development.

Comparative politics in a new setting

Methodological implications

The discipline of comparative politics is built on the idea that 'comparison is the methodological core of the scientific study of politics' (Almond *et al.* 2004: 31). Political systems exist within the framework of sovereign states; for this reason comparison is understood to be comparison between countries (i.e. sovereign states). The principle that comparative politics compares countries is so entrenched that major introductions to the discipline (e.g. Almond *et al.* 2004; Landman 2003) do not find it necessary to explain why that is the case—it is considered self-evident. Similarly, a dominant view in the discipline of international relations is that the international system is a system of sovereign states—they are the basic components of the international system (e.g. Waltz 1999).

Both disciplines have a point. As Chapter 4 shows, almost every individual on earth is the citizen or subject of a state. Whether or not people are provided with basic social values—security, wealth, welfare, freedom, order, justice— strongly depends on the ability of the state to ensure them. Furthermore, states have not withered away because of globalization and other forces. They continue to be overwhelmingly important for the lives of people. It is not attractive to live in a very weak or 'failed' state; it can even be mortally dangerous. Therefore states continue to be extremely significant for any kind of political or social analysis.

At the same time, states are constantly in a process of change. Therefore it is always relevant to ask questions about the current major modalities of statehood, not least because such modalities help explain how and why states are able or unable to provide basic social values. During the Cold War, the prevalent distinction was between the advanced capitalist states in the First World, the communist states in the Second World, and the remaining states in the Third World. With the collapse of most communist states, some use a distinction between the rich countries of the North and the poor countries of the South. This is not a very precise categorization. This chapter has suggested a different one: (1) the advanced capitalist states are in a process of transition from modern to post-modern statehood; (2) the weak post-colonial states display a serious lack of 'stateness'—and they are by no means on a secure path to the development of more substance; (3) the modernizing states are different combinations of these three ideal types. Of course, even this categorization can be further refined.

The typology suggested here is not meant to replace any other possible distinction. It will remain relevant— depending on the research question—to differentiate between large and small states, nation-states and non-nation-states, old and new states, states from various regions and sub-regions, and so on. However, the modalities put forward here help to explain how sovereign states have transformed in the context of globalization. It has also been emphasized that 'globalization' is itself a complex entity that must be explained; it is not an anonymous force that throws states around at will. To the extent that 'globalization' applies pressures on single states, that pressure often originates in actions undertaken by other states, as demonstrated by several examples given in this chapter.

Thus the first recommendation to comparativists is to be aware of the larger context in which political, economic, and other processes play out. This is not a very dramatic proposition as awareness of context is nothing new in comparative politics. The second recommendation goes further: it is to accept that 'international' and 'domestic' are intimately connected and this requires that both elements are taken into the analysis of the development and change of sovereign statehood. The proposition can be translated into two practical guidelines for future study.

1. Proceed on the assumption that the core values pursued by states, i.e. security, wealth, welfare, freedom, order, and justice, each contain 'domestic' as well as 'international' aspects. None of these values can be reduced to a purely 'domestic' or a purely 'international' issue.

2. Therefore avoid purely 'systemic' or purely 'domestic' analysis. Put the international–domestic interplay at the centre of inquiry and ask questions about 'outside–in' and 'inside–out' relationships.

Conclusion

Let us focus on contemporary problems of democracy; that will demonstrate the need to include 'domestic' as well as 'international' aspects in the analysis. Historically, democratic rule has always developed within the context of independent states. But the emergence of multilevel governance raises the question of whether and how that new context can be democratic. According to one view, 'the only forum within which genuine democracy occurs is within national boundaries' (Kymlicka 1999: 124). The reasoning is that outside that context there is no obvious *demos*, no well-defined political or moral community. An opposing view argues that such a community can be created, just as it had to be created within national boundaries in the early phases of sovereign statehood (Habermas 1999). In any case, the emergence of multilevel governance means that the previously well-defined national context for democracy is being replaced by a new context that integrates 'domestic' and 'international' elements in a different kind of polity.

Some optimistic liberal scholars argue that democratic problems in this new setting can be relatively easily confronted by designing international institutions in such a way as to 'preserve as much space as possible for domestic political processes to operate' (Nye 2001: 3). For those who more strongly emphasize the changes invoked by globalization, however, a whole new structure of cosmopolitan democracy must be created, based on an ensemble of organizations at different levels, bound by a common framework of cosmopolitan democratic law with a charter of rights and obligations (Held 1995).

In weak states, institutions at the national level are fragile and ineffective. They are controlled by state elites who do not primarily seek to provide public or collective goods. At the global level, international institutions and stronger states increasingly attempt to constrain, influence, and direct policy measures in weak states. Their ticket to influence is the high level of external dependence, economically and otherwise, of weak states. Again, political developments including attempts at democratization are decided in an interplay between 'domestic' and 'international' elements.

The economic basis of sovereign statehood has also been transformed. In the modern state, there was a segregated national economy, self-sustained in the sense that it comprises the main sectors needed for its reproduction. The major part of economic activity took place at home. In the post-modern state, national economies are much less self-sustained than previously because of 'deep integration' and major parts of economic activity are embedded in cross-border networks. In other words, the economic basis of the post-modern state contains a 'domestic' as well as an 'international' component. That creates a new setting for the provision of wealth and welfare—a key feature of mass democracy (see Chapter 21). When 'national' economies are integrated to an extent where opting out of the world market is no longer a viable option, there must be substantially higher vulnerability. Such vulnerability has been a permanent characteristic of weak post-colonial states, because they were always highly dependent on the global economy.

The changes discussed here are reflected in the transformation of the institution of sovereignty. In the context of the modern state, sovereignty is closely connected with the 'golden rule' of non-intervention (Jackson 1990). But multilevel governance is quite the opposite of non-intervention; it is systematic *intervention* in national affairs by supra-national and international institutions. It means something else to be sovereign under conditions of multilevel governance than it did under traditional conditions of national government. In weak states, sovereignty has changed as well. Traditionally, sovereignty means international legal equality: equal rights and duties of member-states in the international system. But weak states are highly *unequal* so they need help from the developed world. A number of weak states are unable to take care of themselves, but sovereignty, which they have, assumes that they can. They possess sovereignty without being able to meet its requirements. That is what lies behind new practices of 'humanitarian intervention' and trusteeship. In short, the institution of sovereignty changes to make room for a situation where 'domestic' and 'international' affairs can no longer be easily separated.

In conclusion, the sovereign state is alive and doing well. By no means has it been obliterated by forces of globalization. But it has been transformed in ways which closely connect 'domestic' and 'international'. That insight must be taken on board when conducting comparative analysis of political systems.

KEY POINTS

- States continue to be extremely significant for any kind of political or social analysis. But states are constantly in a process of change. It is necessary to ask questions about the current modalities of statehood, not least because such modalities help explain how and why states are able or unable to provide basic social values.

- Changes in statehood places the discipline of comparative politics in a new setting. In particular, it is necessary to accept that 'international' and 'domestic' are intimately connected.

- The core values pursued by states, i.e. security, wealth, welfare, freedom, democracy, order, and justice, each contain 'domestic' as well as 'international' aspects. That insight must be taken on board when conducting comparative analysis of political systems.

 Questions

1. Set out the standard image of the modern state. Does that image apply to your own country?

2. What is globalization? Why is there such an intense debate about globalization and its consequences?

3. What are the major aspects of statehood that are relevant in a debate about globalization and states?

4. Describe the changes involved in the transformation from modern to post-modern statehood. Identify three states that you would consider post-modern.

5. Are identities changing so that we are increasingly becoming citizens of the world rather than nationals belonging to our countries?

6. Identify the characteristics of weak post-colonial statehood. Where can we find such states?

7. Are weak post-colonial states on the road to development or are they on the road to further breakdown and 'state failure'? Discuss examples.

8. Will modernizing states gain from participating in economic globalization or will it further aggravate their problems? Discuss the case of China.

9. Can multilevel governance be democratic? Why or why not?

10. Will the process of state transformation lead to a more peaceful and prosperous world?

Further reading

Dicken, P. (2011) *Global Shift: Mapping the Changing Contours of the World Economy* (New York: Guilford Press). Provides a detailed introduction to all major aspects of economic globalization.

Held, D. and McGrew, A. (2007) *Globalization/ Anti-Globalization* (Cambridge: Polity). Presents the pro- and anti-views in the debate on globalization and state transformation.

Brock, L., Holm, H.-H., Sørensen, G., and Stohl, M. (2011). *Fragile States. Violence and the Failure of Intervention* (Cambridge: Polity Press). Defines fragiles states, examines their characteristics, and explains their development from pre-colonial times to the present day.

Scholte, J. A. (2005) *Globalization: A Critical Introduction* (2nd edn) (Basingstoke: Palgrave Macmillan). Presents a sociological overview of all major dimensions of globalization.

Sørensen, G. (2001) *Changes in Statehood: The Transformation of International Relations* (Basingstoke: Palgrave Macmillan). Explains the dynamics of state transformation and the emergence of post-modern and weak post-colonial states.

Weiss, L. (1998) *The Myth of the Powerless State* (Ithaca, NY: Cornell University Press). Argues that states remain strong and able to regulate the development of economic globalization.

Web links

http://www.globalpolicy.org/
A comprehensive collection of links on sovereignty, provided by Global Policy Forum.

http://europa.eu/index_en.htm
The official website of the European Union.

http://plato.stanford.edu/entries/nationalism/
Provides a thorough introduction to nationalism. The site is maintained by Stanford University.

Websites with data on globalization

www.worldbank.org/data
Extensive website of World Bank 'Data and Statistics' including World Development Indicators. The 'Data by Country' and 'Data by Topic' pages also have good links to other sources of data. See also the 'World Ban Group Inequality Around the World' data page, and the 'Research Datasets'.

http://www.developmentgateway.org/
Development Gateway provides an extensive set of links, possibly all one could ever want.

www.wto.org/
World Trade Organization 'Trade Statistics'.

www.undp.org/poverty/
UNDP's 'World Income Inequality'.

http://utip.gov.utexas.edu/
University of Texas Inequality Project (UTIP) with Galbraith's data sets on inequality based on industrial pay rates.

http://www.childinfo.org/
Website of UNICEF Progress for Children. Includes child survival and health, water and sanitation, education, and maternal health.

http://unctad.org/en/Pages/Statistics.aspx
UNCTAD 'Statistics Overview' with price, trade, and trade barrier data available through their statistical databases.

www.fao.org/waicent/portal/statistics_en.asp
Food and Agriculture Organization (FAO) 'Statistics' with data on agriculture, fisheries, and nutrition.

http://papers.nber.org/papersbyprog/ITI_archive.html
National Bureau of Economic Research ('International Trade and Investment Archive').

www.gtap.agecon.purdue.edu/default.asp
Global Trade Analysis Project Purdue. The GTAP produces a publicly available and regularly updated data set and CGE model tailored for the analysis of trade policy changes.

www.cid.harvard.edu/cidtrade/index.html
Global Trade Negotiations homepage at the Center for International Development, Harvard University.

www.princeton.edu/~deaton/
Angus Deaton's homepage on 'Poverty in the World and in India'.

www.iie.com/research/globalization.htm
The globalization page of the Institute for International Economics.

For additional material and resources, please visit the Online Resource Centre at:
online resource centre **www.oxfordtextbooks.co.uk/orc/caramani3e/**

CHAPTER 25

Supporting democracy

Peter Burnell

Chapter contents

Reader's guide

Of all the issues in comparative and international politics, few are more controversial than those surrounding efforts to spread democracy. The subject lies at the juncture between the study of politics and the worlds of public policy and actors promoting democracy. This chapter explains what 'supporting democracy' means and the controversies around it. It compares policy drivers, institutions, actors, and methods of promotion. The record of supporting democracy is noted, notwithstanding the difficulties of making evaluations. The chapter charts the backlash in the last decade followed by the reinvigoration that the 'Arab revolution' might bring. It concludes by dwelling on whether democracy support is now fit for purpose in a world where the economic performance of established democracies is faltering and the international presence of China and Russia looks set to grow.

Introduction: comparing definitions

The increasing number of democracies in the world is a distinctive feature of recent decades, although from around 2005 progress seemed to stop. These developments have not come about entirely by chance. From the late 1980s onwards democratic change has been supported to a degree and in ways that have no historical precedent (see Box 25.1). The term 'support for democracy' is gradually coming to replace what used to be known as, and sometimes still is called, democracy promotion. The confusing association of democracy promotion with the forcible removal by the US of regimes, most notably that of Saddam Hussein in Iraq, bears partial responsibility. The switch also reflects changed thinking, such as recognition of the limits to what can be achieved by international agency and the primacy of internal drivers and long-term determinants of political change.

Basic vocabulary

Because the vocabulary of democracy support is not universally familiar, some key terms must be clarified first.

The idea of supporting democracy has an active and a passive sense, corresponding to the distinction between the support of democracy and democracy being supported. The *active* sense comprises deliberate actions undertaken with a view to achieving a democratic purpose. There is intentionality. This frames questions about which democracy support actors are doing what, how, and to what effect. The *passive* sense orients us more towards how far democratic trends are occurring in prospective, emerging, and new democracies, the kind of democracy that is emerging, and, crucially, whether these developments are being influenced by outside actors and international events.

Intentionality is central to the active sense of supporting democracy. In the passive sense, however, democratic impulses could emerge as a by-product of exposure to the world outside. For example, political developments taking place inside other countries can have 'spillover' effects. Terms like demonstration effect, democratization by emulation, and (perversely given that democracy has such positive normative connotations) 'contagion' all reflect this. These are part of the international diffusion of democratization.

The intentional support of democracy employs various methods or approaches. An initial distinction is between direct and indirect support. **Direct support** targets some defining political characteristics of democracy, whether political values, norms, and principles or more concrete institutions. **Indirect support** addresses the conditions for democratization, such as the socio-economic requisites and need for social peace. Direct approaches must embody some idea about what democracy means and its manifestations. Liberal democracy has been dominant, but Hobson and Kurki (2012) argue that democracy promotion should now embrace alternative conceptualizations which might be better suited to the variety of circumstances and democratic aspirations of different societies. Indirect approaches demand an understanding of what makes democracy possible and how it comes about—a theory of democratization, where competing accounts exist. For example, disagreements exist over why economic development matters, although it seems less important to democratic transition than to democratic consolidation.

This chapter concentrates on **political** strategies for supporting democracy. But other approaches that proceed via cooperation on furthering economic and social development have gained ground as the political strategies now encounter more resistance than hitherto and often fail. The idea of mainstreaming democracy support in development aid, in ways that make development aid more sensitive to its implications for democratic advance sounds appealing. But the political effects may be hard to demonstrate or accrue only in the longer term.

Democracy support

The political instruments or methods that are employed in supporting democracy directly can be placed along a continuum running from **soft power** to **hard power** (Nye 2005). However, if power means coercion, then the full continuum spans assistance, persuasion, influence, and incentives on the one side. On the other side it includes pressure (e.g. 'diplomatic pressure'), political conditionalities, especially negative conditionalities that

Box 25.1 Democracy and democracy support in the twenty-first century

The idea of democracy as a universal commitment is quite new, and it is quintessentially a product of the twentieth century ... While democracy is not yet universally practiced, nor indeed uniformly accepted, in the general climate of world opinion, democratic governance has now achieved the status of being taken to be generally right. (Sen 1999: 5)

Democracy promotion as a foreign policy goal has become increasingly acceptable throughout most of the international community ... an international norm embraced by other states [than the US], transnational organizations, and international networks ... in the community of democratic states the normative burden has shifted to those not interested in advocating democracy promotion. (McFaul 2004: 148, 158)

embody threats in the event of non-compliance (not the positive conditionalities that stress incentives or inducements), economic and other sanctions (threatened or actual), and, possibly, covert or overt military intervention. In practice, different methods or approaches are often in play simultaneously, or they may be employed in sequence depending on the political circumstances and trajectory of the country on the receiving end. Thus assistance may be offered for democracy-building projects after external pressure has replaced autocracy, as in post-Gadhafi Libya.

The democracy supporters comprise different kinds of organization—governmental, inter-governmental, semi-autonomous, and non-governmental—varying greatly in their mandates and access to diverse instruments for supporting democracy. United Nations (UN) initiatives can employ a form of international legitimacy that other actors lack. Governments among the established democracies have more tools at their disposal than the private political foundations or institutes that specialize in democracy assistance projects.

Democracy assistance

Democracy assistance is usually consensual: it comprises grant-aided support that can take the form of technical, material, or financial assistance to pro-democracy initiatives. Assistance includes what Carothers (2004) calls 'institutional modelling'—attempts to transfer blueprints of democratic practice, procedure, and organizations that resemble working models borrowed from the established democracies. For Carothers, assistance should also extend to helping pro-democracy activists in their efforts to challenge authoritarian and semi-authoritarian rulers. This approximates to direct involvement in domestic political struggles. It moves closer to harder forms of power when combined with the application of external pressure on rulers to open up political space.

The financial value of all democracy assistance is hard to gauge; reporting practices vary and lack precise or standardized definitions. There are questions about whether human rights programmes and support for better governance should be included. For example, the US Agency for International Development (USAID) provides spending figures for good governance, civil society, and rule of law (totalling over $2 billion for fiscal year 2011–12), the United Nations Development Programme's (UNDP) budget for 'democratic governance' was $1.3 billion in 2012, and the budget of the European Commission's European Instrument for Democracy and Human Rights (EIDHR) was around €1 billion for the period 2007–13 (proposals exist for a substantial increase in the period 2014–20). All in all, the grand total of all democracy assistance, very loosely defined, ranges upwards of $5 billion annually—dwarfed by international development aid from all donors of around $160 billion

annually. Nevertheless the amounts spent may be a less important guide to effective democracy support than its timing, quality, and suitability.

Political conditionality

The European Union (EU) has been a major exponent of **political conditionality** as a distinctive approach to supporting democracy. The EU's Copenhagen criteria (1993) lay down conditions referring to 'stability of institutions guaranteeing democracy, the rule of law, human rights and respect for the protection of minorities' in exchange for eligibility for membership. The EU 'speaks softly and carries a big carrot' is one way of describing this approach. A broad consensus exists that this conditionality has helped push the democratization of post-communist countries in Central and Eastern Europe.

Although conditionality can be deployed on its own, some scholars have also attached considerable weight to what has been called 'normative power Europe' (Manners 2002). This refers to the claim that the EU helps spread certain values which in turn translate into liberal democratic principles and processes, while stopping short of exporting some particular institutional model, such as parliamentary democracy. Socialization or social learning can change attitudes and beliefs or, at minimum, behaviour. The result may lead newly adopted democratic practices to become deeply embedded, even when the prize offered by positive conditionality such as EU membership has been secured already. In recent years, however, the EU's commitment to projecting normative power has been brought into question because of the competition from other foreign objectives such as security (Youngs 2010). There are serious reservations about the EU's ability to make an effective deployment of political conditionalities (either incentives or deterrent) towards countries unlikely ever to be offered EU membership, such as those that took part in the 'Arab revolution' in North Africa.

The United States and the European Union

The US government and its instruments have tended to enjoy the larger profile in supporting democracy around the globe. The US is the one country with the capacity and political will to deploy the full range of methods or approaches, including the harder forms of power where the US has a comparative advantage. From the time of President Reagan's interest in furthering democracy as a way of combating Soviet influence, to President G. W. Bush making freedom (in the Middle East especially) central to his foreign policy rhetoric after 9/11, the US has tended to set agendas in democracy support. This has not been wholly beneficial, as indicated by the widely held view that democracy promotion has been tainted by its association with regime change. Europeans have often struggled to know how to relate to the US's efforts, outside of the EU accession process. This remains true even now that President Obama, after initially distancing his stance from that of his predecessor, is embracing greater multilateralism and policies that are sensitive to democracy's developmental needs, which moves closer to the European position.

KEY POINTS

- Supporting democracy abroad has developed over the last twenty-five years, with the US and Europe taking the lead.

- The active support of democracy is intentional but is not bound to succeed; democratic trends may be influenced by a range of international factors, including passive democracy promotion.

- Although active democracy support employs both soft and harder forms of power, the use of military force is challenged on ideological and practical grounds.

- The EU prides itself on dialogue and partnership with governments, but its greatest successes stem from political conditionality in EU accession. Although its more 'muscular' approach has moderated under President Obama, the US remains more willing to actively support the political opposition to autocrats in places where vital US interests are not jeopardized (Carothers 2012).

Explaining democracy support

Since 1945 a strong sense of the value of democracy and a desire to see it spread far and wide have never been absent from the Western world. The dismantling of European empires in Africa and Asia saw attempts to implant formal democratic structures, many of them not very durable. But the end of the Cold War saw a dramatic new willingness to adopt democracy support as a foreign policy objective. The erosion of Soviet influence followed by the collapse of the Soviet Union made it safer for Western governments to demand democracy, human rights, and good governance in countries that previously were valued primarily as Western allies. Former client states of the USSR became more vulnerable to Western political pressure. These international developments were enabling factors.

At the same time sizeable mobilizations of support for political change began to take place inside many so-called Second and Third World countries. Often this was spurred as much by social and economic discontent as by political grievances. International support of democracy gained legitimacy from this *pull-factor*—demands for political reform by people living in societies with non-democratic regimes—even though certain *push-factors* or foreign policy goals in the West also supplied major policy drivers.

Idealism

Idealism offers one possible reason for supporting democracy. The intrinsic value of freedom and democracy may be considered so great that societies which claim to enjoy these already are obliged to help other societies share them too. It is a disinterested act, even when not tinged with missionary zeal. Historians see a close association of the US and democratic idealism dating to the presidency of Woodrow Wilson (1913–21). One view is that the US is 'born to lead'; advancing freedom and democracy is the 'manifest destiny' of the US. Other views are sceptical and even link US policy to imperialism (explored in Cox *et al.* 2000).

Democracy support and US imperialism

A critical view traditionally states that the US defines its aims in such a way as to pursue global hegemony. When backed by all the resources available to the US, the furtherance of democracy abroad can sometimes serve the purpose of US imperialism. It is true that in the 1980s efforts to support democratization were part of a strategy to confront the Soviet Union. That situation no longer exists. And it is not obvious why the many countries that now endorse the idea of democracy would do so if the effect is US domination. Undoubtedly, governments shape their foreign policies in accord with their national interest. However, public opinion studies continue to show that many citizens in the West support efforts to spread democracy, complicating any simple notion that the endeavour is largely a power play by Western leaders.

Developmental arguments

Paradigms depicting the relationships between development in the developing world and democracy or democratization underwent a double shift from the 1980s onwards. Before then, the dominant reasoning was economistic, maintaining that developing countries must address their economic needs before they could expect to sustain democracy. By trying to democratize prematurely they would place their development in peril. What made this 'cruel choice' seem inevitable was the belief that economics determines politics. In so far as some particular kind of political rule is most favourable to development, authoritarian regimes have the edge. The economic 'miracle' of East Asia's 'dragons' lent support.

However, this chain of reasoning came to be questioned. Many non-democracies in Africa were not developing. Social science saw the rise of the proposition that politics can make a difference. This was connected with a recognition that institutions and agency do matter. Not everything is determined by structural 'causes'. Furthermore, development came to be understood not just as economic growth but as improved social conditions and human development (for data on education and literacy see Comparative table 7 at the end of this volume). Attention turned to how governance, democracy, and human rights might benefit development and, even, the incorporation of such values as dignity and freedoms within the very definition of development itself. The double-paradigm shift, away from an 'economics first' approach towards a 'politics does matter' approach, lent plausibility to democracy support. Fortuitously it offered to help developing countries graduate from international aid.

Some major international development agencies like the World Bank continue to emphasize above all the importance of better governance, not democracy. This builds on arguments that the rule of law and secure property rights are fundamental for development. The relationship between democracy and good governance is variable: furthering one of them does not necessarily advance the other, except perhaps in the long run (Emmerson 2012). Moreover, in some countries rectifying state weakness and state fragility demands a higher priority. So although the developmental case for spreading democracy was never universally agreed, and may even have lost some support in recent years, the case for aiding development as a way of supporting stable democracy has, if anything, gained new vitality, in part reflecting the needs of countries post-Arab revolution. Lipset's (1959) thesis that stable democracy is more difficult to maintain in the absence of social modernization and economic development commands universal support. Egypt is one country where broadly based socio-economic progress could be far more critical to building democracy than the very limited direct support for democracy that its government is willing to accept (Burnell 2013).

Democracy support and international capitalism

Arguments originating in neo-Marxist and Gramscian perspectives explain democracy support as an instrument of global capitalism. And it is true that the kind of democracy that democracy support usually promotes resembles what Marxists criticize as bourgeois democracy, lacking the full popular participatory content and truly egalitarian ideals of visions that speak more about empowering the people than safeguarding individual rights. Therefore democracy support has been portrayed as a handmaiden of capital, whether national, international,

or transnational (Robinson 1996). It is likened to a Trojan horse for the kind of selective economic liberalization that serves corporate interests best. It is seen to target regimes that have populist welfare pretensions, like President Hugo Chávez's rule in Venezuela, and some of the countries with the oil that the West needs, like Saddam's Iraq and Gadhafi's Libya. Yet, as the economic success of China among others shows, capitalist forces can thrive even in a non-democracy. Capitalism might be essential to Western ideas of democracy, but democracy does not appear to be essential to capitalism. This is problematic for the idea that democracy is supported as an instrument of capitalism.

Democratization, international peace, and national security

The **democratic peace thesis** has regularly featured in the policy rationales of most official actors. This long-standing thesis maintains that democracies do not go to war with one another. Thus, everyone gains as more states become democratic.

The democratic peace thesis has generated much controversy. One objection is that it holds only under limiting conditions, such as a restrictive definition of war, or during the Cold War era, or when most democracies were economically advanced. There is little agreement on why democracies only rarely go to war with democracies, and of course democracies sometimes initiate wars against non-democracies. Democratization can increase the likelihood of internal turmoil, which in turn might fracture external relations, as happened with the bloody transformation of former Yugoslavia.

Nevertheless, views resembling the democratic peace thesis continue to feature in the justifications for supporting democracy. Furthermore, after the terrorist events of 9/11 and the US government's espousal of a freedom agenda in the Middle East, the spread of democracy came to be presented as an antidote to international terrorism. But the reasoning was always suspect. In some places oppressive rule might provoke a violent response in society, but the primary 'causes' lie elsewhere. Rival interpretations highlight the radicalizing effects of poverty and resentment at global social injustice, or the militant tendencies inherent in extremist religious and nationalist views. Thus it is plausible to argue that a satisfactory resolution to the Israel–Palestinian conflict is a necessary condition for ending the perceived threat to the West posed by Islamic terrorism, al-Qaeda included.

The possibility that non-fraudulent elections could bring about an elected government that itself appears to sponsor terrorism cannot be discounted. It looks likely that democratically elected governments in North Africa will adopt less accommodating policies towards Israel, and this could damage relations with the US and Europe. Western governments undermine the credibility of their own support for democracy when they appear to support the electoral process only when they feel comfortable with the electorate's choice. Maintaining friendly relations with undemocratic regimes that are useful allies against international terrorism or possess strategically valuable resources like oil also makes them look inconsistent. Large arms sales to Saudi Arabia by both the UK and the US, and their passivity when Saudi military involvement helped crush anti-government protests in Bahrain in 2011, place question marks against their true commitment to democracy abroad (Hopkins 2013).

Nevertheless, new thinking about democracy support has been forced onto foreign policy agendas in the West as a result of failing to foresee the timing, nature, and spread of the 2011 'Arab revolutions', along with realizing that their former stance of valuing present political stability in these countries instead of pressing strongly for democratic change was misguided, and now looks a failure.

KEY POINTS

- No single theory captures well all the actors and/or covers all years, not least because the actors do not wholly agree on what they are trying to achieve and why.

- After 9/11 the contribution of democratization to securing peace within and between nations gained some prominence in the rhetoric of politicians but their actions in support of democracy proved inconsistent.

- A lesson of the 'Arab revolutions' is that democracy support should not be dictated by short-term expediency at the expense of a longer-term assessment about likely political developments in foreign countries.

Suppliers of democracy support

The international 'democracy–industrial complex' has grown over the last twenty-five years to include different kinds of organization: governmental, inter-governmental, autonomous but largely publicly funded, and genuinely non-governmental actors, some of whom are not-for-profit and others who are commercially motivated.

One way of distinguishing between the actors is in terms of those for whom democracy support is but one of several activities, such as the UNDP, and those where it provides the sole rationale, like the UK's Westminster Foundation for Democracy (WFD). Another is to distinguish between the kinds of activities they engage in: giving grants, offering technical support, or being operational. Different again is the inter-governmental International Institute for Democracy and Electoral Assistance (IDEA), based in Sweden, whose goal is to assemble and share knowledge with democracy builders.

Inter-governmental actors

The UN is the one truly multilateral organization of great note that is prominent in democracy support. Its contribution ranges from broad statements of support for democratic values by the Office of the Secretary-General through to considerable experience in helping stage, monitor, and observe elections, especially in new states. The UNDP is one of the largest actors within the UN family. It spends around half of its democratic governance budget on making governing institutions more accountable and around a third on 'inclusive participation'. A separate UN Democracy Fund, established in 2005, has attracted voluntary donations from 39 states. It funds mainly civil society initiatives.

Regional-level organizations that express a commitment to democracy in their member-states include the Organization of American States (OAS), and the African Union, through its New Partnership for Africa's Development (NEPAD) and African Peer Review Mechanism. The Commonwealth offers some practical assistance to its members, such as by exchanging experiences in matters like parliamentary training and legislative oversight of the executive. The Organization for Security and Co-operation in Europe (OSCE) Office for Democratic Institutions and Human Rights monitors elections but over the years has faced increasing obstruction by Russia and its allies (Fawn 2006).

Governmental actors

The governments of established democracies support democracy through various channels, including their foreign ministries and other ministries, embassies, and development aid agencies, and by funding formally autonomous democracy institutes or foundations, examples being in the US, the UK, Australia, the Netherlands, and Germany.

USAID has developed a major presence in the area of democracy and governance, although this accounts for only a tiny fraction of its overall budget. The National Endowment for Democracy (NED), a private organization funded by the US Congress and its grantee organizations, including the National Democratic Institute for International Affairs (NDI) and the International Republic Institute (IRI), have smaller funds.

Stiftungen and foundations

Democracy institutes and foundations in countries like the US, the Netherlands, and the UK, and Germany's political foundations or *Stiftungen*, usually have private non-profit status and formal autonomy alongside public funding and some contract-based income. The relationships between their activities and the foreign-policy-making of the government are not always wholly

Box 25.2 The *Stiftungen* are close to Germany's political parties

Friedrich Ebert *Stiftung*	Social Democratic Party
Konrad Adenauer *Stiftung*	Christian Democratic Union
Heinrich Böll *Stiftung*	Green Party (*Bundnis 90/Grune*)
Friedrich Naumann *Stiftung*	Free Democratic Party
Hans Seidel *Stiftung*	Christian Social Union
Rosa Luxemburg *Stiftung*	Left Party.PDS (*Linkspartei.PDS*, Left Party/Party of Democratic Socialism

transparent, but their collective experience in offering practical support is considerable.

In Germany, after a political party has been represented in the federal Parliament for two consecutive elections, it is entitled to receive government funding for civic education work at home and certain international activities. Each one of the *Stiftungen* is close to one of the main parties (see Box 25.2). Together they have long experience in developing contacts abroad at the non-governmental level (e.g. the Friedrich Ebert *Stiftung* was founded in 1925). The foundations work with civil society groups and in some cases political parties. They are unusual in that they establish permanent field offices in countries abroad. Their reputation for developing partisan links with local partners should not be exaggerated, and anyway can be hard to achieve in places like Africa and former Yugoslavia where many parties invoke ethnic or ethno-nationalist sentiment and lack strong or distinct ideological identity.

Germany's foundations have accounted for over three-quarters of the combined annual overall budget spent by Europe's political foundations on democracy-related work (van Wersch and de Zeeuw 2005).

Elsewhere in Europe there is the Olof Palme Foundation linked to Sweden's Social Democratic Party, the WFD which is funded by the Foreign and Commonwealth Office in Britain, and the Netherlands Institute for Multiparty Democracy (NIMD) which, like Australia's Centre for Democratic Institutions (CDI), shows interest in supporting the development of parties and harmonious party systems in some post-conflict situations. The independent European Partnership for Democracy (EPD) was created by civil society actors in 2008, with strong support from Václav Havel, former president of the Czech Republic. It seeks to press the EU to build a stronger presence in democracy support outside the EU. It should not be confused with the European Endowment for Democracy (EED)—a new organization that gained high-level support in the EU in response to the 'Arab revolution'. The EED will initially depend on voluntary funding by member states, and is envisaged to enjoy more political flexibility than such mechanisms as the EIDHR.

The European Union

As was made clear in Chapter 23, the EU is not a state and analysts are not convinced that the lens of foreign policy can be used to illuminate the EU's external behaviour. However, the EU has moved towards the adoption of a common foreign and security policy; as well as being one of the largest foreign aid donors. The EU's commitment to the idea of supporting democracy has grown apace; one of the most established institutional expressions is the EIDHR, which disburses grants to civil society projects in over 30 countries.

The EU's political and diplomatic role in supporting democratic political reform in Central and East European countries in the 1990s, through the accession process, has already been noted. This has been no disinterested act. Just as many people in the post-communist societies saw democratization as an aid to recovering national independence—freedom from authoritarian rule and from political domination by the Soviet Union (Russia)—so Western Europeans saw democratic reform in the 'near abroad' as advantageous to their own security. And EU expansion appealed to many members, although not all for the same reasons. The EU in the past had a strong dynamic of its own: increase in membership could help the institution to become a more powerful actor in world affairs. Democracy support itself could be presented as a symbol and tool of powerful actor status in world affairs. And by expressing its support for democracy in ways that chime with the principles and values of freedom and democracy rather than by force, the EU reaffirms the kind of identify that Europeans now claim for Europe.

The European Neighbourhood Policy (ENP) offers about sixteen neighbours privileged bilateral ties that build on a supposedly mutual commitment to common values such as democracy, human rights, and rule of law. It seems to have been fairly ineffective as a tool for furthering democratic progress. The same is even more true of the Union for the Mediterranean, which succeeded the earlier Euro-Mediterranean Partnership in 2008. Taken by surprise by the 'Arab revolution' in 2011, senior EU figures realized that substantial reform of EU external relations foreign policies was essential. This has led among other things to an initiative offering EU partners 'more for more'—concessions like greater market access to the EU and investment in return for seeing democratic progress. In short, positive conditionality is being revitalized. However, it remains to be seen whether either the EU or its partners can deliver (Burnell 2013).

Finally, there is the conviction that Europe offers a model of political harmony both within and among states that speaks to the needs of some other regions, not least the zones of conflict. This model shows how to rise above long periods of inter-state violence—Europe having been at the heart of two 'world wars' and one 'cold war' in the twentieth century alone. The political values on which this stability in Europe has been constructed are for Europe to demonstrate and share by engaging in 'partnership' and ideological suasion. However, the political strains opened up in Europe by the Eurozone financial crisis and major disagreements among EU states over how to tackle it will now put that model to the test. The crisis draws attention to major shortcomings in financial regulation and economic management by Europe's democratically elected politicians while at the same time absorbing their political attention that might otherwise be channelled to supporting democracy abroad.

Democracy support by new democracies

So far, the newer democracies and large developing-world democracies have in the main disappointed democracy's main supporters in the West by their reluctance to make strong political and practical commitments to democracy support (Carothers and Youngs 2011). Even their voting support for international human rights initiatives led by the US or EU countries in UN forums has been very patchy. The reasons range from the concern of former colonies, including India, to maintain the principles of sovereignty and non-interference intact, emulating positions taken by China and Russia on this issue, to suspicions about the West's inconsistent approach to democracy promotion and its underlying agendas, which are perceived to further the interests of Western powers, especially the US (see Box 25.3).

Box 25.3 Democracy support by rising democracies

Case of India

India, a democracy since independence in 1947 and the world's largest democracy, is, along with Brazil, Russia and China, one of the original BRIC states. But apart from being a notable funder of the UN Democracy Fund, India has shown little enthusiasm for supporting democracy in its bilateral foreign relations. This has been explained by its traditional non-aligned stance in world politics and a sensitivity towards colonialist and imperialist adventures, the strategic importance of maintaining stable relations with neighbouring China and Pakistan, while at the same critical of US support for Pakistan's military rulers in the past, and the commercial and economic benefits derived from maintaining good relations with non-democracies like Myanmar. The exceptional case of Indian support for Nepal's peaceful transition to democracy in 2005–8 signified a desire to promote stability and prevent China gaining influence, not a goal of supporting democracy (Destradi 2012).

Case of Turkey

Turkey is sometimes presented as a model of democracy-building for Islamic societies in the region. Turkey's ruling Justice and Development Party (AKP) historically has Islamist roots and is easily the most popular party. By keeping the military in the barracks and showing allegiance to liberal democratic principles, Turkey and the AKP could encourage, inform, and support pro-democracy forces in North Africa and the Middle East.

Turkey is beginning to respond to Arab requests for democracy support, and might believe that this should advance its claims to become a member of the EU. However, both the exact model that Turkey offers and its provenance are contested. First, Turkey has a strong state, unlike countries such as Yemen. Second, Turkey is a secular state, and the AKP hews to secularism in governance. The Arab countries in transition differ among themselves. Third, Turkey has long-standing ties with the US and aspires to join the EU, whereas Egypt, for example, is very ambivalent about the US and claims no European identity. Fourth, the military's political interventions before 2002 might be construed as instrumental in preparing for today's seemingly secure democracy, having promoted secularism and a largely unifying (but not anti-Western) nationalism. But in Egypt the armed forces could yet frustrate democracy-building. Fifth, the global economic problems since 2007 mean that Turkey's economic boom in the last decade—a positive force for social and political stability and democratization there—looks unlikely to be replicated in the wider region, where even Libya's oil wealth could prove a curse if it breeds corruption. Finally, although Turkey has made progress in human rights, critics still question the AKP's commitment to liberal democracy in the longer term. Major challenges lie ahead in the shape of reconfiguring Turkey's constitution to forestall the drawbacks of a dominant party state and make the political order more inclusive of the country's sizeable Kurdish minority (Ülgen 2011).

Notable exceptions within an EU context have been the new democracies of Poland and the Czech Republic. Petrova (2012) sees Poland's efforts to support democracy, especially in countries to the east, almost as an exemplar. Poland's President Kraśniewski played a leading role in resolving the political crisis in Ukraine in 2004, where mass demonstrations protested against the fraudulent electoral victory claimed by Viktor Yanukovych. An election re-run gave victory to the West's preferred candidate, Viktor Yushchenko. This episode became known as the 'Orange Revolution' (Åslund and McFaul 2006). But the fact that Ukraine's political situation now is seen in the West as retreating from liberal democracy, especially since Viktor Yanukovych became the democratically elected president in 2010, shows how fragile democratic gains can be. The EU might be criticized for not having offered Ukraine a strong incentive to make further democratic progress by promising a conditional offer of accession to the EU at some future date. But political developments inside Ukraine since the 'Orange Revolution' warn against overestimating the importance of democracy support and underestimating domestic political determinants. The precedent should inform expectations about the political future of countries that were caught up in the 'Arab revolution' and the thinking about how to help maintain democratic progress there.

KEY POINTS

- Different kinds of organization are involved in supporting democracy. International development agencies value 'democratic governance' whereas democracy institutes and foundations support democracy for its own sake.

- New sources of democracy support from outside the US and Western Europe are emerging only gradually.

- While the Obama administration rebuilds US leadership, conflicts between its apparent national interests and democracy support exist towards countries like China and Saudi Arabia. The EU experiences difficulty in replicating its contribution to democratization outside the EU zone.

The demand for democracy support

The demand for democracy support is not the same as the demand for democracy. Both can be difficult to gauge, especially where people are oppressed and feel unable to express themselves freely. Demands for authoritarian rulers to step down are often bound up with economic discontents. Even where strong demands for dignity and freedom are clearly present, as in the Arab world, this does not necessarily mean much knowledge of, or indeed

appetite for, Western style liberal democracy (see Hobson and Kurki 2012), let alone for receiving democracy support. Iran's leading pro-reform activists seem to want to retain fundamental political elements of Iran's status as an Islamic state dating from the 1979 Islamic Revolution. Nevertheless, democracy supporters assume that there is popular hunger for democracy almost everywhere and that international support can play a constructive role. Establishing which countries are not democracies or where people have fewest freedoms should not be difficult. However, there is no strong fit between the data for this and the actual patterns of allocation of democracy support.

Over time, major changes in the market for democracy support have followed national political trends. Thus, whereas in the first half of the 1990s countries from the former Second World were at the forefront, many of the European examples have now 'graduated'. Some others, like those in Central Asia, seem more firmly resistant to change. States in the Balkans became candidates for democracy support as they emerged from the violent break-up of Yugoslavia and envisaged eventual membership of the EU. But Russia under President Putin led the 'backlash' against democracy support, and its sensitivity to Western (specifically American) influence in neighbouring countries like Ukraine and Georgia not only constrains their freedom to join NATO but also, and more arguably, their chances of making strong democratic progress (the diffusion of autocracy is an emerging new research agenda e.g. Bader *et al.* 2012). Elsewhere, Africa is a significant recipient of all kinds of assistance, but some countries like Ghana and South Africa, which appear to be consolidating stable democracy, have little need for democracy support except for specialized purposes, such as parliamentary strengthening in Ghana which has a lengthy relationship with the Parliamentary Centre of Canada. Other countries like Angola and Sudan seem impossible to reach, and the dramatic growth of China's financial and commercial engagement with many countries in Africa in recent years is seen to make their governments less dependent on, and less willing to be influenced by, traditional partners in the West. In China itself the challenge of helping persecuted dissidents to improve China's human rights record is enormous, and must mean that questions about the popular demand for democracy and what support to offer are very problematic (see Breslin 2010). In Latin America and the Caribbean, where most countries are democracies, the Organization of American States (OAS) offers a regional inter-governmental forum for giving support to democracy. Its diplomatic interventions to arrest military coups are more notable than its ability to respond to citizens' concerns about the poor performance of their democratically elected rulers in respect of good governance, security from violent crime (escalating in Mexico), and equitable growth, where prolonged dissatisfaction makes democracy vulnerable to populism and more serious threats.

So the region that is now most prominent as a potential growth area for democracy support is North Africa and the Middle East. Iraq's political future remains deeply uncertain and is not a strong advertisement for successful democracy support, but the 'Arab revolution' has created opportunities elsewhere. Another country where political change could be creating new openings for democracy support is Myanmar. After exhibiting initial confusion over how to respond to the Arab revolution, there is some evidence that democracy supporters are now willing to try to learn from their past failures in this region in particular and pursue different democracy support policies in the future. Among other things this means approaching each country differently, rather than conceiving uniform packages of assistance, and listening more intently to what the pro-democratic forces themselves say they want. This chimes with recent survey findings about how the partners of democracy assistance view the assistance they receive and the improvements they want to see (Barkan 2012).

KEY POINTS

- The true demand for democracy support is hard to fathom but the importance of consulting the intended beneficiaries is generally recognized.

- Democracy support has never corresponded very closely to patterns of greatest democratic deficit, and this is not expected to change significantly.

- The actual allocations of democracy support have changed over time, partly because support responds opportunistically to political developments on the ground. For example, places like Russia are now far more restrictive.

Democracy support strategies

Democracy support faces questions of strategy, namely what to do and how to go about it. There are choices to be made.

Constraints on intervention

Democracy support is not licence to do anything in the name of advancing the cause. There are constraints in international law. Not even the UN is legally entitled to try to impose democracy by force. The limited circumstances whereby the UN Security Council may authorize military intervention in the internal affairs of a country against its government's will were narrowly defined at a time when ideas of state sovereignty were paramount. In the first instance they require that the country be regarded as a threat to others, such as exporting instability to the surrounding region. The post-Cold War world saw academic discussions of the rights that peoples have to democratic government. That the UN might have a responsibility to protect and enforce those rights is one possible corollary, but is hugely contentious. The UN or other inter-governmental actors such as the North Atlantic Treaty Organization (NATO) have tended to intervene militarily only where there has been massive abuse of human rights (e.g. in the Balkans) and even then not in every case. In 2011 the UN Security Council approved the use by UN states of 'all necessary measures' to protect Libya's civilians under threat of attack by Colonel Gadhafi's forces, but there was no mention of supporting transition to democracy. And Russian and Chinese perceptions that NATO's intervention subsequently overstepped the UN resolution hardened their resolve to oppose UN-authorized interventions in Syria where state-sponsored violence accelerated in 2012.

Spreading democracy at gunpoint is an unpromising strategy, anyway. Pei and Kasper (2003) calculated that of sixteen US military interventions abroad since 1898, democracy was sustained ten years after the departure of US forces in only four cases. More recent experience in Afghanistan and Iraq hardly improves the record. But military intervention to end internal war can contribute to peace-building and thereby offer a service to democracy-building. For example, UK military deployment in Sierra Leone from 1999 was critical to ending its civil war and restoring elected civilian rule.

Types of democracy assistance

Although governmental and inter-governmental actors share a comparative advantage in having access to the widest range of approaches to supporting democracy, democracy assistance is the one method that is available to the greatest number and variety of actors, the foundations included. Assistance also tends to be much more visible than diplomatic dialogue or pressure. Carothers (2004) offers a useful categorization of democracy assistance in the shape of a 'democracy template'. This distinguishes three sectors: electoral process, state institutions, and civil society. For each sector there are sector goals and related forms of assistance. Boxes 25.4 and 25.5 present concrete examples of how UNDP and USAID, respectively, classify their activities.

Broadly speaking, democracy assistance has evolved along a path from electoral support through an emphasis on civil society to an increased willingness in some circles to view support for party strengthening as essential to democracy-building. For international development agencies who believe that better governance is essential to development, strengthening the capacity of legislatures to hold the executive to account (especially over public expenditure) is another area of growing interest. These trends reflect progress in our understanding of democratization as well as its relationship to development.

Box 25.4 United Nations Development Programme democratic governance

Main services: responding to the requests and needs of developing countries, UNDP offers support in the following focus areas:

- access to information and e-governance
- access to justice and rule of law
- anti-corruption
- civic engagement
- electoral systems and processes
- human rights
- local governance and local development
- parliamentary development
- public administration
- women's empowerment

Source: UNDP, *Democratic Governance Focus Areas* (2011).

Box 25.5 USAID's democracy support toolbox: illustrative and concrete examples of how USAID says it supports democratization

Promoting justice and human rights through the rule of law

Improve laws, institutions, and the judiciary as checks on the executive.
Support due process, non-discrimination, and representation of all segments of society.

Strengthening the institutions of democratic and accountable governance

Encourage effective, transparent provision of goods and services; avenues for participation and oversight; separation of powers with checks and balances.
Support anti-corruption in all institutions and sectors.
Strengthen effective oversight and democratic functioning of authorities responsible for security.

Expanding political freedom and competition

Promote free, fair, transparent multiparty elections.
Promote representative, accountable political parties.

Engaging society through the voice, advocacy, and participation of citizens

Promote effective private voluntary associations and a strong civil society.
Promote vigorous independent media.

Source: USAID, *At Freedom's Frontiers: A Democracy and Governance Strategic Framework* (December 2005).

A lesson grasped fairly early on was that elections alone do not make a democracy, even where international election observation contributes to the impression of a fairly free and fair process on the day of the election (Kelley (2012) contests the reliability of monitoring, after studying 1324 national elections and 600 monitoring missions). Of course fraudulent elections themselves can be a catalyst for unstoppable popular protest, as in Ukraine's 'Orange Revolution', which then creates new openings for democracy support. But although elections can be instrumental for a transition to democracy (Lindberg 2009), this is only one of several possible outcomes. And in the case of what Levitsky and Way (2010) call competitive authoritarian regimes, other domestic political factors and international engagement in trying to level the playing field of political competition must be present as well.

Partly because the electoralist fallacy gained wide recognition, civil society support became a growth area for democracy assistance. The attraction for democracy supporters was that it seemed to avoid direct interference in a country's internal politics. However, the more that resources were directed to trying to create and strengthen institutional capacity in civil societies, the greater was the realization of the risks. Much evidence of donor dependency came to light—civic groups that were unlikely to be sustained after foreign support ceased. Many such groups tend to comprise elites who were neither very representative nor committed to developing extensive roots in society. In some situations support attracts increased government repression or a tightening straitjacket of regulations, as has happened in Putin's Russia and as seemed to occur in Egypt in 2012. Therefore support to civil society can bring disadvantages (Christensen and Weinstein 2013).

Arguments for trying to help strengthen democratic political parties and legislatures are gradually coming more to the fore, even though acting on this can be just as challenging as any recommendation that party support and international election observation should work together in closer synergy (Burnell 2011; Burnell and Gerrits 2012). The arguments are seen to have strong application to Arab countries, where most parties are very weak and some Islamist groupings are suspected of harbouring illiberal designs, and historically the power of the executive, especially the president, has been excessive. But the very reasons that have always weighed against closer involvement with parties and legislature—it resembles foreign interference at the very heart of domestic politics—will probably continue to impede more effective action. However, a new area of interest for democracy support that is receiving growing attention, because of the role that social media played in mobilizing popular protest during the 'Arab revolutions', involves embracing new communications technology in ways that will help democracy activists while at the same time countering its political use by authoritarian regimes to their own advantage.

Democracy support and state-building

Democracy support's greatest challenges include societies coming out of violent conflict, especially those where the state is fragile or ineffective, such as the Democratic Republic of the Congo. In the Arab world, Libya now poses a test case and in time Syria might become one.

Sub-state violence, or at minimum weak governance, is placed under the spotlight that previously focused on threats of large-scale inter-state war and East–West conflict in particular. Where multiple weaknesses exist, the solutions tend to be interconnected, even though they are often not well understood. The challenges may include not just state-building (or rebuilding) and improving the quality of governance but also nation-building, economic reconstruction and development, and even resolution of humanitarian crises. The correct order of priorities, the trade-offs, and sequencing issues between these requirements and installing stable democracy are complex issues for the societies themselves, and also for international actors. The issues lie at the interstices of different discourses and international policy communities having different mandates, competencies, and expertise that are not well joined up.

Democratization vs. state-building

One of the larger theoretical questions is whether state-building should take precedence when public order is weak, especially if political instability also endangers (democracy in) neighbouring countries. Insisting on moving rapidly towards a participatory and competitive political system can risk mobilizing uncivil elements into the political process. Populist leaders take advantage and align political cleavages with the ethnic, racial, religious or sectarian divisions that can (re)ignite violent conflict. Some hallmarks of stateness, monopoly of the means of violence for instance, might be difficult to achieve, especially where competing politicians threaten to make use of private militias. External encouragement to adopt some form of political decentralization may end up handing power to regional warlords and local despots.

However, the alternative of pursuing a 'state first' approach that concentrates on strengthening the powers of central government and trying to establish the rule of law ahead of building democracy is no perfect solution. It can create vested interests in power concentration; the force of path dependence then takes over, making democratization and a deconcentration of power more difficult later on. International actors must be sensitive to these dilemmas. When advising the institutional architecture for building democracy amid pressures for fragmentation, they should take account of the influence that such parameters as electoral systems and party system constellations can have over whether the new political order becomes inclusive and harmonious or, conversely, exclusionary and divisive (Reilly and Nordlund 2008). Bastian and Luckham (2003) highlighted the difficulties of alighting on the right solution even in countries, such as Sri Lanka, which once looked set to become stable democracies but descended into bloody conflict and high-handed rule. International actors often stand accused of making insufficient resources available to address all the issues, especially where the country lacks strategic importance. But the capacity of any country, especially one emerging from violence, to put international help, including democracy support, to good use is limited. For example, the material aid that may be essential to rebuilding the economic foundations may fuel corruption and bad governance. In extreme cases which resemble international trusteeship or administration, such as Kosovo and Bosnia Herzegovina, political self-determination (and hence democracy) may be significantly compromised (e.g. Nenadović 2012).

KEY POINTS

- Civil society seems to offer politically safe opportunities for foreign assistance, but this can be largely illusory.

- Concentrating on elections and civil society limits what democracy support might achieve, but strengthening legislatures and political parties can prove even more problematic.

- Where violent internal conflict exists, because oppression, discrimination, and human rights abuse are rife, the idea that support for establishing peace and building democracy go together seems obvious. But firmly establishing peace and democracy can both be challenging even with substantial international support.

The record of supporting democracy

Supporting democracy has lasted long enough for it to be reasonable to ask 'does it work?' Although the short answer is that its performance has probably been modest, the question is actually far too simple, for the following reasons.

What should be evaluated?

In addressing questions about what should be evaluated, the distinction between an active and passive sense of democracy support is highly relevant. The first involves intentionality, where performance can be assessed against the stated objectives. The second refers to where democracy is affected by many different kinds of external influence, such as the encouragement that might come from living in a 'good neighbourhood'. Evaluators must determine the yardsticks for measuring democracy's trajectory and then set benchmarks against which to measure progress.

Another important distinction is between the consequences for democracy and the contribution democracy makes to serving further goals: economic development, international peace and security, and so on. There is no guarantee that effective support to democratization will procure all these ends, some of which might be better served in some places by maintaining a non-democratic regime for the immediate future.

How to evaluate?

Evaluating democracy assistance is fraught with methodological difficulties. They are relatively trivial when compared with the challenge of assessing democracy support *tout court*, where the methods are so diverse as to defy easy comparison—just note the differences between money, technical know-how, pressure, and 'political capital' for example, or between quiet diplomacy and political conditionality-based threats of coercion.

Compared with international development cooperation, the art of evaluating democracy assistance (and even more so democracy support) remains in its infancy. Inability to attribute causality with any great certainty is a major conundrum. Impact assessment must take in any unintended or negative effects, and somehow predict the long-term effectiveness of assistance. For instance, the number of election observers who have been 'trained' or the number of civic associations that have been launched can be counted easily. But the contribution these make to democratization is harder to assess. Many influences will have a bearing on that. And assigning attribution to a specific instance of democracy support while discounting all the others is tricky where there have been multiple democracy support interventions. Naturally the counterfactual—what would have been the outcome in the absence of intervention—cannot be known.

A sensitive comparison of interventions would take account of differences in the degree of difficulty or obstacles encountered *en route*. Eroding an authoritarian regime, encouraging a process of political liberalization, supporting democratic transition, aiding democratic consolidation, helping secure a fragile democracy against subversion, and combating headlong democratic reversal are all different. What might be considered a very modest achievement in the context of one country could be a major break-through in the context of another.

Why evaluate?

Evaluation is always done for some purpose. The reasons vary but they invariably shape the assessment design and attitude to the results. Accountancy-style audits of expenditure are the least ambitious, but give no clues to achievement. Democracy assistance practitioners can value the process of evaluation as a learning tool—an opportunity to discover what worked or did not work well and the reasons why—rather than as a means of holding them to account. In publicly funded bodies evaluation may also serve as a defence against the kinds of politically motivated interference that would distract democracy support from its true objectives.

Finally, there is a view that evaluations of democracy assistance must themselves be democratic. They should demonstrate fundamental democratic values, in particular a participatory approach that involves partners and 'stakeholders' in the receiving country. How extensive should that participation be: designing and implementing the questionnaires? analysing the findings? writing the conclusions and proposing policy recommendations? The findings that emerge from consulting civil society recipients of support, for example, send some conflicting messages: desires for more generous and sustained funding but less financial dependence on donors; less outside political interference in the country but more international pressure on the regime to reform.

The evaluation findings to date

The largest and technically most sophisticated study of effectiveness is of the democracy and governance (DG) assistance programmes of USAID, covering 195 countries in the period 1990–2003 (Finkel *et al.* 2007). This quantitative study claimed to find a consistent and clear positive impact of democracy assistance (but not human rights assistance) with lagged and cumulative effects. The findings do not refute Carothers' (2004) more qualitative assessment that internal factors generally outweigh external factors. There are no comparable European assessments. However, the future is likely to see more, not less, political pressure to evaluate as US and European governments address the financial need to reduce public expenditure and remain creditworthy. Political and bureaucratic obstacles will probably still govern whether the lessons from *ex post* assessment of democracy assistance are incorporated into the *ex ante* appraisal of policies and strategies for supporting democracy more generally.

Growing challenges

Of the various challenges facing democracy support, the word globalization seems to encompass many of them. The meaning of globalization and its consequences are much debated. For some, globalization is reducible to global economic integration powered by the ascendancy of neoliberal economics and the increasing domination of social relations by market forces. This could have profoundly anti-democratic consequences, in so far as the disequalizing economic and social effects translate into substantial inequalities of political power and influence. Political self-determination may be made more difficult for whole societies or for specific groups, such as women in poverty.

The cultural side of globalization could be no less pernicious. For instance, there is the spread of individual consumerism which displaces the civic engagement and public service ethos on which the strength and depth of liberal democracies depend.

An even more expansive notion of globalization says that in the current era power is being redistributed away from national states to non-state institutions of multi-level governance. Although not accountable to ordinary people, these institutions take decisions that have major consequences for people's livelihoods and even lives. Of course, globalization is not happening at the same pace everywhere, and so the haemorrhage of power affects some states more than others. But just as for a long time developing-country analysts drew attention to the power of both national and international financial institutions to influence politics, indirectly bringing down governments or at least confining their policy choices in welfare and economics, somewhat similar scenarios now seem to exist among established democracies in the developed world, such as Greece. So how democratic are even these democracies, and is their 'soft power' to spread democracy being eroded?

Democracy support does not have and does not pretend to offer solutions to these and other developments that could tarnish democracy's reputation—and that might leave the formal entitlement of voters in new democracies to replace previously autocratic rulers look worthless as steps towards real democratic self-determination. But if democracy support is to maximize its credibility, the idea and practice of it must provoke ways of responding to these challenges. These could range from doing more to meet the demands of people for social justice, such as by exploring arrangements for social democracy that will counterbalance the anti-democratic effects of free economic markets, to scaling up the application of democratic norms and procedures to institutions of regional and global governance, such as the Bretton Woods institutions.

Conclusion

Following the end of the Cold War and collapse of Soviet power, the international support of democracy became a significant feature of international politics. The US and European actors are the most prominent but not the only contributors. The different actors have individual characteristics. The working relationships between government sponsors and notionally autonomous organizations are not wholly transparent. This reflects the confusion of purpose behind democracy support.

A large market for democracy support still exists in the sense that many people do not live in democracies, let alone liberal democracies. The presumption that the majority would welcome more freedom and the chance to hold their government to account may well be correct. However, that does not necessarily mean that they endorse Western-style liberal democracy or agree with all the methods of democracy support.

Although different explanations have been offered for the increase in democracy support after the 1980s, none cites principled idealism alone. They link it to agendas of national interest of the democracy-supporting countries, defined in various ways. These range from economic considerations to a reduced exposure to state-led aggression and other security threats. A measured judgement is that strategic analysis and direction have tended to be weak. Democracy assistance projects or programmes especially have attracted considerable attention, but their actual contribution to democratization should not be exaggerated. There is still much to learn about impact; the methodological challenges of comparing the effectiveness of such different objectives as reforming organizational structures, altering attitudes, and changing behaviour, each with different time spans, is daunting. Political debates over what is the right balance are not new, but their relevance could become even sharper if funding for democracy support is now entering lean years.

Democracy support has worked best where the conditions were favourable or democratic momentum was already under way—in short, where it was least needed. The most receptive countries have now become democracies. In global terms democracy's progress over recent years has stagnated, making democracy support probably more challenging than at any time since the 1980s. The region where political ferment is currently greatest, the Arab world, struggles to take the democratic impulses of 2011 forward and is facing economic and social as well as political hurdles. The kind of democracy that can be expected to develop there and the implications for international support now merit more attention. Structural developments in the global political economy are impacting on democratic political self-determination even in countries that are established democracies, in western Europe for example. The US's claim to be a leader of the free world must address geopolitical shifts that are likely to see China and possibly Russia—no friends of democracy support—become more powerful actors in international politics, not least in developing countries where China's impressive development looks so attractive. Although democracy support will not disappear and opportunities to exert some positive effect will continue to exist, its overall profile compared with all the other determinants of politics is likely to be modest.

Questions

1. How do the different ways of supporting democracy compare with one another?

2. Why did democracy support lose momentum in the first decade of the twenty-first century, and can the 'Arab revolution' now give it a new lease of life?

3. What lessons must democracy support learn from its own past performance if it is to be fit for purpose in the future?

4. Should the international community concentrate on helping to preserve or re-establish state power rather than simultaneously build democracy in societies that have recently experienced violent conflict?

5. Why is measuring the impact of democracy support difficult?

6. Is democracy support now challenged more by globalization or by the growing international presence of some leading authoritarian and semi-authoritarian powers?

7. Why do the US and EU continue to be the main sources of democracy support when there are so many more democracies around the world?

8. Could efforts to improve the democratic credentials and economic credibility of established democracies now be the best way to support democracy's progress elsewhere in the world?

9. Should democracies support ideas or models of democracy significantly different from liberal democracy in the West, for example those that accommodate political Islam?

Further reading

Ambrosio, T. (2008) *Authoritarian Backlash* (Farnham: Ashgate). Russia's strategies for countering democracy promotion.

Barany, Z. and Moser, R. (2009) *Is Democracy Exportable?* (Cambridge: Cambridge University Press). Offers what the Introduction calls 'benevolent skepticism' in addressing the question posed by the book's title.

Burnell, P. (2011) *Promoting Democracy Abroad. Policy and Performance* (New Brunswick, NJ: Transaction). Critically examines major issues.

Burnell, P. and Youngs, R. (eds) (2008) *New Challenges to Democratization* (London: Routledge). Explores interdependent challenges to democratization and democracy promotion.

Burnell, P. and Gerrits. A. (eds) (2012) *Promoting Party Politics in Emerging Democracies* (Abingdon: Routledge). Exposes problems of party support.

Carothers, T. (2004) *Critical Mission: Essays on Democracy Promotion* (Washington, DC: Carnegie Endowment for International Peace). Reflections on US democracy promotion.

de Zeeuw, J. and Kumar, K. (eds) (2006) *Promoting Democracy in Post-Conflict Societies* (Boulder, CO: Lynne Rienner). Examines democracy assistance programmes in ten countries.

Hobson, C. and Kurki, M. (eds) (2012) *The Conceptual Politics of Democracy Promotion* (Abingdon: Routledge). Argues that a more pluralistic conception of democracy than liberal democracy should be adopted by democracy promotion, of which social democracy is one example.

Kelley, J. (2012) *Monitoring Democracy*. Shows that international monitoring can improve election quality but most of the time has not—it is broken but worth fixing.

Magen, A., Risse, T., and McFaul, M. (eds) (2009) *Promoting Democracy and the Rule of Law* (Basingstoke: Palgrave). Growing convergence between EU and US approaches.

Youngs, R. (eds) (2010) *The European Union and Democracy Promotion* (Baltimore, MD: Johns Hopkins University Press). Europe's performance as a normative power advancing democracy is critically assessed against the experience.

 Web links

www.ned.org
The National Endowment for Democracy is the leading private non-profit organization in the US for promoting democracy. The website gives access to *Democracy Newsletter*, World Movement for Democracy, and much more.

www.idea.int
The International Institute for Democracy and Electoral Assistance bridges research on strengthening new democracies and democratization. *Evaluating Democracy Support. Methods and Experiences* (ed. P. Burnell, 2007) can be downloaded from this site.

www.usaid.gov
Gateway to the pioneering 2006 report by S. Finkel, A. Pérez-Liñán, and A. Seligson, with D. Azpuru, *Effects of US Foreign Assistance on Democracy Building: Results of a Cross-National Quantitative Study*.

www.ndi.org
National Democratic Institute, a prominent affiliate of the National Endowment for Democracy, supporting democratic initiatives around the world.

www.wfd.org
Westminster Foundation for Democracy, a UK government funded independent public body for promoting democracy.

www.undp.org/governance
UN Development Programme democratic governance programme.

online resource centre For additional material and resources, please visit the Online Resource Centre at: **www.oxfordtextbooks.co.uk/orc/caramani3e/**

Comparative data and world trends

Country profiles

Country Profile Argentina

Argentine Republic (*República Argentina*)

State formation

Argentina was first explored by Europeans in 1516, became a Spanish colony in 1580, and part of the Viceroyalty of the Rio de la Plata in 1776. After two unsuccessful invasions by the British Empire in 1806 and 1807, the First Government Junta was established in Buenos Aires when King Ferdinand VII had been overthrown by Napoleon in 1810 (May Revolution). Formal independence was gained on 9 July 1816. *Constitution* 1853; amended many times.

Form of government

Presidential republic.
Head of state: President and Vice President elected on the same ticket; term of 4 years (renewable once).
Head of government: The President.
Cabinet: Ministers appointed by the President.
Administrative subdivisions: 23 provinces and 1 autonomous city.

Legal system

Mixture of US and West European legal systems.

Legislature

Bicameral National Congress (*Congreso Nacional*).
Lower house: Chamber of Deputies (*Cámara de Diputados*): 257 seats; staggered elections; term of 4 years.
Upper house: Senate: 72 seats; staggered elections (one-third of the members elected every 2 years); term of 6 years.

Electoral system (lower house)

Proportional representation.
Formula: D'Hondt. A third of the candidates of each party must be women.
Constituencies: 24 multimember constituencies corresponding to the provinces.
Barrier clause: 3 per cent votes of the registered voters in the multimember constituencies.
Suffrage: Universal and compulsory, 18 years.

Direct democracy

Optional but binding legislative referendum can be called by Parliament. Other non-binding referenda can be called by the President or the Congress. A non-binding legislative popular initiative is possible.

Party system Results of the 2009 legislative elections (Chamber of Deputies):

Electorate	27,797,930	100.0%
Voters:	20,123,715	72.2%

Party	Valid votes	%	Seats
Alternative for a Republic of Equals	3,794,853	19.8	28
Republican Proposal	3,391,391	17.7	20
Justicialist Party	2,778,326	14.5	19
Provincial parties	1,872,360	9.8	19
Front for Victory	1,679,084	8.8	14
Others	1,271,081	6.6	8
Radical Civic Union	639,818	3.3	4
Project South	437,634	2.3	4
Justicialist Front	415,405	2.2	6
New encounter	402,502	2.1	2
Front of Everyone	381,067	2.0	3
Others	2,070,566	10.8	0
Total	**19,134,087**	**100.0**	**127**

Source: Adam Carr's website.

Country Profile Australia

Commonwealth of Australia

State formation

James Cook took possession of eastern Australia in the name of Great Britain in 1770. Beginning in 1788, six colonies were successively established that federated and became the Commonwealth of Australia in 1901. *Constitution* 1900, effective 1901.

Form of government

Federal state.

Head of state: English monarch, represented by a Governor General. The monarchy is hereditary.

Head of government: Prime Minister appointed by Parliament.

Cabinet: Ministers appointed by the Prime Minister, responsible to Parliament.

Administrative subdivisions: 6 states and 2 territories.

Legal system

English common law with a High Court (the chief justice and six other justices are appointed by the Governor General).

Legislature

Bicameral Parliament.

Lower house: House of Representatives: 150 members; term of 3 years.

Upper house: Senate: 76 members (12 from each of the 6 states and 2 from each of the 2 territories); staggered elections (one-half of state members are elected every 3 years by popular vote; territory members are elected every 3 years); term of 6 years.

Electoral system (lower house)

Alternative vote system (referred to as 'preferential vote' in Australia).

Formula: Absolute majority (of first preferences or, if necessary, of first preferences plus preferences for eliminated candidates in subsequent counts).

Constituencies: 148 single-member constituencies plus 2 territories.

Barrier clause: None.

Suffrage: Universal and compulsory, 18 years.

Direct democracy

Constitutional referendum must be initiated through a parliamentary bill. Requirement of double majority of states/territories and voters. In addition, non-binding 'plebiscites' are held on non-constitutional matters.

Party system Results of the 2010 legislative elections (House of Representatives):

Electorate	14,088,260	100.0%
Voters	13,131,668	93.2%

Party	Valid votes	%	Seats
Liberal National Coalition	5,408,631	43.6	73
Australian Labor Party	4,711,363	38.0	72
Australian Greens	1,458,998	11.8	1
Family First Party	279,330	2.3	0
Others	544,042	4.4	4
Total	**12,419,863**	**100**	**150**

Notes: Category 'Others' includes parties with less than 1% of the votes nationwide and no seats.

Source: IFES Election Guide; Australian Election Commission.

Country Profile Brazil

Federative Republic of Brazil (*República Federativa do Brasil*)

State formation

Gained independence from Portugal in 1822. The Republic was established in 1889. An authoritarian regime prevailed from 1930 to 1945. Democratization took place after the Second World War, but in 1964 the military overthrew the President and Brazil was ruled by a succession of military governments that suspended constitutional guarantees. Civilian government was restored in 1985.
Constitution 1988; amended many times.

Form of government

Presidential, federal republic.
Head of state: President and Vice President elected on the same ticket with a two-ballot system (run-off between the two candidates with most votes in first ballot); term of 4 years.
Head of government: The President.
Cabinet: Appointed by the President.
Administrative subdivisions: 26 states and 1 federal district.

Legal system

Civil law based on Roman and Germanic traditions.

Legislature

Bicameral parliament: National Congress (*Congresso Nacional*).
Lower house: Chamber of Deputies (*Câmara dos Deputados*): 513 members; term of 4 years.
Upper house: Federal Senate (*Senado Federal*): 81 members (3 members from each constituency, majority vote); staggered elections (one-third elected after 4 years, two-thirds elected after the next 4 years); term of 8 years.

Electoral system (lower house)

Proportional representation.
Formula: Hare quota and highest average, closed non-blocked lists, and preferential voting within lists.
Constituencies: 27 (the states and federal district).
Barrier clause: 5 per cent nation-wide (since 2006).
Suffrage: Universal and compulsory, 18 years; voluntary between 16 and 18 years and over 70; military conscripts do not vote.

Direct democracy

The National Congress can call non-binding referenda and plebiscites. Legislative popular initiative is not binding either.

Party system Results of the 2010 legislative elections (Chamber of Deputies):

Electorate:	135,523,536	100.0%
Voters:	111,038,704	81.9%

Party	Valid votes	%	Seats
Partido dos Trabalhadores (PT)	16,508,091	16.8	87
Partido do Movimento Democratico Brasileiro (PMD)	12,681,654	12.9	78
Partido da Social Democracia Brasileira (PSDB)	11,479,666	11.7	53
Partido da Republica (PR)	7,359,093	7.5	40
Democratas (Dem)	7,301,471	7.4	43
Partido Progressista (PP)	7,209,976	7.3	44
Partido Socialista Brasileiro (PSB)	6,880,252	7.0	35
Partido Democrático Trabalhista (PDT)	4,952,723	5.0	26
Partido Trabalhista Brasileiro (PTB)	4,111,139	4.2	22
Partido Verde (PV)	3,709,647	3.8	14
Partido Social Cristão (PSC)	3,056,208	3.1	17
Partido Comunista do Brasil (PC do B)	2,748,290	2.8	15

Country Profile Brazil (*continued*)

Party	Valid votes	%	Seats
Partido Popular Socialista (PPS)	2,536,809	2.6	12
Partido Republicano Brasileiro (PRB)	1,760,396	1.8	8
Partido Socialismo e Liberdade (PSOL)	1,144,216	1.2	3
Partido da Mobilização Nacional (PMN)	1,108,787	1.1	4
Others	3,673,802	3.7	12
Total	**98,222,220**	**100.0**	**513**

Notes: Category 'Others' includes parties with less than 1% nation-wide and no seats.

Source: electionresources.org; Adam Carr's website

Country Profile **Chile**

Republic of Chile (*República de Chile*)

State formation

Spanish conquerors arrived in the sixteenth century and founded the city of Santiago in 1541. Chile became part of the Spanish Viceroyalty of Peru. In 1810, when the Spanish throne had been toppled by Napoleon, a national junta was formed that proclaimed Chile an autonomous republic within the Spanish monarchy. Warfare continued until the royalists were defeated in 1817. Independence was formally proclaimed in 1818.
Constitution 1980, effective 1981; amended many times.

Form of government

Presidential republic.
Head of state: Directly elected President; term of 4 years.
Head of government: The President.
Cabinet: Ministers appointed by the President.
Administrative subdivisions: 13 regions.

Legal system

Derived from Spanish, French, and Austrian law; criminal justice system modelled on the US system.

Legislature

Bicameral National Congress (*Congreso Nacional*).
Lower house: Chamber of Deputies (*Cámara de Diputados*): 120 seats; term of 4 years.
Upper house: Senate (*Senado*): 38 seats; staggered elections (roughly half renewed every 4 years); term of 8 years.

Electoral system (lower house)

Closed non-blocked lists and preferential voting within one list.
Formula: The majority party is entitled to the two seats of a constituency if it obtains more than two-thirds of the valid votes cast; otherwise the second seat goes to the second-placed party.
Constituencies: 60 two-member constituencies.
Barrier clause: Not applicable.
Suffrage: Universal, 18 years; compulsory.

Direct democracy

Optional constitutional referendum can be called by the President if he/she has rejected a constitutional modification proposed by the Congress but the Congress insists on that modification.

Party system Results of the 2009 legislative elections (Chamber of Deputies):

Electorate	8,285,186	100.0%
Voters	7,179,762	86.7%

Party		Valid votes	%	Seats
List A	Christian Democratic Party	918,379	14.2	19
	Party for Democracy	827,774	12.8	18
	Socialist Party of Chile	647,533	10.0	11
	Social Democratic Radical Party	247,486	3.8	5
	Communist Party of Chile	115,453	1.8	3
	Independents in List A	114,616	1.8	1
	Total List A ('Democratic Concertation')	**2,871,241**	**44.3**	**57**
List B	Independent Democratic Union	1,507,011	23.3	37
	National Renewal	1,165,679	18.0	18
	Independents in List B	168,634	2.6	3
	Chile First	17,749	0.3	-
	Total List B ('Coalition for Change')	**2,859,073**	**44.2**	**58**

Country Profile Chile (continued)

Party		Valid votes	%	Seats
List C	Independents List C	200,731	3.1	0
	Humanist Party	94,216	1.5	0
	Ecologist Party of Chile	3,818	0.1	0
	Total List C ('New Majority')	**298,765**	**4.6**	**0**
List D	Regionalist Party of Independents	251,206	3.9	3
	Independents List D	48,211	0.7	0
	Broad Social Movement	26,121	0.4	0
	Total List D ('Clean Chile. Vote Happy')	**325,538**	**5.0**	**3**
	Independents	119,934	1.9	2
Total		**6,474,551**	**100**	**120**

Source: Servicio Electoral, Adam Carr's website, Inter-Parliamentary Union (electorate and voters).

Country Profile China

People's Republic of China (*Zhōnghuá Rénmín Gònghéguó*)

State formation

The first unification under the Qin Dynasty dates back to the year 221BC. A Republic of China was established in 1912 after the unsuccessful Qing Dynasty had been overthrown, but no political stability was achieved. From 1927 to 1950 the Kuomindang (or Nationalist Party) opposed the Chinese Communist Party in a civil war. The People's Republic was established under Mao Zedong, the leader of the latter party, in 1949.
Constitution 1982; amended several times.

Form of government

Communist state.
Head of state: President and Vice President elected by the National People's Congress; term of 5 years (renewable once).
Head of government: Prime Minister, nominated by the President and confirmed by the National People's Congress.
Cabinet: State Council appointed by the National People's Congress.
Administrative subdivisions: 23 provinces, 5 autonomous regions, and 4 municipalities. Hong Kong and Macau have the status of Special Administrative Regions.

Legal system

Derived from Soviet and continental European civil code.

Legislature

Unicameral National People's Congress (*Quánguó Rénmín Dàibiao Dàhuì*): about 3,000 members elected by municipal, regional, and provincial people's congresses; term of 5 years. There is also a Chinese People's Political Consultative Conference which is not anchored in the constitution but in some sense fulfils the functions of an advisory upper house.

Electoral system

A six-month-long series of layered indirect elections is conducted, beginning from local popularly elected people's congresses up to the National People's Congress. In practice the selection of members for the higher people's congresses is controlled by the Communist Party. Approximately one-third of the seats of the National People's Congress are informally reserved for non-party members such as technical experts and members of the smaller allied parties.
Constituencies: The delegates from each of the 34 administrative subdivisions form a delegation.
Suffrage: Universal, 18 years.

Direct democracy

None.

Party system Results of the 2007–2008 elections:

Electorate	Not available	100.0%
Voters	Not available	Not available

Party		Valid votes	%	Seats
Communist Party of China		n.a.	n.a.	2,987
Registered allied parties	Revolutionary Committee of the Kuomintang	n.a.	n.a.	n.a.
	China Democratic League	n.a.	n.a.	n.a.
	China Democratic National Construction Association	n.a.	n.a.	n.a.
	China Association for Promoting Democracy	n.a.	n.a.	n.a.
	Chinese Peasants' and Workers' Democratic Party	n.a.	n.a.	n.a.
	Zhigongdang of China	n.a.	n.a.	n.a.
	Jiusan Society	n.a.	n.a.	n.a.
	Taiwan Democratic Self-Government League	n.a.	n.a.	n.a.

Country Profile China (*continued*)

Party	Valid votes	%	Seats
Non-Partisans	n.a.	n.a.	n.a.
China Green Party (seeking to become a political party)	n.a.	n.a.	n.a.
Total	**n.a.**	**100.0**	**2,987**

Note: Besides the dominant Communist Party of China, eight registered minor parties exist which, however, do not form any political opposition.

Source: Wikipedia.

Country Profile Egypt

Arab Republic of Egypt (*Jumhuriyat Misr al-Arabiya*)

State formation

An Ottoman viceroyalty since 1805, the country was informally controlled by Great Britain from 1882 and became a British protectorate in 1914. Following a revolution in 1919 and constant insurgency, Egypt was declared independent by Great Britain in 1922 but largely remained under British control until Colonel Gamal Abdel Nasser seized power in 1956, following a military *coup d'état* and the establishment of the Republic in 1953. In January 2011 demonstrations and riots broke out in Cairo and other cities. After several weeks of mounting bloodshed, the Army withdrew support from President Mubarak and he resigned on 11 February. After the fall of Mubarak, political parties were legalized ahead of multistage elections in November and December 2011. The Constitution of the Arab Republic of Egypt was signed into law on 26 December 2012.

Form of government

Semi-presidential republic.
Head of state: President, directly elected (since the 2012 Constitution); maximum of two 4-year terms. There is no Vice President.
Head of government: The President nominates the Prime Minister. If the Prime Minister is not confirmed by parliament, the President nominates a candidate from the strongest party in parliament. If this candidate is also not confirmed by parliament, the parliament nominates the Prime Minister.

Cabinet: Appointed by the President.
Administrative subdivisions: 27 governorates.

Legal system

Based on European models, especially the French civil code, and Sharia law; family law corresponds to Islamic or Christian norms depending on the individual concerned.

Legislature

Bicameral Parliament.
Lower house: People's Assembly (*Majlis Ash-Sha'ab*): 498 members, directly elected, secret public ballot; term of 5 years if not dissolved earlier.
Upper house: Advisory Council (*Majlis Ash-Shura*): at least 150 members, directly elected by secret ballot; staggered elections (half of the elected members renewed every 3 years); term of 6 years.

Electoral system (lower house)

Formula: Mixed-member electoral system for parliamentary elections of 2011 and 2012. Two-thirds of seats elected on party lists, one-third via majority rule according to the Hare quota. Half the seats in parliament are guaranteed to peasants and workers.
Constituencies: Two-member constituencies in plurality elections and multimember constituencies in PR.

Direct democracy

Referendum.

Party system Results of the 2011 legislative elections (People's Assembly):

Electorate	ca. 51 million	100.0%
Voters	27,832,919	ca. 54%

Party	Valid votes	%	Seats
Freedom and Justice Party	10,131,542	36.4	232
Party of Light (al-Nour)	7,532,694	27.1	121
New Delegation Party (al-Wafd)	2,479,819	8.9	40
Egyptian Bloc	2,466,126	8.9	35
New Centre Party (al-Wasat)	987,484	3.6	10
Revolution Continues Alliance	743,477	2.7	10
Reform and Development Party	604,348	2.2	10
Egyptian National Party	424,973	1.5	6

Country Profile Egypt (*continued*)

Party	Valid votes	%	Seats
Freedom Party	514,016	1.9	4
Egyptian Citizen	279,275	1.0	4
Others	1,669,165	5.8	26
Total	**27,832,919**	**100.0**	**498**

Note: Category 'Others' includes parties with less than 1% vote nation-wide.

Source: Inter-Parliamentary Union.

Country Profile Germany

Federal Republic of Germany (*Bundesrepublik Deutschland*)

State formation

The German Empire was unified in 1871. After the Second World War, Germany was divided into four zones of occupation administered by the UK, the US, the USSR, and France. The Federal Republic of Germany, which included the former UK, US, and French zones, was proclaimed in 1949. The former USSR zone became the German Democratic Republic and joined the Federal Republic in 1990.

Constitution Basic Law of 1949; became constitution of the united Germany in 1990 but is still referred to as the Basic Law.

Form of government

Federal republic.

Head of state: President elected by a Federal Convention, including all members of the Federal Assembly and an equal number of delegates elected by the state parliaments; term of 5 years (renewable once).

Head of government: Chancellor elected by an absolute majority of the Federal Assembly; term of 4 years.

Cabinet: Federal Ministers appointed by the President on the recommendation of the Chancellor.

Administrative subdivisions: 16 states (*Länder*).

Legal system

Civil law system; judicial review of legislative acts in the Federal Constitutional Court.

Legislature

Bicameral parliament.

Lower house: Federal Assembly (*Bundestag*): 622 seats; term of 4 years.

Upper house: Federal Council (*Bundesrat*): 69 members (each state government has 3–6 of the total 69 seats and must vote as a block).

Electoral system (lower house)

Mixed system of plurality vote and proportional representation.

Formula: Sainte-Laguë/Schepers. The number of deputies elected in the individual constituencies is subtracted from the total of the seats to which their party is entitled. The remaining seats are allocated to the candidates on the party list, in the order enumerated. 'Overhang mandates' (additional seats in the constituencies than a party is entitled to according to the results of the proportional calculation) have been abolished.

Constituencies: 299 single-member constituencies and 16 multimember constituencies corresponding to the states.

Barrier clause: 5 per cent unless at least 3 candidates of the party in question have been elected in single-member constituencies.

Suffrage: Universal, 18 years.

Direct democracy

None.

Party system Results of the 2009 legislative elections (Federal Assembly):

Electorate	62,168,498	100.0%
Voters	44,005,575	70.8%

Party	Valid votes	%	Seats
Christian Democratic Union	11,828,277	27.3	194
Social Democratic Party	9,990,488	23.0	146
Free Democratic Party	6,316,080	14.6	93
The Left	5,155,993	11.9	76
Alliance '90/The Greens	4,643,272	10.7	68
Christian Social Union	2,830,238	6.5	45
Others	2,605,591	6.0	0
Total	**43,371,190**	**100**	**622**

Note: In the federal institutions, the Christian Social Union (from the state of Bavaria) forms a joint faction with the Christian Democratic Union (present in all of the other states).

Source: Statistisches Bundesamt.

Country Profile India

Republic of India (*Bhārat Gaṇarājya*)

State formation

From the sixteenth century, Indian colonies were established by several European countries. By 1856, most of the country was under the control of the British East India Company. It became a colony of the British Empire after a failed insurrection in 1857. In the twentieth century, the Indian National Congress and other political organizations engaged in a non-violent struggle for independence, which was finally won in 1947. However, India lost the territories that became independent Pakistan and, later, Bangladesh; over 7 million Indian Muslims moved to these countries after the partition, with another 7 million Hindus and Sikhs moving the other way. *Constitution* 1949, effective 1950; amended many times.

Form of government

Federal republic.
Head of state: President elected by an electoral college (elected members of both houses of Parliament and the legislatures of the states); term of 5 years (no term limits).
Head of government: Prime Minister, chosen by the members of Parliament in the majority party.
Cabinet: Appointed by the President on the recommendation of the Prime Minister.

Administrative subdivisions: 28 States and 7 Union Territories.

Legal system

Based on English common law; judicial review of legislative acts.

Legislature

Bicameral parliament (*Sansad*).
Lower house: People's Assembly (*Lok Sabha*): 545 seats (543 elected by popular vote, 2 appointed by the President); term of 5 years.
Upper house: Council of States (*Rajya Sabha*): 250 members (up to 12 appointed by the President, the remainder chosen by the elected members of the state and territorial assemblies); term of 6 years.

Electoral system (lower house)

Plurality
Constituencies: 543 single-member constituencies.
Barrier clause: Not applicable.
Suffrage: Universal, 18 years.

Direct democracy

None.

Party system Results of the 2009 legislative elections (People's Assembly):

Electorate	716,676,063	100.0%
Voters	417,156,494	57.5%

Party	Valid votes	%	Seats
Total 'National Democratic Alliance'	102,689,312	24.6	159
Total 'United Progressive Alliance'	153,482,356	36.8	262
Total 'Third Front'	88,174,229	21.1	79
Others and independents (with seats)	48,603,056	11.7	43
Others (less than 1% nation-wide and no seats)	24,207,541	5.8	0
Total	**417,156,494**	**100**	**543**

Note: Each of the alliances consists of a leading party (the Baharatiya Janata Party, the Indian National Congress, and the Communist Party of India (Marxist), respectively) and a number of smaller parties which cannot be listed in the textbook for reasons of space.

Source: Election Commission of India.

Country Profile Israel

State of Israel (*Medinat Yisra'el*)

State formation

In the late nineteenth century, the Austro-Hungarian Jew Theodor Herzl founded the Zionist movement that strived for the establishment of a national Jewish state. By the end of the Second World War, some 500,000 Jews had immigrated to Palestine, mostly from Russia and Europe following pogroms and outbreaks of anti-semitism. Palestine became a League of Nations mandate administered by Britain in 1920. Independence was gained in 1948.

Constitution No formal constitution. A parliamentary committee has been working on a draft constitution since 2003.

Form of government

Parliamentary democracy.

Head of state: President elected by Parliament, term of 7 years (no term limits).

Head of government: Prime Minister assigned by the President; traditionally the leader of the party that holds most of the seats in parliament.

Party system Results of the 2013 legislative elections:

Cabinet: Ministers selected by the Prime Minister and approved by Parliament.

Administrative subdivisions: 6 districts.

Legal system

Mixture of English common law, British Mandate regulations, and Jewish, Christian, and Muslim legal systems.

Legislature

Unicameral parliament (*Knesset*): 120 seats, term of 4 years.

Electoral system

Proportional representation.

Formula: Hare quota and highest average.

Constituencies: One multimember constituency for 120 seats.

Barrier clause: 2 per cent nation-wide.

Suffrage: Universal, 18 years.

Direct democracy

None.

Electorate:	5,656,705	100.0%
Voters:	3,833,646	67.8%

Party	Valid votes	%	Seats
Likud Yisrael Beitenu	885,163	23.3	31
Yesh Atid	543,458	14.3	19
Israel Labor Party	432,118	11.4	15
Habayit Hayehudi	345,985	9.1	12
Shas	331,868	8.8	11
United Torah Judaism	195,892	5.2	7
Hatenua	189,167	5.0	6
Meretz	172,403	4.5	6
United Arab List	138,450	3.7	4
Hadash	113,439	3.0	4
National Democratic Assembly	97,030	2.6	3
Kadima	78,974	2.1	2
Otzma Leyisrael	66,775	1.8	0
Am Shalem	45,690	1.2	0
Green Leaf—Liberal List	43,734	1.2	0
Others	112,596	3.0	0
Total	**3,792,742**	**100**	**120**

Note: Category 'Others' includes parties with less than 1% nation-wide and no seats.

Source: Knesset, Israel Ministry of Foreign Affairs, Electionresources.org.

Country Profile Italy

Italian Republic (*Repubblica Italiana*)

State formation

The Kingdom of Italy was proclaimed in 1861; Italy was finally unified in 1870. The monarchy was abolished by a popular referendum in 1946.
Constitution 1947, effective 1 January 1948; amended many times.

Form of government

Parliamentary republic.
Head of state: President elected by an electoral college consisting of both houses of Parliament and 58 regional representatives, term of 7 years (no term limit).
Head of government: President of the Council of Ministers, appointed by the President and confirmed by Parliament.
Cabinet: Council of Ministers, nominated by the Prime Minister and approved by the President.
Administrative subdivisions: 15 regions and 5 autonomous regions.

Legal system

Civil law system; judicial review under certain conditions in Constitutional Court.

Legislature

Bicameral Parliament.
Lower house: Chamber of Deputies (*Camera dei Deputati*): 630 seats, with the winning national coalition receiving 54 per cent of them; term of 5 years.

Upper house: Senate (*Senato*): 315 seats, with the winning coalition in each region receiving 55 per cent of that region's seats.

Electoral system (lower house)

Proportional representation.
Formula: If the political coalition or party with the highest number of votes fails to win 340 seats, it is given 'bonus' seats to meet the 340-seat requirement. The 277 remaining seats are distributed among the other coalitions or lists using the whole number quota and highest remainders method.
Constituencies: 26 multimember constituencies for 617 seats, one single-member constituency and one multimember constituency for Italians abroad.
Barrier clause: 10 per cent nation-wide for a coalition, 2 per cent for a party within a coalition, 4 per cent for an independent party; for language minority lists, 20 per cent of the votes cast in their constituency. A list obtaining the highest number of votes among all lists and which fails to win 2 per cent of the votes cast is also entitled to a seat.
Suffrage: Universal, 18 years (25 in senatorial elections).

Direct democracy

A consultative referendum can be called by Parliament, and an abrogative referendum (with a quorum of participation of 50 per cent) can be called by 500,000 citizens or 5 Regional Councils. An optional constitutional referendum has never been practised.

Party system Results of the 2013 legislative elections (Chamber of Deputies):

Electorate:	50,399,841	100.0%
Voters:	36,375,530	72.2%

Party	Valid vote	%	Seats
Partito Democratico	8,932,615	25.5	297
Left, Ecology, Liberty	1,106,748	3.2	37
Democratic Centre	167,072	0.5	6
South Tyrolean People's Party	146,804	0.4	5
Total 'Coalizione Bersani'	**10,353,275**	**29.6**	**345**
People for Freedom	7,478,796	21.4	98
Northern League	1,390,014	4.0	18
Brothers of Italy	665,830	1.9	9
Others in coalition	534,034	1.5	0
Total 'Coalizione Berlusconi'	**10,068,674**	**28.8**	**125**

Country Profile Italy (*continued*)

Party	Valid vote	%	Seats
Five Star Movement coalition	**8,784,499**	**25.1**	**109**
Civic Choice with Mario Monti	3,004,739	8.6	39
Union of the Center	608,739	1.7	8
Others in coalition	159,332	0.5	0
Total 'Coalizione Monti'	**3,772,281**	**10.8**	**47**
Others (outside coalitions)	2,006,122	5.7	4
Total	**34,984,851**	**100.0**	**630**

Source: Ministry of Interior; Adam Carr's website.

Country Profile Japan

Japan (*Nihon-koku/Nippon-koku*)

State formation

The foundation of Japan dates back to the Emperor Jimmu, 660BC. After defeat in the Second World War, Japan adopted a democratic and pacifist constitution. *Constitution* 1947, effective 1 January 1948; amended many times.

Form of government

Constitutional monarchy.
Head of state: Emperor; the monarchy is hereditary.
Head of government: Prime Minister, usually the leader of the majority party or coalition.
Cabinet: Appointed by the Prime Minister.
Administrative subdivisions: 47 prefectures.

Legal system

Modelled on European civil law system with some English and American ingredients; judicial review of legislative acts in the Supreme Court.

Legislature

Bicameral Parliament (*Diet* or *Kokkai*).
Lower house: House of Representatives (*Shugi-in*): 480 seats; term of 4 years.

Upper house: House of Councillors (Sangi-in): 242 seats; term of 6 years; staggered elections (half renewed every 3 years).

Electoral system (lower house)

Mixed system: 300 seats allocated by plurality, 180 seats allocated by proportional representation.
Formula: D'Hondt method for the 180 seats allocated by propotional representation. Candidates may run in both the single-seat constituencies and the proportional representation poll. However, the single-seat constituency must be located within their proportional representation constituency. Candidates running in single-seat constituencies must obtain at least one-sixth of the number of valid votes.
Constituencies: 300 single-member constituencies (plurality vote) and 11 multimember or 'block' constituencies (proportional representation vote).
Barrier clause: None.
Suffrage: Universal, 20 years.

Direct democracy

None.

Party system Results of the 2012 legislative elections (House of Representatives):

Electorate:	103,959,866	100.0%
Voters:	61,669,473	59.3%

Party	Valid votes	%	Seats
Liberal Democratic Party	16,624,457	27.6	294
Democratic Party of Japan	9,628,653	16.0	57
Japan Restoration Party	12,262,228	20.4	54
New Komeito	7,116,474	11.8	31
Your Party	5,245,586	8.7	18
Tomorrow Party of Japan	3,423,915	5.7	9
Japanese Communist Party	3,689,159	6.1	8
Social Democratic Party	1,420,790	2.4	2
New Party Daichi	346,848	0.6	1
Kokumin Shinto (People's New Party)	70,847	0.1	1
Independents	n.a.	n.a.	5
Others	350,931	0.6	0
Total	**60,179,888**	**100.0**	**480**

Notes: Category 'Others' includes parties with less than 1% nation-wide and no seats, and seats won in single-member plurality vote by independent candidates. Votes refer to PR vote, seats to total seats allocated in proportional representation and plurality vote.

Source: Inter-Parliamentary Union, Adam Carr's website, Electionresources.org.

Country Profile Mexico

United Mexican States (*Estados Unidos Mexicanos*)

State formation

Spain occupied what is now known as Mexico in 1519 and conquered the Aztec capital in 1521. Mexican independence was declared in 1810, when Spain was occupied by Napoleon's army, but only recognized after a long war in 1821. The first republic was established in 1824. *Constitution* 1917.

Form of government

Federal presidential republic.
Head of state: President, elected by popular vote; term of 6 years (not renewable).
Head of government: The President.
Cabinet: Appointed by the President; the appointment of the Attorney General requires approval of the Senate.
Administrative subdivisions: 31 states.

Legal system

Mixture of civil law system and US constitutional theory; judicial review of legislative acts.
Legislature
Bicameral National Congress (*Congreso de la Unión*).
Lower house: Chamber of Deputies (*Cámara de Diputados*): 500 seats; term of 3 years.

Upper house: Senate (*Cámara de Senadores*): 128 seats; 96 members are elected in 32 multimember constituencies in the federal entities with the plurality vote; 32 members are elected by PR in a single national constituency according to the Hare quota and highest remainder; term of 6 years.

Electoral system (lower house)

Mixed system: 300 seats allocated by plurality, 200 seats allocated by PR.
Formula: Simple quota plus greatest remainder for the 200 seats allocated by PR. However, the majority party cannot obtain more than 300 seats (or 315 with more than 60 per cent of popular vote).
Constituencies: 300 single-member constituencies (plurality vote) and 5 multimember or 'block' constituencies (PR vote).
Barrier clause: 2 per cent of the votes in the multimember constituencies.
Suffrage: Universal and compulsory (but not enforced), 18 years.

Direct democracy

Referendums on constitutional matters, administrative reforms, and political issues.

Party system Results of the 2009 legislative elections (Chamber of Deputies):

Electorate:	77,481,874	100.0%
Voters:	34,677,991	44.8%

Party	Valid votes	%	Seats
Institutional Revolutionary Party (PRI)	12,809,395	39.1	241
National Action Party (PAN)	9,714,180	29.7	147
Party of the Democratic Revolution (PRD)	4,228,623	12.9	72
Green Party	2,326,045	7.1	17
Labour Party	1,268,151	3.9	9
New Alliance Party	1,186,875	3.6	8
Convergence	854,311	2.6	6
Social Democratic Party	358,485	1.1	0
Total	**32,746,065**	**100**	**500**

Notes: Votes refer to PR vote, and seats to total seats allocated in proportional representation and plurality vote.

Source: Instituto Federal Electoral.

Country Profile Nigeria

Federal Republic of Nigeria

State formation

Nigeria was run by the British Royal Niger Company until 1900, when it came under the rule of the British government. The country was formally united in 1914. Following the Second World War, successive constitutions legislated by the British government increased the autonomy of Nigeria. Independence was finally gained in 1960. From 1966, Nigeria was ruled by military regimes (except the Second Republic from 1979 to 1983); it returned to democracy in 1999.
Constitution 1999; an amendment that would have allowed its president to serve more than two terms was blocked in 2006.

Form of government

Federal republic.
Head of state: President, term of 4 years, renewable once.
Head of government: The President.
Cabinet: Federal Ministers appointed by the President.
Administrative subdivisions: 36 states and 1 Federal Capital Territory.

Legal system

Based on English common law, Sharia law (in 12 northern states), and traditional law.

Legislature

Bicameral National Assembly.
Lower house: House of Representatives: 360 seats; term of 4 years.
Upper house: Senate: 109 seats (the number of seats per state is determined by population); term of 4 years. Both chambers elected at the same time.

Electoral system (lower house)

Plurality.
Constituencies: 360 single-member constituencies.
Barrier clause: Not applicable.
Suffrage: Universal, 18 years. According to observers, elections fall short of international standards.

Direct democracy

None.

Party system Results of the 2011 legislative elections (House of Representatives):

Electorate	n.a.	100.0%
Voters:	n.a.	n.a.

Party	Valid votes	%	Seats
People's Democratic Party (PDP)	n.a.	n.a.	205
Action Congress (AC)	n.a.	n.a.	69
Congress for Progressive Change (CPC)	n.a.	n.a.	36
All Nigeria People's Party (ANPP)	n.a.	n.a.	28
Labour Party (LP)	n.a.	n.a.	9
All Progressives Grand Alliance (AGPA)	n.a.	n.a.	6
Accord (Acc)	n.a.	n.a.	5
Democratic Peoples Party (DPP)	n.a.	n.a.	1
Peoples Party of Nigeria (PPN)	n.a.	n.a.	1
Others	n.a.	n.a.	0
Total	n.a.	**100.0**	**360**

Note: The INEC website has failed to give usable figures for 85 seats, making it impossible to calculate national or state vote totals.

Source: African Elections Database, Independent National Electoral Commission, Adam Carr's website.

Country Profile Russia

Russian Federation (*Rossiyskaya Federatsiya*)

State formation

Independence 24 August 1991 (from Soviet Union). *Constitution* 1993.

Form of government

Federation.

Head of state: President, 6-year term with the option of one consecutive re-election (further re-election possible after a pause lasting at least one term). There is no Vice President; the Prime Minister serves as acting president until a new presidential election is held.

Head of government: Prime Minister appointed by the President with the approval of the Duma.

Cabinet: Appointed by the President.

Administrative subdivisions: 46 oblasts, 21 republics, 9 krays, 4 autonomous okrugs, 2 federal cities, and 1 autonomous oblast.

Legal system

Based on civil law system; judicial review of legislative acts.

Legislature

Bicameral Federal Assembly (*Federalnoye Sobraniye*).

Lower house: State Duma (*Gosudarstvennaya Duma*): 450 seats; term of 6 years.

Upper house: Federation Council (*Soviet Federatsii*): 178 seats (members appointed by the top officials in each of the 88 federal administrative units); term of 4 years.

Electoral system (lower house)

Proportional representation. From 2007, all seats are elected by PR and only parties are allowed to contest the election.

Constituencies: The whole country is one multimember constituency consisting of 450 parliamentary seats.

Barrier clause: 7 per cent. Parties that win between 5 and 6 per cent of votes get one mandate; parties that win between 6% and 7% get two mandates. The 7% threshold applies under the condition that at least two parties passed it, winning at least 60 per cent of votes. If one of the two conditions is not fulfilled, seats are allocated to parties winning less than 7 per cent until the 60 per cent of votes cast is fulfilled and until at least two parties satisfy criteria for entering parliament.

Suffrage: Universal, 18 years.

Direct democracy

The constitution provides the possibility for the President to call an extraordinary referendum under procedures established by federal constitutional law.

Party system Results of the 2011 legislative elections (State Duma):

Electorate:	109,233,695	100.0%
Voters:	65,836,181	60.3%

Party	Valid votes	%	Seats
United Russia	32,529,450	50.2	238
Communist Party	12,606,882	19.5	92
Liberal Democratic Party	7,670,478	11.8	56
Fair Russia	8,712,162	13.4	64
Russian Democratic Party (Yabloko)	2,252,000	3.5	0
Others	1,031,776	1.6	0
Total	**64,802,748**	**100**	**450**

Notes: Category 'Others' includes parties with less than 1% nation-wide and no seats. Seat figures include both 225 district seats (including 74 that were won by non-partisan candidates) and the 225 list seats.

Source: Russian Election Commission; Adam Carr's website.

Country Profile Saudi Arabia

Kingdom of Saudi Arabia (*Al-Mamlaka al-Arabiyya as-Saūdiyya*)

State formation

The Kingdom of Saudi Arabia is characterized by a strong alliance of secular and clerical structures that was initiated in 1744 by Muhammad bin Saud. During the first decades of the twentieth century, Abdul Aziz bin Saud was able to settle some regional rivalries by the successive conquest of important parts of the Arabian peninsula. He became the first King of Nejd and Hejaz, recognized by the UK in 1927. The Kingdom of Saudi Arabia was founded in 1932 when the regions of Al-Hasa and Qatif joined the realm.

Constitution Formally the Qur'an; a Basic Law of Government, promulgated in 1992, articulates the government's rights and responsibilities.

Form of government

Monarchy.

Head of state: The King, chosen by the royal family from among its members and approved by the clergy (*ulema*).

Head of government: The King is also the Prime Minister.

Cabinet: Council of Ministers, appointed by the monarch every 4 years; includes many members of the royal family.

Administrative subdivisions: 13 provinces.

Legal system

Sharia law; several civil and commercial codes exist.

Legislature

Council of Ministers (*Majlis ash-Shura*): 150 members and a chairman, appointed by the monarch; term of 4 years. However, the Council of Ministers is not an actual legislature, for its resolutions have to be ratified by royal decree. Its main function is to advise the King.

Electoral system

To date, no national elections have been held. Municipal elections were held for the first time in 2005.

Suffrage: Males; 21 years.

Direct democracy

None.

Party system No political parties exist except the clandestine Green Party; political opposition is generally prevented.

Country Profile South Africa

Republic of South Africa

State formation

Dutch settlement at the Cape of Good Hope started with the foundation of a station by the Dutch East India Company in 1652. The region was seized by Great Britain in 1797 and annexed in 1805, but the Boers (of Dutch origin) resisted British rule throughout the nineteenth century. The second Anglo-Boer War ended in 1902, with Great Britain assuming sovereignty over the South African republics. In 1910, the Union of South Africa was created. From 1948 to 1990, the country was ruled under a regime of segregationist legislation (apartheid); the first multi-racial elections were held in 1994. *Constitution* 1996, effective 1997 (but implemented in successive phases).

Form of government

Presidential socialist people's republic.
Head of state: President elected by the National Assembly; term of 5 years (renewable once).
Head of government: The President.
Cabinet: Appointed by the President.
Administrative subdivisions: 9 provinces.

Legal system

Based on Roman-Dutch law and English common law.

Legislature

Bicameral Parliament.
Lower house: National Assembly: 400 seats; term of 5 years.
Upper house: National Council of Provinces: 90 seats, 10 members elected by each of the 9 provincial legislatures; term of 5 years.

Electoral system (lower house)

Proportional representation.
Formula: Four seats for each percentage of the nation-wide vote; 200 members chosen from national party lists, and the other 200 members chosen from regional party lists.
Constituencies: 9 multimember constituencies (4–43 seats).
Barrier clause: None.
Suffrage: Universal, 18 years.

Direct democracy

Three referendums have been held on the constitution and the reform process.

Party system Results of the 2009 legislative elections (National Assembly):

Electorate:	23,181,998	100.0%
Voters:	17,919,966	77.3%

Party	Valid votes	%	Seats
African National Congress (ANC)	11,650,748	65.9	264
Democratic Alliance (DA)	2,945,829	16.7	67
Congress of the People (COPE)	1,311,027	7.4	30
Inkatha Freedom Party (IFP)	804,260	4.5	18
Independent Democrats (ID)	162,915	0.9	4
United Democratic Movement (UDM)	149,680	0.8	4
Freedom Front Plus (VF+)	146,796	0.8	4
African Christian Democratic Party (ACDP)	142,658	0.8	3
United Christian Democratic Party (UCDP)	66,086	0.4	2
Pan Africanist Congress (PAC)	48,530	0.3	1
Minority Front (MF)	43,474	0.2	1
Azanian People's Organisation (AZAPO)	38,245	0.2	1
African Peoples☒ Convention (APC)	35,867	0.2	1
Others	134,614	0.8	0
Total	**17,680,729**	**100**	**400**

Notes: Category 'Others' includes parties with less than 1% nation-wide and no seats.

Source: Adam Carr's website.

Country Profile **Switzerland**

Swiss Confederation (*Schweizerische Eidgenossen-schaft/ Confédération Suisse/Confederazione Svizzera*)

State formation

The Swiss Confederation was founded as a defence alliance in 1291. Switzerland gained independence from the German Empire in 1499 and became a republic in 1848, turning from an alliance to a federal state. *Constitution* 1999, effective 2000 (a revised version of the 1874 constitution).

Form of government

Federal parliamentary republic.
Head of state: President and Vice President elected by the Federal Assembly from among the 7 members of the cabinet; term of 1 year (no consecutive terms).
Head of government: The President.
Cabinet: Federal Council (*Bundesrat/Conseil Fédéral/ Consiglio Federale*) elected by the Federal Assembly from among its members; term of 4 years.
Administrative subdivisions: 26 cantons including 6 half-cantons.

Legal system

Civil law system influenced by customary law; judicial review of legislative acts, except with respect to federal decrees of general obligatory character.

Legislature

Bicameral Federal Assembly (*Bundesversammlung/ Assemblee Fédérale/Assemblea Federale*).
Lower house: National Council (*Nationalrat/Conseil National/Consiglio Nazionale*): 200 seats; term of 4 years.

Upper house: Council of States (*Ständerat/Conseil des Etats/Consiglio degli Stati*): 46 seats (2 representatives from each canton and 1 from each half-canton); term of 4 years.

Electoral system (lower house)

Proportional representation, but plurality system for 5 single-member constituencies (2 cantons, 3 half-cantons).
Formula: Hagenbach–Bischoff method, with remaining seats being distributed according to the rule of highest average, in multimember constituencies. Each elector can vote for a list as it stands or modify it by crossing out or repeating names appearing on it; moreover voters can split their vote between different lists ('panachage') or select names from different lists on a blank ballot paper.
Constituencies: 26 multi- or single-member constituencies corresponding to the country's 20 cantons and 6 half-cantons.
Barrier clause: None.
Suffrage: Universal, 18 years.

Direct democracy

Mandatory referendum on constitution and international treaties; optional referendum on laws. Popular initiatives for the total or partial revision of the constitution. The 'general popular initiative' (introduced with a vote in 2003) allows 100,000 citizens to put not only constitutional changes, but also the implementation and modification of federal laws, on the political agenda.

Party system Results of the 2011 legislative elections (National Council):

Electorate:	5,124,034	100.0%
Voters:	2,485,403	48.5%

Party	Valid votes	%	Seats
Swiss People's Party	641,094	26.6	54
Social Democratic Party	451,236	18.7	46
Free Democratic Party	363,855	15.1	30
Christian Democrats	296,420	12.3	28
Green Party	203,365	8.4	15
Green Liberal Party	130,042	5.4	12
Conservative Democratic Party	130,885	5.4	9

Country Profile **Switzerland** (*continued*)

Party	Valid votes	%	Seats
Evangelical People's Party	48,261	2.0	2
Ticino League	18,956	0.8	2
Christian Social Party	15,023	0.6	1
Federal Democratic Union	30,729	1.3	0
Swiss Labour Party	12,915	0.5	0
Solidarities	8,119	0.3	0
Swiss Democrats	4,839	0.2	0
Others	55,740	2.3	0
Total	**2,411,479**	**100**	**200**

Notes: Category 'Others' includes parties with less than 1% nation-wide and no seats.

Source: Federal Assembly; Swiss Federal Statistical Office; Electionresources.org.

Country Profile **Turkey**

Republic of Turkey (*Türkiye Cumhuriyeti*)

State formation

After defeat in the First World War, the constitutional Republic of Turkey succeeded the 600-year-old Ottoman Empire under the leadership of its founder and first president Mustafa Kemal (honorifically rebaptized Atatürk, Father of the Turks, in 1934). Since the establishment of a multiparty system in 1945, the country has suffered several military *coups d'état*; the current constitution was ratified by popular referendum during a military junta that lasted until 1983. *Constitution* 1982, amended many times.

Form of government

Republican parliamentary democracy.
Head of state: President, elected by the National Assembly; term of 7 years.
Head of government: Prime Minister appointed by the President from among the members of parliament.
Cabinet: Council of Ministers appointed by the President on the nomination of the Prime Minister.

Administrative subdivisions: 81 provinces.

Legal system

Civil law system derived from various European continental legal systems.

Legislature

Unicameral Grand National Assembly of Turkey (*Türkiye Büyük Millet Meclisı*): 550 seats; term of 5 years.

Electoral system

Proportional representation.
Formula: D'Hondt.
Constituencies: 79 multimember constituencies.
Barrier clause: 10% nation-wide.
Suffrage: Universal, 18 years.

Direct democracy

Since the 1982 constitutional referendum, two more referenda have been held, most recently in 1988.

Party system Results of the 2011 legislative elections (Grand National Assembly):

Electorate:	50,339,596	100.0%
Voters:	43,913,276	87.2%

Party	Valid votes	%	Seats
Justice and Development Party (AKP)	21,440,702	49.9	326
Republican People's Party (CHP)	11,130,832	25.9	135
Nationalist Movement Party (MHP)	5,578,844	13.0	53
Others	4,823,358	11.2	36
Total	**42,973,736**	**100**	**550**

Source: Adam Carr's website.

Country Profile United Kingdom

United Kingdom of Great Britain and Northern Ireland

State formation

England has existed as a unified entity since the tenth century. The union with Wales was first formalized in 1536; in 1707, England and Scotland joined as Great Britain. The union of Great Britain and Ireland was implemented in 1801 (United Kingdom of Great Britain and Ireland). After the partition of Ireland in 1921, six northern Irish counties remained part of the United Kingdom. *Constitution* Unwritten; partly statutes, common law, and practice.

Form of government

Constitutional monarchy.
Head of state: The monarchy is hereditary.
Head of government: Prime Minister, usually the leader of the majority party in the lower house.
Cabinet: Cabinet of Ministers appointed by the Prime Minister.
Administrative subdivisions: England: 47 boroughs, 36 counties, 29 London boroughs, 12 cities and boroughs, 10 districts, 12 cities, 3 royal boroughs. Northern Ireland: 24 districts, 2 cities, 6 counties (historic). Scotland: 32 council areas. Wales: 11 county boroughs, 9 counties, 2 cities and counties.

Legal system

Common law tradition with early Roman and modern continental influences; non-binding judicial review of Acts of Parliament.

Legislature

Bicameral parliament.
Lower house: House of Commons: 646 seats; term of 5 years unless the House is dissolved earlier.
Upper house: House of Lords: approximately 500 life peers, 92 hereditary peers, and 26 clergy. No elections (but in 1999 elections were held to determine the 92 hereditary peers; elections are held only as vacancies in the hereditary peerage arise).

Electoral system (lower house)

Simple majority vote (plurality).
Constituencies: 646 single-member constituencies.
Barrier clause: Not applicable.
Suffrage: Universal, 18 years.

Direct democracy

Every referendum needs a special *ad hoc* law.

Party system Results of the 2010 legislative elections (House of Commons):

Electorate	45,597,461	100.0%
Voters	29,687,604	65.1%

Party	Valid votes	%	Seats
Conservative Party	10,703,654	36.1	306
Labour Party	8,606,517	29.0	258
Liberal Democratic Party	6,836,248	23.0	57
UK Independence Party	919,471	3.1	0
British National Party	564,321	1.9	0
Scottish National Party	491,386	1.7	6
Green Party	285,612	1.0	1
Sinn Féin	171,942	0.6	5
Democratic Unionist Party	168,216	0.6	8
Plaid Cymru	165,394	0.6	3
Social Democratic and Labour Party	110,970	0.4	3
Ulster Conservatives and Unionists–New Force	102,361	0.3	0

Country Profile **United Kingdom** (*continued*)

Party	Valid votes	%	Seats
Alliance Party	42,762	0.1	1
Respect–Unity Coalition	33,251	0.1	0
Speaker	22,860	0.1	1
Independent Community and Health Concern	16,150	0.1	0
Others	446,489	1.5	1
Total	**29,687,604**	**100**	**650**

Source: The Electoral Commission, Inter-Parliamentary Union, Electionresources.org.

Country Profile United States

United States of America

State formation

American colonies were founded by Spanish, French, and English settlers starting in the sixteenth century. The US was founded by 13 colonies declaring their independence from Great Britain in 1776. It expanded to the western coast of the continent and has since been receiving more immigrants than the rest of the world combined.
Constitution 1787, effective 1789; amended 27 times.

Form of government

Federal republic.
Head of state: President and Vice President elected on the same ticket by a college of representatives who are elected directly from each state; term of 4 years (renewable once).
Head of government: The President.
Cabinet: Appointed by the President with approval of the Senate.
Administrative subdivisions: 50 states and 1 district.

Legal system

Based on English common law; each state has its own legal system; judicial review of legislative acts.

Legislature

Bicameral Congress.
Lower house: House of Representatives: 435 seats; term of 2 years.
Upper house: Senate: 100 seats (2 members from each state); staggered elections (one-third renewed every 2 years); term of 6 years.

Electoral system (lower house)

Simple majority vote in one round (absolute majority in the states of Georgia and Louisiana).
Constituencies: 435 single-member constituencies. Each representative represents roughly the same number of citizens, provided that each state has at least one representative.
Barrier clause: Not applicable.
Suffrage: Universal, 18 years.

Direct democracy

Referendums at state level.

Party system Results of the 2012 legislative elections (House of Representatives):

Electorate:	221,925,820	100.0%
Voters:	121,500,638	54.7%

Party	Valid votes	%	Seats
Republican Party	57,972,629	47.7	234
Democratic Party	59,536,235	49.0	201
Libertarian	1,388,588	1.1	0
Independent	1,273,389	1.1	0
Others	1,329,797	1.1	0
Total	**121,500,638**	**100**	**435**

Notes: Category 'Others' includes parties with less than 1% nation-wide and no seats.

Sources: US House of Representatives; US Elections Project, George Mason University, Ballot-Access.org.

Comparative tables and world trends

Comparative table 1 Communication

Country	Telephone lines per 1,000 people (2011)	Internet users per 1,000 people (2011)	Mobile subscriptions per 1,000 people (2011)	Roads, total network (km) (2009)	Rail lines, total route (km) (2010)	Airports (2012)
Albania	105	490	964	18,000[b]	423	5
Algeria	85	140	990	11,2039	3,512	142
Argentina	249	477	1,349	231,374[b]	25,023	1,149
Australia	466	789	1,083	817,089	8,615	467
Austria	403	797	1,548	106,840	5,066	52
Belgium	431	762	1,166	153,872	3,578	43
Brazil	219	450	1,232	1,751,868[b]	29,817	4,105
Canada	479	827	753	1,409,000	58,345	1,453
Chile	195	539	1,297	78,425	5,352	476
China	212	384	732	3,860,823	66,239	497
Colombia	152	404	985	129,485	1,672[a]	1,724
Costa Rica	315	421	922	39,039	278[b]	153
Cyprus	363	577	977	12,380	n.a.	15
Czech Republic	209	729	1,216	128,512[b]	9,569	128
Denmark	451	900	1,265	73,330	2,131	89
Egypt, Arab Republic	106	356	1,011	100,472	5,195	84
Estonia	351	765	1,390	58,382	787	18
Finland	201	893	1,660	78,925	5,919	148
France	559	768	1,050	951,260	33,608	473
Germany	630	834	1,323	643,969	33,708	541
Greece	499	534	1,065	116,929	2,552	82
Hungary	294	590	1,173	197,518	7,893	41
Iceland	584	966	1,061	12,889	n.a.	99
India	26	101	720	3,320,410[b]	63,974	352
Indonesia	159	180	977	476,337	3,370[b]	676
Iran, Islamic Republic	371	210	749	192,685	6,073	324
Ireland	452	775	1,084	96,602[b]	1,919	39
Israel	463	682	1,217	18,318	1,034	47
Italy	346	568	1,518	487,700[b]	18,011	130
Japan	511	787	1,027	1,207,867	20,035	175
Korea, Republic	609	815	1,085	104,983	3,379	114
Latvia	230	724	1,029	69,148	1,897	42
Lebanon	211	520	786	6,970[b]	401	7
Lithuania	219	672	1,513	81,331	1,767	81

Comparative table 1 Communication (*continued*)

Country	Telephone lines per 1,000 people (2011)	Internet users per 1,000 people (2011)	Mobile subscriptions per 1,000 people (2011)	Roads, total network (km) (2009)	Rail lines, total route (km) (2010)	Airports (2012)
Luxembourg	541	907	1,483	5,227[b]	275	2
Malta	549	690	1,249	2227[b]	n.a.	1
Mexico	171	362	824	366,807	26,704	1,724
Netherlands		921		136,827	3,016	27
New Zealand	426	862	1,092	94,301	4,128[b]	122
Nigeria	4	284	586	193,200[b]	3,528[c]	53
Norway	427	935	1,168	93,853	4,114	98
Peru	111	365	1,104	126,500	2,020	191
Philippines	72	290	920	201,910[b]	479[b]	247
Poland	181	650	1,285	384,103	19,702	125
Portugal	423	556	1,149	82,900[b]	2,843	65
Romania	219	441	1,092	198,817[b]	13620	53
Russian Federation	309	493	1,793	982,000	85,292	1,218
Senegal	27	175	733	14,825	906[b]	20
Slovak Republic	193	749	1,093	43,879	3,587	37
Slovenia	429	714	1,066	38,927	1,228	16
South Africa	82	209	1,268	362,099[b]	22,051	567
Spain	423	679	1,142	681,224[b]	15,317	152
Sweden	487	909	1,186	582,950	9,957	230
Switzerland	608	830	1,301	71,371	3,543	64
Syrian Arab Republic	209	224	632	68,157	2,139	99
Turkey	207	421	887	362,660	9,594	98
Ukraine	281	303	1,230	169,495	21,705	412
United Kingdom	532	817	1,308	419,665	31,471	462
United States	479	782	1,059	6,545,839	228,513	15,079
Uruguay	285	516	1,408	77,732[b]	2,993[b]	94
Venezuela, RB	249	404	978	96,155[b]	336[b]	492
Vietnam	115	355	1,434	222,179[b]	2,347	44

[a]2009; [b]2008; [c]2007

Notes: Telephone lines are fixed telephone lines that connect a subscriber's terminal equipment to the public switched telephone network and that have a port on a telephone exchange. Integrated services digital network channels and fixed wireless subscribers are included. Internet users are people with access to the worldwide network. Mobile cellular telephone subscriptions are subscriptions to a public mobile telephone service using cellular technology, which provides access to the public switched telephone network. Post-paid and pre-paid subscriptions are included. Total road network includes motorways, highways, and main or national roads, secondary or regional roads, and all other roads in a country. A motorway is a road designed and built for motor traffic that separates the traffic flowing in opposite directions. Rail lines are the length of railway route available for train service, irrespective of the number of parallel tracks.

Source: World Bank Data.

Comparative table 2 Religion

Country	Majority religion (% of total)		Second religion (% of total)		Third religion (% of total)		Other religions (% of total)	
Albania	Muslim	70.0	Orthodox	20.0	RomanCatholic	10.0	Other/None	
Algeria	Muslim	99.0	Christian	0.5	Jewish	0.5	Other/None	
Argentina	Roman Catholic	92.0	Protestant	2.0	Jewish	2.0	Other/None	4.0
Australia	Roman Catholic	26.4	Anglican	20.5	Other Christian	20.5	Other/None	32.6
Austria	Roman Catholic	73.6	Protestant	4.7	Muslim	4.2	Other/None	17.5
Belgium	Roman Catholic	95.0					Other/None	5.0
Brazil	Roman Catholic	73.6	Protestant	15.4	Spiritualist	1.3	Other/None	9.7
Canada	Roman Catholic	42.6	Protestant	23.3	Other Christian	4.4	Other/None	29.7
Chile	RomanCatholic	70.0	Evangelical	15.1	Jehovah	1.1	Other/None	13.8
China	Buddhist	43.0	Daoist	20.0			Other/None	37.0
Colombia	Roman Catholic	90.0					Other/None	10.0
Costa Rica	Roman Catholic	76.3	Evangelical	13.7	Jehovah	1.3	Other/None	8.7
Cyprus	Orthodox	78.0	Muslim	18.0			Other/None	4.0
Czech Republic	Roman Catholic	26.8	Protestant	2.1	Other Christian	12.1	Unaffiliated	59.0
Denmark	Evangelical	95.0	Other Christian	3.0	Muslim	2.0		
Egypt, Arab Rep.	Muslim	90.0	Coptic	9.0	Other Christian	1.0		
Estonia	Evangelical	13.6	Orthodox	12.8	Other Christian	1.4	Other/None	72.2
Finland	Lutheran	84.2	Orthodox	1.1	Other Christian	1.1	Other/None	13.6
France	Roman Catholic	85.0	Muslim	7.5	Protestant	2.0	Other/None	5.5
Germany	Protestant	34.0	Roman Catholic	34.0	Muslim	3.7	Other/None	28.3
Greece	Orthodox	98.0	Muslim	1.3	Other Christian	0.7	Other/None	0.7
Hungary	Roman Catholic	51.9	Calvinist	15.9	Lutheran	3.0	Other/None	29.2
Iceland	Lutheran	87.6	Roman Catholic	2.0	Other Christian	2.7	Other/None	7.7
India	Hindu	80.5	Muslim	13.4	Christian	2.3	Other/None	3.8
Indonesia	Muslim	86.1	Protestant	5.7	Roman Catholic	3.0	Other/None	5.2
Iran, Islamic Rep.	Muslim	98.0					Other/None	2.0
Ireland	Roman Catholic	88.4	Other Christian	4.6			Other/None	7.0
Israel	Jewish	76.4	Muslim	16.0	Other Christian	2.1	Other/None	5.5
Italy	Roman Catholic	90.0					Other/None	10.0
Japan	Buddhist	84.0					Other/None	16.0

	Religion 1	%	Religion 2	%	Religion 3	%		%
Korea, Rep.	Christian	26.3	Buddhist	23.2			Other/None	50.5
Latvia	Lutheran	55.0	Roman Catholic	24.0	Russian Orthodox	9.0	Other/None	12.0
Lebanon	Muslim	59.7	Christian	39.0			Other/None	1.3
Lithuania	Roman Catholic	79.0	Russian Orthodox	4.1	Protestant	1.9	Other/None	15.0
Luxembourg	Roman Catholic	87.0					Other/None	13.0
Malta	Roman Catholic	98.0					Other/None	2.0
Mexico	Roman Catholic	76.5	Protestant	6.3			Other/None	17.2
Netherlands	Roman Catholic	31.0	Reformed	13.0	Calvinist	7.0	Other/None	49.0
New Zealand	Anglican	14.9	Roman Catholic	12.4	Presbyterian	10.9	Other/None	61.8
Nigeria	Muslim	50.0	Christian	40.0	Indigenous	10.0	Other/None	
Norway	Church of Norway	85.7	Pentecostal	1.0	RomanCatholic	1.0	Other/None	12.3
Peru	Roman Catholic	81.0	7th Day Adventist	1.4	Other Christian	0.7	Other/None	16.9
Philippines	RomanCatholic	80.9	Muslim	5.0	Evangelical	2.8	Other/None	11.3
Poland	RomanCatholic	89.8	Orthodox	1.3	Protestant	0.3	Other/None	8.6
Portugal	RomanCatholic	84.5	Other Christian	2.2			Other/None	13.3
Romania	Orthodox	86.8	Protestant	7.5	Roman Catholic	4.7	Other/None	1.0
Russian Federation	Russian Orthodox	17.5	Muslim	12.5	Other Christian	2.0	Other/None	68.0
Senegal	Muslim	94.0	Christian	5.0	Indigenous	1.0	Other/None	
Slovak Republic	Roman Catholic	68.9	Protestant	10.8	Greek Catholic	4.1	Other/None	16.2
Slovenia	Roman Catholic	57.8	Muslim	2.4	Orthodox	2.3	Other/None	37.5
South Africa	Zion Christian	11.1	Pentecostal	8.2	Roman Catholic	7.1	Other/None	73.6
Spain	Roman Catholic	94.0					Other/None	6.0
Sweden	Lutheran	87.0					Other/None	13.0
Switzerland	Roman Catholic	41.8	Protestant	35.3	Muslim	4.3	Other/None	18.6
Syrian Arab Rep.	Muslim	90.0	Christian	10.0			Other/None	
Turkey	Muslim	99.8					Other/None	0.2
Ukraine	Orthodox	45.7	Greek Catholic	6.0			Other/None	48.3
United Kingdom	Christian	71.6	Muslim	2.7	Hindu	1.0	Other/None	24.7
United States	Protestant	52.0	RomanCatholic	24.0	Mormon	2.0	Other/None	22.0
Uruguay	Roman Catholic	66.0	Protestant	2.0	Jewish	1.0	Other/None	31.0
Venezuela, RB	Roman Catholic	96.0	Protestant	2.0			Other/None	2.0
Vietnam	Buddhist	9.3	Roman Catholic	6.7	Hoa Hao	1.5	Other/None	82.5

Source: CIA World Fact Book.

Comparative table 3 Language

Country	Majority language (% of total)		Second language (% of total)		Third language (% of total)		Other languages (% of total)	
Albania	Albanian	94.4	Romani	4.5	Macedonian	1.1		
Algeria	Arabic	86.8	Kabylish	6.7	Tamazight	3.3	Other	3.2
Argentina	Spanish	62.3	Aimara	9.7	Quechua	2.5	Other	25.5
Australia	English	96.5	Italian	2.7	Chinese	0.5	Other	0.3
Austria	German	98	Turkish	1	Croatian	0.6	Other	0.4
Belgium	Dutch	52.7	French	39.2	Italian	4.9	Other	3.2
Brazil	Portuguese	96.7					Other	3.3
Canada	English	59.3	French	23.2			Other	17.5
Chile	Spanish	92	Indian	7.2			Other	0.8
China	Mandarin	87.6	Zhuang	1.1	Tibetish	0.4	Other	10.9
Colombia	Spanish	87.5	Indian	12.5				
Costa Rica	Spanish	85.7	English	2.9			Other	11.4
Cyprus	Greek	80	Turkish	19.8			Other	0.2
Czech Republic	Czech	94.3	Slovak	4.9	German	0.5	Other	0.3
Denmark	Danish	96.9					Other	3.1
Egypt, Arab Rep.	Arabic	98.9					Other	1.1
Estonia	Estonian	67.3	Russian	29.7			Other	3
Finland	Finnish	90	Swedish	9.6			Other	0.4
France	French	94.6					Other	5.4
Germany	German	93.6	Turkish	3			Other	3.4
Greece	Greek	96.1	Albanian	1.9			Other	2
Hungary	Hungarian	92.3	Romani	5	German	2	Other	0.7
Iceland	Icelandic	99					Other	1
India	Hindi	35.8	Marathi	7.2	Bengali	6.1	Other	50.9
Indonesia	Indonesian	83.7					Other	16.3
Iran, Islamic Rep.	Farsi	52	Aserbaidshanian	30.1	Kurdish	11.5	Other	6.4
Ireland	English	70.3	Irish	29.7				
Israel	Hebrew	65.4	Arabic	25	Russian	8.3	Other	1.3
Italy	Italian	97.2	German	0.9	Slovene	0.2	Other	1.7
Japan	Japanese	99.1	Korean	0.8	Chinese	0.1		
Korea, Rep.	Korean	100						

Country	Language 1	%	Language 2	%	Language 3	%	Other	%
Latvia	Latvian	61	Russian	38.8			Other	0.2
Lebanon	Arabic	92.9	Armenian	5.7	Kurdish	1.4		
Lithuania	Lithuanian	82.4	Russian	14.8	Belorussian	2.7	Other	0.1
Luxembourg	Luxembourgish	69.1	German	23.8	French	7.1		
Malta	Maltese	95.5	English	4.5			Other	2.2
Mexico	Spanish	90.7	Indian/Maya	7.1			Other	1.3
Netherlands	Dutch	92.3	Frisian	6.4			Other	2.4
New Zealand	English	95	Maori	2.6			Other	61.6
Nigeria	Hausa	16.7	Igbo	15	Fulfulde	6.7	Other	0.4
Norway	Norwegian	98.5	Saamish	1.1			Other	0.4
Peru	Spanish	87.5	Quechua	12.1			Other	48
Philippines	Cebuano	21.3	Tagalog	20	Hiligaynon	10.7	Other	0.8
Poland	Polish	95.3	German	2.6	Ukrainian	1.3	Other	0.1
Portugal	Portuguese	99.9					Other	1.2
Romania	Romanian	91	Hungarian	6.7	Romani	1.1	Other	0.8
Russian Federation	Russian	94.4	Tatarian	3.4	Ukrainian	1.4	Other	22.3
Senegal	Wolof	44.4	Serere-Sine	22.2	Fulacunda	11.1	Other	3.8
Slovak Republic	Slovak	83.9	Hungarian	10.5	Romani	1.8	Other	0.4
Slovenia	Slovenian	92.6	Serbo-Croat	4.5	German	2.5	Other	45.3
South Africa	Zulu	23.8	Xhosa	17.6	Afrikaans	13.3	Other	2.9
Spain	Spanish	73.1	Catalan	17	Galician	7	Other	0.9
Sweden	Swedish	98.4	Finnish	0.7			Other	9.4
Switzerland	German	63.7	French	20.4	Italian	6.5	Other	23.3
Syrian Arab Rep.	Arabic	66.7	Kurdish	6.7	Armenian	3.3	Other	3
Turkey	Turkish	80	Kurdish	15	Arab	2	Other	2
Ukraine	Ukrainian	70.5	Russian	27.5			Other	1.3
United Kingdom	English	97	Hindi	1.7			Other	1.2
United States	English	88.1	Spanish	10.7			Other	4.8
Uruguay	Spanish	99.2	Portuguese	0.8				
Venezuela, RB	Spanish	94.7	Indian	5.3				
Vietnam	Vietnamese	93.2	Khmer	1.3	Mandarin	0.7	Other	

Notes: Languages spoken; percentages indicate first languages disregarding whether or not people also speak other languages.

Source: Lewis *et al.* (2013).

Comparative table 4 Demography

Country	Total population (2011)	Total population in millions (2011)	Population projection 2020 in millions	Aged 65+ (%) (2011)	Fertility rate (2012)	Life expectancy at birth (years) (2012)	Infant mortality per 1,000 births, (2011)
Albania	3,215,988	3.2	3.3	9.9	1.5	77.2	12.8
Algeria	35,980,193	36.0	40.2	4.6	2.1	73.4	25.6
Argentina	40,764,561	40.8	43.9	10.7	2.2	75.6	12.6
Australia	22,620,600	22.6	25.2	13.7	1.9	81.4	4.1
Austria	8,419,000	8.4	8.5	17.9	1.3	80.6	3.5
Belgium	11,008,000	11.0	11.0	17.6	1.8	79.6	3.5
Brazil	196,655,014	196.7	210.4	7.2	1.8	73.1	13.9
Canada	34,482,779	34.5	37.2	14.4	1.7	80.4	4.9
Chile	17,269,525	17.3	18.5	9.5	1.8	78.4	7.7
China	1,344,130,000	1,344.1	1,387.8	8.4	1.6	73.6	12.6
Colombia	46,927,125	46.9	52.2	5.8	2.3	73.5	15.4
Costa Rica	4,726,575	4.7	5.3	6.7	1.8	78.6	8.6
Cyprus	1,116,564	1.1	1.2	11.8	1.5	79.7	2.6
Czech Republic	10,546,000	10.5	10.7	15.2	1.5	77.7	3.2
Denmark	5,574,000	5.6	5.7	16.9	1.9	78.6	3.1
Egypt, Arab Rep.	82,536,770	82.5	94.8	5.2	2.6	73.5	18
Estonia	1,340,000	1.3	1.3	17.3	1.7	74.4	2.8
Finland	5,387,000	5.4	5.5	17.8	1.9	79.8	2.3
France	65,436,552	65.4	65.9	17.1	2.0	80.9	3.4
Germany	81,726,000	81.7	81.0	20.6	1.5	80.2	3.3
Greece	11,304,000	11.3	11.6	18.7	1.5	79.8	3.7
Hungary	9,971,000	10.0	9.8	16.7	1.4	74.3	5.4
Iceland	319,000	0.3	0.4	12.2	2.1	81.5	1.7
India	1,241,491,960	1,241.5	1,386.9	5.0	2.5	65.8	47.2
Indonesia	242,325,638	242.3	262.6	5.6	2.1	69.9	24.8
Iran, Islamic Rep.	74,798,599	74.8	81.0	5.3	1.6	73.2	21.1
Ireland	4,487,000	4.5	5.0	11.9	2.1	80.4	3.2
Israel	7,765,700	7.8	8.7	10.6	2.9	81.3	3.5
Italy	60,770,000	60.8	61.3	20.6	1.5	81.4	3.2
Japan	127,817,277	127.8	124.8	23.4	1.4	82.4	2.4
Korea, Rep.	49,779,000	49.8	49.8	11.5	1.4	80.2	4.1
Latvia	2,220,000	2.2	2.2	17.8	1.5	73.3	7.1
Lebanon	4,259,405	4.3	4.5	7.3	1.8	72.8	8
Lithuania	3,203,000	3.2	3.2	16.2	1.5	72.5	4.7
Luxembourg	517,000	0.5	0.6	13.9	1.7	79.8	2.3
Malta	419,000	0.4	0.4	14.6	1.3	79.6	5.1
Mexico	114,793,341	114.8	125.9	6.5	2.2	76.6	13.4
Netherlands	16,696,000	16.7	17.0	15.7	1.8	80.5	3.4
New Zealand	4,405,200	4.4	4.8	13.3	2.1	80.2	4.7

Comparative table 4 Demography (*continued*)

Country	Total population (2011)	Total population in millions (2011)	Population projection 2020 in millions	Aged 65+ (%) (2011)	Fertility rate (2012)	Life expectancy at birth (years) (2012)	Infant mortality per 1,000 births, (2011)
Nigeria	162,470,737	162.5	203.9	3.4	5.4	52.5	78
Norway	4,952,000	5.0	5.2	15.0	1.9	80.9	2.6
Peru	29,399,817	29.4	32.4	6.2	2.4	73.8	14.1
Philippines	94,852,030	94.9	109.7	3.7	3.1	69.2	20.2
Poland	38,216,000	38.2	38.4	13.8	1.4	76.0	4.9
Portugal	10,637,000	10.6	10.6	18.2	1.3	79.5	2.7
Romania	21,390,000	21.4	21.0	15.0	1.4	74.1	10.8
Russian Federation	141,930,000	141.9	141.0	12.8	1.5	68.8	9.8
Senegal	12,767,556	12.8	16.0	2.4	4.6	59.8	46.7
Slovak Republic	5,440,000	5.4	5.5	12.3	1.4	75.5	6.5
Slovenia	2,052,000	2.1	2.1	16.7	1.5	79.1	2.1
South Africa	50,586,757	50.6	52.6	4.8	2.4	53.6	34.6
Spain	46,235,000	46.2	48.7	17.1	1.5	81.2	3.5
Sweden	9,453,000	9.5	9.9	18.6	1.9	81.2	2.2
Switzerland	7,907,000	7.9	7.9	17.0	1.5	81.8	4
Syrian Arab Rep.	20,820,311	20.8	24.1	4.0	2.8	76.1	13.2
Turkey	73,639,596	73.6	80.8	6.1	2.0	74.3	11.5
Ukraine	45,706,100	45.7	43.0	15.4	1.5	68.8	8.7
United Kingdom	62,641,000	62.6	65.8	16.8	1.9	79.8	4.4
United States	311,591,917	311.6	337.1	13.3	2.1	78.0	6.4
Uruguay	3,368,595	3.4	3.5	13.8	2.0	76.7	8.7
Venezuela, RB	29,278,000	29.3	33.3	5.8	2.4	74.3	12.9
Vietnam	87,840,000	87.8	96.4	6.0	1.8	75.2	17.3

Notes: Population aged 65 and above as a percentage of the total population. Population is based on the *de facto* definition of population, which counts all residents regardless of legal status or citizenship—except for refugees not permanently settled in the country of asylum, who are generally considered part of the population of their country of origin. Total fertility rate represents the number of children that would be born to a woman if she were to live to the end of her childbearing years and bear children in accordance with current age-specific fertility rates. Life expectancy at birth indicates the number of years a newborn infant would live if prevailing patterns of mortality at the time of its birth were to stay the same throughout its life. Infant mortality rate is the number of infants dying before reaching 1 year of age per 1,000 live births in a given year.

Sources: World Bank Data; UN Department of Economic and Social Affairs.

Comparative table 5 Development

Country	Human Development Index (HDI) (2011)	Public debt as % of GDP (2011)	Lowest 10% (2000–2011 [latest available])	Highest 10% (2000–2011 [latest available])	Inequality measures highest 10%/lowest 10% (2000-2011 [latest available])
Albania	0.739	58.9	3.53	28.99	8.21
Algeria	0.698	9.9	2.8	26.9	9.61
Argentina	0.797	44.2	1.46	32.3	22.12
Australia	0.929	22.9	2	25.4	12.70
Austria	0.885	72.2	3.34	23.05	6.90
Belgium	0.886	98.5	3.42	28.1	8.22
Brazil	0.718	66.2	0.77	42.93	55.75
Canada	0.908	85.0	2.63	24.79	9.43
Chile	0.805	9.9	1.53	42.77	27.95
China	0.687	25.8	1.79	31.97	17.86
Colombia	0.71	34.7	0.87	44.43	51.07
Costa Rica	0.744	30.8	1.23	39.5	32.11
Cyprus	0.84	71.8	n.a.	n.a.	n.a.
Czech Republic	0.865	41.5	4.3	22.7	5.28
Denmark	0.895	46.4	2.6	21.3	8.19
Egypt, Arab Rep.	0.644	76.4	3.96	26.58	6.71
Estonia	0.835	6.0	2.71	27.7	10.22
Finland	0.882	48.6	4.02	22.57	5.61
France	0.884	86.3	2.8	25.1	8.96
Germany	0.905	81.5	3.22	22.07	6.85
Greece	0.861	163.3	2.55	26.04	10.21
Hungary	0.816	80.4	3.54	25.44	7.19
Iceland	0.898	99.2	n.a.	n.a.	n.a.
India	0.547	68.1	3.75	28.26	7.54
Indonesia	0.617	25.0	3.67	28.51	7.77
Iran, Islamic Rep.	0.707	12.7	2.62	29.63	11.31
Ireland	0.908	105.0	2.91	27.23	9.36
Israel	0.888	74.3	2.14	28.8	13.46
Italy	0.874	120.1	2.3	26.8	11.65
Japan	0.901	229.8	4.8	21.7	4.52
Korea, Rep.	0.897	34.1	2.9	22.5	7.76
Latvia	0.805	37.8	2.64	28.1	10.64
Lebanon	0.739	136.2	n.a.	n.a.	n.a.
Lithuania	0.81	39.0	2.63	29.1	11.06
Luxembourg	0.867	20.8	3.5	23.77	6.79
Malta	0.832	70.9	n.a.	n.a.	n.a.
Mexico	0.77	43.8	1.81	38.68	21.37
Netherlands	0.91	66.2	2.5	22.9	9.16
New Zealand	0.908	37.0	2.2	27.8	12.64
Nigeria	0.459	17.9	1.75	38.23	21.85

Comparative table 5 Development (*continued*)

Country	Human Development Index (HDI) (2011)	Public debt as % of GDP (2011)	Lowest 10% (2000–2011 [latest available])	Highest 10% (2000–2011 [latest available])	Inequality measures highest 10%/lowest 10% (2000-2011 [latest available])
Norway	0.943	49.6	3.86	23.38	6.06
Peru	0.725	21.6	1.39	36.11	25.98
Philippines	0.644	40.5	2.59	33.62	12.98
Poland	0.813	55.4	3.26	27.05	8.30
Portugal	0.809	106.8	2	29.8	14.90
Romania	0.781	33.0	3.38	23.5	6.95
Russian Federation	0.755	9.6	2.75	31.68	11.52
Senegal	0.459	40.6	2.5	30.14	12.06
Slovak Republic	0.834	44.6	4.36	22.41	5.14
Slovenia	0.884	47.3	3.38	24.6	7.28
South Africa	0.619	38.8	1.17	51.69	44.18
Spain	0.878	68.5	2.57	26.61	10.35
Sweden	0.904	37.4	3.58	22.18	6.20
Switzerland	0.903	48.6	2.88	25.91	9.00
Syrian Arab Republic	0.632	18.6[a]	3.36	n.a.	n.a.
Turkey	0.699	39.4	2.11	29.35	13.91
Ukraine	0.729	36.5	4.2	22.04	5.25
United Kingdom	0.863	82.5	2.1	28.5	13.57
United States	0.91	102.9	1.88	29.85	15.88
Uruguay	0.783	54.2	1.91	34.36	17.99
Venezuela, RB	0.735	45.5	1.2	32.7	27.25
Vietnam	0.593	38.0	3.18	28.21	8.87

[a]2010

Notes: The first Human Development Report introduced a new way of measuring development by combining indicators of life expectancy, educational attainment, and income into a composite human development. Percentage share of income or consumption is the share that accrues to subgroups of population indicated by deciles or quintiles. Ratio of percentage share of income or consumption of richest 10% to poorest 10%.

Sources: United Nations Development Programme; IMF World Economic Outlook Database; World Bank Data; World Development Indicators.

Comparative table 6 Economy

Country	GDP per capita (US$) (2011)	GDP growth (% change) 1995–2011	GDP per capita, PPP (US$) (2011)	Inequality (Gini index) (2001–2011 [latest available])
Albania	4,030	5.7	8,866	34.5
Algeria	5,244	3.5	8,655	35.3
Argentina	10,942	3.8	17,554	45.8
Australia	60,979	3.4	39,721	35.2
Austria	49,609	2.2	42,196	29.1
Belgium	46,663	1.9	38,768	33.0
Brazil	12,594	3.2	11,640	53.9
Canada	50,345	2.6	40,370	32.6
Chile	14,394	4.5	17,310	52.1
China	5,445	9.9	8,400	41.5
Colombia	7,104	3.4	10,033	58.5
Costa Rica	8,647	4.5	12,157	50.3
Cyprus	30,670	3.2	32,254	n.a.
Czech Republic	20,579	3.0	26,208	25.8
Denmark	59,852	1.5	40,908	24.7
Egypt, Arab Rep.	2,781	4.8	6,281	32.1
Estonia	16,533	5.0	21,995	36.0
Finland	48,823	2.9	37,464	26.9
France	42,377	1.7	35,246	32.7
Germany	44,060	1.4	39,491	28.3
Greece	25,622	2.0	25,850	34.3
Hungary	14,044	2.2	21,663	31.2
Iceland	43,969	2.9	36,485	n.a.
India	1,489	7.0	3,627	36.8
Indonesia	3,495	4.2	4,636	36.8
Iran, Islamic Rep.	4,525[b]	4.6	11,508[b]	38.3
Ireland	48,423	4.9	41,682	34.3
Israel	31,282	4.0	27,825	39.2
Italy	36,103	1.0	32,647	36.0
Japan	45,903	0.8	34,314	24.9
Korea, Rep.	22,424	4.5	30,286	31.6
Latvia	12,726	4.3	17,569	35.7
Lebanon	9,413	4.0	14,609	n.a.
Lithuania	13,339	4.6	20,321	37.6
Luxembourg	114,508	3.6	89,012	30.8
Malta	21,209	2.9	27,284	n.a.
Mexico	10,047	2.6	15,266	51.7
Netherlands	50,076	2.2	42,772	30.9
New Zealand	36,254	2.4	30,057	36.2
Nigeria	1,502	5.3	2,533	42.9
Norway	98,102	2.3	60,405	25.8

Comparative table 6 Economy (*continued*)

Country	GDP per capita (US$) (2011)	GDP growth (% change) 1995–2011	GDP per capita, PPP (US$) (2011)	Inequality (Gini index) (2001–2011 [latest available])
Peru	6,018	5.0	10,234	48.0
Philippines	2,370	4.4	4,119	44.0
Poland	13,463	4.6	21,261	34.2
Portugal	22,316	1.8	25,372	38.5
Romania	8,405	2.7	15,139	31.2
Russian Federation	13,089	3.4	21,246	42.3
Senegal	1,119	4.1	1,967	39.2
Slovak Republic	17,646	4.4	23,910	25.8
Slovenia	24,142	3.1	26,954	31.2
South Africa	8,070	3.3	10,960	57.8
Spain	31,943	2.6	32,045	34.7
Sweden	57,091	2.8	41,467	25.0
Switzerland	83,383	1.8	51,262	33.7
Syrian Arab Rep.	2,892[a]	4.2	5,251[a]	35.8
Turkey	10,524	4.5	17,110	39.7
Ukraine	3,615	1.7	7,208	27.5
United Kingdom	39,038	2.3	35,657	34
United States	48,112	2.5	48,112	40.8
Uruguay	13,866	2.9	15,078	42.4
Venezuela, RB	10,810	2.8	12,749	43.5
Vietnam	1,407	7.2	3,412	37.6

[a]2010; [b]2009

Notes: GDP per capita is GDP divided by mid-year population. GDP is the sum of gross value added by all resident producers in the economy plus any product taxes and minus any subsidies not included in the value of the products. It is calculated without making deductions for depreciation of fabricated assets or for depletion and degradation of natural resources. Annual percentage growth rate of GDP at market prices is based on constant local currency. Aggregates are based on constant 2000 US dollars. GDP per capita based on purchasing power parity (PPP) is gross domestic product converted to international dollars using purchasing power parity rates. An international dollar has the same purchasing power over GDP as the US dollar has in the United States. GDP at purchaser's prices is the sum of gross value added by all resident producers in the economy plus any product taxes and minus any subsidies not included in the value of the products. It is calculated without making deductions for depreciation of fabricated assets or for depletion and degradation of natural resources. Data are in current international dollars. Gini index measures the extent to which the distribution of income or consumption expenditure among individuals or households within an economy deviates from a perfectly equal distribution. A Gini index of zero represents perfect equality, while an index of 100 implies perfect inequality.

Sources: The World Bank Data; United Nations Development Report 2011; CIA World Factbook.

Comparative table 7 Environment

Country	Per capita carbon dioxide emissions from the consumption of energy (metric tons of carbon dioxide per person) (2010)	Share of world total (%) (2010)
Albania	1.64	0.0
Algeria	3.21	0.4
Argentina	4.11	0.6
Australia	18.84	1.3
Austria	8.46	0.2
Belgium	12.20	0.3
Brazil	2.26	1.2
Canada	16.25	1.7
Chile	4.11	0.2
China	6.26	25.6
Colombia	1.64	0.2
Costa Rica	1.42	0.0
Cyprus	8.39	0.0
Czech Republic	8.90	0.4
Denmark	8.33	0.2
Egypt, Arab Rep.	2.44	0.7
Estonia	15.92	0.1
Finland	10.35	0.2
France	6.24	1.2
Germany	9.65	2.4
Greece	8.65	0.3
Hungary	5.04	0.2
Iceland	10.87	0.0
India	1.45	6.6
Indonesia	1.60	1.5
Iran, Islamic Rep.	7.28	2.0
Ireland	8.76	0.1
Israel	9.56	0.2
Italy	7.16	1.3
Japan	9.18	3.7
Korea, Rep.	11.90	1.7
Latvia	4.09	0.0
Lebanon	3.69	0.1
Lithuania	4.51	0.0
Luxembourg	21.71	0.0
Malta	7.66	0.0
Mexico	3.96	1.5
Netherlands	15.70	0.6
New Zealand	9.31	0.1
Nigeria	0.53	0.2

Comparative table 7 Environment (*continued*)

Country	Per capita carbon dioxide emissions from the consumption of energy (metric tons of carbon dioxide per person) (2010)	Share of world total (%) (2010)
Norway	8.94	0.2
Peru	1.40	0.2
Philippines	0.86	0.2
Poland	7.90	1.0
Portugal	4.79	0.2
Russian Federation	11.72	5.2
Romania	3.57	0.3
Senegal	0.54	0.0
Slovak Republic	6.31	0.1
Slovenia	8.70	0.1
South Africa	9.47	1.7
Spain	6.80	1.0
Sweden	6.91	0.1
Switzerland	5.95	0.1
Syrian Arab Rep.	2.84	0.2
Turkey	3.39	0.9
Ukraine	6.07	0.9
United Kingdom	8.50	1.6
United States	18.08	17.6
Uruguay	2.07	0.0
Venezuela, RB	5.82	0.6
Vietnam	1.26	0.5

Notes: Carbon dioxide emissions are those stemming from the burning of fossil fuels and the manufacture of cement. They include carbon dioxide produced during consumption of solid, liquid, and gas fuels and gas flaring.

Sources: US Energy Information Administration.

Comparative table 8 Gender

Country	Labour force participation rate female (2009)	Seats in national parliament (% female) (2012)	Ratio of female to male income (2011)
Albania	49.3	16.4	0.53
Algeria	37.2	7.0	0.16
Argentina	52.4	37.8	0.49
Australia	58.4	28.3	0.71
Austria	53.2	28.3	0.41
Belgium	46.7	38.5	0.60
Brazil	60.1	9.6	0.61
Canada	62.7	24.9	0.66
Chile	41.8	13.9	0.49
China	67.4	21.3	0.65
Colombia	40.7	13.8	0.62
Costa Rica	45.1	38.6	0.57
Cyprus	54.3	12.5	0.59
Czech Republic	48.8	21.0	0.48
Denmark	60.3	38.0	0.75
Egypt, Arab Rep.	22.4	n.a.	0.26
Estonia	54.8	19.8	0.65
Finland	57.0	42.5	0.71
France	50.5	20.0	0.63
Germany	53.1	31.7	0.60
Greece	42.9	17.3	0.53
Hungary	42.5	9.1	0.66
Iceland	71.7	42.9	0.65
India	32.8	10.7	0.27
Indonesia	52.0	18.0	0.42
Iran, Islamic Rep.	31.9	2.8	0.21
Ireland	54.4	11.1	0.56
Israel	51.9	19.2	0.65
Italy	38.4	20.3	0.49
Japan	47.9	13.6	0.47
Korea, Rep.	50.1	14.7	0.40
Latvia	54.3	20.0	0.71
Lebanon	22.3	3.1	0.25
Lithuania	50.2	19.1	0.71
Luxembourg	48.0	20.0	0.54
Malta	31.6	8.7	0.52
Mexico	43.2	25.5	0.45
Netherlands	59.5	37.8	0.68
New Zealand	61.8	33.6	0.71
Nigeria	39.2	7.3	0.57
Norway	63.0	39.6	0.78

Comparative table 8 Gender (*continued*)

Country	Labour force participation rate female (2009)	Seats in national parliament (% female) (2012)	Ratio of female to male income (2011)
Peru	58.2	27.5	0.61
Philippines	49.2	21.5	0.60
Poland	46.2	17.9	0.57
Portugal	56.2	27.4	0.58
Romania	45.4	9.8	0.68
Russian Federation	57.5	11.5	0.62
Senegal	64.8	29.6	0.58
Slovak Republic	51.2	16.0	0.58
Slovenia	52.8	10.8	0.62
South Africa	47.0	42.7	0.55
Spain	49.1	34.7	0.58
Sweden	59.3	45.0	0.79
Switzerland	60.6	27.6	0.62
Syrian Arab Rep.	21.1	12.4	0.15
Turkey	24.0	9.1	0.30
Ukraine	52.0	8.0	0.61
United Kingdom	55.3	21.0	0.68
United States	58.4	16.8	0.63
Uruguay	53.8	14.6	0.57
Venezuela, RB	51.7	17.0	0.50
Vietnam	68.0	25.8	0.69

Notes: Labour force participation rate is the proportion of the population aged 15 and older that is economically active: all people who supply labour for the production of goods and services during a specified period.

Sources: United Nations Development Programme (Human Development Statistical Tables); WEF Global Gender Gap Report.

Comparative table 9 Labour

Country	Unemployment rate (2009/2010)	Labour force sector: agriculture (%) (2007–2011 [latest available])	Labour force sector: industry (%) (2007–2011 [latest available])	Labour force sector: service (%) (2007–2011 [latest available])
Albania	13.8	44.1	19.9	36.0
Algeria	11.4	20.7[e]	26.0[e]	53.1[e]
Argentina	8.6	1.2	23.1	75.2
Australia	5.2	3.3	21.1	75.5
Austria	4.4	5.2	24.9	69.9
Belgium	8.3	1.4	23.4	75.3
Brazil	8.3	17.0	22.1	60.7
Canada	8.0	2.4	21.5	76.5
Chile	8.1	11.2	23.2	65.6
China	4.3	39.6[e]	27.2	33.2
Colombia	11.6	17.9	20.0	62.0
Costa Rica	7.8	12.3	21.6	62.2
Cyprus	6.2	3.8	20.8	75.3
Czech Republic	7.3	3.1	38.0	58.9
Denmark	7.4	2.4	19.6	77.7
Egypt, Arab Rep.	9.4	31.6	23.0	45.3
Estonia	16.9	4.2	30.1	65.1
Finland	8.4	4.4	23.2	71.9
France	9.3	2.9	22.2	74.5
Germany	7.1	1.6	28.4	70.0
Greece	12.5	12.5	19.7	67.7
Hungary	11.2	4.5	30.7	64.9
Iceland	7.6	5.5	17.9	75.2
India	4.4[d]	51.1	22.4	26.5
Indonesia	7.1	38.3	19.3	42.3
Iran, Islamic Rep.	10.5[a]	21.2	32.2	46.5
Ireland	13.5	4.6	19.5	75.5
Israel	6.6	1.7	20.4	77.1
Italy	8.4	3.8	28.8	67.5
Japan	5.0	3.7	25.3	69.7
Korea, Rep.	3.7	6.6	17.0	76.4
Latvia	18.7	8.8	24.0	66.9
Lebanon	9.2[b]	n.a.	n.a.	n.a.
Lithuania	17.8	9.0	24.4	66.2
Luxembourg	4.4	1.0	12.0	81.1
Malta	6.9	1.3	24.6	72.9
Mexico	5.3	13.1	25.5	60.6
Netherlands	4.5	2.8	15.9	71.6
New Zealand	6.5	6.6	20.9	72.5
Nigeria	4.9[a]	44.6[e]	11.5[e]	41.7[e]

Comparative table 9 Labour (*continued*)

Country	Unemployment rate (2009/2010)	Labour force sector: agriculture (%) (2007–2011 [latest available])	Labour force sector: industry (%) (2007–2011 [latest available])	Labour force sector: service (%) (2007–2011 [latest available])
Norway	3.6	2.5	19.7	77.6
Peru	6.3	0.8	24.4	74.8
Philippines	7.4	35.2	14.6	50.3
Poland	9.6	12.8	30.2	56.9
Portugal	10.8	10.9	27.7	61.4
Romania	7.3	30.1	28.7	41.2
Russian Federation	7.5	9.7	27.9	62.3
Senegal	10.0[c]	33.7[c]	14.8[c]	36.1[c]
Slovak Republic	14.4	3.2	37.1	59.6
Slovenia	7.2	8.8	32.5	58.3
South Africa	23.8	5.1	25.0	69.8
Spain	20.1	4.3	23.1	72.6
Sweden	8.4	2.1	19.9	77.7
Switzerland	4.2	3.3	21.1	70.9
Syrian Arab Rep.	8.4	14.9	32.2	52.8
Turkey	11.9	23.7	26.2	50.1
Ukraine	8.8	15.8	23.4	60.7
United Kingdom	7.8	1.2	19.1	78.9
United States	9.6	1.6	16.7	81.2
Uruguay	7.3	11.0	21.7	67.2
Venezuela, RB	7.6	8.5	23.0	68.3
Vietnam	2.4[a]	51.7[c]	20.2[c]	28.2[c]

[a]2008; [b]2007; [c]2006; [c]2005; [e]2004.

Notes: Unemployment refers to the share of the labour force that is without work but available for and seeking employment. Definitions of labour force and unemployment differ by country.

Sources: World Bank Data; ILO.

Comparative table 10 Migration

Country	Net migration rate (2012) (migrants per 1,000 population)
Albania	−3.33
Algeria	−0.27
Argentina	0
Australia	5.93
Austria	1.79
Belgium	1.22
Brazil	−0.09
Canada	5.65
Chile	0.35
China	−0.33
Colombia	−0.66
Costa Rica	0.86
Cyprus	10.75
Czech Republic	0.97
Denmark	2.36
Egypt, Arab Rep.	−0.2
Estonia	−3.33
Finland	0.62
France	1.10
Germany	0.71
Greece	2.32
Hungary	1.37
Iceland	0.53
India	−0.05
Indonesia	−1.08
Iran, Islamic Rep.	−0.11
Ireland	1.69
Israel	1.94
Italy	4.67
Japan	0
Korea, Rep.	0
Latvia	−2.34
Lebanon	−12.08
Lithuania	−0.73
Luxembourg	8.15
Malta	2.00
Mexico	−3.11
Netherlands	2.02
New Zealand	2.26
Nigeria	−0.22
Norway	1.69

Comparative table 10 Migration (*continued*)

Country	Net migration rate (2012) (migrants per 1,000 population)
Peru	−3.03
Philippines	−1.27
Poland	−0.47
Portugal	2.90
Romania	−0.26
Russian Federation	0.29
Senegal	−1.82
Slovak Republic	0.29
Slovenia	0.39
South Africa	−6.22
Spain	5.02
Sweden	1.65
Switzerland	1.27
Syrian Arab Repub.	−27.82
Turkey	0.50
Ukraine	−0.08
United Kingdom	2.59
United States	3.62
Uruguay	−1.45
Venezuela, RB	0
Vietnam	−0.34

Notes: Difference between the number of persons entering and leaving a country during the year per 1,000 persons (based on mid-year population). An excess of persons entering the country is referred to as net immigration (e.g. 3.56 migrants/1,000 population); an excess of persons leaving the country is referred to as net emigration (e.g. −9.26 migrants/1,000 population). The net migration rate indicates the contribution of migration to the overall level of population change. The net migration rate does not distinguish between economic migrants, refugees, and other types of migrants, nor does it distinguish between lawful migrants and undocumented migrants.

Sources: CIA World Factbook.

Comparative table 11 Military

Country	Military expenditure (% of GDP)		Conventional arms transfers (1990 prices)	
	1995	2011	Imports (million US$) (2011)	Exports (million US$) (2002–2011 [latest available])
Albania	2.1	1.5	5	n.a.
Algeria	3.0	4.6	783	n.a.
Argentina	1.5	0.7	15	1
Australia	2.1	1.9	1,749	126
Austria	1.1	0.9	6	30
Belgium	1.6	1.1	22	111
Brazil	1.9	1.4	266	27
Canada	1.6	1.4	342	292
Chile	3.1	3.2	323	100
China	1.7	2.0	1,112	1356
Colombia	2.8	3.3	155	5
Costa Rica	n.a.	n.a.	n.a.	n.a.
Cyprus	3.2	2.2	38	n.a.
Czech Republic	1.8	1.2	79	11
Denmark	1.7	1.5	1	20
Egypt, Arab Rep.	3.9	1.9	545	n.a.
Estonia	1.0	1.7	2	n.a.
Finland	1.5	1.5	97	47
France	3.0	2.2	43	2,437
Germany	1.6	1.3	112	1,206
Greece	3.2	2.7	177	23
Hungary	1.6	1.0	11	9
Iceland	n.a.	0.1[b]	n.a.	n.a.
India	2.6	2.6	3,582	8
Indonesia	0.8	0.7	201	4
Iran, Islamic Rep.	1.8	1.9[c]	94	45
Ireland	1.0	0.6	1	1
Israel	8.9	6.8	76	531
Italy	1.7	1.6	311	1,046
Japan	0.9	1.0	254	40
Korea, Rep.	3.0	2.8	1,422	225
Latvia	0.9	1.0	5	n.a.
Lebanon	6.4	4.2	68	45
Lithuania	0.5	1.0	37	3
Luxembourg	0.7	0.6[d]	0.29	0
Malta	0.9	0.7	7	10
Mexico	0.6	0.5	179	n.a.
Netherlands	1.9	1.4	145	538
New Zealand	1.4	1.1[a]	13	0

Comparative table 11 Military (*continued*)

Country	Military expenditure (% of GDP)		Conventional arms transfers (1990 prices)	
	1995	2011	Imports (million US$) (2011)	Exports (million US$) (2002–2011 [latest available])
Nigeria	0.7	1.0	82	19
Norway	2.4	1.6	650	108
Peru	1.9	1.2	74	5
Philippines	2.3	1.1	69	4
Poland	2.0	1.9	144	8
Portugal	2.3	2.0	115	0
Romania	2.8	1.2	96	1
Russian Federation	4.4	3.9	12	7,874
Senegal	1.7	1.6[a]	13	n.a.
Slovak Republic	3.2	1.1	8	8
Slovenia	1.6	1.4	38	n.a.
South Africa	2.1	1.3	175	61
Spain	1.4	1.0	248	927
Sweden	2.3	1.3	71	686
Switzerland	1.5	0.9	19	297
Syrian Arab Rep.	7.0	3.9[a]	291	25
Turkey	3.9	2.3	1,010	6
Ukraine	2.8	2.5	n.a.	484
United Kingdom	3.0	2.6	412	1,070
United States	3.8	4.7	946	9,984
Uruguay	2.7	1.9	26	n.a.
Venezuela, RB	1.6	0.8	560	40
Vietnam	2.6[d]	2.2	1,009	14

[a]2010; [b]2009; [c]2008; [d]2007

Notes: Military expenditures data from SIPRI are derived from the NATO definition, which includes all current and capital expenditures on the armed forces, including peacekeeping forces, defence ministries, and others. Figures are SIPRI Trend Indicator Values (TIVs) expressed in million US dollars at constant (1990) prices. For more information, see http://www.sipri.org/databases/armstransfers/background.

Sources: World Bank Data; SIPRI.

Comparative table 12 Trade

Country	Imports of goods and services (% of GDP) (2011)	Exports of goods and services (% of GDP) (2011)	Manufactured exports (% of exports) (2008–2011 [latest available])	High-technology exports (% of exports) (2010)
Albania	56.0	33.8	60.1	0.9
Algeria	21.5[a]	30.8[a]	2.0	0.5
Argentina	19.5	21.8	32.4	7.5
Australia	19.8	21.3	14.6	11.9
Austria	54.0	57.3	80.3	11.9
Belgium	83.1	84.3	73.2	10.5
Brazil	12.6	11.9	34.1	11.2
Canada	32.4	31.2	46.2	14.0
Chile	34.7	38.1	13.8	5.5
China	27.3	31.4	93.3	27.5
Colombia	20.1	19.0	17.3	5.1
Costa Rica	41.6	37.4	60.4	40.0
Cyprus	46.6[a]	40.1[a]	43.6	37.3
Czech Republic	68.5	72.5	88.4	15.3
Denmark	48.2	53.4	60.6	14.2
Egypt, Arab Rep.	30.2	23.3	44.4	0.9
Estonia	87.6	91.5	63.0	9.0
Finland	41.4	40.7	73.7	10.8
France	29.8	27.0	76.4	24.9
Germany	45.1	50.2	83.2	15.3
Greece	33.1	25.1	38.3	10.1
Hungary	84.9	92.3	80.8	24.2
Iceland	50.8	59.3	14.0	20.9
India	29.8	24.6	62.2	7.2
Indonesia	24.9	26.3	34.2	11.4
Iran, Islamic Rep.	21.5[d]	32.2[d]	15.6	4.5
Ireland	84.3	106.6	86.4	21.2
Israel	37.8	36.9	93.3	14.7
Italy	30.3	28.8	82.2	7.2
Japan	16.1	15.2	89.1	18.0
Korea, Rep.	54.1	56.2	85.9	28.7[b]
Latvia	63.2	59.3	55.5	7.6
Lebanon	50.4	23.7	66.9	12.8
Lithuania	79.3	77.8	52.6	10.6
Luxembourg	145.3	176.5	79.0	8.4
Malta	93.1	98.0	84.7	59.6
Mexico	33.0	31.7	72.3	16.9
Netherlands	74.1	83.0	56.9	21.3
New Zealand	28.7	30.0	19.9	9.0
Nigeria	35.6	39.6	6.7	1.1

Comparative table 12 Trade (*continued*)

Country	Imports of goods and services (% of GDP) (2011)	Exports of goods and services (% of GDP) (2011)	Manufactured exports (% of exports) (2008–2011 [latest available])	High-technology exports (% of exports) (2010)
Norway	28.3	42.1	15.4	16.1
Peru	24.8	28.7	13.7	6.6
Philippines	36.0	31.0	58.8	67.8
Poland	43.5[a]	42.2[a]	78.0	6.7
Portugal	39.3	35.5	75.3	3.4
Romania	29.1	22.3	77.8	10.9
Russian Federation	22.3	31.1	14.3	8.8
Senegal	44.2	24.5	44.1	1.2
Slovak Republic	86.4	89.1	84.7	7.1
Slovenia	71.3	72.3	82.9	5.5
South Africa	29.4	28.8	64.3	4.3
Spain	31.1	30.3	72.5	6.4
Sweden	43.7	49.9	74.4	13.7
Switzerland	40.4	51.2	86.9	24.8
Syrian Arab Rep.	35.8[a]	35.3[a]	24.7	21.6[d]
Turkey	32.6	23.7	78.3	1.9
Ukraine	59.2	53.8	63.5	4.3
United Kingdom	34.1	32.5	68.2	20.9
United States	17.8	14.0	63.4	19.9
Uruguay	27.3	27.1	25.5	5.8[b]
Venezuela, RB	19.7	29.9	68.0	5.1
Vietnam	91.2	87.0	64.7	6.2[b]

[a]2010; [b]2009; [c]2008; [d]2007

Notes: Imports of goods and services represent the value of all goods and other market services received from the rest of the world. They include the value of merchandise, freight, insurance, transport, travel, royalties, license fees, and other services, such as communication, construction, financial, information, business, personal, and government services. They exclude compensation of employees and investment income (formerly called factor services) and transfer payments. Exports of goods and services represent the value of all goods and other market services provided to the rest of the world. They include the value of merchandise, freight, insurance, transport, travel, royalties, license fees, and other services, such as communication, construction, financial, information, business, personal, and government services. They exclude compensation of employees and investment income (formerly called factor services) and transfer payments. High-technology exports are products with high R&D intensity, such as in aerospace, computers, pharmaceuticals, scientific instruments, and electrical machinery.

Sources: World Bank Data.

Comparative table 13 Globalization

Country	Freedom House ranking 2012	Corruption Perception Index 2012	Overall Globalization Index (KOF) 2009
Albania	3	33	58.4
Algeria	5.5	34	54.9
Argentina	2	35	58.9
Australia	1	85	81.6
Austria	1	69	90.6
Belgium	1	75	92.8
Brazil	2	43	59.4
Canada	1	84	85.5
Chile	1	72	73.3
China	6.5	39	59.4
Colombia	3.5	36	56.3
Costa Rica	1	54	63.1
Cyprus	1	66	86.6
Czech Republic	1	49	85.8
Denmark	1	90	88.1
Egypt, Arab Rep.	5.5	32	59.4
Estonia	1	64	79.3
Finland	1	90	84.3
France	1	71	84.1
Germany	1	79	81.5
Greece	2	36	81.3
Hungary	1.5	55	87.4
Iceland	1	82	73.0
India	2.5	36	51.9
Indonesia	2.5	32	56.3
Iran, Islamic Rep.	6	28	40.7
Ireland	1	69	92.0
Israel	1.5	60	77.2
Italy	1	42	81.0
Japan	1.5	74	64.1
Korea, Rep.	1.5	56	62.4
Latvia	2	49	66.3
Lebanon	4.5	30	64.1
Lithuania	1	54	66.6
Luxembourg	1	80	86.0
Malta	1	57	76.4
Mexico	3	34	60.0
Netherlands	1	84	90.9
New Zealand	1	90	78.3
Nigeria	4	27	58.0
Norway	1	85	83.2

Comparative table 13 Globalization (*continued*)

Country	Freedom House ranking 2012	Corruption Perception Index 2012	Overall Globalization Index (KOF) 2009
Peru	2.5	38	64.5
Philippines	3	34	56.7
Poland	1	58	80.8
Portugal	1	63	86.7
Romania	2	44	74.9
Russian Federation	5.5	28	67.3
Senegal	3	36	54.5
Slovak Republic	1	46	83.8
Slovenia	1	61	77.7
South Africa	2	43	64.4
Spain	1	65	84.4
Sweden	1	88	88.2
Switzerland	1	86	86.6
Syrian Arab Rep.	7	26	42.8
Turkey	3	49	70.0
Ukraine	3.5	26	68.5
United Kingdom	1	74	85.5
United States	1	73	74.9
Uruguay	1	72	65.7
Venezuela, RB	5	19	50.9
Vietnam	6	31	47.0

Notes: Freedom in the World, Freedom House's flagship publication, is the standard-setting comparative assessment of global political rights and civil liberties. Published annually since 1972, the survey ratings and narrative reports on 195 countries and 14 related and disputed territories are used by policy-makers, the media, international corporations, civic activists, and human rights defenders to monitor trends in democracy and track improvements and setbacks in freedom worldwide. The Freedom in the World data and reports are available in their entirety on the Freedom House website. The Corruption Perceptions Index ranks countries and territories based on how corrupt their public sector is perceived to be. A country or territory's score indicates the perceived level of public sector corruption on a scale of 0–100, where 0 means that a country is perceived as highly corrupt and 100 means it is perceived as very clean. A country's rank indicates its position relative to the other countries and territories included in the index. 2012 index includes 176 countries and territories. The KOF Index of Globalization measures the three main dimensions of globalization: economic, social, and political. In addition to three indices measuring these dimensions, an overall index of globalization and sub-indices refers to actual economic flows, economic restrictions, data on information flows, data on personal contact, and data on cultural proximity. Data are available on a yearly basis for 208 countries over the period 1970–2009.

Sources: Freedom House; Transparency International; KOF.

WORLD TRENDS

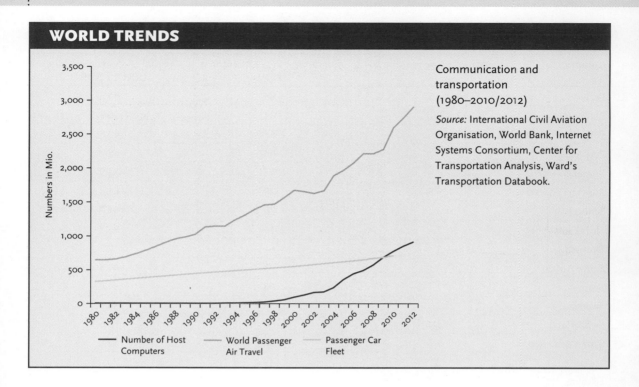

Communication and transportation (1980–2010/2012)

Source: International Civil Aviation Organisation, World Bank, Internet Systems Consortium, Center for Transportation Analysis, Ward's Transportation Databook.

WORLD TRENDS

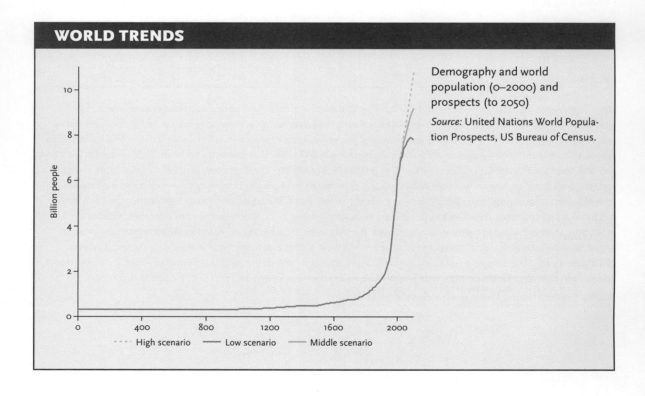

Demography and world population (0–2000) and prospects (to 2050)

Source: United Nations World Population Prospects, US Bureau of Census.

WORLD TRENDS

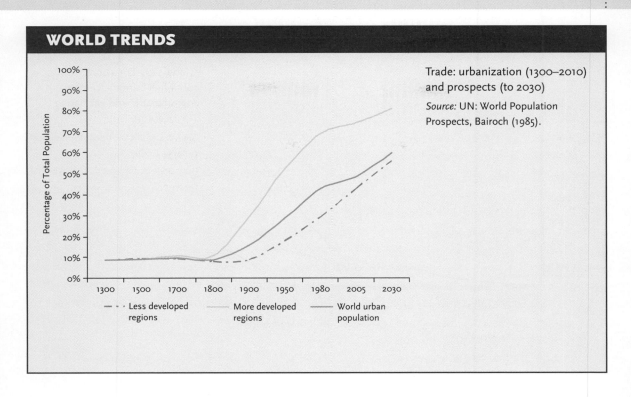

Trade: urbanization (1300–2010) and prospects (to 2030)

Source: UN: World Population Prospects, Bairoch (1985).

- – · – Less developed regions
- —— More developed regions
- —— World urban population

WORLD TRENDS

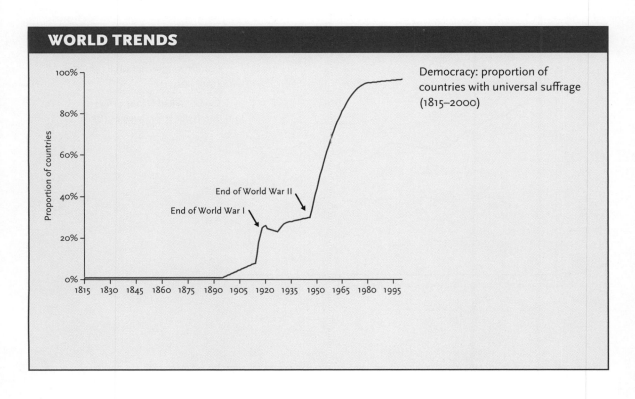

Democracy: proportion of countries with universal suffrage (1815–2000)

WORLD TRENDS

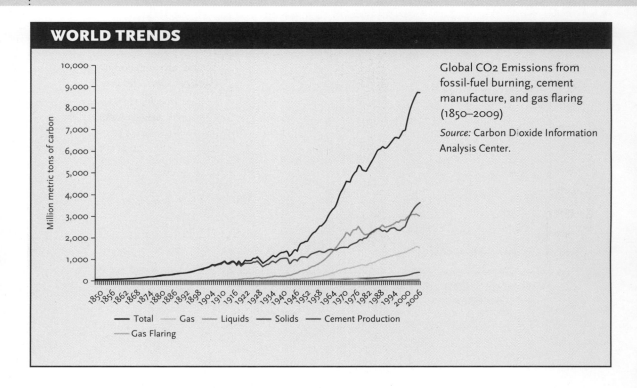

Global CO2 Emissions from fossil-fuel burning, cement manufacture, and gas flaring (1850–2009)

Source: Carbon Dioxide Information Analysis Center.

WORLD TRENDS

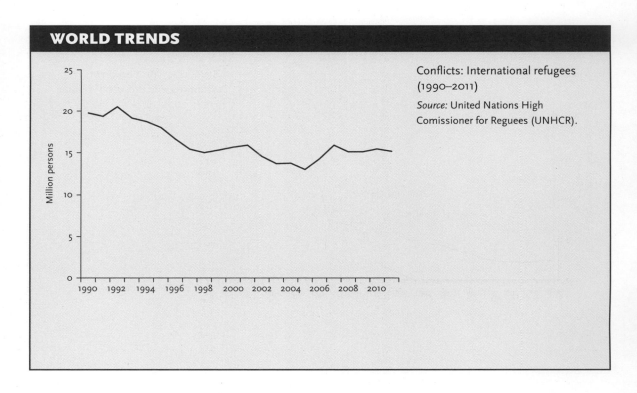

Conflicts: International refugees (1990–2011)

Source: United Nations High Comissioner for Reguees (UNHCR).

WORLD TRENDS

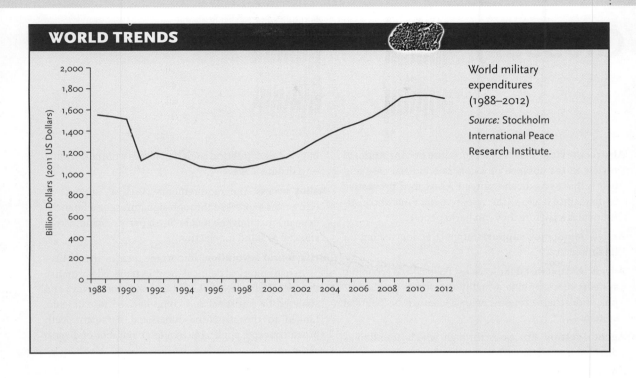

World military expenditures (1988–2012)

Source: Stockholm International Peace Research Institute.

WORLD TRENDS

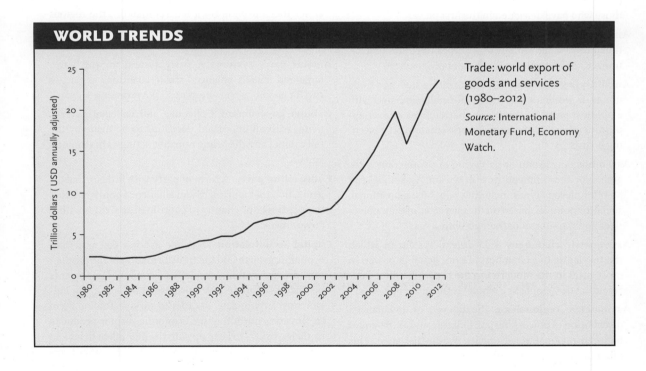

Trade: world export of goods and services (1980–2012)

Source: International Monetary Fund, Economy Watch.

online resource centre

For additional material on world trends, please visit the Online Resource Centre at:
www.oxfordtextbooks.co.uk/orc/caramani3e/

Glossary

Abstract review Refers to a procedure of constitutional review in the absence of a concrete judicial case and before the law has been enforced. Also called 'preventive review', since it allows the system to filter out unconstitutional laws before they can harm people.

Active democracy support Support action resting on intentionality.

Advanced capitalist democracies Political and economic systems that combine a highly developed (industrial/post-industrial) economy with a democratic political system.

Agenda-setting Processes through which attention is directed towards a particular public problem.

Agents In the context of political science, institutions or persons to whom power is delegated. Trustees are a particular kind of agent possessing the power to govern those who have delegated in the first place.

American judicial review A model of judicial constitutional review carried out by all types of courts (decentralized) expected to be fundamentally concrete.

Ancillary organization An organization such as a trade union or women's club that is formally affiliated with a political party through such mechanisms as overlapping memberships or formal representation on governing boards.

Assembly Any group or gathering of people drawn together for a common purpose or reason. Assemblies can be of numerous types including religious, educational, social, or political, based on the character of their objectives and the subject of their activities.

Asymmetric chambers A bicameral system in which the two legislative chambers are not equal in power. In most cases in the modern era the lower chamber (representing the people as a whole) is the more powerful.

Asymmetric regionalism The uneven or imbalanced distribution of powers, responsibilities, and/or revenues between regional governments within that state. This often occurs in states with politicized ethno-territorial minorities or minority nations that consistently demand a range of powers and responsibilities which differs from those exercised by other regional governments populated by members of the ethno-linguistic majority.

Audience democracy Term coined by Bernard Manin (1997) to indicate a contemporary form of democracy in which citizens are not actively engaged in the process but view their political leaders as if they were performing on a distant stage.

Ballot access The requirements (such as support of electors as expressed through signatures, or a financial deposit) that must be met before a party or candidate is allowed to stand for election.

Behavioural revolution Important turn in the 1940s–50s when empirical political theories replaced normative theories. Data were collected by means of surveys and analysed by statistical and computerized instruments. Linked to the structural–functional paradigm, with broad concepts applicable to a large number of diverse cases.

Bicameral legislature A legislature that consists of two chambers, with a lower chamber that represents the people as a whole and an upper house that represents either the sub-units (in a federal system), the regions within a country, or even a particular class or group in society.

Bipolar party systems A party system in which two large and equally balanced stable coalitions of parties run for elections and alternate in government.

Cabinet government Collective and collegial government, with all important decisions to be made by the full cabinet and the prime minister acting as first among equals.

Cadre (elite) party A form of party with little formal organization that is primarily an alliance of politicians and their patrons (or clients) to coordinate activities within government.

Capital accumulation Dynamic process that underlies economic growth and the transformation of the production process within a capitalist economy. This occurs because the competitive business units within capitalism must 'accumulate' in order to survive, forcing them to reinvest a portion of the economic surplus produced by their workers to keep up with the new efficiencies and technological breakthroughs being made by other firms in the national and global economy.

Catch-all party A form of party characterized by appeals, for both votes and material support, that cross cleavage lines and by a shedding of the 'ideological baggage' associated with the mass party model.

Centralization The policy undertaken by a political entity in order to restrict and eliminate the extent to which other, peripheral, regional entities seek to preserve their traditional entitlements, and thus limit its own initiative and its own disposition over political practices and resources.

Central–local relations The way in which relations between central and local governments are organized. These differ in different types of state (federal/unitary) and in different state traditions (Anglo-Saxon, French, Scandinavian). Today, local authorities are less constrained by central governments and are given greater freedom over policy choices and forms of organization.

Centrifugal and centripetal competition Alternative dynamics of competition with parties either distancing themselves from the centre of the left–right axis towards the extremes or converging toward the centre and increasingly resembling each other.

Christian democracy Political movement that is inspired by the Christian faith and has as its main goal the provision of order in society by promoting a harmonious relationship between all classes and layers of society.

Citizenship Historically variable set of rights and obligations which, in the course of modernization, individuals come to possess *vis-à-vis* the state.

Civic culture Type of political culture that emphasizes social activism, participation in networks of free associations, democracy, and a vibrant civil society.

Clash of civilizations Theory stating that cultural, ethnic, and religious differences have replaced the ideological division of the Cold War as the primary source of international conflict.

Classification Process and result of grouping cases by minimizing differences within each class and maximizing differences between classes, according to a dimension or property. Classes are mutually exclusive and jointly exhaustive.

Cleavage A division of interest and values within a polity opposing groups structurally, culturally, and organizationally.

Co-decision procedure The main legislative procedure of the EU under which the Commission makes legislative proposals and legislation must be passed by a majority of MEPs and a qualified-majority vote in the Council.

Collective action Type of action in which more than one individual is required to contribute to an effort in order to pursue a goal or achieve an outcome.

Collective action paradox Mancur Olson's argument that under certain conditions it is not rational for individuals to join interest groups, as they can enjoy the benefits that stem from the group's existence without having to pay the cost to create or maintain the organization (i.e. they can free-ride).

Comparative method Method for testing against empirical evidence alternative hypotheses (and thereby either corroborate or reject them) about necessary and sufficient conditions for events to occur based on the association between configurations of values of different independent variables across cases, and the values of the dependent variable.

Comparison The inquiry of similarities and differences. It is a tool for building empirically falsifiable explanatory theories. In the course of scientific development, systematic and inductive comparison has replaced anecdotal and deductive approaches.

Conceptual stretching Distortion occurring when a concept developed for one set of cases is extended to additional cases to which the features of the concept do not apply.

Concrete review When an ordinary judge refers, within a specific litigation, to a constitutional question.

Congress General term for a legislative assembly within a separation-of-powers political system. Congresses can consist of one chamber or two; if bicameral they may be symmetrical or asymmetrical.

Consensus democracy Form of democracy in which the emphasis is placed on the inclusion of all social groups at all stages in the decision-making process and in which the most widespread possible agreement is sought for public policies and programmes.

Consociationalism Consociationalism is a mode of governing in which political elites representing different communities coalesce around the need to govern, even in the face of intense divisions across their communities.

Constituency The unit, usually defined territorially, into which the country is divided for electoral purposes and from which MPs are returned. Single-member constituencies return just one MP, whereas multimember constituencies return several MPs.

Constitution Statute in which the fundamental political institutions, procedures, and principles of a state are established and in which the basic rights are guaranteed.

Constitutionalism Refers on the one hand to the commitment of a political community to accept the legitimacy of constitutional rules and principles and, on the other hand, to an understanding of government that is derivable from a specific constitutional order. Typical examples are federalism and checks and balances.

Constructivism Basic assumption that social realities are not primordially given but constructed in the course of history.

Control Process through which the influence of some variables on the relationship between operational (independent and dependent) variables is reduced or entirely eliminated (*ceteris paribus* clause).

Conventional and unconventional participation Conventional participation is expressed within accepted institutional channels. Unconventional participation takes place through activities that range from public events to direct physical attacks on property or people.

Corporatism Institutionalized patterns of linkage between social interests and the state, focusing especially on the legitimate role of social interests in influencing policy.

Coup A *coup d'état* is literally a blow by/of the state, but is typically an attack by the military arm of the state against its own government and aimed at seizing power, whether as a 'corporate' coup by the military as a united corporate body or as a 'factional' coup by part of the military.

Decentralization A process whereby power is transferred from the central level of government and/or administration to other levels.

Democracy assistance Concessionary and largely consensual provision of support for democracy and democratization from a state or international organization by way of projects and programmes.

Democracy support Attempts to influence democratization by a variety of methods and approaches that can include linkage and leverage and various measures of soft and hard power.

Democratic deficit The notion that the EU institutions are not as democratically accountable as national institutions. Common allegations associated with the democratic deficit are that the European Commission is appointed rather than elected, that Council decision-making is not as transparent as it could be, and that national parliaments cannot control their governments when they do business in Brussels.

Democratic disguise The disguise that an authoritarian regime uses to hide the fact that it is a non-democratic regime—a disguise that now typically involves the use of semi-competitive multiparty elections.

Democratic peace thesis Statement that democracies tend not to go to war with one another.

Democratization The process by which non-democratic institutions or polities become democratic.

Descriptive analysis Type of analysis aimed at establishing empirical patterns: the degree to which phenomena occur, variations between cases, and change over time.

Devolution Process by which political, administrative, and/or judicial powers are transferred from central state authorities to regional authorities. Whereas decentralization or deconcentration results in no diminution of central state authority, devolution does involve a reduction of power and authority for the centre and more political autonomy for the region.

Digital communication The transmission of digital data through independent new sources that rival mainstream media channels.

Direct support of democracy Action employing political methods and engaging with political institutions.

Disguised military rule The military's rule can be disguised either by civilizing the regime or by ruling indirectly through behind-the-scenes influence upon a puppet civilian government.

District magnitude The number of MPs returned per constituency.

Divided government Configuration of power in which at least one of the chambers of the legislature is controlled by a party that does not hold the presidency.

Electoral market Hypothetical space where political parties present programmes and policies (offer) and voters choose on the basis of their preferences (demand), with the former aiming at maximizing votes and the latter aiming at maximizing utility deriving from specific policies.

Electoral system The set of rules that structure how votes are cast at elections and how these votes are then converted into the allocation of offices/seats.

Empirical research Type of research based on evidence from the real world and disjoined from any type of moral, normative, or value judgement.

Equivalence Feature of concepts and properties whose connotation is similar for all the cases compared.

European model of constitutional review A model of judicial constitutional review carried out by constitutional courts (centralized 'Kelsenian' courts) which are allowed to be abstract.

Evaluation (of policy) Procedure asking whether the output of a given public policy has attained the intended goals.

Explanatory analysis Type of analysis that relates two or more variables (phenomena) with the aim of formulating general causal statements about their relationship. Also referred to as multivariate analysis.

Extension (or denotation) Set (or class) of cases to which a concept refers.

External (extra-parliamentary) origin (of parties) Parties of external origin were founded outside government in order to contest elections and thereby first make demands on government and ultimately elect officials from among their own ranks.

Federal state State where sovereignty is shared across several levels of government and in which one level may not intervene in defined areas of competence of the other. There are different kinds of federal states (e.g. dual federalism in the US and cooperative federalism in Germany).

Flexicurity Combination of flexibility and social protection. In a narrow version, this refers to the combination of liberal employment protection, generous social protection, and active labour-market policies. In a broader version, it refers to a multitude of combinations between different modes of flexibility and security.

Fractionalization Degree of fragmentation in a party system. The higher the number of parties, the higher the fragmentation in a party system.

Free-rider problem A problem faced when public non-excludable goods are provided. Free-riders are individuals who consume a good, but let others pay for its production.

Freezing hypothesis Consolidation of party alternatives and electoral alignments from the 1920s until the 1970s due to the saturation of the electoral market caused by full franchise and PR electoral systems.

Functionalism The functionalist approach aimed at identifying the necessary activities (functions) of all political systems and then comparing the manner in which these functions were performed. This theoretical paradigm, coupled with structuralism and systems theory, aimed at bridging diverse empirical contexts but it was built on assumptions that turned out to be closely related to the Western democratic model.

Fused-powers system Regime in which the executive is selected by the legislature, usually from those within the legislature, and is dependent upon the 'confidence' of the legislature to remain in power. In many cases the executive may also dissolve the legislature by calling for new elections.

Generalizations Law-like statements about relationships between social and political phenomena independent of the specific spatial or temporal context.

Ghent system A system of voluntary unemployment insurance which is administered by trade unions. The name of the system comes from the Belgian town Ghent, where it was first introduced.

Global economy, globalization Terms that refer to the increasing interdependencies between national economies that challenge existing domestic social policy arrangements.

Good governance A commonly used term in the development discourse which, in its most expansive meaning, embraces inclusive and participatory democracy and at a minimum is used to denote freedom from corruption.

Governance Approach in comparative politics interested in the roles that social actors may play in the process of making and implementing governmental decisions.

Hard power A country's military and economic might.

Human development index The UNDP's human development index is a summary measure comprising life expectancy, adult literacy rate, and a decent standard of living measured in income per capita terms. It falls short of the definition provided.

Implementation The conversion of new laws and programmes into practice.

Incomplete contract Contract allowing for uncertainty as to the precise nature of commitments (e.g. the rights and obligations of the parties under the contract).

Indirect support of democracy Action focusing on conditions or preconditions for democratization that may be described as non-political (e.g. economic variables).

Initiative (popular) Referendum held at the behest of a prescribed number of ordinary citizens.

Institutional competitiveness The fact that different regimes develop different comparative advantages. There is not a single road to competitiveness (or to employment), but different strategies that fit into different institutional contexts.

Institutional complementarity Clusters or configurations of (policy) institutions that are mutually supportive (for instance, combinations of various welfare arrangements, or combinations of regulation of the economy).

Institutionalism Set of approaches focusing on the central role of structures in shaping politics and individual behaviour. As well as formal institutional patterns, institutions may be defined in terms of their rules and their routines, and thus emphasize the normative structure of the institutions.

Institutions Formal rules of political decision-making and less formal standard operating procedures. These serve to reduce complexities inherent in the policy-making process, shaping the behaviour of actors and the use of policy instruments.

Intention (or connotation) Set of properties shared by cases to which a concept applies.

Inter-governmentalism One of the two main modes of EU decision-making. Key features of inter-governmentalism are that decisions are reached by unanimous agreement between the EU governments, the European Parliament plays a consultative rather than a legislative role, and the European Court of Justice does not have full judicial review power.

Internal (inter-parliamentary) origin (of parties) Parties of internal origin were originally organized within parliament to coordinate the activities of their members (MPs) in pursuing legislative goals and supporting or opposing cabinets.

International leverage Vulnerability of authoritarian governments to external democratizing pressure. Three important determinants are the state's raw size and military and economic strength, the existence of competing issues on Western foreign policy agendas, and access to support from an alternative regional power.

International linkage Concept composed of five dimensions: economic; geopolitical; social; communication; and transnational civil society. Linkage raises the cost of authoritarianism.

Internationalization (of policies) Describes the processes of policy diffusion, policy transfer, and cross-national policy convergence.

Iron law of oligarchy 'Who says organization, says oligarchy.' The fact of organization leads all parties, including those that proclaim themselves to be democratic, to be dominated by their leaders.

Iron triangle Depiction of the role of interest groups in policy-making. Within a given issue area, a subsystem consisting of a key bureaucrat, a key legislator, and a key interest group would form and set the contours of governmental policy, allowing for little input from outside this group of three.

Judicial review See American judicial review.

Judicialization of politics Process through which the influence of courts on legislative and administrative power develops over time.

Junta Spanish term for a council or committee which is used by political scientists to describe the political committee of military leaders that is formed during a coup to represent the military in its new role as a ruling organization.

Labour movement Social movement that began during the industrial revolution, fighting for better working conditions and higher living standards for industrial workers. For this purpose, it was organized in labour and trade unions.

Ladder of generality Representation of the relation between intension and extension obeying a law of inverse variation. The larger the extension (and the smaller the intension), the higher the level of abstraction of a concept.

Legislature A kind of assembly in which individuals and/or groups are gathered together for explicitly political purposes. At least one of the political goals of a legislature will entail policy-making or legislating.

Liberalism A complex of political values and principles which, through varied constitutional arrangements, seeks to lay relatively narrow boundaries on the activities of the state, committing them first and foremost to respecting and fostering the autonomy of private individuals in their capacity as economic actors.

List systems The most common method of implementing the principle of proportional representation; voters choose between lists of candidates presented by different parties.

Majoritarian democracy Form of democracy in which the emphasis is placed on one side winning an outright (if also temporary) victory over the other, and in which success at the polls offers political control over all the key institutions.

Majority (system) government The parties represented in government hold at least 50 per cent of the seats plus one in parliament.

Mass party (of integration) A party form characterized by the formal dominance of the extra-governmental membership organization, and a strategy of mobilization and encapsulation aimed at a well-defined social constituency (the *classe gardée).*

Media system The social and technological systems through which information is created, gathered, processed, and disseminated.

Merit system Access to the administration is not restricted to particular segments of society; selection and promotion aim at appointing the best-qualified individuals.

Method of Agreement Logic of comparison of cases with similar values on as many variables as possible in order to account for the variation in the dependent variable through the association with independent variables that also vary.

Method of Difference Logic of comparison with cases with different values on as many variables as possible in order to account for the invariance in the dependent variable through the association with invariant independent variables.

Ministerial government Type of government in which decision-making power is dispersed among the individual cabinet members ('fragmented government').

Minority government Type of government in which the parties represented in government hold less than 50 per cent of the seats plus one.

Minority nations Cultural minority groups deprived of their own state (or stateless nations) within a country in which another group is majoritarian and with whom they share the state institutions.

Misappropriation of power (by a party) Usurpation arising when (1) a democratic election victory gives a party access to the key public offices and then (2) the party misappropriates its newly acquired public offices by misusing public powers to ensure that it cannot be defeated in any future elections.

Mixed system Electoral system in which some MPs are returned by plurality or majority from local (usually single-member) constituencies and others by PR from national or regional lists (usually multimember).

Mobilization Attempts by political entrepreneurs (in parties, interest groups, and social movements) to encourage political participation of others.

Most Different Systems Design Research design in which the cases selected are characterized by different values on a large number of independent variables.

Most Similar Systems Design Research design in which the cases selected are characterized by similar values on a large number of independent variables.

Multinational state Type of country comprised of a populace that has two or more ethnically differentiated, culturally distinct, and territorially concentrated political communities that have historical claims to nationhood.

Multiparty systems A party system in which many parties exist, with at most only one party approaching the absolute majority of seats, and therefore need to form coalitions to support a government that are negotiated after the elections.

Nation A political community may be considered a nation when it is unified not only by the shared subjection to a system of rule but also by a complex and historically variable set of social and cultural bonds of diverse nature (commonalities of ethnic origins, language, religion, customs, historical experience, political values) which generate among individuals a significant feeling of affinity and distinctiveness.

National and industrial 'revolutions' Concepts indicating broad political changes in the nineteenth century in politics (formation of nation-states and the democratization and secularization of political systems) and in economy (industrialization and urbanization, and the emergence of a working class).

Nationalism An ideology and political movement based on the nation-state principle in which those who consider themselves to be members of a nation seek to obtain an independent state. A distinction may be made between 'majoritarian nationalism', which refers to established nation-states such as France or Germany, and 'minority nationalism' which refers to stateless nations such as Scotland or Catalonia.

Nation-building Sometimes conflated with state-building, refers to attempts to bring a common sense of national belonging and solidarity to plural communities who reside in the same state.

Nation-state A form of political organization, first advocated during the French Revolution, which links together 'state' and 'nation', whereby each nation should have a single state and each state should correspond to a nation.

Neo-institutionalism Theory that puts forward the role of institutions and norms. Institutions are sets of rules and structures that shape individual behaviour. Other types of institutionalism stress the incentives that institutions set for individual behaviour. In a historical perspective, institutions persist over time and determine future choices (path dependence).

Neoliberalism School of thought that promotes private property rights and free-market capitalism through the deregulation of business activities, the limitation of workers' collective bargaining rights, the retrenchment of the welfare state, and the privatization of public utilities.

Networks Corporatist patterns of linkage between social interests and the state are being replaced by more loosely defined relationships such as networks.

New constitutionalism New model of democratic state legitimacy, based on the following three elements: a written constitution, a charter of rights;, and a judicial review mechanism.

New Public Management The application of market mechanisms in the public sector: fixed-term contracts, 'internal markets' and competition, encouragement of managerialism and entrepreneurship, and performance-related contracts.

New social movements Social movements since the mid-1960s which departed from the 'old' labour movement. These movements include the ecology, peace, solidarity, women's rights, human rights, and squatters' movements, as well as various other movements mobilizing for the rights of discriminated minorities (such as the gay movement).

One-party rule This arises when a political party rules dictatorially as some form of open or disguised one-party state and operates a communist, fascist, or Third World type of one-party rule.

Open military rule The open form of military rule occurs when the military seizure of power leads to military officers openly taking over the governing of the country, such as by establishing a junta or appointing one of themselves as president or prime minister.

Outside lobbying Refers to more recent techniques, such as grass-roots campaigns, in which elites attempt to use mass memberships or the public more broadly to influence key political players.

Over-determination Insufficient number of cases to test for all potentially relevant independent variables (low degree of freedom).

Over/under-representation Distortion between the proportion of votes parties receive and the proportion of seats they are allocated, caused by different types of electoral systems. Through over-representation large parties receive a share of seats that is larger than their share of votes, and through under-representation small parties receive a share of seats that is smaller than their share of votes.

Paradigm Dominant mainstream approach including a set of assumptions and possible research questions. Of the evolutionary stages of comparative politics, only the dominance of the 'behavioural revolution' came close to Kuhn's idea of a paradigm change.

Parliament A legislative assembly within a fused-powers system. Parliaments can consist of one chamber or two; if bicameral, they may be symmetrical or asymmetrical.

Parliamentary systems Regimes in which the executive is not directly elected by the citizens, but is placed in office and held accountable to parliament, which is directly elected.

Party government Regime in which the actions of office-holders are determined by values and policies derived from their party.

Party system Set of political parties within a democratic system competing with each other for the largest share of the electoral vote, with the aim of winning elections and controlling government.

Passive democracy support Type of democratization influenced by external and international forces which do not have democratic outcomes as their aim.

Path dependence Concept originally developed in institutional economics, referring to the large political, as well as practical, costs of changing policy. In addition to this strict notion of path dependence as a theory, with emphasis on mechanisms, one also finds 'softer' versions that apply path dependence as a perspective.

Personal dictatorship The leader of a military or party that has seized or misappropriated power but instead of acting as its representative has established a personal dictatorship.

Pluralism A school of thought that argues that groups within society form to influence government through a process of competition. Individuals themselves are believed to belong to multiple and competing groups, thus further ensuring the stability of the system.

Policy adoption The formal acceptance of a policy.

Policy feedback Concept covering feedback effects from output and outcomes of policies to new input to policies. It includes path dependence, policy learning, policy diffusion, and changing power relations between political actors.

Policy formulation The definition, discussion, acceptance, or rejection of feasible courses of action for coping with policy problems.

Policy learning A 'change in thinking' about a specific policy issue.

Policy paradigms Overall worldview underlying policies. The notion of paradigm is borrowed from the study of revolutions in the worldview of natural sciences (e.g. from a geocentric to a heliocentric paradigm). Policy paradigms provide particular problem definitions, and to a large extent solutions.

Political action committees PACs are vehicles formed by entities such as corporations and unions that bundle contributions from their employees or members and then distribute them to politicians running for office in the US. PACs are necessary because corporations and unions are not legally allowed to contribute directly to candidates.

Political conditionality Attachment of democracy, human rights, and governance conditions to offers of assistance to development. Certain political conditions may also be applied to membership entitlement to inter-governmental organizations like the European Union and Organization of American States.

Political culture The orientation of the citizens of a nation towards politics, and their perceptions of political legitimacy and the traditions of political practice. Set of values, attitudes, and beliefs related to state authority and the political system.

Political entrepreneurs Individuals who instigate collective action without receiving selective benefits, but often induce others with such benefits to participate in the mobilization.

Political opportunity structures The degree to which social movements have access to the political system.

Political process approach Approach that interprets social movements as a form of mass politics. The chances of the movement achieving success are discussed in terms of the 'opportunities' that are available.

Politics, policy, polity Politics is the struggle for power within a system of rules, institutions, and norms (polity) to be exercised (policies) in order to achieve given outcomes.

Polyarchy Term developed primarily by Robert Dahl (1971) to indicate a system of government that is the closest that real existing polities come to democracy. Polyarchies offer inclusive participatory rights to citizens and also guarantee full and fair competition between alternative groups and leaders.

Population An ensemble of human individuals which reproduces itself biologically and which normally occupies the same territory over several generations.

Post-materialism Value orientation that emphasizes quality of life, social equality, protection of the environment, and participation in social and political life, and is expressed in a number of new social movements such as pacifism and feminism.

Prediction Scientific statements about the relationship between social and political phenomena should include elements of prediction, i.e. statements about outcomes if certain conditions are fulfilled.

Preferential voting Opportunity, under some list systems, for voters to cast a preference vote for an individual candidate on a list rather than just for the list as a whole.

Presidential systems Systems in which the chief executive, usually an individual political leader, is directly elected by the citizens and enjoys a fixed term of office.

Presidentialization of politics Strengthening of the chief executive in his/her party and executive functions and increasingly leadership-centred electoral processes.

Prime ministerial government Monocratic decision-making by the prime minister by taking up issues at will, or by deciding key issues with subsequent implications on government policy, or by defining a governing ethos which generates solutions to most policy problems.

Procedural democracy Form of democracy in which the definition emphasizes the process by which political leaders are elected and held accountable rather than the political or ideological goals that are set by the regime.

Professionalization The social process by which the communication occupation transforms itself into a true profession and by which the qualified are demarcated from unqualified amateurs.

Proportional representation The principle that the distribution of seats among parties brought about by an election should closely correspond to the distribution of votes among those parties. This principle can be effected by a wide range of different specific methods.

Proportionality Degree of correspondence between parties' vote shares and their shares of seats.

Protest events Means for social movements to draw attention to their cause. They range from petitions, festivals, and demonstrations to violent confrontations.

Public interest groups Groups that seek to achieve a non-self-interested collective goal (e.g. clean air) that will benefit society at large and not just the members of the interest groups.

Public policies A long series of actions carried out to solve societal problems. They are the main output of political systems.

Public sphere A large number of autonomous individuals find themselves enabled by the resources they possess, activated by their interests, and authorized by the existing constitutional arrangements to communicate to one another their opinions on political issues and policies, to articulate both their disagreements and their agreements, and to align themselves accordingly.

Qualified-majority voting System of weighted-voting in the EU Council, where each member state government has a number of votes in proportion to its population.

Quasi-experimental research design The comparative method is called 'quasi-experimental' because conclusions are inferred from empirically informed comparisons and not from experiments.

Rational choice A set of (more or less formal) deductive models based on assumptions of rationality: ordering of preferences, maximization of utility, and full information.

Rationalization The tendency to engage in action, individual or collective, in a deliberate manner, so as to optimize its bearing on one's interests and preferences. In the case of political and administrative activity, the attempt to optimize the relationship between costs and benefits of public activity by rendering that activity as far as possible uniform, predictable, and economical.

Redistribution Reallocation of both social risks and material resources either from one social group to another or over the life-course.

Referendum Vote held not to elect a parliament but to decide on some specific issue.

Regional autonomy The location of state powers and responsibilities with authorities and institutions at the regional level. The extent of regional autonomy varies from state to state and constitutes a key element of power-sharing arrangements in both federal and non-federal countries.

Regional policy Range of policies, programmes, and fiscal arrangements with the objective of reducing economic and social disparities between regions within a nation-state, a sub-national state, or an affiliated group of nation-states.

Regionalism The social, cultural, economic, and political expression of a spatially distinct pattern of values, attitudes, orientations, opinions, behaviours, preferences, interests, and/or actions that reflect the sense of belonging or attachment to, and the personal and community interests that are vested in, a particular territorial space distinct from either local or nation-state level.

Registration requirements Obligations in order to receive the right to vote. They increase the cost of voting. The low turnout in the US can be partly explained by the time-consuming registration requirements compared with other rich democracies.

Rejective referendum Type of referendum in which the people vote on a proposal that some measure of government or parliament should be rejected.

Repertories of contention The means groups choose to protest. Includes demonstrations, general strike actions, or civil disobedience.

Research design Basic organization of a research programme which formulates hypotheses concerning the relationship between variables, identifies the relevant indicators, selects cases and data, discusses measurement and comparability problems, and identifies suitable techniques for data analysis.

Resource mobilization The amount of people, money, and media coverage that a particular social movement can mobilize.

Riskiness of participation Attribute to classify political participation by the sanctions political authorities might impose on it, from monetary fines and minor harassments to incarceration and death.

Ruling monarchy A ruling monarch exercises the same sort of power as a personal dictator and, unlike a reigning monarch, is not a constitutional and largely ceremonial head of state.

Secularization The decline of religious values as well as the institutional separation of state and church.

Selection bias (1) Distortion affecting the inference from sample to population arising from the non-random inclusion in the analysis of a number of cases chosen from a larger pool that are not representative of the population (external validity); (2) over-representation of cases at one end or the other of the distribution of the dependent variable (internal validity).

Selective incentives 'Private' benefits that political entrepreneurs can direct to those who help to overcome the free-rider problem in the production of a collective good. These incentives can be material (e.g. a gift), expressive (e.g. a sense that one is doing the right thing), or solidarity (e.g. the comfort that comes from being part of the group).

Semi-competitive elections Low level of democratic competition between the official party and one or more other parties, but the dictatorship ensures by various subtle or not so subtle means that its official party will win the elections.

Separation-of-powers system Regime in which the legislative and executive branches are selected independently from one another and neither can dismiss the other (with certain rare exceptions for criminal activity or incapacitation). Both branches are generally elected by citizens through distinct votes.

Single market A single market to replace the separate markets of the member-states is the main aim and achievement of the EU. The creation of the single market involved the removal of technical, physical, and fiscal barriers to the free movement of goods, services, capital, and labour in Europe.

Social capital Positive outcomes generated by the networks that bind a community together. The more of these there are and the stronger they are, the greater the social and political benefits they generate and hence civil society and quality of life have a higher potential to flourish. Social capital is a key component for building and maintaining democracy.

Social democracy Political movement that has as its main goal the material and immaterial improvement of the position of workers and employees in capitalist society by stressing equality.

Social movement Streams of public collective unconventional participation that target demands at policymakers primarily through community, street, and media events, often involving disruption of regular social life, e.g. through blockades and sit-ins.

Social movement organization (SMO) Conscious, collective, organized groups that attempt to bring about, or resist, large-scale change in the social order by non-institutionalized means.

Social networks Connection of several individuals tied by one or more types of relation, such as values, partisanship, or friendship. Social networks are thought of as enabling political participation in various ways (mobilization, group pressure, monitoring).

Social risks Risks that are shared by many people and affect the welfare of society as a whole that are interpreted as a threat to certain strata of society, and are beyond the control of any individual.

Socially embedded growth model Various institutional and political economy theories about the new regionalism. The emphasis within this model is on the internal or endogenous social and economic factors responsible for regional economic success, such as the character and quality of a region's human, social, and cultural capital.

Soft power Strategy based on attraction and persuasion rather than coercion. It arises from the attractiveness of a country's culture, political ideals, policies, and practices, both domestic and as displayed in how it conducts external relations.

Sovereignty A principle originally articulated by rulers involved in early state-making who (1) claimed that within their territories their political faculties and prerogatives overrode all those claimed by lesser powers, and (2) acknowledged no centre of rule operating outside those territories as having political faculties and prerogatives superior to their own.

Spoils system System through which the victorious party appoints large layers of the administration after each election, with the jobs going to party trustees.

Staatslehre Originally a subfield of legal studies, it was among the precursors of modern political science. However, its affirmative, somewhat metaphysical, focus on the state was soon left behind.

State A polity which claims in law (and is able to assert in fact) that within a given portion of the Earth its properly constituted organs are exclusively entitled to practice legitimate violence in the pursuit of political interests, beginning with the maintenance of public order and defence of the territory from foreign encroachments.

State-building Activities intended to create the essential conditions for, and the substance of, a state, defined in terms of a monopoly of the means of violence and an ability to procure certain basic functions like security throughout the territory.

State subventions Subsidies from the public treasury to support the activities of political parties.

Supra-nationalism One of the two main modes of EU decision-making involving a monopoly on legislative initiative by the European Commission, co-equal power in the adoption of legislation by the governments (in the Council) and the European Parliament (under the co-decision procedure), and judicial review of EU legislation by the European Court of Justice.

Symmetric chambers Bicameral legislatures in which both chambers have exactly the same powers, both in terms of investiture/censure of the government and as regards the policy-making process.

Systemic functionalism Theoretical paradigm based on the functions of structures within a social or political system.

Systems theory General empirical theory replacing the narrow concept of state and its institutions with the broader concept of the political system as a set of structures (institutions and agencies) whose decision-making function is to reach the collective and authoritative allocation of values *(output,* i.e. public policies) receiving support as well as demands *(inputs)* from the domestic as well as the international *environment* which it shapes through outputs in the *feedback loop.*

Territoriality Each states rules over a clearly bounded portion of land (and the adjoining waters), and its commands and other practices of rule apply in principle to all individuals operating, at a given time, over that territory.

Third wave Term coined by Samuel Huntington (1991) to distinguish the wave of democratic transition that took place between 1974 and 1990 from earlier waves of democratic transition that took place between 1828 and 1926 and between 1942 and 1962.

Threshold Level of support (usually expressed as a percentage of the total vote) that a party must reach in order to achieve representation.

Traditions Cultural elements inherited from the past and maintained through recurrent rituals.

Transnational social movements Deal with issues that exceed the local and national level and that are trans-boundary or 'global' in their character. Typical examples are ecology or human rights movements.

Triangulation Research strategies aiming at exploring the same set of data with several alternative theories or to go into the field with alternative approaches in mind in order to become more open to unexpected findings.

Trust Type of social relationship based on reliance. The relationship can be horizontal (trust in fellow citizens) as well as vertical (trust in political, cultural, social, and economic elites and authorities).

Turnout The ratio of voters to the electorate. The electorate can be defined in different ways: all residents in a polity, all citizens, or all citizens who are also registered to vote.

Two-party system A party system with two equally balanced parties that receive almost all votes and alternate in power, forming single-party governments.

Unicameral legislature A legislature that consists of only one chamber. Unicameral legislatures are never found in federal political systems and are often associated with smaller, more homogeneous societies.

Unified government All three branches of presidential government—the presidency and both houses of the legislature—are under the control of the same party.

Union state A pre-modern form of state organization constructed through 'acts of union' between political entities.

Unitary state State in which sovereignty is concentrated at the level of a single central government. Unitary states may be centralized, decentralized, or regionalized.

Variables A property or attribute that has been made measurable.

Varieties of capitalism Different methods of coordination between economic actors. The concept is parallel to the welfare regime concept, but the cornerstone is the interest of firms in using the market vs. negotiations and public regulation as the main instance of coordination.

Welfare regime Specific configuration of state, market, and family that nations adopt in their pursuit of work and welfare and the management of social risks. Three or more such clusters are usually identified: conservative, liberal, social democratic.

Welfare state Type of democratic state, influenced by Keynesianism, which offers (some) protection to its citizens against the hardships of the (labour) market (e.g. unemployment) and life (e.g. sickness).

Welfare state reform Generic term to refer to political interventions that are meant to adjust existing welfare arrangements to changing social (e.g. ageing) and economic (e.g. globalization) conditions, ranging from the incremental fine-tuning and correction of policy instruments to radical measures such as the abolition of old social programmes and the introduction of new ones.

Endnotes

Introduction

[1] Not all authors would agree with such a division of disciplines, stressing that fields like public administration, policy analysis, political behaviour, and political economy are not part of comparative politics (see, for example, the titles of the volumes in the *Oxford Handbooks of Political Science* listed in the 'Further reading' section of this Introduction). More importantly, this division into three main disciplines disregards methodology as a separate field. However, opinions diverge as to whether or not methods should be considered within the fields of political science, as they largely overlap with methods in other sciences, such as economics and sociology.

[2] In these years the first studies on political culture were published (see, e.g., Banfield 1958), followed by others stressing the differences in political cultures other than the Anglo-Saxon culture—namely based on clientelism and patronage. For an example of cultural analysis see Putnam (1993).

[3] Numbers are a universal language and thus, from a comparative point of view, the least problematic level of measurement of phenomena in diverse contexts.

[4] Within the new-institutionalist theory different positions have emerged and have been summarized by Hall and Taylor (1996): (1) *historical new-institutionalism* devotes attention to the time dimension and the constraints set by past developments (path dependence) with a strong impact on policy analysis; (2) *sociological new-institutionalism* stresses how institutions model politics, and influence preferences by narrowing expectations and orientations; (3) *rational choice new-institutionalism* focuses on how institutions result from the aggregation of individual preferences and on institutions' contribution to solving collective action problems.

[5] These cycles correspond to what are named pre-modern and post-modern comparative politics in Chapter 1 or what Chilcote (1994) calls traditional, behavioural, and post-behavioural comparative politics.

[6] Charles Tilly's critique of Stein Rokkan's model points precisely to Rokkan's failure to genuinely analyse the *interactions* between countries (Tilly 1984: 129)

Chapter 2

[1] This classification of research types comes from Arend Lijphart's seminal article (Lijphart 1971).

[2] A great deal of political science theory has been developed in reference to the US, given the size and importance of the political science profession there. However, a good deal of that theory does not appear relevant beyond the boundaries of the US (in some cases not within those boundaries either).

[3] This is something of an oversimplification of the assumptions of rational choice approaches, but the central point here is not the subtlety of some approaches but rather the reliance on individual-level explanations. For a more extensive critique of the assumptions see Box 13.5 in Chapter 13.

[4] That is, if we could reject more theories and models then we could focus on the more useful ones. As it is, we are overstocked with positive findings and theories that have credible support.

[5] The classic example of a study that uses triangulation explicitly is Allison (1971). However, this book uses multiple theories but it does not verify the results through multiple research methods.

[6] See, for example, Adcock and Collier (2001) who stress the need for common standards of validity for all varieties of measurement, as well as the interaction of those forms of measurement.

[7] Lijphart (1999) has provided a slightly different conceptualization by distinguishing between majoritarian and consensual political systems (see Chapter 5 on 'Democracies'). Some parliamentary systems, such as the Westminster system, are majoritarian, designed to produce strong majority governments that alternate in office. Others, such as in the Scandinavian countries, may have alternation in office but the need to create coalitions and an underlying consensus on many policy issues results in less alternation in policy.

[8] These shifts are to some extent a function of changes in political culture, especially the movement towards 'post-industrial politics' (Ingelhart 1990).

[9] This is more true for American than for European political science. Discourse theory and the use of rhetorical forms of analysis have been of much greater relevance in Europe than they have in North America, and qualitative methodologies remain more at the centre of European political analysis.

Chapter 3

[1] In comparative politics the term 'cross-*national* research' is often used to depict the cases for comparative analysis (e.g. Landman 2003). Here I use the term 'cross-*system* analysis' to avoid the idea that only 'nations' are cases in a comparative politics (Lijphart 1975: 166).

[2] There are many names in use for independent variables: exogenous, effect-producing, antecedent variables, etc. They all have in common that a change in X affects Y. In this chapter we use the term dependent (Y) and independent (X) variables.

[3] In Table 21.2 the comparative analysis is based on evidence of 18 democracies.

[4] Another way of developing a causal argument is counterfactual analysis, asking *what if* a variable is omitted from the equation. In this example: what if 'politics' does *not* play a role?

[5] A more radical argument is the view that language or (hi) stories and numbers (or music notation) are not different at all: the way it is written may be different but whatever notation is used, its analytical value remains basically the same (see Budge and Keman 1990: 34).

[6] Figure 3.1 is a way to handle spuriousness: by controlling for social and economic factor X_1, one could estimate the *relative* influence of politics X_2 in terms of a direct relationship.

[7] Boolean algebra presents formal relations between variables. In Fuzzy Set Logic/QCA variables are dichotomized to analyse multiple causal relations (see Caramani 2009).

Chapter 4

[1] One often speaks, today, of 'failed' states (see Chapter 25).

[2] The same rules of delimitation apply to the sea.

[3] However, they mostly do that without depriving those individuals and bodies of their private resources and their status advantages.

[4] Since not only more significant faculties and responsibilities correspond to higher offices but also greater material and status rewards, the hierarchical structure we have talked about also constitutes a career system. It is a ladder which office-holders can climb to satisfy their legitimate ambitions.

Chapter 5

[1] See the Freedom House report *Democracy's Century: A Survey of Global Political Change in the 20th Century*, published on 7 December 1999. See also Box 5.1.

[2] This famous observation is also from Linz, and seems to have first been used in a 1990 essay (Linz 1990*b*: 158).

[3] The explosion was also reflected in the successful launch of two new journals devoted to the comparison of democracies and democratization: the *Journal of Democracy*, founded in 1990, and *Democratization*, founded in 1993.

[4] The combination of the criteria proposed by Dahl and by O'Donnell also comes close to the lengthy list of political and civil liberties used by Freedom House in its contemporary ratings of polities across the world. See also Coppedge and Reinicke (1990).

[5] Although even Schumpeter accepted the need for elections in democracy to be free and fair, and also accepted that this required at least some degree of institutional pluralism (Schumpeter 1947: 292–3).

[6] In a recent assessment, Perry Anderson (2007: 10) cites the Russian observer Dmitry Furman who defines the contemporary regime in Russia as 'managed democracy'—a system in which 'elections are held, but the results are known in advance; courts hear cases, but give decisions that coincide with the interests of the authorities; the press is plural, yet with few exceptions dependent on the government'. See also Ekiert *et al.* (2007).

[7] In a similar approach to Dahl's, but also one that is more narrowly specified, Lipset and Rokkan (1967: 26ff.) have traced the relationship between the sequencing of democratic developments in the different polities of Western Europe and the character of the party system that subsequently developed in these polities (see also Chapter 13).

[8] Note also Przeworski's (1991: 10) widely cited definition of democracy as 'a system in which parties lose elections'. Dahl's milestones can also help to make sense of the European Union as a quasi-democratic polity: one that affords the rights of participation and representation but that limits the scope for organized opposition *within* the institutions (see Mair 2007).

[9] Lijphart developed the term 'consociationalism' from the work of the late Reformation philosopher Johannes Althusius who had argued in the early seventeenth century for a form of federalism in which distinct communities within a single polity could work together by retaining a large degree of autonomy (see Hueglin 1979).

[10] In the 1984 version of his new framework, Lijphart included a reference to the number of dimensions of party competition, and, by extension, the cleavage structure, as one of the eight relevant characteristics of the two models of democracy. All other features were strictly political and/or institutional. This feature is not included in the more extended version of the models in 1999, however, even though it is used to help explain variation in party numbers, which remains one of the relevant characteristics. In other words, by 1999 social factors are no longer seen to play a direct role in distinguishing between the two forms of democracy.

[11] This is also sometimes true even when comparing a more limited range of institutions, as the confusion over the classification of presidential, semi-presidential, and parliamentary systems testifies (see e.g. Elgie 1998).

[12] For a review and discussion of the European evidence, see Mair (2006*c*), from which some of the following paragraphs are drawn.

Chapter 6

[1] Innovative ideologies or structures had already appeared in Turkey and Mexico in the 1930s, with visionary military dictators seeking to Westernize the former and to civilianize the latter's military-dominated politics into democratically disguised one-party rule.

[2] Reversing the principal–agent relationship is not sufficient, though, to produce absolutist personal rule if the dictator's party or military is a relatively weak institution. For example, Mussolini's fascist party was too weak to control or counterbalance Italy's military and reigning monarch.

[3] Civilianization and indirect rule have also been favourite strategies of military *personal* rulers in the Middle East and Latin America, respectively.

[4] The military's temporary vanguard role was converted into a civilianized presidential monarchy for Nasser, who was succeeded by his deputy, ex-Colonel Sadat, who was in turn succeeded by his own deputy, ex-General Mubarak, who continued to rule Egypt as a third-generation civilianized presidential monarchy until overthrown in the 2011 Arab Spring.

[5] The military's control mechanisms can be exploited by a military leader establishing and maintaining a *personal* dictatorship. Two particularly useful mechanisms are (1) the official party in the military version of a one-party state and (2) the appointment of officers to positions in the civil service and other civilian posts.

Chapter 7

[1] Currently Saudi Arabia and Myanmar (Burma) are the only two internationally recognized countries that do not have some form of legislature.

[2] The term is also related to the Anglo-Latin 'parliamentum', although the French *'parlement'* predates this construction (Harper 2001).

[3] There are a number of institutional structures that can increase or decrease the ease with which a legislature can successfully adopt a motion of no confidence, such as the requirement for all such motions to include a simultaneously adopted motion for the investiture of a new executive (the German **constructive vote of no confidence**). In some parliamentary systems use of censure votes is very rare (Germany, the UK), in others it occurs more regularly (France), while in still others use of the

mechanism is so common as to cause concern for the system as a whole (Italy pre-1994).

[4] Entitlements, as opposed to discretionary funds, are pre-existing financial commitments that cannot be withdrawn or decreased.

[5] For example, under the previous apartheid regime South Africa had a tripartite legislature with each chamber's membership drawn from a distinct racial group.

[6] The British House of Lords is a well-known example.

[7] This dichotomy ignores the existence of hybrid systems such as the French semi-presidential model.

[8] Even in the case of a venal pursuit of power, within a democratic system policy outcomes will become important to the extent that they influence the probability of re-election. Thus the two goals are inextricably linked.

Chapter 8

[1] Another meaning of 'government' refers to the political science sub-discipline that takes its name from the subject of its study, i.e. government in its broadest meaning. Thus this chapter is a contribution to 'Comparative government'.

Chapter 9

[1] Some social scientists adopt a narrow perspective: any rule that binds actors into a stable system of cooperation with one another, and thus enables them to achieve joint gains and purposes, should be considered 'constitutional'. Thus the rule of reciprocity in a trade regime is a constitutional rule (Hermann-Pillath 2006), and so might be 'thou shalt not lie to or cheat on your neighbours' in a community without a formal state or law (see, generally, Taylor 1982). Consider the 'constituting' role of the Ten Commandments of the Old Testament. I am generally sympathetic to this idea (see Stone Sweet 1999), but will not explore it further here.

[2] A 'complete' contract 'would specify precisely what each party is to do in every possible circumstance and arrange the distribution of realized costs and benefits in each contingency so that each party individually finds it optimal to abide by the contract's terms' (Milgrom and Roberts 1992: 127).

[3] In the past, the legislator and the judge were often one and the same, as when the king or feudal lord or corporate body both made law and resolved disputes.

[4] In this chapter, I do not discuss the extent to which appointment procedures, the partisan affiliation of judges, have influenced the development of constitutional law around the world. These factors have surely mattered, but how much remains a mystery. To date, no sophisticated comparative work on the topic has been produced.

[5] Civil Rights Cases, 109 US 3 (1883); *Plessy* v. *Ferguson,* 163 US 537 (1896).

[6] The data set was compiled by Christina Andersen and the author of this chapter. It includes 196 states. It excludes Brunei and the Central African Republic for which no adequate information is available.

Chapter 12

[1] The importance of the referendum is one of the factors underlying the Swiss practice of entrusting executive power to an apparently permanent coalition of *all* the major parties. As Lehner and Homann (1987) explain, given the threat that any parliamentary decision can be overturned by referendum, the ruling parties are at pains to assemble overwhelming majorities in the hope of deterring any referendum in the first place (see also Chapter 10).

[2] To date, the only women's party that has had any lasting success was the Icelandic Kvinnalistinn (Women's List), which existed from 1983 to 1999, and at the height of its success (1987) won more than 10 per cent of the national vote, and six of sixty-three seats in parliament. In 1999, the Women's List merged into a more general left-wing alliance.

[3] The term 'genetic myth' is used here in the same sense that the term 'stylized' is often used in rational choice theory to suggest the essence of a story without claiming that it fits the details of any particular case.

[4] Or with different terms, but equivalent meaning, they might define the interest of their particular class *to be* the national interest.

[5] There is no inherent reason why a cadre party must be on the right, but as history developed they were generally parties of the propertied classes—who were the only ones who could vote under the *régimes censitaires*.

[6] It should be noted that these regulations apply only to federal parties, which are organizationally distinct from provincial parties, even when they apparently have the same name. For example, the Liberal Party of Quebec has not been affiliated with the Liberal Party of Canada since 1955, and indeed when Jean Charest resigned the leadership of the federal Progressive Conservative Party in 1998, it was to become leader of the Quebec Liberal Party.

[7] Exceptions include some schemes for media access (as well as the British free mailing of electoral addresses) that allocate resources equally among parties or candidates without regard to prior electoral success, schemes that base support at least in part on numbers of members rather than voters, and schemes of (partial) public matching of privately raised contributions.

Chapter 13

[1] In the US two-party systems exist largely because of the rules for forming a party which make it difficult for third parties to present candidates. For this reason there is not a high disproportionality between votes and seats in Table 13.3 (LSq index).

[2] The literature on the positive sides of multiparty systems insists on a different decision-making mode based on consensus. This literature includes Rustow (1955), Daalder (1966), Lorwin (1966a,b), Lijphart (1968a,b), McRae (1974), and Steiner (1974), all stressing accommodation, agreement, and compromise.

[3] In the Federal Republic of Germany a rule of the Constitutional Court banned both Communist and Nazi parties.

[4] 1958 marks the beginning of the Fifth Republic in France with the new 'Gaullist' constitution and a two-ballot majority system in single-member constituencies.

[5] If the effective number of parties is calculated on votes, this is usually referred to as 'effective number of elective parties' (ENEP), whereas if it is calculated on seats it is called 'effective number of parliamentary parties' (ENPP).

[6] Additional causes of distortion between votes and seats are the rules to form a party and present candidates, the size of parliamentary groups, the threshold of representation, the type of quota (Hare, Droop, Imperiali, etc.) and the number of tiers (i.e. various levels of constituencies for the allocation of seats).

[7] A further assumption is that if a voter prefers ideological position 60 over 70, then the voter will also prefer 60 over 80, 90, etc. (transitivity). This is an assumption of single-peakedness of voter preferences, i.e. if a voter prefers 60 then the further away the position is from 60 the less it is liked.

[8] Such a modification of the left–right distribution through new voters is unique. Later 'waves' of enfranchisement—namely, when women and younger generations were enfranchised with the lowering of the voting age— did not have a similar effect.

[9] As a response to the criticism about full information, rational choice theorists argue that it is not rational to spend a lot of time gathering political information (the costs outweigh benefits). This is a free-rider attitude.

Chapter 17

[1] Secular values are measured on the basis of twelve items, indicating a secular distance from the sacred authorities of religion, the nation, the state, and group norms. Each of these items is recoded in such a way that the least secular position is coded zero and the most secular position 1.0. Distance from the authority of religion is measured by three items asking if the respondent considers religion important, defines him/herself as religious, and how frequently he/she practices religion. Distance from state authority is measured by three items asking how much confidence the respondent has in the army, the police, and the courts. Distance from national authority is measured by three items asking how much national pride the respondent has, if he/she is willing to fight for the country in case of war, and whether more respect of authority is needed. Distance from the authority of group norms is measured by three items asking the respondent how justifiable he/she finds taking a bribe, evading taxes, and claiming benefits for which one is not entitled. A respondents' final score on secular values is the average score over all twelve items. As shown in detail by Welzel (2013), dimensional analyses across individuals and nations justify this summary of items.

[2] Emancipative values are measured on the basis of twelve items. Each of these items is recoded in such a way that the least emancipative position is coded zero and the most emancipative position 1.0. Three of the twelve items refer to important child qualities and can be used to measure how much emphasis respondents place on 'autonomy' depending on whether they indicate 'independence' and 'imagination' as important child qualities but do not indicate 'obedience' as such a quality. Another three items address goals that a country's government should pursue. These items are used to measure how much emphasis respondents place on 'voice', depending on whether they assign first, second, or no priority to the goals of 'protecting freedom of speech', 'giving people more say in important government decisions', and 'giving people more say about how things are done at their jobs and in their communities'. The next three items refer to the status of women relative to men and are used to measure how much emphasis respondents place on 'equality', depending on how strongly they disagree with the statements that 'education is more important for a boy than a girl', 'when jobs are scarce, men should have priority over women to get a job', and 'men make better political leaders than women'. The last set of three items addresses life choices and is used to measure how much emphasis respondents place on 'choice', depending on how acceptable they find 'divorce', 'abortion', and 'homosexuality'. A respondent's final score on emancipative values is the average score over all twelve items. As shown in detail by Welzel (2013), dimensional analyses across individuals and nations justify this summary of items.

Chapter 18

[1] We cannot delve into the complications of the interaction between voluntary decentralized coordination and central political authority in human cooperation. Encompassing systems of voluntary exchange organized as markets do not evolve spontaneously, but presuppose some coercive political authority to protect property rights and guarantee the voluntary non-violent character of contractual relations.

[2] For a summary evaluation of research on political opportunity structures in democracies and political participation, see McAdam (1996), Tarrow (1996), and Goodwin (2001). See also Chapter 16.

[3] Trail-blazing contributions were those of Powell (1986) and Jackman (1987) as well as the meticulous study by Franklin (2004). For a comprehensive meta-analysis, on which we rely here, see Geys (2006).

[4] On the difference between the organizational requisites and strategic dilemmas of monological and dialogical interest association, see Offe and Wiesenthal (1980).

[5] Examples are the French Ecologistes of the 1970s or 1980s or the Swedish Miljopartiet in the early 1990s. Both efforts failed, but not because of electoral system (institutions) or strategic configuration (no established party had fully occupied the potential 'place' of Greens). In the case of the unsuccessful British Green Party, its failure may be overdetermined by the single-member-district electoral system.

[6] For this section, see especially Brady *et al.* (1995) and Verba *et al.* (1995). For an overview, see Schlozman (2002).

[7] Time sovereignty refers to the capacity to determine when and where to work, not the absolute amount of free time beyond one's professional life. Highly educated people may have more time sovereignty, but less free time, than people with less education.

Chapter 19

[1] See the UNESCO *Media Development Indicators* (MDI) framework endorsed by the Intergovernmental Council of the International Programme for the Development of Communication (IPDC) at its 26th Session (26–8 March 2008).

[2] EuroStat. (2007) *Internet Usage in 2007 Households and Individuals* http://epp.eurostat.ec.europa.eu. For the EU policy background see EuroActiv (http://www.euractiv.com/en/infosociety/bridging-digital-divide-eu-policies/article-132315).

[3] UNESCO (www.UNESCO.org). The latest available year for all these estimates is 2005.

[4] World Bank (2007) *Development Indicators 2007*, Washington, DC: World Bank, Tables 5.10 and 5.11.

[5] International Telecommunications Union (http://www.itu.int/ITU-D/ict/statistics/ict/index.html).

[6] For more methodological details and results, see Freedom House (2007) *Global Press Freedom 2007* (www.freedomhouse.org). The IREX *Media Sustainability Index* provides another set of indicators (http://www.irex.org/resources/index.asp/.

[7] Reporters sans Frontières (2007) 'At least five journalists arrested in Rangoon, including Japanese daily's correspondent.' 30 Sept 2007. (http://www.rsf.org/article.php3?id_article=23837).

[8] Reporters sans Frontières (2007) *Syria Annual Report 2007* (http://www.rsf.org/country-43.php3?id_mot=143&Valider=OK).

[9] Joel Campagna (2001) 'Press Freedom Reports: Stop signs.' Committee to Protect Journalists. http://www.cpj.org/Briefings/2001/Syria_sept01/Syria_sept01.html.

[10] Human Rights Watch (http://hrw.org/english/docs/2007/10/08/syria17024.htm)

[11] Freedom House (2008) *Global Press Freedom 2008* (http://www.freedomhouse.org/uploads/fop08/FOTP2008Tables.pdf).

Chapter 22

[1] This was avoided in a few countries where demand-stimulating policies were combined with tight incomes policies, for example Austria (see Scharpf 1987; Hemerijck *et al.* 2000).

[2] Esping-Andersen (1990) initially spoke of 'welfare *state* regimes' but because of increasing emphasis on the relationship between the state and the family in provision of care, this was substituted by welfare regimes (Esping-Andersen 1999).

[3] The Netherlands is typically pictured as being closer to a conservative ideal type, but has been more of a hybrid in several respects. This is why it has sometimes served as representative of a social democratic regime.

Chapter 24

[1] I have discussed the subject in two books (Sørensen 2001, 2004). Some formulations in this chapter draw on those works.

References

Aboura, S. (2005) 'French Media Bias and the Vote on the European Constitution', *European Journal of Political Economy*, 21(4): 1093–8.

Acemoglou, D., and Robinson, J. A. (2006) *Economic Origins of Dictatorship and Democracy* (Cambridge: Cambridge University Press).

Adams, M. (2003) *Fire and Ice: The Myth of Converging Values in the United States and Canada* (Toronto: Penguin).

Adcock, R., and Collier, D. (2001) 'Measurement Validity: A Common Standard for Quantitative and Qualitative Research', *American Political Science Review*, 95: 529–46.

Adema, W. and Ladaique, M. (2005) *Net Social Expenditure*. OECD Social, Employment and Migration Paper 29 (Paris: OECD).

Adema, W. and Ladaique, M. (2009) *How Expensive is the Welfare State? Gross and Net Indicators in the OECD Social Expenditure Database (SOCX)*, OECD Social, Employment and Migration Working Paper 92 (Paris: OECD).

Adema, W., Fron, P. and Ladaique, M. (2011) *Is the European Welfare State Really More Expensive? Indicators on Social Spending, 1980–2012*, OECD Social, Employment and Migration Working Papers 124 (Paris: OECD).

Adorno, T. W., Frenkel-Brunswik, E., Levinson, D. J., Sanford, R. N. (1950) *The Authoritarian Personality* (New York: Norton).

Alber, J. (1982) *Vom Armenhaus zum Wohlfahrtsstaat. Analysen zur Entwicklung der Sozialversicherung in Westeuropa* (Frankfurt am Main: Campus).

Albrow, M. (1996) *The Global Age: State and Society Beyond Modernity* (Cambridge: Polity Press).

Aldrich, J. H. (1993) 'Rational Choice and Turnout', *American Journal of Political Science*, 37(1): 246–78.

Aldrich, J. H. (1995) *Why Parties? The Origin and Transformation of Political Parties in America* (Chicago, IL: University of Chicago Press).

Alexander, G. (2002) *The Sources of Democratic Consolidation* (Ithaca, NY: Cornell University Press).

Allison, G. T. (1971) *Essence of Decision* (Boston, MA: Little, Brown).

Almond, G. A. (1958) 'Research Note: A Comparative Study of Interest Groups and the Political Process', *American Political Science Review*, 52(1): 270–82.

Almond, G. A. (1956) 'Comparative Political Systems', *Journal of Politics*, 18(3): 391–409.

Almond, G. A. (1978). *Comparative Politics: System, Process, and Policy* (Boston, MA: Little, Brown).

Almond, G. A. (1990) *A Discipline Divided: Schools and Sects in Political Science* (London: Sage).

(1996) *Political Science: The History of the Discipline*, in R. E. Goodin and H.–D. Klingemann (eds), *A New Handbook of Political Science* (Oxford: Oxford University Press), 50–96.

Almond, G. A. and Powell, G. B.,Jr (1966) *Comparative Politics: A Developmental Approach* (Boston, MA: Little, Brown).

Almond, G. A., and Verba, S. (1963) *The Civic Culture: Political Attitudes and Democracy in Five Nations* (Princeton: Princeton University Press).

Almond, G. A., and Verba, S. (eds) (1980) *The Civic Culture Revisited* (Boston, MA: Little, Brown).

Almond, G. A., Powell, G. B., Jr, Strøm, K., and Dalton, R. J. (2004) *Comparative Politics Today: A World View* (8th edn) (New York: Pearson Longman).

Alter, P. (1994) *Nationalism* (2nd edn) (London: Edward Arnold).

Alvarez, R. M., Garrett, G., and Lange, P. (1991) 'Government Partisanship, Labor Organization, and Macroeconomic Performance', *American Political Science Review*, 85(2): 539–56.

Amadae, S. M., and Bueno de Mesquita, B. (1999) 'The Rochester School: The Origins of Positive Political Economy', *Annual Review of Political Science*, 2: 269–95.

Amalrik, A. A. (1970) *Kann die Sowjetunion das Jahr 1984 erleben?* (Zurich: Diogenes).

Amenta, E. (2003) 'What We Know about the Development of Social Policy: Comparative and Historical Research in Comparative and Historical Perspective', in J. Mahoney and D. Rueschemeyer (eds), *Comparative Historical Analysis in the Social Sciences* (Cambridge: Cambridge University Press), 91–130.

Ames, B. (2002) *The Deadlock of Democracy in Brazil* (Ann Arbor, MI: Michigan University Press).

Amin, A. (1999) 'An Institutionalist Perspective on Regional Economic Development', *International Journal of Urban and Regional Research*, 23(2): 365–78.

Andersen, J. G. (2002) 'Work and Citizenship: Unemployment and Unemployment Policies in Denmark, 1980–2000', in J. G. Andersen and P. H. Jensen (eds), *Changing Labour Markets, Welfare Policies and Citizenship* (Bristol: Policy Press), 59–84.

Andersen, J. G. and Christiansen, P. M. (1991) *Skatter uden velfcerd* (Copenhagen: Jurist-og Økonomforbundets Forlag).

Andersen, T.M., Holmström, B., Honkapohja, S., Korkman, S., Söderström, H., and Vartiainen, J (2007). *The Nordic Model. Embracing Globalization and Sharing Risk* (Helsinki: ETLA).

Anderson, B. (1983) *Imagined Communities: Reflections on the Origin and Spread of Nationalism* (London: Verso).

Anderson, B. (1991) *Imagined Communities: Reflections on the Origin and Spread of Nationalism* (rev. edn) (London: Verso).

Anderson, C. (1998) 'When in Doubt, Use Proxies: Attitudes towards Domestic Politics and Support for European Integration', *Comparative Political Studies*, 31(5): 569–601.

Anderson, C. J., and Beramendi, P. (2008) 'Income Inequality and Electoral Participation', in P. Beramendi and C. J. Anderson (eds), *Democracy, Inequality and Representation* (New York: Russell Sage Foundation).

Anderson, J. E. (2003) *Public Policymaking* (Boston, MA: Houghton Mifflin).

Anderson, L. (1991) 'Absolutism and the Resilience of Monarchy in the Middle East', *Political Science Quarterly*, 106(1): 1–15.

Anderson, P. (2007) 'Russia's Managed Democracy', *London Review of Books*, 29(2).

Andeweg, R. (1997) 'Collegiality and Collectivity: Cabinets, Cabinet Committees and Cabinet Ministers', in P. Weller, H. Bakevits, and R. A. W. Rhodes (eds), *The Hollow Crown: Countervailing Trends in Core Executives* (London: Macmillan).

Andeweg, R. (2008) 'The Netherlands: The Sanctity of Proportionality', in M. Gallagher and P. Mitchell, *The Politics of Electoral Systems* (Oxford: Oxford University Press), 491–510.

Anduiza, E., Cristancho, C., and Sabucedo, J. M. (2012) 'Mobilization through Online Social Networks: The Political Protest of the Indignados in Spain' (http://www.protestsurvey.eu/publications/1344588239.pdf).

Apter, D. E. (1965) *The Politics of Modernization* (Chicago, IL: University of Chicago Press).

Arentsen, M. J. (2003) 'The Invisible Problem and How to Deal with it: National Policy Styles in Radiation Protection Policy in the Netherlands, England and Belgium', in M.-L. Bemelmans-Videc, R. C. Rist, and E. Vedung (eds), *Carrots, Sticks and Sermons: Policy Instruments and their Evaluation* (Piscataway, NJ: Transaction Publishers), 211–30.

Armingeon. K. (2002) 'Interest Intermediation: The Cases of Consociational Democracy and Corporatism', in H. Keman (ed.), *Comparative Democratic Politics: A Guide to Contemporary Theory and Research.* (London: Sage), 143–65.

Armingeon. K. and Giger, N. (2008) 'Conditional Punishment. A Comparative Analysis of the Electoral Consequences of Welfare State Retrenchment in OECD Nations, 1980–2003', *West European Politics*, 31(3): 558–80.

Arts, W., and Gelissen, J. (2002) 'Three Worlds of Welfare Capitalism or More? A State-of-the-Art Report', *Journal of European Social Policy*, 12(2): 137–58.

Ashford, D. (1977) 'Political Science and Policy Studies: Toward a Structural Solution', *Policy Studies Journal*, 5: 570–83.

Áslund, A. and McFaul, M. (eds) (2006) *Revolution in Orange: The Origins of Ukraine's Democratic Breakthrough* (Washington, DC: Carnegie Endowment for International Peace).

Atkinson, A. B. (1999) *The Economic Consequences of Rolling back the Welfare State* (Cambridge, MA: MIT Press).

Auer, P. (2000) *Employment Revival in Europe: Labour Market Success in Austria, Denmark, Ireland and the Netherlands* (Geneva: ILO).

Ayoob, M. (1995) *The Third World Security Predicament* (Boulder, CO: Lynne Rienner).

Baccaro, L. and Heeb, S. (2012) 'Tripartite Responses to the Global Crisis: A Qualitative Comparative Analysis', *Swiss Journal of Sociology*, 38(3), 349–74.

Bache, I., and Flinders, M. (2004) *Multi-Level Governance* (Oxford: Oxford University Press).

Bachrach, P., and Baratz, M. S. (1962) 'Two Faces of Power', *American Political Science Review*, 56: 947–52.

Bader, J. Grävingholt, J., and Kästner, A. (2012) 'Would Autocracies Promote Autocracy? A Political Economy Perspective on Regime-Type Export in Regional Neighbourhoods', in P. Burnell and O. Schlumberger (eds) (2012) *International Politics and National Political Regimes. Promoting Democracy—Promoting Autocracy* (Abingdon: Routledge): 81–100

Bagehot, W. (1889) *The Works of Walter Bagehot* (Hartford, CT: Travelers Insurance Companies).

Bairoch, P. (1985) *De Jéricho à Mexico: Villes et économie dans lhistoire* (Paris: Gallimard).

Balassa, B. (1961) *The Theory of Economic Integration* (Homewood, IL: Richard D. Irwin).

Baldwin, P. (1990) *The Politics of Social Solidarity: Class Bases of the European Welfare State 1875–1975* (Cambridge: Cambridge University Press).

Balkin, J. (2005) 'Wrong the Day it was Decided: Lochner and Constitutional Historicism', *Boston University Law Review*, 85: 677–725.

Balme, R. and Chabanet D. (2008) *European Governance and Democracy: Power and Protest in the EU* (Plymouth: Rowman & Littlefield).

Bamber, G.J., Landsbury, R.D., and Wailes, N. (2011) *International and Comparative Employment Relations: Globalisation and Change* (London: Sage).

Banfield, E. (1958) *The Moral Basis of a Backward Society* (New York: Free Press).

Banisar, D. (2006) *Freedom of Information Around the World 2006: A Global Survey of Access to Government Records Laws* (www.freedominfo.org).

Bannerji, H. (2000) *The Dark Side of Nation: Essays on Multiculturalism and Gender* (Toronto: Canadian Scholar's Press).

Barach, P. and Baratz, M. S. (1969) 'Two Faces of Power', in W.E. Connolly (ed.) *The Bias of Pluralism* (New York: Atheron Press), 51–64.

Barber, J. D. (1992) *Presidential Character: Predicting Performance in the White House* (4th edn) (Englewood Cliffs, NJ: Prentice-Hall).

Bardach, E. (1976) 'Policy Termination as a Political Process', *Policy Sciences*, 7: 123–31.

Bardach, E. (1977) *The Implementation Game: What Happens After a Bill Becomes a Law* (Cambridge, MA: MIT Press).

Barkan, J. (2012) 'Democracy Assistance: What Recipients Think', *Journal of Democracy*, 23(1): 129–37.

Barnes, S. H. and Kaase, M. (1979) *Political Action: Mass Participation in Five Western Democracies* (London: Sage).

Barnett, G. A. (2001) 'A Longitudinal Analysis of the International Telecommunication Network, 1978–1996', *American Behavioral Scientist*, 44: 1638–55.

Barnett, G. A. and Choi, Y. (1995) 'Physical Distance and Language as Determinants of the International Telecommunications Network', *International Political Science Review*, 16: 249–65.

Barnett, G. A., Jacobson, T., Choi, Y., and Sun-Miller, S. (1996) 'An Examination of the International Telecommunications Network', *Journal of International Communication*, 32: 19–43.

Barnett, G. A., Salisbury, J., Kim, C., and Langhorne, A. (1999) 'Globalization and International Communication Networks:

An Examination of Monetary, Telecommunications, and Trade Networks', *Journal of International Communication*, 62: 7–49.

Barros, R. (2002) *Constitutionalism and Dictatorship: Pinochet, the Junta, and the 1980 Constitution* (Cambridge: Cambridge University Press).

Bartolini, S. (1993) 'On Time and Comparative Research', *Journal of Theoretical Politics*, 5(2): 131–67.

Bartolini, S. (2000) *The Political Mobilization of the European Left, 1860–1980: The Class Cleavage* (Cambridge: Cambridge University Press).

Bartolini, S. and Mair, P. (1990) *Identity, Competition and Electoral Availability: The Stabilisation of European Electorates 1885–1985* (Cambridge: Cambridge University Press).

Bastian, S. and Luckham, R. (eds) (2003) *Can Democracy be Designed? The Politics of Institutional Choice in Conflict-Torn Societies* (London: Zed Books).

Bates, R. H. (1981) *Markets and States in Tropical Africa: The Political Basis of Agricultural Policies* (Berkeley, CA: University of California Press).

Bates, R., Greif, A., Levi, M., Rosenthal, J.-L., and Weingast, B. (2002) *Analytic Narratives* (Princeton, NJ: Princeton University Press).

Bauer, R. A. and Jones, B. D. (1993) *Agendas and Instability in American Politics* (Chicago, IL: University of Chicago Press).

Bauer, R. A. and Jones, B. D. (2009). *Agendas and Instability in American Politics* (2nd edn) (Chicago, IL: University of Chicago Press).

Bauer, R. A., Breunig, C., Green-Pedersen, C., *et al.* (2009) 'Punctuated Equilibrium in Comparative Perspective', *American Journal of Political Science*, 53(3): 602–19.

Bechtel, M. and Tosun, J. (2009) 'Changing Economic Openness for Environmental Policy Convergence: When Can Bilateral Trade Agreements Induce Convergence of Environment Regulation', *International Studies Quarterly*, 53(4): 931–53.

Beck, U. (2002) 'Losing the Traditional: Individualization and "Precarious Freedoms"', in U. Beck and E. Beck-Gernsheim (eds), *Individualization* (London: Sage), pp. 1–21.

Beer, S. H. and Ulam, A. B. (eds) (1958) *Patterns of Government: The Major Political Systems of Europe* (New York: Random House).

Béland, D. (2006) 'The Politics of Social Learning: Finance, Institutions, and Pensions Reform in the United State and Canada', *Governance*, 19(4): 559–83.

Bell, D. (1965) *The End of Ideology: On the Exhaustion of Political Ideas in the Fifties* (Glencoe, IL: Free Press).

Bell, D. (1973) *The Coming of Post-Industrial Society* (New York: Basic Books).

Bendix, R. (1960) *Max Weber: An Intellectual Portrait* (Garden City, NY: Doubleday).

Benedetto, G., and Hix, S. (2007) 'The Rejected, the Dejected and the Ejected: Explaining Government Rebels in the 2001–05 British House of Commons', *Comparative Political Studies*, 40: 755–81.

Bennett, C. (1991) 'What is Policy Convergence and What Causes it?', *British Journal of Political Science*, 21: 215–33.

Bennett, C. J., and Howlett, M. (1992) 'The Lessons of Learning: Reconciling Theories of Policy Learning and Policy Change', *Policy Sciences*, 25 (3): 275–94.

Benoit, K. and Laver, M. (2006) *Party Policy in Modern Democracies* (Abingdon: Routledge).

Bentley, A. F. (1908) *The Process of Government: A Study of Social Pressures* (Chicago, IL: University of Chicago Press).

Bentley, A. F. (1949) *The Process of Government: A Study of Social Pressures* (Evanston, IL: Principia Press).

Berglund, S., and Thomsen, S. (eds) (1990) *Modern Political Ecological Analysis* (Åbo: Åbo Akademis Förlag).

Bergman, T., Ecker, A. and Müller, W. C. (2013) 'How Parties Govern—Political Parties and the Internal Organization of Government', in W. C. Müller and H. M. Narud (eds), *Party Governance and Party Democracy* (New York: Springer).

Berg-Schlosser, D. and de Meur, G. (1996) 'Conditions of Authoritarianism, Fascism, and Democracy in Interwar Europe: Systematic Matching and Contrasting of Cases for "Small N" Analysis', *Comparative Political Studies*, 29(4): 423–68.

Berman, L. (2006) *The Art of Political Leadership: Essays in Honor of Fred I. Greenstein* (Lanham, MD: Rowman & Littlefield).

Bernstein, S., and Cashore, B. (2000) 'Internationalization and Domestic Policy Change: The Case of Eco-forestry Policy Change in British Columbia, Canada', *Canadian Journal of Political Science*, 33(1): 67–99.

Berry, J. M. (1977) *Lobbying for the People: The Political Behavior of Public Interest Groups* (Princeton, NJ: Princeton University Press).

Bertola, G., Boeri, T., and Cazes, S. (1999) *Employment Protection and Labour Market Adjustments in OECD Countries: Evolving Institutions and Variable Enforcement*, Employment and Training Papers, 48 (Geneva: Employment and Training Department, ILO).

Besley, T. and Burgess, R. (2002) 'The Political Economy of Government Responsiveness: Theory and Evidence from India', *Quarterly Journal of Economics*, 117(4): 1415–51.

Best, R. E. (2012) 'The Long and the Short of It: Electoral Institutions and the Dynamics of Party System Size, 1950–2005', *European Journal of Political Research*, 51(2): 141–65.

Betz, H.-G. (1994) *Radical Right-Wing Populist in Western Europe* (New York: St Martin's Press).

Bevir, M. and Rhodes, R. A. W. (2010) *The State as Cultural Practice* (Oxford: Oxford University Press).

Beyme, K. von (1998) *The Legislator. German Parliament as a Centre of Political Decision-Making* (Aldershot: Ashgate).

Bickerton, J. (1990) *Nova Scotia, Ottawa, and the Politics of Regional Development* (Toronto: University of Toronto Press).

Bickerton, J. (2007) 'Between Integration and Fragmentation: Political Parties and the Representation of Regions', in A.-G. Gagnon and B. Tanguay (eds), *Canadian Parties in Transition* (3rd edn) (Peterborough, Ontario: Broadview Press), 411–35.

Bickerton, J. Gagnon, A.-G., and Smith, P. (1999) *Ties that Bind: Parties and Voters in Canada* (Toronto: Oxford University Press).

Bieler, A. and Lindberg, I., (eds.), (2010). *Global Restructuring, Labour and the Challenges for Transnational Solidarity* (Abingdon: Routledge).

Biezen, I. van (2003) *Political Parties in New Democracies: Party Organization in Southern and East-Central Europe* (Basingstoke: Palgrave Macmillan).

Biezen, I. van and Caramani, D. (2006) '(Non)Comparative Politics in Britain', *Politics*, 26: 29–37.

Biezen, I. van, Mair, P. and Poguntke, T. (2012) 'Going, going, … gone? The decline of party membership in contemporary Europe', *European Journal of Political Research*, 51(1): 24–56.

Binder, S. H. (2003) *Stalemate* (Washington, DC: Brookings Institution Press).

Binzer Hobolt, S. (2009) *Europe in Question: Referendums on European integration* (Oxford: Oxford University Press).

Birch, A. H. (1967) *Representative and Responsible Government* (London: Allen & Unwin).

Björn, L. (1979) 'Labor Parties, Economic Growth, and Redistribution in Five Capitalist Countries', *Comparative Social Research*, 2: 93–128.

Blais, A. and Dion, S. (eds) (1991) *The Budget-Maximizing Bureaucrat: Appraisals and Evidence* (Pittsburgh, PA: University of Pittsburgh Press).

Blais, A., Massicotte, L., and Dobrzynska, A. (1997) 'Direct Presidential Elections: A World Summary', *Electoral Studies*, 16(4): 441–55.

Blanchard, O. and Katz, L. F. (1996) 'What We Know and Do Not Know about the Natural Rate of Unemployment', *Journal of Economic Perspectives*, 11(1): 51–72.

Blanchard, O. and Summers, L. H. (1986) 'Hysteresis and the European Unemployment Problem', in S. Fischer (ed.), *NBER Macroeconomics Annual*, 1 (Fall): 15–78.

Block, F. (2007) 'Understanding the Diverging Trajectories of the United States and Western Europe: A Neo-Polanyian Analysis', *Politics and Society*, 35(1) 3–33.

Blondel, J. (1970) 'Legislative Behaviour: Some Steps toward a Cross-National Measurement', *Government and Opposition*, 5(1): 67–85.

Blondel, J. (1988) 'Introduction: Western European Cabinets in Comparative Perspective', in J. Blondel and F. Müller-Rommel (eds), *Cabinets in Western Europe* (London: Macmillan).

Blondel, J. and Cotta, M. (eds) (1996) *Party and Government* (London: Macmillan).

Blondel, J. and Cotta, M. (eds) (2000) *The Nature of Party Government* (Basingstoke: Palgrave).

Blumler, J. G. and Gurevich, M. (1975) 'Towards a Political Framework for Political Communication Research', in S.H. Chaffee (ed.), *Political Communication; Issues and Strategies for Research* (Beverly Hills, CA: Sage), 165–93.

Blumler, J. G. and Gurevich, M. (1995) *The Crisis of Communication* (London: Routledge).

Blyth, M. (2002) *Great Transformations: Economic and Institutional Change in the Twentieth Century* (Cambridge: Cambridge University Press).

Boccalini, T. (1614) *Ragguagli di Parnaso: Centuria Prima* (Milan: Battista Bidelli).

Bogaards, M. (2000) 'The Uneasy Relationship between Empirical and Normative Types in Consociational Theory', *European Journal of Political Research*, 12: 395–423.

Bogdani, M. and Loughlin, J. (2007) *Albania and the European Union: The Tumultuous Journey towards Integration and Accession* (London: Tauris).

Boix, C. (1999) 'Setting the Rules of the Game: The Choice of Electoral Systems in Advanced Democracies', *American Political Science Review*, 93(3): 609–24.

Bonoli, G. (2000) *The Politics of Pension Reform* (Cambridge: Cambridge University Press).

Bonoli, G. (2001) 'Political Institutions, Veto Points, and the Process of Welfare State Adaptation', in P. Pierson (ed.), *The New Politics of the Welfare State* (Oxford: Oxford University Press), 238–64.

Bonoli, G. and Natali, D. (eds) (2012) *The Politics of the New Welfare State* (Oxford: Oxford University Press).

Botero, G. (1589) [1948] *Della Ragion di Stato* (Turin: UTET).

Bouwen, P. (2002) 'Corporate lobbying in the European Union: The Logic of Access', *Journal of European Public Policy*, 9(3): 365–90.

Bovens, M., t'Hart, P., and Peters, B. G. (eds) (2001) *Success and Failure in Public Governance* (Cheltenham: Edgar Elgar).

Bowler, S., Farrell, D. M., and Pettit, R. T. (2005) 'Expert Opinion on Electoral Systems: So Which Electoral System is "Best"?', *Journal of Elections, Public Opinion, and Parties*, 15(1): 3–19.

Brady, D. (2005) 'The Welfare State and Relative Poverty in Rich Western Democracies, 1967–1997', *Social Forces*, 83(4): 1329–64.

Brady, H. D., and Collier, D. (eds) (2004) *Rethinking Social Enquiry: Diverse Tools, Shared Standards* (Lanham, MD: Rowman & Littlefield).

Brady, H. E., Verba, K., and Schlozman, L. (1995) 'Beyond SES: A Resource Model of Political Participation', *American Political Science Review*, 89: 271–94.

Bratton, M. and Mattes, R. (2000) 'Support for Democracy in Africa', British Journal of Political Science, 31: 447–74.

Braun, D. (ed.) (2000) *Public Policy and Federalism* (Aldershot: Ashgate).

Braun, D. and Busch, A. (1999) *Public Policy and Political Ideas* (Cheltenham: Edward Elgar).

Braun, D. and Gilardi, F. (2006) Taking Galton's Problem Seriously: Towards a Theory of Policy Diffusion', *Journal of Theoretical Politics*, 18(3): 298–322.

Bräuninger, T. and Debus, M. (2009) *Legislative Agenda-Setting in Parliamentary Democracies, European Journal of Political Research*, 48(6): 804–39.

Bräuninger, T. and König, T. (1999) 'The Checks and Balances of Party Federalism: German Federal Government in a Divided Legislature', *European Journal of Political Research*, 36(6): 207–34.

Bredgaard, T., Larsen, F., and Madsen, P. K. (2005) *The Flexible Danish Labour Market: A Review*, CARMA Research Papers, 1 (Aalborg: Aalborg University).

Brenner, N., Jessop, B., Jones, M., and Macleod, G. (eds) (2003) *State/Space: A Reader* (Oxford: Basil Blackwell).

Brenner, R. (1977) 'The Origin of Capitalist Development: A Critique of Neo-Smithian Marxism', *New Left Review*, 104(July-August): 25–92.

Breslin, S. (2010), 'Democratizing One-party Rule in China', in P. Burnell and R. Youngs (eds), *New Challenges to Democratization* (Abingdon: Routledge): 134–52.

Brock, L, Holm, H.-H., Sørensen, G., and Stohl M. (2011) *Fragile States. Violence and the Failure of Intervention* (Cambridge: Polity Press).

Brooker, P. (1997) *Defiant Dictatorships: Communist and Middle-Eastern Dictatorships in a Democratic Age* (Basingstoke: Palgrave Macmillan).

Brooker, P. (2009) *Non-Democratic Regimes* (rev. edn) (Basingstoke: Palgrave Macmillan).

Brooker, P. (2014) *Non-Democratic Regimes* (3rd edn) (Basingstoke: Palgrave Macmillan).

Brooks, S. M. (2005) 'Interdependent and Domestic Foundations of Policy Change: The Diffusion of Pension Privatization around the World', *International Studies Quarterly*, 49(2): 273–94.

Brouillaud, C. (2005) 'La Ligue du Nord et les politiques publiques italiennes: Influence, instrumentalisation et échecs (1991–2004)', in *Les Partis Régionalistes en Europe: Des Acteurs en Développement?* (Brussels: Éditions de l'Université de Bruxelles), 119–46.

Brusis, M. (2002) 'Between EU Requirements, Competitive Politics and National Traditions: Recreating Regions in the Accession Countries of Central and Eastern Europe', *Governance*, 15(4): 531–59.

Brym, R. (ed.) (1986) *Regionalism in Canada* (Richmond Hill, Ontario: Irwin).

Buchanan, J. M. (1977) 'Why does Government Grow?', in T. Borcherding (ed.), *Budgets and Bureaucrats: The Sources of Government Growth* (Durham, NC: Duke University Press) 3–18.

Budge, I. (2000) 'Deliberative Democracy versus Direct Democracy—Plus Political Parties!', in M. Saward (ed.) *Democratic Innovation* (London: Routledge).

Budge, I. and Keman, H. E. (*1990*) *Parties and Democracy: Coalition Formation and Government Functioning in 22 Democracies* (Oxford: Oxford University Press).

Budge, I. and Klingemann, H.-D. (2001) 'Finally! Comparative Over-Time Mapping of Party Policy Movement', in I. Budge, H.–D. Klingemann, A. Volkens, J. Bara, and E. Tanenbaum (eds), *Mapping Policy Preferences: Estimates for Parties, Electors and Governments 1945–1998* (Oxford: Oxford University Press), 75–90.

Budge, I., Klingemann, H.-D., Volkens, A., Bara, J., and Tanenbaum, E. (2001) *Mapping Policy Preferences: Estimates for Parties, Electors, and Governments, 1945–1998* (Oxford: Oxford University Press).

Buechler, S. M. (2004) 'The Strange Career of Strain and Breakdown Theories of Collective Action', in D. A. Snow, S.A. Soule, and H. Kriesi (eds), *The Blackwell Companion to Social Movements* (Malden, MA: Blackwell), 47–66.

Burch, M. and Holliday, I. (1996) *The British Cabinet System* (London: Prentice-Hall/Harvester Wheatsheaf).

Burgess, K. and Levitsky, S. (2003) 'Explaining Populist Party Adaptation in Latin America: Environmental and Organizational Determinants of Party Change in Argentina, Mexico, Peru, and Venezuela', *Comparative Political Studies*, 36(8): 881–911.

Burgess, M. (ed.) (1986) *Federalism and Federation in Western Europe* (London: Croom Helm).

Burgess, M. (2011) 'Success and Failure in Federation: Comparative Perspectives', in T. Courchene, J. Allan, C. Leuprecht, and N. Verelli (eds), *The Federal Idea: Essays in Honour of Ronald L. Watts* (Montreal/Kingston: McGill-Queen's University Press), 189–206.

Burgess, M. and Gagnon, A.-G. (eds) (1993) *Comparative Federalism and Federation: Competing Traditions and Future Directions* (Harlow: Harvester Wheatsheaf).

Burke, E. (1770) [1889] 'Thoughts on the Present Discontents', in *The Works of the Right Honourable Edmund Burke* (9th edn) (Boston, MA: Little, Brown), 433–551. *Contemporary Politics*, 14 (1): 37–52.

Burnell, P. (2011) 'Does Political Party Aid Compensate for the Limitations of International Elections Observation?', Representation, 47 (4): 383–97.

Burnell, P. (2011) *Promoting Democracy Abroad. Policy and Performance* (Piscataway, NJ: Transaction Publishers).

Burnell, P. (2013) 'Democratisation in the Middle East and North Africa: Perspectives from Democracy Support', *Third World Quarterly*, 34(5): 838–55.

Burnell, P. and Gerrits, A. (eds) (2012) *Promoting Party Politics in Emerging Democracies* (Abingdon: Routledge).

Burnham, P., Gilland, K., Grant, W., and Layton-Henry, Z. (2004) *Research Methods in Politics* (Basingstoke: Palgrave Macmillan).

Bussemaker, J. and van Kersbergen, K. (1994) 'Gender and Welfare States: Some Theoretical Reflections', in D. Sainsbury (ed.), *Gendering Welfare States* (London: Sage) 8–25.

Butler, D., and Ranney, A. (1994) 'Practice', in D. Butler and A. Ranney (eds), (Basingstoke: Palgrave Macmillan), 1–10.

Cairns, A. (1968) 'The Electoral System and the Party System in Canada, 1921–1965', *Canadian Journal of Political Science*, 1(1): 55–80.

Caldeira, G. A. and Gibson, J. L. (1995) 'The Visibility of the Court of Justice in the European Union', *American Political Science Review*, 89(2): 356–76.

Calmfors, L., and Driffill, J. (1988) 'Bargaining Structure, Corporatism and Macroeconomic Performance', *Economic Policy*, 6(1): 12–61.

Cameron, D. R. (1978) 'The Expansion of the Public Economy: A Comparative Analysis', *American Political Science Review*, 72(4): 1243–61.

Cameron, D. R. (1984) 'Social Democracy, Corporatism, Labor Quiescence and the Representation of Economic Interests in Advanced Capitalist Society', in J. H. Goldthorpe (ed.), *Order and Conflict in Contemporary Capitalism* (Oxford: Oxford University Press), 143–78.

Camia, V. and Caramani, D. (2011) 'Family Meetings: Ideological Convergence Within Party Families Across Europe, 1945–2009', *Comparative European Politics*, 10(1): 48–85.

Cammack, P. (1997) 'Globalisation and Liberal Democracy', *European Review*, 6(2): 249–63.

Campbell, J. L. (1998) 'Institutional Analysis and the Role of Ideas in Political Economy', *Theory and Society*, 27: 377–409.

Capoccia, G. (2002) 'Anti-System Parties: A Conceptual Reassessment', *Journal of Theoretical Politics*, 14(1): 9–35.

Capoccia, G. (2005) *Defending Democracy: Reactions to Extremism in Interwar Europe* (Baltimore, MD: Johns Hopkins University Press).

Caramani, D. (2000) *Elections in Western Europe since 1815: Electoral Results by Constituencies* (supplemented with CD-ROM) (London: Palgrave).

Caramani, D. (2004) *The Nationalization of Politics: The Formation of National Electorates and Party*

Systems in Western Europe (Cambridge: Cambridge University Press).

Caramani, D. (2009) *Introduction to the Comparative Method with Boolean Algebra* (Beverly Hills, CA: Sage).

Carey, J. M. and Shugart, M. S. (eds) (1998) *Executive Decree Authority* (Cambridge: Cambridge University Press).

Carney, J. (1980) 'Regions in Crisis: Accumulation, Regional Problems and Crisis Formation', in J. Carney, R. Hudson, and J. Lewis (eds), *Regions in Crisis: New Perspectives in European Regional Theory* (London: Croom Helm), 28–59.

Carothers, T. (2004) *Critical Mission: Essays on Democracy Promotion* (Washington, DC: Carnegie Endowment for International Peace).

Carothers, T. (2012) *Democracy Policy Under Obama: Revitalization or Retreat?* Carnegie Report (Washington, DC: Carnegie Endowment for International Peace).

Carothers, T. and Youngs, R. (2011) *Looking for Help. Will Rising Democracies Become International Democracy Supporters?* Democracy and Rule of Law Paper (Washington, DC: Carnegie Endowment for International Peace).

Castells, M. (1998) *The Power of Identity* (Oxford: Blackwell).

Castles, F. G. (1978) *The Social Democratic Image of Society: A Study of the Achievements and Origins of Scandinavian Social Democracy in Comparative Perspective* (London: Routledge & Kegan Paul).

Castles, F. G. (1985) *The Working Class and Welfare: Reflections on the Political Development of the Welfare State in Australia and New Zealand, 1890–1980* (London: Allen & Unwin).

Castles, F. G. (1987) 'Comparative Public Policy Analysis: Problems, Progress and Prospects', in F. G. Castles, F. Lehner, and M. G. Schmidt (eds), *Managing Mixed Economies* (Berlin: de Gruyter), 197–224.

Castles, F. G. (1989) 'Social Protection by Other Means: Australia's Strategy of Coping with External Vulnerability', in F. G. Castles (ed.) *The Comparative History of Public Policy* (Cambridge: Polity Press), 16–55.

Castles, F. G. (1996) 'Needs-Based Strategies of Social Protection in Australia and New Zealand', in G. Esping-Andersen (ed.), *Welfare States in Transition: National Adaptations in Global Economies* (London: Sage) 88–115.

Castles, F. G. and Mitchell, D. (1992) 'Identifying Welfare State Regimes: The Links between Politics, Instruments and Outcomes', *Governance*, 5(1): 1–26.

Castles, F. G. and Wildenmann, R. (eds) (1986) *Visions and Realities of Party Government* (Berlin: de Gruyter).

Caulfield, J. (2000) 'Local Government Finance in OECD Countries', paper presented at 'Local Government at the Millenium' International Seminar, University of New South Wales, 19 February 2000.

Chambers, W. N. (1967) *The American Party Systems: Stages of Political Development* (New York: Oxford University Press).

Chehabi, H. E. and Linz, J. J. (1998) *Sultanistic Regimes* (Baltimore, MD: Johns Hopkins University Press), Chapters 1 and 2.

Cheibub, J. A. (2007) *Presidentialism, Parliamentarism, and Democracy* (Cambridge: Cambridge University Press).

Cheibub, J. A., Przeworski, A., and Saiegh, S. M. (2004) 'Government Coalitions and Legislative Success under Presidentialism and Parliamentarism', *British Journal of Political Science*, 34: 565–87.

Chhibber, P. and Kollman, K. (2004) *The Formation of National Party Systems: Federalism and Party Competition in Canada, Great Britain, India, and the United States* (Princeton, NJ: Princeton University Press).

Chilcote, R. H. (1994) *Theories of Comparative Politics: The Search for a Paradigm Reconsidered* (2nd edn) (Boulder, CO: Westview Press).

Christensen, D. and Weinstein, J. (2013) 'Defunding Dissent: Restrictions on Aid to NGOs', *Journal of Democracy*, 24(2): 77–91.

Chua, A. (2003) *World on Fire: How Exporting Free Market Democracy Breeds Ethnic Hatred and Global Instability* (New York: Doubleday).

Chwe, M. S.-Y. (2001) *Rational Ritual: Culture, Coordination, and Common Knowledge* (Princeton, NJ: Princeton University Press).

Cigler, A. J. and Loomis, B. A. (eds) (2011) *Interest Group Politics* (8th edn) (Washington, DC: CQ Press).

Clark, G. (1980) 'Capitalism and Regional Disparities', *Annals of the American Association of Geographers*, 70(2): 521–32.

Clasen, J. and Clegg, D. eds. (2011). *Regulating the Risk of Unemployment. National Adaptations to Post-Industrial Labour Markets in Europe* (Oxford: Oxford University Press).

Clasen, J. and Siegel, N. A. (2007) *Investigating Welfare State Change. The 'Dependent Variable Problem' in Comparative Analysis* (Cheltenham: Edward Elgar).

Clayton, R. and Pontusson, J. (1998) 'Welfare-State Retrenchment Revisited: Entitlement Cuts, Public Sector Restructuring, and Inegalitarian Trends in Advanced Capitalist Societies', *World Politics*, 51(1): 67–98.

Clement, S. A. and Andersen, J. G. (2007) *Unemployment and Incentives: What do we Know? Micro-Level Evidence from Scandinavian Surveys*, CCWS Working Papers.

Cobb, R. W. and Elder, C. D. (1972) *Participation in American Politics: The Dynamics of Agenda-Building* (Baltimore, MD: Johns Hopkins University Press).

Cobb, R. W., Ross, J.-K., and Ross, M.-K. (1976) 'Agenda Building as a Comparative Political Process', *American Political Science Review*, 70: 26–138.

Coen, D. (1997) 'The Evolution of the Large Firm as a Political Actor in the European Union', *Journal of European Public Policy* 4(1): 91–108.

Coen, D. (2010) 'European Business-Government Relations', in D. Coen, W. Grant, and G. Wilson (eds) *The Oxford Handbook of Business and Government* (Oxford: Oxford University Press).

Coen, D. and J. Richardson (2009) *Lobbying in the European Union: Institutions, Actors, and Issues* (Oxford: Oxford University Press).

Cohen, M., March, J., and Olsen, J. (1972) 'A Garbage Can Model of Organizational Choice', *Administrative Science Quarterly*, 17(1): 1–25.

Cohen, J. and Rogers J. (eds) (1995) *Associations and Democracy* (London: Verso).

Colley, L. (1992) *Britons: Forging the Nation, 1707–1837* (New Haven, CT: Yale University Press).

Collier, D. (1991) 'New Perspectives on the Comparative Method', in D. A. Rustow and K. P. Ericksen (eds), *Comparative Political Dynamics: Global Research Perspectives* (New York: Harper & Collins), 7–31.

Collier, D. and Levitsky, S. P. (1997) 'Democracy with Adjectives', *World Politics*, 49(3): 430–51.

Collier, D. and Mahon, J. E., Jr., (1993) 'Conceptual Stretching Revisited: Adapting Categories in Comparative Analysis', *American Political Science Review*, 87(4): 845–55.

Collier, R. B. (1999) *Paths toward Democracy: The Working Class and Elites in Western Europe and South America* (Cambridge: Cambridge University Press).

Collier, R. B. and Collier, D. (1991) *Shaping the Political Agenda: Critical Junctures, the Labor Movement and Regime Dynamics in Latin America* (Notre Dame, IN: University of Notre Dame Press).

Colomer, J. and Negretto, G. L. (2005) 'Can Presidentialism Work like Parliamentarianism?', *Government and Opposition*, 40(1): 60–89.

Connolly, W. E. (1969) 'Challenge to Pluralist Theory' in: W.E. Connolly (ed.) *The Bias of Pluralism* (New York: Atheron Press), 3–34.

Conrad, C. R. and Golder, S. N. (2010) 'Measuring Government Duration and Stability in Central Eastern European Democracies', *European Journal of Political Research*, 49(1): 119–50.

Converse, P. E. (1964) 'The Nature of Belief Systems in Mass Publics', in David Apter (ed.), *Ideology and Discontent* (Glencoe: Free Press).

Cooke, F. L. (2011) 'Employment relations in China', in G. J. Bamber, R. D. Landsbury, and N. Wailes (eds) *International and Comparative Employment Relations. Globalisation and Change* (London: Sage), 307–329.

Coppedge, M., and Reinicke, W. H. (1990) 'Measuring Polyarchy', *Studies in Comparative International Development*, 25: 51–72.

Council of Europe (1985) *The European Charter of Local Self-Government* (http://conventions.coe.int/Treaty/EN/Reports/HTML/122.htm).

Council of Europe (2000) *The Financial Resources of Local Authorities in Relation to their Responsibilities: A Litmus Test for Subsidiarity*, Fourth General Report on Political Monitoring of the Implementation of the European Charter of Local Self-Government, rapporteur Jean-Claude Frécon, Strasbourg, 20 April 2000.

Cox, G. (1997) *Making Votes Count: Strategic Coordination in the World's Electoral Systems* (Cambridge: Cambridge University Press).

Cox, G. and Morgenstern, S. (2002) 'Epilogue: Latin America's Reactive Assemblies and Proactive Presidents', in S. Morgenstern and B. Nacif (eds), *Legislative Politics in Latin America* (Cambridge: Cambridge University Press).

Cox, M., Ikenberry, J. and Inoguchi, T. (eds) (2000) *American Democracy Promotion: Impulses, Strategies, and Impacts* (Oxford: Oxford University Press).

Cox, R. H. (2001) 'The Social Construction of an Imperative: Why Welfare Reform Happened in Denmark and the Netherlands But Not in Germany', *World Politics*, 53(3): 463–98.

Crafts, N. and Toniolo, G. (1996) 'Postwar Growth: An Overview', in N. Crafts and G. Toniolo (eds), *Economic Growth in Europe since 1945* (Cambridge: Cambridge University Press), 1–37.

Crombez, C. (1997) 'Policy Making and Commission Appointment in the European Union', *Aussenwirtschaft*, 52(1–2): 63–82.

Crossman, R. H. S. (1963) 'Introduction', in W. Bagehot, *The English Constitution* (Glasgow: Collins).

Crossman, R. H. S. (1972) *The Myths of Cabinet Government* (Cambridge, MA: Harvard University Press).

Crouch, C. (1999) *Social Change in Western Europe* (Oxford: Oxford University Press).

Crouch, C. (2000) 'The Snakes and Ladders of Twenty-first Century Trade Unionism', *Oxford Review of Economic Policy* 16(1): 70–83.

Crouch, C. (2004) *Post-democracy* (Cambridge: Polity).

Crouch, C. (2009) 'Privatised Keynesianism: An Unacknowledged Policy Regime', *British Journal of Politics & International Relations*, 11(3): 382–99.

Crouch, C. (2010) 'The Global Firm', in D. Coen, W. Grant, and G. Wilson (eds), *The Oxford Handbook of Business and Government* (Oxford: Oxford University Press).

Crouch, C. (2011) *The Strange Non-Death of Neo-Liberalism* (Cambridge: Polity).

Crouch, C. and Pizzorno A. (1978) *The Resurgence of Class Conflict in Western Europe since 1968. Vol. 2: Comparative Analysis* (New York: Holmes and Meier).

Crozier, M., Huntington, S. P., and Watanuki, J. (1975) *The Crisis of Democracy* (New York: New York University Press).

Currinder M., Green J. C., and Conway M. M. (2007) 'Interest Group Money in Elections', in A. J. Cigler and B. A. Loomis (eds) *Interest Group Politics* (Washington, DC: CQ Press), 182–211.

Cutright, P. (1965) 'Political Structure, Economic Development and National Social Security Programs', *American Journal of Sociology*, 70(5): 537–50.

Daalder, H. (1966) 'The Netherlands: Opposition in a Segmented Society', in R. Dahl (ed.), *Political Oppositions in Western Democracies* (New Haven, CT: Yale University Press), 188–236.

Daalder, H. (1991) *Paths towards State Formation in Europe: Democratization, Bureaucratization and Politicization*, Working paper 1991/20, Madrid Instituto Juan March de Estudios e Investigaciones.

Daalder, H. (2002) 'The Development of the Study of Comparative Politics', in H. Keman (ed.) *Comparative Democratic Politics: A Guide to Contemporary Theory and Research* (London: Sage), 16–31.

Dahl, R. A. (1956) *A Preface to Democratic Theory* (Chicago, IL: University of Chicago Press).

Dahl, R. A. (ed.) (1966) *Political Oppositions in Western Democracies* (New Haven, CT: Yale University Press).

Dahl, R. A. (1971) *Polyarchy* (New Haven, CT: Yale University Press).

Dahl, R. A. (1982) *Dilemmas of Pluralist Democracy: Autonomy vs. Control* (New Haven, CT: Yale University Press).

Dahl, R. A. (1989) *Democracy and its Critics* (New Haven, CT: Yale University Press).

Dahl, R. A. (2000) 'A Democratic Paradox?', *Political Science Quarterly*, 115(1): 35–40.

Dahl, R. A. (2002) *How Democratic is the American Constitution?* (New Haven, CT: Yale University Press).

Dalacoura, K. (2012) 'The 2011 uprisings in the Arab Middle East: political change and geopolitical implications', *International Affairs*, 88(1): 63–79.

Dalton, R. J. (1991) 'Comparative Politics of the Industrial Democracies: From the Golden Age to Island Hopping', in W. Crotty (ed.), *Political Science* (Evanston, IL: Northwestern University Press), 15–43.

Dalton, R. J. (ed.) (2004) *Democratic Challenges, Democratic Choices: The Erosion of Political Support in Advanced Industrial Democracies* (Oxford: Oxford University Press).

Dalton, R. J. and Kuechler, M. (eds) (1990) *Challenging the Political Order* (Cambridge: Polity Press)

Dalton, R. J. and Wattenberg, M. (eds) (2000) *Comparing Democracies: Elections and Voting in Global Perspective* (Thousand Oaks, CA: Sage).

Dalton, R. J. and Weldon, S. A. (2005) 'Public Images of Political Parties: A Necessary Evil?', *West European Politics*, 28: 931–51.

Dalton, R. J. and Welzel, C. (2013) *The Civic Culture Transformed: From Allegiant to Assertive Citizenship* (New York: Cambridge University Press).

Dalton, R. J., Baker, K. L., and Hildebrandt, K. (1987) Germany Transformed (Boston: Harvard University Press).

Dalton, R. J., Flanagan, S., and Beck, P. A. (1985) *Electoral Change in Advanced Industrial Democracies: Realignment or Dealignment?* (Princeton, NJ: Princeton University Press).

Dalton, R. J., van Sickle. A., and Weldon, S. (2010) 'The Individual-Institutional Nexus of Protest Behavior', *British Journal of Political Science* 40: 51–73.

Darcy, R. and Laver, M. (1990) 'Referendum Dynamics and the Irish Divorce Amendment', *Public Opinion Quarterly*, 54(1): 1–20.

Davieri, F. and Tabellini, G. (2000) 'Unemployment, Growth and Taxation in Industrial Countries', *Economic Policy*, 30(1): 49–90.

Debus, M. (2007) *Pre-Electoral Alliances, Coalition Rejections, and Multiparty Governments* (Baden-Baden: Nomos).

de la Porte, C., Pochet, P., and Room, G. (2001) 'Social Benchmarking, Policy Making and the Instruments of New Governance', *Journal of European Social Policy*, 11(4): 291–307.

della Porta, D. (1999) *Social Movements: An Introduction* (Oxford: Blackwell).

della Porta, D. and Caiani M. (2009) *Social Movements and Europeanization* (Oxford: Oxford University Press).

della Porta, D., Kriesi, H., and Rucht, D. (eds) (1999) *Social Movements in a Globalizing World* (London: Macmillan).

Delli Carpini, M. X. and Keeter, S. (1996) *What Americans Know about Politics and Why it Matters* (Yale: Yale University Press).

Delwitt, P. (2005) 'Les Partis régionalistes, des acteurs politico-électoraux en essor? Performances électorales et participations gouvernementales', in *Les Partis Régionalistes en Europe: Des Acteurs en Développement?* (Brussels: Éditions de l'Université de Bruxelles), 51–84.

Deng, Y. (1998) 'The Chinese Conception of National Interests in International Relations', *China Quarterly*, 154: 308–29.

De Smaele, H. (1999) 'The Applicability of Western Media Models on the Russian Media System', *European Journal of Communication*, 14(2): 173–89.

Destradi, S. (2012) 'India as a democracy promoter? New Delhi's Involvement in Nepal's Return to Democracy', *Democratization*, 19(2): 286–311.

Deudney, D. and Ikenberry, G. J. (1999) 'The Nature and Sources of Liberal International Order', *Review of International Studies*, 25(2): 179–96.

Deutsch, K. (1966a) *Nationalism and Social Communication: An Inquiry into the Foundations of Nationality* (Cambridge, MA: MIT Press).

Deutsch, K. (1966b) *The Nerves of Government: Models of Political Communication and Control* (New York: Free Press).

Deutsch, K., Lasswell, H. D., Merritt, R. L., and Russett, B. M. (1966) 'The Yale Political Data Program', in R. Merritt and S. Rokkan, S. (eds), *Comparing Nations* (New Haven, CT: Yale University Press), 81–94.

De Winter, L. (2008) 'Belgium: Empowering Voters or Party Elites?', in M. Gallagher and P. Mitchell (eds), *The Politics of Electoral Systems* (Oxford: Oxford University Press), 417–32.

Diamond, L. (1999) *Developing Democracy* (Baltimore, MD: Johns Hopkins University Press).

Diamond, L. and Morlino, L. (eds) (2005) *Assessing the Quality of Democracy* (Baltimore, MD: Johns Hopkins University Press).

Diani, M. and Bison, I. (2004) 'Organizations, Coalitions, and Movements', *Theory and Society*, 3: 281–309.

Dicken, P. (2011) *Global Shift: Mapping the Changing Contours of the World Economy* (New York: Guilford Press).

DiMaggio, P. J. and Powell, W. W. (1991) 'The Iron Cage Revisited: Institutionalised Isomorphism and Collective Rationality in Organizational Fields', in P. J. DiMaggio and W. W. Powell (eds), *The New Institutionalism in Organizational Analysis* (Chicago, IL: Chicago University Press), 63–82.

Dippel, H. (2005) 'Modern Constitutionalism: A History in the Need of Writing', *Legal History Review*, 73(1–2): 153–70.

Disney, R. (2000) *Fiscal Policy and Employment. I: A Survey of Macroeconomic Models, Methods and Findings* (Washington, DC: IMF).

Dobbin, F. (1994) *Forging Industrial Policy: The United States, Britain, and France in the Railway Age* (Cambridge: Cambridge University Press).

Dogan, M. and Pelassy, D. (1990) *How to Compare Nations: Strategies in Comparative Politics* (2nd edn) (Chatham, NJ: Chatham House).

Dogan, M. and Rokkan, S. (eds) (1969) *Quantitative Ecological Analysis in the Social Sciences* (Cambridge, MA: MIT Press).

Dolowitz, D. (1997) 'British Employment Policy in the 1980s: Learning from the American Experience', *Governance*, 10(1): 23–42.

Dolowitz, D. and Marsh, D. (2000) 'Learning from Abroad: The Role of Policy Transfer in Contemporary Policy Making', *Governance*, 13: 5–24.

Donovan, T. and Bowler, S. (1998) 'Responsive or Responsible Government?', in S. Bowler, T. Donovan, and C. Tolbert (eds), *Citizens as Legislators* (Columbus, OH: Ohio State University Press), 249–73.

Donovan, T. and Karp, J. A. (2006) 'Popular Support for Direct Democracy', *Party Politics*, 12(5): 671–88.

Dorenspleet, R. (2000) 'Reassessing the Three Waves of Democratization', *World Politics*, 52(3): 384–406.

Doorenspleet, R. (2005) *Democratic Transitions: Exploring the Structural Sources of the Fourth Wave* (Boulder, CO: Lynne Rienner).

Döring, H. (ed.) (1995) *Parliaments and Majority Rule in Western Europe* (Frankfurt: Campus).

Döring, H. (2001) 'Parliamentary Agenda Control and Legislative Outcomes in Western Europe', *Legislative Studies Quarterly*, 26: 145–66.

Douglas, M. (1978) *Cultural Bias* (London: Royal Anthropological Institute).

Downs, A. (1957) *An Economic Theory of Democracy* (New York: Harper & Row).

Downs, A. (1967) *Inside Bureaucracy* (Boston, MA: Little, Brown).

Drezner, D. W. (2001) 'Globalization and Policy Convergence', *International Studies Review*, 3: 53–78.

Droysen, J. G. (1858) [1969] *Historik* (Darmstadt: Wissenschaftliche Buchgesellschaft).

Ducheyne, S. (2008) 'J. S. Mill's Canons of Induction: From True Causes to Provisional Ones', *History and Philosophy of Logic*, 29(4): 361–76.

Dunleavy, P. and Bastow, S. (2001) 'Modelling Coalitions that Cannot Coalesce: A Critique of the Laver-Shepsle Approach', *West European Politics*, 24: 1–26.

Dunleavy, P. and Rhodes, R. A. W. (1990) 'Core Executive Studies in Britain', *Public Administration*, 68: 3–28.

Dür, A. (2008) 'Interest Groups in the EU: How Powerful Are They?', *West European Politics*, 32(1) 1212–30.

Durkheim, É. (1950) *Les Règles de la Méthode Sociologique* (11th edn) (Paris: PUF).

Durkheim, É. (1964) [1893] *The Division of Labor in Society* (New York: Free Press).

Durkheim, É. (1988 [1893]) *Über soziale Arbeitsteilung* [On Social Division of Labor]. (Frankfurt a. M., Germany: Suhrkamp).

Duverger, M. (1954) *Political Parties* (New York: Wiley).

Duverger, M. (ed.) (1988) *Les Régimes Sémi-Présidentiels* (Paris: PUF).

Dye, T. R. (1966) *Politics, Economics, and the Public: Policy Outcomes in the American States* (Chicago, IL: Rand McNally).

Dye, T. R. (2005) *Understanding Public Policy* (Upper Saddle River, NJ: Pearson/Prentice-Hall).

Dye, T. R., Schubert, L. and Zeigler, H. (1970) *The Irony of Democracy* (Boston: Wadsworth).

Dyson, K. (1980). *The State Tradition in Western Europe: A Study of an Idea and Institution* (Oxford: Martin Robertson).

Easton, D. (1953) *The Political System: An Inquiry into the State of Political Science* (New York: Knopf).

Easton, D. (1957) 'An Approach to the Study of Political Systems', *World Politics*, 9(5): 383–400.

Easton, D. (1965*a*) *A Framework for Political Analysis* (Englewood Cliffs, NJ: Prentice-Hall).

Easton, D. (1965*b*) *A Systems Analysis of Political Life* (New York: Wiley).

Ebbinghaus, B. (2006). *Reforming Early Retirement in Europe, Japan and the USA*. Oxford: Oxford University Press.

Ebbinghaus, B. (ed.) (2011). *The Varieties of Pension Governance. Pension Privatization in Europe* (Oxford: Oxford University Press).

Ebbinghaus, B. and Manow, P. (eds) (2001) *Comparing Welfare Capitalism: Social Policy and Political Economy in Europe, Japan and the USA* (London: Routledge).

Eckstein, H. (1966) A *Theory of Stable Democracy* (Princeton: Princeton University Press).

Eisinger, P. K. (1973) 'The Conditions of Protest Behavior in American Cities', *American Political Science Review*, 67: 11–28.

Ekiert, G., Kubik, J., and Vachudova, M. A. (2007) 'Democracy in the Post-Communist World: An Unending Quest?', *East European Politics and Societies*, 21(1): 7–30.

Elazar, D. J. (ed.) (1991) *Federal Systems of the World: A Handbook of Federal, Confederal and Autonomy Arrangements* (Harlow: Longman Current Affairs).

Elazar, D. J. (1995) *Federalism: An Overview* (Pretoria: HSR).

Elgie, R. (1998) 'The Classification of Democratic Regime Types: Conceptual Ambiguity and Contestable Assumptions', *European Journal of Political Research*, 33(2): 219–38.

Elgie, R. (ed.) (1999) *Semi-Presidentialism in Europe* (Oxford: Oxford University Press).

Elgie, R. (ed.) (2001) *Divided Government in Comparative Perspective* (Oxford: Oxford University Press).

Elgie, R. (2008) 'France: Stacking the Deck', in M. Gallagher and P. Mitchell (eds), *The Politics of Electoral Systems* (Oxford: Oxford University Press), 119–36.

Elkins, D. and Simeon, R. (1974) 'Regional Political Cultures in Canada', *Canadian Journal of Political Science*, 6(3): 397–437.

Elkins, D. and Simeon, R. (1979) 'A Cause in Search of an Effect: Or What does Political Culture Explain?', *Comparative Politics*, 11: 127–45.

Elkins, D. and Simeon, R. (eds) (1980) *Small Worlds: Provinces and Parties in Canadian Political Life* (Agincourt, Ontario: Methuen).

Elmeskov, J. and MacFarland, M. (1993) *Unemployment Persistence*, OECD Economic Studies 21 (Paris: OECD), 59–88.

Elmeskov, J., Martin, J., and Scarpetta, S. (1998) 'Key Lessons for Labour Market Reforms: Evidence from OECD Countries' Experiences', *Swedish Economic Policy Review*, 5(2): 205–52.

Emmenegger, P., Häusermann, S., Palier, S., and Seeleib-Kaiser, S. (eds) (2012) *The Age of Dualization. The Changing Face of Inequality in Deindustrializing Societies* (Oxford: Oxford University Press).

Emmerson, D. (2012) 'Minding the Gap Between Democracy and Governance', *Journal of Democracy*, 23(2): 62–73.

Enyedi, Z. (2006) 'Party Politics in Post-Communist Transition', in R. S. Katz and W. Crotty (eds), *Handbook of Party Politics* (London: Sage), 228–38.

Epp, C. (1998) *The Rights Revolution: Lawyers, Activists, and Supreme Courts in Comparative Perspective* (Chicago, IL: University of Chicago Press).

Epstein, L. D. (1986) *Political Parties in the American Mold* (Madison, WI: University of Wisconsin Press).

Erne, R. (2008) *European Unions: Labor's Quest for a Transnational Democracy* (Ithaca, NY: Cornell University Press).

Erne, R. (2012*a*) 'European Unions after the Global Crisis', in L. Burroni, M. Keune, and G. Meardi (eds), *Economy and Society in Europe: A Relationship in Crisis* (Cheltenham: Edward Elgar), 124–139.

Erne, R. (2012*b*) 'European Industrial Relations after the Crisis. A Postscript', in S. Smismans (ed.), *The European Union and Industrial Relations. New Procedures, New Context* (Manchester: Manchester University Press), 225–235.

Esping-Andersen, G. (1985*a*) *Politics Against Markets: The Social Democratic Road to Power* (Princeton, NJ: Princeton University Press).

Esping-Andersen, G. (1985*b*) 'Power and Distributional Regimes', *Politics and Society*, 14: 223–56.

Esping-Andersen, G. (1990) *The Three Worlds of Welfare Capitalism* (Cambridge: Polity Press).

Esping-Andersen, G. (1996) 'After the Golden Age? Welfare State Dilemmas in a Global Economy', in G. Esping-Andersen (ed.), *Welfare States in Transition. National Adaptations in Global Economies* (London: Sage), 1–31.

Esping-Andersen, G. (1999) *Social Foundations of Post-Industrial Economies* (Oxford: Oxford University Press).

Esping-Andersen, G. (2000) 'Who is Harmed by Labour Market Regulations?', in G. Esping-Andersen and M. Regini (eds), *Why Deregulate Labour Markets?* (Oxford: Oxford University Press), 66–98.

Esping-Andersen, G. (ed.) (2002) *Why We Need a New Welfare State* (Oxford: Oxford University Press).

Esser, F. and Pfetsch, B. (eds) (2004) *Comparing Political Communication: Theories, Cases, and Challenges* (New York: Cambridge University Press).

Estevez-Abe, M., Iversen T., and Soskice D. (2001) 'Social Protection and the Formation of Skills: A Reinterpretation of the Welfare State', in P. A. Hall and D. Soskice (eds), *Varieties of Capitalism: The Institutional Foundations of Comparative Advantage* (Oxford: Oxford University Press), 145–83.

European Commission (2004) The Social Situation in the European Union 2004, (Luxembourg: European Commission).

European Industrial Relations Dictionary (2010) *Fixed-term work* (www.eurofound.europa.eu/areas/industrialrelations/dictionary/definitions/fixed-termwork.htm).

Evans, P. B. (1995) *Embedded Autonomy: States and Industrial Transformation* (Princeton, NJ: Princeton University Press).

Falter, J., and Klingemann H.-D. (1998) 'Die deutsche Politikwissenschaft im Urteil der Fachvertreter', in M. T. Greven (ed.), *Demokratie eine Kultur des Westens?* (Wiesbaden: Westdeutscher Verlag), 306–41.

Farago, P. (1985) 'Regulating milk markets: Corporatist arrangements in the Swiss dairy industry' in W. Streeck and P. C. Schmitter, P. C. (eds), *Private Interest Government: Beyond Market and State* (London: Sage), 168–81.

Farrell, D. M. (2010) *Electoral Systems: A Comparative Introduction* (2nd edn) (Basingstoke: Palgrave Macmillan).

Farrell, D. M. and McAllister, I. (2008) 'Australia: The Alternative Vote in a Compliant Political Culture', in M. Gallagher and P. Mitchell (eds), *The Politics of Electoral Systems* (Oxford: Oxford University Press).

Fawn, F. (2006) 'Battle Over the Box: International Election Observation Missions, Political Competition and Retrenchment in the Post-Soviet Space', *International Affairs*, 82(6): 1133–53.

Fearon, J. D. and Laitin, D. D. (1996) 'Explaining Interethnic Cooperation', *American Political Science Review*, 90(4): 715–35.

Ferree, M. M., and McClurg Mueller, C. (2004) 'Feminism and the Women's Movement: A Global Perspective', in D. A. Snow, S. A. Soule, and H. Kriesi, H. (eds), *The Blackwell Companion to Social Movements*, Blackwell Companions to Sociology (Malden, MA: Blackwell), 576–607.

Ferree, M. M., Gamson, W. A., Gerhards J., and Rucht, D. (2002) *Shaping Abortion Discourse: Democracy and the Public Sphere in Germany and the United States* (Cambridge: Cambridge University Press).

Ferrera, M. (1996) 'The "Southern Model" of Welfare in Social Europe', *Journal of European Social Policy*, 6(1): 17–37.

Ferrera, M. (1997) 'Introduction Génerale', *MIRE: Comparer les Systèmes de Protection Sociale en Europe du Sud* (Paris: Ministère Affaire Sociales), 15–26.

Finer, S. E. (1970) *Comparative Government* (London: Allen Lane).

Finer, S. E. (1976) [1962] *The Man on Horseback: The Role of the Military in Politics* (Harmondsworth: Penguin,).

Finer, S. E. (1999) *The History of Government* (Oxford: Oxford University Press).

Finkel, S., Pérez-Liñán, A., and Seligson, M. (2007) 'The Effects of U.S. Foreign Assistance on Democracy Building, 1990–2003', *World Politics*, 59(April): 404–39.

Finnemore, M., and Sikkink, K. (2001) 'Taking Stock: The Constructivist Research Program in International Relations and Comparative Politics', *Annual Review of Political Science*, 4: 391–416.

Fiorina, M. (1996) *Divided Government* (2nd edn) (Boston, MA: Allyn & Bacon).

Fischer, F. (2003) *Reframing Public Policy: Discursive Politics and Deliberative Practices* (Oxford: Oxford University Press).

Flanagan, S. (1987) 'Value Change in Industrial Society', *American Political Science Review*, 81: 1303–19.

Flanagan, S. and Lee, A.-R. (2003) 'The New Politics, Culture Wars, and the Authoritarian-Libertarian Value Change in Advanced Industrial Democracies', Comparative Political Studies, 36: 235–70.

Flora, P. (1974) *Modernisierungsforschung: Zur empirischen Analyse der gesellschaftlichen Entwicklung* (Opladen: Westdeutscher Verlag).

Flora, P. (1977) *Quantitative Historical Sociology: A Trend Report and Bibliography* (The Hague: Mouton).

Flora, P. (ed.) (1986) *Growth to Limits: The Western European Welfare States since World War II* (Berlin: de Gruyter).

Flora, P. and Alber, J. (1981) 'Modernization, Democratization, and the Development of Welfare States in Western Europe', in P. Flora and A. J. Heidenheimer (eds), *The Development of Welfare States in Europe and America* (Piscataway, NJ: Transaction Publishers), 37–80.

Flora, P. and Heidenheimer, A. J. (1981) 'Introduction', in P. Flora and A. J. Heidenheimer (eds), *The Development of Welfare States in Europe and America* (Piscataway, NJ: Transaction Publishers), 17–34.

Florida, R. (2003) *The Rise of the Creative Class* (New York: Basic Books).

Flynn, J. R. (2009) *What Is Intelligence? Beyond the Flynn Effect* (New York: Cambridge University Press).

Foley, M. (1993) *The Rise of the British Presidency* (Manchester: Manchester University Press).

Foley, M. (2000) *The British Presidency: Tony Blair and the Politics of Public Leadership* (Manchester: Manchester University Press).

Føllesdal, A. and Hix, S. (2006) 'Why there is a Democratic Deficit in the EU: A Response to Majone and Moravcsik', *Journal of Common Market Studies*, 44(3): 533–62.

Forbes, E. (1979) *The Maritime Rights Movement, 1919–1927: A Study in Canadian Regionalism* (Montreal/Kingston: McGill-Queen's University Press).

Förster, M. and d'Ercole, M. M. (2005) *Income Distribution and Poverty in OECD Countries in the Second Half of the 1990s*, OECD Social, Employment and Migration Working Paper 22 (Paris: OECD).

Forsyth, M. (1981) *Union of States: The Theory and Practice of Confederation* (Leicester: Leicester University Press).

Foucault, M. (1969) *L'Archéologie du savoir* (Paris: Gallimard).

Franklin, M. N. (1992) 'The Decline of Cleavage Politics', in M. N. Franklin, T. Mackie, and H. Valen (eds), *Electoral Change: Responses to Evolving Social and Attitudinal Structures in Western Countries* (Cambridge: Cambridge University Press), 383–405.

Franklin, M. N. (2004) *Voter Turnout and the Dynamics of Electoral Competition in Established Democracies since 1945* (Cambridge: Cambridge University Press).

Freeman, G. P. (1985) 'National Styles and Policy Sectors: Explaining Structured Variation', *Journal of Public Policy*, 5(4): 467–96.

Freud, S. and Bullitt, W. C. (1967) *Thomas Woodrow Wilson: A Psychological Portrait* (Boston, MA: Houghton Mifflin).

Friedrich, C. J. (1950) *Constitutional Government and Democracy: Theory and Practice in Europe and America* (Boston, MA: Ginn).

Friedrich, C. J. (1963) *Man and His Government* (New York: McGraw-Hill).

Fukuyama, F. (1992) *The End of History and the Last Man* (New York: Free Press).

Gabel, M. J. (1998) *Interests and Integration: Market Liberalization, Public Opinion, and European Union* (Ann Arbor, MI: University of Michigan Press).

Gagnon, A.-G. and Hérivault, J. (2007) 'The Bloc Québécois: Charting New Territories?', in A.-G. Gagnon and A. B. Tanguay (eds), *Canadian Parties in Transition* (Peterborough, Ontario: Broadview Press), 111–36.

Gagnon, A.-G. and Lachapelle, G. (1996) 'Québec Confronts Canada: Two Competing Projects Searching for Legitimacy', *Publius*, 26(3): 177–91.

Gagnon, A.-G. and Tully, J. (eds) (2001) *Multinational Democracies* (Cambridge: Cambridge University Press).

Galbraith, J. K., Conceicao, P., and Ferreira, P. (1999) 'Inequality and Unemployment in Europe: The American Cure', *New Left Review*, 237 (Sept.-Oct.): 28–51.

Gallagher, M. (1991) 'Proportionality, Disproportionality, and Electoral Systems', *Electoral Studies*, 10(1): 33–51.

Gallagher, M. (1996) 'Conclusion', in M. Gallagher and P. V. Uleri (eds), *The Referendum Experience in Europe* (Basingstoke: Palgrave Macmillan), 226–52.

Gallagher, M. (2008a) 'Conclusion', in M. Gallagher and P. Mitchell (eds), *The Politics of Electoral Systems* (Oxford: Oxford University Press), 535–78.

Gallagher, M. (2008b) 'Ireland: The Discreet Charm of PR-STV', in M. Gallagher and P. Mitchell (eds), *The Politics of Electoral Systems* (Oxford: Oxford University Press), 511–32.

Gallagher, M., Laver, M., and Mair, P. (2005) *Representative Government in Modern Europe* (4th edn) (New York: McGraw-Hill).

Gallie, D. (1983) *Social Inequality and Class Radicalism in France and Britain* (Cambridge: Cambridge University Press).

Gallie, D. and Paugam, S. (eds) (2000a) *Welfare Regimes and the Experience of Unemployment in Europe* (Oxford: Oxford University Press).

Gallie, D. and Paugam, S. (eds) (2000b) 'The Experience of Unemployment in Europe: The Debate' in D. Gallie and S. Paugam (eds), *Welfare Regimes and the Experience of Unemployment in Europe* (Oxford: Oxford University Press), 1–24.

Gambetta, D. (1993) *The Sicilian Mafia: The Business of Private Protection* (Cambridge, MA: Harvard University Press).

Gambetta, D. (2005) *Making Sense of Suicide Missions* (Oxford: Oxford University Press).

Gamson, W. (1975) *The Strategy of Social Protest* (Homewood, IL: Dorsey).

Gamson, W. and Meyer, D. S. (1996) 'Framing Political Opportunity', in D. McAdam, J. D. McCarthy, and M. N. Zald (eds), *Comparative Perspectives on Social Movements: Political Opportunities, Mobilizing Structures, and Cultural Framings* (Cambridge: Cambridge University Press), 275–90.

Gamson, W., Croteau, D., Hoynes, W., and Sasson, T. (1992) 'Media Images and the Social Construction of Reality', *Annual Review of Sociology*, 18: 373–93.

Ganz, M. (2000) 'Resources and Resourcefulness: Strategic Capacity in the Unionization of California Agriculture, 1959–1966', *American Journal of Sociology*, 105(4): 1003–62.

Gardbaum, S. (2001) 'The New Commonwealth Model of Constitutionalism', *American Journal of Comparative Law*, 49(4): 707–61.

Garon, S. (1987) *The State and Labor in Modern Japan* (Berkeley, CA: University of California Press).

Garrett, G. (1998) *Partisan Politics in the Global Economy* (Cambridge: Cambridge University Press).

Garrett, G. and Nickerson, D. (2005) 'Globalization, Democratization, and Government Spending in Middle-Income Countries', in M. Glatzer and D. Rueschemeyer (eds) *Globalization and the Future of the Welfare State* (Pittsburgh, PA: University of Pittsburgh Press), 23–48.

Gat, A. (2006) *War in Human Civilization* (New York: Oxford University Press).

Genschel, P. and P. Schwarz (2011). 'Tax Competition: A Literature Review'. *Socio-Economic Review* 9(2): 339–70.

Gerring, J., Thacker, S. C., and Moreno, C. (2005) 'Centripetal Democratic Governance: A Theory and Global Inquiry', *American Political Science Review*, 99(4): 567–81.

Gerston, L. N. (2004) *Public Policy Making: Process and Principles* (Armonk, NY: M. E. Sharpe).

Geva-May, I. (2004) 'Riding the Wave Opportunity: Termination in Public Policy', *Journal of Public Administration Research and Theory*, 14: 309–33.

Geys, B. (2006) 'Explaining Voter Turnout: A Review of Aggregate-Level Research', *Electoral Studies*, 25(4): 637–63.

Gibbins, R. (2004) 'Regional Integration and National Contexts: Constraints and Opportunities', in S. Tomblin and C. Colgan (eds), *Regionalism in a Global Society: Persistence and Change in Atlantic Canada and New England* (Peterborough, Ontario: Broadview Press), 37–56.

Gibbins, R. (2005) 'Early Warning, No Response: Alan Cairns and Electoral Reform', in G. Kernerman and P. Resnick (eds), *Insiders and Outsiders: Alan Cairns and the Reshaping of Canadian Citizenship* (Vancouver: University of British Columbia Press), 39–50.

Giddens, A. (1990) *The Consequences of Modernity* (Cambridge: Polity Press).

Ginsburg, T. (2003) *Judicial Review in New Democracies: Constitutional Courts in Asian Cases* (Cambridge: Cambridge University Press).

Gilardi, F. (2008) *Delegation in the Regulatory State: Independent Regulatory Agencies in Western Europe* (Cheltenham: Edward Elgar).

Gilbert, N. (2002) *Transformation of the Welfare State: The Silent Surrender of Public Responsibility* (Oxford: Oxford University Press).

Gilland Lutz, K. and Hug, S. (2010). *Financing Referendum Campaigns* (Basingstoke: Palgrave Macmillan).

Gilpin, R. (2002) 'The Nation-State in the Global Economy', in D. Held and A. McGrew (eds), *The Global Transformations Reader* (Cambridge: Polity Press), 349–58.

Giugni, M. G. (1998) 'Was it Worth the Effort? The Outcomes and Consequences of Social Movements', *Annual Review of Sociology*, 98: 171–93.

Giugni, M. G., McAdam, D., and Tilly, C. (eds) (1999) *How Social Movements Matter* (Minneapolis, MN: University of Minnesota Press).

Glatzer, M., and Rueschemeyer, D. (eds) (2005) *Globalization and the Future of the Welfare State* (Pittsburgh, PA: University of Pittsburgh Press).

Goetschy, J. and Jobert, A. (2011) 'Employment relations in France', in G.J. Bamber, R.D. Landsbury, and N. Wailes (eds) *International and Comparative Employment Relations. Globalisation and Change* (London: Sage), 169–95.

Goldthorpe, J. H. (ed.) (1984) *Order and Conflict in Contemporary Capitalism: Studies in the Political Economy of Western European Nations* (Oxford: Oxford University Press).

Goldthorpe, J. (2000) *On Sociology: Numbers, Narratives, and the Integration of Research and Theory* (Oxford: Oxford University Press).

Goodin, R. E. and LeGrand, J. (1987) *Not Only the Poor: The Middle Classes and the Welfare State* (London: Allen & Unwin).

Goodin, R. E., Headey, B., Muffels, R., and Dirven, H.-J. (1999) *The Real Worlds of Welfare Capitalism* (Cambridge: Cambridge University Press).

Goodstadt, L. F. (2005) *Uneasy Partners: The Conflict Between Public Interest and Private Profit in Hong Kong* (Hong Kong: Hong Kong University Press).

Goodwin, J. (2001) *No Other Way Out: States and Revolutionary Movements, 1945–1991* (Cambridge, MA: Cambridge University Press).

Goodwin, J. and Jasper, J. M. (1999) 'Caught in a Winding, Snarling Vine: The Structural Bias of Political Process Theory', *Sociological Forum*, 14(1): 27–92.

Grant, T.D. (2005) *Lobbying, Government Relations and Campaign Financing Worldwide. Navigating the Law, Regulations and Practices of National Regimes* (New York: Oxford University Press).

Graz, J.-C. and Nölke, A. (2008) *Transnational Private Governance and its Limits* (Abingdon: Routledge).

Green, D. and Shapiro, I. (1994) *Pathologies of Rational Choice: A Critique of Applications in Political Science* (New Haven, CT: Yale University Press).

Green-Pedersen, C. (2001) 'Welfare-State Retrenchment in Denmark and the Netherlands, 1982–1998: The Role of Party Competition and Party Consensus', *Comparative Political Studies*, 34(9): 963–85.

Green-Pedersen, C. (2004) 'The Dependent Variable Problem within the Study of Welfare-State Retrenchment: Defining the Problem and Looking for Solutions', *Journal of Comparative Policy Analysis*, 6(1): 3–14.

Green-Pedersen, C. (2007) 'The Conflict of Conflicts in Comparative Perspective: Euthanasia as a Political Issue in Denmark, Belgium, and the Netherlands', *Comparative Politics*, 39(3): 273–91.

Green-Pedersen, C. and Haverland, M. (2002) 'The New Politics and Scholarship of the Welfare State', *Journal of European Social Policy*, 12(1): 43–51.

Greenwood, J. (2011) *Interest Representation in the European Union* (3rd edn) (Basingstoke: Palgrave Macmillan).

Griffin, L. J., O'Connell, P. J., and McCammon, H. J. (1989) 'National Variation in the Context of Struggle: Postwar Class Conflict and Market Distribution in the Capitalist Democracies', *Canadian Review of Sociology and Anthropology*, 26: 37–68.

Gros, J.-G. (1996) 'Towards a Taxonomy of Failed States in the New World Order', *Third World Quarterly*, 17(3): 455–71.

Gross, A. M. (1998) 'The Politics of Rights in Israeli Constitutional Law', *Israel Studies*, 3: 80–118.

Grossman, S. J. and Hart, O. D. (1983) 'An Analysis of the Principal-Agent Problem', *Econometrica*, 51(1): 7–46.

Gruner, E. (1956) *Die Wirtschaftsverbände in der Demokratie. Vom Wachstum der Wirtschaftsorganisationen im Schweizerischen Staat* (Erlenbach: E. Rentsch).

Grzymala-Busse, A. (2006) 'The Discreet Charm of Formal Institutions: Postcommunist Party Competition and State Oversight', *Comparative Political Studies*, 39(3): 271–300.

Guéhenno, J.-M. (1995) *The End of the Nation-State* (Minneapolis, MN: University of Minnesota Press).

Guibernau, M. (1996) *Nationalisms: The Nation-State and Nationalism in the Twentieth Century* (Cambridge: Polity).

Guibernau, M. (2012) 'Calls for independence in Catalonia are part of an evolution of Spain's democracy that the country's constitution may have to come to accommodate' (http://blogs.lse.ac.uk/europpblog/2012/10/08/catalonia-independence-spain-constitution/).

Gunther, R. and Mughan, A. (eds) (2000) *Democracy and the Media: A Comparative Perspective* (New York: Cambridge University Press).

Gunther, R., Sani, G., and Shabad, G. (1986) 'Micronationalism and the Regional Party Systems of Euskadi, Catalunya, and Galicia', in R. Gunther, G. Sani, and G. Shabad (eds), *Spain After Franco: The Making of a Competitive Party System* (Berkeley, CA: University of California Press).

Gurr, T. (1970) *Why Men Rebel* (Princeton, NJ: Princeton University Press).

Guttmann, A., and Thompson, D. (2004) *Why Deliberative Democracy?* (Princeton, NJ: Princeton University Press).

Haas, E. B. (1958) *The Uniting of Europe: Political, Social and Economic Forces 1950–1957* (London: Stevens).

Haas, E. B. (1961) 'International Integration: The European and the Universal Process', *International Organization*, 15(3): 366–92.

Haas, P. M. (1992) 'Introduction: Epistemic Communities and International Policy Coordination', *International Organization*, 46(1): 1–37.

Habermas, J. (1999) 'The European Nation-State and the Pressures of Globalization', *New Left Review*, 235: 46–59.

Hacker, J. S. (2002) *The Divided Welfare State: The Battle over Public and Private Social Benefits in the United States* (New York: Cambridge University Press).

Hacker, J. S. (2004). 'Privatizing Risk without Privatizing the Welfare State: The Hidden Politics of Social Policy Retrenchment in the United States', *American Political Science Review*, 98(2): 243–60.

Hage, J., Hanneman, R., and Gargan, E. T. (1989) *State Responsiveness and State Activism: An Examination of the Social Forces and State Strategies that Explain the Rise in Social Expenditure in Britain, France, Germany and Italy 1870–1968* (London: Unwin Hyman).

Hahn, R. W. (1990) 'The Political Economy of Environmental Regulation: Towards a Unifying Framework', *Public Choice*, 65(1): 21–47.

Hainsworth, P. (2006) 'France Says No: The 29 May 2005 Referendum on the European Constitution', *Parliamentary Affairs*, 59(1): 98–117.

Hall, P. A. (1989) *The Political Power of Economic Ideas* (Princeton, NJ: Princeton University Press).

Hall, P. A. (1993) 'Policy Paradigms, Social Learning and the State', *Comparative Politics*, 25(3): 275–96.

Hall, P. A. (2004) 'Beyond the Comparative Method', *APSA-Comparative Politics Newsletter*, 15(2): 1–4.

Hall, P. A. and Soskice, D. (2001*a*) 'An Introduction to Varieties of Capitalism', in P. A. Hall and D. Soskice (eds), *Varieties of Capitalism: The Institutional Foundations of Comparative Advantage* (Oxford: Oxford University Press), 1–70.

Hall, P. A. and Soskice, D. (eds) (2001*b*) *Varieties of Capitalism: The Institutional Foundations of Comparative Advantage* (Oxford: Oxford University Press).

Hall, P. A. and Taylor, R. (1996) 'Political Science and the Three New Institutionalisms', *Political Studies*, 44 (5): 936–57.

Hallin, D. C. and Mancini, P. (2004) *Comparing Media Systems: Three Models of Media and Politics* (Cambridge: Cambridge University Press).

Hammond, T. H. (1986) 'Agenda Control, Organizational Structure, and Bureaucratic Politics', *American Journal of Political Science*, 30: 379–420.

Hammond, T. H. and Knott, J. (1996) 'Who Controls the Bureaucracy? Presidential Power, Congressional Dominance, Legal Constraints, and Bureaucratic Autonomy in a Model of Multi-Institutional Policy-Making', *Journal of Law, Economics, and Organization*, 12: 119–66.

Hamrin, C. L. (1992) 'The Party Leadership System', in K. G. Lieberthal and D. M. Lampton (eds), *Bureaucracy, Politics, and Decision Making in Post-Mao China* (Berkeley, CA: University of California Press).

Hancké, B. (ed.) (2009) *Debating Varieties of Capitalism. A Reader* (Oxford: Oxford University Press).

Hardin, R. (1982) *Collective Action* (Baltimore, MD: Johns Hopkins University Press).

Harper, D. (2001) *The Online Etymology Dictionary* (www.etymonline.com/).

Hartz, L. (1955) *The Liberal Tradition in America* (New York: Harcourt, Brace & World).

Hartz, L. (ed.) (1964) *The Founding of New Societies* (New York: Harcourt, Brace & World).

Harvey, D. (2005) *A Brief History of Neoliberalism* (Oxford: Oxford University Press).

Hayes-Renshaw, F. and Wallace, H. (2006) *The Council of Ministers* (2nd edn) (Basingstoke: Palgrave Macmillan).

Hayward, J. E. S. (1983) *Governing France: The One and Indivisible Republic* (2nd edn) (London: Weidenfeld & Nicolson).

Haywood, T. (1995) *Info-Rich, Info-Poor: Access and Exchange in the Global Information Society* (New Providence, NJ: Bowker).

Heath, A., Glouharova, S., and Heath, O. (2008) 'India: Two-Party Contests within a Multiparty System', in M. Gallagher and P. Mitchell (eds), *The Politics of Electoral Systems* (Oxford: Oxford University Press), 137–56.

Hechter, M. (1975) *Internal Colonialism: The Celtic Fringe in British National Development, 1536–1966* (Berkeley, CA: University of California Press).

Heclo, H. (1974) *Modern Social Politics in Britain and Sweden: From Relief to Income Maintenance* (New Haven, CT: Yale University Press).

Heclo, H. (1977) *A Government of Strangers* (Washington, DC: Brookings Institution Press).

Heclo, H. and Madsen, H. J. (1986) *Policy and Politics in Sweden* (Philadelphia, PA: Temple University Press).

Heidenheimer, A. J., Heclo, H., and Adams, C. T. (1975) *Comparative Public Policy: The Politics of Social Choice in Europe and America* (New York: St Martin's Press).

Held, D. (1995) *Democracy and the Global Order* (Cambridge (UK): Polity Press).

Held, D., and McGrew, A. (2002) *Globalization/Anti-Globalization* (Cambridge: Polity).

Helms, L. (2013) *Oxford Handbook of Political Leadership* (Oxford: Oxford University Press).

Hemerijck, A.C. (2013) *Changing Welfare States* (Oxford: Oxford University Press).

Hemerijck, A.C. and Schludi, M. (2000) 'Sequences of Policy Failures and Effective Policy Responses', in F. W. Scharpf and V. A. Schmidt (eds), *Welfare and Work in the Open Economy*, Vol. I (Oxford: Oxford University Press), 125–228.

Hemerijck, A.C., Unger, B., and Visser, J. (2000) 'How Small Countries Negotiate Change: Twenty-Five Years of Policy Adjustment in Austria, the Netherlands, and Belgium', in F. W. Scharpf and V. A. Schmidt (eds), *Welfare and Work in the Open Economy*, Vol. II (Oxford: Oxford University Press), 175–263.

Henderson, A. (2007) *Nunavut: Rethinking Political Culture* (Vancouver: University of British Columbia Press).

Herb, M. (1999) *All in the Family: Absolutism, Revolution, and Democratic Prospects in the Middle Eastern Monarchies* (Albany, NY: State University of New York Press).

Herrmann-Pillath, C. (2006) 'Reciprocity and the Hidden Constitution of World Trade', *Constitutional Political Economy*, 17(3): 133–63.

Hewitt, C. (1977) 'The Effect of Political Democracy and Social Democracy on Equality in Industrial Societies: A Cross-National Comparison', *American Sociological Review*, 42(1): 450–64.

Hibbing, J. and Theiss-Morse, E. (2002) *Stealth Democracy: Americans' Beliefs about How Government should Work* (Cambridge: Cambridge University Press).

Hicks, A. M. (1999) *Social Democracy and Welfare Capitalism: A Century of Income Security Politics* (Ithaca, NY: Cornell University Press).

Hicks, A. M. and Swank, D. H. (1984) 'On the Political Economy of Welfare Expansion: A Comparative Analysis of 18 Advanced Capitalist Democracies, 1960–1971', *Comparative Political Studies*, 17(1): 81–119.

Hicks, A. M., Swank, D. H., and Ambuhl, M. (1989) 'Welfare Expansion Revisited: Policy Routines and their Mediation by Party, Class and Crisis, 1957–1982', *European Journal of Political Research*, 17(4): 401–30.

Higgins, W. and Apple, N. (1981) *Class Mobilization and Economic Policy: Struggles over Full Employment in Britain and Sweden* (Stockholm: Arbetslivcentrum).

Higley, J. and Gunther, R. (1992) *Elites and Democratic Consolidation in Latin America and Southern Europe* (Cambridge: Cambridge University Press).

Hill, L. (2006) 'Low Voter Turnout in the United States: Is Compulsory Voting a Viable Solution?', *Journal of Theoretical Politics*, 18 (2): 207–32.

Hill, M. (2006) *Social Policy in the Modern World* (Malden, MA: Blackwell).

Hirschl, R. (2001) 'The Political Origins of Judicial Empowerment through Constitutionalization: Lessons from Israel's Constitutional Revolution', *Comparative Politics*, 33 (3): 315–36.

Hirst, P. (1990) *Representative Democracy and its Limits* (Cambridge: Polity Press).

Hirst, P. and Thompson, G. (2000) *Globalization in Question* (2nd edn) (Cambridge: Polity Press).

Hix, S. (2002) 'Constitutional Agenda-Setting through Discretion in Rule Interpretation: Why the European Parliament Won at Amsterdam', *British Journal of Political Science*, 32 (2): 259–80.

Hix, S. (2005) *The Political System of the European Union* (2nd edn) (Basingstoke: Palgrave Macmillan).

Hix, S., Noury, A., and Roland, G. (2007) *Democratic Politics in the European Parliament* (Cambridge: Cambridge University Press).

Hoberg, G. (2001) 'Globalization and Policy Convergence: Symposium Overview', *Journal of Comparative Policy Analysis: Research and Practice*, 3: 127–32.

Hobsbawm, E. (1977) 'Some Reflections on "The Breakup of Britain"', *New Left Review*, 105: 3–23.

Hobson, C. and Kurki, M. (eds) (2012) *The Conceptual Politics of Democracy Promotion* (Abingdon: Routledge).

Hoffmann, S. (1966) 'Obstinate or Obsolete? The Fate of the Nation State and the Case of Western Europe', *Daedalus*, 95(4): 862–915.

Hoffmann, S. (1982) 'Reflections on the Nation-State in Western Europe Today', *Journal of Common Market Studies*, 21 (1–2): 21–37.

Hofstede, G. (2001) *Culture's Consequences: Comparing Values, Behaviors Institutions and Organizations* (Thousand Oaks, CA: Sage).

Holm, H. H. and Sørensen, G. (eds) (1995) *Whose World Order? Uneven Globalization and the End of the Cold War* (Boulder, CO: Westview).

Holmes, L. (1986) *Politics in the Communist World* (Oxford: Oxford University Press).

Holmlund, B. (1998) 'Unemployment Insurance in Theory and Practice', *Scandinavian Journal of Economics*, 100: 113–41.

Holzinger, K. (2002) 'The Provision of Transnational Common Goods: Regulatory Competition for Environmental Standards', in A. Héritier (ed.), *Common Goods: Reinventing European and International Governance* (Lanham, MD: Rowman & Littlefield), 59–82.

Holzinger, K. (2003) 'Common Goods, Matrix Games, and Institutional Solutions', *European Journal of International Relations*, 9: 173–212.

Holzinger, K. (2008) Transnational Common Goods: Strategic Constellations, Collective Action Problems, and Multi-Level Provision (New York: Palgrave Macmillan).

Holzinger, K. and Knill, C. (2005) 'Causes and Conditions of Cross-National Policy Convergence', *Journal of European Public Policy*, 12 (5): 775–96.

Holzinger, K., and Knill, C., and Arts, B. (eds.) (2008) *Environmental Policy Convergence in Europe? The Impact of International Institutions and Trade* (Cambridge: Cambridge University Press).

Hood, C. (2000) *The Art of the State: Culture, Rhetoric and Public Management* (Oxford: Oxford University Press).

Hooghe, L. (ed.) (1996) *Cohesion Policy and European Integration: Building Multi-Level Governance* (Oxford: Oxford University Press).

Hooghe, L. (2001) *The European Commission and the Integration of Europe: Images of Governance* (Cambridge: Cambridge University Press).

Hooghe, L. and Marks, G. (2001) *Multi-Level Governance and European Integration* (Lanhan, MD: Rowman & Littlefield).

Hopkin, J. (2008) 'Spain: Proportional Representation with Majoritarian Outcomes', in M. Gallagher and P. Mitchell (eds), *The Politics of Electoral Systems* (Oxford: Oxford University Press), 375–94.

Hopkin, J., and Paolucci, C. (1999) 'New Parties and the Business Firm Model of Party Organization: Cases from Spain and Italy', *European Journal of Political Research*, 35(3): 307–39.

Hopkins, N. (2013) 'UK approved £112m of arms exports to Saudi Arabia last year', *The Guardian*, 20 May 2013.

Horn, L. (2012) *Regulating Corporate Governance in the EU. Towards Marketization of Corporate Control* (Basingstoke: Palgrave Macmillan).

Hotelling, H. (1929) 'Stability in Competition', *Economic Journal*, 29(1): 41–57.

Howard, C. (1993) 'The Hidden Side of the American Welfare State', *Political Science Quarterly*, 108(3): 403–36.

Howlett, M. (1991) 'Policy Instruments, Policy Styles and Policy Implementation', *Policy Studies Journal*, 19(2): 1–21.

Howlett, M., Ramesh, M., and Pearl, A. (2009) *Studying Public Policy: Policy Cycles and Policy Subsystems* (Oxford: Oxford University Press).

Huber, E. and Stephens, J. D. (2000) 'Partisan Governance, Women's Employment, and the Social Democratic Service State', *American Sociological Review*, 65(3): 323–42.

Huber, E. and Stephens, J. D. (2001) *Development and Crisis of the Welfare State: Parties and Policies in Global Markets* (Chicago, IL: University of Chicago Press).

Huber, J. D. (1996) *Rationalizing Parliament* (Cambridge: Cambridge University Press).

Huckshorn, R. (1984) *Political Parties in America* (Monterey, CA: Brooks/Cole).

Hueglin, T. (1979) 'Johannes Althusius: Medieval Constitutionalist or Modern Federalist?', *Publius*, 9(4): 9–41.

Hueglin, T. (2003) 'Federalism at the Crossroads: Old Meanings, New Significance', *Canadian Journal of Political Science*, 36(2): 275–94.

Hug, S. (2003) 'Endogenous Preferences and Delegation in the European Union', *Comparative Political Studies*, 36(1–2): 41–74.

Hume, D. (1741) *Essays, Literary, Moral, and Political* (Edinburgh: Kincaid).

Huntington, S. P. (1968) *Political Order in Changing Societies* (New Haven, CT: Yale University Press).

Huntington, S. P. (1991) *The Third Wave: Democratization in the Late Twentieth Century* (Norman, OK: University of Oklahama Press).

Huntington, S. P. (1996) *The Clash of Civilizations and the Remaking of World Order* (New York: Simon & Schuster).

Husa, J. (2000) 'Guarding the Constitutionality of Laws in the Nordic Countries: A Comparative Perspective', *American Journal of Comparative Law*, 48(3): 345–81.

Hyden, G., Leslie, M., and Ogundimu, F. F. (eds) (2002) *Media and Democracy in Africa* (Uppsala: Nordiska Afrikainstitutet).

Hyman, R. (1975) *Industrial Relations: A Marxist Introduction* (London: Macmillan).

Hyman, R. (1999) 'Imagined Solidarities: Can Trade Unions Resist Globalisation?' in P. Leisink (ed.), *Globalisation and Labour Relations* (Cheltenham: Edward Elgar) 94–115.

Hyman, R. (2001) *Understanding European Trade Unionism: Between Market, Class and Society*. London: Sage.

Hyman, R. (2010) 'Trade Unions and "Europe": Are the Members Out of Step?', *Relations Industrielles Industrial Relations* 65(1): 3–29.

Inglehart, R. (1977) *The Silent Revolution: Changing Values and Political Styles among Western Publics* (Princeton, NJ: Princeton University Press).

Inglehart, R. (1990) *Culture Shift* (Princeton, NJ: Princeton University Press).

Inglehart, R. (1997) *Modernization and Postmodernization: Cultural, Economic and Political Change in 43 Societies* (Princeton, NJ: Princeton University Press).

Inglehart, R. (2003). 'How Solid is Mass Support for Democracy – And How Do We Measure It?', *PS: Political Science and Politics*, 36: 51–7.

Inglehart, R. and Baker, W. E. (2000) 'Modernization, Cultural Change, and the Persistence of Traditional Values', *American Sociological Review*, 65: 19–51.

Inglehart, R. and Norris, P. (2003) *Rising Tide: Gender Equality and Cultural Change around the World* (Cambridge: Cambridge University Press).

Inglehart, R. and Welzel, C. (2005) *Modernization, Cultural Change, and Democracy: The Human Development Sequence* (Cambridge: Cambridge University Press).

Inglehart, R. and Welzel, C. (2010) 'Changing Mass Priorities: The Link between Modernization and Democracy', *Perpectives on Politics*, 8(2): 551–67.

Inglehart, R., Foa, R., Peterson C., and Welzel, C. (2008) 'Development, Freedom and Rising Happiness: A Global Perspective 1981–2006', *Perpectives on Psychological Science* 3(4): 264–85.

Inkeles, A. (1969) 'Participant Citizenship in Six Developing Countries', American Political Science Review, 63: 112–41.

Inkeles, A. and Smith, D. (1974) Becoming Modern (Cambridge: Harvard University Press).

Iversen, T. (2005) *Capitalism, Democracy and Welfare* (Cambridge: Cambridge University Press).

Iversen, T. (2006) 'Capitalism and Democracy', in D. Wittman and B. R. Weingast (eds), *Oxford Handbook of Political Economy* (New York: Oxford University Press), 601–23.

Iversen, T. and Cusack, T. R. (2000) 'The Causes of Welfare State Expansion: Deindustralization or Globalization?', *World Politics*, 52(3): 313–49.

Iversen, T. and Soskice, D. (2001) 'An Asset Theory of Social Policy Preferences', *American Political Science Review*, 95(4): 875–93.

Iversen, T. and Wren, A. (1998) 'Equality, Employment, and Budgetary Restraint: The Trilemma of the Service Economy', *World Politics*, 50(4): 507–46.

Jackman, R. (1998) 'European Unemployment: Why Is It So High and What Should Be Done About It?', in G. Debelle and J. Borland (eds), *Unemployment and the Australian Labour Market* (Sydney: Reserve Bank of Australia), 39–63.

Jackman, R., Layard, R., and Nickell, S. (1996) 'Combating Unemployment: Is Flexibility Enough?', presented at OECD

Conference on Interactions between Structural Reform, Macroeconomic Policies and Economic Performance (London: LSE).

Jackman, R. W. (1975) *Politics and Social Equality: A Comparative Analysis* (New York: Wiley).

Jackman, R. W. (1986) 'Elections and the Democratic Class Struggle', *World Politics*, 39(1): 123–46.

Jackman, R. W. (1987) 'Political Institutions and Voter Turnout in the Industrial Democracies', *American Political Science Review*, 81(2): 405–24.

Jackson, R. (1990) *Quasi-States: Sovereignty, International Relations and the Third World* (Cambridge: Cambridge University Press).

Jackson, R. and Rosberg, C. G. (1982) *Personal Rule in Black Africa: Prince, Autocrat, Prophet, Tyrant* (Berkeley, CA: University of California Press).

Jahn, D. (2006) 'Globalization as Galton's Problem: The Missing Link in the Analysis of Diffusion Patterns in Welfare State Development', *International Organization*, 60(2): 401–31.

James, A. (1999) 'The Practice of Sovereign Statehood in Contemporary International Society', *Political Studies*, 47(3): 457–74.

James, B. (ed.) (2006) *Media Development and Poverty Eradication* (Paris: UNESCO).

James, J. (2008) 'Digital Divide Complacency: Misconceptions and Dangers', *Information Society*, 24(1): 54–61.

James, S. (1999) *British Cabinet Government* (2nd edn) (London: Routledge).

Janis, I. L. (1972) *Victims of Groupthink* (Boston, MA: Houghton Mifflin).

Jann, W. and Wegrich, K. (2006) 'Theories of the Policy Cycle', in F. Fischer, G. Miller, and M. Sidney (eds), *Handbook of Public Policy Analysis: Theory, Politics, and Methods* (Boca Raton, FL: CRC Press), 43–62.

Jeffery, C. (ed.) (1997) *The Regional Dimension of the European Union: Towards a Third Level in Europe?* (London: Frank Cass).

Jeffery, C. (ed.) (2011) 'Problems of Territorial Finance: UK Devolution in Perspective' in T. Courchene, J. Allan, Ch. Leuprecht, and N. Verelli (eds), *The Federal Idea: Essays in Honour of Ronald L. Watts* (Montreal/Kingston: McGill-Queen's University Press) 379–94.

Jensen, C. (2011) 'Conditional Contraction: Globalisation and Capitalist Systems', *European Journal of Political Research*, 50(2): 168–189.

Jessop, B. (2002) *The Future of the Capitalist State* (Cambridge: Polity).

John, P. (2001) *Local Governance in Western Europe* (London: Sage).

Johnston, R. (2005) 'The Electoral System and the Party System Revisited', in G. Kernerman and P. Resnick (eds), *Insiders and Outsiders: Alan Cairns and the Reshaping of Canadian Citizenship* (Vancouver: UBC Press), 51–64.

Jones, B. D. and Baumgartner, F. R. (2004) 'Representation and Agenda-Setting', *Policy Studies Journal*, 32(1): 1–24.

Jones, B. D. and Baumgartner, F. R. (2005) 'A Model of Choice for Public Policy', *Journal of Public Administration Research and Theory*, 15(3): 325–51.

Jones, E. L. (1981) *The European Miracle: Environments, Economies, and Geopolitics in the History of Europe and Asia* (Cambridge: Cambridge University Press).

Jones, M., and Mainwaring, S. (2003) 'The Nationalization of Parties and Party Systems: An Empirical Measure and an Application to the Americas', *Party Politics*, 9(2): 139–66.

Jordan, G. and Maloney, W. A. (2007) *Democracy and Interest Groups: Enhancing Participation* (Basingstoke: Palgrave Macmillan).

Julius, D. (1997) 'Globalization and Stakeholder Conflicts: A Corporate Perspective', *International Affairs*, 73(3): 453–69.

Kalathil, S. and Boas, T. C. (2001) *The Internet and State Control in Authoritarian Regimes: China, Cuba and the Counterrevolution, Global Policy Program No. 21* (Washington, DC: Carnegie Endowment for International Peace).

Kangas, O. (1991) *The Politics of Social Rights: Studies on the Dimensions of Sickness Insurance in OECD Countries* (Stockholm: Swedish Institute for Social Research).

Kanter, R. M. (1995) *World Class: Thriving Locally in the Global Economy* (New York: Simon & Schuster).

Kapstein, E. B. (1993) 'Territoriality and Who is "US"', *International Organization*, 47: 501–3.

Karmis, D. and Norman, W. (2005) 'The Revival of Federalism', in D. Karmis and W. Norman (eds), *Theories of Federalism: A Reader* (Basingstoke: Palgrave Macmillan).

Katz, R. S. (1986) 'Party Government: A Rationalistic Conception', in F. W. Scharpf and V. A. Schmidt (eds), *Welfare and Work in the Open Economy* (Oxford: Oxford University Press).

Katz, R. S. (1990) 'Party as Linkage: A Vestigial Function?', *European Journal of Political Research*, 18: 143–61.

Katz, R. S. (1997) *Democracy and Elections* (Oxford: Oxford University Press).

Katz, R. S. (2003) 'Europeanization and the Decline of Partisan Political Activity', presented at the 2003 General Conference of the European Consortium for Political Research, Marburg, Germany.

Katz, R. S. and Mair, P. (1995) 'Changing Models of Party Organization and Party Democracy: The Emergence of the Cartel Party', *Party Politics*, 1(Jan.): 5–28.

Katzenstein, P. J. (1984) *Corporatism and Change: Austria, Switzerland and the Politics of Industry* (Ithaca, NY: Cornell University Press).

Katzenstein, P. J. (1985) *Small States in World Markets: Industrial Policy in Europe* (Ithaca, NY: Cornell University Press).

Kaufmann, D., Kraay, A., and Mastruzzi, M. (2006) *Governance Matters: Aggregate and Individual Governance Indicators for 1996–2005*, World Bank Policy Research Working Paper 4012, (Washington, DC: World Bank).

Kautto M. and Kvist J. (2002) 'Parallel Trends, Persistent Diversity—Nordic Welfare States in the European and Global Context', *Global Social Policy*, 2(2): 189–208.

Keating, M. (1997) 'The Political Economy of Regionalism', in M. Keating and J. Loughlin (eds), *The Political Economy of Regionalism* (London: Routledge), 17–40.

Keating, M. (1998a) 'Is There a Regional Level of Government in Europe?', in P. LeGalès and C. Lequesne (eds), *Regions in Europe* (London: Routledge), 11–29.

Keating, M. (1998b) *The New Regionalism in Western Europe: Territorial Restructuring and Political Change* (Cheltenham: Edward Elgar).

Keating, M. (2004) 'Introduction', in M. Keating (ed.), *Regions and Regionalism in Europe* (Cheltenham: Edward Elgar), xi–xv.

Keck, M. E. and Sikkink, K. (1998a) *Articles Beyond Border: Networks in International Politics* (Ithaca, NY: Cornell University Press).

Keck, M. E. and Sikkink, K. (1998b) 'Transnational Advocacy Networks in the Movement Society', in D. S. Meyer and S. Tarrow (eds), *The Social Movement Society: Contentious Politics for a New Century* (Lanham, MD: Rowman & Littlefield), 217–38.

Kelley, J. (2012) Monitoring Democracy. When International Election Observation Works, and Why It Often Fails (Princeton and Oxford: Princeton University Press).

Kelly, M., Mazzoleni, G., and McQuail, D. (eds) (2004) *The Media in Europe: The Euromedia Research Group* (3rd edn) (London: Sage).

Keman, H. (1988) *The Development Toward Surplus Welfare: Social Democratic Politics and Policies in Advanced Capitalist Democracies (1965–1984)* (Amsterdam: CT Press).

Keman, H. (1990) 'Social Democracy and the Politics of Welfare Statism', *Netherlands Journal of Social Sciences*, 26(1): 17–34.

Keman, H. (1993) 'Comparative Politics: A Distinctive Approach to Political Science?', in H. Keman (ed.), *Comparative Politics: New Directions in Theory and Method* (Amsterdam: VU Press), 31–57.

Keman, H. (ed.) (1993b) *Comparative Politics: New Directions in Theory and Method* (Amsterdam: VU Press).

Keman, H. (ed.) (2002a) *Comparative Democratic Politics: A Guide to Contemporary Theory and Research* (London: Sage).

Keman, H. (2002b) 'Comparing Democracies: Theory and Evidence', in H. Keman (ed.), *Comparative Democratic Politics: A Guide to Contemporary Theory and Research* (London: Sage), 32–61.

Keman, H. (2013) 'Political Science and History: Symbiosis or Synthesis?', in A. Zimmer (ed.), *Civil Societies Compared: Germany and the Netherlands* (Baden Baden: Nomos Verlaggesellschaft), 43–65.

Kenworthy, L. (1999) 'Do Social-Welfare Policies Reduce Poverty? A Cross-National Assessment', *Social Forces*, 77(3): 1119–40.

Kenworthy, L. (2004) *Egalitarian Capitalism: Jobs, Incomes and Growth in Affluent Countries* (New York: Russell Sage Foundation).

Kerr, C., Dunlop, J. T., Harbison, F. H., and Myers, C. A. (1973) *Industrialism and Industrial Man* (London: Penguin).

Kershaw, I. (2001) *Hitler 1936-45: Nemesis* (London: Penguin).

Key, V. O., Jr (1964) *Politics, Parties, and Pressure Groups* (New York: Crowell).

King, A. (1973) 'Ideas, Institutions, and the Policies of Government: A Comparative Analysis', *British Journal of Political Science*, 3: 291–313.

King, A. (1975) 'Executives', in F. I. Greenstein and N. W. Polsby (eds), *Handbook of Political Science. V: Governmental Institutions and Processes* (Reading, MA: Addison-Wesley).

King, G. (1997) *A Solution to the Ecological Inference Problem* (Princeton, NJ: Princeton University Press).

King, G., Keohane, R. D., and Verba, S. (1994) *Designing Social Inquiry* (Princeton, NJ: Princeton University Press).

King, G., Rosen, O., and Tanner, M. A. (2004) *Ecological Inference: New Methodological Strategies* (Cambridge: Cambridge University Press).

King, P. (1982) *Federalism and Federation* (London: Croom Helm).

Kingdon, J. W. (2003) *Agendas, Alternatives, and Public Policies* (Harlow: Longman).

Kirchheimer, O. (1966) 'The Transformation of West European Party Systems', in J. LaPalombara and M. Weiner (eds), *Political Parties and Political Development* (Princeton, NJ: Princeton University Press).

Kitschelt, H. (1986) 'Political Opportunity Structures and Political Protest: Anti-Nuclear Movements in Four Democracies', *British Journal of Political Science*, 16: 57–85.

Kitschelt, H. (ed.) (1994) *The Transformation of European Social Democracy* (Cambridge: Cambridge University Press).

Kitschelt, H. (1995) *The Radical Right in Western Europe* (Ann Arbor, MI: University of Michigan Press).

Kitschelt, H. (2001) 'Partisan Competition and Welfare State Retrenchment: When Do Politicians Choose Unpopular Policies?', in P. Pierson (ed.), *The New Politics of the Welfare State* (Oxford: Oxford University Press), 265–302.

Kitschelt, H., Marks, G., Lange, P., and Stephens, J. D. (eds) (1999) *Continuity and Change in Contemporary Capitalism* (Cambridge: Cambridge University Press).

Kittel, B. (1999) 'Sense and Sensitivity in Pooled Analysis of Political Data', *European Journal of Political Research*, 35: 225–53.

Klandermans, B. (1997) *The Social Psychology of Protest* (Oxford: Blackwell).

Kleinman, M. (2001) *A European Welfare State? European Union Social Policy in Context* (London: Palgrave Macmillan).

Klingemann, H.-D. (1999) 'Mapping Political Support in the 1990s', in P. Norris (ed), Critical Citizens (New York: Oxford University Press).

Klingemann, H.-D., Volkens, A., Bara, J., Budge, I. and McDonald, M. (2006) *Mapping Policy Preferences II: Estimates for Parties, Electors, and Governments in Eastern Europe, European Union and OECD, 1990–2003* (supplemented with CD-ROM) (Oxford: Oxford University Press).

Klug, H. (2000) *Constituting Democracy: Law, Globalism, and South Africa's Political Reconstruction* (New York: Cambridge University Press).

Knill, C. (2001) *The Europeanisation of National Administration: Patterns of Institutional Change and Persistence* (Cambridge: Cambridge University Press).

Knill, C. (2005) 'Introduction: Cross-National Policy Convergence: Concepts, Approaches and Explanatory Factors', *Journal of European Public Policy*, 12(5): 764–74.

Knill, C. and Tosun, J. (2012). *Public Policy—A New Introduction*. Basingstoke: Palgrave Macmillan.

Knill, C., Tosun, J., and Bauer, M.W. (2009) 'Neglected Faces of Europeanization: The Differential Impact of the EU on the Dismantling and Expansion of Domestic Policies', *Public Administration*, 87(2): 519–37.

Kobach, K. W. (2001) 'Lessons Learned in the Participation Game', in A. Auer and M. Bützer (eds), *Direct Democracy: The Eastern and Central European Experience* (Aldershot: Ashgate), 292–309.

Kohler-Koch, B., De Biévre, D., and Maloney, W. (2008) *Opening EU-Governance to Civil Society—Gains and Challenges*, Connex Report Series No. 5 (www.mzes.uni-mannheim.de/projekte/typo3/site/index.php?id=641).

Kohler-Koch, B. and Quittkat, C. (2011) *Die Entzauberung partizipativer Demokratie. Zur Rolle der Zivilgesellschaft bei der Demokratisierung von EU-Governance* (Frankfurt: Campus).

Kohnle-Seidl, R. and Eichhorst, W. (2008) 'Does Activation Work?', in W. Eichhorst, O. Kaufmann, and R. Kohnle-Seidl (eds), *Brining the Jobless into Work? Experiences with Activation Schemes in Europe and the US* (Heidelberg: Springer Verlag).

König, T., Tsebelis, G., and Debus, M. (eds) (2010) *Reform Processes and Policy Change: Veto Players and Decision-Making in Modern Democracies*. New York: Springer.

Kooiman, J. (2003) *Governing as Governance* (London: Sage).

Koopmans, R. (1992) *Democracy from Below: New Social Movements and the Political System in West Germany* (Boulder, CO: Westview).

Koopmans, R. (2001) 'Better Off by Doing Good: Why Antiracism Must Mean Different Things to Different Groups', in M. Giugni and F. Passy (eds), *Political Altruism? Solidarity Movements in International Perspective* (Lanham, MD: Rowman & Littlefield), 111–32.

Koopmans, R. and Statham, P. (1999) 'Ethnic and Civic Conceptions of Nationhood and the Differential Success of the Extreme Right in Germany and Italy', in M. G. Giugni, D. McAdam, and C. Tilly (eds), *How Social Movements Matter* (Minneapolis, MN: University of Minnesota Press), 225–52.

Kornhauser, W. (1959) *The Politics of Mass Society* (Glencoe, IL: Free Press).

Korpi, W. (1983) *The Democratic Class Struggle* (London: Routledge & Kegan Paul).

Korpi, W. (1985) 'Economic Growth and the Welfare State: Leaky Bucket or Irrigation System?', *European Sociological Review*, 1(2): 97–118.

Korpi, W. (1989) 'Power, Politics, and State Autonomy in the Development of Social Citizenship: Social Rights during Sickness in Eighteen OECD Countries since 1930', *American Sociological Review* 54(3): 309–28.

Korpi, W. (2002) 'The Great Trough in Unemployment: A Long-Term View of Unemployment, Strikes, and the Profit/Wage Ratio', *Politics and Society*, 30(3): 365–426.

Korpi, W. (2006) 'Power Resources and Employer-Centered Approaches in Explanations of Welfare States and Varieties of Capitalism', *World Politics*, 58(2): 167–206.

Korpi, W. and Palme, J. (1998) 'The Paradox of Redistribution and Strategies of Equality: Welfare State Institutions, Inequality, and Poverty in Western Countries', *American Sociological Review*, 63(5): 661–87.

Korpi, W. and Palme, J. (2003) 'New Politics and Class Politics in the Context of Austerity and Globalization: Welfare State Regress in Eighteen Countries, 1975–1995', *American Political Science Review*, 97(3): 425–46.

Kreppel, A. (2001) *The Development of the European Parliament and Supranational Party System* (Cambridge: Cambridge University Press).

Kriesi, H. (1995) 'The Political Opportunity Structure of New Social Movements: Its Impact on their Mobilization', in J. C. Jenkins and B. Klandermans (eds), *The Politics of Social Protest: Comparative Perspectives on States and Social Movements* (Minneapolis, MN: University of Minnesota Press), 167–98.

Kriesi, H. (1998) 'The Transformation of Cleavage Politics', *European Journal of Political Research*, 33(1): 165–85.

Kriesi, H. (2004) 'Political Context and Political Opportunity', in D. A. Snow, S. A. Soule, and H. Kriesi, H. (eds), *The Blackwell Companion to Social Movements*, Blackwell Companions to Sociology (Malden, MA: Blackwell), 67–90.

Kriesi, H. (2013) 'The populist challenge', *West European Politics* (forthcoming).

Kriesi, H., Koopmans, R., Duyvendak, J. W., and Giugni, M. G. (eds) (1995) *New Social Movements in Western Europe: A Comparative Analysis* (Minneapolis, MN: University of Minnesota Press).

Krouwel, A. (2006) 'Party Models', in R. S. Katz and W. Crotty (eds), *Handbook of Party Politics* (London: Sage), 249–69.

Krugman, P. (1990) 'Policy Problems of a Monetary Union', in P. de Grauwe and L. Papademos (eds), *The European Monetary System in the 1990's* (London: Longman).

Küchenhoff, E. (1967) *Möglichkeiten und Grenzen begrifflicher Klarheit in der Staatsformenlehre* (Berlin: Duncker & Humblot).

Kühner, S. (2007) 'Country-Level Comparisons of Welfare State Change Measures: Another Facet of the Dependent Variable Problem within the Comparative Analysis of the Welfare State?', *Journal of European Social Policy*, 17(1): 5–18.

Kuhnle, S. (ed.) (2000) *Survival of the European Welfare State* (Abingdon: Routledge).

Kuran, T. (1991) 'The East European Revolution of 1989: Is It Surprising That We Were Surprised?', *American Economic Review*, 81(2): 121–5.

Kurian, G., Longley, T. L. D., and Melia, T. O. (1998) *World Encyclopedia of Parliaments and Legislatures* (Washington, DC: Congressional Quarterly).

Kuruvilla, S., Lee, C.L., and Gallagher, M.E. (eds.) (2011) *From Iron Rice Bowl to Informalization: Markets, Workers, and the State in a Changing China.* (Ithaca, NY: Cornell University Press).

Kymlicka, W. (1998) *Finding our Way: Rethinking Ethnocultural Dimensions in Canada* (Toronto: Oxford University Press).

Kymlicka, W. (1999) 'Citizenship in an era of globalization', in I. Shapiro and C. Hacker-Cordón (eds), *Democracy's Edges* (Cambridge: Cambridge University Press), 112–27.

Laakso, M. and Taagepera, R. (1979) 'Effective Number of Parties: A Measure with Application to West Europe', *Comparative Political Studies*, 12: 3–27.

Lancaster, T. and Lewis-Beck, M. (1989) 'Regional Vote Support: The Spanish Case', *International Studies Quarterly*, 33(1): 29–43.

Landman, T. (2003) *Issues and Methods in Comparative Politics: An Introduction* (Abingdon: Routledge).

Larsen, C. A. (2002) 'Policy Paradigms and Cross-National Policy (Mis-)Learning from the Danish Employment Miracle', *Journal of European Public Policy*, 9(5): 715–35.

Lasswell, H. D. (1936) *Politics: Who Gets What, When, How* (New York: McGraw-Hill).

Lasswell, H. D. (1951) Democratic Character (Glencoe, IL: Free Press).

Lasswell, H. D. (1956). *The Decision Process: Seven Categories of Functional Analysis* (College Park, MD: University of Maryland Press).

Lasswell, H. D. (1960) *Psychopathology and Politics: A New Edition with Afterthoughts by the Author* (New York: Viking Press.).

Lasswell, H. D. (1968) 'The Future of the Comparative Method', *Comparative Politics* 1: 3–18.

Latham, E. (1965) *The Group Basis of Politics: A Study in Basing-Point Legislation* (New York: Octagon).

Lavenex, S. (2002) 'EU Enlargement and the Challenge of Policy Transfer', *Journal of Ethnic and Migration Studies*, 28(4): 701–21.

Laver, M. and Hunt, W. B. (1992) *Policy and Party Competition* (London: Routledge).

Laver, M. and Schofield, N. (1990) *Multiparty Government* (Oxford: Oxford University Press).

Laver, M. and Shepsle, K. A. (1990) 'Coalitions and Cabinet Government', *American Political Science Review*, 84: 873–90.

Laver, M. and Shepsle, K. A. (1991) 'Divided Government: America is Not Exceptional', *Governance*, 4: 250–69.

Laver, M. and Shepsle, K. A. (eds) (1994) *Cabinet Ministers and Parliamentary Government* (Cambridge: Cambridge University Press).

Laver, M. and Shepsle, K. A. (1996) *Making and Breaking Governments: Cabinets and Legislatures in Parliamentary Democracies* (Cambridge: Cambridge University Press).

Laver, M., Benoit, K., and Garry, J. (2003) 'Extracting Policy Positions from Political Texts Using Words as Data', *American Political Science Review*, 97(2): 311–31.

Lecours, A. and Moreno, L. (2003) 'Paradiplomacy: A Nation Building Strategy? A Reference to the Basque Country', in A.-G. Gagnon, M. Guibernau, and F. Rocher (eds), *The Conditions of Diversity in Multinational Democracies* (Montreal/Kingston: IRPP/McGill-Queen's University Press).

LeDuc, L. (2003) *The Politics of Direct Democracy: Referendums in Global Perspective* (Peterborough, Ontario: Broadview Press).

LeDuc, L., Niemi, R. G., and Norris, P. (eds) (2002) *Comparing Democracies 2* (London: Sage).

Lee, C. (2007) 'We Are All Comparativists Now: Why and How Single Country Scholarship Must Adapt and Incorporate the Comparative Politics Approach', *Comparative Political Studies*, 39: 1084–1108.

Lee Kaid, L. and Holtz-Bacha, C. (1994) *Political Advertising in Western Democracies: Parties and Candidates on Television* (London: Sage).

Lee Kaid, L. and Holtz-Bacha, C. (2004) *The Sage Handbook of Political Advertising* (London: Sage).

Leeke, M., Sear, C., and Gay, O. (2003) *An Introduction to Devolution in the UK*, Research Paper 03/84 (London: Parliament and Constitution Centre, House of Commons Library).

LeGrand, J. (1982) *The Strategy of Equality* (London: Allen & Unwin).

Lehmbruch, G. (1967) *Proporzdemokratie* (Tubingen: Mohr).

Lehner, F. and Homann, B. (1987) 'Consociational Decision-Making and Party Government in Switzerland', in R. S. Katz (ed.), *Party Governments: European and American Experiences* (Berlin: de Gruyter), 243–69.

Lenaerts, K. (1990) 'Constitutionalism and the Many Faces of Federalism', *American Journal of Comparative Law*, 38: 205–63.

Lenschow, A., Liefferink, D., and Veenman, S. (2005) 'When Birds Sing: A Framework for Analysing Domestic Factors Behind Policy Convergence', *Journal of European Public Policy*, 12(5): 764–74.

Léonard, E., Erne R., Marginson P., and Smismans S. (2007) *New Structures, Forms and Processes of Governance in European Industrial Relations*. (Brussels: Office for the Official Publications of the European Communities) (www.eurofound.europa.eu/publications/htmlfiles/ef0694.htm).

Levitsky, S. and Way, L. (2010) *Competitive Authoritarianism: Hybrid Regimes After the Cold War* (Cambridge: Cambridge University Press).

LeVan, A. (2011) 'Power Sharing and Inclusive Politics in Africa's Uncertain Democracies', *Governance*, 24, 31–53.

Levy, J. D. (1999) 'Vice into Virtue? Progressive Politics and Welfare Reform in Continental Europe', *Politics and Society* 27(2): 239–74.

Lewis, J. (1992) 'Gender and the Development of Welfare Regimes', *Journal of European Social Policy*, 2(3): 159–73.

Lewis, M. P., Simons, G.F., and Fennig, C. D. (eds.) (2013) *Ethnologue: Languages of the World* (17th edn) (Dallas, TX: SIL International).

Lichbach, M. I. (1995) *The Rebel's Dilemma, Economics, Cognition, and Society* (Ann Arbor, MI: University of Michigan Press).

Leibfried, S. and Pierson, P. (1995) 'Semisovereign Welfare States: Social Policy in a Multitiered Europe', in S. Leibfried and P. Pierson (eds), *European Social Policy: Between Fragmentation and Integration* (Washington, DC: Brookings Institution).

Lijphart, A. (1968a) *The Politics of Accommodation: Pluralism and Democracy in the Netherlands* (Berkeley, CA: University of California Press).

Lijphart, A. (1968b) 'Typologies of Democratic Systems', *Comparative Political Studies*, 1(1): 3–44.

Lijphart, A. (1971) 'Comparative Politics and Comparative Method', *American Political Science Review*, 65: 682–93.

Lijphart, A. (1975) 'The Comparable-Cases Strategy in Comparative Research', *Comparative Political Studies*, 8: 158–77.

Lijphart, A. (1977) *Democracy in Plural Societies: A Comparative Exploration* (New Haven, CT: Yale University Press).

Lijphart, A. (1984) *Democracies: Patterns of Majoritarian and Consensus Government in Twenty-One Countries* (New Haven, CT: Yale University Press).

Lijphart, A. (ed.) (1992) *Parliamentary versus Presidential Government* (Oxford: Oxford University Press).

Lijphart, A. (1994) *Electoral Systems and Party Systems: A Study of Twenty-Seven Democracies, 1945–1990* (Oxford: Oxford University Press).

Lijphart, A. (1996) 'The Puzzle of Indian Democracy: A Consociational Interpretation', *American Political Science Review*, 90: 258–68.

Lijphart, A. (1999) *Patterns of Democracy: Government Forms and Performance in Thirty-Six Countries* (New Haven, CT: Yale University Press).

Lijphart, A. (2000) 'Varieties of Nonmajoritarian Democracy', in M. M. L. Crepaz, T. A. Koelble, and D. Wilsford (eds), *Democracy and Institutions: The Life Work of Arend Lijphart* (Ann Arbor, MI: University of Michigan Press).

Lijphart, A. (2008) *Thinking about Democracy: Power Sharing and Majority Rule in Theory and Practice* (Abingdon: Routledge).

Lijphart, A. and Waisman, C. (eds) (1996) *Institutional Design in New Democracies* (Boulder, CO: Westview Press).

Lindbeck, A. and Snower, D. (1988) *The Insider-Outsider Theory of Unemployment* (Cambridge, MA: MIT Press).

Lindberg, L. N. (1963) *The Political Dynamics of Economic Integration* (Oxford: Oxford University Press).

Lindberg, S. (2009) *Democratization by Elections. A New Mode of Transition* (Baltimore, MD: Johns Hopkins University Press).

Lindblom, C. E. (1959) 'The Science of Muddling Through', *Public Administration Review*, 19(2): 79–88.

Lindblom, C. E. (1977) *Politics and Markets: The World's Political-Economic Systems* (New York: Basic Books).

Lindert, P. H. (2004a) *Growing Public: Social Spending and Economic Growth since the Eighteenth Century*. I: *The Story* (Cambridge: Cambridge University Press).

Lindblom, C. E. (2004b) *Growing Public Social Spending and Economic Growth since the Eighteenth Century: Further Evidence* (Cambridge: Cambridge University Press).

Linz, J. (1970) [1964] 'An Authoritarian Regime: Spain', in E. Allardt and S. Rokkan (eds), *Mass Politics* (New York: Free Press).

Linz, J. (1978) *The Breakdown of Democratic Regimes: Crisis, Breakdown and Equilibration* (Baltimore, MD: Johns Hopkins University Press).

Linz, J. (1990a) 'The Perils of Presidentialism', *Journal of Democracy*, 2: 131–45.

Linz, J. (1990b) 'Transitions to Democracy', *Washington Quarterly*, 13(3): 143–64.

Linz, J. (1992) 'Change and Continuity in the Nature of Contemporary Democracies', in G. Marks and L. Diamond (eds), *Reexamining Democracy: Essays in Honor of Seymour Martin Lipset* (Beverly Hills, CA: Sage).

Linz, J. (1994) 'Presidential or Parliamentary Democracy: Does it Make a Difference?', in J. Linz and A. Valenzuela (eds), *The Failure of Presidential Democracies*. I: *Comparative Perspectives* (Baltimore, MD: Johns Hopkins University Press).

Linz, J. and Stepan, A. (1996) *Problems of Democratic Transition and Consolidation: Southern Europe, South America, and Post-Communist Europe* (Baltimore, MD: Johns Hopkins University Press).

Linz, J. and Valenzuela, A. (eds) (1994) *The Failure of Presidential Democracies*. I: *Comparative Perspectives* (Baltimore, MD: Johns Hopkins University Press).

Lipset, S. M. (1959) 'Some Social Requisites of Democracy: Economic Development and Political Legitimacy', *American Political Science Review*, 53(1): 69–105.

Lipset, S. M. (1960) *Political Man: The Social Bases of Politics* (Garden City, NY: Doubleday).

Lipset, S. M. (1968) [1950] *Agrarian Socialism: The Cooperative Commonwealth Federation of Saskatchewan: A Study in Political Sociology* (Garden City, NY: Doubleday).

Lipset, S. M. (1990) *Continental Divide: The Values and Institutions of the United States and Canada* (New York: Routledge).

Lipset, S. M. and Rokkan, S. (1967) 'Cleavage Structures, Party Systems, and Voter Alignments: An Introduction', in S. M. Lipset and S. Rokkan (eds), *Party Systems and Voter Alignments* (New York: Free Press), 1–64.

Lipsky, M. (1971) 'Street Level Bureaucracy and the Analysis of Urban Reform', *Urban Affairs Quarterly*, 6: 391–409.

Lipsky, M. (1980) *Street-Level Bureaucracy: The Dilemmas of Individuals in the Public Service* (New York: Russell Sage Foundation).

Ljungkvist, L. and Sargent, T. J. (1998) 'The European Employment Dilemma', *Journal of Political Economy*, 106(3): 514–50.

Lohmann, S. (1994) 'The Dynamics of Informational Cascades: The Monday Demonstrations in Leipzig, East Germany, 1989–91', *World Politics*, 47(1): 42–101.

Lorwin, V. (1966a) 'Belgium: Religion, Class, and Language in National Politics', in R. A. Dahl (ed.), *Political Oppositions in Western Democracies* (New Haven, CT: Yale University Press), 147–87.

Lorwin, V. (1966b) 'Segmented Pluralism, Ideological Cleavages and Political Cohesion in the Smaller European Democracies', *Comparative Politics*, 3: 141–75.

Loughlin, J. (1986) 'Regionalist and Federalist Movements in Contemporary France', in M. Burgess (ed.), *Comparative Federalism and Federation* (London: Croom Helm), 76–98.

Loughlin, J. (1989) *Regionalism and Ethnic Nationalism in France: A Case Study of Corsica* (Florence: European University Institute).

Loughlin, J. (2004a) 'The "Transformation" of Governance: New Directions in Policy and Politics', *Australian Journal of Politics and History*, 50(1): 8–22.

Loughlin, J. (2004b) *Subnational Democracy in the European Union: Challenges and Opportunities* (Oxford: Oxford University Press).

Loughlin, J. (2007a) 'Les Nationalismes Britannique et Français Face aux Défis de l'Européanisation et de la Mondialisation', in A.-G. Gagnon, A. Lecours, and G. Nootens (eds), *Les Nationalismes Majoritaires Contemporains: Identité, Mémoire et Pouvoir* (Montréal: Québec Amérique), 193–215.

Loughlin, J. (2007b) *Subnational Government: The French Experience* (Basingstoke: Palgrave Macmillan).

Loughlin, J. and Martin, S. (2003) *International Lesson on Balance of Funding Issues: Initial Paper* (London: Office of the Deputy Prime Minister).

Loughlin, J. and Mazey, S. (eds) (1995) *The End of the French Unitary State? Ten Years of Regionalization in France* (London: Frank Cass).

Loughlin, J. and Peters, B. G. (1997) 'State Traditions, Administrative Reform and Regionalization', in M. Keating and J. Loughlin (eds), *The Political Economy of Regionalism* (London: Routledge), 41–62.

Loughlin, J., Kincaid. J., and Swenden W. (eds) (2013) *Routledge Handbook of Regionalism and Federalism* (London: Routledge).

Loughlin, J., Lidstrom, A., and Hudson, C. (2005) 'The Politics of Local Taxation in Sweden: Reform and Continuity', *Local Government Studies*, 31(3): 334–68.

Lowi, T. (1964) 'American Business, Public Policy, Case Studies, and Political Theory', *World Politics*, 16: 677–715.

Lowi, T. (1969*a*) *The End of Liberalism: Ideology, Policy and the Crisis of Public Authority* (New York: W. W. Norton).

Lowi, T. (1969*b*) 'The Public Philosophy: Interest-Group Liberalism' in: W.E. Connolly (ed.) *The Bias of Pluralism* (New York: Atheron Press), 81–122.

Lucas, R. E. (1972) 'Expectations and Neutrality of Money', *Journal of Economic Theory*, 4(2): 103–24.

Lucas, R. E. (1973) 'Some International Evidence on Output-Inflation Tradeoffs', *American Economic Review*, 63(3): 326–34.

Luebbert, G. M. (1991) *Liberalism, Fascism or Social Democracy: Social Classes and the Political Origins of Regimes in Interwar Europe* (Oxford: Oxford University Press).

Luhmann, N. (1970) *Soziologische Aufkldrung* (Cologne: Westdeutscher Verlag).

Lukes, S. (1974) *Power: A Radical View* (London: Macmillan).

Lupia, A. and Johnston, R. (2001) 'Are Voters to Blame? Voter Competence and Elite Maneuvers in Referendums', in M. Mendelsohn and A. Parkin (eds), *Referendum Democracy: Citizens, Elites and Deliberation in Referendum Campaigns* (Basingstoke: Palgrave Macmillan), 191–210.

Lupia, A. and McCubbins, M. D. (1998) *Can Citizens Learn What They Need to Know?* (New York: Cambridge University Press).

Lustick, I. (1997) 'The Discipline of Political Science: Studying the Culture of Rational Choice as a Case in Point', *Political Science and Politics*, 30: 175–9.

Lusztig, M., James, P., and Kim, H., (2003) 'Signaling and Tariff Policy: The Strategic Multistage Rent-Reduction Game', *Canadian Journal of Political Science*, 36(4): 765–89.

Luxemburg, R. (2008) [1906] *The Mass Strike, the Political Party and the Trade Unions* (ww.marxists.org/archive/luxemburg/1906/mass-strike/index.htm).

McAdam, D. (1982) *Political Process and the Development of Black Insurgency, 1930–1970* (Chicago, IL: University of Chicago Press).

McAdam, D. (1996) 'Conceptual Origins, Current Problems, Future Directions', in D. McAdam, J. D. McCarthy, and M. N. Zald (eds), *Comparative Perspectives on Social Movements: Political Opportunities, Mobilizing Structures, and Cultural Framings* (Cambridge: Cambridge University Press), 23–40.

McAdam, D., McCarthy, J. D., and Zald, M. N. (eds) (1996) *Comparative Perspectives on Social Movements: Political Opportunities, Mobilizing Structures, and Cultural Framings* (Cambridge: Cambridge University Press).

McAdam, D., Tarrow, S., and Tilly, C. (2001) *Dynamics of Contention* (Cambridge: Cambridge University Press).

McBride, S. (1980) *Many Voices One World* (London: Kogan Page).

McCarthy, J. D. and Zald, M. N. (1977) 'Resource Mobilization and Social Movements: A Partial Theory', *American Journal of Sociology*, 82(6): 1212–41.

McCarthy, N. and Meirowitz, A. (2007) *Political Game Theory: An Introduction* (Cambridge: Cambridge University Press).

McClosky, H. and Brill, A. (1983) *Dimensions of Tolerance* (New York: Russell Sage).

McDonald, M. D. and Budge, I. (2005) *Elections, Parties, Democracy* (Oxford: Oxford University Press).

McFaul, M. (2004) 'Democracy Promotion as a World Value', *Washington Quarterly*, 28(1): 147–63.

McKay, D. (1996) *Rush to Union: Understanding the European Federal Bargain* (Oxford: Clarendon Press).

McLean, I. (2000) 'Review Article: The Divided Legacy of Mancur Olson', *British Journal of Political Science*, 30(4): 651–68.

McMenamin, I. (2013) *If Money Talks, What Does it Say? Corruption and Business Financing of Political Parties* (Oxford: Oxford University Press).

McQuail, D. (1994) *Mass Communication Theory* (3rd edn) (London: Sage).

McQuail, D. (2005) *Mass Communication Theory* (5th edn) (London: Sage).

McQuail, D. (2009) *Media Performance: Mass Communications and the Public Interest* (London: Sage).

McQuail, D. (2010) *Mass Communication Theory* (6th edn) (London: Sage).

McRae, K. (1964) 'The Structure of Canadian History', in L. Hartz (ed.), *The Founding of New Societies* (New York: Harcourt, Brace & World).

McRae, K. (1974) *Consociational Democracy: Political Accommodation in Segmented Societies* (London: McClelland & Stewart).

Mackie, T. T. and Rose, R. (1991) *The International Almanac of Electoral History* (London: Macmillan).

Mackintosh, J. P. (1977) *The British Cabinet* (London: Stevens).

McMillan, J. (1991) *Napoleon III* (Harlow: Longman).

Macpherson, C. (1953) *Democracy in Alberta: The Theory and Practice of a Quasi-Party System* (Toronto: University of Toronto Press).

Macridis, R. (1955) *The Study of Comparative Government* (New York: Random House).

Maddison, A. (1995) *Monitoring the World Economy: 1820–1992* (Paris: OECD).

Madsen, P. K. (2002) 'The Danish Model of Flexicurity: A Paradise—With Some Snakes', in H. Sarfati and G. Bonoli (eds), *Labour Market and Social Protection Reforms in International Perspective: Parallel or Converging Tracks?* (London: Ashgate), 243–65.

Magleby, D. B. (1994) 'Direct Legislation in the American States', in D. Butler and A. Ranney (eds), *Referendums around the World: The Growing Use of Direct Democracy* (Basingstoke: Palgrave Macmillan), 218–57.

Magraw, R. (1992) *A History of the French Working Class.* Vol. 1: *The Age of Artisan Revolution 1815–1871* (Oxford: Blackwell).

Mahler, G. (1998) 'Israel', in G. Kurian (ed.), *World Encyclopedia of Parliaments and Legislatures* (Washington, DC: Congressional Quarterly Press), 352–9.

Mahoney, C. and Baumgartner F. R. (2008) 'Converging Perspectives on Interest-Group Research in Europe and America' *West European Politics*, 31(6): 1251–71.

Mahoney, J. and Rueschemeyer (eds) (2003) *Comparative Historical Analysis in the Social Sciences* (Cambridge: Cambridge University Press).

Mahoney, J. and Thelen, K. eds. (2010) *Explaining Institutional Change. Ambiguity, Agency, and Power* (Cambridge: Cambridge University Press).

Mainwaring, S. and Shugart, M. S. (eds) (1997) *Presidentialism and Democracy in Latin America* (Cambridge: Cambridge University Press).

Mair, P. (1995) 'Political Parties, Popular Legitimacy and Public Privilege', *West European Politics*, 18(3): 40–57.

Mair, P. (1996) 'Comparative Politics: An Overview', in R. E. Goodin and H.-D. Klingemann (eds), *A New Handbook of Political Science* (Oxford: Oxford University Press), 309–35.

Mair, P. (2002) 'Populist Democracy vs. Party Democracy', in Y. Mény and Y. Surel (eds), *Democracies and the Populist Challenge* (Basingstoke: Palgrave Macmillan), 81–98.

Mair, P. (2006*a*) 'Party System Change', in R. S. Katz and W. J. Crotty (eds), *Handbook of Political Parties* (London: Sage), 63–73.

Mair, P. (2006*b*) 'Sistemi Partitici e Alternanza al Governo, 1950–1999', in L. Bardi (ed.), *Partiti e Sistemi di Partito* (Bologna: Il Mulino), 245–64.

Mair, P. (2006*c*) 'Ruling the Void: The Hollowing of Western Democracy', *New Left Review*, 42: 25–51.

Mair, P. (2007) 'Political Opposition and the European Union', *Government and Opposition*, 42(1): 1–17.

Mair, P. and Biezen, I. van (2001) 'Party Membership in Twenty European Democracies, 1980–2000', *Party Politics*, 7(1): 5–21.

Maiz, R. and Losada, A. (2011) 'The Erosion of Regional Powers in the Spanish "State of Autonomies" ' in F. Requejo and K.-J. Nagel (eds) *Federalism beyond Federations: Asymmetry and Processes of Resymmetrisation in Europe* (Farnham: Ashgate), 81–107.

Majone, G. (1993) 'The European Community between Social Policy and Social Regulation', *Journal of Common Market Studies*, 31(2): 153–70.

Majone, G. (1994) 'The Rise of the Regulatory State in Europe', *West European Politics* 17(3): 77–101.

Majone, G. (1996) *Regulating Europe* (London: Routledge).

Manin, B. (1997) *The Principles of Representative Government* (Cambridge: Cambridge University Press).

Manners, I. (2002) 'Normative Power Europe: A Contradiction in Terms?', *Journal of Common Market Studies*, 40(2): 235–58.

Manow, P. (2004) *The Good, the Bad, and the Ugly: Esping-Andersen's Regime Typology and the Religious Roots of the Western Welfare State*, MPIfG Working Paper 3 (Bonn: Max-Planck-Institut für Gesellschaftsforschung).

March, J. G. and Olsen, J. P. (1984) 'The New Institutionalism: Organizational Factors in the Political Life', *American Political Science Review*, 78(3): 734–49.

March, J. G. and Olsen, J. P. (1989) *Rediscovering Institutions* (New York: Free Press).

March, J. G. and Olsen, J. P. (2008) 'Elaborating the "New Instituionalism" ', in R. A. W. Rhodes, S. A. Binder, and B. A. Rockman (eds), ' *The Oxford Handbook of Political Institutions*, (Oxford: Oxford University Press), 3–20.

Margetts, H. (2006) 'Cyber Parties', in R. S. Katz and W. Crotty (eds), *Handbook of Party Politics* (London: Sage), 528–35.

Marks, G. (1992) 'Rational Sources of Chaos in Democratic Transition', *American Behavioral Scientist*, 35: 397–421.

Marks, G., Hooghe, L., and Blank, K. (1996) 'European Integration from the 1980s: State-Centric v. Multi-Level Governance', *Journal of Common Market Studies*, 34(3): 341–78.

Markusen, A. (1987) *Regions: The Economics and Politics of Territory* (Lanham, MD: Rowman & Littlefield).

Marmor, T. L., Mashaw, J. L., and Harvey, P. L. (1990) *America's Misunderstood Welfare State: Persistent Myth, Enduring Realities* (New York: Basic Books).

Marsh, A. (1990) *Political Action in Europe and the USA* (Basingstoke: Palgrave Macmillan).

Marsh, M. (2007) 'Referendum Campaigns: Changing What People Think or Changing What They Think About?', in C. de Vreese (ed.), *The Dynamics of Referendum Campaigns* (Basingstoke: Palgrave Macmillan, 63–83.

Marshall, T. H. (1950) *Citizenship and Social Class, and Other Essays* (Cambridge: Cambridge University Press).

Marshall, T. H. (1965) *Class, Citizenship and Social Development* (New York: Anchor).

Martin, J. P. (2000) *What Works among Active Labour Market Policies: Evidence from OECD Countries' Experiences*, OECD Economic Studies 30 (Paris: OECD).

Martin, L. and Simmons, B. (1998) 'Theories and Empirical Studies of International Institutions', *International Organization*, 52: 729–57.

Martin, L. W. and Vanberg, G. (2004) 'Policing the Bargain: Coalition Government and Parliamentary Scrutiny', *American Journal of Political Science*, 48: 13–27.

Martin, L. W. and Vanberg, G. (2011) *Parliaments and Coalitions* (Oxford: Oxford University Press).

Mattson, I. (1995) 'Private Members Initiatives and Amendments', in H. Döring, (ed.), *Parliaments and Majority Rule in Western Europe* (Frankfurt: Campus), 448–87.

Massey, D. (1978) 'Regionalism: Some Current Issues', *Capital and Class*, 6: 106–25.

Massicotte, L. (2008) 'Canada: Sticking to First-Past-the-Post, for the Time Being', in M. Gallagher and P. Mitchell (eds), *The Politics of Electoral Systems* (Oxford: Oxford University Press), 99–118.

Mattila, M. (2004) 'Contested Decisions: Empirical Analysis of Voting in the European Union Council of Ministers', *European Journal of Political Research*, 43(1): 29–50.

Mayhew, D. R. (1991) *Divided we Govern* (New Haven, CT: Yale University Press).

Mayntz, R. (1979) 'Public Bureaucracies and Policy Implementation', *International Social Science Journal*, 31(4): 633–45.

Mazmanian, D. and Sabatier, P. (1983) *Implementation and Public Policy* (Glenview, IL: Scott Foresman).

Meier, K. J. (2000) *Politics and the Bureaucracy: Policymaking in the Fourth Branch of Government* (New York: Harcourt College).

Meier, K. J. and Bohte, J. (2001) 'Structure and Discretion: The Missing Link in Representative Bureaucracy', *Journal of Public Administration Research and Theory*, 11: 455–70.

Meltzer, A. H. and Richard, S. F. (1981) 'A Rational Theory of the Size of Government', *Journal of Political Economy*, 89(5): 914–27.

Mény, Y., and Surel, Y. (eds) (2002) *Democracies and the Populist Challenge* (Basingstoke: Palgrave Macmillan).

Merkel, W., Puhle, H.-J., Croissant, A., Eicher, C., and Thiery, P. (2003) *Defekte Demokratie* (Opladen: Leske & Budrich).

Merritt, R., and Rokkan, S. (eds) (1966) *Comparing Nations* (New Haven, CT: Yale University Press).

Meseguer Yebra, C. (2009) *Learning, Policy Making, and Market* (Cambridge: Cambridge University Press).

Meyer, D. S., and Tarrow, S. (1998*a*) 'A Movement Society: Contentious Politics for a New Century', in D. S. Meyer and S. Tarrow (eds), *The Social Movement Society: Contentious Politics for a New Century* (Lanham, MD: Rowman & Littlefield), 1–28.

Meyer, D. S., and Tarrow, S. (eds) (1998*b*) *The Social Movement Society: Contentious Politics for a New Century* (Lanham, MD: Rowman & Littlefield).

Meyers, P. and Vorsanger, J. (2005) 'Street Level Bureaucracy', in B. G. Peters and J. Pierre (ed.), *Handbook of Public Administration* (London: Sage).

Mezey, M. (1979) *Comparative Legislatures* (Durham, NC: Duke University Press).

Michels, R. (1915) *Political Parties: A Sociological Study of the Oligarchical Tendencies of Modern Democracy* (London: Jarrold).

Milgrom, P. and Roberts, J. (1992) *Economics, Organization and Management* (Englewood Cliffs, NJ: Prentice-Hall).

Mill, J. S. (1843) [1959] *A System of Logic* (London: Longman), 55–89 ; also in *John Stuart Mill on Politics and Society* (London: Fontana, 1976).

Mill, J. S. (1859) 'M. de Tocqueville and Democracy in America', in *Dissertations and Discussions* (London: John W. Parker).

Miller, E. A. and Banaszak-Holl, J. (2005) 'Cognitive and Normative Determinants of State Policymaking Behavior: Lessons from the Sociological Institutionalism', *Publius*, 35(2): 191–216.

Mills, C. W. (1956) *The Power Elite* (New York: Oxford University Press).

Milne, S. (2004). *The Enemy Within. The Secret War against the Miners* (3rd edn) (London: Verso).

Milner, H. (1989) *Sweden: Social Democracy in Practice* (Oxford: Oxford University Press).

Minns, J. (2006) *The Politics of Developmentalism: The Midas States of Mexico, South Korea and Taiwan* (Basingstoke: Palgrave Macmillan).

Mitchell, D. (1990) 'Income Transfer Systems: A Comparative Study Using Microdata', Ph.D. thesis, Australian National University.

Mitchell, P. (2008) 'United Kingdom: Plurality Rule under Siege', in M. Gallagher and P. Mitchell (eds), *The Politics of Electoral Systems* (Oxford: Oxford University Press), 157–84.

Molina, O. and Rhodes, M. (2002) 'Corporatism: The Past, Present and Future of a Concept' *Annual Review of Political Science*, 5: 305–31.

Møller, J. (2007) 'The Gap between Electoral and Liberal Democracy Revisited: Some Conceptual and Empirical Qualifications', *Acta Politica*, 42(4): 380–400.

Montesquieu (1721) [1973] *Persian Letters* (Harmondsworth: Penguin).

Moore, B. (1966) *Social Origins of Dictatorship and Democracy: Lord and Peasant in the Making of the Modern World* (Boston, MA: Beacon Press).

Morales, L. (2009) *Joining Political Organizations: Institutions, Mobilization, and Participation in Western Democracies* (London: European Consortium for Political Research Press).

Moravcsik, A. (1991) 'Negotiating the Single European Act: National Interests and Conventional Statecraft in the European Community', *International Organization*, 45(1): 19–56.

Moravcsik, A. (1993) 'Preferences and Power in the European Community: A Liberal Intergovernmentalist Approach', *Journal of Common Market Studies*, 31(4): 473–524.

Moravcsik, A. (1998) *The Choice for Europe: Social Purpose and State Power from Messina to Maastricht* (Ithaca, NY: Cornell University Press).

Moravcsik, A. (2002) 'In Defense of the "Democratic Deficit": Reassessing the Legitimacy of the European Union', *Journal of Common Market Studies*, 40(4): 603–34.

Morel, N., Palier, B., and Palme, J. (eds) (2012). *Towards a Social Investment Welfare State?Ideas, Policies and Challenges* (Bristol: Policy Press).

Moreno, L. (2001) *The Federalization of Spain* (London: Frank Cass).

Morgan, K. J. (2002) 'Forging the Frontiers between State, Church and Family: Religious Cleavages and the Origins of Early Childhood Education in France, Sweden, and Germany', *Politics and Society*, 30(1): 113–48.

Morgan, K. J. (2003) 'The Politics of Mothers' Employment', *World Politics*, 55(2): 259–89.

Morgan, K. J. (2006) *Working Mothers and the Welfare State: Religion and the Politics of Work-Family Policies in Western Europe and the States* (Stanford, CA: Stanford University Press).

Morgenstern, S. and Nacif, B. (eds) (2002) *Legislative Politics in Latin America* (Cambridge: Cambridge University Press).

Moustafa, T. (2007) *The Struggle for Constitutional Power: Law, Politics, and Economic Development in Egypt* (Cambridge: Cambridge University Press).

Mudde, C. (2004) 'The Populist *Zeitgeist*', *Government and Opposition*, 39(3): 541–63.

Mueller, D. C. (2003) *Public Choice III* (Cambridge: Cambridge University Press).

Muller, E. N. (1989) 'Distribution of Income in Advanced Capitalist States: Political Parties, Labour Unions, and the International Economy', *European Journal of Political Research*, 17(4): 367–400.

Muller, P. (1984) *Le Technocrate et le Paysan* (Paris: Éditions Ouvriéres).

Müller, W. C. (1994) 'Models of Goverment and the Austrian Cabinet', in M. Laver and K. A. Shepsle (eds), *Cabinet Ministers and Parliamentary Government* (Cambridge: Cambridge University Press).

Müller, W. C. and Narud, H. M. (eds.) (2013) *Party Governance and Party Democracy* (New York: Springer).

Müller, W. C. and Strøm, K. (eds) (2000) *Coalition Governments in Western Europe* (Oxford: Oxford University Press).

Müller-Rommel, F. and Poguntke, T. (eds) (2002) *Green Parties in National Governments* (London: Frank Cass).

Munck, G. L. (2001) 'Game Theory and Comparative Politics: New Perspectives and Old Concerns', *World Politics*, 53(2): 173–204.

Mundell, R. (1961) 'A Theory of Optimal Currency Areas', *American Economic Review*, 51: 657–65.

Munger, M. C. (2000) *Analyzing Policy: Choices, Conflicts, and Practices* (New York: W. W. Norton).

Mungiu-Pippidi, A. (2005) 'The Unbearable Lightness of Democracy: Is Good Quality Democracy Possible in a Post-Communist Environment?', in L. Diamond and L. Morlino (eds), *Assessing the Quality of Democracy* (Baltimore, MD: Johns Hopkins University Press).

Muñoz, J. and Guinjoan i Cesena, M. (2013) 'Accounting for internal variation in nationalist mobilization: unofficial referendums for independence in Catalonia (2009–11)', *Nations and Nationalism*, 19(1): 44–67.

Murray, C. (1984) *Losing Ground: American Social Policy 1950–1980* (New York: Basic Books).

Myles, J. (1989) *Old Age in the Welfare State: The Political Economy of Public Pensions* (rev. edn) (Lawrence, KS: University Press of Kansas).

Myles, J. and Pierson, P. (2001) 'The Comparative Political Economy of Pension Reform', in P. Pierson (ed.), *The New Politics of the Welfare State* (Oxford: Oxford University Press), 305–33.

Myrdal, G. (1957) *Economic Theory and Underdeveloped Regions* (London: Gerald Duckworth).

Nairn, T. (1977) *The Break-up of Britain: Crisis and Neo-nationalism* (London: New Left Books).

Naisbitt, J. (1994) *The Global Paradox* (New York: Avon).

Ndegwa, S. N. (1997) 'Citizenship and Ethnicity: An Examination of Two Transition Moments in Kenyan Politics', *American Political Science Review*, 91(3): 599–617.

Neidhardt, F. (1994) 'Öffentlichkeit, öffentliche Meinung, soziale Bewegungen', in F. Neidhardt (ed.), *Öffentlichkeit, öffentliche Meinung, soziale Bewegungen,* Kölner Zeitschrift Sonderheft 34 (Opladen: Westdeutscher Verlag), 7–41.

Nenadović, M. (2012) 'An Uneasy Symbiosis: the Impact of International Administrations on Political Parties in Post-conflict Countries', in P. Burnell and A. Gerrits (eds), *Promoting Party Politics in Emerging Democracies* (Abingdon: Routledge): 89–111.

Nevitte, N. (1996) *Decline of Deference* (Toronto: University of Toronto Press).

Newton, K. and van Deth, J. W. (2010) *Foundations of Comparative Politics* (Cambridge: Cambridge University Press).

Nickell, S. (1997) 'Unemployment and Labor Market Rigidities: Europe versus North America', *Journal of Economic Perspectives*, 11(3): 55–74.

Nickell, S. and Layard, R. (1999) 'Labour Market Institutions and Economic Performance', in O. Ashenfelter and D. Card (eds), *Handbook of Labour Economics* (Amsterdam: North Holland), 3029–84.

Nickell, S., Nunziata, L., and Ochel, W. (2004) 'Unemployment in the OECD since the 1960s: What do we Know?', *Economic Journal*, 115(1): 1–27.

Nijeboer, A. (2005) 'The Dutch Referendum', *European Constitutional Law Review*, 1(3): 393–405.

Nikolenyi, C. (2004) 'Cabinet Stability in Post-Communist Central Europe', *Party Politics*, 10: 123–50.

Niskanen, W. A. (1971) *Bureaucracy and Representative Government* (Chicago, IL: Aldine Atherton).

Nolan, P. and Lenski, G. E. (1999) *Human Societies: An Introduction to Macrosociology* (New York: McGraw-Hill).

Nordlinger, E. A. (1977) *Soldiers in Politics: Military Coups and Governments* (Englewood Cliffs, NJ: Prentice-Hall).

Norris, P. (1999) 'Introduction: The Growth of Critical Citizens', in P. Norris (ed.), *Critical Citizens: Global Support for Democratic Government* (Oxford: Oxford University Press), 1–27.

Norris, P. (2000) *A Virtuous Circle: Political Communications in Postindustrial Societies* (Cambridge: Cambridge University Press).

Norris, P. (2001) *Digital Divide* (New York: Cambridge University Press).

Norris, P. (2002) *Democratic Phoenix: Reinventing Political Activism* (Cambridge: Cambridge University Press).

Norris, P. (2004) *Electoral Engineering: Voting Rules and Political Behaviour* (Cambridge: Cambridge University Press).

Nye, J. S., Jr (2001). 'Globalizations's Democratic Deficit', *Foreign Affairs*, 80: 2–6.

Nye, J. S., Jr (2002) *The Paradox of American Power* (Oxford: Oxford University Press).

Nye, J. S., Jr (2005) *Soft Power: The Means to Success in World Politics* (New York: Public Affairs).

Oberschall, A. (1973) *Social Conflict and Social Movements* (Englewood Cliffs, NJ: Prentice-Hall).

Obinger, H. and Schmitt, C. (2011). Guns and Butter? Regime Competition and the Welfare State during the Cold War, *World Politics*, 63(2): 246–70.

Obinger, H., Leibfried, S., and Castles, F. (eds.) (2005) *Federalism and the Welfare State: New World and European Experiences* (Cambridge: Cambridge University Press).

O'Connor, J. (1973) *The Fiscal Crisis of the State* (New York: St Martin's Press).

O'Connor, J., Orloff, A., and Shaver, S. (1999) *States, Markets, and Families: Gender, Liberalism and Social Policy in Australia, Canada, Great Britain and the United States* (New York: Cambridge University Press).

O'Donnell, G. (1973) [1979] *Modernization and Bureaucratic Authoritarianism: Studies in South American Politics* (Berkeley, CA: Institute of International Studies/University of California).

O'Donnell, G. (1994) 'Delegative Democracy', *Journal of Democracy*, 5(1): 55–69.

O'Donnell, G. (1996) 'Illusions about Democracy', *Journal of Democracy*, 7(2): 34–51.

O'Donnell, G. and Schmitter, P. (1986) *Transitions from Authoritarian Rule: Tentative Conclusions about Uncertain Democracies* (Baltimore, MD: Johns Hopkins University Press).

OECD (1994) *The OECD Jobs Study: Evidence and Explanations.* Part I: *Labour Market Trends and Underlying Forces of Change;* Part II: *The Adjustment Potential of the Labour Market* (Paris: OECD).

OECD (1997) *The OECD Jobs Strategy: Implementing the OECD Jobs Strategy. Member Countries' Experiences. and Making Work Pay: Taxation, Benefit, Employment and Unemployment* (Paris: OECD).

OECD (2006) *OECD Employment Outlook: Boosting Jobs and Incomes* (Paris: OECD).

OECD (2008*a*) *OECD Employment Outlook* (Paris: OECD).

OECD (2008*b*) *Growing Unequal? Income Distribution and Poverty in OECD Countries* (Paris: OECD).

OECD (2011). *Divided We Stand. Why Inequality Keeps Rising* (Paris: OECD).

Offe, C., and Wiesenthal, H. (1980) 'Two Logics of Collective Action', *Political Power and Social Theory*, 1: 67–115.

Offe, C., and Wiesenthal, H. (1985) 'Two Logics of Collective Action: Theoretical Notes on Social Class and Organizational Form', in C. Offe, *Disorganized Capitalism: Contemporary Transformations of Work and Politics* (Cambridge: Polity), 175–220.

Ohmae, K. (1993) 'The Rise of the Region State', *Foreign Affairs*, 72(2): 78–87.

Ohmae, K. (1995) *End of the Nation State: The Rise of Regional Economies* (London: HarperCollins).

Okun, A. M. (1975) *Equality and Efficiency: The Big Tradeoff* (Washington, DC: Brookings Institution Press).

Olson, D. (1980) *The Legislative Process: A Comparative Approach* (New York: Harper & Row).

Olson, M. (1965) *The Logic of Collective Action* (Cambridge, MA: Harvard University Press).

Orloff, A. (1993) 'Gender and the Social Rights of Citizenship', *American Sociological Review*, 58(3): 303–28.

Ostrom, E. (2007) 'Institutional Rational Choice: An Assessment of the Institutional Analysis and Development Framework', in P. A. Sabatier (ed.), *Theories of the Policy Process* (2nd edn) (Boulder, CO: Westview Press), 21–64.

Oversloot, H. and Verheul, R. (2006) 'Managing Democracy: Political Parties and the State in Russia', *Journal of Communist Studies and Transition Politics*, 22(3): 383–405.

Page, E. and Goldsmith, M. (eds) (1987) *Central and Local Government Relations: A Comparative Analysis of West European Unitary States* (London: Sage).

Page, E. and Wright, V. (eds) (1999) *Bureaucratic Élites in Western European States* (Oxford: Oxford University Press).

Page, E. and Wright, V. (eds) (2007) *From the Active to the Enabling State* (Basingstoke: Palgrave Macmillan).

Palfrey, J., Zittrain, J., Deibert, R., and Rohozinski, R. (2008) *Access Denied: The Practice and Policy of Global Internet Filtering* (Cambridge, MA: MIT Press).

Palier, B. (ed.) (2010) *A Long Goodbye to Bismarck? The Politics of Welfare Reforms in Continental Europe* (Amsterdam: Amsterdam University Press).

Panebianco, A. (1988) *Political Parties: Organization and Power* (Cambridge: Cambridge University Press).

Panitch, L. (1980) 'Theorizations of Corporatism: Reflections on a Growth Industry' *British Journal of Sociology*, 31(2): 159–87.

Paquin, S. (2003) 'Paradiplomatie Identitaire et Diplomatie en Belgique Fédérale: Le Cas de la Flandre', *Revue Canadienne de Science Politique*, 36(3): 621–42.

Parkinson, C. N. (1958) *Parkinson's Law: The Pursuit of Progress* (London: John Murray).

Parsons, T. (1968) *The Structure of Social Action* (2nd edn) (New York: Free Press).

Pedersen, S. (1990) 'Gender, Welfare, and Citizenship in Britain during the Great War', *American Historical Review*, 95(4): 983–1006.

Pedersen, S. (1993) *Family Dependence and the Origin of the Welfare State, Britain and France, 1914–1945* (Cambridge: Cambridge University Press).

Peeters, P. (2007) 'Multinational Federations: Reflections on the Belgian State', in M. Burgess and J. Pinder (eds), *Multinational Federations* (Abingdon: Routledge), 31–49.

Pei, M. and Kasper, S. (2003) *Lessons from the Past: The American Record on Nation Building*, Policy Brief 24 (Washington, DC: Carnegie Endowment for International Peace).

Pennings, P., Keman, H., and Kleinnijenhuis, J. (2006) *Doing Research in Political Science: An Introduction to Comparative Methods and Statistics* (2nd edn) (London: Sage).

Pérez-Liñán, A. (2010) *Presidential Impeachment and the New Political Instability in Latin America* (Cambridge: Cambridge University).

Perroux, F. (1950) 'Economic Space: Theory and Applications', *Quarterly Journal of Economics*, 64: 89–104.

Peters, B. G. (1998) *Comparative Politics: Theory and Methods* (Basingstoke: Palgrave Macmillan).

Peters, B. G. (2011) *Institutional Theory in Political Science: The New Institutionalism* (London: Continuum).

Peters, B. G. and Pierre, J. (eds) (2001) *Politicians, Bureaucrats, and Administrative Reform* (Abingdon: Routledge).

Peters, B. G., Pierre, J., and King, D.S. (2005) 'The Politics of Path Dependency: Political Conflict in Historical Institutionalism', *Journal of Politics*, 67(4), 1275–1300.

Petrova, T. (2012) 'How Poland Promotes Democracy', *Journal of Democracy*, 23(2): 133–47.

Pierre, J. and Peters, B. G. (2000) *Governance, Politics and the State* (Basingstoke: Palgrave Macmillan).

Pierson, C. (2003) 'Learning from Labor? Welfare Policy Transfer between Australia and Britain', *Commonwealth and Comparative Politics*, 41(1): 77–100.

Pierson, P. (1994) *Dismantling the Welfare State? Reagan, Thatcher, and the Politics of Retrenchment* (New York: Cambridge University Press).

Pierson, P. (1996) 'The Path to European Integration: A Historical Institutionalist Analysis', *Comparative Political Studies*, 29(2): 123–63.

Pierson, P. (1998) 'Irresistible Forces, Immovable Objects: Post-Industrial Welfare States Confront Permanent Austerity', *Journal of European Public Policy*, 5(4): 539–60.

Pierson, P. (2000) 'Increasing Returns, Path Dependence, and the Study of Politics', *American Political Science Review*, 94(2): 251–67.

Pierson, P. (2001a) 'Coping with Permanent Austerity: Welfare State Restructuring in Affluent Democracies', in P. Pierson (ed.), *The New Politics of the Welfare State* (Oxford: Oxford University Press), 411–56.

Pierson, P. (ed.) (2001b) *The New Politics of the Welfare State* (Oxford: Oxford University Press).

Pierson, P. and Skocpol, T. (2002) 'Historical Institutionalism in Contemporary Political Science', in I. Katznelson and H. V. Milner (eds), *Political Science: The State of the Discipline* (New York/Washington, DC: W. W. Norton/American Political Science Association), 693–721.

Piore, M. J. and Sabel, C. F. (1984) *The Second Industrial Divide: Possibilities for Prosperity* (New York: Basic Books).

Pitkin, H. (1967) *The Concept of Representation* (Berkeley, CA: University of California Press).

Pizzorno, A. (1978) 'Political Exchange and Collective Identity', in C. Crouch and A. Pizzorno (eds), *The Resurgence of Class Conflict in Western Europe Since 1968*. Vol. 2: *Comparative Analysis* (London: Macmillan), 277–98.

Poggi, G. (1999) *The State: Its Nature, Development and Prospects* (Cambridge: Polity Press).

Poguntke, T. and Webb, P. (eds) (2005) *The Presidentialization of Politics* (Oxford: Oxford University Press).

Polanyi, K. (2001) [1944] *The Great Transformation: The Political and Economic Origins of Our Time* (Boston, MA: Beacon).

Pollack, M. A. (1997) 'Delegation, Agency and Agenda Setting in the European Community', *International Organization*, 51(1): 99–134.

Pollack, M. A. (2003) *The Engines of European Integration: Delegation, Agency, and Agenda Setting in the EU* (Oxford: Oxford University Press).

Polsby, N. W. (1975) 'Legislatures', in F. I. Greenstein and N. Polsby (eds), *Handbook of Political Science* (Reading, MA: Addison-Wesley).

Pontusson, J. (1995) 'From Comparative Public Policy to Political Economy: Putting Institutions in their Place', *Comparative Political Studies*, 27: 117–47.

Pontusson, J. (2005) *Inequality and Prosperity: Social Europe vs. Liberal America* (Ithaca, NY: Cornell University Press).

Pope Leo XIII (2010) [1891] *Rerum Novarum. Encyclical of Pope Leo XIII on Capital and Labor* (www.vatican.va/holy_father/leo_xiii/encyclicals).

Popitz, H. (1992) *Phänomene der Macht* (2nd edn) (Tübingen: Mohr).

Popkin, S. L. (1979) *The Rational Peasant: The Political Economy of Rural Society in Vietnam* (Berkeley, CA: University of California Press).

Popper, K. R. (1971 [1962]) *The Open Society and Its Enemies* (two volumes) (Princeton: Princeton University Press).

Porter, B. D. (1994) *War and Rise of the State: The Military Foundations of Modern Politics* (New York: Free Press).

Porter, M. E. (1990) *The Comparative Advantages of Nations* (New York: Free Press).

Posner, R. A. (2004) *Catastrophe: Risk and Response* (Oxford: Oxford University Press).

Post, R. (2000) *Democratic Constitutionalism and Cultural Heterogeneity*, Working Paper 2000–8 (Berkeley, CA: University of California at Berkeley, Institute of Governmental Studies).

Powell, G. B. (1982) *Contemporary Democracies: Participation, Stability and Violence* (Cambridge, MA: Harvard University Press).

Powell, G. B. (1986) 'American Voter Turnout in Comparative Perspective', *American Political Science Review*, 80(1): 17–43.

Powell, G. B. (2000). *Elections as Instruments of Democracy: Majoritarian and Proportional Vision* (New Haven, CT: Yale University Press).

Powell, W. W. (1991) 'Expanding the Scope of Institutional Analysis', in W. W. Powell and P. J. DiMaggio (eds), *The New Institutionalism in Organizational Analysis* (Chicago, IL: University of Chicago Press), 183–203.

Pressman, J. L. and Wildavsky, A. (1973) *Implementation: How Great Expectations in Washington are Dashed in Oakland* (Berkeley, CA: University of California Press).

Preuß, U. (1996) 'The Political Meaning of Constitutionalism', in R. Bellamy (ed.), *Constitutionalism, Democracy, and Sovereignty* (Aldershot: Avebury Press).

Przeworski, A. (1991) *Democracy and the Market: Political and Economic Reforms in Eastern Europe and Latin America* (Cambridge: Cambridge University Press).

Przeworski, A. (2004) 'Institutions Matter?', *Government and Opposition*, 39(4): 527–40.

Przeworski, A. and Sprague, J. D. (1986) *Paper Stones: A History of Electoral Socialism* (Chicago, IL: University of Chicago Press).

Przeworski, A. and Teune, H. (1970) *The Logic of Comparative Social Inquiry* (New York: Wiley Interscience).

Pryce, S. (1997) *Presidentializing the Premiership* (Basingstoke: Palgrave Macmillan).

Pryor, F. L. (1968) *Public Expenditure in Communist and Capitalist Countries* (London: Allen & Unwin).

Pülzl, H. and Treib, O. (2006) 'Policy Implementation', in F. Fischer, G. Miller, and M. Sidney (eds), *Handbook of Public Policy Analysis: Theory, Politics, and Methods* (Boca Raton, FL: CRC Press), 89–107.

Putnam, R. D. (1976) *The Comparative Study of Political Elites* (Englewood Cliffs, NJ: Prentice-Hall).

Putnam, R. D. (1992) Making Democracy Work (Princeton: Princeton University Press).

Putnam, R. D. (1993) *Making Democracy Work: Civic Traditions in Modern Italy* (Princeton, NJ: Princeton University Press).

Putnam, R. D. (1995) 'Tuning in, Tuning out: The Strange Disappearance of Social Capital in America', *PS: Political Science and Politics*, 28(4): 664–83.

Putnam, R. D. (2000) *Bowling Alone: The Collapse and Revival of American Community* (New York: Simon & Schuster).

Pye, L. (1968) 'Introduction', in L. Pye (ed.), *Political Culture and Political Development* (Princeton, NJ: Princeton University Press).

Qvortrup, M. (2005) *A Comparative Study of Referendums: Government by the People* (2nd edn) (Manchester: Manchester University Press).

Radaelli, C. (2005) 'Diffusion Without Convergence: How Political Context Shapes the Adoption of Regulatory Impact Assessment', *Journal of European Public Policy*, 12(5): 924–43.

Rae, D. W. (1971) *The Political Consequences of Electoral Laws* (2nd edn) (New Haven, CT: Yale University Press).

Ragin, C. (1987) *The Comparative Method: Moving Beyond Qualitative and Quantitative Strategies* (Berkeley, CA: University of California Press).

Ragin, C. (2008) *Redesigning Social Inquiry. Fuzzy Sets and Beyond* (Chicago, IL: University of Chicago Press).

Rahat, G. (2011) 'The Politics of Electoral Reform: The State of Research', *Journal of Elections, Public Opinion and Parties* 21(4): 523–43.

Rahat, G. and Hazan, R. Y. (2008) 'Israel: The Politics of an Extreme Electoral System', in M. Gallagher and P. Mitchell (eds), *The Politics of Electoral Systems* (Oxford: Oxford University Press), 333–52.

Rakove, J. N. (1996) *Original Meanings: Politics and Ideas in the Making of the Constitution* (New York: Knopf).

Ranney, A. (1962) *The Doctrine of Responsible Party Government* (Urbana, IL: University of Illinois Press).

Raunio, T. (2008) 'Finland: One Hundred Years of Quietude', in M. Gallagher and P. Mitchell (eds), *The Politics of Electoral Systems* (Oxford: Oxford University Press), 473–90.

Rawlings, R. (2001) 'Law, Territory and Integration: A View from the Atlantic Shore', *International Review of Administrative Sciences*, 67(3): 479–504.

Reed, S. R. (2008) 'Japan: Haltingly toward a Two-Party System', in M. Gallagher and P. Mitchell (eds), *The Politics of Electoral Systems* (Oxford: Oxford University Press), 277–94.

Rehfeldt, U. (2009) 'La concertation au sommet toujours d'actualité face à la crise? Théorie du néocorporatime et analyse comparée des relations professionnelles en Europe.' *Chronique International de l'IRES*, 121 (November): 40–9.

Reilly, B. and Nordlund, P. (eds) (2008) *Political Parties in Conflict-Prone Societies* (New York: United Nations University Press).

Renwick, A. (2010). *The Politics of Electoral Reform: Changing the Rules of Democracy* (Cambridge: Cambridge University Press).

Requejo, F. (2005) *Multinational Federalism and Value Pluralism: The Spanish Case* (London: Routledge).

Reynolds, A., Reilly, B., and Ellis, A. (2005) *Electoral System Design: The New International IDEA Handbook* (Stockholm: International IDEA).

Rhodes, M. (1998) 'Globalisation, Labour Markets and Welfare States: A Future of "Competitive Corporatism"?, in M. Rhodes and Y. Meny (eds), *The Future of European Welfare: A New Social Contract?* (London: Palgrave Macmillan), 178–203.

Rhodes, R. A. W. (1995) 'From Prime Ministerial Power to Core Executive', in R. A. W. Rhodes and P. Dunleavy (eds), *Prime Minister, Cabinet and Core Executive* (Basingstoke: Palgrave Macmillan).

Rhodes, R. A. W. (1997) *Understanding Governance: Policy Networks, Governance, Reflexivity and Accountability* (Buckingham: Open University Press).

Rhodes, R. A. W. and Dunleavy, P. (eds) (1995) *Prime Minister, Cabinet and Core Executive* (Basingstoke: Palgrave Macmillan).

Richardson, J. (ed.) (1982) *Policy Styles in Western Europe* (London: Allen & Unwin).

Rieger, E., and Leibfried, S. (1998) 'Welfare State Limits to Globalization', *Politics and Society*, 26(3): 363–90.

Rieger, E., and Leibfried, S. (2001) *Welfare State Mercantilism: The Relations between Democratic Social Policy and the World Market Order* (Frankfurt: Suhrkamp).

Riggs, F. W. (1994) 'Thoughts about Neoidealism vs. Realism: Reflections on Charles Kegley's ISA Presidential Address', *International Studies Notes*, 19 (Winter): 1–6.

Riker, W. H. (1982) *Liberalism against Populism* (San Francisco: Freeman).

Riker, W. H. (1990) 'Political Science and Rational Choice', in J. E. Alt and K. A. Shepsle (eds), *Perspectives on Positive Political Economy* (Cambridge: Cambridge University Press), 163–81.

Rimlinger, G. V. (1971) *Welfare Policy and Industrialization in Europe, America and Russia* (New York: Wiley).

Ringen, S. (2006) *The Possibility of Politics: A Study in the Political Economy of the Welfare State* (Piscataway, NJ: Transaction Publishers).

Risse-Kappen, T. (1995) 'Bringing Transnational Relations Back In: Introduction', in T. Risse-Kappen (ed.), *Bringing Transnational Relations Back In: Non-State Actors, Domestic Structures, and International Institutions* (Cambridge: Cambridge University Press), 3–33.

Robinson, W. (1950) 'Ecological Correlations and the Behavior of Individuals', *American Sociological Review*, 15: 351–7.

Robinson, W. I. (1996) *Promoting Polyarchy. Globalization, US Intervention and Hegemony* (Cambridge: Cambridge University Press).

Roche, W. K., and Cradden, T. (2003) 'Neo-Corporatism and Social Partnership', in M. Adshead and M. Millar (eds) *Public Administration and Public Policy in Ireland* (Abingdon: Routledge), 69–90.

Rodgers, D. T. (2000) *Atlantic Crossings: Social Politics in a Progressive Age* (Cambridge, MA: Harvard University Press).

Rodrik, D. (1996) *Why do More Open Economies have Bigger Governments?*, NBER Working Paper Series 5537 (Cambridge: NBER).

Rogers, E. M. (1995) *Diffusion of Innovations* (New York: Free Press).

Rogowski, R. (1989) *Commerce and Coalitions: How Trade Affects Domestic Political Alignments* (Princeton, NJ: Princeton University Press).

Rohrschneider, R. (2002) 'The Democratic Deficit and Mass Support for an EU-Wide Government', *American Journal of Political Science*, 46(2): 463–75.

Rokeach, M. (1968) Beliefs, Attitudes and Values (San Francisco: Jossey-Bass).

Rokkan, S. (1966) 'Norway: Numerical Democracy and Corporate Pluralism', in R. A. Dahl (ed.), *Political Oppositions in Western Democracies* (New Haven, CT: Yale University Press), 70–115.

Rokkan, S. (1970) *Citizens, Elections, Parties* (Oslo: Universitetsforlaget).

Rokkan, S. (1980) 'Territories, Centres and Peripheries: Toward a Geoethnic, Geoeconomic, Geopolitical Model of Differentiation within Western Europe', in J. Gottman (ed.), *Centre and Periphery: Spatial Variation in Politics* (Beverly Hills, CA: Sage), 163–204.

Rokkan, S. and Urwin, D. (eds) (1982) 'Introduction: Centres and Peripheries in Western Europe' in S. Rokkan and D. Urwin (eds), *The Politics of Territorial Identity: Studies in European Regionalism* (London: Sage), 1–17.

Romano, S. (1947) *Principii di Diritto Costituzionale Generale* (Milan: Giuffe).

Rose, R. (1969) 'The Variability of Party Government: A Theoretical and Empirical Critique', *Political Studies*, 17: 413–45.

Rose, R. (1976) *The Problem of Party Government* (Harmondsworth: Penguin).

Rose, R. (1991) 'What is Lesson-Drawing?', *Journal of Public Policy*, 11: 3–30.

Rose, R. (1993) *Lesson Drawing in Public Policy: A Guide to Learning Across Time and Space* (Washington, DC: CQ Press).

Rose, R. and Chull Shin, D. (2000) 'Democratization Backward', British Journal of Political Science, 31: 331–75.

Rosenau, J. N. (1993) 'Citizenship in a Changing Global Order', in J. N. Rosenau and E.-O. Czempiel (eds), *Governance without Government: Order and Change in World Politics* (Cambridge: Cambridge University Press), 272–95.

Rosenfeld, M. (ed.) (1994) *Constitutionalism, Identity, Difference, and Legitimacy: Theoretical Perspectives* (Durham, NC: Duke University Press).

Ross, F. (2000) ' "Beyond Left and Right": The New Partisan Politics of Welfare', *Governance*, 13(2): 155–83.

Rothstein, B. (2011) The Quality of Government: Corruption, Social Trust, and Inequality in International Perspective (Chicago: University of Chicago Press).

Rousseau, J. J. (1973) [1762] *The Social Contract: and Discourses* (London: Everyman); also available at http://ebooks.adelaide. edu.au/r/rousseau/jean_jacques/r864s/

Rozell, M. J., Wilcox, C., and Madland, D (2006) *Interest Groups in American Campaigns* (Washington, DC: CQ Press).

Rueda, D. (2005) 'Insider-Outsider Politics in Industrialized Democracies: The Challenge to Social Democratic Parties', *American Political Science Review* 99(1): 61–74.

Rueschemeyer, D., Huber, E., and Stephens, J. D. (1992) *Capitalist Development and Democracy* (Cambridge: Polity Press).

Russett, B., Alker, H. R., Deutsch, K. W., and Lasswell, H. D. (1964) *World Handbook of Political and Social Indicators* (New Haven, CT: Yale University Press).

Rustow, D. (1955) *The Politics of Compromise: A Study of Parties and Cabinet Government in Sweden* (Princeton, NJ: Princeton University Press).

Saalfeld, T. (2008) 'Germany: Stability and Strategy in a Mixed-Member Proportional System', in M. Gallagher and P. Mitchell (eds), *The Politics of Electoral Systems* (Oxford: Oxford University Press), 209–30.

Saalfeld, T. (2013) 'Economic Performance, Political Institutions and Cabinet Durability in 28 European Parliamentary Democracies, 1945–2011', in W. C. Müller and H. M. Narud (eds), *Party Governance and Party Democracy* (New York: Springer).

Sabatier, P. A. (1988) 'An Advocacy-Coalition Framework of Policy Change and the Role of Policy-Oriented Learning Therein', *Policy Sciences*, 21: 129–68.

Sabatier, P. A. (1998) 'The Advocacy Coalition Framework: Revisions and Relevance for Europe', *Journal of European Public Policy*, 5(1): 98–130.

Sabatier, P. A. and Jenkins-Smith, H. (eds) (1993) *Policy Change and Learning* (Boulder, CO: Westview Press).

Sadurski, W. (2005) *Rights Before Courts: A Study of Constitutional Courts in Postcommunist States of Central and Eastern Europe* (Dordrecht: Kluwer Academic).

Saich, T. (2011) *Governance and Politics of China* (Basingstoke: Palgrave Macmillan).

Sainsbury, D. (ed.) (1994) *Gendering Welfare States* (London: Sage).

Sainsbury, D. (ed.) (1996) *Gender and Welfare State Regimes* (Oxford: Oxford University Press).

Salisbury, R. H. (1969) 'An Exchange Theory of Interest Groups', *Midwest Journal of Political Science*, 13(1), 1–32.

Sandholtz, W. and Stone Sweet, A. (eds) (1998) *European Integration and Supranational Governance* (Oxford: Oxford University Press).

Sandholtz, W. and Zysman J. (1989) '1992: Recasting the European Bargain', *World Politics*, 42(1): 95–128.

Sandmo, A. (1991) 'Presidential Address: Economists and the Welfare State', *European Economic Review*, 35(2–3): 213–39.

Sartori, G. (1965) *Democratic Theory* (New York: Frederick Praeger).

Sartori, G. (1970) 'Concept Misformation in Comparative Politics', *American Political Science Review*, 65: 1033–53.

Sartori, G. (1976) *Parties and Party Systems: A Framework for Analysis* (Cambridge: Cambridge University Press).

Sartori, G. (1986) 'The Influence of Electoral Systems: Faulty Laws or Faulty Method?', in B. Grofman and A. Lijphart (eds), *Electoral Laws and their Political Consequences* (New York: Agathon Press), 43–68.

Sartori, G. (1987) *The Theory of Democracy Revisited* (Washington, DC: CQ Press).

Sartori, G. (1991) 'Comparing and Miscomparing', *Journal of Theoretical Politics*, 3: 243–57.

Sartori, G. (1994) *Comparative Constitutional Engineering: An Inquiry into Structures, Incentives and Outcomes* (New York/ Basingstoke: New York University Press/Palgrave Macmillan).

Sartori, G. (1997) *Comparative Constitutional Engineering: An Inquiry into Structures, Incentives and Outcomes* (2nd edn) (New York/Basingstoke: New York University Press/Palgrave Macmillan).

Saur, K. G. and Wresch, W. (1996) *Disconnected: Haves and Have-Nots in the Information Age* (New Brunswick, NJ: Rutgers University Press).

Savoie, D. (1986) *Regional Economic Development: Canada's Search for Solutions* (Toronto: University of Toronto Press).

Sbragia, A. M. (ed.) (1992) *Euro-Politics: Institutions and Policymaking in the 'New' European Community* (Washington, DC: Brookings Institution).

Scarpetta, S. (1996) 'Assessing the Role of Labour Market Policies and Institutional Settings on Unemployment: A Cross-Country Study', *OECD Economic Studies*, 26: 43–98.

Scarrow, S. E. (2003) 'Making Elections More Direct? Reducing the Role of Parties in Elections', in B. E. Cain, R. J. Dalton, and S. E. Scarrow (eds), *Democracy Transformed? Expanding*

Political Opportunities in Advanced Industrial Democracies (Oxford: Oxford University Press), 44–58.

Schain, M. and Menon, A. (2007) *Comparative Federalism* (Oxford: Oxford University Press).

Scharpf, F. W. (1984) 'Economic and Institutional Constraints of Full Employment Strategies: Sweden, Austria and Germany, 1973–1982', in J. H. Goldthorpe (ed.), *Order and Conflict in Contemporary Capitalism* (Oxford: Oxford University Press), 275–90.

Scharpf, F. W. (1987) *Sozialdemokratische Krisenpolitik in Europa* (Frankfurt: Campus).

Scharpf, F. W. (1988) 'The Joint-Decision Trap: Lessons from German Federalism and European Integration', *Public Administration*, 66(3): 277–304.

Scharpf, F. W. (1997*a*) 'Economic Integration, Democracy and the Welfare State', *Journal of European Public Policy*, 4(1): 18–36.

Scharpf, F. W. (1997*b*) *Employment and the Welfare State: A Continental Dilemma*, MPIfG Working Paper 97/7 (Bonn: Max-Planck-Institut für Gesellschaftsforschung).

Scharpf, F. W. (1997*c*) *Games Real Actors Play: Actor-Centered Institutionalism in Policy Research* (Boulder, CO: Westview).

Scharpf, F. W. (1997*d*) 'Introduction: The Problem-Solving Capacity of Multi-level Governance', *Journal of European Public Policy*, 4: 520–38.

Scharpf, F. W. (2000) 'Economic Changes, Vulnerabilities, and Institutional Capabilities', in F. W. Scharpf and V. A. Schmidt (eds), *Welfare and Work in the Open Economy*. I: *From Vulnerability to Competitiveness* (Oxford: Oxford University Press), 21–124.

Scharpf, F.W. and Schmidt, V. A. (eds) (2000) *Welfare and Work in the Open Economy* (Oxford: Oxford University Press).

Schattschneider, E. E. (1942) *Party Government* (New York: Holt, Rinehart & Winston).

Schattschneider, E. E. (1975) [1960] *The Semisovereign People: A Realist's View of Democracy in America* (London: Harcourt Brace Jovanovich).

Schattschneider, E. E. (1988) [1960] *The Semi-Sovereign People: A Realist's View of Democracy in America* (London/New York: Wadsworth/Holt, Rinehart & Winston).

Scheinin, M. (ed.) (2001) *Welfare State and Constitutionalism: Nordic Perspectives* (Copenhagen: Nordic Council of Ministers).

Scheppele, K. L. (2005) 'Democracy by Judiciary (or Why Courts can Sometimes be More Democratic than Parliaments)', in W. Sadurski, M. Krygier, and A. Csarnota (eds), *Rethinking the Rule of Law in Post Communist Europe: Past Legacies, Institutional Innovations, and Constitutional Discourses* (Budapest: CEU Press).

Scheufele, D. and Tewksbury, D. (2006) 'Framing, Agenda Setting, and Priming: The Evolution of Three Media Effects Models', *Journal of Communication*, 57(1): 9–20.

Schimmelfennig, F. and Sedelmeier, U. (2005) *Europeanization of Central and Eastern Europe* (Ithaca, NY: Cornell University Press).

Schlesinger, J. (1991) *Political Parties and the Winning of Office* (Ann Arbor, MI: University of Michigan Press).

Schlozman, K. L. (2002) 'Citizen Participation in America: What Do We Know? Why Do We Care?', in I. Katznelson and

H. V. Milner (eds), *Political Science: The State of the Discipline* (New York: W. W. Norton and American Political Science Association).

Schmidt, M. G. (1982) *Wohlfahrtsstaatliche Politik unter biirgerlichen und sozialdemokratischen Regierungen* (Frankfurt: Campus).

Schmidt, M. G. (1983) 'The Welfare State and the Economy in Periods of Economic Crisis', *European Journal of Political Research*, 11(1): 1–26.

Schmidt, M. G. (1998) *Sozialpolitik in Deutschland Historische Entwicklung und internationaler Vergleich* (Opladen: Leske & Budrich).

Schmidt, M. G. (2002) 'The Impact of Parties, Constitutional Structures and Veto Players on Public Policy', in H. Keman (ed.) *Comparative Democratic Politics. A Guide to Contemporary Theory and Research* (London: Sage).

Schmidt V. A. (2002) 'Does Discourse Matter in the Politics of Welfare State Adjustment?', *Comparative Political Studies*, 35(2): 168–93.

Schmitter, P. C. (1974) 'Still the Century of Corporatism?', *Review of Politics*, 36: 85–131.

Schmitter, P. C. (1974) 'Still the Century of Corporatism?' reprinted in P. C. Schmitter and G. Lehmbruch (eds) (1979) *Trends Towards Corporatist Mediation* (London: Sage), 7–52.

Schmitter, P. C. (1981) 'Interest Intermediation and Regime Governability in Contemporary Western Europe and North America' in S. Bergers (ed.) *Organizing Interests in Western Europe. Pluralism, Corporatism and the Transformation of Politics* (Cambridge: Cambridge University Press), 285–327.

Schmitter, P. C. (1989) 'Corporatism is Dead! Long Live Corporatism', *Government and Opposition*, 24: 131–57.

Schmitter, P. C. (1993) 'Comparative Politics', in J. Krieger (ed.), *The Oxford Companion to Politics of the World* (Oxford: Oxford University Press), 171–7.

Schmitter, P. C. and Grote, J.R. (1997) *The Corporatist Sisyphus: Past, Present and Future*, European University Institute Working Paper SPS 97/4 (http://cadmus.iue.it/dspace/bitstream/1814/284/1/97_4.pdf).

Schmitter, P. C. and Karl, T. (1991) 'What Democracy Is and Is Not', *Journal of Democracy*, 2(3): 75–88.

Schmitter, P. C. and Lehmbruch, G. (eds) (1979) *Trends toward Corporatist Intermediation* (London: Sage).

Schmitter, P. C. and Trechsel, A. H. (eds) (2004) *The Future of Democracy in Europe: Trends, Analyses and Reforms* (Strasbourg: Council of Europe).

Scholten, P. and Timmermans, A. (2010) 'Setting the Immigrant Policy Agenda: Expertise and Politics in the Netherlands, France and the United Kingdom'. *Journal of Comparative Policy Analysis: Research and Practice* 12(5): 527–44.

Schumpeter, J. A. (1943) *Capitalism, Socialism and Democracy* (New York: Harper & Row).

Schumpeter, J. A. (1947) *Capitalism, Socialism, and Democracy* (2nd edn) (New York: Harper & Brothers).

Schumpeter, J. A. (1962) *Capitalism, Socialism and Democracy* (New York: Harper & Row).

Schwartz, H. (2001) 'Round Up the Usual Suspects! Globalization, Domestic Politics, and Welfare State Change', in P. Pierson (ed.), *The New Politics of the Welfare State* (Oxford: Oxford University Press), 17–44.

Scruggs, L. (2002) 'The Ghent System and Union Membership in Europe, 1970–1996', *Political Research Quarterly*, 55(2): 275–97.

Scruggs, L. and Allan, J. (2006a) 'The Material Consequences of Welfare States: Benefit Generosity and Absolute Poverty in Sixteen OECD Countries', *Comparative Political Studies*, 39(7): 880–904.

Scruggs, L. and Allan, J. (2006b) 'Welfare State Decommodification in Eighteen OECD Countries: A Replication and Revision', *Journal of European Social Policy*, 16(1): 55–72.

Seeliger, R. (1996) 'Conceptualizing and Researching Policy Convergence', *Policy Studies Journal*, 24: 153–72.

Segura-Ubiergo, A. (2007) *The Political Economy of the Welfare State in Latin America: Globalization, Democracy, and Development* (New York: Cambridge University Press).

Seldon, S. C. (1997) *The Promise of Representative Bureaucracy* (Armonk, NY: Sharpe).

Sen, A. (1999) 'Democracy as a Universal Value', *Journal of Democracy*, 10(3): 3–17.

Setälä, M. (1999) *Referendums and Democratic Government: Normative Theory and the Analysis of Institutions* (Basingstoke: Palgrave Macmillan).

Shalev, M. (1983) 'The Social Democratic Model and Beyond: Two Generations of Comparative Research on the Welfare State', *Comparative Social Research*, 6: 315–51.

Shapiro, M. (1964) *Law and Politics in the Supreme Court: Studies in Political Jurisprudence* (Glencoe, IL: Free Press).

Shapiro, M. and Stone Sweet, A. (1994) 'The New Constitutional Politics of Europe', *Comparative Political Studies*, 26: 397–420.

Sharpe, L. (1993a) 'The European Meso: An Appraisal', in L. Sharpe, *The Rise of Meso Government in Europe* (London: Sage), 1–39.

Sharpe, L. (1993b) *The Rise of Meso Government in Europe* (London: Sage).

Sharpe, L. and Newton, K. (1984) *Does Politics Matter? The Determinants of Public Policy* (Oxford: Clarendon Press).

Shaw, J. (1999) 'Post-National Constitutionalism in the EU', *Journal of European Public Policy*, 6(4): 579–97.

Shepsle, K. A. (2006) 'Rational Choice Institutionalism', in R. A. W. Rhodes, S.A. Binder, and B. a. Rockman (eds), *Oxford Handbook of Political Institutions* (Oxford: Oxford University Press), 23–38.

Shepsle, K. A. and Weingast, B. (1987) 'The Institutional Foundations of Committee Power', *American Political Science Review*, 81(1): 85–104.

Shepsle, K. A. and Bonchek, M. S. (1997) *Analyzing Politics* (New York: W. W. Norton).

Shils, E. (1975) *Center and Periphery: Essays in Macrosociology* (Chicago, IL: University of Chicago Press).

Shoemaker, P. J. and Cohen, A. A. (2006) *News Around the World* (Abingdon: Routledge).

Shugart, M. S. (2008) 'Comparative Electoral Systems Research: The Maturation of a Field and New Challenges Ahead', in M. Gallagher and P. Mitchell (eds), *The Politics of Electoral Systems* (Oxford: Oxford University Press), 25–56.

Shugart, M. S. and Carey, J. M. (1992) *Presidents and Assemblies* (Cambridge: Cambridge University Press).

Shugart, M. S. and Wattenberg, M. P. (eds) (2003) *Mixed-Member Electoral Systems: The Best of Both Worlds?* (Oxford: Oxford University Press).

Shugart, M. S., Valdini, M. E., and Suominen, K. (2005) 'Looking for Locals: Voter Information Demands and Personal Vote-Earning Attributes of Legislators under Proportional Representation', *American Journal of Political Science*, 49(2): 437–49.

Siaroff, A. (1999) 'Corporatism in Twenty-four Industrial Democracies: Meaning and Measurement', *European Journal of Political Research*, 36: 175–205.

Siavelis, P. M. (2008) 'Chile: The Unexpected (and Expected) Consequences of Electoral Engineering', in M. Gallagher and P. Mitchell (eds), *The Politics of Electoral Systems* (Oxford: Oxford University Press), 433–52.

Siebert, F. S., Peterson, T., and Schramm, W. (1956) *Four Theories of the Press* (Chicago, IL: University of Illinois Press).

Sieder, R., Schjolden, L., and Angell, A. (2005) *The Judicialization of Politics in Latin America* (New York: Palgrave Macmillan).

Silver, B. J. (2003) *Forces of Labor: Workers Movements and Globalization Since 1870* (Cambridge: Cambridge University Press).

Simeon, R. (1977) 'Regionalism and Canadian Political Institutions', in J. Meekison (ed.), *Canadian Federalism: Myth or Reality?* (Toronto: Methuen), 293.

Simmel, G. (1984 [1908]) *Das Individuum und die Freiheit: Essays* [*The Individual and Freedom*] (Berlin, Germany: Duncker & Humblodt).

Simmons, B. A. and Elkins, Z. (2004) 'The Globalization of Liberalization: Policy Diffusion in the International Political Economy', *American Political Science Review*, 98: 171–89.

Simon, H. A. (1955) 'A Behavioral Model of Rational Choice', *Quarterly Journal of Economics*, 69(1): 99–118.

Simon, H. A. (ed.) (1957) *Models of Man: Social and Rational* (New York: Wiley).

Simonton, D. K. (1993) 'Putting the Best Leaders in the White House: Personality, Policy and Performance', *Political Psychology*, 14: 537–48.

Singh, N. and Srinivasan, T. N. (2003) *Can India Survive Globalization?* (www.project-syndicate.org/commentary/nsingh1).

Sinnott, R. (2010) 'The electoral system', in J. Coakley and M. Gallagher (eds), *Politics in the Republic of Ireland* (5th edn) (Abingdon: Routledge Press), 111–36.

Sinyai, C. (2006) *Schools of Democracy. A Political History of the American Labor Movement* (Ithaca, NY: Cornell University Press).

Skocpol, T. (1979) *States and Social Revolution: A Comparative Analysis of France, Russia and China* (Cambridge: Cambridge University Press).

Skocpol, T. (ed.) (1984) *Visions and Methods in Historical Sociology* (Cambridge: Cambridge University Press).

Skocpol, T. (1985) 'Bringing the State Back In: Strategies of Analysis in Current Research', in P. Evans, D. Rueschenmeyer, and T. Skocpol (eds), *Bringing the State Back In* (Cambridge: Cambridge University Press), 3–37.

Skocpol, T. (1992) *Protecting Soldiers and Mothers: The Political Origins of Social Policy in the United States* (Cambridge, MA: Belknap Press).

Skocpol, T. (2003) *Diminished Democracy: From Membership to Management in American Civic Life* (Norman, OK: University of Oklahoma Press).

Skocpol, T. and Amenta, E. (1986) 'States and Social Policies', *Annual Review of Sociology*, 12: 131–57.

Skocpol, T. and Orloff, A. S. (1986) 'Explaining the Origins of Welfare States: A Comparison of Britain and the United States, 1880s–1920s', in S. Lindenberg, J. S. Coleman, and S. Nowak (eds), *Approaches to Social Theory: Proceedings of the W. I. Thomas and Florian Znaniecki Memorial Conference on Social Theory* (New York: Russell Sage Foundation), 229–54.

Slaughter, A.–M. (1997). 'The Real New World Order', *Foreign Affairs*, 76: 183–97.

Smeeding, T. M. (2005) 'Public Policy, Economic Inequality, and Poverty: The United States in Comparative Perspective', *Social Science Quarterly*, 86 (Suppl): 955–83.

Smeeding, T. M. and Gottschalk, P. (1999) 'Cross-National Income Inequality: How Great Is It and What Can We Learn From It?', *International Journal of Health Services*, 29(4): 733–41.

Smeeding, T. M., O'Higgins, M., and Rainwater, L. (1990) *Poverty, Inequality and Income Distribution in Comparative Perspective: The Luxembourg Income Study (LIS)* (New York: Harvester Wheatsheaf).

Smelser, N. J. (1962) *Theory of Collective Behavior* (New York: Free Press).

Smelser, N. J. (1966) 'Mechanisms of Change and Adjustment to Change', in J. Finkle and R. Gable (eds), *Political Development and Social Change* (New York: Wiley).

Smismans, S. (ed.) (2006) *Civil Society and Legitimate European Governance* (Cheltenham: Edward Elgar).

Smith, D. (1985) 'Party Government, Representation and National Integration in Canada', in P. Aucoin (ed.), *Party Government and Regional Representation in Canada* (Toronto: University of Toronto Press), 1–68.

Smith, M. J. (1993) *Pressure, Power and Policy: State Autonomy and Policy Networks in Britain and the United States* (Pittsburgh, PA: University of Pittsburgh Press).

Smith, M. J. (1999) *The Core Executive in Britain* (Basingstoke: Palgrave Macmillan).

Smithies, A. (1941) 'Optimum Location in Spatial Competition', *Journal of Political Economy*, 49: 423–39.

Sniderman, P. (1975) Personality and Democratic Politics (Berkeley: University of California Press).

Snow, D. A., Soule, S. A., and Kriesi, H. (2004) *The Blackwell Companion to Social Movements, Blackwell Companions to Sociology* (Malden, MA: Blackwell).

Soja, E. (1989) *Postmodern Geographies: The Reassertion of Space in Critical Social Theory* (New York: Verso).

Somit, A. and Tanenhaus, A. (1964) *American Political Science: A Profile of a Discipline* (New York: Atherton).

Sørenson, E. and Torfing, J. (2007) *Theories of Democratic Network Governance* (Basingstoke: Palgrave Macmillan).

Sørensen, G. (2001) *Changes in Statehood: The Transformation of International Relations* (Basingstoke: Palgrave Macmillan).

Sørensen, G. (2004) *The Transformation of the State: Beyond the Myth of Retreat* (Basingstoke: Palgrave Macmillan).

Soysal, Y. N. (1994) *Limits of Citizenship: Migrants and Postnational Membership in Europe* (Chicago, IL: University of Chicago Press).

Spruyt, H. (1994) *The Sovereign State and its Competitor: An Analysis of Systems Change* (Princeton, NJ: Princeton University Press).

Stan, S. (2005) *L'agriculture roumaine en mutation. La construction sociale du marché* (Paris: Éditions CNRS).

Starke, P. (2006) 'The Politics of Welfare State Retrenchment: A Literature Review', *Social Policy and Administration*, 40(1): 104–20.

Starke, P., Obinger, H., and Castles, F.G. (2008) 'Convergence Towards Where: In What Ways, If Any, Are Welfare States Becoming More Similar?', *Journal of European Public Policy*, 15(7): 975–1000.

Steenbergen, M. and Marks, G. (2007) 'Evaluating Expert Judgments', *European Journal of Political Research*, 46: 347–66.

Steiner, J. (1974) *Amicable Agreement versus Majority Rule: Conflict Resolution in Switzerland* (Chapel Hill, NC: University of North Carolina Press).

Steinmo, S., Thelen, K., and Longstreth, F. (eds) (1992) *Structuring Politics: Historical Institutionalism in Comparative Analysis* (Cambridge: Cambridge University Press).

Stepan, A. (1971) *The Military in Politics: Changing Patterns in Brazil* (Princeton, NJ: Princeton University Press).

Stephens, J. D. (1979) *The Transition from Capitalism to Socialism* (Champaign, IL: University of Illinois Press).

Stephens, J. D. (2005) 'Economic Internationalization and Domestic Compensation: Northwestern Europe in Comparative Perspective', in M. Glatzer and D. Rueschemeyer (eds) (2005) *Globalization and the Future of the Welfare State* (Pittsburgh, PA: University of Pittsburgh Press), 49–74.

Stevenson, G. (1980) 'Canadian Regionalism in Continental Perspective', *Journal of Canadian Studies*, 15(2): 16–27.

Stiglitz, J. (2010) *Freefall: Free Markets and the Sinking of the Global Economy* (London: Penguin Group).

Stohr, W. (ed.) (1990) *Global Challenge and Local Response: Initiatives for Economic Regeneration in Contemporary Europe* (London: Continuum Publishing).

Stolleis, M. (2003) 'Judicial Review, Administrative Review, and Constitutional Review in the Weimar Republic', *Ratio Juris*, 16(2): 266–80.

Stone, A. (1990) *The Birth of Judicial Politics in France: The Constitutional Council in Comparative Perspective* (Oxford: Oxford University Press).

Stone, D. (2005) *Capturing the Political Imagination: Think Tanks and the Policy Process* (London: Frank Cass).

Stone Sweet, A. (1999) 'Judicialization and the Construction of Governance', *Comparative Political Studies*, 32(2), 147–84.

Stone Sweet, A. (2000) *Governing with Judges: Constitutional Politics in Europe* (Oxford: Oxford University Press).

Stone Sweet, A. (2002) 'Constitutional Courts and Parliamentary Democracy', *West European Politics*, 25: 77–100.

Stone Sweet, A. and Thatcher, M. (2002) 'The Politics of Delegation: Non-Majoritarian Institutions in Europe', *West European Politics*, 25(1): 1–22.

Storper, M. (1995) 'The Resurgence of Regional Economies, Ten Years Later: The Region as a Nexus of Untraded Interdependencies', *European Urban and Regional Studies*, 2(3): 191–221.

Stouffer, S. A. (1955) Communism, Conformity and Civil Liberties (New York: Doubleday).

Strang, D. and Meyer, J. (1993) 'Institutional Conditions for Diffusion', *Theory and Society*, 22: 487–511.

Strang, D. and Soule, S. A. (1998) 'Diffusion in Organizations and Social Movements: From Hybrid Corn to Poison Pills', *Annual Review of Sociology*, 24: 265–90.

Strange, S. (1996) *The Retreat of the State: The Diffusion of Power in the World Economy* (Cambridge: Cambridge University Press).

Streeck, W. (1996) 'Neo-Voluntarism: A European Social Policy Regime?', in G. Marks, F. W. Scharpf, P. C., and W. Streeck (eds), *Governance in the European Union* (London: Sage).

Streeck, W. (2006) 'The Study of Organised Interests: Before "The Century" and After', in C. Crouch and W. Streeck (eds) *The Diversity of Democracy: Corporatism, Social Order and Political Conflict* (Cheltenham: Edward Elgar), 3–45.

Streeck, W. and Schmitter, P. C. (eds) (1985) *Private Interest Government: Beyond Market and State* (London: Sage).

Streeck, W. and Schmitter, P. C. (1991) 'From National Corporatism to Transnational Pluralism: Organized Interests in the Single European Market', *Politics and Society*, 19(2): 133–64.

Streeck, W. and Thelen, K. (2005) 'Introduction: Institutional Change in Advanced Political Economies', in W. Streeck and K. Thelen (eds), *Beyond Continuity: Institutional Change in Advanced Political Economies* (Oxford: Oxford University Press), 1–39.

Streisand, B. (2010) 'Elections Should be Won—Not Bought', *Huffington Post*, 23 February 2010 (www.huffingtonpost. com/barbra-streisand/elections-should–be-won_b_ 473481.html).

Strøm, K. (1990) *Minority Government and Majority Rule* (Cambridge: Cambridge University Press).

Strøm, K. and Swindle, S. M. (2002) 'Strategic Parliamentary Dissolution', *American Political Science Review*, 96: 575–91.

Strøm, K., Müller, W. C., and Bergman, T. (eds) (2003) *Delegation and Accountability in Parliamentary Democracies* (Oxford: Oxford University Press).

Strøm, K., Müller, W. C., and Bergman, T. (eds) (2008) *Cabinets and Coalition Bargaining: The Democratic Life Cycle in Western Europe* (Oxford: Oxford University Press).

Strøm, K., Müller, W. C., and Smith, D. M. (2010) 'Parliamentary Control of Coalition Governments', *Annual Review of Political Science*, 13: 517–35.

Strömbäck, J. and Lee Kaid, L. (2008) *The Handbook of Election News Coverage* (Abingdon: Routledge).

Suleiman, E. N. (2003) *Dismantling Democratic States* (Princeton, NJ: Princeton University Press).

Sundberg, J. (1987) 'Exploring the Basis of Declining Party Membership in Denmark: A Scandinavian Comparison', *Scandinavian Political Studies*, 10(1), 17–38.

Surel, Y. (2000) 'The Role of Cognitive and Normative Frames in Policy-Making', *Journal of European Public Policy*, 7(4): 495–512.

Swank, D. (2001) 'Political Institutions and Welfare State Restructuring: The Impact of Institutions on Social Policy Change in Developed Democracies', in P. Pierson (ed.), *The New Politics of the Welfare State* (Oxford: Oxford University Press), 197–237.

Swank, D. (2002) *Global Capital, Political Institutions, and Policy Change in Developed Welfare States* (Cambridge: Cambridge University Press).

Swank, D. and Hicks, A. (1985) 'The Determinants and Redistributive Impacts of State Welfare Spending in the Advanced Capitalist Democracies, 1960–1980', in N. J. Vig and S. E. Schier (eds), *Political Economy in Western Democracies* (New York: Holmes & Meier), 115–39.

Swenson, P. (2004) 'Varieties of Capitalist Interest: Power, Institutions, and the Regulatory Welfare State in the United States and Sweden', Studies in American Political Development, 18: 1–29.

Swenson, P. (2002) *Capitalists Against Markets* (Cambridge: Cambridge University Press).

Taagapera, R. and Shugart, M. (1989) *Seats and Votes: The Effects and Determinants of Electoral Systems* (New Haven, CT: Yale University Press).

Tajfel, H. and Turner, J. C. (1979) 'An Integrative Theory of Intergroup Conflict', in S. Worchel and W. G. Austin (eds), *The Social Psychology of Intergroup Relations* (Chicago: Nelson-Hall) pp. 33–47.

Tallberg, J. (2006) *Leadership and Negotiation in the European Union* (Cambridge: Cambridge University Press).

Tarrow, S. (1977) *Between Center and Periphery: Grassroots Politicians in Italy and France* (New Haven, CT: Yale University Press).

Tarrow, S. (1988) 'Old Movements in New Cycles of Protest: The Career of an Italian Religious Movement', *International Social Movement Research*, 1: 281–304.

Tarrow, S. (1994) *Power in Movement: Social Movements, Collective Action and Politics* (Cambridge: Cambridge University Press).

Tarrow, S. (1996) 'States and Opportunities: The Political Structuring of Social Movements', in D. McAdam, J. D. McCarthy, and M. N. Zald (eds), *Comparative Perspectives on Social Movements: Political Opportunities, Mobilizing Structures, and Cultural Framings* (Cambridge: Cambridge University Press), 41–61.

Tarrow, S. (2005) *The New Transnational Activism* (New York: Cambridge University Press).

Taylor, C. (1993) 'The Deep Challenge of Dualism, in A.-G. Gagnon (ed.) *Quebec: State and Society* (2nd edn) (Toronto: University of Toronto Press), 82–95.

Taylor, C. L. and Hudson, M. C. (1972) *World Handbook of Political and Social Indicators* (2nd edn) (New Haven, CT: Yale University Press).

Taylor, C. L. and Jodice, D. A. (1983) *World Handbook of Political and Social Indicators* (3rd edn) (New Haven, CT: Yale University Press).

Taylor, P. (1982) 'Intergovernmentalism in the European Communities in the 1970s: Patterns and Perspectives', *International Organization*, 36(4): 741–66.

Tepe, S. (2006) 'When and How does Electoral Competition Moderate Religious Parties?', paper presented at the 2006 Annual Meeting of the American Political Science Association, Philadelphia, PA.

't Hart, P. (1990) *Groupthink in Government* (Amsterdam: Swets & Teitlinger).

Thatcher, M. and Stone Sweet, A. (eds) (2002) *The Politics of Delegation: Non-Majoritarian Institutions in Europe*, special issue of *West European Politics*, 25(1): 1–219.

Thelen, K. A. (1999) 'Historical Institutionalism in Comparative Politics', *Annual Review of Political Science*, 2: 369–404.

Thelen, K. A. (2004). *How Institutions Evolve. The Political Economy of Skills in Germany, Britain, the United States, and Japan* (Cambridge: Cambridge University Press).

Thelen, K. A. and Steinmo, S. (1992) 'Historical Institutionalism in Comparative Politics', in S. Steinmo, K. Thelen, and F. Longstreth (eds) (1992) *Structuring Politics: Historical Institutionalism in Comparative Analysis* (Cambridge: Cambridge University Press), 1–32.

Therborn, G. (1977) 'The Rule of Capital and the Rise of Democracy', *New Left Review*, 103: 3–42.

Therborn, G. (1989) ' "Pillarization" and "Popular Movements": Two Variants of Welfare State Capitalism: The Netherlands and Sweden', in F. G. Castles (ed.), *The Comparative History of Public Policy* (Cambridge: Polity), 192–241.

Thies, M. F. (2001) 'Keeping Tabs on Partners: The Logic of Delegation in Coalition Governments', *American Journal of Political Science*, 45: 580–98.

Thomson, E. P. (1963) *The Making of the English Working Class* (London: Gollancz).

Tilly, C. (1978) *From Modernization to Revolution* (New York: Random House).

Tilly, C. (1984) *Big Structures, Large Processes, Huge Comparisons* (New York: Russell Sage Foundation).

Tilly, C. (1990) *Coercion, Capital, and European States AD 990–1990* (Oxford: Blackwell).

Tilly, C., and Tarrow, S. G. (2007) *Contentious Politics* (London: Paradigm Publishers).

Tilly, C., Tilly, L., and Tilly, R. (1975) *The Rebellious Century, 1830–1930* (Cambridge, MA: Harvard University Press).

Timmermans, A. I. (2003) *High Politics in the Low Countries* (Aldershot: Ashgate).

Timmermans, A. I. (2006) 'Standing Apart and Sitting Together: Enforcing Coalition Agreements in Multiparty Systems', *European Journal of Political Research*, 45: 263–83.

Titmuss, R. M. (1958) *Essays on the Welfare State* (London: Allen & Unwin).

Titmuss, R. M. (1974) *Social Policy: An Introduction* (edited by B. Abel-Smith and K. Titmuss) (New York: Pantheon Books).

Tocqueville, A. de (2006*a*) [1835] *Democracy in America*, Vol 1, Project Gutenberg ebook (www.gutenberg.org/etext/815).

Tocqueville, A. de (2006*b*) [1840] *Democracy in America*, Vol 2, Project Gutenberg ebook (www.gutenberg.org/etext/816).

Tocqueville, A. de (1961) [1835] *De la Démocratie en Amérique,Oeuvres complétes*, Vol.1 (Paris: Gallimard).

Tolbert, C. J., Lowenstein, D. H., and Donovan, T. (1998) 'Election Law and Rules for Using Initiatives', in in S. Bowler, T. Donovan, and C. Tolbert (eds), *Citizens as Legislators* (Columbus, OH: Ohio State University Press), 27–54.

Tönnies, F. (1955 [1887]) *Community and Association* (London: Routledge and Kegan Paul).

Tosun, J. (2013). *Environmental Policy Change in Emerging Market Democracies: Central and Eastern Europe and Latin America Compared.* Toronto: University of Toronto Press.

Traxler, F. and Unger B. (1994) 'Industry or Infrastructure? A Crossnational Comparison of Governance, Its Determinants and Economic Consequences in the Dairy Sector', in J. R. Hollingworth, P. C. Schmitter, and W. Streeck (eds), *Governing Capitalist Economies: Performance and Control of Economic Sectors* (Oxford: Oxford University Press), 183–214.

Traxler, F., Blaschke, S., and Kittel, B. (2001) *International Labour Relations in Internationalized Markets: A Comparative Study of Institutions, Change and Performance* (Oxford: Oxford University Press).

Triandis, H. C. (1995) *Individualism and Collectivism* (Boulder: Westview Press).

Trigilia, C. (1991) 'The Paradox of the Region: Economic Regulation and the Representation of Interests', *Economy and Society*, 20(3): 306–27.

Troeltsch, E. (1922) [1961] *Der Historismus und seine Probleme* (Aalen: Scientia).

True, J. L., Jones, B. D., and Baumgartner, F. R. (2007) 'Punctuated-Equilibrium Theory: Explaining Stability and Change in American Policymaking', in P. A Sabatier (ed.), *Theories of the Policy Process* (2nd edn) (Boulder, CO: Westview Press).

Truman, D. B. (1971) [1951] *The Governmental Process: Political Interests and Public Opinion* (New York: Knopf).

Tsebelis, G. (1990) *Nested Games: Rational Choice in Comparative Politics* (Berkeley, CA: University of California Press).

Tsebelis, G. (1994) 'The Power of the European Parliament as a Conditional Agenda-Setter', *American Political Science Review*, 88(1): 128–42.

Tsebelis, G. (1995) 'Decision Making in Political Systems: Veto Players in Presidentialism, Parliamentarism, Multicameralism and Multipartism', *British Journal of Political Science*, 25: 289–325.

Tsebelis, G. (2000) 'Veto Players and Institutional Analysis', *Governance*, 13: 441–74.

Tsebelis, G. (2002) *Veto Players: How Political Institutions Work* (Princeton, NJ: Princeton University Press).

Tsebelis, G. and Money, J. (1997) *Bicameralism* (Cambridge: Cambridge University Press).

Turner, R. A. and Killian, L. (1987) *Collective Behavior* (3rd edn) (Englewood Cliffs, NJ: Prentice-Hall).

Uleri, P. V. (1996*a*) 'Introduction', in M. Gallagher and P. V. Uleri (eds), *The Referendum Experience in Europe* (Basingstoke: Palgrave Macmillan), 1–19.

Ülgen, S. (2011) *From Inspiration to Aspiration. Turkey in the New Middle East*, Carnegie Paper (Washington, DC: Carnegie Endowment for International Peace).

UN (United Nations) (1997) *World Investment Report 1997* (New York: United Nations).

UNCTAD (United Nations Conference on Trade and Development) (1993) *World Investment Report 1993: Transnational Corporations and Integrated International Production* (New York: United Nations).

UNDP (United Nations Development Programme) (2005) *Human Development Report 2005* (New York: Oxford University Press).

UNDP (2011). *Human Development Report 2011* (Basingstoke: Palgrave Macmillan).

Urwin, D. (1998) 'Modern Democratic Experiences of Territorial Management: Single Houses, But Many Mansions', *Regional and Federal Studies*, 8(2): 81–110.

Uslaner, E. M. (2002) *The Moral Foundations of Trust* (New York: Cambridge University Press).

van der Eijk, C. and Franklin, M. (eds) (1996) *Choosing Europe? The European Electorate and National Politics in the Face of Union* (Ann Arbor, MI: University of Michigan Press).

van der Velden, S., Dribbusch, H., Lyddon D., and Vandaele, K. (eds) (2007) *Strikes Around the World, 1968–2005: Case Studies of 15 Countries* (Amsterdam: Aksant).

Van Deth, J. W. (ed.) (1998) *Comparative Politics: The Problem of Equivalence* (London: Routledge).

Van Deth, J. W. and Scarbrough, E. (1995) *The Impact of Values* (Oxford: Oxford University Press).

Vanhanen, T. (1997) *Prospects of Democracy: A Study of 172 Countries* (New York: Routledge).

van Kersbergen, K. (1995) *Social Capitalism: A Study of Christian Democracy and the Welfare State* (London: Routledge).

van Kersbergen, K. (2002) 'The Politics of Welfare State Reform', *Swiss Political Science Review*, 8(2): 1–19.

van Oorschot, W. (2006) 'Making the difference in social Europe: deservingness perceptions among citizens of European welfare states', *Journal of European Social Policy*, 16(1), 23–42.

van Thiel, S. (2006) 'Styles of Reform: Differences in Quango Creation between Policy Sectors in the Netherlands', *Journal of Public Policy*, 26(2): 115–39.

van Waarden, F. (1995) 'Persistence of National Policy Styles', in B. Unger and F. van Waarden (eds), *Convergence or Diversity?* (Aldershot: Ashgate), 333–72.

van Wersch, J., and de Zeeuw, J. (2005) *Mapping European Assistance*, Working Paper 36 (The Hague: Netherlands Institute of International Relations).

Verba, S. (1985) 'Comparative Politics: Where Have We Been, Where Are We Going?', in H. J. Wiarda (ed.), *New Directions in Comparative Politics* (Boulder, CO: Westview Press) 26–38.

Verba, S., Schlozman, K. L., and Brady, H. (1995) *Voice and Equality: Civic Voluntarism in American Politics* (Cambridge, MA: Cambridge University Press).

Verma, S. K. and Kumar, K. (eds) (2003) *Fifty Years of The Supreme Court of India: Its Grasp and Reach* (New Delhi: Oxford University Press).

Vilar, P. (1977) *Catalunya en la Espana moderna* (Barcelona: Ed. Critica).

Vile, M. J. C. (1967) *Constitutionalism and the Separation of Powers* (Oxford: Oxford University Press).

Vis, B. and van Kersbergen, K. (2007) 'Why and How do Political Actors Pursue Risky Reforms?', *Journal of Theoretical Politics*, 19(2): 153–72.

Vis, B., Woldendorp, J., and Keman, H. (2007) 'Do Miracles Exist? Economic Performance of Nineteen OECD Democracies 1975–1999', *Journal of Business Research*, 60: 531–8.

Vogel, D. J. (1995) *Trading Up: Consumer and Environmental Regulation in a Global Economy* (Cambridge, MA: Harvard University Press).

Volcansek, M. (ed.) (1997) *Law Above Nations: Supranational Courts and the Legalization of Politics* (Gainesville, FL: University of Florida Press).

Voltmer, K. (ed.) (2006) *Mass Media and Political Communication in New Democracies* (Abingdon: Routledge).

Vowles, J. (2008), 'New Zealand: The Consolidation of Reform?', in M. Gallagher and P. Mitchell (eds), *The Politics of Electoral Systems* (Oxford: Oxford University Press), 295–312.

Wagemann, C. (2012) *Breakdown and Change of Private Interest Governments* (Abingdon: Routledge).

Wagschal, U. (2000) 'Besonderheiten der gezügelten Sozialstaaten', in U. Wagschal and H. Obinger (eds), *Der gezügelte Wohlfahrtsstaat. Sozialpolitik in reichen Industrienationen* (Frankfurt: Campus), 37–72.

Walgrave, S., Varone, F., and Dumont, P. (2006) 'Policy With or Without Parties? A Comparative Analysis of Policy Priorities and Policy Change in Belgium, 1991 to 2000', *Journal of European Public Policy*, 13(7): 1021–38.

Walker, N. (1996) 'European Constitutionalism and European Integration', *Public Law* (Summer): 266.

Wallerstein, I. (1979) *The Capitalist World Economy* (Cambridge: Cambridge University Press).

Waltz, K. N. (1999) 'Globalization and Governance', *PS: Political Science and Politics*, 32(4): 693–700.

Wang, G., Goonasekera, A., and Servaes, J. (eds) (2000) *The New Communications Landscape: Demystifying Media Globalization* (Abingdon: Routledge).

Wannop, U. (1997) 'Regional Planning and Urban Governance in Europe and the USA', in M. Keating and J. Loughlin (eds), *The Political Economy of Regionalism* (London: Routledge), 139–70.

Warshaw, S. A. (1996) *Powersharing: White House Cabinet Relations in the Modern Presidency* (Albany, NY: State University of New York Press).

Wattenberg, M. P. (2006) *Is Voting for Young People?* (New York: Pearson).

Watts, R. (1996) *Comparing Federal Systems in the 1990s* (Kingston, Ontario: Institute of Intergovernmental Relations, Queen's University).

Weaver, D. (1998) *The Global Journalist* (New York: Hampton Press).

Weaver, R. K. and Rockman, B. A. (1993). 'Assessing the Effects of Institutions', in R.K. Weaver and B. A. Rockman (eds), *Do Institutions Matter? Government Capabilities in the United States and Abroad* (Washington, DC: Brookings Institution), 1–41.

Weber, M. (1920) *Gesammelte Aufsätze zur Religionssoziologie* (Tübingen: Mohr).

Weber, M. (1947) *The Theory of Social and Economic Organization* (New York: Free Press).

Weiler, J. H. H. (1991) 'The Transformation of Europe', *Yale Law Journal*, 100: 2403–83.

Weiler, J. H. H., Haltern, U., and Mayer, F. C. (1995) 'European Democracy and its Critique', *West European Politics*, 18(4): 4–39.

Weingast, B. R. (2002) 'Rational Choice Institutionalism', in I. Katznelson and H. V. Milner (eds), *The State of the Discipline* (New York/Washington, DC: W. W. Norton/American Political Science Association), 660–92.

Weingast, B. R., Shepsle, K. A., and Johnsen, C. (1981) 'The Political Economy of Benefits and Costs: A Neoclassical Approach to Distributive Politics', *Journal of Political Economy*, 89(4): 642–64.

Weiss, L. (1998) *The Myth of the Powerless State* (New York: Cornell University Press).

Welzel, C. (2007) 'Are Levels of Democracy Influenced by Mass Attitudes? *International Political Science Review*, 28(4): 397–424.

Welzel, C. (2010) 'How Selfish Are Self-Expression Values: A Civicness Test', *Journal of Cross Cultural Psychology*, 41(March): 2–23.

Welzel, C. (2013) *Freedom Rising: Human Empowerment and the Quest for Emancipation* (New York: Cambridge University Press).

Welzel, C. and Inglehart, R. (2010) 'Values, Agency, and Well-Being: A Human Development Model', *Social Indicators Research*, 97(1): 43–63.

Welzel, C., Inglehart, R., and Deutsch, F. (2005) 'Social Capital, Voluntary Associations, and Collective Action', *Journal of Civil Society*, 1: 121–46.

Wen, D. (2005) *China Copes with Globalization* (San Francisco, CA: International Forum on Globalization).

Western, B. (1997) *Between Class and Market: Postwar Unionization in the Capitalist Democracies* (Princeton, NJ: Princeton University Press).

Weyland, K. (2005) 'Theories of Policy Diffusion: Lessons from Latin American Pension Reform', *World Politics*, 57(2): 262–95.

Weyland, K. (2006) *Bounded Rationality and Policy Diffusion: Social Sector Reform in Latin America*. Princeton, NJ: Princeton University Press.

Wheare, K. (1963) *Federal Government* (4th edn) (Oxford: Oxford University Press).

Whiteley, P., Clarke, H. D., Sanders, D., and Stewart, M. C. (2012) 'Britain Says NO: Voting in the AV Ballot Referendum', *Parliamentary Affairs*, 65: 301–22.

Wildavsky, A. (1964) *The Politics of the Budgetary Process* (Boston, MA: Little, Brown).

Wilensky, H. L. (1975) *The Welfare State and Equality: Structural and Ideological Roots of Public Expenditures* (Berkeley, CA: University of California Press).

Wilensky, H. L. (1981) 'Leftism, Catholicism, and Democratic Corporatism: The Role of Political Parties in Recent Welfare State Development', in P. Flora and A. J. Heidenheimer (eds), *The Development of Welfare States in Europe and America* (Piscataway, NJ: Transaction Publishers), 345–82.

Wilensky, H. L. and Lebeaux, C. N. (1965) *Industrial Society and Social Welfare: The Impact of Industrialization on the Supply and Organization of Social Welfare Services in the United States* (New York: Macmillan).

Wilkinson, R. G. and Pickett, K. (2009) *The Spirit Level: Why More Equal Societies Almost Always Do Better* (London: Allen Lane).

Wilson, C. and Dunn, A. (2011) 'Digital Media in the Egyptian Revolution: Descriptive Analysis from the Tahrir Data Sets', *International Journal of Communication*, 5: 1248–72.

Wilson, G. K. (1990) *Interest Groups* (Oxford: Basil Blackwell).

Wilson, J. (1983) 'On the Dangers of Bickering in a Federal State: Some Reflections on the Failure of the National Party System', in A. Kornberg and H. Clarke (eds), *Political Support in Canada: The Crisis Years* (Durham, NC: Duke University Press), 171–222.

Wilson, J. Q. (1973) *Political Organizations* (Beverly Hills, CA: Sage).

Wilson, J. Q. (1989) *Bureaucracy* (New York: Basic Books).

Wilson, J. Q. (1995) *Political Organizations* (Princeton, NJ: Princeton University Press).

Wilthagen, T. (1998) *Flexicurity: A New Paradigm for Labour Market Policy Reform?*, WZB Discussion Paper (Berlin: FSI).

Wilthagen, T., Tros, F., and van Lishout, H. (2003) 'Towards "Flexicurity": Balancing Flexicurity and Security in EU Member States', paper presented at the 13th World Congress of IIRA, Berlin.

Windhoff-Héritier, A. (1980) *Politikimplementation: Ziel und Wirklichkeit politischer Entscheidungen* (Königstein: Anton Hain).

Wiseman, N. (1981) 'The Pattern of Prairie Politics', *Queen's Quarterly*, 88: 298–315.

Wolin, S. S. (1989) *The Presence of the Past: Essays on the State and the Constitution* (Baltimore, MD: Johns Hopkins University Press).

World Bank (2006) *World Development Report 2006* (New York: Oxford University Press).

Wren, A. (ed.) (2013) *The Political Economy of the Service Transformation* (Oxford: Oxford University Press).

Wriston, W. B. (1992) *The Twilight of Sovereignty: How the Information Revolution is Transforming our World* (New York: Charles Scribner's Sons).

Wyler, R. (2012) *Schweizer Gewerkschaften und Europa* (Münster: Westfälisches Dampfboot).

Young, A. and Wallace, H. (2000) *Regulatory Politics in the Enlarging European Union: Weighing Civic and Producer Interests* (Manchester: Manchester University Press).

Yu, L. (2006) 'Understanding Information Inequality: Making Sense of the Literature of the Information and Digital Divides', *Journal of Librarianship and Information Science*, 38(4): 229–52.

Young, L. and Archer, K. (eds) (2002) *Regionalism and Party Politics in Canada* (Don Mills, Ontario: Oxford University Press).

Youngs, R. (eds) (2010) *The European Union and Democracy Promotion* (Baltimore, MD: Johns Hopkins University Press).

Zakaria, F. (1997) 'The Rise of Illiberal Democracy', *Foreign Affairs*, 76(6): 22–43.

Zaller, John R. (1992) *The Nature and Origin of Mass Opinion* (Cambridge: Cambridge University Press).

Zürn, M. (1998) *Regieren jenseits des Nationaalstaates: Globalisierung und Denationalisierung als Chance* (Frankfurt: Suhrkamp).

Other sources

Amsterdam Institute for Advanced Labour Studies (2011) 'CTWSS: Database on Institutional Characteristics of Trade Unions, Wage Setting, State Intervention and Social Pacts in 34 countries.' dataset no. 3 (http://www.uva-aias.net/207).

Afrobarometer (2002) Afrobarometer data, round 1 (see web links).

ANES (2004) American National Election Study 2004 (see web links).

CAWP (2006) Center for American Women and Politics (see web links).

CSES (2006) Comparative Study of Electoral Systems (see web links).

Comparative Study of Electoral Systems, 'CSES Module 1: 1996–2001', www.cses.org, 2001.

Comparative Study of Electoral Systems, 'CSES Module 2: 2001–2006', www.cses.org, 2005.

Corporate Europe Conservatory, www.corporateeurope.org/.

European Values Study Group and World Values Survey Association, 'European and World Values Surveys Four-Wave Integrated Data File, 1981–2004 (V.20060423)', www.worldvaluessurvey.org, 2006.

Elections in Euskadi (2006) (see the Online Resource Centre).

EUSTAT (2006) Instituto Vasco de Estadística (see web links).

Foreign Policy and Kearney, A. T. (2006) 'The Globalization Index', *Foreign Policy*, November/December: 26–36.

Freedom House (2006) *Freedom in the World 2006: The Annual Survey of Political Rights and Civil Liberties* (Lanham, MD: Rowman & Littlefield).

Freedom House (2012) *Freedom in the World 2012* (New York: Freedom House).

German Marshall Fund of the US (2005) *Transatlantic Trends 2005* (http://gmfus.org).

Huber, E., Ragin, C., and Stephens, J. D. 'The Comparative Welfare States Data Set' (www.lisproject.org/publications/welfaredata/welfareaccess.htm), 1997.

IDEA, International Institute for Democracy and Electoral Assistance, 'Voter Turnout' (http://www.idea.int/vt/), 2006.

ILO, 'Statistics of Trade Union Membership: Data for 47 Countries Taken Mainly from National Statistical Publications', 2006.

ILO (2013) 'Ratification by Convention', in NORMLEX Information System (http://www.ilo.org/dyn/normlex/en/f?p=1000:12001:0).

Inter-Parliamentary Union (2006) 'Women in National Parliaments' (see web links).

NILT (2004) Northern Ireland Life and Times Survey 2004 (see web links).

Index